Nineteenth-Century
Literature Criticism

Guide to Gale Literary Criticism Series

For criticism on	Consult these Gale series
Authors now living or who died after December 31, 1999	*CONTEMPORARY LITERARY CRITICISM (CLC)*
Authors who died between 1900 and 1999	*TWENTIETH-CENTURY LITERARY CRITICISM (TCLC)*
Authors who died between 1800 and 1899	*NINETEENTH-CENTURY LITERATURE CRITICISM (NCLC)*
Authors who died between 1400 and 1799	*LITERATURE CRITICISM FROM 1400 TO 1800 (LC)* *SHAKESPEAREAN CRITICISM (SC)*
Authors who died before 1400	*CLASSICAL AND MEDIEVAL LITERATURE CRITICISM (CMLC)*
Authors of books for children and young adults	*CHILDREN'S LITERATURE REVIEW (CLR)*
Dramatists	*DRAMA CRITICISM (DC)*
Poets	*POETRY CRITICISM (PC)*
Short story writers	*SHORT STORY CRITICISM (SSC)*
Black writers of the past two hundred years	*BLACK LITERATURE CRITICISM (BLC)* *BLACK LITERATURE CRITICISM SUPPLEMENT (BLCS)*
Hispanic writers of the late nineteenth and twentieth centuries	*HISPANIC LITERATURE CRITICISM (HLC)* *HISPANIC LITERATURE CRITICISM SUPPLEMENT (HLCS)*
Native North American writers and orators of the eighteenth, nineteenth, and twentieth centuries	*NATIVE NORTH AMERICAN LITERATURE (NNAL)*
Major authors from the Renaissance to the present	*WORLD LITERATURE CRITICISM, 1500 TO THE PRESENT (WLC)* *WORLD LITERATURE CRITICISM SUPPLEMENT (WLCS)*

ISSN 0732-1864

Volume 98

Nineteenth-Century Literature Criticism

Excerpts from Criticism of the
Works of Novelists, Philosophers, and Other
Creative Writers Who Died between 1800
and 1899, from the First Published Critical
Appraisals to Current Evaluations

Juliet Byington
Thomas J. Schoenberg
Lawrence J. Trudeau
Editors

GALE GROUP

THOMSON LEARNING

Detroit • New York • San Diego • San Francisco
Boston • New Haven, Conn. • Waterville, Maine
London • Munich

STAFF

Library of Congress Catalog Card Number
ISBN 0-7876-4553-2
ISSN 0732-1864
Printed in the United States of America

10 9 8 7 6 5 4 3 2 1

Contents

Preface vii

Acknowledgments xi

Preface

Since its inception in 1981, *Nineteeth-Century Literature Criticism* (*NCLC*) has been a valuable resource for students and librarians seeking critical commentary on writers of this transitional period in world history. Designated an "Outstanding Reference Source" by the American Library Association with the publication of is first volume, *NCLC* has since been purchased by over 6,000 school, public, and university libraries. The series has covered more than 300 authors representing 29 nationalities and over 17,000 titles. No other reference source has surveyed the critical reaction to nineteenth-century authors and literature as thoroughly as *NCLC*.

Scope of the Series

NCLC is designed to introduce students and advanced readers to the authors of the nineteenth century and to the most significant interpretations of these authors' works. The great poets, novelists, short story writers, playwrights, and philosophers of this period are frequently studied in high school and college literature courses. By organizing and reprinting commentary written on these authors, *NCLC* helps students develop valuable insight into literary history, promotes a better understanding of the texts, and sparks ideas for papers and assignments. Each entry in *NCLC* presents a comprehensive survey of an author's career or an individual work of literature and provides the user with a multiplicity of interpretations and assessments. Such variety allows students to pursue their own interests; furthermore, it fosters an awareness that literature is dynamic and responsive to many different opinions.

Every fourth volume of *NCLC* is devoted to literary topics that cannot be covered under the author approach used in the rest of the series. Such topics include literary movements, prominent themes in nineteenth-century literature, literary reaction to political and historical events, significant eras in literary history, prominent literary anniversaries, and the literatures of cultures that are often overlooked by English-speaking readers.

NCLC continues the survey of criticism of world literature begun by Gale's *Contemporary Literary Criticism* (*CLC*) and *Twentieth-Century Literary Criticism* (*TCLC*).

Organization of the Book

An *NCLC* entry consists of the following elements:

- The **Author Heading** cites the name under which the author most commonly wrote, followed by birth and death dates. Also located here are any name variations under which an author wrote, including transliterated forms for authors whose native languages use nonroman alphabets. If the author wrote consistently under a pseudonym, the pseudonym will be listed in the author heading and the author's actual name given in parenthesis on the first line of the biographical and critical information. Uncertain birth or death dates are indicated by question marks. Single-work entries are preceded by a heading that consists of the most common form of the title in English translation (if applicable) and the original date of composition.

- The **Introduction** contains background information that introduces the reader to the author, work, or topic that is the subject of the entry.

- A **Portrait of the Author** is included when available.

- The list of **Principal Works** is ordered chronologically by date of first publication and lists the most important works by the author. The genre and publication date of each work is given. In the case of foreign authors whose works have been translated into English, the list will focus primarily on twentieth-century translations, selecting those works most commonly considered the best by critics. Unless otherwise indicated, dramas are dated by first performance, not first publication. Lists of **Representative Works** by different authors appear with topic entries.

■ Reprinted **Criticism** is arranged chronologically in each entry to provide a useful perspective on changes in critical evaluation over time. The critic's name and the date of composition or publication of the critical work are given at the beginning of each piece of criticism. Unsigned criticism is preceded by the title of the source in which it appeared. All titles by the author featured in the text are printed in boldface type. Footnotes are reprinted at the end of each essay or excerpt. In the case of excerpted criticism, only those footnotes that pertain to the excerpted texts are included. Criticism in topic entries is arranged chronologically under a variety of subheadings to facilitate the study of different aspects of the topic.

■ A complete **Bibliographical Citation** of the original essay or book precedes each piece of criticism.

■ Critical essays are prefaced by brief **Annotations** explicating each piece.

■ An annotated bibliography of **Further Reading** appears at the end of each entry and suggests resources for additional study. In some cases, significant essays for which the editors could not obtain reprint rights are included here. Boxed material following the further reading list provides references to other biographical and critical sources on the author in series published by Gale.

Indexes

Each volume of *NCLC* contains a **Cumulative Author Index** listing all authors who have appeared in a wide variety of reference sources published by the Gale Group, including *NCLC*. A complete list of these sources is found facing the first page of the Author Index. The index also includes birth and death dates and cross references between pseudonyms and actual names.

A **Cumulative Nationality Index** lists all authors featured in *NCLC* by nationality, followed by the number of the *NCLC* volume in which their entry appears.

A **Cumulative Topic Index** lists the literary themes and topics treated in the series as well as in *Classical and Medieval Literature Criticism, Literature Criticism from 1400 to 1800, Twentieth-Century Literary Criticism,* and the *Contemporary Literary Criticism* Yearbook, which was discontinued in 1998.

An alphabetical **Title Index** accompanies each volume of *NCLC*, with the exception of the Topics volumes. Listings of titles by authors covered in the given volume are followed by the author's name and the corresponding page numbers where the titles are discussed. English translations of foreign titles and variations of titles are cross-referenced to the title under which a work was originally published. Titles of novels, dramas, nonfiction books, and poetry, short story, or essay collections are printed in italics, while individual poems, short stories, and essays are printed in roman type within quotation marks.

In response to numerous suggestions from librarians, Gale also produces an annual paperbound edition of the *NCLC* cumulative title index. This annual cumulation, which alphabetically lists all titles reviewed in the series, is available to all customers. Additional copies of this index are available upon request. Librarians and patrons will welcome this separate index; it saves shelf space, is easy to use, and is recyclable upon receipt of the next edition.

Citing *Nineteenth-Century Literature Criticism*

When writing papers, students who quote directly from any volume in the Literary Criticism Series may use the following general format to footnote reprinted criticism. The first example pertains to material drawn from periodicals, the second to material reprinted from books.

Kim McQuaid, "William Apes, Pequot: An Indian Reformer in the Jackson Era," *The New England Quarterly,* 50 (December 1977): 605-25; excerpted and reprinted in *Nineteenth-Century Literature Criticism,* vol. 73, ed. Janet Witalec (Farmington Hills, Mich.: The Gale Group, 1999), 3-4.

Richard Harter Fogle, *The Imagery of Keats and Shelley: A Comparative Study* (Archon Books, 1949), 211-51; excerpted and reprinted in *Nineteenth-Century Literature Criticism,* vol. 73, ed. Janet Witalec (Farmington Hills, Mich.: The Gale Group, 1999), 157-69.

Suggestions are Welcome

Readers who wish to suggest new features, topics, or authors to appear in future volumes, or who have other suggestions or comments are cordially invited to call, write, or fax the Managing Editor:

Managing Editor, Literary Criticism Series
The Gale Group
27500 Drake Road
Farmington Hills, MI 48331-3535
1-800-347-4253 (GALE)
Fax: 248-699-8054

Acknowledgments

The editors wish to thank the copyright holders of the excerpted criticism included in this volume and the permissions managers of many book and magazine publishing companies for assisting us in securing reproduction rights. We are also grateful to the staffs of the Detroit Public Library, the Library of Congress, the University of Detroit Mercy Library, Wayne State University Purdy/Kresge Library Complex, and the University of Michigan Libraries for making their resources available to us. Following is a list of the copyright holders who have granted us permission to reproduce material in this volume of *NCLC*. Every effort has been made to trace copyright, but if omissions have been made, please let us know.

COPYRIGHTED EXCERPTS IN *NCLC*, VOLUME 98, WERE REPRODUCED FROM THE FOLLOWING PERIODICALS:

The American Historical Review, v. 92, June 1987 for "The Making of an American Prophet: Emerson, His Audiences and the Rise of the Culture Industry in Nineteenth-Century America" by Mary Kupiec Cayton. © 1987, The American Historical Review. Reproduced by permission of The American Historical Association and the author.—*American Literature,* v. 66, September, 1994; v. 70, September, 1998. Copyright © 1994, 1998 by Duke University Press, Durham, NC. Reproduced by permission.—*American Transcendental Quarterly,* v. 8, December, 1994. © 1994 by the University of Rhode Island. Reproduced by permission.—*Annali d'Italianistica,* v. 3, 1985. Reproduced by the permission of the University of North Carolina at Chapel Hill.—*Arizona Quarterly,* v. 49.3, 1993. Copyright © 1993 by the Regents of the University of Arizona. Reproduced by permission.—*ESQ: A Journal of the American Renaissance,* v. 40, 2nd Quarter, 1994 for "'Too Pathetic, Too Pitiable': Emerson's Lessons in Love's Philosophy" by Eric Murphy Selinger; v. 41, 1995 for "'Living Property': Emerson's Ethics" by James M. Albrecht; v. 43, 1997 for "Fate, Power, and History in Emerson and Nietzsche" by Herwig Friedl. Reproduced by permission of Washington State University and the authors.—*Forum Italicum,* v 35, Spring 1991. Reproduced by permission of State University of New York at Stoney Brook, Center for Italian Studies.—*Legacy,* v. 14, 1997. © 1997 by Pennsylvania State University. Reproduced by permission of the Nebraska Press.—*Modern Language Notes,* v. 101:1, 1986; 113:1, 1998. © 1986, 1998 The Johns Hopkins University Press. Reprinted with the permission of The Johns Hopkins University Press.—*Modern Language Review,* v. 87, October, 1992 for "Manzoni After 1848: An 'Irresolute Utopian?'" by Mark Davie. Reproduced by permission of the Modern Humanities Research Association and the author.—*The New England Quarterly,* vol. 66, September 1993 for "Negotiating a Self: The Autobiography and Journals of Catharine Maria Sedgwick," by Mary Kelley. Copyright held by The New England Quarterly. Reproduced by permission of the publisher and the author, Mary Brinsmead Wheelock.—*Philosophy and Rhetoric,* v. 29, 1996. © 1996 by The Pennsylvania State University. Reproduced by permission of the publisher.—*Renascence: Essays on Values in Literature,* v. 38, Spring, 1986. © copyright, 1986, Marquette University Press. Reproduced by permission.—*Revista di Studi Ilaliani,* v. 3, December, 1985. Reproduced by permission of the University of Toronto, Department of Italian Studies.—*Romance Studies,* v. 19, 1991. Reproduced by permission of the University of Wales, Swansen.—*Short Stories in Fiction,* v. 27, Fall, 1990. © 1990 by Newberry College. Reproduced by permission.—*Studies in the Literary Imagination,* v. 27:1, 1994. © 1994 Department of English, Georgia State University. Reproduced by permission.—*Studies in Romanticism,* v. 29, Winter, 1990. Copyright 1990 by the Trustees of Boston University. Reproduced by permission.—*Women's Writing,* v. 2, 1995 for "'She Could Make a Cake as Well as Books...': Catherine Sedgwick, Anna Jameson, and the Construction of the Domestic Intellectual," by Maria LaMonaca. Reproduced by permission of Triangle Journals Ltd. and the author.—*Yale Journal of Criticism,* v. 12:1, 1999. © The Johns Hopkins University Press. Reproduced by permission of The Johns Hopkins University Press.

COPYRIGHTED EXCERPTS IN *NCLC*, VOLUME 98, WERE REPRODUCED FROM THE FOLLOWING BOOKS:

Barricelli, Gian Piero. From "Provident Ill-Fortune," in *Alessandro Manzoni.* Twayne Publishers, 1976. Reproduced by permission.—Goodman, Russell. From "Ralph Waldo Emerson," in *American Philosophy and the Romantic Tradition.* Cambridge University Press, 1990. Reproduced by permission of Cambridge University Press.—Gould, Philip. From "Catherine Sedgwick's 'Recital' of the Pequot War," in *Covenant and Republic: Historical Romance and the Politics of Puritanism.* Cambridge University Press, 1996. Reproduced by permission of Cambridge University Press.—Lopez, Michael. From "The Anti-Emerson Tradition," in *Emerson and Power: Creative Antagonism in the Nineteenth Century.*

Ralph Waldo Emerson
1803-1882

American essayist and poet. For additional information on Emerson's life and works, see *NCLC,* Volumes 1 and 38.

INTRODUCTION

Universally regarded as one of the most influential American writers of the nineteenth century, Ralph Waldo Emerson was one of the founders of the Transcendental movement, a group of New England literary figures who believed deeply in the presence of the divine in human beings. The Transcendentalists asserted that each individual must determine what is morally correct regardless of religious dogma, and Emerson's essays are regarded as some of the most important and commanding literary expressions of this philosophy. In addition, Emerson is also widely regarded as one of the most effective architects of a distinctly American philosophy embracing optimism, individuality, and mysticism, and he is noted for his influence on such authors as Herman Melville, Henry David Thoreau, Nathaniel Hawthorne, and Emily Dickinson.

BIOGRAPHICAL INFORMATION

Emerson was born in Boston to a long line of Unitarian ministers and it was there that he spent a sheltered childhood. He graduated from Harvard University in 1821, taught school in Boston for four years, and began attending Harvard Divinity School in 1825. The following year, he became a minister and was ordained pastor of Boston's Second Church in 1829. At this time he also married his first wife, Ellen Tucker, whose death in 1831 left Emerson with an inheritance that secured his financial future. Despite his traditional academic career, Emerson was familiar with numerous modern religious influences, including ideas regarding Romantic subjectivity, a philosophy that was just then beginning to reach America from Europe. Additionally, his years at Harvard had exposed him to the publications of the German Higher Critics, as well as translations of Hindu and Buddhist poetry. Thus, even while he assumed the pastorate of his church, Emerson brought with him many doubts concerning traditional Christian belief. Unable to stem these growing misgivings, in 1832 Emerson resigned his position as pastor after expressing objections to the traditional meaning and function of the Communion ritual. Following his resignation, Emerson spent the next year traveling in Europe, where he met such writers as William Wordsworth, Samuel Taylor Coleridge, and Thomas Carlyle. During these years he also visited the botanical gardens at the Jardin des Plantes in Paris, an ex-

perience he claimed inspired his interest in the mystical significance of nature. He returned to America in 1833 and settled in Concord, Massachusetts, where he began his career as a lecturer. He soon established his reputation as one of the most successful speakers on the country's new lyceum circuit. During the late 1830s and early 1840s Emerson published several works that presented his thought at its most idealistic and optimistic. His first published work, an essay entitled *Nature* (1836), repudiated traditional religion, declaring nature to be the divine example of inspiration, as well as the source of boundless possibilities of human fulfillment. This work in particular is believed to have helped found what would later become known as the Transcendental Club, a group of intellectuals that included Thoreau, Hawthorne, and Margaret Fuller. Emerson frequently contributed poetry to the group's journal, the *Dial,* and later served as its editor. It was also during this time that Emerson wrote and delivered two of his most important lectures: "The American Scholar" (1837), an address delivered to Harvard's Phi Beta Kappa Society, widely regarded as a call for a distinct school of American intellectualism that was independent of European influence; and "The Divinity School Address" in which he caused tremendous controversy by challenging the tenets of traditional Christianity and defined Transcendental philosophy in terms of the "impersoneity" of God. Emerson undertook a second journey to Europe in 1847, which included a lecture tour in England. This trip also resulted in the publication of his *English Traits* (1856), a work that was hailed by contemporaries as an accurate evaluation of contemporary English society. For the next two decades, Emerson continued to write and lecture and was often referred to as the "Sage of Concord." He died in Concord in 1882.

MAJOR WORKS

Emerson wrote essays and poetry over several decades, but most of his thoughts regarding Transcendentalism were laid out in his earliest works, including *Nature* and his lectures "The American Scholar" and "The Divinity School Address." The doctrines he formulated in these early works were later expanded and elaborated upon in *Essays* (1838) and *Essays: Second Series* (1844). From these collections, the essays "Self-Reliance," "The Over-Soul," and "The Poet" are among the best known. The philosophical and religious outlook of Emerson's works are traced to many sources, including the Unitarian religion, German Philosophical Idealism, the work of Swedish scientist and mystic Emmanuel Swedenborg, the poetry of Wordsworth and Coleridge, and the Hindu scriptures, all of which emphasize the unity of nature, humanity, and God. Much of Emerson's Transcendental philosophy is encapsulated in *Nature,* a work in which he argued that nature is a symbolic language that can reveal the mind of God, and that through the experience of oneness with nature, a communion with God is possible. In addition to his essays, Emerson was a prolific contributor of poetry to the *Dial* and later issued many of his poems in *Poems* (1847) and *May-Day, and Other Pieces* (1867). Well-known poems in these collections include "The Rhodora," "The Sphinx," "Brahma," "The Humble Bee," and one of his earliest works, the "Concord Hymn." Scholars have charted a steady decline in Emerson's idealism in his poetry and prose works following his contributions to the *Dial* and the publication of his *Essays: Second Series.* The most noted example of his humanistic acquiescence to the reality of circumstances surrounding mortal limitations is *The Conduct of Life* (1860). Other important works include *Representative Men* (1850), a series of essays on the men who most closely fit Emerson's ideal, and another collection titled *Society and Solitude* (1870). Emerson spent the last years of his life in Concord, writing little, but enjoying national recognition throughout America as a central figure of the American Renaissance.

CRITICAL RECEPTION

Emerson left a large literary legacy and is widely acknowledged as one of the most influential writers of the nineteenth century. However, critics have found it difficult to agree on which facet of Emerson's work deserves the most attention and where his influence has been most profoundly felt. Filled with maxims, his writings offer encouragement and consoling wisdom, which has gained him an enduring place in American popular culture. On the other hand, he has also been openly acknowledged by scholars as one of the most important influences in the fields of poetry and philosophy. Although he published a large number of poems in his lifetime, Emerson's poetry has often been regarded as secondary to his prose writing. In fact, it wasn't until the 1990s that a collected edition of his poems was issued and it is only in the last few years that any significant critical analyses of his poetry have become available. According to Saundra Morris, a balanced overview of Emerson's work is impossible without a significant emphasis on his verse. Morris states that Emerson identified himself primarily as a poet and that as a poet-essayist he has exerted an enormous influence on other poets. While Emerson's writing was well received by most nineteenth-century scholars, he fell out of favor with critics during the 1920s and 1930s, many of whom charged that his works lacked unity and logical structure. More recent criticism, however, has repudiated this charge, noting a dialectical structure in Emerson's philosophy that unifies his otherwise disparate statements. Regardless of his critical reception, his poetry and theories regarding writing have been often cited as vitally influential to the work of authors such as Thoreau and Walt Whitman. In fact, Emerson the poet is now lauded as a theorist and goal-setter, and is revered for the creation of a distinctly American tradition in poetry. In recent years, Emerson and his writings have enjoyed renewed critical attention, including a re-evaluation of the artistic and philosophic merits of his work. In fact, during the 1980s and 1990s, Emerson's writing was acknowledged as a complex mixture of deeply resonant rhetoric that goes far beyond the traditional representations of his work. Now seen as one of the founding figures in the American philosophical tradition, Emerson's prose and poetry reflect the many contradictory mantles he assumed in his work, including those of Transcendentalist, philosopher, prose stylist, theorist, and social commentator.

PRINCIPAL WORKS

Nature (essay) 1836

An Oration, Delivered Before the Phi Beta Kappa Society at Cambridge (essay) 1837; also published as *The American Scholar* 1901

Essays (essays) 1838; also published as *Essays: First Series* 1854

Essays: Second Series (essays) 1844

Poems (poetry) 1847

Nature, Addresses, and Lectures (essays) 1849

Representative Men: Seven Lectures (essays) 1850

English Traits (essays) 1856

The Conduct of Life (essays) 1860

May-Day and Other Pieces (poetry) 1867

Society and Solitude (essays) 1870

Letters and Social Aims (essays) 1876

Fortune of the Republic. Lecture Delivered at the Old South Church (essay) 1878

Lectures and Biographical Sketches (essays and biographies) 1884

Natural History of the Intellect, and Other Papers (essays) 1893

The Complete Works of Ralph Waldo Emerson. 12 vols. (essays and poetry) 1903-21

The Letters of Ralph Waldo Emerson. 6 vols. (letters) 1939

Journals and Miscellaneous Notebooks. 16 vols. (journals and notebooks) 1960-82

The Complete Sermons of Ralph Waldo Emerson 4 vols. (sermons) 1989-92

The Topical Notebooks of Ralph Waldo Emerson 3 vols. (notebooks) 1990-94

Emerson's Antislavery Writings (essays) 1995

The Later Lectures of Ralph Waldo Emerson 2 vols. (essays) 2000

CRITICISM

Mary Kupiec Cayton (essay date 1987)

SOURCE: "The Making of an American Prophet: Emerson, His Audiences, and the Rise of the Culture Industry in Nineteenth-Century America," in *Ralph Waldo Emerson: A Collection of Critical Essays,* edited by Lawrence Buell, Prentice Hall, 1993, pp. 77-100.

[*In the following essay, originally published in 1987, Cayton offers an assessment of Emerson's cultural impact in the context of contemporary media.*]

. . . The case of Ralph Waldo Emerson, one of the most celebrated of American intellectuals, can shed light on the ways in which meanings are made in intellectual discourse and what those meanings have to do with those people not filling the role of intellectual within the culture. Historians have never known precisely how to categorize Emerson. Perry Miller saw him as the heir and transformer of Edwardsian Puritanism. F. O. Matthiessen saw in him the founder of American literary romanticism and termed his the "age of Emerson." Others (notably Stanley Elkins) have seen him as a prime mover in a generation of reformers, with Transcendentalism being a dangerously uncompromising Emersonian movement for social reform. He was also, according to various scholars, a democratic philosopher, an incipient Darwinist, and a pragmatic mystic.[1] Reception theory suggests that Emerson's cultural impact may have depended less on what he intended than on what key communities of interpreters made of him.

If reaction in the popular and religious press and in the journals of the literary community is any gauge, Emerson attained a limited, local notoriety in his native new England during the 1830s. He was born in Boston in 1803, the son of a prominent Unitarian minister who died young. Prior to 1825, Emerson seems to have viewed himself (to judge by his journals and letters) primarily as a fledgling poet who hoped to make his mark on the world of *belles-lettres.* In need of both money and a socially sanctioned way of indulging his proclivities for philosophizing, he entered upon the study of the ministry, eventually assuming the pastorate of the Second (Unitarian) Church, Boston. He resigned in 1832: his ministerial colleagues and his congregation interpreted the role of the Lord's Supper celebration in the spiritual life of the church in a way he had come to view as intolerable. After a period of travel, he returned to his ancestral home of Concord, lecturing occasionally, substituting for local ministers, and preaching from time to time in vacant pulpits. Freed from immediate financial pressure by his wife's legacy, he also spent time during the period 1834-36 reading, thinking, and writing his challenge to the epistemology of the time, *Nature.*

Prior to 1836, Emerson seems to have been viewed by his contemporaries much as one might expect: a somewhat unorthodox clergyman whose eccentricities and devotion to literature were within the bounds of acceptability for the Unitarian ministry. Joel Myerson and Robert Burkholder, in their comprehensive Emerson bibliography, have listed fifteen published works, mainly in the religious press, that speak of or implicitly refer to Emerson during the period 1829-35. Nearly all refer to ecclesiastical, literary, or civic activities that would have been well within the province of a Unitarian minister of the day. With the publication of *Nature,* attention to Emerson increased but remained within the elite circles of institutional Unitarianism and its literary adjuncts, the Harvard-dominated literary journals of the Boston area.[2] Part of a culture in which literature still functioned principally as a mode of spiritual discourse, the reviewers of *Nature* analyzed something they named philosophical and aesthetic discourse, but, clearly, they meant to read through these in order to see its religious and moral implications.[3]

Emerson emerged as a recognizable national figure in the decade and a half following the publication of *Nature* because his message shifted from being heard in religious and literary terms to being heard as discourse pertaining to something else. That something else seemed to move beyond the conventions of religious or literary discussion and provide a framework that included both. It would not be entirely accurate to call Emerson's message "secular" in contrast to "religious," since both he and his audiences perceived something spiritual in his utterances. Nor am I willing to use the term "popularization," since the process was not necessarily one of simplification and homogenization of a complex, determinate message for a non-expert audience. Rather, something happened from 1836 to 1850 that made Emerson accessible and appealing to a new audience who, because of its own circumstances, was able to hear him in a new and different way.

In lyceums and Mechanics' Institutes, knowledge that had formerly been defined only as religious, literary, or scientific began to be defined also as practical or pragmatic. The lyceum movement in its early days depended mostly on local speakers who had regional reputations. As Donald Scott has noted, early lyceum speakers were usually people with training and connections in other areas of public performance—law or the ministry, for instance—and their drawing power may have been proportional to the audience's familiarity with their other public roles.[4] Some speakers may also have been known through locally printed and distributed sermons, speeches, essays, or textbooks. Speakers not immediately familiar to the audience were probably arranged for by local ministers, lawyers, and other intellectuals, who tended to be part of networks that, in some cases, crossed regions. Emerson's course on "The Times," in New York, 1842, for instance, was arranged by his brother William, a New York lawyer. The new "popular" audience for the lyceums grew out of pre-existing networks of intellectuals who began to be heard in new contexts.[5]

The existence of a new popular press, growing in conjunction with a burgeoning commercial economy, eventually provided a vehicle that made these early word-of-mouth connections superfluous and masked the origins of the speakers in the religious or legal communities. At first, in the major publishing centers of Boston and New York, coverage of lecturers in newspapers was minimal, lest summaries of lectures steal the speaker's "product" and render it unusable with other audiences. The only evidence in the Boston *Daily Advertiser* of Emerson's lecture course on "Human Life" in Boston in the winter of 1838 took the form of paid advertisements: two in October announcing a course of "ten or more Lectures" and soliciting subscriptions; and individual announcements printed the day of each lecture, advertising its topic, time, location, and price.[6] This neglect of Emerson was neither unique nor the consequence of his late notoriety over the **"Divinity School Address."** Wendell Phillips's lecture in 1839 at the Boston Lyceum on "The History of Inventions" was announced with much the same lack of fanfare.[7]

Before long, the situation changed, at least in some newspapers. An article in the Boston *Daily Advertiser,* reprinted from the New York *Evening Post,* commented that other newspapers had responded to the public's desire for press coverage of lectures. The *Post* spoke of "the practice which certain newspapers have recently adopted, of reporting the lecture made before the different societies of the city" and felt compelled to explain why it had not covered lectures.[8] The *Post's* misgivings notwithstanding, a number of New York newspapers and literary periodicals began to afford Emerson significant coverage in the mid-1840s. New York controlled the publishing market, and what New Yorkers wrote about, other parts of the country usually read about. "The eastern papers had said much of Mr. Emerson, and we get an eastern mail every day," wrote a Cincinnati correspondent on Emerson's first visit there in 1850.[9] Perhaps the most important paper to cover lectures was Horace

Greeley's New York *Tribune,* said to be "the most influential newspaper in the country."[10] Greeley's coverage of the "isms" of the day, sensational in their own way, sold newspapers and rocketed the *Tribune* to a position of importance in the world of the New York press.[11]

In Boston, the *Daily Advertiser* wholeheartedly endorsed the New York *Evening Post's* position and refused to publish accounts of lectures. Perhaps in recognition of Emerson's rising popularity as a lecturer, it nevertheless accorded *Essays, First Series,* themselves print versions of the lectures, a lengthy front-page review.[12] This article treated Emerson as part of a literary community and evaluated *Essays* in literary terms. The review was far from flattering; the writer found Emerson's *Essays* tough, distorted, inharmonious, opaque, ponderous, and labored. Yet he expended time and attention on the book, he explained, because, "from its intellectual tendencies, it may be viewed as the representative of a class of works (chiefly of foreign importations) which have met with some success in 'Young England.'"[13]

The British connection the *Advertiser* refers to provides a second clue to the sources of Emerson's early notice as a public figure in the United States. Although Emerson had enjoyed substantial popularity among a certain group of educated, patrician, Unitarian-bred young men in New England, a transatlantic connection contributed significantly to the furthering of Emerson's reputation as a literary figure. The Boston reviewer who took Emerson to task for *Essays,* for example, began his article by noting that the preface to Emerson's book had been written by Thomas Carlyle. Emerson "is brought before the reading public by one of the 'observed' of the day," the reviewer remarked, "and may thus gain a degree of notice, which, we will venture to affirm, he would not else have attracted."[14] Emerson had done Carlyle the service of overseeing the American publication of Carlyle's works and ensuring that he received royalties for them; Carlyle in turn arranged for the publication of a British edition of 750 copies of the *Essays* and wrote a preface. The anonymous reviewer of the *Advertiser* was responding not to the American edition of Emerson's work but to the British edition, published almost half a year after its American counterpart under the patronage of an established British literary figure. The British edition of Emerson's work proved popular enough to be pirated. Beginning with the British publication of *Essays, First Series,* British periodicals began to review Emerson, frequently pairing his name with that of Carlyle. ("A Yankee pocket edition of Carlyle," some called him.)[15] Although the reviews in Great Britain were far from uniform, Emerson was generally noted, whatever his faults, to be a characteristically American product.[16]

Emerson's lecture tour of Britain in 1847-48 increased his standing as a public figure there, and British periodicals took note of him, for better or worse. The several American periodicals that reprinted British literary gleanings—the *Eclectic* or *Littell's Living Age,* for example—picked up the British literary assessments.[17] Emerson made no money from any of his books until after his celebrated tour of England; *English Traits,* published in 1850, was the first to make a profit. An anecdotal example of the role of British publicity in expanding Emerson's reputation beyond his region appears in the autobiography of Moncure Daniel Conway, the young Virginian who became Emerson's hagiographer and his publicist in Cincinnati. Studying law in Warrenton, Virginia, in December of 1847, Conway stumbled on an article about Emerson with extracts from his essays in *Blackwood's,* the Scottish literary review.[18] Conway traveled to a bookstore in Fredericksburg, where a copy of Emerson's **"Arithmetic"** was in stock but Emerson's *Essays* unheard of. Ordering a copy and remarking on his new literary find to his cousin John, Conway learned that the increased attention to Emerson had prompted John to write an article about him for the Richmond *Examiner.*[19]

Between a growing notice in the New York press, whose literary editors were often originally from New England, and a reputation in British literary periodicals, which persisted in influencing American literary opinion, Emerson's name was becoming familiar by the late 1840s to a class of readers who kept up with literary affairs. Characterization of him in the British popular press during his 1847-48 lecture tour, however, provided him with an image more readily transferable to popular American audiences. Townsend Scudder's work contains substantial evidence that the British press, in presenting Emerson to audiences of the Mechanics' Institutions, substantially de-emphasized the literary and religious aspects of his discourse in order to portray him as an already highly acclaimed American of prophetic stature. He was a man who spoke directly to the heart, not subject to the ordinary canons of logic. Both literary and religious criticism of Emerson continued to be produced, and, in fact, critics frequently evaluated his writing in either negative or decidedly mixed fashion. Even these appraisals, however, began to betray the influence of the popular press: this man was not to be evaluated strictly according to the rules defining literary or theological discussion. Rather, he was to be seen as a radical of some sort, whose message was to be judged according to some new, and as yet unarticulated, rules governing "feeling" and "spirit," and whose exemplary Americanness was defined as somehow crucial to audience reception of his message.[20]

Although dissenters and young Oxford intellectuals formed part of Emerson's audience, by far the majority of those who heard him in Mechanics' Institutions were not mechanics at all, but "clerks, shopkeepers, apprentices, &c . . . professional men, merchants, warehousemen, schoolboys."[21] The new commercial classes coalesced around Emerson despite the fact that they remained relatively oblivious to his notions of theology, metaphysics, society, and government. What such an audience made of Emerson is a perplexing question. Its primary concern lay neither with literature nor theology. Yet, to understand the making of Emerson as a "popular" intellectual, it is crucial to know the mind of his audience. Between 1840 and 1855,

Emerson began to be seen not primarily as a religious or literary figure but as something else, and the coalescence of a bourgeois mercantile audience via the press had much to do with this redefinition of role.

The importation of eastern lecturers such as Emerson in the 1850s marked a new phase of the lyceum and lecturing movement in the midwestern United States. The formation of audiences for these lecturers suggests a good deal about the ways in which the emerging American commercial classes "made" Emerson and gave a cultural imprimatur to particular aspects of his message. Over time, various parts of Emerson's message became obscured through the sheer inability of his listeners to comprehend them as relevant to their own situations. Other parts became exaggerated, probably beyond anything Emerson ever intended, as a result of the coalescing audience's ability to fit them into discourse patterns and experiences that it brought to its experience of the speaker. Emerson's audience had come to a sense of group identity long before his arrival, and hearing him seems to have played a part in heightening its self-consciousness as a group. Before examining in detail how this audience heard his message, it is important to look closely at who his listeners were and the common experience they brought to their interpreting.

Nearly every town had its own lyceum by the mid-1830s. Cincinnati's lyceum was founded in 1830, Cleveland's in 1832; the Columbus Reading Room and Institute was organized in 1835, and the one in Indianapolis sometime before that year.[22] These lyceums were part of the national movement begun by Josiah Holbrook in 1829 to promote dissemination of useful information, discussion, and debate. Lyceums began to languish within a decade, however, and were forced to change their form of organization. It was to the second form of this lyceum movement that Emerson was eventually invited to speak, and in the character of these newer organizations lie the clues to the nature of Emerson's audience in the Midwest.

Throughout the young cities of the region, Literary Societies, Young Men's Societies, and Young Men's Mercantile Libraries rapidly displaced lyceums, These new organizations were explicitly established by and for the young mercantile classes of the cities. The urban centers of the newer region contained a disproportionate number of young, unmarried men, most of whom lived in boarding houses. In Chicago in 1850, for example, 94 percent of the male population was under the age of fifty, two-thirds were under thirty, and half ranged from fifteen to twenty-nine years of age.[23] Mostly migrants from rural areas, these young clerks, salesmen, bookkeepers, and banktellers were potentially cut off from the influences of family, friends, and church that might have held them in the path of virtue at home. Many writers saw these young men in danger of slipping into vicious habits such as gambling, drinking, theater-going, brothel-visiting, and Sabbath-breaking. A steady stream of advice manuals and tracts poured forth to advise them on the formation and maintenance of character and the path to social acceptability in their new environment.[24] In the cities of the Midwest, the Young Men's Societies provided an alternative gathering-place to taverns and theaters for the young members of the mercantile class. These groups also afforded young men the opportunity to acquire the practical knowledge and debating and speaking skills necessary for social and professional advancement.[25]

The Young Men's Associations, like the lyceums themselves, were anchored in the tenets of the self-culture movement. Self-culture as an ideal originated in urban centers, from the desire of artisans and mechanics to acquire an education in practical and theoretical knowledge of scientific and technical matters. The notion of self-culture quickly took on wider implications: the apostles of the self-culture movement began to advocate the cultivation of an internalized system of morality especially fitted to the newly commercialized portions of the country, particularly, urban areas. Introspective self-examination of conduct would provide highly mobile young men of the urban centers, isolated from traditional institutional bolsters of morality, the means for maintaining character in a disorienting environment.[26] Within the philosophy, however, a tension existed: the young man had to be self-reliant and independent of external influences but only so that he could remain true to a collective standard of morality in time of trial. "Self-culture" was, in short, an articulation of the *process* whereby moral character might be maintained. The "culture" that succeeded it—and that Emerson's lecturing did its part to promote—focused on the *definition* of collective standards of morality and acceptable behavior.[27]

The self-culture movement in the Midwest was intimately linked to city boosters and businesspeople, those who had the greatest interest in maintaining moral order among the young male migrants to the city. In the Midwest, the gradual commercial development of eastern cities was compressed into a few years, as cities rapidly appeared out of the prairie. As a result of this rapid economic development, the midwestern merchants played a larger part in civic affairs than their counterparts in the East. Because the merchant—not the minister, the lawyer, the politician or the college professor—was the representative civic figure, the culture movement in the Midwest was, almost from its inception, dominated by the merchant classes.[28] Over and over in their official biographies, successful merchants had their good fortune attributed to self-education and self-culture.[29] It is not surprising that they dominated the foundation of a new lecture movement in the Midwest designed to inculcate certain moral values in their protégés. When Emerson came to Pittsburgh in 1851, merchants closed their shops early so that young clerks could go to hear him.[30] The sorts of messages he and other eastern lecturers brought to the platform fit the aims of a mercantile version of the self-culture ideal. In it, recommended activities and ways of thinking led not only to improvement of character but directly to business success.[31]

While sponsoring self-culture activities such as debating, public speaking, and literary study, the Young Men's Or-ganizations also served to consolidate the young business class of a city by introducing them to one another and giving them a common set of cultural activities that, by their very definition, built "character." The reading rooms that flourished with these organizations were regarded as "a pleasant resort and an agreeable place to introduce one's friends and also respectable strangers who visit the city."[32] These organizations provided the setting for Emerson's lectures in the Midwest during the 1850s. Although they shaped the character of popular response to him, he in his turn acted as a catalyst for the cultural consolidation already underway in the region. Emerson's reception in one important midwestern city—Cincinnati—illustrates how these business-oriented audiences helped create an Emerson in line with commercial values.[33]

The primary impetus for Emerson's first trip to Cincinnati in 1850 was literary. Emerson's reputation at this time still rested principally on his print production. In October of 1849, twelve young men—lawyers, clerks, and teachers, none of whom were over twenty-five years of age—formed the Cincinnati Literary Club. These men lived close together and gathered on Friday nights in the rooms of Ainsworth Rand Spofford, a clerk at a Cincinnati bookstore, to eat, drink, and debate slavery, the tariff, and free will. The group combined the aims of self-culture and conviviality that typically characterized Young Men's Associations. It met weekly "to promote the wider culture of our intellectual, moral, and social powers," with one night a month set aside for formal debate and another for the "Informal": songs, light verse, and drinking.[34] As was the case with Young Men's Organizations elsewhere, the young men of the Literary Club could not afford to guarantee Emerson's expenses, so they turned to the "solid men of Cincinnati," lawyers, ministers, and merchants, to underwrite his expenses. The merchants responded by pledging one hundred and fifty dollars toward the course of lectures.[35]

Emerson came to deliver his course of lectures in May of 1850, to a city decidedly unclear as to what to believe about him. He already had a large enough reputation for the *Daily Cincinnati Gazette* to note on 15 May that "the movement for a course of lectures from RALPH WALDO EMERSON, to which we alluded sometime since, has proved successful, and . . . Mr. Emerson will arrive in Cincinnati in a few days, and commence a course of five lectures here early next week." The *Gazette* thought he would have "'a few' people to hear him, at least."[36] "In this don't-care-much-for-genius sort of latitude," a Cincinnati correspondent of the Salem *Register* wrote after Emerson's first lecture, "the town was on tip-toe of 'look out' to see what kind of reception would be extended to him, what class of people would attend, and, finally, what would be thought of him. No one could come to any conclusion upon either point from what the daily papers said in advance; for it was observed that they had not been *paid* in advance, and consequently the 'Locals' were as silent as an oyster, excepting so far as they felt called upon to draw attention to his advertisement, &c.—and that, by the way, with the same adjectives that informed us that a *notable* fat boy was exhibiting at the Museum, &c."[37] For the majority of Cincinnatians outside the small literary and professional circles that issued the invitation, the popular attitude was one of wait-and-see. Emerson was but one more presumably famous name, of whom many might have heard but from whom few knew what to expect.

Press reception of Emerson on his first appearance in Cincinnati is significant both because it illustrates the process of public image-making and because it set the tone for Emerson's visits to the region throughout the decade that followed. In the race with other growing cities of the region for resources, midwestern newspapers, which were even more intimately connected with the mercantile community than those of the East, became "civic cheerleaders."[38] Extensive journalistic treatment of the individual lecturers, including Emerson, contributed toward the shaping of a corporate response to the speaker, as had been the case in Britain during Emerson's 1847-48 tour there.

By far the most common response to Emerson was to wonder why all the fuss about his transcendentalism. "Judging Mr. Emerson's matter and manner, by this single lecture," the *Gazette* reporter wrote, "we should write so differently of both, from what we have seen written by others, that the same man could not be recognized as the subject of the several descriptions . . . [H]e is so far, in his intellectual and oratorical lineaments, from resembling the newspaper portraits above which we have at various times seen his name written, that we half incline to think the wrong man has come along, and attempted to play off a hoax upon us backwoods people." "Gothamite scribes have certainly mistaken Mr. Emerson for somebody else, and given descriptions of him which will not be recognized in this region," the *Gazette* concluded, referring to descriptions of Emerson that emphasized his religious deviation and his impractical and unintelligible philosophy.[39] Another reviewer, "perfectly satisfied by the Lecture of Wednesday evening," insisted that "a great deal more nonsense has been written about him by Gilfillan and others, than they have written about other people." George Gilfillan reviewed Emerson in 1848 for *Tait's Magazine,* a British periodical, and the *Gazette* reviewer's familiarity with the British review is perhaps as significant as his disagreement with Gilfillan, who attacked Emerson for triteness, mistiness, and worship of man disguised as nature.[40]

Although Cincinnatians persisted in looking for evidence of Emerson's vaunted unorthodoxy and fuzzy philosophical doctrines, they could not find it. "In that portion of the discourse which might be placed under the didactic head," wrote the correspondent for the Cincinnati *Daily Commercial,* after Emerson's second lecture, "no theory was introduced which would appear to present the lecturer in the character of a 'new light.'" He was "as unpretending as . . . a good old grandfather over his Bible," the *Gazette* reported, and "his most remarkable trait is that of plain *common sense.*" The *Columbian and Great West* reported that "the *transcendentalism* didn't come, longingly as we

looked for it from the beginning, and stoutly as many, who professed to have heard the course before, declared that it would be along by-and-by." When Emerson's planned course of lectures met with success, he was persuaded to give a second course of three, **"The Natural History of Intellect," "The Identity of Thought with Nature,"** and **"Instinct and Inspiration."** In these, it was judged, "our people will get something more of what is *peculiar* in Mr. Emerson's mind, and philosophical views, than was obtained from the first course." Still, newspapers found no sign of a threatening religion or philosophy.[41]

A comparison of the print essays **"Aristocracy," "Eloquence," "Books,"** and **"Instinct and Inspiration"** with reportage of the lectures that formed their basis offers some idea of what Emerson's audiences thought they heard if it was not transcendentalism. It is noteworthy that in none of his lectures of the first course did Emerson speak directly about religious or philosophical opinion as he had in lectures of the late 1830s and early 1840s. Rather, he adapted his philosophy to the needs of the popular audience by choosing topics that communicated through concrete and homely metaphors his attitude toward these subjects without ever approaching them directly. His audience believed itself to be getting "common sense, humor, and truth; the second time, humor, truth, and common sense; the third time, truth, common sense, and humor."[42] The texts of the essays show that the audiences of the lectures were still receiving, albeit indirectly, the characteristic Emersonian depiction of the universe as a series of laws that transcended social convention, tradition, or proscriptive statute. In other words, Emerson's underlying philosophy and his religious stance in these lectures had not changed substantially from the more controversial **Nature** and **"Divinity School Address,"** but Emerson was no longer explicitly using the languages of philosophy or religion to make his points.

By applying those laws to subjects that were ostensibly nonpolitical and nonreligious, Emerson seemed to his listeners to be merely passing along practical advice on practical subjects—the epitome of self-culture. In Cincinnati, the talks that received the most enthusiastic responses included **"Eloquence"** and **"England." "Eloquence"** contained what conventionally came to be called "gems" or "pearls of wisdom": aphoristic sayings that encapsulated the practical laws of human life in a novel way. **"England"** was praised as "one of the most graphic and interesting pieces of descriptive narration that we have listened to."[43] It was treated as a catalogue of observations rather than as a coherent piece of thought. If the audience was pleased by Emerson's "common sense," it was because his compelling images drawn from everyday life could be understood in a practical, materialist way as well as in the metaphorical, idealist sense in which Emerson probably intended them. Emerson "don't *say* at all—he *hints* or *intimates* or walks around about what he *would* say but *don't* say," the young Rutherford B. Hayes, a member of the Cincinnati Literary Club, astutely observed in a letter to a friend.[44]

Ironically, one of the least successful of Emerson's lectures in Cincinnati was concerned with literary culture itself, the area in which Emerson had presumably made his mark. **"Books"** was pronounced "above the range and without the best of the great majority of the auditory." His lectures on **"The Natural History of the Intellect,"** of a more overtly philosophical character, were "of too abstruse a nature, and altogether too comprehensive in their method, to be characterized in a newspaper paragraph or two, at all events from a single hearing." **"Instinct and Inspiration,"** which the printed text shows to be one of the most overtly philosophical and least anecdotal of his lectures, flowed right past the audience. It was what the British and American reviewers would have called "misty"; the Cincinnati audience, at least, the commercial elements of it whose opinions tended to be reflected in newspapers, were by that time prepared for a frontier philosopher rather than a dangerous transcendentalist. Listeners found the lecture difficult and waited for something more to their liking. As Emerson's lectures grew more philosophical and the novelty of having him in town wore off, attendance at his lectures fell.[45]

Throughout the 1850s, midwestern newspapers that reported on Emerson's discourses exhibited some difficulty in summarizing his lectures as coherent wholes. Although audiences were described as "strongly impressed" or "profoundly attentive," reporters often found it "impossible to give a synopsis of the lecture," no matter how favorably impressed.[46] The organizing principles escaped them. Of **"The Conduct of Life"** in Cincinnati in 1857, for example, the *Daily Enquirer's* front-page story stated: "The lecture was listened to with profound attention, though, from its epigrammatic and somewhat abrupt and disconnected style, it was a matter of extreme difficulty to follow the thread of the discourse."[47] Rutherford Hayes's description of his impression of an Emerson lecture echoes the responses of most newspaper reviewers. "Logic and method, he has none," Hayes wrote, "but his bead-string of suggestions, fancies, ideas, anecdotes, and illustrations, delivered in a subdued, earnest manner, is as effective in chaining the attention of his audience as the most systematic discourse could be."[48] Emerson's philosophy of composition, natural law, and organic growth are clearly articulated elsewhere, and his treatment of individual subjects in the western lectures are without a doubt illustrative of his philosophical framework as he had sketched it in earlier writings. Because he focused on concrete topics for the popular audience, however, the system behind the anecdotes remained implicit and suggestive rather than explicit and logically developed. Audiences frequently reached the conclusion that, in his talks, there was no point at all.

When reporters did summarize Emerson's lectures for their readers, the result was frequently a disjointed series of remotely connected sentences. The following selection, taken from the Cincinnati *Gazette's* summary in 1852 of Emerson's **"Wealth,"** conveys some of the difficulty listeners had in finding an overarching framework in which to put Emerson's anecdotes and aphorisms:

One of the most natural enquiries about a person, but partially known, was "what has been his *success* in life?" The first question asked with regard to a stranger is, "*How does he get his living?*" All men are consumers, and all ought to be producers. Man is an expensive animal and ought to be rich. Wealth has its source in the application of mind to nature. The most intimate ties subsist between thought and nature. The art of getting rich consists, not in industry, but in being at the right spot for such getting, and in the right application of forces. Steam was as abundant 100 years ago as now, but it was not put to so good a use as now. (Applause.) The grass and wheat rots in Michigan, until the active men screw steam power to that hay and flour and whirl it into New York and London. Coals have been rightly called black diamonds. Coal is a portable climate and transports itself. (Applause.) But coal and water were useless in England, till Watt and Stephenson and Brunel came, and then how quickly transformed to wealth![49]

This summary also affords an interesting comparison of what the audiences heard and what the speaker actually said. The essay **"Wealth"** from *The Conduct of Life* parallels the lecture in every respect, yet it is fascinating to notice how the newspaper interpretation compares with this printed text:

As soon as a stranger is introduced into any company, one of the first questions which all wish to have answered, is, How does that man get his living? And with reason. He is no whole man until he knows how to earn a blameless livelihood. Society is barbarous until every industrious man can get his living without dishonest customs.

Every man is a consumer, and ought to be a producer. He fails to make his place good in the world unless he not only pays his debt but also adds something to the common wealth. Nor can he do justice to his genius without making some larger demand on the world than a bare subsistence. He is by constitution expensive, and needs to be rich.

Wealth has its source in applications of the mind to nature, from the rudest strokes of spade and axe up to the last secrets of art. Intimate ties subsist between thought and all production; because a better order is equivalent to vast amounts of brute labor. The forces and the resistances are nature's, but the mind acts in bringing things from where they abound to where they are wanted; in wise combining; in directing the practice of the useful arts, and in the creation of finer values by fine art, by eloquence, by song, or the reproduction of memory. Wealth is in applications of mind to nature; and the art of getting rich consists not in industry, much less in saving, but in a better order, in timeliness, in being at the right spot. One man has stronger arms or longer legs; another sees by the course of streams and growth of markets where land will be wanted, makes a clearing to the river, goes to sleep and wakes up rich. Steam is no stronger now than it was a hundred years ago; but it is put to better use. A clever fellow was acquainted with the expansive force of steam; he also saw the wealth of wheat and grass rotting in Michigan. Then he cunningly screws on the steam-pipe to the wheat-crop. Puff now, O Steam! The steam puffs and expands as before, but this time is dragging all Michigan at its back to hungry New York and hungry England.[50]

Some immediately apparent differences between the two texts include a treatment of material facts (steam, wheat, grass, coal) as a more prominent part of the message in the lecture summary and as the substance of the message rather than as illustrative of higher theory. The audience appears to have been expecting instruction in empirical truth, and that is what they found in Emerson's address. The applause would indicate that the audience responded more readily to the illustrations than to the point of those illustrations: that wealth, both material and moral, consists in the discovery of a "better order" to the one currently in use. Moreover, the newspaper's concern with success is as a how-to proposition rather than as a moral issue having a bearing on one individual's relationship to the social order. For Emerson, the issue is how "every industrious man can get his living without dishonest customs." For the reviewer, it is merely the issue of getting a living. Finally, the newspaper account flattens the double sense of Emerson's utterances. "Every man is a consumer, and ought to be a producer," says Emerson, echoing themes introduced in **"The American Scholar,"** the **"Divinity School Address,"** *Nature,* and **"Self-Reliance."** In the newspaper summary, the question becomes purely a material one. Emerson's "He is by constitution expensive, and *needs* to be rich," becomes "Man is an expensive animal and *ought* to be rich" (emphasis added). For Emerson, "rich" stands as material metaphor for a spiritual and moral state; in the context in which the reviewer places it, it seems to have predominantly material and economic references.

Emerson meant to inculcate moral reformation through his lecture topics, and he proposed to draw in his audience through a choice of topics that seemed familiar and practical. Some of the titles in his western course, **"The Conduct of Life,"** indicate the nature of the audience to whom he was accommodating himself stylistically—**"Power," "Wealth,"** and **"Culture."** Each title can be read as praise of the commercial culture as practiced in the United States or, as Emerson intended, a subtle indictment of its shortcomings. Emerson's attempt to restructure his mercantile audience's vision of the institutions they were creating to define their lives might easily be mistaken for endorsement of the existing order. For example, when Emerson says in his lecture on **"Power"** that "life is a search after power," the audience who heard common sense but no organizing idea may have interpreted the comment as sanction for an aggressive economic expansionism they could readily recognize as a part of their current practice. The organizing idea of the lecture is, however, Emerson's advocacy of a power that derives from a moral understanding of the laws of nature and a "sympathy with the course of things."[51] His larger message has little to do with economics. His analogies, which include much practical advice to young men, are nevertheless taken from the realm of affairs with which his audience was familiar—business.

Emerson may have been systematically misconstrued by his audience. Several instances of newspaper reportage of lectures reveal the same tendencies as are apparent in the Cincinnati *Gazette's* report on **"Wealth"**: a summary of the individual propositions from the lecture without a sense of underlying structure, an inclination to take Emerson's statements at face value as common sense, and a failure to acknowledge Emerson's reasoning by analogy from the material to the moral sphere.[52] Other newspapers flatly refused to summarize Emerson's discourses and explained their failure to do so in terms that are very suggestive of misunderstanding. The Alton *Weekly Telegraph* (Illinois) is a case in point: "Concerning the matter of Mr. Emerson's lectures, we shall not attempt to speak, as a synopsis of anything so closely condensed would be almost impossible. Each sentence seemed separate and distinct, perfect in itself. On his views, however, of culture, that of polishing our manners so as to suppress all natural and spontaneous emotions—making men mere cultivated automatons—was rather in advance of his audience. They may be capable of being educated to such a point;—but we question its desirability."[53] The irony is, so did Emerson. The discussion either obscures or distorts Emerson's point; from the summary, it is not entirely clear which.

Audience claims that Emerson used no logic in constructing his lectures appear to have been another way of saying that his mercantile audiences could not see the logical structure of the discourses. Stephen Toulmin has analyzed the structure of an argument as consisting of claims (assertions about what is true), grounds (the underlying foundation that assures the claim to be solid and reliable), and warrants (the connection that exists between ground and claim).[54] Emerson's warrant for the assertions of his "common sense" lectures was the radically idealist cosmology sketched out in *Nature* and further elaborated in the spoken and published lectures of the early period. Whatever language or analogies he employed to reach his audience, he saw himself as preaching a message of moral reform whose warrant was a unique spiritual understanding of nature and nature's laws. His audience heard the warrant to be a set of already familiar, pragmatic, common-sense rules for attaining individual financial and social success. The Emerson whose anecdotes and aphorisms are understood but whose larger method is not becomes the epitome of the commercial values prized by the audiences who invited him.

Often presented in the same lecture series with such pragmatic materialists as P. T. Barnum, Emerson's lectures resembled in import, if not in style, Barnum's "Art of Money-Getting," or "Success in Life."[55] Emerson's presence and message became implicated in the expansion of the commercial culture that sponsored his visits. As the lecture system of which he was part became more solidly entwined with the making of the urban commercial order, his lecture performances came to be part of a canon of acquired learning that defined the parameters of knowledge and behavior within the new international bourgeois way of life, and he himself the representative *par excellence* of "culture."

Emerson lecturing in Concord during a meeting of the Summer School of Philosophy.

The transition in the Midwest from institutions for self-culture to institutions for the spread of culture can be seen in microcosm in the transformation of the lecture into a form of popular entertainment. The process mirrored a larger one, in which "culture" was becoming a form of consumption necessary for the maintenance of one's class standing. Although originating in the ideals of personal empowerment implicit in the self-culture movement, the new culture industry was signaled by appreciation of emerging icons of culture who apparently supported mercantile values. Emerson's reputation as American prophet became firmly established in tandem with the rise of a national culture industry that created and perpetuated obedience to social hierarchy.[56] Speakers like Emerson began to be publicized in newspapers and competed with the theater, concerts, panoramas, and wax museums for public audiences. Lecturers were introduced to the public in the same way as other performers.

One criterion that audiences increasingly used to evaluate the worth of performers was the national or international reputation of the performer or amusement in question. P. T. Barnum's extraordinary engineering of a public reception for Jenny Lind in the United States in 1850 illustrates the influence that journalistic coverage of a public figure could have on a career. Barnum distributed widely a biography of Lind emphasizing her international fame, her piety, character, and philanthropy. Crowds who had not heard of her a few months before mobbed her upon arrival in New York. "All of this extraordinary enthusiasm . . . had developed before Jenny Lind had sung a note in America," wrote Neil Harris. "In a sense the musical performances, tumultuously received as they were, formed only an anticlimax."[57]

Lind's remarkable success as a result of Barnum's promotion was one version of a national trend toward celebrity-making, which capitalized on gossipy anecdotes designed to reveal the inmost characters of performers. As Emerson entered a company of "distinguished performers and well known names" in Cincinnati, for example, he began to receive a familiar kind of attention in the local press heretofore rare. One "Anecdote of Mr. Emerson" the *Gazette* published during Emerson's visit to the city depicted Emerson as at once disingenuous, familiar, and eccentric—in short, as a "personality." His journal was called "a kind of intellectual and scientific rag-bag" in the popular press, his wife an amazed observer of a genius she little understood. The significance of stories such as these lies not so much in any real information they imparted to audiences as in the way their personification of Emerson and performers like him met the needs of audiences for personalities (not belief systems) with whom to identify and on whom to model themselves.[58]

Newspapers began to comment frequently on the physical appearance of the speaker as if it were equal in importance to anything he might say. Emerson surprised audiences with his gaunt and homely appearance, his narrow forehead, and his long, hooked nose. In his habitual "plain suit of ill-fitting black," he was "not unlike a New England schoolmaster." He was by turns bashful, ungraceful, embarrassed, and half-apologetic, but each designation only added to his mystique as an uncalculating soul of pure wisdom and character. "He rarely looks his hearers full in the face," the *Gazette* observed, "but at emphatic expression has a habit of turning his eyes backward as if to look in at himself." Here was no trickster or partisan but a single-hearted purveyor of truth.[59]

Response to great individuals became the index of culture in a city, and evidences of "cultured" responses to them became in turn proof of the speaker's own worthiness. The newspapers announced one of a new course of Emerson lectures in 1857 with the assurance that it had been "delivered with great effect before a very cultivated Boston audience." In Chicago, in February of 1854, the *Tribune* prepared the city for Emerson's arrival by reprinting a laudatory excerpt about him from the *Edinburgh Review,* for Chicago, a foreign literary journal of impeccable reputation. Such notices served a dual function: while drumming up interest in a particular speaker, they also reaffirmed for booster-conscious cities their connection with a larger world of "culture" outside the region. Awareness and appreciation of people who had captivated the better sort of audiences elsewhere testified to the tone and quality of the city itself.[60]

The emphasis on a speaker's wide reputation enabled the promoters to clear a profit and established the city's claim to fame as a member of the cultural *avant-garde* but led to the demise of speakers of purely local reputation. As a city's participation in a national system of culture grew, local notables declined in status and authority on the lecture circuit. When the Reverend Francis Vinton of New York came to Cincinnati to lecture on "The Gentlewoman," the *Enquirer* regretted the small crowd in attendance. "The reverend lecturer has not the particular kind of notoriety which, we regret to say, is most attractive here." Cincinnati's own Rev. C. M. Butler lectured on "Sir Philip Sidney" in his home city, and the *Enquirer* took the opportunity to fulminate on the pervasiveness of the celebrity lecture system and its "imported trash."[61] So prevalent did well-known, highly paid speakers become on the western lecture circuit that some newspapers began self-consciously to try to stem the tide and restore the old regional system. In 1855, the Sandusky *Register* and the *Genius of the West* both published lists of western lecturers in the hope that the region would begin to employ its own.[62] They were not successful. Westerners continued for the most part to look to those of established reputation, that is, to easterners, to occupy their lecture platforms.

Along with describing visiting speakers in inflated terms, newspapers offered glowing descriptions of the audiences who partook of the high-toned intellectual fare. The more famous the speaker, the more elaborate the description of the audience. "The audience to-night will no doubt be the most brilliant and fashionable that has been drawn together for some time," ran the announcement of a Cincinnati concert of Ole Bull, a Norwegian violinist of renown, and Maurice Strakosch, a pianist, in 1852. Theodore Parker's fame attracted "the select many" to his lecture on "The Progress of Mankind." With Emerson, the praise awarded the audience grew with his national reputation. His first course of lectures in Cincinnati in 1850 attracted an "audience intellectual as well as large." "The literati and the fashion of our Queen city" were expected in December of 1852.[63] By 1857, Emerson's lectures were "largely and brilliantly attended," and it was apparent to the reviewer that "the intellectual aristocracy of the city has seldom been so well represented as in this audience." In Milwaukee, too, Emerson's audience was certified "very large and brilliant." After the Civil War, when Emerson had become a household word as literary figure and popular lecturer, newspaper accounts increasingly congratulated audiences on their wisdom in appreciating such a great man, "The literary public of Cincinnati honored themselves last night, in honoring perhaps the finest scholar and most profound thinker of the country," the *Gazette* reported in the first sentence of its review. "The most elegant assemblages we remember to have seen on any occasion in this city" welcomed him. When Emerson gave his final lecture in Chicago in 1871, it was the audience reaction, not the quality of the lecture, that was at issue. "It is needless to say that it [the lecture] was well received. The applause was discreetly timed, and bespoke the culture of the audience."[64]

The press continually reinforced the renown of the speaker before, during, and after his arrival and thus promoted the notion that the audience was cultured and brilliant. The "justly celebrated Emerson" was praised; journalists were certain that "the fame of the lecturer will undoubtedly draw a crowded hall"; "the poet and philosopher, who is universally recognized as one of the great thinkers of the age" was coming to speak.[65] This newspaper promotion could not have created talent where there was none, but it did establish a cycle whereby the repute of the speaker drew self-defined "intellectual" and "cultivated" audiences, and "cultivation" itself began to be defined as attendance on and acquaintance with certain famous cultural figures. Self-culture, the active expansion of one's faculties and the promoting of self-awareness, was becoming transformed into culture, the conspicuous consumption of the performances of people who were nationally and internationally defined as important intellectuals. Emerson became one of the first symbols of this culture, newly defined as the awareness and mastery of a certain body of knowledge. Culture was a state to be achieved, a status to be acquired, no longer a process of self-awareness and introspection.[66]

Emerson the public personality contributed to a national system of culture that was effectually the consumption of well-known texts and performances. Indeed, his lectures, in an oft-repeated phrase, came to be known as "intellectual treats," tidbits of wisdom dispensed by the wise man to the public at large. Thomas Wentworth Higginson perhaps best expressed this representative image Emerson had come to hold for most midwesterners as he repeated the assessment of a booking agent for western tours: Emerson's continued popularity rested "not on the ground that the people understand him, but that 'they think such men ought to be encouraged.'"[67] "He impresses one with the idea of long years of study, of many nights of toil, of incessant diligence in the fields of art, science and literature," another commented.[68] Emerson had become the professional embodiment of Man Thinking, the archetype set forth in his own **"American Scholar"** address of 1837. Ironically, however, in becoming a representative man, he seemed set apart, superhuman—no longer an inspiration to individual thought but an embodiment of the best that had already been thought and was known to be true. As Emerson himself remarked of Horace Greeley, the people liked him because he did their thinking for them.[69]

Nearly half a century after Emerson's decade of western lecturing, Thorstein Veblen observed that, in all known civilizations, the people place an esoteric knowledge of truth and reality in the keeping of a select body of specialists; scientists, scholars, savants, clerks, priests, shamans, folk healers. "In the apprehension of the group in whose life and esteem it lives and takes effect," Veblen wrote, "this esoteric knowledge is taken to embody a systematization of fundamental and eternal truth; although it is evident to any outsider that it will take its character and its scope from the habits of life of the group, from the institutions with which it is bound in a web of give and take."[70] Even though Emerson had not necessarily intended to do so, even though, in fact, such a system of culture as an end in itself was at odds with some of the cardinal tenets of his philosophy, he became its high priest. By 1860, it was generally agreed that Emerson was "one of the most remarkable men in America." He embodied values that his audience took to be vital to their way of life. He was "original, self-reliant, bold in thought and utterance," yet he seemed to threaten none of the customs or institutions that had become comfortable. He was "unpretending and simple in manners," yet he became a standard by which to measure one's own intellectual and moral sophistication. "He says many things that the majority of people either misunderstand or intelligently disapprove," yet his audience could tell, from his impeccable character and apparent approval of the mores of society—of wealth, power, aristocracy—that he did not really mean these things.[71] He became the image of the seer and prophet whose double-edged moral message could be taken materially if it made more sense to do so. The embodiment of the democratic scholar, he helped to consolidate for an economically defined community a notion of culture that reinforced boundaries between the cultivated and the uncultivated. He represented the paradox of a dominant culture that claimed to be dedicated to self-improvement but that increasingly took self-improvement to mean adherence to an ever-more-clearly defined body of standards and behaviors sanctioned by the mercantile and professional groups who sponsored him.

Emerson could become this powerful national symbol because the structure of the lecture system encouraged speakers and audiences alike to view what happened on the lecture platform as unbiased and apolitical.[72] The moral knowledge dispensed from the platform by the guileless speaker could shape a national consensus. Especially in the Midwest, where the proliferation of religious denominations provided some measure of ideological division, Emerson's ideas were bled of any philosophical, political, or religious implications and used as the basis for a secular faith that focused on a materially defined progress, unlimited wealth, and conspicuous social achievement within the framework of a stable and proscriptive set of moral values. If professional and mercantile people dominated the values of this new consensus, if the moral orientation of the mercantile community and its Young Men's Associations was generalized and taken to be impartial and unbiased knowledge, it was not through hypocrisy. The intentions of the groups were sincere, even if the result was to extend their own hegemony over American culture as a whole.

Certainly, this is not the whole story of Emerson or the whole story of what audiences made of him. There remains the question of what he may have thought of his audience's misapprehension of him. In general, he seems to have believed that a person had to speak the truth and maintain a studied oblivion toward what hearers might or might not make of it.[73] Other audiences contested for the right to interpret his words definitively, among them, religious scholars, philosophers, literary critics, historians, and radical reformers, who did not cease to appropriate his discourse to their own ends, despite the popular triumph of the mercantile Emerson. Because he claimed to speak a truth that transcended context, Emerson may also be a particularly blatant example of the process by which an intellectual may be "made" by the interpretive stance of a specific discourse community. With other intellectuals, the process may not be nearly so clear cut.

A view of the mercantile Emerson nevertheless helps sort out many of the apparent contradictions within Emerson scholarship, as scholars may belong to more than one discourse community at a time. It reminds us that there is one Emerson but many discourse communities to hear his message. It is not only the speaker who represents a battleground in which conflicting cultural tensions or differing discourse communities strive for reconciliation; the text itself is debated and interpreted by various publics. Groups that are catalyzed into new forms of self-consciousness as a result of hearing texts that resonate for them receive ways not only of naming the world for themselves but also of seeming to share a common vision with others who share the text. No matter that the same words may be recognized in a wholly different way by other communities of listeners or readers. If Emerson has come down to us as a cultural prophet, it is not necessarily evidence that we all share a common culture founded on a common intellectual philosophy—only that the words themselves are common to enough cultural groups that we are willing to overlook the sometimes radically different ways in which we hear them.

Notes

1. Perry Miller, "From Edwards to Emerson," *New England Quarterly,* 13 (1940): 589-617; F. O. Matthiessen, *American Renaissance: Art and Expression in the Age of Emerson and Whitman* (New York, 1941); Stanley M. Elkins, *Slavery: A Problem in American Institutional and Intellectual Life* (Chicago, 1976). For a variety of views on Emerson spanning 150 years, see *Critical Essays on Ralph Waldo Emerson,* Robert E. Burkholder and Joel Myerson, eds. (Boston, 1983). Some of the major biographies of Emerson include Ralph L. Rusk, *The Life of Ralph Waldo Emerson* (New York, 1949); Joel Porte, *Representative Man: Ralph Waldo Emerson in His Time* (New York, 1979); Maurice Gonnaud, *Individu et société dans l'oeuvre de Ralph Waldo Emerson* (Paris, 1964); Stephen E. Whicher, *Freedom and Fate: An Inner Life of Ralph Waldo Emerson* (Philadelphia, Pa., 1953); Gay Wilson Allen, *Waldo Emerson: A Biography* (New York, 1981); and John McAleer. *Ralph Waldo Emerson: Days of Encounter* (Boston, 1984).

2. Robert E. Burkholder and Joel Myerson, *Emerson: An Annotated Secondary Bibliography* (Pittsburgh, Pa., 1985).

3. See Burkholder and Myerson, *Bibliography,* 12-27; and selected reactions to *Nature* in *Emerson's Nature—Origin, Growth, Meaning,* Merton M. Sealts, Jr., and Alfred R. Ferguson, eds. (New York, 1969), 74-110.

4. Donald M. Scott, "The Popular Lecture and the Creation of a Public in Mid-Nineteenth-Century America," *Journal of American History,* 66 (1980): 791-809. On the lyceum movement, see Carl Bode, *The American Lyceum: Town Meeting of the Mind* (New York, 1956); and David Mead, *Yankee Eloquence in the Middle West: The Ohio Lyceum, 1850-1870* (East Lansing, Mich., 1951).

5. Until 1835, even publication was predominantly a local matter, with few materials marketed outside the area where the bookseller had printed and bound them. Of the lecturers during the first decade of the lyceum in Salem, Massachusetts, for example, fewer than half resided in Salem itself. The rest included locally prominent politicians, ministers, and college professors, such as William Sullivan, Edward and Alexander H. Everett, and Henry Ware, Jr. See William Charvat, "James T. Fields and the Beginnings of Book Promotion, 1840-1855," *Hun-*

tington Library Quarterly, 8 (1944-45): 76; and *Historical Sketch of the Salem Lyceum, with a List of the Officers and Lectures since its Formation in 1830* (Salem, Mass., 1879), rpt. in Kenneth Walter Cameron, ed., *The Massachusetts Lyceum during the American Renaissance* (Hartford, Conn., 1969), 15-17.

6. *Boston Daily Advertiser,* 21, 22, and 26 October 1838.

7. *Boston Daily Advertiser,* 21 February 1839.

8. To publish accounts of lectures, or even to describe the lecturer so as possibly to misrepresent him, the *Post* argued, was tantamount to robbing him of his daily bread, because it precluded his right to give the lecture again and to receive remuneration for it. Excerpts from this article are reprinted in the *Boston Daily Advertiser and Patriot,* 7 December 1841.

9. *Salem Register* (Massachusetts), 3 June 1850, p. 2, rpt. in Kenneth Walter Cameron, ed., *Literary Comment in American Renaissance Newspapers* (Hartford, Conn., 1977), 19.

10. William Alexander Linn, *Horace Greeley* (New York, 1912), 71.

11. Emerson met Greeley in 1842; throughout the decade, Greeley published sympathetic reports of what had come to be called "transcendentalism." In 1844, Emerson's stock undoubtedly rose further as Greeley hired Margaret Fuller as his regular literary editor. Her first piece for the *Tribune* was a review of Emerson's *Essays, Second Series.* George Ripley, late of Brook Farm, followed her as the *Tribune's* literary critic in 1849. See Linn, *Horace Greeley,* 71-109; Greeley, *Recollections of a Busy Life* (New York, 1869), 169-91; James Parton, *The Life of Horace Greeley* (Boston, 1855), 219-28; and Glyndon G. Van Deusen, *Horace Greeley: Nineteenth-Century Crusader* (Philadelphia, Pa., 1953). Charvat indicated that, during the period of the commercialization of the book trade (1840-55), an author's "literary and social contacts"—and those of the publisher—were instrumental in getting books reviewed in the popular press ("Fields and the Beginnings of Book Promotion," 77-78). Hence the contact of Emerson's friends with the influential world of New York periodicals seems particularly significant. Charvat's *Literary Publishing in America, 1790-1850* (Philadelphia, Pa., 1959) provides a fuller description of the way in which publishing networks in the United States operated during this period.

12. *Boston Daily Advertiser,* 7 December 1841.

13. *Boston Daily Advertiser,* 16 December 1841.

14. *Boston Daily Advertiser,* 16 December 1841.

15. See, for example, George Gilfillan, "Ralph Waldo Emerson; or The 'Coming Man,'" *Tait's Magazine,* rpt. in *Littell's Living Age,* 17 (April 1848). This

article is in turn reprinted in Kenneth Walter Cameron, ed., *Emerson among His Contemporaries* (Hartford, Conn., 1967), 15-19.

16. In addition to Gilfillan's article, see "Emerson," *Blackwood's Magazine,* rpt. in *Eclectic Magazine,* 13 (February 1848): 145-58, in turn rpt. in Cameron, *Emerson among His Contemporaries,* 8-14; "Mr. Emerson's Lectures," *Jerrold's Newspaper,* rpt. in *The Daguerrotype,* 2 (12 August 1848): 467-73, and in Cameron, 20-24; "The Emerson Mania," *The English Review,* 12 (September 1849): 139 and following, rpt. in *The Eclectic Magazine,* 23 (December 1849): 546-53, in *Littell's Living Age,* 25 (6 April 1850): 37-38, and in Cameron, 38-39; "Review of Representative Men," *British Quarterly Review,* 11 (1 May 1850): 281-315, rpt. in *Littell's Living Age,* 26 (6 July 1850): 1-16, and in Cameron, 45-56. On the wide notice taken of Emerson in British periodicals from 1840-50, see William J. Sowder, *Emerson's Impact on the British Isles and Canada* (Charlottesville, Va., 1966), 1-28.

17. E. Douglas Branch, *The Sentimental Years, 1836-1860: A Social History* (New York, 1934), 111.

18. The article is almost certainly "Emerson," *Blackwood's Edinburgh Magazine,* 62 (December 1847): 643-57. This was the first article on Emerson published in *Blackwood's.*

19. Moncure Daniel Conway, *Autobiography, Memories and Experiences,* 2 vols. (London, 1904), 1:68-70.

20. Evidence is both summarized and quoted at length in Townsend Scudder, "Emerson's British Lecture Tour, 1847-1848," *American Literature,* 7 (1935): 166-80.

21. Robert Chambers, "Mechanics' Institutions," *Papers for the People* (Philadelphia, Pa., 1851), 3: 197-228, quoted in Scudder, "Emerson's British Lecture Tour," 35. For more extensive remarks on the nature of Emerson's British audiences, see Scudder, 15-36; see also David D. Hall, "The Victorian Connection," in *Victorian America,* Daniel Walker Howe, ed. (Philadelphia, Pa., 1976), 84.

22. John J. Rowe, "Cincinnati's Early Cultural and Educational Enterprises," *Bulletin of the Historical and Philosophical Society of Ohio,* 8 (1950): 304-06; Elbert Jay Benton, *Cultural Study of an American City: Cleveland,* Part II (Cleveland, Ohio, 1944), 38-39; William Alexander Taylor, *Centennial History of Columbus and Franklin County, Ohio,* 2 vols. (Chicago and Columbus, 1909), 1: 241; W. R. Holloway, *Indianapolis: A Historical and Statistical Sketch of the Railroad City* (Indianapolis, Ind., 1870), 50. Mead, *Yankee Eloquence,* provides the fullest account of the growth of the lecture system in Ohio.

23. Paul Boyer, *Urban Masses and Moral Order in America, 1820-1920* (Cambridge, Mass., 1978), 109.

24. See Boyer, *Urban Masses,* 108-20; Irvin G. Wyllie, *The Self-Made Man in America: The Myth of Rags to Riches* (New Brunswick, N.J., 1954), 34-54; and Karen Halttunen, *Confidence Men and Painted Women: A Study of Middle-Class Culture in America, 1830-1870* (New Haven, Conn., 1982), 1-32. On the moral dangers inherent in the theater, see Claudia D. Johnson, "That Guilty Third Tier: Prostitution in Nineteenth-Century American Theaters," in Howe, *Victorian America,* 111-20.

25. William Ellery Channing, in *Self-Culture* (1838) noted the importance of "Utterance"—not only because he considered speaking in public a prime way of improving one's intellect but also because "to have intercourse with respectable people we must speak their language." He noted that social rank and social advancement depended on this fluency. See *Self-Culture* (rpt. edn., New York, 1969), 27-28.

26. Wyllie, *Self-Made Man,* 21-54 and 94-115; and John G. Cawelti, *Apostles of the Self-Made Man* (Chicago, 1965), 39-98.

27. On character as a defense of virtue against the corrupt, see Halttunen, *Confidence Men and Painted Women,* 1-55.

28. This is not to suggest that the mercantile classes of eastern cities were not also influential in the establishment of its cultural institutions. The leisure and professional classes nevertheless seem to have been more strongly represented there than in the West. See Ronald Story, "Class and Culture in Boston: The Athenaeum, 1807-1860," *American Quarterly,* 27 (1975): 178-99. An example of mercantile leadership in cultural affairs that I take to be fairly typical in the Midwest was the organization of the St. Louis Mercantile Library Association, the organization that sponsored Emerson's visit in 1852. It was established and funded by merchants and businessmen. Convinced by mercantile journals such as *Hunt's Merchant Magazine* that their young clerks needed to be educated beyond practical matters of business to do their jobs well, merchants took pride in the "inestimable value" that the new association would offer "the young men connected with commerce" by sponsoring lectures and discussions as well as providing books. *Missouri Reporter* (St. Louis), 6 January 1846. The typical founder of the association tended to be an older and established merchant involved in business dealings with the New York financial market and with markets outside St. Louis. He had probably migrated to St. Louis in his youth in search of "a wider field of enterprise," as the stock phrase for the sort of ambition that was positively evaluated went. He looked on himself as a self-made man whose thirst for self-culture led to his success. A canny businessman as well as a morally responsible employer, he took personal responsibility for promoting the reputation of his city as a cultural center. See Brad

Luckingham. "A Note on the Significance of the Merchant in the Development of St. Louis Society as Expressed in the Philosophy of the Mercantile Library Association, 1846-1854," *Missouri Historical Review,* 57 (1963): 184-98.

29. For the St. Louis case as one example, see Richard Edwards and M. Hopewell, *Edward's Great West and Her Commercial Metropolis, Embracing a General View of the West, and a Complete History of St. Louis, from the Landing of Ligueste, in 1764, to the Present Time* (St. Louis, Mo., 1860), 389, which lists thirty-six individuals instrumental in the establishment of the Mercantile Library Association.

30. Anne Louise Hastings, "Emerson's Journal at the West, 1850-1853" (Ph.D. dissertation, Indiana University, 1942), 8.

31. This is the traditional notion of the self-made man, as opposed to the ideal of self-culture. It is discussed at length in Wyllie, *Self-Made Man*; and Cawelti, *Apostles of the Self-Made Man.*

32. Taylor, *Centennial History,* 241.

33. Although the responses to Emerson's visits to Cincinnati had at times their own character, they are, so far as I can tell, fairly typical of the range of reaction he received elsewhere in the region. I base this judgment mainly on a wealth of accounts of Emerson's lecture tours in the Middle West and his reception there that rely heavily on local periodicals for documentation: Mead, *Yankee Eloquence,* 24-61; Willard Thorpe, "Emerson on Tour," *Quarterly Journal of Speech,* 16 (1930): 19-34; Samuel P. Orth, *A History of Cleveland, Ohio,* 3 vols. (Chicago and Cleveland, 1910), 1: 491-93; Owen Philip Hawley, *Orient Pearls at Random Strung: Mr. Emerson Comes to Marietta* (Marietta, Ohio, 1967); C. J. Wasung, "Emerson Comes to Detroit," *Michigan History Magazine,* 29 (1945): 59-72; Russel B. Nye, "Emerson in Michigan and the Northwest," *Michigan History Magazine,* 26 (1942): 159-72; Donald F. Tingley, "Ralph Waldo Emerson on the Illinois Lecture Circuit," *Journal of the Illinois State Historical Society,* 64 (1971): 192-205; Paul Russell Anderson, "Quincy, An Outpost of Philosophy," *Journal of the Illinois State Historical Society,* 34 (1941): 54-57; Robert R. Hubach, "Illinois, Host to Nineteenth Century Authors," *Journal of the Illinois State Historical Society,* 38 (1945): 454-59; Hubert H. Hoeltje, "Ralph Waldo Emerson in Iowa," *Iowa Journal of History and Politics,* 25 (1927): 236-76; Hubert H. Hoeltje, "Notes on the History of Lecturing in Iowa, 1855-1885," *Iowa Journal of History and Politics,* 25 (1927): 62-131; Luella M. Wright, "Culture through Lectures," *Iowa Journal of History and Politics,* 38 (1940): 115-62; Brad Luckingham, "The Pioneer Lecturer in the West: A Note on the Appearance of Ralph Waldo Emerson in St. Louis, 1852-1853," *Missouri Historical Review,* 58 (1963): 70-88; "Emerson in In-dianapolis," *Indiana History Bulletin,* 30 (1953): 115-16; Lynda Beltz, "Emerson's Lectures in Indianapolis," *Indiana Magazine of History,* 60 (1964): 269-80; Hubert H. Hoeltje, "Emerson in Minnesota," *Minnesota History,* 11 (1930): 145-59; and C. E. Schorer, "Emerson and the Wisconsin Lyceum," *American Literature,* 24 (1953): 462-75. Louise Hastings, "Emerson in Cincinnati," *New England Quarterly,* 11 (1930): 443-69, focuses on Emerson's reception in this city.

34. Cincinnati Literary Club, Minutes, vol. 1, MS., Cincinnati Public Library. On the Cincinnati Library Club, see Hastings, "Emerson's Journal at the West," 6-7; James Albert Green, *The Literary Club and Cincinnati in 1849* (Cincinnati, Ohio, 1931), 3; and Eslie Asbury, "The Literary Club," *Cincinnati Historical Society Bulletin,* 32 (1974): 105-21.

35. Ainsworth Rand Spofford, "Address Delivered at the Literary Club's 50th Anniversary," *Minutes of the Literary Club,* 28 October 1899, quoted in Hastings, "Emerson in Cincinnati," 443.

36. *Daily Cincinnati Gazette,* 15 May 1850.

37. *Salem Register,* 3 June 1850.

38. Carl Abbott, *Boosters and Businessmen: Popular Economic Thought and Urban Growth in the Antebellum Middle West* (Westport, Conn., 1981), 39. On the booster mentality on the midwestern frontier, see also Don Harrison Doyle, *The Social Order of a Frontier Community: Jacksonville, Illinois, 1825-70* (Urbana, Ill., 1978), 62-91.

39. "Emerson's Lectures," *Daily Cincinnati Gazette,* 22 May 1850.

40. *Daily Cincinnati Gazette,* 24 May 1850.

41. *Cincinnati Daily Commercial,* 23 May 1850; *Daily Cincinnati Gazette,* 24 May 1850, *Columbian and Great West,* 1 June 1850; *Daily Cincinnati Gazette,* 30 May 1850.

42. *Columbian and Great West,* 1 June 1850.

43. *Daily Cincinnati Gazette,* 30 May 1850. For a complete text of "Eloquence," see *W* 1: 59-100.

44. *Diary and Letters of Rutherford Birchard Hayes,* Charles Richard Williams, ed., 5 vols. (Columbus, Ohio, 1922), 1: 315.

45. *Daily Cincinnati Gazette,* 30 May 1850, 3 June 1850. For the printed essay versions of these lectures, see *W* 7: 187-222 ("Books"), and 12: 65-89 ("Instinct and Inspiration").

46. *Chicago Tribune,* 23 January 1857.

47. *Cincinnati Daily Enquirer,* 28 January 1857.

48. *Diary and Letters of Hayes,* 301. For a similar reaction, see the commentary of William Cullen Bryant a decade earlier, who, as he listened to Emerson in New York, explicitly listened for transcendentalism: "In regard to the peculiar doctrines of Mr. Em-

erson, we hardly consider ourselves qualified to judge. We cannot say that we precisely apprehend what they are. Now and then, in listening to his discourses, or reading his essays, we have fancied that we caught glimpses of great and novel truths"; *New York Evening Post,* 3 March 1842, rpt. in Charles I. Glicksberg, "Bryant on Emerson the Lecturer," *New England Quarterly,* 12 (1939): 530-34.

49. *Daily Cincinnati Gazette,* 13 December 1852.

50. *W* 6: 85-86.

51. *W* 6: 55, 58.

52. Instances in which parallel texts can be compared include reportage on "Power" in the *Daily Cincinnati Gazette,* 10 December 1852, with "Power" in *The Conduct of Life (W* 6: 51-82); and a summary of "Power" in *The Illinois Journal,* 13 January 1853, rpt. in Robert R. Hubach, "Emerson's Lectures in Springfield, Illinois, in January, 1853," *American Notes and Queries,* 6 (1947): 164-67. Compare a summary of "Books" in *The Independent* (New York), 4 April 1850, with "Books" in *Society and Solitude (W* 7: 187-221). Compare "Social Aims" and "Resources," summarized in *Boston Semi-Weekly Advertiser,* 30 November 1864, with the essays of those titles in *Letters and Social Aims* (*W* 8: 77-108, 135-54). Summaries of lectures for which I have not yet 30 November 1864; "The Man of the World," *Cincinnati Daily Gazette* [same periodical as *Daily Cincinnati Gazette*], 15 March 1867; "Economy," *Daily Cincinnati Gazette,* 14 December 1852; "Culture," *Chicago Daily Tribune,* 4 February 1854.

53. 20 December 1867, rpt. in Paul O. Williams, "Emerson in Alton, Illinois", *ESQ [Emerson Society Quarterly*], 47 (1967): 98. Among those who declined to synopsize because of the "condensed nature" of the utterance were the *Daily Cincinnati Gazette,* 5 June 1850; and the *Cincinnati Daily Enquirer,* 1 February 1857.

54. Stephen Toulmin, Richard Rieke, and Allan Janik, *An Introduction to Reasoning* (New York, 1979), 25-26.

55. On Barnum, see Neil Harris, *Humbug: The Art of P. T. Barnum* (Boston, 1973), 154-58, 193-95.

56. I have borrowed the term "culture industry" from Max Horkheimer and Theodor W. Adorno, *The Dialectic of Enlightenment* (New York, 1969), 120-67.

57. Harris, *Humbug,* 121.

58. *Daily Cincinnati Gazette,* 22 November 1852; 15 December 1852. On the tendency toward the creation of media personalities, see Richard Sennett, who, in *The Fall of Public Man* (New York, 1976), made the case that, by the nineteenth century in Western culture, privatization of experience led to a distorted emphasis on personality of public figures rather than attention to their social roles.

59. *Daily Cincinnati Gazette,* 28 January 1857. Halttunen, *Confidence Men and Painted Women,* 56-152, has commented on the use of dress and mannerisms during this period to communicate an image of personal sincerity.

60. *Daily Cincinnati Gazette,* 31 January 1857; *Chicago Daily Tribune,* 4 February 1854.

61. *Cincinnati Daily Enquirer,* 25 January 1857.

62. *Sandusky Commercial Register,* 24 October 1855. Mead, *Yankee Eloquence,* 194-95, discussed the growing disenchantment with eastern lecturers by the end of the 1850s; W. H. Venable, *Beginning of Literary Culture in the Ohio Valley: Historical and Biographical Sketches* (New York, 1949), 251-53, lists the eastern and western lectures being promoted by the various factions.

63. Daily Cincinnati Gazette, 23 and 30 November 1852; 22 May 1850; and 8 December 1852. *Cincinnati Daily Times,* 8 December 1852, printed the only mixed description of an audience I have come across. The auditors were mixed in character, it observed, and "people who never had a Father, and do not possess a thousand dollars in the world to bless themselves and progeny" took the front seats.

64. *Cincinnati Daily Commercial,* 3 February 1857; *Milwaukee Daily Sentinel,* 8 February 1854; *Daily Cincinnati Gazette,* 15 March 1867; *Cincinnati Daily Commercial,* 15 March 1867; *Chicago Tribune,* 28 November 1871.

65. *Daily Cincinnati Gazette,* 10 December 1852; *Chicago Tribune,* 2 February 1854; *Cincinnati Daily Commercial,* 27 January 1857.

66. This definition of culture as acquisition of a certain body of knowledge and style is suggested by Alan Trachtenberg, *The Incorporation of America: Culture and Society in the Gilded Age* (New York, 1982), 140-81; and Burton J. Bledstein, *The Culture of Professionalism: The Middle Class and the Development of Higher Education in America* (New York, 1976), 1-45.

67. Thomas Wentworth Higginson, "The American Lecture-System," *Every Saturday,* 5 (18 April 1868): 494.

68. *Cincinnati Daily Enquirer,* 1 February 1857.

69. *Chicago Daily Tribune,* 4 February 1854.

70. Thorstein Veblen, *The Higher Learning in America: A Memorandum of the Conduct of Universities by Business Men* (New York, 1957), 1.

71. *Cincinnati Daily Gazette,* 2 February 1860.

72. The Cincinnati Young Men's Mercantile Library Association, for example, took pains to prevent discussion of anything "political" in its lecture program. Orestes Brownson caused a ruckus in 1852 when he made inflammatory remarks about Louis Kossuth. See David Mead, "Brownson and Kossuth

at Cincinnati," *Bulletin of the Historical and Philo-sophical Society of Ohio,* 7 (1949): 90-93. Henry Ward Beecher was invited to St. Louis in 1860 on the condition that he "eschew all subjects pertain-ing either to politics or religion"; *Daily Cincinnati Gazette,* 2 February 1860. He refused the invita-tion. Emerson himself received some difficulty in the press in Cincinnati after he had publicly spoken elsewhere in praise of John Brown. See *Cincinnati Daily Times,* 1 February 1860; and *Cincinnati Daily Commercial,* 2 February 1860.

73. On Emerson's attitude toward audience reception, see John H. Sloan, "'The Miraculous Uplifting': Emerson's Relationship with His Audience," *Quar-terly Journal of Speech,* 52 (1966): 10-15. Passages in Emerson's own writing that are illuminating in-clude *L* 5: 4 and *JMN* 9: 10-11, 50, 225, 258, 430; 10: 315.

Russell B. Goodman (essay date 1990)

SOURCE: "Ralph Waldo Emerson," in *American Philoso-phy and the Romantic Tradition,* Cambridge University Press, 1990, pp. 34-57.

[In the following essay, Goodman provides an overview of Emerson's philosophical beliefs as expressed in his writ-ings.]

Emerson is a direct link between American philosophy and European Romanticism. Soon after leaving his minis-try in the Unitarian church (in part because he no longer believed in the "divine authority and supernatural effi-cacy"[1] of the communion he administered), Emerson trav-eled to Europe where he met his heroes Wordsworth, Col-eridge, and Carlyle. There is little doubt of their influence on his thought or of Emerson's founding role in American Romanticism. As Harold Bloom observed, "Emerson is to American Romanticism what Wordsworth is to the British or parent version."[2]

What is less clearly established is Emerson's importance as a philosopher. His thought plays a minor role in many histories and surveys of American philosophy,[3] perhaps be-cause it has no obvious connection with the major Ameri-can movement of pragmatism. Yet one pragmatist, John Dewey, thought that Emerson was "the one citizen of the New World fit to have his name uttered in the same breath with that of Plato,"[4] and another, William James, thought enough of Emerson to deliver an address to the Emerson centenary celebrations (after rereading his entire corpus), in which he called him a "real seer . . . [who] could per-ceive the full squalor of the individual fact, but . . . also . . . the transfiguration."[5] In recent years, Stanley Cavell, Barbara Packer, David Van Leer, and Cornel West have worked at establishing Emerson's philosophical creden-tials.[6]

In this chapter I shall focus on Emerson's philosophical views, particularly on his epistemology and metaphysics.[7]

In Emerson's writings, the ideas and projects of the Euro-pean Romantics—"the feeling intellect," the "marriage of self and world," the human mind as a shaper of experi-ence, the criticism and expansion of empiricism, and the naturalization and humanization of the divine—developed in a philosophically distinctive way on American soil.

Emerson, then, is America's first Romantic philosopher. His relation to those who follow him is both significant and complex. He actually met the young William James in the James family home in New York, where he was a fre-quent visitor of William's father, Henry James, Sr. There is, as Richard Poirier has shown us, a deep Emersonian layer in James's thought. But it was John Dewey and, later, Stanley Cavell who better enunciated Emerson's philosophical importance.[8] Dewey saw Emerson as a phi-losopher of experience, an "idealist" who traced the exist-ence of ideals not to a transcendental realm but to their sources in human life. Cavell treats him as an "episte-mologist of moods" who teaches the Romantic doctrine that our feelings are as objective and revelatory of the world as are our thoughts or sensations. All the American philosophers whom I shall examine criticize and attempt to move beyond what Emerson calls "paltry empiricism."[9]

I. FREEDOM

Emerson's views on the metaphysical topic of freedom serve as a convenient introduction to his philosophy. In general, Emerson is not so much interested in analyzing the concept of freedom (though some of his remarks are relevant to such analyses) as he is in exploring ways in which human beings are or can be free and, correspond-ingly, ways in which we—by either our own wills or the forces of fate—are less free than we might be. I shall look to Emerson's earlier essays and addresses for his outlook on freedom and to some of his later ones to show the se-vere constraints on freedom that he discerns. This is not to say that he ignores such constraints in his earlier essays nor that he abandons belief in or hope for freedom later on. Indeed, most of Emerson's ideas that concern us in this chapter are expressed throughout his career. Emer-son's vision does darken, however, especially after the death of his son Waldo,[10] and this fact is reflected in the comparative ease with which one can find discussions of freedom in the earlier works and discussions of limitations on freedom in the later ones.

In his first writings, *Nature* (1836) and **"The American Scholar"** (1837),[11] Emerson is concerned with our free-dom from the traditions and institutions of the past. It is not that he sees no value in them—books are of great value if well used—but that valuable as they are, they can prevent our enjoying what he calls in *Nature* "an original relation to the universe." Why, he begins that work by asking, should we not enjoy such a relation? "Why should not we have a poetry and philosophy of insight and not of tradition, and a religion by revelation to us, and not the history of theirs?"[12]

"The American Scholar" amplifies this message. Emer-son criticizes traditional scholarship precisely because of its slavishness. He warns against "the restorers of read-ings, the emendators, the bibliomaniacs of all degrees."[13] These idolizers of books may know all that they contain, page by page, but they lack what Emerson calls "their own sight of principles," the source of all good thinking and writing. (There is an obvious connection here with Wordsworth's injunction to "close up those barren leaves" and "Come forth . . . with . . . a heart / That watches and receives." However, Emerson stresses the active, as op-posed to the receptive, powers of humanity more than does Wordsworth.)[14] Emerson criticizes his contemporary "meek young men" who "grow up in libraries" and who feel duty bound to find out and follow the dictates of the works they worship. Such duty is that of the slave: The "guide" has become a "tyrant."[15]

Emerson accordingly puts forward a different conception of the scholar, one that depicts him or her as self-reliant, not dependent, exploratory, not tied to already-discovered truth. The true purpose of books, he tells us, is "to in-spire," not to promote imitation or idolization. Their power may be misused: "I had better never see a book than to be warped by its attraction clean out of my own orbit." Emer-son is confident that within each man or woman lies a "genius," a unique capacity. As he later stated in **"Self-Reliance"**: "The power which resides in him is new in na-ture, and none but he knows what that is which he can do, nor does he know until he has tried."[16] True scholarship sets this genius free: discovering, developing, and relying on it.

Emerson's idea of self-reliance, so prominent in his early addresses and essays, is explicitly connected with freedom in **"The American Scholar"**: "In self-trust, all the virtues are comprehended. Free should the scholar be,—free and brave. Free even to the definition of freedom, 'without any hindrance that does not arise out of his own constitution.' Brave; for fear is a thing which a scholar by his very func-tion puts behind him."[17] This passage shows Emerson thinking of freedom as a virtue, like courage. He is not, then, treating freedom or its lack as a metaphysical condi-tion affecting all people equally but as something of which people can have more or less. By enjoining his readers to become self-reliant, Emerson evinces his belief that we can control, to some extent at least, our freedom, that—to use "free" in the more usual philosophical sense—we are free to become more free by becoming more self-reliant.

Although Emerson's aim is toward freedom—forward rather than backward as he says[18]—**"The American Scholar"** both implicitly and explicitly records our fail-ures to act freely. "We are the cowed," he writes, "the trustless."[19] Using images that remind one of his admirer Nietzsche, he characterizes human existence as like that of bugs or spawn or, as in the following case, as that of a herd: "Men in history, men in the world of to-day . . . are called 'the mass' and 'the herd.'"[20] Yet **"The American Scholar"** is suffused with confidence that a new day is at hand and that humankind, and particularly Americans, are ready to slough off the past. Emerson writes in the first paragraph that "our day of dependence, our long appren-ticeship to the learning of other lands, draws to a close," and in the last paragraph he predicts that "we will walk on our own feet; we will work with our own hands; we will speak our own minds."[21]

If **"The American Scholar"** urges the abandonment of slavish scholarship for the self-reliant and creative life of **"Man Thinking,"** Emerson's **"Divinity School Address"** urges the abandonment of slavish religion for the free ap-prehension of a divinity that "is, not was."[22] As scholars idolize books, so do Christians idolize Christ: "The lan-guage that describes Christ to Europe and America is not the style of friendship and enthusiasm to a good and noble heart, but is appropriated and formal,—paints a demigod, as the Orientals or the Greeks would describe Osiris or Apollo."[23] Emerson's shocking moral is that we should try not to imitate Christ but to achieve our own original spiri-tual relationship to the universe.[24] Each of the Harvard Di-vinity College graduates to whom he is speaking is "a newborn bard of the Holy Ghost," who must "cast behind you all conformity, and acquaint men at first hand with Deity." The imitator is hopelessly mediocre; he "bereaves himself of his own beauty, to come short of another man's."[25] Once again, one is to be free from all external reliance, even on so good a model as Jesus or Moses. Our religion is characterized by a "soul-destroying slavery to habit." Still, Emerson maintains, "it is not to be doubted, that all men have sublime thoughts; that all men do value the few real hours of life."[26] (Emerson's assertion that all men have sublime thoughts is an indication of the demo-cratic impulse that Dewey so admired in him.[27] Although it might seem to conflict with his portrayal of our domina-tion by herdlike instincts, one should remember that the hours of sublime thought are "few.")

It is these "few real hours" that Emerson constantly seeks. In **"Circles,"** published as one of his first series of essays in 1841, he identifies these hours with those times in our lives when we cast off the old, whether in the form of a model (like Christ or Locke or, a philosopher might add today, Wittgenstein or Husserl or Derrida) or a habit. "Our life is an apprenticeship to the truth, that around every circle another can be drawn."[28] Each new circle represents freedom from the constriction of the old one, but each will harden into a new constriction: "It is the inert effort of each thought, having formed itself into a circular wave of circumstance,—as, for instance, an empire, rules of an art, a local usage, a religious rite,—to heap itself on that ridge, and to solidify, and hem in the life." Our real hours are our original ones, when "the heart refuses to be impris-oned"[29] and we burst through to a new circle, thereby abandoning the old.

In **"Circles"** this idea of abandoning our old forms begins to assume the status of a metaphysical principle, as when Emerson writes: "The way of life is wonderful: it is by abandonment."[30] Abandonment of the old imprisoning circle is, Emerson asserts, both the way in which "life" ac-tually proceeds (though not the way in which human life is conducted) and an ideal of human conduct, as if we become real (enjoy our few real hours) only in such transitions. Although Emerson's links to the Platonic (including the Neoplatonic) tradition are important, he is not, like Plato, a follower of Pythagoras, who maintained that the real is the unchanging. Emerson is a Heraclitean rather than a Pythagorean on this issue, maintaining that the real is the changing: "In nature, every moment is new; the past is always swallowed and forgotten; the coming only is sacred. Nothing is secure but life, transition, the energizing spirit. . . . No truth so sublime but it may be trivial tomorrow in the light of new thoughts. People wish to be settled: only as far as they are unsettled, is there any hope for them."[31]

Emerson applies his notion of radical human freedom to the moral domain in **"Circles,"** again foreshadowing Nietzsche.[32] "The great man will not be prudent in the popular sense; all his prudence will be so much deduction from his grandeur."[33] In the idea of deducing his virtues from the grandeur of his character, Emerson expresses the thought that the great man is responsible only to himself, that he is, as Nietzsche would say, a creator of values. A consequence of this view is that the great man is not limited even to commonly and deeply accepted virtues (of which prudence is a minor example). For Emerson all virtues are, as he puts it, "initial." "The terror of reform," he continues, "is the discovery that we must cast away our virtues, or what we have always esteemed such, into the same pit that has consumed our grosser vices." Not only may we abandon good; we also may abandon, or transcend, evil: "It is the highest power of divine moments that they abolish our contritions also."[34]

That Emerson's notion of freedom is akin to those of philosophers like Nietzsche, Kierkegaard, and Heidegger is suggested also by Cavell's analysis of a key passage in **"Self-Reliance"** in his complex and provocative paper "Being Odd, Getting Even: Threats to Individuality."[35] The passage in question is this one: "Man is timid and apologetic; he is no longer upright; he dares not say 'I think,' 'I am,' but quotes some saint or sage."[36] Once he points it out, one must be struck, as Cavell is, by the seeming allusion to Descartes's classical argument in the Second Meditation in which he proves his own existence. Cavell reminds us of the importance in the Cartesian argument of actually saying or thinking "I am, I exist" and examines the ways in which, for Emerson, saying becomes a metaphor for existing, and quoting a metaphor for herdlike, conforming, "ghostly" nonexistence. Just as saying or thinking in Descartes's account is necessary for certain knowledge of my own existence, so for Emerson, saying becomes a metaphor for the enactment of my existence. Here "existence" is used in the existentialists' sense of a way of human life that one does not have merely by virtue of being a live human being but that one must acquire (Kierkegaard's word for this is "choosing").[37] We are beings, Cavell interprets Emerson as meaning, for whom their existence is an issue and who must claim or enact it for it to occur.[38] Quotation, the opposite of saying, is the

equivalent of the "warping out of one's orbit" that Emerson warns against in **"The American Scholar"** and **"Divinity School Address."** In **"Self-Reliance"** Emerson is saying that our quotation, our slavery to others (even to our own past sayings and doings), robs us of our existence. The only real existence is a free one (i.e., "without any hindrance that does not arise out of his own constitution"). "Imitation," as he stated, "is suicide."[39]

If Emerson hopes for a constantly renewed "original relation to the universe," he is not unaware of the barriers to, and the general unlikelihood of, such relations taking place. In **"Experience,"** published in his second series of essays in 1844, he records his disenchantment with even those people who seem least conforming and hidebound:

> There is an optical illusion about every person we meet. In truth, they are all creatures of given temperament, which will appear in a given character, whose boundaries they will never pass: but we look at them, they seem alive, and we presume there is impulse in them. In the moment, it seems impulse; in the year, in the lifetime, it turns out to be a certain uniform tune which the revolving barrel of the music-box must play.[40]

Life moves by expanding circles, he had written, but here in **"Experience"** he pictures people who only "seem alive" (i.e., in Kierkegaardian terms, who seem to exist) and whose "boundaries" will never expand. "Temperament shuts us in a prison of glass,"[41] a prison we cannot even see.

Emerson notes restrictions on our freedom in all his writing, maintaining even in the ebullient **"Self-Reliance,"** for example, that through our conformity to society we are "as it were, clapped into jail by [our] consciousness."[42] In his later essays, however—as in the preceding quotation—he comes to emphasize the extent to which these restrictions are not under our control. Nowhere is this recognition more apparent than in his late essay **"Fate,"** published in 1860 in *The Conduct of Life.* There, fate becomes a name for "whatever limits us,"[43] and Emerson provides a veritable catalogue of forces that limit our ability to find or express ourselves: earthquakes, climatic changes, disease, sex, "organization tyrannizing over character."[44] Emerson seems to be talking about his earlier thought when he explains: "Once we thought positive power was all. Now we learn that negative power, or circumstance, is half. Nature is the tyrannous circumstance, the thick skull, the sheathed snake, the ponderous, rock-like jaw."[45] Even when he stresses our human influence over events, Emerson's moral seems to be that this too is fated and that such influence comes unconsciously, unintelligently, like bodily secretions:

> Each creature puts forth from itself its own condition and sphere, as the slug sweats out its slimy house on the pear leaf, and the woolly aphides on the apple perspire their own bed, and the fish its shell. In youth we clothe ourselves with rainbows and go as brave as the zodiac. In age we put out another sort of perspiration,— gout, fever, rheumatism, caprice, doubt, fretting and

avarice. . . . A man will see his character emitted in the events that seem to meet, but which exude from and accompany him.[46]

At the end of **"Fate,"** Emerson offers a "solution to the older knots of fate, freedom, and foreknowledge." But it is difficult to make sense of this. It lies, he tells us, in "the propounding . . . of the double consciousness." His idea seems to be not that the universe is essentially dual—for he speaks of it as a "Blessed Unity"[47]—but that our consciousness of it is. We vary, he explains, in the way we handle the dictates of fate.[48] A person may be "the victim of his fate," but he ought then (and this would presumably be the alternative or double consciousness of which Emerson speaks) "to rally on his relation to the Universe, which his ruin benefits. Leaving the daemon who suffers, he is to take sides with the Deity who secures universal benefit by his pain."[49] Note that "his ruin" remains, and so Emerson is not talking about escape to another (e.g., a transcendental or noumenal) "world." We are stuck with this one, but we can, he seems to hold, accommodate ourselves to it.

So far, this sounds like typical Stoic doctrine. Emerson departs from this position, however, by saying that we can, after all, "offset the drag of temperament," that we are compensated for "taking sides with the Deity" by an access of "sudden power. When a god wishes to ride, any chip or pebble will bud and shoot out winged feet and serve him for a horse."[50] Fate becomes something that we can control. Whether this position makes sense is questionable; a fuller examination of it must await our examination of Emerson's idealism. It is in any case characteristic of Emerson both to set out the limitations on our power and to testify to their being overcome. Perhaps the fairest summary of Emerson's position is that offered earlier in **"Fate"** and just quoted: "Circumstance is half," but "positive power" is the other half. And although his talk of "impulse" might make it seem as if Emerson posits a contracausal notion of freedom, it seems just as easy to make him out to be a Humean on this question (if on few others), his list of the forces arrayed against us just a catalogue of those "chains"[51] that we must and can avoid if we wish to be free.

II. IDEALISM

Emerson's idealism is a blend of many elements: Neoplatonic, Hindu, Kantian, Coleridgean, and others. These philosophies share a sense of the immense power of the human mind in determining both reality and our knowledge of it. In this respect, Emerson is an inheritor of Kant, who stressed this power of the mind. Like Kant and his followers (including Coleridge), but unlike Berkeley, Emerson is not a simple idealist. He does not hold that reality is only mental, and he gives substantial play (as in the idea of fate) to the idea that there are objective forces beyond our influence. Emerson's idealism does not come neatly packaged, however, so that our task is to distinguish some of its main parts.

ILLUSION VERSUS REALITY

We begin with the Platonic/Neoplatonic/Hindu strain, which we met when discussing **"Fate."** In that essay, Emerson sets out the forces of fate arrayed against us but maintains that by an access of sudden power it can be transcended. In such places in his writing, Emerson comes close to the Platonic view that the world we inhabit is (like the shadows on the wall of Plato's cave) an illusion and that we can transcend that illusion, breaking out to reality. In **"Experience,"** for example, after discussing the limitations brought about by temperament, Emerson writes:

> On its own level . . . temperament is final. . . . But it is impossible that the creative power should exclude itself. Into every intelligence there is a door which is never closed, through which the creator passes. The intellect, seeker of absolute truth, or the heart, lover of absolute good, intervenes for our succor, and at one whisper of these high powers we awake from ineffectual struggles with this nightmare. We hurl it into its own hell, and cannot again contract ourselves to so base a state.[52]

Emerson suggests that the world we see (or the way we see the world) is dreamlike or, worse, nightmarish. It is in any case base and ghostly, not solid or elevated. We may hope to wake up to "reality."

Emerson tends to identify the reality with which we come in touch in the elevated moments he describes as "ours," the "soul's," or that of some cosmic "self." This makes his position similar to the Hindu view that behind all phenomena lies an "atman," or world-soul. The poem with which **"Experience"** begins, for example, lists the forms of experience Emerson calls the "lords of life" (which include "Temperament," "Dream," "Succession," and "Surprise"), but though these lords appear to tower over the "little man, least of all," they are in fact just his creations or emanations:

> "To-morrow they will wear another face,
> The founder thou! these are thy race!"

More Neoplatonic in tone is Emerson's remark, again in **"Experience,"** that "the consciousness in each man is a sliding scale, which identifies him now with the First Cause, and now with the flesh of his body; life above life, in infinite degrees."[53] Again, "man" can be identified with divinity, with the "First Cause" that created the world.

Although Emerson shares the idea of the soul's waking up to a higher order of things with Hindus and Platonists, there are important differences. The Platonic Ideas are timeless, unchanging, and the soul that ascends to them becomes more steady and settled (as in the *Phaedo*).[54] Emerson offers, however, a Heraclitean rather than a Pythagorean outlook, what he calls a philosophy of "fluxions."[55] "God offers to every mind its choice between truth and repose," he writes in **"Intellect."** "Take which you please,—you can never have both."[56]

Again, Emerson does not think that one can make a direct assault on truth—as the geometer does in piling up one reliable truth on another, or the yogi by years of meditation. For Emerson reality comes in flashes and gleams, and it is these "few real hours" of our lives for which he searches. These gleaming moments may not be only in the past, as in Wordsworth's poetry, but they are equally rare: "Reason, the prized reality, the Law, is apprehended now and then for a serene and profound moment amidst the hubbub of cares and works which have no direct bearing on it;—is then lost, for months or years, and again found, for an interval, to be lost again. If we compute it in time, we may, in fifty years, have half a dozen reasonable hours."[57]

Finally, we should note that the dualism (of dream and reality) that Emerson seems to embrace is countered by an equally strong sense that this world, the world we experience, contains all the divinity we shall ever need or find. "Life wears to me a visionary face," he reports in **"Experience."**[58] And earlier, in a passage from **"The American Scholar"** that Cavell rightly connects with the Wordsworthian (and Wittgensteinian) interest in the "ordinary" or "common," Emerson writes:

> I embrace the common, I explore and sit at the feet of the familiar, the low. Give me insight into today, and you may have the antique and future worlds. . . . The meal in the firkin; the milk in the pan; the ballad in the street; the news of the boat; the glance of the eye; the form and the gait of the body;—show me the ultimate reason of these matters; show me the sublime presence of the highest spiritual cause lurking, as always it does lurk, in these suburbs and extremities of nature . . . and the world lies no longer a dull miscellany and lumber-room, but has form and order.[59]

Although Emerson calls for us to awake from our nightmare, it is not to a separate, transcendent world that he calls us, but to a vision of "the sublime presence" at work in the "familiar" phenomena of our lives.

SUBJECTIVE IDEALISM

Emerson flirts with the subjective idealism of Berkeley, particularly in **Nature.** According to Berkeley, the world just is our ideas of it, so that reality is made up entirely of ideas and the selves who experience them. Emerson clearly has Berkeley in mind when he treats idealism as the view that "matter is a phenomenon, not a substance." But he criticizes this view: It "leaves me in the splendid labyrinth of my perceptions, to wander without end. Then the heart resists it, because it baulks the affections in denying substantive being to men and women. . . . This theory makes nature foreign to me, and does not account for that consanguinity which we acknowledge to it."[60] Berkeley's theory "makes nature foreign" because it makes it just a set of ideas, whereas I am not a set of ideas. Emerson insists that on the contrary, nature, including the "men and women," are consanguineous—of the same blood—with me. The subjective idealist errs in saying that they are ideas and I am substantial. For Emerson, we all are equally substantial.

Emerson counters in another way the solipsistic implications of his flirtation with Berkelian idealism in **Nature,** by speaking of a relationship between mind and world that, like those depicted in Wordsworth's and Coleridge's poetry, resembles a marriage. "I am the lover of uncontained and immortal beauty," he writes at the end of **Nature**'s first chapter:

> In the wilderness, I find something more dear and connate than in streets or villages. In the tranquil landscape, and especially in the distant line of the horizon, man beholds somewhat as beautiful as his own nature.

> The greatest delight which the fields and woods minister is the suggestion of an occult relation between man and the vegetable. I am not alone and unacknowledged. They nod to me, and I to them. . . . Yet it is certain that the power to produce this delight does not reside in nature, but in man, or in a harmony of both.[61]

This passage emphasizes our relations with nature, though its vision is a shifting one. The first paragraph praises the wilderness and opposes it to the "I" by portraying it as "distant" and by contrasting it with one's "own nature." But the ultimate praise offered the wilderness is that it is as beautiful as man's own nature, which suggests a link between it and ourselves. And the first clause of the last sentence veers toward subjectivism in asserting that "this delight"—presumably the beauty of nature—resides "in man." Yet on the other hand, the pronouncement, or phenomenological report, that "I am not alone and unacknowledged" is surely not the language of the solipsist. Further complicating Emerson's view is the alternation contained in the last sentence: The power resides in man and not in nature, its first half tells us, but the second adds, "or in a harmony of both."

Although Emerson is talking about beauty here, and not about the world *in toto,* his suggestions and withdrawals or qualifications of idealism are entirely typical.[62] This same section of **Nature,** in which he asserts the alternatives of the self's dominance over, or harmony with, nature also includes the famous (and in some quarters, infamous)[63] "transparent eyeball" passage, which postulates the disappearance of the self: "Standing on the bare ground—my head bathed by the blithe air, and uplifted into infinite space,—all mean egotism vanishes. I become a transparent eyeball; I am nothing; I see all; the currents of the Universal Being circulate through me; I am part or parcel of God." (Note, however, that it is only "mean" egotism that vanishes.)

Although in **Nature** Emerson rejects idealism, at least of a solipsistic sort, he does admit that it is "a useful introductory hypothesis." In later writings he continues to suggest, if not to assert, the insubstantiality of the "men and women" who surround us: "Let us treat the men and women well," he writes in **"Experience,"** "treat them as if they were real: perhaps they are."[64]

TRANSCENDENTAL IDEALISM

Emerson wants both to assert the vast powers of the human mind in forming our experience and to acknowledge the objectivity or substantiality of the world that this mind encounters. These two ideas come together in a form of idealism that was available to Emerson through his knowledge of Coleridge, the transcendental idealism developed by Kant.

Stanley Cavell has attempted, beginning with his 1978 paper "Thinking of Emerson" and in later papers, to assess Emerson's place in a Romantic Kantian tradition.[65] (Van Leer's *Emerson's Epistemology* also argues, though in a rather different way than Cavell does, for Emerson's basic Kantianism.)[66] In "Thinking of Emerson" Cavell contends that Emerson revises Kant's scheme of categories beyond Kant's twelve pure concepts of the Understanding, by countenancing more ways of knowing or making the world than did Kant. (This would presumably be part of Emerson's active opposition to what he refers to as "paltry" empiricisms.)[67] Just as Kant is trying to justify our claims to necessary knowledge of geometry, arithmetic, and Newtonian physics, so Emerson is trying to justify claims to other necessary knowledge, for example, that centering on our moods. **"Experience,"** Cavell maintains, "is about the epistemology, or say the logic, of moods."[68]

For moods to deserve a transcendental deduction or exploration, they would have to constitute a form of knowledge, just as geometry, arithmetic, or physics is knowledge. That they do is a point Cavell wants to confirm: "The idea is roughly that moods must be taken as having at least as sound a role in advising us of reality as sense-experience has."[69]

But should we take moods as revelatory? There is no established science of moods as there is a science of physics or geometry. Here it must be said that Emerson is as much interested in discovering as in justifying the truths about moods he treats; his essay contains penetrating observations about the operation of moods in our knowledge of the world. In this respect, he does more than Kant does in the *Critique of Pure Reason*. There Kant relies on Euclid and Newton to provide his sciences of geometry and physics (though in the moral and political realms, Kant has a greater claim to be a discoverer of truth, for example, the Categorical Imperative). Many of the most important laws on which Emerson relies are those he has observed himself (which is not to say that he does not look to science or literature for such laws). Emerson is at once an empiricist (insofar as he relies on observations), a transcendental idealist (insofar as he attempts to justify their validity by invoking some structure in us), and an experimenter (insofar as he discovers truths).

What truths, then, does Emerson investigate? In **"Experience,"** he observes that it "depends on the mood of the man whether he shall see the sunset or the fine poem"[70] and adds that the universe "inevitably . . . wear[s] our color. . . . As I am, so I see."[71] (The word "inevitably" marks the truth as necessary, thus signaling the need for a transcendental explanation.) Emerson indicates an area of experience about which Wittgenstein wrote in the *Tracta-*

tus when he said that "the world of the happy man is a different one from that of the unhappy man."[72] Wittgenstein's way of phrasing it coheres with Emerson's in stressing the global (and hence for a Kantian categorial or formal) extent of such "moody" structures: The whole world is "colored." In his treatment, Cavell maintains that "sense-experience is to objects what moods are to the world."[73] This means, first, that moods reveal the world (as our senses reveal objects) but, second, that "the world" is to be distinguished from "objects." "The world" is to be understood as indicated by our whole sense of things, what William James calls those "dumb responses" or "*consents,*" which seemed to him, as they did to Emerson, to be "our deepest organs of communication with the nature of things."[74] "Mood" in this context is much like "will," as discussed in Chapter 1: It is both subjective and revelatory. Coleridge wrote that "all true reality has both its ground and its evidence in the *will,*" thereby regarding the will as having both the metaphysical ("ground") and epistemological force ("evidence") that Emerson and Cavell ascribe to mood. Kant sets the stage for these claims with his view that other (if less obviously) subjective structures—such as space, time, and causality—both determine and furnish us with knowledge of the world.

Another candidate for a synthetic a priori truth about moods is Emerson's remark in **"Circles,"** that "our moods do not believe in each other."[75] It is not just that our moods vary but that they affect what Emerson calls the whole "tissue of facts and beliefs"[76] we encounter, so that (as in the difference between Wittgenstein's happy and unhappy world) they bring about a radical discontinuity of outlook and being. Our problems look different in the middle of a sleepless night than they do in the bright morning. "Our life is March weather," Emerson notes in **"Montaigne,"** "savage and serene in one hour. We go forth . . . believing in the iron links of Destiny . . . but a book . . . or only the sound of a name, shoots a spark through the nerves, and we suddenly believe in will. . . . All is possible to the resolved mind. Presently, a new experience gives a new turn to our thoughts; common sense resumes its tyranny."[77]

To the extent that Emerson is a Kantian, he would want to stress not only our (subjective) role in experience but also the objectivity of the knowledge with which experience furnishes us. Cavell admits that many of Emerson's remarks (e.g., that the universe "wears our color") sound subjective but responds that "whether you take this to be subjective or objective depends upon whether you take the successive colors or moods of the universe to be subjective or objective." Emerson, Cavell argues, "is out to destroy the ground on which such a problem takes itself seriously, I mean interprets itself as a metaphysical fixture. The universe is as separate from me, but as intimately part of me, as one on whose behalf I contest, and who therefore wears my color. We are in a state of 'romance' with the universe (to use a word from the last sentence of [**"Experience"**])."[78] This "intimate separation" between ourselves and the universe is what Wordsworth and Coleridge call a "marriage" of self and world. Some such vision is characteristic of each of the American Romantic philosophers.

Another way in which Emerson incorporates objectivity into his epistemology of mood is to stress the receptive, rather than the active, element in knowing. The treatment of our organizing powers as receptive rather than active is, according to Cavell, Emerson's "most explicit reversal of Kant," for in Kant one knows by synthesizing—gathering together and shaping. But at the end of **"Experience"** Emerson concludes: "All I know is reception; I am and I have: but I do not get, and when I have fancied I had gotten anything, I found I did not. I worship with wonder the great Fortune."[79] Emerson here describes a mode of apprehending the world that is receptive, not active (not "getting"), but also subjectively influenced, "moody" in its "worship" and "wonder." Cavell links this receptive mode of apprehension with the thought of Heidegger, who stresses "listening" and who connects truth with an attitude he calls "thinking," but equally "thanking."

THE LORDS OF LIFE

If one follows up Cavell's suggestion that one can "hear Kant working throughout Emerson's essay **'Experience,'**"[80] then one must be struck by the "lords of life" that are the essay's ostensible subject. Emerson lists them in the essay's last section—"Illusion, Temperament, Succession, Surface, Surprise, Reality, Subjectiveness"—and speaks of them as "threads on the loom of time." The metaphor suggests that they are woven into time, just as Kant's categories weave objects by synthesizing, weaving together, the temporalized material furnished through our faculty of sensibility. Each lord, then, would be a way of weaving temporalized material, a Kantian category.[81]

There is much that is attractive about this view, though there are important problems with it as well. One problem is that some of the lords seem more plausible as categories than do others. For example, because Temperament is subjective yet also yields us knowledge (of a person, of the world as seen through or responding to a person), it is a plausible candidate for a category. But Illusion seems distinctly implausible, for it seems on its face not to give us knowledge, something a category must do. Again, Reality seems hard to construe as a category both because it is not an epistemological notion but a metaphysical one and because it seems, especially as Emerson uses it, too objective, not subjective enough to be traced to a faculty of our mind. That is, Emerson seems at times to mean by Reality something nonphenomenal.

Another problem with the list of lords is that moods—for which Cavell provides the compelling argument that they function as Kantian categories and which, because of their shifting nature, are clearly temporalized—are not on Emerson's list of lords, even though they are a dominant subject of **"Experience"** and other of Emerson's essays. We can handle this problem by noting that Emerson's list is

only an approximate one, that moods do concern him, and that the case for moods as categories is as strong as that produced for any named lord. Indeed, the list at the end of **"Experience"** does not match the list given in the poem that begins the essay. Van Leer sees the list of seven lords at the end as corresponding to the essay's seven sections, and there is some textual evidence for this, but there is also evidence against it. For example, Emerson makes the important general claim that "life is a series of surprises" not in the section Van Leer identifies as being about surprise but in the one that he takes to be about Surface.[82] Again, Emerson remarks that "our friends early appear to us as representative of certain ideas which they never pass or exceed," a remark about character in the section Van Leer regards as about succession,[83] and all sections of the essay treat Reality in some way. Sharon Cameron seems to be on more solid ground in claiming that "these designations seem divorced from, and seem only arbitrarily to apply to, discrete portions of the essay."[84] In any case, it is instructive to treat at least some of the lords of life as Emerson's extensions of Kantian categories and to look not just to **"Experience"** but to other of Emerson's essays for help in understanding how this is so.

Temperament. In connection with Emerson's views on freedom, we discussed temperament and its associated notion of character. Like the category of causality or the form of space, temperament provides limits to reality, boundaries that a person "will never pass," a "uniform tune which the revolving barrel of the music-box must play." (As with moods, Emerson indicates necessity here by his use of the word "must.")[85] In an inversion that we can now recognize as characteristic, Emerson does allow that "it is impossible that the creative power should exclude itself,"[86] but temperament is clearly a powerful force hemming it in.

Sometimes temperament issues in the kind of potent character Emerson discusses in the essay of that title. A hero or genius like Napoleon or Washington is "destined" to organize events: "He encloses the world, as the patriot does his country, as a material basis for his character, and a theatre for action."[87] The unswerving force of temperament is as effectual in the world as a law of physics: "It is of no use to ape it, or to contend with it. . . . The hero sees that the event is ancillary: it must follow *him*."[88]

Emerson's talent for observation is at work in his many reports of the pervasive force of character in human life. To one person—but to no one else we have ever met—we will reveal secrets that normally make us "wretched either to keep or to betray."[89] To others we cannot speak at all; our bodies "seem to lose their cartilage." Our friends exert a positive force on us just by their characters, refreshing and energizing us just by their presence: "The entrance of a friend adds grace, boldness, and eloquence."

Temperament and the character in which it issues are forces for Emerson, but like gravity, they both shackle and enable us to act. Temperament is responsible for "the power and furniture of man" and makes possible that "profound good understanding"[90] that arises between friends. But it operates implacably even when we wish it would not, so that we become the prey of our personalities or temperaments. "Character teaches above our wills. Men imagine that they communicate their virtue or vice only by overt actions and do not see that virtue or vice emit a breath every moment."[91]

Surface. We "emit" our characters constantly, Emerson holds, in the ways we sit or walk, respond or ignore, talk or laugh: We lie exposed to view. But that exposure does not reveal all there is to know about us. We may be able to tell that "this or that man is fortunate" just by meeting him, but we cannot discover "the reason why."[92] Indeed, just at the point a person is most self-reliant, most himself or herself, Emerson sees a mystery: "A man will not be observed in doing that which he can do best. There is a certain magic about his properest action, which stupefies your powers of observation, so that though it is done before you, you wist not of it."[93] (Think of Wittgenstein "doing philosophy," of Larry Bird playing basketball.)

Emerson finds such hiddenness or obliqueness, which can be assigned to the lord Surface but also in some respects to Dream and Illusion, to be a characteristic of all human experience: "Nature does not like to be observed, and likes that we should be her fools and playmates. We may have the sphere for our cricket-ball, but not a berry for our philosophy. Direct strokes she never gave us power to make; all our blows glance, all our hits are accidents. Our relations to each other are oblique and casual." We can give a cricket ball a good whack, but we cannot touch—except by accident—any of our philosophical berries, cannot grasp or understand life. The context for this remark, as indeed for the entire essay in which it appears, is the death of Emerson's son Waldo.

> It does not touch me: something which I fancied was a part of me, which could not be torn away without tearing me, nor enlarged without enriching me, falls off from me, and leaves no scar. . . . The Indian who was laid under a curse, that the wind should not blow on him, nor water flow to him, nor fire burn him, is a type of us all. The dearest events are summer-rain, and we the Para coats that shed every drop."[94]

Although the inaccessibility of, or our obliqueness to, experience takes on a deeply personal tone in **"Experience,"** Emerson in fact uses Waldo's death to register a more general complaint, about the essential "evanescence and lubricity" of all phenomena. This is the dark side, the darker mood of the inaccessibility praised when it was manifested in the form of the genius, doing what "he can do best." Now, in **"Experience,"** Emerson laments that the tendency for things to "slip through our fingers then when we clutch hardest [is] the most unhandsome part of our condition."[95]

Surface, Illusion, and Dream thus emerge in Emerson's account as phenomenal, or phenomenological terms, describing not something arrived at as a conclusion from an argument (as in Plato or Descartes) but a characteristic of human experience. Descartes argued that dreams do not have a dreamlike quality, for if they did, we could tell them from waking experiences and refute radical skepticism.[96] But Emerson is saying that waking experiences have a dreamlike quality: "Dream delivers us to dream, and there is no end to illusion."[97]

Surprise. There is still, as always in Emerson, another mood, another side to the play of surfaces: "In liberated moments, we know that a new picture of life and duty is already possible."[98] Such moments, which must also be recognized as part of the "succession of moods or objects," come as surprises to us. Emerson records some of them in **Nature**: "The waving of the boughs in the storm, is new to me and old. It takes me by surprise, and yet is not unknown."[99] Again, in a famous passage employed by both James and Dewey:[100] "Crossing a bare common, in snow puddles, at twilight, under a clouded sky, without having in my thoughts any occurrence of special good fortune, I have enjoyed a perfect exhilaration. I am glad to the brink of fear."[101] These surprising insights may be brought about by a person, by art rather than nature: "In the thought of genius there is always a surprise." Or they may come about for no clearly assignable reason, with the mere passage of time: "The results of life are uncalculated and uncalculable. The years teach much which the days never know. The persons who compose our company, converse, and come and go, and design and execute many things, and somewhat comes of it all, but an unlooked for result. . . . It turns out somewhat new."[102]

Surprise is essential to Emerson's conception of life as a set of concentric circles, around every one of which another can be drawn. When it is drawn, the limitations and possibilities of life take on an entirely different aspect. Emerson concludes **"Circles"** in his hopeful voice, stressing the surprise of overcoming rather than the routine of confinement:

> Life is a series of surprises. We do not guess to-day the mood, the pleasure, the power of to-morrow, when we are building up our being. . . . The masterpieces of God, the total growths and universal movements of the soul, he hideth; they are incalculable. . . . The one thing which we seek with insatiable desire, is to forget ourselves, to be surprised out of our propriety, to lose our sempiternal memory, and to do something without knowing how or why; in short, to draw a new circle.[103]

The last sentence here portrays surprise not as a limitation that, as it were, causes us to lose our way by disorienting us but, rather, as something that is helpful in forming our expanding series of circles and so leads us on our way to what we desire. (The last sentence is interesting too for its blending of the Platonic and Neoplatonic image of desire—felt by the soul for the Ideas in Plato's *Phaedo* and *Symposium,* for example—with the Romantic and Kantian idea that knowledge and the reality it discloses (Emerson's new circle) are constructed by us, are things that we draw.)[104]

The form of experience Emerson wants to explain by positing a category of Surprise is expressed not only in such general pronouncements as "life is a series of surprises"[105] but also in his frequently stated thought that what we know comes, as it were, in our side glances, by the wayside. Emerson writes in **"Intellect,"** for example: "You cannot, with your best deliberation and heed, come so close to any question as your spontaneous glance shall bring you, whilst you rise from your bed, or walk abroad in the morning after meditating the matter before sleep, on the previous night."[106] Truth comes in glimpses, for Emerson, not in a total and finished product. He searches widely for these genuinely new ideas or insights, finding "every surmise and vatication of the mind . . . entitled to a certain respect. . . . We learn to prefer imperfect theories, and sentences which contain glimpses of truth, to digested systems which have no one valuable suggestion."[107] The surprising and indirect character of truth requires the special epistemological attitude that Emerson sees in his self-reliant heroes: "A man should learn to detect and watch that gleam of light which flashes across his mind from within, more than the lustre of the firmament of bards and sages." But there is a darker, even tragic side to the claim that truth comes only by surprise: We cannot be surprised twice by the same object. One must thus, Emerson advises, leave a picture forever, after seeing it well once: "You shall never see it again." This is a painful discovery, one that "murmurs" a "plaint of tragedy" to us "in regard to persons, to friendship and love."[108]

With Surprise, we reach a feature of experience that is problematic when seen as a category. For although one might say there are synthetic a priori truths about surprise (e.g., that life is a series of surprises), it is implausible to say that those surprises come from us. Indeed, the surprises of life give us the sense of how much we do not determine, how much of our experience is not up to us.[109] Nevertheless, no matter how Emerson wishes to account for the surprising newness we find from time to time in our experience, he clearly wishes to record his strong sense of it. More than Wordsworth (who wrote in *The Prelude* of a "gentle shock of mild surprise") or Dewey, with whom he shares it, Emerson has a vast appreciation for the role that the unexpected or novel plays in our life and thought.

III. EMERSON'S EXPERIMENTALISM

Even when he lists the lords of life, Emerson is careful to put them forward tentatively or experimentally:

> Illusion, Temperament, Succession, Surface, Surprise, Reality, Subjectiveness,—these are threads on the loom of time, these are the lords of life. I dare not assume to give their order, but I name them as I find them in my way. I know better than to claim any completeness for my picture. I am a fragment, and this is a fragment of me. I can very confidently announce one or another law, which throws itself into relief and form, but I am too young yet by some ages to compile a code. I gossip for my hour concerning the eternal politics."[110]

Emerson shares an open-ended, experimental attitude with the pragmatists James and Dewey. They all leave room for the possibility that the true account of a given matter is quite different even from what they are convinced of. James distinguishes himself from Hegel on this point, for example, by finding the "completed" Hegelian system "suffocating" (see Chapter 3). Because he is an "idealist," it might seem that Emerson must be committed to the idea, which attracted Hegel and Plato, of a completed and unchanging account of the world. But Emerson is committed to experimentation; his idealism is, as Dewey's was to be, experimental.

The idea of testing is essential both to the meaning of the words "experience" and "experiment" and to Emerson's use of them. The English word "experience," deriving from the French *expérience* (the word used by Montaigne in his essay on experience), in turn comes from the Latin verb meaning "to try, to put to the test." ("Experiment" is derived from the same verb.) It may seem odd to think of Emerson as a tester rather than a speculator, spinning ideas out of his head, but that is perhaps because we associate experience with the Lockean (and Humean, Russellian, etc.) account, according to which experience consists primarily of sensation.

Like traditional empiricists, Emerson values the senses and the natural world they reveal. As a young man he was excited more by the discoveries of geologists or botanists than by the world of art. In Paris in 1833 (on the trip during which he met Wordsworth, Coleridge, and Carlyle) he was "only mildly excited" by the Louvre but had "memorable experiences in the Musée Nationale d'Histoire Naturelle and the Jardin des Plantes." There he confronted what he called in his journal "the inexhaustible riches of nature."[111] When he returned from Europe he continued his study of astronomy, thermodynamics, and geology and gave lectures on these topics.[112] "I have no hostility to nature, but a child's love to it," he writes in *Nature*. "I expand and live in the warm day like corn and melons."[113] But Emerson does want to "expand and live" in that nature, not to be confined in his experience of it. He complains in **"The Poet"** that "too feeble fall the impressions of nature on us to make us artists." The word "impressions" here marks his awareness of his connection with the experiential philosophy of Locke and Hume, whereas his search for an artistic way through the world marks his Romantic criticism of their unimaginative account of human life.

Emerson enacts his commitment to observation and experiment by his use of the essay form, a form invented by his hero Montaigne. An essay is, etymologically, a trial or test of something, an examination. Such an inquiry need not present the final and unrevisable word on some issue, as so many philosophical and religious texts (e.g., Hegel's *Logic,* Wittgenstein's *Tractatus*) claim to do. Emerson pays homage to the spirit of open inquiry that he finds in Montaigne's essays in his own essay **"Montaigne; or the Skeptic,"** published in 1850 as part of *Representative Men*:

I weary of these dogmatizers. I tire of these hacks of routine, who deny the dogmas. I neither affirm nor deny. I stand here to try the case. I am here to consider, σκεπτειν, to consider how it is. . . . Why pretend that life is so simple a game, when we know how subtle and elusive the Proteus is? Why think to shut up all things in your narrow coop, when we think there are not one or two only, but ten, twenty, a thousand things, and unlike? Why fancy that you have all the truth in your keeping? There is much to say on all sides.[114]

Skepticism is not Emerson's most considered stance: He sees it as something to be incorporated but also transcended in a larger truth: "The new philosophy must take [skepticisms] in and make affirmations outside of them."[115] But in **"Montaigne,"** Emerson gives voice to a part of his outlook that, because of its naturalistic sense of uncertainty and risk combined with its emphasis on our great human powers, coheres especially well with the pragmatic projects of James and Dewey. Emerson values Montaigne's sense that the uncertainty of the universe is a spur to do better, not a reason for resignation. The following passage from Montaigne's great essay "On Experience" captures—as it surely inspired—the spirit in which Emerson conducts his inquiries: "There is no end to our investigations. . . . No generous spirit stays within itself. . . . If it does not advance and push forward . . . it is only half alive. Its pursuits have no bounds or rules; its food is wonder, search, and ambiguity."[116] Emerson accepts "the clamor and jangle of contrary tendencies," but he finds among them patches and places of insight: "The seer's hour of vision is short and rare," and the "authentic utterances of the oracle" are sparingly distributed even among the works of Plato and Shakespeare. But these are what the experimenter seeks.[117]

Emerson's incipient pragmatism emerges in such early essays as **"Man the Reformer,"** in which he holds that "manual labor is the study of the external world," and in **"The American Scholar,"** in which he maintains that without action "thought can never ripen into truth." "Only so much do I know," he continues, "as I have lived."[118] When Dewey defines knowing as "a form of doing" and holds that we in part constitute the objects we know by the actions we take in knowing them, he takes a path prepared by Emerson.[119]

The dwarflike, still-emerging man that Emerson describes in *Nature* is just learning to guide the changes of nature: "We do not know the uses of more than a few plants, as corn and the apple, the potato and the vine."[120] In the chapters "Commodity" and "Discipline" Emerson sets out the project of understanding nature by influencing it. And even though he follows his Romantic forebears Wordsworth and Coleridge in giving a primary role to the imagination, he gives it a practical cast: "The imagination may be defined to be, the use which the Reason makes of the material world."[121] In later essays, Emerson continues to ascribe not only insight to his heroes but power as well: "the thought and the publication."[122]

Emerson extends his experimentalism to our reading, anticipating Cavell's development of the thought that our ex-perience takes special and important forms in the realm of literature. Books can speak to us, although they may, depending on our attitude or background, be entirely mute. Emerson aspires to write such telling books. "There is some awe mixed with the joy of our surprise," he writes in **"The American Scholar,"** "when this poet, who lived in some past world . . . says that which lies close to my own soul, that which I also had well-nigh thought and said." But, he warns, "one must be an inventor to read well," a creative reader as well as a creative writer. Emerson's wide-ranging discussions of the classics of East and West are as much records of his experience as is Hume's discussion of the collision of two billiard balls. In commenting on Emerson, John Dewey was surely correct in stressing the basic experientialism of his philosophy: "I fancy he reads the so-called eclecticism of Emerson wrongly who does not see that it is a reduction of all the philosophers of the race, even the prophets like Plato and Proclus, whom Emerson holds most dear, to the test of trial by the service of the present and immediate experience."[123]

Emerson's experimentalism infiltrates not only his religion, epistemology, and metaphysics but also, as Poirier and West have seen, his philosophy of language. "All symbols are fluxional," he states in **"The Poet,"** indicating the impermanence he sees even in those instruments with which we order change. Furthermore, he believes that "all language is vehicular and transitive, and is good, as ferries and horses are, for conveyance, not as farms and houses are, for homestead." He thus treats language as an instrument needed for some result, not as mirroring some preexisting reality. Emerson's position anticipates those of the pragmatists: James's view, for example, that truth is what we can "ride" and that "essences" are not "the copying, but the enrichment of the previous world," or Dewey's claims that ideas are operations and that "essences are provisional."[124]

In concluding **"Circles,"** Emerson writes:

> But lest I should mislead any when I have my own head, and obey my own whims, let me remind the reader that I am only an experimenter. Do not set the least value on what I do, or the least discredit on what I do not, as if I pretended to settle any thing as true or false. I unsettle all things. No facts are to me sacred; none are profane; I simply experiment, an endless seeker with no Past at my back.[125]

Emerson here gives us a rule for interpreting all of his pronouncements. He does not lack conviction or passion, but he commits himself to the possible overturning of even those convictions that he feels most strongly. Emerson is open to phenomena. He embraces the surprises that experience brings. Yet he is a "seeker" of truth, even as he claims to "settle" nothing.

IV. HUMANISM

There was only one thought which could set him aflame, and that was the unfathomed might of man.

John Jay Chapman

Emerson's heroes are experimenters, confident, as he remarked in **"The American Scholar,"** "in the unsearched might of man."[126] If Emerson was a "transcendentalist," his transcendentalism was, as Firkins states, "in essence, a disclosure of possibilities; it showed vistas within man."[127] The Unitarianism of Emerson's day postulated a supernatural rather than a deified Christ, an intrusion or eruption from beyond the human and natural.[128] But Emerson advances a natural and human supernaturalism in **"The Divinity School Address,"** stressing not the divinity but the humanity of Christ. He argues that "we degrade" Christ's life and dialogues by making them transcendental and that we should rather "let them lie as they befel, alive and warm, part of human life, and of the landscape, and of the cheerful day."[129] He understands religion to be in partnership with the natural world, maintaining (in language clearly reminiscent of "Tintern Abbey") that "faith should blend with the light of rising and of setting suns, with the flying cloud, the singing bird, and the breath of flowers." Where in this divine natural world, he asks, "sounds the persuasion, that by its very melody imparadises my heart, and so affirms its own origin in heaven?"[130]

Emerson's experiments require a human contribution, as in his idea that to be a good reader one must also be a creative one. Here Emerson embraces what we called in Chapter 1 a voluntarist picture of knowledge: To know something (in this case, the book one is reading) one must do something (read creatively), take a special attitude or stance. Coleridge took such attitudes to be produced by the will, and some of Emerson's language describing the power of the human mind clearly derives from Coleridge. For example, he writes: "Such is the constitution of all things, or such the plastic power of the human eye, that the primary forms, as the sky, the mountain, the tree, the animal, give us a delight *in and for themselves*."[131] The "plastic power" of the human eye echoes Coleridge's account of the imagination as an "esemplastic power," that is, as a power of shaping.[132] Coleridge's idea of the human mind "giving form to a yielding material" (which is the first Oxford English Dictionary meaning of "plastic") derives from Kant, whose forms and categories do just that. But Coleridge and, following him, Emerson depict such shaping not as automatic operations of the faculties of sensibility, imagination, and understanding, as in Kant, but as, to some degree at least, under our control, subject to our will. Emerson follows Coleridge in complaining of "the wintry light of the understanding" and in placing redemptive hopes in an "educated Will."[133]

In **"Experience"** Emerson asserts that the universe "inevitably wear[s] our color," that character and mood determine the world we experience. These ideas and some of the same language go back to *Nature,* in which Emerson claims: "Nature always wears the colors of the spirit." Some of Emerson's most Coleridgean expressions of the mind's plastic powers occur in *Nature*: "The sensual man conforms thoughts to things; the poet conforms things to his thoughts. The one esteems nature as rooted and fast; the other, as fluid, and impresses his being thereon. To him, the refractory world is ductile and flexible; he invests dust and stones with humanity, and makes them the words of the Reason."[134] From the standpoint of someone who believes that there are things-in-themselves, a possibly inaccessible set of facts or truths against which our human "facts" or "truths" are measured, Emerson's talk of ductility and fluidity will seem like a glorification of illusion and of the poetic embroidery of illusion. But it is important to see that Emerson associates such ductility with truth. Like Kant, who defends the reality of the humanized or phenomenal, or James, who writes that "the trail of the human serpent is . . . over everything," Emerson denies that we can separate the human from the real.[135] When properly employed, the plastic powers of the human mind gain us access to, as they shape, the only world about which we can possibly gain truth.

A great part of what seems idealistic in Emerson is his development of this Romantic doctrine of the shaping power of the individual mind. It is easy to take him as being some sort of solipsist, with the Oversoul perhaps as the single cosmic entity, spinning off the world from itself or creating it *ex nihilo*. The shaping metaphor, on the contrary, suggests that the mind works on and with its material. "We want men and women," he states in **"Self-Reliance,"** "who shall renovate life and our social state."[136] Although Emerson clearly glorifies the individual, he does not call for isolation. He envisions a society reconstituted, not eliminated, in which men and women will "sit apart as the gods, talking from peak to peak all round Olympus." But he warns of the dangers of "an excess of fellowship" and counsels "lovers" to "guard their strangeness."[137]

Emerson's claim is that we are not sufficiently aware of our powers, not sufficiently noble. "Man," he notes in *Nature,* "is the dwarf of himself." This striving and transformative man emerges further in the work of William James and John Dewey, who participate in the formation of the new human-oriented Romantic myth described by Frye and in "the act of discovery that is also a making" which Bloom sees as essential to Romanticism.[138] Dewey's theory of education, for example, is a recipe for producing an active and imaginative human being, not the narrow and skulking "dwarf" diagnosed by Emerson. Both James and Dewey follow Emerson in focusing on the shaping power of the human mind, holding that the world we know is a malleable product of our pragmatically determined concepts. James particularly stresses the role of temperament in forming our vision of things, especially our philosophical visions. James and Dewey follow Emerson in criticizing the paltry notion of experience with which empiricism traditionally operates. Whether through their interest in feeling, in religious experience, in imagination, or in the shaping powers of the mind, the American Romantic philosophers seek to expand the narrow focus of classical empiricism while retaining the empiricist commitment to human experience for our knowledge of the world.

Notes

1. Gay Wilson Allen, *Waldo Emerson* (New York: Penguin, 1982), p. 187.

2. Harold Bloom, *The Ringers in the Tower* (Chicago: University of Chicago Press, 1971), p. 297. See also Bloom's discussion of "Romanticism and the Rational," pp. 323-38 of *The Ringers*; his discussion of "Emerson and His Influence," in his *A Map of Misreading* (New York: Oxford University Press, 1975), pp. 160-76; and B. L. Packer, *Emerson's Fall* (New York: Continuum, 1982), *passim.* On Emerson's use of the marriage metaphor for expressing the mind-world relationship, see Eric Cheyfitz, *The Trans-Parent: Sexual Politics in the Language of Emerson* (Baltimore: Johns Hopkins University Press, 1981), pp. 69 ff.

3. See notes 2 and 3 in the Preface.

4. John Dewey, *The Middle Works* (Carbondale: Southern Illinois University Press, 1976-83), 3:191 (hereafter cited as *MW*).

5. William James, *Essays in Religion and Morality* (Cambridge, Mass.: Harvard University Press, 1982), p. 114.

6. Stanley Cavell, "Thinking of Emerson" and "An Emerson Mood," in *The Senses of Walden* (San Francisco: North Point Press, 1981), hereafter cited as *SW*; "Genteel Responses to Kant? In Emerson's 'Fate' and Coleridge's *Biographia Literaria*," *Raritan* 3 (1985):34-61; hereafter cited as *GR*; and "Being Odd, Getting Even: Threats to Individuality," *Salmagundi* no. 67 (Summer 1985):97-128, hereafter cited as *BO* (the two previous papers are reprinted in Cavell's *In Quest of the Ordinary: Lines of Skepticism and Romanticism* (Chicago: University of Chicago Press, 1988); David Van Leer, *Emerson's Epistemology* (Cambridge, England: Cambridge University Press, 1986), Cornel West, *The American Evasion of Philosophy: A Geneology of Pragmatism* (Madison: University of Wisconsin Press, 1989); and Packer, *Emerson's Fall.* See also Julie Ellison, *Emerson's Romantic Style* (Princeton, N.J.: Princeton University Press, 1984); and Evan Carton, *The Rhetoric of American Romance: Dialectic and Identity in Emerson, Dickinson, Poe, and Hawthorne* (Baltimore: Johns Hopkins University Press, 1985) for application of the deconstructive philosophy of Barthes and Derrida to Emerson's works.

7. Emerson is often treated as a moral philosopher. See, for example, Ellen Kappy Sukiel, "Emerson on the Virtues," in Marcus G. Singer, ed., *American Philosophy* (Cambridge, England: Cambridge University Press, 1985), pp. 135-52. West understands him to be a political philosopher who "evades" traditional epistemological issues.

8. For a comparison of Dewey's and James's evaluations of Emerson, see John McDermott, "Spires of Influence: The Importance of Emerson for Classical American Philosophy," in his *Streams of Experience* (Amherst: University of Massachusetts Press, 1986), pp. 29-43. Poirier argues in *The Renewal of Literature: Emersonian Reflections* (New York: Random House, 1986)—convincingly in my view—that whether or not he acknowledged it, James was profoundly influenced by Emerson, for example, in his focus on action and transition (pp. 9-17).

9. *The Collected Works of Ralph Waldo Emerson,* ed. Robert E. Spiller et al. (Cambridge, Mass.: Harvard University Press, 1971-), 3:48; hereafter cited as *CW*.

10. See the interpretation of "Experience," provided by Sharon Cameron in "Representing Grief: Emerson's Experience," *Representations* 15 (Summer 1986):15-41.

11. Emerson, *CW*, 1:7-70.

12. Ibid., 1:7.

13. Ibid., 1:56.

14. A point stressed by Ellison, *Emerson's Romantic Style, passim.*

15. Emerson, *CW*, 1:56.

16. Emerson, *CW*, 2:28. For the idea that the scholar's freedom is essentially interpretive, see Ellison, *Emerson's Romantic Style,* pp. 97-104.

17. Emerson, *CW*, 1:63-4.

18. Such forward looking is a link between Emerson and the pragmatists. "Genius looks forward," Emerson stated, "The eyes of man are set in his forehead, not in his hindhead. Man hopes. Genius creates" (Ibid., 1:57).

19. Ibid., 1:64.

20. Ibid., 1:65.

21. Ibid., 1:52, 70.

22. Ibid., 1:89.

23. Ibid., 1:82.

24. For the contemporary reaction to the address, see Allen, *Waldo Emerson,* pp. 316 ff. Emerson was attacked for his "infidelity, pantheism, and atheism" (p. 322).

25. Emerson, *CW,* 1:90.

26. Ibid.

27. See his essay on Emerson.

28. Emerson, *CW,* 2:179.

29. Ibid., 2:180-1.

30. Ibid., 2:190. I broach the subject of Emerson's transitional metaphysics in my paper "Freedom in the Philosophy of Ralph Waldo Emerson, *Tulane Studies in Philosophy* 35 (1987):7.

31. Emerson, *CW,* 2:189. On the notion of transition or flux in Emerson, see Poirier, *The Renewal of Lit-*

erature, passim; West, *The American Evasion*, pp. 15 ff.; and my paper "Reconstructing American Philosophy: Emerson and Dewey," given at a conference, "Frontiers in American Philosophy," in June 1988 and forthcoming in *Texas A & M Studies in American Philosophy*. Cf. Friedrich Schlegel's idea that becoming is the essence of Romantic poetry, in *Friedrich Schlegel's Lucinde and the Fragments*, trans. Peter Firchow (Minneapolis: University of Minnesota Press, 1971), p. 173 (Athenaeum Fragment 116); and the discussion in Philippe Lacoue-Labarthe and Jean-Luc Nancy, *The Literary Absolute: The Theory of Literature in German Romanticism* (Albany: State University of New York Press, 1988), p. 43.

32. For some treatments of Emerson and Nietzsche, see Van Leer, *Emerson's Epistemology*, p. 217, n. 52.

33. Emerson, *CW*, 2:186.

34. Ibid., 2:187.

35. See note 6.

36. Emerson, *CW*, 2:38. Van Leer's discussion of this passage suggests his unfamiliarity with the Cartesian source, for he maintains that Emerson's statement of it lacks a "therefore" (Van Leer, *Emerson's Epistemology*, p. 136). "I think, therefore I am" occurs in the *Discourse on the Method* but not in the *Meditations*, in which Descartes writes "'I am, I exist' is necessarily true whenever I utter it or conceive it in my mind," using exactly the words that Emerson reproduces.

37. See Søren Kierkegaard, *Concluding Unscientific Postscript* (Princeton, N.J.: Princeton University Press, 1941). For a brief account of Kierkegaard's picture of human existence, see Section III of my paper "How a Thing Is Said and Heard: Wittgenstein and Kierkegaard," *History of Philosophy Quarterly* 3 (July 1986): 335-53.

38. Cavell, *BO*, p. 102.

39. Emerson, *CW*, 2:27.

40. Emerson, *CW*, 3:31.

41. Ibid.

42. Emerson, *CW*, 2:29.

43. Ralph Waldo Emerson, *The Conduct of Life* (Boston: Houghton Mifflin, 1904), p. 20; hereafter cited as *CL*. A classic discussion of Emerson's dialectic of freedom and fate occurs in Stephen Whicher's *Freedom and Fate: An Inner Life of Ralph Waldo Emerson* (Philadelphia: University of Pennsylvania Press, 1953).

44. Emerson, *CL*, pp. 8-9.

45. Ibid., p. 15; for the view that Emerson is not talking about his earlier thought in this passage, see Cavell, *GR*, p. 43.

46. Emerson, *CL*, pp. 41-2.

47. Ibid., p. 48.

48. But, one might ask, why shouldn't the way we handle it be part of fate, as our temperament is?

49. Emerson, *CL*, p. 47.

50. Ibid., pp. 47-8.

51. David Hume, *An Inquiry Concerning Human Understanding* (Indianapolis: Bobbs-Merrill, 1955), p. 104.

52. Emerson, *CW*, 3:32.

53. Ibid., 3:42.

54. The Heraclitean side of Plato emerges, however, in such dialogues as the *Phaedrus* and *Symposium*.

55. Emerson, *CW*, 4:91.

56. Ibid., 2:202.

57. Ibid., 4:101.

58. Ibid., 3:48.

59. Cavell's discussion is in Cavell, *SW*, pp. 142-3.

60. Emerson, *CW*, 1:37-8.

61. Ibid., 1:10.

62. Ellison argues that these are essential to Emerson's "aggressive" project of mastering the universe by interpreting it.

63. Allen, *Waldo Emerson*, p. 278.

64. Emerson, *CW*, 3:35.

65. See note 6.

66. Van Leer comes at Emerson's Kantianism independently of Cavell's work, producing an original argument about the Kantian claims of *Nature* and also enlightening discussions of many other Emersonian texts.

Although he is familiar with many philosophical sources, Van Leer's understanding of philosophical literature is somewhat shaky. For example, in discussing criticisms of Emerson for missing the distinction between "transcendental" (a priori and in some sense human) and "transcendent" (apart from all determination by what is human, beyond "the bounds of sense") in Kant, he misstates that very distinction by understanding transcendent principles as "organizing mental principles that are inaccessible to experience." For Kant they are illusions, not existing but inaccessible principles. The point of them (in the illusory tale, as it were) is that they are not mental and not subjective but, rather, that they reflect things as they are in themselves. Again, Van Leer takes transcendental idealism to mean that space and time are illusions; for example, he speaks of the rapidity with which "time and space vanish . . . in Kant's Aesthetic" (*Emerson's Epistemology*, p. 40) and maintains that "transcendental idealism ensures that experience will always be illusion, a tempest of fancies" (p. 163). Kant's project was to justify the objectivity of space and time.

More technically, Van Leer confuses entailment with identity (p. 91), gives an account of transcendental argument in which that notoriously difficult notion amounts merely to showing entailments ("that certain concepts are logically built into other concepts," p. 112); misses Austin's notion of a performative, for example, by saying that "performatives are oughts" (p. 243, n. 91); (If I insult you, I do not necessarily command you; only some performatives are "oughts"); and is unreliable on Wittgenstein—remarking (p. 175) that "a pain is not a possessing or even a content of any kind, but a behavioral act" or (p. 176) that in Wittgenstein's parable of the beetle in the box, pain drops out like the beetle (which misses Wittgenstein's point that this is so only if we "construe" pain "on the model of object and designation").

67. Emerson, *CW,* 3:48. Cf. Cavell, *SW,* p. 126.

68. Cavell, *SW,* p. 126.

69. Ibid., p. 125. This is a point that Van Leer fails to consider, for example, when he interprets Emerson's discussions as having moved beyond epistemology when they reach a sentiment such as Romantic joy (*Emerson's Epistemology,* p. 92). Van Leer, in fact, has an extremely puzzling notion of epistemology, maintaining for example, that Emerson's essay "Montaigne; or the Skeptic" is not about an epistemological topic (pp. 194-5). He appears to believe that if one regards faith or mystical experience (or, as one might say, a certain mood) as superseding doubt and as leading to truth, as Emerson does in "Montaigne" (and elsewhere), then one has somehow passed beyond the domain of epistemology. But this is to restrict epistemology, the theory of knowledge, to certain kinds of knowledge.

70. Emerson, *CW,* 3:30.

71. Ibid., 3:30, 45-6.

72. Ludwig Wittgenstein, *Tractatus Logico-Philosophicus* (London: Routledge & Kegan Paul, 1961), para. 6.43.

73. Cavell, *SW,* p. 125.

74. William James, *The Principles of Psychology* (Cambridge, Mass.: Harvard University Press, 1981), p. 1182.

75. Emerson, *CW,* 2:182.

76. Ibid., 4:99.

77. Ibid.; here the "common" is not to be embraced but avoided.

78. Cavell, *SW,* p. 128.

79. Emerson, *CW,* 3:48.

80. Cavell, *SW,* p. 126.

81. Cavell does not actually suggest this use of the "lords" in *SW,* though his interpretation of Emerson led me to it. Cf. Stanley Cavell, *This New Yet Un-*approachable America: Lectures After Emerson After Wittgenstein (Albuquerque, N.M.: Living Batch Press, 1989), p. 88. Van Leer also treats the lords as Kantian categories or forms in his discussion of "Experience" (*Emerson's Epistemology,* pp. 150-87).

82. Emerson, *CW,* 3:39; Van Leer, *Emerson's Epistemology,* p. 158.

83. Emerson, *CW,* 3:33.

84. Cameron, "Representing Grief," p. 21.

85. Emerson, *CW,* 3:31.

86. Ibid., 3:32.

87. Ibid., 3:57.

88. Ibid., 3:61, 57.

89. As Milly Theale does to Lord Mark in Henry James's *The Wings of the Dove.*

90. Emerson, *CW,* 3:64.

91. Ibid., 2:34.

92. Ibid., 3:54.

93. Ibid., 3:40.

94. Ibid., 3:29-30.

95. Ibid.

96. "There is no mark by which we can tell dreaming from waking." René Descartes, *Meditations on First Philosophy,* trans. Donald A. Cress (Indianapolis: Hackett, 1979). Cf. J. L. Austin, *Sense and Sensibilia* (New York: Oxford University Press, 1962), pp. 48-9.

97. Emerson, CW, 3:30.

98. Ibid., 3:43.

99. Ibid., 1:10.

100. James in *Varieties of Religious Experience,* and Dewey in *Democracy and Education.* See Chapters 3 and 4 in this text.

101. Emerson, *CW,* 1:10.

102. Ibid., 3:40.

103. Ibid., 2:189-90.

104. The contrast between the Platonic idea of knowledge as recollection and Emerson's idea of losing our memory is also striking.

105. Emerson, *CW,* 3:189 ("Circles"); *CW,* 3:39 ("Experience").

106. Ibid., 2:195.

107. Ibid., 1:41.

108. Ibid., 3:33.

109. Van Leer makes this point (*Emerson's Epistemology,* p. 165), though he does not seem to see the problem it raises for his claim that surprise is a category.

110. Emerson, *CW,* 3:47.

111. Allen, *Waldo Emerson,* p. 209.

112. Gay Wilson Allen, "A New Look at Emerson and Science," in Robert E. Burkholder and Joel Myerson, eds., *Critical Essays on Ralph Waldo Emerson* (Boston: G. K. Hall, 1983), pp. 339-40.

113. Emerson, *CW,* 1:35.

114. Ibid., 4:89. The last sentence is Montaigne's famous slogan in *Essays,* bk. 1, chap. 47.

115. Ibid., 3:43.

116. Montaigne, "On Experience," in *Selected Essays* (New York: Penguin, 1958), p. 348.

117. Emerson, *CW,* 1:58.

118. Ibid., 1:59, 150.

119. *The Later Works of John Dewey,* ed. Jo Ann Boydston (Carbondale: Southern Illinois University Press 1981-), 4:164-5.

120. Emerson, *CW,* 1:39.

121. Ibid., 1:31.

122. Ibid., 2:198.

123. Dewey, *MW,* p. 3

124. Emerson, *CW,* 3:20; William James, *Pragmatism* (Cambridge, Mass.: Harvard University Press, 1979), p. 34; *The Later Works of John Dewey,* 4:92; and R. W. Sleeper, *The Necessity of Pragmatism* (New Haven, Conn.: Yale University Press, 1986), p. 69. Cf. Poirier, *The Renewal of Literature,* pp. 33, 58; and West, *The American Evasion,* p. 36.

125. Emerson, *CW,* 2:188.

126. Ibid., 1:69.

127. Oscar W. Firkins, *Ralph Waldo Emerson* (Boston: Houghton Mifflin, 1915), p. 68.

128. Ibid., p. 33.

129. Emerson, *CW,* 1:83.

130. Ibid., 1:85. There is a voluntarist structure of evidence here, in that "my heart" provides the criterion of "origin in heaven."

131. Ibid., 1:12.

132. Samuel Taylor Coleridge, *Biographia Literaria,* ed. James Engell and Walter Jackson Bate (Princeton, N.J.: Princeton University Press, 1983), chap. 13. On the links with Coleridge, see Packer, *Emerson's Fall.*

133. Emerson, *CW,* 1:44.

134. Ibid., 1:31.

135. James, *Pragmatism,* p. 37. Cf. Hilary Putnam, *The Many Faces of Realism* (La Salle, Ill.: Open Court, 1987).

136. Emerson, *CW,* 2:43.

137. Ibid., 3:80-1.

138. Bloom, *The Ringers,* p. 337.

David Jacobson (essay date 1990)

SOURCE: "Vision's Imperative: 'Self-Reliance' and the Command to See Things As They Are," in *Studies in Romanticism,* Vol. 29, No. 4, Winter, 1990, pp. 555-70.

[In the following essay, Jacobson explores Emerson's early theories on self-reliance, explaining that for Emerson, self-reliance leads to an emancipation of the will, allowing for a clearer understanding of the universe.]

Emerson sets down the practical imperative of his early thought in the opening paragraph of **"Self-Reliance"** when he writes, "To believe your own thought, to believe that what is true for you in your private heart, is true for all men,—that is genius. Speak your latent conviction and it shall be the universal sense."[1] He describes a hyperbolic conception of freedom, freedom conceived as the unmediated expression of personal conviction unconstrained by regulations or rules. However, Emerson does not merely embrace the premise of pure expressivity; he goes on to assert in these lines that free expression affirms, shall affirm, "the universal sense." Here we find what is peculiar and what is characteristic about Emerson's idea of self-reliance: its claim that radical freedom shall issue of necessity in universal value, that the hyperbolically private shall issue in a universal sense. The peculiarity of this belief can be emphasized by comparing it to its most obvious precedent, Kant's Categorical Imperative. Emerson's statement in some respects repeats, and may even be intended to evoke, Kant's famous assertion that freedom is the basis of universal value. When placed side by side, the two formulations show their similarity: "Speak your latent conviction and it shall be the universal sense" echoes Kant's command to "Act only on the maxim through which you can at the same time will it should become a universal law."[2] Moreover, Kant recognized the essential oddness of his thought: "The thing is strange enough," he writes in reference to the Categorical Imperative, "and has no parallel in the remainder of practical knowledge. For the a priori thought of the possibility of giving universal law, which is thus merely problematic, is unconditionally commanded as a law without borrowing anything from experience or from any external will."[3]

Kant's moral thought rests on the intuition that pure freedom itself can be the transcendental condition of moral action.[4] And in this respect Emerson follows him. It is well known, however, that Kant mitigates the peculiarity of the impulse toward the Categorical Imperative by asserting that the transformation of pure freedom to universal law occurs through the mediation of reason—freedom legislates universal laws by appeal to the forms of reason. If the faculty of freedom overlooks all particular practical maxims, for Kant it does not overlook the structure of rational thought itself. On the contrary, it works through the structure of reason, and only thereby does Kant believe it returns freedom to practical efficacy. Thus the practical imperative in Kant's thought is finally no more or less than the command to be rational. Emerson, on the other hand, resists this and all limitation. He maintains the uncanniness of his intuition by refusing to retreat from the hyperbole of radical freedom to any definitive mediating structure, any antecedent criterion of value. Self-reliance thus consists of a skeptical release of the will from antecedent conditions, including especially the conditions of rational thought. It grows from the form of thought that Emerson identifies in **Nature** as *matutina cognitio,* the morning thought of forward-directed will that ignores a backward glance to prior limits of action and finds its value in what Emerson calls onwardness. As this suggests, self-reliance consists in an unlimited will, a will that knows no formal conditions. Emerson's early thought is founded on a skeptical will that, as he writes in his 1837 journal, comes "armed and impassioned to parricide thus murderously inclined ever to traverse and kill the Divine Life."[5] Insofar as recent criticism has focused on Emerson's representation and justification of conditionless will, it has accurately reflected that the individual for Emerson consists of the health of the will, the state of being oriented toward onwardness itself.

However, the emancipation of will does not entail for Emerson an essentially critical posture in the world, nor does it define an attitude that initiates or stands for the negation of meaning and value. That self-reliance affirms the universal sense makes clear that, for Emerson at least, the skeptical release of the will does not institute a negative method. It goes without saying that the emancipation of will involves a destructive moment. But Emerson found in skepticism the possibility for a fundamental affirmation, and it is in this respect that his imperative reminds us of Kant, that it has its Kant-like moment. However much self-reliance contrasts with Kant's rational Categorical Imperative, Emerson nonetheless shares with Kant a faith in the efficacy of a unified transcendental will. It is not enough, then, to infer from the destructive elements of Emerson's thought, from his skepticism in general, that his theory merely overthrows meaning, or that it leads to a prolific indeterminacy, or least of all, that it leads to some sort of broad deconstructionist position.[6] The challenge for readers of Emerson's early essays and lectures is rather to understand how his deep and far-reaching skepticism can be reconciled with an equally far-reaching affirmation: how skepticism can signify the infinite self.

I would urge that we can meet this challenge by recognizing that Emerson's skepticism does not function within the limits of the epistemological project that largely defines modern philosophical thought, and that it thus reflects less a strategy of rational thought than an attitude of will. For modern rationalism, skepticism is limited to either providing a tactical means to locate the sure grounds of knowledge, or, when this fails, to becoming the spearhead of a nihilistic assault on the forms of rational thought itself. In the latter case, the destructive moment in skepticism be-

comes the endpoint of thought, finding its destiny in the subversion of constructions of meaning. The history of modern philosophy consists in part of the portrayal of this destiny. But, as I have indicated, it does not represent the value skepticism holds for Emerson. If his writings refute modern philosophical positions, his skepticism nonetheless is not aimed principally at argumentation. Or put otherwise, it is not limited to a rationalist project. Aligning Emerson's position with radical *epistemological* skepticism thus runs a sizeable risk: that of inappropriately situating Emerson's thought in a context he would not recognize as his own. More importantly, it has the effect of de-emphasizing, even eliding, the "vast affirmative" at the core of his early thought, and replacing it with a negative thesis.

Emerson is rightly read in the context of religious thought, as a writer who recognized the power of human will to manifest the world, and thus gave to human will the revelatory power displaced by Christian ideology to the otherworldly will of God. Emersonian skepticism serves this humanist thesis insofar as he conceives of it as the attitude of will, the way of being in the world, that describes the central causality of human will, returning to it the capacity, not merely to act freely, but by doing so to bring the world to appearance, to speak the universal sense of the world. Emerson's purpose in **"Self-Reliance,"** and in all of his early lectures and essays, is to describe such infinite power of human will, and thereby to recognize the centrality of Man in the world, a centrality veiled behind myths of the omnipotence of God or nature.

My principal concern in this article is to demonstrate that self-reliance is linked to a phenomenological capacity, to the ability to *see truly*; and that only thereby can it speak the universal sense. I will do so first by showing that self-reliance and skepticism are closely related, that the freedom of the self-reliant individual is not isolated or unprecedented in Emerson's writings, but rather intersects with and can be articulated through the terms Emerson attributes to the skeptical attitude. The vigor and life—the transcendent virtue—of self-reliance can thus be seen to consist, not of mere randomness of will, but rather of the activity of living skeptically in the world. I will then go on to show that the skeptical attitude implies the phenomenological capacity to see truly by willing the transparency of the world. The imperative to self-reliance thereby shows itself to involve two discernible elements: the performances of emancipated will, and the consequent universal transparency of the world before a healthy will. In the first respect, self-reliance stands directly opposed to the essentially contemplative posture at the core of reflective thought, and as such, opposed to the project of epistemology, a fact that I will develop by following Stanley Cavell's reading of the essay.[7] Cavell's essay on **"Self-Reliance"** well demonstrates the performative nature of Emerson's skepticism, and by extension of self-reliance, and thereby distances Emerson from the tradition of modern reflective philosophy. The universal sense, however, can be understood only insofar as we recognize the phenomenological power of performative will. Therefore, I will trace the conjunction of self-reliance and the skeptical attitude to the capacity to bring the world to presence. Doing so will provide an explanation of Emerson's early thought that accommodates both the command to radical freedom and the insistence that free utterance establishes the universal sense. Moreover, it will allow me to specify the ways in which Emerson remains faithful to Kant's transcendental project, and the ways in which he revises it.

2

The most engaging of Emerson's descriptions of self-reliance is found a short way into the essay, where he writes, "The nonchalance of boys who are sure of a dinner, and would disdain as much as a lord to do or say aught to conciliate one, is the healthy attitude of human nature" (**CW** II: 29). Emerson raises through this description the image of an attitude of indifference that accords with an unconditioned will. He goes on to fill out the idea:

> A boy is in the parlour what the pit is in the playhouse; independent, irresponsible, looking out from his corner on such people and facts as pass by, he tries and sentences them on their merits, in the swift summary way of boys, as good, bad, interesting, silly, eloquent, troublesome. He cumbers himself never about consequences, about interests: he gives an independent, genuine verdict.
>
> (**CW** II: 29)

As a description of self-reliance, this statement is dominated by the sense of a will emancipated from crippling responsibility and released to the indifference that characterizes the boy's attitude before he is "clapped into jail by his consciousness" (**CW** II: 29). It undoubtedly reflects the unconditioned spontaneity most often associated with self-reliance. However, the statement is more interesting for the capacity of evaluation that it connects to the boy's attitude. Indifference is set out as a posture of immediate judgment, and moreover, the posture from which *genuine* verdicts derive. If the boy's attitude is one of irresponsibility, then the effect of his attitude is evaluation of the most authentic kind. The most remarkable aspect of this description, then, is the relation it establishes between a conditionless will and genuine or right evaluation.

When, a few sentences later, Emerson characterizes the boy's attitude as the posture of "neutrality," he provides the means necessary to link the boy's healthy attitude to the meaning of skepticism that he elaborates over the course of his writings. Neutrality carries precisely the sense of the suspension of judgment that Emerson identifies in **"Montaigne"** as the principle of skepticism. The boy is neither a critic nor a believer, his back is turned on the conditions of criticism and belief, and he stands, like the skeptic, as an "innocent" observer in the midst of the world. We can hear an echo of the description of the boy in Emerson's later depiction of the skeptic: "I neither affirm nor deny," Emerson's skeptic says, "I stand here to try the case. I am here to consider, *skopein,* to consider how it is."[8]

In neither the instance of self-reliance nor of skepticism does neutrality indicate a broad indifference to value, the mere negation entailed by universal doubt. Rather, in each case it stands for a specific indifference to antecedent criteria of value, and thereby represents the capacity for giving genuine verdicts, a capacity enabled by the scope that indifference or neutrality implies. It is not at all correct then to see neutrality as incapacitating or merely playful whim; evaluations that issue from neutrality, from a position of "unaffected, unbiassed, unbribable, unaffrighted innocence," are not inconsequential or frivolous. On the contrary, they "must always be formidable" (**CW** II: 29). Emerson says he writes whim on the lintels of his doorpost to protect his genius, not to disarm it. The boy and the skeptic alike are marked by the unprecedented capacity to observe, to "look out" from their corner of the world, and to give value to the world without blame or prejudice. Although the statement comes from **"Montaigne,"** Emerson could as well have written of the self-reliant individual that "Every thing that is excellent in mankind . . . he will see and judge" (**W** 4: 161).[9]

What interests me here, at least first of all, is the connection between self-reliance and skepticism, and the implication that skepticism runs through and is essential to all of Emerson's thought. Stanley Cavell has recognized the central place of the skeptical attitude in Emerson's thought, and has developed its role. There is good reason, then, to turn to his work on **"Self-Reliance"** in order to sharpen our understanding of the meaning of Emersonian skepticism.

Cavell develops his reading by juxtaposing Emerson's notion of self-reliance to Descartes' skeptical cogito in order to note in Emerson's writings a rejection of the contemplative model of reason that stands at the core of reflective philosophy, and then to replace it with a performative model of reason. He thereby situates Emerson's thought in an emerging tradition of theories of action that dismiss material and ideal bases of value and engender the value of the self and nature through an act of will. Cavell's interpretation of **"Self-Reliance"** is important because he shows that the skeptical subject is essentially performative.

Cavell argues that Descartes' theory is weakened by its failure to show the dependence of self-identity on individual performance, or to be more precise, on the issuance of a skeptical attitude in an evaluative stance in the world. Cavell brings this issue to a discussion of **"Self-Reliance"** by focusing on Emerson's description of the upright position as a willingness to dare to say "I think, I am," taking this statement to be a direct allusion to Descartes' famous epistemological formulation, "I think, therefore I am." Unlike Descartes, Cavell argues, Emerson recognized the necessity of action for the description of the cogito. In Emerson's use of it, the fundamental axiom of modern epistemology, as well as the set of problems it initiates, gives way to issues of action. Thus, if Emerson quotes Descartes, he does not quote him exactly. Or at least in quoting him he affirms, as Descartes hadn't, the *moral* imperative in the epistemological assertion, and with it the necessity of performance for the acknowledgement of the value of the self.

However, Cavell's critique of Descartes (as well as his consequent defense of Emerson) involves more than the suggestion that the self-reliant individual is active. More importantly, he indicates that within a skeptical method like Emerson's true individuality, or as he would have it, self-acknowledgement, is possible only to the extent that a context of otherness is itself acknowledged. "Because," he writes, "it turns out that to gain the assurance, as Descartes had put it, that I am not alone in the world has turned out to require that I allow myself to be known" (Cavell 293). Descartes failed to make this clear. His "use of [the "I"] arises exactly in a context in which there are no others to distinguish himself (so to speak) from. So the force of the pronoun is in apparent conflict with its sense" (Cavell 280). The challenge to skeptical thought as Cavell describes it is to provide the means of locating one's skepticism in a context of otherness, for only thereby is effective or postural self-identity enabled. The figure of the upright individual attracts him, not only because it indicates action but because it is precisely an effective posture, a figure that is defined in relation to the world, that has value as a posture in the context of the world. It implies for him the position of standing, or of standing *for,* something—and thus indicates conviction as a function of one's position in some context of action. The "imperative of human existence," he writes, "[is] that it must prove or declare itself," which means it must bear responsibility for itself in a community of others (Cavell 279). The crucial fact of self-reliance for Cavell is that by acting—by daring to act—we dispose ourselves in a context of otherness, and thereby can be acknowledged.

Cavell's discussion sets our reading of Emerson on the right track; it is useful for its explication of the problem of self-reliance in terms of skepticism, of performance and effective value; for his insistence that self-reliance describes an active individual and reveals the individual in relation to the world, as it is disposed in the world, and as it thereby bears responsibility for itself. By drawing a connection between a formal cogito and Emerson's idea of individuality, Cavell convincingly demonstrates that Emerson's skeptical approach is rooted in a performance that enables the recognition of the self in the world. He indicates that the individual is thus present as an instance of becoming, a transitional moment, or as he says, "a transience of being, a being of transience" (Cavell 284). However, my sense is that Cavell does not sufficiently emphasize the phenomenological core of the performative act, the fact that for Emerson the boy "looks on" the world and the skeptic "*sees* and judges." For Emerson, there is a profound intimacy between skepticism and sight, which is to say, between performance and sight. Later I will suggest why I believe that Cavell's failure to emphasize this intimacy leads him to misconstrue Emerson's meaning in an important way, but first I want to point out that even the upright position, which Cavell treats as a figure of a

postural and dispositional individual, in fact refers to the process of sight.

Emerson derived the figure of uprightness from Milton in the seventh book of *Paradise Lost,* where it refers to the attitude of man at his creation. But more importantly, he calls it up in this essay from his own earlier writings, which show that he clearly understood the human attitude as a way of seeing. In his 1835 journals Emerson wrote: "I ought to have no shame in publishing the records of one who aimed only at the upright position more anxious that the thing should be truly seen than careful what thing it was" (*JMN* V: 43). The statement indicates that to be in the upright posture means for Emerson to be in a condition or attitude of seeing truly, to be identified with and to find oneself as the process of sight.

Cavell's emphasis on performance is thus only half of the story of self-reliance. For *to do* in Emerson principally means to make visible; to speak is to lay out the appearance of nature. To be sure, the appearance of nature presents an effective context in which self and otherness are mutually disposed—indeed the relations between them are rendered transparent. But it is important to recognize that the essential individual in Emerson's early writings is not the self found in a dispositional relation to otherness; rather, the act of self-reliance consists of a fundamental trust in one's vision, and the authentic individual is recognized as the prolific capacity to bring nature to appearance. What Emerson has in mind in **"Self-Reliance"** is a phenomenological account of individuality for which the "Trustee," the "aboriginal Self on which a universal reliance may be grounded" consists of such a phenomenological power (*CW* II: 37). In the very paragraph of **"Self-Reliance"** that refers to the final trustee as Instinct or Spontaneity—i.e. unconditioned will—Emerson completes his thought by describing the "involuntary perceptions" to which "a perfect faith is due" (*CW* II: 37). The final trustee of the individual is the phenomenological capacity of unconditioned will, the involuntary, inevitable, unmediated illumination of the world, and secondarily, our place in it.

If we wish to understand Emerson's "philosophy of the erect position," we should then take a lively interest in what he means when he says "the thing should be truly seen."[10] It goes without saying that he does not mean seeing either what is objectively there or what is subjectively-represented as being there. That epistemological distinction is not relevant to Emerson. That a thing be truly seen means that it be recognized before the eye of an emancipated will, transparent for *matutina cognitio.* Here we see the importance that Emerson places in uprightness; it is a skeptical attitude and a phenomenological power—an attitude that consists in the power of vision. Uprightness is Emerson's principal figure for a specific manner of being in the world, i.e. as the human power to manifest the world. Self-reliance consists of a phenomenological way of being in the world. It consists of unconditioned will *in the service of* a phenomenological method. Insofar as uprightness is the proper figure of Emersonian individuality, it suggests that the self-reliant individual consists of a causal power to manifest the world anew, that it names an orientation of thought that is directed away from any predictable appearance, and enables the appearance of a plurality of natural effects. Uprightness converges for Emerson with the boy's attitude and means the capacity to see without shame, to *observe* innocent of prior conditions. The boy's "formidable" verdicts stem from thus seeing, willing, things as they are.

That Emerson believed in the possibility of skeptical sight to manifest the sheer and unmediated effects of the world is suggested as early as the end of *Nature* in his well-known assertion that "The ruin or blank, that we see when we look at nature, is in our own eye. The axis of vision is not coincident with the axis of things" (*CW* I: 43). The coincidence of the axis of vision and the axis of things, enabled by the forward orientation of *matutina cognitio,* describes unmediated vision of the world as a natural unfolding of the effects of emancipated will. This statement in *Nature* is an early indication of Emerson's turning away from a rationalist approach to the value of self and nature, an approach he believed necessarily intervened in the relation between seer and nature, rendering the latter through fixed categories of thought and alienating the former from the consequent static world. The figure of the coincidence of vision and nature graphically illustrates Emerson's conception of the immediacy of the relation between will and *phusis.* It also suggests the essentially pragmatic nature of Emerson's insight; pragmatic, that is, inasmuch as the figure of twin axes places emphasis on the integrity of natural effects, and indicates that the value of self and world, for Emerson, will be found in the visible effects of nature.[11] The central causality of human will knows itself and has value for Emerson in and through the world it manifests. Emerson thus calls on us to be in the world as the occasion of the pragmatic manifestation of the world. The "transparent eyeball," described early in *Nature,* is an effective figure of the idea of pragmatic sight. It well describes the location of the value of self and world in the appearance and gathering of nature's effects. Moreover, it identifies the eye and individuality without asserting the epistemological subjectivity of the eye. Emerson makes clear that all categories that could define subjectivity and objectivity are lost in the sheer manifestation of nature, and the individual is taken to be no more than the occasion of nature's presence. The individual does not mediate or condition nature's appearance so much as it is, to use a Heideggerian term, the "clearing" in which nature appears.

The conception of individuality as sight does not indicate a static manifestation of nature, however, but the process of nature's coming to appearance; this is the core meaning of the figure of the coincidence of the axes of vision and things. Emerson best reflects the fluidity and transitional nature of sight in **"Circles"** by representing the imperative to overcome any single horizon of the eye. The horizon of the eye establishes the limit of the appearance of nature. The eye's horizon is then the first and the only circle; it demarcates the space within which natural effects appear. However, the constancy of any single horizon of the eye establishes a fixed economy of value according to which natural presence is determined and rendered static. More importantly, within the economy of any horizon the individual is diminished to functional self-identity. Emerson's Orphic poet in *Nature* speaks of such dwarfing of ourselves (*CW* I: 42). The economic disposition effected by the horizon of the eye fixes the self in opposition to nature, subverts the coincidence of vision and things, and introduces an artificial divide between self and nature. The sedimentation and repetition of a particular order, as revealed within the eye's view, acts to construct normative and theoretical values that effectively constitute one's lived experience. Emerson's embrace of a performative phenomenological capacity is the foundation for his attacks on conventions and more broadly on all circumstantial limits. He views the delimitation of sight to a particular horizon of the eye as the consequence of foreclosing the coincidence of vision and things, denying the performance of the individual or turning away from the forward orientation of a healthy will.

Time and again, in **"Circles"** and elsewhere, Emerson characterizes the phenomenological destruction and progressiveness essential to his thought. He insists in a litany of phrases and sentences that his central value is the manifestation of pure onwardness: "There are no fixtures to men," "no Past at my back," "Life is a series of surprises," "The continual effort to raise himself above himself, to work a pitch above his last height, betrays itself in a man's relations," and most characteristically, "We can never go so far back as to preclude a still higher vision" (*CW* II: 182, 188, 189, 182, 183). Everything emerges within the eye's horizon, but equally, there is no limit to what we can see, and therefore to how we can find ourselves: "There is no outside, no enclosing wall, no circumference to us" (*CW* II: 181). Here Emerson advocates a phenomenological attitude of evaluation that consists of the sheer activity of overcoming one's limits, of recognizing that "the only sin is limitation" (*CW* II: 182). In order to stand upright as the focal point of nature's gathering and appearance, the individual must overcome its self-diminution within any circle and find a new generalization, a new horizon of sight. Emerson conceives no end to this process; it is not as though eventually the true horizon of the eye, and thus of nature and the individual, will be found. Rather, the true horizon is found each time a previous economy is overcome; the *true* horizon is the emergent horizon that reveals the individual as the clearing that enables the appearance of nature. Seeing beyond is thus to see truly, to be in the upright posture, to think, to dare. And the practical activity that enables right vision is the process of overcoming self- and natural determination.

If the upright position implies a phenomenological power, then it should be added that recognizing this fact is crucial to our understanding of the universal sense. This point can be emphasized by thinking again about Cavell's article, for the universal sense is explicable only on the terms of the phenomenological thesis, and I would suggest Cavell's reading falls short of explaining Emerson's early thought, and specifically **"Self-Reliance,"** on just this point. Insofar as uprightness speaks the transparent appearance of the world as the body of relations that fall in place around acts of will, it lays out the universal sense of the world; it represents the fundamental capacity that Emerson attributes to human will, the power to bring the world to appearance, to enclose nature within the horizon of the eye, and thereby to effect the universal sense. Although he rightly emphasizes the active, performative nature of the upright position, Cavell overlooks its phenomenological value, and is led, therefore, to locate the self-reliant individual *in the world*, rather than noting the causality of the individual for the world's appearance. Specifically, Cavell depicts the individual as situated in a larger field of value, stating that the individual dares to think and to act up against the terms of an overwhelming external power, the sort of power that Emerson would later speak of as fate. By so doing Cavell places truth, or at least the provisional terms of true value, outside the individual and beyond the efficacy of human will. The revolution that Emerson conceived of under the sign of self-reliance consists, however, of recognizing the universality of authentic human will, of the essential life above the "running sea of circumstance" (*CW* II: 70). I do not want to overstate my differences with Cavell, for there can be little doubt that by emphasizing the performative nature of the Emersonian individual he has established important terms for considering self-reliance, directing attention toward the individual's way of being in the world, the quality of his existence. But there is nonetheless an important point to be made here: in a fundamental respect Cavell's interpretation skews Emerson's early thought, turns Emerson on his head. Because he ignores the phenomenological causality of the individual, Cavell disposes the individual in an essentially alien world. Having done so, he can only construe the universal sense in formal terms, casting Emerson's thought as more rhetorical than it is, and finally asserting that the command to speak one's latent conviction is a "proposed therapy," no more than "a fantasy of finding your own voice" (Cavell 286, 288).

It is not adequate to Emerson's early thought, however, to give to human will a merely rhetorical power, the power to create formal transparency. Emerson's early insight is not partial or limited, but rather consists of a profound belief in the universal power of human being to will the world's appearance, a belief in the possibility of the coincidence of vision and things. It is essential to recognize the phenomenological core of uprightness, its intersection with the argument of **"Circles,"** because thereby we see that uprightness provides the foundation for the utterance of the universal sense, and that it figures forth the cause of the real, living appearance of nature. It is a well known fact that Emerson would soon enough reject his early faith in the centrality of human will, but if we are to understand the imperative of the early thought—and indeed, the significance of his later turn to fate—we must recognize the phenomenological power that Emerson attributes to human will.[12] When we do, it is clear that the imperative of Emerson's early thought is not simply to acknowledge ourselves—though doing so is certainly an aspect of Emer-

son's concern, and the phenomenological thematics of the figure of uprightness hardly obstruct the illumination of the relations of self and otherness. The imperative, however, is to recognize the individual as the sole principle and occasion of nature's appearance, and thus to disclose nature, to act in such a way as to bring nature from behind the concealments that are put in place by the imposition of prescriptive conditions on the will. Emerson's imperative to speak your latent conviction is thus a command to see the world as it is, to discover the world you have built and your place in it.

Emerson's principal concern in **"Self-Reliance,"** as in all of the early essays, is to describe the meaning and manner of unconcealing nature, of being with nature. He doesn't naively ignore that we make reasoned decisions about our role in society, that we operate through the terms of conventions and norms. But he denies that doing so is the meaning of self-reliance. On the contrary, it shows the ultimate dependence of identity—the account we give of ourselves—on antecedent evaluative structures, broadly, the structures of society that he says are in conspiracy against the individual. Emerson describes a performative individual that bespeaks his coincidence with nature and thereby his engagement of Being; not the subjective domination or construction of nature, but human activity that discloses the nearness of human and natural being under the causality of emancipated will. The authentic speech he has in mind is not bound by the customs of social language; it speaks the plurality of value opened by the individual, by the individual's immediate relation to the proliferation of nature. Such speech has very little to do with being responsible to society in the narrow sense of rational reckoning, a fact that Emerson's critics have often pointed out. Emerson struggled, however, to convince his readers that it has everything to do with being responsible to human being in the broad sense, in the sense of recognizing the quality of our being in the world. The latter sort of responsibility implies Emersonian transcendentalism, a capacity that eludes appropriation by conventional forms of thought, and thereby affords a direct relation to Being.

3

I began this article by suggesting that Emerson shared Kant's intuition of the basis of moral value in freedom but substantially altered the conception of transcendence attached to it, maintaining the immediate transformation of private will into the universal sense. It is now possible to articulate the difference in Emerson's notion of transcendence by using the terms of the central imagery of sight. Emerson understood transcendence as the clearing of the eye, the space opened up within the horizon of the eye. His then is a phenomenological transcendence, not a rational one. It is height, the upright posture, understood as the activity of rising above normative conventions—which for Emerson means all principled determinations of thought—and seeing truly. To see truly is to establish a phenomenological opening in which nature and the self appear, and moreover, in which they appear immediately as manifest value. Transcendence, the upright posture and height are all comprehensible as nothing but this phenomenological opening.

If so, then Emerson altered the meaning of transcendence mainly by indicating that it is a matter of action, not contemplation, by inverting the traditional priority of theory over practice and rendering universality finite. The imperative in Emerson's thought is to act, rather than to deliberate; specifically, to act in such a way as to establish the eye's opening, to clear the area of the eye's horizon, to manifest nature. **"Self-Reliance"** compels us to action that destroys the mediate forms of thought that conceal nature and diminish the individual. Action accordingly precedes and enables thought. The fundamental imperative standing behind **"Self-Reliance"** is not Kant's imperative on freedom to legislate rationally, an imperative that presupposes thought's priority over action, but the Emersonian command to act freely and thus give rise to thought as the presence of the world; i.e. to ignore the external language of grounds and principles and to "Speak rather of that which relies, because it works and is" (*CW* II: 40). The imperative of early Emersonian thought is to act out of innocence *in order to* think, to see, clearly. Emerson often spoke of his imperative as abandonment. In **"Spiritual Laws,"** for example, he noted that our public speaking "has not abandonment." Here oratory only figures forth Emerson's larger claim about authenticity. "Somewhere," he wrote, "not only every orator but every man should let out all the length of all the reins; should find or make a frank and hardy expression of what force and meaning is in him" (*CW* II: 83). Emersonian transcendence, figured by the decisiveness of speech, manifests being by following no pre-given path and having no definite goal, and thereby enables the universal sense as the authentic effect of actions by which the individual brings the world to appearance. The teleological structure assumed by rationalism locates universality in a discursive final cause. Advocating the willful abandonment of rational teleology, Emerson effectively reconceives the meaning of universal causality, construing it not as a formal and alien law but as a quality of life, the recognition of one's causality in nature, one's coincidence with the directionality, the onward appearance of nature, and thus one's manifestation of the universal sense of nature.

Critics who understand self-reliance strictly in terms of the imperative to abandonment are in an important sense not mistaken. Genuine verdicts do reflect the utterance of an unconditioned will. From the perspective of rationalist conventions of thought they are evaluations made without aim, random shots in the dark. The boy's attitude gives value—achieves self- and natural determination—without purpose or goal, as scattered assertions whose only intent is "the shooting of the gulf . . . the darting to an aim," and whose only end is illuminating the unknown transition, "advancing on Chaos and the Dark" (*CW* II: 40, 28). However, Emersonian transcendence, although emancipated from formal reason and impelled by the activity of abandonment, nonetheless identifies unified individuality,

not the dispersal and fragmentation of the will, and it does so because assertion situates a phenomenological clearing, and speech articulates the boundary of sight. Self-reliance is therefore not only a feeling of onwardness, an affect of the will's power and freedom, but the presence, the universal sense, of the world as the effect of the will's authenticity. The act of speech lays out the terms of a decision that gives presence to the world and defines the individual. Insofar as decision consists of the pure act of severing or cutting off one's vision, the unity of the individual emerges through the decisive act of speech. Choice implies no rational deliberation and presupposes no a priori structure of identity, but it results in the unity of phenomenological resolution: the individual understood as the gathering of the transparent relations of self and nature. It involves a fundamental trust in one's own vision; to decide—and thereby to identify oneself—means both to believe your private heart, your latent convictions, and to speak their appearance as the emergence of the world, as the ever-new definition of the individual given by the willed manifestation of the world.

Emerson's phenomenological transcendentalism thus converges with the meaning of individuality, it returns the individual in the nonchalance of the boy's attitude, an attitude of abandonment that *as such* signifies the appearance of the world, an attitude that passes genuine verdicts and speaks truly out of its innocent observation, an attitude of will that speaks the involuntary perception given to it. Thus, when Emerson asks in his journal "Who can define to me an individual? . . . armed and impassioned to parricide thus murderously inclined, ever to traverse and kill the Divine Life," he has already his answer (*JMN* V: 336-37). The individual is defined when we recognize our power to *decide* to blend with nature's appearance, to speak the truth of nature, and to identify ourselves as the occasion of that true appearance. Out of his skepticism, out of the death of God, Emerson found the possibility of practical transcendence and individuality in the decision that thus heeds the "awful invitation . . . to blend with [the dawn's] aurora" (*JMN* V: 337).

Notes

1. Ralph Waldo Emerson, *The Collected Works of Ralph Waldo Emerson,* ed., Alfred R. Ferguson, et al. (Cambridge: Harvard UP, 1971) II: 27; hereafter cited as *CW,* with volume and page number.

2. Immanuel Kant, *The Groundwork of the Metaphysic of Morals,* ed., H. J. Paton (London: The Mayflower Press; Hutchinson University Library, 1947) 88.

3. Kant, *Critique of Practical Reason,* ed., Lewis White Beck (Chicago: U of Chicago P, 1949) 142.

4. Cf. "Instead of this vainly sought deduction of the moral principle something entirely different and unexpected appears: the moral principle itself serves as a principle of the deduction of an inscrutable faculty . . . the faculty of freedom" (Kant, *Critique of Practical Reason,* cited in Robert J. Benton, *Kant's Second Critique and the Problem of Tran-*

scendental Arguments [The Hague: Martinus Nijhoff, 1977]) 55.

5. Emerson, *The Journals and Miscellaneous Notebooks of Ralph Waldo Emerson,* ed., William H. Gilman, et al. (Cambridge: Harvard UP, 1960) v: 337; hereafter cited as *JMN,* with volume and page number.

6. See, for example, Barbara Packer, "Uriel's Cloud: Emerson's Rhetoric," *Georgia Review* 31: 322-42; Harold Bloom, "Emerson: The American Religion," in *Agon: Toward a Theory of Revision* (New York: Oxford UP, 1982); Julie Ellison, "The Laws of Ice Cream: Emerson's Irony and 'The Comic'" *ESQ* 30 (2): 73-82. My reading of Emerson corresponds in some respects to the work of each of these writers, and I do not support the sort of return to epistemological readings that David Van Leer puts forward in his recent book (*Emerson's Epistemology: The Argument of the Essays* [New York: Cambridge UP, 1986]). However, for Emerson the disruption of epistemological categories of thought yields an affirmative potential, rather than a negative, deconstructive or merely ironic value. I will urge in this article that a complete interpretation of Emerson's thought requires a recognition of the identity of will and sight and thus of a consequent affirmative phenomenology. By noting the phenomenological core of the early thought, we not only enrich our reading of "Self-Reliance," but also provide the terms necessary to comprehend the changes that occur in Emerson's philosophical method during and after the 1840's.

7. Stanley Cavell, "Being Odd, Getting Even: Threats to Individuality," in *Reconstructing Individualism: Autonomy, Individuality and the Self in Western Thought,* ed., Thomas C. Heller, Morton Sosna, David E. Wellbery (Stanford: Stanford UP, 1986); hereafter cited as Cavell, with page number.

8. Emerson, *The Complete Works of Ralph Waldo Emerson,* ed., Edward Emerson (Cambridge: Houghton Mifflin, 1903) iv: 156; hereafter cited as *W,* with volume and page number.

9. If the self-reliant boy and the skeptic share the capacity of innocent sight, they nonetheless mark quite different roles for that capacity in Emerson's thought. "Self-Reliance" is Emerson's most powerful humanist statement, which is to say he identifies sight and judgment as human capacities. By the time he writes "Montaigne" Emerson has revised his theory, turning to a method of philosophical anti-humanism. The principal effect this has on human nature is to render it representative, typical. Thus, whereas the boy's innocence reflects the universal sense of individual authenticity, the skeptic's is a delimited, representative capacity. It is nonetheless wrong to conclude that no continuity exists between skepticism and the self-reliant attitude. On the contrary, both are motivated by the central en-

during fact of Emerson's thought: his meditation on skeptical sight.

10. The development of the "philosophy of the erect position" can be traced over a number of years (*JMN* iv: 333). It refers to Emerson's theory of judgment and reason, which consist of the phenomenological exposition of the relations initiated and engaged by an active will. The treatment of uprightness as sight receives its most detailed development in "Circles," where uprightness and individuality are explicitly identified with the figure of the eye.

11. Peirce formulates the pragmatic maxim this way: "Consider what effects, that might conceivably have practical bearings, we conceive the object of our conception to have. Then, our conception of these effects is the whole of our conception of the object" (*The Collected Papers of Charles Sanders Peirce,* ed., Charles Hartshorne and Paul Weiss [Cambridge: Harvard UP, 1931] 5: 402).

12. Emerson's later thought is philosophically antihumanist. But, this point will continue to be overlooked until we give due weight to the universal phenomenological causality of human will in the early essays, and thus are able to recognize that the turn to fate is predicated on a rejection of the phenomenological power of human will.

Eduardo Cadava (essay date 1993)

SOURCE: "The Nature of War in Emerson's 'Boston Hymn,'" in *Arizona Quarterly,* Vol. 49, No. 3, Autumn, 1993, pp. 21-58.

[*In the following essay, Cadava traces the link between nature and politics, in addition to examining Emerson's views on war in the context of his poem "The Boston Hymn."*]

Less than five years before the outbreak of the Civil War, Emerson announces a crisis in the structures of political and linguistic representation. "Language has lost its meaning in the universal cant," he writes, "*Representative Government* is misrepresentative; *Union* is a conspiracy against the Northern States which the Northern States are to have the privilege of paying for; the *adding of Cuba and Central America* to the slave marts is *enlarging the area of Freedom. Manifest Destiny, Democracy, Freedom,* fine names for a ugly thing."[1] He makes this statement within the context of the controversy over the Kansas-Nebraska Act. This Act had repealed the Missouri Compromise and legislated that the question of slavery be determined by individual state constitutions rather than by a national policy of exclusion. For Emerson, that slavery is to be preserved and extended signals a contradiction in the meaning of America, a contradiction that is dissimulated within a rhetoric of representation, democracy, and freedom. Declaring the rhetorical and historical basis of the virtues upon which America was to be founded, Emerson here predicts the crisis of representation that would define the issues over which the coming war would be fought.[2] These issues included debates over who could claim the right to representation and over the relations of power existing between state and federal governments within the system of representation. The crisis to which Emerson refers is therefore a crisis written into the history of America, insofar as America was itself conceived in various efforts to rethink and define the nature and concept of representation.

As Emerson suggests, however, this crisis in political representation is inseparable from the acts of representation that would soon render, and sometimes justify, the suffering and death brought on by the war. What interests him are the various rhetorical means whereby the war or its ideological implications are legitimated. Throughout the war, his lectures, essays, poems, and journal entries persistently challenge the tendencies of contemporary representations of the war either to justify the effects of its violence or to have them disappear in the name of the ideological discourses that helped both the North and the South negotiate the meaning of the war even before it had ended. We should not be surprised if, within this arena of representation, Emerson's attention focuses upon the recourse to a rhetoric of nature. Both Union and Confederate soldiers and civilians enlisted nature in the service of legitimating their respective causes as well as the war's violence. Moreover, the rhetoric of nature was central to the constitution of a nationalist ideology in the antebellum period. Insofar as this rhetoric attempts to dissimulate the violence that has been effected in its name, the historical issues and questions that have led to the civil crisis, or the death and violence of the war, Emerson positions himself against it.

Nevertheless, amidst the brutality and terror of the Civil War, Emerson's own appeal to the virtues of liberty and justice converges with an appeal to a rhetoric of nature. Aroused by the dangers of the war, by the danger that the ethical dimension of the war might be attenuated by the colossal carnage and suffering that define the struggle's most visible effects, he consistently mobilizes his efforts in the direction of stirring up enthusiasm for the war and its moral benefits. Nothing characterizes these efforts more than his use of natural imagery. Men and women need to be moved to act, he argues. They need to be persuaded to make sacrifices in the name of justice and freedom. And nothing moves or persuades people better than the evocation of nature. The idiom of nature is in fact everywhere in Emerson. If he seems to use the same rhetoric used by others to justify the war, though, he uses it in order to trace its operations within the many efforts to define the meaning of the war: he uses this rhetoric in order to mobilize it in another direction. Only in this way, he says, may we take a step in the direction of justice.

The war itself is of course such a step, but Emerson suggests at least two more such steps in his poetry written during this time, each in their own way a turning point for the war—Lincoln's Emancipation Proclamation and the recruitment of black soldiers into the Union Army. In his **"Boston Hymn"** he celebrates the occasion and significance of the Proclamation and in **"Voluntaries"** he eulogizes the heroism of the Massachusetts 54th regiment, perhaps the most renowned black regiment of the war.[3] In both poems, Emerson names the revolutionary forces of emancipation with natural metaphors. In the first, he turns to the natural phenomena of snow to figure the gathering momentum of the Northern drive toward freedom. In the second, he joins this same climatic metaphor to a meteorological one, the aurora borealis, in order to emphasize the moral center around which the North, having welcomed black soldiers into its army, is now magnetized. In the process, the metaphors of snow and the aurora take on specific historical, political, theological, and literary connotations that require us to turn to the relationship between these domains and questions of language. Always in Emerson, the urgency that we align ourselves with the laws of nature corresponds to the necessity that we be attentive to the rhetorical dimension of our historical and political existence. In what follows, I wish to trace the link between nature and politics as it manifests itself in his **"Boston Hymn."** If the political agenda of this poem sometimes seems to support Unionism, it at the same time works to criticize the political and rhetorical assumptions that might ground such support. This work of criticism can often be read more easily in the actual practice of Emerson's writing, that is to say, in its staging and treatment of the rhetoric of slavery and war, than in any explicit and straightforward arguments. This is why much of what follows will involve tracking the history sealed within the language of Emerson's poem. In the long run, this approach hopes to contribute to the recent reevaluations of Emerson's relation to this same history.[4]

. . . . .

Emerson delivered his **"Boston Hymn"** on January 1, 1863, the effective date of the Emancipation Proclamation, at a "Jubilee Concert" in the Boston Music Hall. He praises the Proclamation for having inaugurated the dawning of a new day in the meaning of America and challenges his audience to meet the responsibilities this new day and meaning entail. For him, the Proclamation revises America's legacy and thereby renews the legacy's power and promise. It declares a promise that is also a rethinking of the promise of America's settlement, its revolution and future. This is to say, however, that the Proclamation draws its social and political force from the history it wishes to overcome. If the Proclamation is not to repeat the sins of this history, if it is to realize its promise of political and social change, it must convey the promise of its own truth to all peoples. But this can only happen if the declaration at the same time encourages people to take responsibility for their own history. Men and women must risk thinking the history that has made this declaration necessary. Only in this way may they be prepared to respond to the demands of emancipation. What is at stake for Emerson as he writes his poem is the possibility of translating the truth of the

Proclamation into the minds and hearts of his audience. The hymn rehearses the history of the proclamation, of its terms and conditions—in its present form as well as in its Puritan form—and encourages the audience to commit itself to realizing the proclamation within history. Such commitment is necessary because the mere declaration of a promise may never be its realization. The revolutionary emancipation of the slave can only begin with this act and can only take place if it is continually renewed by every individual who receives the force of its truth. "Every revolution," he explains in his essay **"History,"** is "first a thought in one man's mind, and when the same thought occurs to another man, it is the key to that era" (***Works*** 2: 3). The Proclamation itself attests to this necessity. From the beginning of the war, abolitionists had individually and collectively called for emancipation as a war policy. As the conflict grew in intensity, the exigencies of war began to convince more and more Northerners that emancipation was the only means to victory. Coming as a powerful means of persuasion, the war itself declared what was necessary.

The task of abolitionists and anti-slavery Republicans was, in a fundamental and essential way, a rhetorical one: the North had to be convinced that slavery was the issue of the war. "The negro is the key of the situation," Douglass pronounced in September of 1861, "the pivot upon which the whole rebellion turns. . . . To fight against slaveholders, without fighting against slavery, is but a half-hearted business, and paralyzes the hands engaged in it."[5] Emancipation was presented as a "military necessity." This phrase became the watchword for abolitionists in subsequent months and was eventually cited by Lincoln as the primary reason for his Proclamation. Despite opposition to emancipation within the administration, there was a dramatic increase of emancipationist sentiment in the weeks following the North's defeat at Bull Run. Even the *New York Tribune* and the *New York Times* revised their earlier stances and began to hint at emancipation. Still discouraged by Lincoln's reluctance to forward a resolution for emancipation and by conservative hostility toward their cause, however, abolitionists began a broad program of popular education aimed at moving public opinion toward the abolition of slavery. This new organization, tentatively called the Boston Emancipation League, was to distribute articles and editorials by prominent abolitionists to newspapers all over the North. The campaign was to be kept temporarily under cover because of the prevailing prejudice against abolitionists. This battle of words was supplemented by well-advertised speeches by Charles Sumner, William Garrison, Wendell Phillips and others during the months of October through November. The campaign was successful and on December 16, because of the growing support of emancipation and the consequent increase in the prestige of abolitionists, the Emancipation League brought their organization into the open. In the winter and spring of 1861-62 the number of emancipation organizations and lecture associations grew rapidly.[6] Pressured by the continued defeats of the North and the growing forces of the abolitionist movement, Lincoln finally issued a preliminary Emancipation Proclamation on September 22, 1862.

Although the terms of the proclamation still provoked disappointment and suspicion amongst the abolitionists, most believed that the deliberateness with which Lincoln had finally announced his decision indicated that the President had every intention of putting his promise into effect. Garrison and Phillips encouraged abolitionists to use their forces to influence public opinion in favor of emancipation rather than to denounce the weakness of the administration's announcement. Garrison, for example, after having expressed his concern that the emancipation would not be immediate, that it was only confined to the rebelling states, and that once again it was coupled with Lincoln's favorite scheme of gradual, compensated emancipation, publicly rejoiced in the Proclamation as "an important step in the right direction, and an act of immense historic consequence."[7] Within a few days, abolitionists arranged a rally in Boston at which Emerson was asked to speak. Emerson's speech is traversed by the political and rhetorical exigencies of the moment. Linking the Proclamation to such acts as "the plantation of America . . . the Declaration of Independence in 1776, and the British emancipation of slaves in the West Indies," he calls the act "poetic" and encourages his audience to recognize its "great scope." In his famous opening sentences, he writes:

> In so many arid forms which states encrust themselves with, once in a century, if so often, a poetic act and record occur. These are the jets of thought into affairs, when, roused by danger or inspired by genius, the political leaders of the day break the else insurmountable routine of class and local legislation, and take a step forward in the direction of catholic and universal interests. Every step in the history of political liberty is a sally of the human mind into the untried Future. . . . This act makes a victory of our defeats. Our hurts are healed; the health of the nation is repaired. With a victory like this, we can stand many disasters. . . . We have recovered ourselves from our false position, and planted ourselves on a law of Nature.
>
> (***Works*** 11: 315, 320)

Emphasizing the poetic and moral force of an act of thought that follows the laws of Nature, Emerson points to the revolutionary character of the Proclamation. The Proclamation is in fact revolutionary because it aligns itself with the forces of Nature, the forces of transformation. The very act of its declaration propels the country beyond the prejudice and legislation that until now had so forcefully determined national sentiment against emancipation. But now "the cause of disunion and war has been reached and begun to be removed" (***Works*** 11: 321-22). Lincoln's edict reveals its force, its transformative power, by committing the country to justice. In doing so, it promises political and social changes that call forth "a new public . . . to greet the new event" (***Works*** 11: 316). Clearing the way for an "untried Future," the proclamation recalls the American people to their founding in Nature. Both a promise and a memory, it indicates the nation's health. "In the light of this event," Emerson says, "the public distress begins to be removed" (**Works** 11: 321). Whatever we might have thought of as Lincoln's shortcomings, "every mistake, every delay," may now be called "endurance, wisdom, magnanimity." "Liberty is a slow fruit," Emerson explains, "It comes, like religion, for short periods, and in rare conditions. . . . We are beginning to think that we have underestimated the capacity and virtue which the Divine Providence has made an instrument of benefit so vast" (**Works** 11: 315, 317).[8]

Emerson's invocation of organic and religious imagery is far more than a spontaneous response to an act whose moral aspect seems unquestionable. In joining an act of great political and national significance with the movement of religious history, Emerson's rhetoric exploits the pervasive sense among many Northerners that God's hand could be recognized in Lincoln's edict.[9] In this edict, religious and political mission are brought together through the promise of their ultimate realization. January 1, 1863, marks a new era in the history of America—an era in which injustice and oppression would be forced to flee before the divine principles of justice and righteousness. The Proclamation itself bears witness to the sacred cause of the war. The justice of the Northern cause turns the Civil War from a crisis of national legitimacy into a conflict with eschatological significance.

For Emerson, the Emancipation Proclamation plays a decisive role within the history of this transformation. It is precisely this role and this history that are the subjects of his **"Boston Hymn."** Written for the specific purpose of celebrating the moral and historical importance of the Proclamation, the poem opened the festivities at the Music Hall. It was read to a wildly enthusiastic audience that included many former slaves.[10] In the poem, Emerson dramatizes the importance of the pronouncement by inscribing it within the form of a jeremiad that presents in small the history of American as "the great charity of God to the human race" (**Works** 11: 540). Choosing to frame his poem within the jeremiad form in fact enables him to respond to the heterogeneity of his audience. The jeremiad had frequently been adapted by abolitionist and black political writing in order both to reproach a country that had been unfaithful to its sacred beginnings and to recall the promise upon which American was founded.[11] Providing a lesson in national genealogy, Emerson's sermon sets out the sacred history of the New World and describes the typology of the American mission. By situating the significance of the Proclamation within a history that claims to reveal the nation's divine mission, Emerson emphasizes the historical significance of the Proclamation and the political and cultural significance of this Puritan history. He also entwines this history with the motifs of black emancipation and national regeneration at work within antebellum black rhetoric. This joining of the history of recent events with the history of the meaning of America requires that we read every line of the poem according to a double register. For Emerson, whatever significance we may attribute

to the force of Lincoln's pronouncement, this significance can only be read through the history of similar pronouncements, each of which, in their own way, have worked to link the destinies of America's peoples.

Still, within the movement of the poem, the particular pronouncement to which Lincoln's is compared is that of God to his chosen people. In both cases, the pronouncement takes the form of a promise, the promise of freedom. If the Emancipation Proclamation has the force of God's edict, it is because it is the promised realization of God's will. What is most striking about this particular jeremiad, however, is that both it, and by implication, the Proclamation, are spoken by God himself. It is God who laments the tyranny and the selfishness of the Old World and who reveals the terms of his promise to his listeners—the Pilgrims mentioned in the poem certainly, but also their descendants, including all Americans of the year 1863:

> The word of the Lord by night
> To the watching Pilgrims came,
> As they sat by the seaside,
> And filled their hearts with flame.
>
> God said, I am tired of kings,
> I suffer them no more;
> Up to my ear the morning brings
> The outrage of the poor.
>
> Think ye I made this ball
> A field of havoc and war,
> Where tyrants great and tyrants small
> Might harry the weak and poor?
>
> My angel,—his name is Freedom,—
> Choose him to be your king;
> He shall cut pathways east and west
> And fend you with his wing.
>
> Lo! I uncover the land
> Which I hid of old time in the West
> As the sculptor uncovers the statue
> When he has wrought his best.
>
> (**Works** 9: 201)

Emerson's sources for this emergent allegory of the history of America are the writings of the early colonists.[12] These opening stanzas identify what was perhaps the single most important element in the formation of the colonists' collective identity: their typological reading of history, a reading that both presumes and accounts for their strong identification with the covenanted people of Israel. As Philip Gura has suggested, the New England Puritans defined their community "not so much through its political or territorial integrity as through a common ideology: specifically, their incessant rhetorical justification of what they regarded as their divinely ordained purpose."[13] For the Puritans, the typological relationship that existed between the New Testament and the Old linked the progressive unfolding of history to the possibility of redemption in this world.[14] At the same time, since the New Testament speaks of things still to be realized, when events in England transformed the New England Puritans' relation to their homeland, they came to believe that they alone were left to fulfill Biblical prophecy. It is no accident, then, that the model for the Great Migration to which Emerson alludes here is the Biblical exodus. Guided by the hand of Providence, the pilgrims, like the Hebrews, abandon an oppressive monarchy for a new promised land. The Puritan God delivers the Pilgrims from the rod of tyranny and oppression and leads them to America.[15] Although this country is the latest found, it is also the earliest. Both the New Canaan and the New Jerusalem, this Columbia "Of clouds and the boreal fleece" is integral to God's sacred design. In giving the pilgrims a new opportunity, He calls upon His people to renew their covenant with Him.

The poem's next six stanzas outline the conditions of the covenant, the rules for this alliance between God and his chosen people. He promises to divide his goods. He promises expansion and growth for all of humanity. He offers to all, without distinction of color or creed, the infinite variety of America's natural resources. In return, he asks that the people build schools and churches in his name, govern the land and sea with just laws, not give way to selfish or proud rulers, refuse to swerve away from what is right, and, most of all, never bind another man or woman into their service. For Emerson, the measure of the degree to which the Puritans and their descendants have lived up to their end of the promise, have followed the laws of the covenant, is nothing less than the entire history of America—from the settlement of New England up to the pronouncement he now celebrates. Emerson's judgment here is decisive. Rather than suggest in any explicit fashion what this history has been, he brings his audience to the moment within which they are listening to him deliver his poem:

> Lo, now! if these poor men
> Can govern the land and sea
> And make just laws below the sun,
> As planets faithful be.

> And ye shall succor men;
> 'T is nobleness to serve;
> Help them who cannot help again:
> Beware from right to swerve.

> I break your bonds and masterships,
> And I unchain the slave:
> Free be his heart and hand henceforth
> As wind and wandering wave.

(***Works*** 9: 203)

Fusing the legacy of the Puritan founders with the present—according to a law of reading that recalls the law that governs the pilgrims' reading of their own special place within history—Emerson implies a typological relationship between the promise of the Puritan settlement of America and its fulfillment in the enactment of the Emancipation Proclamation. If the first half of his poem evokes the "birth" of this legacy, the second half will serve to call upon his audience, or rather to have God call upon his au-

dience, to recognize that it is within its support of the Proclamation that the renewal of His promise will take place. But if God's "Lo, now!" calls attention to the present, it at the same time expresses a kind of surprise at what God sees, almost as though He had, in growing even wearier than before in the face of continued disappointment, come to wonder whether or not men could ever "govern the land and sea" with justice. Nevertheless, the Proclamation is presented as a profound indication that "these poor men" can "make just laws."

The directness with which both Emerson and God turn to this act as the fulfillment of the alliance between God and the pilgrims, however, makes it difficult not to notice their silence upon the years that intervene between these two "events." This silence is hardly an omission. Rather it is a quiet condemnation of everything that, within the history of America, has betrayed or breached this special alliance. It is especially an indictment of those transgressions that occurred in the name of this promise, that justified themselves within the rhetoric and claim of God's grace. If Emerson begins his poem by having God give voice to the terms and conditions of the covenant, he does so not only to draw a link between the covenant and its realization in Lincoln's edict, but also to draw attention to the very rhetoric with which the Puritan founders attempted to conquer and transform the New World in God's name. In giving voice to the story of the covenant, God tells the story of the Puritans as well. That is to say, he tells to the Puritans their own story, the story that they themselves told in order to rationalize the often violent means whereby they settled their new home. The America whose history goes unspoken in Emerson's poem has also been "A field of havoc and war," a place where "tyrants great and small" have consistently oppressed "the weak and poor." The Puritan understanding of the nation's eschatological significance installed an understanding of the sanctity of the national union that in turn enabled the pilgrims to justify westward expansion, slavery, the extermination of the native population, the marginalization of cultural diversity in general, and the idea of manifest destiny. In carrying the notion of America as God's chosen westward, the Puritans and their descendants felt obliged to subdue, transform, and overcome nature. The strong sense of their place within this sacred history gave them license to "cut down trees in the forest / And trim the straightest boughs." The settlement of America, while it may have at one time promised a beneficent reunion with Nature, now revealed the more selfish and material impulses that the vision of a "free" and "prosperous" land proffered.

For Emerson, the Puritan capacity to appropriate anything before them within the rhetoric of the covenant indicates the power of this rhetoric as well as the Puritan will to authority. The legitimacy accorded to their rhetoric, for example, enabled them to determine in advance what belonged to the chosen community and what did not. This rhetoric in fact demanded the marginalization or assimilation of immigrants and other groups who did not fit into their conception of American nationality. In addition to the exclusion of other cultures, this nationalistic dimension of Puritan thought worked to bring the wide range of theological opinion in the colonies within the boundaries of what Gura has called "the internal development of Puritan doctrine." Although there was no unified community of Puritan thought, the unity of purpose and mission claimed by the New England Puritans was not only essential to their social and political organization, but also defended by recourse to the covenant.[16] This unity was then used to require submission to the authority of the founding fathers and their laws, conformity to convention, and reverence for the sacred moral purpose of whatever this community might deem necessary to further its special mission—even if such purpose might in truth go against every one of the terms of the covenant. For Emerson, such respect, conformity, and reverence works against the virtue of independence in the name of which the New World was founded. If Emerson and God turn from the terms and conditions of the covenant directly to the effective date of the Emancipation Proclamation, it is in part because each wishes to suggest that, until this day, the rhetoric of God's promise has been used primarily to promote interests that betray the letter of this same promise. That is to say: since the plantation of America there have been no truly just laws. There have been no laws which protect the divine rights of all men. Only with this Proclamation does America redeem itself; only with this act does it meet the conditions of God's promise.[17] This act works to purify the covenant as it has been passed down from generation to generation, to recover the promise of an America without slavery. Within the terms of Emerson's poem, the emancipation of the slaves will revise older concepts of manifest destiny, concepts which, emerging from the Puritan rhetoric of mission and errand, took their currency, at least implicitly, from the expansion of the southern slaveholding system.[18]

If the powerful ethical force of the Proclamation corresponds with the justice of divine law, it is also because, as Emerson states, in pronouncing this law, men have planted themselves on "a law of Nature." God himself seconds this point when he claims that as long as men "make just laws" they remain as faithful to the divine order of nature as do the planets.[19] Such claims are by no means surprising, however. For over two hundred years eschatological and prophetic images within Puritan rhetoric had been inseparable from natural metaphors. One could now find figurations of divine order not only through the figurative expressions that appear in the Bible, but also through the seemingly more direct revelation of the divine principle in the activities of the natural world. "Every natural fact," Emerson writes, "is a symbol of some spiritual fact" (*Works* 1: 26). What is surprising, though, is the recognition that God's words already echo Emerson's own language. The matter becomes immediately more complicated when we notice that nearly every single stanza in the second half of the poem alludes in some way to the various speeches, lectures, essays, and even poems that Emerson had written on the question of freedom, that is, on the question of emancipation. Drawing in particular from Emerson's speeches on the **"Emancipation Proclamation"**

(1862), on **"American Civilization"** (1861), on **"American Slavery"** (1855), and on "the **"Emancipation of the British West Indies"** (1844), Emerson's God speaks Emerson's language.[20] The "Lo, now!" of January 1, 1863, merges the voice of the Puritan God with the voice of Emerson's God, with that of men who speak in the name of "just laws." "If a man is at heart just," Emerson proclaims in his **"Divinity School Address,"** "then in so far is he God; the safety of God, the immortality of God, the majesty of God do enter that man with justice" (*Works* 1: 122). The Puritan God is not the God of To-day. The God of To-day is man himself. The God of To-day is the man who, refusing to swerve from right, proclaims this act of emancipation, revealing in this way the divinity that lies within his heart and his hands. Breaking away from the God of Puritan tradition and rhetoric, this man finds the presence of God within his own soul.[21] This man is not only Lincoln; rather, he is any man who recognizes the divinity of Lincoln's edict and chooses to serve its cause of universal freedom. If the Emancipation Proclamation is the fulfillment of God's promise, the Proclamation is itself a promise requiring fulfillment. This is why the act cannot accomplish the work of its promise all alone. Emerson tells us that this measure will not "be suddenly marked by any signal result" (*Works* 11: 319) on the slaves or on the rebel masters. Rather, this declaration—if it is not to be "a paper proclamation"—will require that men "succor" each other. Not only will Lincoln have to "repeat and follow up his stroke," but the nation will be asked to "add its inevitable strength." "If the ruler has duties," Emerson says, "so has the citizen. . . . What right has any one to read in the journals tidings of victories, if he has not bought them with his own valor, treasure, personal sacrifice, or by service as good in his own department" (*Works* 11: 321).

. . . . .

The effectuation of the proclamation within history depends upon the acts and thoughts of men and women whom every day and every hour renew their alliance with the declaration's revolutionary truth. This Proclamation is in fact a declaration of independence truer to the spirit of the revolution than that of the revolutionary fathers because it remembers a people whom they had forgotten. If the edict fulfills the promise of God's covenant, it also realizes the promise of the revolutionary struggle for freedom. From the beginning of the war, abolitionists and others had evoked the rhetoric of the revolution in order to further their cause. By the early 1860s the revolution had become a trope of persuasion within the war's new crusade for freedom. In an editorial entitled "The Second American Revolution," written less than three weeks after the attack on Fort Sumter, William Goodell pronounced: "It has begun. It is in progress . . . The Revolution must go on, to its completion—*A National Abolition of Slavery*. . . . What . . . can long delay the proclamation, inviting the slave to a share in *the glorious second American Revolution*."[22] The virtue of this second revolution was that it revealed what had always been the nation's "fatal weakness." In *The Rejected Stone*, a book which went through three editions in 1861-62, Conway argued that when the founding fathers constructed the edifice of the Union they cast aside one essential "foundation stone." That stone, he suggested, was "essentially, *Justice*." "The form in which it stands for us," he went on to say, "IS THE AFRICAN SLAVE."[23]

It was on the basis of such arguments that abolitionists refused to recognize the Southern rebellion as a revolution. Only the North was in a position to fight a revolution of freedom. "The revolution is on our side," Conway argued, "and as soon as the nation feels that, and acts upon it, the strength of the South is gone. . . . WE ARE THE REVOLUTIONISTS."[24] But if "we are the revolutionists" because we break the "bonds and masterships" of all Americans, including those of the slave, for Emerson we are also the revolutionists because we break these bonds and chains before God does. By the time that God declares His own emancipation proclamation in stanza 14, He has already acknowledged in stanza 12 that men have preceded Him in this act. If the hand of God is really at work within Lincoln's Proclamation, it is because the Proclamation, as an image of our creativity and freedom, is already divine. If God is preceded in this act, it is because he has also been preceded in other, perhaps more fundamental, ways. From the moment that His voice merges with the voice through whom He speaks on January 1, 1863, He speaks in a voice other than His own—in the same way that He had earlier spoken in the voice attributed to Him by the Puritan pilgrims. This is to say at least two things: i) the God of To-day speaks in a voice that is different from the voice in which He spoke to the pilgrims; and ii) the 1863 Emancipation Proclamation precedes the proclamation of To-day's God by fulfilling the promise of the Puritan God, but in a way that questions the Puritan conception of God. From the moment that Emerson has God address the present, God's voice is one with Emerson's.

This is not to say that God speaks the words that Emerson has Him speak solely because He is a persona within Emerson's poem. Instead, we need to recognize that Emerson does not speak for God; he speaks as God. The force of Emerson's rhetoric lies in its assumption of divinity. Emerson's thought is "ejaculated as Logos, or Word" (*Works* 3: 40). Whenever God says "I," Emerson says "I." Whenever God speaks, He quotes Emerson. Emerson's God is an emanation of Emerson's own rhetoric, a figure for Emerson's ambitions as a powerful political orator. Moreover, in having God speak within his language, Emerson sets up a typological relationship between the revolutionary promise of his earlier writings and the Proclamation as the fulfillment of this promise. In a certain sense, God's voice makes the potentiality within Emerson's language real. If God's rhetoric depends upon Emerson's, Emerson's is in turn enhanced through its being spoken by God. Emerson subsumes his own voice, his own rhetoric, within the voice of God in order to lend it more authority, in order to better persuade his audience of the virtue of the Proclamation as well as the necessity to constantly renew one's commitment to its promise of justice. In the passage from which God derives the sentence He speaks in stanza 13, Emerson claims that "God is God because he is the servant of all"

(*Works* 11: 298). God has served the Puritan founders. Now, in this poem, God serves Emerson as a figure of persuasion. We can only imagine the impact that Emerson's rhetoric would have had upon his audience. Having been recalled to their present moment by the "Lo, now!" of the twelfth stanza, his listeners could not have overlooked the powerful fusion of God's "I" with Emerson's.

We will never know the tone or force with which Emerson read this poem—a poem whose themes had been his for over thirty years—but anyone familiar with Emerson's writings would have certainly heard his voice within the following four stanzas:

> I cause from every creature
> His proper good to flow:
> As much as he is and doeth,
> So much he shall bestow.
>
> But, laying hands on another
> To coin his labor and sweat,
> He goes in pawn to his victim
> For eternal years in debt.
>
> To-day unbind the captive,
> So only are ye unbound;
> Lift up a people from the dust,
> Trump of their rescue, sound!
>
> Pay ransom to the owner
> And fill the bag to the brim.
> Who is the owner? The slave is owner,
> And ever was. Pay him.
>
> (*Works* 9: 203-4)

God speaks here in the voice of the Emersonian Poet whose task it is to liberate all men. Like the Poet, God breaks the chains that prevent men from recognizing and realizing their divine potential—that "proper good" which determines who man is and what he does.[25] He takes on the Poet's "office of announcement and affirming" (*Works* 3: 13) and declares the necessity and rectitude of emancipation. Relying on the language of Emerson's essay **"American Civilization,"** He explains that the moment a man lays his hands upon another person and tries to transform this person's "labor and sweat" into "coin," into money, he reverses the "natural sentiments of mankind" (*Works* 11: 297). In the opening paragraph to this essay, Emerson had already argued that, in accordance with the laws of nature, "man coins himself into his labor; turns his day, his strength, his thought, his affection into some product which remains as the visible sign of his power" (*Works* 11: 297). To secure this labor for the laborer, this should be "the object of all government." Insofar as the slaveholder presumes that "the well-being of a man" consists "in eating the fruit of other men's labor," however, he not only prevents the establishment of a just government, but he also goes against Nature (*Works* 11: 297). Betraying nature, he betrays himself. In exploiting the slave's labor he becomes eternally indebted to him, eternally subjected to the institution of slavery. Emerson had delineated this argument almost twenty years earlier in his address on the

"Emancipation of the British West Indies," suggesting that it had in fact played an important role in the history and events that contributed to that emancipation. "It was shown to the planters," he explains, "that they, as well as the negroes, were slaves. . . . The oppression of the slave recoiled on them. . . . Many planters have said, since the emancipation, that, before that day, they were the greatest slaves on the estates" (**Works** 11: 125). This argument both follows and anticipates those made by Phillips and Sumner as they tried to persuade both the North and the South of the insidiousness of slavery. Slaveholding, they argued, especially corrupted the manners and morals of white Southerners, since it presented their children with examples of brutal violence and despotism.[26] Phillips, in his speech on the "Right of Petition" (1837), had already emphasized national complicity in the issue of slavery. "Our fate is bound up with that of the South," he said, "so that they cannot be corrupt and we sound; they cannot fail and we stand."[27] In his own speech, Emerson hints at the planters' exaggeration of their own suffering in relation to that of the slave and then links Phillips' point to an older, more philosophical issue: "The civility of no race can be perfect whilst another race is degraded. It is a doctrine alike of the oldest and of the newest philosophy, that man is one, and that you cannot injure any member, without a sympathetic injury to all the members. America is not civil, whilst Africa is barbarous" (**Works** 11: 145).[28] Since "Every man is an inlet to the same and to all of the same" (**Works** 2: 3), no man can commit a violence upon another without committing a similar violence upon himself. If any man is a slave every man is a slave. For Emerson, this consideration leaves no choice for the country's conscience. In the name of respect, for both ourselves and others, we must rid ourselves of slavery. As he states in his 1851 address on the Fugitive Slave Act, "Everything invites emancipation" (**Works** 11: 208).

Emerson's God invites emancipation as well. But if His invitation is made in Emerson's language, this language takes a turn in stanza 18 against Emerson's earlier statements—in his addresses on the West Indies, the Fugitive Slave Law, and especially his 1855 speech on **"American Slavery"**—on the necessity of compensating slaveholders for their losses upon emancipation. Following the example of the British emancipation of the West Indies, Emerson argues in these speeches that Southern slaveholders ought to be paid a kind of "ransom" for their slaves. In his 1851 address against the Fugitive Slave Law, for example, he proclaims: "Why not end this dangerous dispute on some ground of fair compensation on one side, and satisfaction on the other to the conscience of the free states? It is really the great task fit for this country to accomplish, to buy that property of the planters, as the British nation bought the West Indian slaves. I say buy,—never conceding the right of the planter to own, but that we may acknowledge the calamity of his position, and bear a countryman's share in relieving him; and because it is the only practicable course, and is innocent" (**Works** 11: 208).[29] Such claims were prevalent in the North in the late 1840s and 1850s and were generally made either in the name of preserving

the Union or in the name of admitting some shared responsibility in the matter. If Emerson argues for disunion after the passing of the Fugitive Slave Act, we may still question his willingness to risk reinforcing the claim that slaves were property owned by the slaveholders. Indeed, many abolitionists were hostile to compensation for just this reason. Nevertheless, after the outbreak of the war, while Lincoln and others were still making similar arguments in the interest of effecting some kind of wartime compromise, Emerson claimed that such a suggestion was no longer either "practicable" or "innocent." His **"Boston Hymn"** records this turn of mind. If stanza 18 begins by referring to Emerson's earlier appeals to his countrymen to "Pay ransom to the owner / And fill the bag to the brim," it ends by questioning the appeal's assumption that the slave could be considered as property. "Who is the owner?" God asks. "The slave is owner, / And ever was," comes the answer, "Pay him."[30] These lines implicate an earlier Emerson in the outrages the Proclamation wishes to overcome. The poem is at this point a confession of Emerson's shared guilt, a renunciation of his earlier position, and a passionately challenging exhortation that no one ever forget again that the slave has always owned his or her own labor.

This admonishment and appeal are particularly pertinent at a time when many abolitionists were wondering whether the Proclamation had itself been purchased at too great a cost. What disturbed them most was their sense that Lincoln's edict was based upon the argument of "military necessity" rather than upon a concern for the rights of the black man as a person. Although he later changed his position, even Sumner himself had claimed that abolition was not "the object of the war, but simply one of its agencies." He repeated this point in a letter of November 10, 1861, to John Jay, arguing that emancipation "is to be presented strictly as a measure of military necessity, and the argument is to be thus supported rather than on grounds of philanthropy."[31] For both Sumner and Jay, the argument for emancipation based upon "military necessity" was a strategic, that is to say, rhetorical one. They, as did many others, assumed that the administration would respond more quickly to this argument than to the moral issues they had already been promoting for over thirty years. Some abolitionists strongly questioned these tactics, however. Emancipation would be worth very little, they argued, if it did not proceed from a strong commitment to justice and human rights. As Lydia Maria Child solemnly proclaimed, "This entire absence of a moral sense on the subject, has disheartened me more than anything else. Even should they be emancipated, merely as a 'war necessity,' everything *must* go wrong, if there is no heart or conscience on the subject. . . . It is evident that a great moral work still needs to be done."[32] Douglass expressed the same fear in a speech he delivered at Cooper Union on February 6, 1863, five weeks after the enactment of the Proclamation. "Much as I value the present apparent hostility to Slavery at the North," he said, "I plainly see that it is less the outgrowth of high and intelligent moral conviction against Slavery, as such, than because of the trouble its friends have brought upon country. I would have Slavery hated for that and more. A man that hates Slavery for what it does to the white man, stands ready to embrace it the moment its injuries are confined to the black man, and he ceases to feel those injuries in his own person."[33]

These arguments would have had special force for the Emerson who insists that everything be thought according to first principles. He might have been particularly moved by Douglass's remarks since he had himself opened his 1854 speech on the Fugitive Slave Law by admitting that until this law had been passed he had lived all his life "without suffering any known inconvenience from American Slavery." "I never saw it," he says, "I never heard the whip; I never felt the check on my free speech and action, until, the other day, when Mr. Webster, by his personal influence, brought the Fugitive Slave Law on the country" (*Works* 11: 219). Although these sentences would need to be read as part of the rhetorical pose that Emerson takes in this speech, we can still say that they at least dramatize his awareness of the ease with which we can neglect suffering that does not touch our own person. In drawing attention to these arguments in his poem, Emerson reveals his shared concern over the possibility that the Proclamation might become a dead letter if it is not taken up into the hearts and minds of individuals willing to commit themselves to the difficult struggle of genuine emancipation. His insistence that the slave be treated as a person rather than as property serves as a powerful reminder of the tremendous moral stakes involved in this struggle. They are nothing less than the integrity of the self-reliant individual. If compensation should go to anyone, it should therefore go to the slave. But this compensation can only take the form of true emancipation. This is to say that the slave may only be truly compensated through a task of thinking: a thinking whose task it is to think the slave as a person rather than as a thing.

This task will involve a confrontation with the painful and distressing history that has led to the necessity of this moral reevaluation. Emerson encourages his listeners to begin this task by offering his own sense of this history. Racing against time, because going against the embattled history of America, emancipation must be immediate, but genuine.[34] Emerson's God commands the slaves to arise and run to meet the challenge of their newly pronounced freedom. In the poem's final two stanzas, He calls upon peoples of all races to carry His purpose forth into the world. He then ends his speech by turning, in a properly Emersonian fashion, to the force and efficacy of His own rhetoric:

> Come, East and West and North,
> By races, as snowflakes,
> And carry my purpose forth,
> Which neither halts nor shakes.
>
> My will fulfilled shall be,
> For, in daylight or in dark,
> My thunderbolt has eyes to see
> His way home to the mark.

(*Works* 9: 204)

God's Word works as a force of provocation and gathering. He enjoins all races to come together and carry his declaration of emancipation into the slaveholding South—as snowflakes. Coming in accordance with the laws of nature, these peoples come as snowflakes—that is to say, in one of the figure's many connotations, in *numbers*—to realize the will of God. "Every spark of intellect," Emerson tells us in his speech on the Proclamation, "every virtuous feeling, every religious heart, every man of honor, every poet, every philosopher, the generosity of cities, the health of the country, the strong arms of the mechanic, the endurance of farmers, the passionate conscience of women, the sympathy of distant nations" (*Works* 11: 320)—all rally to the support of this edict. A host of different peoples and sentiments shall draw together in this "great and good work" of emancipation.

But what exactly does it mean for them to draw together *as* snowflakes? What could it mean for Emerson's God to associate men and women of different colors to an element of nature known by its single color—especially when, within the context of questions of slavery and race, this color is hardly an innocent one? In calling for men and women from different races rather than from a single race, God suggests that these questions may not be as black and white as they seem. The figural connotations of snowflakes within such a context are in fact multiple and in no way simple. Within the Biblical and theological traditions to which both God and Emerson belong, snow and snowflakes have borne an array of rhetorical significances—all of which have some figural relationship to God's will. For example, in H. W. Beecher's "Teachings of Snow," the movement of snowflakes is seen as a figure for the movement of God's hosts in battle.[35] Wafting down from the sky like the thoughts of God, snowflakes fight to realize the will of God. They conceal in their beauty a great power of annihilation and in their color a means of purification. Covering the land and thereby changing the whole aspect of nature, they represent a powerful force of conversion. It "tends to mitigate the severity of winter" and, when it melts, it serves as a powerful force of regeneration.[36] As a figure for the will of God, it figures the hand of God in Matthew 10: 29-30 and the Word of God itself. In Isaiah 55: 29-30, for example, God says: "as the rain cometh down, and the snow from heaven, and returneth not thither, but watereth the earth, and maketh it bring forth and bud, that it may give seed to the sower, and bread to the eater: So shall my word be that goeth forth out of my mouth: it shall not return unto me void, but it shall accomplish that which I please, and it shall prosper *in the thing* whereto I sent it."

When God demands that the men and women of all races come together as snowflakes for the purpose of enacting his will, His language evokes each and all of these connotations. Coming to battle slavery in the name of God, these peoples will purify the sin that has beset America from its beginning. "Announced by all the trumpets of the sky" (*Works* 9: 41), like the snow in Emerson's poem **"The Snow-Storm,"** they are architects of a new union, fierce artificers of a new revolution. Rebuilding the edifice of America according to the principles of nature and in re-alization of the divine potential of man's creative capacity for reform, these snowflakes shall inaugurate a new era. The snowflake is, as Emerson says elsewhere, "Freedom's star."[37] Led by the light of this star, God's hosts are to ful-fill simultaneously the Word of God, the Words of Emer-son's God, the Emancipation Proclamation, and the words of Lincoln, who, in 1854, had already pronounced the ne-cessity that would eventuate in his 1863 Proclamation. "Our republican robe is soiled, and trailed in the dust," he said, "Let us repurify it. Let us turn and wash it white, in the spirit, if not the blood, of the Revolution. . . . Let us re-adopt the Declaration of Independence, and with it, the practices and policies which harmonize with it. Let north and south—let all Americans—let all lovers of liberty ev-erywhere—join in the great and good work."[38] The snow falling downward from the heavens—like the races which, coming from the East and the West and the North accord-ing to God's directive, move southward—represents the descent of the thought which will become the new ground for a new Declaration of Independence. Transforming the landscape of American history, the snowflake brings men and women to rethink their relation to both nature and his-tory.

Like the God whose word it figures, the snowflake is a force of provocation and emancipation. It gains its force as a trope through the religious and literary associations at-tributed to it by the same men and women it now wishes to mobilize. If history has as its goal the process of moral justice and freedom, that process can only be achieved, ac-cording to Emerson, by the forces of Nature; and simi-larly, if Nature is the means to human justice and freedom, its end is to be found in human action and human history. If the Proclamation is a poetic act, it is precisely because it joins human history with natural history. As Emerson writes in *Nature,* "Natural history by itself has no value; it is like a single sex. But marry it to human history, & it is poetry" (**Works** 1: 28; *Journals* 4: 311). God's poetry works to define the grounds and necessity of this coopera-tion. Emerson himself had proclaimed this necessity in the final sentence of his 1854 speech on the Fugitive Slave Act. There, forcefully encouraging his audience to believe in the amelioration that "will not save us but through our own cooperation," Emerson prophesizes the end of slavery (**Works** 11: 244). No matter how much he may evoke the necessity of self-reliant deeds, "free doers" are bound to-gether in a community of believers whose votes must co-operate with the work of emancipation—which is to say that, for Emerson, the burden of self-reliance is the burden of cooperation.[39] The difficulty of taking on this responsi-bility, however, is not due to any contradiction here. Emer-son's doctrine of "self-reliance" is inseparable from its commitment to social and political reform. The self-reliant individual is from the very beginning "related and en-gaged" with others (**Works** 11: 217). In the very act of de-livering this poem, Emerson himself keeps this engage-ment and fulfills this relation. Engaging his audience through the force of his rhetoric, Emerson transforms his

exhortation into a commitment—his as well as his audi-ence's—toward emancipation. Emerson and his God pro-nounce the virtues and necessity of having everyone sup-port Lincoln's edict. This edict breaks "bonds" and "masterships" and unchains the slave by binding "lovers of liberty" into a community that can cooperate in revolt against the institution of slavery as well as against its own guilt in this institution—for who among us, Emerson seems to suggest, has not at one time or another relied on an idea of America that includes the possibility of slavery within its language. What is necessary, he argues, is a renewal of the community of the covenant that remains vigilant to-ward the various ways in which the covenant can at the same time become a means of enslavement. Rather than fleeing before the demands of the revolution, we should become "guides, redeemers, and benefactors" who, "obey-ing the Almighty effort and advancing on Chaos and the Dark," do not fear entering the struggle for emancipation (**Works** 2: 47).

We should all race to become snowflakes—agents of co-operation and regeneration. To say this is to admit the role of rhetoric within the process of emancipation. God uses the trope of the snowflake precisely in order to persuade His listeners to meet the challenges of freedom. Like Em-erson, He knows that "Nothing so works on the human mind . . . as a trope" (**Works** 7: 90). He condenses the ur-gency and necessity of His message of freedom into the figure of the snowflake and, in doing so, expects to move all men and women in the direction of this freedom. As Emerson tells us in **"The Poet,"** the use of tropes "has a certain power of emancipation and exhilaration for all" (**Works** 3: 30). It is within this context that we should un-derstand Lincoln's Proclamation as a powerful act of lan-guage. The necessarily rhetorical dimension of any such Proclamation answers to the demand that men and women of all races be persuaded to act in the name of this act.

The importance of the rhetorical dimension of the poem is high-lighted in a striking and unmistakable fashion in its final sentence, as Emerson's God announces the irresist-ible force of His rhetoric: "My will fulfilled shall be, / For, in daylight or in dark, / My thunderbolt has eyes to see / His way home to the mark." God's unerring flash of light-ning recalls the Puritan use of thunder and lightning as signals of God's voice. This topos is pervasive within Bib-lical literature and commentary and is quite common in Massachusetts literature from the seventeenth-century on. In Michael Wigglesworth's *God's Controversy with New England,* for example, thunder is the voice of God repri-manding the sins of the Puritan pilgrims: "The Air became tempestuous; / The wilderness gan quake: / And from above with awfull voice / Th' Almighty thundring spake."[40] The image also recurs in sermons such as Cotton Mather's "Brontologia Sacra," included in the *Magnalia Christi Americana,* and Jonathan Edwards's *Personal Narrative.* As Mitchell Breitweiser reminds us, Mather's sermon was in fact given "extemporaneously upon the occasion of a thunderstorm in September 1694."[41] "The omnipotent God in the thunder," Mather explained to his audience, "speaks to those hardy Typhons, that are found fighting against him." In Edwards's narrative, the association between thunder and God's voice is made within a discussion of his present understanding of the thunder's significance. "Before," he writes, "I used to be uncommonly terrified with thunder, and to be struck with terror when I saw a thunder storm rising; but now, on the contrary, it rejoiced me. I felt God, so to speak, at the first appearance of a thunder storm; and used to take the opportunity to . . . hear the majestic and awful voice of God's thunder."[42] God's claim for the inevitable power of His rhetoric in the poem's last sentence should be read against the background of this Puritan rhetoric. This is to say that the poem ends where it began—by recalling the rhetoric of the Puritan God. It is framed by the burning words of the God that had earlier filled the Pilgrim's hearts with flame and that now wishes to enflame men and women of all races toward the difficult but necessary work of emancipation.

But the apocalyptic language of the God of 1863 takes a different form than that of the God of the early seventeenth century. The meaning of His covenant has been altered to meet the challenges of the Civil War and of the slave's emancipation. Now the voice of the Puritan God merges with the voice of Emerson's God and together their target is at least fourfold. The primary target is of course emancipation for the slave, but this emancipation can only occur through the cooperation of the audience listening to Emerson and God within the walls of the Music Hall, the men and women called together in stanza 21 to fulfill the terms of God's covenant, and finally the slave himself—although we might say that this last target is implied in each of the other three. That the slave is a mark internal to the others is made clear in the end rhyme of lines two and four in the poem's last stanza—in the rhyme, that is, between "dark" and "mark." The slave is the "dark mark" of God's word. God's word shall reach the ears of the black man and pronounce his freedom. As in stanza 20, God encourages the slave to take part in his own emancipation.[43] In this instance, however, He at the same time condemns the interpretations of the Biblical curse of Canaan and of the exile of Cain sometimes used to justify the black man's color and enslavement.[44] He distinguishes the dark mark to which His voice is now directed from the "dark mark" which, according to these interpretations, His voice had earlier condemned. In the Biblical account, when the drunken Noah realizes that his son, Ham, has been staring at his naked body, he curses Ham's son, Canaan. He condemns Canaan to servitude and, according to Talmudic and Midrashic sources, tells Ham that his seed will from then on "be ugly and darkskinned." As David Brion Davis suggests, these explanations for the black man's enslavement were most likely intensified by religious cosmologies that "envisioned spiritual progress as the triumph of the children of light over the pagan or infidel children of darkness."[45] For Emerson, however, the difficulty that the issue of slavery poses for people who understand America's mission as furthering the cause of divine truth and enlightenment is precisely that of distinguishing between the forces of light and those of darkness. The rhetoric of this mission has too often been used to reinforce rather than to undo patterns of enslavement among both blacks and whites for such a distinction to be clear. The conditions of genuine emancipation ought to include a reconsideration of the implications of this difficulty. As Emerson declares in his speech on the **"Emancipation of the British West Indies,"** at the moment of emancipation, all "disqualifications and distinctions of color" cease and "men of all colors have equal rights in law. . . . If you have man, black or white is an insignificance" (*Works* 11: 121, 144).

Rather than curse the black man for any original sin, God prophesies his redemption and emancipation from the sins committed against him in the name of a justice determined by color. If the black man is still marked, he is now marked for freedom rather than punishment. He is marked for inclusion within the family of man.[46] Like the snowflake—whose angles "are invariable" but whose forms exhibit "the greatest variety and beauty"[47]—the black man has a share in what is universal in man's nature, even as he maintains the singularity of his history and existence. God's rhetoric displays its force by re-marking the marks of Cain and Canaan in the direction of a more just understanding of the divinity that the black man shares with all men. In this, God also questions the rhetoric within which both the North and the South described the Civil War as a fratricidal conflict. Each tried to mark the other with the brand of Cain. Each claimed that it was the righteous brother—trying to defend the legacy bequeathed to the nation by the Founding Fathers.[48] Within the context of the poem's last sentence, such branding coincides with the rhetoric and logic of exclusion that has justified and thereby maintained the institution of slavery. If God's thunderbolt does indeed see its way home to the mark, it does so by striking against any rhetoric and logic that would privilege any mark over another.

The authority of God's Word therefore cannot be separated from His vision of emancipation. His thunderbolt has eyes that enable it to see its way home to its mark and His voice has eyes that enable it to see its way toward expressing His Will. God's speech is visionary and His vision can be communicated. The Word of God and the vision of God are, as Emerson writes in a journal entry of 1835, "not two acts but one. The sight commands, the command sees" (*Journals* 5: 272). The poem's last stanza can be read as a tribute to the inexorable force of God's visionary rhetoric. But to stop here would be to miss what is now the poem's trademark: God's Word and vision gain their power from the force of Emerson's own visionary rhetoric. God and Emerson steal each other's thunder. This is to say that the poem's last stanza is also a tribute to Emerson's marksmanship. Not only because God continues to evoke arguments that Emerson has already made, but also because, in this case, He cites Emerson speaking eloquently on the importance and power of eloquence. God takes his final sentence from a passage in Emerson's **"The Celebration of Intellect,"** an address that Emerson delivered before the students of Tufts College on July 10, 1861, less than four months after the firing of Fort Sumter. In the address, Emerson encourages his audience not to be swayed away from the urgent tasks of thinking that the present times of "arraignment," "trial," and "judgment" require. Rather than be taken in by the "fracas of politics" and the "brute noise of the cannon," we should instead think the principles that motivate both politics and cannons. For even though the "brute noise of the cannon" has "a most poetic echo in these days when it is an instrument of freedom and the primal sentiments of humanity . . . it is but representative and a far-off means" (***Works*** 12: 113). We should think the creative cause of the war's fracas and brute noise, the "sanctity and omnipotence of Intellectual Law." "The whole battle is fought in a few heads," he says (***Works*** 12: 121).

To think the relationship between the laws of the intellect and the laws of politics, however, requires us to think the place of rhetoric within these laws. For as we have already seen, nothing moves the minds of men and women or affects the direction of politics more than rhetoric does. But to say this is to say as well that nothing moves people or affects politics more than history does, since, for Emerson, rhetoric is essentially historical. What gives force to a trope like that of the snowflake, for example, are the myriad associations that have been attributed to the crystal within history. If there is, and Emerson says there is, a relationship between questions of politics, history, and language, the issue becomes one of how to direct one's rhetoric toward the accomplishment of moral effects. The issue becomes one of how one's rhetoric may see its way home to the mark when the figures one uses may include, within their history, connotations that lead one's argument away from its intended end. It is within this context that Emerson declares the passage from which God will draw His final sentence. "I wish you to be eloquent," he says:

> to grasp the bolt and to hurl it home to the mark. I wish to see that Mirabeau who knows how to seize the heart-strings of the people and drive their hands and feet in the way he wishes them to go, to fill them with himself, to enchant men so that their will and purpose is in abeyance and they serve him with a million hands just as implicitly as his own members obey him. But I value it more when it is legitimate, when the talent is in true order, subject to genius, subject to the total and native sentiment of the man, and therefore in harmony with the public sentiment of mankind. Such is the patriotism of Demosthenes, of Patrick Henry and of what was best in Cicero and Burke; not an ingenious special pleading, not the making of a plausible case, but strong by the strength of the facts themselves. Then the orator is still one of the audience, persuaded by the same reasons which persuade them, not a ventriloquist, not a juggler, not a wire-puller paid to manage the lobby and caucus.

(***Works*** 12: 119-20)

Emerson encourages his audience to become eloquent by providing them with examples of the power a skilled orator may have over his listeners. The orator who knows his art well knows how to seduce and direct the hearts and minds of the people. Giving free reign to his creative and transformative power, the orator thereby claims his rightful identity. The truth he offers is the effect of a language powerful enough to persuade his listeners to believe that it is transparent to a Power beyond that language. Whether this orator is a Mirabeau, a Demosthenes, a Henry, a Cicero, a Burke, or even God, he has the capacity to direct people to the fulfillment of his will rather than theirs. He has the power "to grasp the bolt" of rhetoric and "hurl it home to the mark." But the orator's singular power may quickly become despotic if it is not "legitimate." The orator risks tyrannizing over his audience whenever he simply effects "an ingenious special pleading," or constructs "a plausible case," in order to realize his own personal aims. To say that an orator's eloquence is legitimate, however, is not to say that he may do just about anything with language, as long as he remains fully aware of the misleading power of his rhetoric. Rather, his rhetoric is legitimate only if it is: i) in true order, that is to say, in accord with the laws of nature, with the demand that we think the rhetoricity of nature; ii) subject to genius, that is to say, subject to the particularity of the orator's own history as well as to all of history; and iii) subject to the native sentiment of man. The orator must, as Emerson explains in the opening paragraph of **"American Civilization,"** think, speak, and act in a way that respects the self-reliance of each of his listeners. Only by meeting these conditions may an orator remain "in harmony with the public sentiment of mankind." Only in this way are "the spells of persuasion, the keys of power . . . put into his hands."

These are the directives that guide Emerson's hand as he writes the **"Boston Hymn."** He wishes to celebrate the Emancipation Proclamation, to encourage his listeners to pledge their support for emancipation, but without imposing his own particular will upon them. Directing his efforts toward emancipation and self-reliance rather than enslavement and dependence, he remains "one of the audience." He too must promise to keep the promise of the Proclamation. For although the Proclamation comes, as the Fugitive Slave Law did, like "a sheet of lightning at midnight" to strike the truth of emancipation into the hearts and minds of the populace, even though it affects the country with the suddenness and revelatory force of God's Word, as Emerson well knows, "the habit of oppression will not be destroyed by a law and a day of jubilee" (***Works*** 11: 117). What is required is that we rethink the meaning of emancipation, while remaining vigilant to the ways in which the promise of freedom can easily become a means to enslavement. We should consider the habits of thinking that determine our "habit of oppression," habits that include the rhetoric of nationalism, cultural difference, and racial superiority. As the Puritan God set out the conditions and terms of His promise, the Emersonian Poet must set out the terms and conditions of the task of thinking his audience must meet if the Proclamation is to be fulfilled. While this is a difficult task, the Poet may find help by drawing from a source of energy that is larger than he is. He may abandon himself to "the nature of things" (***Works*** 3: 26).

"Besides his privacy of power as an individual man," Emerson explains, "there is a great public power on which he can draw, but unlocking, at all risks, his human doors, and suffering the ethereal tides to roll up into the life of the universe, his speech is thunder, his thought is law" (**Works** 3: 26-27). If Emerson chooses to subsume his voice within the authority and "ethereal tides" of God's voice, he does so because he knows that, within the nature of things, God has "a great public power," a great power over the public. He knows that when God speaks, people listen. He speaks as God not only because he wishes to indicate the divine creative potential he believes exists within us all, but also because he may then appropriate God's "public power" as his own—by surrendering himself to its effects. Using God as a powerful trope of persuasion, Emerson mobilizes God's "public power" in the direction of emancipation. Abandoning himself to this trope of power, Emerson transforms his voice into thunder and his thought into law. He becomes "the mere tongue of the occasion and the hour, and says what cannot but be said." He surrenders himself to "the principle on which he is horsed, the great connection and crisis of events, thunder in the ear of the crowd" (**Works** 7: 49). The power of Emerson's strategy becomes evident when we recognize that the force of his poem may remain intact regardless of whom his audience thinks is speaking—God or Emerson as God. In either case, God's thunder reaches its mark—for once it enters the ear of the crowd, it matters little whose thunder it was; it becomes the listener's responsibility. Lincoln's edict may only be realized if men and women of all races take on the challenge of Self-reliance—a reliance on the Self that, as we know from Emerson's second "Fugitive Slave Law Address," is nothing else than a reliance on God (**Works** 11: 235). To rely on the "public power" of God is to rely on one's self—because one's self is already infused with the power that is God. This is the recognition upon which emancipation depends. Emerson writes the **"Boston Hymn"** in order to proclaim the conditions for realizing the promise of emancipation, to signal the divinity that defines our potential for freedom. Like the voice of God that calls forth men and women to realize His will as snowflakes, the poem creates the audience that is to hear it by speaking to it as if it could already hear. The thunderbolt that it is sees its way home to the mark insofar as it brings forth the possibility of a future. This future lies in the hands of the races who, coming like snowflakes, commit themselves to its chances. The **"Hymn"** celebrates an emancipation that does not yet exist but is already occurring in the form of a promise—a promise that has always magnetized American desire.

Rather than distance itself aesthetically from the war, Emerson's **"Boston Hymn"** registers the traces that the Civil War has left upon it. The concern that it expresses over its own status as an act of representation is one and the same with its analysis of the varied cultural and political attempts to invent and enforce a particular image of America. Linking its language to the events of its time, evoking their various contexts and enacting the way in which history informs its own movement, the poem also suggests the way in which texts inform the practices of history. If the poem—with its figures, emblems, and symbols—is linked to America's capacity to institute, within a general network of representation, the political experience of its citizens, Emerson wishes it to reflect critically on efforts to evade the historical issues that had led to the civil crisis and to legitimate the war and its violence by recourse to the rhetoric against which the war is being fought. In recalling these issues and this history, in evoking the genealogy of the rhetorics within which his listeners thought about their place within this same history, the poem works to encourage a rethinking of our relation to the meaning of America, to an America that realizes its promise of emancipation.

Notes

1. *The Complete Works of Ralph Waldo Emerson,* Centenary Edition (Boston: Houghton Mifflin, 1903-4) 11: 259. Further citations from Emerson's essays are to this edition unless otherwise noted.

2. Compare this point with Timothy Sweet's recent book, *Traces of War: Poetry, Photography, and the Crisis of the Union* (Baltimore: Johns Hopkins University Press, 1990).

3. Emerson was not alone in granting such importance to these two steps. In a public letter of August 26, 1863, attacking opponents of emancipation, Lincoln himself proclaimed that "Some of the commanders of our armies in the field who have given us our most important successes, believe the emancipation policy, and the use of colored troops, constitute the heaviest blow yet dealt to the rebellion." See *The Collected Works of Abraham Lincoln,* ed. Roy P. Basler (New Brunswick, New Jersey: Rutgers University Press, 1953) 6: 408.

4. I refer here to the efforts of, among others, Len Gougeon, Carolyn Porter, Michael Gilmore, John Michael, and Maurice Gonnaud, to demonstrate Emerson's preoccupation with the central political and social issues of his time, and to do so against what critics such as F. O. Matthiessen, Stephen Whicher, R. W. B. Lewis, Irving Howe, and Harold Bloom, and historians such as Anne Rose and George Frederickson have seen as the ahistorical character of Emerson's writings. In tracing the connections between Emerson and the domain of history, these efforts have helped to revise the perception of Emerson as a writer who retreated from history and politics. See Gougeon, *Virtue's Hero: Emerson, Antislavery, and Reform* (Athens: University of Georgia Press, 1990); Porter, *Seeing and Being: The Plight of the Participant Observer in Emerson, James, Adams, and Faulkner* (Middletown, Conn.: Wesleyan University Press, 1981); Gilmore, *American Romanticism and the Marketplace* (Chicago: University of Chicago Press, 1988); Michael, *Emerson and Skepticism: The Cipher of the World* (Baltimore: Johns Hopkins University Press, 1988); and Gonnaud, *An Uneasy Solitude:*

Individual and Society in the Work of Ralph Waldo Emerson, trans. Lawrence Rosenwald (Princeton, N.J.: Princeton University Press, 1987). Although the reading of "Boston Hymn" that follows has certain relays with this ongoing reassessment of Emerson's relation to history, it differs in its effort to integrate the methods of rhetorical reading with the materials and concerns of the more "external" historicism evident in the above-mentioned works. It assumes that Emerson's rhetoric takes place between what we might call "internal," formal or conceptual difficulties and the "external" conditions and forces it addresses. It requires, and in fact is, a kind of commentary that situates rhetoric materially within the political and historical moment of its production.

5. *Douglass Monthly,* September 1861.

6. The Washington Lecture Association was perhaps one of the most effective of these organizations, perhaps because of its location in the nation's capital. The Association sponsored more than twenty lectures in the hall of the Smithsonian Institute during the winter. Emerson's speech on "American Civilization" was delivered within this series.

7. *The Liberator,* Sept. 26, 1862; cited in James M. McPherson, *The Struggle for Equality* (Princeton, N.J.: Princeton University Press, 1964) 119. Although always for total and immediate abolition, Garrison himself, as late as in the fall of 1861, had written a widely circulated petition in which he urged Congress to decree abolition under the war power, but also recommended giving fair compensation to *loyal* masters "as a conciliatory measure, and to facilitate an amicable adjustment of difficulties" (see *The Struggle for Equality* 93). The petition, although resisted by some because of the inclusion of compensation, was nevertheless signed by most abolitionists. This is just another indication of the difficult contradictions that were so pervasive within the rhetoric of abolition certainly, but also within any of the efforts attempting to confront the incalculability of the war's outcome.

8. Emerson had already been arguing for emancipation as early as the fall of 1861 and in January of 1862, in "American Civilization," a lecture he delivered before the Smithsonian Institution in Washington, D.C., he proclaimed its immediate necessity:

> If the American people hesitate, it is not for want of warning or advice. The telegraph has been swift enough to announce our disasters. The journals have not suppressed the extent of the calamity. . . . We cannot but remember that there have been days in American history, when, if the free states had done their duty, slavery had been blocked by an immovable barrier, and our recent calamities forever precluded. The free states yielded, and every compromise was sur-

render and invited new demands. Here again is a new occasion which heaven offers to sense and virtue. It looks as if we held the fate of the fairest possession of mankind in our hands, to be saved by our firmness or to be lost by hesitation. Emancipation is the demand of civilization. That is a principle; everything else is an intrigue. . . . Congress can, by edict, as a part of the military defense which it is the duty of Congress to provide, abolish slavery. . . .

> (*Works* 11: 300, 303-5)

With Lincoln's pronouncement of his preliminary Proclamation, however, Emerson, along with other abolitionists who had also criticized Lincoln for his hesitation to support such an act, chooses to praise the act in order to help see it through. Given the exigencies of the moment, he temporarily puts aside his doubts for the sake of drawing up support for the proclamation. Finding himself in a similar position as he speaks on the "Emancipation of the British West Indies," he explains that although "There are other comparisons and other imperative duties which come sadly to mind . . . I do not wish to darken the hours of this day by crimination; I turn gladly to the rightful theme, to the bright aspects of the occasion" (*Works* 11: 135).

9. See David Brion Davis, *Slavery and Human Progress* (New York: Oxford University Press, 1984) 268-70; and Leon F. Litwack, *Been in the Storm So Long: The Aftermath of Slavery* (New York: Knopf, 1979) 64-103, 169.

10. For a summary of the reactions to Emerson's reading see the January 8, 1863, issue of *The Liberator* and the February 1863 issue of the *Douglass Monthly.*

11. For an account of the role and place of the jeremiad sermon form within black rhetoric, see David Howard-Pitney's *The Afro-American Jeremiad: Appeals for Justice in America* (Philadelphia: Temple University Press, 1990).

12. See Sacvan Bercovitch, *The American Jeremiad* (Madison: University of Wisconsin Press, 1978), and *The Puritans Origins of the American Self* (New Haven: Yale University Press, 1975); Nathan Hatch, *The Sacred Cause of Liberty: Republican Thought and the Millennium in Revolutionary New England* (New Haven: Yale University Press, 1977); and Emory Elliott, *Power and the Pulpit in Puritan New England* (Princeton, N.J.: Princeton University Press, 1975).

13. See *A Glimpse of Sion's Glory: Puritan Radicalism in New England, 1620-1660* (Middletown, Conn.: Wesleyan University Press, 1984) 215.

14. On this point, see Gura, *A Glimpse of Sion's Glory,* especially Part II. Gura is particularly useful in discussing the evolution of this myth during the first two decades of the settlement.

15. In late summer of 1860, Emerson cites a passage from a letter of Humboldt to Varnhagen von Ense in his journal. The passage is itself already a citation and I cite it here because it serves as a source for the first line that God speaks to the pilgrims: "God getting tired of Kings. Antonio Perez quotes a wise counsellor of Philip II. who said to him, 'Should God once get tired of monarchies, he will give another form to the political world'" (*Journals* 14: 356). It is rather unusual for God to be speaking in the form of a jeremiad, but, as this citation makes clear, God is not speaking in his own voice. In fact one of the main questions within the "Hymn" is precisely that of what gets said in the name of God.

16. On the heterogeneity that characterized the colony's religious life, see Gura, *A Glimpse of Sion's Glory*; Darrett Rutman, *American Puritanism: Faith and Practice* (Philadelphia: Lippincott, 1970) and *Winthrop's Boston: A Portrait of a Puritan Town: 1630-1649* (1965; rpt. New York: W. W. Norton, 1972); and William K. B. Stoever, "*A Faire and Easie Way to Heaven*": *Covenant Theology and Antinomianism in Early Massachusetts* (Middletown, Conn.: Wesleyan University Press, 1978). Each of these writers in one way or another challenge Perry Miller's conclusions about the existence of a unified body of thought called "American Puritanism." As Gura suggests, "A full understanding of seventeenth-century New England Puritanism depends on an acknowledgement that many of those who migrated to America did not share a fixed ideology or commitment to an agreed-upon ecclesiastical program as much as a common spiritual hunger and a disenchantment with the Church of England's refusal to address the nation's spiritual famine" (*A Glimpse of Sion's Glory* 8).

17. Although in his speech on the "Emancipation Proclamation" Emerson links the Proclamation to the Declaration of Independence, his omission here is perhaps not without significance. More than once Emerson points to the ambiguities within a declaration that pretends to speak for everyone but in truth only speaks for a limited few. Neither the South's declaration of independence through secession nor the revolutionaries' declaration of independence from British rule made provisions for the independence of the black man.

18. As Davis explains, "Early expansionists like William Gilmore Simms had hailed black slavery as 'the medium & great agent for rescuing and recovering to freedom & civilization all the vast tracts of Texas, Mexico, & c.' See *Slavery and Human Progress* 271.

19. The use of the motion of the planets as a metaphor for one's fidelity to the Law was pervasive during the seventeenth and eighteenth centuries in both England and America and corresponds to the attempt to join the tenets of theology with those emerging from Newtonian and Keplerian physics. As Emerson notes in his sermon on "Astronomy":

the science of astronomy has had an irresistible effect in modifying and enlarging the doctrines of theology. . . . Cheered by these results we come to feel that planet gravitates to planet and star attracts star, each fulfilling the last mile of its orbit as surely in the round of space as the bee which launches forth for the first time from its dark cell into light, and wandering amidst flowers all day, comes back at eve with unerring wing to the hive. It is the same invisible guide that pilots the bee and pilots the planet, that established the whole and perfected the parts, that giveth to all beauty, and order, and life, and usefulness. And thus I say, my friends, that to the human race the discoveries have reconciled the greatness to the greatness of the mind.

See *Young Emerson Speaks: Unpublished Discourses on Many Subjects,* ed. Arthur Cushman McGiffert, Jr. (Port Washington, N.Y.: Kennikat Press, Inc., 1968) 173, 176. The planetary metaphor goes back at least to Milton who, in his *The Reason of Church Government,* in a discussion of the freedom consequent upon reading the Gospels, claims that man may therefore become "as it were an invariable Planet of joy and felicity." See *Works* (New York: Columbia University Press, 1931) 186. See also Mitchell Breitweiser, *Cotton Mather and Benjamin Franklin: The Price of Representative Personality* (Cambridge: Cambridge University Press, 1984) 33-34; and Mason I. Lowance, *The Language of Canaan: Metaphor and Symbol in New England from the Puritans to the Transcendentalists* (Cambridge, Mass.: Harvard University Press, 1980).

20. For example, stanzas 13 and 16 come directly from the opening of "American Civilization." There Emerson writes:

Use, labor of each for all, is the health and virtue of all beings. *Ich dien,* I serve, is a truly royal motto. And it is the mark of nobleness to volunteer the lowest service, the greatest spirit only attaining to humility. Nay, God is God because he is the servant of all . . . now here comes this conspiracy of slavery,—they call it an institution, I call it a destitution . . . standing on this doleful experience, these people have endeavored to reverse the natural sentiments of mankind, and to pronounce labor disgraceful, and the well-being of a man to consist in eating the fruit of other men's labor. Labor: a man coins himself into his labor; turns his day, his strength, his thought, his affection into some product which remains as the visible sign of his power; and to protect that . . . is the object of all government.

(*Works* 11: 297)

Stanzas 16-18 are indebted to "Emancipation of the British West Indies" and "American Slavery" (*Works* 11: 125-26, 145, 469). For stanza 18 see also "American Civilization" (*Works* 11: 310-11). Stanza 22 is indebted to "The Celebration of the Intellect" (*Works* 12: 119, 121). Other references are perhaps less direct although one can hear echoes of "Self-Reliance," "The American Scholar," and "Over-Soul" in stanzas 14-15, and 17.

21. Compare the following passage from Emerson's "Over-Soul": "When we have broken our god of tradition, and ceased from our god of rhetoric, then may God fire the heart with his presence" (*Works* 2: 292).

22. Cited in McPherson, *The Struggle for Equality* 65.

23. *The Rejected Stone: or Insurrection vs. Resurrection in America* (Boston, 1861) 23-24.

24. *Rejected Stone* 110. No doubt the situation was more complex and difficult than Conway wished it to be. As Anne Norton notes:

> When the South seceded, declaring its independence of the Union, those who disputed the legality of the act, Lincoln among them, named their independence mere rebellion. But Lincoln knew, as much as any other man, that there could no longer be mere rebellion in America. The nation's revolutionary origins had granted all such popular upheavals a kinship with creative authority. The Rebellion had at least a family resemblance to the Revolution. . . . Confederates engaged in the active emulation of that enterprise recognized that this aspect of reenactment brought not merely legitimacy, but grandeur and sanctity to their cause.
>
> (*Alternative Americas: A Reading of Antebellum Political Culture* [Chicago: University of Chicago Press, 1986] 240)

Nevertheless, the necessity of emancipation compelled many abolitionists to overlook their own earlier attacks upon the North's support of slavery. Not wishing to detract from the administration's movements towards emancipation, these freedom fighters, Emerson included, threw their weight in support of the northern cause.

25. Compare the following from Emerson's essay "The Poet": "With what joy I begin to read a poem which I confide in as an inspiration! And now my chains are to be broken: I shall mount above these clouds and opaque airs in which I live,—opaque, though they seem transparent,—and from the heaven of truth I shall see and comprehend my relations. . . . Poets are thus liberating gods" (*Works* 3: 12, 30).

26. See especially Sumner, *The Landmark of Freedom: Speech of Hon. Charles Sumner, against the Repeal of the Missouri Prohibition of Slavery* (Boston, 1854).

27. *Speeches, Lectures, and Letters,* 2nd Series, ed. Rev. Theodore C. Pease (Boston, 1900) 5.

28. Compare with the following, even earlier argument in his essay "Politics": "Whenever I find my dominion over myself not sufficient for me, and undertake the direction of his also, I overstep the truth, and come into false relations to him . . . it is a lie, and hurts like a lie to both him and me" (*Works* 3: 214).

29. Emerson expands this argument in a remarkable passage at the end of his speech on "American Slavery." I quote it in its entirety:

> We shall one day bring the States shoulder to shoulder, and the citizens man to man, to exterminate slavery. It was said a little while ago that it would cost a thousand or twelve hundred millions, now it is said it would cost two thousand millions; such is the enhancement of property. Well, was there ever any contribution that was so enthusiastically paid as this will be? The United States will be brought to give every inch of their public lands for a purpose like this. Every State will contribute its surplus revenue. Every man will bear his part. We will have a chimney tax. We will give up our coaches and wine and watches. The church will melt her plate. The father of his country shall wait, well pleased, a little longer for his monument;— Franklin will wait for his; the Pilgrim Fathers for theirs; and the patient Columbus, who waited all his mortality for justice, shall wait a part of immortality also. . . . The rich shall give of their riches; the merchants of their commerce; the mechanics of their strength; the needlewomen will give, and children can have a Cent Society. If, really, the thing could come to a negotiation and a price were named, I do not think that any price, founded upon an estimate that figures could fairly represent, would be unmanageable. Every man in this land would give a week's work to dig away this accursed mountain of slavery, and force it forever out of the world."
>
> (*Works* 9: 469)

30. That these lines may have had particular resonance for the former slaves in Emerson's Music Hall audience can be gathered from a letter of January 1864 from Thomas Westworth Higginson to Emerson. In the letter, Higginson, a leader of a regiment of black troops, tells Emerson that his surgeon, Doctor Rogers, had recently read the "Boston Hymn" to his black soldiers and that "they understood every word of it . . . I recall vividly the thrill that went through me as he read the grand verse beginning 'Pay ransom to the owner,' and thought that these were the owners before us." Cited in Gougeon, *Virtue's Hero* 305-6.

31. See Edward L. Pierce, *Memoir and Letters of Charles Sumner,* 4 vols. (Boston, 1877-94) 4: 49.

32. *Liberator,* January 17, 1862.

33. Cited in McPherson, *The Struggle for Equality* 93.

34. At the end of "American Civilization" Emerson makes it clear that he supports immediate rather than gradual emancipation. He writes: "If Congress accords with the President, it is not yet too late to begin the emancipation; but we think it will always be too late to make it gradual. All experience agrees that it should be immediate" (*Works* 11: 310-11).

35. See *Cloud Crystals: A Snowflake Album, Collected and Edited by a Lady* (New York: D. Appleton & Company, 1864) 53.

36. *Early Lectures of Ralph Waldo Emerson,* ed. Stephen E. Whicher, Robert E. Spiller, and Wallace E. Williams (Cambridge, Mass.: Belknap Press of Harvard University, 1961) 1: 59.

37. *Journals and Miscellaneous Notebooks of Ralph Waldo Emerson,* ed. William H. Gilman, et al. (Cambridge: Harvard University Press, 1960-) 15: 250.

38. *Collected Works* 2: 276.

39. On this point see Gertrude Reif Hughes, *Emerson's Demanding Optimism* (Baton Rouge: Louisiana State University Press, 1984), especially chapter 4.

40. This figure also reappears in Wigglesworth's *The Day of Doom.* See Harrison T. Messerole, ed., *Seventeenth Century American Poetry* (New York: New York University Press, 1968) 46, 56.

41. See *Cotton Mather and Benjamin Franklin* 210.

42. See Mather, *Magnalia Christi Americana* (New York: Russell and Russell, 1967) 2: 368; and Edwards, *Works* (New York: G. & C. & H. Carvill, 1830) 1: 62.

43. This participation is the subject of Emerson's poem "Voluntaries," a poem written in celebration of the Massachusetts 54th regiment, one of the first black regiments in the Union army.

44. See, for example, Thomas F. Gossett, *Race: The History of an Idea in America* (Dallas, Texas: Southern Methodist University Press, 1963) 5; Davis, *The Problem of Slavery in Western Culture* (Ithaca, N.Y.: Cornell University Press, 1966) 63-64, 316-17; *Slavery and Human Progress* 21-22, 42-43, 86-87; *The Problem of Slavery in the Age of Revolution: 1770-1823* (Ithaca, N.Y.: Cornell University Press, 1975) 539-41; and Winthrop Jordan, *White over Black: American Attitudes Toward the Negro, 1550-1812* (Chapel Hill: University of North Carolina Press, 1968) 18-19, 35-37, 41-42, 54-56.

45. *Slavery and Human Progress* 39.

46. Compare this statement from his speech on the emancipation of the British West Indies: "a man is added to the human family" (*Works* 11: 140). Emerson suggests the necessity of this inclusion in a journal entry from 1846 and does so within the context of the Cain story. Indicating his awareness of the association between the curse of Cain and the black man, he writes: "Nature loves to cross her stocks. A pure blood, Bramin on Bramin, marrying in & in, soon becomes puny & wears out. Some strong Cain son, some black blood must renew & refresh the paler veins of Seth" (*Journals* 9: 365).

47. *Early Lectures* 1: 64.

48. On this point, see Norton, *Alternative Americas* 299.

David M. Robinson (essay date 1993)

SOURCE: "Toward a Grammar of Moral Life," in *Emerson and the Conduct of Life: Pragmatic and Ethical Purpose in the Later Work,* Cambridge University Press, 1993, pp. 181-201.

[*In the following excerpt, Robinson provides an assessment of Emerson's later career, noting that the author's personal struggles with authorship should prompt caution in too closely analyzing these texts as true examples of Emerson's ideas and writing.*]

The Universal Cipher

"I am of the oldest religion"

(*W,* 12:16).

The assessment of Emerson's later career is complicated by the gradual decline in creative order that he was able to bring to his work after *Society and Solitude.* The pattern of revision and rearrangement of journal and lecture material into book form that had begun in the 1830s served him well in many respects, but the final process of selection, organization, and revision was always a burden to him, perhaps because it seemed further removed from the original moment of inspiration and lacked the immediacy of a potential living audience.[1] Emerson's personal struggles with authorship were exacerbated in the 1860s by the emotional burdens and material constrictions of the Civil War, and his will and capacity to bring his papers into book form declined precipitously after a fire at his home in 1872.[2] The resulting situation, in which James E. Cabot took charge of editing much of the later work, prompts caution in analyzing these texts, but less for their validity as Emerson's ideas than for the authority of their combination and arrangement. "There is nothing here that he did not write, and he gave his full approval to whatever was done in the way of selection and arrangement," Cabot explained, adding, as I pointed out in Chapter 8, "but I cannot say that he applied his mind very closely to the matter" (*W,* 8:xiii).

Emerson's failure to push toward book completion should not, however, overshadow his intellectual vigor in the 1860s, and the decline in his creative power during the next decade should not obscure the significance of a number of later pieces. Several later texts authoritatively express Emerson's continuing orientation toward the ethical expression of spirituality and extend the pragmatic direction of his work in the 1850s. Emerson's exploration of the interplay of spiritual enlightenment with ethical action continued in *Natural History of Intellect,* **"Poetry and Imagination,"** and **"Character."** These works chart the resurgence of Emerson's long-held faith in the moral sentiment, which the political experience of the 1850s and 1860s had confirmed and revivified. Emerson composed by accretion, and the roots of his later texts are usually deep in his journals and lectures. But the later texts indicate clearly that moral philosophy permeated all aspects of his thought. Although Emerson could arguably be labeled a moral philosopher throughout his career, that is emphatically true of his final productive decades.

We have noted how the tour of England in 1847-8 had a significant impact on Emerson's shift, the most tangible result of which was *English Traits.* But England jolted Emerson in another way, by rekindling an attraction to science that had long been part of his intellectual outlook. With fresh exposure to current work in empirical science, Emerson undertook the ambitious project of translating the paradigm of the scientific study of nature into an inquiry into the processes of mind and spirit. *Natural History of Intellect* was the title Emerson gave to this essentially uncompleted project, a compilation of loosely related speculations that in their present form exemplify what Nancy Craig Simmons has termed the "synthetic" texts Cabot had a hand in arranging.[3] But despite its long and tangled history, the work still suggests the original intellectual stimulus that was first embodied in lectures presented in England in 1848. Struck anew by the power of English science, Emerson hoped that the same observation, classification, and generalization that had made "natural history" a revolutionary intellectual discipline might be harnessed in the profounder work of the inner life.[4]

This compelling philosophical project has been largely overlooked in Emerson studies, its state of incompletion contributing to the general assessment of failure and waning intellectual force in his later work. But *Natural History of Intellect* is significant as a point of reference for Emerson's attempt to correlate knowledge with ethical action. The term *natural history,* when applied to the mind, implied that the same laws of genesis and development that controlled organic nature also operated on mental processes. If mind and nature operated by the same laws and could be understood with the same rigor, Emerson felt that these laws could be put to work to derive an ordered economy of mental power. But it was the hope, not the finally unpersuasive demonstration, that was intellectually fertile. In a formative journal entry for the project, written shortly before he departed for England in 1847, he noted that "the highest value of natural history & mainly of these new & secular results like the inferences from geology, & the discovery of parallax, & the resolution of Nebulae, is its translation into an universal cipher applicable to Man viewed as Intellect also" (*JMN,* 10:136). The mind

and nature were different manifestations of a seamless whole, and nature stood as the "cipher" of that reality, the means by which the mind could pursue a knowledge that ultimately coincided with self-determination.

The promise of science had a formative influence on Emerson's early career, but he increasingly felt that a more rigorous attempt might be made to specify the correlations that existed between the physical world and the mind. In entertaining the idea of applying a scientific model to the mind, Emerson implied that the success of pure observation, the mark of scientific advancement, might also characterize self-reflexive knowledge. The scientist observes and compiles facts, and from these observations, classifications and laws emerge. Emerson was confident that similar results would obtain if the mind were closely observed, and when he heard lectures by Richard Owen and Michael Faraday in England, and attended meetings of the Geological Society of London, that conviction was renewed. Science became again, at least for a time, his paradigm for philosophical speculation.[5] Emerson measured himself, with a sense of vulnerability, against the scientific example that he saw: "One could not help admiring the irresponsible security and happiness of the attitude of the naturalist; sure of admiration for his facts, sure of their sufficiency" (*W,* 12:3). To be "sure"—this was a quality that appealed to the Emerson of the late 1840s, when certainty had become a scarce commodity.

Natural history seemed to offer this promise of stable knowledge at a crucial moment, when Emerson had been battling with skepticism about the capacity of the self to make an impact on the world through willed choice. The subject of nature, and the example of the naturalist, offered an alternative to the introspection inevitable to the philosophy of self-culture, while also suggesting that certainties, even in the inner life, might be approached. It was a welcome and provocative stimulus to the Emerson who had risked so much of himself in the introspective probings of **"Experience."** It is therefore significant to find, in the aftermath of **"Experience,"** an important credo: "I believe in the existence of the material world as the expression of the spiritual or the real, and in the impenetrable mystery which hides (and hides through absolute transparency) the mental nature, I await the insight which our advancing knowledge of material laws shall furnish" (*W,* 12:5). But it is a credo that admits "impenetrable mystery" and thus suggests the bounds of its own capacity to know fully.

Emerson's reaction to the claims of science to certainty was the basis of that credo. He wondered whether "a similar enumeration" might not "be made of the laws and powers of the Intellect." Would these not "possess the same claims on the student"? Enthralled by the power of facts, he was driven to search for them in the more problematic realm of the intellect: "Could we have, that is, the exhaustive accuracy of distribution which chemists use in their nomenclature and anatomists in their descriptions, applied to a higher class of facts; to those laws, namely, which are common to chemistry, anatomy, astronomy, geometry, intellect, morals and social life;—laws of the world?" (*W*, 12:3-4). Emerson's list is carefully structured to move from the more concrete and factual objects of study to the more abstract and subjective ones. Anatomy yields to astronomy, also a physical science, but of greater compass, which in turn yields to geometry, a discipline with a different, though no less compelling, aura of certainty. But the move from the physical solidity of astronomy to the abstract mathematical truths of geometry prepares him for the greater leap from geometry to intellect; his progressions into morals and social life are deeper forays into the regions in which speculation must replace empiricism. It is here, of course, that we find the seeds of his project's failure—but also its enormous challenge and appeal. His assumption, finally, was that the "certainty" of empirical observation was one manifestation of a system of symbolic resonances that constituted our perception of the world. The scientist's capacity to move from fact to law was the evidence that the spiritual world showed itself in the material.

That such correlations between the material and the spiritual existed, Emerson had never doubted. His immersion in scientific reading in the early 1830s, leavened by his background in natural theology, Platonism, and his new reading of the Swedenborgian Sampson Reed, had helped him to develop a theory of corresponding levels of reality, in which the phenomena of the physical world were reflections of a deeper series of spiritual laws.[6] Nature thus became the means for the education of the mind, and the key intellectual task was to perceive and express the analogy between physical and spiritual phenomena. Such perception, and its correlative expression, were problematic, standing at the crossroads between ecstatic intuition, symbolic perception, metaphysical speculation, and exact scientific observation. But the conviction that in certain moments a glimpse of unified being might be available, a perception that would prove the connection between the physical and the spiritual, was the motivating promise of much of his intellectual career.

The revelation of the spirit through the processes of nature served Emerson best as a working hypothesis, or a basis from which to reason by analogy. Its fragility as a philosophical concept is suggested by the eventual failure of *Natural History of Intellect,* which he himself also seemed to feel. The most persuasive part of the project is the statement of the method and assumptions, not the effort to work them out. Emerson's premise that laws and operations of the mind could be mastered in the way that the forms of nature had been was far from a dry statement of procedural assumptions; it was the evidence of a hope in the mind's growing comprehension of being. Ironically, as Emerson's conviction of the possibility of specifying the identity of nature and the mind grew, building a momentum for a more thorough analysis, the suggestive potential of the doctrine decreased. Reality, he thought at times, could be conceived as a continuum between mind and matter, or perhaps a series of ascending planes of signifi-

cance, or a material surface under which depths of spiritual truths were to be found. All of these poetic images served well as a framework for speculation, even though they could not sustain the weight of minute and detailed analysis.

An important moment in the initial development of his project was recorded in a journal entry of 1848 (*JMN*, 10:316-17), written under the influence of a recent visit to the British Museum. The renewed exposure to science had reinforced Emerson's sense of the monistic unity of matter and mind, and he expressed that insight in terms of a unifying power. "One power streams into all natures," he noted, pursuing the implications of that law into an analysis of mind. "Mind is vegetable, & grows thought out of thought as joint out of joint in corn." This was the first of several analogies in which mental processes were considered in terms of the natural world. "Mind is chemical, & shows all the affinities & repulsions of chemistry, & works by presence." The analogy of chemistry is followed by the notations "Mind grows, crystallizes, electricity," as Emerson stretches to capture the suggestions of the mind's conformity to natural law. This insight might be regarded as the starting point for his speculation on natural history, but it marks its end point as well. Even though it illumined the dark connection between spirit and matter, it was a flash of insight hard to sustain. The entry continues in an abbreviated but fascinating recapitulation of Emerson's entire structure of metaphysical belief:

> This all comes of a higher fact, one substance
>   Mind knows the way because it has trode it before
>   Knowledge is becoming of that thing
>   Somewhere sometime some eternity we have played this game
>   before
>   Go thro' British Museum & we are full of occult sympathies
>   I was azote

The curious sense of completion contained in the bare bones of this sketch suggests the problem of the entire project—the prosaic analysis and descriptions of exactly how the mind is "vegetable" or "chemical" constitute a significant reduction of intellectual intensity from the initial recognition of the similarity. These poetic assertions have greater impact when they remain suggestive, free of heavy explanatory comment.

The last statement is a three-word summation of what Emerson defined a decade later (1857) as the laws of his "philosophy": "1. *Identity,* whence comes the fact that *metaphysical faculties & facts are the transcendency of physical.* 2. Flowing, or transition, or shooting the gulf, the perpetual striving to ascend to a higher platform, the same thing in new & higher forms" (*JMN*, 14:191-2). The identity of the human self with so distant a form as the mineral is the telling exemplification of the law of identity.[7] The capacity to sense that identity is itself the evidence of the series of similarly patterned levels of reality that for Emerson was the form of the universe. "Mind knows the way because it has trode it before."

But to read *Natural History of Intellect* is a frustrating experience. It is permeated with the Neoplatonism that marks the preceding journal entry, but also claims a skepticism of all metaphysics: "I confess to a little distrust of that completeness of system which metaphysicians are apt to affect. 'Tis the gnat grasping the world. All these exhaustive theories appear indeed a false and vain attempt to introvert and analyze the Primal Thought" (*W,* 12:12). One of the attractions the scientific method held for Emerson was its seeming release from rational systematization. Its inductiveness suggested a certain pragmatic humility and reemphasized close observation as a key to the truth. "We have invincible repugnance to introversion, to study of the eyes instead of that which the eyes see," he wrote, seeing in rational and deductive metaphysical systems a damaging solipsism. For Emerson, "the natural direction of the intellectual powers is from within outward" (*W,* 12:12). *Natural History of Intellect* shares with *Nature* the belief that natural objects serve as a symbol or cipher of a larger reality, but this devaluation of the introspective and the deductively rational sets quite a different tone. *Nature* had devolved ultimately to the moral and pragmatic injunction "Build, therefore, your own world" (*CW,* 1:45). Similarly, *Natural History of Intellect* is finally less a treatise of philosophical speculation or scientific observation than a search for usable truth for the conduct of life. "My metaphysics are to the end of use," Emerson declared. "I wish to know the laws of this wonderful power [mind], that I may domesticate it." The object of observing the mind, as one would observe the facts of the natural world, is "to learn to live with it wisely, court its aid, catch sight of its splendor, feel its approach, hear and save its oracles and obey them." And just as he had given the final and authoritative words of *Nature* to his figure of the "Orphic Poet," he admits in *Natural History of Intellect* that philosophy "will one day be taught by poets"—the poet "is believing; the philosopher, after some struggle, having only reasons for believing" (*W,* 12:13-14).

Emerson's plan of observing the intellect thus subtly becomes a plea for the moral advantages of its cultivation and an argument for the greater social valuation of intellectual pursuits. Moreover, he aspires not only to describe the mind, but to offer a practical guidebook for intellectual development. His remark on "instinct," which he has described as the groundwork of the intellect, typifies the nature of his pragmatic orientation toward epistemology. "To make a practical use of this instinct in every part of life constitutes true wisdom, and we must form the habit of preferring in all cases this guidance, which is given as it is used" (*W,* 12:67). The applications of this attitude amount to no more, really, than the development of a habit for the instinctual and a faith that acting out of it will increase its availability. Emerson has instinct enough to know that the further specification of the means of intellectual cultivation would be reductive, narrowing the appeal to openness that he is trying to broaden. This limitation offers one example of the irony of *Natural History of Intellect.* Despite its rhetoric of scientific specificity and close observation of

the factual, the work's greatest accomplishment is its demonstration of the impenetrable mystery of the intellect.

We might borrow the very terms that Emerson uses to describe the basis of the intellect to indicate how the work thus undercuts itself. For Emerson, all intellectual power is a reduction to instinct, the individual's access to the fundamental power of being. Contact with that source of power requires a constant discarding of impediments, a perpetual turning back to an unobstructed rediscovery of one's primary orientation. Similarly, the reader of *Natural History of Intellect* finds that Emerson's rational accounts of the working of the mind are less impressive than his images of its mystery. Emerson's desire to describe the intellect in the terms he has set forth is thus undermined by the operation of the very power he has described, instinct, when the reader directs it to the text. I have in mind in particular Emerson's strangely compelling presentation of the metaphor of the stream of consciousness: "In my thought I seem to stand on the bank of a river and watch the endless flow of the stream, floating objects of all shapes, colors and natures; nor can I much detain them as they pass, except by running beside them a little way along the bank. But whence they come or whither they go is not told me" (*W,* 12:16). This image of the self helplessly witnessing the processes of the mind overpowers most of the talk about the precise observation and practical use of intellect. Emerson's adept dramatization of the desperation involved in running for a closer look drains the text of its assurance of power. Where is the surety that he has envied in the scientist? In the face of such absolute mystery, talk of certainty seems out of place. This eruption of vulnerability clouds the whole enterprise of tracing the mind's "natural history," but it stands as one of the valuable lessons of this divided and revealing work. Emerson stressed instinct as the primary power of intellect because he saw it as the entry to "that unknown country in which all the rivers of our knowledge have their fountains, and which, by its qualities and structure, determines both the nature of the waters and the direction in which they flow" (*W,* 12:33). The metaphor of the stream is extended to include the mysterious source of the waters, emphasizing that the value of instinct is its contiguity with this fundamental mystery.

Emerson's motivating paradigm of scientific observation is thus inadequate to the elucidation of the mind, but he is left with other means of binding his observations together, loci of value rather than observations or categories. Primary among them is a faith in the essential identity of reality, the assumption that has underlain his entire project. "There is in Nature a parallel unity which corresponds to the unity in the mind and makes it available." That this unity has a mysterious source does not weaken Emerson's conviction that "without identity at base, chaos must be forever" (*W,* 12:19-20). This faith in a final order compensates for the vulnerability of our limited knowledge, and is closely related to a valuation of "impressionability," the constant openness to perception, as an ethical quality. This is the same value that he expounded in **"Success,"** when he turned the definition of successful living to a renewed attention to the quality of open sensitivity. In *Natural History of Intellect* he bolsters that idea with reference to our sense of our place in the larger cosmic order. "The universe is traversed by paths or bridges or stepping-stones across the gulfs of space in every direction. To every soul that is created is its path, invisible to all but itself" (*W,* 12:42). The responsibility of the intellect is to maintain those paths and thus retain a vital connection with the order of things, which is, after all, a part of ourselves, as we are a part of that order. "The conduct of Intellect must respect nothing so much as preserving the sensibility," alive to the nuances that confirm the complexity and richness of reality. Everything of which we remain sensible, after all, helps us to discover or reconfirm another part of ourselves, so that self-knowledge and open impressionability become one and the same. "That mind is best," Emerson declared, "which is most impressionable" (*W,* 12:43).

Daily life must be imbued with this kind of heightened sensibility, which can show itself as the capacity to value the ordinary as a revelation. "There are times when the cawing of a crow, a weed, a snow-flake, a boy's willow whistle, or a farmer planting in his field is more suggestive to the mind than the Yosemite gorge or the Vatican would be in another hour" (*W,* 12:43). This catalog of the homely and rural elevates the quality of the day and the hour to a quest for divinity in the ordinary conduct of life, but made extraordinary through a consecrated openness of the senses and the mind. Such "suggestive" moments become occasions in which the assumption of faith in a holistic order is reconfirmed through symbolic seeing.

The valuation of "impressionability" entails a similar emphasis on "transition," an energetic capacity to change and adapt. Although *impressionability* is a word with passive connotations, it has a latent orientation toward the seizure of the world in perception. "Transition is the attitude of power," Emerson asserted, thus emphasizing the necessity of an impressionability turned active. This is the mood of **"Circles,"** and it emerges fresh in Emerson's later analysis of the mind's response to uncertainty and illusion. "The universe exists only in transit, or we behold it shooting the gulf from the past to the future" (*W,* 12:59). Richard Poirier's persuasive meditation on the Emersonian attitude of "transition" has suggested the fundamental importance of Emerson's distrust of stasis in any form and its continuing value as an example.[8] It is telling that Emerson sounded this note well beyond **"Circles."** Embedded in *Natural History of Intellect,* the thrust of which was to reduce the operations of mind to factual laws, we find this energetic declaration: "A fact is only a fulcrum of the spirit. It is the terminus of a past thought, but only a means now to new sallies of the imagination and new progress of wisdom" (*W,* 12:59). Facts, as tools, are only the means by which we work.

The method of science never functions in *Natural History of Intellect* as a true methodology, but only as a scaffolding, discarded when Emerson's meditation on intellect be-

comes self-supporting. It metaphorically suggests the fundamental connection between nature and the mind, but as metaphor rather than as method, it is enabling, returning him by a different route to his old faith in energy. Since it is the leap itself that Emerson values, he honors whatever brings him to the edge. In *Nature,* the energy for movement was derived from the mystical charge best described in the transparent eyeball passage. In *Natural History of Intellect* the mysticism has largely evaporated, leaving the complex promise of natural history, and the desire to employ a corresponding economy of mind and spirit, as the remaining source of power.

THE TROPE OF PERCEPTION

"For the value of a trope is that the hearer is one: and indeed Nature itself is a vast trope, and all particular natures are tropes"

(*W,* 8:15).

Despite its empiricist rhetoric, *Natural History of Intellect* was at bottom a poetic project, a consideration of the relation of power to the creation and recognition of symbolic forms. It aimed to achieve a deeper symbolic knowing, an apprehension of the correspondence and ultimate unity of the physical and the mental. This aim was a restatement through the metaphor of science of the centrality of poetic knowledge. This recurring emphasis on symbolic perception in Emerson's later work is important, for as he replaced the wilder voice of his earlier work with a more tempered and pragmatic one, he reduced the potential of his work for emotional nurture. His pragmatic emphasis, as we have seen, was in part an attempt to compensate for the scarcity and unreliability of the ecstatic moment, and he continued to explore ways of reaffirming truths that he had earlier asserted by vision. The claim of symbolic knowledge, and of poetry in particular, thus remained a crucially stable element in Emerson's transition from mystic visionary to pragmatic moralist.

Among Emerson's most significant explorations of the nature of symbolic knowledge and its connection to moral action is **"Poetry and Imagination,"** an essay whose significance has been recently noted by both Barbara Packer and Ronald A. Bosco. Like *Natural History of Intellect,* the essay has its roots in the late 1840s and developed over the next two decades in Emerson's lecturing.[9] The epistemological concern fundamental to *Natural History of Intellect* also drives **"Poetry and Imagination,"** which begins its exploration of the symbolic consciousness with an acknowledgment that "the perception of matter is made the common sense, and for cause." As in *Nature,* the perception of matter is shown to be only the first stage of perception, but crucial in the development of the individual's capacity to establish a relation with the order of things. "We must learn the homely laws of fire and water; we must feed, wash, plant, build. These are ends of necessity, and first in the order of Nature. Poverty, frost, famine, disease, debt, are the beadles and guardsmen that hold us to common sense. The intellect, yielded up to itself, cannot supersede this tyrannic necessity" (*W*, 8:3). We might compare this passage with the discussion of the use of nature as "Commodity" in *Nature* to understand the rather significant change of focus in Emerson's later work. *Nature* had stressed the successful use of the world to solve human material needs; **"Poetry and Imagination"** describes, with less confidence and considerably more gravity, the "tyrannic" and threatening qualities of material necessity that the "common sense" reinforces.

Although this depiction of the tragic limitations of human experience is consonant with the more somber strains of **"Experience"** and **"Fate,"** it has a larger purpose in Emerson's description of the working of the symbolic imagination. The common sense, as he calls it, is the first and most elemental reminder that intellectual power is a power of synthesis. The mind has no power outside the range of possible convergences that nature represents. One manifestation of romanticism, represented in its extremest form by Poe, posited the power of intellect as arrayed against the material world, and the poet as one who struggles against the restraints that materiality and empiricism represent.[10] Emerson's opening acknowledgment of the material "ends of necessity" is a recognition not only that rebellion against nature is finally impossible but that it is undesirable as well, for the nature of its impossibility is self-destruction. Common sense respects "the existence of matter, not because we can touch it or conceive of it, but because it agrees with ourselves, and the universe does not jest with us, but is in earnest, is the house of health and life" (*W*, 8:3). Materiality is thus the most fundamental expression of the governing laws that establish our identity, and the limitations represented by these laws are in this sense forms of self-expression.

Emerson's project in **"Poetry and Imagination"** is to develop this insight about material knowing into a recognition that symbolic knowing is also a form of self-knowledge. The limits imposed by materiality are, as Emerson reads them, the signs of a fundamental cosmic unity, and the apprehension of this unity is the work of poetry. The imagination is not, however, simply an echo of the life of the senses or of empirical knowledge. Emerson stresses "the independent action of the mind" with its "strange suggestions and laws," and describes a quality of thought that resonates with his opening discussion of matter: "a certain tyranny which springs up in his own thoughts, which have an order, method and beliefs of their own, very different from the order which this common sense uses" (*W*, 8:6). Emerson's recurrence to the term *tyranny* to describe the workings of the mind implies that its laws are as ironclad as those of matter, and his reference to the "order, method and beliefs" of the mind suggests a uniform structure of mental activity that was the fundamental assumption of *Natural History of Intellect.*

But Emerson develops his theory of mind less in terms of its static structural elements than in terms of process and metamorphosis, arguing that the tyranny of mind is its persistent movement toward unity. Commenting on the ten-

dency of science to rise to ever higher and more inclusive general classifications, he concludes that "all multiplicity rushes to be resolved into unity" (*W*, 8:7). It is this perceptual "rush" that Emerson finds at the basis of symbolic perception, a process in which the mind discerns the metamorphosis of a physical form into part of a larger pattern or order, the form serving as the entry into that order. Poetic knowledge is thus the pursuit of the larger contextual pattern that will make sense of an individual object by demonstrating its relation to the whole. Emerson takes reading itself as a metaphor for perception, a striking moment in which the reader is asked to perceive metaphorically the process of metaphor: "Natural objects, if individually described and out of connection, are not yet known, since they are really parts of a symmetrical universe, like words of a sentence; and if their true order is found, the poet can read their divine significance orderly as in a Bible." The relation between the establishment of a scientific order and the workings of language confirms the assumption that "identity of law, perfect order in physics, perfect parallelism between the laws of Nature and the laws of thought exist," or more simply that "there is one animal, one plant, one matter and one force" (*W*, 8:8-9).

This pervasive unity suggests the limits of the empirical method of science, which attempts to isolate a phenomenon rather than find its larger context and is therefore "false by being unpoetical" (*W*, 8:10). Poetic knowing, which is fundamentally a recognition that perception is connection, strives not to isolate objects from each other or the object of perception from the perceiving subject. Emerson's recognition of the self-referential element of symbolic perception makes the perceiver of a symbol also a symbol, an argument that is crucial to his eventual reading of poetic perception as a form of the moral imagination. "For the value of a trope is that the hearer is one: and indeed Nature itself is a vast trope, and all particular natures are tropes" (*W*, 8:15). In the resonant ambiguity of Emerson's phrase, "the hearer" is "one," a trope, that is, in the sense of being similar to what he or she perceives. But the hearer is also "one" in the sense of having achieved oneness with the object of perception, and with the unity that is the fundamental quality of the cosmos. Symbolic perception is a means of transcending the self through participating momentarily in the rush of energy that defines both the natural order and the pattern of the mind. "The endless passing of one element into new forms, the incessant metamorphosis, explains the rank which the imagination holds in our catalogue of mental powers. The imagination is the reader of these forms." It is significant that Emerson again uses reading to represent this participation in the widening of a consciousness of our larger context, expanding it into an image of the cosmos as a vast language. The "productions and changes of Nature" come to be viewed by the poet "as the nouns of language" (*W*, 8:15). Used "representatively" they provide interpretive access to the same grammar that provides and defines the poet's identity as well.

There is pleasure as well as knowledge in reading this text of nature. Emerson's testimony to that pleasure is striking, particularly in light of the waning of his dependence on mystical ecstasy that we have traced. "Every new object so seen"—seen, that is, as part of the vocabulary of natural unity—"gives a shock of agreeable surprise" (*W,* 8:15). Emerson's description of the experience of recognizing that the identity of one thing slides perennially into the identity of another, in an ever-enlarging whole, is permeated with a sense of bodily excitement and emotional intensity that is, many readers might be tempted to say, positively un-Emersonian. If he has found the ecstasy of mystical rapture fleeting and precarious, his closest emotional substitute has become the Bacchanalian quality of the peak moment of poetic insight, the perception of the collapse of individual identity into a newer form: "The act of imagination is ever attended by pure delight. It infuses a certain volatility and intoxication into all Nature. It has a flute which sets the atoms of our frame in a dance. Our indeterminate size is a delicious secret which it reveals to us. The mountains begin to dislimn, and float in the air" (*W,* 8:18). This dizzying rapture that seems to threaten the solidity of the material world is a result of experiencing the flow of energy that confirms the unity of nature, a flow Emerson had identified earlier as the principal law or quality of the mind.

Emerson denotes the experiential apprehension of this law as imagination, and his description of the phenomenon of imaginative perception stresses the sense in which it is a form of knowing in which mind and object are both encompassed in a comprehensive energy: "The imagination exists by sharing the ethereal currents." Such a phenomenon is essentially one of process rather than stasis; knowing is an event, one that defines the knower as it reveals the world. The "central identity" moves "with divine flowings, through remotest things." This is also the movement of the mind in symbolic perception. The poet "can detect essential resemblances in natures . . . because he is sensible of the sweep of the celestial stream, from which nothing is exempt." As Emerson emphasizes, that inclusiveness extends to the poet or perceiver, whose act of perception is a surrender to the "celestial stream" of identity. "His own body is a fleeting apparition,—his personality as fugitive as the trope he employs" (*W,* 8:21).

Yet as ethereal as this description of symbolic perception seems—"In certain hours we can almost pass our hand through our own body" (*W,* 8:21)—it is, like the pursuit of scientific perception in *Natural History of Intellect,* ultimately linked to a moral imperative. The capacity of the self to blend into a larger flow of cosmic identity is at bottom a moral quality for Emerson, indicating the larger possibilities of the self and the grounding of moral decisions in self-transcendence. In moving from the description of the symbolic perception essential to poetry to a consideration of the effects of poetry in a larger social framework, Emerson argues that the value of poetry lies in its capacity to address human possibility: "All writings must be in a degree exoteric, written to a human *should* or *would,* instead of to the fatal *is*: this holds even of the bravest and sincerest writers" (*W,* 8:30-1). The poet's ad-

dress to human potential is grounded in the recognition that the human mind is linked to vastly larger powers, a revelation that the moment of symbolic insight has provided. The ethereal sense of the self's evaporation into a larger stream of natural energy thus gives way to the recognition that larger power is always the power *to do* and that poetry is finally a pragmatic discipline. "To the poet the world is virgin soil; all is practicable; the men are ready for virtue; it is always time to do right." Poetry is the expression of the reality and immediacy of moral choice, for the poet "affirms the applicability of the ideal law to this moment and the present knot of affairs" (*W,* 8:31).

Poetry is vision, but as Emerson describes it here, it is completed only in the grounding of that vision in practical power. "None of your parlor or piano verse, none of your carpet poets, who are content to amuse, will satisfy us. Power, new power, is the good which the soul seeks" (*W,* 8:63). Emerson associates that power with the concept of "metamorphosis," another term, like "transition," that captured his sense of reality as process. Such terms became increasingly crucial in his later philosophical vocabulary. Metamorphic energy comes to represent the condition of human possibility. "The nature of things is flowing, a metamorphosis. The free spirit sympathizes not only with the actual form, but with the power or possible forms." Although he admits the conservative tendency to "rest on today's forms," he sees that inertia as a contributing element to the rush of energy that accompanies the renewed recognition of change. "Hence the shudder of joy with which in each clear moment we recognize the metamorphosis, because it is always a conquest, a surprise from the heart of things" (*W,* 8:71). The term *conquest* suggests initially the poet's triumphant perception, but its more lasting implication is that in the act of perception the individual is conquered, overtaken by power that had been heretofore unknown.

That sense of surprised surrender is finally the product of the nature of perception as a series of enlarging generalizations in which the mind is carried from the particular to an inclusive whole. "Power of generalizing differences men," Emerson argues, equating the capacity "of not pausing but going on" with "the Divine effort in a man" (*W,* 8:72). He discusses this as a form of aesthetic energy, in which the poet is elevated by a larger capacity for generalization, but this aesthetic energy is a form of the moral energy that is required in the transcendence of the limited desires and perspectives of the self into a larger will for the benefit of the whole. **"Poetry and Imagination"** reminds us how closely Emerson had interwoven his aesthetic concerns with his moral perspective, and of the increasingly important role his aesthetics of symbolic perception played in the growing predominance of the ethical in his later outlook.

THE HABIT OF ACTION

"The progress of religion is steadily to its identity with morals"

(*JMN,* 16:209).

As noted earlier, Emerson had turned to the concept of character in *Essays: Second Series* (1844) to express the increasingly social and moral grounding of his spirituality. The renewed emphasis on moral theory that resulted from his pragmatic turn permeates most of his work from the middle 1840s on and is encapsulated in a second essay on character, published in the *North American Review* in 1866.[11] Relegated to deep obscurity in the general neglect of his later work, **"Character"** is nevertheless a significant text for assessing Emerson's transformation of the doctrine of self-culture under the pressures of fleeting mysticism and rising ethical responsibility. The essay reflects Emerson's renewed emphasis on ethical action, and its tone of earnest determination reflects his response to the nation's moral and political crisis. The essay makes it clear that purpose and commitment are central values, and the threats of introspective paralysis and constitutional restriction enunciated in **"Experience"** and **"Fate"** seem to have lost some of their urgency. Although the essay is not explicitly political, its edge of hard-won confidence in moral fortitude reflects an attempt to find and maintain moral bearings in the aftermath of the antislavery struggle and the Civil War. The "steadfastness" that Emerson praises as essential to the moral character (*W,* 10:102) has not been abstractly deduced but has proved itself as both a personal and national resource in difficult times.

"Character" is most significant for the force with which it restates Emerson's doctrine of the moral sentiment, the foundation of his earliest thinking and the most important point of continuity in his thinking from first to last. He had identified it in a sermon of 1827 as "the main, central, prominent power of the soul" (*CS,* 1:116), and it had remained a crucial point of reference, the various depictions of his vision of self-development always circling back to this fundamental quality of the self. His explication of the concept of character as a version of the moral sentiment marks no new philosophical departure, but it is a good example of Emerson's later emphatic dependence on the ethical as the subsuming spiritual category. Called in 1867 to address an organizational meeting of the religious radicals who were forming the Free Religious Association, he made clear his conviction that religion was less a matter of speculation than action: "Pure doctrine always bears fruit in pure benefits. It is only by good works, it is only on the basis of active duty, that worship finds expression" (*W,* 11:480). He had come to feel that "the progress of religion is steadily to its identity with morals" (*JMN,* 16:209), and the moral category had become the means of testing and confirming both religious experience and perceptual validity.

Even though **"Character,"** with its exposition of the moral sense, marks no major philosophical departure, it does suggest how the national crisis had confirmed Emerson's faith. The antislavery movement and the Civil War were crusades that had tested and might restore the moral fiber of American culture. Emerson's evocation of qualities such as steadfastness, stability, and determination represents an important tonal shift from the aggressive defiance

of earlier texts like the **"Divinity School Address"** and **"Self-Reliance."** Emerson describes character as the representation of the moral sense in the cumulative action of the individual, "the habit of action from the permanent vision of truth" (*W,* 10:120). It is the product of two potentially contradictory factors, namely, the exercise of the will and the orientation of the self toward a universal rather than a personal good. The construction of character is a result of perpetual work in both these directions, in each of which it is vulnerable to a different form of skepticism: a surrender to fate or a narrowing pursuit of selfish ends. The battle against these forms of skepticism, the obstacles to the achievement of character, constitutes the narrative of Emerson's later work.

Emerson locates the work of character building in the perpetual necessity of choice, the condition of life that gives to every moment a moral quality. The fatalism that loomed as such a pressing issue in **"Experience"** and **"Fate"** has been displaced in **"Character"** by an unequivocal affirmation of the freedom of human moral expression: "Morals implies freedom and will. The will constitutes the man." Emerson argues that the distinction of humanity among the species lies in this capacity for choice: "Choice is born in him; here is he that chooses" (*W,* 10:91-2). The cumulative lesson of the 1850s and 1860s, decades saturated with political challenge and struggle, has been to reaffirm the centrality of will. "For the world is a battleground; every principle is a war-note, and the most quiet and protected life is at any moment exposed to incidents which test your firmness" (*W,* 10:87), he wrote in **"Perpetual Forces,"** another late essay with close affinities to **"Character."** **"Character"** reflects that shift in moral vision with its emphasis on will, choice, and action as the fundamental expressions of the moral sentiment.

Emerson is careful, however, to specify that "will, pure and perceiving, is not wilfulness" (*W,* 10:92), a distinction that allows the power of choice to be insulated from narrowly individualistic ends: "Morals is the direction of the will on universal ends. He is immoral who is acting to any private end. He is moral,—we say it with Marcus Aurelius and with Kant,—whose aim or motive may become a universal rule, binding on all intelligent beings." The consideration of universal ends thus lies at the foundation of all human virtues, which are "special directions of this motive" (*W,* 10:92). The cooperative enterprise that the antislavery movement and the Civil War represented had demonstrated how the individual will might be conjoined into a larger social movement with an end that went beyond the individual. That possibility had not been excluded from his moral reasoning in the 1830s, of course, but his problem then had been a different one—to separate the individual from a suffocating social identity, whose moral ends were questionable.

In **"Character,"** Emerson points to unrestrained individualism as the fundamental moral challenge. A deeper problem for the moral life than fatalism is the fundamental antagonism between "the wishes and interests of the individual" who "craves a private benefit," and the pursuit of an "absolute good." The individual's cultivation of the capacity to renounce private interest in deference to a larger good is "the moral discipline of life" (*W,* 10:94). Despite the renunciatory and ascetic nature of this principle, the essay communicates a celebratory quality, according with the energetic rush of fulfillment associated with symbolic perception in **"Poetry and Imagination."** The moral sentiment "puts us in place. It centres, it concentrates us. It puts us at the heart of Nature, where we belong, in the cabinet of science and of causes, there where all the wires terminate which hold the world in magnetic unity, and so converts us into universal beings" (*W,* 10:95). The imagery of circuitry suggests both the instantaneous unity and mysterious power of the moral sense, but we should not overlook Emerson's use of a term drawn from an entirely different world of discourse, the suggestion of conversion. He is cognizant of a resistance to a religion of morals alone, arising from the "fear that pure truth, pure morals, will not make a religion for the affections" (*W,* 10:119). All the emotional dynamics concentrated in the Protestant concept of conversion are therefore lent to the action of the moral sentiment. Although Emerson notes that "Truth, Power, Goodness, Beauty, are its varied names," he also ties the moral sense to more specific and historically resonant religious terminology: "the light, the seed, the Spirit, the Holy Ghost, the Comforter, the Dæmon, the still, small voice" (*W,* 10:95-7). The burden of this assertion is not only to establish the universality of the moral sense but to imbue it with the emotional and spiritual coloration that will save it from being perceived as mere legalism.

From this perspective, religious forms represent the mythical expression of an enduring moral energy. "The religions we call false were once true. They also were affirmations of the conscience correcting the evil customs of their times." Although the comment seems at first to affirm religious forms and institutions, its deeper strategy is to undermine a belief in the stability of any particular historical manifestation of religion, including, of course, Protestant Christianity as most of Emerson's readers would have known it. "The populace drag down the gods to their own level, and give them their egotism; whilst in Nature is none at all, God keeping out of sight, and known only as pure law, though resistless" (*W,* 10:103-4). Emerson thus offers an assurance of religious development based on the capacity of the moral sentiment to evoke perpetually a critique of the religious forms in which it is periodically embodied. "Men will learn to put back the emphasis peremptorily on pure morals, always the same, not subject to doubtful interpretation, with no sale of indulgences, no massacre of heretics, no female slaves, no disfranchisement of woman, no stigma on race; to make morals the absolute test, and so to uncover and drive out the false religions" (*W,* 10:114). The progression of religious abuses is notable, for it equates the modern movements for feminism and racial equality with the struggle against the most egregious historical examples of religious bigotry. The immediate relevance of the working of this law is clear: "It

is only yesterday that our American churches, so long silent on Slavery, and notoriously hostile to the Abolitionist, wheeled into line for Emancipation" (*W,* 10:114). These reform movements have thus become the gauges of the workings of the moral sentiment.

This analysis of the course of American religion articulates Emerson's larger concern about the social context within which the development of character must occur, and it suggests his concern about the moral condition of the new American culture that was emerging from the war. Emerson's sense that a new and less institutionalized form of religion was emerging was much in accord with the spirit of the Free Religious Association, which hoped to foster a "radical" religion based on noncreedal theological speculation and a decentered, individualized worship through ethical commitment and moral work.[12] Emerson recognized that during the 1840-60 period, American culture's moral impetus had passed from the churches to the reform movements. "The churches are obsolete," he wrote in 1859, because "the reforms do not proceed from the churches" (*JMN,* 14:236). The sign of that cultural shift was confirmed for him in the growing schism between the church and the intellectuals. "Every intellectual man is out of the old Church," he noted in 1867. "All the young men of intelligence are on what is called the radical side" (*JMN,* 16:72). **"Character"** and other writings that reflect the experience of the 1850s and 1860s suggest that Emerson had been profoundly impressed with the coalescence of the ethical imperative of antislavery with the national political purpose, and that this conjunction of events had a renewing effect on his moral confidence. "We see the dawn of a new era," he wrote in 1865, "worth to mankind all the treasure & all the lives it has cost, yes, worth to the world the lives of all this generation of American men, if they had been demanded." He noted the cost in lives, but he argued that the war "has made many lives valuable that were not so before" and has effectively "*moralized* cities & states" (*JMN,* 15:64). Although he worried, prophetically, that in the war's aftermath "the high tragic historic justice which the nation with severest consideration should execute, will be softened & dissipated & toasted away at dinner-tables" (*JMN,* 15:459), his final phase of thought emphasized the ethical renewal that he found in the unavoidable commitment that the slavery crisis and the war had forced on the nation. He had, through experience, come to stake all on a single proposition: "The only incorruptible thing is morals" (*JMN,* 15:471).

THE PRAGMATIC STANCE

"Will is always miraculous, being the presence of God to men"

(*W,* 12:46).

In an address at Waterville College in 1863, Emerson remarked on the "dark, but heroic" times: "The times develop the strength they need" (*W,* 10:258). This faith in the nation's moral resolve during the war was conditioned by his own experience of renewed strength as he brought his philosophy into working relationship with the moral demands of his day. Although the war confirmed that strength for him, it had been secured well before in the ethical emphasis that had marked a turn in his work in the 1840s. Emerson had needed strength to believe in the possibility of the "transformation of genius into practical power" (*CW,* 3:49), and the narrative of his work after **"Experience"** focuses on the growth of that faith in will, power, and moral action. This pragmatic turn entailed, especially as the slavery crisis deepened and the war approached, a circling back to his early vocabulary of the moral sense. But by the 1860s, Emerson was not simply parroting the terminology of his college texts, but expounding a position he had earned with some difficulty. No, we do not find in his later texts the buoyancy we associate with *Nature* or **"The American Scholar."** But the burden of the later texts has its own value, especially when placed in the context of Emerson's career.

The persistence of Emerson's moral-sense terminology, from very early to very late in his career, also helps us understand with wider reference the five-year burst of expression, from 1836 to 1841, that has been historically regarded as his most important phase. The version of philosophical idealism and the concomitant exploration of mystical experience that characterize that period were motivated in large part by his earlier conviction that the soul grasped moral imperatives without mediation—apart from, and perhaps in opposition to, institutionalized religious forms and socially defined moral codes. The mystical and transcendental Emerson, the Emerson American literary scholars have come to accept as the "real" or "important" Emerson, was from the beginning in the process of exploring the connection of morals with intuitive enlightenment. He had combined, in the supple concept of self-culture, his belief in the moral sense, inherited from the Unitarian theological milieu, with an intense personal commitment to religious experience as a form of ecstasy, an inheritance from the larger tradition of New England congregationalism. That synthesis kept elements of the moral and the mystical in a delicate balance for a while, but when Emerson began to see ecstasy as an increasingly problematic and unreliable concept in the early 1840s, he entered a new phase of his thinking. It was in some respects a crisis in epistemology, centering on the difficulty of assurance in perception. But it was also a crisis in moral philosophy, a reassessment of the capabilities of the will. Emerson's essentially pragmatic answer to his problem, an emphasis on action and work, led him to see that action could generate new experience, and thus bolster faith. His experience in the later 1840s and the 1850s helped him formulate in the notions of will and work a broad conception of moral action that integrated the inner life and the social world. These efforts represent a patient attempt to understand the moral sense as the expression of a comprehensive but progressive natural unity, a unity best revealed through moral action that subsumed the individual for a larger end.

Talk of moral sense or moral law inevitably seems rigid and rulebound, but Emerson's final stance is really an appeal to a life less of settled patterns and relations than of "very mutable" circumstances, in which the individual must "carry his possessions, his relations to persons, and even his opinions, in his hand, and in all these to pierce to the principle and moral law, and everywhere to find that." Such a stance, fundamentally open, relational, and dynamic, is also a position of faith, for in assuming it, one stands "out of the reach of all skepticism" (*W,* 10:213-14).

Notes

1. For the argument that the journal was fundamental, see Lawrence Rosenwald, *Emerson and the Art of the Diary.*

2. There seems to have been a struggle involved in bringing each of Emerson's books to print, but it is especially notable in the cases of *English Traits* and *Society and Solitude.* With *Letters and Social Aims,* the difficulties became insurmountable, and the book was finally arranged with the help of James E. Cabot.

3. See Nancy Craig Simmons, "Arranging the Sibylline Leaves," pp. 335-89. For further analysis of Emerson's later compositional practice, and the resulting textual problems, see Ronald A. Bosco, "'Poetry for the World of Readers' and 'Poetry for Bards Proper.'"

4. Emerson began to gather notes for his "Natural History of Reason" as early as 1838 (*JMN,* 5:482), and the first and most significant gestures toward its completion were made in the 1848 lecture series "Mind and Manners of the Nineteenth Century," delivered in England. On the earliest delivery of these lectures and their English context, see Larry J. Reynolds, *European Revolutions and the American Literary Renaissance,* pp. 38-40. Versions of the lectures were delivered in various contexts in the 1850s and 1860s, the period in which Emerson was also working through the ethical pragmatism that marks his later work. Of particular interest are the lectures "Powers and Laws of Thought" (1848-50, Houghton Library, Harvard University, b MS Am 1280.200 [3], [4], and [5]) and "Relation of Intellect to Natural Science" (1848-50, b MS Am 1280.200 [6] and [7]). The project was culminated in Emerson's lectures in the Harvard philosophy department in 1870. *Natural History of Intellect* as we now have it in James E. Cabot's arrangement is a good example of the textual problem presented by Emerson's later work. I do not believe that anything absolutely definitive can be written of this and other such later texts until the later volumes of Emerson's *Collected Works* are completed and we have an edition of his later lectures. Even so, these later texts cannot be absolutely ignored either, containing as they do powerful passages that reveal important aspects of Emerson's thought.

5. See Ralph L. Rusk, *The Life of Ralph Waldo Emerson,* pp. 341-6, and Gay Wilson Allen, *Waldo Emerson,* p. 509.

6. On the intellectual influences on *Nature,* see Kenneth Walter Cameron, *Emerson the Essayist.*

7. See Robert D. Richardson, Jr.'s discussion of the expanded sense of the "organic" in *Henry David Thoreau: A Life of the Mind,* pp. 310-13.

8. Richard Poirier, *The Renewal of Literature,* pp. 47-8.

9. In "Ralph Waldo Emerson," p. 390, Barbara Packer termed "Poetry and Imagination" a "brilliant" essay. In "'Poetry for the World of Readers' and 'Poetry for Bards Proper,'" Ronald A. Bosco characterized it as "the unrecognized fullest statement by Emerson of poetic theory" (p. 280). As Bosco demonstrates, the essay is closely connected with the development of Emerson's late poetry anthology *Parnassus.* For other details on the essay's evolution, see *W,* 8:357-8.

10. The example of Poe is delineated in Joseph J. Moldenhauer, "Murder as Fine Art: Basic Connections Between Poe's Aesthetics, Psychology, and Moral Vision."

11. See *JMN,* 15:468-71, for Emerson's notes on the essay. "Character" concluded a series of lectures at the Parker Fraternity in 1864-5 (*W,* 10:531).

12. On the Free Religious Association, see Stow Persons, *Free Religion: An American Faith,* and David Robinson, *The Unitarians and the Universalists,* pp. 107-22.

Abbreviations

The following abbreviations are cited parenthetically in the text to refer to various editions of Emerson's writings.

CEC The Correspondence of Emerson and Carlyle. Edited by Joseph Slater. New York: Columbia University Press, 1964.

CS The Complete Sermons of Ralph Waldo Emerson. Edited by Albert J. von Frank et al. 4 volumes. Columbia: University of Missouri Press, 1989- .

CW The Collected Works of Ralph Waldo Emerson. Edited by Alfred R. Ferguson et al. 4 volumes to date. Cambridge, Mass.: Belknap Press of Harvard University Press, 1971- .

EL The Early Lectures of Ralph Waldo Emerson. Edited by Robert E. Spiller, Stephen E. Whicher, and Wallace E. Williams. 3 volumes. Cambridge, Mass.: Harvard University Press, 1959; Belknap Press of Harvard University Press, 1964, 1972.

JMN The Journals and Miscellaneous Notebooks of Ralph Waldo Emerson. Edited by William H. Gilman et al. 16 volumes. Cambridge, Mass.: Belknap Press of Harvard University Press, 1960-82.

L The Letters of Ralph Waldo Emerson. Edited by Ralph L. Rusk (Volumes 1-6) and Eleanor Tilton (Volumes 7-8). 8 volumes to date. New York: Columbia University Press, 1939- .

W The Complete Works of Ralph Waldo Emerson (Centenary Edition). Edited by Edward Waldo Emerson. 12 volumes. Boston: Houghton Mifflin, 1903-4.

Ronald Bosco (essay date 1994)

SOURCE: "'What poems are many private lives': Emerson Writing the American Plutarch," in *Studies in the Literary Imagination,* Vol. 27, No. 1, Spring, 1994, pp. 103-29.

[*In the following essay, Bosco examines Emerson's views on the link between biography and history in the context of his two biographical works,* Representative Men *and* Lectures and Biographical Sketches.]

> The world looks poor & mean so long as I think only of its great men; most of them of spotted reputation. But when I remember how many obscure persons I myself have seen possessing gifts that excited wonder, speculation, & delight in me . . . when I consider the absolute boundlessness of our capacity . . . [when] I recollect the charms of certain women, *what poems are many private lives,* each of which can fill our eye if we so will . . . then I feel the riches of my inheritance in being set down in this world gifted with organs of communication with this accomplished company.
>
> (*JMN* 4:353-54; emphasis added)

I

Suffering from the trauma of witnessing his house burn in July, 1872, Ralph Waldo Emerson began to dictate his "last wishes" concerning his extensive collection of manuscript journals, notebooks, and related papers. During a recuperative journey, he gave specific instructions to his daughter Ellen Emerson. Writing from Waterford, Maine, on 22 August, Ellen Emerson shared the instructions with her sister Edith Emerson Forbes:

> [Father] seems to return to the thought that this is possibly the end. . . . Just now he came in to tell me where the money is. . . . And he gives me directions about his books and M.SS. which ought to be written and I'll write them now to you. Then we shall both know, and two depositions are safer than one. 'What to do with them?' he keeps saying. 'They are invaluable to anyone like me.' . . . The M.S. books date way back to 1820. [T]he . . . early ones are worthless and must be burnt without exception, also all the sermons for what was good in them has been extracted for the Essays &c. . . . Then come the large quarto books, A, B, and D, &c. Those are valuable. Those are of the date 1834 and later. S. and Z. are collections of good stories, not his but collected. . . . Among [others] . . . are WO, (which is filled with sketches of Webster all taken from life at the moment, and good, and other matter, collected while for a long time he had the idea of writing . . . a History of Liberty from the beginning and therein are recorded obscure anecdotes bearing on it, small and important steps). ED (which is about England contains the record of his interviews with Car-

lyle, Tennyson and others, precious material not to be used in their lifetime, and more). . . . Another time he said he had material for beautiful lives of Mr. Channing [the younger] and Mr. Alcott, and it would be a pity if they outlived him, for the world would miss two very good chapters, but he spoke as if nothing could be done about it.

(2:690-91)

This neglected letter raises an important point for students of Emerson's biography. Ellen's juxtaposition of the shocking effects of the fire with her father's anguish over his papers provides insight into Emerson's state of mind during the vexed last decade of his life. While it is clear that he wanted Edward, his son, to inherit his manuscripts—"they would be a mine of riches to him"—regrettably Edward was not "a scholar by profession." At the same time, Ellen reported Emerson's "dread" that Moncure Conway, Franklin Sanborn, "or anyone like that should get hold of them." He feared the kind of biographical trifle they might make out of them. Although Emerson mentioned that Frederic Henry Hedge or James Elliot Cabot could be trusted to do justice to such and to prepare a sensible account of his life, in 1872 he was reluctant to impose on their good will (2:690).

Ellen Emerson's letter shows that her father considered his manuscripts valuable for their relevance to his already composed or anticipated lives of other worthies. Suggestions in the letter about what constitute the proper materials for biography—good stories, obscure anecdotes, character sketches, reports of "life at the moment"—in fact match literary techniques Emerson routinely employed in journal and notebook entries, lectures, and essays. His insistence that a biographer respect the privilege of conversations with those around him and protect it until the death of his subject undoubtedly served as a liberating influence on conversations between Emerson and those in his ever-expanding circle of literary, philosophical, and social acquaintances. It certainly explains how Emerson came to possess the mass of factual and anecdotal detail preserved in his manuscripts about the lives of such famous or obscure contemporaries as his brothers Charles and William, Aunt Mary Moody Emerson, and step-grandfather Ezra Ripley, his Concord intimates Thoreau, Margaret Fuller, William Ellery Channing, and Bronson Alcott, and his distant correspondents Philip Physick Randolph and Thomas Carlyle. Emerson's opinion that the lives of worthy figures make "very good chapters" in the history of mankind is an understated characterization of his long-held view of the function of biographical writing. Believing in a necessary relation between the lives of worthy figures and the history of the race, he held that biography and history are indistinguishable.

Emerson applied a distinctive theory of biography to the lives of persons featured in his 1835 "Biography" lectures, *Representative Men* (1850), and *Lectures and Biographical Sketches,* a posthumous miscellany of biographical lectures, memorial addresses, and essays published in 1884

by James Elliot Cabot. Few of the nearly one thousand recent studies of Emerson have been concerned with his theory and practice of biography. Informing the present essay is a reading of Emerson's theory of biography drawn principally from his journals and notebooks, a theory heretofore acknowledged only in the occasional headnote or explanatory note.[1] Emerson's theory of biography takes him from an aspiring Plutarchan-style biographer in his sermons and lectures of the early to mid-1830s, to a biographer whose idealism dating from the late 1830s through the end of his career in the 1870s encouraged him to challenge Plutarchan biographical tradition first in theory and then in practice. Emerson challenged Plutarchan theory wherein history is defined as a discrete reality consisting of a finite number of representational lives that all adhere to a prescribed formula for greatness. By collapsing the distinction between the exemplary heroes of Plutarchan biography, historical *"Bigendians"* such as Plato and Napoleon, and his own *"Littleendians"* such as Alcott and Thoreau, Emerson enlarged on what had traditionally constituted individual greatness. He reassessed those "great men" who might exert a claim on their own and succeeding generations, and he reexamined the extent to which emulation of them was desirable or even possible.[2]

Evidence of Emerson's ambition to write biography occurs throughout his early journals, often in conjunction with his reading of history, particularly his re-reading of Plutarch's *Lives.* In 1832, noting that "the modern Plutarch is yet to be written," Emerson imagined that he might undertake biographies of Sir Thomas More, George Fox, Luther, Milton, the elder John Adams, and Sir Walter Scott, among others. He would write their lives "from love & from seeing the beauty that was to be desired in them." Like Plutarch, he pledged that "I would draw characters, not write lives. I would evoke the spirit of each [while] their relics might rot. . . . I would walk among . . . dry bones & wherever on the face of the earth I found a living man I would say here is life & life is communicable" (*JMN* 4:35). In funeral sermons, the "Biography" lectures of 1835, and lectures on English writers in 1835-36, Emerson relied on the Plutarchan definition of temporal distance and exemplariness in identifying greatness. He relied on the Plutarchan view of biography and history as fixed, finite realities, varying from one age to another only in the accidents of time and place.

However, during the fifteen years between these works and the appearance of his next major biographical endeavor, *Representative Men,* he departed from Plutarch's theory. Between 1836 and 1844, in essays such as *Nature,* **"History," "Self-Reliance," "Circles," "The Method of Nature,"** and **"Nominalist and Realist,"** in lectures such as **"The Present Age," "Heroism," "Genius,"** and **"The Poet,"** and in numerous journal passages, Emerson brought the key terms of his idealistic system to bear upon his ideas concerning biography and history. Emphasizing spirit, thought, universality, and human achievement, he challenged the Plutarchan concept of greatness. As he explained in **"Nominalist and Realist,"** he would allow any whose lives bear witness to one or more of these ideal features of experience into the select Emersonian class of great men: "[T]here is somewhat spheral and infinite in every man. . . . [E]very man is a channel through which heaven floweth. . . . Nature keeps herself whole, and her representation complete in the experience of each mind" (*CW* 3:142).

Just as he defined biography as the record of the "deep and sublime" ("History," *CW* 2:12), he also defined history anew. Rejecting mere physical and practical advancements, he now defined history as the record of the "one mind common to all individual men." He discerned within that unified record "the intellectual step, or short series of steps . . . [in effect] the spiritual act" as the "precious" element whereby the race progressively constitutes and advances itself ("History," *CW* 2:3; "The Method of Nature," *CW* 1:120). Emerson thus supplanted the old view of history as fixed and finite with a view of history as "fluid and true" ("History," *CW* 2:12). With biography newly defined as "deep and sublime" and history as "fluid and true," biographers and historians could no longer merely string together events in chronological narrative. From the 1830s on, Emerson argued that biography and history had to be read and written "in the light of these two facts, namely, that the mind is One, and that nature is its correlative. . . . History . . . walk[s] incarnate in every just and wise man" ("History," *CW* 2:21-22; "Introductory," *The Philosophy of History, EL* 2:19.). Emerson had merged separate ideas and disciplines into a single ideal discipline. He proclaimed in 1839:

> There is no history: There is only Biography. The attempt to perpetuate, to fix a thought or principle, fails continually. You can only live for yourself: Your action is good only whilst it is alive,—whilst it is in you. The awkward imitation of it by your child or your disciple, is not a repetition of it, is not the same thing but another thing. The new individual must work out the whole problem of science, letters, & theology for himself [and he] can owe his fathers nothing. . . .
>
> There is no history, only biography. The private soul ascends to transcendental virtue. Like Very, he works hard without moving hand or foot; like Agathon, he loves the goddess & not the woman; like Alcott he refuses to pay a debt without injustice; but this liberty is not transferable to any disciple[,] no nor to the man himself when he falls out of his trance & comes down from the tripod.

(*JMN* 7:202, 216; "History," *CW* 2:6)[3]

A long span of time separates Emerson's formulation of an idealistic theory of biography from the appearance of *Representative Men*. An even greater span of time separates Emerson's theory from his numerous biographical miscellanies. These intervals between theory and practice exasperated one of his closest friends, and they possibly account for occasional misjudgments of Emerson's accomplishments in biography. In the first instance, after receiving Emerson's gift of "The Method of Nature," Carlyle, who seems to have read the piece as a treatment of biogra-

phy and its relation to history, sympathized with the first audience who, on hearing the piece as an address, cried "Whitherward? What? What?" Writing on 19 November 1841, Carlyle complained to Emerson that his theory was "all spirit-like, aeriform, aurora-borealis like." He wondered, "[w]ill no *angel* body himself out of that; no stalwart Yankee *man*, with colour in the cheeks of him, and a coat on his back!" Observing that without application to the lives and works of real men Emerson's merger of biography and history would remain an idealist's dream, Carlyle writes that "I . . . desiderate some *concretion* of these beautiful *abstracta*. It seems to me they will never be right otherwise; that otherwise they are but as prophecies yet, not fulfilments" (Emerson, *Correspondence* 312-13).

Carlyle is not alone in misunderstanding Emerson's method. More recently, failing to notice that the lives of *Representative Men* and the figures Emerson developed in other biographical addresses and essays represent applications of his own idealistic philosophy, Edmund G. Berry in *Emerson's Plutarch*, the sole book-length treatment of Emerson as a biographer, considers Emerson's biographical writings nothing more than variations on Plutarch's *Lives*. Similarly, ignoring Emerson's assertion of an operative idealism in the lives of real men and women, Emersonians have failed to credit Emerson with erecting, through the imperfection and obscurity of his biographical subjects, a theoretic defense against the anarchy and pessimism of material culture.[4]

Napoleon, Swedenborg, Thoreau, and Bronson Alcott confirmed for Emerson how "the great object" of biography and history would be "commensurate with the object of life": "to teach self-trust; to inspire . . . man with an interest in himself; with a curiosity touching his own nature; to acquaint him with the resources of his mind, and to teach him that there is all his strength, and to inflame him with a piety towards the Grand Mind in which he lives" ("Education," *W* 10:135). Unlike exemplary heroes in Plutarchan biography, Emerson's real men and women ministered "balm and consolation and immortality" to those who struggled with the dire realities of his age. As early as 1832, Emerson invested biography with a sacramental function. He commented that biographers could and should speak with the authority of Christ, who "truly said," "life is communicable . . . my flesh is meat . . . I am the bread" (*JMN* 4:35-35). Years later, describing how "graces and forces" of individuals can elevate domestic life, Emerson complained that "our negligence of these fine monitors [biographers]" makes religion "cold" and life itself "low" ("The Sovereignty of Ethics," *W* 10:198).

Except for some Plutarchan techniques and didactic tonalities, Emerson was not a Plutarchan biographer.[5] His idealism eliminated the distance imposed by Plutarch between modern readers and exemplary figures either from the past or from his own time. For both Emerson and Plutarch the surest biographical method is one that relies on the subject's thought and action to illustrate his "permanent vision of truth."

II

What is it that interests us in biography? Is there not always a silent comparison between the intellectual & moral endowments portrayed & those of which we [in our own minds] are conscious? . . . [W]e take the picture for a standard Man, and so let every line accuse or approve our own ways of thinking & living by comparison. . . .

[M]aterials . . . exist for a Portraiture of Man which should be at once history & prophecy. Does it not seem as if a perfect parallelism existed between every great & fully developed man & every other?

There are ever & anon in history expressions uttered that seem to be fourfold-visaged & look with significant smile to all the quarters of time.

(*JMN* 4:256, 336-37, 339)

Employing a modified Plutarchan method in the "Biography" lectures, Emerson emphasized universality of mind, history, and the affections. Subjects such as Michel Angelo, Luther, Milton, George Fox, and Edmund Burke transcend time and place; their character is timeless, worthy of inspiring others for whom they serve as "types" of mankind (*JMN* 4:354). In **"John Milton,"** for instance, Milton does not appear as a Puritan poet or author of influential tracts on liberty and education. Instead, he "stands erect, commanding . . . [and] visible as a man among men, [a man who] read the laws of the moral sentiment to the newborn race." Emerson's Milton is a "commissioned spirit," a sacramental oracle: "Better than any other he has . . . raise[d] the idea of Man in the minds of his contemporaries and of posterity,—[he has] drawn after nature a life of man, exhibiting such a composition of grace, of strength, and of virtue, as poet had not described nor hero lived" (*EL* 1:149). Milton actualized capacities of the mind and imagination. Milton's virtues—bravery, purity, temperance, toil, independence, angelic idealism—are virtues for all time (*EL* 1:163).

In **"Martin Luther,"** Luther lives as "a simple erect Man . . . [and] because his head and heart are sound, [he is] a sort of Adam, one of that class of standard men in which . . . unsophisticated humanity seems ever and anon to be reproduced in its first simplicity, as model and leader of new generations." Emerson emphasizes Luther's "good humor" in facing religious debates, "sanity" in the face of fanaticism, and "humanity" in liking music and a joke. Even so, Emerson prudently reports that Luther was a most "earnest man" in an "earnest age" (*EL* 1:138, 140, 142).

Like Milton, Luther served Emerson's auditors as a man who pursued the ideal and thus taught that any individual may flourish in relation to the universal mind. Emerson pauses early in **"Martin Luther"** to lavish extravagant praise on Luther's poetic consciousness:

Luther was a Poet but not in the literary sense. He wrote no poems, but he walked in a charmed world. Everything to his eye assumed a symbolical aspect. All

occurrences, all institutions, all natural agents, God in a personal form, angels, Satan, and his devils are never out of his mind's eye. All objects, all events are transparent. He sees through them the love or malignity which is working behind them.

(*EL* 1:132)

Luther's talent for discovering symbolic truths is a talent available to everyone. Emerson humanizes the distant Luther as an ideal hero:

He believed and therefore spake, hit or miss, please or sting whom it might. If you tickled him, he would laugh,—if you pricked him, he would bleed. He loved, he hated, he feared God, he dared the world and the devils, he prayed, he sang, he desponded, he married, he served his prince, he abhorred dependence and became free, he erred, and repented, he worked unceasingly, he advanced unceasingly.

(*EL* 1:142)

Lectures on Milton and Luther extend Plutarch's method. They also develop Emerson's own ideas, particularly his 1835 theory of biography with its assumptions about history. For Emerson, an ideal or "perfect sympathy" transcends time, place, and personality (*JMN* 5:11). Each figure portrays one who enabled a hero for the common man, a fulfillment of the commonplace. Each figure emblematizes the race, the capacity to move from facts to spirit. To credit facts with "a symbolical aspect," hardly a Plutarchan principle, is indeed quintessentially Emersonian.

Ironically, a non-Plutarchan principle of Emerson's method apparent in the "Biography" lectures allows the biographer to speak with a kind of Plutarchan authority. Many subjects are measured against some classical figure whose ideals they appear to recreate. Although Edmund Berry considered this feature among the most compelling proofs that Emerson practiced Plutarchan biography (262-68), another explanation for this feature is more likely. Without referring to Plutarch, Emerson asserted that the sympathy between similar minds assists the reader to come to terms with his own values and ideas and also to discover his own self-identity. He observes that

the faintest sentiments which we have shunned from fear of singularity are older than the oldest institutions,—are eternal in man"; consequently, in biography "we can find ourselves, our private thoughts, our preferences, & aversions, & our moral judgments perhaps . . . truly matched in an ancient Lombard, or Saxon, or Greek."

(*JMN* 5:11)

Emerson's system of classical typology represents an original, non-Plutarchan strategy for reducing the distance between a biographer and his audience, between the audience and the figures readers must measure themselves against. Emerson's classical typology enhances the human qualities of his biographical subjects, underscoring their timelessness, and elevating the attractiveness of their ideal character. Readers who do in fact identify themselves with the biographical subjects enjoy the pleasure of admiring their own character:

> We recognize with delight a strict likeness between . . . [the] noblest impulses [of biographical subjects] & our own. We are tried in their trial. By our cordial approval we conquer in their victory. We participate in their act by our . . . understanding of it. . . . These affinities atone to us for the narrowness of our society, & the prison of our single lot, by making the human race our society, & the vast variety of human fortune the arena of actions on which we . . . take part.
>
> (*JMN* 5:11-12)

In its application, Emerson's classical typology serves equally well the author and the reader. When Emerson describes Milton's possessing "the senses of a Greek" and "the prudence of the Roman soldier," or when he introduces a litany of Milton's virtues, or when he states that "[they] remind us of what Plutarch said of Timoleon's victories, that they resembled Homer's verses, they ran so easy and natural," he virtually guarantees the authority of his own remarks on Milton, he stresses the timeless appeal of Milton's most noteworthy qualities, and he humanizes Milton's character for the reader (*EL* 1:151, 154, 156).

More extravagantly drawn, Emerson's portrait of Luther produces comparable results. Shortly after characterizing Luther as "a sort of Adam . . . of new generations," Emerson summarizes Luther's universality by reference to two pairs of ancients, one from the Middle Ages and one from modern times: "[Luther] is to us in the German age what Homer is in the Greek; Moses in the Hebrew; Alfred in the Saxon; Washington in the American epoch" (*EL* 1:138). Elsewhere, to humanize and elevate Luther's defining talents, Emerson remarks that Luther was a scholar and philosopher comparable to "Isaiah or Ezekiel among the ancient Hebrews"; like them, a Prophet and Poet; he possessed "the will of Attila or Napoleon"; and took delight in the satisfaction and honor his fight for conscience brought to his family and the memory of his parents (*EL* 1:132, 140, 141).

III

> And it seems as if nature, contemplating the long geologic night behind her, when at last in five or six millenniums she had turned out five or six men,—say, Phidias, Plato, Menu, Columbus, was nowise impatient of the millions of disgusting blockheads she had spawned along with them, but was well contented with these few.
>
> (*JMN* 11:167; **"Plato: New Readings,"** *CW* 4:45)

> Nature has as seldom a success in her machines, as we in ours. There is almost never good adjustment between the spring & the regulator, in a man. He only is a well made man, who has a good determination. Now, with most men, it does not appear for what they were made, until after a long time.
>
> (*JMN* 11:197-98; **"Culture,"** *W* 6:134, and **"Society and Solitude,"** *W* 7:8)

While the exemplary lives of "Biography" illustrate Emerson's early dependence upon Plutarchan theory and method, the flawed personalities and misapplied virtues of the specific **Representative Men** designated "*Bigendians*" illustrate his own contributions to his own theory. The idealistic biography Emerson writes in **Representative Men** expresses his conviction that a biographical figure need not be a Milton or a Luther to prove that "every man is a channel through which heaven floweth." It is responsive to Carlyle's complaint that theory without practical application represents only "prophecies yet, not fulfilments." In **"Uses of Great Men,"** the preface to **Representative Men,** and in scattered authorial intrusions, Emerson calls attention to the realism of his lives of Plato, Swedenborg, Montaigne, Shakespeare, Napoleon, and Goethe. He notes that while his candid portrayals of materialism, egotism, narrow-mindedness, or self-delusion may preclude his subjects from uncritical emulation, they are worthy of admiration for having actualized the universal. He also acknowledges that the variance between his idealistic theory and his flawed characters may be construed as itself a flaw. In **"Montaigne, or the Skeptic,"** Emerson admits that the "astonishment of life, is, the absence of any appearance of reconciliation between the theory and practice of life," between the "largest promise of ideal power" and the actual "shabby experience" (*CW* 4:101, 104). Nevertheless, he insists, the seeming absence of reconciliation between the promise and the experience need not mean that the theory is flawed. He cryptically adds: "needles are nothing; the magnetism is all" (*CW* 4:104).

"*Bigendians*" portrayed in **Representative Men** predictably represent the ideal power of the human race. As "needles," Milton and Luther or Shakespeare and Montaigne point to "the qualities of primary nature, admit us to the constitution of things." However, their real significance lies in their being illuminators of that "magnetism" which introduces "moral truths into the general mind" (*CW* 4:12-13). Ideal power (spirit, "magnetism," moral truth) in **Representative Men** shows forth in Plato's, Shakespeare's, or Goethe's command of human aspirations, or Napoleon's political spirit, or Montaigne's or Swedenborg's transforming abstractions into thought and conduct. Flaws inherent in these representative men are diminished in proportion to their ideal "largeness." He explains: "I look on Swedenborg as on Kant, Newton, Leibnitz, Goethe, Humboldt, men of a larger stature than others, & possessing very great advantages in that preternatural size. He & Newton were both cracked or bursten; yet 'tis easier to see the reflection of the sphere in globes of this magnitude, cracked or not, than in the common minute globe" (*JMN* 11:91).

Similarly, in **"Uses of Great Men,"** he justified subjects of mixed reputation by arguing that their reputation is less important than their "mental and moral force."

> Men are helpful through the intellect and the affections. Other help I find a false appearance. If you affect to give me bread and fire, I perceive that I pay for it the full price, and at last it leaves me as it found me, nei-

ther better nor worse; but all mental and moral force is a positive good. . . . This is the moral of biography.

(*CW* 4:8-9)

Emerson thus invoked a transcendentalist's anticipation of reader-response theory, inviting readers to infer at will and to "supply many chasms" in his reports of blemished lives. Years before, he legitimated this kind of reading in **"Nominalist and Realist,"** when, describing his own general style of reading, he stated, "What is well done, I feel as if I did; what is ill done, I reck not of. . . . I read Proclus, and sometimes Plato, as I might read a dictionary, for a mechanical help to the fancy and the imagination. I read for the lustres, as if one should use a fine picture in a chromatic experiment, for its rich colors. 'Tis not Proclus, but a piece of nature and fate . . . I explore" (*CW* 3:137). Only by wilfully reading for "lustres" can one lay claim to the readerly joy available in literature. For Emerson, it is a greater joy to see the "author's author, than himself" (*CW* 3:137); reading for "lustres" in biography means reading for the operations of spirit. Emerson expected his readers to fashion out of the "mechanical" materials of imperfect but large personalities or misapplied values, coupled with momentous actions, a biography even better than Emerson's own heuristic version:

> The history of the universe is symptomatic, and life is mnemonical. No man in all the procession of famous men is reason or illumination, or that essence we are looking for. . . . The study of many individuals leads us to an elemental region wherein the individual is lost, or wherein all touch by their summits. Thought and feeling that break out there, cannot be impounded by any fence of personality.
>
> The vessels on which you read sacred emblems, turn out to be common pottery, but the sense of the pictures is sacred, and you may still read them transferred to the walls of the world.

(*CW* 4:18-19)

"*Bigendians*" represent a balance between the "sacred" (spirit) and the "common pottery" (masks of human nature); thus Emerson preserves the enchantment of the world. Readers can achieve a "sense" of the prevalence of spirit in thoughts and actions, but with varying degrees of success. In *Representative Men,* for example, Emerson creates a distinct hierarchy, with Shakespeare, Goethe, and Montaigne representing the highest degree of correspondence between spirit and human nature, whereas Plato, Swedenborg, and Napoleon represent the lowest.

In Shakespeare, Emerson finds the best conceivable balance between spirit and human nature. Emerson recites an extended litany of praise. Shakespeare's poetic imagination "dilates the closet he writes in to the world's dimension, crowds it with agents in rank and order, [and] quickly reduces . . . reality to the glimpses of the moon." Shakespeare is "inconceivably wise," possessing a unique "executive faculty, for creation" and an "omnipresent humanity [that] coordinates all his faculties"; he "has no

discoverable egotism: the great he tells greatly, the small subordinately [so that he] is wise without emphasis or assertion . . . [and] strong as nature is strong"; he exudes supreme "cheerfulness, without which no man can be a poet, for beauty is his aim"; and because "[h]e loves virtue, not for its obligation, but for its grace[,] . . . the spirit of joy and hilarity, he sheds over the universe" (*CW* 4:118-19, 121-23). Emerson's admiration of Shakespeare's art as a literary extension of the greatness of the man is no less extravagant. He asks, "What point of morals, of manners, of economy, of philosophy, of religion, of taste, of the conduct of life, has [Shakespeare] not settled [in it]?" (*CW* 4:120).

> [H]e drew the man of England and Europe; the father of the man in America: he drew the man, and described the day, and what is done in it: he read the hearts of men and women, their probity, and their second thought and wiles; the wiles of innocence, and the transitions by which virtues and vices slide into their contraries: he could divide the mother's part from the father's part in the face of the child, or draw the fine demarcations of freedom and fate: he knew the laws of repression, which makes the police of nature: and all the sweets and all the terrors of human lot lay in his mind as truly but as softly as the landscape lies on the eye.

(*CW* 4:121)

With only slightly less enthusiasm, Emerson portrays Montaigne, who commands an ideal equanimity with which one must read and respond to the world. Emerson avows that all men are "natural believers" in the principle that men and events and life come to us "connected by a common thread," even if experience usually "scatters or pulls down" that which "affirms, connects, preserves" (*CW* 4:96). Thinking men must confront such reality and decide how they will respond to it. Those of a philosophic bent choose optimism. Men of toil and trade and "luxury" choose materialism. Still others, whose attraction to materialism "runs into indifferentism, and then into disgust," choose cynicism (*CW* 4:85-88).

Against these three typical responses to disruptive or chaotic reality, Emerson measures Montaigne, who took the moral high road mapped out by "a wise skepticism." Skepticism is a philosophy "of consideration, of selfcontaining, not at all of unbelief, not at all of universal denying, nor of universal doubting . . . [and] least of all, of scoffing, and profligate jeering at all that is stable and good." Its practitioner is "the Considerer, the prudent, taking in sail, counting stock, husbanding his means, believing that a man has too many enemies, than that he can afford to be his own." He very nearly embodies Nature's own philosophy of "fluxions and mobility" (*CW* 4:89-91). Emerson takes personal delight in the way Montaigne's skepticism blends pragmatism and idealism. Montaigne "labours to plant his feet, to be the beam of . . . balance[;] . . . he stands for the intellectual faculties, a cool head, and whatever serves to keep it cool: no unadvised industry, no unrewarded self-devotion, no loss of the brains in toil[;] . . . [he knows] that human strength is not [found] in [espousing philosophic] extremes, but in avoiding extremes" (*CW* 4:88-89). Montaigne conducted his affairs in a manner "[d]ownright and plaindealing" and he "abhorr[ed] to be deceived or to deceive." He was "esteemed . . . for his sense and probity."

Taking up even menial tasks with earnestness, Montaigne encouraged comparable action in those around him which produced at least one tangible effect that might reduce a materialist to envy: he "made his farms yield the most." In time of war, he alone could keep "his gates open, and his house without defence," for "his courage and honor [were] universally esteemed." "[A] biblical plainness coupled with a most uncanonical levity" in his conversation as in his writing made Montaigne "the frankest and honestest of all" men (*CW* 4:93). Because "[t]he sincerity and marrow of the man reache[d] to his sentences," Montaigne's essays, like Shakespeare's plays, serve Emerson as texts of life:

> Montaigne talks with shrewdness, knows the world, and books, and himself, and uses the positive degree: never shrieks, or protests, or prays; no weakness, no convulsion, no superlative: does not wish to jump out of his skin, or play any antics, or annihilate space or time, but is stout and solid; tastes every moment of the day; likes pain, because it makes him feel himself, and realize things; as we pinch ourselves to know that we are awake. He keeps the plain; he rarely mounts or sinks; likes to feel solid ground, and the stones underneath. His writing has no enthusiasms, no aspiration; contented, selfrespecting, and keeping the middle of the road.

> (*CW* 4:95-96)

Neither Shakespeare nor Montaigne entirely escapes censure in *Representative Men*. Emerson must have felt that he had to lessen Shakespeare's allure so that this "bard and benefactor" could be reduced to parity with surrounding figures. Reaching back to his "Biography" lecture on Milton in which he had praised Milton at Shakespeare's expense by pointing to the latter's "mean and jocular way of life," Emerson concludes **"Shakespeare, or the Poet"** by remarking sadly that "the best poet led an obscure and profane life, using his genius for the public amusement" (*EL* 1:161; *CW* 4:125). In Montaigne's case, Emerson's censure is more severe, but with good reason. Even if Montaigne's "wise skepticism" surpasses some other responses to reality, it does not completely avoid suspicions of petty egotism. "The ground occupied by the skeptic," Emerson states, is merely "the vestibule to the temple" of "moral sentiment," which as a rebuke to reality's compromising the ideal, "never forfeits its supremacy" (*CW* 4:97, 103). Although in the sensible ebb and flow of his thought the skeptic comes closer than most men to portraying Nature's own philosophy of "fluxions and mobility," he does not actually replicate "the thought that is parent of the universe: that the masses of nature do undulate and flow" (*CW* 4:103). Paradoxically, Montaigne the skeptic is an imperfect representative of the ideal, but for Emerson he reaffirms the enchantment of the universe:

> The expansive nature of truth comes to our succour, elastic, not to be surrounded. Man helps himself by larger generalizations. The lesson of life is practically to generalize, to believe what the years and the centuries say against the hours; to resist the usurpation of particulars; to penetrate to their catholic sense. Things seem to say one thing, and say the reverse. . . .

> Let . . . man learn to look for the permanent in the mutable and fleeting; let him learn to bear the disappearance of things he was wont to reverence, without losing his reverence; let him learn that he is here not to work, but to be worked upon, and, that, though abyss open under abyss, and opinion displace opinion, all are at last contained in the eternal Cause.

> (*CW* 4:104-105)

"[G]reat men exist," Emerson asserts at the conclusion of **"Uses of Great Men,"** "that there may be greater men." Because "[t]he destiny of organized nature is amelioration" to which, ideally, there is no limit, the service great men provide is to glimpse mankind's achieved glory and to improve upon such glory (*CW* 4:20). Although the world still lacks its poet-priest, a "reconciler who shall not trifle," in Shakespeare the world has a model by which to test the claims of pretenders. Although the world has yet to espouse an Emersonian system of romantic contrarities, the world has in Montaigne a model by which to test responses to reality inferior to a "wise skepticism" (*CW* 4:103-104, 125).

Emerson's second-rank representative men exhibit an unresolved tension between the operations of spirit and the accidents of human nature. Even here, though, Swedenborg and Napoleon deserve recognition as "great men," as heroes, if not "in the high sense" (*CW* 4:120). Believing "[t]he world has a sure chemistry by which it extracts what is excellent in its children, and lets fall the infirmities and limitations of the grandest mind," in his portraits of Swedenborg and Napoleon, Emerson is interested in selectively drawing traits and habits that appeal broadly to "the intellect and the affections" (*CW* 4:8, 70). Swedenborg's appeal is exclusively intellectual. A "colossal soul" in the mystic tradition of Plotinus, Porphyry, Bunyan, and Pascal, who executed an extended review of "the atmosphere of moral sentiment" and its relation to nature, Swedenborg wrote "a sufficient library to . . . [the] athletic student," nearly fifty books which, "by the sustained dignity of thinking," are "an honour to the human race" (*CW* 4:54, 58, 60). "[V]isionary and elixir of moonbeams" to his countrymen, Swedenborg's "varied and solid knowledge" taxes and baffles the minds of any who come his way. This includes Emerson, who admits that it is a life's work to master the cosmology, metaphysics, and theology that Swedenborg assimilated into his own thought (*CW* 4:56, 59-60). To study nature as he captured its "points and shooting spicula of thought" is to discover oneself alive on "one of those winter mornings when the air sparkles with crystals" (*CW* 4:60).

As Swedenborg appeals to the intellect, Napoleon appeals to the affections. He is "the incarnate Democrat," actualizing the virtue, vice, spirit, and aim of the rising middle class. Emerson states, "precisely what is agreeable to the heart of every man in the nineteenth century, this powerful man possessed. . . . Bonaparte was the idol of the common man, because he had in transcendent degree the qualities and powers of common men" (*CW* 4:130-31). The "qualities and powers" exhibited by Napoleon comprise a litany of attributes which outnumber those of any other figure in *Representative Men.* "[A] man of stone and iron," Napoleon is "not embarrassed by any scruples," and "[w]ith him is no miracle, and no magic"; he is "a worker in brass, in iron, in wood, in earth, in roads, in buildings, in money, and in troops, and a very consistent and wise master workman"; he is "never weak and literary, but acts with the solidity and the precision of natural agents," nor has he "lost his native sense and sympathy with things"; he is "compact, instant . . . prudent, and of a perception which did not suffer itself to be baulked or misled by any pretenses of others, or any superstition or any heat or haste of his own"; he is "a realist, terrific to all talkers and confused truth-obscuring persons"; he is "strong in the right manner, namely, by insight" and "inspires confidence and vigor by the extraordinary unity of his action"; and he is "firm, sure, self-denying, self-postponing, sacrificing everything to his aim,—money, troops, generals, and his own safety also, to his aim; not misled, like common adventurers, by the splendour of his own means" (*CW* 4:132-34).

Whereas Shakespeare and Montaigne appeal to intellect and affections, Swedenborg and Napoleon erred as persons and hence are flawed by their inability to rise above the accidents of human nature. They have not integrated the commanding intellect or military genius into the larger requirements of idealism. They exemplify one of the deficiencies (asymmetry) that damage potentially ideal men.

> Great men or men of great gifts you shall easily find, but symmetrical men never. When I meet a pure intellectual force, or a generosity of affection, I believe, here then is man; and am presently mortified by the discovery, that this individual is no more available to his own or to the general ends, than his companions; because the power which drew my respect, is not supported by the total symphony of his talents. All persons exist to society by some shining trait of beauty or utility, which they have. We borrow the proportions of the man from that one fine feature, and finish the portrait symmetrically; which is false; for the rest . . . is small or deformed. . . . All our poets, heroes, and saints, fail utterly in some one or in many parts to satisfy our idea, fail to draw our spontaneous interest, and so leave us without any hope of realization but in our own future.
>
> ("**Nominalist and Realist,**" *CW* 3:134)

Swedenborg and Napoleon exhibit defects of character. Poet-priests and mystics may find in Swedenborg's complex symbols a precedent to build on, but they will also find a narrow "theological bias." Swedenborg overvalues form, so he lacks "central spontaneity" and is unable to incorporate the "apparatus of poetic expression" into his philosophy (*CW* 4:67-68, 74, 80). Swedenborg and his sys-

tem are too cerebral. The vision of nature is "dynamic[,] not vital, and lacks the power to generate life." (*CW* 4:74-75).

Swedenborg's excessive intellection is matched by Napoleon's unparalleled power, identification with social class, physical might, and military genius having run amok without the least constraints of conscience (*CW* 4:147). Napoleon's lack of moral sentiment deprives him of ultimate or ideal victory. In a burst of uncharacteristic rage, Emerson launches an extended attack:

> Bonaparte was singularly destitute of generous sentiments. The highest placed individual in the most cultivated age . . . of the world, he has not the merit of common truth and honesty. He is unjust to his generals, egotistic, and monopolizing; meanly stealing the credit of their great actions. . . . He is a boundless liar . . . [who] sat in his premature old age . . . coldly falsifying facts and dates and characters, and giving to history a theatrical éclat. . . . His doctrine of immortality is simply fame. His theory of influence is not flattering. [As he himself writes,] "There are two levers for moving men, interest and fear. Love is a silly infatuation. . . . Friendship is but a name. I love nobody." . . . He was thoroughly unscrupulous. He would steal, slander, down, and poison, as his interest dictated. He had no generosity, but mere vulgar hatred: he was intensely selfish; he was perfidious: he cheated at cards: he was a prodigious gossip; . . . and delighted in his infamous police. . . . His manners were coarse: He treated women with low familiarity. . . . In short, when you have penetrated through all the circles of power and splendour, you [are] not dealing with a gentleman at last, but with an impostor and a rogue.
>
> (*CW* 4:145-46)

Despite the unresolved tension between the sacred and the mundane in Swedenborg and Napoleon, both figures belong with Shakespeare and Montaigne because they too represent a "type" of mankind. Their lives of exploit and achievement encourage fresh resolve in observers to improve upon their own performance. Even their failures prove useful to the idealist: recorded failures of poets and heroes, saints and sinners, prove that the last word on advancement has not been written.

Things balance out. In *Representative Men,* Napoleon's embodiment of nineteenth-century crassness is offset by Shakespeare's poetic genius. Montaigne's equanimity in the face of war reduces the allure of Napoleonic militarism, and his genial warmth asserts, by contrast with Swedenborg, that a life of the mind does not preclude humane love or openness to nature. Emerson drew on his essential idealism, doctrine of self-reliance, and sense of Nature's constancy as a solid basis for confidence in symmetrically great men. These saviors would possess rare gifts and poetic talents to be drawn upon in "our own future."

IV

Our reading is mendicant and sycophantic. In history, our imagination plays us false. Kingdom and lordship, power and estate are a gaudier vocabulary than private John and Edward in a small house and common day's work: but the things of life are the same to both: the sum total of both is the same. Why all this deference to Alfred . . . and Gustavus? Suppose they were virtuous: did they wear out virtue? As great a stake depends on your private act to-day, as followed their public and renowned steps. When private men shall act with original views, the lustre will be transferred from the actions of kings.

("Self-Reliance," *CW* 2:36; *JMN* 5:394-98)

Given Emerson's progressive application of biographical theory from the exemplary lives of "Biography" to the imperfect lives of **Representative Men,** together with his belief that the "talent and means which operate great results . . . are common to all men," formal attention to the lives of "obscure persons . . . that excited wonder, speculation, & delight" would seem inevitable. Emerson could only believe that individuals from the past were not entirely adequate to his own time, particularly the materialism and pessimism he documented in **English Traits** (1856) and **The Conduct of Life** (1860). Montaigne could exemplify a class of enlightened minds and generous hearts capable of thwarting materialism and pessimism, but Emerson conceded that such examples were, after all, centuries old and not altogether pertinent to the crisis of values in the mid-nineteenth century. In an aside in **"Uses of Great Men,"** he admitted as much.

> [I]t is hard for departed men to touch the quick like our own companions, [even those] whose names may not last as long. What is he whom I never think of? whilst in every solitude are those who succour our genius, and stimulate us in wonderful manners. There is a power in love to divine another's destiny better than that other can, and by heroic encouragements hold him to his task. What has friendship so signal as its sublime attraction to whatever virtue is in us? We will never think more cheaply of ourselves or of life. We are piqued to some purpose.
>
> (*CW* 4:9)

In quantity, the written record of Emerson's attraction to the conduct, values, and heroism of his contemporaries is almost staggering. His journals from the 1820s to the 1870s contain entries on individuals with whom he claimed intimate acquaintance and who served him as "types" of mankind representing noble aspirations. His spouse, children, siblings, other relatives, neighbors, friends, correspondents, and companions of the mind and heart—all appealed to Emerson by their character and insight, by their submission to the ideal spirit. Emerson's journal accounts of their opinions, activities, and relation to him constitute an informal and personalized type of biography. Some special ones proved particularly attractive. As early as the 1840s he extracted anecdotes about, details of personal contacts with, and character descriptions of several persons from his journals, entering them, together with excerpts from their writings and conversation, into individualized topical notebooks.

Emerson's aim, as reported by his daughter in 1872, was to produce some "very good chapters" of human history out of notebooks devoted to Mary Moody Emerson, Thoreau, Charles King Newcomb, Bronson Alcott, and others. The type of biography represented by these accounts is more formal than the journals. Emerson's method endows each subject with life-like integrity and coherence.[6]

Lives memorializing Emerson's contemporaries are perhaps surprisingly similar to those of great men from the past. Emerson portrays his *Littleendian* heroes as exerting a moral claim on his audience by their representation of spirit, actualization of ideas, conduct, and universal values. Rhetorical strategies, literary devices, and authorial tone in the essays are virtually indistinguishable from those in Emerson's biographical lectures and writings of the 1830s and 1840s. The only discernible difference is predictable, given that Emerson was actually living among his subjects. It is perhaps reasonable to expect that he would demonstrate authorial approbation in part by means of gracious and generous turns of description.

Despite Mary Moody Emerson's well-known idiosyncracies, her nephew portrays her as an inspiring character who "had a deep sympathy with genius," one who "gave high counsels" to the minds of those, like young Emerson and his brothers, entrusted to her care (*W* 10:403, 432). Reading through her papers, Emerson is impressed by her acumen and personal genius: "Plato, Aristotle, Plotinus,— how venerable and organic as Nature they are in her mind." On a par with Dante, Aunt Mary excites her biographer with wonder at her biblical authority and ability to create "paraphrases to signify with more adequateness Christ or Jehovah" than the inspired texts themselves (*W* 10:402). Conversant with Marcus Antoninus, Milton, Young, Jonathan Edwards, Locke, and even Byron, Aunt Mary's lively mind and fertile imagination confirm the idealism of **"The Method of Nature"**: "An individual . . . is a fruit which it cost all the foregoing ages to form and ripen" (*CW* 1:128). Her sensibility made her feel at home "in the fiery depths of Calvinism, [with] its high and mysterious elections," but she could just as easily become a Transcendentalist, "driven," as she was at times, "to find Nature her companion and solace" (*W* 10:403, 411). Aunt Mary also draws praise as being a good Greek: "Our Delphian," one who could tame and be tamed "by large and sincere conversation"; one always attendant to expressions of "thought and eloquence"; one whose life and mind "burned . . . [with] the glow of . . . pure and poetic spirit" (*W* 10:408). In sum, she was a modern Cassandra, uttering "to a frivolous, skeptical time, the arcana of the Gods" by representing the great Christian truth, "Faith alone, Faith alone" (*W* 10:433).

In contrast to Emerson's sketch of his aunt, drawn against the background of late-eighteenth-century Puritan New England, his essays on Samuel Hoar and Thoreau measure his subjects against contemporary America. To these might be added a proposed but unfinished life of Bronson Alcott. Emerson would have written it had not, as Ellen Emerson reported in 1872, his own declining health and Alcott's longevity interfered. Alcott material in his journals, together with a brief account of Alcott's character preserved in notebook "A[mos] B[ronson] A[lcott]," suggest that Emerson's portrayal of this *Littleendian* Plato would have been consistent with his essays on Hoar and Thoreau. Taken together, the essays on Hoar and Thoreau and the one he intended to write on Alcott would form a trilogy dramatizing an intellectual and imaginative bulwark against mid-century materialism and pessimism.

Like Mary Moody Emerson, attorney Samuel Hoar has personally tapped the moral reserves of character—integrity, honesty, manliness, personal conviction, naturalness, simplicity, and clear perception. He remains his own man in a world of convention and conformity. According to Emerson,

> [Hoar] was a very natural, but a very high character; a man of simple tastes, plain and true in speech, with clear perception of justice, and a perfect obedience thereto in his action; of a strong understanding, precise and methodical. . . . The severity of his logic might have inspired fear, had it not been restrained by his natural reverence, which made him modest and courteous. . . . He combined a uniform self-respect with a natural reverence for every other man.
>
> (*W* 10:439)

Hoar becomes "our old Roman," a Christian Cato who exemplifies ideals present in the universal mind ranging from truth and justice to self-reliance and charity.

> He was born under a Christian and humane star, full of mansuetude and nobleness, honor, and charity; and, whilst he was willing to face every disagreeable duty, whilst he dared to do all that might beseem a man, his self-respect restrained him from any foolhardiness. The Homeric heroes, when they saw gods mingling in the fray, sheathed their swords. So did not he feel any call to make it a contest of personal strength with mobs or nations; but when he saw the day and the gods went against him, he withdrew, but with unaltered belief. All was conquered *praeter atrocem animum Catonis.*
>
> (*W* 10:437)

By virtue of practicing the law, Hoar stands out among Emerson's subjects as a man of the world. Nonetheless, he is a vigorous model of Emerson's ideal, proving that no matter what profession or place one fills, one may possess the capacity to integrate operations of spirit with one's own conduct.

Writing about his friend Thoreau, Emerson portrays his subject as representing an ideal response to materialism and pessimism and thus as personifying an ideal version of life for nineteenth-century America. Thoreau the man is indistinguishable from his ideals: he is the ideal actualized.

> Thoreau was sincerity itself, and might fortify the convictions of prophets in ethical laws, by his holy living.

It was an affirmative experience which refused to be set aside. A truth-speaker he, capable of the most deep and strict conversation; a physician to the wounds of any soul; a friend knowing not only the secret of friendship, but almost worshipped by those few persons who resorted to him as their confessor and prophet, and knew the deep value of his mind and great heart. He thought that without religion or devotion of some kind, nothing great was ever accomplished. . . . Himself of a perfect probity, he required not less of others. . . . He praised wild mountains and winter forests for their domestic air; in snow and ice, he would find sultriness; and commended the wilderness for resembling Rome and Paris. . . . [He possessed a] tendency to magnify the moment, to read all the laws of nature in the one subject or one combination under [his] eye.

> (**"Emerson's 'Thoreau'"** 52)

Thoreau's habits and social relations in and around Concord sound forth as a panegyric to one who has perhaps uniquely fulfilled Emerson's program. Thoreau was a student of nature, and his study of nature, "a perpetual ornament to him[,] . . . inspired his friends with curiosity to see . . . through his eyes." In society, he "interrogated every custom, and wished to settle all his practice on an ideal foundation." In matters religious, he "was a protestant *à outrance,* and few lives contain so many renunciations." In a world devoted to commerce, industry, and material gain, he "had no temptations to fight against; no appetites, no passions, no taste for elegant trifles"; in a world that glorified the dandy, he was always "somewhat military in his nature, not to be subdued, always manly and able." His intellectual and imaginative needs define him as an Emersonian type for "man thinking": "[h]e wanted a fallacy to expose, a blunder to pillory." Although sometimes hermit-like and stoic, Thoreau was susceptible to the whole range of good feelings that could move a heart. He was "fond of sympathy, and threw himself heartily and childlike into the company of young people whom he loved, and whom he delighted to entertain." In sum, Thoreau "was a speaker and actor of the truth" (**"Thoreau"** 37-39, 53).

Emerson's extravagant praise of Thoreau stands out as unique among his biographical sketches. Likewise, he contradicts one of his cardinal principles with regard to specificity of personal detail: "Man helps himself by larger generalizations. The lesson of life is practically to generalize" (*CW* 4:104). In **"Thoreau,"** Emerson developed his subject with an unexpected degree of specificity. In keeping perhaps with his nationalistic theme, Thoreau is not only an ideal man but also an ideal *American* man.

Considerable space is devoted to a sympathy and symmetry between Thoreau's physical traits and the landscape of Concord, where he roams and where he prepares his charts and communes with nature. Emerson notes that Thoreau was adapted to the environment much like James Fenimore Cooper's character Natty Bumpo.

> He was short of stature, firmly built. . . . His senses were acute, his frame well-knit and hardy, his hands

strong and skilful in the use of tools. And there was a wonderful fitness of body and mind. He could pace sixteen rods more accurately than another man could measure them with rod and chain. He could find his path in the woods at night . . . better by his feet than his eyes. He could estimate the measure of a tree very well by his eye; he could estimate the weight of a calf or pig, like a dealer. . . . He was a good swimmer, runner, skater, boatman, and would probably out-walk most countrymen in a day's journey. And the relation of body to mind was still finer than we have indicated.

("Emerson's 'Thoreau'" 41)

Like Bumpo, Emerson's real-life hero is a born naturalist whose feeling for natural history was so "organic," so "very deep in his mind," that he refused to define "the meaning of Nature." Thoreau let "[e]very [natural] fact lay in glory in his mind, a type of the order and beauty of the whole" (46-7). Thoreau confessed that he sometimes felt like a hound or a panther, and, "if born among Indians, would have been a fell hunter." Too civilized actually to take up bow and arrow or tomahawk, he nevertheless enjoyed a prelapsarian familiarity with the creatures of the land: "[s]nakes coiled round his leg; the fishes swam into his hand, and he took them out of the water; he pulled the woodchuck out of its hole by the tail, and took the foxes under his protection" (47). Emerson also remarks on the authority one commands in politics, society, and moral debate achieved by such an identification with the natural environment.

> [So] much knowledge of Nature's secret and genius few others possessed; none in a more large and religious synthesis. For not a particle of respect had he to the opinions of any man or body of men, but homage solely to the truth itself. . . . He grew to be revered and admired by his townsmen, who had at first known him only as an oddity. The farmers who employed him as a surveyor soon discovered his rare accuracy and skill, his knowledge of their lands, of trees, of birds, of Indian remains and the like, which enabled him to tell every farmer more than he knew before of his own farm. . . . They felt, too, the superiority of character which addressed all men with a native authority.
>
> (47)

As a fitting conclusion to a native life so well lived, Emerson revisits Thoreau's privileged relation to transcendent Nature and native landscape. Thoreau was a "commissioned spirit," a human voice ordained by Nature to advertise and protect the landscape and the ideal vision it offers to right-minded, poetic human beings. Thoreau's lament in the following passage resembles Natty Bumpo's lament at the destruction of nature.

> [Thoreau] delighted in echoes, and said, they were almost the only kind of kindred voices that he heard. He loved nature so well, was so happy in her solitude, that he became very jealous of cities, and the sad work which their refinements and artifices made with man and his dwelling. The axe was always destroying his forest—"Thank God," he said, "they cannot cut down

the clouds. All kinds of figures are drawn on the blue ground, with this fibrous white paint."

> (53)

Bronson Alcott is a very different case in contrast to Samuel Hoar, who exists in a world of commerce and law, and to Thoreau, the child of nature and mediator between nature's facts and the thoughts they signify. Alcott is an impractical reformer who lives immediately in and for his quasi-Platonic mind. Although he shares with Hoar and Thoreau the Plutarchan and Emersonian trait of natural largeness, he espouses a philosophy which, to the extent that it has become his "biography," frustrates any attempt to extract a system out of his life or to capture his essence for general emulation. Like a "gold ore in great abundance in which the gold is in combination with such elements that no chemistry has yet been able to separate it without great loss[,] Alcott is a man of unquestionable genius, yet no doctrine or sentence or word or action of his which is excellent can be detached & quoted" (*JMN* 11:51; **ABA** 18, 27-28). As much as Hoar and Thoreau are defined by versions of mid-nineteenth-century American life which they represent, Alcott may be defined only by subjective worlds where his friends find solace by finding in him representations of themselves. Alcott has the capacity to fathom and reflect back onto those in his little circle their own best intellectual and imaginative abilities. Alcott's good nature is foremost in Emerson's mind when he describes their own personal relationship.

> Alcott is a certain fluid in which men of a certain spirit can easily expand themselves & swim at large, they who elsewhere found themselves confined. He gives them nothing but themselves. Of course, he seems to them the only & wise man. But when they meet people of another sort, critics & practical, & are asked concerning Alcott's wisdom, they have no books to open, no doctrines to impart, no sentences or sayings to repeat, and they find it quite impossible to communicate to these their good opinion.
>
> Me he has served . . . in that way; he was the reasonable creature to speak to, that I wanted.
>
> (*JMN* 11:19; **ABA** 25)

Emerson would never write his life of Alcott, yet without any doubt he highly prized Alcott's generative powers or, as he once called them, "spermatic" powers, that is, his setting in motion countless ideas and ethical resolutions. In the privacy of his journals Emerson entered a sexual simile that best characterized Alcott: "[Alcott] was like a vigorous cock let into the coop of a farm house. He trod the hundred hens of the barnyard, and the very partridges for a mile round, and for the next fortnight the whole country side was filled with cackle over the eggs which they laid." Any "eggs" fathered by Alcott would assuredly have run counter to expectations of orthodox nineteenth-century political wisdom, such hatchings hardly ever yielding financial profit or title to large tracts of land. Yet, for Emerson, Alcott is valuable because he ushers his companions out of modern meanspiritedness and back to the

"Chaldaean, Egyptian, or Teutonic ages, when man was not featherbrained . . . or servile, but, if he stooped, he stooped under Ideas: times when the earth spoke & the heavens glowed, when the actions of men indicated vast conceptions . . . [and showed] that is only real which men love & rejoice in,—not the things which starve & freeze & terrify them" (*JMN* 8:6-7). Alcott provides a vision of "the first monks and anchorets without [one's having to cross] seas or centuries." He verifies the thesis of **"History"**: "all History becomes subject & repeats itself. . . . [N]ow Alcott with his hatred of labor & commanding contemplation, a haughty beneficiary, makes good to the 19th Century Simeon the Stylite & the Thebaid, & the first Capuchins" (*JMN* 7:211; **ABA** 27; *CW* 2:16). In sum, Alcott is a "singular person, a natural Levite, a priest forever after the order of Melchizedek," and though Emerson admits that were Alcott to be "a founder of a family or institution," Emerson himself would not endeavor to raise funding, he believes Alcott's service is so crucial to the well-being of those he touches that "all good persons [should] readily combine . . . to maintain [Alcott] as a priest by voluntary contribution to live in his own cottage[,] literary, spiritual, and choosing his own methods of teaching & action" (*JMN* 8:300-301; **ABA** 19).

By virtue of his conversational and speculative abilities which transcend time and place, Alcott invites others to enjoy the inheritance of virtue and thought from earlier ages. Alcott is thus out of step with his time. To an age that believes in material progress only, Alcott stands as a philosophic anachronism, a defiant anomaly. He measures progress by its inherent "folly," and he finds common labor "a cruel waste of time [that] depresse[s] his spirits even to tears" (*JMN* 8:211-12). Emerson might have praised Alcott as philosophic and defiant, as "the magnificent dreamer, brooding as ever on the . . . reedification of the social fabric after ideal law, heedless that he ha[s] been uniformly rejected by every class [except by his intimates] to whom he has addressed himself" (*JMN* 9:50; **ABA** 19). Conceding that Alcott "dissatisfies . . . & disgusts many" because "it is speculation which he loves & not action," Emerson would have characterized him as an "intellectual Torso," a "celestial mind incapable of offence, of haste, of care, of inhospitality, of peeping, of memory, incapable of being embarrassed, incapable of discourtesy, treating all with a sovereign equality" (*JMN* 8:212, 9:164; **ABA** 20-21, 26). Finally, however, because Alcott believes in the soul, Emerson would have lavished on him the praise which he reserved for those special persons who elevate joy and hope in the hearts of those they encounter, whose "actions are poetic and miraculous," and in whose presence "one believes in . . . immortality" (**"Character,"** *W* 10:101). Because it was Alcott's belief in the soul that attracted Emerson to his company, it is likely that in his intended biography Emerson would have returned to a definitive description written in 1838, of Alcott's character and value.

> I think he has more faith in the Ideal than any man I have known. Hence his welcome influence. A wise woman said to me that he has few thoughts, too few.

She could count them all. Well. Books, conversation, discipline will give him more. But what were many thoughts if he had not this distinguishing Faith, which is palpable proclamation out of the deeps of nature that God yet is? With many thoughts, & without this, he would be only one more of a countless throng of lettered men; but now you cannot spare the fortification that he is.

> (*JMN* 7:34; **ABA** 18)

V

We dissect Kant and Hegel, but the wonder is not explained. The central life we do not touch. It remains a miracle as astounding now as at the beginning of Philosophy. . . . I think . . . persons who are most impressive to us interest us without reference to their education. They have an insight we cannot explain. People who have been particularly attractive to me are those of whom I can give no account. They have neither families nor circumstances. They show qualities.

(Emerson at the Examiner Club, 7 March 1870)[8]

If interpreted only as discrete character studies, Emerson's lives of Hoar and Thoreau and his intended life of Alcott may be taken to represent three biographical contrasts between native Emersonian great men who do not, finally, disprove the wisdom of the realist's complaint: "Great men or men of great gifts you shall easily find, but symmetrical men never" (*CW* 3:134). Read this way, these accounts extend the discontinuity between the theoretical promise of ideal, great men and one's "shabby experience" of real men which Emerson conceded in **Representative Men.** At this level, the only difference between the figures of **Representative Men** and those of the biographical miscellanies is the poignancy with which the latter in effect insult the idealist by forcing him to make concessions about theory based not on his "sense" of "departed men" who lived on a grand but distant scale, but on his experience of his own dearest companions (see *CW* 4:9). Read as discreet character studies, these accounts also may be said to depict men of Emerson's age representing by their idiosyncrasy the exclusionary factions warring for dominance in mid-nineteenth-century America. In the first instance there is Samuel Hoar, man of business and the law, who as spokesperson for progress would seem to have little interest in the qualities—to him, more likely, the affectations and nuisances—attributed to Thoreau, and no interest whatsoever in Alcott's celestial dreams. Then there is Thoreau, who as creature of nature may find in a figure like Hoar a subject deserving his contempt and scorn and, except for noticing his coziness with rats and mice, may find he has little in common with a figure like Alcott who was never associated with even the minutest bit of physical exertion. And, finally, there is Alcott, who as pure intellect personified blithely living off the largesse of others takes delight in poking fun at the folly of men who, like Hoar, seem encumbered by their notions of progress and may wonder at the sense of those who, like Thoreau, find satisfaction in allowing snakes to curl around their legs or in pulling woodchucks by their tails.

Yet evidence from his journals as well as from the sketches themselves shows that Emerson never intended his writ-

ings on these obscure persons who excited wonder, speculation, and delight in him, and whose lives were lived poems to him, to be read this way; instead, he considered the
lives of Hoar, Thoreau, Alcott, and those many others to
whom he was attracted as, so Ellen Emerson remarked,
very good chapters of human history. Although he portrays
in each figure a trait derived from his vocation that sets
him completely apart from the others, he also portrays in
each an essential, attractive quality—a moral center—
which all three share in common. For Emerson, Hoar is
the New World's gentleman-businessman-democrat—a
Napoleon *with* a conscience combined with a Montaigne
without skepticism—who, by virtue of his conscience, has
the ability to effect enlightened change in society and tame
the crassness of the rising middle class through the exercise of will complemented by moral vision. Although he
does not specifically address this aspect of Hoar's character and value in the printed sketch, in his journal for 1844
Emerson did address it in a paragraph he eventually
adapted for use in **"Montaigne, or the Skeptic"**:

> Men are edificant or otherwise. Samuel Hoar is to all
> men's eyes conservative & constructive: his presence
> supposes a well ordered society, agriculture, trade, large
> institutions & empire. If these things did not exist, they
> would begin to exist through his steady will & endeav-
> ours. Therefore he cheers & comforts men, who feel all
> this in him very readily. The reformer, the rebel, who
> comes by, says, all manner of unanswerable things
> against the existing republic, but discovers to my grop-
> ing Daemon no plan of house or empire of his own.
> Therefore though Samuel Hoar's town & state are a
> very cheap and modest commonwealth men very rightly
> go for him & flout the reformer.

(*JMN* 9:113-14; *CW* 4:96-97)

By contrast, in Thoreau's naturalistic, physical, and moral
vigor Emerson discovered the traits most needed in the
New World environment in which Nature would proceed
with her design of an ideal race. And, finally, Alcott is, for
Emerson, the New World's Socratic *agent provocateur,*
Nature's "commissioned spirit" who must be cultivated,
sounded, and, literally, fed, because his intellectual and
moral vigor is a necessary complement to Hoar's activism
and Thoreau's environmentalism.

Thus if, as Emerson predicted in **English Traits,** "the elas-
ticity and hope of mankind" reside in the ideas, poetry, cities, institutions, and spirit of America's evolving self-
reliant men (*W* 5:314), then it is only because of the moral
self-sufficiency which joins these three men together that
the promise of the ideal in society will never be destroyed
by the anarchy of material culture nor the advantages of
idealism ever be outweighed by the decadent indulgences
of pessimism. In Hoar, Thoreau, and Alcott, Emerson
found his surest evidence that intellect and virtue had not
been exhausted by the great men of earlier ages, that the
sacred had not been permanently offset by the mundane.
Indeed, in his lives of such *"Littleendians,"* Emerson reaffirmed the "riches of [his] inheritance in being set down in
this world" and thus ironically realized his ambition of
writing the American Plutarch.

Notes

1. Except for studies by Berry and Roberson, or edito-
rial introductions by Bosco (Emerson, "'Blessed'"),
Myerson (Emerson, "Emerson's 'Thoreau'"), and
Williams, or Sarah Wider's paper "Inventing a Life:
The Example of the Sermons," at the American Lit-
erature Association, Washington, D. C., 29 May
1991 and my own papers "Emerson's *Littleendians*:
A Hedge against the Anarchy of Material Culture,"
Modern Language Association of America, New
York, 27 December 1989 and "The Anarchy of Ma-
terial Culture: An Unspoken Side of Emerson's Na-
tionalism," American Literature Association, San
Diego, 28 May 1992, most detailed commentary on
Emerson's theory and practice of biography has occurred within discussions of his Christology, skepticism, and philosophy of history. See Michael, Mott,
Neufeldt, Nicoloff, Richardson, Robinson (*Apostle*
and "Sermons"), and Whicher.

2. In 1849, Emerson established a correspondence between the figures developed in *Representative Men*
and those who would represent the ideal in his proposed biographical essays. Thereby, he would preserve idealism from the vagaries of human conduct.
Under the respective headings *"Bigendians"* and
"Littleendians" he paired Plato with Alcott, Swedenborg with Jones Very, Shakespeare with Charles
King Newcomb, Montaigne with Ellery Channing,
Goethe with himself, and Napoleon with Thoreau
(*JMN* 11:173). The editors of *JMN* volume 11
judged Emerson's juxtaposition of Napoleon and
Thoreau unclear. Subsequently, drawing on Emerson's unpublished notebook "Auto," Nancy Simmons recently observed that late in life Emerson removed Thoreau from the comparison with Napoleon
and inserted James Elliot Cabot and Samuel Gray
Ward. He replaced himself in the comparison with
Goethe by substituting both Carlyle and Thoreau
(1). However these pairings are construed, for Emerson they represented a continuity between the accomplishments of great men from the past and the
promise of his own contemporaries.

3. Many historical and biographical writings influenced Emerson's thought. Extensive reading in and
journal commentary on an "organic" model of history show the influence of Coleridge, Goethe, and
Friedrich von Schlegel. In his journals, Emerson
debated assumptions about history and biography
advanced by Carlyle and the French philosopher
Victor Cousin. He assimilated Carlyle's definition
of history as "the essence of innumerable biographies" into his own evolving idealistic system. At
the same time, ideas from Cousin's *Introduction a
l'histoire de la philosophe* (1828), which Emerson
owned in an English translation, shaped or colored
Emerson's ideas on the relation between history
and biography as well as issues he raises in *Nature,*
"The Method of Nature," "Circles," and "Nominalist and Realist." A typical Cousin passage:

What is the business of history? . . . What is the stuff of which it is made? Who is the personage of history? Man: evidently man and human nature. There are many different elements in history. What are they? Evidently again, the elements of human nature. History is therefore the development of humanity, and of humanity only; for nothing else but humanity develops itself, for nothing else than humanity is free. . . . We must begin with seeking the essential elements of humanity, and proceed by deriving from the nature of these elements their fundamental relations, and from these the laws of their development; and finally we must go to history and ask if it confirms or rejects our results.

(Cited in *EL* 2:3)

Emerson's debt to Cousin has attracted little critical attention, but his debt to Carlyle has been extensively reviewed. See particularly Harris (70-96), Nicoloff (70-90), and Williams (xix-xxi).

4. Michael, Nicoloff, Whicher, and Williams take up Emerson's putative loss of idealism. They have contributed to what Neufeldt identifies as an "efficient assumption" (12) governing our understanding of Emerson's career. The "efficient assumption" is this: between the mid-1840s, when he began preparing the "Representative Men" lectures, and the appearance successively of *English Traits* (1856), *The Conduct of Life* (1860), and *Society and Solitude* (1870) Emerson moved away from idealism toward realism, skepticism, and naturalism. I do not subscribe to this theory of such an "efficient assumption." Emerson frequently rejected realism, skepticism, and naturalism (*JMN* 11:95; *W* 6:48; *JMN* 13:229).

5. Techniques Emerson and Plutarch share have been summarized by Berry: (1) at most, facts surrounding the life of the subject are briefly mentioned either at the beginning or the end of a biographical sketch or formal essay; (2) character, the biographical and moral center of the subject, is elaborated through anecdote, epigram, second-hand or third-hand accounts, and personal material such as letters, poems, diaries, and essays; and (3) sentiments and values most appropriate to an individual of noteworthy character are idealism, self-reliance, integrity, simplicity, manliness, and high principle (258-59ff).

6. *Lectures and Biographical Sketches,* as first compiled by Cabot, is Volume 10 of Emerson's *Complete Works* (*W*). Emerson's biographical notebooks on his brother Charles, Margaret Fuller, and Thoreau have been printed in *JMN* 6:255-86, 9:455-509, and 15:483-92, respectively; his recently published notebook on Alcott is cited below. His notebooks C[harles] K[ing] N[ewcomb] and multivolume M[ary] M[oody] E[merson] remain unpublished in the Houghton Library, Harvard University.

Notebooks on Mary Moody Emerson and Thoreau, both of whom predeceased Emerson, proved handy resources for memorial lectures immediately upon their deaths. Posthumously, in essays collected by his executors as *Lectures and Biographical Sketches,* Emerson would produce his most formal biographical accounts of contemporary "*Littleendians.*" As with the pieces on Mary Moody Emerson and Thoreau, before being collected in 1884, essays on Ezra Ripley, Samuel Hoar, Carlyle, and George L. Stearns had done service variously as a funeral oration, an address before an interested society, or a magazine publication, but each, regardless of its prior service, was substantially drawn from materials Emerson had preserved in journals and topical notebooks.

7. *JMN* 11:134. In the *JMN* entry this anecdote is used to describe the otherwise unidentified "M." However, in journal indices in ABA (19), Emerson's keyed reference to Alcott's "spermatic powers" refers to this entry. The reference is a coarse pun on the original spelling of the Alcott name, which during the previous century-and-a-half had evolved from "Alcock" to "Alcocke" to "Alcox" before Bronson finally changed it to "Alcott."

8. Emerson's remarks, together with a brief history of his association with the Examiner Club and a transcription of the minutes of the Club's meeting on 7 March 1870, will appear in Litton's forthcoming article "Emerson and the Examiner Club." I am grateful to Professor Litton for sharing his work with me in advance of its publication.

Works Cited

Berry, Edmund G. *Emerson's Plutarch.* Cambridge: Harvard UP, 1961.

Emerson, Ellen Tucker. *The Letters of Ellen Tucker Emerson.* Ed. Edith E. W. Gregg. 2 vols. Kent: Kent State UP, 1982.

Emerson, Ralph Waldo. "'Blessed Are They Who Have No Talent:' Emerson's Unwritten Life of Amos Bronson Alcott." Ed. Ronald A. Bosco. *ESQ: A Journal of the American Renaissance* 36.1 (1990): 1-36. Cited as ABA.

———. *The Collected Works of Ralph Waldo Emerson.* Eds. Alfred R. Ferguson, Joseph Slater, et al. 4 vols. to date. Cambridge: Harvard UP, 1971-. Cited as *CW.*

———. *The Complete Works of Ralph Waldo Emerson.* Ed. Edward Waldo Emerson. 12 vols. Boston: Houghton, Mifflin, 1903-1904. Cited as *W.*

———. *The Correspondence of Emerson and Carlyle.* Ed. Joseph Slater. New York: Columbia UP, 1964.

———. *The Early Lectures of Ralph Waldo Emerson.* Eds. Stephen E. Whicher, Robert E. Spiller, and Wallace E. Williams. 3 vols. Cambridge: Harvard UP, 1959-71. Cited as *EL.*

————. *The Journals and Miscellaneous Notebooks of Ralph Waldo Emerson.* Eds. William H. Gilman, Ralph H. Orth, et al. 16 vols. Cambridge: Harvard UP, 1960-82. Cited as *JMN.*

————. "Emerson's 'Thoreau': a New Edition from Manuscript." Ed. Joel Myerson. *Studies in the American Renaissance 1979.* Boston: G. K. Hall, 1979. 17-92.

Harris, Kenneth Marc. *Carlyle and Emerson: Their Long Debate.* Cambridge: Harvard UP, 1978.

Litton, Alfred G. "Emerson and the Examiner Club: An Unpublished Conversation." *New England Quarterly* [forthcoming 1994].

Michael, John. *Emerson and Skepticism: The Cipher of the World.* Baltimore: Johns Hopkins UP, 1988.

Mott, Wesley T. *The Strains of Eloquence: Emerson and His Sermons.* University Park: Pennsylvania State UP, 1989.

Neufeldt, Leonard. *The House of Emerson.* Lincoln: U of Nebraska P, 1982.

Nicoloff, Philip L. *Emerson on Race and History: An Examination of* English Traits. New York: Columbia UP, 1961.

Richardson, Robert D., Jr. "Emerson on History." *Emerson: Prospect and Retrospect.* Ed. Joel Porte. Cambridge: Harvard UP, 1982. 49-64.

Roberson, Susan L. "Young Emerson and the Mantle of Biography." *American Transcendental Quarterly.* N. S. 5 (1991): 151-68.

Robinson, David M. *Apostle of Culture: Emerson as Preacher and Lecturer.* Philadelphia: U of Pennsylvania P, 1982.

————. "The Sermons of Ralph Waldo Emerson: An Introductory Historical Essay." *The Complete Sermons of Ralph Waldo Emerson.* Ed. Albert J. von Frank et al. 4 vols. Columbia: U of Missouri P, 1989-92. I:1-32.

Simmons, Nancy Craig. "Thoreau as Napoleon; or A Note on Emerson's Big, Little, and Good Endians." *Emerson Society Papers* 4.1 (1993): 1-4.

Whicher, Stephen E. *Freedom and Fate: An Inner Life of Ralph Waldo Emerson.* Philadelphia: U of Pennsylvania P, 1953.

Williams, Wallace E. "Historical Introduction." *Representative Men. The Collected Works of Ralph Waldo Emerson.* Eds. Wallace E. Williams and Douglas Emory Wilson. 4 vols. to date. Cambridge: Harvard UP, 1987. IV:xi-lxv.

Barbara Ryan (essay date 1994)

SOURCE: "Emerson's 'Domestic and Social Experiments': Service, Slavery, and the Unhired Man," in *American Literature,* Vol. 66, No. 3, September, 1994, pp. 485-508.

[*In the following essay, Ryan outlines Emerson's ideas on abolition, examining the development of these views in the context of the writer's own domestic arrangements.*]

> I hope New England will come to boast itself in being a nation of servants, & leave to the planters the misery of being a nation of served.
>
> —R. W. Emerson, *Journal C* (1837)

Len Gougeon has shown that Ralph Waldo Emerson traveled a long way between 1837, when he made his first "abolitionist" speech, and 1844, when he affirmed his opposition to chattel slavery. The first effort, Gougeon notes, disappointed Emerson's friends because it was more a defense of free speech than a denunciation of American slavery; indeed, the great idealist had recommended tolerance for slaveholders' views. Yet by 1844 Emerson made a stirring antislavery speech which, according to Gougeon, found him speaking "with an emotional as well as an intellectual appreciation" he had not demonstrated earlier. Gougeon explains this dramatic shift with reference to developments in Emerson's philosophy and sense of vocation.[1]

Here, I propose another perspective on Emerson's decision to advocate abolition precisely when, and on the terms, he did. This perspective helps explain three related phenomena: how a series of "domestic & social experiments" helped shape Emerson's published views on American slavery; how hard reformers had to struggle against prevailing notions of mastery, domestic service, and the home; and how Emerson's slow conversion to antislavery was part and parcel of his dwindling enthusiasm for the once-feted Henry Thoreau.

The linchpin holding these phenomena together is Emerson's unphilosophical vexation with America's "servant problem." That much-discussed concern was a response to, and affirmation of, changing social patterns in the industrializing Northeast. From Puritan days through the eighteenth century, servants had been understood as members, or almost-members, of the families in which they served. But by the 1820s, that time-tested trope looked less pertinent to domestic patterns in America's industrializing areas. One change was that industrialization separated home and work, a shift that made waged co-residents seem anomalous. Another was that altered legal structures gave waged domestic workers increased mobility, a freedom their disgruntled employers deplored as upsetting their hearths and homes. Third, and perhaps most worrisome, dense urban populations eroded many served Americans' sense that non-kin domestic workers were, or could be made, familial co-residents who could be trusted within their ostensibly "privatized" abodes.[2] Pinpointing these anxieties, Caroline Howard Gilman, an anti-abolitionist, wrote gleefully that a new waged servant was "a forlorn hope—one of those experiments that New-England ladies are so constantly obliged to make of the morals and dispositions of strangers."[3] Gilman's subtlety lies in her implicit comparison to the affectionate bonds supposed to exist between slaveholders and petted house chattel. The expression a "family white and black" usually included chattel field hands. But "family" feelings were thought especially likely among those house slaves who enjoyed long-term, intimate, and supposedly affectionate relationships with those they served. Those slaves, whom I call "chattel servants" or "house chattel," were routinely praised as more loving, efficient, and loyal than the North's waged domestic workers.

Beginning in the 1830s, propagation of the notion of a "plantation family" invited middling homemakers of all regions to contrast the service relations extant on the two sides of the Mason-Dixon. In response to mounting abolitionist activity, proslavery propagandists boosted the idea that loving, childlike chattel, born and raised within sight of the Big House, would grow into more familial attendants than wage-hungry "strangers" ever could. These same writers also promoted the idea that affection foundered on waged relations. As everyone recognized, house chattel served without benefit of wages while waged servants were apt to leave if cash were not forthcoming. Under these circumstances, it was hard for wage-payers to claim "family" feeling, and proslavery writers were quick to seize the emotive edge. George Fitzhugh smirked: "we love our slaves, and we are ready to defend, assist and protect them; you hate and fear your white servants."[4] Much of Fitzhugh's popularity was due to such canny thrusts: this jibe reproduced exactly many wage-payers' own anxieties and envies.

Today, of course, Fitzhugh's claims appear disingenuous, rhetorical posturing in aid of repugnant political goals. But in the early years of the nineteenth century, many believed that slaveholders had found a better form of service. Those wage-payers who had never owned chattel servants, such as Waldo Emerson, would have been especially likely to believe that an extended and nonwaged "family" was the best model yet devised for providing comfortable and mutually beneficial service relations.

Emerson did not hope to reinstitute slavery in Massachusetts. But he did try, between 1837 and 1844, to establish "family-style" domestic service, as if to show that slaveholders were not the only ones who could create or maintain familial bonds. Only after a series of experiments had been tried and found wanting did he accede to friends' pleas to oppose slavery publicly. Then, like most antislavery speakers, he had most to say about the field hand. But it is noteworthy that when he did turn his attention to chattel servants, Emerson was particularly impressed by the "silent obedience" he thought those workers would supply.

Demands for silence were far from Emerson's mind when he first set up housekeeping at Bush, a large private home in Concord, in 1835. Before that date, Emerson did not recognize a servant problem, probably because, during his first marriage, he had "boarded out." But when he married for a second time, Emerson was forced to confront the do-

mestic workers he had once paid landladies to manage. By 1838, he thought the issues agitating American society to be: "War, Slavery, Alcohol, animal food, Domestic hired service, Colleges, Creeds, & now at last Money."[5] By 1840, he would come to see servants and slaves as more closely related; in his lecture **"Religion,"** given that same year, he publicly praised those who worked for "the freedom of the servant and the slave."[6] Later still, Emerson would retreat from this radical conflation: by the late 1840s, waged domestic servants were accepted as fixtures in the Emersons' home.

It is the interim period that interests me here, the years during which Emerson came to realize that waged relations offered savvy homemakers certain advantages. Lidian Emerson had always thought so: though an early and unwavering advocate of antislavery, she was happy to employ domestic assistants. Thus she had written in 1822: "I don't see how you can get along with so many 'to make & mend for' and bad help. I see but one remedy against being hurried all the time out of your wits, and that is to hire work enough done to enable you to get along easy. What is expense in comparison with the comfort of one's life and the improvement of ones mind."[7] Lidian did not share her husband's dis-ease with waged domestics. Indeed, she was willing to contend, acerbically, with a neighbor she thought had "stolen" a servant promised to the Emerson home.[8]

Servants, she recognized, were simple necessities, at least in a home as large and hospitable as Bush. But they were also encumbrances, especially for an inexperienced bride. According to Ellen Tucker Emerson's memoir of her mother, the erstwhile *religieuse* predicated her agreement to marry on her suitor's realization that she had not been trained to run a home. "[S]he foresaw," wrote Ellen Emerson, "that with her long life wholly aside from housekeeping she should not be a skillful mistress of a house and that it would be a load of care and labour from which she shrank and a giving up of an existence she thoroughly enjoyed and to which she had become exactly fitted, and she could not undertake it unless he was sure he loved her and needed her enough to justify her in doing it."[9] Waldo inevitably replied that he *was* sure, and the reluctant housekeeper accepted his hand, his home, and the management of his mother's servants.

Newly arrived at Bush, Lidian gushed to her sister, Lucy Jackson Brown, "This Nancy of the Emerson's is indeed a treasure. I will when I have time write you particulars concerning her—such a rare blessing as wise and faithful help, is worth writing about" (*SL*, 34). Unfortunately, relations with Nancy Colesworthy did not run smoothly for long. Though Lidian gained confidence in housekeeping as she grew accustomed to staff management, Waldo recorded his wife's confession, in 1838, that "when she gives any new direction in the kitchen she feels like a boy who throws a stone & runs" (*JMN*, 5:479).

Waldo was alternately charmed by his wife's efforts and irritated by poor household management. In a genial mood,

Emerson's study.

he could write: "The common household tasks are agreeable to the imagination: they are the subjects of all the Greek gems"; though another day would find him wishing: "my housekeeping should be clean & sweet & . . . it should not shame or annoy me" (*JMN,* 7:242 and 229). He usually vented his impatience on the servants whom he saw as causing the distress, but he could also indict his wife's incompetence. According to Waldo, "literary men" who marry should take a "shrew for a wife, a sharp-tongued notable dame who can & will assume the total economy of the house, and having some sense that her philosopher is best in his study suffers him not to intermeddle with her thrift" (*JMN,* 7:420).

Most advice manuals supported a husband's distance from servant problems.[10] But when that husband was a clergyman, he was even less obliged to do household work: at least two advice books of the 1830s taught that domestic servants should minister to ministers. In one, a reluctant waged serving maid is persuaded that a servant is not "a low and a mean thing to be," since "if there were no mechanics and no servants, then preachers and writers, and all such as have gained a good education, would have to

get their own food and clothes, and do housework for themselves. And that would keep them busy all day long, and every day; so that they would not have time to preach and write books, and spread knowledge and religion, however fit and able they might be to do it; so there would be little or no good done." "Yes," this fictional servant-to-be concludes happily, "I see that servants help to get the gospel taught."[11]

Her ideas were seconded by William Andrus Alcott, a popular and prolific writer of domestic advice manuals and, not incidentally, Bronson Alcott's cousin. In *The Young Woman's Guide to Excellence,* Alcott offered his own version of the preceding story, with his anecdote of a servant whose labors rivaled that of any missionary. "She is an ordinary domestic—and no more," Alcott wrote, but because her employer is a teacher, her influence extends unto the multitude. "And if ninety millions," he perorated, "or even one tenth that number of citizens should, in the course of the next two centuries, reap the benefit of his labors, and become lights in the world, is it too much to say that she has been an important aid in accomplishing the work?"[12]

Considering the popularity of this notion, Waldo Emerson may be excused for thinking devoted service his due. But he would also have known that most households did without servants and that many considered reliance on waged servants enervating, anti-Christian, and unrepublican. Despite these fears, Alcott admitted servants to selected homes, especially those with sick inmates and those which entertained frequently. This last condition may have soothed Waldo's doubts about his home's reliance on waged non-kin: in the early years of his second marriage, he kept open board for his admirers.

Of course Southerners were famous for hospitality, too. The difference in the South, at least in proslavery literature, was that domestic staffs were assumed to be always present, willing, and numerous, qualities sometimes lacking in the staff at Bush. With *Swallow Barn* (1832), *Sheppard Lee* (1836), and other plantation fantasies much in evidence, Emerson must have succumbed to a few sideways glances: that is, his views on slavery would have affected his dawning sense of a "servant problem" just as much as his gripes about waged service influenced his thoughts on chattel labor. With portraits of a loving, immobilized plantation "family" being promoted on all sides, any American homemaker could have found restless co-residents disturbing. But the point was particularly acute for the lecturer who proclaimed that the "constant progress of Culture is to a more interior life, to a deeper Home."[13] Obviously, with waged co-residents coming and going just as they pleased, this desideratum was out of step with most domestic employers' realities. William Gilmore Simms probed this wound succinctly in 1837. "Envy of the North by the South!" he snorted. "The boot is on the other leg, perhaps."[14]

The progress of Emerson's thought suggests that Simm's mockery was well founded: during the period in which he abstained from abolition, Emerson directed his energies toward establishing a waged domestic staff as familial and immobilized as any slaveholder could boast. To accomplish the goal of a family-like serving force would have been a home-lover's triumph in a day when great spiritual value was attributed to a stable and stabilizing domestic realm. Emerson accepted these values: in his lecture **"Home,"** he grieves over the family in which a homemaker "had supposed a perfect understanding and intimate bonds subsisted," only to find "with surprise that in proportion to the force of character existing all are in a degree strangers to and mutually observant of each other's acts" (*EL,* 32). To counteract domestic strangeness, this harried householder suggests that men become more involved in the domestic sphere: "He is not yet a man," this same lecture asserts, "if he have not learned the Household Laws, if he have not learned how in some way to labor for the maintenance of himself and others" (*EL,* 33). This struggle to fit men into domestic life (still ongoing in some American homes) had its roots in the same home/market split that gave rise to the "servant problem."

For if home was essentially woman's sphere, then where did men *or* servants fit within its sacralized boundaries? It

is much to Emerson's credit that he tried to find himself domestic duties; it is much to his credit, too, that he saw servants' position in a non-kin family as ripe for reform. But his greatest imaginative leap was to see what most domestic employers refused to consider: that waged domestic service was not wholly different from Southern slavery.

In **"Reforms,"** another pre-Brook Farm lecture, this thinker reveals the conceptual proximity of waged and chattel service. "[I]n a community where labor was the point of honor," he claims, "the vain and the idle would labor. What a mountain of chagrins, inconveniences, diseases, and sins would sink into the sea with the uprise of this one doctrine of labor. Domestic hired service would go over the dam. Slavery would fall into the pit. Shoals of maladies would be exterminated, and the Saturnian Age revive" (*EL,* 264).[15] By 1839, then, Emerson was arguing that, in a better world, both forms of service would disappear. He expected, as did his friends George and Sophia Ripley, that the rethinking or revaluing of menial labor would put an end to both these abuses against the home.

Yet neither rethinking nor revaluing would help Lidian with what she dubbed the "Martha-like care of wine & custards" (*SL,* 62). Idealists could say that housekeeping itself was the real problem: hence Waldo's scorn of domestic fripperies and repeated calls for simpler housekeeping. But it is easy to imagine Lidian's reaction to such dreamy heights: her housekeeping was not arduous by choice. The more practical option, therefore, especially as one's family grew, might be to make servants seem more like kin.

This strategy explains why Waldo Emerson began, in 1840, a series of domestic reforms intended to make waged servants extended "family." Only after these efforts failed did Emerson agree to speak out against slavery. In other words, he did not commit his energies to abolition until he had found, for himself, that servants could not be immobilized or made less disturbing simply by employers' treating them as members of one united household. It suggests a nice sense of honor—or bullheadedness—that Emerson refrained from attacking Southerners' domestic service while he tried to devise better labor arrangements within his own home.

Lidian, already committed to antislavery, thought at least one of her husband's domestic proposals "a wild scheme."[16] Her pragmatic scorn—or nineteenth-century gender roles—may explain why her husband most often discussed service reforms in the voice of the first person singular. For instance, in the letter expressing his half-apologetic decision not to join Brook Farm, Waldo tries to let the Ripleys down lightly, claiming to be "so ignorant & uncertain in my improvements that I would fain hide my attempts & failures in solitude where they shall perplex none or very few beside myself."[17] He adds, as if his wife played no part in such domestic efforts, "The ground of my decision is almost purely personal to myself" and "I think that all I shall solidly do, I must do alone" (*Letters,* 2:369-70).[18]

But the best explanation for Emerson's self-portrayed solitude is that his experiments were all attempts to establish more fully the so-called privatized home. Brook Farm was no solution, then, for the theorist of the single-family hearth. "I think," suggests one version of this important apologia, "that my present position has even greater advantages than yours would offer me for testing my improvements in those small private parties into which men are all set off already throughout the world" (**Letters,** 2:370). This same letter makes it clear that service relations are the rub. "The principal particulars in which I wish to mend my domestic life," Emerson declares, "are in acquiring habits of regular manual labor, and in ameliorating or abolishing in my house the condition of hired menial service. . . . But surely I need not sell my house & remove my family to Newton in order to make the experiment of labor & self help. I am already in the act of trying some domestic & social experiments which my present position favors" (2:370). This refusal of communitarian living includes the substitution of the words "ameliorating or abolishing" for the original "discontinuing." There is little practical difference between "discontinuing" and "abolishing," though the latter obviously echoes antislavery rhetoric. But there is a good deal of room between "ameliorating" and "abolishing," and Emerson's real movement was toward the former.

Yet it is easy to see why the Ripleys thought the Emerson family a likely candidate for Brook Farm: in the late 1830s, Waldo was wont to proclaim the beauties of communal labor. In **"Domestic Life,"** a lecture delivered during these servant-conscious years, he sounds egalitarian and even gender-neutral, when he scoffs that "this voice of communities and ages, 'Give us wealth, and the good household shall exist,' is vicious, and leaves the whole difficulty untouched. It is better, certainly, in this form, 'Give us your labor, and the household begins.' I see not how serious labor, the labor of all and every day, is to be avoided." Going further, he advises his audience that "the reform that applies itself to the household must not be partial. It must correct the whole system of our social living. It must come with plain living and high thinking; it must break up caste, and put domestic service on another foundation."[19] This sentiment, no doubt well intended, proved deceptive: as the Ripleys would find, this thinker preferred to mind his own hen-coop.[20]

Within that confined space, Emerson's first foray was the "hiring" of Alexander McCaffery, younger brother of a servant employed at William Emerson's home. In mid-March 1840, Emerson decided to "make the experiment for a few months. If we find that he is not good help for us, we can let him come back" (**Letters,** 7:375). Precisely why he calls this employment an "experiment" is not clear: it was common practice to hire from the family of an already familiar servant as a shortcut to establishing appropriate relations within one's home. Emerson's sense of risk may have resulted from McCaffery's youth, gender, or religious training. He advised Lidian that McCaffery was "to go to Church with us, & to Sunday School," but does not mention who set these terms (**Letters,** 7:375).

But Emerson's sense of an "experiment" could also have been due to the fact that McCaffery's "hiring" was difficult to place within the usual categories of service. The boy was nothing if not a domestic servant, since most of his work was with Lidian and the Emerson children.[21] On the other hand, he apparently spent most of his time at school, and was not paid: "I have made no other bargain with his sister," Emerson wrote, "than that I will board & clothe him at present" (**Letters,** 7:375). Just how the Emersons viewed this arrangement is unclear, but it is close to the pattern of the "bound orphan" and thus a variation on that estate, the condition of human chattel.

Though the Emersons would have been horrified at the suggestion that they had "bought" McCaffery, the terms of the boy's co-residence had much in common with slaves' estate. A master's obligation to offer his slaves religious training marks one similarity; so does McCaffery's limited remuneration. From Emerson's point of view, though, McCaffery's co-residence was probably a blow against chattel conditions and a challenge to abolitionists' importunings. In one of his most famous essays, Emerson could have been talking about McCaffery when he disparaged muchpublicized reform efforts as so much self-righteous obfuscation. The quotation is now well known: "If an angry bigot assumes," he writes in **"Self-Reliance,"** "this bountiful cause of Abolition, and comes to me with his last news from Barbadoes, why should I not say to him, 'Go love thy infant; love thy woodchopper . . . and never varnish your hard, uncharitable ambition with this incredible tenderness for black folk a thousand miles off. Thy love afar is spite at home.'"[22] These lines admit the extent to which "self-reliance" depended on hired workers; they also suggest that when McCaffery arrived, Emerson hoped to love this woodchopper—that is, to make him part of the Bush "family." If he could do so, this quotation suggests, he would have shown up Northern abolitionists' outcries as wrong-headed, self-aggrandizing, and remarkably blind to problems in their own backyards—or kitchens.

But of course, there were significant differences between Alexander McCaffery and, say, the young Frederick Douglass—namely, each worker's legal mobility. The flaw in Waldo Emerson's plan to make McCaffery "family" was that a free worker could not easily be held to a given post. Emerson was not, finally, allowed to enact the benevolent "good" master of plantation literature: though he took his duties in loco parentis seriously, he could not prevent Mrs. McCaffery from removing her son from his place at Bush. Sounding more than a little peeved at his waged servant's mobility, Emerson groused that "boys must not be expected to come & go like sheets of lightning. . . . [W]e had intended to keep the boy" (**Letters,** 2:382).[23]

In a more elevated tone, the philosopher admitted: "I should willingly have kept him & made him a partaker of what new experiments we shall try," and Lidian thought him "my idea of what we should desire in a servant-boy, being quick & skilful as well as pleasant and orderly" (**Letters,** 2:386; SL, 86). Their contentment was not shared by McCaffery's mother, who preferred her son to learn a trade. Unfortunately for the Emersons' domestic comforts, she had the right to reclaim her offspring. Alexander's thoughts on his removal are not recorded.

Almost as soon as McCaffery was gone, Emerson tried another domestic "experiment," this time an attempt to heal class divisions between servers and served. In March 1841, he expressed a yearning for family-style intimacy by inviting the cook and "second girl" to share his family's table. The impetus for such a gesture is suggested by related anecdotes. In one, Waldo Emerson expressed discomfort with the sense that servants and masters lived parallel lives within one "family" residence. Thus he noted with chagrin in 1837 that Nancy Colesworthy had felt the need to apologize for using the front door to go to church (*JMN,* 5:338). A few years later, when his first son was just a toddler, the concerned father recognized that class consciousness developed early. Asked one day to stay at home with a domestic servant, Waldo Jr. cried and refused. Ellen Emerson's memoir quotes the young boy as wailing: "'I do not want to go with Mrs Hill! Because she has red on her face and red on her arms, and she eats at a table which is not painted [that is, not mahogany] and she is not beautiful'" (*Life,* 78-79). In Waldo Emerson's journal, a very similar tale has Waldo Jr. refusing to accompany a servant to church "because," he reportedly told her, "you live in the kitchen" (*JMN,* 7:541).[24]

Waldo Jr.'s reference to separate dining arrangements must have smote his father's idealism: the great shibboleth of America's "servant problem" was that servants were not welcome (to sit) at their employers' tables. In the "old days," liberal Americans liked to recall, waged and indentured servants had eaten with those they worked for and with; by the 1840s, though, genteel authorities forbade that practice. The realization that his young son had already noted and affirmed such class divisions likely influenced Emerson's thoughts on co-residential service. But as if unwilling to confront this thought too directly, he explained the famous invitation to his servants to share the family table (which coincided with the Ripleys' move to Roxbury) with reference not to labor reform but to a happier past. That is, he explained his second "experiment" in domestic service as an attempt to turn servants back into the familial workers associated with a rural age:

> You know Lidian & I had dreamed that we would adopt the country practice of having but one table in the house. Well, Lidian went out the other evening & had an explanation on the subject with the two girls. Louisa accepted the plan with great kindness & readiness, but Lydia, the cook, firmly refused—A cook was never fit to come to table, &c. The next morning Waldo was sent to announce to Louisa that breakfast was ready but she had eaten already with Lydia & refuses to leave her alone.
>
> (*Letters,* 2:389)

This account is not supplemented, unfortunately, by any records from Lydia or Louisa, yet its testimony is sugges-

tive of in-house workers' different status and even power. For instance, while Lidian and the affectionate Louisa apparently concurred with this reform, the cook—a worker with much more clout—did not.

Though the ill-fated invitation is often recounted with a snicker, it provides important evidence that Emerson was trying to make non-kin servants seem familial. This was no easy task in a privatized home, where only one person could be master. Though Emerson admired communal imagery—"We are all boarders at one table," notes a journal entry from July 1840, "White man, black man, ox and eagle, bee, & worm"—his son's tears remind us that, at this time, he maintained two tables in his own home (*JMN,* 7:382).

Emerson noted the contradiction but thought that abolitionists generally did not. "My dear little abolitionist," he wrote in late October 1841, "do not puff & swell so; I am afraid our virtue is a little geographical and that there are sins nearer home that will one day be found of the self-same dye as this scarlet crime of the Virginians" (*JMN,* 8:138). His next attempt to deal with one of those sins would have consequences for American letters: this time, Emerson chose a servant who shared his own philosophy and who enjoyed an unusually excellent education. While the strategy was still to relieve ruling-class anxiety by making servants familial, new issues arose when the servitor was a thoughtful Harvard man who was also remarkably handy about the house.[25]

In April 1841, only a few weeks after McCaffery left and less than a month after the Ripleys moved to Roxbury, Emerson crowed: "Henry Thoreau . . . may stay with me a year. . . . [H]e is to have his board &c for what labor he chooses to do: and he is thus far a great benefactor & physician to me for he is an indefatigable & a very skilful laborer & I work with him as I should not without him. . . . Thoreau is a scholar & a poet & as full of buds of promise as a young apple tree" (*Letters,* 2:402). As this praise indicates, Thoreau, who moved into Bush as an adult and a disciple, was not called a servant. Nonetheless, he took on gardening, home repairs, and child care, jobs that Waldo Emerson professed to enjoy but found little time to do.

Thoreau's duties were not those of the ordinary servant. Instead, resident in the Emersons' home, responsible for duties they and their female staff could not manage, Thoreau was expected, biographer Robert Richardson writes, "to look after things while Emerson was away on his now-frequent lecture tours. . . . His was a very special position, the friend who is closer than many members of the family, an addition to the inner family group, certainly not a 'hired man' or a 'boarder.'"[26] I would argue, though, that Richardson's implied "mere" indicates the extent to which many still want relations within the home to rest on familial affection. For of course, Thoreau *was* a boarder, if not a hired hand: receiving only room and board, he was closer, as Sherman Paul asserts, to "the status of a poor relation."[27] Considering, though, that mentor and student preferred to dispense with wages, and that Thoreau was not really kin, one way to explain the younger man's presence is within the terms of "disciple service," serving one's mentor without wages.[28]

Disciple service would explain a point every biographer questions: the puzzle of why Thoreau did not just live at home and walk to Bush as needed.[29] On Emerson's side, the answer would seem to lie in his desire to inculcate family-like relations among all the residents of his home, coupled with his self-image as a patron for younger Transcendentalists. For Thoreau, the advantages were somewhat different: as Sherman Paul has pointed out, his journals of this period "are full of passages on the desire to serve."[30]

It was during this period, of course, that Thoreau essayed the fumbling inquiry called "The Service." Margaret Fuller, editing the *Dial* in December 1840, rejected this essay, despite Emerson's praise. Twentieth-century scholars have agreed with her assessment: the essay does not represent Thoreau's greatest literary skill. But when Thoreau's willingness to live at Bush is considered alongside his juvenilia, it is plain that the young man was groping for a life mission, one he viewed in terms of dignified self-abnegation. "The Service" was one attempt to determine what that mission might be. The braver attempt, a term at disciple service in a sage's home, was typically Thoreauvian in its insistence that the explorer not write about, but experience, a serving life.

Before moving into the Emersons' home, this stalwart had written: "All those contingences which the philanthropist, statesman, and housekeeper write so many books to meet are simply and quietly settled in the intercourse of friends."[31] One such "contingence" was the masterservant relationship, which Thoreau hoped to realize and improve upon through friendship. This aim Emerson would no doubt have applauded. Unfortunately, the homemaker's ideals could not keep pace with his need for service—nor, perhaps, with his taste for domestic mastery.

This lapse was not entirely Emerson's fault: he could not have known how swiftly his neighbor would come to find service uncomfortable, nor that reigning cultural notions of service would infect even Thoreau's independent mind. Nor, in all likelihood, could Emerson have fully realized how much his expectations had been shaped by a desire for non-kin coresidents who knew and kept their "place." If either man was susceptible to reigning notions of his day—and it seems quite likely that both were—then good intentions were unlikely to paper over the unpalatable truth that one of the two was the servant, and one the master.

Relations no doubt looked placid enough on the surface: "Henry Thoreau," Emerson wrote in early 1842, had been "one of the family for the last year" (*JMN,* 8:165). But Thoreau himself seems to have been troubled: "I want to go soon," he had written, a few weeks earlier, "and live

away by the pond" (*JHDT,* 299). One source of his disease is suggested by Emerson's letters home, which do not demonstrate the equal friendship Thoreau had moved in to find. Not that Emerson ignored his unhired man: indeed, he was punctilious about sending Thoreau his regards. If those regards sometimes sound like the slaveholder's "Howdy to the servants," that patronizing echo is pertinent. So is the paucity of reference to Thoreau's happiness or housework, though Emerson probably did not intend a slight. As Paul has noted, the Harvard-trained servant was quickly "taken for granted, superserviceable, the perfect transcendental handy man."[32] According to the domestic advice guides of the day, invisibility was desirable: "good" servants were prized for their near-ectoplasmic attendance. This was one of the reasons many wage-payers imagined slaves made better servants (while those with first-hand experience of chattel servants had their doubts). But the more important reason to consider chattel unintrusive was that, like disciple servants, they did not bring waged relations into the home.

"Sisters & brothers," Emerson opined to Caroline Sturgis, "must not pay each other money, must they?" (**Letters,** 7:481). His decision to "adopt" rather than employ Thoreau was based on this same credo; what's more, his disciple fully agreed, at least in principle. One of Thoreau's favorite mottos from the Hindu teacher Menu was that the pure man "must avoid service for hire."[33] So it was not oppression or exploitation that caused Thoreau to be less remunerated than most chattel servants. On the contrary, his unhired status was undoubtedly a mutual decision, pleasing both to the servant-conscious Emerson and the service-conscious Thoreau. It was precisely because this wagelessness helped Emerson to conceive of his disciple as poised somewhere between "servant" and "family member," paid employee and class equal, that Thoreau could seem to "solve" his guru's servant problem. He did not solve Lidian's staffing troubles: she continued to employ waged domestic servants the whole time Thoreau served at Bush. More to the point, he did not solve his own. In fact, it seems to have been his uncertain siting that most bothered Thoreau about disciple service.

The doubts began almost immediately. In a journal entry written on his first night at Bush and headed "At R. W. E.'s," Thoreau wrote: "the civilized man has the habits of the house. His house is a prison, in which he finds himself oppressed and confined, not sheltered and protected. He walks as if he sustained the roof; he carries his arms as if the walls would fall in and crush him, and his feet remember the cellar beneath. His muscles are never relaxed. It is rare that he overcomes the house, and learns to sit at home in it" (*JHDT,* 253). The resentment, verging on fear, of this startling passage indicates more than first-night jitters. As Thoreau's letters and journals of this period indicate, his uneasy position continued to irritate: soon, he would dissociate himself from his menial post. Writing to Lidian's sister, Lucy Jackson Brown, he planned to erect barriers: "I shall hold the nobler part at least out of the service."[34]

Of course, Thoreau was not everyone's idea of an easy co-resident. As another neighbor, Nathaniel Hawthorne, noted, "Mr. Emerson appears to have suffered some inconveniency from his experience of Mr. Thoreau as an inmate. It may well be that such a sturdy and uncompromising person is fitter to meet occasionally in the open air, than to have as a permanent guest at table and fireside."[35] The observation should be taken with a grain of salt: Hawthorne was a man so devoted to his privacy that he might have projected his insularity onto Emerson. Yet it is true that Emerson began to question Thoreau's "buds of promise" during the very period he turned the erstwhile apple tree into a servant. This was not because Thoreau worked badly or shirked: when Waldo set out for Europe in 1847, Lidian asked that Henry return to Bush, though this time in the dignified role of secretary. She must have known about the discomfort he denied to Waldo Emerson; she probably recognized, too, that things would run more smoothly if the mentor were too far away to ruffle his disciple's feathers.[36]

For whatever Thoreau told Emerson—"I am well and happy in your house," the disciple wrote—the Sage was not able to help his neighbor investigate the ideal friendship much on Thoreau's mind in his serving days (*Correspondence,* 84). Emerson probably thought he did, but Thoreau himself held a different view: in writings intended for other readers, he portrayed himself as a god forced to serve a king.[37]

Apollonian imagery could have been a laconic joke, but its implication of cosmic imbalance strongly indicates Thoreau's dis-ease. At the same time, of course, Apollonian imagery is rather arrogant, the consequence, perhaps, of seeing through inflated illusions. "I am constrained," Thoreau wrote Lucy Jackson Brown, "to live a strangely mixed life" in which "all I hear about brooms and scouring and taxes and house keeping [reminds me that] even Valhalla might have its kitchen" (*Correspondence,* 76). Such a room in the Emerson home should not have surprised the practical Thoreau; that it did so suggests the degree of glamor with which he had once invested a servant's role. The glamor soon faded, though Thoreau served faithfully for over a year. When he left, he published two accounts of disciple service while living far from the precincts of Valhalla.[38]

The first account was a mocking review of J. A. Etzler's *The Paradise Within the Reach of All Men, Without Labor, by Powers of Nature and Machinery.* As might be expected, Thoreau scorns those who evaded labor, even when the servant-surrogates were not human. "We saw last summer," the essay recalls, "a dog employed to churn for a farmer's family, travelling upon a horizontal wheel, and though he had sore eyes, an alarming cough, and withal a demure aspect, yet their bread did get buttered for all that."[39] Dismissing Etzler's claims that, with proper technological design, "kitchen business" could be simplified to reduce domestic staff, the erstwhile Apollo suggests that those who would eat should cook for themselves. Calling for moral, not mechanical, reform, Thoreau spoke highly

of manual labor, and insisted that fuzzy dreamers knuckle down to practical work.

It was a most Thoreauvian message, and one with which Emerson might have agreed. Yet the veiled criticism of the young man's next essay might have raised hackles back at Bush. In "The Landlord," it is clearer that non-kin co-residence could have inspired resentment in a servant's breast, for in this essay, published in October 1843, Thoreau portrays the great-souled hero as one characterized by his welcoming home. Whether "The Landlord" is a Transcendentalist is open to question, but he is certainly one who dissolves social rankings in his all-encompassing bonhomie.

The ideal landlord, wrote the Emerson's ex-boarder, "is a man of more open and general sympathies, who possesses a spirit of hospitality which is its own reward, and feeds and shelters men from pure love of the creatures."[40] So far, this sounds like the man Emerson wanted to be: in fact, it is easy to imagine the Sage reading this and feeling pleased at such graceful praise. But "such universal sympathies" could have their drawbacks for co-residents, when "so broad and genial a human nature . . . would fain sacrifice the tender but narrow ties of private friendship to a broad, sunshiny, fair-weather-and-foul friendship for his race." As Thoreau could have learned from his time at the Emersons', "the farthest-traveled is in some measure kindred to him who takes him into the bosom of his family," while "he treats his nearest neighbor as a stranger."

Since Thoreau was one of Emerson's nearest neighbors, both spiritually and geographically, this sentiment hints at grievances based on overwork or neglect. In one of the ironies of the Emerson marriage, Waldo Emerson's calls for a simpler, more private domestic life were contradicted by the open board he kept during the hectic period Lidian called "Transcendental times." In fact, both Lidian and her domestic staff were exhausted by his hospitality: Nancy Colesworthy, one of the most obstreperous Bush servants, once threatened to post a sign saying, "This House is not a Hotel" (*Life,* 71-72). Thoreau, who was not obstreperous, may have posted his version of the sign for her and let him who had eyes to read it, read.

Though he does not mention it in "The Landlord," Thoreau's own home (that is, his parents'), often took in boarders. So he may have been referring to his kinfolk's virtues when he described the ideal home as one in which all guests were welcomed by a host whose hands are callused. Emerson's hands, despite good intentions, were not hardened by manual labor. Nor was his home a place in which a "traveler steps across the threshold, and lo! he too is master," at least not if that traveler was a Concord rambler abruptly transformed into a servant.[41] But if the threshold was not a servant's place, the once-surprising kitchen might be. "[W]hy," this essay asks, "should we have any serious disgust at kitchens? Perhaps they are the holiest recess of the house."

Back at Bush, where Emerson may not have been privy to the "Valhalla" sentiment, there is no sure evidence that the householder read his disciple's essays as an attack. But we do know that the two men's friendship began to decline between 1842 and 1843 and that Emerson was wont to remark that his neighbor did not live up to early promise.[42] What is less frequently noted is that Emerson was changing, too, perhaps most significantly by resolving to appear in public as an abolitionist. In his 1844 speech on the emancipation of West Indian slaves, delivered only a few months after the appearance of Thoreau's Etzler review and "The Landlord," Emerson openly sympathizes with the slave. He shows a good deal less fellow-feeling for the waged domestic servant: according to this homemaker, waged service relations are "precarious."[43]

He was as grudging, privately, in his attitude toward abolitionists: he described them, in a journal entry, as "an altogether odious set of people, whom one would be sure to shun as the worst of bores & canters" (*JMN,* 9:120). Nor was he persuaded that antislavery had solved the servant question: "Two tables in every house!" he groaned, in an entry from 1844. "Abolitionists at one & *servants* at the other! It is a calumny that you utter" (*JMN,* 9:127). But he seems to have been convinced, after Thoreau's departure, that he himself could do no better, an admission that could have helped push him, albeit reluctantly, into supporting abolition. In the speech that announced that support, Emerson argued from expediency, stating that it was "cheaper to pay wages than to own the slave."

Obviously, moral punning is important: the "wages" indicated here are not to be equated with mere money. In part, Emerson meant to indicate a surcease of guilt: "Whilst we sit here talking & smiling," he noted, after Thoreau's departure, "some person is out there in field & shop & kitchen doing what we need, without talk or smiles" (*JMN,* 9:127). At the same time, though, the more grievous cost could have been to this reserved man's self-esteem or public persona. This personal exaction suggests that, when Emerson publicly extolled "the picturesque luxury of [chattel] vassalage . . . their silent obedience, their hue of bronze, their turbaned heads," aesthetic pleasure is only one advantage slaves provide. The other, perhaps more important to a middling householder, was that he thought well-treated chattel provided "silent" service.

Whatever his racist tendencies, Emerson could not have been referring here to legal strictures on slaves' ability to testify in court. More probably, he was alluding to his era's demand for ideally inaudible domestic staff. Thoreau was unlikely to have been so unobtrusive while he lived at Bush; more to the point, he had been noticeably chatty after he left. Depending on how Emerson viewed his one-time co-resident, the Etzler piece, and especially "The Landlord," were either Transcendental roman à clef, like *The Blithedale Romance,* or that bane of the private household, an airing of backstairs gossip. Either way, Thoreau's decision to broadcast his views of the erstwhile "master" could well have offended and alarmed the notoriously reserved, even standoffish, Waldo Emerson. But what could the outraged homeowner have done to protect his privacy?

Because wages had not passed between Thoreau and those he served, there was far less moral ground on which to chastise the one-time "servant" for publicizing domestic relations within the Emersons' "private" home.

Overall, then, whatever the drawbacks of waged attendance, Emerson had learned that wages kept masters masters. He did not advocate the enforced silence slaveholders visited upon their slaves. But he did believe in the maintenance of certain social ranks, such as those between a servant and the people in whose home he served. Emerson, in short, had come to see that payment of wages helped maintain hierarchies pertinent to privacy, mastery, and publication rights; that wages enforced distance, by insisting on the relative power of server and served; and that, at least for a capitalist, wages relieved guilt. Wages therefore offered a more moral, though still "precarious," foundation for in-house service relations. To say so was to move a long way from the idealism of the 1830s. But it was also to foretell where Americans' thoughts on non-kin domestic service were headed.

Notes

1. Len Gougeon, *Virtue's Hero: Emerson, Antislavery, and Reform* (Athens: Univ. of Georgia Press, 1990), 46-57, 75.

2. These shifts are explained at greater length in my dissertation, "The Uneasy Relation of Domestics: Servants in the Nineteenth-Century American Family." Briefly, though, I will point out that the split between "productive" and domestic labor is outlined in Jeanne Boydston, *Home and Work: Housework, Wages, and the Ideology of Labor in the Early Republic* (New York: Oxford Univ. Press, 1990); servants' mobility is explained in Robert J. Steinfeld, *The Invention of Free Labor: The Employment Relation in English and American Law and Culture, 1350-1870* (Chapel Hill: Univ. of North Carolina Press, 1991). Finally, the best single study of waged domestic service in the American nineteenth century is Faye E. Dudden's *Serving Women: Household Service in Nineteenth-Century America* (Middletown, Conn.: Wesleyan Univ. Press, 1983). All have been important in my formulations of antebellum thoughts on domestic service.

3. Mrs. Clarissa Packard [Caroline Howard Gilman], *Recollections of a Housekeeper* (New York: Harper & Brothers, 1834), 130.

4. Fitzhugh's claim appears in *Cannibals All! or, Slaves without Masters,* ed. C. Vann Woodward (Cambridge: Harvard Univ. Press, 1960), 220.

5. See *The Journals and Miscellaneous Notebooks of Ralph Waldo Emerson,* 16 vols. ed. William H. Gilman et al. (Cambridge: Harvard Univ. Press, 1960-1982), 7:115. Hereafter, journal citations appear parenthetically as *JMN.*

6. "Religion" was delivered in Boston on 22 January, and in Concord on 24 April 1840. See *The Early*

Lectures of Ralph Waldo Emerson, Volume III, ed. Robert E. Spiller and Wallace E. Williams (Cambridge: Harvard Univ. Press, 1972), 275. Volume III is hereafter abbreviated as *EL.*

7. *The Selected Letters of Lidian Jackson Emerson,* ed. Delores Bird Carpenter (Columbia: Univ. of Missouri Press, 1987), 7. Hereafter abbreviated as *SL.*

8. See her letters to William Whiting from February and March of 1848, in the Emerson Family Papers at the Houghton Library, Harvard University. The first is reprinted in *SL,* 139-41.

Because this article treats both the public and the private Ralph Waldo Emerson and includes references to Lidian Emerson and other members of the family, I have used first names when referring to the actions of the Emersons in the private sphere and "Emerson" or "Waldo Emerson" when discussing the lecturer and public figure most familiar to scholars of American literature.

9. Ellen Tucker Emerson, *The Life of Lidian Jackson Emerson,* ed. Delores Bird Carpenter (Boston: Twayne Publishers, 1980), 48. Hereafter abbreviated as *Life.* I have amended an "of of" printed in Carpenter's text.

10. This point is most apparent in advisors' silence on husbands' household duties. But for a strong statement of the wives' domestic sway, see Charles Butler, *The American Lady* (Philadelphia: Hogan & Thompson, 1836), 218-19.

11. American Sunday-School Union, *Ann Connover* (Philadelphia: American Sunday-School Union, 1835), 20-21.

12. To keep social ranks in their proper position, Alcott concludes: "I will not, indeed, say that any thing like as much credit is due to her as to him; but I may say, and with truth, that she was an important auxiliary in producing the results that have been mentioned." See William Alcott, *The Young Woman's Guide to Excellence* (Boston: Charles H. Peirce, 1847), 35-37.

The book, written in 1836, was held back for eleven years; that is, neither Lidian nor Waldo were likely to have read it until after their experiments were concluded. I would argue, though, that its ideas were probably in circulation before Alcott published them, if only through friendly intercourse among the Alcott cousins and the Emersons.

13. Emerson delivered "Home" in Boston on 12 December 1838, and in Concord on 20 March 1839. See *EL,* 23, 31.

14. William Gilmore Simms, "The Morals of Slavery," as reprinted in *The Pro-Slavery Argument; as maintained by the most distinguished writers of the Southern States* (Charleston: Walker, Richards & Co., 1852), 214. The essay, an attack on Harriet

Martineau's comments about the South, appeared in the *Southern Literary Messenger* in 1837, and was reprinted as a pamphlet in 1838.

15. This lecture was delivered in Boston on 15 January 1840 and in Concord on 22 April 1840; see *EL,* 256. The last cited comment virtually quotes a Notebook "D" entry dated 28 June 1839; see *JMN,* 7:220.

16. Annie Russell Marble says that this was Lidian's judgment on the idea of boarding with the Alcotts, a hint that Abba Alcott's discomfort with Emerson's wife could have been returned, or at least perceived. See *Thoreau: His Home, Friends and Books* (New York: Thomas Y. Crowell, 1902), 112.

17. Ralph Waldo Emerson to George Ripley, 15 December 1840, *The Letters of Ralph Waldo Emerson,* 9 vols., ed. Ralph L. Rusk and Eleanor Tilton (New York: Columbia Univ. Press, 1939-1994), 7:437. Hereafter abbreviated as *Letters.*

18. Eleanor Tilton, editor of volume 7 of *Letters,* describes the Volume 7 version as an early draft of the letter finally sent, and suggests that Rusk's version, in *Letters* 2, may be closer to what the Ripleys finally received. I have used passages from both drafts because each provides a slant on Emerson's doubts about joining Brook Farm. Note that the "solidly do" sentence appears in both.

19. "Domestic Life," *The Complete Works of Ralph Waldo Emerson,* 12 vols., (Boston: Houghton Mifflin Company, 1870), 7:116-17.

20. Glenna Matthews comments perceptively on what she calls Emerson's attempt "to combat the application of invidious caste distinctions to domestics." She points out, for instance, that while there is much to praise in his intentions at this time, it is not at all clear how his "distinctions" are going to be dissolved. See Matthews's critique in *"Just a Housewife": The Rise and Fall of Domesticity in America* (New York: Oxford Univ. Press, 1987), 37.

21. See Waldo's instructions to Lidian that the boy's chores were to be yardwork, carpentry, care of poultry and horses, and childminding (*Letters,* 7:375). Waldo expected "the girls," that is the cook and maid, to do in-house chores while a part-time gardener did heavy work in the yard.

In practice, Waldo's staff management was as uncertain as his wife's had been. One month after McCaffery arrived in Concord, Waldo admitted: "The cold weather until yesterday has given me at least no appetite for gardening & its preliminaries, so that I have still left him to the women, & have not summoned him to my side" (*Letters,* 2:279).

22. *Works,* 2:52-53.

23. Emerson's sense of ownership, or at least guardianship, was common among benevolent employers.

See, for instance, the ways in which the Salem Female Charitable Society ignored its charges' parents as it thought best, in Carol S. Lasser, "A 'Pleasingly Oppressive' Burden: The Transformation of Domestic Service and Female Charity in Salem, 1800-1840," *Essex Institute Historical Collections* 116 (July 1980): 156-75.

24. It is tempting to read these two stories as versions of one incident; as far as I could learn, though, there is little evidence either way. In both, the proposed outing has to do with attending church, though in Ellen's tale the boy is left behind and in her father's the boy is being offered a chance to go. Additionally, two different servants are referred to in the incidents. Because Waldo Sr.'s account was written on or near the date of his son's tears, and Ellen's is obviously family legend, the former is probably the more reliable anecdote, but both, of course, are instructive.

25. An earlier attempt to accomplish the same end was the suggestion, broached just after Emerson wrote Ripley declining to join Brook Farm, that the Bronson Alcott family move in at Bush. It is no accident that this letter repeats phrases he used in writing to the Roxburyites: "I am quite intent on trying the experiment of manual labor to some considerable extent & of abolishing or ameliorating the domestic service in my household. Then I am grown a little impatient of seeing the inequalities all around me, am a little of an agrarian at heart and wish sometimes that I had a smaller house or else that it sheltered more persons. So I think that next April we shall make an attempt to find house room for Mr Alcott & his family under our roof." Though the Alcotts were not invited to work as domestic servants, their presence was obviously expected to relieve Waldo's guilt about his comfortable living arrangements. For instance, Emerson planned to reduce his home's domestic staff from four or five to one full-time and one part-time worker, plus of course Abba May Alcott and Lidian Emerson. This scheme never got further than the planning stages, because Abba May had a "kink" against non-kin co-residence and perhaps no great liking for Lidian. See *Letters,* 2:371; and Madelon Bedell, *The Alcotts: Biography of a Family* (New York: Clarkson N. Potter, 1980), 160-61.

26. Robert D. Richardson Jr., *Henry Thoreau: A Life of the Mind* (Berkeley and Los Angeles: Univ. of California Press, 1986), 103.

27. See Sherman Paul, *The Shores of America: Thoreau's Inward Exploration* (Urbana: Univ. of Illinois Press, 1958), 95. Paul cites Sanborn's comment that Thoreau lived at Bush like a "younger brother or a grown-up son," a formulation that would probably have pleased Emerson. Thoreau's views, however, come across more clearly in the references to himself as Apollo, and in the texts he produced while living at Bush.

28. It may be this experiment that led Carl J. Guarneri to state that "Distrust of the cash nexus made [Emerson] forgo house servants." Although it is clear that Emerson *wished* to do away with such workers in his home, this paper shows that his attempts to do so were short-lived. See Guarneri, *The Utopian Alternative: Fourierism in Nineteenth-Century America* (Ithaca: Cornell Univ. Press, 1991), 48.

29. Annie Russell Marble claims that Thoreau moved to Bush to oblige the Emersons (92), and Walter Harding suggests that access to his mentor's library could have appealed to the voracious reader (*The Days of Henry Thoreau* [New York: Alfred A. Knopf, 1966], 130). Sherman Paul proposes that it was an experiment in Transcendental friendship, but also a way to devise a freer schedule which gave greater scope to Thoreau's individualist nature (94).

30. Paul, 18.

31. See *The Journal of Henry David Thoreau, Volume I,* ed. Bradford Torrey and Francis H. Allen (Salt Lake City: Peregrine Smith Books, 1984), 190. The abbreviation *JHDT* indicates Volume I.

32. Paul, 96.

33. He also liked Menu's caste-minded dictum that menial work could not humble a Brahmin, whose soul was "transcendently divine." Thoreau's selections from this Asian code, or scripture, were published as "The Laws of Menu," *The Dial* (January 1843): 331-40. Sherman Paul believes Thoreau had read Menu by December 1839—that is, as he was formulating "The Service" and before he went to Bush (71).

34. *The Correspondence of Henry David Thoreau,* ed. Walter Harding and Carl Bode (New York: New York Univ. Press, 1958), 47. Hereafter cited in text and abbreviated *Correspondence.*

35. Nathaniel Hawthorne, *The American Notebooks,* ed. Randall Stewart (New Haven: Yale Univ. Press, 1932), 176. Stewart suggests that Emerson was uncomfortable with Thoreau's brusque manner and points out places in which he lamented the same.

36. I would note, in passing, that this second stay found Thoreau somewhat bolder, at least in letters to the absent Waldo. Not only did he address his mentor by his first name, but he also essayed a rather pointed humor concerning the absent man's family circle. In one letter he boasts: "Lidian and I make very good housekeepers. . . . [and Edward, the Emersons' youngest son] very seriously asked me, the other day, 'Mr. Thoreau, will you be my father?'. . . . So you must come back soon, or you will be superseded." Though Waldo would have known, presumably, how to interpret Thoreau's wit, he would probably also have recognized, at some level, the pitfalls of affectionate co-residence.

The cited letter is dated 14 November 1847; that is, while Waldo was in England, and unable to return "soon." An earlier and milder jibe at Emerson's absences appears in a letter from Thoreau's first residence, in which the wandering affections are Edith Emerson's. See *Correspondence,* 189 and 76.

37. Walter Harding and Carl Bode call the story of Apollo and Admetus "one of Thoreau's favorite symbols," but do not observe that he used it most frequently during his term as a domestic servant (see, for instance, *Correspondence,* 47 and 76). Note, too, Emerson's use of the imagery in 1836 (*JMN,* 5:208-09).

38. Thoreau was even less at ease in the Staten Island home of William and Susan Emerson. Part of his discomfort there was that he did not believe he aided his host-employers. "I do not feel myself especially serviceable," he wrote to his mentor, "to the good people with whom I live, except as inflictions are sanctified to the righteous" (*Correspondence,* 112).

39. According to Wendell Glick, Thoreau reviewed the book at Emerson's request. The review, intended for the *Dial,* eventually appeared in the *United States Magazine and Democratic Review* in November 1843. See Glick, "Paradise (To Be) Regained: Textual Introduction," *Reform Papers* (Princeton: Princeton Univ. Press, 1973), 275. Thoreau's remark about canine service appears on page 23.

40. Henry David Thoreau, "The Landlord," *The Writings of Henry David Thoreau,* 20 vols. (Boston: Houghton and Mifflin, 1906), 5:153. Subsequent quotations from this essay appear on 154-56.

41. If that traveler were a fellow-boarder, the situation might be different: in 1846, the Emersons turned Bush into a boardinghouse under the management of Mrs. E. C. Goodwin. This final experiment was successful to the extent that relations with the new housekeeper were cordial during and after her co-residence, and that the Emersons shared their private home with assorted non-kin. It was noticeably less successful in relieving Lidian of household cares. Ellen remembered that "keeping the entries & doorsteps and parlour free from litter" somehow became her mother's duty, "for Mrs Goodwin with all her children and the boarders was very busy attending to the providing and the chambers." See *Life,* 106-07 and *Letters,* 3:331, 398, 411, and 456.

42. Robert Sattelmeyer, "'When He Became My Enemy': Emerson and Thoreau, 1848-49," *New England Quarterly* 62 (June 1989): 192. Sattelmeyer comments that the early rift simmered for several years, finally bursting into explicit conflict after Thoreau's second residence at Bush.

43. "Emancipation in the British West Indies," *Works* 11:101. All quotations from this address are on page 101 of this edition.

Eric Murphy Selinger (essay date 1994)

SOURCE: "'Too Pathetic, Too Pitiable': Emerson's Lessons in Love's Philosophy," in *ESQ: A Journal of the American Renaissance* Vol. 40, No. 2, 2nd Quarter, 1994, pp. 139-82.

[*In the following essay, Selinger examines Emerson's view on marriage and love, and the friction between earthly love and a more divine love.*]

I take my title from **"Illusions,"** the final essay in *The Conduct of Life.* Emerson has just named women as "the element and kingdom of illusion," and defied anyone to "pluck away the . . . effects and ceremonies, by which they live." In a moment he will announce with chilling calm that "[w]e are not very much to blame for our bad marriages." The pivot between these statements comes in a punning interjection that discovers or exposes the illusions of matrimony, not in men's or women's actual faults, but encoded in the letters that name the space between them, the married state: "Too pathetic, too pitiable, is the region of affection, and its atmosphere always liable to *mirage.*"[1] In this essay I want to dwell not on **"Illusions"** per se but on the lines of thought about affection and illusion, marriage and mirage, friendship and love that connect this essay to earlier Emersonian texts. What would it mean to take such observations seriously? What ethic and epistemology of love would it take for Emerson to mean them in the way we now grant he means the more general philosophical investigations of, say, **"Self-Reliance," "Circles,"** or **"Experience"**?[2] And how do these lessons in love's philosophy respond to Puritan and sentimental strains in nineteenth-century New England culture, especially to its continuing concern with amorous idolatry?

Critics as a rule shy away from Emerson's thoughts on love, dismissing them as the bristlings of a congenitally cold fish or writing them off as mere moralizing expressions of Platonic piety. John McCormick, for example, tugs in embarrassment at the "bland blanket of transcendental uplift" in the "published, public, quasi-philosophical" work. He is relieved to find a "much more human figure" lurking in the journals, one with a "pulsing, emotional and often torn spirit" we pity and understand, if not necessarily admire.[3] In a book-length study of love, sex, and marriage in Emerson, Erik Ingvar Thurin feels compelled to reassure us that Emerson "married twice, and some of his best friends were women."[4] Even Emerson himself, rereading "Love," laments, "I . . . have much more experience than I have written there, more than I will, more than I can write" (*JMN,* 7:368).

Some critics take this journal entry as an invitation to psychobiography, to a patient recovery of that unnamed experience.[5] It is tempting to account for Emerson's ideas through references to his "one first love" and second marriage or to the hopes and frustrations he found in his friendships with, among others, Margaret Fuller and Caroline Sturgis, and in doing so lose sight of the independent complexity of the ideas themselves. Like David Van Leer, I "find such accounts convincing, [but] I do not feel . . . that Emerson's meaning is all that clear," and while I share the impulse to "read through to the why of Emerson's statements," I too "find myself all too often stuck on the preliminary question of what."[6] We need to read **"Love"** and **"Friendship"** more closely as texts, with more attention to structure and wordplay than the essays seem at first to demand, and set them in a context of other works on similar subjects, both earlier and later. Perhaps the "much more experience" Emerson could not record in **"Love"** finds its way, not just into the journals and letters, but into the essay that he finally called **"Experience,"** with its hardest of sayings on human relations. In **"Love"** (1841), two people are "shut up in one house to spend in the nuptial society forty or fifty years" (*CW*, 2:109); in the later **"Experience"** (1844), "[m]arriage (in what is called the spiritual world)" is declared "impossible, because of the inequality between every subject with every object"; and even outside the spiritual world, "[t]he great and crescive self . . . ruins the kingdom of mortal friendship and love" (*CW*, 2:44). The earlier essay seems a little self-conscious, but here in the mordant, memorable passages of **"Experience,"** we learn that self-consciousness, "the discovery we have made, that we exist[,] . . . is called the Fall of Man"; and that since this fall our dearest loves are mere "idolatries," since love itself can never "make consciousness and ascription equal in force" (*CW*, 3:43, 44).

These bracing admonitions trust in Kant, not the Bible. The gulf between noumenal subjects and phenomenal objects, and not the second commandment, chastens our desires. But in the same manner that Emerson describes "the subject" as "the receiver of Godhead" (*CW*, 3:44), so does he powerfully and suggestively infuse other philosophical terms with theology. This conjunction of Puritan love-doctrine, romantic solipsism, and American individualism, which we find, in one way or another, throughout Emerson's published works, marks him as an important and unrecognized theorist of human affections. Spanning the "failure of continuity" Bernard Duffey sees between the colonial and postromantic American imaginations, Emerson restates the Calvinist discrimination between human and divine loves that haunted Anne Bradstreet and other early American writers in terms that have preoccupied American poets ever since. Walt Whitman and Emily Dickinson, Marianne Moore, Wallace Stevens, and Adrienne Rich—all respond, directly or indirectly, to what the deeply Emersonian feminist Elizabeth Cady Stanton calls "our Protestant idea" of "the Solitude of Self." All wonder what can and will happen when that sole self falls in love.[7]

1

To understand Emerson's lessons in love's philosophy, we must first appreciate the continuing force of certain Puritan notions of love in nineteenth-century America. As historians Karen Lystra, Ellen K. Rothman, and others maintain, the inclination to idolatry troubled lovers and ministers, poets and novelists, long after the colonial period. "I beg

you, my dearest Mary," wrote Samuel Francis Smith in an 1834 love letter, "see that you do not worship any image of clay—and pray that I may be kept from similar idolatry." "Daily you occupy a portion of my thoughts," Mary Holyoke Pearson wrote to Ephraim Abbot in 1812, "too large a share, I fear. Could I love my Creator in proportion to the creature, I should be happier."[8] Jonathan Edwards, by then a half-century dead, would have been pleased with her qualms. "The primary object of virtuous love is *being*, simply considered," he argues in *The Nature of True Virtue*. "No exercise of love, or kind affection to any one *particular* being," whether one's self or a suitor, a husband, wife, or child, "has *anything* of the nature of true virtue," although from a benevolence toward and consent to "being in general," which will come in the end to mean God, "may arise exercises of love to particular beings, as objects are presented and occasions arise."[9]

Popular poet Martin F. Tupper's warning to husbands in 1854, "Take heed lest she love thee before God; that she be not an idolator," thus uses a familiar discourse. But how serious is he when a few pages earlier in *Proverbial Philosophy* he defines love as "a sweet idolatry enslaving all the soul, / A mighty spiritual force, warring with the dullness of matter," with no worry at all about the contradiction.[10] Admittedly, Tupper is not much of a poet, and British at that, but his awkward lines illuminate an important development in American romantic culture; as Lystra writes, "[T]he metaphorical distance between God and man . . . was collapsing" in the nineteenth century. Though human romance once provided a vocabulary to describe the soul's romance with God, that metaphorical relation was reversed, so that Nathaniel Hawthorne tells Sophia in 1839, "I have really thought sometimes, that God gave you to me to be the salvation of my soul." Stanley Cavell speaks of the "horror" expressed by Hawthorne, as by Poe, that "marriage cannot bear up under its metaphysical burden": a burden of "ensuring the existence of one's other."[11] In practice, as Lystra shows, this might entail the burden of acting as another's "symbol of ultimate significance,"[12] say by forgiving all of another's sins—an absolution that no earlier intercessor in Protestant America had been licensed to give.

"Within the context of the nineteenth-century religion of romantic love," writes Lystra, "Milton's lines must be changed to reflect a different emotional logic: 'he for God in her, she for God in him.'"[13] Likewise the Puritan strictness that saw an end to marriage at death and death as God's final check on our impulse to idolatry drifts out of focus through the colonial and post-revolutionary periods. For every Gusta Hallock who agonizes over the way love for another person displaces her love for God, so that God takes him away with no hope of reunion, we find many lovers, diarists, and poets who insist on the sanctity of fervent love below and its continuation above.[14] Annis Boudinot Stockton damns death in her 1780 "Extempore Ode in a Sleepless Night by a Lady Attending on Her Husband in a Long and Painful Illness": "[T]hou canker-worm of human joy! / Thou cruel foe to sweet domestic peace!" She ignores the consequent need to wean affections, just as she avoids expressing those "doubts, and gloomy fears" an earlier Puritan poet would have worked through to reach a pious acceptance of loss by the end of the poem.[15] In an amatory acrostic "Oh, may propitious Heaven," published in the mid-eighteenth century, Martha Brewster restates the Puritan distinction between mundane and heavenly pleasures and rewards, although with no apparent conflict between "Injoying ev'ry lawful Sweet below" and "Viewing by Faith, the Fountain whence they Flow." But Brewster's final prayer for God to "Renew our Love to Thee, and Love us up to Heaven" implies that the couple will be carried up as such, a proposition that the Puritan Bradstreet, while tempted, scrupled to suggest.[16] In "To a Lady on the Death of Her Husband" (1773), Phillis Wheatley is still more explicit in her vision of a heavenly reunion:

> There fix thy view, where fleeter than the wind
> Thy *Leonard* mounts, and leaves the earth behind.
> Thyself prepare to pass the vale of night
> To join for ever on the hills of light:
> To thine embrace his joyful spirit moves
> To thee, the partner of his earthly loves;
> He welcomes thee to pleasures more refin'd,
> And better suited to th' immortal mind.[17]

There may be no marriage in the hereafter, but in the "new domestic heaven" of these poems, couples are rejoined just as mothers and children meet "beyond" in the elegies for children increasingly common by the early nineteenth century.[18]

We do not insult these poems by calling them sentimental, for they unabashedly champion the force and value of human sentiment against the chill of strict theology. They anticipate the "feminization of American culture" that Ann Douglas traces in the nineteenth century, a group of related shifts in the political, theological, and literary realms. And though this feminization is evident in the increasing presence and popularity of women authors, we find its effects in the writing of men as well. The heaven Wheatley envisions in 1773 may still distinguish between earthly pleasures and those enjoyed by the "immortal mind," but in its companionable domesticity, it looks forward to the one detailed by Congregationalist minister George Cheever in 1853: "[N]ot the dim incomprehensible universality of omnipresence merely, but a place for our abode . . . with as intimate a home circle, as the dearest fireside on this earth can have, nay incomparably more intimate and personal and definitely local in our Father's House."[19]

Against this grandly sentimental ground a few figures stand out, startling in their contrast. We find some women—Mary Moody Emerson and Margaret Fuller most memorably—who announce a feminist suspicion of romantic union. They suspect its idealizations, the overvaluation of men by women lovers or the etherealization of women by their men. And they suspect erotic attraction, which leads to the entanglements of marriage and children and to a loss of self, a life lived purely through and for another. "[L]iberty is a better husband than love to many of

us," noted Louisa May Alcott in her diary on Valentine Day, 1868.[20] Though Fuller may have longed in private for "a full, a godlike embrace from some sufficient love," in public she disavowed the constraints of such desire.[21] We can "live too much in relations," she warns, falling into "distraction, or imbecility, from which [we] can only be cured by a time of isolation." Hence her praise of celibacy, of the "old bachelors and old maids" whose numbers (in percentage of the population) rose throughout the nineteenth century. Hence also her praise for the thought of "a wise contemporary" who observed that "union is only possible to those who are units. To be fit for relations in time, souls, whether of man or woman, must be able to do without them in the spirit."[22]

Is this unnamed contemporary Emerson, who called himself "I whose name is Unit" in an 1840 letter to Fuller (*L,* 2:258)? Certainly he had made similar pronouncements. If religion tells us "'[i]t is not good for man to be alone,'" he told the Second Church congregation in 1829, "[i]t says also, 'Go into thy closet and shut thy door.'" "These are not two laws but one," he continues, for "no man is fit for society who is not fit to stand alone" (*CS,* 2:84).[23] In his later **"Historic Notes of Life and Letters in New England,"** Emerson looks back on a trend from 1820 to 1840 directly opposed to the rising importance of human love in sentimentalism, one that binds him to Fuller in a common cultural protest. He writes, "It seemed a war between intellect and affection," a war that intellect won. "Instead of the social existence which all shared, was now separation. . . . The young men were born with knives in their brain," ready to cut all social ties through "introversion, self-dissection, anatomizing of motives," and "driven to find all [their] resources, hopes, rewards, society and deity within the self" (*W,* 10:325, 329). In 1839 Hawthorne unself-consciously courted Sophia as "Mine own self," and attests that he felt "as if [his] being were dissolved, and the idea of [Sophia] were diffused throughout it. Am I writing nonsense?" he demands. *Yes,* one imagines Emerson's young men would reply. As Emerson himself grew up to testify, the truest love has nothing to do with such "maudlin agglutinations."[24] At the heights of affection all forms indeed dissolve into one, but lovers are not mingled:

> Plain and cold is their address,
> Power have they for tenderness;
>
> . . . . .
>
> They can parley without meeting;
> Need is none of forms of greeting;
> They can well communicate
> In their innermost estate;
> When each the other shall avoid,
> Shall each by each be most enjoyed.

> (*W,* 9:117)

That last couplet of **"Celestial Love,"** wonderfully perverse, cuts against the sentimental grain. And it typifies Emerson's pronouncements on love. Too much the skeptic to extol sentimental enthusiasms below, he is equally scathing on the dream of domesticity above. In a journal entry from November 1840, later used in **"Swedenborg; or, The Mystic,"** he chides the Swedish visionary for his "attempt to fix & eternize the fireside & nuptial chamber[,] to fasten & enlarge these fugitive clouds of circumstance[,] these initial pictures through which our first lessons are prettily conveyed." A relationship of "one to one, married & chained through the eternity of Ages, is frightful . . . & is no more conceivable to the soul than the permanence of our little platoon of gossips, Uncles, Aunts, & cousins." Rather, in heaven "[w]e meet & worship an instant under the temple of one thought & part as though we parted not, to join another thought with other fellowships of joy" (*JMN,* 7:532).[25] This motility applies to earthly loves as well. Cupid, Emerson's figure for "Initial Love," has a mincing, insinuating approach. "[H]is wish is intimacy, / Intimater intimacy, / And a stricter privacy" in which "The impossible shall yet be done, / And, being two, shall still be one." But erotic unions do not last, for

> As the wave breaks to foam on shelves,
> Then runs into a wave again,
> So lovers melt their sundered selves,
> Yet melted would be twain.
>
> (*W,* 9:108-9)

Hence the poet's decree in **"Give All to Love"** that the lover even on earth must

> Keep . . . to-day,
> To-morrow, forever,
> Free as an Arab
> Of thy beloved.
>
> (*W,* 9:92)

Ideal affections may light on two and even join them into one, but they always flicker elsewhere, onward and upward. A Platonic ladder of affection leads from human loves to a union with what he calls in **"The Over-Soul"** "the Lonely, Original, and Pure" (*CW,* 2:174) and elsewhere simply the "gods":

> Though thou loved her as thyself,
> As a self of purer clay,
> Though her parting dims the day,
> Stealing grace from all alive;
> Heartily know,
> When half-gods go,
> The gods arrive.
>
> (*W,* 9:92)

As a love poet, Emerson is uninspiring. He calls himself "cold because [he is] hot,—cold at the surface only as a sort of guard & compensation for the fluid tenderness of the core," but he found few ways to embody either that tenderness or the keen brilliance of his colder self in verse (*JMN,* 7:368). Neoplatonism is hardly a poetically restrictive philosophy—not for the Elizabethans or the Italian poets of the sweet new style, not for his contemporary Poe—and when Emerson expresses his faith that we are all essentially one man, one mind, at best longing to be alone with the alone, as an apology for his erotic attraction

to a woman in **"To Eva,"** we glimpse the compositional potential. Similarity acts across the threatening difference of sexes, granting a license to love:

> Ah! let me blameless gaze upon
> Features that seem at heart my own;
>   Nor fear those watchful sentinels,
> Who charm the more their glance forbids,
> Chaste-glowing, underneath their lids,
>   With fire that draws while it repels.
>
> (*W,* 9:95)

But this man who calls himself "a photometer" and not "a stove" is unable to get much heat into his measures (*L,* 4:33). Perhaps even philosophical intensities have too erotic a tone, derived from the loves that nourish them, for Dame Philosophy as much devours as consoles her admirers:

> Philosophers are lined with eyes within,
> And, being so, the sage unmakes the man.
> In love, he cannot therefore cease his trade;
> Scarce the first blush has overspread his cheek,
> He feels it, introverts his learned eye
> To catch the unconscious heart in the very act.
> His mother died,—the only friend he had,—
> Some tears escaped, but his philosophy
> Couched like a cat sat watching close behind
> And throttled all his passion. Is't not like
> That devil-spider that devours her mate
> Scarce freed from her embraces?
>
> (*W,* 9:374-75)

The most affecting moments in Emerson's love poetry are those in which philosophy has not yet pounced on and throttled or devoured her sage, as in unpublished poems to his first wife, Ellen—those he wrote before her untimely death seventeen months into their marriage, which though clumsy move us in their vain hope for "graybeard years" together,[26] and especially the less artful, more anguished lines he wrote in the first weeks after her death:

> In yonder ground thy limbs are laid
> Under the snow
> And earth has no spot so dear above
> As that below
>
> And there I know the heart is still
> And the eye is shut & the ear is dull
>
> But the spirit that dwelt in mine
> The spirit wherein mine dwelt
> The soul of Ellen the thought divine
> From God, that came—for all that felt
>
> Does it not know me now
> Does it not share my thought
> Is it prisoned from Waldo's prayer
> Is its glowing love forgot
>
> (*JMN,* 3:228)

The ignorance confessed in the last lines, which keeps their author from too quick a compensation for his loss, holds philosophy at bay. As in **"Dirge,"** the well-paced and achingly restrained elegy for his brothers, these lines for Ellen do not reject the ascent of souls promised in Plato and Plotinus. But they speak their piece from "the middle of the mount": not the proud, uncrowded heights of **"Celestial Love"** but a "lonely field" and wooded valley, a Concord fall's "long sunny afternoon" (*W,* 9:145).

Emerson would concern us far less if he were more or less maritally unhappy, more or less erotically repressed, more or less consistently a Neoplatonist poet bucking the age's sentimental trend. Mary E. Hewitt has a poem, tediously brief, in which Plato sets aside philosophy to hymn the wrinkles of his "fair friend, Archeanassa."[27] That Emerson reclaims such philosophy for verse marks an interesting nineteenth-century tug-of-war, but little more. But when we turn from the primarily Neoplatonic poems to the more complex fabric of Puritan, romantic, and transcendental ideas in the sermons, lectures, and essays, we find a more interesting struggle underway in which the Hamlet-like self-consciousness mourned in **"Philosopher"** is found to be an unhandsome and incurable philosophical condition and not a more or less pitiable psychological case, one where the most moving moments come after philosophy, not before it. I do not suggest that these texts form a seamless garment of Emersonian thought. But when we look back with the hard sayings of **"Experience"** and other late essays in mind, a pattern or development emerges in which an old fear of idolatry is secularized into a skeptical, scrupling epistemology of love.

2

Emerson's early sermons frequently extol both Platonic and sentimental pieties, with little public worry over the tension between them. In December 1827, shortly before the twenty-four-year-old minister met his first wife-to-be, he preached to her church that "by the strong cords of friendship and love God invested the fireside with its sacred delights"; Rusk notes that a year later in another sermon to her church, Emerson explained a contrasting Platonic progress whereby "the affections . . . tended to expect perfection in the loved person, and from seeking perfection in the human friend were led to seek it in God."[28] As Joel Porte observes, the sermons also show that Emerson maintained an inordinate attachment to Puritan ideas of sin and innate depravity, to the sublime rhetorical claims of Edwardsian Calvinism, and to the demands of a "great preeminent unpartaken relation" with "his Maker" (*CS,* 2:84).[29] "Our religion takes the individual out of the mass and reminds him of the burden he must bear alone," Emerson observes in 1829, six weeks after his wedding to Ellen. "It recommends the duties of self-command, of the connexion of the soul with God;—it teaches that to each soul is its own destiny which is stript of all connexions and friendships—the soul hath neither father nor mother nor wife nor sister," so that "before God we are solitary unrelated men" (*CS,* 2:82, 84). This isolating Puritan strain will be my first concern.

I will focus on Sermon CIV, preached on 12 January 1831, a month before Ellen's death, for in it the tension between

the connection of the soul with God and the interhuman "web of relations" that should "awaken [the] heart and [the] conscience amid the present despondency" is particularly notable (*CS,* 3:84). Addressing members of a Unitarian philanthropic group, the Howard Benevolent Society, Emerson chose as his text Luke 10:27: "Thou shalt love the Lord thy God with all thy heart, and thy neighbor as thyself." An appropriate passage, no doubt, given the audience, but a thorny one as well: will love for God turn out to be the same as, a model for, a part of, or the actual substance of our love for one another? Reformed theology held that inasmuch as our love is human, it is suspect. "Adam Rent in himselfe from his Creator," as John Winthrop put it, and thus "rent all his posterity allsoe one from another, whence it comes that every man is borne with this principle in him, to love and seeke himselfe onely."[30] "No one is able to love God from his whole heart, etc., and his neighbor as himself," writes Luther. This commandment is "an impossible law."[31] Emerson's immediate theological precursor, William Ellery Channing, denied the doctrine of original sin on which such charges are based. Jesus came to "set free our imprisoned energy for love"; and it is *our* love, in its potential "largeness and liberty," that both Channing and Jesus, in Channing's view, address.[32] According to Robert Lee Patterson, Channing believes that "[t]he affections of the home, . . . are intended to overflow until they embrace the entire human race." And yet even for Channing love for God is the only love commensurate with, and able to repay, the soul's true yearnings. "In language which reminds us of Edwards," Patterson writes, "he warns us that fellow human beings will disappoint us by their imperfections, and sometimes their disloyalty." But Channing does not take the common orthodox step of Edwards, who moves from this observation to "the conclusion that God is, not the supreme, but the *only* legitimate object of love."[33] As a founding gesture, proving himself at once more conservative and more radical than Channing, Emerson will so move.

At the start of his sermon Emerson promises to "present the principle on which the great class of social duties depends." He sifts through a number of possible grounds for neighborly duty, echoing in his progress the *via negativa* logic of Edwards's *Nature of True Virtue.* "[S]elf love well calculated," for example, will not do. "In any common use of the word self," he argues, "in any sense less than that infinite sense in which self-love loses itself in the love of God and the Universe," it will not suffice. Nor will our divinely commanded love for our neighbors. "[I]n that degree of strength in which the sentiment is ordinarily found," he observes, it cannot "be safely trusted as the support of such various and incessantly returning duties as we owe to others" (*CS,* 3:84, 85, 86). Not that we cannot love *anyone* properly: the sermon admits, as Luther will not, that "[t]he love of our neighbor is a principle of wonderful force where it really acts." But our love is "too capricious and discriminating," he writes, "too selfish" (*CS,* 3:87, 86). A good decade before **"Self-Reliance,"** Emerson will not sanction questioning a sense of responsibility for our neighbors.

At this point in the sermon we might expect a turn to Christ as the teacher of benevolence, since his command to "love . . . thy neighbor" prompts a lawyer to demand to know who his neighbors are, and the parable of the Good Samaritan is Christ's answer. Yet instead of a Unitarian Jesus who sets our love-energy free, Emerson offers a vision of men glorified in their dependence on deity, and he does so in such terms that we can hardly recall his earlier admission of some partial value in the love for neighbors we muster on our own. The neighbor's claim is "through God," Emerson declares, and he expands by shifting into a sublime rhetorical register that owes more, once again, to Edwards than to Channing. "The Scriptures teach us that nothing is more intimate than our relation to Him," he explains. "They teach that we are God's children, not by any metaphor but in a far stricter sense than we are the children of men. *We are made of him—we live but in him,* as the leaf lives in the tree" (*CS,* 3:87; emphasis added).[34] All love collapses into love of God; indeed, for the next four paragraphs we hear nothing of neighbors at all.

But who in love actually acts? Who loves? When we keep divine commandments we "all but identify" with God, says Emerson—an unsteady distinction, and the effort to maintain it forces him into a revealing syntactical strain. "We shall be parts of God," he writes, "as the hand is part of the body, if only the hand had a will." That "if only" reads at once as plaintive (if only it could, or did) and as mocking the very possibility. Emerson remains Unitarian enough to cling to some notion of will. But "free agency" does no good. "We are made of God as the urn is made of clay," he explains, "but separated from our great Parent by our free agency. . . . Whenever we act from self, we separate ourselves from God; when we do right, we consent to his action by our hands" (*CS,* 3:88). For Edwards, true virtue consists of a "consent, propensity and union of heart" with "being in general," rather than lying in any partial or personal affection;[35] likewise here love for a neighbor consists of allowing "a full consent between God in him and God in [us]" (*CS,* 3:89). Commandments to be holy, merciful, and perfect as our father in Heaven are otherwise not merely "impossible," as Luther said. They are incomprehensible. As for self-love, "[t]here is not an inch of ground in the Creation left" for it to stand on. "We are not," Emerson preaches, "our own" (*CS,* 3:88, 90).[36]

The sermon backs down from these rhetorical heights, chatting of fathers and brethren and even (in a cancelled passage) of an angel's voice that tells the human race, "Little Children[,] love one another." This nervous and infantilizing return to the interpersonal, to speaking of love of each other "for God's sake" and "for our own sake" (*CS,* 3:311, 91), as though the second were not just a limited vision of the first, seems required not just by the expectations of Emerson's audience, but by an internal logic as well. Though Scriptures "teach us that we are God's children . . . in a far stricter sense than we are the children of men," such strictness would seem unbearable after a while—a perspective that we cannot deny, yet which denies us the power to love of our own volition, even to love

each other in any ordinary sense of the phrase (*CW,* 3:87). Without the paternal metaphor's support, after all, impartial benevolence "for God's sake" is hard to recognize as human love.[37] The love of God's children for each other is a divinely sanctioned version of the love of parents and spouses Emerson admits might occasionally work (such love as he clearly felt for his young wife). By contrast, God's love for himself through us leaves us part of the circuit but finally out of the picture.

Throughout Emerson's career he proposes that "the ardors of piety agree at last with the coldest skepticism," shunting us away from merely social affections (*CW,* 3:40). Yet his texts vary as to precisely when these ardors or doubts will be acknowledged and how (or how closely) we may be reunited with one another. In Sermon CIV we start with the social, and when God returns as a person, a father, we fall into place as his children, our lives together restored and reassured. We find a new, less certain structure in the "Human Culture" lecture called **"The Heart,"** written in 1838, seven years after the sermon. The period between witnessed Ellen's death, Emerson's resignation from the Second Church, his travels in Europe and return to Concord, his marriage to Lidian Jackson, the deaths of Edward and Charles, the birth of Waldo, and the start of friendships with Fuller, Thoreau, and Carlyle. In the lecture Emerson struggles to make cold ardors and human warmth meet on adult grounds: grounds called "the impersonal" (*EL,* 2:279), a Platonic goal that stands opposed to any sentimental vision of domestic, fireside bliss.[38] One thinks of Emerson's unnerving journal entry, five years into his second marriage: "I marry you for better but not for *worse.* I marry impersonally" (*JMN,* 7:336). If by the 1830s, as Lystra observes, the "worst fears of early American religious leaders" were coming to pass, as "the personhood of the loved one . . . had become a powerful rival to God as the individual's central symbol of ultimate significance,"[39] Emerson does his best to undo that rivalry, and not simply by reasserting a personal God's first claim on our affections. "Personhood" turns out to be a questionable term in any context, social or religious: well before Emerson resigned his ministry he had stopped thinking of God in personal terms, and this loss of personality somehow also applies to us and to those neighbors we are admonished to love.[40]

When the loss appears in **"The Heart"** and later texts, it is flagged by the phrase "in strict science" or "in strictness." Echoing the words "far stricter sense" of Sermon CIV, these phrases hint that this impersonality comes at some cost—we must be strict, enforce it on ourselves—and that the cost is associated with a language whose tone is ungraceful, merciless, philosophical, and pure. Examining "the social relation, the powers of affection" in **"The Heart,"** Emerson is first obliged to outline a doctrine that sounds quite asocial, hardly affectionate:

> In strictness we ought to say, the soul seems to be insulated. With persons pure soul has nothing to do. . . . In strictness the soul does not respect men as it respects itself. It looks at a continual unfolding of the imper-

sonal, at a total infusion, impenetration of its own essence by the nature of justice, of truth; it postpones
persons, all persons, to this contemplation of the impersonal, the One.

(*EL,* 2:278-79)

Faced with such a blur of assertions, it helps to imagine
Emerson's concerns. What would the photographic negative of these strict assertions resemble? The soul would respect others as much, perhaps more, than it respects itself;
it would be tangled up in persons. And in the religious
more than the philosophical sense, God's disrespect of the
personal would be true. We would in fact have to love our
neighbors, and ourselves, as a condition of loving a personal God; and such affection would stem at most from a
partial infusion of our souls by the divine. This mixture of
our own and God's efforts, of eros and agape, is characteristic of the sentimental synthesis of love and religion that
developed in the early nineteenth century, recalling Thomas Aquinas, who maintains "that charity proceeds from
an intrinsic principle while still being 'added to human nature[,] . . . perfecting the will.'"[41] This vision of caritas,
rejected by the Reformation, is not the essential sameness
of human and divine affections in Channing or its symmetrical opposite, the "full consent between God in him
and God in me" of the Edwardsian moments in Sermon
CIV (*CS,* 3:89).

Emerson thus implicitly recasts the argument of Sermon
CIV in Platonic or Plotinian terms. But "strict and stern
science" teaches us a lonelier lesson than the "strict sense"
of the sermon. Our neighbors now "must" appear as em-
bodiments of our thoughts, repetitions of self: a solipsistic,
narcissistic threat we did not face when we were images
of God. And strict science requires us to confess something new, "that all persons, the very nearest and dearest,
underlie the same condition of an infinite remoteness." Before our neighbors crowded in too close; now they flee
from us, fall away, vanish.[42] "[L]over and enemy," Emerson now contends, "can never enter by infinity the precincts of selfhood." This lack of access, and not our inability to love properly en masse, makes our relations
"partial," a situation our lecturer calls "pathetic" (*EL,*
2:279).

The word "pathetic" seems to me carefully chosen against
an alternative designation of our relations as *tragic,* the vision, according to Cavell, of *King Lear* and *Othello.*
"[S]kepticism's 'doubt,'" he explains, "is motivated not by
(not even where it is expressed as) a (misguided) intellectual scrupulousness but by a (displaced) denial, by a self-
consuming disappointment that seeks world-consuming revenge."[43] The sources of Emerson's disappointment are not
hard to find: the loss of Ellen ("[S]he never disappointed
me except in her death" [*L,* 1:376]); the quotidian losses
of his marriage to Lidian ("The husband loses his wife in
the cares of the household") and a consequent sense of
"incongruities[,] defects . . . [,] surprise, regret, strife"
coming between them; and perhaps the insufficiency he
felt in the "affections & consuetudes that gr[e]w near

[him]" and in his inability to respond to them (*JMN,* 5:297,
322). In his 19 May 1837 journal entry, used in **"The
Heart,"** Emerson utilized a phrase that reappears in **"Experience."** He laments the disappointments of his connection to any ideal friend, in this case Carlyle. "We never
touch but at points," he complains.

> I am led on from month to month with an expectation
> of some total embrace & oneness with a noble mind, &
> learn at last that it is only so feeble & remote & hiant
> action as reading a Mirabeau or a Diderot paper, & a
> few the like. This is all that can be looked for. . . .
> Baulked soul! It is not that the sea & poverty & pursuit
> separate us. Here is Alcott by my door,—yet is the
> union more profound? No, the Sea, vocation, poverty,
> are seeming fences, but Man is insular, and cannot be
> touched. Every man is an infinitely repellent orb, &
> holds his individual being on that condition.

(*JMN,* 5:328-29)

The "innavigable sea" and fast-held "poverty" that isolate
in the later essay **"Experience"** (*CW,* 3:29, 46) are metaphorical restatements of the literal "seeming fences" that
Emerson dismisses here, and the later loss of Waldo might
have reminded him that while "[t]here is nothing so easy
as to form friendships & connexions," "a Tragedy" will inevitably come to give "protection" to the "helpless" gulf
between us (*JMN,* 5:17).[44]

Emerson's losses, failures, and frustrations, however,
hardly prompt the revenge Cavell describes. It is as if to
avoid such an impulse that Emerson quickly contrasts the
"absolute condition" he describes at the start of **"The
Heart"** with "the relative and actual" condition of "our
position in nature." In the latter, having to do with acts
and relations, we are "tenderly alive to love and hatred,"
"woven all over" with a vital "net" of emotions that recalls the "web of relations" (reminiscent of George Eliot)
named early in Sermon CIV (*EL,* 2:280; *CS,* 3:84). And
these loves, fears, hopes, and regrets *respect other men*
as the soul, we have read, does not (*EL,* 2:280; emphasis
added). If there are sacred "precincts of selfhood," there
are equally sacred "precincts of actual life" where "we
know ourselves as partial and social creatures." And this
partiality now opens the way to connection. "We see that
our being is shared by thousands," Emerson explains, "who
live in us and we in them." Or is it, as once was claimed
in theological terms, that something common lives in us
all? "[O]ver all men and through all men is diffused an affection"; "[i]t is an element they all breathe," which "informs each of the presence, of the brotherhood, of the
wants of the other" (*EL,* 2:279, 281).[45] While Sermon CIV
has a three-step trajectory (from comfort to strictness to
home), **"The Heart"** alternates between these absolute
and relative claims. We might call them moods of strictness and kindness, as when Emerson drops the aside that
"in general there is a great deal [of kindness] that makes
the earth habitable," while by implication strictness, which
is never "in general," would make the world uninhabit-
able, unlivable, deathly. (Indeed, "[t]he moment we indulge our affections, the earth is metamorphosed," bring-

ing it back to life.) Theology calls these moods justice and mercy. We cannot simply choose one, nor can we blithely unite them—how live in two moods at once? And yet the desire persists.[46] As when the syntax of Emerson's sermon reveals the tension between the individual and the divine will, so here we find a too-insistent phrase, an overstated case: "The Heart is as I have said a community of nature which *really does* bind all men into a consciousness of one brotherhood" (*EL*, 2:282, 290, 283; emphasis added).

Perhaps uncertain of this assertion of brotherhood—especially since earlier in the lecture conversation proves too unsatisfying, too evanescent a relation to prove its existence—Emerson tries a second and equally unsatisfying proof. He looks to glances, which intertwist like Donne's "eye-beames" to unite self and other.[47] When our gazes intersect, he writes, we realize "that all men have one soul," thus proving "the radical unity" of our nature. "We look into the eyes to know if this other form is another self; and the eyes will not lie, but they give a faithful confession what inhabitant is there" (*EL*, 2:283; cf. *JMN*, 5:8). This knowledge of the other as "another self" sits poorly, though, with what we have already heard. "[A]ll persons that surround you," Emerson says early in the lecture, "must seem to you as the thoughts, opinions, emotions, affections which have taken body and on which . . . the student soul reads . . . its own nature and law" (*EL*, 2:279). Is it "the rounding mind's eye" then, as he later puts it (*CW*, 3:44), that looks in and fills out the eyes of another? I find such concerns, attributed to the later, openly skeptical essays, implicit in two comments from **"The Heart."** "Every man meets glances," Emerson writes, "which shall illustrate for him all that he hath heard of the terrors and beauty of the Cherubim"—cherubim, linked with knowledge and perception, strictness and solitude, and not seraphim, who figure abandonment to love. And "the unity, the community of men," he insists, is grounded in "perception and acknowledgment of a strictly identical nature of which all the individuals are organs"; but that key term "strictly" reminds us of solitary, solipsistic heights, not of heavenly agape (*EL*, 2:284). Identical, he means, to *me*: moral education does not consist of discerning an *equivalent* center in you, but in finding that center is *the same* as my own.[48]

Acknowledging the one soul between us thus seems the first effort to name an adult version of "Little Children[,] love one another." But in practice, as in the poem **"To Eva,"** it seems prompted primarily by the fear that someone's "sweet dominion" over the will might be caused by something other than "[a] sympathy divine" (*W*, 9:95). Questions of narcissism, subjectivism, even idolatry arise. Am I recognizing the god in you, or just treating you like the god in me? These are difficult, unhappy questions, since the intersection of strictness and indulgence, where the soul seeks "to domesticate these rare and lofty satisfactions," has the "two societies of Marriage and Friendship" for its social site.[49] There we may be entirely satisfied by "the indulgence of affection toward one soul," Emerson assures us, because of the "infinite nature of one

soul." But are those two single souls the same? And if they are distinct, which proves the infinite nature: that of the object, or that of the indulger? "In the highest friendship," he explains, "we form a league with the Idea of the man who stands to us in that relation, not with the actual person. We deal with him as with a just, true, pure, and universal soul and make him therefore a representative to us of the entire Humanity." Such statements mark the Neoplatonist Emerson we suspect, more comfortable with ideas than with other people. And they imply, as the author himself seems discomfited to find, that our relations are not reciprocal but ascriptive, not my acknowledgment of something within you, but a deal struck, within me, with the universal soul. The lecture moves on to praise "conversation . . . the first office of friendship" and "heartiness" as "inspiration," but the cheerfulness rings a little hollow. The last word, we sense, has already been spoken: "We walk alone in the world" (*EL*, 2:288, 292, 294).

3

Less than a year after first delivering **"The Heart,"** Emerson lectured on **"Love."** In this lecture too we find allusions to "strict philosophy," according to which "there is a quite infinite distance between our knowledge of our own existence and the evidence we have for the existence of nature including that of persons"; and here too we find that since "[p]ersons are love's world," we must "descend from the high ground of absolute science and converse with things as they appear" in order to "treat of Human Life," the subject of this new lecture series (*EL*, 3:56). I will pass over this lecture, however, in favor of Emerson's revision as it appears in *Essays: First Series*. For in this version of **"Love,"** implicitly paired with **"Friendship,"** Emerson once again considers the question of love's ascriptive impulse—the "illusion" that "attributes to the beloved person all which that person shares with his or her family, sex, age or condition, . . . with the human mind itself," so that while it is "these which the lover loves, . . . Anna Matilda gets the credit of them" (*W*, 6:319). He also explores the scandal of succession, the losses and alterations that chasten our idolatries and, as he will say in **"Experience,"** make us all idealists. Recall the Puritan admonishment: "[L]et this caution be minded, that they don't love inordinately, because death will soon part them."[50] The object of my affections may vanish, but I remain, and the guilt of outlasting the one-to-one relation of love casts what the essay calls a "certain stain of error" (in the lecture it is "a certain slime" [*EL*, 3:54]) over every autobiography. "Every thing is beautiful seen from the point of the intellect, or as truth," he explains. "But all is sour, if seen as experience. . . . With thought, with the ideal, is immortal hilarity, the rose of joy. Round it all the muses sing. But grief cleaves to names, and persons, and the partial interests of to-day and yesterday" (*CW*, 2:100).

We can give the names Ellen, Edward, and Charles to those mournful "partial interests." Indeed, in the journal source for this passage, the "remembering & remembering talk with Lidian" recalled on 4 March 1838, Emerson does just that (*JMN,* 5:456). Likewise he seems to take his own sad experience—an initial and short-lived ideal love followed by a long-lasting and pragmatic "modulated" affection in which "the trick of solitariness" remains uneased—to be the human norm (*L,* 1:434, 4:33). As David Leverenz charges, Emerson "universalizes his self-pity and his inability to love Lidian," although he does so in the faith that his audience can summon up their own sad names and interests and errors, just as Whitman assumes we all have a "secret silent loathing and despair" that we long to confess.[51] Emerson may be correct, at least in a general sense, and part of the critical resistance to **"Love"** comes from a certain sentimentalism, a continuing "erotic faith" that love is aroused by the qualities of a particular beloved and that a passionate and inextricable merger of two into one can be accomplished in this life and will survive, somehow, after the grave.[52] Emerson tells us that love is prior to and superior to its objects, that we confuse the occasion of our happiness (call it Charles, Edward, Ellen, Lidian) with its efficient cause, which can be found elsewhere, within; and he holds to the line that the true union to be desired—indeed, the only one possible—is the union of the soul with the good and the beautiful, and that to attribute those ultimate virtues to any person is a snare and a delusion, a brilliant and painful mistake.[53] But Emerson has his reservations about stepping "on this ladder of created souls" up to divinity (*CW,* 2:106). We find them expressed in the essay on **"Intellect,"** a little later in the same collection, where the intellect, "void of affection," leaves each truth "eviscerated of care" (*CW,* 2:193, 194). We find the same reservations in the structure of the essay on **"Love,"** where Emerson relates a love story in three veins: sentimental, Platonic, and only finally Emersonian, this last a view that encompasses the others, but only if we read the following essay, **"Friendship,"** as the conclusion to **"Love."**

Since love begins, according to Emerson, with "a private and tender relation of one to one" (*CW,* 2:99), let us begin by examining that phrase. "Tender" has been Emerson's word for a stance toward other persons that permits or even produces connection.[54] In **"Love,"** for the first time, the word is associated with youth as well as connection, and stands contrasted with "mature philosophy." The "palpitations of joy and sorrow" that mark "the meaning of the Heart" at *any* age in **"The Heart"** (*EL,* 2:281) are here the "throbbing experience" of "every youth and maid," which Emerson the philosopher begs leave not to portray in "vivid tints" (*CW,* 2:99). More than memories of Ellen are encoded in that phrase. Although Emerson writes of tenderness earlier, "private" has no long history in the same works, and its appearance here signals a new insistence, not on love as a violation of public mores, but on its *interiority,* as though it occurs entirely within an isolated subject. Love, writes Emerson, "is a fire that, kindling its first embers in the narrow nook of a private bosom, caught from a wandering spark out of another private heart, glows and enlarges until it warms and beams upon multitudes of men and women, upon the universal heart of

all, and so lights up the whole world and all nature with its generous flames" (*CW,* 2:100). "How high that highest candle lights the dark"—until one remembers that the fire beams out, as in Wallace Stevens's poem, from the interior of a private bosom still.[55]

With that tenderness and privacy in mind, Emerson now begins the love story. The "rude village boy" and the "school girls who . . . talk half an hour about nothing, with the broad-faced, good-natured shop-boy" are characters in his quick comic sketch of a "novel of passion" replete with puns and rhetorical extravagance. But as the boy sees one particular girl and "instantly" feels "as if she remove[s] herself from him infinitely, and [is] a sacred precinct," Emerson's tone grows more serious. We read of the precinct of selfhood in **"The Heart,"** into which no other could enter, but here a distance inserts itself at the first moment of affection, as though it were a precondition for relationship. "[O]ne alone distances him," he writes; "and these two little neighbors that were so close just now, have learned to respect each other's personality" (*CW,* 2:100, 101). That respect so distances them that the beloved hardly appears, or seems needed, when Emerson describes

> the visitations of that power to [the youth's] heart and brain, which created all things new; which was the dawn in him of music, poetry and art; which made the face of nature radiant with purple light . . .; when a single tone of one voice could make the heart bound[;] when he became all eye when one was present, and all memory when one was gone; when the youth becomes a watcher of windows, and studious of a glove . . .; when no place is too solitary, and none too silent for him who has richer company and sweeter conversation in his new thoughts, than any old friends, though best and purest, can give him.
>
> (*CW,* 2:102)

The youth seems most enraptured when alone with ever-available nature, confessing his affection to a sympathetic cloud or a tree. Then a sudden shift of perspective leaves the boy a "fine madman" who merely "soliloquizes" (*CW,* 2:103). Like one of Freud's "ancient" theorists of love (like Freud himself, for that matter), Emerson cares less about the qualities of the beloved than about the character of "that power" itself.[56] Love in this essay, unlike the affections in **"The Heart,"** seems fundamentally antisocial: for all that it gives the lover to another, "it still more gives him to himself." No longer does the lover belong to family or society; rather "*he* is somewhat; *he* is a person; *he* is a soul" (*CW,* 2:104).

With this declaration Emerson closes the first part of the essay, turning from sentimental to Platonic reflections to consider "the nature of that influence" so potent over youth, naming it "Beauty" ("the flowering of virtue"). "The ancient writers," "Plato, Plutarch, and Apuleius[,] . . . Petrarch, Angelo, and Milton," are his avowed source (*CW,* 2:104, 106), those who believed that "the Deity sends the glory of youth before the soul, that it may avail itself

Emerson reads by the fireside.

of beautiful bodies as aids to its recollection of the celestial good and fair" (*CW,* 2:105-6). But how seriously does Emerson believe, for example, that "[i]n the particular society of his mate" the lover "attains a clearer sight of any spot, any taint, which her beauty has contracted from this world, and is able to point it out, and this with mutual joy that they are now able without offence to indicate blemishes and hindrances in each other, and give to each all help and comfort in curing the same" (*CW,* 2:106)? Perhaps Hawthorne thought Emerson was serious, since a counter to those lines seems to underlie the plot of "The Birth-mark." But in fact, while Emerson says this "dream of love" will serve to counteract the "subterranean prudence" of most marriages, he does *not* endorse the idea entirely and proves as bothered as Hawthorne by this unbelievable process of mutual improvement (*CW,* 2:107, 106).

Now that the ancient writers have had their say, Emerson supplies the final position that both supplements and corrects the sentimental and Platonic stances. He first disposes of the bulk of the "novel of passion." The lovers glance at one another, a moment of radical connection and unity both in **"The Heart"** and in Emerson's journals (cf. *JMN,* 5:8), little knowing "the precious fruit" to come of "this new, quite external stimulus." The plot quickens: "From exchanging glances, they advance to acts of courtesy, of gallantry, then to fiery passion, to plighting troth

and marriage." Even the wedding night appears in the account, albeit obliquely: "Passion beholds its object as a perfect unit. The soul is wholly embodied, and the body is wholly ensouled." This unity encompasses the lovers as well. "Does that other see the same star, . . . read the same book, feel the same emotion, that now delight me?" the lovers wonder, but only when they are physically apart, the distance between them quite different from the ontological unseen gulf that intellect and strict science finds between every self and other, lover and beloved. They are, by Emerson's account, quite happy, "discovering that willingly, joyfully, they would give all as a ransom for the beautiful, the beloved head, not one hair of which shall be harmed" (*CW,* 2:107, 108). A companionable ideal that may have been Emerson's model was an instance of "recorded loneliness . . . during his absence from Ellen."[57]

"But the lot of humanity is on these children," the next sentence grimly announces; and while we are hardly surprised—they seem "tender" in both senses of the word—we must wonder which lot? Mutability? Isolation? Considering both the text and Emerson's biography, the first seems the obvious answer. "Danger, sorrow, and pain arrive to them, as to all"; and in a phrase that sounds to me as sad as "Jesus wept," we learn the inevitable result: "Love prays." But these prayers make "covenants with Eternal Power in behalf of [a] dear mate" (*CW,* 2:108). As "means to effect a private end," these prayers are not the "contemplation of the facts of life from the highest point of view" that Emerson commends in **"Self-Reliance"** (1841), where they are rather seen as "vicious" expressions of "meanness and theft" (*CW,* 2:44). The union such prayer brings in this essay (whether it is with God or the beloved we cannot be sure) is "yet a temporary state," because the lover's soul will soon learn that neither God nor the beloved is as personal as once thought. "[A]rous[ing] itself . . . from these endearments, as toys," the soul "aspires to vast and universal aims"—a "mature philosophy" (*CW,* 2:108, 99). This recapitulates the earlier and absurdly easy progress toward divinity, where lovers could point out one another's blemishes "without offence" (*CW,* 2:106), but now the results turn sour. "The soul which is in the soul of each," Emerson writes, "craving a perfect beatitude, detects incongruities, defects, and disproportion in the behavior of the other." Hence arise, not "mutual joy," but "surprise, expostulation, and pain" (*CW,* 2:108; cf. *JMN,* 5:297).

The couple has reached the limits of both sentimental love, with its vision of fireside union, and Platonic love. One imagines them retreating to the verse of Hewitt or a cold draft of Plotinus for relief. We have returned to the moment in Emerson's lecture where "the heart" is "repelled" by the multitude as such and by each individual as "an infinitely repellent orb" (*EL,* 2:288, 279)—the moment when it finds itself "betrayed" and rallied in marriage or friendship, "concentrating its desire . . . on one." But in **"Love"** the painful surprise comes from within the private and tender relation, and it brings back with renewed force the questions that plagued us earlier. Is "[t]he drawing of the entire satisfactions of the heart from the indulgence of affection toward one soul" allowed by "the infinite nature" of the indulger or of the soul beheld? Are these souls in fact the same? Does forming a "league with the Idea . . . not with the actual person" in order to "make him a representative to us of the entire Humanity" mean we never truly deal with him at all (*EL,* 2:288)? Emerson must somehow allow for the mundane experience of being, in his brutally unsentimental phrase, "shut up in one house to spend in the nuptial society forty or fifty years," despite the soul's new maturity and aspiration to universals (*CW,* 2:109).

As if in response to these questions, Emerson distinguishes the "signs of loveliness, signs of virtue" that drew the lovers together (and that appear and reappear through time) from "the substance" of virtues. "[T]he regard changes," he writes—we are meant to think both of the physical glance and of the new estimation of these lovers for one another's virtues—and this new regard "repairs the wounded affection." And "as life wears on, . . . a game of permutation and combination of all possible positions" enables the pair "to employ all the resources of each, and acquaint each with the strength and weakness of the other" in a distinct, but complementary, process (*CW,* 2:108). Not "the infinite nature of one soul" as in **"The Heart,"** but the nature of this relationship, which in its temporal duration makes a virtue of mutability's wear, can provide the employment and acquaintance that **"Love"** endorses in place of mere "satisfactions" (*EL,* 2:288). The two "resign each other, without complaint, to the good offices which men and women are severally appointed to discharge *in time*" (*CW,* 2:109; emphasis added). Furthermore, Emerson suggests that we can know nothing but our idea of the other: "All that is in the world which is or ought to be known, is cunningly wrought into the texture of man, of woman." He abandons metaphors of politics and commerce in favor of a little couplet on taste, Locke's and Edwards's favorite trope for the incorrigibility of sense. "The person love does to us fit," he quotes Abraham Cowley, "Like manna, has the taste of all in it" (*CW,* 2:108-9).

There is something unsatisfying about this resolution, for it fails to resolve the tension between nuptial society and the solitary love of virtue, the moods of indulgence and strictness, of experience and intellect, that Emerson has tried to reconcile in structure and in substance since Sermon CIV. **"The Heart"** offers one vision of balance—"[t]he highest conversation," which "seems to be a marriage of the intellect and the affections" (*EL,* 2:292). But in this essay, conversation is undercut by misunderstandings and subjectiveness, and such a marriage seems forced as a best-case scenario.

What Emerson suggests as an alternative, or at least as a firmer foundation for conversations to come, is something called "the real marriage." After surprise and expostulation, after the wounded affections' repair, after a certain chastening, as the couple's "once flaming regard is sobered by time in either breast, and . . . becomes a thorough good understanding," the lovers "exchange the pas-

sion which once could not lose sight of its object, for a cheerful, disengaged furtherance, whether present or absent, of each other's designs." The pun on "disengaged" seems to me one of Emerson's finest. Only after leaving off "engagement," after all, can we be truly married. Year by year, he writes, this exchange of passion for loving disengagement involves a "purification of the intellect and the heart" (*CW,* 2:109). This twofold purification comes as the lovers of **"Love,"** if not Ralph Waldo and Lidian Jackson Emerson, turn into friends.[58] And "celestial" friendship, not romantic or prudential or "natural" marriage, will turn out to be the ground for their progress toward divinity as well (*EL,* 2:288).

4

In her extensive treatment of the **"Love"** and **"Friendship"** essays, Mary Kupiec Cayton describes what she calls Emerson's third "stage" of love, the stage that involves these purifications, as "thin and unconvincing." Following Carl F. Strauch, and for solid biographical reasons, she reads the essay on friendship as exploring a social alternative to Emerson's unsatisfying marriage to Lidian, one based on his "Concord Experiments" (as Cayton's punning chapter title puts it) with a community of friends centered on Fuller and Sturgis. "If marriage did not completely fulfill his need for relation," Cayton observes, "friendship—at least in 1839 and 1840—seemed to." Yet even friendship proved to have its crises and limits, provoked in part by the difference between Victorian men's and women's expectations of what friendship would involve; and, she concludes, "[t]he fear that like everything else in life, friendship will prove 'phenomenal' forces him to ascend to a spiritual plane," where in some ideal state, "the feeling that 'the *not mine is mine*'" might last, and friendship "overcome the gap between 'the ME and the NOT ME' (as Emerson had put it in *Nature*)."[59] I cannot quarrel with Cayton's overall sense of the essay and its context. Yet her glancing reference to the "phenomenal" nature of friendship touches on what is to me the heart of the essay, its epistemological claims.

Unlike Sermon CIV, the lecture, or the essay on **"Love,"** **"Friendship"** gives an overt philosophical framework for its assertions, one in which words like "phenomenal" must be read as terms of art. Emerson is not only a Neoplatonic but also a romantic philosopher, and when he writes in **"Love"** that the lovers must "exchange the passion that once could not lose sight of its object" he means the word "object" in its full post-Kantian force (*CW,* 2:109). Not only does passion, with its eye on an "object" or end, use the other as a means, it must treat the other as an object inasmuch as he or she remains in the phenomenal and not the noumenal realm, an object of perceiving subjectivity. Emerson repeats what he wrote in **"The Heart"**: "In strictness, the soul does not respect men as it respects itself." But in **"Friendship,"** he also provides a metaphysical foundation for this lesser respect:

> I cannot choose but rely on my own poverty, more than
> on your wealth. I cannot make your consciousness tan-

tamount to mine. . . . I cannot deny it, O friend, that the vast shadow of the Phenomenal includes thee, also, in its pied and painted immensity,—thee, also, compared with whom all else is shadow. Thou art not Being, as Truth is, as Justice is,—thou art not my soul, but a picture and effigy of that.

(*CW*, 2:116)

My assurance of your substantial identity, in the philosophical sense, has fallen away. "I who alone am" know only phenomena, not things (let alone persons) in themselves, and I "see nothing in nature whose existence I can affirm with equal evidence to my own." Indeed here, "the Deity in me . . . usually connives" to raise "thick walls of individual character, relation, age, sex, circumstance" between us—that is to say (as **"The Heart"** does not) that the condition of insularity by which we hold our individual being is in general a function of the God in me, and not something that he serves to counteract (*CW*, 2:120, 115).

The purification of the heart thus involves exchanging a passion for objects for the knowledge of the other's phenomenality.[60] We must leave off clutching, wean our affections, grow out of our proprietary interests in one another, and learn to "hold [this relation] by simple affinity" of "virtue with itself," which allows the interior deity to negate the walls it helped raise (*CW*, 2:115). This connection can yield the "higher self-possession" that, Emerson claims in **"The Over-Soul,"** we attain through "common nature" and "unity of thought"; and it anticipates the alluring independence that he describes in **"Swedenborg,"** where "it is only when you leave and lose me by casting yourself on a sentiment which is higher than both of us, that I draw near" (*CW*, 2:165, 4:72). Yet Emerson knows full well that in practice our virtues will not often coincide: like the "high freedom of great conversation," where two souls become as one, this coincidence is "an evanescent relation,—no more." In strictness, in the world of intellect, we will always be reminded of the concern that arises in **"The Heart,"** namely, that a friend's or beloved's virtues are in the eye of the beholder. "We overestimate the conscience of our friend," he writes; we feel "a property in his virtues," as if they were our own, and in time we realize that they are in some sense our own, since we "bestow" virtues and "afterwards worship the form to which we have ascribed this divine inhabitation" (*CW*, 2:122, 115, 116).

On these epistemological grounds, Emerson revives the lingering Puritan fear of loving creation more than its creator, of "idolatry" with its "adulterate passion" and "perpetual disappointment" in the other (*CW*, 2:126, 117). We need no theology to warn us of these dangers, he seems to say, but theology gives us the precise, prophetic term for mistaking our own creative power, bestowals, and amorous imagination for another's intrinsic virtues. And we cannot easily evade Emerson's argument, even through appeals to his own biographical frustrations. At stake, after all, is the danger that love will make us proclaim another's sovereign selfhood as real to us as our own, only to find

ourselves ignored or undermined, ready for a fall. If "idolatrous love attributes an absolute value to the loved one," this "first falsity" inevitably leads to "searing disappointment" and "bitter solitude," so observes not Emerson but Simone de Beauvoir, a century later and a continent away.[61]

As we realize that we have forgotten our own strength, that we have slipped from bestowing virtues to worshipping our creation, our hearts may be purified, albeit painfully. Yet this purification might well prompt the intellect to retreat from the social realm altogether, to rally elsewhere and alone in the solipsistic heights of virtue and "strict science." To ward off this retreat the intellect too must be purified. Musing on this second purification, Emerson names "two elements that go to the composition of friendship," each of them equally "sovereign." The second he names "Tenderness," a word that reminds us of the couple in **"Love."** The first, "Truth," which receives more attention, involves the moral sense, as it appears in the "municipal virtues of justice, punctuality, fidelity and pity." Solipsism necessarily betrays these social virtues, and by insisting on their continued claim Emerson restrains the intellect, both in its enthusiasms and its potential disappointment (*CW*, 2:119, 121).

At the close of **"Friendship,"** Emerson turns to a third modulating force, one that we have not seen before: the power of seeming, of the heart's imagination. "True love transcends the unworthy object," he writes in the final paragraph, because all objects as such are unworthy of the way we must treat them for true friendship to take place, which is "as a god," or as a "receiver of Godhead" as he puts it in **"Experience"** (*CW*, 2:127, 3:44). But such love is not necessarily delusional: it may be a self-consciously fictive gift, one that does not infantilize us and that is too well aware of the powerful and performative nature of its praise to be idolatrous. Intellect demands that we sacrifice the passionate love-object on the altar of strict science, that we confess it is in some sense sinful, a lie. To bring the love-object back, as the heart desires, we impute selfhood, virtue, divinity to the other. "Friendship demands a religious treatment," Emerson writes, and in this essay it receives one. Through an erotic economy of love and disappointment we have returned to a gracious economics of salvation, where both strictness and indulgence, justice and mercy, can be satisfied (*CW*, 2:123).

In the **"Love"** and **"Friendship"** essays Emerson seems confident that such imaginative satisfactions will suffice, in part because they imitate God. "It never troubles the sun that some of his rays fall wide and vain into ungrateful space," Emerson writes, revising Matthew 5:45 (*CW*, 2:127). As gratuitous bestowers of value, we are likewise enlarged by so shining.[62] Later in his career the dicta are more bitter. "Never can love make consciousness and ascription equal in force," he asserts in **"Experience,"** since "[t]he soul is not twin-born, but the only begotten, . . . admitting no co-life" (*CW*, 3:44, 45). While I am tempted to explain this shift in tone by referring to a biographical event (the death of Waldo is an obvious candidate), I suspect that it stems from the ambivalence inherent in Emerson's philosophy of love. The self-enlarging bestowals at the end of **"Friendship"** are only one of Emerson's proposed solutions to our epistemological solitude. "The one thing which we seek with insatiable desire, is to forget ourselves," he writes at the end of **"Circles"**—that is, among other things, to forget the stateliness, deference, and poise incumbent on our separateness (the heart of his later essay on **"Manners"**) and be "surprised out of our propriety" by the "flames and generosities of the heart" (*CW*, 2:190). On the other hand, if the "evanescence and lubricity of all objects" turns out to be "the most unhandsome part of our condition," perhaps with more of Emerson's restraint we might find our condition "handsome" indeed, which is to say *attractive*, drawing objects and persons to us without the need to clutch at them and hold them fast (*CW*, 3:29).[63] Finally, Emerson's theory of bestowal is unavoidably complicated by his continuing assumption that love must be deserved, a mathematically proportionate response to the worth of the beloved: a bestowal of virtues that is then valued, rather than, as in Whitman, a bestowal of value itself.[64] When M. Wynn Thomas speaks of the "cold emotional logic" of the end of **"Friendship,"**[65] he has this underlying structure of appraisal in mind—the essayist's solar expansiveness so different, in tone if not in metaphor, from Whitman's appreciative "[l]ove like the light silently wrapping all."[66] In bestowing virtues, doesn't Emerson simply make a gift and then marry for the money? Both shame the beloved, and the telling makes it worse.

If I risk distorting the tone of the record, however, I do so for two reasons. First, while Emerson is unable to maintain the poise of, or write a love poetry commensurate with, his theory of bestowal, I believe Whitman does, extolling its pleasures and its therapeutic value. And despite my reservations, there seem to be strong grounds for admiring not only the logic of Emerson's doctrine but its ethic as well. I will close with these grounds, since they involve a summary of Emerson's progress from the theology of love where we began to the "too pathetic, too pitiable" world of affection and illusion that **"Love," "Friendship,"** and the later essays confront.

In Sermon CIV Emerson retreats from his strongest assertions, based on a God that dwells in the human heart, to a comforting rhetoric of father and child. Behind this segregation and hierarchy of the human and divine lies a need to keep God, who mediates between us, both above us and distinct from us. For if love for neighbors is "through God," then something of the machinery of the "'triangular' desire" René Girard describes in the opening sentence of *Deceit, Desire, and the Novel* must come into play: "Don Quixote has surrendered to Amadis the individual's fundamental prerogative: he no longer chooses the objects of his own desire—Amadis must choose for him." Emerson's sermon suggests that Christians cannot choose their poor: God chooses for them. And yet, as Girard also points out, "[t]he impulse toward the object is ultimately an impulse toward the mediator," so much so that "the desiring sub-

ject wants to become his mediator; he wants to steal from the mediator his very being of 'perfect knight' or 'irresistible seducer.'" As long as the mediator, in this case God, stays fundamentally distinct from the desiring subject, or the man who wants to love his neighbor, no rivalry can ensue. But in "internal mediation," where the distinction dissolves (say, when God takes up his seat within the soul), "the subject is torn between two opposite feelings toward his model, the most submissive reverence and the most intense malice. This is the passion we call hatred."[67]

Girard's description illuminates Miles Standish's feelings toward John Alden, or Dickinson's (on occasion) toward Christ, perhaps better than any specific moment of ambivalence in Emerson. Yet he names a threat that Emerson must check: that as God becomes less a father above than an internalized god, one's access to the other or even to the god in the other will be thwarted, paling by comparison to the access granted to that god, or to put it philosophically, the access to one's own existence. This is the threat we left behind many pages ago, when we touched on the potential for tragedy in Emerson's epistemological isolation. The skeptic may end up like Othello, who (in Gerald L. Bruns's commentary on Cavell's reading of the play) "wants to possess, and can never have . . . Desdemona's own self-certainty of her fidelity. . . . [H]e wants to not-doubt Desdemona as she not-doubts herself, as Descartes could not-doubt his own existence."[68] Skepticism in *Othello* leads to murder: a tragic case Emerson is at pains to avoid. (As we have seen, he anticipates and counters, before Hawthorne, the deathly trajectory of "The Birthmark"). I would love to say that the "true marriage" of **"Love"** and **"Friendship"** presents us with a comic alternative, perhaps something like the screwball comedy of remarriage that Cavell describes in *Pursuits of Happiness* and elsewhere.[69] But while points of similarity emerge—the importance of conversation, of being "alert and inventive," to "add rhyme and reason" to the drudgery and "daily needs" of life together (*CW*, 2:121)—Emerson's vision seems never so shared, so reciprocal as Cavell's. He makes his student the philosopher seem unabashedly sentimental, for when "the air clears and the cloud lifts" as at the end of **"Illusions,"** the scene contains only one mortal and "the gods": "they alone with him alone" (*W*, 6:325).

Between tragedy and comedy, though, comes pathos, the "too pathetic, too pitiable" world. For Emerson never gives up his faith in the moral sense and returns again and again to those "municipal virtues of justice, punctuality, fidelity and pity" (*CW*, 2:121) where the heart finds its mature, philosophical home.[70] Since effusions of affection (as in Whitman) are rather less common than tales of submission or revenge or the "metaphysically desperate degree of private bonding" in tragic romance (to which Cavell refers), the return to and revision of Calvinist theology in Emerson may be no more radical than it is admirable.[71] If never two were one, then surely the "municipal virtues" need to have their say. And is there nothing noble in the scene as Emerson's lovers, "really" married through friendship, by ascription deified, through Concord take their solitary way?

Notes

1. *The Complete Works of Ralph Waldo Emerson,* ed. Edward Waldo Emerson, 12 vols. (Boston: Houghton Mifflin, 1903-4), 6:315-16. Quotations from "Illusions" and other essays in *The Conduct of Life,* from "Historic Notes of Life and Letters in New England," and from Emerson's poems are taken from this edition and are cited in the text as *W,* with volume and page number. Other Emerson texts quoted in this essay, cited parenthetically by volume (when appropriate) and page number, are as follows:

   CS The Complete Sermons of Ralph Waldo Emerson, ed. Albert J. von Frank, 4 vols. (Columbia: Univ. of Missouri Press, 1989-92).

   CW The Collected Works of Ralph Waldo Emerson, ed. Alfred R. Ferguson and Joseph Slater et al., 4 vols. to date (Cambridge: Harvard Univ. Press, Belknap Press, 1971-).

   EL The Early Lectures of Ralph Waldo Emerson, ed. Stephen E. Whicher, Robert E. Spiller, and Wallace E. Williams, 3 vols. (Cambridge: Harvard Univ. Press, Belknap Press, 1959-72).

   JMN The Journals and Miscellaneous Notebooks of Ralph Waldo Emerson, ed. William H. Gilman and Ralph H. Orth et al., 16 vols. (Cambridge: Harvard Univ. Press, Belknap Press, 1960-82); deletions Emerson made in the process of writing have been ignored in the interest of readability.

   L The Letters of Ralph Waldo Emerson, ed. Ralph L. Rusk, 6 vols. (New York: Columbia Univ. Press, 1939).

2. The major figure in a twentieth-century reevaluation of Emerson as an American philosopher, or as one who calls for an American philosophy, is Stanley Cavell. See "Thinking of Emerson" and "An Emerson Mood," in *The Senses of Walden* (San Francisco: North Point, 1981), 121-60; "Emerson, Coleridge, Kant (Terms as Conditions)," chap. 2 of *In Quest of the Ordinary: Lines of Skepticism and Romanticism* (Chicago: Univ. of Chicago Press, 1990), 27-49; and the lectures collected in *This New Yet Unapproachable America* (Albuquerque: Living Batch Press, 1989).

3. John McCormick, "'The Heyday of the Blood': Ralph Waldo Emerson," in *American Declarations of Love,* ed. Ann Massa (New York: St. Martin's Press, 1990), 35.

4. Erik Ingvar Thurin, *Emerson as Priest of Pan: A Study in the Metaphysics of Sex* (Lawrence: Regents Press of Kansas, 1981), 21. Only outside the literary world, it seems, has this side of Emerson been approached with due consideration. Philosopher Irving Singer finds a place for him in his three-volume history of *The Nature of Love* as a transitional thinker between romantic and modern notions. The essay "Love," Singer argues, "com-

bines Hegelian, Neoplatonic, and Christian elements in a way that reveals why each of these is so unsatisfactory from our contemporary perspective" (*The Nature of Love,* 3 vols. [Chicago: Univ. of Chicago Press, 1984], 2:484). But even Singer gives Emerson only a paragraph and a half of explication, hardly time to explore the subtleties of this one essay, let alone the several that make up his *ars amatoria.* For the sort of attention these issues deserve (taking Emerson at his words), we would turn to Cavell, but though he has written about Emerson and about love and skepticism, he has not yet done both at the same time.

5. See, for example, the efforts of biographers like Ralph L. Rusk (*The Life of Ralph Waldo Emerson* [New York: Charles Scribner's Sons, 1949]); Henry F. Pommer (*Emerson's First Marriage* [Carbondale: Southern Illinois Univ. Press, 1967]); Gay Wilson Allen (*Waldo Emerson: A Biography* [New York: Viking Press, 1981]); and John McAleer (*Ralph Waldo Emerson: Days of Encounter* [Boston: Little, Brown, 1984]). See also the work of Carl F. Strauch ("Hatred's Swift Repulsions: Emerson, Margaret Fuller, and Others," *Studies in Romanticism* 7 [1968]: 65-103); and the more recent critical work of Mary Kupiec Cayton (*Emerson's Emergence: Self and Society in the Transformation of New England, 1800-1845* [Chapel Hill: Univ. of North Carolina Press, 1989]).

6. David Van Leer, *Emerson's Epistemology: The Argument of the Essays* (Cambridge: Cambridge Univ. Press, 1990), xiii. I suspect that my agreement with Van Leer stems from our common debt to Michael Colacurcio.

7. Bernard Duffey, *Poetry in America: Expression and Its Values in the Times of Bryant, Whitman, and Pound* (Durham: Duke Univ. Press, 1978), xiii; Elizabeth Cady Stanton, "The Solitude of Self," in *Elizabeth Cady Stanton, Susan B. Anthony: Correspondence, Writings, Speeches,* ed. Ellen Carol Du Bois (New York: Schocken, 1981), 247.

   American love poets continue to display the influence, direct or indirect, of Emersonian ideas on love. Gertrude Reif Hughes notes that "there is something deeply Emersonian about Rich's severe renunciation of her lovers' union" in the poem "Origins and History of Consciousness" ("'Imagining the Existence of Something Uncreated': Elements of Emerson in Adrienne Rich's *The Dream of a Common Language,*" in *Reading Adrienne Rich,* ed. Jane Roberta Cooper [Ann Arbor: Univ. of Michigan Press, 1984], 152-53). Virginia M. Kouidis sees Marianne Moore and Mina Loy as quarreling, in love poems and other poems, with the claims of "Experience." See her "Prism into Prison: Emerson's 'Many-Colored Lenses' and the Woman Writer of Early Modernism," in *The Green American Tradition: Essays and Poems for Sherman Paul,* ed. H. Daniel Peck

(Baton Rouge: Louisiana State Univ. Press, 1989), 115-34. I have traced this tradition of response in readings of Walt Whitman, Hart Crane, and John Ashbery in "When I'm Calling You: Reading, Romance, and Rhetoric in and around Hart Crane's 'Voyages,'" *Arizona Quarterly* 47 (winter 1991): 85-118, and I have recently finished a larger study, *What Is It Then Between Us? Traditions of Love in American Poetry,* in which it plays an important role.

8. Quotes are taken from Karen Lystra, *Searching the Heart: Women, Men, and Romantic Love in Nineteenth-Century America* (New York: Oxford Univ. Press, 1989), 243; and Ellen K. Rothman, *Hands and Hearts: A History of Courtship in America* (New York: Basic Books, 1984), 19.

9. Jonathan Edwards, *The Works of Jonathan Edwards,* vol. 8, *Ethical Writings,* ed. Paul Ramsey (New Haven: Yale Univ. Press, 1989), 544, 541; emphasis added.

10. Martin F. Tupper, *Proverbial Philosophy* (London: Thomas Hatchard, Picadilly, 1854), 162, 159.

11. Lystra, *Searching the Heart,* 240; Nathaniel Hawthorne, *The Letters, 1813-1843,* ed. Thomas Woodson, L. Neal Smith, and Norman Holmes Pearson, vol. 15 of the Centenary Edition of *The Works of Nathaniel Hawthorne* (Columbus: Ohio State Univ. Press, 1984), 330; Stanley Cavell, "Two Cheers for Romance," in *Passionate Attachments,* ed. Williard Gaylin and Ethel Person (London: Macmillan, 1988), 91.

12. Lystra, *Searching the Heart,* 252.

13. Lystra, *Searching the Heart,* 258.

14. See Lystra, *Searching the Heart,* 252-57.

15. Annis Boudinot Stockton's poem was published in Rev. Samuel Stanhope Smith's *Funeral Sermon on the Death of the Hon. Richard Stockton* (1780). It has been brought back to print in *The Heath Anthology of American Literature,* ed. Paul Lauter et al. (New York: Heath, 1990), 1:658.

16. Martha Brewster, "An Acrostick for My Husband," in *Poems on Divers Subjects* (Boston: Edes and Gill, 1757), 33; Anne Bradstreet, "To My Dear and Loving Husband," in *The Works of Anne Bradstreet,* ed. John Harvard Ellis (New York: Peter Smith, 1932), 394.

17. *The Collected Works of Phillis Wheatley,* ed. John C. Shields (New York: Oxford Univ. Press, 1988), 30 (spelling modernized).

18. The phrase "new domestic heaven" is from Ann Douglas, *The Feminization of American Culture* (New York: Knopf, 1977), 214; see also 204.

19. George Cheever, *The Powers of the World to Come* (New York, 1853), 221.

20. Quoted in Lee Virginia Chambers-Schiller, *Liberty, a Better Husband: Single Women in America, The*

Generations of 1780-1840 (New Haven: Yale Univ. Press, 1984), xi.

21. Quoted by Emerson in *JMN,* 11:500.

22. Margaret Fuller, *Woman in the Nineteenth Century,* in *The Essential Margaret Fuller,* ed. Jeffrey Steele (New Brunswick: Rutgers Univ. Press, 1992), 312, 298. For more on celibacy, see Chambers-Schiller, *Liberty,* 3, 29-45. In *Summer on the Lakes,* Fuller mourns the wasted love and energy of a young alterego, Mariana, whose "large impulses are disproportioned to the persons and occasions she meets, and which carry her beyond those reserves which mark the appointed lot of woman." "Such women as Mariana are often lost," she writes, "unless they meet some man of sufficiently great soul to prize them," a man "man enough to be a lover!" But since men like Philip Van Artevelde, her example from *Summer on the Lakes,* (or like Giovanni Angelo Ossoli) "come not so often as once an age, their presence should not be absolutely needed to sustain life" (*Essential Margaret Fuller,* 131, 132).

23. Emerson echoes these comments on love in "Friendship": "The condition which high friendship demands, is, ability to do without it. . . . There must be two, before there can be very one" (*CW,* 2:123).

24. Hawthorne, *Letters,* 316. The phrase "maudlin agglutinations" is Emerson's, from "The Uses of Great Men" (*CW,* 4:15).

25. This vision of the hereafter proposes as spiritual counsel the whimsical independence Emerson's first wife, Ellen Tucker, declares in a poem that begins "When we're angels in heaven":

I shan't keep a carriage
My wings will be strong
And our earthly marriage
Will be vain as a song.

I therefore shall use them
As I may see fit
And tea out and dine out
Nor mind you a bit.

(*One First Love: The Letters of Ellen Louisa Tucker to Ralph Waldo Emerson,* ed. Edith W. Gregg [Cambridge: Harvard Univ. Press, Belknap Press, 1962], 157.)

26. Tucker, *One First Love,* 14.

27. Mary E. Hewitt, *Poems: Sacred, Passionate, and Legendary* (New York: Lamport, Blakeman, 1854), 196.

28. *Young Emerson Speaks: Unpublished Discourses on Many Subjects by Ralph Waldo Emerson,* ed. Arthur Cushman McGiffert Jr. (Boston: Houghton Mifflin, 1938), 19; Rusk, *Life,* 134. Although Emerson "was doubtless abashed" at preaching this Pla-

tonic sermon to Ellen's church, Rusk asserts that the sermon "served to restore the dignity of his philosophy, which had proved so unreliable in her presence" (133).

29. See Joel Porte, *Representative Man: Ralph Waldo Emerson in His Time* (New York: Columbia Univ. Press, 1988), 169-71.

30. John Winthrop, "A Model of Christian Charity," in *Winthrop Papers,* vol. 2, *1623-1630,* ed. Stewart Mitchell (New York: Russell and Russell, 1968), 290.

31. Martin Luther, *Weimar Auflage,* quoted in Anders Nygren, *Agape and Eros,* trans. Philip S. Watson (New York: Harper and Row, 1969), 695.

32. Quoted in Robert Lee Patterson, *The Philosophy of William Ellery Channing* (New York: Bookman Associates, 1952), 169. "Love," Channing observes, "may prove our chief woe, if bestowed unwisely, disproportionately, and on unworthy objects; if confined to beings of imperfect virtue, with whose feelings we cannot always innocently sympathize, whose interests we cannot always righteously promote, who narrow us to themselves instead of breathing universal charity, who are frail, mutable, exposed to suffering, pain, and death" (quoted in Patterson, *Philosophy,* 236).

33. Patterson, *Philosophy,* 169, 236, 237. "The difficulty," Patterson goes on, "can be solved, if at all, only by showing not only that human love leads on to the love of God, but also that the love of God augments and fosters human love. Such a solution, however, we do not find in the thought of Channing" (238). We can find it in Aquinas, in what Nygren calls his "caritas-synthesis" (*Agape and Eros,* 476-558, 613-58). A different solution is worked through by Emerson.

34. Cf. Edwards: "The whole is *of* God, and *in* God, and *to* God; and God is the beginning, middle, and end in this affair. And though it be true that God has respect to the creature in these things; yet his respect to himself, and to the creature in this matter, are not properly to be looked upon as a double and divided respect of God's heart" ("Concerning the End for Which God Created the World," in *Ethical Writings,* 531).

35. Edwards, *Ethical Writings,* 540.

36. Cf. John Calvin: "We are not our own; therefore, neither is our own reason or will to rule our acts and counsels. We are not our own; therefore, let us not make it our end to seek what may be agreeable to our carnal nature. We are not our own; therefore, as far as possible, let us forget ourselves and the things that are ours" (*Institutes of the Christian Religion,* trans. Henry Beveridge [Grand Rapids: Wm. B. Eerdmans, 1972], 2:7).

37. The phrase "human love" bears for me an overtone of imperfection, of faithlessness and tender disappointment, as in W. H. Auden's "Lay your sleeping head, my love, / Human on my faithless arm" ("Lullaby," in *Collected Poems,* ed. Edward Mendelson [New York: Random House, 1976], 131). I draw it here, though, from Patterson's discussion of love and benevolence. "It has been urged by the atheistic idealist, McTaggart," he writes,

> that the fundamental defect of theism is that it sets, and must set, a low value upon human love. The point of this criticism will not be duly appreciated until the distinction be grasped between love and benevolence. Benevolence is basically volitional in character; it does not, indeed, exclude emotion, but that emotion is of an impersonal variety. Theists of all faiths and in all ages have concurred in emphasizing the value of benevolence. When it comes, however, to personal affection and devotion, such as engages the whole personality, theists have habitually told us that this in its purest and intensest form belongs to God alone, that the creatures are to be loved "for God's sake" rather than for themselves. In no Christian thinker is this characteristic more pronounced than in Channing's predecessor, Edwards. Love, Edwards maintains, should be proportionate to its object. God, the Supreme Good, alone deserves the fullness of one's love; to bestow this upon any finite being would be idolatry.

(Philosophy, 268)

38. While the years between Sermon CIV and "The Heart" are extraordinarily eventful, even before Emerson's marriage to Ellen he imagined an effort at self-culture that would lead one from interhuman affections to the "sublime" world of love for God. See *JMN,* 3:146.

39. Lystra, *Searching the Heart,* 241-42.

40. Emerson's push toward "the impersonal" will thus force a few revisions on Cavell's history of skepticism, in which "the philosophical problem of the other" appears "as the trace or scar of the departure of God." For Emerson, God ("the god," "the gods," the "Over-soul," or "Spirit") can never be said to depart, but as at the close of "Give All To Love," functions mainly to drive off lesser lovers. The simultaneous loss of personality in God and man gives new resonance to Cavell's question, "[C]ouldn't the other suffer the fate of God?" (*The Claim of Reason* [New York: Oxford Univ. Press, 1979], 470). I find this linkage as compelling as the sociopolitical explanation offered by David Leverenz, where "solitary male freedom," which presumes the "depersonalized servitude" of others, vitiates the self (*Manhood and the American Renaissance* [Ithaca: Cornell Univ. Press, 1989], 44).

41. Singer, *Nature of Love,* 1:320-21, quoting Thomas Aquinas, *On Charity (De Caritate),* trans. Lottie H. Kendzierski (Milwaukee: Marquette Univ. Press, 1960), 21.

42. According to Michael Fischer, Cavell's work suggests that "the sense of a gap between us and others originates in our wishing to give up responsibility for maintaining those shared forms of life linking us" to them (*Stanley Cavell and Literary Skepticism* [Chicago: Univ. of Chicago Press, 1989], 64). Given the constricting social web in America between 1820 and 1840 and Emerson's depiction of the contemporary "war between intellect and affection," there may be this sort of wish-fulfillment in his skeptical and individualistic claims. The importance of gender in this drive to separation is easily overstated. Compare, for example, Mary Moody Emerson's exultation in "the advantage of loneliness," quoted in Phyllis Cole, "The Advantage of Loneliness: Mary Moody Emerson's Almanacks, 1802-1855," in *Emerson: Prospect and Retrospect,* ed. Joel Porte (Cambridge: Harvard Univ. Press, 1982), 10.

43. Stanley Cavell, *Disowning Knowledge in Six Plays of Shakespeare* (Cambridge: Cambridge Univ. Press, 1987), 6.

44. "Many of the questions [of 'Experience'] seem familiar," Van Leer explains, "and offer recognizable (if not entirely predictable) reformulations of earlier problems. . . . If psychologically Emerson shows an unsuspected willingness to treat the authentic facts of experience, philosophically he merely develops the next stage of his epistemological argument," including, I would add, his argument over the epistemology of love (*Emerson's Epistemology,* 143).

45. Emerson calls this "common soul" a sort of ether, "an element" of love, and his litany of its attributes surely echoes Paul's Corinthian hymn to agape. "This common soul plunges into water to save the drowning man; seizes the bridle of the rearing horse; runs over the burning rafters of the flaming house to rescue the child," Emerson writes. "It takes counsel only of itself; sneers never; imputes never a low motive. . . . No King was ever yet able to kill or root it out" (*EL,* 2:281).

46. We might compare this to the Puritan desire to "live in the world but not of the world," one of the goals of weaning one's affections (Douglas Anderson, *A House Undivided: Domesticity and Community in American Literature* [Cambridge: Cambridge Univ. Press, 1990], 3).

47. John Donne, "The Exstasie," in *John Donne: The Elegies and the Songs and Sonnets,* ed. Helen Gardner (Oxford: Clarendon Press, 1965), 59.

48. For more on the difference between the cherubim and seraphim, that "old politics of the skies," see "Intellect" (*CW,* 2:204). In a letter to Fuller (25 September 1840), Emerson tries to finesse their differences by claiming that they "are not inhabitants of one thought of the Divine Mind, but of two thoughts, that [they] meet & treat like foreign states, one maritime, one inland, whose trade & laws are essentially unlike" (*L,* 2:336). I find this "two thought" system rather unconvincing; yet when Emerson explains in the lecture how, other than etymologically, "Courage is of the Heart," he dares us to deny that we, too, do not act on a similar faith. "If we believed in the existence of strict *individuals,*" he writes, "natures, that is, not radically identical but unknown, unmeasurable we should never dare to fight" (*EL,* 2:285). The same perhaps might be confessed of our "daring" to love.

49. Why are marriage and friendship the issue, and not general social duty? "The Heart," Emerson insists, "truly regards all men as its neighbor" because, we may assume, it sees itself, or the god in it, in them. Still, "in the actual state of society it presently finds abundant obstacle to the indulgence of sympathy. It is chilled and sneered at and betrayed" (*EL,* 2:288). Our affections, repelled by the multitude as such, and from each individual as "an infinitely repellent orb," will "rally in some one object," Emerson writes; and the heart accommodates itself "by concentrating its desire of helping and comforting upon one" (*EL,* 2:279, 288).

50. Benjamin Wadsworth, *The Well-Ordered Family* (Boston, 1712), 26; quoted in Edmund S. Morgan, *The Puritan Family: Religion and Domestic Relations in Seventeenth-Century New England* (New York: Harper and Row, 1966), 49.

51. Leverenz, *Manhood,* 69; Walt Whitman, "Song of the Open Road," in *Leaves of Grass: A Textual Variorum of the Printed Poems,* ed. Sculley Bradley et al., 3 vols., in *The Collected Writings of Walt Whitman* (New York: New York Univ. Press, 1980), 1:236. It is worth noting that Emerson's journals often work on the same level of abstraction, so that his observations about a husband who "loses the wife in the cares of the household" and who "cannot rejoice with her in the babe for by becoming a mother she ceases yet more to be a wife" are drawn only loosely (or in the second case, not at all) from his own experience (*JMN,* 5:297).

52. See Robert M. Polhemus, *Erotic Faith: Being in Love from Jane Austen to D. H. Lawrence* (Chicago: Univ. of Chicago Press, 1990), esp. 1-27.

53. "Marriage unites the severed halves and joins characters which are complements to each other," Emerson writes in the lecture on "Love" (*EL,* 3:62), sounding a bit like Aristophanes in Plato's *Symposium*; but this vision of union disappears when he revises the lecture into an essay.

54. In Sermon CIV a "tender reverence for our mutual nature, divine in its origin," properly grounds "all

our dealings with mankind" (*CS,* 3:89). In "our position in nature," Emerson writes in "The Heart," "[w]e are tenderly alive to love and hatred"; shortly thereafter we are warned not to "wrong the truth and [our] own experience by too stiffly standing on the cold and proud doctrine of self-sufficiency" (*EL,* 2:280). In "Historic Notes of Life and Letters in New England," Emerson puns on the word "tender" again, though with a different set of senses. "There grew a certain tenderness on the people," he writes in the second sentence of the piece; a few pages later the notion that "the individual is the world" gives people "a neck of unspeakable tenderness; it winces at a hair" (*W,* 10:325, 326, 327).

55. Wallace Stevens, "Final Soliloquy of the Interior Paramour," in *The Collected Poems* (New York: Vintage, 1982), 524.

56. According to a footnote Freud added in 1910 to his "Three Essays on the Theory of Sexuality," "[t]he ancients laid the stress upon the [sexual] instinct itself, whereas we . . . emphasize its object" (*The Standard Edition of the Complete Psychological Works of Sigmund Freud,* vol. 7, *1901-1905,* ed. James Strachey [London: Hogarth Press, 1953], 149). I am grateful to Deborah Garfield for pointing out this connection.

57. Pommer, *Emerson's First Marriage,* 82.

58. Emerson sounds quite stoutly Victorian in his emphasis on exchanging passionate marital relations for companionable ones. But unlike the advice writers cited by Steven Seidman, he will not propose marriage as a site of both self-realization and perfect emotional union. See Seidman's *Romantic Longings: Love in America, 1830-1980* (New York: Routledge, 1991), 30-32. Whether his purifications are sublimations of sexuality seems to me an arguable and not very interesting point. Lest I seem merely soft-hearted here, let me adduce textual evidence that friendship is what "true marriage" means. A "cheerful, disengaged furtherance," Emerson calls it in "Love" (*CW,* 2:109); and in "The Heart," a "manly furtherance" appears as one of the "stern conditions . . . of friendship" (*EL,* 2:289). While love begins as a "private and tender relation of one to one," friendship appears in "Friendship" as "a just and firm encounter of two" in which we "dignify to each other the daily needs and offices of man's life"—the same sort of "offices" to which the married couple resigned one another a moment ago (*CW,* 2:99, 114, 121). Finally, the tale of friendship with a "commended stranger" in the opening pages of "Friendship" recapitulates all the crucial stages of "Love," as though to suggest, in fact, that the lovers were at best strangers to each other from the start (*CW,* 2:114).

59. Cayton, *Emerson's Emergence,* 200, 208, 209, 210.

60. Unlike Sartre, Emerson is never bothered by the fact that he is just as phenomenal, just as much an

object and not a subject, to the perceiving other as the other is to him.

61. Simone de Beauvoir, *The Second Sex,* ed. and trans. H. M. Parshley (New York: Alfred A. Knopf, 1993), 687.

62. Singer also speaks of the way bestowing value will "augment one's own being as well as the beloved's" (*Nature of Love,* 1:7).

63. For a discussion of this pun on handsomeness and attraction, see Cavell, *This New Yet Unapproachable America,* 87.

64. See Walt Whitman, "A Song for Occupations," in *Leaves of Grass,* 1:83-98.

65. See M. Wynn Thomas, "A Comparative Study of Emerson's 'Friendship' and Whitman's 'Calamus,'" *ATQ* 55 (1985): 57.

66. Whitman, "Song of the Universal," in *Leaves of Grass,* 3:681.

67. René Girard, *Deceit, Desire, and the Novel: Self and Other in Literary Structure,* trans. Yvonne Freccero (Baltimore: Johns Hopkins Press, 1985), 1, 10, 54, 10. "We shall speak of *external mediation,*" Girard explains, "when the distance is sufficient to eliminate any contact between the two spheres of *possibilities* of which the mediator and the subject occupy the respective centers. We shall speak of *internal mediation* when this same distance is sufficiently reduced to allow these two spheres to penetrate each other more or less profoundly" (9).

68. I quote Gerald L. Bruns, "Stanley Cavell's Shakespeare," *Critical Inquiry* 16 (1990): 614. For Cavell's reading of *Othello,* see "Othello and the Stake of Other," chap. 3 of *Disowning Knowledge,* 125-42.

69. Stanley Cavell, *Pursuits of Happiness: The Hollywood Comedy of Remarriage* (Cambridge: Harvard Univ. Press, 1981); see esp. the chapters "Knowledge as Transgression: *It Happened One Night*" (71-109) and "The Importance of Importance: *The Philadelphia Story*" (133-60).

70. The "simple and childish virtues of veracity and honesty," Emerson puts it in "Illusions," are still "the root of all that is sublime in character" (*CW,* 6:322).

71. Cavell, *Disowning Knowledge,* 10.

James M. Albrecht (essay date 1995)

SOURCE: "'Living Property': Emerson's Ethics," in *ESQ: A Journal of the American Renaissance,* Vol. 41, No. 3, 1995, pp. 177-247.

[*In the following essay, Albrecht examines Emerson's ethical philosophy in the context of such essays as "Self-Reliance" and "Experience."*]

[T]hat which a man is, does always by necessity acquire, and what the man acquires is living property.

—Emerson, **"Self-Reliance"**

What a man does, that he has. What has he to do with hope or fear? In himself is his might. Let him regard no good as solid but that which is in his nature, and which must grow out of him as long as he exists. The goods of fortune may come and go like summer leaves; let him scatter them on every wind as the momentary signs of his infinite productiveness.

—Emerson, **"Spiritual Laws"**

"When will you mend Montaigne?" Emerson challenged himself in 1835: "Where are your Essays? Can you not express your one conviction that moral laws hold?"[1] Ironically, his philosophy, intended to affirm "moral laws," has often been criticized as an amoral ethics of individualized activity. Emerson typically is accused of a "transcendentalist" fascination with the absolute that ignores or subsumes the tragic limitations of our material existence; curiously, this supposed absolutism has been described as taking two nearly contradictory forms. As the title of Stephen E. Whicher's influential study *Freedom and Fate* indicates,[2] critics have charted in Emerson's thought a shift from a naïve affirmation of individual power, in his early works, to a more sober focus, in his later works, on the forces that limit the autonomy and power of human acts. The "early" Emerson posited in this widely accepted narrative celebrates absolute power as a goal to which individuals should aspire—thereby blaming tragic inequities on individual failings instead of on social or political forces. The "late" Emerson, in contrast, celebrates the absolute forces that determine our human identities and acts—thereby linking individualism with a fatalistic acceptance of limitation and a renunciation of political action. Much recent criticism has set out to describe Emerson's amorality in historical, ideological terms, often arguing that his individualism endorses the amoral logic of laissez-faire capitalism and discourages collective political action. However, most assessments of his politics reinforce, even as they reformulate, the major contours of Whicher's reading. For example, Sacvan Bercovitch's argument that Emerson shifted from a "utopian" critique of capitalism to an "ideological" apology for capitalism updates Whicher's opposition of an early and a late Emerson. Myra Jehlen also emerges from Whicher's opposition, arguing that Emerson's assertion of absolute individual power paradoxically implies a negation of individual will.[3]

Emerson's ethics, I want to maintain, do not reflect these absolutist extremes of autonomy and determinism; rather, they extend his balanced, proto-pragmatic analysis of the power and limitation of individual acts.[4] For Emerson, creative change is a process of *limited* transcendence—in which people turn inherited cultural tools to new uses, exceeding their previous reality only by facilitating the emergence of another, also limited, reality. Insisting that creative acts are constrained by both the cultural media with which they must be articulated and the environment they strive to reshape, Emerson views individuals as alienated

from both the sources and the products of their acts. He therefore locates value in the act of doing: "The one thing in the world of value, is, the active soul," he provocatively asserts in **"The American Scholar"** (*CW*, 1:56). Emerson's transcendentalism thus anticipates two fundamental attitudes of William James's pragmatism, namely, that ideas are limited human tools and that their "truth" lies in their ability to facilitate human acts.[5] This emphasis on activity or work that lies at the heart of Emerson's ethics cannot easily be reconciled with traditional capitalist ideology, which locates value in accumulated (and alienated) wealth and profit. To reassert the pragmatic basis of Emerson's ethics is to gain a renewed understanding of the writer who inspired Thoreau in *Walden* and "Civil Disobedience" by articulating an "economy" of living measured in terms of creative experience and activity. However, in thus distinguishing Emerson's ethics from traditional capitalist ideology, it is crucial to address other recalcitrant ethical dilemmas posed by his thought, primarily the anti-communicative and anti-communitarian implications of his emphasis on action. Indeed, these dilemmas are hardly avoidable, for Emerson not only confronts them frankly but exploits them as central issues in such essays as **"Self-Reliance"** and **"Experience."**

Emerson's pragmatic focus on action reflects his complex analysis of how culture both *enables* individual acts that may result in creative change and *limits* the degree to which any creative result expresses individuality. Invention—truly new perception or utility—occurs when the tools inherited from the past are used to transcend the horizon of perception and utility defined by those tools:

> The useful arts are but reproductions or new combinations by the wit of man, of the same natural benefactors. He no longer waits for favoring gales, but by means of steam, he realizes the fable of Aeolus's bag, and carries the two and thirty winds in the boiler of his boat. To diminish friction, he paves the road with iron bars, and, mounting a coach with a ship-load of men, animals, and merchandise behind him, he darts through the country, from town to town, like an eagle or a swallow through the air.
>
> (*CW*, 1:11-12)

This passage, from the "Commodity" chapter of ***Nature***, describes all new creations as quotations of nature's forms and forces and of previous human works.[6] Yet invention is not mere reproduction; it is a kind of metaphoric translation or turning that Emerson frequently calls troping:[7] the railroad tropes a sailing ship by using iron rails to recreate the fluidity of water, carrying a "ship-load" on land. The steam engine retropes the sail, and both engine and sail retrope the fable of Aeolus's bag—the idea of catching and harnessing the wind.

However, though an individual's acts may facilitate invention, any true invention is by definition different from previous utility and perception, and thus beyond merely individual intention:[8]

> I pursue my speculations with confidence & tho' I can discern no remoter conclusion I doubt not the train I

commence extends farther than I see as the first artificer of glass did not know he was instructing men in astronomy & restoring sight to those from whom nature had taken it. There is no thought which is not seed as well as fruit. It spawns like fish.

(*JMN*, 2:387)

Invention here consists in making something the full use of which you cannot know, in disrupting or transcending utility. This nonintentional aspect of action, which Emerson often describes in such terms as "reception," "whim," and "abandonment,"[9] can literally reinvent our reality: the "first artificer of glass" could not *foresee* how the telescope would change how *we see* the universe, nor could the inventor of the steam engine intend all the changes in the "realities" of space and time brought by the railroad.

Inherited culture is thus a collection of tools that enables individual creative acts and at the same time requires a surrender of individuality. Emerson expresses this duality in **"Shakespeare; or, The Poet"**: Culture provides tremendous power—"The world has brought him thus far on his way. . . . Men, nations, poets, artisans, women, all have worked for him." However, this power also determines and constrains the direction of an individual's acts:

Choose any other thing, out of the line of tendency, out of the national feeling and history, and he would have all to do for himself: his powers would be expended in the first preparations. Great genial power, one would almost say, consists in not being original at all; in being altogether receptive; in letting the world do all, and suffering the spirit of the hour to pass unobstructed through the mind.

(*CW*, 4:110)

Similarly, culture is both a rich mine for invention and a medium that makes true invention extremely difficult. Creative acts depend on inherited tools; they escape the utility defined by those tools only to have any new result reappropriated as a new utility. Invention is a disruption of utility, an act of "abandonment" or "whim," that occurs as a liminal moment between old and new utility. Emerson distinguishes invention from utility in **"The Method of Nature"**: "I look on trade and every mechanical craft as education also. But let me discriminate what is precious herein. There is in each of these works one act of invention, one intellectual step, or short series of steps taken; that act or step is the spiritual act: all the rest is mere repetition of the same a thousand times" (*CW*, 1:120-21). True invention here is strikingly restricted. It is only "one intellectual step," an "act" within the "work." The railroad, once repeated and used, is no longer invention but only "mere repetition" and "routine" (*CW*, 1:121). Extending this logic, even the first prototype model steam engine is not wholly invention; the "work" is not the same as the "spiritual act." Returning to the "Aeolus's bag" passage, the act of invention might be no more than the mental act of troping, the thought of a new application that "realizes the fable." Invention thus described is a kind of synonym for genius as Richard Poirier defines it in Emerson: a po-

tential or energy for change that ceases to be itself as soon as it begins to take form in a medium.[10]

Two central, and related, facets of this theory of invention are crucial for understanding the aims and priorities of Emerson's ethics: first, his acute awareness that individuals are inescapably limited by the media with which and on which they must act, and second, his consequent portrayal of originality or creativity as extremely tenuous and elusive. These aspects of Emerson's pragmatism challenge the persistent idea that he naïvely affirms the sufficiency and power of individual action, thus ignoring its tragic limits. Indeed, his ethics are essentially a response to limitation: his pragmatic stress on individual action is an attempt to locate value that is not subject to alienation. However, though this emphasis on action distinguishes Emerson's pragmatism from the amorality of laissez-faire capitalism, it leads him into another type of amorality. By locating value in the individual's activity, Emerson problematizes the communication of value and, by extension, the fulfillment of communal responsibility. Similarly, his complex and conflicted attitudes toward political reform do not correspond neatly to laissez-faire capitalism but, rather, logically extend his pragmatic valorization of activity over established or codified cultural forms.

"HERE OR NOWHERE": THE TRAGIC ETHICS OF ACTION IN THE MATERIAL WORLD

In town I also talked with Sampson Reed, of Swedenborg & the rest. "It is not so in your experience, but is so in the other world."—"Other world?" I reply, "there is no other world; here or nowhere is the whole fact; all the Universe over, there is but one thing,—this old double, Creator-creature, mind-matter, right-wrong."

—Emerson's journal, June-July 1842

Emerson's "transcendentalism" has often been equated with a desire to transcend the material world and its tragic limits. The charge that he lacks a sense of tragedy is a familiar one, running from Herman Melville through influential twentieth-century critics like F. O. Matthiessen, Stephen Whicher, and Myra Jehlen.[11] This indictment is typically based on the following assumptions: first, that Emerson defines nature as the perfect embodiment of an ideal truth existing beyond it; second, that he believes human action can potentially exert unbounded control over nature; and third, that his fascination with unlimited individual power at best leads him to disregard the material consequences of particular actions (valuing, instead, intuitive apprehensions of the "absolute"), and at worst leads him to insist that our failure to achieve total control over nature reflects our own vice. Jehlen offers a powerful reformulation of this traditional reading. She suggests that Emerson defines truth as wholly independent of human actions: we have access to truth only through our preexisting harmony with or intuition of nature; our actions merely express or replicate nature's absolute truth. This severe proscription of human creativity provides, according to Jehlen, a powerful metaphysical support for the amorality of capitalism: it simultaneously removes any responsibility for political action (since nature does not need human re-forms or revolutions) and authorizes economic and nation-alist expansion (since nature comprehends all such activity).[12]

Jehlen cogently traces possible ideological implications of the way Emerson traditionally has been read, but Emer-son's ethics need to be reassessed, I think, on the basis of alternative readings. Ultimately, Emerson's pragmatic theory of invention cannot be made to fit conventional views of transcendentalism. His ruminations on Shakes-peare and on the "first artificer of glass" demonstrate that Emersonian intuition or "reception" is not incompatible with creative action. Rather, intuition is only one aspect or phase of invention; it is the new perception that cannot be intended by the human actor but that depends upon his or her acts. Jehlen's contention that Emersonian action can-not create anything original is true only in the broadest possible terms: for example, that God created humans, their faculties, and the world, and thus created all potential human acts; or in secular terms, that people are part of na-ture, which thus comprehends all changes wrought by hu-man arts. Emerson himself makes this latter argument in his 1844 essay **"Nature."**[13] But this does not mean, as Je-hlen concludes, that Emerson defines human acts and truths as predetermined, confined to replicating an already abso-lute perfection. He insists that truth and reality are limited human constructs, products of culturally mediated percep-tions of our environment and thus contingent upon human acts. Emerson's entire theory of invention stands on the premise that human action does matter, that people can and must re-create their reality: "[H]istory and the state of the world at any one time," he asserts in **"Circles,"** is "di-rectly dependent on the intellectual classification then ex-isting in the minds of men. . . . A new degree of culture would instantly revolutionize the entire system of human pursuits." However, as that essay insists, each limited real-ity is exceeded only by the emergence of yet another lim-ited reality: "[E]ach thought[,] having formed itself into a circular wave of circumstance," begins to "solidify, and hem in the life" (*CW*, 2:184, 180-81). Thus Emerson ap-provingly notes one woman's definition of transcendental-ism as "[a] *little* beyond" (*JMN*, 5:218; my emphasis).

In claiming that Emerson's universe is "infinitely benevo-lent,"[14] Jehlen is insufficiently attentive to this crucial dis-tinction of scope—that is, to the difference between, on the one hand, God or nature as the ground of possibility for all human action and, on the other, human reality as defined by particular acts. When Emerson insists that the universe is benevolent, that there is an immutable justice or balance in nature, he is describing a systemic balance that transcends any merely individual or even human mea-sure of fairness or justice. When he affirms that the results of human action are moral, he is not asserting that the world is wholly answerable to human will and that failures and suffering thus reflect human vices. Instead, he is as-serting that our limited ability to transform the world around us is an accurate reflection of our limited position in a nature that is not organized according to human con-cepts of justice.

This ethic of *accepting* the limited control human beings have over their environment is implicit in Emerson's theory of invention. Creative acts that transcend or disrupt our current horizon of utility can yield unintended new perceptions and utilities. Thus, in **"Self-Reliance,"** Emer-son expresses his desire to "write on the lintels of the door-post, *Whim*," in the hope it will be "somewhat better than whim at last." But creative acts at best allow us to re-create our otherwise determining surroundings: "[P]ercep-tion is not whimsical, but fatal," Emerson insists a few pages later (*CW*, 2:30, 38). Disruptive acts of "whim" can facilitate new perception, yet such perception is "fatal," a term that for Emerson specifically refers to the external circumstances that determine us.[15] Already implicit in *Na-ture*'s claim that "[e]very spirit builds itself a house; and beyond its house, a world; and beyond its world, a heaven" (*CW*, 1:44) is the corollary Emerson voices in **"Fate"**: "Every spirit makes its house; but afterwards the house confines the spirit" (*W*, 6:9).[16] Even while our acts may change our environment, they then become part of a new environment or "circle," a new context that re-acts upon us. As Kenneth Burke argues, tragedy expresses exactly this kind of relation between self and environment:

> The act, in being an assertion, has called forth a counter-assertion in the elements that compose its con-text. And when the agent is enabled to see in terms of this counter-assertion, he has transcended the state that characterized him at the start. In this final state of tragic vision, intrinsic and extrinsic motivations are merged. That is, although purely circumstantial factors partici-pate in his tragic destiny, these are not felt as exclu-sively external, or scenic; for they bring about a *repre-sentative* kind of accident, the kind of accident that belongs with the agent's particular kind of character.[17]

Instead of ignoring the tragedy of existence, Emerson's ethics express a tragic logic of human action in the mate-rial world. He is able to affirm the justice of nature only through a tragic transcendence of scope, through accepting nature's nonhuman balance. And he affirms the morality of human acts by accepting the imperfect results of those acts as accurate representations of people's circumscribed posi-tion in nature.

"Compensation" articulates the tragic ethics implicit in Emerson's theory of invention. And yet, along with the "Discipline" chapter of *Nature*, it is often interpreted to mean that Emerson affirms the benevolence of the uni-verse by asserting that people deserve the suffering they receive.[18] Consider Jehlen's discussion of "Discipline":

> I do not suggest that in writing *Nature* Emerson schemed to co-opt dissent. But effective defenses are seldom consciously invented, arising rather from con-viction of more or less global rectitude. Emerson's as-sumption of his world's rectitude was absolutely glo-bal. So although he was not coldly calculating how to control opposition, he was thinking politically in this section, as seems clear from his making here the most directly political statement of the essay, the assertion that "Property and its filial systems of debt and credit,"

along with space, time, climate, and the animals, are nature's benevolent guides to intellectual truths. . . . In "Discipline" Emerson brings up the two strongest objections to the notion of a transcendentally benevolent world: poverty and death. . . . [T]hese are the classical reasons for rebellion—one the oldest justification to rise against the human order, the other to rail at the divine.

The function of "Discipline" is to disarm these reasons. . . . After this section come "Idealism," "Spirit," and "Prospects," in which Emerson can assert the possibility of transcendence—of freedom and omnipotence—because "Discipline" has co-opted the material reality of limits and powerlessness. The facts that some are indebted to others and that all owe the final debt of mortality have been made to testify to the primacy and infinite power of the individual in an infinitely benevolent universe.[19]

If **"Compensation"** is read as an extension of Emerson's theory of invention, this so-called "global rectitude" becomes more complex than Jehlen seems to allow. **"Compensation"** does not "co-opt . . . the material reality of limits" so as to "assert the possibility of transcendence" to a state in which the individual enjoys "infinite power"; instead, it opens by explicitly rejecting the notion of any justice beyond the material world. Emerson criticizes a sermon he has heard on the Last Judgment:

> Yet what was the import of this teaching? What did the preacher mean by saying that the good are miserable in the present life? Was it that houses and lands, offices, wine, horses, dress, luxury, are had by unprincipled men, whilst the saints are poor and despised; and that a compensation is to be made to these last hereafter, by giving them the like gratifications another day,—bank-stock and doubloons, venison and champagne? This must be the compensation intended; for, what else? Is it that they are to have leave to pray and praise? to love and serve men? Why, that they can do now. The legitimate inference the disciple would draw was,— 'We are to have *such* a good time as the sinners have now;'—or, to push it to its extreme import,—'You sin now; we shall sin by and by; we would sin now, if we could; not being successful, we expect our revenge tomorrow.'

The "fallacy" of this sermon's logic, Emerson concludes, lies "in the immense concession that the bad are successful; that justice is not done now" (*CW,* 2:56). This is hardly an assertion that the material world perfectly rewards individual merit. Rather, in rejecting the notion of a transcendent justice, Emerson by extension rejects the notion that our material world *should* perfectly reward us, for the latter idea is implicit in the former: the very concept of a heavenly compensation implies the need to overcome the imperfections of worldly rewards and suffering. Emerson's satire on heaven suggests that banishing justice to an ideal realm does not transcend the moral limits of our world; it implicitly reproduces them. Far from desiring transcendence and infinite individual power, **"Compensation"** insists we must accept our material world and the tragic limits of our control over it.

Crucially, Emerson portrays this acceptance as a gain of meaning, not a loss. The denial of any transcendent truth invests the material world with all the meaning we shall ever have.[20] "Thus is the universe alive. All things are moral" (*CW,* 2:60). This "morality" expresses the full significance of all the facts and forces that determine our existence, not just those that fit our human concepts of merit and desert. As Emerson describes it in the journal account of his exchange with Sampson Reed, the "whole fact" of our world exceeds the terms of human morals—it is "right-wrong." Whether just or not, the circumstances of our environment, both by responding to and resisting our control, reflect our limited position within nature. Thus an individual "comes at last to be faithfully represented by every view you take of his circumstances" (**"Spiritual Laws,"** in *CW,* 2:86). It is this very limitation that gives us our individuality: "We must have an antagonism in the tough world for all the variety of our spiritual faculties, or they will not be born" (**"Man the Reformer,"** in *CW,* 1:150). It is only against the resistance and limitation of material media that we know, express, and develop our creative power. The circumstances of the world that restrict, thwart, and eventually kill us are also what prompt Emerson's expressions of gratitude, notably in **"Experience."** His ethics value limitations, presenting them as occasions for the circumscribed acts and performances that define us as humans, not "co-opting" them, as Jehlen contends, in an affirmation of total transcendence.

Having insisted that morality must be found in the material world, **"Compensation"** then affirms that this morality, though imperfect, is ensured by the way media both respond to *and resist* human acts: "The league between virtue and nature engages all things to assume a hostile front to vice. The beautiful laws and substances of the world persecute and whip the traitor" (*CW,* 2:67). Emerson's theory of invention assumes our alienation from the tools and products of our own labor. For him, invention is a process of turning inherited tools to new uses not fully intended or controlled, a process in which each creative result in turn becomes part of a new if still confining environment. Thus true property, or inalienable value, exists only in the exercise and development of human faculties: "The thief steals from himself. The swindler swindles himself. For the real price of labor is knowledge and virtue, whereof wealth and credit are signs. These signs, like paper money, may be counterfeited or stolen, but that which they represent, namely, knowledge and virtue, cannot be counterfeited or stolen" (*CW,* 2:66-67). It is important to note the limits of Emerson's claim. People, he allows, can be unjustly deprived of the material products of their labor, but the person who so deprives others achieves a merely material gain at the cost of a much higher good, the development and exercise of his or her own self: "[H]e has resisted his life, and fled from himself, and the retribution is so much death" (*CW,* 2:61-62). The alien and resistant status of material media, often viewed as the sign of the world's injustice, actually guarantees a certain degree of justice, for it ensures that the value of action must be earned and cannot be stolen. That Emerson clearly turns necessity into virtue only underscores the way in which **"Compensation"** is frequently misread. He does not affirm the perfect justice of material fortunes and thereby support the capitalist status quo. His definition of value, as the experience of action that cannot be stolen, explicitly discourages faith in capitalism's goal of accumulated property. **"Compensation"** warns that fulfillment should be sought neither in heaven nor in the material products of labor, but in activities that express human will and develop human talents.

"WORSE COTTON AND BETTER MEN":
REASSESSING EMERSONIAN INDIVIDUALISM

> The common experience is, that the man fits himself as well as he can to the customary details of that work or trade he falls into, and tends it as a dog turns a spit. Then is he a part of the machine he moves; the man is lost. Until he can manage to communicate himself to others in his full stature and proportion, he does not yet find his vocation.

—Emerson, **"Spiritual Laws"**

Because capitalism and Marxism have been the two dominating social models from Emerson's time to our own, the task of assessing Emerson's ethics has often entailed deciding how his philosophy supports one camp against the other, eliding his difference from both.[21] Emerson's ethics reflect his pragmatic analysis of how individual acts utilize cultural resources and facilitate cultural processes of change. The ethical implications of his analysis cannot easily be subsumed under either side of the capitalist/Marxist dichotomy of political economy: Both systems focus on the accumulation of wealth, capitalism maintaining that trade is a process of comparative advantage that enriches all, and Marxism that it is a process of class exploitation. In contrast, Emerson's acute sense of our fundamental alienation from the tools and products of action leads him to locate value in the experience of action and to measure value in terms of the quality of experience.

Like his near-contemporary Marx, Emerson is obsessed with the alienation of value.[22] In the passage from **"Spiritual Laws,"** he warns of how easily "the man is lost" in the "machine" of culture, work, and wealth; in **"Self-Reliance,"** he criticizes people for having "looked away from themselves and at things so long" (*CW,* 2:83, 49). But Emerson is primarily a writer, not an economist, and his economic ideas derive largely from his sense of the affinities between language, money, and material property as cultural media for creative action.[23] For him, alienation does not begin with any particular mode of economic production; it is fundamental to our cultural, linguistic intelligence, to the fact that we live our lives with and against words, tools, ideas, and values that we inherit.[24] Since Emerson focuses on how individual acts facilitate cultural processes of change, his pragmatism has unquestionable affinities to capitalist arguments about market efficiencies. But he pragmatically insists that the only true "property" people have in material media is in the experience of using them, which leads him to reject accumulated wealth as

the standard for judging economic efficiencies. He supports such institutions as private property and the division of labor only to the extent that these allow people to exercise and develop their particular talents.

The ethical implications of Emersonian individualism follow directly from the central tenets of the pragmatic theory of invention announced in the opening paragraphs of *Nature*: namely, that the present must be created out of the materials inherited from the past, that any original action must utilize cultural media that are by definition *un*original. Inherited concepts threaten not only to obstruct our imagination of new relations to the world but also to deprive us of the action that is our only inalienable property. As Emerson asserts in **"History,"** "Every mind must know the whole lesson for itself": "What the former age has epitomized into a formula or rule for manipular convenience, it will lose all the good of verifying for itself, by means of the wall of that rule. Somewhere, sometime, it will demand and find compensation for that loss by doing the work itself" (*CW,* 2:6-7). This explains why Emerson in **"Self-Reliance"** claims that "[s]ociety everywhere is in conspiracy against the manhood of every one of its members" (*CW,* 2:29); culture is a threat because it provides such powerful benefits, because it offers to do so much for us. There is an ethical imperative to resist conventional ideas, values, and lifestyles, not because they have no enduring value (Emerson insists they do),[25] but because the utility and power they provide deprive us of the more valuable experience of forging our own active relation to the world.

Here it becomes evident that Emerson's pragmatism differs radically from both Marxism and capitalism. Consider the description from **"Spiritual Laws,"** where the man becomes "a part of the machine he moves." Emerson and Marx share a concern with the dehumanizing effects of the alienation of value. Marx stresses how private property and commodity exchange transform relations between people into market relations between products, and how wage laborers become mere parts of a production "machine" designed to accumulate capital for someone else.[26] To prevent this alienation of value, Marx endorses a revolution in the ownership of the means of production.[27] In contrast, Emerson focuses not on the alienation of economic production and exchange but on the alienation inherent in all culture (beginning with language itself). Thus he is concerned less with the potential loss of wealth than with the loss of active self-development and expression. Far from desiring to *secure* alienable value, he argues that culture everywhere makes us *too* secure: he calls for a radical reform in the location of value, exhorting us to seek an active expression of self that can be achieved only by rejecting the security of accumulated value:

> If our young men miscarry in their first enterprizes, they lose all heart. If the young merchant fails, men say he is *ruined*. . . . A sturdy lad from New Hampshire or Vermont, who in turn tries all the professions, who *teams it, farms it, peddles,* keeps a school, preaches, edits a newspaper, goes to Congress, buys a

township, and so forth, in successive years, and always, like a cat, falls on his feet, is worth a hundred of these city dolls. He walks abreast with his days, and feels no shame in not 'studying a profession,' for he does not postpone his life, but lives already.

("**Self-Reliance**," in *CW,* 2:43)

This passage demonstrates how Emerson's support for a division of labor rejects a capitalist motive of accumulated wealth: he insists that value must not be alienated from self-expression and development, that instead of postponing life, we must live. This is a direct consequence of his assertion that self-expression lies in the *way* we use the material and cultural tools that never really belong to us. Providing a sociological model of Emerson's assertion in "**Self-Reliance**" that "[p]ower ceases in the instant of repose" but "resides in the moment of transition from a past to a new state" (*CW,* 2:40), his "sturdy lad" exemplifies success not as accumulated wealth but as *succession,* as the expression of self achieved in exploring different activities "in turn" over "successive years." Emerson insists that the cultural resources for specialized activity must be turned to noncapitalist ends.

Emerson's statements on the economic issues of his day consistently express this pragmatic logic, complicating attempts to define him against the ideological poles of capitalism and Marxism. Consider the issue of division of labor. In *Capital,* Marx insists that any division of labor is a social division that establishes social relations and creates a social product. Under a system of private property, such social interdependence is expressed only in the alienated form of commodity exchange, which obscures the social basis of value. Market value is viewed as inherent in the product itself, not as an expression of the social labor costs of different products. Socially created value is falsely attributed to the individual producer, and social obligation is limited to payment of this false standard of individual desert.[28] In the 1844 lecture "**New England Reformers**," Emerson expresses a surprisingly similar view, while also indicating his radical difference from Marxist political economy:

Who gave me the money with which I bought my coat? Why should professional labor and that of the counting-house be paid so disproportionately to the labor of the porter, and woodsawyer? This whole business of Trade gives me to pause and think, as it constitutes false relations between men; inasmuch as I am prone to count myself relieved of any responsibility to behave well and nobly to that person whom I pay with money, whereas if I had not that commodity, I should be put on my good behavior in all companies, and man would be a benefactor to man, as being himself his only certificate that he had a right to those aids and services which each asked of the other. Am I not too protected a person? is there not a wide disparity between the lot of me and the lot of thee, my poor brother, my poor sister? Am I not defrauded of my best culture in the loss of those gymnastics which manual labor and the emergencies of poverty constitute?

(*CW,* 3:151-52)

Recall that in "**Compensation**" Emerson fully acknowledges that the material products of wealth can be exploited; here he concedes that division of labor and commodity exchange facilitate such exploitation: "Why should professional labor . . . be paid so disproportionately to the labor of the porter, and woodsawyer?" Yet Emerson attacks this alienation by stressing the value of action, a value that *cannot* be stolen. Instead of emphasizing how cultural specialization leaves us vulnerable to being exploited by others, he argues that culture leaves us "too protected." His main concern with the division of labor is that, if we defraud others, we defraud ourselves of our "best culture," the activity and work that is our primary property in life. He attacks the capitalist logic of comparative advantage by articulating an economy, not of profits or wealth, but of life lived as action: if the division of labor merely serves to extract or exploit wealth from others, the supposed beneficiary has "resisted his life, and fled from himself, and the retribution is so much death" ("**Compensation**," in *CW,* 2:61-62).

Yet Emerson celebrates individuals who can utilize cultural resources supplied by others, as indicated by his description in *Nature* of the "private poor man" and in "**Shakespeare; or, The Poet**" of the "greatest genius" as "the most indebted man" (*CW,* 4:109).[29] Indeed, he suggests that division of labor is inherent in the cultural constitution of human intelligence: no person can perform all the actions culture makes available; each must choose a specialized scope of activity. If a genius like Shakespeare did not utilize cultural resources and facilitate cultural tendencies, "his powers would be expended in the first preparations" (*CW,* 4:110). Similarly, in "**Man the Reformer**," Emerson argues that "[i]f we suddenly plant our foot" in a principled "isolation from the advantages of civil society" that we "do not know to be innocent, . . . we shall stand still" (*CW,* 1:155). Thus he endorses a division of labor for its efficiency—because it facilitates creative individual acts by allowing each person to concentrate on particular areas of aptitude: the true "advantages which arise from the division of labor" are that "a man may select the fittest employment for his peculiar talent" ("**Man the Reformer**," in *CW,* 1:149).

Though Emerson's focus on the problem of alienation differs from Marx's, he shares the conviction that any division of labor implies social relations and responsibilities; indeed, Emerson argues that the social interdependence inherent in culture makes all actions socially indebted. In focusing our energies, we must engage in some meaningful activity, "stand in primary relations with the work of the world" ("**Man the Reformer**," in *CW,* 1:152): "No, it is not the part & merit of a man to make his stove with his own hands, or cook & bake his own dinner: Another can do it better & cheaper; but it is his essential virtue to carry out into action his own dearest ends, to dare to do what he believes and loves" (*JMN,* 9:189). By utilizing cultural resources provided by specialized labor, you can "multiply your presence," but "in labor as in life there can be no cheating" ("**Compensation**," in *CW,* 2:66). Ethically, a person may take advantage of cultural resources only if he or she uses this advantage to focus on meaningful work: "This were all very well if I were necessarily absent, being detained by work of my own, like theirs,—work of the same faculties" (**"Man the Reformer,"** in *CW,* 1:150). For Emerson, the choices of vocation that culture offers are essentially moral choices: the division of labor inherent in culture must not be used to exploit and live off others, but to enable each of us to work more vitally.

Believing that cultural specialization carries ethical responsibilities and that such specialization is inescapable, Emerson argues that individualized activity must and can be turned to moral purposes:

> You may fulfil your round of duties by clearing yourself in the *direct,* or, in the *reflex* way. Consider whether you have satisfied your relations to father, mother, cousin, neighbor, town, cat, and dog; whether any of these can upbraid you. But I may also neglect this reflex standard, and absolve me to myself. I have my own stern claims and perfect circle. It denies the name of duty to many offices that are called duties. But if I can discharge its debts, it enables me to dispense with the popular code. If any one imagines that this law is lax, let him keep its commandments one day.
>
> (**"Self-Reliance,"** in *CW,* 2:42)

This strident assertion of the morality of individual acts, even those that seem to disregard social obligations, reflects economic calculations of both efficient means and valuable ends. The sheer variety of social relatedness that makes every act socially indebted also, somewhat paradoxically, frees individuals to appropriate the resources of cultural specialization: it would be far too inefficient, if not impossible, to consider all the responsibilities incurred in the most basic human acts. Emerson makes this point humorously by running his list of household and civic duties to "cousin, neighbor, town, cat, and dog." However, if it is impossible to measure all the moral responsibilities implied in the cultural *sources* of our acts, Emerson insists that we can and must measure the *use* to which those resources are put, the aim of our individual pursuits. His claim "I may . . . absolve me to myself" does not reject moral accountability but asserts that people must pay their social debt in this "*direct*" way.

Yet Emerson's defense of specialized labor on the grounds of its efficiency is secondary to his belief that diversified, individualized activity is a moral end in itself. When he claims "I may . . . absolve me to myself," he is also endorsing a radical shift in our location of value: as in **"Compensation,"** he insists that we seek "salvation" neither in heaven nor in the alienable products of our labor but in the experience of action—experience that is radically subjective. While Emerson asserts that action must be moral, his definition of value as the active expression and development of self means that "moral" activity comprehends a potentially unlimited spectrum of human pursuits. His economics thus are based on a logic of maximizing vital experience: he asserts the value of people exercising differ-

ent talents, enjoying different aspects of life, keeping different possibilities of experience alive. His writings are full of exhortations to expand human consciousness by exploring through our actions new relations to the world: **"The American Scholar,"** for example, declares, "So much of nature as he is ignorant of, so much of his own mind does he not yet possess" (*CW,* 1:55); and **"Self-Reliance"** avers, "The eye was placed where one ray should fall, that it might testify of that particular ray" (*CW,* 2:28). Emerson asserts the morality of allowing people the freedom to pursue their own interests, even in extravagant, luxurious ways. "Man" is "by constitution expensive": "He is born to be rich. He is thoroughly related" (**"Wealth,"** in *W,* 6:85, 88). This redefinition of morality is undeniably an "amoral" consequence of Emerson's pragmatism. Yet this "amorality" is itself a moral and economic calculation—the decision that since life is never safe or secure, moral activity should mean not merely preserving life but living it: "I do not wish to expiate, but to live. My life is for itself and not for a spectacle" (**"Self-Reliance,"** in *CW,* 2:31).

It is critical to see how this Emersonian "amorality" differs radically from the amoral logic of capitalism, in which the self-interested pursuit of profit facilitates market efficiencies that allegedly increase wealth for all. Emerson exhorts us to harness the efficiencies of culture so as to maximize creative opportunities, but he is willing to see a reform of capitalist institutions whenever these thwart our creative faculties: "I would not have the laborer sacrificed to the splendid result,—I would not have the laborer sacrificed to my convenience and pride, nor to that of a great class of such as me. Let there be worse cotton and better men" (**"The Method of Nature,"** in *CW,* 1:121).

"I SHALL KNOW YOU": THE
ANTI-COMMUNITARIAN COMMUNICATION OF SELF

The claim "I may . . . absolve me to myself" marks another ethical dilemma posed by Emerson's pragmatism. By locating value in the experience of action, he problematizes the communication of value and thus the concept of a communitarian standard of morality.[30] Inherited culture both threatens and enables the active expression of self that, for Emerson, is our primary property in life. "[C]onforming to usages that have become dead to you . . . scatters your force," he writes in **"Self-Reliance"**: "[U]nder all these screens, I have difficulty to detect the precise man you are." But in the next breath he claims, "[D]o your work, and I shall know you" (*CW,* 2:31-32). Since all human acts must be articulated in cultural media, this "work" that communicates a true "knowledge" of self to others can only be the new *use* to which we put inherited ideas. Any original self-expression requires retroping, disrupting, or rejecting conventional meanings and morality; hence **"Self-Reliance"** calls on us to "speak the rude truth," preach the "doctrine of hatred," and "write on the lintels of the door-post, *Whim*" (*CW,* 2:30).

It would seem, then, that the active expression of self that Emerson defines as our primary moral value and responsibility opposes any concept of community based on con-ventional communication, on the sharing of codified val-ues. The opening paragraph of **"Self-Reliance,"** for example, describes expression in strange terms of asser-tion and domination. Emerson begins by sounding a confi-dent, and often-quoted, definition of genius: "To believe your own thought, to believe that what is true for you in your private heart, is true for all men,—that is genius." Despite this image of accord, it soon appears that truth, for Emerson, is less a knowledge to be shared than an occa-sion for action that *cannot* be shared. "Speak your latent conviction and it shall be the universal sense," he exhorts, implying that one cannot really *have* a conviction until it is spoken, that an inward belief is merely "latent" until re-alized in action. To have another person give voice to and confirm "precisely what we have thought and felt all the time" does not create an encouraging solidarity of convic-tion; rather, it deprives us of the act of speaking that latent conviction, forcing us "to take with shame our own opin-ion from another" (*CW,* 2:27). Emerson thus arrives at the peculiar position that expressive acts are necessary, not to communicate with others, but to prevent them from com-municating with you, since if they did they might deprive you of, or distract you from, your own expressive acts: "A preoccupied attention is the only answer to the importu-nate frivolity of other people" (**"Experience,"** in *CW,* 3:47); "church and old book mumble and ritualize to an unheeding, preöccupied and advancing mind" (**"The Tran-scendentalist,"** in *CW,* 1:215).

The self-expression that Emerson values most highly is limited to a performative presence: the "act" within the "work" that he describes in **The Method of Nature,"** a shaping energy or tendency of mind. Thus he claims that the "real value" of great works of art "is as signs of power" (**"Art,"** in *CW,* 2:215). Original works need not dominate us or deprive us of our own action; instead, they can ap-prise us of our own capacity to re-create our relation to the world: "Therefore we love the poet, the inventor, who in any form . . . has yielded us a new thought. He un-locks our chains, and admits us to a new scene" (**"The Poet,"** in *CW,* 3:19). But because the primary value of ac-tivity lies in the experience of the actor, that value can be "communicated" only if an action provokes others to emu-lative or antagonistic acts of their own:

> There is at this moment for you an utterance brave and grand as that of the colossal chisel of Phidias, or trowel of the Egyptians, or the pen of Moses, or Dante, but different from all these. Not possibly will the soul all rich, all eloquent, with thousand-cloven tongue, deign to repeat itself; but if you can hear what these patri-archs say, surely you can reply to them in the same pitch of voice: for the ear and the tongue are two or-gans of one nature.
>
> (**"Self-Reliance,"** in *CW,* 2:47)

This is perhaps the most optimistic image of communica-tion and community compatible with Emerson's location of value in the experience of action. However, his tropes of conversation here also acknowledge limits: to respond in the same "pitch" of voice is not necessarily to share the same meanings or values, perhaps not even to have a com-mon language. Rather, it is to emulate the spirit or energy of other people's creative acts by doing something decid-edly "different from all these."

This anti-communicative aspect of Emerson's pragmatism leads to an ethical conclusion that many readers find re-pugnant—an individualism that seems to scorn the needs and infirmities of others:

> And we cannot say too little of our constitutional ne-cessity of seeing things under private aspects, or satu-rated with our humors. And yet is the God the native of these bleak rocks. That need makes in morals the capi-tal virtue of self-trust. We must hold hard to this pov-erty, however scandalous, and by more vigorous self-recoveries, after the sallies of action, possess our axis more firmly. The life of truth is cold, and so far mourn-ful; but it is not the slave of tears, contritions, and per-turbations. It does not attempt another's work, nor adopt another's facts. It is a main lesson of wisdom to know your own from another's. I have learned that I cannot dispose of other people's facts; but I possess such a key to my own, as persuades me against all their denials, that they also have a key to theirs. A sym-pathetic person is placed in the dilemma of a swimmer among drowning men, who all catch at him, and if he give so much as a leg or finger, they will drown him. They wish to be saved from the mischiefs of their vices, but not from their vices. Charity would be wasted on this poor waiting on the symptoms. A wise and hardy physician will say, *Come out of that,* as the first condi-tion of advice.
>
> (**"Experience,"** in *CW,* 3:46-47)

Faced with a passage of such troubling (and troubled) elo-quence, readers often are tempted to conflate Emerson's argument with a capitalist blame-the-victim ideology (the type often applied to welfare recipients), which presumes that individuals have opportunities not, in fact, provided by society. But Emerson's logic here is explicitly *non*-capitalist: he is again articulating a critical response to the alienation of value, an alienation on which capitalism de-pends.

Emerson in this passage honestly assesses the costs and benefits of his location of value in the experience of ac-tion; for if it allows him to focus on value that cannot be alienated, it also forces him to acknowledge that such value cannot be given to others. This is the central mes-sage of **"Compensation"**: true value cannot be stolen, but it also must be earned. Emerson insists, without apology, that each person must earn his or her own value in life, for he believes that "seeing things under private aspects" is a "constitutional necessity": our alienation from all media is the basis of our self-conscious, symbol-making intelli-gence.[31] He acknowledges that alienation and the radical subjectivity of value can be "mournful," but he also attests that this "poverty" brings into play the mitigating "virtue of self-trust." **"Compensation"** argues that accepting the limits of worldly action makes the universe "alive" with meaning; similarly, accepting our own lives and actions as the only value we will ever have encourages us to see our actions as sufficient. Even if Emerson seems to be scorning others, the underlying logic is one of empowerment. To insist that others must help themselves is also to insist that they *can*: "I have learned that I cannot dispose of other people's facts; but I possess such a key to my own, as persuades me against all their denials, that they also have a key to theirs."

This statement provides another description of the limits and possibilities of Emersonian community: though we cannot directly communicate or share value, we can know that every person has his or her own life and work, different from ours, yet equally valuable. Thus, the anti-communicative implications of Emerson's philosophy imply a communitarian ethos of pluralism. Far from being scornful toward others, Emerson's individualism affirms that each person possesses the talents sufficient to lead a morally significant life. This is a positive *moral* consequence of Emerson's "amoral" defense of the full spectrum of specialized, individual activity. Emerson's thought encourages not simply a tolerance but a celebration of diversity.

THE "NECESSARY FOUNDATIONS" OF REFORM

I now want to address the issues of political action and reform and to consider the familiar charge, renewed most recently by Sacvan Bercovitch and Cornel West, that Emerson's individualism precludes collective political action.[32] There is no question that the anti-communitarian aspects of his pragmatism imply a deep distrust of political institutions. However, I want to complicate the conclusion that this distrust makes his philosophy politically impotent. Emerson's critique of political institutions must be seen in the context of his pragmatic attitude toward culture: just as he locates value in activity and not in products, so he locates morality in behavior and not in codes, laws, or institutions. If this view extends to a utopian, anarchist critique of political institutions, it also translates into a practical political mandate to examine human behavior critically and reform it.

By rejecting an emphasis on accumulated wealth, Emerson's pragmatism offers an important alternative to both capitalist and Marxist attitudes toward culture. The mixture of practical and utopian strains in his views on political action reflects his pragmatic analysis of culture:

> It is handsomer to remain in the establishment better than the establishment, and conduct that in the best manner, than to make a sally against evil by some single improvement, without supporting it by a total regeneration. Do not be so vain of your one objection. Do you think there is only one? Alas! my good friend, there is no part of society or of life better than any other part. All our things are right and wrong together. The wave of evil washes all our institutions alike. Do you complain of our Marriage? Our marriage is no worse than our education, our diet, our trade, our social customs. Do you complain of the laws of Property? It

is a pedantry to give such importance to them. Can we not play the game of life with these counters, as well as with those; in the institution of property, as well as out of it.

> **("New England Reformers,"** in *CW*, 3:154-55)

Somewhat paradoxically, this perspective portrays culture as simultaneously more and less alienated than Marxism does. Emerson laments not only the alienation of property or wealth but also the alienation of all cultural media. For Emerson, every word, statement, or idea is an alien and constricting tool: "Every thought is also a prison; every heaven is also a prison," he claims in **"The Poet"** (*CW*, 3:19). Yet this assumption of a universal alienation leads Emerson to portray culture as *more* responsive to human action than does Marxism. By focusing on the alienation of wealth, Marxism develops its traditional view of culture as ideology, as a totalizing system of domination that serves to perpetuate existing inequalities of wealth. In contrast, Emerson implies it is pedantic to assume that culture could ever *not* be alienated, or to locate the alienation of culture in any particular institution. Assuming alienation as the norm, Emerson views culture not as a totalizing system of control but as a medium that allows for and requires performance: though we are alienated from all cultural media, they can be turned to our purposes. It is crucial to see that this perspective rejects not only a traditional Marxist view of culture as ideology but also the capitalist doctrine that the efficiencies of cultural specialization can transform the self-interested pursuit of profit into the moral result of increased wealth for all. Instead, Emerson stresses how culture both limits and enables our action: it neither guarantees morality nor prevents it. This duality is expressed in his question "Can we not play the game of life with these counters, as well as with those . . .?" Culture allows for moral action, but morality is achieved only through our acts, through the *way* we "play the game of life" with the cultural tools we inherit.

A related dualism lies at the core of Emerson's attitude toward politics, government, and reform. On the one hand, he insists that political change is desirable and inevitable; on the other, he shows an indifference to and even cynicism about the reform of legal codes and institutions. An understanding of this dualism again depends on seeing Emerson's ethics as an outgrowth of his theory of invention. In the opening lines of *Nature,* he articulates a central axiom of this theory: the inexorability of change. These famous lines, often read as a complaint against history, actually portray history as a process of inevitable and revitalizing change. Emerson does complain that he and his contemporaries "buil[d] the sepulchres of the fathers," "grope among the dry bones of the past," and "put the living generation into masquerade out of its faded wardrobe"; however, he then asserts: "The sun shines to-day also. There is more wool and flax in the fields" (*CW,* 1:7). Emerson's tropes insist that the burdensome obsolescence of inherited culture is inseparable from the vital process of change: the passage of time that kills the fathers brings us life today; the same sun that dries their bones and fades their wardrobes creates new flax for us to weave our own garments. We continually turn the cultural tools we inherit to new uses, thereby reinventing the present and rendering obsolete those same inherited systems of ideas.

Using language that echoes the beginning lines of *Nature,* Emerson in **"Man the Reformer"** describes political change as an inevitable result of this creative change wrought by human activity: "[T]he world not only fitted the former men, but fits us. . . . What is man born for but to be a Reformer, a Re-maker of what man has made" (*CW,* 1:156).[33] Political change is inevitable because people are constantly re-forming society by changing the quality and focus of their pursuits:

> [T]he old statesman knows that society is fluid; there are no such roots and centres; but any particle may suddenly become the centre of the movement, and compel the system to gyrate round it, as every man of strong will, like Pisistratus, or Cromwell, does for a time, and every man of truth, like Plato, or Paul, does forever. But politics rest on necessary foundations, and cannot be treated with levity. Republics abound in young civilians, who believe that the laws make the city, that grave modifications of the policy and modes of living, and employments of the population, that commerce, education, and religion, may be voted in or out; and that any measure, though it were absurd, may be imposed on a people, if only you can get sufficient voices to make it a law. But the wise know that foolish legislation is a rope of sand, which perishes in the twisting; that the State must follow, and not lead the character and progress of the citizen; the strongest usurper is quickly got rid of; and they only who build on Ideas, build for eternity; and that the form of government which prevails, is the expression of what cultivation exists in the population which permits it. The law is only a memorandum. We are superstitious, and esteem the statute somewhat: so much life as it has in the character of living men, is its force. The statute stands there to say, yesterday we agreed so and so, but how feel ye this article today? Our statute is a currency, which we stamp with our own portrait: it soon becomes unrecognizable, and in process of time will return to the mint. Nature is not democratic, nor limited-monarchical, but despotic, and will not be fooled or abated of any jot of her authority, by the pertest of her sons: and as fast as the public mind is opened to more intelligence, the code is seen to be brute and stammering. It speaks not articulately and must be made to. Meantime the education of the general mind never stops.
>
> (**"Politics,"** in *CW,* 3:117-18)

This passage illustrates Emerson's dual attitude toward reform. On the one hand, political change is inevitable: laws, like coins, are "stamped" "with our own portrait"; they reflect "man" as defined by the system of human pursuits in the period from which they emerge. As human activity continually changes, along with the range of pursuits that shape "man" and society, laws grow obsolete; the coin grows "unrecognizable" and must "return to the mint." However, the corollary of Emerson's belief that human ac-

tivity *guarantees* political change is his assertion that it also imposes limits: real political change must be based in the behavior of a society's citizens. Thus, he combines an affirmation of the inevitability of reform with a skepticism toward it.

Crucially, Emerson's insistence that reform must accompany social and behavioral change does *not* translate into a renunciation of political action. The idea that individuals can facilitate and even impel broad forces of creative change obtains in the realm of politics as well as invention: persons who understand the tendencies of an era can articulate those tendencies and galvanize others behind new moral purposes. Indeed, a new idea can "revolutionize the entire system of human pursuits" (**"Circles,"** in *CW,* 2:184); poets utter ideas that "become the songs of the nations" (**"The Poet,"** in *CW,* 3:6), and each institution appears as "the lengthened shadow of one man" (**"Self-Reliance,"** in *CW,* 2:35). Again, however, this assertion that people can change society through the power of ideas carries a reverse assertion: in order to compel meaningful political change, ideas must effect a real change in people's habits. Thus, in the passage from **"Politics,"** the "old statesman," the actor whose creative medium is government, "knows that society is fluid" and that a new idea may "compel the system to gyrate round it." However, he also knows that "politics rest on necessary foundations": policies must be based in the "modes of living, and employments of the population"; and thus reform must "follow, and not lead the character and progress of the citizen."

This dualism at the center of Emerson's attitude toward politics undoubtedly has a utopian element. As the unabashedly utopian flight in the closing pages of **"Politics"** shows, Emerson's insistence that reforms be based in the behavior of citizens, if carried to its logical conclusion, results in anarchism. However, if his theory of reform admits of anarchist extensions, it also has practical political applications. He found only too much confirmation of his political theories in the central political event of his lifetime: the sectional struggle over slavery that came to a head for him in the Compromise of 1850.[34] In the willingness of Massachusetts legislators and judges to enforce the Fugitive Slave Law, he found embittering evidence that morality cannot be codified or legislated but must exist in the actions of citizens:

> I wish that Webster & Everett & also the young political aspirants of Massachusetts should hear Wendell Phillips speak, were it only for the capital lesson in eloquence they might learn of him. This, namely, that the first & the second & the third part of the art is to keep your feet always firm on a fact. They talk about the Whig party. There is no such thing in nature. They talk about the Constitution. It is a scorned piece of paper. He feels after a fact & finds it in the money-making, in the commerce of New England, and in the devotion of the Slave states to their interest, which enforces them to the crimes which they avow or disavow, but do & will do.
>
> (*JMN,* 9:136-37)

Cotten thread holds the union together, unites John C. Calhoun & Abbott Lawrence. Patriotism for holidays & summer evenings with music & rockets, but cotten thread is the union.

(*JMN,* 9:425)

The sectional crisis forced Emerson to apply his political theories to American democracy. The level of liberty in America could not be guaranteed by the rights asserted in the Constitution or by the form of government established there. Political freedom was determined by the actions of Americans—by the will of legislators and judges to preserve the liberty promised in the law, and by the will of citizens to pay the price of true reform. The crisis of 1850 showed that this political will did not exist in Massachusetts: the primary political reality was revealed as the "cotten thread" uniting the manufacturing and commercial economy of New England to Southern planters. Emerson was compelled to abandon the notion of combining a principled opposition to slavery with support for union with the slave states. The political reality of the union was complicity with slavery: "Here is a measure of pacification & union. What is its effect? that it has made one subject, one only subject for conversation, & painful thought, throughout the Union, Slavery. We eat it, we drink it, we breathe it, we trade, we study, we wear it" (*JMN,* 11:361).

It is the context of these attitudes toward political reform that the basis for and extent of Emerson's rejection of collective politics must be assessed. Emerson does not oppose collective interests or action per se; rather, he distrusts the institutional *vehicles* of collective will. This distrust stems from a central tenet of his thought, that inherited culture threatens to obstruct the creative change that is crucial to the vitality of our individual and social lives:

> Parties are also founded on instincts, and have better guides to their own humble aims than the sagacity of their leaders. They have nothing perverse in their origin, but rudely mark some real and lasting relation. We might as wisely reprove the east wind, or the frost, as a political party, whose members, for the most part, could give no account of their position, but stand for the defence of those interests in which they find themselves. Our quarrel with them begins, when they quit this deep natural ground at the bidding of some leader, and, obeying personal considerations, throw themselves into the maintenance and defence of points, nowise belonging to their system. A party is perpetually corrupted by personality. Whilst we absolve the association from dishonesty, we cannot extend the same charity to their leaders. They reap the rewards of the docility and zeal of the masses which they direct. Ordinarily, our parties are parties of circumstance, and not of principle; as, the planting interest in conflict with the commercial; the party of capitalists, and that of operatives; parties which are identical in their moral character, and which can easily change ground with each other, in the support of many of their measures. Parties of principle, as, religious sects, or the party of free-trade, of universal suffrage, of abolition of slavery, of abolition of capital punishment, degenerate into personalities, or would in-

spire enthusiasm. The vice of our leading parties in this country (which may be cited as a fair specimen of the societies of opinion) is, that they do not plant themselves on the deep and necessary grounds to which they are respectively entitled, but lash themselves to fury in the carrying of some local and momentary measure, nowise useful to the commonwealth.

("**Politics,**" in *CW,* 3:122)

It is crucial that Emerson affirms the concept of political association, not only for parties of "principle," but even for those based on the frankly material grounds of "the defence of those interests in which [people] find themselves," for such association reflects "some real and lasting relation."[35] Indeed, somewhat surprisingly, he argues that collective interests form the valid basis for parties, and that the threat of political corruption comes from mere individualism or "personality." Yet if Emerson asserts the fundamental legitimacy of collective interests, he fears that collective political institutions (like all cultural institutions) threaten to become distorting and stifling. Parties, he declares, are too susceptible to the ambitions and interests of their leaders; they become focused on goals that have more to do with the perpetuation of institutional power than with any thoughtful application of principle. Emerson's theory of invention asserts that vital change is maximized when individuals exercising their own particular talents utilize and facilitate cultural resources and processes. Thus, he finds the remedy for the monolithic and inflexible aims of political institutions in individualized activity.

This pragmatic critique of collective institutions undeniably problematizes political action. When Emerson attempts to imagine collective interests defined not through distorting institutional channels but by the vital interests of individual activity, his utopian formula betrays the impossibility of completely realizing this goal: "The union is only perfect, when all the uniters are isolated. . . . The union must be ideal in actual individualism" (**"New England Reformers,"** in *CW,* 3:157).[36] Yet, as I have suggested, the practical possibilities of his political philosophy do not reduce to its utopian limits. His critique of collective politics is only one aspect of his belief that morality cannot be guaranteed in forms or codes but exists only in practice—a belief that provides a practical mandate to transform our behavior.

In Conclusion

Emerson's ethics reject the standard of accumulated wealth that defines the capitalist/Marxist axis of traditional economics, articulating instead an economics of maximizing vital, self-expressive activity. Seeing alienation as a problem common to all media of human action, Emerson endorses a radical reform in ethical standards, locating value in the experience of action, in the active expression and development of self. Since his pragmatism stresses the cultural sources of individual acts, he insists that all action carries a social responsibility that can be fulfilled by using those resources for a moral end. However, his redefinition of value also expands the definition of "moral" activity to include the full spectrum of possible creative activities. Though these ethics imply a rejection of communitarian standards of morality, they simultaneously imply a pluralist basis for community.

These priorities place Emerson's philosophy firmly within the broad tradition of "liberalism." Of course, scholars take differing views on the value or limitations of Emerson's liberalism. One influential judgment, by Bercovitch, is that Emerson exemplifies how American "dissent" holds a fundamentally ambiguous status between subversion and co-optation. Liberal democracy socializes individuals, Bercovitch contends, "not by repressing radical energies but by redirecting them, in all their radical potential, into a constant conflict between self and society." As a theory of this conflict, Bercovitch concludes, Emerson's individualism is "not . . . a form of co-optation [but] a form of utopia developed within the premises of liberal culture and therefore especially susceptible to co-optation by liberal strategies of socialization." He claims that Emerson failed to challenge the premises of liberal culture because his inability to endorse the collective methods of socialism forced him to halt his early utopian critique at *"the edge of class analysis."*[37] It is worth remembering, however, that in any form of consensual government dissent has a similar "ambiguity": people must decide what degree and kind of freedom they demand in return for submitting to society's laws. Like any social or political theory, Emerson's ethics confront conflicts and trade-offs between the goals of individual freedom and social responsibility. I have tried to show why assessments of Emerson's ethics must address the pragmatic analyses and priorities behind his positions on these conflicts. An understanding of how his ethics differ from traditional political economy allows us to reconsider how "susceptible" his thought is to "co-optation" by capitalist ideology.

Notes

1. *The Journals and Miscellaneous Notebooks of Ralph Waldo Emerson,* ed. William H. Gilman and Ralph H. Orth et al., 16 vols. (Cambridge: Harvard Univ. Press, Belknap Press, 1960-82), 5:40; hereafter cited parenthetically as *JMN,* with volume and page number. In the interest of readability, deletions Emerson made in the process of writing have been ignored, and minor punctuation marks added by the *JMN* editors have been included. Other Emerson editions quoted in this essay, cited parenthetically by volume and page number, are as follows:

   CW The Collected Works of Ralph Waldo Emerson, ed. Alfred R. Ferguson and Joseph Slater et al., 5 vols. to date (Cambridge: Harvard Univ. Press, Belknap Press, 1971-).

   W The Complete Works of Ralph Waldo Emerson, ed. Edward Waldo Emerson, 12 vols. (Boston: Houghton Mifflin, 1903-4).

2. Stephen E. Whicher, *Freedom and Fate: An Inner Life of Ralph Waldo Emerson* (Philadelphia: Univ. of Pennsylvania Press, 1953).

3. See Sacvan Bercovitch, "Emerson, Individualism, and the Ambiguities of Dissent," *South Atlantic Quarterly* 89 (1990): 623-62. In an argument of impressive breadth, Bercovitch places Emerson in a transatlantic debate between "individualism" as an "ideological" apology for capitalism and "individuality" as a locus of "utopian" dissent. Bercovitch argues that because Emerson was unable to endorse the socialist experiments of the 1840s, he shifted increasingly to an ideological affirmation of capitalism. Also see Myra Jehlen, *American Incarnation: The Individual, the Nation, and the Continent* (Cambridge: Harvard Univ. Press, 1986), especially pages 82 and 84, where she discusses how her reading builds on Whicher's.

4. My interpretation extends the important revisionary work that has already been done on Emerson and pragmatism. See, in particular, Kenneth Burke, "I, Eye, Ay—Emerson's Early Essay 'Nature': Thoughts on the Machinery of Transcendence," in *Emerson's "Nature"—Origin, Growth, Meaning,* ed. Merton M. Sealts Jr. and Alfred R. Ferguson, 2nd ed. (Carbondale: Southern Illinois Univ. Press, 1979), 150-63, and "William James, Emerson, Whitman," in *Attitudes toward History* (Los Altos, CA: Hermes, 1959), 3-33; Harold Bloom, "Emerson: The American Religion," in *Agon: Towards a Theory of Revisionism* (New York: Oxford Univ. Press, 1982), 145-78; Stanley Cavell, "Thinking of Emerson" and "An Emerson Mood," chaps. 2 and 3 in *The Senses of Walden: An Expanded Edition* (San Francisco: North Point, 1981), 123-38, 141-60; and Richard Poirier, *Poetry and Pragmatism* (Cambridge: Harvard Univ. Press, 1992), *The Renewal of Literature: Emersonian Reflections* (New York: Random House, 1987), and *A World Elsewhere: The Place of Style in American Literature* (London: Oxford Univ. Press, 1966; Madison: Univ. of Wisconsin Press, 1985), esp. 50-70, 90-91.

5. Ideas, James insists, "become true just in so far as they help us to get into satisfactory relation with other parts of our experience" ("What Pragmatism Means," in *The Writings of William James: A Comprehensive Edition,* ed. John J. McDermott [New York: Random House, 1967; Chicago: Univ. of Chicago Press, 1977], 382). This definition of truth leads James, like Emerson, to place a primary value on activity: "[A word] appears less as a solution, then, than as a program for more work" (380).

6. As Emerson writes in "Quotation and Originality," "We quote not only books and proverbs, but arts, sciences, religion, customs, and laws; nay, we quote temples and houses, tables and chairs by imitation" (*W,* 8:178-79).

7. See Poirier on this connection between troping and "turning" (*Renewal of Literature,* 13).

8. James observes that "concepts are abstracted from experiences already seen or given, and he who uses

them to divine the new can never do so but in ready-made and ancient terms. Whatever actual novelty the future may contain . . . escapes conceptual treatment altogether" ("Percept and Concept—Some Corollaries," in *Writings of William James,* 253).

9. See, for example, the following usages: "All I know is reception" ("Experience," in *CW,* 3:48). "Great genial power, one would almost say, consists in not being original at all; in being altogether receptive" ("Shakspeare; or, The Poet," in *CW,* 4:110). "I would write on the lintels of the door-post, *Whim.* I hope it is somewhat better than whim at last, but we cannot spend the day in explanation" ("Self-Reliance," in *CW,* 2:30). "The one thing which we seek with insatiable desire, is to forget ourselves, to be surprised out of our propriety, to lose our sempiternal memory, and to do something without knowing how or why; in short, to draw a new circle. Nothing great was ever achieved without enthusiasm. The way of life is wonderful: it is by abandonment" ("Circles," in *CW,* 2:190).

10. Poirier characterizes Emersonian genius as an energy that becomes distorted as soon as it must take form in the medium of language (*Renewal of Literature,* 79-82).

11. Melville's marginal comments in his copy of *Essays: Second Series* accuse Emerson of blithely dismissing the existence of evil (*The Portable Melville* [New York: Viking, 1952], 600-601). F. O. Matthiessen set the direction for most subsequent twentieth-century criticism by arguing that Emerson rejected tragedy, while Hawthorne and especially Melville made it central to their art (*American Renaissance: Art and Expression in the Age of Emerson and Whitman* [New York: Oxford Univ. Press, 1941], esp. 634, 180-86, 337-51, 435-59, 467-84, and 500-514). The central theme of Whicher's study is that "[a]lthough Emerson refused to conceive of life as tragedy," he nonetheless developed an increasing "recognition of the limits of mortal condition [that] meant a defeat of his first romance of self-union and greatness" (*Freedom and Fate,* 109). Matthiessen's distinction survives in different forms today. For example, Jehlen contends that Emerson believed in "a transcendentally benevolent world" (*American Incarnation,* 109), while she titles her chapter on Melville's *Pierre* "The Rebirth of Tragedy." For an opposing view, one that is largely in accord with the reading I offer here, see Michael Lopez, "Transcendental Failure: 'The Palace of Spiritual Power,'" in *Emerson: Prospect and Retrospect,* ed. Joel Porte (Cambridge: Harvard Univ. Press, 1982), 121-53. Lopez argues that Emerson, far from lacking a sense of tragedy or evil, portrays "failure" as a central and indispensable fact of life, for it provides the necessary "antagonist" or resistance against which human will expresses itself.

12. See Jehlen, *American Incarnation,* esp. chap. 3, "Necessary and Sufficient Acts," 76-122. Jehlen asserts that for Emerson, "willful intervention either to hasten the future's advent or, worse still, to redefine it, can only distort the perfect order that already exists implicitly, and thus delay its explicit realization. Not only are deeds and revolutions not needed, they are forbidden, doomed to failure and worse." Yet this conviction paradoxically "frees the builders for pure activity": "By believing that his acts enact the universal purpose, the Emersonian actor feels free, not only from the tax of ethical or political considerations, but free to invoke all the powers that be, to his and nature's end" (85, 84).

13. In "Nature," Emerson undercuts the dichotomy of nature versus art: "We talk of deviations from natural life, as if artificial life were not also natural. . . . If we consider how much we are nature's, we need not be superstitious about towns, as if that terrific or benefit force did not find us there also, and fashion cities. Nature who made the mason, made the house" (*CW,* 3:106).

14. Jehlen, *American Incarnation,* 110.

15. "Whatever limits us we call Fate" ("Fate," in *W,* 6:20).

16. Similarly, *Nature*'s claim that every spirit builds its own heaven is best understood in light of Emerson's provocative axiom from "The Poet": "Every thought is also a prison; every heaven is also a prison" (*CW,* 3:19).

17. Kenneth Burke, *A Grammar of Motives* (New York: George Braziller, 1945; Berkeley and Los Angeles: Univ. of California Press, 1969), 38-39.

18. "Discipline" is an incipient version of the argument Emerson makes in "Compensation." It is in "Discipline" that he first claims "[a]ll things are moral" (*CW,* 1:25), a claim repeated with much greater detail and clarity in "Compensation." For a representative reading of the later work, see Whicher, who argues that "Compensation" posits a naïve or extreme model of "automatic moral compensation" which "is without question the most unacceptable of Emerson's truths," for it confronts "two classic human problems—the relation of virtue to happiness, and the problem of evil, and seemingly proceeds to deny that they *are* problems" (*Freedom and Fate,* 36). Also see Michael Gilmore's contention that "'Compensation' reveals an Emerson already well on his way to becoming an apologist for commercial and industrial capitalism," who perversely applies "economic categories" to "the operations of the Soul" (*American Romanticism and the Marketplace* [Chicago: Univ. of Chicago Press, 1985], 31, 30).

19. Jehlen, *American Incarnation,* 108-10.

20. My phrasing here echoes Wallace Stevens's poem "Sunday Morning": "And shall the earth / Seem all

of paradise that we shall know?" (*The Collected Poems of Wallace Stevens* [1954; New York: Vintage, 1982], 68). This parallel reveals a major line of influence reaching back from Emerson to Stevens, in whose poems the loss of a belief in any God behind nature can make earthly reality explode with human significance.

21. Consider, for example, Bercovitch's view that Emerson's skepticism toward socialism led him to embrace capitalism, to renounce "utopian" social critique in favor of "ideological" apology. Also see Gilmore's *American Romanticism and the Marketplace,* 18-34. Gilmore argues that early works like "The Transcendentalist" and "Self-Reliance" contain strong criticisms of the marketplace's pervasive and constricting effects, while works like "Compensation" and "Wealth" signal Emerson's shift into the stance of an "apologist" for capitalism (31).

22. Emerson lived from 1803 to 1882, Marx from 1818 to 1883.

23. Much recent criticism has considered how the "economic" logics and metaphors in Emerson's philosophy relate to the realities and ideologies of America's capitalist economy. Perhaps the most influential work is Gilmore's *American Romanticism and the Marketplace,* which locates the familiar Whicherian pattern of "early" radicalism and "late" conservatism in Emerson's attitudes toward capitalism. Christopher Newfield ("Emerson's Corporate Individualism," *ALH* 3 [1991]: 657-84) suggests that the affinities between Emersonian individualism and the corporation illustrate the "[b]enevolent despotism" of American democracy (657), which, Newfield argues, substitutes oligarchy and consumerism in place of any meaningful collective control. Howard Horwitz ("The Standard Oil Trust as Emersonian Hero," *Raritan* 6 [spring 1987]: 97-119) also explores the connections between Emersonian self-transcendence and the corporate trust, but warns against conflating the possibilities of Emerson's philosophy with the actualities of American society. The establishment of the trusts as oligarchies, Horwitz reminds us, was a historical event, the result of a specific power struggle, and as such does not "disclose the implied and total political agenda of [Emerson's] thought": "[N]or should we think that because the trust was formally a transcendentalist institution [Emerson's] ideal of selfhood can only serve monopolistic interests" (118). Also see Richard A. Grusin, "'Put God in Your Debt': Emerson's Economy of Expenditure," *PMLA* 103 (1988): 35-44; and William Charvat, "American Romanticism and the Depression of 1837," in *The Profession of Authorship in America, 1800-1870: The Papers of William Charvat,* ed. Matthew Bruccoli (Columbus: Ohio State Univ. Press, 1968; New York: Columbia Univ. Press, 1992), 49-67.

24. For Kenneth Burke's explanation of this view (one that demonstrates the pragmatic roots of his own thought), see "Priority of the 'Idea,'" in *A Rhetoric of Motives* (New York: Prentice-Hall, 1950; Berkeley and Los Angeles: Univ. of California Press, 1969), 132-37.

25. Emerson asserts the value of inherited cultural conventions in "The Conservative": "Reform converses with possibilities, perchance with impossibilities; but here is sacred fact. This also was true, or it could not be: it had life in it, or it could not have existed; it has life in it, or it could not continue. . . . This will stand until a better cast of the dice is made" (*CW,* 1:188).

26. "Division of labour within the workshop implies the undisputed authority of the capitalist over men, that are but parts of a mechanism that belongs to him" (Karl Marx, *Capital: A Critique of Political Economy,* ed. Frederick Engels, trans. Samuel Moore and Edward Aveling [New York: Random House, Modern Library, 1906], 391).

27. Marx envisions a society in which "the means of production" are owned "in common" and the "total product of [the] community" is acknowledged as a "social product," with each individual's "share in the part of the total product destined for individual consumption" "determined by his labour-time" (*Capital,* 90-91).

28. See Marx, *Capital,* 82-84, 83-87, 94-96. According to Marx, a "definite social relation between men . . . assumes, in their eyes, the fantastic form of a relation between things" (*Capital,* 83). He insists that the value of a product is a function of the amount of human labor required to produce it: "[I]n the midst of all the accidental and ever fluctuating exchange-relations between the products, the labour-time socially necessary for their production forcibly asserts itself like an over-riding law of nature." Thus the value of the product of any individual producer is a socially produced value—a function of the society's division of labor—and the fluctuations of market value should be viewed as reflecting the "quantitative proportions in which society requires" "all the different kinds of private labour" (*Capital,* 86). The most just way to distribute wealth is on the basis of the individual's share in the total labor-time of society (*Capital,* 90-91).

The capitalist form of commodity exchange portrays this social value as the private property of the individual—as the private product of his or her labor: "It is, however, just this ultimate money form of the world of commodities that actually conceals, instead of disclosing, the social character of private labour, and the social relations between the individual producers" (*Capital,* 87). Marx argues that this alienation of social value is further exacerbated by wage labor and capitalist production. Unlike an independent producer who owns the means of production and sells a commodity, a wage laborer owns only his or her own labor-power, and the capitalist who owns the means of production sells the commodity produced by the worker's labor (*Capital*, 389-91). In this capitalist mode of production, the value of a worker's labor is not measured by the market value of a commodity sold by that worker, but specifically by the ability to produce surplus labor (capital) for an employer: hence, "to be a productive labourer is . . . not a piece of luck, but a misfortune" (*Capital*, 558).

29. In the "Commodity" chapter of *Nature*, Emerson describes the "private poor man" as able, like Shakespeare, to utilize a wealth of cultural benefits (*CW*, 1:12).

30. Donald E. Pease's *Visionary Compacts: American Renaissance Writings in Cultural Context* (Madison: Univ. of Wisconsin Press, 1987) argues that Emerson, like other antebellum writers, did not (as is commonly assumed) envision freedom in the exclusively negative terms of rejecting social conventions and traditions, but sought visions of communal involvement consistent with the principles and ideals of "America." George Kateb offers Emerson as a prime example of an American strain of "democratic individualism" that opposes only certain aspects of communitarian thought (*The Inner Ocean: Individualism and Democratic Culture* [Ithaca, NY: Cornell Univ. Press, 1992], esp. 222-29). Kateb contends that Emerson's brand of democratic individualism does not reject social relations; rather, it scrutinizes and reformulates those relations. Such scrutiny is consistent with a democratic notion of community, which stresses the explicitly conventional and consensual status of human bonds (226).

31. At the opening of this section on "subjectiveness," several pages earlier, Emerson declares: "It is very unhappy, but too late to be helped, the discovery we have made, that we exist. That discovery is called the Fall of Man. Ever afterwards, we suspect our instruments. We have learned that we do not see directly, but mediately, and that we have no means of correcting these colored and distorting lenses which we are, or of computing the amount of their errors" (*CW*, 3:43).

32. Bercovitch, for example, argues that Emerson rejects the collectivist *methods* of socialism, although he admires its reformist and utopian goals ("Emerson, Individualism, and the Ambiguities of Dissent," esp. 641-52). And Cornel West, in *The American Evasion of Philosophy: A Genealogy of Pragmatism* (Madison: Univ. of Wisconsin Press, 1989), concludes that Emerson's commitment to the "moral transgression" of individual nonconformity, his mystical celebration of "individual intuition over against collective action," and his fatalistic or "organic conception of history" doom him to the politically impotent position of a "petit bourgeois libertarian, with at times anarchist tendencies

and limited yet genuine democratic sentiments" (17, 18, 34, 40).

33. Emerson's phrasing in "Man the Reformer" also recalls two other sentences from the first paragraph of *Nature*: "Why should not we also enjoy an original relation to the universe?" and "There are new lands, new men, new thoughts. Let us demand our own works and laws and worship" (*CW*, 1:7).

34. Emerson's political opposition to slavery grew over time, yet he never became a radical abolitionist. As West argues, Emerson's journals show that he was by no means free from racist prejudices against African Americans (*American Evasion of Philosophy*, 28-35). However, his journals also show that slavery always was deeply abhorrent to him (see, for example, *JMN*, 5:15, 2:57-58). Emerson opposed the Annexation of Texas and the Kansas-Nebraska Act, both of which extended slavery into new regions beyond the boundaries set in the Compromise of 1820 (see Len Gougeon, *Virtue's Hero: Emerson, Antislavery, and Reform* [Athens: Univ. of Georgia Press, 1990], 20, 191). His support for the abolitionist movement strengthened throughout the 1840s; yet like many Northerners, he only slowly came to consider that citizens of free states might morally be required to take direct political action to abolish slavery where it already existed. The crisis over the Fugitive Slave Law forced Emerson to acknowledge how both commercial and Constitutional ties made the free states complicit with Southern slavery. In his first speech on that law, in 1851, he insisted that Northerners were morally obligated to break it, and further suggested that they follow the example of the British and buy the freedom of the slaves from Southern slaveholders ("The Fugitive Slave Law," in *W*, 11:186-98, 208-10). Elsewhere, he argued that preserving the union was not worth participating in slavery (*JMN*, 11:348-49). In 1859-60, Emerson proclaimed insurrectionist John Brown a hero (see his two public speeches on Brown in *W*, 11:265-81), and he eventually came to see the war as an inevitable struggle between free and slave societies, a struggle whose goal had to be the complete abolition of slavery (*JMN*, 15:299-302). In 1862, he hailed the Emancipation Proclamation, which for the first time made emancipation the direct object of the war (see his speech on the proclamation in *W*, 11:313-26).

35. For example, Emerson's theory of invention led him to believe that all people are served by principles of both conservatism and reform—by acknowledging the value of existing conventions and the necessity of change. See the companion lectures "The Conservative" and "The Transcendentalist," in *CW*, 1:184-216.

36. Bercovitch offers a detailed reading of this statement as it first appears in Emerson's journals ("Emerson, Individualism, and the Ambiguities of Dissent," esp. 628-30).

37. Bercovitch, "Emerson, Individualism, and the Ambiguities of Dissent," 655, 656, 650-51, 641. In contrast to Bercovitch, see Kateb's *Inner Ocean,* which presents Emerson as a theorist of rights-based individualism, a democratic philosophy that Kateb considers "the best way of honoring . . . the equal dignity of every individual" (1).

Michael Lopez (essay date 1996)

SOURCE: "The Anti-Emerson Tradition," in *Emerson and Power: Creative Antagonism in the Nineteenth Century,* Northern Illinois University Press, 1996, pp. 19-52.

[*In the following essay, Lopez traces the critical reception of Emerson's philosophical writings through the decades in an attempt to define his place in American critical thinking.*]

> Melville and Whitman persuasively strive to give us the substance promised by their titles: grass and a whale, earth and the sea are delivered. . . . But Emerson? Is there not something cloudy at the center of his reputation, something fatally faded about the works he has left us? When, I ask myself, did I last read one of his celebrated essays? How much, indeed, are Emerson's works even assigned in literary courses where the emphasis is not firmly historical?
>
> —*John Updike, "Emersonianism" (1984)*

In 1982 Alfred Kazin worried that criticism had for too long underestimated or overlooked entirely Ralph Waldo Emerson's "central concern with power": "There is no book that truly does justice to Emerson's sense of power"; "[T]here is no satisfactory book on Emerson's mind itself and his relation to the romantic, bourgeois, 'progressive' sense of individual power that became the stock gospel of the nineteenth century." A scant five years later, in a reinterpretation of Emerson, Richard Poirier complained that the study of "power"—indeed, the word itself—had become a cliché: "Thanks mostly to Foucault and his followers, the word 'power' has become tiresomely recurrent in discussions of cultural forms or the order of things." But, Poirier hastened to add—and his own "Emersonian reflections" are cogent testimony—power is "nonetheless unavoidable in any consideration of Emerson."[1]

Such diverse progress reports indicate how much has been happening inside the "Emerson industry" in the past decade and a half. The 1980s mark a definite turning point for Emerson criticism. The changes that have taken place in our understanding and valuation of his work might well, as Lawrence Buell has noted, astonish even those who would once have considered themselves Emerson's defenders.

SALUTATION AND DISMISSAL

The revived emphasis on "Emerson's stature as a pivotal American cultural hero" is one manifestation of that trans-

formation. For Kazin, Emerson is "the father of us all"—the "teacher of the American tribe." For Harold Bloom, Emerson is "the mind of our climate; he is the principal source of the American difference in poetry and criticism and in pragmatic post-philosophy. . . . [He] is the inescapable theorist of virtually all subsequent American writing. From his moment to ours, American authors either are in his tradition, or else in a countertradition originating in opposition to him." Emerson's influence has been so extensive, Poirier argues, "that his works now constitute a compendium of iconographies that have gotten into American writers who may never have liked or even read him." For Denis Donoghue and Joel Porte, Emerson remains "the founding father of nearly everything we think of as American in the modern world": "To the extent to which the sentiments of power, self-reliance, subjectivity, and independence attract to themselves a distinctly American nuance, its source is Emerson." For Stanley Cavell, Emerson is, along with Thoreau, the ("repressed") "founder" of American thinking. "When we trace the history of American literature or of American ideas," John Michael writes, "we retrace the influence of Emerson." He was, David Bromwich suggests, simply one of history's great men who irrevocably altered American culture.[2]

Such testimonials may sound, Buell writes, "pushed to an extreme." But they are not new. Emerson was only thirty-five years old and the author of one slim book when Harriet Martineau reported back to her English and European readers that it was not "too much to say that the United States cannot be fully known" without knowing Emerson. In 1850 Theodore Parker dubbed him "the most American of our writers" and the one with the greatest reputation. Walt Whitman called him "the actual beginner of the whole procession," the writer who would always be "nearest" to his country. "Mr. Emerson always draws," James Russell Lowell remarked of his popularity as a lecturer; "Few men have been so much to so many." In the 1880s Matthew Arnold surveyed the century that was drawing to a close and pronounced Wordsworth's "the most important work done in verse" and Emerson's *Essays* "the most important work done in prose."[3]

Emerson is, John Dewey said at the turn of the century, "the prophet and herald of any system which democracy may henceforth construct . . . when democracy has articulated itself, it will have no difficulty in finding itself already proposed in Emerson." To John Jay Chapman, Emerson seemed "the first modern man," looming "above his age like a colossus . . . towering like Atlas over the culture of the United States." Henry James would speak of him as "the first, and the one really rare, American spirit in letters." He is, George Woodberry claimed in 1907, "the only great mind that America has produced in literature." Even during the Modernist decades, when T. S. Eliot proposed that Emerson be "carved joint from joint," it was still not difficult to argue that he had "obtained a recognition such as no other of his countrymen can claim." "It becomes more and more apparent," Paul Elmer More wrote in 1921, "that Emerson, judged by an international or even by a true national standard, is the outstanding figure of American literature." "The leader of these minds," Lewis Mumford said five years later—referring to the writers of that epoch that F. O. Matthiessen would call "the American Renaissance"—"the central figure of them all, was Ralph Waldo Emerson."[4]

From the late 1830s on, Emerson has always been perceived as an American cultural hero, although our willingness to accept such putative heroes has varied dramatically. (Heroes, Emerson was well aware, are destined to become bores.) But there seems never to have been a time when Emerson's critics have questioned for very long his historical importance or have forgotten his significance as either a benign or a destructive influence on other American writers. ("America produced him," Barrett Wendell wrote in 1900, "and whether you like him or not, he is bound to live." "We must take Emerson into the bargain," Charles Feidelson conceded in 1953, "whether we like it or not.") Emerson has always been accorded what D. H. Lawrence called "museum-interest."[5]

What has changed over the years is, quite simply, the complexity that critics have been willing to ascribe to Emerson's writing and ideas. If, a quarter-century ago, the contours of Emerson scholarship were "reassuringly clear" (even, as Buell puts it, "cozy," like a Brahmin parlor), then those contours have been and continue to be radically stretched and refashioned or abandoned altogether. The boundaries that seemed, in the mid-1960s, firmly to prescribe both the value accorded his work and the historical context in which he was to be comprehended have been so expanded that it is now possible to say, as Emerson scholars do increasingly, that there appears to be much in Emerson that has been blunted, much that has still to surface, much that we have not been able or willing to see. Emerson is, Cavell writes, still far from "settled." Or, as David Marr puts it, "it is at least possible that much of Emerson's significance has eluded us, that there is [still] a literary-philosophical narrative of Emersonianism to be written." We need, Peter Carafiol writes, to find "other terms" and "a new place for Transcendentalism, or a new notion of Transcendentalism to go in the old place."[6]

The transformations that have occurred in Emerson criticism can all be described, it seems to me, as playing some part in that broad movement that Buell has christened the "de-Transcendentalizing" of Emerson. That Emerson's de-transcendentalizing has gone hand in hand with an increasing respect for his work is no accident, for the perception of Emerson as essentially "Transcendentalist"—always the predominant public image of him, an image still stubbornly embedded in much Emerson scholarship—has always been what Porte calls "a positive hindrance" to the appreciation of his writing. Porte put it this way, in a remarkable admission, in 1973:

> What I am prepared to state categorically is that the familiar rubrics of Emersonian thought, the stock in trade of most Emerson criticism, though undeniably there, are a positive hindrance to the enjoyment of Emerson's

writing. Though some Emersonians will undoubtedly continue until the end of time to chew over such concepts as Compensation, the Over-Soul, Correspondence, Self-Reliance, Spiritual Laws, et id genus omne, the trouble with such things is that they are not very interesting. They make Emerson seem awfully remote, abstract, and—yes—academic. My experience has been that when these topics are mentioned the mind closes, one's attention wanders.[7]

That one of Transcendentalism's preeminent scholars never doubted, some twenty years ago, that such dullness does indeed lie at the heart of Emerson's thought says much about our main tradition of Emerson scholarship. Even more telling is the failure of Porte's critique to elicit, as far as I am aware, even a single direct response or rejoinder from Emerson scholars. It could still simply be taken for granted, in 1973, that much of Emerson's thought was a closed book—essentially "transcendental" (easily classifiable under the familiar Transcendentalist catchwords) and too tedious to merit any serious reflection (though continuing to supply the material for an endless succession of scholarship).

"As any candid teacher of American literature can report," Porte concluded, "[Emerson] has manifestly *not* made his way 'on the strength of his message.' He has become the least appreciated, least enjoyed, least understood—indeed, least read—of America's unarguably major writers." (Emerson is, William Dean Howells concluded in 1900, "the most misunderstood man in America.") In other words, a great deal is still to be done in arguing for Emerson's inherent worth. In these "new historical" days such "recanonizing," as Cavell speaks of it, may appear distinctly old-fashioned, but the ambivalent way in which Emerson has been canonized makes it necessary.[8]

My point is not that Porte was imperceptive or even wrong, for he actually records a valuable perception about the way our major tradition of Emerson criticism has dehistoricized, simplified, and devalued Emerson and has made him seem dull, much more parochial, and much less complicated than he is. The same tradition that has ensured Emerson's continuing canonization, while never failing to uphold his historical importance, has, when it turned to his work itself, generally found little reason for *any longer* taking Emerson seriously as a writer or a thinker. There exists, David Robinson notes, "the uneasy feeling among historians of American thought and literature that Emerson's influence outdistances his achievement." Porte puts succinctly the value most critics have accorded Emerson "the Transcendentalist": worthy of preservation as the source of historical attention, but inherently objectionable or uninteresting. This attitude underlies most Emerson criticism, whether it is the outright condemnation by his enemies or the patronizing or vague disapproval of his friends. ("We turn to him," one Emerson scholar writes, "as to an amiable lunatic who seems to tell us whatever it is we think we want to hear.")[9]

In his canonization, as in so many things, Emerson presents a productive test case for the various theory and culture wars now being waged. Emerson is indeed a well-canonized American writer. But what does that mean? Is there a difference between canonization in one's own lifetime (early in it) and canonization after one's death? What are the ramifications of a canonization that is also, as it undoubtedly has been in Emerson's case, a "sanctification" as "the unshakably serene and satisfied," the "bloodless or nebulous" Sage of Concord?[10] Is there a difference between literary reputation in America and canonization in, say, England or France? Does canonization imply appreciation or condescension, or both? Does it impede or quicken public and academic understanding?

Emerson is, O. W. Firkins concluded in 1915, "at the same time honored and forsaken." Or, as he dryly restated it in 1933: "[Emerson] is certain of the due toll of inscriptions, invocations, appraisements, and obeisances—of that form of greeting from posterity which combines salutation with dismissal." Peter Carafiol reaches the same conclusion in a more recent backward glance at Emerson scholarship. The ambivalent terms in which Emerson's so-called Transcendentalism has been received may, Carafiol goes on to suggest, lie more "in the peculiarities of scholarship about Transcendentalism . . . than in Transcendentalism itself."[11]

> Assertions of Emerson's centrality and discomfort with it have gone hand in hand in Transcendentalist scholarship from the start. In 1876, O. B. Frothingham argued that "by sheer force of genius Emerson anticipated the results of the transcendental philosophy, defined its axioms and ran out their inferences to the end." But he complained that "Mr. Emerson's place is among poetic, not among philosophic minds." In one of the first "academic" studies, H. C. Goddard found Emerson's writing marred by absurd and unpoetic figures, and subsequent scholars have seen him as too abstract, too detached, or lacking in philosophical rigor. Even the most respected of Transcendentalism's modern commentators sometimes seem to hold the subject in something not far short of contempt. Lawrence Buell, for example, chastises the Transcendentalists for their "awkward and inchoate style" and "half-baked content," and the editors of Emerson's Works seem uncertain about how to evaluate him. They praise his earlier writing for its "absolute literary merit" but seem uncomfortable with the "excesses" of its "irrational eloquence." They apparently prefer the "dispassionate depth and balance" of the later work.[12]

According him equal parts reverence and contempt was a well-established convention in Emerson's own time, and it has continued, through a long line of distinguished scholars, to the present. *Almost* everyone," as Cavell remarks, "gets around to condescending to Emerson." Orestes Brownson's 1838 defense of Emerson's controversial **"Divinity School Address"** is a notable, early example of that traditional condescension: Brownson defended Emerson's good intentions and benevolent influence but apologized for "the puerility of his concepts," "the affectations of his style," and "the unphilosophical character of his speculations." Such backhanded compliments continued in John Morley's conclusion, in 1881, that "Emersonian transcen-

dentalism" must be regarded as "gospel" rather than "philosophy proper" and in W. C. Brownell's concession that Emerson had no artistry, "no sense of composition."[13]

T. S. Eliot launched a forthright attack on Transcendentalist foolishness, but there was no less disdain in Perry Miller's remark, in 1940, that Emerson's ideas were "too utterly fantastic to be any longer taken seriously." In the 1950s, Leslie Fiedler characterized Emerson as a writer of considerable historical "though not often sympathetic interest, who erected a notable monument to an insufficient view of life." More recently, Lawrence Buell has concluded that "Emerson and his circle *are* more important for historical reasons than for the quality of their achievements in art, philosophy, and theology." "It is hard to suppose," Irving Howe remarked in 1986, "that anyone could now take Emerson as a sufficient moral or philosophical guide—and impossible to suppose that anyone could find him very helpful in understanding the span of Western history between the time of his death and the present."[14]

Emerson's canonization has been, then, double-edged. Always granted museum-interest, he has in the same ambivalent motion been raised to the pedestal as a Transcendentalist-idealist saint and put down as, in William Dean Howells's phrase, "a national joke" ("all that was most hopelessly impossible, . . . the type of the incomprehensible, the byword of the poor paragrapher"). This is not only, as Howells saw it, Emerson's image in "the popular mind" but also the foundation for most Emerson criticism. It has resulted in what Cavell justly identifies as that still "fixated critical gesture toward Emerson both on the part of his friends and of his enemies."[15]

That gesture is twofold. It consists of "denying to Emerson the title of philosopher" (even, in most cases, the title of serious or morally complex thinker) and of describing Emerson's prose as, on the whole, a second- or third-rate failure, "a kind of mist or fog." In 1903 Dewey was already impatient with this "old story" that "puts away" Emerson as neither an artist nor a philosopher. That fixated critical gesture has been repeated so often by so many of Emerson's "friends" that it is not too much to say that Emerson's canonization has been a curse as well as a blessing and not an exaggeration to characterize the dominant tradition of Emerson criticism as also an anti-Emerson tradition. It is as if Emerson scholarship has thoroughly internalized, consciously or unconsciously, T. S. Eliot's caveat that Emerson was not "individually," or intrinsically, "very important" and "ought to be made to look very foolish."[16]

A long, venerable, and continuing critical tradition has decided that Emerson is primarily not a philosopher, thinker, or writer but the preacher of a New England gospel (a semimystical figure steeped in the atmosphere of religion). This idealizing, moralizing, transcendentalizing Emerson is the patron saint of those who seek to retire upward to a life of the spirit—to a "spiritual transcendence," as Philip Gura puts it, that takes us away from our "surroundings," away from "the things of this world." ("Transcendentalism" has, of course, always been a highly problematic description. In chapter 6 I shall have more to say about it and about the "Transcendentalist Image" of Emerson to which I refer here.) It is important to demarcate clearly and keep in mind this interpretation of Emerson, for it would seem, as Cavell notes, that "[i]f you insist on this view you will seem to find a world of evidence to support it." (And if you have settled on this definition of Emerson, then it is no longer necessary, or even very interesting, to ask again what Emerson thought. More important, then, are biographical questions, questions of textual history, questions about the immediate theological or social history that surrounds him.)[17]

But a crucial question needs to be raised. Can we say that a scholarly tradition has given an author a fair hearing, a hearing fair enough to establish what can be called a standard or canonical evaluation, if the interpretation it offers habitually denies the intrinsic value of his work? Does a critical tradition that has, for more than a century and a half, relegated "the quality of [Emerson's] achievement in art, philosophy, or theology" to secondary importance deserve to remain the dominant approach? Did it ever?

For there have been important counterstrains in the history of Emerson's reception, responses to what Porte calls "the problem of Emerson" that represent major alternatives. These approaches have judged Emerson's writing to have the highest intrinsic value aesthetically, philosophically, culturally, even politically, and have stressed an Emerson far different from the idealist-organicist-Transcendentalist preacher. The past quarter-century of the Emerson "revival" has witnessed the rapid expansion of those countertraditions, and it is now clear that a new canonization of Emerson is under way, that a new narrative of his importance as an artist and thinker is being written. The goal is still to answer the prolix, Emerson sphinx: Emerson as ungraspable (Henry James Sr.), as "elusive, irreducible" (Henry James Jr.), as a writer "who retains so much secrecy" (Cavell). The goal is still, as Jonathan Bishop phrased it in 1964, to identify "a central core of imaginative activity that will throw into intelligible relief the multitudinous details of doctrine and rhetoric" among "the broken sequences of essays, the scattered poems, the large numbers of letters and journals, the overlapping continuities of published and manuscript material."[18]

What has changed is what criticism has taken as that central core. Emerson the Transcendentalist prophet of the (young, history-evading, American) soul increasingly gives way to Emerson the redoubtable writer, Emerson the mainstream nineteenth-century (and pre-twentieth-century) thinker, Emerson the philosopher, Emerson the theorist of power, Emerson the pragmatist (an allusion often made but infrequently explored), Emerson the "cultural critic," Emerson the (still-timely) literary theorist ("essentially a philosopher of language and literature"), Emerson the still-vital defender of the "theory of free being" (an achievement that is still underestimated, overshadowed as it has

been by the perception of Emerson as an idealizing escapist), Emerson the vitally historical thinker who views experience not in terms of the individual's "transcendent relation to his surroundings" (Gura) but "in terms of [the] relations and interactions" of this world (Cornel West).[19]

Porte, for example, helped to redirect that major tradition of Emerson criticism that finds insufficient artistic sense in his work by emphasizing Emerson's brilliant "manipulations of language and figure." Emerson's "interest and appeal," Porte argued, "reside in the imaginative materials and structure of his writing—in his tropes and topoi, his metaphors and verbal wit, in the remarkable consistencies of his conceiving mind and executing hand."[20] Porte's *Representative Man: Ralph Waldo Emerson in His Time* (1979) was followed closely by Barbara Packer's *Emerson's Fall: A New Interpretation of the Major Essays* (1982) and by the works of a number of critics who have returned successfully to the intricacies of Emerson's writing with the kind of sensitivity to metaphor and language that would once have been considered irrelevant in the face of Emerson's allegedly inartistic style.

"Why has America never expressed itself philosophically? Or has it—in the metaphysical riot of its greatest literature?" That was the groundbreaking question first posed by Stanley Cavell in *The Senses of Walden* (originally published in 1972). Thoreau's masterpiece was, Cavell suggested, "a book of sufficient intellectual scope and consistency to have established or inspired a tradition of thinking." At first put off by Emerson in the way most twentieth-century critics have been ("[Emerson] kept sounding to me like a second-hand Thoreau"), Cavell soon renounced his original bias and turned his attention to recovering Emerson as a "founding" American thinker and a central nineteenth-century mind. Cavell's commitment to putting Emerson into the company of Wittgenstein, Heidegger, Spengler, Freud, Descartes, Kant, or Nietzsche represents a notable breakthrough—not because Emerson has never been paired with most of these writers but because Cavell's powerful essays have none of the condescension toward Emerson that heretofore characterized such comparisons.[21]

Generally, the dominant (and anti-Emerson) critical tradition, as I have characterized it, has felt comfortable chiding Emerson for misinterpreting Kant or for temperamentally lacking the profundity of a Coleridge or Nietzsche. Even more predictable is the still almost inevitable comparison that finds Emerson incapable of the moral complexity of a Melville, Hawthorne, or Henry James. Emerson scholarship has traditionally looked skeptically on the importation of foreign names onto New England soil. (It still comes as a surprise to many Americanists that Nietzsche ever admired or even read Emerson.) But, as Cavell reminds us, Nietzsche's lifelong engagement with Emerson's essays may well be considered a conduit for Emerson's influence on later European intellectual tradition (Heidegger especially), just as Coleridge's or Carlyle's engagement with German writing was originally a conduit for Kant or Fichte into England and America.[22] Since his first essay on Emerson in 1978, Cavell has made it possible to approach the question, "What did Emerson think?" with a seriousness never before maintained. He has pushed the issue of Emerson as a philosopher (and the requestioning of what philosophy is or can be) to the forefront of Emerson criticism, and he has argued that the tone and terms of the discussion will need to be more sophisticated than ever before.

In the wake of Cavell's work there have appeared several studies, most notably by Poirier, that, if not directly indebted to Cavell, have avoided the patronizing tone of most previous criticism and, without apology, have taken Emerson as a central resource in what Giles Gunn calls our current "culture of criticism." Several complex social, literary, and academic factors have contributed to this revival. If the reediting of Emerson's journals, essays, lectures, letters, and sermons that began in 1959 constitutes its foundation, then the widespread revaluation of Romantic thought and writing (exemplified in the work of Northrop Frye, M. H. Abrams, Paul de Man, Geoffrey Hartman, Harold Bloom, and, most recently, Cavell) has provided an atmosphere in which Emerson can be reaffirmed (in what Hartman calls a counter-"emigration of ideas from within") as a key American answer to the massive influence of Continental and post-Modernist theory. European and deconstructive theorists, situated within the context of an American, Emersonian tradition, can appear as "belatedly catching up with the illuminating discoveries of our great creative writers."[23]

The most vulnerable side to the dominant tradition of Emerson criticism has always been its provincialism. "Emerson scholarship," Kazin writes, "is fiercely local. . . . [It] is intense and minuscule." Emerson's stolid Transcendentalist image and our underestimation of American culture generally have made us reluctant to count him among those "North Atlantic cultural critics who set the agenda and terms for understanding the modern world." The commitment to recovering Emerson's place in American tradition has too often merged confusedly with the misperception of Emerson as a timeless "mystagogue" (James Russell Lowell's word) and has denied his work a place in the mainstream of nineteenth-century thought. That denial has exerted such a tenacious hold that even some of our most formidable critics continue to see Emerson as at heart a displaced, first-century Christian or as a New England anachronism with little or nothing to tell us about the larger course of post-Enlightenment thought or history.[24] Cornel West puts well the point I wish to make. Those approaches, he writes, that have stressed Emerson's American context (and have emphasized Emerson's "flight from history, his rejection of the past, his refusal of authority") have, however valuable in themselves, helped to blind us to Emerson's broader significance.

> Unfortunately, these influential . . . readings of Emerson hide the degree to which Emerson's perspective is infused with historical consciousness; they also conceal his seminal reflections on power. These interpretive

blindnesses result, in part, from situating Emerson in the age of the American literary renaissance (along with Hawthorne, Melville, Thoreau, and Whitman) rather than relating him to the European explosions (both intellectual and social) that produced Karl Marx, John Stuart Mill, Thomas Carlyle, and Friedrich Nietzsche. We can no longer afford or justify confining Emerson to the American terrain. He belongs to that highbrow cast of North Atlantic cultural critics who set the agenda and the terms for understanding the modern world.[25]

At the same time that Emerson the "representative American" comes to seem "acutely marginal" from the polemical perspective of the new historicism, he is being recanonized as an inexpendable participant in that mid- and late-nineteenth-century debate over power, culture, and history waged by writers like Carlyle, Marx, Nietzsche, or Henry Adams. It is a detranscendentalizing, a redemption from an insular Transcendentalist image that has for too long postponed our appreciation of Emerson's significance and artistry. West postulates an Emerson important for his "seminal reflections on power," an Emerson important for his preoccupation with determining "the scope of human powers and the contingency of human societies," an Emerson who struggled (exactly as Carlyle had) to find his vocation as a new kind of "cultural critic" or "theorist of power" (an intellectual vocation unprecedented before the nineteenth century) and then attempted to formulate "a conception of power" that could enable "himself and others to respond to the crises of his day."[26]

Emerson is significant, West argues, for his influential, pragmatic evasion of a transcendental/epistemology-centered philosophy as "antiquated, anachronistic, and outdated" in a century that needed a new kind of "philosopher of power."[27] West is thus the latest in a series of critics who have de-emphasized Emerson as a seeker of a transcendent truth or cosmic unity and stressed instead the essentially agonistic nature of his thought. Emerson was committed, Carolyn Porter writes, "not [to] a soaring transcendence, but a perpetual resistance." "The Emersonian quest," Gertrude Hughes concludes, is "after power, not after truth"; "Emerson's essays are designed to empower rather than to instruct." Charles Feidelson believed that Emerson's "characteristic form" was "an autonomous series of visionary events." But the Emersonian "self," as Poirier contends, does not come about in an autonomous or visionary act of "reflection" or transcendence. It is pressured into existence as a reaction to something else: "The self can . . . be located here and now, not by reflection but, so far as Emerson and William James are concerned, by virtue of 'acts.' These acts are variously named—'resistance,' 'antagonism,' 'transition,' 'abandonment.' None has to do with compliance. They are *re*active." Or, as Donoghue puts it, writing of **Nature**: "Not knowledge but power is its aim; not truth but command." Emerson is, Eric Cheyfitz observes, our "devout psychologist of power": "throughout his work the term ['power'] is as omnipresent as the Deity itself." "Power," Bloom writes, is "Emerson's key term."[28]

This mid-nineteenth-century "theoretician of power" (as Bloom calls him) is my subject. Clearly the time has been right for several years now for the collective reinterpretation of Emerson committed to clarifying that synthesis of disparate, often warring, elements that accounts for what Edmund Wilson called the "dynamic" nature of Emerson's thought. The time is propitious for a rereading of Emerson's work in light of his unchanging conviction that "Power is the first good" (**W,** 8:272)—and for a recovery of what Richard Grusin calls "the structure of Emersonian action."[29]

The poststructuralist obsession with demystification and deidealizing has, to be sure, helped to make possible Emerson's detranscendentalization. The post-Foucauldian obsession with the study of history and texts as scenes of power struggles has made power the latest ("tiresomely recurrent") catchword. The present moment might, in fact, be defined by its "disenchantment with transcendental conceptions of philosophy"—a skepticism that "has led to a preoccupation with the relation of knowledge and power" and a "small-scale intellectual renascence . . . under the broad banner of pragmatism."[30] Because such transformations have done much to generate a renewed concern for Emerson the pragmatic philosopher of power, it is important to make clear—without denying the influence of poststructuralist thought—that I believe the detranscendentalizing of Emerson I advocate is an act of historical recovery. I do not regard it as merely a social construction of the late twentieth century, as the product of the latest-model deidealizing in order to squeeze out one more in an infinite number of possible Emersons. My approach, in short, though it will explore central strains in Emerson's thought that may be called antitranscendental or deconstructive or antifoundationalist, is in itself quite foundationalist. I believe, in other words, that there really exists a primary and definitive aspect of Emerson's thought that has been, as Cavell and Poirier put it, "repressed" by the critical-philosophical establishment.

Equally foundationalist is my assumption that there was such a thing as "Romanticism" and that there is a family of intellectual problems and tendencies which define a distinctively nineteenth-century (more accurately, a post-Kantian) tradition. It is a presupposition of this study that "there arose significantly new forms of thought and standards for evaluation in the post-Enlightenment period, and that these not only marked a radically new epoch in intellectual history but came to dominate almost all schools of European thought for something over one hundred years."[31] It is necessary to insist on such a context because Emerson has so often been left out of it.

Henry James, Santayana, Dewey

Interpretations of Emerson as most vitally a theorist of action or power have existed since the nineteenth century, though they have always been kept in check as critical countertraditions by the weight of the Transcendentalist image or that Modernist/New Critical, anti-Romantic

prejudice that has only given way, as far as Emerson is concerned, in the last twenty-five years. Surely there is some significance in the ability of Nietzsche, William James, and Dewey (major proponents or inheritors of that nineteenth-century transnational tradition that produced philosophies of will) to place a far greater value on both Emerson's art and thought than has that line of scholars who have accepted Emerson as a Transcendentalist.

Nietzsche saluted Emerson as one of the century's "masters of prose" (GS, 92) and regretted that America lacked an academic culture capable of providing "some strict discipline, a really scientific education" in philosophy. Nietzsche's lament—"As it is, in Emerson, we have *lost a philosopher*"—is quite the opposite of the common scholarly conclusion that finds Emerson temperamentally or intellectually incapable of philosophical thought. Indeed, for Nietzsche, Emerson was a "brother soul," an intellectual twin. "Never have I felt so much at home in a book," he wrote of Emerson's essays, "and in *my* home, as—I may not praise it, it is too close to me." Emerson was, he declared, "the author who has been richest in ideas in this century so far."[32]

For Matthew Arnold, Emerson's prose was, as it has been for so many critics since, an embarrassment: "Unsound it is, indeed, and in a style almost impossible to a born man of letters." Henry James returned a similar verdict: Emerson never found his proper "form"; his writings "were not composed at all." But for William James, Emerson was, above all, a consummate *writer*: "[I]f we must define him in one word, we have to call him Artist"—"[his] mission culminated in his style." "No previous literary artist," James claimed, had achieved "such penetratingly persuasive tones." Even the essence of Emerson's message (that "the point of any pen can be an epitome of reality") was best captured, for James, in a writer's metaphor.[33]

Dewey, too, championed Emerson's "concentration of form and effect." Dewey's brief, but astute, 1903 defense of Emerson has remained, until Emerson's recent revival, the most serious argument for Emerson's continuing importance.[34] It is today remembered primarily for its description of Emerson as "the Philosopher of Democracy" (the whole phrase is "not only a philosopher, but . . . the Philosopher of Democracy"), but it merits far closer attention than it has received. It is particularly relevant for my own argument because Dewey begins in the recognition that Emerson is, first of all, in need of defense from both literary critics and philosophers. Any appreciation of Emerson, Dewey insists, must begin with a clear sense of the false limitations imposed by Emerson's reception-history. Anticipating Cavell's hypothesis of a twofold "fixated critical gesture toward Emerson," Dewey suggests that we must first avoid "the condescending patronage by literary critics"—the usual, easy accusations of incoherence—as well as the habitual rejection of the possibility that Emerson's writing could constitute philosophy. The problem, Dewey argues, lies not in any "lack of method" or artistry on Emerson's part but in the stupidity of critics and professors of philosophy.[35]

Dewey continues his defense by dissociating Emerson from the "remotenesses" of "the transcendentalists." Emerson only borrows from them, Dewey says, certain idioms, "certain pigments and delineations." Emerson was not a "Platonist" or "idealist" but achieved a new kind of synthesis that "reduced" the names and ideas associated with those movements to a new philosophy—he put them to use in the service of his own experiential, pragmatic interests, put them to "the test of trial by the service rendered the present and immediate experience." Plato and Platonism may appear as elements in Emerson's writing, but it would be wrong to take Emerson's thought as, therefore, immaculately or chiefly Platonic or transcendental: Emerson was not interested in "the immanence of absolute ideas in the world," in "any Reality that is beyond or behind or in any way apart," or in "the reputed transcendental worth of an overweening Beyond and Away."[36]

To claim him for the Transcendentalist-Idealist party amounts, in Dewey's eyes, to Emerson's unjustified appropriation by a conservative, Brahmin class: it means "embezzling" him away from the democratic and pragmatic tradition ("the common man" and "the common store") to which he properly belongs. The misrepresentation of Emerson's thought as transcendentalism not only robs his work of sustaining interest and artistic credibility but also leaves him vulnerable to unfair moral and political attack. Emerson, Dewey insists, "drew the line which marks him off from transcendentalism—which is the idealism of a Class."[37]

Dewey's vision of an ongoing battle between a democratic and an elite, "embezzling" class—with Emerson's reputation at stake—undoubtedly reflects his own commitment to civic activism. Dewey opposed any philosophy or intellectual tradition that could deteriorate into "an esthetic appreciation carried on by a refined class or a capitalistic possession of a few learned specialists."[38] Clearly much could be gained if Dewey, still early in his career, could demonstrate that Emerson was not the fastidious idealist—as Emerson's critics were painting him—but Dewey's true pragmatic and "instrumentalist" precursor. It would be wrong, however, to construe his essay as merely "a creative misreading of Emerson," an attempt to dress Emerson "in Deweyan garb."[39] For Dewey's portrait of Emerson (first delivered in the same month as William James's speech at Concord and as Santayana's Harvard address on "Emerson the Poet") needs to be set in the context of that pivotal, still influential, reassessment of Emerson's legacy that was being waged throughout the three or four decades after his death. That "second stage" of Emerson studies, which began in 1882, had already witnessed an even more intense apotheosization of an otherworldly Emerson than had occurred in his own lifetime; it would culminate in 1911, when Santayana eloquently banished Emerson's memory to the pale regions of "the genteel tradition"—an association that has stuck securely to the Emerson image.[40]

Dewey was, in 1903, waging a rear-guard but necessary battle. He was attempting to counter the burgeoning mystical-transcendental image of Emerson, attempting to rescue and articulate for the twentieth century an Emerson who was disappearing behind the relentless characterizations of him as provincial, clerical, Brahminical, the declaimer of a fragile or empty idealism.

Empty, vacant—the image is invoked repeatedly in Henry James's and Santayana's portrayals of Emerson. For James, Emerson's memory evoked an unforgettable series of "impressions" of New England's cultural barrenness. "Emerson's personal history," he recalled, could be "condensed into the single word Concord, and all the condensation in the world will not make it look rich." He continued, in his 1888 essay, to associate Emerson with the "terrible paucity of alternatives," the "achromatic picture" his environment presented him. As far as James was concerned, the whole "Concord school" had, as Matthiessen notes, "enacted a series of experiments in the void." Emerson's "special capacity for moral experience"—which for James meant Emerson's "ripe unconsciousness of evil," his inability "to look at anything but the soul"—was the result of his coming to maturity in a community that "had to seek its entertainment, its rewards and consolations, almost exclusively in the moral world." The "decidedly lean Boston." of Emerson's day was self-enclosed, an island above the extremes of common human experience.[41]

Emerson's limited moral world was, like the "New England [of] fifty years ago," sealed off, perpetually untested by the "beguilements and prizes" of experience. Boston existed serenely, James writes (and he means Boston to stand for Emerson), "like a ministry without an opposition." It was no surprise, then, that his eyes were "thickly bandaged" to all "sense of the dark, the foul, the base," no surprise that there was "a certain inadequacy and thinness in [Emerson's] enumerations" and "quaint animadversion[s]." "We get the impression," James concludes, "of a conscience gasping in the void, panting for sensations, with something of the movement of the gills of a landed fish."[42]

Santayana was even more explicit about the hermetic nature of Emerson's life and thought. He had "a certain starved and abstract quality . . .; [he] fed on books. . . . And to feed on books, for a philosopher or poet, is . . . to starve. . . . [Emerson] was employed in a sort of inner play, or digestion of vacancy." Once again Emerson was depicted as a mind weakened and starved by its narrow circumstances. (T. S. Eliot would use the same imagery a few years later, associating Emerson's outdated volumes with gentility, Boston aunts, and "the barren New England hills" in his early satire, "Cousin Nancy.") By the end of the nineteenth century Emersonian Transcendentalism had indeed come to seem, as Irving Howe puts it, "toothless, a genteel evasion." The document that best expressed and further propagated that version of Emerson was Santayana's hugely influential critique of "the genteel tradition." Santayana reintroduced Emerson to the twentieth century as the "detached, unworldly, contemplative" spokesman for a moribund nonphilosophy that subsisted in the modern world as a "sacred mystery only."[43]

Santayana hoped that America's "genteel tradition" would one day give way to a new, more "naturalistic" morality. "Only a morality frankly relative to man's nature," he warned, "is worthy of man, being at once vital and rational, martial and generous; whereas absolutism smells of fustiness." Its debilitating "moral absolutism"—the same untested "conception of the moral life" James had cited as Emerson's (dubious) "great distinction"—was, Santayana charged, the very "essence" of the genteel tradition. (The year after Santayana's famous address, Irving Babbitt would again employ Emerson as the great "absolutist" counterweight to the relativism of Sainte-Beuve. Emerson had "lost himself," Babbitt would later conclude, "in a mystical-transcendental mist, where it was impossible to follow him." That Emerson embodied a misty absolutism, as opposed to the naturalist-experiential thought of a Melville or a Twain, would remain, until recent years, one of the axioms of Emerson scholarship.)[44]

Santayana's conception of Emerson may well have evolved as he considered and reconsidered him in his 1886 essay on "The Optimism of Ralph Waldo Emerson," the chapter on Emerson in *Interpretations of Poetry and Religion* (1900); his 1903 address on "Emerson the Poet;" and the extended meditation on Emerson's legacy offered in his 1936 novel, *The Last Puritan.* But in each work Emerson is once again invoked as a genteel, distant cleric, a mystic rather than a philosopher, a chilly pantheist whose beloved nature was a convenient escape from "human life." "He is never a philosopher," Santayana contended in 1886, "but always Emerson philosophizing." He preached "the lesson of indifference to circumstances." He "walked this earth with a bland and persistent smile." He was "in no sense a prophet or herald for his age or country," Santayana wrote in 1900 (in an essay with which Dewey must surely have been familiar)—he "was not primarily a philosopher, but a Puritan mystic." (And even in this, as Santayana noted in 1886, he was often "the mystic turned dilettante.") "Reality eluded him." Unequivocally an "idealist," Emerson stood "aside from the life of the world" in the quasi-Platonic, quasi-Oriental, "abstract sphere" of mysticism. His "single theme" was "imagination." He was "a poet whose only pleasure was thought," and "he showed in his life and personality the meagerness, the constraint, the frigid and conscious consecration which belonged to his clerical ancestors."[45]

"He's simply a distinguished-looking old cleric with a sweet smile and a white tie," Jim Darnley remarks in *The Last Puritan,* "he's just honourable and bland and as cold as ice." As one minor character states it earlier in the novel: "Emerson served up Goethe's philosophy in ice-water." Santayana's later, no less sardonic description of Oliver Alden and Mario Van de Weyer's pilgrimage to Concord comes as no surprise: "They looked at the dreadful little house in which Emerson lived, and at his cold little sitting-room; and then they looked at each other. Could such great things leave such mean traces?" (Emerson appears to have permanently lowered the temperature everywhere he went. Oliver remembers his room

at the Harvard Divinity School—the room once occupied by Emerson—as "a beastly hole: impossibly far from everywhere, and impossibly cold.")[46]

In 1903 Santayana spoke of the "political thinker" ("a moralist interested in institutions and manners, a democrat and Puritan") that lay behind the pantheist. But, Santayana continued, "chiefly what lay there was a mystic, a moralist athirst for some superhuman and absolute good." Emerson's glance "sometimes . . . rested on human life, but more often and far more lovingly on Nature. . . . The love of nature was Emerson's strongest passion."[47]

Now Santayana was keenly aware that "transcendentalism"—in either its German or American variety—was but an outgrowth of the Protestant spirit and that however mystical or Neoplatonic its rhetoric, it fundamentally shunned "the endless battle of metaphysics" (what Dewey called the "overweening Beyond and Away") for a more pragmatic "philosophy of enterprise." Santayana was well aware that Emerson had at least one foot in this tradition—well aware that Emerson was, like William James, like Dewey, radically concerned with "the Here and Now" of common experience and committed to the use and testing of the life one confronts "on the highway." In a review of Dewey's *Experience and Nature* (1925), Santayana suggested that Emerson, William James, and Dewey all asked the same pragmatic question. "In order to get to the bottom and to the substance of anything," Santayana phrased it, describing Dewey's pragmatism, "we must still ask with Emerson, What is this *to me?* or with William James, What is this *experienced as?*" Pragmatism shared with transcendentalism and empiricism the conceit that the universe exists "to subserve the interests of mankind," the conviction that mankind has "a right to treat the world as its field of action." American pragmatism was, Santayana said, "the most close-reefed of philosophical craft[s], most tightly hugging appearance, use, and relevance to practice today and here."[48] But it is precisely the pragmatic, experiential thinker—the Emerson who proposed "the great doctrine of Use" (**CW,** 1:26), defined "wisdom" as the "return" for "fit actions" (**CW,** 1:60), spurned "inaction" as "cowardice," and condemned "every opportunity of action past by, as a loss of power" (**CW,** 1:59)—it is this confrontational theoretician of human power who all but vanishes in James's or Santayana's accounts.

There are, finally, scattered through Santayana's books and essays, two quite distinct Emersons (and two Transcendentalisms); their coexistence he never adequately explained. The dominant Emerson—the figure depicted in those essays in which Santayana considered Emerson specifically—is the genteel Transcendentalist, disincarnate and naive, removed from the real forces at work in nineteenth-century America. But in Santayana's asides on Emerson, in his perceptive comments on the Promethean/Faustian nature of Romantic literature as a whole, a different figure emerges. When Santayana turned his attention to the Romantic movement in general, he had no difficulty situating Emerson in a German-Anglo-American, Protestant tradition that enshrined the exercise of the human will and perpetually ached for new trials of its strength. Transcendence in the context of this tradition meant not Buddhistic withdrawal but what Emerson—and, later, Nietzsche—called the "incorporation" or "assimilation" of the world. This Protestant "appetite for action" (Hegel called it the "appetitive relation to the external world") devoted its energies not to pantheism or the life of the spirit but to "world-building."[49] It was mystical only in its "faith in will and action." Ironically, it was in his appraisal of European tradition, in the introductory comments to *Three Philosophical Poets,* that Santayana offered his most astute summation of Emerson's thought. His remarks, though brief, cover a great deal of territory in capturing what Kazin calls the neglected "romantic, bourgeois, 'progressive,' sense of individual power" underlying Emerson's work. The "Teutonic races," Santayana wrote in 1910,

> turn successively to the Bible, to learning, to patriotism, to industry, for new objects to love and fresh worlds to conquer; but they have too much vitality, or too little maturity, to rest in any of these things. A demon drives them on; and this demon, divine and immortal in its apparent waywardness, is their inmost self. It is their insatiable will, their radical courage. Nay, though this be a hard saying to the uninitiated, their will is the creator of all those objects by which it is sometimes amused, and sometimes baffled, but never tamed. Their will summons all opportunities and dangers out of nothing to feed its appetite for action; and in that ideal function lies their sole reality. Once attained, things are transcended. Like the episodes of a spent dream, they are to be smiled at and forgotten; the spirit that feigned and discarded them remains always strong and undefiled; it aches for new conquests over new fictions. This is romanticism. . . . It was adapted by Emerson and ought to be sympathetic to Americans; for it expresses the self-trust of the world-building youth, and mystical faith in will and action.[50]

THE CONDUCT OF LIFE

In his earliest essay on Emerson, Santayana had raised the specter of this Faustian thinker, an Emerson who hardly sounded "detached, unworldly, contemplative," when he quoted one of Emerson's many passages welcoming war, temptation, and antagonism as heroic forms of self-overcoming—as the very foundation of nature, the cosmos, culture, art, religion, and history.[51] Santayana quotes three sentences from the following paragraph in "Considerations By the Way," one of the many meditations on power that make up *The Conduct of Life* (1860). But the paragraph is worth citing in its entirety. It is surely one of the many Emersonian precursors of Nietzsche's doctrine that culture and selfhood are born not in the escape from time and history but in "creative tension and fruitful struggle."[52] It makes conspicuous the Emerson suppressed in James's and Santayana's rendering of a ministerial mystic, quaintly unconscious of evil or conflict. (This is an objection that would be repeated endlessly in the twentieth century and still stands as one of the clichés of Emerson criticism.)

> In front of these sinister facts, the first lesson of history is the good of evil. Good is a good doctor but Bad is

sometimes a better. The oppressions of William the Norman, savage forest laws and crushing despotism made possible the inspirations of Magna Charta under John. Edward I. wanted money, armies, castles, and as much as he could get. It was necessary to call the people together by shorter, swifter ways,—and the House of Commons arose. To obtain subsidies, he paid in privileges. In the twenty-fourth year of his reign he decreed "that no tax should be levied without consent of Lords and Commons;"—which is the basis of the English Constitution. Plutarch affirms that the cruel wars which followed the march of Alexander introduced the civility, language and arts of Greece into the savage East; introduced marriage; built seventy cities, and united hostile nations under one government. The barbarians who broke up the Roman Empire did not arrive a day too soon. Schiller says the Thirty Years' War made Germany a nation. Rough, selfish despots serve men immensely, as Henry VIII. in the contest with the Pope; as the infatuations no less than the wisdom of Cromwell; as the ferocity of the Russian czars; as the fanaticism of the French regicides of 1789. The frost which kills the harvest of a year saves the harvests of a century, by destroying the weevil or the locust. Wars, fires, plagues, break up immovable routine, clear the ground of rotten races and dens of distemper, and open a fair field to new men. There is a tendency in things to right themselves, and the war or revolution or bankruptcy that shatters a rotten system, allows things to take a new and natural order. The sharpest evils are bent into that periodicity which makes the errors of planets and the fevers and distempers of men, self-limiting. Nature is upheld by antagonism. Passions, resistance, danger, are educators. We acquire the strength we have overcome. Without war, no soldiers; without enemies, no hero. The sun were insipid if the universe were not opaque. And the glory of character is in affronting the horrors of depravity to draw thence new nobilities of power; as Art lives and thrills in new use and combining of contrasts, and mining into the dark evermore for blacker pits of night. What would painter do, or what would poet or saint, but for crucifixions and hells? And evermore in the world is this marvellous balance of beauty and disgust, magnificence and rats. Not Antoninus, but a poor washer-woman said, "The more trouble, the more lion; that's my principle."

(W, 6:253-55)

It is difficult not to remain silent in the face of such an astonishing passage—especially astonishing if one comes to it after James's and Santayana's judgment that Emerson, either through provincialism or through mystic withdrawal, managed to avoid the nineteenth century. It is even more difficult to hold off citing all those equivalent passages in Emerson that deserve to be placed beside it. (The conception of culture Emerson presents here is—to cite just one example—condensed into one extraordinary line, a line worthy of Nietzsche at his best, in the aphoristic theory of Christianity's evolution Emerson advances in *English Traits.* "The violence of the northern savages," he writes, "exasperated Christianity into power" [ET, 139].) Santayana, however, passed quickly over such characteristically Emersonian thinking about the place of evil and the power of blackness, about the origin of culture and morality, about the physical laws of polarity. He dismissed such moments as digressions, unrepresentative of Emerson's main concerns: "The title under which these remarks appear ["**Considerations By the Way**"] is for once appropriate. . . . To give these views a fundamental importance would be to misunderstand Emerson."[53]

Yet there is sufficient evidence in this paragraph alone to suggest the extreme partiality and inadequacy of the James/Santayana image of Emerson. There is, for one thing, nothing provincial about it. The thick package of allusions—to Greece, Rome, and "the Savage East"; to English law and history; to the Cromwellian and French Revolutions; to the Thirty Years' War; to contemporary Russia—suggests that Emerson did not stand outside time and that he had not left history behind him. Nor is there anything to suggest that Emerson ignores evil. One can hear the relish with which he plunges into the dark, foul, and base; the prose is as tautly balanced as Nietzsche's aphoristic "dynamite."

It was Emerson's verse Santayana had in mind when he concluded that Emerson's passion for nature "was sincere adoration, self-surrendering devotion . . . not qualified or taken back by any subsumption of nature under human categories"; but there are no grounds in this passage, in all of *The Conduct of Life,* and in most of Emerson's prose, for ascribing to him so self-effacing a form of pantheism.[54] The "subsumption of nature under human categories" is precisely what *Nature,* what *The Conduct of Life,* champions. It was not nature's "inhuman perfection" Emerson adored (as Santayana claims) but nature's ultimate usefulness as a "tool chest," a "field of action," for human "appetites" (**W,** 6:88-90, 246). The "deferential," "universal passive hospitality" that James found in Emerson's personality (and that, James seems to imply, is also the hallmark of his thought) is manifestly not the point in this exhortation to self-strengthening.[55]

The question of whether Emerson was a mystic hinges, of course, on the definition of mysticism one accepts. But clearly the ascetic withdrawal Santayana imputes to Emerson fails to account for so fervent an invocation of "resistance." And it is at least an open question whether this vision of the terrible process by which "things right themselves" is merely another instance of that blandly optimistic and familiar Emersonian rubric, **"Compensation,"** or something more akin to Nietzsche's definition of "the sublime" as "the artistic taming of the horrible" (BT, 7) or to the Nietzschean conception of civilization as the beautiful balance of brutally warring oppositions. Is such a passage evidence of Emerson's naïveté, his "cheerful Monism" (as Robert Frost called it)?[56] Or does it suggest an "optimism" closer to Nietzsche's ideal: the Hellenic capacity for looking "boldly right into the terrible destructiveness of . . . world history as well as the cruelty of nature" and, in the face of such suffering, for overcoming the mystic's "longing for a Buddhistic negation of the will" in order to achieve the "blissful affirmation of existence that seeks to discharge itself in actions" (BT, 7, 15). "The blos-

som of the Apollonian culture," Nietzsche writes, sprang "from a dark abyss, as the victory which the Hellenic will . . . obtains over suffering" (BT, 17). "What terrible questions are we learning to ask!" (**W,** 6:318) Emerson says: "Let us replace sentimentalism by realism, and dare to uncover those simple and terrible laws which, be they seen or unseen, pervade and govern" (**W,** 6:215). However one chooses to approach this passage, it is no longer possible to ignore or dismiss it in the way James or Santayana did.

Nor is it possible to argue that such moments are atypical of Emerson. It is baffling and, finally, testament to the pernicious way in which Emerson's ministerial image has blinded us to his words themselves, that Santayana could ever have thought so. Santayana's equation of transcendentalism and idealism with Emersonianism—and those chestnuts that have been taken as the too familiar rubrics of Emersonian thought (Compensation, the Over-Soul, Organicism, Pantheism, Absolutism, Monism, Passivity)—need to be balanced, ultimately reconceived, and redefined, in light of the tendencies (call them Nietzschean) that are so overt in the above paragraph.

We might label these, using only Emerson's own language, "the good of evil," the good of war, antagonism, resistance, education, the search for strength, overcoming, affronting, the search for power (the "combining of contrasts" in the search for new power), the use of darkness. We might expand this list, still confining our terminology to the language of *The Conduct of Life,* to include the command to "know the realities of human life" (p. 261), to "taste the real quality of existence" (p. 323), and to "try the rough water" (p. 162). "Nature," Emerson writes, "forever puts a premium on reality" (p. 189). And we might continue this list with the addition of the Emersonian terms and concepts emphasized in the following passages from the same book (further evidence that the Nietzschean strain beneath Emersonian "optimism" is anything but a digressive anomaly). These concepts are the ever-present imperatives of power, use (using what is near), resistance, testing, and overcoming (and confronting temptation—like the possibility of suicide), the perpetual friction ("perpetual tilt and balance") between man and nature, giving "form and actuality" to thought (p. 93), execution, instrumentation (tools), knowing, command ("command of nature" [p. 95]), "taking things up" into one's self/conversion/absorption/incorporation/transmutation ("the assimilating power" [p. 142]), conquest, vigor, action, will, "working up," "the extension of man" (p. 284), building, taking advantage, the charm and power of practicality (p. 317).

> [Man's] instincts must be met, and he has predisposing power that bends and fits what is near him to his use. . . . As soon as there is life, there is self-direction and absorbing and using of material.
>
> (p. 38)

> Everything is pusher or pushed; and matter and mind are in perpetual tilt and balance.
>
> (p. 43)

The friction in nature is so enormous that we cannot spare any power. It is not question to express our thought, to elect our way, but to overcome resistances of the medium and material in everything we do.

(p. 79)

[Man] is tempted out by his appetites and fancies to the conquest of this and that piece of nature, until he finds his well-being in the use of his planet, and of more planets than his own. . . . [T]he elements offer their service to him. . . . The world is his tool-chest, and he is successful, or his education is carried on just so far, as is the marriage of his faculties with nature, or the degree in which he takes up things into himself.

(pp. 88-90)

Kings are said to have long arms, but every man should have long arms, and should pluck his living, his instruments, his power and his knowing, from the sun, moon and stars.

(p. 95)

Man was born to be rich, or inevitably grows rich by the use of his faculties.

(p. 99)

[T]he student we speak to must have a mother-wit invincible by his culture,—which uses all books, arts, facilities, and elegancies of intercourse, but is never subdued or lost in them. . . . And the end of culture is not to destroy this, God forbid! but to train away all impediment and mixture and leave nothing but pure power.

(p. 134)

Man's culture can spare nothing, wants all the material. He is to convert all impediments into instruments, all enemies into power. The formidable mischief will only make the more useful slave. . . . [W]e shall dare affirm that there is nothing he will not overcome and convert, until at last culture shall absorb the chaos and gehenna. He will convert the Furies into Muses, and the hells into benefit.

(p. 166)

I have no sympathy with a poor man I knew, who, when suicides abounded, told me he dare not look at his razor.

(p. 201)

Yet vigor is contagious, and whatever makes us either think or feel strongly, adds to our power and enlarges our field of action.

(p. 246)

We learn geology the morning after the earthquake. . . . In our life everything is worked up and comes in use,—passion, war, revolt, bankruptcy, and not less, folly and blunders, insult, ennui and bad company.

(p. 262)

Alchemy, which sought to transmute one element into another, to prolong life, to arm with power,—that was in the right direction. . . . [A] man is a fagot of thunderbolts. All the elements pour through his system; he is the flood of the flood and fire of the fire; he feels the

antipodes and the pole as drops of his blood; they are the extension of his personality. His duties are measured by that instrument he is.

(pp. 282-83)

[I]f a man can build a plain cottage with such symmetry as to make all the fine palaces look cheap and vulgar; can take such advantages of nature that all her powers serve him; making use of geometry, instead of expense; tapping a mountain for his water-jet; causing the sun and moon to seem only the decorations of his estate;—this is still the legitimate dominion of beauty.

(p. 302)

The Conduct of Life, Emerson's last great book, may well be the work in which his speculations on the search for power, the antagonism of fate, the service of culture, the force of behavior, worship, and wealth are most explicit. *The Conduct of Life* is, as Porte suggests, obsessed with power.[57] It is obsessed with "the sovereignty of power" (p. 63), with "coarse energy" (p. 64), with "the excess of virility" (p. 69) and the "man of force" (p. 58), "the charm of practical men" (p. 317) and men of superior will (p. 248), with health, "recuperative force" (p. 61), and "the advantage of a strong pulse" (p. 56), with "personal power" and "the enormous elements of strength which . . . make our politics unimportant" (p. 61), with "aboriginal might," "hairy Pelasgic strength," "*plus* or positive power" (pp. 71-73) and "beast-force" (p. 252). But it must be emphasized (because the common perception of distinct early and late periods in Emerson's thought would seem to deny it) that the concern for power, for use and command, and the predominance of the Emersonian pattern of overcoming are not at all new.

Although *The Conduct of Life* was not published until 1860, the lectures that form its basis were first delivered in 1851. The anxiety over the ebb of vital force, the compensating obsession with power, the "underlying psycho-physiological anxiety" over the proper expending and conservation of energy, and the attendant "fantasies of size, power, violence, debauchery, and fertility"—all, as Porte argues, can be traced back to the journal entries of the 1840s.[58] But one needs only to return to Emerson's first book, in 1836, to find exactly the same founding patterns reexpressed so vehemently in *The Conduct of Life.* There is, in *Nature,* the same call for "the kingdom" (or "dominion") of "man over nature" (**CW**, 1:45), the same stress on the "endless exercise" of all human "faculties" (**CW**, 1:37), the same affirmation of "new activity" (**CW**, 1:41), "new creation" (**CW**, 1:16) (as opposed to "barren contemplation"), the same "doctrine of Use" (**CW**, 1:26), the same concern for "self-command" and "the varying phenomenon of Health" (**CW**, 1:27), the same push to grasp "the keys of power" (**CW**, 1:21), to transmute "unconscious truth" into "the domain of knowledge" where it may become "a new weapon in the magazine of power" (**CW**, 1:23). There is the same emphasis on "heroic action," "the energy of [man's] thought and will" (**CW**, 1:15), and the necessity of work (**CW**, 1:12).

"At present," Emerson complains, "man applies to nature but half his force" (**CW**, 1:42). *Nature* is the prophecy of man's "resumption of power," his taking advantage of nature "with his entire force" and building his world (**CW**, 1:43). "By the time he composed *Nature*," Leo Marx notes, "Emerson had adapted the rhetoric of the technological sublime to his purposes." The "submerged metaphor" in *Nature*, Marx suggests, was technology; it is submerged—rendered obscure or ambiguous—in the heavy counterpresence of traditional idealist terminology and Christian imagery:[59]

> The exercise of the Will or the lesson of power is taught in every event. From the child's successive possession of his several senses up to the hour when he saith, "thy will be done!" he is learning the secret, that he can reduce under his will, not only particular events, but great classes, nay the whole series of events, and so conform all facts to his character. Nature is thoroughly mediate. It is made to serve. It receives the dominion of man as meekly as the ass on which the Saviour rode. It offers all its kingdoms to man as the raw material which he may mould into what is useful. Man is never weary of working it up. He forges the subtle and delicate air into wise and melodious words, and gives them wing as angels of persuasion and command. More and more, with every thought, does his kingdom stretch over things, until the world becomes, at last, only a realized will,—the double of the man.
>
> (**CW**, 1:25)

This is the vision of the world as tool chest and field of action for the extension of man that would inform all of Emerson's subsequent work. (This passage, like many of those I have cited from *The Conduct of Life*, is also a good example of a point I shall stress in chapter 2. Emerson is, for all the emphasis that has been placed on his faith in intuition, a philosopher of tuition. He generally defines man in precisely the same terms he uses in the above passage—as a perpetual student in a universal school of power.) Marx is undoubtedly correct in noting the allusion to technological power in this passage, but it might be more accurate to include technology as part of a broader Emersonian project that anticipates Dewey's rejection of "the spectator theory of knowledge." That project is the attempt to approach the world not as a spectator who knows things at a distance but as a worker or user for whom nature and materials are known only as they become "*tools* and *instruments,* with which we can do things and satisfy our desires."[60]

Maurice Mandelbaum identifies such an approach as the "pragmatic-economical view of the human mind" that first became prominent in the latter decades of the nineteenth century.[61] But that pragmatic perspective is certainly apparent, in greater and lesser degrees, throughout the post-Kantian era: in Fichte and the German tradition; in Carlyle; and, most centrally, in Emerson.[62] "Our nineteenth century," Emerson said—summing up his fundamental point of view as aptly as any single sentence could—"is the age of tools" (**W**, 7:157). "Without tools," Carlyle had earlier insisted, in *Sartor Resartus*, "[man] is nothing, with Tools he is all."[63]

Johann Gottlieb Fichte, the German philosopher who may well have had an important, if indirect, hand in shaping Emerson's thought, proposed, in 1800, that man's vocation was "Not merely TO KNOW but . . . TO DO." "Not for idle contemplation of thyself," Fichte argued, "not for brooding over devout sensations;—no, for action art thou here; thine action, and thine action alone, determines thy worth."[64] In his own Fichtean defense of the scholar class, Emerson upheld a similar ideal: "The preamble of thought, the transition through which it passes from the unconscious to the conscious, is action. Only so much do I know, as I have lived. . . . [H]e who has put forth his total strength in fit actions, has the richest return of wisdom" (**CW**, 1:59-60). The problem of the times, as he diagnosed it in 1841, was that men were inclined not "to a deed, but to a beholding. . . . [They] are paralyzed by the uncertainty what they should do" (**CW**, 1:179). "Metaphysics," as he later restated it, "is dangerous as a single pursuit. . . . The inward analysis must be corrected by rough experience. Metaphysics must be perpetually reinforced by life; must be the observations of a working man on working men . . . the record of some law whose working was surprised by the observer in natural action" (**W**, 12:13).

The remarkable image in that last phrase, difficult to forget once it has been noticed, suggests that metaphysical truth, or knowledge, can only be grasped at, captured, or surprised—like an animal observed or hunted—in the midst of some active pursuit, an action that must be natural. Emerson's ambiguous syntax suggests that both the observer and the law or truth that is surprised are in states of action. Knowledge, in other words, begins in reciprocal action or what Emerson elsewhere calls friction. "By how much we know, so much we are," Emerson says a few pages earlier (**W**, 12:10): and what we know, what we are, comes about only in antagonism or *re*action. Our knowledge, our identity, must be "corrected" and "perpetually reinforced" by a life and experience that are *rough*—that push back. "Intelligence," as Dewey put it, "must throw its fund out again into the stress of life; it must venture its savings against the pressure of facts."[65]

We are now better prepared to appreciate Dewey's crucial, turn-of-the-century defense of Emerson. Dewey was, as I have said, endeavoring to refute those interpretations that relegated Emerson to the transcendentalist-genteel camp. Upholding Emerson as the prophet and herald of modern democracy appears to be a direct rebuttal of Santayana's belief that Emerson was "in no sense a prophet for his age or country"; Dewey's insistence that Emerson's philosophy not be misunderstood as the nostalgic "idealism of a Class" even anticipates Santayana's charge that Emerson was anachronistically "genteel." But Dewey was trying to suggest something even more significant than this. His famous praise for Emerson as "the philosopher of Democracy," the philosopher of "any system which democracy may *henceforth* construct" (my italics), was the attempt to recover Emerson (at a time when he was entering the twentieth century in the white smile and tie of the New England saint) as a distinctively modern mind—a mind whose strikingly original contribution (clouded as it was behind its surface, absolutist pigments) was still not fully apparent, was "just now dawning" and still difficult to classify. Its validity as a "new type of literary art" and "method of knowledge," its relevance to the modern world, would, Dewey argued, become clearer—like the significance of Platonic thought for the Old World—in retrospect.[66]

Cornel West suggests that it is precisely Emerson's swerve away from metaphysical idealism to a new kind of "cultural criticism" that defines Emerson's modernity; it was precisely this pragmatic and pioneering "evasion of philosophy" that Dewey inherited from Emerson—and it was this central, still underappreciated Emersonian legacy that Dewey was attempting to pull from beneath Emerson's confusing, Platonic language and his Transcendentalist image. Emerson's claim that "philosophy is still rude and elementary . . . [and] will one day be taught by poets" (generally taken by scholars as further evidence of Emerson's desire to escape into poetry's idealisms) was welcomed by Dewey as a path-breaking "more-than-philosophy," commendable precisely because it preferred to work "by art, not by metaphysics." As West puts it: "Dewey understands Emerson's evasion of modern [metaphysical, epistemology-centered] philosophy . . . as a situating of philosophical reflection and poetic creation in the midst of quotidian human struggles for meaning, status, power, wealth, and selfhood."[67] Emerson, "the philosopher of democracy," was—to put it another way—not transcendental "man in the open air" (that "pure, will-less, painless, timeless knowing subject" Nietzsche hoped to abolish [GM, 3:12]) but a mind committed above all to reaction—committed to finding ways of coping with those natural and cultural forces that made life in mid-nineteenth-century America (and in any future democratic society) a "quotidian struggle."

West is, I think, right. Emerson is "like Friedrich Nietzsche . . . , first and foremost a cultural critic obsessed with ways to generate forms of power." "Cultural critic," however (and Stanley Cavell has recently made a similar claim), is, like power, problematic. Its meaning and nineteenth-century context can be further clarified. We can note, first of all, that Emerson anticipated Dewey's pragmatic insistence that philosophical debate (the discourse, as Emerson portrayed it, of "four or five noted men") resolve itself "into a practical question of the conduct of life. How shall I live?" (**W**, 6:3). Dewey reinstated Emerson's priorities in 1917 in his key essay, "The Need for a Recovery of Philosophy"; he condemned any philosophical tradition that existed as "an ingenious dialectic exercised in professorial corners by a few who have retained ancient premises, while rejecting their application to the conduct of life." Dewey wanted philosophy to be the democratic medium for "releas[ing] the powers of individuals for cultural expression"—a philosophy premised on the necessity of "an active coping with conditions," committed to "the possibilities of action."[68]

He was not the only one to feel that the modern mind required a new kind of education in the possibilities of hu-

man power. In his popular 1917 essay, "The Energies of Men," William James called for a new theory of human power as a basis for reconstructing the system of "individual and national education" in the twentieth century:

> The two questions, first, that of the possible extent of our powers; and, second, that of the various avenues of approach to them, the various keys for unlocking them in diverse individuals, dominate the whole problem of individual and national education. We need a topography of the limits of human power. . . . We need also a study of the various types of human being with reference to the different ways in which their energy-reserves may be appealed to and set loose.[69]

The history of Henry Adams's struggle to measure "man as a force" would finally be published a year later. Modern education, Adams theorized, "should try to lessen the obstacles, diminish the friction, invigorate the energy, and should train minds to react, not at haphazard, but by choice, on the lines of force that attract their world." Adams claimed that his vocation had been the attempt of the mind "to invent scales of force" for all those nonhuman powers that surround and threaten it. "A new avalanche of unknown forces," he warned, had fallen upon the mind and "required new mental powers to control."[70] But Adams's vocation as a "student of force" was not new—though his example as a mind lost in the attempt to find new scales for new forces and viable scales for old ones may stand as a paradigm by which we can measure the aims and achievements of minds like Emerson, Nietzsche, or Carlyle (or for that matter, Marx, Darwin, and Freud, who were similarly committed to finding the "scale of force" that could best explain to an energy-obsessed age the fundamental forces that set individuals and societies in motion).

Adams may not have sensed it in the way Dewey, William James, or Nietzsche did. But the nineteenth-century penchant for seeing the world *sub specie vis* had already found its first American spokesman in Emerson. It was Emerson who first spoke of himself as the "geometer of [human] forces" (**EJ**, 507). "There is not yet," he announced in the opening sentence of his essay on **"Power,"** "any inventory of a man's faculties" (**W**, 6:53). We lack, as he put it in his lecture, **"Aristocracy,"** an "anthropometer"—a quintessentially Emersonian coinage to describe his vision of a machine that would improve society by providing every man with a true appraisal of the degree of power he could be trusted to "carry and use" (**W**, 10:49). It was Emerson who first saw himself (as Nietzsche would later see himself) as a source of cultural strength—the hero who could restore the balance of power between man and his environment, the modern prophet who could "enumerate the resources we can command," "reinforce [man's] self-respect, show him his means, his arsenal of forces, physical, metaphysical, immortal" (**W**, 10:69).

Emerson was, as West puts it, one of the century's first "grand valorizer[s] of human power."[71] Culture, Emerson said, must replenish that "pure power" and "mother-wit" that allows the student to use "all books, arts, facilities, and elegancies of intercourse" without becoming "subdued" by them or "lost in them" (**W,** 6:134). Our current "habit of thought" is "poor and squalid"; our "common experience" a (genteel) "egg-shell existence" (**W,** 6:271). What was needed "to add somewhat to the well-being of men" (and give us "the courage to be what we are") (**W,** 6:278) was a teacher who could remind his readers of their "magical powers over nature and man" and inspire "new ways of living, new books, new men" (**W,** 6:271).

Emerson's last important book ends, like his first, with the prophecy that man will one day liberate himself from those illusions that blind him to his "elemental power" (**CW,** 1:42). Emerson's vision of a teacher who can awaken in his audience new energies, energies capable of "renovat-[ing] life and our social state" (**CW,** 2:43), capable of rising to the resistances and impediments offered by nature and history, stakes out a new kind of intellectual or cultural vocation. It is one of many similar self-portraits.

We may call this new vocation a kind of "cultural criticism" concerned with securing the balance of human and nonhuman powers. Or we may define it as pragmatism—devoted to "the Here and Now," to the testing of truth by immediate experience, to promoting (in Alexander Bain's phrase) "an attitude or disposition of preparedness to act."[72] Or we may feel that pragmatism is too limiting a label (for it localizes Emerson within American tradition) and stress its broader connections to concurrent European philosophies of will. Whatever we may decide to call this new way of thinking, this new vocation, it was largely neglected by Emerson scholarship until the middle of this century.

Not that Emerson's devotion to will and action went unnoticed. It was noted repeatedly: in a series of articles on Emerson and pragmatism, or Emerson and Nietzsche, in Kenneth Burke's perception that "Emerson's brand of transcendentalism was but a short step ahead of out-and-out pragmatism," in Eduard Baumgarten's prescient linking of Emerson, James, Dewey, and Nietzsche as founders of a pragmatic *"Philosophie der Macht,"* in Matthiessen's comparison of Emerson's ideal individual and "the hard-willed [Nietzschean] *Übermensch,"* in Perry Miller's remarks on the Napoleonic propensities beneath Emerson's worship of genius, in Daniel Aaron's discussion of Emerson as "the seer of *laisser-faire* capitalism and the rampant individual."[73]

But "theoretician of power" was always seen as one of Emerson's "lesser roles."[74] Emerson remained chiefly what he had been in Santayana's portrait of "the Genteel Tradition": fundamentally a literary anachronism, whose ideas were for the most part sufficiently distant that they could be easily classified as Platonic or Neoplatonic, as transcendental organicism or pantheism, as Puritan (or Oriental) mysticism. In the works of Matthiessen, Hopkins, Paul, Miller, Feidelson, and others, Emerson remained primarily the influential expounder of a transcendental (often

mystical) aesthetic. If that aesthetic seemed anachronous, it was because Emerson continued to be perceived as awkwardly attempting "to describe an ancient way of seeing [a nonrational, organic vision] by means of a modern vocabulary which had been designed to repress it."[75]

That aspect of Emerson's thought that seemed more intrinsically (and troublesomely) modern—his "attraction . . . toward every form of power"[76]—the critical establishment of the time could only begin to identify as the most drastic form of Nietzscheanism. Emerson's "Nietzschean strain" existed, when it surfaced, as the disturbing underside of the Transcendentalist image—and almost always it was defused by that very image. Emerson's fascination with power was treated as anomalous, a temporary extravagance amid his overall moral mildness, the exception that proved the Transcendentalist rule. Thus Matthiessen noted the connection between Emerson's "ideal man of self-reliant energy" and "the brutal man of Fascism." "It is no long step," Matthiessen wrote, "from [Emerson's] indiscriminate glorification of power to the predatory career of Henry Ford." But Emerson's temperate monistic image could finally not be reconciled with what appeared to be a Nietzschean vision of *Machtpolitik*; the potential link had to be acknowledged but defined as simply the denaturing or degradation of true ("unworldly") Emersonianism. "The sentiments of such essays as those on **'Wealth'** and **'Power,'"** Matthiessen said, "working on temperaments less unworldly than their author's, have provided a vicious reinforcement to the most ruthless elements in our economic life."[77]

What was lost between the extremes of these two perspectives—Emerson as upholder of an ancient holism, Emerson as harbinger of an all-too-modern fascism—was the much more prominent middle ground recent criticism has sought to recover: Emerson as Nietzschean (and quintessentially of his time) in his omnipresent rhetoric of "power" (one of the central, ambiguous tropes or "master signs" of the nineteenth century generally);[78] Emerson as Nietzschean in his persistent patterns of resistance, overcoming, and incorporation; Emerson as pragmatic in his commitment to testing and use; Emerson as Nietzschean "geometer of force," committed to the generation and extension of human energies.

STEPHEN WHICHER'S *FREEDOM AND FATE*

Stephen Whicher's *Freedom and Fate: An Inner Life of Ralph Waldo Emerson,* first published in 1953 and still considered by many the single most important and revolutionary critical work on Emerson, changed the course of scholarship in several ways. For one thing, it redirected critical attention to Emerson's startlingly original reflections on power; that emphasis would have important consequences for the criticism of the next forty years. Unfortunately, Whicher also did much to keep alive many of the central tenets of the anti-Emerson tradition. Because his ideas and, even more significantly, his methodology have exerted so controlling an influence on later scholarship, they are worth considering here.

Freedom and Fate is a masterful job of summary and synthesis. It remains one of the most sensitive studies of an American writer ever written. Out of what had always been "a distressingly sprawling topic," Whicher presented, more forcefully than had any previous critic, the portrait of a dramatic evolution: Emerson moved from an early, apocalyptic rebellion in the name of an emancipated individualism to a chastened acquiescence before fate and experience.[79] But Whicher's evolutionary paradigm—his very insistence that Emerson had a dramatic development—though intended to rescue Emerson from an even shallower, hagiographic image, has resulted in an overly schematic and still pejorative perception of his thought. That perception has made it possible to continue speaking of Emerson in simplistic either-or terms: Emerson as either optimistic or pessimistic, revolutionary or acquiescent, idealistic or skeptical, nonconformist or conservative, and so forth.

Such overschematizing is the major difficulty inherent in any attempt to impose on Emerson anything like the usual evolutionary thesis that finds distinct early and late periods in a writer's career. It is all too likely that the standard biographical rubrics of youth and age (and the built-in value judgments they impose) will only perpetuate the traditional prejudices against Emerson as intellectually and artistically naive and underdeveloped. An evolutionary paradigm that posits an artist's growth from youthful illusion to mature disillusionment is implicitly anti-Romantic; the earlier idealistic, revolutionary, or Romantic period will, in the framework of such a scheme, always be associated with immaturity. Such an approach, in other words, seems predisposed to repeat, consciously or not, the Arnoldian or Eliotic bias that finds Romantic literature inherently immature, blind to experience or evil, and in need of some further growth or knowledge before it can be, morally and artistically, of the highest seriousness. Whicher's thesis of a drastic development in Emerson's thought has thus, as Poirier remarks, "helped perpetuate the view that when [Emerson] is not naively wide-eyed he is only reluctantly sensible." It has helped preserve, Hughes notes, "the chiding solicitousness with which readers [have] regarded the unfolding of Emerson's work." Julie Ellison justly speaks of it as "the hypothetical divide in Emerson's career that has plagued us for decades."[80]

The temptation to simplify Emerson's thought in this way remains a potential obstacle for any chronological interpretation of his work; and until recently criticism has been reluctant to consider Emerson's ideas in any context *but* a chronological one. No one, of course, can or would want to argue with a biographical approach to a writer's thought. But Emerson's case is more complicated than it might appear. When the critical tradition has been largely antipathetic to a writer's work, as I have tried to suggest it has been in Emerson's case, one has reason to be suspicious of criticism that seems ever anxious to balance (or shore up) one strain (or phase) of thought with another, as if the ideas or style of a single essay or book were somehow not enough in themselves or were intellectually embarrassing

taken on their own. At what point does an insistently chronological perspective on Emerson become something other than just respectable scholarship—become, rather, another reflex action in that fixated, critical need to highlight, apologize, and account for Emerson's failings? At what point does chronology become yet another aspect of Emerson scholarship to act as a positive hindrance to appreciation?

Whicher's method—the employment of a broad, biographical framework for assessing not just Emerson's life but his *ideas*—has been repeated so often now, over several decades, that it has become virtually de rigueur. This method—committed to getting at Emerson through the identification of phases and periods—has been the explicit or implicit foundation for most criticism of the last forty years. It has dictated, in large measure, the shape of most book-length studies, which generally move from early to late stages, mapping out transitions and crisis points, identifying the various degrees of Emersonian "optimism." Even books like Bishop's, which have tried to focus on a single topic and have attempted to abstract "the essence of the Emersonian achievement . . . from the whole body of his work," have based their interpretations on some version of development, and have defined Emerson in terms of immature or mature degrees of idealism.[81]

The Whicherian method is, as Ellison has argued, disposed to finding growth (or surrender) and attempts at resolution rather than repetition or complex, persisting tensions. Its origin, as a method, lies in a perception of Emerson that is basically impatient with his actual work; it therefore lends itself most readily to overviews, to biography, not to thorough explorations of ideas or to the kind of intensive pressing or leaning on lines and passages that recent critics have practiced. Whicher's method does not encourage attempts to recover or argue for, in any extensive or systematic way, an Emersonian philosophy. It depends on the assumption that "optimism" (loaded term that it is) and "idealism"—or the lack of them—are adequate parameters for fixing and defining Emerson's thought. Whicher, Bishop, and Emerson's readers generally have assumed that they were; but recent scholarship has not.[82] These limitations are part of the general and, finally, crippling weakness underlying Whicher's entire approach—that is, the basically deprecatory or apologetic attitude that Whicher, in 1953, was obliged to take toward his subject or, more specifically, to his subject's ideas.

"It is only," Whicher claimed, "as we see [Emerson] *sub specie temporis* that we can justly estimate his quality as a writer." That central statement of method may sound unobjectionable. Who would not wish to understand an author *sub specie temporis?* But the operative word (as the context of Whicher's argument makes clear) is that qualifying *only*. So we need to ask, "Why won't **'Self-Reliance'** or **'Experience'** in and of itself vouch for Emerson's 'quality as a writer'?" Or, to push the point, what negative presumptions are at work if we insist that the only way for estimating, say, Nietzsche's or Shakespeare's quality is in the context of comprehensive appraisals of evolution over a lifetime of work? Can't the examination of a single play or, say, Nietzsche's publications in 1886 and 1887 provide sufficient evidence of the intrinsic merit of their author's achievement? Whicher assumes that in any other approach Emerson will not come off well, that his ideas are intrinsically moribund, and that only a procedure that can bring to life again the large, chronological outline of Emerson the man can make his readers overcome their aversion to his work itself. "Increasing numbers of critics and readers," Whicher remarks, "conclude that [Emerson] is, in Eliot's phrase, 'already an encumbrance.'"[83]

The conclusion of *Freedom and Fate,* while upholding Emerson's "craftsman's skill," reasserts the traditional charges. Emerson's optimistic faith is irritating in a modern age; his ideas are irrevocably anachronistic ("the story of his thought seems an episode from a vanished past"); and—the central charge leveled by Santayana, John Morley, and so many others—they are essentially a form of gospel thinly disguised as "modern philosophy."[84]

One could garner several such disparaging remarks from Whicher, from Bishop's *Emerson on the Soul* (1964), and especially from Feidelson's *Symbolism and American Literature* (published in the same year as *Freedom and Fate*). (Feidelson's influential study is, like others that followed it, a sustained use of Emerson as a bad example, a foil to the more complex modernity of Melville.) These books have routinely been considered key contributions to a mid-century resurrection of Emerson. They might, with equal reason, be described as central works in the last important generation of criticism to replicate, in various degrees, the negative presuppositions of the James/Santayana version of Emerson.

But if *Freedom and Fate* retained much that was characteristic of the anti-Emerson tradition, it also broke new ground. Most significant, at least in terms of the influence Whicher would have on Emerson's current revival, is the renewed emphasis placed on the centrality of power in Emerson's thought. No topic receives greater space in Whicher's index than power, and there is an additional lengthy entry under "vital force." (It should be noted, for purposes of comparison, that the subject is not even indexed in Feidelson, in Vivian Hopkins's *Spires of Form* [1951], Sherman Paul's *Emerson's Angle of Vision* [1952], Ralph Rusk's *The Life of Ralph Waldo Emerson* [1949], or F. I. Carpenter's *Emerson Handbook* [1953].) What is most striking, however, about *Freedom and Fate*'s discussion of Emerson's "radically anarchic" devotion "not [to] virtue, but freedom and mastery" is that it reasserts not the James or Santayana version of Emerson but a response that recalls Dewey's.[85]

Whicher does, in closing, characterize the Nietzschean strain in Emerson as merely the obsolescent, "final eruption of protestant perfectionism." But his main discussion of Emerson's philosophy of power or action otherwise resembles Dewey's. The way Whicher presents this genu-

inely revolutionary aspect of Emerson's thought—and the same thing can be said of Dewey's essay—recalls Ezra Pound's remark that "Artists are the antennae of the race." For this new and surprising commitment to an agonistic vision of human power and the total "emancipation of man" seems to emerge in Emerson's thinking semiconsciously, obliquely, in response to pressures of which Emerson is himself only half aware. Like Dewey, Whicher sees this concern for action, for mastery or use as the source of Emerson's true originality.[86]

It is, Whicher writes, "one of the most startlingly new notes . . . ever to be struck in American literature." Whicher finds traces of this new strain in Emerson in an inherited, Edwardsean vitalism, in an even older tradition of Antinomianism (the "discovery of the God within"), in the Ideal theories of Platonic tradition as well as "the Locke-Berkeley-Hume tradition." But he associates it most closely with what was still the major philosophical tradition of its time: the German conception of philosophy (or the Romantic union of philosophy and poetry) as the revolutionary medium for *Selbsttätigkeit* (self-activity) and freedom ("the liberation of humanity," as Matthew Arnold called it). And it is his commitment to this tradition—not his conventional ethical thought or moralistic language, not the vestiges of mysticism or Platonic idealism—that makes Emerson, Whicher suggests, still significant, still impressive.[87]

Whicher's discussion of this radical, still half-emergent core of Emerson's thought has had a central and continuing influence on Emerson scholarship. His emphasis on Emerson's concern with mastery and power was reapplied, repeatedly and variously, through the 1970s: in Bloom's essays on Emerson's assertions of "the autonomy of the imagination" (1971), in Quentin Anderson's attack on Emerson's "pseudopodial" self (1971), in Lewis Simpson's analysis of Emerson's discovery of "the Archimedean Self" (1971), in Laurence Holland's suggestion that Emerson's writings constitute "a hymn to power" (1978), in Porte's examination of the broad significance of vital force in Emerson's thought (1979).[88] By the end of the decade, the ground had been securely laid for Emerson's "detranscendentalizing," for that renewed emphasis on a pragmatic, agonistic (not a monistic, organicist) Emerson that would mark the criticism of the 1980s.

Like Dewey, Whicher is certain that there is something new and unique in Emerson's emphasis on power but is uncertain what to call it. We are faced with the same problem. Whicher speaks of Emerson's Nietzschean side; yet—although the Emerson-Nietzsche connection is undoubtedly more significant than criticism has generally recognized—Nietzschean is an unsatisfactory description (though I shall continue to use it), if only because Emerson came first. Dewey identifies this side of Emerson as the precursor of an American "new individualism," the preeminent herald of pragmatism and Deweyan "instrumentalism." Whicher associates it with a Germanic "transcendental egoism" or "self-centeredness" that is part of Romantic philosophy's longing for "the emancipation of man."[89]

But Whicher also speaks of Emersonian power as "the Power present and agent in the soul"—a description that leaves open another, very different possibility. It suggests that such power may ultimately be divine in origin, that Emerson is really only giving fresh expression to a God-intoxication older than Christendom. Firkins long ago summed up this theocentric view of Emersonian power when he proposed that Emerson's claim on posterity, his "whole secret," could be defined as the ubiquitous "experience of God"—"the successful practice," as Firkins phrased it, "of unbroken commerce with omnipresent deity." The essentially anachronistic nature of such conviction Firkins made clear in a memorable image. "Emerson in the history of religion," he concluded, "was a guest of honor who reached a party at the moment when its members were dispersing. His arrival evoked a brief sensation—on the doorstep, as it were—but did not finally reconstitute the party."[90]

If this view of Emerson is correct—and it is certainly part of Emerson's commonly accepted Transcendentalist image—then there is, in substance, really little that is new about Emerson's adoration of a power that is essentially divine or spiritual. Firkins finds "the notion of unbroken spiritual commerce" an audacious and "a novel thing"; but such fundamentally pantheistic and mystical God-intoxication (Firkins hails Emerson as "the first of mystics") can be traced back to, among others, Spinoza, Plotinus, and the English Christian Platonists. Thus Henry Bamford Parks reasoned that Emerson was a "pseudo-mystic," a throwback to the middle ages without "any unusually deep insight into reality."[91]

We have arrived, however, at a fundamental paradox: Emerson provides, apparently, sufficient evidence for reading him as both a late-arriving Plotinus and an early Nietzsche or William James. It is a paradox familiar to students of Emerson, one of which Dewey and Whicher were keenly aware. "Emerson was," Denis Donoghue remarks, "just as readily available to Pragmatism as to Transcendentalism." Or, as Gay Wilson Allen observes: "One of the paradoxes in Emerson's Idealism is that he grounds it on empiricism." "What is puzzling about Emerson's writing," Anthony Cascardi notes, "is his simultaneous attraction to and repulsion from idealism." We shall return to this paradox again. What I wish to emphasize here is that it is Emerson's startlingly new, not easily identifiable ruminations on power and action in "the Here and the Now" that draws both Dewey and Whicher. Emerson's "voluntarism" and "vocabulary of Will," as Donoghue has more recently concluded, founded "a pragmatics of the future."[92]

Notes

1. Alfred Kazin, "The Father of Us All," *New York Review of Books,* 21 January 1982, 3; Richard Poirier, *Renewal of Literature,* 141. The epigraph is from "Emersonianism," originally published in *The New Yorker,* 4 June 1984, and reprinted in John Updike, *Odd Jobs: Essays and Criticism* (New York: Knopf, 1991), 148-68.

2. Lawrence Buell, "The Emerson Industry in the 1980s: A Survey of Trends and Achievements," *ESQ: A Journal of the American Renaissance* 30 (1984):118; Kazin, "Father of Us All," 3; Harold Bloom, "Mr. America," *New York Review of Books,* 22 November 1984, 19; Richard Poirier, *A World Elsewhere: The Place of Style in American Literature* (New York: Oxford University Press, 1966), 56; Joel Porte, *Representative Man: Ralph Waldo Emerson in His Time,* 2d ed. (New York: Columbia University Press, 1988), x; Denis Donoghue, *Reading America: Essays on American Literature* (Berkeley: University of California Press, 1988), 37; Stanley Cavell, *In Quest of the Ordinary: Lines of Skepticism and Romanticism* (Chicago: University of Chicago Press, 1988), 27-28; John Michael, *Emerson and Skepticism: The Cipher of the World* (Baltimore, Md.: Johns Hopkins University Press, 1988), ix; David Bromwich, *A Choice of Inheritance: Self and Community from Edmund Burke to Robert Frost* (Cambridge, Mass.: Harvard University Press, 1989), 148.

3. Buell, "Emerson Industry," 118; Harriet Martineau, *Retrospect of Western Travel* (1838; rpt. Haskell House, 1969), vol. 2, 203; Theodore Parker, in *The Transcendentalists: An Anthology,* ed. Perry Miller (Cambridge, Mass.: Harvard University Press, 1950), 415-16; Walt Whitman, in *The Shock of Recognition,* ed. Edmund Wilson (1943; rpt. New York: Octagon Books, 1975), vol. 1, 272; James Russell Lowell, in *Literary Criticism of James Russell Lowell,* ed. Herbert Smith (Lincoln: University of Nebraska Press, 1969), 206, 213; Matthew Arnold, in *The Recognition of Ralph Waldo Emerson,* ed. Milton R. Konvitz (Ann Arbor: University of Michigan Press, 1972), 73.

4. John Dewey, "Ralph Waldo Emerson," in *Emerson: A Collection of Critical Essays,* ed. Milton Konvitz and Stephen Whicher (Englewood Cliffs, N.J.: Prentice-Hall, 1962), 29; John Jay Chapman, "Emerson," in *Shock of Recognition,* vol. 1, 596, 657; Henry James, *The American Scene* (1907; Bloomington: Indiana University Press, 1968), 264; George Woodberry, *Ralph Waldo Emerson* (1907; rpt. New York: Haskell House, 1968), 176; T. S. Eliot, in *Shock of Recognition,* vol. 2, 855; Paul Elmer More, *Shelburne Essays in American Literature,* ed. Daniel Aaron (New York: Harcourt, Brace, and World, 1963), 173; Lewis Mumford, *The Golden Day: A Study in American Literature and Culture* (1926; New York: Dover, 1968), 45.

5. Barrett Wendell, in *Recognition of Ralph Waldo Emerson,* 118; Charles Feidelson, *Symbolism and American Literature* (Chicago: University of Chi-

cago Press, 1953), 120; D. H. Lawrence, in *Recognition of Ralph Waldo Emerson,* 169.

6. Buell, "Emerson Industry," 117; Stanley Cavell, *This New Yet Unapproachable America: Lectures after Emerson after Wittgenstein* (Albuquerque, N.Mex.: Living Batch Press, 1989), 107; David Marr, *American Worlds Since Emerson* (Amherst: University of Massachusetts Press, 1988), 9; Peter Carafiol, "Reading Emerson: Writing History," *Centennial Review* 30 (Fall 1986), 450.

7. Joel Porte, "The Problem of Emerson," in *The Uses of Literature,* ed. Monroe Engel (Cambridge, Mass.: Harvard University Press, 1973), 94.

8. Ibid., 92-93; William Dean Howells, *Literary Friends and Acquaintances,* ed. David F. Hiatt and Edwin H. Cady (Bloomington: Indiana University Press, 1968), 56; Cavell, *This New Yet Unapproachable America,* 3.

9. David Robinson, *Apostle of Culture: Emerson As Preacher and Lecturer* (Philadelphia: University of Pennsylvania Press, 1982), 1; Kenneth Marc Harris, *Carlyle and Emerson: Their Long Debate* (Cambridge, Mass.: Harvard University Press, 1978), 170. Lawrence Buell, *Literary Transcendentalism: Style and Vision in the American Renaissance* (Ithaca, N.Y.: Cornell University Press, 1973) remains an important attempt "to find better ways of measuring the qualities of [Transcendentalist] works" (2)—though its opening page alone provides ample evidence of the usual condescension. See also, as particularly telling examples of the broad, negative presuppositions that underlie Emerson scholarship, Paul K. Conkin, *Puritans and Pragmatists: Eight Eminent American Thinkers* (New York: Dodd, Mead, 1968), 151-90, and Alfred S. Reid, "Emerson's Prose Style: An Edge to Goodness," in *Style in the American Renaissance: A Symposium,* ed. Carl Strauch (Hartford, Conn.: Transcendental Books, 1970), 37-42. Important direct denunciations of Emerson include James Truslow Adams, "Emerson Re-Read," in *Recognition of Ralph Waldo Emerson,* 182-93; Yvor Winters, "Jones Very and R. W. Emerson: Aspects of New England Mysticism" and "The Significance of *The Bridge* by Hart Crane, or What Are We to Think of Professor X?" in *In Defense of Reason* (Chicago: Swallow Press, 1937); Quentin Anderson, *The Imperial Self: An Essay in American Literary and Cultural History* (New York: Knopf, 1971); Russell Kirk, *The Conservative Mind: From Burke to Santayana* (Chicago: Henry Regnery, 1953), 209-13; A. Bartlett Giamatti, "Power, Politics and a Sense of History," in *The University and the Public Interest* (New York: Atheneum, 1981), 166-79; and John Updike, "Emersonianism."

10. Maurice Gonnaud, *An Uneasy Solitude: Individual and Society in the Work of Ralph Waldo Emerson,* trans. Lawrence Rosenwald (Princeton, N.J.: Princeton University Press, 1987), 262, 116.

11. O. W. Firkins, *Ralph Waldo Emerson* (1915; rpt. New York: Russell and Russell, 1965), 373; O. W. Firkins, "Has Emerson a Future?" in *Selected Essays* (Minneapolis: University of Minnesota Press, 1933), 80-81; Carafiol, "Reading Emerson: Writing History," 432.

12. Carafiol, "Reading Emerson: Writing History," 432.

13. Cavell, "Emerson's Aversive Thinking," in *Romantic Revolutions: Criticism and Theory,* ed. Kenneth Johnston et al. (Bloomington: Indiana University Press, 1990), 243; Brownson's essay is reprinted in *Transcendentalists: An Anthology,* 198-200; John Morley, in *Recognition of Ralph Waldo Emerson,* 76; W. C. Brownell, *American Prose Masters,* ed. Howard Mumford Jones (1909; Cambridge, Mass.: Harvard University Press, 1963), 126-27.

14. T. S. Eliot, in *Shock of Recognition,* vol. 2, 859; Perry Miller, "From Edwards to Emerson," in *Errand into the Wilderness* (Cambridge, Mass.: Harvard University Press, 1956), 186; Leslie Fiedler, "American Literature," in *Contemporary Literary Scholarship: A Critical Review,* ed. Lewis Leary (New York: Appleton-Century-Crofts, 1958), 174; Buell, *Literary Transcendentalism,* 1-2; Irving Howe, *The American Newness: Culture and Politics in the Age of Emerson* (Cambridge, Mass.: Harvard University Press, 1986), 14.

15. Howells, *Literary Friends and Acquaintances,* 56; Cavell, *This New Yet Unapproachable America,* 78.

16. Cavell, *This New Yet Unapproachable America,* 78; Dewey, "Ralph Waldo Emerson," 24; T. S. Eliot, in *Shock of Recognition,* vol. 2, 859.

17. Philip F. Gura, *The Wisdom of Words: Language, Theology, and Literature in the New England Renaissance* (Middletown, Conn.: Wesleyan University Press, 1981), 103-4; Cavell, *This New Yet Unapproachable America,* 79. See, as an example of this approach, Ellen Kappy Suckiel's recent conclusion that Emerson remains "first and foremost . . . a preacher" ("Emerson and the Virtues," in *American Philosophy: Royal Institute of Philosophy Lecture Series: 19,* ed. Marcus Singer [New York: Cambridge University Press, 1985], 152). Bruce Kuklick recommends, in the same volume, that further attempts to interpret Emerson's thought be replaced by the study of its local contexts ("Does American Philosophy Rest On a Mistake?" in *American Philosophy,* 187).

18. For Henry James Sr.'s famous response to Emerson—"Oh you man without a handle!" see F. O. Matthiessen, *The James Family* (New York: Knopf, 1961), 43; Henry James, "Emerson," in *Partial Portraits* (1888; rpt. Ann Arbor: University of Michigan Press, 1970), 25; Cavell, *This New Yet Unapproachable America,* 107; Bishop, *Emerson on the Soul,* 1.

19. See Poirier, *Renewal of Literature,* 33; George Kateb, "Thinking About Human Extinction (I) Ni-

etzsche and Heidegger," *Raritan* 6 (Fall 1986):1-28, and "Thinking About Human Extinction (II) Emerson and Whitman," *Raritan* 6 (Winter 1987):1-22; Gura, *Wisdom of Words,* 104; Cornel West, *The American Evasion of Philosophy: A Genealogy of Pragmatism* (Madison: University of Wisconsin Press, 1989), 74.

20. Porte, "Problem of Emerson," 94.

21. Cavell, *The Senses of Walden: An Expanded Edition* (San Francisco: North Point Press, 1981), 33, 124. Joel Porte likewise apologized for an earlier anti-Emerson bias in his preface to the first edition of *Representative Man* (New York: Oxford University Press, 1979), xxi.

22. Cavell, *This New Yet Unapproachable America,* 80.

23. Giles Gunn, *The Culture of Criticism and the Criticism of Culture* (New York: Oxford University Press, 1987); Geoffrey Hartman, *Criticism in the Wilderness: The Study of Literature Today* (New Haven, Conn.: Yale University Press, 1980), 9; William Cain, *The Crisis in Criticism: Theory, Literature, and Reform in English Studies* (Baltimore, Md.: Johns Hopkins University Press, 1984), 240.

24. Kazin, "Father of Us All," 3; James Russell Lowell, "A Fable For Critics," in *Shock of Recognition,* vol. 1, 46. Emerson is, Kazin concluded in 1984, essentially "a revenant from early ages of faith—a primordial, 'aboriginal' kind of early Christian" (*An American Procession* [New York: Knopf, 1984], 39).

25. West, *American Evasion of Philosophy,* 11. Two other recent arguments for resituating Emerson in the mainstream of European thought, not simply within the confines of New England tradition, are Russell B. Goodman, *American Philosophy and the Romantic Tradition* (New York: Cambridge University Press, 1990); and Lawrence Buell, "Emerson in His Cultural Context," in *Ralph Waldo Emerson: A Collection of Critical Essays,* ed. Lawrence Buell (Englewood Cliffs, N.J.: Prentice-Hall, 1993), 48-60.

26. See Eric Cheyfitz's foreword to Gonnaud, *Uneasy Solitude,* xviii; and West, *American Evasion of Philosophy,* 10-11. Philip Rosenberg points out that Carlyle's role as cultural critic was largely unprecedented in the English tradition (*The Seventh Hero: Thomas Carlyle and the Theory of Radical Activism* [Cambridge, Mass.: Harvard University Press, 1974], vii, 33, 52-53).

27. West, *American Evasion of Philosophy,* 36. Harold Bloom makes a similar point: "The relation of Emerson to both Nietzsche and William James suggests that Emersonian Transcendentalism was already much closer to pragmatism than to Kant's metaphysical idealism" (*Agon: Towards a Theory of Revisionism* [New York: Oxford University Press, 1982], 20).

28. Carolyn Porter, *Seeing and Being: The Plight of the Participant Observer in Emerson, James, Adams, and Faulkner* (Middletown, Conn.: Wesleyan University Press, 1981), 94; Gertrude Reif Hughes, *Emerson's Demanding Optimism* (Baton Rouge: Louisiana State University Press, 1984), 162, 18; Feidelson, *Symbolism and American Literature,* 135; Poirier, *Renewal of Literature,* 171; Eric Cheyfitz, *The Trans-Parent: Sexual Politics in the Language of Emerson* (Baltimore, Md.: Johns Hopkins University Press, 1981), xi, 15; Donoghue, *Reading America,* 36; Harold Bloom, *Figures of Capable Imagination* (New York: Seabury Press, 1976), 60.

29. Bloom, "Mr. America," 20; Wilson, *Shock of Recognition,* vol. 1, 596; Richard Grusin, "Revisionism and the Structure of Emersonian Action," *American Literary History* 1 (Summer 1989), 404-31.

30. West, *American Evasion of Philosophy,* 3.

31. Maurice Mandelbaum, *History, Man, and Reason,* 5.

32. See Walter Kaufmann's discussion of the Emerson-Nietzsche relationship in his introduction to Nietzsche, *Gay Science,* 7-13; see also Frederic Ives Carpenter, *Emerson Handbook* (New York: Hendricks House, 1953), 244-49.

33. Arnold, in *Recognition of Ralph Waldo Emerson,* 70; Henry James, *Partial Portraits,* 32; William James, "Address at the Emerson Centenary in Concord," in *Emerson: A Collection of Critical Essays,* 19, 23.

34. Dewey's essay is, F. O. Matthiessen noted in 1941, "in strong opposition to the usual academic dismissal of Emerson's thought" (*American Renaissance: Art and Expression in the Age of Emerson and Whitman* [New York: Oxford University Press, 1941], 4).

35. Dewey, "Ralph Waldo Emerson," 24.

36. Ibid., 27-28.

37. Ibid.

38. Dewey, cited in West, *American Evasion of Philosophy,* 97.

39. West, *American Evasion of Philosophy,* 74, 85.

40. The "second phase of Emerson studies" is Bliss Perry's description, in *Emerson Today* (Princeton, N.J.: Princeton University Press, 1931), 5.

41. Henry James, *Partial Portraits,* 2, 7-10; the Matthiessen quotation is from *James Family,* 429.

42. Henry James, *Partial Portraits,* 8, 31, 15.

43. The Santayana quotations are from "The Genteel Tradition in American Philosophy," in *Santayana on America,* ed. Richard Lyon (New York: Harcourt, Brace, and World, 1968), 40, 45, 54; Irving Howe, "The American Voice—It Begins on a Note of Wonder," *New York Times Book Review,* 4 July 1976, 2.

44. Santayana, "The Genteel Tradition at Bay," in *Santayana on America,* 158, 138; Babbitt and Warner G. Rice, cited in René Wellek, "Irving Babbitt, Paul More, and Transcendentalism," in *Transcendentalism and Its Legacy,* ed. Myron Simon and Thornton H. Parsons (Ann Arbor: University of Michigan Press, 1966), 192-193, 197.

45. Santayana, "Emerson the Poet," in *Santayana on America,* 271; Santayana, "The Optimism of Ralph Waldo Emerson," in *George Santayana's America,* 83, 73, 81; Santayana, "Emerson," in *Santayana on America,* 267, 266, 259, 260. For the evolution of Santayana's opinion of Emerson, see Porte, *Representative Man* (1979), 16-31.

46. Santayana, *The Last Puritan: A Memoir in the Form of a Novel* (New York: Scribner's, 1936), 201, 126, 404, 445.

47. Santayana, "Emerson the Poet," 275, 271.

48. Santayana, "Dewey's Naturalistic Metaphysics," in *Santayana on America,* 111-12, 121, 116, 125.

49. Hegel, *German Aesthetic and Literary Criticism: Kant, Fichte, Schelling, Schopenhauer, Hegel,* 211. See Eugene Goodheart, *The Cult of the Ego: The Self in Modern Literature* (Chicago: University of Chicago Press, 1968), 118-19, for a discussion of Nietzsche and this German, Protestant tradition of the "I" as appropriator and consumer.

50. Santayana, *Three Philosophical Poets* (1910; rpt. New York: Cooper Square Publishers, 1970), 7-8.

51. Santayana, "Optimism of Ralph Waldo Emerson," 73.

52. John Burt Foster, *Heirs to Dionysus: A Nietzschean Current in Literary Modernism* (Princeton, N.J.: Princeton University Press, 1981), 51.

53. Santayana, "Optimism of Ralph Waldo Emerson," 73.

54. Santayana, "Emerson the Poet," 273.

55. Henry James, *Partial Portraits,* 17.

56. "Cheerful Monist" is Frost's description in *Emerson: A Collection of Critical Essays,* 12.

57. Porte, *Representative Man* (1979), 229.

58. Ibid., 258-59, 234.

59. Leo Marx, *The Machine in the Garden: Technology and the Pastoral Idea in America* (New York: Oxford University Press, 1967), 230.

60. I quote Robert Solomon's description of Heidegger's philosophy in *In the Spirit of Hegel,* 389. The traditional description of Emerson as "a philosopher of intuition," Cavell notes, "uniformly fails to add that he is simultaneously the teacher of tuition" (*In Quest of the Ordinary,* 115).

61. Mandelbaum characterizes the "pragmatic-economical view of the human mind" as the theory that defines intelligence "in terms of its usefulness in satisfying needs." According to this view, all that we consider knowledge or truth or regard "as an order fixed by nature itself" may be defined, instead, as "a product of our own tendencies to arrange and summarize experience in a manner useful to us." See Mandelbaum, *History, Man, and Reason,* 16-17.

62. Robert Solomon suggests the shared emphasis on "action as knowledge" that links Fichte and Hegel to the pragmatism of William James and Dewey (*In the Spirit of Hegel,* 10-11).

63. Carlyle, *Carlyle Reader,* 152.

64. Johann Fichte, *The Vocation of Man,* trans. William Smith (1931; rpt. Chicago: Open Court, 1940), 94.

65. Dewey, cited in West, *American Evasion of Philosophy,* 82.

66. Dewey, "Ralph Waldo Emerson," 29.

67. West, *American Evasion of Philosophy,* 73.

68. Ibid., 211; Dewey quotations from ibid., 100-101, 104, 92, 91. Cavell approaches Wittgenstein and Emerson as "philosophers of culture" in *This New Yet Unapproachable America.*

69. William James, *The Energies of Men* (New York: Moffat, Yard, 1917), 38.

70. Henry Adams, *The Education of Henry Adams,* ed. Ernest Samuels (Boston: Houghton Mifflin, 1973), 314, 463, 461.

71. West, *American Evasion of Philosophy,* 25.

72. Poirier, *Renewal of Literature,* 59.

73. Kenneth Burke, "I, Eye, Ay—Emerson's Early Essay 'Nature': Thoughts on the Machinery of Transcendence," in *Transcendentalism and Its Legacy,* 9; Eduard Baumgarten, *Der Pragmatismus: R. W. Emerson, W. James, J. Dewey* (Frankfurt, 1938); Matthiessen, *American Renaissance,* 368; Perry Miller, *Nature's Nation* (Cambridge, Mass.: Harvard University Press, 1967), 171; Daniel Aaron, *Men of Good Hope: A Story of American Progressives* (New York: Oxford University Press, 1951), 8. Emerson, Hermann Hummel concluded in 1946, "must be regarded as the teacher and master rather than as a 'précurseur' of Nietzsche" ("Emerson and Nietzsche," *New England Quarterly,* 19 [March 1946]:84). But scholarship on the Emerson-Nietzsche connection has been sparse. The handful of articles in English, as well as European studies, are catalogued in Carpenter, *Emerson Handbook,* 254-58. See also William Salter, *Nietzsche the Thinker* (New York: Holt, 1917).

74. Aaron, *Men of Good Hope,* 8.

75. Feidelson, *Symbolism and American Literature,* 126.

76. Gonnaud, *Uneasy Solitude,* 355.

77. Matthiessen, *American Renaissance,* 367-68, 4.

78. Jon Klancher defines "master sign" as a single, to-talizing concept that takes on, in the hands of a critic-seer like Carlyle, sufficient heuristic power to explain a diverse array of social, philosophical, po-litical, and cultural problems (*Making of English Reading Audiences,* 71-73).

79. See Gonnaud's introduction to Stephen Whicher, *Freedom and Fate: An Inner Life of Ralph Waldo Emerson,* 2d ed. (Philadelphia: University of Penn-sylvania Press, 1971), x.

80. Poirier, *Renewal of Literature,* 33; Hughes, *Emer-son's Demanding Optimism,* 70; Julie Ellison, "The Edge of Urbanity: Emerson's *English Traits,*" *ESQ: A Journal of the American Renaissance* 32 (1986):104.

81. Bishop, *Emerson on the Soul,* 165.

82. See, for example, Cheyfitz, foreword to Gonnaud, *Uneasy Solitude,* xv; Marr, *American Worlds Since Emerson,* 70-71; and Harold Bloom's introduction to *Modern Critical Interpretations: Henry James's 'The Portrait of a Lady'* (New York: Chelsea House, 1987), 6.

83. Whicher, *Freedom and Fate,* 172-73.

84. Ibid.; see also 179.

85. This central passage from *Freedom and Fate* is on pp. 55-56.

86. Ibid., 172.

87. See *Freedom and Fate,* 56, 53, 44; Arnold described Heinrich Heine as a "soldier in the war of libera-tion of humanity" (cited in Peter Allan Dale, *The Victorian Critic and the Idea of History: Carlyle, Arnold, and Pater* [Cambridge, Mass.: Harvard Uni-versity Press, 1977], 63).

88. Harold Bloom, *The Ringers in the Tower: Studies in Romantic Tradition* (Chicago: University of Chi-cago Press, 1971), 224; Anderson, *Imperial Self,* 130; Lewis P. Simpson, *The Man of Letters in New England and the South* (Baton Rouge: Louisiana State University Press, 1973), 81, 65; Laurence Holland, cited in Eric Cheyfitz, *The Trans-Parent,* 15; Porte, *Representative Man* (1979), 209-82 and passim. Leo Marx's analysis (in *Machine in the Garden*) of the complex relationship between Tran-scendentalism and technological power should not be left out as an important example of this trend.

89. Dewey, cited in West, *American Evasion of Phi-losophy,* 103; Whicher, *Freedom and Fate,* 55-56.

90. Whicher, *Freedom and Fate,* 56; Firkins, "Has Em-erson a Future?," 79.

91. Firkins, "Has Emerson a Future?" 79-81; Henry Bamford Parks, in *Emerson: A Collection of Criti-cal Essays,* 126, 124.

92. Dewey called Emerson's ideas "versions of the Here and the Now" ("Ralph Waldo Emerson," 28); Donoghue, *Reading America,* 23, 37; Gay Wilson Allen, *Waldo Emerson* (New York: Viking, 1981), 642; Anthony J. Cascardi, "Emerson on Nature: Philosophy beyond Kant," *ESQ: A Journal of the American Renaissance* 30 (1984):202. Emerson and those in his tradition are, Russell Goodman writes, "as much 'transcendentalist' as 'pragmatic'" (*American Philosophy and the Romantic Tradition,* 33).

Abbreviations

CW *The Collected Works of Ralph Waldo Emerson,* edited by Robert Spiller et al. 4 vols. Cambridge, Mass.: Harvard University Press, 1971-.

EJ *Emerson in His Journals,* edited by Joel Porte. Cam-bridge, Mass.: Harvard University Press, 1982.

ET *English Traits,* edited by Howard Mumford Jones. Cambridge, Mass.: Harvard University Press, 1966.

GM *On the Genealogy of Morals.* In *Basic Writings of Ni-etzsche.*

GS *The Gay Science,* translated by Walter Kaufmann. New York: Random House, 1974.

JMN *The Journals and Miscellaneous Notebooks of Ralph Waldo Emerson,* edited by William H. Gilman et al. 16 vols. Cambridge, Mass.: Harvard University Press, 1960-1982.

W *The Complete Works of Ralph Waldo Emerson,* Cente-nary Edition, edited by Edward Waldo Emerson. 12 vols. Boston: Houghton Mifflin, 1903-1904.

Anthony P. Petruzzi (essay date 1996)

SOURCE: "Emerson, Disclosure, and the Experiencing Self," in *Philosophy and Rhetoric,* Vol. 29, No. 1, 1996, pp. 51-64.

[*In the following essay, Petruzzi contends that the disclo-sive theory of truth allows for a more complete description of Emerson's rhetorical theory than either Enlightenment rhetoric or Romantic rhetoric.*]

INTRODUCTION

Emerson was educated at Harvard at a time when compo-sition and rhetorical theory were dominated by Hugh Blair's "commonsense" rhetoric. The nature of Emerson's rhetorical theory has most often been positioned some-where between the two poles of Scottish "commonsense" and Romantic rhetorics. I will argue that the disclosive theory of truth presents a more complete and richer way to describe Emerson's rhetorical theory than either the En-lightenment rhetoric of "commonsense" or the Romantic rhetoric of "self-expression." For Emerson, the experiencing-self functions to organize discourse and con-struct reality through the continual effort to deconstruct the discourse of public interpretations, what Heidegger calls the "they-self." As the discourse of public interpretations is deconstructed, there is a concomitant action to reconstruct a more authentic, yet always partial and temporary "experiencing-self." The experiencing-self lives "in a system of approximations. Every end is prospective of some other end, which is temporary; a round and final success nowhere" (1940, **"Nature,"** 417). For Emerson, like Heidegger, the nature of truth is "thrown projection"; that is, the experiencing-self discloses both the truth and the untruth.

Glen M. Johnson (1993) argues that Emerson's romanticism was mitigated by the qualities of style that Blair's "commonsense" rhetoric emphasizes: perspicuity, or clarity and economy, as well as ornamentation, or diction and eloquence. Johnson examines the way Emerson revised his manuscripts; he finds that Emerson's writing was neither spontaneous nor automatic. Rather, Emerson's written texts were crafted not only by "selection and arrangement," but also by a "final stage of revision" that was "strictly rhetorical, designed to serve the *communication of meaning*" (171; emphasis in original). Johnson's main point is that Emerson's essays are not "inspired overflow," but rather "the product of exhaustive revision" and "painstaking work" (189). Emerson "often depersonalize[s] or generalize[s] his experience," but equally often he "individualize[s]" and "personalize[s]" his experience as he feels the need to increase the "rhetorical impact" (174). For Johnson, Emerson's writing is not spontaneous self-expression and his rhetoric is not essentially Romantic.

Sheldon W. Liebman (1969) argues that, although the "early" Emerson is a follower of Hugh Blair's "commonsense" school of rhetoric, beginning in 1821 "Emerson's ideas underwent a radical change" (178) because of the influence of "the romantic school." For Liebman, Emerson's "latter" rhetoric is essentially Romantic and it includes the following tenets: "man's principal endeavor is to express himself" (193); "common speech" is elevated to "a position of virtue" while "eloquent" or ornate style is seen as merely "bookish" language (194); automatic writing will break through the acculturated and conventional modes of thought and privileges spontaneity over "conscious deliberation" (196); spontaneity removes "planning and premeditation" (196) as the two major "hindrances to effective writing"; and by removing premeditation and deliberation from the writing process, the writer achieves a "will-lessness" that facilitates a "true" expression of the self.

We can see that Emerson's rhetoric is being defined by the Romantic notion that truth is the "self-expression" of a private and personal vision. According to James Berlin (1984), Emerson is not a Platonist: "Despite his admiration for Plato, Emerson's philosophical idealism is not Platonic. His position is indeed closer to such moderns as Ernst Cassirer and Susanne Langer" (46). Berlin's view is that Emerson is a Social Constructionist: "Reality is a human construction, joining the world of ideas to the material object in the act of creative perception" (46). Berlin aptly points out the relational nature of Emerson's view of truth: "Truth is a product of a relationship; its source is neither subject nor object, but is located at the point of intersection of the two"; the relation is defined for Emerson by "the interaction of the perceiver and that which is perceived" (47). Although Berlin notes both the relational quality of Emerson's view of truth and the important role truth plays in the social and public world, he also insists that "for Emerson the ground of reality is the ideal" (46). Consequently, Berlin argues that for Emerson "[t]ruth remains always and everywhere the same, but new metaphors must be continually generated in order to express it" (53).

Ultimately, I would suggest that none of these theories provide an accurate description of Emerson's rhetoric because they fail to take into consideration Emerson's disclosive notion of truth. Emerson is not a systematic thinker; his interest in Plato as a "representative man" revolves around his identification with Socrates, "that central figure" (1940, **"Plato,"** 487) who typifies the endless search for truth, and also with Plato's notion of philosophy as an unending process.

EMERSON ON PLATO AND THE DISCLOSIVE NATURE OF TRUTH

Although Emerson, like Plato, flirts with a correspondence theory of truth, the most pervasive and important aspect of his thought on the nature of truth is the process of disclosure, what Heidegger calls the process of revealment and concealment. Emerson sees Plato's writing as the work of an active intellect who demonstrates that knowledge is a correspondence: "Things correspond. There is a scale; and the correspondence of heaven to earth, of matter to mind, of the part to the whole, is our guide" (1940, 483). Although Emerson describes a type of correspondence theory, the important thing to note is that here *correspondence* does not imply a mode of static correctness between the absolute and the contingent. Emerson describes truth in terms of relationality; a human being "studies relations in all objects" because he is in the midst of the world: "He is placed in the centre of beings, and a ray of relation passes from every other being to him. And neither can man be understood without these objects, nor these objects without man" (1940, **"Nature,"** 15-16). Understanding exists as a relation between Dasein and the world. For Emerson, the theory of correspondence does not imply that truth is a mode of correctness of representation; rather, it implies a field of relations. The fundamentally interpretative nature of understanding and the expansive or dynamic nature of truth is both revealed and concealed through the difference between understanding the part and projecting a whole: "On seeing the arc we complete the curve, and when the curtain is lifted from the diagram which it seemed to veil, we are vexed to find that no more was drawn than just that fragment of an arc which we first beheld" (1940, **"Nominalist,"** 435). As Emerson notes, the correspondence highlights the difference between the part and the whole; recognition of correspondence is a "guide" for understanding, not an absolute standard to be mirrored.

The kind of intellectual activity about which Emerson is speaking occurs from within a framework of rhetorical action: "The world shall be to us an open book," says Emerson, and because every object in the world has a "hidden" life, like a book the world needs to be interpreted. The "hidden" or "unconscious truth" is made manifest "when interpreted and defined in an object" (1940, **"Nature,"** 20). Interpretation makes an object manifest; it uncovers the object's hidden aspects so that the object stands phenomenologically revealed. The uncovering or revealing of the object itself is the process of truth; the object then enters into or becomes "a part of the domain of knowledge" (20). Interpretation includes both the critical awareness of the forestructure of understanding—"Each truth that a writer acquires is a lantern which he turns full on what facts and thoughts lay already in his mind" (1940, **"Intellect,"** 296)—and the projection of new possibilities and new definitions of the world:

> This defining is philosophy. Philosophy is the account which the human mind gives to itself of the constitution of the world. Two cardinal facts lie forever at the base; the one, and the two. 1. Unity, or Identity; and 2. Variety. We unite all things by perceiving the law which pervades them; by perceiving the superficial differences and the profound resemblances. But every mental act— this very perception of identity or oneness, recognizes the difference of things. Oneness and otherness. It is impossible to speak or to think without embracing both.
>
> (1940, **"Plato,"** 475)

As Berlin correctly notes, Emerson views the world as constructed by the intellect; "all things" are united through perception. Perception is a twofold movement recognizing interaction of resemblances and differences. The discursive process operates from the difference of things; for both speaking and thinking it necessarily embraces the "oneness and otherness" of identity and difference.

Emerson understands Plato's interest in the problem of the one and the many as being central to cognition: "The mind returns from the one to that which is not one, but other and many; from cause to effect; and affirms the necessary existence of variety, the self-existence of both, as each is involved in the other" (1940, **"Plato,"** 476). For Emerson, speculation or thinking is a movement toward or a search for unity while action in the world is a movement "backwards to diversity" (477). While the activity of Man Thinking "melts," "reduces," and "absorbs" the diversity of experience in a search for the One, the search for the One is never successful: "No sentence will hold the whole truth, and the only way in which we can be just, is by giving ourselves the lie. . . . All things are in contact; every atom has a sphere of repulsion; Things are and are not, at the same time . . . therefore I assert that every man is a partialist" (1940, **"Nominalist,"** 446). The search for understanding one human being can be attempted only by understanding the whole: "You must take the whole soci-

ety to find the whole man" (1940, **"American Scholar,"** 46). For Emerson, the circular pattern of understanding revolves around the one and the many, identity and difference: "These two principles reappear and interpenetrate all things, all thought; the one, the many" (1940, **"Plato,"** 477), and, because of the interpenetration of these two principles, understanding can never be complete. This is why Emerson argues that "thinking is a partial act" (1940, **"American Scholar,"** 54).

Emerson's self-conscious exposition of the fragmented nature of the self and concomitant fragmentary nature of discourse results in a qualification that affects all discursive claims or assertions. For Emerson, this qualification in discourse unsettles the nature of knowledge to the degree that it cannot be corrected, even through an attempt to create systematic knowledge. Although Plato recognizes this limitation, Emerson sees that the Platonists have not. The power of Plato's thought does not lie in a systematic construct that "explains" complete or self-evident truth: "[Plato] has not a system. The dearest defenders and disciples are at fault. He attempted a theory of the universe, and his theory is not complete or self-evident. One man thinks he means this, another that; he has said one thing in one place, and the reverse of it in another place . . . but the theory of the world is a thing of shreds and patches" (1940, 491). Emerson sees the problem of understanding Plato as intimately involved with the problem of the interpretative acts of his "dearest defenders and disciples." The real intention of Plato's thought has been obscured by the interpretative acts that have created Platonism. Rather than being led by Plato's example to think of the world as "a thing of shreds and patches," Platonists look for systematic order; rather than attending to the process of the mind that Plato describes, Platonists actually conceal the way the texts of Plato operate; rather than participate in the disclosure of the truth, Platonists participate in the covering up of the truth in Plato's texts.

Emerson recognizes that Plato's "beautiful definitions of ideas, of time, of form, of figure, of the line, [are] sometimes hypothetically given" (1940, **"Plato,"** 494),[1] but from out of the method of hypothesis emerges meanings that are disclosive in nature: "Whatever [Plato] looks upon discloses a second sense, and ulterior senses" (494). Plato's texts actually embody the projective nature of understanding, and they lead to further interpretative acts that uncover new "ulterior senses" of meaning. Emerson chooses Plato as a "representative man," not because he devised a logically irrefutable system, but rather because he represents a "great average man" whose dynamic nature reveals the disclosive approach to truth:

> Plato's thinking does not stand on syllogism, or any masterpieces of the Socratic reasoning, or on any thesis, as for example the immortality of the soul. He is more than . . . the prophet of a peculiar message. He represents the privilege of the intellect, the power, namely, of *carrying up every fact to successive platforms* and so *disclosing in every fact a germ of expansion*. The *expansions* are in the essence of thought.
>
> (493; emphasis added)

Plato's thinking stands on its power to reveal the world, and each new revelation contains possibilities that in turn disclose new expansions. Emerson recognizes that Plato's notion of truth is processual; his constant effort to overturn old truths and to create new truths is a series of interpretative "expansions" that carries "every fact to successive platforms." For Emerson, the impulse to generalize or to be a "universalist" is what creates an individual point of view, but thinking entails the ability to resist generalizing in order to "shift the platform on which we stand" (1940, **"Nominalist,"** 447) so that the "million fresh particulars" (441) of experience can provide new expanded platforms for "all [that] is yet unsaid" (447).

The Nature of the Experiencing-Self

Emerson's essay **"Experience"** describes the partiality or fragmented nature of knowledge as a condition of human experience. The opening image of this essay creates a vivid image of what Heidegger calls Dasein's "throwness." Understanding our relation to others, the fact that we are "thrown" into the middle of life, is what Heidegger calls "being-in-the-world." For Emerson, the experience of being-in-the-world is the starting point of his essay **"Experience"**: "Where do we find ourselves? In a series of which we do not know the extremes, and believe that it has none. We wake and find ourselves on a stair; there are stairs below us, which we seem to have ascended; there are stairs above us, many a one, which go upward and out of sight" (1940, 342). We are always already in the midst of existence, and this means we are in the midst of "old belief," which "gives us lethe to drink" (342). Emerson states the problem again in **"Intellect"**: "All that mass of mental and moral phenomena which we do not make objects of voluntary thought, come within the power of fortune; they constitute the circumstance of daily life" (293). Consequently, Dasein, who is "immersed" in the concerns of everyday life, "cannot see the problem of existence" (1940, **"Intellect,"** 293). For both Emerson and Heidegger, forgetfulness, lethargy, indolence, and sleepiness all threaten our perception of reality and our understanding of self and are the "problems" of existence.

For Emerson, cultural habits, customs, and old beliefs construct a system of illusions that must be deconstructed by thoughtful critical analysis. The analysis consists of conceptual expansions that utilize both "the understanding and the reason" to discover and explore the horizons of thought. Leonard Neufeldt (1971) describes how for Emerson, "Every opinion or knowledge is essentially a new creation, a new understanding or interpretation of the world" (258). The interpretative nature of understanding means two things to Emerson. First, conceptual expansions are an organic process of intellectual development. He uses two images to describe this process: Emerson's first image is exfoliation or unfolding, "All our progress [of the intellect] is an unfolding, like the vegetable bud" (1940, **"Intellect,"** 294); the second image is a constantly expanding circle that "bursts over the boundary on all sides and expands another orbit on the great deep" (1940, **"Circles,"**

281). Emerson's description of the thought process is remarkably close to Gadamer's description of the hermeneutic circle of understanding: "To expand in concentric circles the unity of the understood meaning" (1988, 68). The second aspect of the expansive nature of thought is, as Neufeldt states, that it "reorders what we know" (1971, 259). Because thinking constantly reorders knowledge, Emerson sees himself as "an endless seeker" (1940, **"Circles,"** 288); all thinking is experienced as a process that equally unifies and disrupts the life of the thinker.

Those who see Emerson's rhetoric as an expression of "literary self-reliance" reduce Emerson to a proponent of American individualism. However, a reading such as this fails to understand the ontological concerns of Emerson's thought. Imitation, drills of school education, rules and regulations all operate as existential structures that disguise or, in Heidegger's terms, cover up authentic Being. For Emerson, the fundamental relation of human beings (the being of beings or the Many) with Being (the One) is always of primary importance. Emerson recognizes that the covering up of this relationship is co-original with the revelation of truth. The dynamic of the authentic-self, the self that experiences the covering up as covering up, seeks to make manifest "the system of illusions" that "shuts us in a prison of glass which we cannot see" (1940, **"Experience,"** 346). The reason Emerson constantly emphasizes individual "voice" and "expression" is because he uses experience as the primordial rhetorical model. The expression of an individual's voice both asserts and highlights the difference between the covering up typified by the "they-self" and the discovering of the "authentic-self." In other words, for Emerson, experience is not "self-expression" of some inner and private meaning; rather, what is expressed is the experience, is the being of a voice as it manifests itself in relation to the "prison of glass which we cannot see."

For Emerson, Nature is a philosophical concept: "All that is separate from us, all which Philosophy distinguishes as the NOT ME, that is, both nature and art, all other men and my own body, must be ranked under this name, NATURE" (1940, **"Nature,"** 4; emphasis in original). For Emerson, the self is both plural, a dispersed "us," and individual or separate from "all other men." Nature, or all that is "not me," in and of itself operates to disguise or "fool" the authentic-self: "Nature does not like to be observed, and likes that we should be her fools and playmates" (1940, **"Experience,"** 345). The human experience of Nature is evanescent and has a "lubricity" that lets it "slip through our fingers" (344). Yet, the harder we clutch at an experience of Nature, says Emerson, the more it dodges us and the more we reveal "the most unhandsome part of our condition" (345). The exact nature of our "unhandsome" condition is that, in the attempt to grasp, observe, and control the objects of the everyday world, through moods we deliver ourselves over to our own systems of illusion or dreams. While temperament, the "iron wire on which the beads [of emotion] are strung" (345), provides the structure for the "system of illusions,"

Dream delivers us to dream, and there is no end to illusion. *Life is a train of moods* like a string of beads, and as we pass through them they prove to be many-colored lenses which paint the world their own hue, and each shows only what lies in its focus. . . . We animate what we can, and we see only what we animate. Nature and books belong to the eyes that see them. *It depends on the mood of the man* whether he shall see the sunset or the fine poem.

(345, emphasis added)

For Emerson, moods control the way that the self experiences and understands the everyday world. This means that all perception is colored by moods; moods are the "hues" that focus vision and also determine how we "animate" or bring the world into existence. For Emerson, an individual's state of mind can either "counterfeit" experience or it can disclose the authentic-self or being of the individual: "Every appearance in nature corresponds to some state of the mind, *and that state of the mind can only be described by presenting* that natural appearance as its picture" (1940, **"Nature,"** 15; emphasis added). For Emerson, the only way to describe the ontological state of a mind is to interpret the way that mind constructs the world, but the activity of reception and construction of the world through the intellect is always anterior to the expression of our experience of state-of-mind.

In "Thinking of Emerson" (1993), Stanley Cavell notes that Emerson clearly distinguishes between an analysis of the way sense experience reveals objects and an analysis of the way mood reveals the world. Cavell aptly notes the similarity between Heidegger's and Emerson's "effort[s] to formulate a kind of epistemology of moods" (191). Heidegger describes the way that mood or "state-of-mind" discloses or reveals a kind of "submission to the world"; and in that submission to the "throwness" of the world the authentic-self is fragmented and overtaken by the world: "Dasein constantly surrenders itself to the 'world' and lets the 'world' matter to it in such a way that somehow Dasein evades its very self" (1962, 178). According to Heidegger, Aristotle was the first to recognize that the function of rhetoric was to interpret these moods (178). It is in the second book of Aristotle's *Rhetoric* that Heidegger sees a systematic attempt to understand the public nature of discourse. The public is the way the "they" reveals itself. All discourse speaks both into and out of the moods or states of mind of "they." It is only through an interpretation of state-of-mind that rhetoric can "understand the possibilities of moods in order to rouse them and guide them aright" (178).

Cavell states that he is "startled by the similarities" (1993, 194-95) between Heidegger and Emerson. It seems to me that Cavell is quite right; the connection between these two thinkers runs very deep. Emerson and Heidegger are deeply connected by the way they describe both the nature of experience itself and the important way that the experiencing-self is in a constant struggle to make visible the "prison of glass which we cannot see" (1940, **"Experience,"** 346). For Heidegger, Dasein is in a constant

struggle to overcome its contextual constraints: "The Self of everyday Dasein is the *they-self*, which we distinguish from the *authentic Self*". (1962, 167). Individual human beings are "Self" only in relation to the social world; the self is "dispersed into the they, and must first find itself" (167). In everyday life a human being operates within an internalized mode of understanding that determines how an individual interprets the world. These social and internalized constraints are the illusions of the "they-self." For Dasein to "find itself," it must deconstruct the illusions: the authentic-self discloses itself to itself by "clearing away [the] concealments and obscurities, as a breaking up of the disguises with which Dasein bars its own way" (167). By clearing away the "concealments and obscurities," the authentic-self experiences a disclosure of truth.

DECOMPOSITION IS RECOMPOSITION

Emerson begins **"Intellect"** by stating that the intellect's function is to dissolve "the subtlest unnamed relations of nature" (1940, 292). He uses two terms, intellect receptive and intellect constructive, to describe the activity of the intellect and the explicitly interpretative nature of the "rhetoric of thought":

The thought of genius is spontaneous; but the power of picture or expression, in the most enriched and flowing nature, implies a mixture of will, a certain control over the spontaneous states, without which no production is possible. It is *a conversion of all nature into the rhetoric of thought*, under the eye of judgement, with a strenuous exercise of choice.

(298; emphasis added)

The experiencing-self imposes, through the intellect receptive and intellect constructive, its will and control upon experience in order to transform or convert experience "into the rhetoric of thought." In other words, the rhetoric of thought is the activity of the intellect as it makes interpretative choices that "construct" or compose the "unconscious states" that the receptive intellect opens upon. For Emerson, rhetorical expression implies both an opening to the world and a willful construction of interpretative choices. Interpretation implies both the critical awareness of the forestructure of understanding, and the projection of new possibilities and new definitions of the world; in other words, Emerson's theory of rhetoric is based on the disclosive theory of truth.

The first aspect, the "intellect receptive" opens the mind to its relationship to the 'system of illusion' it exists within; the second is "intellect constructive," which constructs, produces, or composes the systems of relations; in other words, it names the world. The intellect receptive is "anterior to all action or construction" (1940, **"Intellect,"** 292). Emerson argues that contrary to "common" opinion, intellectual activity does not make "abstract truth" (292). Emerson attacks the notion of objective truth, or, in other words, the notion that truth is absolute and separate from the human intellect. When truth is abstracted from the human context it becomes objectified, impersonal, and embalmed. On the contrary, Emerson sees truth as an organic occurrence. Truth is inseparable from human being and lives in the same circular pattern as human beings: life and death, generation and degeneration, decomposition and recomposition, truth and not truth, are all processes of "unfolding, like a vegetable bud" (294).

In order to understand Emerson's conception of the intellect, we first need to see why the intellect receptive is an anterior structure of mind. The intellect receptive is the "common wealth" that is contained in "every man's mind"; the wealth consists of "images, words and facts," which are "scrawled" or written "inscriptions" on the walls of the mind, in other words thoughts (1940, **"Intellect,"** 295). But these thoughts are anterior to intellectual reflection because reflection acts only to focus the mind on "purpose" or "intent." Reflection gives thought direction and an openness or receptivity: "Our thinking is a pious reception. Our truth of thought is therefore vitiated as much by too violent direction given by our will, as by too great negligence. We do not determine what we will think. We only open our senses, clear away as we can all obstruction from the fact, and suffer the intellect to see. We have little control over our thoughts. We are prisoners of ideas" (294). Here again Emerson uses the image of a prison to describe the human condition. As the analysis of experience has shown, Dasein exists only in the midst of a series of relations. Intellectual activity always starts by opening to the fact that thinking is dominated, imprisoned, and obstructed by its historical context. We can note that two dangers here corrupt the truth: the first danger is a willful violence that takes place when one tries to determine what truth is before it has manifested itself, before we have piously received or observed its presence; and the second danger is negligence, that is, that the ideas "so fully engage us" that we make no "effort to make them our own" (294).

The intellect constructive can be defined as the effort to make ideas "our own." When "the truth appears" to the intellect receptive, it needs to be acted upon. Every appearance or revealment of truth is projective in nature: "*Every intellection is mainly prospective. . . . Each truth that a writer acquires is a lantern which he turns full on what facts and thoughts lay already in his mind*" (1940, 296; emphasis added). Reception of truth is not enough; it is the active projection of new possibilities that gives truth its processual nature. The intellect constructive is "the marriage of thought with nature"; it joins the "me" to the "not me." On the one hand, the constructive aspect of mind is "the advent of truth into the world, a form of thought now for the first time bursting into the universe" (297). Yet, on the other hand, the intellect constructive also contributes to the creations of systems of illusion.

As we have noted before, disclosure of truth has a concomitant concealing aspect that Emerson sees as a transformation of truth to untruth: "Truth is our element of life, yet if a man fasten his attention on a single aspect of truth and apply himself to that alone for a long time, the *truth becomes distorted* and not itself but falsehood. . . . Every

thought is a prison also" (emphasis added). Once again Emerson reminds us that human beings live in the "prison" of glass, which surrounds us with an unseen system that distorts truth into falsehood or error. Emerson is like Heidegger who argues in "On the Essence of Truth," that Dasein exists simultaneously within truth and untruth. Heidegger argues that human beings do "not merely fall into error"; they always live in "untruth": "Error is part of the inner structure of *Da-sein,* in which historical man is involved" (1949, 317).

Truth and untruth coexist for Emerson; each contributes in an active way to the revealing and concealing process, which is inherent in the circular pattern of understanding. For Emerson, the disclosive nature of truth is an organic process that exists as a natural phenomenon: "The new continents are built out of the ruins of an old planet; the new races fed out of the decomposition of the foregoing. New art destroys the old" (1940, **"Circles,"** 280). New truths are created as the illusions of past truths are destroyed: "Decomposition is recomposition . . . [they] are only signals of a new creation" (1940, **"Plato,"** 494). Yet, Emerson recognizes that a dominant aspect of human temperament is the constant desire for stability: "People wish to be settled; only as far as they are unsettled is there any hope for them" (1940, **"Circles,"** 289). Once people become "settled," a platform of normative standards is established to codify one's point of view. In other words, once truth is viewed as stable and abiding, truth is transformed into an "old" belief: "Every ultimate fact is only the first of a new series. Every general law only a particular fact of some more general law presently to disclose itself" (281). Truth discloses itself. Yet, when truth is abstracted it dies: "It is eviscerated of care" and then embalmed or transformed into an idol. Emerson proposes a necessary deconstruction of the idols of abstract truth, of the illusions of settled truths: "I unsettle all things. No facts are to me sacred; none are profane; I simply experiment, an endless seeker" (288).

CONCLUSION

For Emerson, the experiencing-self is constituted in discursive action and is always "being towards" the disclosure of a future meaning. The "authentic-self" is constituted in discursive acts and is always "being towards" the disclosure of a future meaning. Self-understanding is projected toward the disclosure of possible meanings. The destruction of everyday understanding provides an interpretation that discloses a self as self-understanding; but any disclosure serves only to reconstruct another, equally temporary, version of "everyday understanding." The disclosive process is the concomitant revealing and concealing of truth. The rhetor reveals meaning through discourse: the meaning of discourse hides or, in Heidegger's terms, is a withdrawing that occurs in the very effort of revealing or arriving at a truth.

Emerson does not conceive of the self as "separate" from truth; rather, he describes the way truths are discursively constructed and always partial. The discovery of truth is an event that occurs only within an experiencing-self; the experiencing-self does not exist outside of its struggle to interpret the world. However, this struggle is not one of "self-expression." Rather, Emerson emphasizes separating the "authentic" voice of the experiencing-self from the dominant discourse of the writer's everyday world. Paradoxically, the separation is both futile and necessary. It is necessary in order to participate in the continual process of revealing truth. It is futile because the process revealing the truth contains the process of concealing the truth with "system of illusion." Emerson recognizes that destroying the illusions of the dominant discourse can be only partially successful: "When each new speaker strikes a new light, emancipates us from the oppression of the last speaker to oppress us with the greatness and exclusiveness of his own thought, then yields us to another redeemer, we seem to recover our rights, to become men" (1940, **"Circles,"** 284). Truth is both oppression and emancipation; it is, in Heidegger's term, "thrown projection." Because of this, rhetoric involves a radical awareness that the nature of truth is a process. As James DiCenso (1990) notes: "The strength of the approach to truth as disclosure is found in its capacity to bring to light these constitutive dimensions of disclosure while maintaining a basis in lived experience or being-in-the-world" (56). Emerson's disclosive notion of truth operates within the field of relations established by an authentic-self experiencing the world.

Note

1. Gadamer's interpretation of Plato recasts what is commonly called either the "Doctrine of Ideas" or the "Theory of Forms" into what he calls the "hypothesis of the *eidos*" (1980, 35). For Gadamer, Plato's *eidos* or Ideas are a hypothesis that unites the manifold aspects of existence within the process of dialogue and dialectic. Gadamer makes an important distinction between the modern "scientific" method of hypothesis and the Platonic method of hypothesizing the *eidos*.

Works Cited

Berlin, James A. *Writing Instruction in Nineteenth-Century American Colleges.* Carbondale: Southern Illinois University Press, 1984.

Cavell, Stanley. "Thinking of Emerson." In *Ralph Waldo Emerson: A Collection of Critical Essays,* ed. Lawrence Buell, 191-98. Englewood Cliffs, N.J.: Prentice Hall, 1993.

DiCenso, James. *Hermeneutics and the Disclosure of Truth: A Study in the Work of Heidegger, Gadamer, and Ricoeur.* Charlottesville: University Press of Virginia, 1990.

Emerson, Ralph Waldo. *The Complete Essays and Other Writings of Ralph Waldo Emerson.* Ed. Brooks Atkinson. Modern Library College Editions. New York: Random, 1940.

Gadamer, Hans-Georg. *Dialogue and Dialectic: Eight Hermeneutical Studies on Plato.* Trans. P. Christopher Smith. New Haven: Yale University Press, 1980.

———. "On the Circle of Understanding." In *Hermeneutics versus Science? Three German Views: Essays,* trans. and ed. John M. Connolly and Thomas Keutner, 68-78. Notre Dame: University of Notre Dame Press, 1988.

Heidegger, Martin. *Existence and Being.* Trans. Werner Brock. South Bend: Gateway Editions, 1949.

———. *Being and Time.* Trans. John Macquarrie and Edward Robinson. New York: Harper, 1962.

Johnson, Glen M. "Emerson's Craft of Revision: The Composition of *Essays* (1841)." In *Ralph Waldo Emerson: A Collection of Critical Essays,* ed. Lawrence Buell, 171-90. Englewood Cliffs, N.J.: Prentice Hall, 1993.

Liebman, Sheldon W. "The Development of Emerson's Theory of Rhetoric, 1821-1836." *American Literature* 41 (1969): 178-206.

Neufeldt, Leonard. "The Vital Mind: Emerson's Epistomology." *Philological Quarterly* 50.2 (1971): 253-70.

Herwig Friedl (essay date 1997)

SOURCE: "Fate, Power, and History in Emerson and Nietzsche," in *ESQ: A Journal of the American Renaissance,* Vol. 43, No. 1-4, 1997, pp. 267-93.

[*In the following essay, Friedl offers a comparison between the philosophical vision and the terminology expounded by Emerson and Nietzsche in some of their best-known essays.*]

1

Radical changes or innovations in the history of thinking—changes that characterize a whole new epoch—usually are not sufficiently accounted for when we limit our attention solely to changing concepts, tenets, propositions, or systems of belief. In his analysis of seventeenth-century rationalism and scientism, Alfred North Whitehead briefly characterized the conditions of the possibility of new modes of thinking in a given historical era:

> There will be some fundamental assumptions which adherents of all the variant systems within the epoch unconsciously presuppose. Such assumptions appear so obvious that people do not know what they are assuming because no other way of putting things has ever occurred to them. With these assumptions a certain limited number of types of philosophic systems are possible, and this group of systems constitutes the philosophy of the epoch.[1]

In drawing attention to the formative potential of unconsciously and unwittingly held beliefs, or unquestioned fundamental assumptions, Whitehead merely adumbrates the problem. We might still want to know whether he believes in an individual or collective subject who or which, however unconsciously, assumes these fundamental assumptions, or whether they do indeed—and this is the way I read Whitehead—simply and contingently occur and thus happen *to* subjects.

Other twentieth-century thinkers have argued the case more decisively. Moving beyond the subject as foundation of historical change or belief, Heidegger has opened the possibility of our appreciating historical modes of thinking as dispensations of Being, as un-grounded challenges to which not only individual thinkers but whole eras feel constrained to respond. According to Whitehead and Heidegger, then, we would be obliged to characterize a radical change in thinking either as an unmediated and contingent occurrence of new, fundamental assumptions or as the emergence of a new dispensation of Being. In both cases the new era would be something that happened and not something humanly authored.

Following Whitehead, Susanne K. Langer has tried to find an appropriate terminology for major historical shifts in thinking. In the first chapter of *Philosophy in a New Key,* she speaks of "basic assumptions," of a "framework of thinking," or even of "common-sense notions about things in general." Arguing that the questions we ask, rather than specified answers in a given philosophical system, determine the prevalent mode of thinking, she posits a "horizon" within which new possibilities of thought, or a new key, for that matter, may arise or be detected. For Langer, there are "tacit, fundamental way[s] of seeing things." A new mode of thinking owes itself to a new and basic idea. Such fundamental ideas, she concludes, "are not theories; they are the terms in which theories are conceived; they give rise to specific questions, and are articulated only in the form of these questions. Therefore one may call them *generative ideas* in the history of thought."[2]

The very profusion of Langer's terminology tends to obscure the fact that she cannot really account for what the sciences or the humanities might describe as a paradigm change. Again, as in the case of Whitehead, the question remains: who thinks these generative ideas, or how and why are they generated? At first sight, Langer's implicit subjectivism seems to exclude the possibility that changes in thinking occur or emerge as challenges or dispensations of Being, as contingent ways the world may show itself in a manner unforeseen by a previous mode of thinking; her very concepts (idea, theory, conception) insinuate a rationalist and metaphysical basis for all kinds of thinking. And yet, in a minor key, Langer's remarkable endeavor also indicates the possibility of a mode of speaking about radical change that goes beyond "basic assumptions" and "generative ideas." Insisting on "*tacit . . .* way[s] of *seeing* things" (emphasis added), she intimates, ever so obliquely, that there must be as-yet-unnamed modes for things to appear before they are conceptualized as ideas. The half-buried terminology of appearing and seeing acknowledges the always possible and unpredictable new manner in which things may make themselves known by showing themselves.

Thus Whitehead's example, Heidegger's interpretation of the history of thinking as a history of the dispensation of

Being, and Langer's very hesitation within the precincts of metaphysical conceptualization, all point in the same direction: changes in thinking that may constitute the beginning of an epoch occur because of the way the *world* or *things* reveal themselves and because of the way they are then seen before they are being questioned or answered. This kind of ontological change is realized by thinkers as a new and basic *intuition* or *vision* provoked by Being rather than as fundamental assumptions or ideas simply and unaccountably generated and then held by subjects.

Emerson and Nietzsche stand at the beginning of one of the most dramatic changes in the history of thinking. In our century, Stanley Cavell was the first to comprehend thoroughly the significant role of Emerson in helping to bring about the *way* or *methodos* of thinking that we have come to understand as the slow erosion and gradual overturning of the possibilities of metaphysical systems. In linking Emerson, Nietzsche, and Heidegger, Cavell also has set the agenda for a new understanding of the relationship between Emerson and Nietzsche.[3] Harold Bloom, Richard Poirier, and most recently George Kateb have followed Cavell's lead in variously reading Emerson from the (sometimes implicit) perspective of the major philosophical changes commonly acknowledged in Nietzsche.[4] This approach has complemented the more traditional extensive research devoted to tracing Emerson's influence on Nietzsche in terms of thematic and sometimes only localized inspirations of single (even if singularly) significant insights in the later thinker. (The majority of attempts to deal with the relationship have concerned themselves with terms, concepts, images, ideas, problems, and opinions shared by the two thinkers.)[5]

If, however, a momentous change in thinking like the beginning of the erosion of metaphysics is due to the way Being addresses thinkers, if a fundamental redirection of thought is due to the way a new and basic vision happens to them, then we may legitimately ask whether there is a common ontological core, a post-metaphysical response to a new dispensation of Being, a primary intuition shared by Emerson and Nietzsche that is not sufficiently recognized if we focus exclusively on common concepts, images, and themes in their thinking. What was it, we may ask, that kept Nietzsche's interest in Emerson alive beyond the fascination with the occasional aphorism or single existential or ethical interpretation of the *conditio humana*?

The ontological revelation and/or vision shared by Emerson and Nietzsche may be circumscribed tentatively by the Emersonian terms "fate," "power," and "history," provided we do not use them as concepts in a metaphysical sense.[6] Emerson himself insists that language is a system of fluxional symbols, "vehicular and transitive . . . good, as ferries and horses are, for conveyance, not as farms and houses are, for homestead" (*E&L,* 463)—an idea that anticipates or projects Nietzsche's description of language as "bewegliches Heer von Metaphern" (a mobile army of metaphors).[7] Philosophical terms and terminologies lose their sharp outlines in the "quicksand" (*E&L,* 476) of illusory references that complicate linguistic orientation in Emerson and, at the same time, widen and invigorate the possibilities of meaning-making, of *poiesis,* in a newly opened ontological realm.[8] The three terms in the title of this essay thus may be said to create a field or to map a territory within which the Emersonian primary intuition of a new dispensation of Being may be articulated or imaged. Nietzsche's "conceptions" of "the eternal return of the same," of "the will to power," and—again—of "history" possibly serve a corresponding function for him without being exact equivalents of words that have no fixed significance in Emerson in the first place.

"The American Scholar" (1837) contains one of the most profound early pronouncements by Emerson on the way nature shows herself to the thinker, the scholar:

> There is never a beginning, there is never an end, to the inexplicable continuity of this web of God, but always circular power returning into itself. Therein it resembles his own spirit, whose beginning, whose ending, he never can find,—so entire, so boundless. Far, too, as her splendors shine, system on system shooting like rays, upward, downward, without centre, without circumference,—in the mass and in the particle, nature hastens to render account of herself to the mind.
>
> (*E&L,* 55)

Nature speaks and the thinker responds; Being reveals itself as both nature and mind, as and through a world of possible correspondences without origin or telos, without center or delimitation. The highest, the supreme being, God himself, is an ambiguous entity, a doubtful agent: does he weave the web, is he identical with the web, or does the web—like the emerging deity of process philosophy—weave God? All beings in this world of natural and mental continuities without destination seem open to the possibility of endless readings or classifications, as Emerson goes on to explain.

Emerson's new awareness foreshadows Nietzsche's famous vision, in *The Will to Power,* of the world as "ein Ungeheuer von Kraft, ohne Anfang, ohne Ende . . . ein Meer in sich selber stürmender und fluthender Kräfte, ewig sich wandelnd, ewig zurücklaufend, mit ungeheuren Jahren der Wiederkehr" (*KSA,* 11:610 [1067]). Nietzsche's powerful oceanic monster without beginning and end, stormily raging within itself, forever changing and returning into itself through immensities of circular time, is nothing but a hyperbolic version of Emerson's earlier interpretation. The core of the primary vision, the fundamental assumption literally pro-voked by a new dispensation of Being, however, is neither Emerson's "web of God" nor Nietzsche's raging sea; the core of this world of nature and mind shows itself in the most original and innovative way as "circular power returning into itself." In this phrase, I would like to maintain, we witness the new dispensation of Being: the very beginning of the momentous implications explored both by Emerson and, responding to the same challenge or following Emerson's vision, by Nietzsche. The phrase "circular power returning into itself"

poses a severe threat to any metaphysical and substantialist ontology—more severe, ultimately, than the denial of beginning and end, of Alpha and Omega, in the same quotation. It is a new and unprecedented way of naming Being.

The first chapter of the second volume of Heidegger's *Nietzsche* is titled "Die ewige Wiederkehr des Gleichen und der Wille zur Macht" (The eternal return of the same and the will to power);[9] his critical interpretation of these concepts aims to show that Nietzsche's way of thinking the Being of beings is the ultimate and disastrous culmination of metaphysics. Even if one disagrees with Heidegger's historical analysis, the basic ontological insight in this chapter illustrates Emerson's and Nietzsche's new departure in thinking Being. The notions of the will to power and the eternal return of the same think the identical ontological factuality according to Heidegger; in this way the traditional difference between *essentia* and *existentia* is overcome, an effect that Heidegger sees as a deficiency, speaking not so much of overcoming as of a forgetting of the difference.[10] However, if the will to power names the *essentia* or *quidditas* (i.e., *what* something is), and if the eternal return of the same thinks this *essentia* in its *existentia* (or the fact *that* it is), then, Heidegger concludes, both terms speak of the "steadying" (*Beständigung*) of becoming in the mode of a continuous—and again "steady"—(self-)overpowering.[11]

Emerson thinks the same thought when he speaks of "circular power returning into itself" as the basic feature of the way the world as nature shows in its Being. He first establishes the continuity, the temporal "steadiness" of becoming through the very circularity of the *essentia* of all beings, namely power. If power, then, is that which or what things are, their that-ness or *existentia* is a constant circular return into their own what-ness or *quidditas* or *essentia* (i.e., power). Power, the Being of beings, we may conclude, is a persistent, a continuous, a steady, self-grounding of beings. The becoming of beings—their Being—is a self-conditioning. By their power, by their assertion of the possibility to become and thus to transcend any of their given states, they paradoxically also return into themselves and ground themselves again and again, incessantly, as radically temporal and yet as steady and continuous in their very becoming, weaving the web of God.

Emerson's response to a new dispensation of Being, his generative idea, his primary vision, differs in only one respect from that of Nietzsche. Emerson does not even articulate the duality of the eternal return and the will to power: the idea of circular power thinks the unity of *essentia* and *existentia* more radically and originally than Nietzsche's tortuous attempt to join and fuse two traditional metaphysical ontological categories like *essentia* (will to power) and *existentia* (the eternal return of the same). Though the earlier thinker, Emerson surpasses Nietzsche in opening the most radical and far-reaching implications of the new response to the new dispensation of Being.

If we look at Emerson's seminal, post-metaphysical de-scription of "circular power returning into itself" from a Heideggerian, ontological perspective, we become aware of the expanse of the field that has been opened for think-ing: (1) beings ground themselves in becoming what they are; they condition themselves, owe themselves to them-selves in their Being as becoming—perhaps we could say, they are their own "fate"; (2) in the foundational, the cre-ative, act of continuously returning to themselves as they become what they are, they show themselves as the very potential of becoming or "power"; and (3) the constant and circular play of a powerful self-conditioning provides for continuity and thus for a self-generated and always in-dividualized "history." The ontological turn beyond meta-physics in Emerson shows itself ontically—that is, in the way he reads so-called real events and things and (human) beings, in his interpretations of fate, power, and history.[12] The essays titled **"Fate"** (1860), **"Power"** (1860), and **"History"** (1841) were among those Nietzsche studied again and again.[13] Thus in reading the central ontological implications of these texts, we may deepen our under-standing, our vision-ary awareness, of the common, the identical, ground of Emerson's and Nietzsche's founda-tional "idea."

2

"Fate" is, in a way, Emerson's ontological *summa philosophiae,* an essay as much about power and history as it is about fate itself. Once we adopt the ontological perspective, **"Power"** may be read as a coda to **"Fate,"** and **"History"** may be read as the prelude to the mature considerations in *The Conduct of Life.* Nietzsche, in 1862, at age eighteen, showed extraordinary appreciation for Emerson's most revolutionary concerns when he wrote two essays, "Fatum und Geschichte" and "Willensfreiheit und Fatum," after reading the German translation of *The Conduct of Life.* Focusing on the terms freedom of the will, fate, and history, Nietzsche responded to Emerson's primary vision of a radically changed dispensation of Be-ing—a vision he continued to share and was never to aban-don throughout his career.[14]

Now Emerson, throughout **"Fate,"** carefully avoids any strict terminology that would create the impression that fate or its seeming opposite, power, stand as metaphysi-cally solidified entities. Fate is often spoken of as neces-sity, determination, nature, or natural history, and power tends to assume the verbal guises or alternatives of free-dom, spirit, and thought. Emerson stresses the fact that power and fate, freedom and necessity, are not even, strictly speaking, pairs in a binary opposition but rather possibilities of naming the way things are in a realm of gradual transitions without metaphysical fixation: "to see how fate slides into freedom, and freedom into fate, ob-serve how far the roots of every creature run, or find, if you can, a point where there is no thread of connection. Our life is consentaneous and far-related. This knot of na-ture is so well tied, that nobody was ever cunning enough to find the two ends" (*E&L,* 961). Every existent being,

and thus also our human life, is determined by consent and relation, by will (the will to yea-saying, we might add, in a Nietzschean vein), and by fate. Like the metaphysical opposites of the one and the many,[15] or the classical posi-tions of metaphysics discussed in Emerson's essay **"Nomi-nalist and Realist,"** such apparent binary antagonists as "freedom and fate," or "power and determination," or "spirit and nature" are really aspects of Being and not (substantial) essences in themselves.

The transgression of the ontological boundaries of *essentia* and *existentia* is echoed in the ontic realm as the literal de-limitation, the un-defining, of that which conditions and the act of conditioning itself. Being as becoming owes it-self to itself: "The planet makes itself. The animal cell makes itself;—then what it wants. Every creature,—wren or dragon,—shall make its own lair. As soon as there is life, there is self-direction, and absorbing and using of ma-terial. Life is freedom,—life in the direct ratio of its amount" (*E&L,* 962). The circular structure of Being as-serts itself in the way beings are conceived in their indi-vidual becoming. The intensity of this becoming depends on the amount of life or power, on the quanta of power, as Nietzsche later put it. One of the central concerns of **"Fate,"** however, is specifically with the human being and with newly envisioned possibilities of becoming who one is.

This crucial existential concern—this *fundamentalontolo-gische* problem concerning the Being of *Dasein,* which is so prominent in Emerson's **"Self-Reliance"** and in Ni-etzsche's late *Ecce Homo* (subtitled *Wie Man wird, was Man ist* [How one becomes one what is; *KSA,* 6:255-374])[16]—may be investigated best under the guidance of two momentous aphoristic propositions in "Fate." The first statement is introduced as a version of the Hindu idea of karma, a conception also advanced, as Emerson notes, by Friedrich Schelling: "in the history of the individual is al-ways an account of his condition, and he knows himself to be a party to his present estate" (*E&L,* 948). The temporal dimension of the Being of *Dasein,* her or his history, liter-ally presents the self with the conditioning factors of that which she or he has become. At the same time, fate, or the conditions of becoming who one is, must be seen as re-sults of (free and powerful) acts of will, and consequently each one is "a party to his present estate." Necessity and freedom, fate and the power of self-fashioning, are variet-ies of reading the self. The past of the self, what Emerson calls its "condition," may be read as fate or it may be read as acts, as a series of active participations. This implies, at the same time, that the self may be said to incorporate an alien other, an "it," which she or he may accept as a yet-to-be-acknowledged phase of self-hood. Returning into "it"-self, the human being may appropriate the alienated or forgotten other that usually shows itself as the natural his-tory of the species. In a powerful act of interpretive will, however,[17] the self may transgress its metaphysical idea of her- or himself as self-contained, as a self contained, and re-appropriate the past that only seems to be mere "condi-tion," or fate, or determination, or the natural history of the species: "We must respect Fate as natural history, but there is more than natural history" (*E&L*, 953). It is power, Emerson asserts, that enables the self to go beyond its dependency on previous conditions. The true self is the one not limited by her or his presence or present estate as a seemingly subjective and enclosed entity. The true self may say yes to its forgotten other: it returns in a circular motion into its own past and thus grounds the self in the it-self while becoming who she or he is. This—as we saw in the passage on "circular power" in **"The American Scholar"**—is the temporal gesture that characterizes (true) Being. In accepting the alienated past as her or his own, the self becomes who she or he is; the self achieves the fullness of Being, becomes a *Dasein*.[18]

A second proposition, again from **"Fate,"** illuminates even more profoundly the new ontological situation within which Emerson and Nietzsche find themselves obliged to re-describe the Being of the human being or *Dasein*:

> Just as much intellect as you add, so much organic power. He who sees through the design, presides over it, and must will that which must be. We sit and rule, and, though we sleep, our dream will come to pass. Our thought, though it were only an hour old, affirms an oldest necessity, not to be separated from thought, and not to be separated from will. They must always have coëxisted.
>
> (*E&L*, 956)

Awareness, knowing, intellect are, as Emerson describes them, agents of ontic, of real, of organic, power. To know is to rule and dominate. Knowing Being, knowing the design of the intimate relationship of and the transitionality between fate and power enables the human being to fulfill her or his existential desire: "our dream will come to pass." The parallelism of "must will" and "must be" asserts that there is only one mode of Being and that true willing, the fully unfolded will to power that is aware of itself, the genuine existential desire, is the same as, is identical with, the necessity of Being. Willing does not oppose fate; it does not battle the past. Willing as the power of the human being may return into its conditioning, into what "must be," and may knowingly will its own becoming in the by-now-familiar, circular ontological structure. In willing fate and in revealing fate as the ossification of past willing,[19] our thought—the human being's existential awareness—"affirms an oldest necessity." This affirmation is the precursor or equivalent of Nietzsche's yea-saying to the eternal return and to the steadiness of becoming; it is the foreshadowing of his un-conditioned ontological assent to what must be, *amor fati*.

3

One of the most intriguing philosophical problems in Nietzsche's *Also sprach Zarathustra* is his meditation on and re-valuation of the meaning of time and thus of history in the ontological sense of the indispensable dimension of becoming.[20] In "Von der Erlösung" (On salvation), chapter 20 in the second part of the work, Zarathustra meditates

on the now and the "has been." He calls their relationship "*mein* Unerträglichstes" (*KSA*, 4:179), his most unbearable thought or burden. The problem for Zarathustra is the fact that the will, the will to power as "der Befreier und Freudebringer" (the liberator and bringer of glad tidings, the new evangelist), seems unable to overcome that which chains it and limits its freedom: the "it was," the past as an immovable fate. The fact that beings owe themselves to an "other," that they are indebted in their very existence to something that seems alien to them—this is the ontological condition of guilt and bad conscience, the melancholy of existing (*KSA*, 4:180) that ultimately results in "Widerwille," in resentment. The chapter culminates in this prophetic pronouncement:

> Alles "Es war" ist ein Bruchstück, ein Räthsel, ein grauser Zufall—bis der schaffende Wille dazu sagt: "aber so wollte ich es!"
>
> —Bis der schaffende Wille dazu sagt: "Aber so will ich es! So werde ich's wollen!"
>
> Aber sprach er schon so? Und wann geschieht diess? Ist der Wille schon abgeschirrt von seiner eignen Thorheit?
>
> Wurde der Wille sich selber schon Erlöser und Freudebringer? Verlernte er den Geist der Rache und alles Zähneknirschen?
>
> Und wer lehrte ihn Versöhnung mit der Zeit, und Höheres als alle Versöhnung ist?
>
> Höheres als alle Versöhnung muss der Wille wollen, welcher der Wille zur Macht ist—: doch wie geschieht ihm das? Wer lehrte ihn auch noch das Zurückwollen?
>
> (*KSA*, 4:181)[21]

The past, Zarathustra explains, is a mere and contingent given unless the will (to power) accepts it and identifies with it as something willed. Then the past is grounded and, we might inelegantly add, it becomes relevant. The will, or power as event, if we use Emerson's rhetoric, has to encompass all dimensions of time: past, present, and future. A true and full existence beyond resentment would have to accept and will its own past otherness and its as yet-unachieved future possibility. Only in this way can the will, Being as power, become reconciled with time; it might even become something higher, namely time itself. Understood as identical with time and its three dimensions, the will to power as the Being of the human being would achieve salvation; it could gladly say yes to its own conditioning and to its as-yet- and forever-open future. This new gospel is the ontological promise that the human being may one day accept her- or himself as Being and time. Being able to "will backwards," the human being is "circular power returning into itself." Nietzsche's Zarathustra's prophecy of salvation is one with Emerson's ontological vision. True Being as becoming grounds itself in returning into its own (alienated) past in order to guarantee the freedom of its future; this is the ultimate realization of self-reliance. Once the human being "must will that which must be," as Emerson says in **"Fate,"** it is indeed true that "freedom is necessary" (*E&L*, 956, 953).

Nietzsche did not gradually *develop* this vision, this response to a new dispensation of Being as time—this response to the identity of will to power and eternal return, to the unity of freedom and fate in their circular interdependence. Rather, he seems, in 1862, to have been struck immediately by Emerson's response to the endless "web of relation" forever linking fate and freedom (*E&L*, 961). He returned to reading Emerson with great intensity in 1881 when he began to compose *Also sprach Zarathustra* and uttered the prophecy of the will's power to "will backwards";[22] and he reaffirmed this generative idea in 1888 when he added his favorite phrase, "How One Becomes What One Is" (or "How to Become Who You Are"), as a subtitle to his last "autobiography," *Ecce Homo.*

In "Fatum und Geschichte," his first essay inspired by Emerson, and written during the Easter vacation of 1862, Nietzsche responds to Emerson's **"History"** and **"Fate,"** the opening texts of *Essays: First Series* and *The Conduct of Life*, respectively.[23] Nietzsche says:

> Was ist es, was die Seele so vieler Menschen mit Macht zu dem Gewöhnlichen niederzieht und einen höhern Ideenaufflug so erschwert? Ein fatalistischer Schädel—und Rückgratsbau, der Stand und die Natur ihrer Eltern, das Alltägliche ihrer Verhältnisse, das Gemeine ihrer Umgebung, selbst das Eintönige ihrer Heimat. Wir sind beeinflußt worden, ohne die Kraft einer Gegenwirkung in uns zu tragen, ohne selbst zu erkennen, daß wir beeinflußt sind.[24]

This passage strongly echoes Emerson in **"Fate"**: "The menagerie, or forms and powers of the spine, is a book of fate: the bill of the bird, the skull of the snake, determines tyrannically its limits. So is the scale of races, of temperaments; so is sex; so is climate; so is the reaction of talents imprisoning the vital power in certain directions" (*E&L*, 946).

Nietzsche at age eighteen had accepted Emerson's putatively bleak view of the determining factors of natural history. The last sentence quoted from Nietzsche's "Fatum und Geschichte" indicates, however, where the solution to such apparent bleakness will be found. If the fatality of the past arises from our not knowing that we have been influenced or determined by the "it was," it follows that a powerful insight may change the depressing, the melancholy, state of affairs, which Nietzsche describes in the passage on salvation from *Zarathustra*. Nietzsche's solution will be, and has to be, Emerson's: "He who sees through the design, presides over it, and must will that which must be" (*E&L*, 956). A late fragment from the so-called *Dionysos-Dithyrambs*, written in the summer of 1888, once again states the solution (Emerson's solution in **"Fate"** and Nietzsche's in *Also sprach Zarathustra*) to the problem posed by the seemingly inflexible and majestically alien past and its antagonism to the free play of Being as the will to power in its now-ness. The solution is indeed none other than that of "circular power returning into itself," now described by Nietzsche in terms of willing and determination:

> so ist's jetzt mein Wille:
> und seit das mein Wille ist,
> geht Alles mir auch nach Wunsche—
> Dies war meine letzte Klugheit:
> ich wollte das, was ich muß:
> damit zwang ich mir jedes "Muß" . . .
> seitdem giebt es für mich kein "Muß." . . . [25]

(*KSA*, 13:553 [20])

Emerson had affirmed the progressive and retroactive self-constituting circularity of both nature and mind in **"The American Scholar."** Nietzsche deepens Emerson's insight by prophetically joining true or authentic (human) Being and time. The ultimate acceptance of the identity of fate and freedom, of power and eternal return, of *essentia* and *existentia*, is seen by both Emerson and Nietzsche as a promise rather than an existential fact.

Emerson's thoughts on the fallen state of humanity—on the fragmentation of the human being in **"The American Scholar,"** on humanity's deficiencies when compared with nature in **"The Method of Nature"**—and his so-called skepticism in **"Experience"** are well matched by Zarathustra's meditations on the deformed and despicable "last" man. Both Emerson and Nietzsche-Zarathustra repeatedly have to remind themselves that they need courage to continue on the arduous road toward the overman or the "*plus* man," as Emerson phrases it in **"Power"** (*E&L*, 973).[26] Nietzsche's recurring "Wohlan! Wohlauf! Altes Herz!" in *Also sprach Zarathustra* is a direct response to, and equivalent of, Emerson's "up again, old heart!" at the end of **"Experience"** (*KSA*, 4:184 ["On Human Prudence," 2.21]; *E&L*, 492). This kind of post-Christian *sursum corda* affirms that the overman and Emerson's "*plus*" man are projected possibilities and that the presently existing human being is, as Nietzsche says in *Zarathustra*, "a rope tied between animal and overman, a rope spanning an abyss" (*KSA*, 4:16 ["Prologue," 4]); the present human being, in Emerson's description, shows her or his promise and power "in the moment of transition from a past to a new state, in the shooting of the gulf, in the darting to an aim" (*E&L*, 271).

The true fulfillment would indeed be self-sufficient circularity. Nietzsche has envisioned this state and thus the true figuration of the overman as the Being of the child: "Unschuld ist das Kind und Vergessen, ein Neubeginnen, ein Spiel, ein aus sich rollendes Rad, eine erste Bewegung, ein heiliges Ja-Sagen" (*KSA*, 4:31 ["On the Three Metamorphoses," 1.1]).[27] This truly self-moved mover, this self-contained ecstasy and play, is a constant beginning and as such it testifies to the will to power as the potentiality of becoming; at the same time she or he constantly grounds her- or himself in a past that is forgotten and overcome *as* past by this act of circular re-appropriation: this person is the innocent wheel of the eternal return or, in Emerson's phrase, circular power who or which does not owe her-, him-, or itself to anything.

Since the primary ontological intuition shared by Emerson and Nietzsche is not limited to the human or any other particular being, however, one must remind oneself that all beings—that nature herself—shares in this identity of Being as becoming and time. In **"The Method of Nature,"** Emerson describes the Being of nature as "a work of *ecstasy,* to be represented by a circular movement" (***E&L,*** 120). "Ecstasy" in Emerson's writing often indicates the tendency of all beings to overpower themselves; it is the word he uses to hint at the way the will to power shows itself. This literal "going beyond" is, however, at the same time, a going back in the sense of a grounding of becoming through reclaiming the past state of the ecstatic being. The wheel, the play of the innocence of becoming, characterizes all beings.

This ontological homology between nature and human being, or *Dasein,* is an important aspect of Emerson's **"Power"**:

> Life is a search after power; and this is an element with which the world is so saturated,—there is no chink or crevice in which it is not lodged,—that no honest seeking goes unrewarded. . . .
>
> All power is of one kind, a sharing of the nature of the world. The mind that is parallel with the laws of nature will be in the current of events, and strong with their strength. One man is made of the same stuff of which events are made; is in sympathy with the course of things; can predict it.
>
> (***E&L,*** 971-72)

Life as becoming is a search after, a desire for, a will to power. Power here appears as the Being of all beings, as that which saturates and permeates every single being. Heraclitus, whom both Emerson and Nietzsche so often quote, said that nature likes to hide (her essential Being),[28] but in Emerson, this tendency of the Being of beings to withdraw cannot match the desire of beings to participate, to be their Being fully and powerfully.

Since power is a participation in the nature or Being of the world, the human being or *Dasein* is seen as ontologically identical with nature as process, as ecstatic unfolding of the will to power. Event and entity, event and human being, are one. In **"Fate"** Emerson writes: "The secret of the world is, the tie between person and event. Person makes event, and event person" (***E&L,*** 962). Being as powerful becoming dissolves the boundaries between entity and eventuality, between "subject" and history. This succinctly describes, analyzes, and thinks what Nietzsche calls the "Rückübersetzung," the literal re-trans-lation of the human being into nature.[29] Karl Löwith has explained this motif in Nietzsche's thinking as his central cosmological—and I would add, ontological—concern:

> Ein "Vorspiel der Philosophie der Zukunft" sind Nietzsches Schriften nicht dadurch, daß er an einen künftigen Wandel im Wesen des Menschen dachte, den man vorbereiten oder gar wollen könnte, und zu dessen Herbeiführung er sich den Uebermenschen erdachte, sondern dadurch, daß er—in Erinnerung der vorsokratischen physikoi—den großen Versuch unternahm, den Menschen in die *Natur* aller Dinge "zurückzuübersetzen."[30]

In reading Emerson's thoughts on the relationship of person and event, Nietzsche could not only perceive the continuity of nature and *Dasein* and the reintegration of the human being into the world as process; he also found reenforcement for his basic intuition of the structure of Being as time: "Person makes event, and event person." If the human being and events are "made of the same stuff," as Emerson says in **"Power"** (***E&L,*** 972), then the circular interdependence of process and human agent is guaranteed ontologically. Emerson's vision reveals that, ultimately, there is only power. Fate now appears merely as a word indicating the insufficiently understood and not-yet appropriated past, a past into which the human being has to be re-translated in order to make it her or his own. In this act of re-translation, the circular and transitional relationship and ultimate identity of event and person, of fate and power, become apparent.

In such passages of Emerson's writings, and in their ontological implications, Nietzsche found a sufficient basis for his critique of the subject as separate entity and, as a consequence, a starting point for his demolition of the idea of determination as a necessitarian interaction of distinct causes and effects.[31] Emerson's ontological interpretation of a world of power transcending the separation of person and event led Nietzsche to the repeatedly stated insight, in *Jenseits von Gut und Böse* (1886; see, for example, *KSA* 5:37 [22]) and in his late notes toward a theory of the will to power, that power does nothing but enact its own ultimate consequences in every moment.

4

If person and event are not only interdependencies but also names for aspects of a continuum, then "person" has to be thought of as one important name for process or for history. In **"Fate,"** Emerson says: "History is the action and reaction of these two,—Nature and Thought;—two boys pushing each other on the curbstone of the pavement. Everything is pusher or pushed: and matter and mind are in perpetual tilt and balance, so" (***E&L,*** 964). Nature, I have suggested, may be the term designating the realm of fate, whereas thought or spirit may indicate the possibilities for the free play of power antagonizing fate. Basically, however, both power and fate, nature and thought, are of the same kind—they are aspects of the Being of the world; the image of the two boys asserts the identity and the difference of these players in a precarious field (the curbstone). Their contingent play is called history: a continuity of persons or events in which the roles assumed (pusher and pushed, action and reaction, fate and power) are "sliding" into each other, as in Emerson's description of freedom and fate, evading the attribution of metaphysical essentials and the fixation of a binary opposition that would misrender the continuities of Being.

Nietzsche's 1862 essay "Fatum und Geschichte" testifies to his fascination with Emerson's conception of history. **"History"** is, in fact, the essay that supplied Nietzsche throughout his career, with the greatest number of direct references to Emerson: the image and idea of the Sphinx reading her own riddle, the motto selected for the first edition of *Die fröhliche Wissenschaft,* the concept of nomadic thinking[32]—these and many other borrowings indicate that Nietzsche took Emerson's vision of history as a central aspect of his own thinking, of his new ontological perspective. Such famous Emersonian statements as "All history becomes subjective; in other words, there is properly no history; only biography" (*E&L,* 240) may well have encouraged Nietzsche to write so often in the autobiographical mode—as a means of ascertaining the historical significance of his own thinking.[33] Emerson's most important ontological insights, however, seem to be contained in two succinct phrases of the essay **"History."** He states, first, that "[w]e must in ourselves see the necessary reason of every fact,—see how it could and must be" (*E&L,* 240). The self is seen here as the place, as the *there* in the sense of *Dasein,* where necessity and possibility, fate and power as freedom, are grounded. The self, however, is also an event, as we saw in reading **"Power."** The Being of *Dasein*—of the human self, as time—is the realm of the interplay of power and fate. This temporally progressive *there,* however, always is focused in the present; the present as a constantly evanescent event is the domain of true Being, as this second major ontological statement in **"History"** asserts: "All inquiry into antiquity . . . is the desire to do away with this wild, savage, and preposterous There or Then, and introduce in its place the Here and the Now" (*E&L,* 241).

Nietzsche included this second passage in the selection of paraphrases from Emerson that he entered into separate notebooks late in 1881 and early in 1882 (*KSA,* 9:618-22, 666-72), while conceiving the central ontological ideas of *Also sprach Zarathustra* and while writing its first two parts. Nietzsche's paraphrase intensifies Emerson's original statement: "Dieses planlose rohe widersinnige Dort und Jetzt soll verschwinden und an seine Stelle das Jetzt und Hier treten" (*KSA,* 9:666).[34] The affirmation of "the Here and the Now" is familiar from Nietzsche's second *Untimely Meditation: Vom Nutzen und Nachtheil der Historie für das Leben* (1874). This *Untimely Meditation* on the uses and disadvantages of history for life asserts the existential prerogative of the present over the past as a possible repository of models, values, and meaning. The appropriation of the past from the perspective of a powerfully asserted present point of view, however, is also the concern of the fully developed ontological interpretations that Emerson offers in **"Fate"** and that Nietzsche proposes in *Also sprach Zarathustra.* In *Zarathustra,* reading and making history become one with true temporal Being. When Emerson says in **"Fate"** that "[h]e who sees through the design . . . must will that which must be" (*E&L,* 956), he deepens the vision of **"History"** and the interpretation of the human being as the origin and place of "could be" and "must be." And when Nietzsche prophesies the possibility of powerfully overcoming the "it was," and of making the will to power "will backwards," he also expands the Emersonian injunction from **"History"** to transform the "There or Then" into "the Here and the Now": he

moves beyond the cultural critique of the second *Untimely Meditation* while unfolding the ontological underpinning, inherited from Emerson, of his earlier work.

5

The map of Being sketched by Emerson uses the flexible terms fate, power, and history to facilitate the experience of thinking a new dispensation of Being—a revolutionary, generative idea. Nietzsche, in reading Emerson throughout his career, returned to his predecessor and, again and again, successfully appropriated Emerson's ontological thought, transforming it into his own authentic achievement. Emerson's vision of the will to power and the eternal return of the same, his version of *amor fati* and the endeavor to become who one is—these were, for Nietzsche, legacies to be acknowledged and overcome. Nietzsche's recognition of his forebear's significance was at the same time generous and secretive.[35] In the privacy of his notebooks, he called Emerson *the thinker* of the nineteenth century, the author whose thought was unsurpassed, though sometimes darkened by the verbal ground glass of German idealism. A philosopher who styled himself the homeless wanderer on icy Alpine heights of thought, Nietzsche yet showed himself overcome by emotion in confessing that Emerson provided a real home for him: Emerson "is too close to me," he said, for words of appropriate praise.[36]

In section 3 of the chapter on *Untimely Meditations* in *Ecce Homo,* Nietzsche suggests that Plato used Socrates as a "semiotics" for Plato, that Plato read his own thought into the older alter ego.[37] And Emerson similarly asserts, in *Representative Men,* that "[o]ther men are lenses through which we read our own minds" (*E&L,* 616). Both characterize the relationship between one writer and another as a uniquely intimate kinship, exactly the kind of deep and complex affinity that Nietzsche expresses for Emerson. Yet the significance of the Emerson-Nietzsche relationship goes beyond even the ineffably profound appreciation one writer can have for another. Nietzsche's encounter with Emerson served as a testing ground for the very ontological revolution they shared. In aphorism 13 of "Skirmishes of an Untimely Man," in *Götzen-Dämmerung,* written during the creative intensity of 1888, Nietzsche describes Emerson's existential disposition—and his own—in a way that goes beyond mere psychology: "Emerson hat jene gütige und geistreiche Heiterkeit, welche allen Ernst entmuthigt; er weiss es schlechterdings nicht, wie alt er schon ist und wie jung er noch sein wird,—er könnte von sich mit einem Worte Lope de Vega's sagen: 'yo me sucedo a mi mismo'" (*KSA,* 6:120).[38] Nietzsche not only celebrates an almost Mediterranean serenity in Emerson's thinking, he above all attributes to Emerson's Being a temporal dimension that reaches far back into the past and extends into an unforeseeable future. He is not merely commenting on Emerson's fame, or the future of his reputation, as the quotation from Lope de Vega might suggest. In Nietzsche's portrait of him, Emerson, as thinker, *is* his own immemorial past, his fate, and—at the same time—the potential, the power of his unlimited future: as thinker, he is the very exemplum of his own existential vision.

Portraying himself in *Ecce Homo* (in section 1 of the chapter titled "Why I Am So Wise") both as a *décadent* and as a new beginning, Nietzsche writes, "Das Glück meines Daseins, seine Einzigkeit vielleicht, liegt in seinem Verhängniss: ich bin, um es in Räthselform auszudrücken, als mein Vater bereits gestorben, als meine Mutter lebe ich noch und werde alt" (*KSA*, 6:264).[39] This passage thinks Nietzsche's own Being, the temporal mode of his existence, in a way that parallels his interpretation of Emerson. Nietzsche envisions himself as reaching back into a seemingly unavailable, dead past (the father); at the same time, this very past (the mother) is the guarantee of an extended future. Nietzsche pictures Emerson and himself as both fated and free, as both determined by the burden of the past and empowered to overcome this affliction; this circular structure, once again, is the very condition of the possibility of their (common) history.

At the end of his wonderfully painstaking study of Nietzsche and Emerson, Stanley Hubbard modestly summarized his insights and concluded that, after all, Emerson was not Nietzsche.[40] If one considers not so much their biographies and their psychological profiles, but dwells, rather, on the essential challenge to and of their thinking, one will have both to agree and disagree with Hubbard. Emerson is not Nietzsche. However, Nietzsche, as a thinker, responding to a new dispensation of Being, could only become who he was by appropriating the fated antecedent other, called Emerson, enacting that significant circular move of a powerful return into a seemingly obstinate past that alone guarantees the possibility of a new history of thinking.

Notes

1. Alfred North Whitehead, *Science and the Modern World* (New York: Free Press, 1967), 48.

2. Susanne K. Langer, *Philosophy in a New Key: A Study in the Symbolism of Reason, Rite, and Art,* 3rd ed. (Cambridge: Harvard Univ. Press, 1979), 36, 8.

3. Stanley Cavell, "Thinking of Emerson," in *The Senses of Walden: An Expanded Edition* (San Francisco: North Point Press, 1981), 121-38.

4. Harold Bloom, "Emerson: Power at the Crossing," in *Ralph Waldo Emerson: A Collection of Critical Essays,* ed. Lawrence Buell (Englewood Cliffs: Prentice Hall, 1993), 148-58; Richard Poirier, *Poetry and Pragmatism* (Cambridge: Harvard Univ. Press, 1992); George Kateb, *Emerson and Self-Reliance* (Thousand Oaks: Sage Publications, 1995).

5. George J. Stack's comprehensive *Nietzsche and Emerson: An Elective Affinity* (Athens: Ohio Univ. Press, 1992) is certainly the first systematic presentation in English of the "many elements" that Nietzsche may have adapted from Emerson. However, contrary to Stack's claim in his preface that this field "has not been explored" (vii), extensive inter-national research since at least 1902 has unearthed practically all the evidence that he now so generously reassembles for the American reader. Major sources of information are Georg Biedenkapp, "Der amerikanische Nietzsche," *Ernstes Wollen* 4 (1902-3): 246-49; Régis Michaud, "Emerson et Nietzsche," *La revue germanique* 6 (1910): 414-21; Charles Andler, *Nietzsche: Sa vie et sa pensée* (Paris: Bossard, 1920-31; Paris: Gallimard, 1958); Julius Simon, *Ralph Waldo Emerson in Deutschland* (Berlin: Junker und Dünnhaupt, 1937); Rudolf Schottlaender, "Two Dionysians: Emerson and Nietzsche," *South Atlantic Quarterly* 39 (1940): 330-43; Fred B. Wahr, "Emerson and the Germans," *Monatshefte für Deutschen Unterricht* 33 (1941): 49-63; Hermann Hummel, "Emerson and Nietzsche," *New England Quarterly* 19 (1946): 63-84; Ernst Robert Curtius, "Emerson," in *Kritische Essays zur europäischen Literatur* (Bern: Francke, 1950), 189-203 (published in English in *Essays on European Literature,* trans. Michael Kowal [Princeton: Princeton Univ. Press, 1973], 211-27); Eduard Baumgarten, "Emerson-Nietzsche," *Internationale Zeitschrift für Erziehung* 8 (1939): 1-16; Baumgarten, "Mitteilungen und Bemerkungen über den Einfluβ Emersons auf Nietzsche," *Jahrbuch für Amerikastudien* 1 (1956): 93-152; Stanley Hubbard, *Nietzsche und Emerson* (Basel: Verlag für Recht und Gesellschaft, 1958); Ingo Seidler, "'Den Blick fernhin auf Nordamerika richten': Zur Amerikaperspektive Nietzsches," in *Amerika in der deutschen Literatur,* ed. Sigrid Bauschinger et al. (Stuttgart: Kohlhammer, 1975), 218-28; Michael Lopez, "Transcendental Failure: 'The Palace of Spiritual Power,'" in *Emerson: Prospect and Retrospect,* ed. Joel Porte (Cambridge: Harvard Univ. Press, 1982), 121-53; Vivetta Vivarelli, "Nietzsche und Emerson: Ueber einige Pfade in Zarathustras metaphorischer Landschaft," *Nietzsche-Studien* 16 (1987): 227-63; Herwig Friedl, "Emerson and Nietzsche: 1862-1874," in *Religion and Philosophy in America,* ed. Peter Freese (Essen: Die Blaue Eule, 1987), 1:267-88; and Michael Payne, "Emerson, Nietzsche, and the Politics of Interpretation," *CEA Forum* 18 (1988): 16-18. Also see Irena S. M. Makarushka, *Religious Imagination and Language in Emerson and Nietzsche* (New York: St. Martin's Press, 1994), which appeared after Stack's study.

6. Michel Haar, "Nietzsche and Metaphysical Language," in *The New Nietzsche,* ed. David B. Allison (Cambridge: MIT Press, 1987), 4-36, offers an excellent analysis of the changes in the function and reach of philosophical terms effected by Nietzsche's post-metaphysical vision.

7. Friedrich Nietzsche, "Ueber Wahrheit und Lüge im außermoralischen Sinne," in *Sämtliche Werke: Kritische Studienausgabe,* ed. Giorgio Colli and Mazzino Montinari, 15 vols. (Munich: Deutscher Taschenbuch Verlag/de Gruyter, 1980), 1:880. This

edition is hereafter cited parenthetically as *KSA,* with volume and page numbers; bracketed references are to part, chapter, section, and/or aphorism numbers in particular works. I will offer my own translations or detailed interpretive paraphrases of non-English originals. This particular well-known quotation from Nietzsche can also be found in *The Portable Nietzsche,* ed. Walter Kaufmann (New York: Viking, 1954), 46.

8. Compare the concept of "troping" used by Richard Poirier in *The Renewal of Literature: Emersonian Reflections* (New Haven: Yale Univ. Press, 1987) and in *Poetry and Pragmatism.*

9. Martin Heidegger, *Nietzsche,* 3rd ed. (Pfullingen: Neske, 1961), 2:7-29.

10. Heidegger, *Nietzsche,* 2:13, 16.

11. Heidegger, *Nietzsche,* 2:14: "Die ewige Wiederkehr des Gleichen trägt gleichsam ihr Wesen als ständigste Beständigung des Werdens des Ständigen vor sich her" [The eternal return of the same propagates—so to speak—its essence as the steadiest steadying of the becoming of steadiness].

12. The terms "ontic[al]" and "ontological" are used here in the senses established by Heidegger, and by Heideggerian criticism, as referring to empirical beings and to the Being of beings, respectively.

13. Thorough and comprehensive information on the phases of Nietzsche's reading of Emerson is found in Baumgarten, "Mitteilungen und Bemerkungen"; and in Hubbard, *Nietzsche und Emerson.* The early phase is analyzed systematically in Herwig Friedl, "Emerson and Nietzsche: 1862-1874." Stack discusses Nietzsche's reading of Emerson, and the detailed and intensive German research on that reading, in *Nietzsche and Emerson* and in "Nietzsche's Earliest Essays: Translation of and Commentary on 'Fate and History' and 'Freedom of Will and Fate,'" *Philosophy Today* 37 (1993): 153-69.

14. Friedl, "Emerson and Nietzsche: 1862-1874," explores all major motifs of Nietzsche's mature thought already to be found in these early exercises in Emersonian thinking. In "Nietzsche's Earliest Essays," Stack provides useful English translations of the two sketches, along with commentary that also emphasizes the many shared motifs.

15. Emerson erodes the binary opposition of the one and the many in his essay on Plato, in *Representative Men,* by using the very word "sliding" to indicate the continuity of these two (one might say, tentative) conceptions rather than their separate essentialist integrity: "each so fast slides into the other, that we can never say what is one, and what it is not" (*E&L,* 638).

16. Stanley Cavell suggests that Nietzsche's subtitle may be a rewording of Emerson's call, in the concluding paragraph of "Considerations by the Way," for the "courage to be what we are" (*E&L,* 1096).

See *A Pitch of Philosophy: Autobiographical Exercises* (Cambridge: Harvard Univ. Press, 1994), 35.

17. An exceptionally thorough and philosophically sophisticated essay on the concepts of the will to power and of interpretation as an assertion of power is Wolfgang Müller-Lauter, "Nietzsches Lehre vom Willen zur Macht," in *Nietzsche,* ed. Jörg Salaquarda (Darmstadt: Wissenschaftliche Buchgesellschaft, 1980), 234-87; first published in *Nietzsche-Studien* 3 (1974): 1-60.

18. Heidegger's familiar term, characterizing the human being from the perspective of a fundamental ontology, literally denotes the place or "there" (*Da*) where Being occurs. Like Emerson, Nietzsche thinks human beings as localized events of circular (self-)grounding.

19. Compare this passage in "Fate": "Every spirit makes its house; but afterwards the house confines the spirit" (*E&L,* 946).

20. There are few really in-depth investigations of the question of time in Nietzsche. I have been encouraged in my own attempts to think through the problem by these two outstanding and quite different interpretations: Joan Stambaugh, *The Problem of Time in Nietzsche,* trans. John F. Humphrey (Lewisburg: Bucknell Univ. Press, 1987); and David Wood, "Nietzsche's Transvaluation of Time," in *Exceedingly Nietzsche: Aspects of Contemporary Nietzsche Interpretation,* ed. David Farrell Krell and David Wood (London: Routledge, 1988), 31-62.

21. All "it was" is a fragment and a riddle, a cruel chance—till the creative will says to it: "but this is the way I willed it!"

—Till the creative will says to it: "But thus I will it! This is the way I will will it!"

But has the will already spoken in this way? And when will this happen? Has the will already been released from the harness of its own stupidity?

Has the will already become its own savior and evangelist? Has it unlearned the spirit of revenge and all grating of teeth?

And who taught it reconciliation with time, and something that is higher than all reconciliation?

The will that is the will to power has to will something higher than all reconciliation—: but how does this happen to it? Who taught it also to will backwards?

22. See Baumgarten, "Mitteilungen und Bemerkungen," 107-9.

23. See Friedl, "Emerson and Nietzsche: 1862-1874," 270-71; and Stack, "Nietzsche's Earliest Essays," 153. Also see Graham Parkes, who has greatly deepened our understanding of the psychological and biographical significance of Nietzsche's early encounter with Emerson in *Composing the Soul: Reaches of Nietzsche's Psychology* (Chicago: Univ. of Chicago Press, 1994), 35-42.

24. Friedrich Nietzsche, "Fatum und Geschichte," in *Frühe Schriften,* ed. Hans Joachim Mette (Munich: C. H. Beck, 1933-40; reprint, 1994), 2:58. My translation does not attempt to gloss over Nietzsche's stylistic awkwardness: "What is it that so powerfully debases the soul of so many people and makes a higher flight of ideas impossible? A fatalistic structure of the skull and the spine, the social status and the nature of their parents, the everyday routine of their condition, the vulgarity of their surroundings, the monotony even of their home. We have been influenced, without bearing within us the power of reaction, without even knowing that we have been influenced and determined."

25. thus it is now my will:
    and since this is my will,
    Everything obeys my wishes and desires—
    This way my ultimate and last prudence:
    I willed that which I must [do or be]
    in this way I forced any "Must" . . .
    ever since there is no "Must" for me. . . .

26. The word "plus," which Nietzsche uses frequently, is one he would have found several times in the German translation of *The Conduct of Life.* See Ralph Waldo Emerson, *Führung des Lebens: Gedanken und Studien,* trans. E. S. von Mühlberg (Leipzig: E. F. Steinacker, 1862), 40, 42, 47, 49.

27. I would suggest the following paraphrase for this passage: the child is innocence and forgetting, a (constant) new beginning, a play, a self-moved wheel, a first (an initial and initiating) movement, a holy yea-saying.

28. See *Heraklit: Fragmente, Griechisch und Deutsch,* ed. Bruno Snell (Munich: Artemis, 1986), fragment B 123: "Das Wesen der Dinge versteckt sich gern" [The essence of things likes to hide].

29. See Friedrich Nietzsche, *Jenseits von Gut und Böse* (Beyond good and evil), in *KSA,* 5:169 [230].

30. Karl Löwith, *Nietzsches Philosophie der ewigen Wiederkehr des Gleichen,* 3rd ed. (Hamburg: Felix Meiner Verlag, 1978), 192. I suggest this translation: "Nietzsche's writings are a 'Prelude to a Philosophy of the Future,' not because he thought of a future change in the essence of man, which one could possibly prepare or even will, and for the realization of which he conceived of the overman, but rather because of the fact that he—remembering the great pre-Socratic *physikoi*—started the great experiment of 're-translating' the human being into the nature of all things."

31. Müller-Lauter has analyzed these critiques insightfully in "Nietzsches Lehre," 261.

32. Nietzsche's references to Emerson are presented in painstaking detail by Baumgarten in "Mitteilungen und Bemerkungen," 101-14.

33. Parkes has explored this connection convincingly in *Composing the Soul,* 35-48.

34. This chaotic and brute and absurd There and Then must disappear and the Here and Now must take its place.

35. See Baumgarten, "Mitteilungen und Bemerkungen," 152.

36. I have paraphrased two notes dated fall 1881. The first reads, "der gedankenreichste Autor dieses Jahrh [underts] ist bisher ein Amerikaner gewesen (leider durch deutsche Philosophie verdunkelt—Milchglas)" (*KSA,* 9:602). And the second, "Emerson—Ich habe mich nie in einem Buch so zu Hause und in meinem Hause gefühlt als—ich darf es nicht loben, es steht mir zu nahe" (*KSA,* 9:588).

37. In the original German, Nietzsche's statement reads, "Dergestalt hat sich Plato des Sokrates bedient, als einer Semiotik für Plato" (*KSA,* 6:320).

38. Emerson possesses that benevolent and spirited serenity that discourages all heavy seriousness; he simply doesn't know how old he is already and how young he will yet be,—he could possibly say of himself, quoting Lope de Vega: "I am my own heir."

39. The good furtune of my existence, maybe its uniqueness, resides in its fatedness. I will express it in the form of a riddle: as my father I have already died, as my mother I am still alive and will grow to be old.

40. Hubbard, *Nietzsche und Emerson,* 178.

Jonathan Bishop (essay date 1998)

SOURCE: "Emerson and Christianity," in *Renascence: Essays on Value in Literature,* Vol. 50, No. 3-4, Spring, 1998, pp. 221-237.

[*In the following essay, Bishop examines Emerson's "Divinity School Address" to locate the "Emersonian alternative" to traditional or "historical Christianity."*]

Emerson and Christianity could seem almost too vague and ideological a topic to some at least among the current cohort of Americanists. A recent review of research by Lawrence Buell for the *Emerson Society Quarterly* observes that much recent work has concentrated either upon the youthful or the aging Emerson. To rediscover the comparative orthodoxy of the first or the adaptive Victorianism of the second is in either case to obscure Emerson the Transcendentalist. The influence of newer modes of criticism might also serve to "call into question," as the phrase goes, the very idea of a central or essential Emerson who might still be identified and confronted. And the monumental new editions of the essays, journals, and lectures would only further reinforce such a disposition, as would the new biographies by Allen, Porte, and McAleer. Emerson can seem in some danger of disappearing back into his contexts, textual or historical.

To be sure the question of Emerson and Christianity might be approached in just this style. A reporter might collect opinions and exhibit attitudes as these are revealed anecdotally through an increasingly well-evidenced lifetime. Such an approach would make what it could of an Aunt Mary's eccentric traditionalism or the attraction of an unbelieving Achille Murat. Or it might count up references in journal or letter to Pope Gregory's blessing, or the mass in St. Augustine or Baltimore, or estimate the tone of certain comments on the influence of Calvinism, or Orestes Brownson, or the Shakers. But these, it is easy to agree, are minor matters. A broader sweep might once again examine the history of religious ideas in New England up through the emergence of Unitarianism and the beginnings of Transcendentalism. But Perry Miller and his several "sons" have already done this more than once. Or one might, less conventionally, pay attention to that curious contrast within the America of the time and since between the ethos represented by Emerson and his friends and the evangelicalism of the heart which in some mysterious way it can seem in cultural equilibrium with. Popular Christianity versus what has more recently been called the human potential movement has been a persistent conflict within our national experience. And the progress of the Emersonian impulse down through its repetitions among the half-baked and eccentric but also the learned and adventurous will always reward attention.

An approach by way of the history of American religion can in any case lead to ambiguities and thence into confusion, as more and more inquiry might demonstrate—not always on purpose. Some modern commentators have in fact found it oddly difficult to distinguish the doctrine advanced in the essays from one or another variety of Christianity. Randall Stewart, to be sure, as a testy Agrarian of old fashioned opinions, could at least repeat earlier judgments to the effect that Emerson is "radically anti-Christian," and "has done more than any other . . . to undermine Christian orthodoxy in America" (33-40). But Robert Ward, writing in another southern journal, subsequently found occasion to rebuke Stewart by name in defense of what he was prepared to call Emerson's fundamental "orthodoxy." Perhaps it needn't surprise us to find an up-to-date New York critic like Steven Donadio unable to disentangle one species of American spirituality from another; or even to discover at least one scholar, Harold Fromm, prepared to affirm a likeness between Emerson and, of all people, Kierkegaard. But surely it should seem odd that a recent *History of American Religion* by William Clesch detects an uninterrupted continuity from Jonathan Edwards through Emerson to William James. There is some reason, then, to re-examine the question in philosophical, not to say theological, terms. And it is most readily faced where Emerson himself deliberately and openly declared what he had to say—which is, of course, the **"Divinity School Address."**

If we return to that central document, we need read no further than the opening paragraphs to find language acutely relevant to the general issue. The opening words of this deliberately contentious announcement to the academic and ecclesiastical powers that were on that Cambridge Sunday evening in mid-July of 1838 offer as good evidence as any to locate the Emersonian alternative to what he and his party were accustomed to call "historical Christianity." He is addressing the graduating class of the first seminary in New England on the occasion of their commencement as Christian preachers. Time, place, and audience could not have been more carefully calculated to throw into relief the purport of his utterance. The only analogue indeed is Jesus teaching in the Temple. And like Jesus, Emerson is speaking not as an apostate from the received faith but what the enemies of both would call a heretic; that is, one who believes himself authorized to announce the real truth of a message which the apparently orthodox have somehow missed. He is claiming to be at the center of rather than outside the circle he would now reconstitute on a new principle—which of course intensifies our interest in what is being said.

Which is, through these opening paragraphs, to outline the possibilities of the ideal human subject, which Emerson calls the "Soul." His first words are deliberately provocative. For he begins with suavely insinuating praise of the high season which prevailed as he spoke, with its delicious burden of flowers, trees, stars, and night. "In this refulgent summer," he says, the "mystery of nature was never displayed more happily." It therefore behooves even such tightly cravatted and black suited folk as their reverend selves to "respect the perfection of this world in which our senses converse" (*Works* I, 76). The words "perfection" and "senses" are loaded with animus: such rhetoric advances the claims of the body in a style which mocks any reasonable expectation of his audience. Here is the Soul, to be sure; but on the level of scent and touch, where its proper "object" is not the moral law but that circumambiant environment within which us children of Adam might always enjoy ourselves—if only we dared. The praise this erotic opportunity as already "perfect," and so virtually "spiritual" in its own right is on the face of it to insult every decent feeling.

Such language is insolent. But though Emerson is more than willing to shock, his tongue is really in his cheek. The point of the joke is lost unless we remember that he is very far from being a sensualist. He is ordinarily more than willing to reinforce the distrust of the flesh normal to his society and profession. Perhaps as a result he suffered, as he occasionally complained, from a certain detachment from his own sensations and feelings. There is besides his eventual reaction to Whitman's very different disposition to recall if we need reminding how Emerson could feel when someone actually proposed doing what he humorously alludes to here. He is shocking, but he is not serious. It would be others who would explore the possibility thus opened out.

The second half of this initial paragraph is devoted to the practical "faculties" of mankind, which make of fruitful soils and navigable seas resources to be worked up into things useful to human kind. This side of nature is worth, he observes, the "pith and heart of great men to subdue and enjoy it." But "commodity," or the practical mode of our engagement with the world, is in this context only a pendant to the sensuous abandon with which Emerson began. It is not on this occasion a topic to be explored on its own account.

A third step up the scale of the faculties which Emerson is climbing in these paragraphs brings us to the mind. When that "opens," he says, the impressions and circumstances which man enjoys or makes use of through the passive or active body "shrink" to mere "illustrations" of that mind's proper objects, the "laws" which define nature as a system of ideas. The world in which our senses converse becomes significant of a universe we understand through the intellect. Emerson had already explored this mode of the Soul in *Nature* and **"The American Scholar,"** and would do so again, several times. The natural history of intellect is one of his most persistent concerns.

But in this context even activity of mind is reduced to a mere "entertainment." Within a religious perspective, the highest in rank among the faculties is not the intellect but what he then goes on to praise, the "sentiment of virtue," or "moral sentiment." It is this interior power that most entirely informs whoever exercises it that the human subject is indeed "without bound"; that he or she (we can always supply the other pronoun, as Margaret Fuller once had to insist) is already "born" to the perfection of the Soul. "That which he [or she] venerates is still his own," the most explicit sentence affirms, "though he has not realized it yet." The deliverances of conscience belong not to an internalized society or external God, but to ourselves as human beings. To *realize* this privilege is accordingly to re-appropriate what may have become alienated from us as most properly our own. By way of the moral sentiment, man becomes God. The subject is altogether unlimited on just this side.

The sources of Emerson's belief in the moral sentiment as at once inborn and infinite can be found in the proposition of less extravagant thinkers. Joel Porte's first book showed the extent to which we could understand Emerson as a descendent of those eighteenth-century British philosophers, Price, Shaftesbury, Hutchinson and Stewart, who had long before proposed an inherent moral sense as the chief faculty in what was to become the standard Bostonian idea of human nature. Daniel Walker Howe and more recently David Robinson have shown how much the Unitarian conscience and the ideal of self-culture organized around it could depend on an optimistic assessment of this resource. The founding texts of this species of moral humanism, read in college, would to that extent make Emerson a pious student of the previous century. We could then appreciate the incitements of Coleridge and through him a misunderstood Kant as latter-day repetitions of an expectation that had already become intellectual second nature. For Emerson like invariably went with like; his reading could only confirm what he knew already, not challenge it. So he

might be understood to have assimilated not just the German idealists but his favorite neo-Platonists and in due course the Orientals.

The idea that the moral sentiment is not only intrinsic and universal but functionally identical with God is already in any case the central thesis of the movement for which Emerson is speaking on this occasion. The same apotheosis of the conscience may be found, if not quite in Channing, at least in Ripley or Brownson or Parker. And Emerson had already made his own agreement clear, most recently in two lectures, one on **"Religion,"** delivered in the series on the Philosophy of History at the Masonic Temple in January of 1837, and another on **"Holiness"** delivered in the series on Human Culture in January of 1838.

The doctrine, then, is by no means new. The differences between other renderings of the key proposition and Emerson's on this occasion is in the first instance rhetorical: he is speaking face to face with those he is challenging on behalf of a declaration which by that very act becomes an either/or that has to be answered in kind. And this rhetorical crisis is itself the manifestation of an emergent spiritual claim. Emerson is not only speaking *for* but also *as* the infinite subject he proclaims. Joel Porte's more recent book has observed that Emerson had recently been reading his father's unfinished *Historical Sketch* of the First Church of Boston, before the elders of which Anne Hutchinson had been brought, exactly two centuries before, to answer a charge he knew might now be raised against himself (Porte 98-101). For to assert that the right of judgment is infinitely exercised while speaking in the name of that power to those who are free to deny it is at the very least to repeat the old Antinomian claim that the elect are each endowed individually with just that Spirit whose authority must prevail over Church and State alike. But it is also a claim to act as the ultimate agent here and now. Emerson makes himself the Christ anew for this occasion. His words translate the same *I am* which, Mark tells us, confronted the high priest and elders of another establishment once upon a time, and which, on that authority, John would make the key motif of his gospel.

It is this revelation—the term would be exact—that determines our understanding of the language at the very end of the **"Address"**, where Emerson somewhat disingenuously calls for a "new Teacher" who should improve upon the oracles of "those Eastern" men who once delivered the holy word. The role of the Baptist apparently adopted here seems a transparent mask. Nor do the parallels with Jeremiah traced by Carol Johnston in a recent article appear sufficient to account for the identity presumed. In fact, we also know, Emerson's friend Jones Very supposed that he was the Messiah here looked for—and came by night to identify himself as just this figure to Henry War (Gittleman 187-92). The result was a forced retreat to Salem, where that unfortunate Greek tutor was to live out the remainder of a melancholy life. But for one moment at least Very had been Emerson's best contemporary hearer—in his own schizophrenic fashion. But a saner un derstanding would have to be equally startling. Who but Emerson himself, and at just this time of speaking, could more reasonably appropriate the identity proposed? He is in fact already the "new born bard of the Holy Ghost" he urges the graduates sitting before him to become. If so, he is competing directly with Jesus on his own elder brother's spiritual as well as social territory. To adopt Harold Bloom's useful language, Jesus is the "precursor" for who Emerson is the "ephebe." The speech is accordingly an agon to decide which of the two shall prevail. At stake, it is not too extravagant to claim, is America's consciousness of itself. For here at last would be a declaration of independence going beyond either the political or the cultural.

If Emerson is adopting a Messianic role, though, it is very much in his own style. The character of his declaration may be thrown into relief by comparing it with some alternative affirmations within the same apocalyptic genre. The most obvious of these would be found within the tradition of German idealism to which Emerson owed so much. This had already made the "Reason" man's highest faculty, and so his access to infinitude. In Fichte or Hegel such a "strong" misreading of Kant would become direct assertion. But in them and the tradition which descends through Husserl to the philosophic day before yesterday, the unlimited subject is regularly understood in cognitive terms. It is Mind that constitutes the universe, and so occupies the place of God. But in Emerson this absolute possibility belongs to the sense of duty. He is a moral, not a rational, idealist. So his I AM is not collective or intellectual but ethical and solitary. The scene is New England, after all, not Germany.

Another contrast just worth making would bear on more current manifestations of the Emersonian inheritance. His literary descendants, creative or academic, have been inclined to honor him as if it were not the moral sentiment or even the intellect that offered an "open channel to the highest life" but the imagination. The imperial self has taken that form for modern men of letters. Harold Bloom's own solipsistical sublime, to cite him once more, is, however grandiose its central encompassments, most centrally the product of an imaginative contest. But Emerson would not, I think, have been pleased with such a metamorphosis of his central claim. The Poet, however capitalized and inspired, is according to him always subordinate to the Preacher—and the **"Address"** is *kerygma*, not poetry.

We might forestall this modern disposition to translate Emerson downward on the scale of the faculties by contrasting his message with other figures or movements which have frankly reversed the psychic hierarchy upon which he depends. Whitman could show, for instance, what might happen if one started at the *other* end of the Soul. On the level of the body, intuition is simply identification; and evidently identification is the first principle of Whitman's poetic project. He too believes in infinitude—and sometimes manifested Messianic tendencies. But on the level of the body infinity presents itself as either intensity or multiplicity, those other angles of the

Whitmanian enterprise. These, though, obliterate or diffuse the solitary ecstasy Emerson values.

The recollection of Whitman could remind us too of another not so distant "newness," when the word "movement" once again bore a religious as well as a political import. Many have since felt the likenesses between the Transcendentalist moment and what we now so familiarly call "the sixties," when the Soul once again awoke in America—only to fall asleep, as before. But the subject that revived in our more recent time of fervor was a manifestation of the Soul's "lower" energies. It was our desires, our feelings, our capacity for group identification that found themselves encouraged. The typical pronoun of the time was accordingly "We" rather than "I." Whitman would have joined in; Emerson, surely, would have held back.

The Soul is hierarchically ordered, then, with the moral sentiment at the top. And it is accessible to individuals, not collectivities. The essential singularity of its manifestations, which Emerson never tires of insisting upon, reinforces both these presuppositions. There is always one Man, one Mind, one Spirit. To be sure this emphasis does not imply a high value for individuals as such. Emerson repeatedly insists that the Soul is no respecter of persons. It can sometimes be hard to believe he means what he says. We are apt to think him a sponsor for individuality in himself and others. And to some extent it clearly is. But strictly speaking his doctrine prohibits what it may in fact have promoted. The various modes of the Soul in action are all anonymous in principle, whatever name tags may be tied to the various instances. These are no more than representations, performances, examples—never the whole of the Subject as such. There are in fact no true selves in the Emersonian universe. No wonder then that his rhetoric always prefers the type, as Poet or Scholar, Transcendentalist or Conservative. This is Emerson's Platonic side, which also explains his insistence that the Soul knows nothing of time or place. It is always essentially identical with itself, whatever the circumstances of its manifestation. History too is degraded to illustration, like biography. The Soul is time-*less*—rather, we may observe, than eternal.

This synchronic impersonal ideality of the Soul goes with Emerson's already old fashioned emphasis on its different "faculties." We may understand this psychology by translating it into somewhat more recent critical jargon as "competence." Emerson would then be inviting us to develop our abilities in whatever spheres of life are open to us. The resulting exhilaration comes from the discovery that we are entitled to exercise one or another of just these powers; that we are old enough to vote, as it were, in so many elections. It is the typical experience of youth. Emerson's vision of possibility can seem a very academic invitation, well suited to an ideal process of education. To be sure, Americans are always in school, and have trouble believing in history. But it is worth stressing that the question—who is the person that disposes of these abilities?—

has in principle not yet been either asked or answered. And this would be as true for the moral sentiment as for the intellect or any lesser power.

The Soul, then, is Anybody, not Somebody. This can have its chilly as well as its encouraging side. Emerson believes that the Soul is immortal; indeed, he must, for the subject as defined in such a way would be accessible to whoever becomes conscious of the opportunity to practice it at any time or place. It is Permanent, not Transient, as Theodore Parker would say. This kind of immortality, though, is little comfort to a mere individual haunted by his own mortality—or to a bereaved lover. The issue was evidently most acute for Emerson immediately before and after the death of his first wife Ellen. They appear to have made a pact that she should reveal herself somehow after death. The Journal contains pathetic pleas to this effect (*JMN* III, 230, 240, 275, 309). We must gather that she did not. It was Ellen's money that proved immortal after all, not her presence.

To be sure there are also advantages to the impersonality of the soul. The distinction between impersonal privilege and its individual manifestation helped preserve Emerson from the madness that has so often overtaken Messianic pretentions. His appreciation of the difference between en- titlement and fact was presently to make up the burden of his wisdom as opposed to his gospel. For this invariably exhibits a controlled acceptance of every diminishment that could ever hinder the exercise of the very powers he begins by celebrating. Infinitude in principle is finitude in practice. "I am God in nature," the familiar sentence from **"Circles"** confesses, "I am a weed by the wall" (*Works* II, 182). Within this skeptical gap his best work as on-going man of letters was shortly to be done—which allows us to admire his personal defeat rather more than the victory of his principle, if we choose.

The perfect Subject, then, is ideally intrinsic, infinite, su- perordinate, and impersonal. It manifests itself most acutely as a timeless moment of human triumph. "They call it Christianity," says a Journal entry of the same year with the **"Address"**: "I call it Consciousness" (*JMN* VII, 28). This makes a neat formulation of his challenge, which should resonate through a variety of modern instances. Should we not always be reducing the tradition to so much of the subject as it can be made to produce? What else are we here for? I shall venture some answers to these ques- tions shortly; but let me go back now to the problem of Jesus, which arises in the middle of the **"Address"**. If the doctrine of the Soul as just outlined is the true meaning of what used to be known as Christianity, what role is left for Emerson's rival on this ground?

In fact the view of Jesus specified in the **"Address"** fol- lows directly from Emerson's general definition of the subject. Jesus too is an avatar, as it were, of the moral sen- timent. He saw once what Emerson now confirms in his own person, the infinite potential of the Soul. "Alone in all history," Jesus "estimated the greatness" not of God but

man. "One man was once" true to what is "already" you and me. Therefore he said, though no more extrav gantly than Emerson is saying now, "I am divine, throu me, God acts; through me, speaks. Would you see G see me; or see thee, when thou thinkest as I now think."

We may feel that this Jesus is an oddly epicene version the figure of whom we can also read in the New Test ment. The second person singular placed in his mouth only Biblical language for Emerson's own views. But th is of course the point. Jesus can be so thoroughly recast Emersonian terms because he has no room, as it were, be otherwise within the scheme of possibility just viewed. Jesus and Emerson alike are no more than figur of Absolute Spirit. For those bold enough to realize much, all other persons, past or present, are therefo prophecies of one's own ideal self. Jesus stands for wh Emerson and any member of his audience (and therefo every reader of the **"Address"** since) *ought* to be. But that case he has no identity or language of his own th need be respected.

Christology is an obvious test for any religious propos that purports to redefine Christianity. Emerson's idea Jesus is accordingly the likeliest point at which to insert critical crowbar, the better to separate the Transcendent ist gospel from its older original. Of course Emerson tak for granted that Jesus is man rather than God. So far he merely Unitarian. He had indeed written a sermon **"Christ Crucified"** ten years before the Address in whi he had elaborated a portrait of Jesus as a model for mo growth and unworldly sublimity of character. His prese doctrine differs from that of his culture and his own earli views chiefly in affirming that the idea of Man includ the possibility of infinitude. But even his newer doctri continues to presume that it is still the human subject th Jesus manifests. Divinity has moved over, as it were, the near side of that old Jewish difference between ma and God. In the process, of course, the gap itself disap pears. There *is* no other, human or divine, in the Emerso ian universe. There is only what the contemporary Fren philosopher Emmanuel Levinas has called *the same*. Th Soul is then a psychic tautology. Jesus is the same as Em erson because that is all there is for anyone to be. Aesthe or hero, he can be no better than Somebody; who is, w have already noticed, no more than Anybody in disguis He cannot possibly be the true other in the correspond ingly capitalized sense, or Somebody Else.

But Somebody Else is indeed who Jesus appears withi the Christian tradition—including, for this occasion, s much Unitarian feeling as might be shocked by Emerson ventriloquism. For to feel distaste would be to experienc in an attenuated form the impropriety of any language tha assumes an immediate identity of Jesus with ourselves The Christian would have to confess on the contrary tha Jesus should be understood as coming to meet us, as were, from the other side of the relation. He is God inca nate; not Man in apotheosis. And if so, his words an deeds acquire an infinite right to be respected. They ha better *not* be preempted by one's own. For in that case they are truly the voice of the Other. And in that recognition, the Other is always God. The Subject, by whatever name, is only Me.

Emerson's absorption of Jesus can be linked with another feature of the opening paragraphs of one **"Address."** It may be observed that the hierarchy of faculties has its linguistic reflection. The so-called "conversation" of the senses with their world is literally pre-verbal. No language mediates that intercourse. The Soul simply "breathes" in the bounty dealt forth in "never-ending silence." Nor do the things grasped by the hand of farmer or mechanic become words. But when the mind opens, this mute environment of the senses and the muscles shrinks, says Emerson, to "an illustration and a fable." Nature becomes a dictionary of symbols. The moral sentiment, though, once one has arrived at that height, turns out to be as far above language as sensation is below it. Infinitude is *post*-verbal. Its laws can*not* be "adequately stated. They will *not* be written out on paper, or spoken by the tongue." Yet once this inner divinity has been realized, words may once again be used on its behalf, to affirm its prevalence—as in the **"Address"** itself.

If we attend to this verbal dimension of the Emersonian scheme we become more aware of what is at stake between him and the authorities of the Divinity School, and so in the end between him and Jesus. The issue is, who shall command the discourse? Does language belong to the Other, or to the Subject? If the Other is understood profanely as society in general, then the struggle is simply between Me and Them. Emerson's literary strategy already enfigures his answer here. To keep a journal is implicitly to take secret possession of discourse in advance. To rewrite its contents in sermon or lecture or essay is to claim for oneself the essential privilege of repetition. Thus writing itself is shifted inside the boundaries of *the same,* where the Subject dominates. So far Emerson is fighting the familiar nineteenth-century war between the individual and society.

But this struggle to command the discourse is most acute when the other is not merely Harvard but Jesus—who is already, by a previous tradition, the word of God himself. Who shall say what Jesus has said—or would say now? We have seen that Emerson feels free to put his own words in Jesus' mouth. He is not the first to do that. But his conquest is in fact incomplete. The apparent willingness to shock is complicated by an unconscious diffidence. This appears in the curious weakness that infiltrates these words. They rather parody Emerson's message than exhibit his power to incorporate the Other. Indeed the same weakness appears whenever Emerson attempts to speak directly on behalf of the moral sentiment. At just these moments his language becomes over-poetical and effete. We must often apply his own objection to those sermons in which is to be heard "no arrows no axes no nectar no growling." His *but I say unto you* lacks evangelic power. A concentration of this debility may be found in what has surely struck many

as the feeblest single sentence in the whole **"Address"**, the definition of a "true conversion, a true Christ" as that which is brought about by, of all things, "the reception of beautiful sentiments." To be sure, the word "beauty" often leads Emerson astray. It cannot be made to mean what he wants it to say. So it represents an erosion from the moral to the aesthetic, and thence to the sentimental. On this ground he is regularly defeated by his own rhetoric.

The question, who shall command the word, had already arisen in a still more acute form six years previously, when Emerson resigned from his church over the issue of the Lord's Supper. The chief document of that event is the sermon Emerson delivered to explain his unwillingness to celebrate this ordinance. In it he examines the relevant Biblical texts with conventional care. It has in fact been discovered that the argumentative middle of this discourse was cribbed from Thomas Clarkson's *Portraiture of Quakerism,* which Emerson borrowed from the Athenaeum for the purpose (McAleer 120). But his proper conclusion really precedes the evidence he so uncharacteristically rehearses. It is that Jesus did not mean to establish a perpetual institution at the last supper. He meant only to offer a parable the significance of which should evaporate on that occasion. We had better understand the words over the bread and wine as an allegory of his teaching, in the style of the sixth chapter of John. In any case the idiom employed is too "oriental" for a civilized congregation (*Essays and Lectures* 429-1140).

We may detect in this last objection the strongest grounds for that "disagreeableness" to his "feelings" upon which Emerson eventually depends. He is not "interested" in the eucharist, to use his word, because the mute bodiliness of bread and wine, not to mention flesh and blood, affronts a sensibility as fastidious as his. A symbol should exhaust itself on its occasion. There is no reason thereafter to repeat the mere vehicle. Besides, to allow this low idiom would be to confess an alien authority. In the Lord's Supper the officiant sinks his own identity in that of his master. He does not speak for himself but as the Other, whose words are confessed to be more efficacious than his own. The rite thus concentrates everything that Emerson most feared in traditional Christianity: carnality, altereity, and subordination.

The struggle between Emerson and Jesus, then, is not only over who shall control the language, but what sort of language is to be used. Emerson claims verbal eloquence for the Soul—in this case with rather less success than his argument requires. Jesus claims the body for God. And this vulgar idiom, we may observe, is not exceptional to the eucharist but typical. The Jesus of the traditional texts is shown proving his case by touching the unclean, the disabled, and the mad. It is sinners and tax collectors who are brought into the kingdom, not scribes and pharisees. And the same principle informs the method by which the kingdom is established; not a military victory but a criminal passion. For Emerson an appeal to the body is at most a polemical joke, as we have seen. For Jesus it seems to have been the key to his strategy. Like Whitman, Jesus reverses the normal hierarchies—but on behalf of the Other rather than *the same.*

To revert to the problem of the Lord's Supper and the implications of the quarrel Emerson had with this ordinance is to become more confident of the case that would need to be made in answer to the **"Address"** so as to disengage Christianity once again from Consciousness. Against immanence one would need to reassert transcendence; against hierarchy, reversal; against abstraction, concreteness; against timelessness, the scandal of persons in history. *For eternity, in the Christian conception, is not the absence but the fullness of time.*

Before continuing our general contrast, though, we should glance at one or two of the particular answers the **"Address"** provoked at the time. For these can now be seen to include elements which should appear in any ideal reply to Emerson's challenge. Henry Ware's sermon on "The Personality of the Deity," for instance, delivered two months later to the same audience, is a public rebuttal to at least one of the heresies announced in the Address. Emerson's depersonalization of the divine being, objects Ware, blends God with his commandments in a moral pantheism. But if there is "no consciousness and power of will and action behind these laws, they cease to apply." Atheism *is,* practically speaking, a denial of God's personality: "There is a personal God, or there is none." For without such a God, to whom I may be related in love or fear, "I am left to myself," and so without a motive to obey the moral law (84-91).

What Ware can be taken as defending in his own pained style is the relevance of relation as such, together with the persons it entails. As we have seen, Emerson's gospel excludes these altogether. There is no relation in his universe, and therefore no real persons, human *or* divine. This aboriginal absence reappears in Emerson's famous refusal to answer Ware's pamphlet version of the sermon on the ground that he could not understand what "arguments mean in reference to any expression of a thought." For argument presupposes at least an intellectual relation. He would prefer, he says, to go on reading the words of others just so far as they "speak my thought, skipping the page that has nothing for me" (**Letters** II, 166-67). Impersonality is in danger here of becoming indistinguishable from solipsism, not for the last time.

Other responses conveniently reprinted in Perry Miller's anthology can also supply material for a retrospective reply to Emerson that might go beyond the intentions either of the original writers or their modern compiler. Andrews Norton's initial reaction in the *Boston Daily Advertiser* for August 27th, some six weeks after the **"Address,"** is not, to be sure, an answer to the case Emerson had proposed. It is simply an expression of scornful disgust that anyone should have been invited to deliver such self-evidently unChristian opinions in the Chapel of the Divinity School to a class of graduating clergymen. Emerson had failed to

recognize his social place. Such a protest displays the collective link between doctrine and manners that Emerson was in part objecting to. The same composite standard is evoked by *The Christian Examiner's* similar reference to the "utterly distasteful . . . notions" which must have been "altogether repugnant" to the feelings of those who listened to the words of "an individual who has no connection with the school whatever. . . . " (Miller 193-96).

But Norton's more considered response, the notorious "The Latest Form of Infidelity," is indeed useful. This essay connects the traditional Unitarian affirmation that miracles are essential to Christianity, which the **"Address"** had almost casually denied, with a rehearsal of the anthropology the argument presupposes. Man is *not* infinite but finite, the "creature of a day, *just* endowed with the capacity of thought, at first receiving all his opinions from those who have preceded him, entangled among numberless prejudices, confused by his passions, perceiving, if the eyes of his understanding are opened, that the sphere of his knowledge is hemmed in by an infinite of which he is *ignorant. . . .* " (Miller 211). So limited a humanity requires a miracle-working God for its enlightenment. According to Norton, Jesus is at least the Moses of a new dispensation. But his authority to teach what God commands requires the confirmation supplied by the wonders he is reported to have done. Belief that the miracles did indeed occur is therefore indispensable to the Christian case. This in turn throws a heavy responsibility on the scholar who, though "*just* endowed with the capacity of thought," can at least make himself reasonably sure that the events reported may be accepted as facts, however long ago and far away.

The weakness of Norton's argument lies in the assumption that though miracles can just be inferred to have occurred in the past, it need not be supposed that any such thing would ever happen in the present. This means in turn that man's relation to God has to be not faith but reason—and reason in the reduced sense of the Coleridgean "understanding," exercised not even upon the sensations of the moment but on the evidences supplied by old texts. The strength which corresponds to this weakness lies in the realization that without the possibility represented by miracle itself, the otherness of God disappears. For a miracle is by definition something only God can do. Thus the Transcendentalist is strong where the Unitarian is weak and vice versa. For Transcendentalism correctly realizes that a God who could once act but is now impotent must be a Deistic figment. A true miracle would have to be possible in the present too. But the Transcendentalist assimilates this possibility to the powers of mankind. In that case, though, miraculousness once again disappears, for the Soul cannot do anything that could be distinguished in principle from the operations of nature. Miracles and otherness stand or fall together.

One position, then, leaves God out of the present; the other assimilates him to the Subject. It is possible to imagine a third position that would admit otherness with the

Unitarian and contemporaneity with the Transcendentalist. In such a scheme, the place filled by exceptions to the laws of nature in first century Palestine might very well be filled with other *pneumena* (to coin a term) either in Emerson's day or ours. The modes by which the infinitely Other is revealed would not have to be limited to what made that kind of sense once upon a time. On the human side too such a third option could realize that both the contending parties omit the possibility of faith. In the place where this might occur, the Unitarian substitutes induction. In the same place the Transcendentalist supplies an experience of the sublime. The quarrel between the parties, scholarship is accustomed to observe, concerns the nature of man. But a detached perspective could add that the nature of man does not really matter—provided the figure in question is related to God. Once that obtains, the amount of change to be found in our psychic pockets scarcely matters.

The objections to the **"Address"** at the time must be eked out, then, to be fully useful. But carefully read, they provide materials out of which to construct an ideal answer to the Emersonian project from the side of Christianity. This had better begin, I have already suggested, with the primary distinction between immanence and transcendence. The first will supply the ground for Emerson's trust in the unlimited possibilities of the human subject. But only the second can be, I suspect, altogether consistent with the Christian gospel as soon as this has been seriously entertained. And from this difference others derive.

If God is transcendent, for example, it would follow that the Other is more instead of less than *the same*. Both sides could agree with Kierkegaard that subjectivity is truth. But Emerson understands subjectivity in the mode of identity. To take the Other seriously is on the contrary to discover that subjectivity is truth only in the mode of relation. In that case Spirit would not be the superlative of Soul but its opposite. Then the central task of the Subject would not be an indefinite expansion of itself but faith. For faith is relation *realized*. And faith, we could also find, would indeed have to be suffered in historical persons, whom it defines. The impersonality of the Emersonian Soul would then have to be replaced by a recovery of the actual individual in exactly the scandalous sense he refuses. *Fides facit personam,* said Luther, who was also one of Emerson's heroes, though not on that ambiguous personage's Christian side: relation produces persons—and persons, stories. This is not to say that a Christian analogue to Emersonian self-reliance would have to be some reassertion of the personal as such. The true alternative, it seems to me, would rather take the form of self-acknowledgment—which could involve either some appropriation of power in virtually the Emersonian style or a thoroughgoing confession of disability, as occasion determined. For in Christianity there is in principle no hierarchy of faculties, as we have seen. Such a self-acknowledgment would then be the reflexive mode of faith.

Obviously the role of Jesus would also have to be very different within any Christian perspective. In most ver-

sions, we may notice, there is a place for him on either side of the relation. To begin and end with, he is on God's side; which is to say, as Somebody Else, not Somebody. It is this uncanny figure whom the various individuals in the gospel stories either accept or deny. It is these needy or antagonistic persons, therefore, who represent the human subject, not Jesus, who throughout stands in for the Other, not *the same*. We may sum up this role in Catholic terms as his sacramental identity. But he also has what may be called his Protestant role on the near side of the relation. As Somebody like and unlike ourselves he represents us not in the positive, like other heroes of the Soul, but in the negative, as victim. Jesus is then either resurrected or afflicted—but never merely exemplary. To look for him in that guise is to gaze into an abyss—or make up some figment, as we see Emerson doing in the **"Address"**. And that process is of course familiar in more orthodox contexts too.

But such implications need not be overdrawn. I need only add, in conclusion, an acknowledgment of my own. It has seemed odd for me to be reviewing the arguments of Emerson and his antagonists as if one were still involved in the issue; even if that has also got to be true. It has felt unacademic, not to say anachronistic, as if one were supplying yet another item to the Miller anthology. This predicament may go with any approach to a "classic." But it still made me uncomfortable. In what century did one live, after all? Besides, it felt ungrateful. How should an old student of this author now speak or write not just in elucidation as once but in objection, as if Emerson still lived a short distance out of town and could receive one more pamphlet not worth answering? It seemed that I needed to restore a decent ambivalence to my own discourse.

Let me in that spirit return accordingly to still another text for a final instance. This is a paragraph in the introductory announcement composed for the *Dial* in 1840, or two years after the **"Address"**, which must, it is agreed, be attributed to Emerson though it did not go out under his name. The paragraph concludes with a survey of those for whom the new journal hoped to speak, who had, though "without pomp, without trumpet, in lonely and obscure places, in solitude, in servitude, in compunctions and privations, trudging beside the team in the dusty road, or drudging a hireling in other men's cornfields, schoolmasters, who teach a few children rudiments for a pittance, ministers of small parishes of the obscurer sects, lone women in dependent condition, matrons and young maidens, rich and poor, beautiful and hard-favored, without concert or proclamation of any kind, have silently given in their several adherence to a new hope, and in all companies do signify a greater trust in the nature and resources of man, than the laws or the popular opinions will well allow" (Miller 249). It is easy, I hope, to find this series poignant. There is love in it, and of an unusual kind. I suppose too that others may feel that the concluding clause, "the nature and resources of man," is something of an anti-climax. The kinds of people mentioned, and vividly enough for us to bring their several predicaments painfully to mind, seem to deserve something better than that. They are like the poor of the Beatitudes, who in a similar series are told that they should consider themselves blessed, for theirs is the kingdom of heaven. These people though are offered instead the "nature and resources of man." It can seem a stone instead of bread. But the momentum built up in the sequence as it proceeds allows us, I think, the option of reading through this diminished formula the fullness of its ghostly original. I think it is this possibility that makes the poignancy of the passage ring true, and not merely occasional or sentimental. In which case even our best criticism of Emerson might become reconstructive at last, leaving us able to admire unreservedly after all—even against the intent of the author. And that might not be so bad in the long run.

Works Cited

Allen, Gay Wilson. *Waldo Emerson*. New York: Viking, 1981.

Buell, Lawrence. "The Emerson Industry in the 1980's: A Survey of Trends and Achievements." *Emerson Society Quarterly* 30 (1984): 117-36.

Clebsch, William A. *American Religious Thought: A History*. Chicago: Chicago UP, 1973.

Donadio, Stephen. "Emerson, Christian Identity, and the Dissolution of the Social Order." *Art, Politics, and Will: Essays in Honor of Lionel Trilling*. Eds. Quentin Anderson, Stephen Donadio, and Steven Marcus. New York: Basic, 1977. 99-123.

Emerson, Ralph Waldo. *The Collected Works*. Ed. Alfred R. Ferguson, et al. Cambridge, MA: Harvard UP, 1971-1983.

———. *Essays and Lectures*. Ed. Joel Porte. New York: Viking, 1983.

———. *The Journals and Miscellaneous Notebooks*. Ed. William Gilman et al. Cambridge, MA: Harvard, UP, 1960-82.

———. *The Letters*. Ed. Ralph L. Rusk. New York: Columbia UP, 1939.

Fromm, Harold. "Emerson and Kierkegaard: the Problem of Historical Christianity." *Massachusetts Review* 9 (1968): 741-52.

Gittleman, Edwin, *Jones Very: The Effective Years*. New York: Columbia UP, 1967.

Howe, Daniel Walker. *The Unitarian Conscience: Harvard Moral Philosophy, 1805-1861*. Cambridge, MA: Harvard UP, 1970.

Johnston, Carol. "The Underlying Structure of the Divinity School Address: Emerson as Jeremiah." *Studies in the American Renaissance* 4 (1980): 41-49.

Levinas, Emmanuel. *Totality and Infinity: An Essay on Exteriority*. The Hague: Nijhoff, 1979.

McAleer, John. *Ralph Waldo Emerson: Days of Encounter*. Boston: Little, Brown, 1984.

Miller, Perry. *The Transcendentalists: An Anthology*. Cambridge, MA: Harvard UP, 1960.

Porte, Joel. *Emerson and Thoreau: Transcendentalists in Conflict*. Middletown: Wesleyan UP, 1966.

———. *Representative Man: Ralph Waldo Emerson in His Time*. New York: Oxford UP, 1979.

Robinson, David. *Apostle of Culture: Emerson as Preacher and Lecturer*. Philadelphia: Pennsylvania UP, 1982.

Stewart, Randall. "Emerson, Asset or Liability." *Tennessee Studies in Literature* 2 (1957): 33-40.

Ward, Robert Stafford. "Still 'Christians,' Still Infidels." *Southern Humanities Review* 2 (1968): 365-74.

Ware, Henry Jr. "The Personality of the Deity." *American Transcendentalist Quarterly* 13 (1972): 84-91.

Len Gougeon (essay date 1998)

SOURCE: "Emerson and the Woman Question: The Evolution of His Thought," in *New England Quarterly*, Vol. 71, No. 4, December, 1998, pp. 570-92.

[*In the following essay, Gougeon summarizes Emerson's views on the women's liberation movement.*]

In a newspaper article celebrating the one-hundredth anniversary of Emerson's birth, Thomas Wentworth Higginson complained that those who knew Mr. Emerson in the light of a reformer, as he surely did, would find precious little information "given in that direction by his biographers."[1] Noting the generally conservative character of the two most influential and popular biographies of Emerson, those by Oliver Wendell Holmes and James Elliot Cabot,[2] Higginson was particularly distressed over their "constitutional reticence" in discussing the philosopher's role in both the antislavery and women's movements. "It was a well-known fact," Higginson observed, "that Mr. Emerson spoke several times at woman suffrage conventions, and this cordially and sympathetically. Yet," he says, "this is not mentioned in Mr. Cabot's memoir." If Higginson were to return today he would find that scant progress has been made in the biographical treatment of Emerson's views on the "Woman Question." While serious efforts have recently been made to recover the record of Emerson's important activities in the antislavery movement, very little is presently known about his contributions to the cause of women's rights.[3] Emerson's only published work on the topic is the well-known lecture he delivered before the women's rights convention in Boston on 20 September 1855. The address, titled simply **"Woman,"** was first published, in part, in the *Woman's Journal* in 1881 and later, in its entirety, in both the 1883 and 1903-4 Centenary Edition of Emerson's **Complete Works.**[4] Our understanding of

Emerson's public views on an important question of his day has, thus, been confined to this single source.

In editing the 1855 **"Woman"** address for publication in the 1903-4 Centenary Edition of his father's writings, Edward Waldo Emerson responded to Higginson's criticism of Cabot's *Memoir.* Cabot, in addition to being Emerson's biographer, was also his literary executor and worked with Edward and Emerson's older daughter, Ellen, in preparing various works for publication both before and after Emerson's death.[5] In his "Notes" to the reprinted version of **"Woman"** in the Centenary Edition, Edward stated that "the only other address on the subject which is known to exist Mr. Cabot did not print probably because Mr. Emerson never delivered it."[6] In fact, the brief address Edward titles "Discours Manqué" and reproduces from manuscript in the Notes (11:627-30) was delivered. On 26 May 1869, at Boston's Horticultural Hall, Emerson joined Wendell Phillips, William Lloyd Garrison, Paulina Wright Davis, and Julia Ward Howe, all prominent advocates of women's rights, and others to celebrate the anniversary of the New England Woman's Suffrage Association. An account of the proceedings, including Emerson's brief speech, is registered in the *Boston Post.*[7] Before turning to the *Post*'s record, however, it is interesting to speculate about what may have led Emerson to that podium by reflecting on the evolution of his thinking on the Woman Question.

. . . . .

Emerson's involvement with the women's movement, although initiated at a later date, approximates the trajectory of his experience with the antislavery movement. Both began with a troubled concern, moved to a reserved commitment, and culminated in unambiguous support. While committed to social reform his entire life, Emerson was always resistant to organized efforts to address a single social ill. He sought a comprehensive reform of American society and this, he felt, could be accomplished only if individuals thoroughly reformed themselves.[8] Thus, in his 1844 lecture **"New England Reformers,"** he stated rather caustically, "when we see an eager assailant of one of these wrongs, a special reformer, we feel like asking him, What right have you, sir, to your one virtue? Is virtue piece-meal? This is a jewel amidst the rags of a beggar."[9]

Emerson also objected to the organizational structure of specific reform efforts. In his view, all organizations tend, by their very nature, to compromise the independence of individual members and also to aggrandize certain leaders. In his 1840 lecture **"Reforms,"** he cautioned, "Accept the reforms but accept not the person of the reformer nor his law. Accept the reform but be thou thyself sacred, intact, inviolable, one whom leaders, one whom multitudes cannot drag from thy central seat. If you take the reform as the reformer brings it to you he transforms you into an instrument."[10] Despite these reservations, however, antislavery drew Emerson irresistibly, and from the mid-1840s to the Civil War, he was an increasingly strong advocate of the cause. Something similar would happen with the women's movement.

The Old Manse, Concord, Massachusetts.

After first experiencing the benefits of organization through their involvement in the antislavery movement, women began to organize to secure their own rights in the late 1840s. The seminal event, of course, was the Seneca Falls Convention in 1848.[11] Thereafter, women began to form activist groups throughout the nation. As the virtual center of the abolition movement, Massachusetts had more than its share. In August 1850, Paulina Wright Davis sent Emerson a copy of a call for the women's rights convention to be held in Worcester, Massachusetts, and appended to it a handwritten note requesting "the sanction of your name and your personal attendance." She signed it, "Yours with much respect, Paulina W. Davis."[12] It is not clear what prompted Davis to solicit Emerson's support at this time, but it is entirely likely that she was aware of his increasingly active role in the antislavery movement and hoped for a similarly sympathetic response to her cause.

Emerson was personally aware of women's special contributions to the antislavery movement. He considered Lucretia Mott a "noble woman," and he had a high regard for Harriet Martineau, the British social reformer and antislavery advocate. His own wife, mother, and, eventually, daughters were early activists in the Women's Anti-slavery Society established in Concord in 1835, and when the Grimké sisters, Angelina and Sarah, lectured on antislavery in Concord, they stayed at the Emersons' home. Emerson's Aunt Mary Moody Emerson, a significant intellectual influence throughout his life, was also an early convert to the cause and encouraged her nephew to make a similar commitment. These women, along with Henry Thoreau's mother and sisters, also members of the Concord Women's Anti-slavery Society, eventually persuaded Emerson to compose his first significant abolition address, **"Emancipation in the British West Indies,"** delivered in Concord on 1 August 1844.[13]

Emerson's reputation as an antislavery advocate was growing throughout the late 1840s, and Davis was undoubtedly aware that his third address celebrating West Indian Emancipation was received in Worcester just a year earlier by a crowd estimated to be over five thousand.[14] Clearly Emerson would be quite a catch for her cause, and Davis's expectations must have mounted as summer waned. On 18 September, Emerson sent his response:

> I have waited a very long time since I had your letter, because I had no clear answer to give, and now I write rather that I may not neglect your letter, than because I have anything very material to say. The fact of the political & civil wrongs of woman I deny not. If women feel wronged, then they are wronged. But the mode of obtaining a redress, namely, a public convention called by women is not very agreeable to me, and the things to be agitated for do not seem to me the best. Perhaps I am superstitious & traditional, but whilst I should vote for every franchise for women,—vote that they should hold property, and vote, yes & be eligible to all offices as men—whilst I should vote thus, if women asked, or if men denied . . . these things, I should not wish women to wish political functions, nor, if granted assume them. I imagine that a woman whom all men would feel to be the best, would decline such privileges if offered, & feel them to be obstacles to her legitimate influence.[15]

Emerson's reservations have nothing to do with the *right* of women to vote, hold property or public office, or generally enjoy the full benefits of citizenship. He fears, rather, that a public role will de-feminize the fairer sex. As Ralph Rusk comments, Emerson "hoped that women would not after all wish an equal share with men in public affairs," for "his imagination balked when he pictured women with masculine aggressiveness wrangling in public."[16] Robert Richardson suggests that in this matter Emerson's views were very similar to Margaret Fuller's. He notes that Fuller had written in "The Great Lawsuit," which was the forerunner of *Woman in the Nineteenth Century,* that "Were they [women] free, were they wise fully to develop the strength and beauty of woman, they would never wish to be men, or man-like."[17] While holding fast to his principles, however, Emerson stopped short of condemning Davis's plan. Indeed, he conceded her right to go forward and pledged a measure of support: "At all events, that I may not stand in the way of any right you are at liberty if you wish it to use my name as one of the inviters of the convention, though I shall not attend it, & shall regret that it is not rather a private meeting of thoughtful persons sincerely interested, instead of what a public meeting is pretty sure to be a heartless noise which we are all ashamed of when it is over."

The following year, 1851, Lucy Stone invited Emerson to another convention for women's rights, also to be held in Worcester. He again declined, but this time he excused himself by noting that he was working on a biography of Margaret Fuller, who had died tragically in May 1850 and whose *Woman in the Nineteenth Century* was already becoming a classic of feminist literature.[18] Expressing full support for the principles of the women's movement in his journal at the time, Emerson observed, "I think that, as

long as they have not equal rights of property & right of voting, they are not on a right footing." He continued, however, "For the rest, I do not think a woman's convention, called in the spirit of this at Worcester, can much avail. It is an attempt to manufacture public opinion, & of course repels all persons who love the simple & direct method." That "simple & direct method" involves the more or less private exercise of the feminine sensibility, the power of sentiment that would, in turn, have a renewing effect on the entire society. Thus, Emerson goes on to comment, "If it were possible to repair the rottenness of human nature, to provide a rejuvenescence, all were well, & no specific reform, no legislation would be needed. For as soon as you have a sound & beautiful woman, a figure in the style of the Antique Juno, Diana, Pallas, Venus, & the Graces, all falls into place, the men are magnetised, heaven opens, & no lawyer need be called in to prepare a clause, for woman moulds the lawgiver."[19] Emerson would later include some of these observations in **"Woman."**

. . . . .

Others attempting to coax Emerson into a more activist position on the Woman Question undoubtedly took heart from the increasing intensity of his public pronouncements on the slavery issue following the passage of the Fugitive Slave Law in September 1850. Emerson's first public response to the law was a letter published in the *Liberator* on 18 April 1851 which urged defiance of "the detestable statute of the last Congress."[20] The next month he delivered an address on the subject, the most vitriolic of his career, which he repeated on several occasions throughout the spring of 1851 as a stump oration in support of John Gorham Palfrey's campaign for Congress on the Free Soil ticket.[21] This highly untypical action by a man who generally avoided the degrading realm of politics reflects the level of Emerson's anxiety over the new aggressiveness of the slave states.

One of those who undoubtedly took notice of Emerson' waxing zeal was Wendell Phillips, the most eloquent of the abolitionist orators, a man Emerson genuinely admired.[22] In January 1853 Phillips wrote to Emerson indicating that it had not been forgotten that he had signed the circular calling for the first women's convention in Massachusetts three years earlier and asking permission to use his name to help draw signatures for a petition to be laid before the state constitutional convention.[23] After considering it, Emerson declined Phillips's request. His explanation is revealing:

> I read the Petition with attention, & with the hope that I should find myself so happy as to do what you bade me. But this is my feeling in regard to the whole matter: I wish that done for their rights which women wish done. If they wish to vote, I shall vote that they vote. If they wish to be lawyers & judges, I shall vote that those careers be opened to them But I do not think that wise & wary women wish to be electors or judges; and I will not ask that they be made such against their will If we obtain for them the ballot, I suppose the best women would not vote. By all means let their rights of

property be put on the same basis as those of men, or, I should say, on a more favorable ground. And let women go to women, & bring us certain tidings what they want, & it will be imperative on me & on us all to help them get it.[24]

In certain respects, Emerson's position resembles the arguments of those who successfully opposed the Equal Rights Amendment in the 1970s.[25] He does not want women forced into accepting the social role and social obligations of males, which today would include being subject to the military draft and in his time involved, more immediately, voting and serving as electors and judges. In other words, Emerson did not feel that the best women would want to participate in the sordid game of politics and, certainly, should not be compelled to do so by the democratic obligations of citizenship. If, however, women decided among themselves that they truly wanted to exercise those rights, Emerson would be moved to support them.

In his response, Phillips addressed Emerson's concerns. "Giving the ballot does not _oblige_ any woman to vote," he reminded the Concordian. "Making women eligible to office does not oblige any one to _take_ office. But _if_ responsibility & interest in great questions be one of the best means of _education_ for the _masses_—we want women to enjoy that advantage as well as men." Phillips goes on to note, "You speak decidedly as to propriety—Is it either _wise_ or _republican_ to make _one class_ or sex dependent for their rights in that respect, on the magnanimity or sense of justice of another class or sex—." Phillips ends his appeal by asking Emerson to forgive him for "troubling you with all this," but, he insists, "It only shows how sincere I believe your note & how confidently I expect your name on some future occasion."[26]

Such appeals, as well as Emerson's accelerating participation in the antislavery movement throughout the early 1850s, undoubtedly had their impact. In June 1855 Paulina Davis once again asked Emerson to participate in the Second Annual New England Women's Rights Convention.

> A meeting was last week held in Boston by several persons engaged in the Woman's Rights Movement at which I was appointed Committee to Correspond with yourself and others relative to a larger meeting to be held in Boston the third week in September. A very unanimous desire was expressed that you should occupy one evening of the day set apart for that gathering, in giving an expression of your views in relation to the great questions involved in this movement in which the whole human race are so deeply interested.
>
> From your well known antecedents we have taken it for granted that your heart is with us, and that you have a message which will aid, cheer, and strengthen us in progress toward perfect freedom and the highest right.[27]

This time Mrs. Davis's appeal fell on a more sympathetic ear, and the result is Emerson's **"Woman"** address. Why he decided to speak on the topic at this time is not perfectly clear, but we might surmise that his continuing in-

volvement in the antislavery movement, in which women played a major role, had something to do with it. Despite the reservations noted earlier, Emerson was becoming less reluctant to speak out on specific social issues, especially the growing slavery crisis. In 1854 he delivered his second address on the Fugitive Slave Law, which was only slightly less vitriolic than the first, and in 1855 he incorporated a major **"Lecture on Slavery"** into his regular lecture offerings, presenting it on several occasions.[28] Of course, issues of individual freedom were involved in the plight of both slaves and women, and Emerson's efforts to articulate that basic human right may be the "well known antecedents" which led Davis to presume a positive response. The convention's roster of major speakers—which included Wendell Phillips, Thomas Wentworth Higginson, Lucy Stone, Caroline Dall, Antoinette L. Brown, and Susan B. Anthony—may also have been persuasive. By this time, Phillips and Higginson had become Emerson's comrades-in-arms in the antislavery movement, and Dall was a protégée of Margaret Fuller's. Moreover, the purpose of the convention was to report, state by state, on the status of New England's laws relating to women's property rights, and Emerson's views on that topic were not in the least ambiguous, as his address, and his earlier comments, make clear.[29]

. . . . .

Emerson's **"Woman"** address has always been somewhat problematic for feminist scholars because in it his emphatic support for the principles of women's rights is matched by equally strong reservations about the wisdom of fully exercising those rights. Women have qualities, he insists, that may prove vulnerable to the hurly-burly of politics. Soon after opening his address, Emerson invokes the authority of the classics. "Plato said, Women are the same as men in faculty, only less in degree. But the general voice of mankind has agreed that they have their own strength; that women are strong by sentiment; that the same mental height which their husbands attain by toil, they attain by sympathy with their husbands. Man is the will, and Woman the sentiment" (11:406-7). For Emerson, the power of sentiment is not insignificant. In fact, it is an expression of mankind's intuitive strength and divinity, one of the core tenets of transcendentalism. For women, this power expresses itself in marriage, art, and education, and through those activities, women play a fundamental part in shaping society. Emerson summarizes this position when he states, "Women are, by this and their social influence, the civilizers of mankind. What is civilization? I answer, the power of good women" (11:409). It is this sensitivity that Emerson fears will be compromised if women pursue a more public role. Still, the essential value of their public participation in the antislavery movement could not be denied. As he notes, "Another step [in the progress of woman in society] was the effect of the action of the age in the antagonism to Slavery. It was easy to enlist Woman in this; it was impossible not to enlist her. But that Cause turned out to be a great scholar. He was a terrible metaphysician. He was a jurist, a poet a divine. Was never a University of Oxford or Göttingen that made such students. It took a man from the plow and made him acute, eloquent, and wise, to the silencing of the doctors. There was nothing it did not pry into, no right it did not explore, no wrong it did not expose. And it has, among its other effects, given Woman a feeling of public duty and an added self-respect" (11:416).

In Emerson's view, women's sympathetic involvement in antislavery had led naturally to their demands for a greater share of rights for themselves as well. He notes, "One truth leads in another by the hand; one right is an accession of strength to take more. And the times are marked by the new attitude of Woman; urging, by argument and by association, her rights of all kinds,—in short, to one half of the world;—as the right to education, to avenues of employment, to equal rights of property, to equal rights in marriage, to the exercise of the professions and of suffrage" (11:416). On all of these issues Emerson is in complete philosophical agreement, and he is unambiguous in his affirmation: Women "have an unquestionable right to their own property. And if a woman demand votes, offices and political equality with men . . . it must not be refused" (11:419). Nonetheless, what is theoretically sound may not be practically so. "The answer that lies, silent or spoken, in the minds of well-meaning persons, to the new claims, is this: that though their mathematical justice is not to be denied, yet the best women do not wish these things; they are asked for by people who intellectually seek them, but who have not the support or sympathy of the truest women; and that, if the laws and customs were modified in the manner proposed, it would embarrass and pain gentle and lovely persons with duties which they would find irksome and distasteful" (11:418-19).

It is not clear with what justification Emerson generalizes his own concerns, expressed earlier in journal comments and letters to Paulina Davis and Wendell Phillips, to "well-meaning persons" at large, but he does go on to answer various specific objections against women's voting, maintaining that the whole process would be much improved through their participation. His concluding comments, however, fall short of a whole-hearted endorsement. "I do not think it yet appears that women wish this equal share in public affairs. But it is they and not we that are to determine it. Let the laws be purged of every barbarous remainder, every barbarous impediment to women. Let the public donations for education be equally shared by them, let them enter a school as freely as a church, let them have and hold and give their property as men do theirs;—and in a few years it will easily appear whether they wish a voice in making the laws that are to govern them" (11:423-24). In the final analysis, Emerson advocates a form of gradualism in the allocation of women's rights. First equal education and property rights, then voting rights, if women so wish. Overall, however, it is women who must dictate the process and the outcome.

Although Emerson's position may appear to be less than liberal by today's standards, during his time he was in the vanguard of women's rights advocates, for he stated un-

equivocally that men have no right to withhold from women the rights they demand. Commentators then and now, however, have shown mixed reactions to the 1855 address. An article appearing in *The Boston Traveller* the next day observed, "The Convention closed last night by a public meeting at the Melodeon, the chief attraction at which consisted in an Address from Ralph Waldo Emerson, and a Poem by Mrs. E. Oakes Smith. The place was crowded, many gentlemen being present who had come with the irreverent motive of laughing at the proceedings." The writer then goes on to note, "Mr. Emerson was introduced, and delivered a very fine oration, full of mythic grandeur and nonsense, but redeemed by passages of great beauty and brilliance. On the whole, it told far more against 'the cause' than for it."[30] Echoing the same sentiment, one contemporary critic describes the address as one which "turned out full of ambivalence and ambiguity and could hardly have satisfied anyone."[31] Another observes that "from a late-twentieth-century perspective, at least, the lecture 'Woman' seems at best condescending."[32] A third critic points out that "this lecture remains obscure even though it is one of the first lectures in support of the woman's movement to be given by a major literary figure." She goes on to note that, "Ironically, but somehow in keeping with this bias, Emerson's lecture has been attacked by feminist critics for its failure to supply a strong foundational 'feminism.'"[33]

Paulina Davis, however, was effusive in expressing to Emerson her gratitude for his address:

> At the close of our meeting I thanked you almost coldly as it seemed to me at the time for your noble words to that audience, but my heart was too full for utterance— There was no language for it but tears and the "public eye" restrained them till in the sacredness of my room I could let them flow while I thanked our Father for his truth and love.

> Our committee met on the following day and I was desired by them to express to you their cordial thanks for your ready compliance with their invitation and for the good service done to our Cause; and at the same time they desired me to request the favor of the address or such parts of it as you might be disposed to have published. . . . We should like to announce that the address will be published should you be so disposed.[34]

In her journal, prominent feminist Caroline Dall, who helped organize and preside over the convention, described Emerson's lecture as "his finished poem." Writing him a short time later, she hoped that he had been properly thanked for his "beautiful address" and that he had been asked to provide a copy for publication. Placing Emerson's words in context, she told him:

> It did not trouble me that some of the papers thought it doubtful, whether you were for us or against us. That was only because they were too heavy to breathe that upper air. Neither was I inclined to quarrel with your estimate of woman per se, though it differs somewhat from my own. In the lowest sense—it has been true of the best women of the past. In one far higher, it may be

true of the best that are to come. That they are fully capable of becoming "innocent citizens" was all we needed you should admit.[35]

It is not clear whether Emerson forwarded his address for publication or not. It is possible that he felt that such occasional forays into the realm of public controversy did not constitute a sufficiently polished example of his social thinking, for he always preferred his more philosophical and circumspect treatments of various subjects such as are represented in his *Essays.* After delivering his 1844 antislavery address, **"Emancipation in the British West Indies,"** for example, he told Thomas Carlyle that "though I sometimes accept a popular call, & preach on Temperance or the Abolition of slavery, as lately on the First of August, I am sure to feel before I have done with it, what an intrusion it is into another sphere & so much loss of virtue in my own."[36] Indeed, many of Emerson's antislavery addresses were not published in his lifetime. One of the most important, the 1855 **"Lecture on Slavery,"** was not published until 1995.[37] It is also possible that Emerson felt that the publication of detailed accounts of his presentation, such as that found in the *Boston Telegraph,* sufficiently indicated his views.[38]

Other than repeating his **"Woman"** address before the Parker Fraternity on 2 December 1860, Emerson apparently offered no further formal public statement on the Woman Question for fourteen years.[39] It is entirely possible that he was preoccupied with his continuing service in the cause of antislavery, which was, in its own way, also the cause of woman. Caroline Dall felt that Emerson's views on the Woman Question continued to liberalize following his 1855 address. On 12 February 1858, Dall addressed a joint committee of the Massachusetts legislature on the subject of women's rights. She was pleased when, some two months later, Emerson complimented her on her presentation, which he had read and admired.[40] In his 1867 **"Progress of Culture"** lecture to the Phi Beta Kappa Society at Harvard, Emerson heralded the women's movement as a sign of America's advancement. "The new claim of woman to a political status," he said, "is itself an honorable testimony to the civilization which has given her a civil status new in history." The progressive development of women's rights, which he had envisioned in his 1855 address, was now nearing its conclusion. "Now that by the increased humanity of law she controls her property, she inevitably takes the next step to her share in power" (8:208). Dall, who attended the event, was delighted when Emerson "turned slightly" towards her while making this comment.[41]

Emerson's evolving views on the Woman Question were undoubtedly influenced by a number of factors. Women's contributions to the campaign against slavery, and their unselfish labors in support of the Union cause, continued to impress him. Moreover, these activist women seemed to suffer no diminution of their sympathetic capacities; in fact, abolitionism seemed to provide them with a proper sphere for exercising those qualities. Thus, early in the

Civil War, in January 1862, when Emerson traveled to Washington to promote emancipation, a Unionist goal that would not be officially declared for another nine months, he acknowledged the vital role of women in the cause. In the context of his speech on **"American Civilization,"** Emerson asserts that there have always been two distinct cultures in America, "the feudal one of the slave States, and the progressive one of the free States." Among the characteristics of the superior civilization of the North, Emerson notes the prevalence of road building, commerce, agriculture, the post office, a cheap press, the division of labor, and "the right position of woman in society." This last point was made emphatically enough that one reporter later commented that "The lecturer had thought that it was a sufficient definition of civilization to term it the influence of good women," a point he had made seven years earlier in his **"Woman"** address.[42] In more specific terms, Emerson was quite aware of the inestimable service rendered by women through the Sanitary Commission, as nurses, administrators, and inspectors; through the Freedman's Bureau, as teachers of emancipated slaves; and through the various "home front" organizations, which provided supplies ranging from clothing to bandages for the Union army. Concord's was one of the most active of these organizations, and all the Emerson women took part in it.[43] In his 1863 address, "Fortune of the Republic," Emerson observed that "the women have shown a tender patriotism, and an inexhaustible charity."[44]

Following the war, the women's suffrage movement continued to gain momentum. The abolition of slavery having been achieved, reformers focused their attentions on a campaign to liberate American women. The similarities between the two causes seemed obvious and compelling to many. Harriet Beecher Stowe, for example, noted in an article on "The Woman Question," published in *Hearth and Home,* that "The position of a married woman, under English common law, is, in many respects, precisely similar to that of the negro slave."[45] Aware, no doubt, of Emerson's notable service in the cause of antislavery, and his previous contributions to the cause of women's rights, activists once more appealed to him for public support. He was persuaded. Emerson agreed to speak, for the second time in his career, on the Woman Question. The complete text of his 1869 speech is as follows:

> Ladies and Gentlemen—It seems unnecessary to add any words to the statements and arguments which you have already heard, and I certainly shall do but little more than to express my sympathy and my delight in the rightness of this movement—the rightness of this action, as it is shown by the discourses which you have just listened to. There seems little to say and it ought directly be put to vote. I think that the action of this Society, the sentiment of this assembly, is by no means a whim; but is an organized policy—slow, cumulative, and reaching a greater height of health and strength than hitherto. I think we all feel the necessity of the admission into our colleges of the two partners in the activity of this world. We look upon the man as the representative of intellect and the woman as the representative of affection; but each shares the charac-

teristics of the other, only in the man one predominates and in the woman the other. We know woman as affectionate, as religious, as oracular, as delighting in grace and order possessed of taste. In all ages woman has been the representative of religion. In all countries it is the women who fill the temples. In every religious movement the woman has been an active and powerful part, not only in those in the most civilized, but in the most uncivilized countries; not less in the Mahommedan than the Greek and Roman religions. She holds a man to religion. There is no man so reprobate, so careless of religious duty, but what delights to have his wife a saint. All men feel the advantages that abound of that quality in a woman. I think it was her instinct in the dark superstitions of the Middle Ages which tempered the hardness of the theology by making the Virgin Mary, the mother of God, the intercessor to whom all prayers were directed. My own feeling is that in all ages woman has held substantially the same influence. I think that superior women are rare as superior men are rare. I think that women feel when they are in the press, as men of genius are said to do among energetic workers,—that they see through all these efforts with finer eyes than their noisy masters. I think that all men in the presence of the best women feel over-looked and judged, and sometimes sentenced. They are the educators in all our society. Through their sympathy and quickness they are the proper mediators between those who have knowledge and those who want it; but what I would say is that in this movement an important part of the history of woman is the history of the Quakers, and then of the Shakers, who gave an equal part of their power to the elderess and the elder, and so made active and instructed workmen and workwomen in social and public affairs. When the great enterprise of recent civilization, the putting down of slavery,—of that institution, so called, was done, it was done, as you know, in this country, by a society whose executive committee was composed of men and women, and every step was taken by both. So they hung together till success was achieved. This was getting instruction of our sisters in the direction and control of important affairs, and now at the moment when we are agitating the question of how to save society from the threatened mischief of the invasion of the purity of the ballot, by corrupt and purchased votes, and thus stultifying the will of the honest community—now, at this moment, woman asks for her vote. If the vote is to be granted to woman, and certainly it must be, then we must arrange to have the voting clean and honest and polite. The State must build houses, instead of dirty rooms and corner shops; the State must build palaces and halls in which women can deposit their votes in the presence of their sons and brothers and fathers. The effect of that reform upon the general voting of the State all can feel. But it isn't for me at this time, after what you have heard, to detain you longer. I only feel the gladness with which such representations as you have heard, such arguments as you have heard, inspire me. It is certain that what is not given to-day will be given to-morrow, and what is asked for this year will be given in the next year; if not in the next year then in the next lustrum. The claim now pressed by woman is a claim for nothing less than all, than her share in all. She asks for her property; she asks for her rights, for her vote; she asks for her share

in education, for her share in all the institutions of society, for her half of the whole world; and to this she is entitled.[46]

Despite his well-known reservations about organized reform efforts, at the conclusion of the meeting Ralph Waldo Emerson allowed himself to be elected a vice-president of the New England Woman's Suffrage Association.[47]

While there are some similarities between the 1869 address and the 1855 **"Woman,"** it is obvious that Emerson's position on the Woman Question had changed significantly. One of the most striking differences between this and the earlier address is the total lack of qualification regarding women's right to full participation in the political process. Emerson leaves no doubt that women, even the best women, want and deserve the right to vote. Indeed, they are not just entitled to but have earned their rights. In the manuscript version of the speech, Emerson refers specifically to the means by which they have done so. "Civilization is progressive," he notes. "One truth leads in another by the hand, & her activity in putting an end to Slavery; & in serving the Hospitals of the Sanitary Commission in the war & in the labors of the Freedman's bureau have opened her eyes to larger rights & duties. They claim now her full rights of all kinds,—to education, to employment to equal laws of property."[48]

In addition to their exemplary service, women had, as Emerson stipulated in his 1855 address, demonstrated their commitment to securing their own rights, and they had done so patiently. "[I]n a few years it will easily appear whether they wish a voice in making the laws that are to govern them" (11:424), Emerson had stated in 1855. The years had passed, and it was now manifest that women, indeed, did want the right to vote, and they had said so consistently and eloquently, both in public and, as Emerson must have surmised from his own experience, in private as well. His wife, Lidian, "became a strong supporter of women's rights," according to Robert Richardson, while daughter Edith was in favor, and only Ellen opposed.[49] Emerson's views of what "the best women" might want as their proper rights having thus altered and the terms for offering his support having been fulfilled, he held true to his promise to affirm women's right to vote without hesitation or qualification.

Following his 1869 address, and to the end of his life in 1882, Emerson was consistently regarded as a friend to the cause of women's rights. Shortly after his address, Harriet Beecher Stowe approached Emerson about the possibility of writing a two-column article on woman suffrage for *Hearth and Home,* for which he would be paid fifty dollars. She indicated in her letter that his name and philosophical balance might win the ear of "fastidious circles" and "take [suffrage] out of the sphere of ridicule into that of rational consideration." Emerson declined the request, citing other commitments that demanded all of his available time.[50]

Numerous articles in the *Woman's Journal,* a suffragist publication, testified over the next several years that Emerson was held in high esteem by the women reformers who knew him.[51] Their admiration is conveyed in a memorial article, written by Julia Ward Howe, which was published in May 1882, just weeks after his death. It stands as a fitting conclusion to our examination of Emerson and the Woman Question.

> Among all of Mr. Emerson's great merits, we of this *Journal* must especially mention his loyalty to woman. As tenderly conservative in nature as he was boldly original in thought, Mr. Emerson would have shrunk most sensitively from any infraction of the sacred sphere of womanhood. He knew and cherished all the feminine graces. But justice, as well as beauty, was to him a feminine ideal. He believed in woman's power to hold and adjust for herself the scales in which character is weighed against attraction. At more than one woman suffrage meeting, he has entered his protest against the political inequality which still demoralizes society. Some of us remember the sweet *naif* manner in which he did this, the sincerity and the measure with which he spoke, as if urged and restrained by a weight of conviction which called for simple and solemn utterance.
>
> He was for us, knowing well enough our limitations and short-comings, and his golden words have done much both to fit us for the larger freedom, and to know that it belongs to us.[52]

Notes

1. "Emerson as the Reformer," *Boston Daily Advertiser,* 23 May 1903, p. 1. Higginson (1823-1911), an 1847 graduate of Harvard Divinity School, left the ministry, in part because of the unpopularity of his strong antislavery views. He participated in the 1854 forceful and unsuccessful attempt to free fugitive slave Anthony Burns from a Federal Court House in Boston, and he served as a colonel in a Negro Regiment during the Civil War. He was, like many abolitionists, a strong supporter of women's rights. In 1896 he presented to the Boston Public Library his "Galatea collection of books relating to the history of women," numbering about one thousand volumes.

2. Oliver Wendell Holmes, *Ralph Waldo Emerson* (Boston: Houghton, Mifflin and Co., 1884); James Elliot Cabot, *A Memoir of Ralph Waldo Emerson,* 2 vols. (Boston: Houghton, Mifflin and Co., 1887).

3. Emerson's substantial contributions to the antislavery movement are documented in detail in my *Virtue's Hero: Emerson, Antislavery, and Reform* (Athens: University of Georgia Press, 1990) as well as my and Joel Myerson's edition of *Emerson's Antislavery Writings* (New Haven: Yale University Press, 1995). Emerson's social reform activities also receive substantial consideration in such recent biographies and studies as Robert Richardson's *Emerson: The Mind on Fire* (Berkeley: University of California Press, 1995); David Robinson's *Emerson and the Conduct of Life* (New York: Cambridge University Press, 1993); Merton M. Sealts, Jr.'s

Emerson on the Scholar (Columbia: University of Missouri Press, 1992); and Barbara Ryan's "Emerson's 'Domestic and Social Experiments': Service, Slavery, and the Unheard Man," *American Literature* 66 (September 1994): 485-508.

The political ramifications of Emerson's reform philosophy are considered in John Carlos Rowe's *At Emerson's Tomb: The Politics of Classic American Literature* (New York: Columbia University Press, 1997); Richard Teichgraeber's *Sublime Thoughts/Penny Wisdom: Situating Emerson and Thoreau in the American Market* (Baltimore: Johns Hopkins University Press, 1995); Stanley Cavell's *Philosophical Passages* (Cambridge: Blackwell, 1995); and George Kateb's *Emerson and Self-Reliance* (Thousand Oaks, Calif.: Sage Press, 1995).

4. See Joel Myerson, *Ralph Waldo Emerson: A Descriptive Bibliography* (Pittsburgh: University of Pittsburgh Press, 1982), pp. 375, 680.

5. For a comprehensive discussion of Cabot's seminal role in shaping, or misshaping, the Emerson canon in the late nineteenth century, see Nancy Craig Simmons, "Arranging the Sibylline Leaves: James Elliot Cabot's Work as Emerson's Literary Executor," in *Studies in the American Renaissance,* ed. Joel Myerson (Charlottesville: University Press of Virginia, 1983), pp. 335-89.

6. *The Complete Works of Ralph Waldo Emerson,* ed. Edward Waldo Emerson, 12 vols. (Boston: Houghton, Mifflin and Co., 1903-4), 11:625-26. All subsequent references to this edition of Emerson's works will appear parenthetically in the text.

7. *Boston Post,* 27 May 1869, p. 1. A brief account of Emerson's address also appears in the *Springfield Republican,* 27 May 1869, p. 2, and the *Boston Daily Advertiser,* 27 May 1869, p. 1.

8. For a detailed discussion of Emerson's philosophy of reform, see my *Virtue's Hero.*

9. *The Collected Works of Ralph Waldo Emerson,* ed. Alfred R. Ferguson et al., 5 vols. to date (Cambridge: Belknap Press of Harvard University Press, 1971-), 3:155.

10. *The Early Lectures of Ralph Waldo Emerson,* ed. Robert Spiller et al., 3 vols. (Cambridge: Harvard University Press, 1959-72), 3:260.

11. For a full accounting of this important gathering, see *The Birth of American Feminism: The Seneca Falls Woman's Convention of 1848,* ed. Virginia Bernhard and Elizabeth Fox-Genovese (St. James, N.Y.: Brandywine Press, 1995).

12. Pauline W. Davis to Ralph Waldo Emerson, [August 1850], bMS Am 1280 (775), Ms. Houghton Library, Harvard University, Cambridge, Mass. Quoted by permission of the Houghton Library and the Ralph Waldo Emerson Memorial Association.

Paulina Wright Davis (1813-76) was a prominent feminist leader who once participated in Margaret Fuller's Boston "Conversations." See Charles Capper, *Margaret Fuller, An American Romantic Life: The Private Years* (New York: Oxford University Press, 1992), p. 306.

13. See my *Virtue's Hero,* pp. 361, 29, 10, 27-28, 25-26. See also Gougeon and Myerson, *Emerson's Antislavery Writings,* p. xxxvii, and, for the 1844 Emancipation Address, pp. 7-33. For a detailed discussion of Mary Moody Emerson's antislavery interests, see Phyllis Cole, *Mary Moody Emerson and the Origins of Transcendentalism* (New York: Oxford University Press, 1998).

14. Gougeon and Myerson, *Emerson's Antislavery Writings,* p. 211. For the complete address, see pp. 47-50.

15. *The Letters of Ralph Waldo Emerson,* ed. Ralph Rusk and Eleanor Tilton, 10 vols. (New York: Columbia University Press, 1939-95), 4:229-30. Excerpts from this letter were published by Cabot in his *Memoir* (pp. 455-56) to indicate Emerson's views on the women's movement generally. Many advocates of women's rights, in addition to Thomas Wentworth Higginson, objected to that choice as a gross misrepresentation.

16. Ralph Rusk, *The Life of Ralph Waldo Emerson* (New York: Columbia University Press, 1949), p. 370.

17. Richardson, *Emerson: Mind on Fire,* p. 533.

18. Gay Wilson Allen, *Waldo Emerson: A Biography* (New York: Viking Press, 1981), p. 559. Emerson's letter to Lucy Stone was published in the *New York Tribune,* 17 October 1851, p. 7. See also *Emerson's Letters,* 8:288.

19. *The Journals and Miscellaneous Notebooks of Ralph Waldo Emerson,* ed. William H. Gilman et al., 16 vols. (Cambridge: Harvard University Press, 1960-82), 11:444.

20. See Gougeon and Myerson, *Emerson's Antislavery Writings,* pp. 51-52, for the letter.

21. For the story of Emerson's only political campaign, see my *Virtue's Hero,* pp. 166-67. For the address, formally titled "An Address to the Citizens of Concord on the Fugitive Slave Law," see Gougeon and Myerson, *Emerson's Antislavery Writings,* pp. 53-72.

22. Wendell Phillips (1811-84) was an early advocate of women's rights as well as abolition. When he attended the world antislavery convention in London in 1840, he openly advocated the eligibility of women as delegates. Emerson was an early admirer of Phillips's abolition efforts and his eloquence. In 1845 Emerson became embroiled in a controversy in his hometown of Concord by insisting, successfully, that Phillips be allowed to speak at the local Lyceum on the topic of slavery. See my *Virtue's Hero,* pp. 95-96.

23. Emerson, *Letters,* 4:345.

24. Emerson, *Letters,* 8:360.

25. For an interesting discussion of this issue, see Janet K. Boles, *The Politics of the Equal Rights Amendment* (New York: Longman, 1979), pp. 170-80.

26. Wendell Phillips to Emerson, 21 February 1853, bMS Am 1280 (2544), Ms. Houghton Library. Quoted with permission of the Houghton Library and the Ralph Waldo Emerson Memorial Association.

27. Paulina Wright Davis to Emerson, 7 June 1855, bMS Am 1280 (7740), Ms. Houghton Library. Quoted with permission of Houghton Library and the Ralph Waldo Emerson Memorial Association.

28. William Charvat, *Emerson's American Lecture Engagements: A Chronological List* (New York: New York Public Library, 1961), pp. 30-31. For the complete text of Emerson's important 1855 "Lecture on Slavery," see *Emerson's Antislavery Writings,* pp. 91-106, where it is published for the first time. For the story of his increasing antislavery activity in the mid 1850s, see my *Virtue's Hero,* pp. 187-249.

29. Richardson, *Emerson: Mind on Fire,* p. 532.

30. Reprinted in *Transcendental Log,* ed. Kenneth Walter Cameron (Hartford: Transcendental Books, 1973), p. 99.

31. Albert J. von Frank, *An Emerson Chronology* (New York: G. K. Hall & Co., 1994), p. 301.

32. Helen R. Deese, "'A Liberal Education': Caroline Healey Dall and Emerson," in *Emersonian Circles: Essays in Honor of Joel Myerson,* ed. Wesley T. Mott and Robert E. Burkholder (Rochester: University of Rochester Press, 1997), p. 248. This excellent essay presents an insightful discussion of Emerson's relationship with one of the most significant feminists of his time.

33. Christina Zwarg, "Emerson's 'Scene' Before the Women: The Feminist Poetics of Paraphernalia," *Social Text* 18 (Winter 1987/88): 133. Zwarg herself presents a generally positive analysis of the address in her insightful essay. See also her *Feminist Conversations: Fuller, Emerson, and the Play of Reading* (Ithaca: Cornell University Press, 1995) for Fuller's feminist influence on Emerson.

34. Davis to Emerson, 29 September 1855, bMS Am 1280 (775), Ms. Houghton Library. Quoted with permission of Houghton Library and the Ralph Waldo Emerson Memorial Association. Davis published *The Una,* "A Paper Dedicated to the Celebration of Woman," in Providence, R.I., from 1853 to 1855. The final issue, published on 15 October 1855 (vol. 3, no. 10), was prepared by Caroline Dall in the absence of Davis. It indicates that reports on

the speeches from the convention would follow in a later edition because "upon examining the phonographic report, it was found that the reporter had given the speakers credit for MS. in several instances where it did not exist. This inadvertent compliment to the fluency of the Convention is extremely inconvenient, inasmuch as it will compel much unexpected labor." Unfortunately, the later edition, in which Emerson's "Woman" most likely would have appeared, never materialized, probably because a number of speakers were unable or unwilling to reconstruct their oral deliveries on paper.

35. Quoted by Deese, in "A Liberal Education," p. 248.

36. *The Correspondence of Emerson and Carlyle,* ed. Joseph Slater (New York: Columbia University Press, 1964), p. 373.

37. Gougeon and Myerson, *Emerson's Antislavery Writings,* pp. 91-106.

38. Eventually, however, at least a portion of the "Woman" address was published by the women. An article in the *Woman's Journal,* 26 March 1881, titled, "Mr. Emerson on Woman Suffrage," states, "In 1862 there was a proposition to establish a Woman Suffrage paper in this city [Boston]. Several articles were contributed for it, but the idea was not carried out, and the papers remained unpublished. The following from Ralph Waldo Emerson is characteristic and as valuable now as then" (p. 100). The article then presents a long excerpt from "Woman" focusing on the suffrage issue. This excerpt was later reprinted as a leaflet titled *A Reasonable Reform* (New York: National Woman Suffrage Publishing Co., 1881).

Also, a later article in the same journal (24 September 1887) complains, as Higginson did, about the misrepresentation of Emerson's views on the women's movement in James Elliot Cabot's *Memoir.* As a corrective, the writer quotes briefly from Emerson's "Woman" address and prefaces the quote with the notation that Emerson "put himself on the record in a statement so admirable that it has been published by the suffragists as a leaflet" (p. 312).

39. See Charvat, *Emerson's Lecture Engagements,* p. 37. Most Boston newspapers took no notice of Emerson's presentation at the time, perhaps because they were preoccupied with numerous reports on secessionist fever, which was beginning to sweep the South. There were also numerous notices of John Brown and anti-John Brown meetings in the Boston area. However, the *Boston Atlas and Bee* of 3 December 1860 ran the following short notice of Emerson's talk: "Mr. Emerson gave a lecture yesterday forenoon, in Music Hall, before Theodore Parker's society, on 'Woman.' It was a characteristic production. The central idea of the lecture was that whatever contributes to the well being and

progress of man, does so to woman. Incidentally he remarked that the 'masculine' woman is not so strong in influence as the lady. He favored so much of the woman's rights movement as to give woman entire justice. If she is to be taxed she should vote" (p. 3).

40. Deese, "A Liberal Education," p. 249.

41. Deese, "A Liberal Education," p. 250.

42. Emerson lectured at the Smithsonian on 31 January 1862. A detailed report of his presentation appeared in the *Washington Evening Star,* 1 February 1862, p. 1, which is the source of the quotations here. The speech was later published as "American Civilization" in the *Atlantic Monthly,* April 1862, pp. 502-11. It was eventually divided into two parts and published as "Civilization" in *Society and Solitude (Complete Works,* 7:19-34) and "American Civilization" in *Miscellanies (Complete Works,* 11:295-311).

43. The "Concord Soldier's Aid Society" was a women's organization which was established in 1861 to supply the needs of soldiers in the Concord Artillery. However, by 1862 the society was preparing boxes of goods to benefit all soldiers served by the U.S. Sanitary Commission. Members included Mrs. Ralph Waldo Emerson, Misses Ellen and Edith Emerson, Mrs. Amos Bronson Alcott, Miss Elizabeth Hoar, and others. The Society raised money through dues, donations, collections at local churches, and benefits such as theatrical productions, tea parties, Fourth of July festivals, dances, etc. (See Concord Soldier's Aid Society Records, 1861-65, Concord Free Public Library, Concord, Mass.)

44. *Emerson's Antislavery Writings,* p. 152.

45. Quoted by Joan D. Hedrick, in her *Harriet Beecher Stowe: A Life* (New York: Oxford University Press, 1994), p. 360.

46. A comparison of this newspaper account with the transcription of the "Discours Manqué" manuscript provided by Edward Waldo Emerson in volume eleven, "Miscellanies," of the Centenary Edition, as well as the original manuscript at the Houghton Library, bMS Am 1280.202 (13), which is somewhat longer, suggests that the "Discours" Edward Emerson and James Elliot Cabot assumed was never delivered served as the basis for Emerson's second address on the Woman Question. The original manuscript and the newspaper account are similar in terms of the major points made. The wording varies in some instances, which could represent Emerson's improvisations at the moment of delivery. Also, some points were repeated from the 1855 "Woman" address, which was considerably longer. These are also materials in the original manuscript which do not appear in the newspaper account and which may have been omitted due to the limitations

of time as suggested by Emerson's desire not to "detain" his audience. Fortunately, a modern and carefully edited edition of both "Woman" and "Discours Manqué" will soon be available in *Emerson's Later Lectures,* edited by Ronald Bosco and Joel Myerson.

47. *Boston Daily Advertiser,* 27 May 1869, p. 1.

48. bMS Am 1280.202 (13), Ms. Houghton Library. Quoted with permission of the Houghton Library and the Ralph Waldo Emerson Memorial Association. See *Complete Works,* 11:629, for Edward's slightly different rendering of this passage.

49. Richardson, *Emerson: Mind on Fire,* p. 534.

50. Hedrick, *Harriet Beecher Stowe,* p. 361. Emerson was also requested in July to make a presentation to the Essex County Woman's Suffrage Association. In his letter declining that invitation, Emerson asks his correspondent to "say to the Essex County Woman's Suffrage Association, that while I think their political claim founded in equity, and though perhaps it does not yet appear to any what precise form in practice it will and ought to take, yet the seriousness and thoughtfulness with which it is urged seem to me to mark an important step in civilization." This letter, which obviously pleased the women, was read at the convention in Newburyport, Mass., and published in both the *Boston Daily Advertiser* and the *New York Times* (*Letters,* 6:77-78). A writer for the *Philadelphia Inquirer* (31 July 1869, p. 4), however, saw the letter as evidence that Emerson "does not regard their claims to vote as at all pressing, and thinks he has work on hand more important than assisting in furthering it." He goes on to express his hope that "the prime movers in this agitation will carefully review their crude and hasty conclusions in the light of Mr. Emerson's short, but pithy letter."

51. *Woman's Journal* was published in Boston, Mass., Chicago, Ill., and St. Louis, Mo., variously, between 1870 and 1912. The following articles from the *Woman's Journal* present very positive views on Emerson and his consistent support of the women's movement. The list is not intended to be exhaustive. "Tested by Time," 1 January 1876, p. 1; "Mr. Emerson on Suffrage," 26 March 1881, p. 100; "Bereaved Nations," 29 April 1882, p. 1; "Obituary: Ralph Waldo Emerson," 6 May 1882, p. 140; "The King Is Dead," 20 May 1882, pp. 158-59; "Concord School of Philosophy," 19 August 1882, p. 257; "Literary Notices, Review of James Elliot Cabot's, *A Memoir of Ralph Waldo Emerson,*" 24 September 1887, p. 312; "Editorial Notes" (complains about the misrepresentation of Emerson's views on woman suffrage in biographies and the popular press).

52. *Woman's Journal,* 6 May 1882, p. 140.

Saundra Morris (essay date 1999)

SOURCE: "'Metre-Making' Arguments: Emerson's Poems," in *The Cambridge Companion to Ralph Waldo Emerson,* edited by Joel Porte and Saundra Morris, Cambridge University Press, 1999, pp. 218-42.

[In the following essay, Morris presents an overview of Emerson's poetical works.]

"I am not the man you take me for."

Consideration of Emerson's writings without significant emphasis on his verse would in some ways produce *Hamlet* without the prince, for Emerson seems to have identified himself primarily as a poet. During his New York lecture tour of March 1842, he wrote to his wife Lidian of feeling alienated from and misunderstood by his dinner companions, the social reformers Horace Greeley and Albert Brisbane:

> They are bent on popular action: I am in all my theory, ethics, & politics a poet and of no more use in their New York than a rainbow or a firefly. Meantime they fasten me in their thought to "Transcendentalism" whereof you know I am wholly guiltless, and which is spoken of as a known & fixed element like salt or meal: so that I have to begin by endless disclaimers & explanations—"I am not the man you take me for."
>
> (*LA* 3: 18)[1]

By "poet," Emerson didn't mean exclusively a writer of verse, but instead a person whose energy was fundamentally both iconoclastic and—as he emphasizes in his lecture and essay **"The Poet"**—affirmative, creative, and imaginative. For Emerson, the best preachers, the best scholars, and even the best social activists are all poets. In the Divinity School **"Address,"** he calls for the preacher to be "a newborn bard of the Holy Ghost" (*LA* 89); in **"Literary Ethics,"** he speaks of "immortal bards of philosophy" (*LA* 98). In **"The Method of Nature,"** whoever seeks to realize his "best insight" becomes one of the "higher poets" (*LA* 131); in **"Heroism,"** the life of the great person is "natural and poetic" (*LA* 376); and the **"Representative Man"** Plato, although not literally a poet, is "clothed with the powers of a poet, stands upon the highest place of the poet" (*LA* 635). This inclusive use of its terminology shows how important Emerson felt poetry to be, and how closely he identified himself with it.

Not only was Emerson consistently referred to and thought of in his own time as a *poet*-essayist, his verse has exerted a persistent influence on other poets. It is so much like that of his admirer Emily Dickinson that readers often mistakenly attributed her anonymously published "Success is counted sweetest" to him.[2] Later, Emerson's fellow poet-essayist George Santayana chose to speak on "Emerson the Poet" during the 1903 Harvard Memorial Week celebration of the centennial of Emerson's birth. An twentieth-century poets who have admired the verse include, among many others, E. A. Robinson, Robert Frost, and A. R. Ammons.

Nonetheless, modern readers and scholars have tended to view his poetry as secondary to the "essential" Emerson. Until very recently, no current edition of the poems was available, and even now just three modern book-length studies of them exist, all dating from the 1970s.[3] This imbalance of attention, however, is beginning to be corrected. New primary material is being published, including the Library of America ***Emerson: Collected Poems and Translations*** and a forthcoming edition of the poems in the Harvard ***Collected Works***; the poems are receiving more extensive representation in anthologies; and significant critical analyses are emerging.

Such "recovery" is fitting. Emerson wrote poetry from the time he was a boy to nearly the end of his life, penning thousands of lines (both original and translated) into his journals and notebooks—particularly into the ***Poetry Notebooks,*** which span half a century.[4] Using much the same method of composition as he did for his prose, Emerson would often record his initial inspiration or a preliminary draft, then later shape the material into finished pieces. He published these gleanings for over half a century, from 1829 to 1880, seeing into print more than 200 poems and translations.

Emerson collected his verse into two major volumes, both published at the urging of his admirers and after his enshrinement as an important literary figure. ***Poems,*** dated 1847 (it actually was printed in December 1946), contains 256 pages, with 56 poems and two translations. ***May-Day and Other Pieces,*** a smaller book of 205 pages, was published 20 years later, in 1867. Many of the poems in both volumes had appeared previously in giftbook anthologies or little magazines—most frequently *The Dial,* edited by Emerson and Margaret Fuller, for ***Poems***; and James Russell Lowell's the *Atlantic Monthly,* for ***May-Day.*** A section of ***May-Day*** had also been published in Emerson's prose collections as individual epigraphs, for, in a virtually unprecedented gesture that I will discuss below, Emerson prefaced many of his essays with original poems.

The first of Emerson's books of poetry, the 1847 ***Poems,*** contains the majority of his most famous pieces—works such as **"The Sphinx," "The Rhodora," "Uriel," "The Snow-Storm," "Bacchus," "Hamatreya," "Threnody,"** and the Concord **"Hymn."** While its earliest text is **"Good-Bye,"** dating from 1823, the volume also includes several significant poems composed in the 1830s (**"Each and All," "The Rhodora,"** and Concord **"Hymn,"** for example).[5] However, most of the compositions were written in the 1840s, during Emerson's editorship of the *The Dial,* and first appeared there (they are thus in a sense "occasional" pieces—done particularly for publication in *The Dial*). The second volume, ***May-Day,*** is generally considered a less groundbreaking work—its poems are smoother and more conventional overall—but it nonetheless contains a substantial number of important texts, among them **"Brahma," "Days," "Voluntaries,"** and **"Terminus."** Of the 30-some poems, excluding translations, that Emerson published but did not collect in these two books, eight appear in the 1876 ***Selected Poems*** that he prepared with his daughter Ellen and his friend James Elliot Cabot, and 15 more are printed as essay epigraphs.

This poetic canon displays considerable range. It contains quatrains and long poems; rhymed, blank, and experimental verse; patriotic tributes, social protest poems, and Romantic lyrics; elegies, free translations, love poems, and hymns. Its tones are alternately comic, meditative, narrative, and oracular. At the same time, the pieces coalesce around a set of recurrent issues and strategies central to a poem that Emerson repeatedly positioned at the thresholds of his volumes of verse, **"The Sphinx."** This piece opens Emerson's 1847 ***Poems,*** his ***Selected Poems,*** and the volume of poetry in the first edition of his collected works.[6] Following Emerson's lead, I, too, begin with **"The Sphinx,"** and employ it in this essay as an interpretive paradigm for Emerson's poetry as a whole, for individual poems, and for the essay epigraphs.[7]

Originally published in the third issue of *The Dial* (January 1841), the 132-line, 17-stanza narrative is quite literally a "metre-making argument"[8] between a contemptuous Sphinx and an indomitably cheerful poet. At the beginning of the poem, the "drowsy" and brooding Sphinx calls for a "'seer'" to answer her "'secret,'" and thereby bring her health and animation. When she goes on to taunt humanity for its ineptitude and impotence, a mysterious "great mother" joins in to lament the condition of her juvenilized "'boy,'" humankind. As though to refute their claims, a cheerful and confident poet appears, who praises and blesses the Sphinx. In response, the Sphinx utters an enigmatic pronouncement and soars away, evanescing into the universe.

Its notable degree of undecidability and the richness of the mythological material upon which it draws combine to make **"The Sphinx"** a highly suggestive choice for what I have called a "threshold poem." I use this term to identify a distinct yet previously unrecognized genre of poetry encompassing various types of introductory verse: initial sonnets, seventeenth-century emblem-book inscriptions, epic invocations to muses, the prothalamion and epithalamion, and other poems of dedication, preface, and prologue. A particular subgroup within this broad, highly self-reflexive tradition are those poems that function, like **"The Sphinx,"** to initiate volumes of poetry.

"The Sphinx" also exemplifies another distinctive (yet overlapping) form of threshold poem. In thematizing the difficulty of poetic expression, it claims a place in the tradition of poems about the inability to write or the absence of inspiration—Milton's sonnet on his blindness, for example, or Coleridge's "Dejection: An Ode." Often these works, like **"The Sphinx,"** function as threshold pieces for volumes of verse. We might think of Sidney's first *As-*

trophil and Stella sonnet, which both begins the sequence and voices anxiety about the poet's ability to begin; or Bradstreet's poetic preface to *The Tenth Muse,* which questions her ability to write poetry even as it introduces the poetry she has written. Since the answer to their dilemma is creation, a remedy provided by the poems themselves, the category is by definition both ironic and paradoxical: these are poems about their own impossibility. Such is, of course, especially the case with *threshold* poems about lack of inspiration, for these texts "answer" blockage both through their own existence and through the verses they introduce. **"The Sphinx"** provides a consummate instance of this variant.

Emerson's threshold poem is also provocative because it participates in a recurrent preoccupation of its time. Nineteenth-century American writers were especially enticed by the Sphinx figure, bestowing upon it the primary regard that we, following Freud, have tended to grant Oedipus. Melville's chapter "The Sphynx" in *Moby-Dick,* for example, depicts the sperm whale's head as a Sphinx; in Poe's riddling short story "The Sphinx," the conundrum is an inscrutable and deadly disease; and Elizabeth Stuart Phelps employs the image of the Sphinx to represent women's struggle for self-expression in her novel *The Story of Avis* (originally entitled *The Story of the Sphinx*). And countless other "Sphinx"es appear in periodical literature of the time.

As befits its subject, Emerson's **"The Sphinx"** has always been considered especially puzzling, even for the notoriously enigmatic Emerson. Despite the abundance of critical attention the poem has received, scholars continue to debate precisely what the Sphinx is supposed to represent, what her question is, and whether the poet's reply to her is astute or absurd.[9] When he encounters her, instead of reinscribing the Sphinx's traditional association with death, the poet affirms her ("'Say on, sweet Sphinx! thy dirges / Are pleasant songs to me'"). He identifies her as idealism, the "'love of the Best'" that paradoxically can silence with castigation, but that is also the only impetus for self-improvement.

The Sphinx responds by confirming the poet's answer and further identifying herself as part of the poet himself—"'I am thy spirit, yoke-fellow / Of thine eye I am eyebeam.'" Animated by poetic acceptance, the Sphinx then soars and disperses into nature. In direct contradistinction to traditional myths, which culminate in her plummeting death, **"The Sphinx"** ends with her ascension. Once "drowsy," "heavy," and brooding, the now "merry" creature silvers, melts, spires, flowers, and flows. And since "metaphor" is "movement," the Sphinx essentially *becomes* both metamorphosis and rhetoric. We find, then, that the answer to the riddle of existence is not so much "man" as "language"—"man" as **"Sphinx"** is fundamentally figuration, metaphor, poetry.

The Sphinx nonetheless leaves the readers and the poet amid uncertainty with her final enigmatic utterance, now

spoken through an equally obscure "universal dame" with "a thousand voices." Emerson, in other words, closes this poem—itself a riddle about a riddle—with yet another puzzle, one that echoes the paradigmatic conundrum of the Hebrew God's self-identification, "I AM THAT I AM" (Exodus 3:14; a locution not unlike "'Of thine eye I am eyebeam'"):

> Thorough a thousand voices
> Spoke the universal dame:
> "Who telleth one of my meanings,
> Is master of all I am."

This "answer" leaves ambiguous the crucial issue of whether or not the poet actually has been this triumphant teller. Thus, just as she seems to assert her own supercession, the Sphinx both returns to her role as riddler and achieves vocality to a hyperbolic, even sublime, extent.

This conundrum is reflected in the poem's structure, for **"The Sphinx"** ends on its most significant formal deviation. Given the established metrical pattern, the poem's last lines form a half stanza—a quatrain instead of an octave. One impression the curtailment produces is that the Sphinx finally stifles Emerson and the poet—that, returning to her role of throttler, she utters a closing quatrain to which the only available response is silence. In this reading, such a thousand-voiced Sphinx, like the thousand-snaked head of Medusa, overcomes the poet with her fecundity, so that the poem breaks off to leave the poet voiceless and a blank where his corresponding quatrain should be. An opposed perspective, though, suggests that this space remains vacant precisely for poetry to fill, so that the rest of the volume represents the poet's reply—all the other poems complete the stanza. In this view, the stanzaic fragment creates an avenue to the following pages. The poem thus replicates the function of the Sphinx at Thebes: it poses a test for readers so that its difficulty will prevent some from proceeding into the subsequent poems, but will open a gateway into the verse for others (rather like Jesus' parables).

As a threshold poem, then, **"The Sphinx"** performs multiple tasks. It provides riddling instructions about how to approach the rest of Emerson's verse. It raises in theme and form issues crucial to the poetry. It offers an intriguing figure for Emerson's life and writings. And, finally, it suggests theories of reading, writing, and intertextuality pertinent to the poems that follow, to Emerson texts generally, and to the act of interpretation itself. By invoking the mythological *topos* of the Sphinx at the threshold, Emerson places readers in the position of the dramatized poet figure and himself in the position of Sphinx, enacting at the portal of his volume a ventriloquistic play that characterizes his poetry and his prose.[10] For **"The Sphinx"** activates crossings and reversals between genders, modes of discourse, forms of rhetoric, writer and reader, and subject and object that disrupt oppositional tendencies central to the cultures whose myths it employs.

In all these ways, the poem shows us how to read the rest of Emerson's verse, functioning as an initiatory riddle whose "meanings" emerge from the poems that ensue. The poem suggests that we approach Emerson's texts as the poet does the Sphinx, admiring their suggestiveness and difficulty rather than seeking to master them, all the while encouraging them to "'say on.'" Readers are to continue through the volume, animated instead of overcome by the inexhaustibility of language and life. The subsequent poems then flow from the ongoing metamorphosis of issues raised in this threshold piece, and embody its multitude of voices and forms.

When we read Emerson's other poems through the interpretive rubric of **"The Sphinx,"** some of their most perplexing moments, structures, and styles are illuminated. Rhetorical strategies and thematic concerns raised by that poem recur throughout *Poems* and *May-Day.* Especially in the earlier volume, the texts are characteristically multivocal, dialogic, puzzling, and elliptical. They are frequently structured according to debate or inquisition. As David Porter and R. A. Yoder have emphasized, a high percentage of Emerson's poems tell the story of a poet figure, his search for voice, and his role as an unriddler. The poems also often explore other aesthetic issues suggested in **"The Sphinx."** In addition, like **"The Sphinx,"** many contain figures of blockage, flow, speech, vision, and ascension.

The most crucial connection between the individual pieces in Emerson's first volume and **"The Sphinx"** is their variously manifested preoccupation with riddling. *Poems* as a whole, single compositions, or sections of texts may be read as additional riddles of the Sphinx, as her oracular utterances, or as responses to her questioning. Such is the case with many of the texts literally from their beginnings, for a number of the titles function as puzzles. Many of the more enigmatic are formed from obscure, misleading, or personal allusions. **"Alphonso of Castile," "Xenophanes," "Hamatreya,"** and **"To J. W.,"** for example, confused many readers. Emerson's **"Merlin"** is not primarily the Arthurian magician, but a lesser-known Welsh bard. And several titles—**"Ghaselle," "Saadi,"** and **"Hafiz"**—refer to Persian poetry, an area no more a part of his readers' usual repertoire of knowledge then than now.[11]

We get past such difficulty only to find that a surprising number of the poems are occasioned by direct or implicit questions. Sometimes these inquiries are stated at the beginnings of the poems, as in **"The Rhodora,"** subtitled "On Being Asked, Whence Is the Flower?" Most of the pieces contain embedded questions, and many end with them: **"Uriel"** closes with the couplet, "And a blush tinged the upper sky, / And the gods shook, they knew not why." Other poems culminate by posing "solutions" that are themselves riddling—as **"The Rhodora"**'s "The self-same Power that brought me there brought you," and the assurances about "gods" and "half-gods" at the end of **"Give All to Love."**

At the same time, dialogue and multivocality are also pervasive, almost definitive qualities of the poems. Their tonal variety and instability may be read as further manifestations of the Sphinx, now speaking "Thorough a thousand voices." Typically, Emerson leaves these tones unreconciled, or, one might say, unappropriated, by other voices in the poems. For Emerson, the poet is one who can hear the locutions of nature and translate them (almost literally "carry" them "across") into verse. One of his most characteristic poetic strategies is to present the speech of natural objects or forces in direct quotation or paraphrase. In **"Woodnotes II,"** we hear the "pine-tree"; in **"Alphonso of Castile,"** the "Earth"; in **"Dirge,"** a "pine-warbler"; in **"Threnody,"** the "deep Heart." In other poems, the narrator quotes himself, as in **"Each and All"** and **"Berrying."** Sometimes, quoted sources quote themselves, as does Monadnoc in its poem. Or the quoted voices quote still others—the Fakirs cite Allah in **"Saadi,"** and the Sphinx, the "great mother" in **"The Sphinx."** And in some of the most slippery texts, such as the **"Ode, Inscribed to W. H. Channing,"** Emerson presents contradictory voices and disparate points of view without using quotation marks either to distinguish between speakers or to privilege a particular one.

Often, opposite interpretations of a poem arise from readers' being persuaded by one or the other contesting voice within a poem, or by readers' posing antithetical solutions to a text's fundamental riddle or conundrum. Some of the most interesting "debatable" issues involve art and sexuality, with poems seeming to posit traditional and orthodox solutions while actually suggesting more presumptuous notions. In **"The Rhodora,"** a poem replete with the language of Romance, the "Power" that motivates the blossom and the observer, traditionally thought to be God, may partake more of sexual than of divine energy. In **"The Snow-Storm,"** the identity of the sculptor is also more vague and threatening than readers often acknowledge. Its identification as a "fierce artificer" echoes a description of Milton's Satan as the "Artificer of fraud" in *Paradise Lost* (4:121). In a more playful note of irony, the wind in the poem might be seen as hanging "Parian wreaths" in derisive burlesque of the nineteenth-century American fad of imitating Greek architecture. And while readers often perceive the creative act of the sculptor as second-rate imitation of nature's, to "mimic" is usually to imitate "Mockingly." The term thus suggests that the artist's imitation of nature is at best ambivalent, and that the two creators agonistically mock one another.

In conjunction with riddling and argument as forms of verbal play, and with the "merry" Sphinx and cheerful poet, the volume also contains lines of even more direct humor, often missed by overly somber readers. **"Fable,"** composed of a quarrel between a mountain and a squirrel, reveals its comic nature through a submerged closing pun. Asserting its own equal value to the mountain, the squirrel ends the poem by claiming, "'If I cannot carry forests on my back, / Neither can you crack a nut.'" The real wit here turns subtly on the adage about a question or riddle being a "hard nut to crack," so that the reader is now expected to be the especially clever animal who can "crack" the "nut" of Emerson's poem. Accordingly, the otherwise unfortunate line in **"Hamatreya"** about a dog—"'I fancy these pure waters and the flags / Know me, as does my dog: we sympathize'"—is of course *meant* to be funny, spoken as it is by a farmer who is fundamentally ridiculous in thinking that he "owns" the earth.

A review of some frequently anthologized pieces in *Poems* indicates how much of the volume develops and expands upon preoccupations initiated by **"The Sphinx." "The Problem,"** for instance, whose title is synonymous with "Sphinx," consummately represents an "argument" with a "metre-making argument." Responding to an implicit indictment of Emerson's own decision to be an artist instead of a preacher, the poem involves debate between two points of view, dramatizes a poet confronting an obstacle to his calling, and relies upon tropes of fluidity and petrifaction. Moreover, the poem both begins with a question and contains imbedded questions—sometimes, as in **"The Sphinx,"** in the form of catalogues.

"Uriel," another quite puzzling poem, concerns many of the same issues. A narrative of a rebellious angel who is essentially a poet figure, this text also represents a sort of indirectly autobiographical *apologia* for the poet. With rhetorical similarities both to **"The Sphinx"** and **"The Problem,"** it not only contains the imbedded voice of Uriel in a riddling quatrain, but also involves argument between Uriel and the gods, speaks of Uriel as "solving," and closes with an emphasis on riddling and mystery. We never truly know Uriel's fate, and in the end the gods still "kn[o]w not why" they reacted to it as they did.

"Hamatreya" represents a literally bipartite rendition of an argument between farmers and the earth over who is more powerful—over, finally, who owns whom. This poem, like **"The Sphinx,"** treats death as a contest between a man and a powerful mythic female figure; contains imbedded interrogation and interpolated voices, including that of a captious female figure; couches enigmas in elliptical and convoluted wordplay that centers upon pronouns ("Mine and yours / Mine not yours"); and culminates in a question that is actually a riddling paradox. In answer to the farmers' assertion of ownership and power, the earth seems to ask a question, but actually poses a conundrum that asserts the grave as the ultimate indication of mastery:

> "How am I theirs,
> If they cannot hold me,
> But I hold them?"

And the poem's title, moreover, is perhaps the most famously enigmatic among Emerson's many cryptic ones—we have yet to establish a definitive linguistic derivation of **"Hamatreya,"** though a surprising number of scholars have tried. My guess is that Emerson coins the riddling locution by conflating "Hamadryad," or "wood-nymph," and "Maitreya," a character in Hindu scripture, perhaps to represent a bonding between two of his own seemingly opposite loves—American nature and Eastern philosophy.

The two halves of **"Merlin,"** one of the best and most frequently read poems of Emerson's, together exemplify the recurrence of figures, structures, rhetorical forms, and concerns that I have been exploring. "Merlin I," addressed to an inadequate poet, echoes the castigating yet instructive voice of the Sphinx as it insists that the poet must "strike . . . hard" the aeolian harp strings of the imagination to create

> Artful thunder, which conveys
> Secrets of the solar track,
> Sparks of the supersolar blaze.

This section of **"Merlin"** receives its momentum from figures of release and ascent. The poet is allowed to "'Pass in, pass in'" to the "'upper doors,'" just as Oedipus was permitted to pass the slain Sphinx to enter Thebes and as readers have been allowed to pass **"The Sphinx"** into the rest of the poems. He is then admonished not to

> ". . . count compartments of the floors,
> But mount to paradise
> By the stairway of surprise."

Emerson often underscores the point he is making in the form of his verse. Here, the poet is told in irregular, oddly rhymed, un"count"ed lines to trust instinct rather than predetermined pattern.

The poem goes on to describe the true poet as one who, when bereft of imagination, need only "Wait his returning strength." And an especially long heptameter line follows to illustrate that the poet will soon be able to soar with his recovered muse:

> Bird, that from the nadir's floor
> To the zenith's top can soar,
> The soaring orbit of the muse exceeds that journey's
> length.

This tone of confidence prevails at the end of "Merlin I," answering the initial castigation. The very doors that had blocked the poet now open of their own agency to divulge their mysteries, even though no external force, however divine, could have budged them:

> Self-moved, fly-to the doors,
> Nor sword of angels could reveal
> What they conceal.

But celebration of limitlessness is only half of the equation. **"Merlin,"** like the Channing **"Ode"** (and, most famously, Emerson's essay **"Experience"**), presents a debate without differentiating between voices or clearly endorsing a perspective. Hence, "Merlin II," complements "Merlin I," providing the counterpoise to the emphasis on freedom (and power) in "Merlin I" to stress form (and balance) instead:

> The rhyme of the poet
> Modulates the king's affairs;
> —Balance-loving Nature

Made all things in pairs.
To every foot its antipode;
Each color with its counter glowed;
To every tone beat answering tones.

With a pun on "answering," the "answer"—in politics, nature, and verse—is polarity itself. Since that polarity creates the bipartite structure of **"Merlin,"** "Merlin II" begins with a metapoetic gesture of self-reflection.

The emphasis on doubleness then reverses to become glorification of union, but, as in **"The Sphinx,"** the language of duality and unity wavers:

Coeval grooms and brides;
Eldest rite, two married sides
In every mortal meet.

Here, Emerson has even more strongly sexualized the harmonizing work of the poet and the nature of existence itself, using figures both of androgyny and of copulation. The entire universe is paired (like the poet's couplets), so that "The animals are sick with love, / Lovesick with rhyme." Even concepts are sexualized:

Thoughts come also hand in hand;
In equal couples mated,
Or else alternated.

For if they remain "Solitary," ideas are doomed to wander aimlessly, "Most like to bachelors. / Or an ungiven maid," and to remain sterile, "Not ancestors, / With no posterity."

Toward the end of "Merlin II," lines treating fate and termination "couple" into iambic pentameter:

And Nemesis,
Who with even matches odd,
Who athwart space redresses
The partial wrong,
Fills the just period,
And finishes the song.

This passage contains a great many puns about writing poetry that connect "Nemesis," this poem's Sphinx figure, and the poet. Nemesis "with even matches odd"—as does Emerson in these lines of alternating dimeter and trimeter. It works "athwart space" to end with a "just period"—as do these lines if they are metrically enjambed. When the poem "matches" them, the lines actually couple into classic iambic pentameter, the form of Milton, master of "period"ic syntax. Yet this closing "couplet" of pentameter rhymes, as Milton's blank verse does not, so that Emerson's prosody also alludes to the neoclassical heroic couplet of Pope, and thus in another way to formal stability.

The final lines of "Merlin II" celebrate spinning sister-poets, the fates. These are threatening female figures like Nemesis and the Sphinx, who sing "subtle rhymes . . . / In perfect time and measure" (as the poem makes a sudden shift into irregularly but heavily rhymed tetrameter). These figures act as divine architect-artists who fashion in-dividuals even while "two twilights," the two thresholds of birth and death, "Fold us music-drunken in." This last image of enclosure makes human life—paradoxically—a wild revelry presided over by benevolent spirits who gently tuck children into bed at night. In the "Sisters," Nemesis, the poet, and the twilights, we find figures of the Sphinx again, now (in 1846, when **"Merlin"** was composed) much like the "Beautiful Necessity" to whom Emerson would have us "build altars" by the time of his 1850 essay **"Fate"** (*LA* 967).

A similar effort to accept fate is central to **"Threnody,"** the penultimate text in *Poems,* a work also composed in the mid-1840s. In this long elegy for his firstborn child, Waldo, Jr., who died suddenly of scarlatina at age five, Emerson confronts one of the most dread Sphinxes of all, the death of his very young son. As he does so, problems traditionally associated with Greek and Egyptian Sphinxes—inscrutability, death, time, family, guilt, and art—converge. **"The Sphinx"** and **"Threnody"** begin with humanity in similar conditions of need, both looking for someone to answer questions about offspring and fate. **"The Sphinx"** is concerned with "Life death overtaking," and **"Threnody"** with the absence of "Life, sunshine, and desire." Finally, both poems seek answers to their dilemmas, but the responses do not so much answer as reconstitute what "answering" means.

The most frequently commented upon, and criticized, feature of **"Threnody"** is its tonal bifurcation. The first 175 lines and seven stanzas represent a heartfelt lamentation for young Waldo—virtually an outpouring of emotion in the voice of the grieving father. The following 114 lines appear as two stanzas of direct quotation in the voice of the "deep Heart" as it responds to the grieving father. **"The Sphinx"** can provide readers a clue about how to read the irresolution within the latter poem, and show how its abrupt shift is actually one of its strengths. For the disparity within **"Threnody"** replicates the debate of poems like **"The Sphinx,"** and the structure of those like **"Merlin":** Emerson allows contradictory perspectives to coexist. **"Threnody"**'s tones of despair and consolation are *both* real, and are fundamentally unreconcilable. The solution in **"Threnody"** is acceptance and love of the universe, as in **"The Sphinx,"** but, as in the earlier poem, love and affirmation remain riddles. For the poem does not allow part two ever to neutralize the pain of part one, and it never explains how one can love a universe arranged so that one's five-year-old child would die.

We find the same philosophical and structural tension between and within two crucial Emerson essays written at the same time as **"Threnody"** and dealing with the same concerns, **"The Poet"** and **"Experience."** These three pieces are, in fact, best read together, with each inflecting the others' perspectives. That interrelationship illustrates how I suggest we read and teach Emerson's work generally—exploring, for example, **"The Snow-Storm"** with the anecdote about the snow storm in the Divinity School **"Address,"** and poems such as **"Uriel"** and **"The Prob-**

lem," with the address itself. My point is that the moods of **"Threnody," "The Poet,"** and **"Experience,"** as well as their structures, share in the preoccupations and rhetorical gestures I have explored throughout the *Poems.* Although we long read **"The Poet"** as one of Emerson's most affirmative essays, and **"Experience"** as one of his most skeptical, we are increasingly coming to appreciate how fully the essays echo one another.[12] Their contiguous placement and their vacillation of tone, especially within **"Experience,"** replicate the bipartite structure and wavering point of view of **"Threnody,"** and, less precisely, of other Emerson poems.

Emerson's *Poems,* then, move from a narrative of overcoming threat and silence to scenes in which death itself has become the primary impulse for the poetry. In the middle, they are composed of a host of voices in a variety of personas. With **"Threnody"** and the poems immediately before and after it, **"Dirge"** and the Concord **"Hymn,"** Emerson closes his first volume of poetry on an elegiac yet triumphant note that brings to a sort of culmination the tension between threat and affirmation that he initiated at the volume's threshold.

The second of Emerson's two primary collections of poetry, *May-Day and Other Pieces,* did not appear until 20 years later, in 1867, and thus represents one of his last significant book-length publications. The volume contains seven parts: two long poems, **"May-Day"** and **"The Adirondacs,"** each of which forms its own section (together about one-fourth of the total volume); three substantial sections of midlength poems, "Occasional and Miscellaneous Pieces," "Nature and Life" (with a posthumously published poem by Emerson's brother Edward), and "Elements"; and two short sections of mostly very brief poems, "Quatrains" and "Translations." Scholars have emphasized that *May-Day,* especially in its title poem, represents the sexagenarian Emerson's answer to his own aging process.[13] The structure of the volume would seem to reinforce this connection, as though the first sections corresponded to Emerson's more productive decades and the final brief segments to the waning of his creative powers. Certainly *May-Day*'s texts are preoccupied, even more than those of *Poems,* with the challenges of confronting limitation and finding rejuvenation.

In addition to reading those concerns as personally reflective ones, however, I suggest that we also view the *May-Day* volume in a way that previous scholarship has not noted.[14] Its 1867 publication, soon after the end of the American Civil War, invites us to read *May-Day* along with Melville's *Battle-Pieces* and Whitman's *Drum-Taps* as part of the literary response to the war itself. A few of the poems in Emerson's volume—**"Freedom," "Ode Sung in Town Hall," "Boston Hymn,"** and **"Voluntaries"**— treat the conflict directly. Many others address it implicitly, either tropically or through such subjects as camaraderie, reconciliation, and restoration.

Some poems, including the volume's titlepiece, call upon the poetic spirit as a salve for wounds and the herald of a new age of greater freedom, with spring as a trope for national renewal. Emerson had made a similar gesture of responding to a political occasion metaphorically, and connecting politics and poetry, years earlier. Len Gougeon has pointed out that Emerson's first answer to the passage of the 1850 Missouri Compromise and its Fugitive Slave Law was in the form of poems he sent to the antislavery annual *The Liberty Bell* at the request of its editor. Ordinarily, material in *The Liberty Bell* treated abolition directly; Emerson's poems, however, translate philosophical Persian texts about poetry and rebirth. The connection of May and springtime with postwar healing (which we find in Whitman's "When Lilacs Last in the Dooryard Bloom'd") is also Emersonian. Eduardo Cadava has shown that Emerson characteristically uses nature imagery in conjunction with political events, as in **"Boston Hymn,"** when he associates snow with the Northern forces, and in **"Voluntaries"** when he employs snow, and the aurora borealis, to represent the North.[15] Emerson's connection of springtime and Reconstruction extends the same strategy.

Even in its concern with the war and its aftermath, however, the volume shares affinities with the earlier *Poems*—a fact that Emerson's repeated use of **"The Sphinx"** as a comprehensive threshold poem implies. For with the war and again following it, America was forced to face the question of national identity—forced (as were Oedipus and the poet when they met their Sphinxes) to confront the issue of who it was. Such a challenge, the titlepiece and the volume imply, can best be met through the power of poetry, which is to bring war-torn yet now-virtuous America the vitality of spring.

Emerson does not, however, start his volume of war poetry with poems that relate to battle, then move to poems that emphasize healing and regeneration, as does Whitman in *Drum-Taps.* Rather, he inverts that more predictable structure, beginning the volume instead with a threshold poem that both describes and provides the balmic equivalent to the "rue, myrrh, and cummin" brought by the poet of **"The Sphinx."** Thus, his readers move immediately to the anodyne of poetry. **"May-Day"**'s simultaneous role as title and threshold poem, reinscribed by the book's serendipitous publication just before May Day (on April 29), attests to the importance of its sexually exuberant celebration of spring. In more than 500 lines of irregularly rhymed tetrameter (mostly in couplets and alternating rhyme),[16] the poem loosely consists of a series of odes that celebrate fertility much like classic Renaissance songs to Hymen. Its subject also makes Emerson's longest single poem a *reverdie,* a verse that welcomes the springtime regreening of the earth, in the long tradition of such poems as the Middle English "Cuckoo Song," the prologue to the *Canterbury Tales,* Shakespeare's "When Daisies Pied," Herrick's "Corinna," many of Dickinson's spring songs, and, in modern times, cummings's "in just." As such, **"May-Day,"** like **"The Sphinx,"** establishes the keynote of its volume.

At the same time, a number of lines in **"May-Day"** allude to the war through martial and emancipation imagery. The passages often employ images of blockage and fluidity to indicate the need for spring, when "the bondage-days are told [i.e., finished], / And waters free as winds shall flow." Because "The world hath overmuch of pain," Emerson writes, it is in particular need of pleasure, a time of "cheer" and "joy" when spring will "Rebuild the ruin, mend defect," just as the poet cured the Sphinx. Spring will create "liberated floods" and "new-delivered streams," bringing in summer, when—as the poem makes explicit the connection of national trauma and sexuality—the world will celebrate a "Hymen of element and race." Then, "one broad, long midsummer day / Shall to the planet overpay / The ravage of a year of war."

Thus, this threshold poem also focuses on the issue most central to the earlier poem and volume—how to respond to the sphinxes of impotence and death with cheer and potency. "May-Day" bears other resemblances to "The Sphinx" as well. It, too, represents a riddling answer to the riddle of existence, unexpectedly (especially for this aging ex-cleric) emphasizing that creativity and renewal derive from an internal "storm of heat" whose release generates life. The subsequent poems and translations illustrate that productivity even as they address it metapoetically, returning again and again to notions of regeneration and recuperation.

Immediately after "May-Day," we find a poem that is in many ways its counterpart, "The Adirondacs," a long narrative piece in a blank verse that complements its lyrical, heavily rhymed predecessor. Like "May-Day," "The Adirondacs" concerns the importance of natural renewal. Unlike "May-Day" and its glorification of heterosexual love, this poem celebrates male bonding.[17] "The Adirondacs" tells of a summer camping trip Emerson took with a group of friends, among them author and *Atlantic Monthly* editor James Russell Lowell and the naturalist Louis Aggasiz, in 1858. Despite its antebellum composition date and publication, the poem's appearance in *May-Day* would have made "The Adirondacs"'s celebration of camaraderie and renewal resonate politically for a nation just having emerged from the strife of brother fighting brother.

Though "The Adirondacs" devotes itself mostly to the tale of the explorers' energizing journey, it closes with the one direct mention of the Sphinx in Emerson's poetry other than in her own eponymous piece. As the men leave the woods to return home, Emerson writes:

And Nature, the inscrutable and mute,
Permitted on her infinite repose
Almost a smile to steal to cheer her sons,
As if one riddle of the Sphinx were guessed.

Thus, a text again culminates with a riddle about a riddle—it is very tentatively "as if" the men (like perhaps the poet in "The Sphinx") had penetrated the silence and mystery of nature.

The next section of *May-Day,* "Occasional and Miscellaneous Pieces," treats the Civil War and emancipation di-

rectly in four of its 11 poems. Emerson composed the first of these political poems, "Freedom," at the request of Julia Griffiths for the December 1853 *Autographs for Freedom,* an antislavery volume to benefit the Rochester (New York) Anti-slavery Society. At first, "Freedom," like the earlier "Ode, Inscribed to W. H. Channing," seems to be essentially an *apologia* for Emerson's lack of direct participation in the fight for freedom. However, both poems also function like classical *praeteritio,* the rhetorical device by which a speaker draws attention to something by announcing its omission ("I'll pass over the fact that the candidate stole millions"). They are thus intrinsically ironic—by virtue of their very existence, they address what they say they will not. What is more, while "Freedom" claims that Emerson is unable to "rehearse / Freedom's paean in my verse," he next proceeds even more directly to do just that. In the following poem, the "Ode Sung in the Town Hall, Concord, July 4, 1857," written to help raise money for Sleepy Hollow Cemetery, Emerson exhorts America to "bid the broad Atlantic roll, / A ferry of the free," and assure that "henceforth, there shall be no chain."

The third of these "freedom" poems, "Boston Hymn, Read in Music Hall, January 1, 1863," is even more explicit. Emerson composed it when another friend, John Sullivan Dwight, asked him to read a poem to begin the celebration for the enactment of the Emancipation Proclamation. "Boston Hymn" became famous immediately, and was sung by the African-American South Carolina regiment commanded by the white literary figure T. W. Higginson. The quatrain that alludes to the then-current debate about how emancipation was to be achieved is especially moving. A proposed solution (one that Emerson himself had supported) called for the government to recompense slaveholders for the "property" they would lose upon emancipation. Now, Emerson forcefully assumes the voice of God, whom he quotes, to command:

Pay ransom to the owner,
And fill the bag to the brim.
Who is the owner? The slave is owner,
And ever was. Pay him.

Finally, later in 1863, Emerson wrote his most frequently anthologized political poem, "Voluntaries," to honor the slain members of the Massachusetts 54th Colored Infantry and their white commander, Col. Robert Gould Shaw. This illustrious group of soldiers is also commemorated by a statue that now stands on Boston Common, and by a number of additional poems, among them the modern elegy "For the Union Dead," by Bostonian Robert Lowell. Emerson himself had earlier spoken at a fund-raising event for the group, with whom he felt a particular connection through his friendship with Col. Shaw's father, Francis Shaw. Emerson sent "Voluntaries" in September of 1863 to Mr. Shaw after the combat deaths, on July 18, of Robert Shaw and nearly half of the soldiers under his command.

"Voluntaries" begins in a mood of reverence by invoking the "Low and mournful" tones of a slave, then goes on to celebrate freedom's new cohabitation with the heroic black race. The poem asserts its faith in the ultimate triumph of the slain Northern soldiers, a victory achieved because of the probity of their cause and evidenced partly, in the Greek and Latin heroic tradition, by their immortalization in this verse. Emerson predicts that the evil Southerners finally will be "Reserved to a speechless fate," while the virtuous dead will be crowned with laurels and honored in song. And Emerson's poem, of course, participates in the commemoration it prophesies.

These war poems indicate that Emerson's concerns in *May-Day* had shifted somewhat from the time of the earlier volume. In addition, these poems are on the whole less riddling in both form and subject than their predecessors. On the other hand, many of the pieces continue a number of structural, rhetorical, and thematic preoccupations of **"The Sphinx." "The Titmouse,"** to cite one example, begins with a question much like that in **"The Sphinx"**—how to overcome lethargy; it is about poet figures (narrator and bird) who cheer; it uses imagery of petrifaction; it contains interpolated voices; and its "solution" involves interaction with nature. **"Days"** is another riddle, and another allegorization. The speaker of this 11-line parable is as overwhelmed by the personified Days as the poet is accused of being in **"The Sphinx,"** and as, in 1867, Emerson and the country were by the Sphinxes of age and war. The poem involves the adequacy of a respondent to mysteriously threatening and scornful female inquisitors, and requires the respondent to *ask* instead of answer—but with a question that is actually a test of her own worth. Its obscurity leads readings even now to remain, like those of **"The Sphinx,"** divided about whether the response was successful.

Finally, two of the most famous poems in the second collection, **"Brahma"** and **"Terminus,"** illustrate the evolution of Emerson's continuing concerns. Positioned at the threshold of its section, **"Brahma"** is the poem in Emerson's canon most often compared to **"The Sphinx,"** in both sympathetic analyses and parodies. Fundamentally a riddle, with an implicit "What am I" as its undertone, the poem assumes the voice of what may loosely be identified as the soul or the oversoul. It begins:

> If the red slayer think he slays,
> Or if the slain think he is slain,
> They know not well the subtle ways
> I keep, and pass, and turn again.

Once more, then, readers receive the voice of a mysterious entity in enigmatic, oracular quatrains. The voice in **"Brahma"** again wants to know its own identity, and again Emerson presents his clues in opposites and paradox: Brahma asserts that "I am the doubter and the doubt," for "When me they fly, I am the wings." And the answer to this riddle is also linguistic, even poetic—Brahma's most direct statement of identity is "I [am] the hymn the Brahmin sings," and the poem itself actually *is* that hymn, in the classic long measure of Christian hymnody. Thus the god, the voice, the Sphinx, and the individual become in fundamental ways both articulation and poetry.

In addition, the readers who hear of the "slayer" and "slain" in **"Brahma"** are those who have just observed North and South in those roles. Although **"Brahma"** was written and published in the late 1850s, for its 1867 readers, the language would have been inflected with events of the war. In this context, **"Brahma"** also becomes a meditation on the insignificance of residual divisiveness, an affirmation of life beyond tragedy, victory, and defeat. Echoing the message of **"May-Day,"** **"Brahma"** suggests that poetry can provide answers to the horrors of "slayer" and "slain."

"Terminus," Emerson's meditative poem on the individual's aging process, along with the three elegiac poems that accompany it, balances **"Brahma"** and **"May-Day"** in the structure of *May-Day*'s central sections much as the closing elegies served as counterparts to **"The Sphinx"** in *Poems*. Its title is another riddle about its allegorized subject—this time the Greek god of bounds. And **"Terminus"** also addresses the questions of how to deal with the Sphinxes of depletion and death: it opens, "It is time to be old, / To take in sail." Emerson's familiar concerns again cluster—the poem thematizes limitation, directly this time; contains figures of flow and blockage; portrays muses as at once helpfully provocative and potentially overwhelming; expresses anxiety about silencing; and contains interpolated voices, including that of a mysterious divinity the meaning of whose closing quatrain once more may be read in diametrically opposed ways. The poem ends by quoting a figure identified simply as "the voice . . . obeyed at prime" that tells the poet she should, even while closing in upon the shore, "'banish fear, / Right onward drive unharmed,'" for "The port, well worth the cruise, is near, / And every wave is charmed.'" This advice, reminiscent of but different from Tennyson's in "Ulysses," seems paradoxical in a poem that ostensibly urges readers "To take in sail."

In a similar gesture of ambivalence, this time a structural one, *May Day* indeed does not "terminate" with these elegies, as *Poems* had, but instead contains three more sections: "Elements," selected essay epigraphs; 30 "Quatrains" (or near-quatrains); and 18 "Translations," all but one, a Michelangelo sonnet, renditions of Persian poetry. The quatrains and translations, by virtue of their length, subject matter, and very existence, are quite sphingine, gnomic utterances. In addition, the translations reveal a method of composition quintessentially Emersonian, for in them Emerson blends the Persian, its German rendition, and his own revisions to create poems that disrupt boundaries between origin and elaboration.[18] That appropriative impulse is also at the heart of the final section of Emerson's verse I want to treat, his essay epigraphs, some of which are collected in the *May-Day* section "Elements." I will close by exploring the existence of these "Elements" and other epigraphs as they stood originally, at the thresholds of Emerson's prose.

For 30 essays in five separate collections Emerson chose to print his own poems as epigraphs. That decision was altogether unconventional, or, more precisely, was *anti*conventional. At the thresholds of prose pieces, as on the lintels of doorways, we expect to see "sacred" text, whether from the Bible, or from Shakespeare, Homer, Dante, or Milton. The tradition is definitively deferential. That Emerson was acutely aware of, and resistant to, this sycophantic and possibly impoverishing tendency of the epigraph convention is evident in a statement from his essay **"Quotation and Originality"**:

> Quotation confesses inferiority. In opening a new book we often discover, from the unguarded devotion with which the writer gives his motto or text, all we have to expect from him. If Lord Bacon appears already in the preface, I go and read the "Instauration" instead of the new book.
>
> (*W* 8: 188)

He is even more adamant in his journal: "I hate quotation. Tell me what you know" (May 1849; *JMN* 11: 110).

In the epigraphs, then, Emerson boldly transposes and appropriates convention. Yet despite their peculiarity, and the fact that they are his verse that Emerson's readers most frequently encounter, the epigraph poems have received very little analytical attention. When teaching the essays and writing about them, we typically act as if the mottoes aren't there at all. It is as though readers are embarrassed by the short-lined, heavily rhymed, enigmatic pieces, and are anxious to get past them into the "important" material that follows. But not only are the epigraphs quite appealing as individual works, their presence before the essays even more insistently invites attention. As original, often lengthy, and sometimes independently printed verse "mottoes," Emerson's epigraphs are generically distinct, significant modifications of both epigraphic and poetic convention. Their peculiarity combined with their own preoccupation with enigma invites us, I think, to imagine the epigraphs themselves as riddling Sphinxes at the thresholds of Emerson's essays.

First, the epigraphs serve as problematic guardians at the gateways, representing distilled challenges that we are to grapple with before we reach the prose. At the same time, the relation of the epigraphs and the essays to their titles is frequently a puzzling, even paradoxical one. The mottoes and essay **"History,"** for instance are not about "History" as much as about the priority of the soul over history. And, to cite a late occurrence of the same tendency, in the companion essays **"Fate"** and **"Power,"** the notion of "Fate" or "Beautiful Necessity" is paradoxical, so that the poem and motto titled **"Fate"** might be said really to be about "Power," and those called **"Power,"** about "Fate." In addition, the epigraphs frequently appear in rhetorical structures and forms that are directly or indirectly based on riddling—paradox, situation *in medias res,* and fragmentary or elliptical syntax, for example. And many of the verses thematize obscurity, thus becoming poems about themselves, the essays they introduce, and what Emerson saw as the ultimate inscrutability of life. Unlike travelers

near Thebes, we may choose to overlook these elusive puzzlers. But then we miss valuable hints about the essays that follow, the pleasure of playing with the runic lines, and the provocation to self-confrontation and self-examination the epigraphs provide.

As he appropriates and extends the epigraph form, Emerson writes two basic types of poems, both related to **"The Sphinx"**: first, a sort of oracular wisdom verse that makes gnomic and riddling yet weighty pronouncements; and, second, fragmented narratives about the development of a poet-hero who can solve the enigmas that plague humankind, actually an externalization of the poetic impulse that Emerson would locate within all individuals. As a group, many of the epigraphs tell of this foundling son of Mother Nature, who in his "answers" to her produces the sort of oracular poetry that other epigraphs embody—prophetic in tone and tendency, but with an element of forbidden mystery.

Consequently, the epigraphs often double the riddle form—are frequently riddles about riddling, mysterious oracles about mystery. We find a good illustration of their terse ambiguity in the second motto to **"History"** (1841 and 1847):

> I am owner of the sphere,
> Of the seven stars and the solar year,
> Of Caesar's hand, and Plato's brain,
> Of Lord Christ's heart, and Shakespeare's strain.

Since the poem never identifies a subject, this quatrain is on one level the "I am" of children's riddles and a tradition extending at least back, for instance, to the Old English *Exeter Book.* The purest such construction among the epigraphs, this is the only motto in the first-person voice of its own subject, a common rhetorical strategy in riddling also employed quite frequently by Emerson's contemporary, Emily Dickinson. As in **"The Sphinx,"** the phrase in this context also recalls the riddling "I am" of God that I mentioned in conjunction with **"The Sphinx,"** and Coleridge's concept of the secondary imagination outlined in *Biographia Literaria,* the creating, synthesizing power of the mind that Coleridge calls "the infinite I AM." Also, especially in the context of this epigraph, the phrase imports considerable theological weight from Eastern traditions. It directly echoes a text very dear to Emerson, the *Bhagavad-Gita,* in which the speaker of the "I am" is the soul: "I am the soul which standeth in the bodies of all beings."[19]

Accordingly, that "soul" is the paradoxical topic of the first **"History"** epigraph, the companion to the poem I have been examining:

> There is no great and no small
> To the soul that maketh all:
> And where it cometh all things are;
> And it cometh everywhere.

This epigraph identifies the soul as the source of creation (and, by extension, poetic creation). And it makes explicit the point of the essay that follows, in which "History" is also really "soul," because "there is properly no history; only biography" (*LA* 240). In a sense, then, Emerson has provided in the first poem the answer to the second.

The lovely motto to the 1860 essay **"Illusions,"** in *The Conduct of Life,* is my own favorite. Although Emerson did not choose to reprint **"Illusions"** as a separate text, the poem is increasingly anthologized. I see it as in some ways the culmination of the epigraphs, combining traits of the aphoristic and the narrative pieces finally to exist in a category of its own. An exploration of ambivalence toward perpetual change, **"Illusions"** finally celebrates the ongoing metamorphosis that occurs at the end of **"The Sphinx."** It begins in syntax that is ambiguously both imperative and declarative:

> Flow, flow the waves hated,
> Accursed, adored,
> The waves of mutation:
> No anchorage is.

These lines exemplify high Romantic apostrophe, in which the poet pretends to command what is manifestly beyond his control. In the course of the poem, these polarities of power and passivity converge: readers are reassured that the wave of progress will also restore what it subsumed. By the end of the piece, we come full circle to find that humanity, too, rides "the wild turmoil" of this threateningly perpetual wave "to power, / And to endurance."

This epigraph and others play an important role in our understanding of the relationship between Emerson's various texts and voices, and, most importantly, between his poetry and his prose. In the essay **"Self-Reliance,"** Emerson issues an arch rejoinder to anyone who might question the value of his vocation: "I shun father and mother and wife and brother, when my genius calls me. I would write on the lintels of the door-post, *Whim.* I hope it is somewhat better than whim at last, but we cannot spend the day in explanation (*LA* 262).[20] Here, an irascible Emerson invokes Deuteronomy's rendition of the Mosaic covenant, in which God cautions Moses to keep the words he has told him that day in his heart, to teach them to his children, to talk of them, and to "write them upon the posts of thy house, and on thy gates" (Deut. 6:9). The doorway also figures prominently in connection with Passover, and with the sacrificial blood of Christ. Emerson's assertion in **"Self-Reliance,"** then, substitutes an arrogant yet fanciful rejoinder of his own for biblical text and the words of God.

Just as in **"Self-Reliance,"** where the word and act of *"Whim"* replace the ancient text, Emerson's own poetry does so before his essays, in the form of the essay epigraphs. They inscribe *"Whim"* upon the lintels of the prose. In this sense, the essays become elaboration, application, even "exegesis" of the initial poetic "scriptures." The epigraphs thus combine the sacred and the jovial in their existence as whimsical pre-liminary conundrums. In a larger sense, we might also imagine the epigraphs and

essays as together figuring the positions of poetry and prose in Emerson's life. Emerson positions the two *together,* establishing between the genres a dialogue in which formal divisions become happily indistinct. This invitation to pause at the thresholds of his essays provides our best hint about how to read the prose that follows—poetically.

Finally, the epigraphs place Emerson himself in the position of the Sphinx and readers in the position of Oedipus. They thus initiate at the gateways to his prose the destabilization of boundaries between author and audience, reader and writer that we have come to associate with Emerson's work. For his verse as a whole asks us to challenge our intellects, imaginations, and assumptions, to *argue* with ourselves, so to speak—as does Emerson's prototypical threshold poem **"The Sphinx,"** the crucial and complex whim upon the lintel of his first volume of verse.

Notes

1. I use the following abbreviations to cite parenthetically from Emerson's texts: *CW, The Collected Works of Ralph Waldo Emerson,* ed. Robert E. Spiller, Alfred R. Ferguson, Joseph Slater, and Jean Ferguson Carr (Cambridge, MA: Harvard University Press, 1971-); *JMN, The Journals and Miscellaneous Notebooks of Ralph Waldo Emerson,* ed. William H. Gilman et al., 16 vols. (Cambridge, MA: Harvard University Press, 1960-82); *LA, Ralph Waldo Emerson: Essays and Lectures,* ed. Joel Porte (New York: Library of America, 1983); *W, The Complete Works of Ralph Waldo Emerson,* Centenary Edition, ed. Edward Waldo Emerson, 12 vols. (Boston and New York: Houghton Mifflin, 1903-4). Unless otherwise indicated, citations from Emerson's poetry are taken from *Emerson: Collected Poems and Translations,* ed. Harold Bloom and Paul Kane (New York: Library of America, 1994). For their help in the preparation of this essay, I am indebted to Julie Vandivere, Catherine Tufariello, Tamar Katz, Cynthia Hogue, and Joel Porte.

2. Richard Benson Sewall, *The Life of Emily Dickinson* (New York: Farrar, Straus and Giroux, 1974), pp. xxvi, 583.

3. Hyatt Waggoner, *Emerson as Poet* (Princeton: Princeton University Press, 1974); R. A. Yoder, *Emerson and the Orphic Poet in America* (Berkeley, Los Angeles, London: University of California Press, 1978); David Porter, *Emerson and Literary Change* (Cambridge, MA, and London: Harvard University Press, 1978).

4. Ralph Waldo Emerson, *The Poetry Notebooks of Ralph Waldo Emerson,* ed. Ralph H. Orth, Albert J. von Frank, Linda Allardt, and David W. Hill (Columbia: University of Missouri Press, 1986).

5. Carl Strauch, groundbreaking scholar of Emerson's poetry, emphasizes the importance of 1834 as "the year of Emerson's poetic maturity" in his article of that title (*Philological Quarterly* 34 [October 1955]: 353-77).

6. Ralph Waldo Emerson, *Selected Poems,* New and Rev. Ed. (Boston: James R. Osgood, 1876); and *Poems,* Vol. 9 of *Emerson's Complete Works,* Riverside Edition, ed. James Elliot Cabot (Boston and New York: Houghton Mifflin, 1903-4). Emerson's son Edward explicitly chose not to begin the Centenary Edition *Poems* with "The Sphinx," choosing instead to start it with a much more accessible early poem, "Good-Bye." This sequence of events gains even further Oedipal inflection when we note that Emerson himself apparently very much disliked "Good-Bye." A letter from Ellen Emerson to Sarah Gibbons Emerson makes clear that Emerson allowed "Good-Bye" to be included in his *Selected Poems* at his family's insistence: "You asked me in one letter how we could let Father leave out 'Good-bye proud world' from the new volume [*Selected Poems*]. We were sorry, and several friends begged for it, but Father disliked it so much himself that all persuasion failed." [Ellen Tucker Emerson, *The Letters of Ellen Tucker Emerson,* ed. Edith E. W. Gregg (Kent, OH: Kent State University Press, 1982), 2: 245.] As justification for his action Edward argues that "The Sphinx" would deter readers at the start rather than entice them to read on:

> Not without serious consideration has the editor removed the poem, which his father put at the beginning of his verse, to a later place. But he has always shared the feeling of regret that Dr. Holmes expressed in his book, that "Emerson saw fit to imitate the Egyptians by placing the Sphinx at the entrance of his temple of song." In the mythology the Sphinx let no man pass who could not solve her riddle; and Emerson's Sphinx has no doubt put off, in the very portal, readers who would have found good and joyful words for themselves, had not her riddle been beyond their powers.

(*W* 9: 403)

7. I discuss the importance of "The Sphinx" in my essay "The Threshold Poem, Emerson, and 'The Sphinx'" (*American Literature* 69.3 [September 1997]: 547-70). Part of this chapter is adapted from that essay.

8. Emerson writes in "The Poet": "For it is not metres, but a metre-making argument which makes a poem" (*LA* 450).

9. Gayle L. Smith surveys the points of disagreement in her excellent essay, "The Language of Identity in Emerson's 'The Sphinx,'" *ESQ: A Journal of the American Renaissance* 29 (3d Quarter 1983): 136-43. While agreeing in many particulars, I take issue with Smith's emphasis on the "identity" of the Sphinx and the poet.

10. Scholars have consistently recognized the propriety of the Sphinx as a figure for Emerson and his work, and modern scholarship has continued this emphasis on Emerson and his writings as Sphinxes. The second chapter of Barbara Packer's book on Emerson's prose is "The Riddle of the Sphinx: *Nature*" [*Emerson's Fall: A New Interpretation of the Major Essays* (New York: Continuum, 1992)], and Yoder stresses the unriddling power of what he identifies as the recurrent Emersonian figure of the American Orphic poet. Emerson jokingly writes of himself as a Sphinx in an 1873 journal entry about his trip to Egypt: "Mrs Helen Bell, it seems, was asked 'What do you think the Sphinx said to Mr Emerson?' 'Why,' replied Mrs Bell, 'the Sphinx probably said to him, 'You're another'" (*JMN* 16: 294).

11. Hafiz, Shams od-Dīn Muhammad Hāfiz (1326?-?1390), of Shiraz; and Sa'di (whose name Emerson spells Saadi, Said, Seyd, and Seid), Mosharref od-Dīn ibn Mosleh od-Dīn Sa'dī, of Shiraz (ca. 1213-92), are two of the most famous Persian poets.

12. See, for example, B. L. Packer, *Emerson's Fall: A New Interpretation of the Major Essays* (New York: Continuum, 1982); Richard Lee Francis, "The Poet and Experience: *Essays: Second Series,*" in *Emerson Centenary Essays,* ed. Joel Myerson (Carbondale: Southern Illinois University Press, 1982, pp. 93-106); David Hill, "Emerson's Eumenides: Textual Evidence and the Interpretation of 'Experience,'" in Myerson, *Emerson Centenary Essays,* pp. 107-21; Joel Porte, "Experiments in Creation," in The *New Pelican Guide to English Literature,* vol. 9: *American Literature,* ed. Boris Ford (London: Penguin, 1988).

13. See, e.g., Porter, pp. 130-33. Porter also emphasizes the title poem's thematization of the poetic process in relation to what he calls Emerson's "crisis of the imagination."

14. Len Gougeon has treated the importance of issues associated with abolition and the Civil War as a part of his emphasis on Emerson as, in the title of Gougeon's book, *Virtue's Hero: Emerson, Antislavery, and Reform* (Athens: University of Georgia Press, 1990); see also Gougeon, "Emerson, Poetry, and Reform," *Modern Language Studies* 19.2 (Spring 1989): 38-49.

15. Eduardo Cadava, *Emerson and the Climates of History* (Stanford: Stanford University Press, 1997), especially pp. 171ff.

16. "May-Day" exists in several versions. The first-edition text, that in the 1876 *Selected Poems,* a third in the Riverside Edition, and a fourth in the Centenary.

17. For a discussion of Emerson and the gendered construction of selves, see Julie Ellison, "The Gender of Transparency: Masculinity and *The Conduct of Life,*" *American Literary History* 4.4 (Winter 1992): 584-606.

18. On Emerson's translations, see *The Topical Notebooks of Ralph Waldo Emerson,* vol. 3, ed. Ronald A. Bosco (Columbia and London: University of

Missouri Press, 1993); Richard Tuerk, "Emerson as Translator—'The Phoenix,'" *Emerson Society Quarterly* 63 (1971): 24-26; and J. D. Yohannan, "Emerson's Translations of Persian Poetry from German Sources," *American Literature* 14 (1943): 407-20.

19. Charles Wilkins, trans., *The Bhagavat-Geeta* (London: C. Nourse, 1785), p. 85.

20. Stanley Cavell has devoted a good deal of attention to this same passage. See especially his two essays on Emerson in *The Senses of Walden: An Expanded Edition* (San Francisco: North Point Press, 1981).

Robert D. Richardson, Jr. (essay date 1999)

SOURCE: "Emerson and Nature," in *The Cambridge Companion to Ralph Waldo Emerson,* edited by Joel Porte and Saundra Morris, Cambridge University Press, 1999, pp. 97-105.

[*In the following essay, Richardson defines Emerson's perception of nature and the role it played in his philosophical thinking and writing.*]

Explicit or implicit in nearly everything Emerson wrote is the conviction that nature bats last, that nature is the law, the final word, the supreme court. Others have believed—still believe—that the determining force in our lives is grace, or that it is the state—the polis, the community—or that it is the past. More recently it has been argued that the central force is economics or race or sex or genetics. Emerson's basic teaching is that the fundamental context of our lives is nature.

Emerson's definition of nature is a broad one. Nature is the way things are. Philosophically, Emerson says, the universe is made up of nature and the soul, or nature and consciousness. Everything that is *not me* is nature; nature thus includes nature (in the common sense of the green world), art, all other persons, and my own body.

Emerson's interest in nature was more than theoretical. Like his friends Alcott and Thoreau, Emerson was passionately attached to the natural world. "The mind," says Alcott, speaking for them all, "craves the view of mountain, ocean, forest, lake and plain, the open horizon, the firmament—an actual contact with the elements." As a boy, Emerson rambled in the woods and fields outside Boston. As a young man, he thought for a while of becoming a naturalist. As a father, he took his children on nature walks and taught them all the flowers and birds and trees. All his life his interest in nature was rooted in his delight in and close observation of nature. Of one sunrise he wrote, "the long slender bars of cloud float like fishes in the sea of crimson light." Of a particularly fine January sunset, he wrote, "The western clouds divided and subdivided themselves into pink flakes modulated with tints of unspeakable softness; and the air had so much life and sweetness, that it was a pain to come within doors. . . .

The leafless trees become spires of flame in the sunset, with the blue east for their background, and the stars of the dead calices of flowers, and every withered stem and stubble rimed with frost contribute something to the mute music."[1]

The decisive moment in Emerson's interest in nature came in 1832, in Paris, when he was 29. He had trained for the Unitarian ministry, and in 1829 became the minister of Boston's Second Church. At about the same time he fell in love with and married a beautiful young woman named Ellen Tucker, who hoped to become a poet. But Ellen died in 1831, after they had been married only a year and a half. This tragic event, together with Emerson's growing interest in science, especially astronomy, led him to question seriously what he called "historical Christianity." In May 1832, he told his congregation, "I regard it as the irresistible effect of the Copernican astronomy to have made the theological scheme of redemption absolutely incredible."[2]

Emerson resigned from his church, gave up his house, sold his furniture, relocated his mother, and sailed for Europe. After an eight-month tour of Italy and a quick trip through Switzerland and France, he found himself in Paris gazing at the vast and wonderful exhibits in the Jardin des Plantes, where he experienced a vocational epiphany. He observed in his journal that "the Universe is a more amazing puzzle than ever as you glance along this bewildering series of animated forms—the hazy butterflies, the carved shells, the birds, beasts, fishes, insects, snakes—& the upheaving principle of life everywhere incipient in the very rock aping organized forms."[3] Not only were the specimens in the exhibits linked to each other, they were also linked to him. Perhaps for the first time since the death of Ellen, Emerson felt an agitated, sympathetic—almost physical—connection with the natural world. He was powerfully stirred. "I feel the centipede in me—cayman, carp, eagle & fox. I am moved by strange sympathies, I say continually 'I will be a naturalist'."[4]

When Emerson returned home and began a new career as a public lecturer, the first subject he took up was science, which he understood as the study of nature. But Emerson never became a scientist, or even a naturalist, not in the semiliterary way Thoreau did, and certainly not in the way his cousin, George B. Emerson, author of a standard botany of Massachusetts, did. Emerson had, however, a daily and a detailed knowledge of the natural world, as his family and friends testified. He taught his children how to recognize the birds by their songs. He knew the names of all the plants; he took daily walks to Walden Pond. He loved the word *lespedeza,* his daughter recalled, and he would say it over and over as a sort of homemade Yankee mantra. Emerson was an avid gardener and orchard keeper. He planted trees to mark his children's birthdays. He grew many varieties of apple, pear, and quince, although he did so with more enthusiasm than skill. His son recalled how the local botanical society launched an inquiry into how Emerson could get such poor results from such splendid stock.

Emerson remained interested in the sciences all his life. He read in geology, astronomy, chemistry, and, above all, botany. He was a friend of Louis Agassiz, who was the leading scientist of his time, and he kept up with new discoveries and controversies. As Dirk Struik, a modern historian of New England's contributions to science, has observed, Emerson's warm interest in science—his hospitable openness to it—was itself a real contribution, because it helped to create an intellectual atmosphere in which there is no necessary gulf between science and the humanities, no structural reason for the existence of the "two cultures" described by C. P. Snow in his famous essay of 1956. What science and the humanities have in common, Emerson argued, is a perennial interest in nature.

The most important result of Emerson's long engagement with nature was the publication in 1836 of the small book he called *Nature.* Its opening paragraph represents a turning point, not only in American literature, but also in his own life. It records the moment when Emerson turned explicitly and self-consciously from biography, history, and criticism to nature for his starting point. Reading the first paragraph of *Nature* has brought about a similar shake-up in many a reader as well. "Our age is retrospective," he begins. "It builds the sepulchres of the fathers. It writes biographies, histories, and criticism." Emerson clears the agenda with a dismissive sweep, pointing out that "the foregoing generations beheld God and nature face to face; we, through their eyes." The question Emerson incites us to ask is "Why should not we also enjoy an original relation to the universe?" The emphasis is on the word *also.* "Why should not *we* have a poetry and philosophy of insight and not of tradition, and a religion by revelation to *us,* and not the history of *theirs*?"[5]

Pursuing his own question, Emerson sets out the main benefits we derive from nature, and from putting nature first. In the chapter called "Commodity," he considers how nature provides the raw material and the energy for everything we build, grow, or eat. Who can fail to be impressed by "the steady and prodigal provision that has been made for his support and delight on this green ball which floats through the heavens?" It was the practical usefulness of nature that Emerson had in mind as he admired a tide-mill, "which, on the seashore, makes the tides drive the wheels and grind corn, and which thus engages the assistance of the moon like a hired hand, to grind, and wind, and pump, and saw, and split stone, and roll iron." And it was a typical leap of imagination for Emerson to draw from this activity his much-repeated injunction to "hitch your wagon to a star," which gains its full force when we see that the emphasis is on the word *your.* But nature as commodity is only the most obvious and most tangible of benefits, and Emerson quickly moves on to the less-material gifts of nature.[6]

In the chapter called "Beauty," he outlines a theory of aesthetics grounded in nature. "Such is the constitution of things, or such the plastic power of the human eye, that the primary forms, as the sky, the mountain, the tree, the animal, give us a delight *in and for themselves.*" Nature provides us our first and most reliable standards of beauty. "Nature is a sea of forms," he says, and "the standard of beauty is the entire circuit of natural forms." This is a fundamental proposition, a given, an "ultimate end." "No reason can be asked or given why the soul seeks beauty," says Emerson. It cannot be explained, but is itself the explanation for other things.

Just as nature provides us with our standard of beauty (Emerson's natural aesthetic can be traced from Henry Thoreau and Horatio Greenough to Frederick Church, Frank Lloyd Wright, and Edward Weston and John Cage), so *Nature* provides us with language and with an explanation of the use of language. Emerson goes further; for him, nature *is* language. "Nature is the vehicle of thought" is his formulation. Certainly for writers—and perhaps for everyone—this is the central chapter of Emerson's central book. To begin with, Emerson shows how "words are signs of natural facts." Not only does "apple" stand for an apple, but most abstractions, when traced to their origins, will be found to have roots in the visible, the concrete, the tangible. *Sierra* means saw, "supercilious" is from the Latin *super cilia,* meaning raised eyebrow. **"Experience"** goes back to Latin *periculum* and so means something won or snatched from danger. So, as Emerson will say later in his essay **"The Poet"** (to which the book *Nature* is linked by the underground river of Emerson's interest in language), language is fossil poetry. It is noteworthy that Emerson's ideas about language were picked up in England by Richard Trench and led, perhaps indirectly, to the undertaking of the *Oxford English Dictionary.*[7]

The next step of Emerson's argument is the most difficult, the most philosophically limiting, and, for the writer, the most exciting point. The writer understands, says Emerson, that "it is not words only that are emblematic; it is things which are emblematic." He fills a paragraph with examples. "Who looks upon a river in a meditative hour, and is not reminded of the flux of all things? Throw a stone into the stream, and the circles that propagate themselves are the beautiful type of all influence." What writers understand is "this immediate dependence of language upon nature." What writers do is "this conversion of an outward phenomenon onto a type of somewhat [something] in human life."[8]

What Emerson understood, and what American writers since Emerson have been able to get from him, is the importance of the primary connection between the writer and nature. Emerson puts it with unusual vehemence. "Hundreds of writers may be found in every long-civilized nation, who for a short time believe, and make others believe, that they see and utter truths, who do not of themselves clothe one thought in its natural garment, but who feed unconsciously on the language created by the primary writers of the country, those, namely, who hold primarily on nature."[9]

The essence of language then is imagery. For this reason "good writing and brilliant discourse are perpetual allegories." The reason we love imagery and respond to it is not just that language is a vast river of images, but also that nature itself is the inexhaustible upstream reservoir and source of all the rivers of language. "The world is emblematic," Emerson says. "Parts of speech are metaphors, because the whole of nature is a metaphor of the human mind." Every mind can claim all of nature for its material.[10]

Emerson is an idealist, a believer that process, purpose, or concept precedes and determines product. The most daring, and to a modern reader, the most challenging aspect of Emerson's nature, is his argument that nature teaches him to look beyond nature. To put it more carefully, he says that the beauty and interrelatedness of physical, outward nature leads him to inquire into the inner laws of nature which determine the outer appearances.

"In my utter impotence to test the authenticity of the report of my senses, to know whether the impressions they make on me correspond with outlying objects, what difference does it make, whether Orion is up there in heaven, or some god paints the image in the firmament of the soul?" Conceding that phenomena are real enough whether they objectively exist or exist only in the mind, Emerson pushes on to contend that "it is the uniform effect of culture [education, consciousness] on the human mind, not to shake our faith in the stability of particular phenomena, as of heat, water, azote [nitrogen]; but to lead us to regard nature as a phenomenon, not a substance; to attribute necessary existence to spirit; to esteem nature [that is, external nature] as an accident and an effect."[11]

The distinction Emerson makes here between the inner, invisible *laws* of nature, and the external, visible *forms* of nature is not a new one. The English Romantic poets, especially Coleridge, recognized a similar distinction between *natura naturans* (nature as a collection of active forces and processes) and *natura naturata* (the finished products of nature, natural objects). Perhaps Emerson's greatest contribution was his account of how these two aspects of nature are interrelated. His lifelong endeavor was to show how the laws and processes of nature are part of mind, and to work out the relation between mind and external nature. Emerson was, finally, a naturalist of mental more than of physical facts. Beginning around 1848, he worked on and off for the rest of his life on a project he called **"Natural History of Intellect."**

Like all thorough romantics, and like the new scientists from Goethe to Lyell and Darwin, Emerson understood that nature is in continuous change or flux. "There are no fixtures in nature," he wrote in **"Circles."** "The universe is fluid and volatile. Permanence is but a word of degrees." He understood nature to be a process rather than a thing. "Thus there is no sleep, no pause, no preservation, but all things renew, germinate and spring." His view of nature as dynamic also explains his preference for nature over history. "In nature every moment is new; the past is always swallowed and forgotten; the coming only is sacred. Nothing is secure but life, transition, the energizing spirit."[12]

As much as Emerson was committed to the idea that all is flux—an idea he called "the metamorphosis"—and as much as he was committed to the pluralistic, the diverse, and the particular, he also understood that there were laws governing appearances and that things in nature are unified and whole, though not always in obvious ways. "Everything in nature contains all the powers of nature," he wrote in **"Compensation."** "Every thing is made of one hidden stuff, as the naturalist sees one type under every metamorphosis."[13]

The central point, the pivot of Emerson's understanding of nature, is his conception of the all-encompassing relationship that exists at all times between the mind—understood as a more or less constant, classifying power—and the infinite variety of external nature. He had read Kant and Schelling and was echoing Kant when he wrote in **"The Oversoul"** that "the sources of nature are in [man's] own mind." He knew Schelling's breathtaking all-inclusive proposal that "nature is externalized mind; mind is internalized nature." In **"The American Scholar"** Emerson said that "nature is the opposite of the soul, answering to it part for part. One is seal and one is print. Its beauty is the beauty of his own mind. Its laws are the laws of his own mind. So much of nature as he [the scholar] is ignorant of, so much of his own mind does he not yet possess." In **"Compensation"** he wrote, "each new form repeats not only the main character of the type, but part for part all the details, all the aims, furtherances, hindrances, energies and whole system of every other. Every occupation, trade, art, transaction, is a compend of the world, and a correlative of every other. Each one is an entire emblem of human life; of its good and ill, its trials, its enemies, its course and its end."[14]

This radical and comprehensive connection between nature and mind is the unwobbling pivot, the fundamental condition of most of Emerson's work, and it explains why he can turn to nature for his starting point on virtually any subject. We can touch here only on a few of the most important.

Nature was Emerson's starting point for a new theology. His rejection, in the Divinity School **"Address,"** of organized—or as he called it, historical—Christianity was a protest not against, but on behalf of, religion. Following the Scottish Common Sense philosophers, Emerson argued that the "moral sentiment," which is found in all human beings, "is the essence of all religions." By religion, Emerson means concrete, personal, religious feelings or experience. "The intuition of the moral sentiment is an insight into the perfection of the laws of the soul." Intuition is, for Emerson, like religion, a matter of actual, present personal experience. "It cannot be received at second hand. Truly speaking it is not instruction, but provocation, that I can receive from another soul. What he announces, I must find true in me, or wholly reject: and on his word, or as his second, be he who he may," be he Jesus or Moses, or Paul, or Augustine, "I can accept nothing." Thus revelation must be revelation to me or to you. "Men have come to speak of the revelation as somewhat [something] long ago given and done, as if God were dead." But if there is a God then he is present now in all of us, Emerson believes. "It is the office of a true teacher to show us that God is, not was, that he speaketh, not spake." Emerson is not interested in secondhand revelations, secondhand gospel. For this reason he never refers to the Bible as an authority. He cares about what he calls the "Gospel of the present moment." He rejects the standard Christian chronological concept of history, the idea that there was one creation, that there will be one day of judgment. Religious convictions and feelings, like all others, exist for Emerson only in the present.

Thus he says "there is no profane history . . . all history is sacred." Creation is continuous. Every day is a day of creation. So, too, with the day of judgment. "No man has learned anything until he has learned that every day is judgment day." Noting that the Hebrew word for prophet is also the word for poet, Emerson insists that the modern poet can do for his people what the old Hebrew prophet-poets did for theirs. (Walt Whitman was listening.) The incarnation means God takes on flesh in every person, not just in one. When Emerson writes that "infancy is the perpetual Messiah," he means that the power of the concept of the Messiah is the hope and promise we feel in every infant. Because we live in nature, Emerson believes we can see God every day, face to face. He will have none of the disabling, through-a-glass-darkly dirge of lamentation. As he expresses it in his finest lyric poem, **"Days,"** the days themselves are gods, bringing to each of us gifts according to our capacity to receive. Every day offers us new kingdoms, powers, and glories. It is on our own heads if we settle out of court for a few herbs and apples.[15]

Nature is also Emerson's practical guide to an ethical life. In this he is a modern stoic. He believed, like Marcus Aurelius and Montaigne, that nature rather than tradition or authority or the state is our best teacher. To live in nature means above all to live in the present, to seize the day. "Life only avails, not the having lived," he says in **"Self-Reliance."** "Power ceases in the instant of repose; it resides in the moment of transition from a past to a new state, in the shooting of the gulf."[16]

Nature for Emerson was a theory of the nature of things—how things are; it was a guide to life, a foundation for philosophy, art, language, education, and everyday living. "Nature is what you may do." It was the green world of gardens and parks, and the wild world of the sea and the woods. Above all, and running through all his thought on the subject, nature was for Emerson the experience of nature. Some of the most often-cited passages in Emerson's writings are accounts of immediate physical experiences. "Crossing a bare common, in snow puddles, at twilight, under a clouded sky, without having in my thought any occurrence of special good fortune, I have enjoyed a perfect exhilaration. I am glad to the brink of fear." Even the famous passage about becoming a transparent eyeball is best understood not as a theory of nature, but as an actual

moment of experience, a feeling. Emerson devoted an entire essay to this aspect of nature. It is called **"The Method of Nature."** To a post-Darwinian reader, the title inevitably suggests a discussion of evolution, or the formation of elements beginning with hydrogen. The essay is, however, about the human experiencing of nature, which is, at its most intense, a state Emerson calls "ecstasy." By ecstasy he does not mean a technical out-of-body experience, but a joyous consciousness of the rich plenitude of existence. He speaks of the "redundancy or excess of life which in conscious beings we call ecstasy." "Surely joy is the condition of life," said Thoreau, and Emerson agreed, saying "Life is an ecstasy." For Emerson the feeling of joy was a state of ecstasy which, in his lexicon, meant nearly the same thing as "enthusiasm," that other key to a fully lived life. "Nothing great was ever achieved without enthusiasm," he said in **"Circles,"** adding that "the way of life is wonderful: it is by abandonment." When we are in this state of heightened awareness, of enthusiasm, of ecstasy, we come as close to the secret heart of nature as we can get. The important thing about your enthusiasm for nature—or for Emerson—is the enthusiasm in you. This is the highest and most valuable teaching of that nature we all agree we cannot do without. As Emerson says in **"Illusions,"** the permanent interest of every person is "never to be in a false position, but to have the weight of nature to back him in all that he does."[17]

Notes

1. Amos Bronson Alcott, "Report of the School Committee, 1861" in *Essays on Education,* ed. Walter Harding (Gainesville, FL: Scholars' Facsimiles and Reprints, 1960), p. 189. R. W. Emerson, *Nature,* in *Essays and Lectures* (New York: Viking Press, The Library of America, 1983), p. 15.

2. R. W. Emerson, *Journals and Miscellaneous Notebooks,* vol. 4, ed. Wm. H. Gilman et al. (Cambridge, MA: Harvard University Press, 1964), p. 26.

3. Cited in Robert D. Richardson, Jr., *Emerson: The Mind on Fire* (Berkeley: University of California Press, 1995), p. 208.

4. *JMN* 4, pp. 198, 199, 200.

5. Emerson, *Nature,* in *Essays and Lectures,* p. 7, emphasis added.

6. R. W. Emerson, "Civilization," in *Society and Solitude* (Cambridge, MA: Riverside Press, 1904), p. 30.

7. Richard Trench, *On the Study of Words,* 22d ed. (New York: Macmillan, 1900, orig. 1851), p. 5. In earlier editions RWE is not named but is identified as "a popular American author."

8. Emerson, *Nature,* in *Essays and Lectures,* pp. 20, 21, 22.

9. Emerson, *Nature,* in *Essays and Lectures,* pp. 22-23.

10. Emerson, *Nature,* in *Essays and Lectures,* pp. 23, 24.

11. Emerson, *Nature,* in *Essays and Lectures,* pp. 32, 33.

12. Emerson, "Circles," in *Essays and Lectures,* pp. 403, 412-13.

13. Emerson, "Compensation," in *Essays and Lectures,* p. 289.

14. Emerson, "The Oversoul," in *Essays and Lectures,* p. 399; "The American Scholar," in *Essays and Lectures,* p. 56; "Compensation," in *Essays and Lectures,* p. 289.

15. Emerson, "An Address . . ." in *Essays and Lectures,* pp. 76, 79, 88; "The Oversoul," in *Essays and Lectures,* p. 400; "Days," in *Collected Poems and Translations* (New York: Viking Press, The Library of America, 1994), p. 178.

16. Emerson, "Self-Reliance," in *Essays and Lectures,* p. 271.

17. Emerson, "Fate," in *Essays and Lectures,* pp. 949, 963; "The Method of Nature," in *Essays and Lectures,* p. 121; "Circles," in *Essays and Lectures,* p. 414; "Illusions," in *Essays and Lectures,* p. 1122.

FURTHER READING

Biography

Tuttleton, James W. "The Drop Too Much: Emerson's Eccentric Circle." In *The New Criterion* 14, No. 9 (1996): 19-27.

    A biographical overview of Emerson's social circle, which included Henry David Thoreau, Edward Thompson Taylor, and several other contemporary intellectuals.

Criticism

Bickman, Martin. "From Emerson to Dewey: The Fate of Freedom in American Education." In *American Literary History* 6, No. 3 (Fall 1994): 385-408.

    A review of Emerson's contributions as an educational thinker, citing examples of his educational principles in his essays.

Bosco, Ronald A. "The 'Somewhat Spheral and Infinite' in Every Man: Emerson's Theory of Biography. In *Emersonian Circles: Essays in Honor of Joel Myerson,* edited by Wesley T. Mott and Robert E. Burkholder. Rochester: University of Rochester Press, 1997, pp. 67-103.

    Outlines Emerson's philosophy of biography in the context of the Plutarchan model.

Burkholder, Robert E. "History's Mad Pranks: Some Recent Emerson Studies." In *ESQ: A Journal of the American Renaissance* 38, No. 3 (1992): 231-63.

    A review of ten Emersonian studies, including several reprints of his sermons and philosophical essays.

Coltharp, Duane. "Landscapes of Commodity: Nature and Economy in Emerson's Poems." In *ESQ: A Journal of the American Renaissance* 38, No. 4 (1992): 265-91.

    Contends that in contrast to Emerson's prose writing which presents a serious examination of social, political, and economic issues, his poetry contains great ambiguities and personal ambivalence.

Gougeon, Len and Joel Myerson. *Emerson's Antislavery Writings.* New Haven: Yale University Press, 1995, 232 p.

    Reprints Emerson's essays regarding antislavery, including textual commentary and an essay providing historical background on the antislavery movement.

Meyer Jr., William E. H. "Faulkner, Hemingway, et al.: The Emersonian Test of American Authorship." In *The Mississippi Quarterly* 51, No. 3 (Summer 1998): 557-71.

    Examines the influence of Emerson's philosophy of American writing on the styles of American writers including Ernest Hemingway.

Kronick, Joseph G. "Emerson and the Divisions of Criticism." In *Review,* ed. James O. Hoge. V. 2 (Charlottesville: University Press of Virginia, 1999): 59-98.

    An overview of varying critical responses to Emerson including a review of several books that examine Emerson's writings in the context of his transcendentalist beliefs.

Levin, Jonathan. "Life in the Transitions: Emerson, William James, Wallace Stevens." In *Arizona Quarterly* 4, No. 4 (Winter 1992): 75-97.

    A comparative analysis of the dynamic processes that infuse the working of language in the works of Emerson, James, and Stevens.

Morris, Saundra. "The Threshold Poem, Emerson, and 'The Sphinx.'" In *American Literature* 69, No. (September 1997): 547-70.

    A review of "The Sphinx" as an overture or "threshold poem" to the material that follows it in Emerson's *Poems.*

Newfield, Christopher. "Controlling the Voice: Emerson's Early Theory of Language." In *ESQ: A Journal of the American Renaissance* 38, No. 1 (1992): 1-29.

    An examination of Emerson's theory of language outlined in his *Nature,* stressing the relationship between invention and imitation.

Porte, Joel and Saundra Morris, editors. *The Cambridge Companion to Ralph Waldo Emerson.* Cambridge: Cambridge University Press, 1999, 280 p.

A collection of critical, biographical, and interpretive essays on Emerson's works, including bibliographical references and indices.

Thomas, Joseph M. "'The Property of My Own Book': Emerson's *Poems* (1847) and the Literary Marketplace." In *New England Quarterly* 69, No. 3 (September 1996): 406-25.

An examination of Emerson's handling of his authorial affairs using the 1847 edition of *Poems* as an example.

Additional coverage of Emerson's life and career is contained in the following sources published by Gale Group: *Concise Dictionary of American Literary Biography 1640-1865; Dictionary of Literary Biography,* **Vols. 1, 59, 73, and 223;** *DISCovering Authors; DISCovering Authors: British; DISCovering Authors: Canadian; DISCovering Authors Modules: Most-Studied Authors* **and** *Poets; Poetry Criticism,* **Vol. 18; and** *World Literature Criticism, 1500 to the Present.*

Alessandro Manzoni
1785-1873

(Full name Alessandro Francesco Tommaso Antonio Manzoni) Italian novelist, playwright, poet, essayist, and critic. For additional information on Manzoni's life and works, see *NCLC,* Volume 29.

INTRODUCTION

Manzoni is remembered as the author of the first great modern Italian novel, *I promessi sposi* (1827; *The Betrothed*). A complex historical narrative of seventeenth-century Italian life, *I promessi sposi* is distinguished by its psychological insight, religious and nationalistic themes, use of common people as protagonists, and introduction of spoken Italian as a medium for literary expression. *I promessi sposi* was widely imitated by subsequent Italian novelists, influencing the evolution of both Italian language and literature and contributing to the rise of Italian nationalism in the nineteenth century. In addition to the novel, Manzoni produced several collections of verse, two dramas, and numerous critical and historical writings that comprise a notable contribution to the development of Italian Romanticism.

BIOGRAPHICAL INFORMATION

Manzoni was born in Milan, the son of wealthy aristocratic parents who separated while he was still a child. His early years were spent in religious schools where he studied Catholic theology, philosophy, history, and Latin and Italian classics. During the period of his formal education, which ended when he was sixteen, Manzoni also began to write poetry. After he left school, Manzoni lived with his father for several years in Milan, where his interest in literature, history, and politics was stimulated by the cultural life of the city. In 1805 he joined his mother in Paris. There he continued to write, composing poems that were influenced in form and diction by eighteenth-century Neoclassicism. In Paris he also met artists and intellectuals who introduced him to the literary trends of the age, particularly Romanticism. Two years later, Manzoni returned to Italy, and in 1810 he experienced a strengthening and renewal of his Catholic faith that was to form the basis for his major literary works. He moved to an inherited estate in the country, and established the sedate and retiring lifestyle he maintained for the rest of his life. During the next fifteen years, he produced his principal works of poetry, drama, and criticism. In 1827 Manzoni published his only novel, *I promessi sposi*. Popular and critical response in Italy was almost unanimously favorable, earning Man-

zoni a respected position in Italian letters and society. During the next few years, prompted by his concern that prose Italian should more closely reflect the language of the common people, Manzoni revised the novel according to the dialect of Tuscany, which he felt was nearer to an ideal Italian idiom. This version appeared in installments from 1840 to 1842. Thereafter, Manzoni primarily wrote essays on various subjects, including linguistics, literature, and politics. His life of quiet study and contemplation was interrupted in 1860, when, as a result of his revered public status, he was made a member of the Italian senate. Manzoni died in 1873.

MAJOR WORKS

Set in seventeenth-century Spanish-dominated Lombardy during the Thirty-Years' War, *I promessi sposi* relates the story of two peasant lovers, Renzo and Lucia, separated before their marriage by the machinations of Don Rodrigo, a local nobleman desirous of Lucia. Fleeing the city to escape Rodrigo, the couple endures many hardships, including famine, war, plague, and the abduction of Lucia, before they are finally wed. Throughout the narrative, Manzoni detailed historical events with meticulous accuracy, presenting realistic descriptions of starving, plague-ridden villages and cities and chronicling the effects of the Thirty Years' War in Italy. The work also demonstrates Manzoni's major themes: the evil of unbridled passions, the necessity of trust in God and in an afterlife, the corruption of religious and political organizations, and the blight of foreign domination. In addition to this well-known novel, Manzoni also produced several notable works of poetry, including his *Inni sacri* (1806; *The Sacred Hymns*), verses on religious subjects, and the nationalistic *Il cinque maggio* (1815; *Ode on the Death of Napoleon*). In his essay *Osservazioni sulla morale cattolica* (1819; *A Vindication of Catholic Morality*) Manzoni offered a defense of the Catholic religion. He also composed two historical verse dramas: *Il conte di Carmagnola* (1820), featuring a proud count wrongly accused of treason, and *Adelchi* (1822), which recounts an era of political intrigue and military turmoil among the Longobards, Franks, and Latins in early Medieval Italy. These tragedies also demonstrate in practice Manzoni's disregard for the Aristotelian unities of time and place, which he stated formally in his *Lettre à M. Chauvet sur les unités de temps et de lieu dans la tragédie* (1823; *A Letter on Dramatic Unities and the Essence of Tragedy*). Like the *Lettre à M. Chauvet*, many of Manzoni's significant critical statements were drafted in epistolary form. Among these, his *Lettera sul romanticismo* (1823), written to the Marchese Cesare D'Azeglio, rejects the subject matter of classical mythology in modern literature.

CRITICAL RECEPTION

Late in life Manzoni repudiated the form of the historical novel because he believed that it failed to satisfy the aims of either history or fiction. Nevertheless, most commentary on Manzoni's work has been concentrated on *I promessi sposi,* which most critics consider his most important work and a masterpiece of world literature. Early critics focused on the relationship of the novel to the historical fiction of Sir Walter Scott and on Manzoni's moral and political concerns, while later critics have emphasized the novel's structure and language. The consensus has been that *I promessi sposi,* in its complex interweaving of plot, characterization, theme, and style, is the culmination of Manzoni's literary career. In addition, critics have observed that Manzoni's characters, both humble and aristocratic, are skillfully portrayed against a finely realized, if revisionist, historical background. Likewise, scholars have noted that Manzoni's integration of spoken and literary Italian aptly delineates his characters and conveys his moral, religious, and patriotic themes. Manzoni's critical, poetic, and dramatic works have also elicited modern scholarly interest as seminal documents of Italian Romanticism. Several contemporary critics have examined the stylistic and thematic significance of Manzoni's historical verse tragedies and have analyzed his political stance,

which blends a devout respect for Catholicism with an overriding belief in the importance of liberal revolution.

PRINCIPAL WORKS

In morte di Carlo Imbonati (poetry) 1806

Urania (poetry) 1809

Inni sacri [*The Sacred Hymns*] (poetry) 1815

Osservazioni sulla morale cattolica [*A Vindication of Catholic Morality*] (essay) 1819

Il Conte di Carmagnola (verse drama) 1820

Il cinque maggio [*Ode on the Death of Napoleon*; also published as *The Napoleonic Ode* and *The Fifth of May*] (poetry) 1821

Adelchi (verse drama) 1822

Discorse sopra alcuni punti della storia longobardica in Italia (history) 1822

Lettera sul romanticismo (criticism) 1823

Lettre à M. Chauvet sur les unités de temps et de lieu dans la tragédie [*A Letter on Dramatic Unities and the Essence of Tragedy*] (criticism) 1823

*I promessi sposi [*The Betrothed*] (novel) 1827

Storia della colonna infame [*The Column of Infamy*] (historical narrative) 1840-42

Dell'invenzione [*A Dialogue of the Artist's Idea*] (dialogue) 1850

Del romanzo storico [*On the Historical Novel*] (essay) 1850

Del trionfo della libertá (poetry) 1878

Tutte le opere. 11 vols. (poetry, verse dramas, novel, historical narrative, letters, criticism, and essays) 1957-70

**Originally titled *Fermo e Lucia,* but never published. The revised version of this novel was published between 1840 and 1842.

CRITICISM

Henry T. Tuckerman (essay date 1851)

SOURCE: "The Novelist: Manzoni," in *Characteristics of Literature Illustrated by the Genius of Distinguished Writers,* Lindsay and Blakiston, 1851, pp. 2-37.

[*In the following excerpt, Tuckerman discusses Manzoni as he represents the nineteenth-century novelist, and comments on the "fidelity to nature" of his *I promessi sposi.*]

As I stood by the taffrail of the little steamer that plies up and down Lake Como, a good-natured fellow-passenger, whose costume and bearing denoted the experienced gentleman, indicated the various points of interest along the beautiful shores. It was a clear, warm day of that enchanting season, in those climates, when spring is just verging into summer. The atmosphere was transparent, and every indentation of the beach had a well-defined relief; the sails of the fishing-boats were reflected in the water as distinctly as if it were a mirror; and the cloudless sky wore the densely azure hue peculiar to that region. My companion urbanely pointed out every object worthy of note, which the shifting landscape afforded; here was the site of Pliny's country-seat, there the former residence of Queen Caroline of England, and now we are directly opposite the villa of Pasta; but there was a more genial animation in his look and voice, as a low promontory loomed in sight, neither remarkable for the cultivation at its base, nor the picturesque beauty of its treeless slope: "Just behind that ridge," said he, "is the road which Don Abbondio followed until he encountered the *bravi* who forbade him to marry the *Promessi Sposi.*" The perfectly natural manner in which the locality of an imaginary scene was thus designated, as if quite as real and more interesting than the abodes of actual persons, struck me as the very best evidence of Manzoni's genius and fame. All genuine creations assert and maintain a distinct personality; and this is, perhaps, the readiest and most faithful test whereby the legitimate characters of fiction may be distinguished from the counterfeit. The most universal triumph of this kind is that of Shakespeare, of whose personages we habitually speak not only as actual, but world-familiar celebrities. It is probable that if the origin of those characters in fiction, which are recognised by the general feeling of mankind as living originals, could be analyzed, it would appear that their essential features were drawn carefully from life. The chief attraction of the novels of the reign of George the Third is said to have been, that the individuals depicted were well known at that period, and this fact gave a relish to the infirmities of character thus revealed. But a more recent instance occurs in regard to several of the best delineations of Dickens, whose Pecksniff, Squeers, brothers Cheeryble, and others, are confidently identified; so that, even if there is an error in the designation, it only shows how nearly the author followed nature. Another convincing proof of the substantial relation to our experience, such daguerreotypes from life bear, is the habit so prevalent of naming our acquaintances from the well-drawn characters of able novelists. To realize the variety of fanciful beings who have been added by modern genius to the world's vast gallery of memorable portraits, it is only requisite to summon before our minds the long array of Scott's familiar creations. Charles Swain has done this in a poem entitled *Dryburgh Abbey*; and the obsequies of no human being were ever graced by so glorious an array of the representatives of human nature, acknowledged as such by the verdict of mankind, as this procession of his own "beings of the mind, and not of clay," which are described as following Sir Walter to the tomb.

An avidity for fabulous narrative seems to have characterized the Oriental races. The indolent life of that dreamy clime naturally induced a necessity of being amused. Professed story-tellers were patronised by those in authority; and doubtless listened to with as earnest an attention as the lazzaroni on the Mole at Naples now bestow upon a reader of Tasso. Pastorals were probably the first improvised tales of rural districts. The more exacting imaginations of Eastern potentates called forth "Arabian Nights;" and, subsequently, when the western world was alive with the lays of troubadours and the thirst for gallant emprise, came the tales of chivalry destined chiefly to be remembered through the genial satire of Cervantes. The supremacy of the Church brought saintly legends in vogue; the spirit of maritime adventure led to the production of countless "*voyages imaginaires*;" civic revolutions, of a later period, gave birth to political romance, of which Utopia is the English type; and the more complicated interests and varied drama of modern society, finds its most welcome and perhaps faithful portraiture in one or another of the diversified species of the novel. Thus it is evident that from the Song of Solomon and the fables of mythology, to the last hot-pressed emanation from Albemarle Street, Fiction has served as a mirror to successive ages, reflecting with more or less truth, events and manners, in hues not so emphatic as the drama, but with greater detail and more elaborate exactitude.

There are few more interesting literary processes than the composition of a novel, artistically wrought and genially inspired. If we analyze the method, it seems to be very like that by which a fine picture is executed. First, there are historical materials to collect,—the costume, manners, and spirit of the time chosen, to be studied and reproduced; then the dramatic incidents or plot to be arranged—corresponding to the action of the subject in pictorial art; the impressive background of history, the just perspective of time, so as to render the illusion complete; with the light and shade of cheerful and solemn feeling. These may all be derived from study and observation, and effectively arranged by skill and taste; but another, and the most vital element—the sentiment, or if the work be too prosaic to admit of such a definition, the sensation of the whole—that vague yet magnetic quality which in nature, in painting, and even in social life, we call atmosphere, must be derived from individual consciousness. This it is which brings us into relation with the story; which essentially attracts or repels; its presence gives life, and its absence makes entirely objective the most patiently finished conception. The other traits of a romance are more or less mechanical, or at least originate in the active intelligence of the writer; but this last and crowning principle emanates from the individual soul: it is that which makes the statue appear to breathe, and the picture to be a conscious reality; which carries the words of the poet into the universal heart of mankind, and causes the characters and scenery of a romance to assimilate themselves, in the imagination, with the actual and the endeared.

The gravest artistic faults or deficiencies may be counterbalanced, in a novel, by the truth, elevation, or delicacy of the sentiment, exactly as warmth and sincerity of character atone for a thousand foibles and even distasteful qualities in a friend. Thus Mackenzie's *Man of Feeling,* and Foscolo's *Jacopo Ortis,* considered as tales, are barren of striking events, wonderful coincidences, or elaborately-drawn characters; yet the one from its gentle and resigned and the other from its thoughtful and impassioned sentiment, apparently warm from a living heart, win and impress us with an indefinite but entrancing interest. Mrs. Radcliffe's novels abound in local mistakes; Southey demonstrates that her description of Skiddaw is entirely untrue; and in *The Sicilian,* she makes her heroine look from the towers of Palermo upon Mount Etna—a geographical impossibility; yet the scenes she depicts are so invested with the sentiment of wonder so largely developed in her nature, that the wizard charm of superstition haunts the reader with its gloomy fascination, notwithstanding the improbabilities of her narrative, the tame solution of her mysteries, and the inexcusable incorrectness of her topography. No one can read *Corinne* without impatience at the inconsistent character of Oswald, and the unsatisfactory reasons assigned for the unhappy course of events; but Madame de Staël has so deeply impregnated the imperfect drama with earnest, acute, and philosophical sentiment, with the sentiment at once of love, of genius, and of Italy, that we pause not to examine and object to the story, in our profound sympathy with the intense feeling and reflection which it sustains, like an unsymmetrical and ill-jointed trellis holding up to the air and sunshine, clusters of purple fruit and masses of autumn-tinted leaves. Some of Hans Andersen's stories, professedly written for children, and quite fantastic in conception, are so sweetly invented and so imbued with genuine humanity, that they charm all who have not outlived heart and imagination. It is, therefore, the idiosyncrasy of the novelist that imparts the zest to his writings; it is the point where his nature overflows, that yields the peculiar charm to his inventions; and it is thus that our real sympathies are awakened. The biographers of Richardson and Mrs. Inchbald let us into the secret of that winsome tenderness that once caused us to hang fondly over *Pamela* and the *Simple Story*; it was their own prevailing characteristic. Godwin, on the same principle, excites metaphysical curiosity; Goldsmith, the sense of domestic enjoyment; Scott, chivalrous and patriotic emotion; Cooper, the zest of adventure; Dickens, convivial, pitiful, and humorous feeling; Irving, agreeable reverie; Beckford, an epicurean delight of the senses; Miss Porter and Maturin, the luxury of heroic self-devotion, and the rich but consuming excitement of ardent passion; Paul de Kock, the vagrant but spirited moods of Parisian adventure; and Balzac, the philosophical and sympathetic interest which anatomizes the inmost life of the heart.

Truth to nature, rather than dramatic effect, was the aim of Manzoni; and, as is ever the case when realized, it secured for his romance a permanent interest and celebrity. There is no attempt at brilliancy in the dialogue, no accumulation of incredible events in the plot, and scarcely a trait of improbability in the characters. Fidelity is the charm upon which the author relies both to enlist the sympathies of the reader and disarm the opposition of the critic. It is as if a well-skilled artist were to roam, during an exciting epoch, over the fertile plains of Lombardy, and transfer scrupulously to his sketch-book, the most characteristic figures of peasant and prelate,—here a picturesque bit of landscape and there an animated group; now a monastery, and again some by-way cottage, vineyard, or shrine,—thus giving us authentic hints whereby we can reproduce in imagination, especially if seconded by memory, a satisfactory conception of all the prevailing features of the scene. The author's manner, to borrow a term so often applied to the old masters in painting, is more that of Murillo and the Flemish school than of Raphael or Correggio: except that the literary execution of Manzoni has a somewhat classical and even pedantic character. Essentially, however, the same artistic principle is relied upon. There is something of Gainsborough and Moreland in the tone of his graphic pictures; he seldom idealizes, but conscientiously represents the actual. His ***Promessi Sposi*** is attractive to Italians on the same ground that the *Vicar of Wakefield* is a favourite with English readers. We are interested in his characters, not because they are perfect, but because they are natural. Renzo, indeed, can scarcely be called a hero, or Lucia a heroine, in the sense in which that term is employed by fanatical novel-readers. Neither exhibit any poetic sentimentalism. Their love is as unromantic as it is honest. He is but a skilful and industrious silk-weaver; and she, as the disappointed Bergamese, who expected to see a wonderful beauty, discovered, is only *"una contadina come tante altre;"*—a peasant girl like so many others. But, then, the attractive simplicity of nature, the affectionate disposition, the child-like faith and rustic truth of these lovers, and especially their excellence as types of a local peasantry, render them, in contrast with the remarkable vicissitudes through which they pass, objects of real and sometimes intense sympathy. There is a kind of elemental human nature about Lucia that is irresistibly charming; the very weakness and ignorance, as well as the faithful attachment and irascible temper of Renzo, are eminently illustrative of the rural population of Lombardy. It is, too, exceedingly characteristic of somewhat advanced women of the middle class of Italians, to affect the wisdom of experience, and nourish their self-esteem by a kind of pretension to knowledge of the world—which is the more diverting from the actual narrowness of their ideas and their obvious superficial knowledge and lack of real confidence. The sage counsels, and desire to have her say, ascribed to poor Agnese, peculiarly belong to her sphere and age. The ecclesiastical portraits are the most carefully laboured of all; and even allowing for the author's strong Catholic partialities, they must be admitted to be most consistent, each with itself, and all with probability and truth. The church that can boast a Fenelon and a Cheverus, doubtless has, from time to time, included priests as exalted in their views as Federigo Borromeo, as true to an expiatory vow as Padre Cristofero, and as timid and time-serving as poor Don Abbondio. Nay, at this very time, whoever has been on familiar terms with the Italian clergy, must have encountered exceptions to the general corruption, in the form of a martyr-like asceticism or a life-devoted benevolence. In some, perhaps isolated regions there are members of the monastic fraternities that are idolized by the common people for their charity; preachers who fill a cathedral by their eloquence, and men of saintly lives whose benediction is received with awe and gratitude. In short, traces of the three prominent ecclesiastics of Manzoni's romance, may be easily detected at the present day; and, in many pious minds, yet excite the sentiments of love and reverence, which, at the period described, united the peasant to the church. It was doubtless the author's main object to vindicate the religious sentiment; to show how the essential principles of Christianity were knit into the well-being of society; and to bring into strong relief, for the advantage of a sceptical and revolutionary era, the consoling, purifying, and happy influences of the church, whose superstitions had become a byword, and whose sovereignty already yielded to military power. We can, indeed, imagine no greater contrast than that which exists between the whole spirit and atmosphere of Manzoni's story and the times in which it appeared. The star of Europe's modern conqueror was rapidly culminating; all that was prescriptive and venerable in usage, form, law, manners, and faith, had either yielded to inexorable reform or was in a transition state; and the primal sentiments of our common nature, without whose prevailing sanction and tender intervention we can scarcely hope for the stability of any human institution, were so violently assailed, that a kind of social chaos seemed inevitable. The triumphs of Napoleon had opened the way for an apparently limitless series of experiments in government; and a fearless challenge of all authority, especially that of religion. The mental activity and civic revolutions incident to this state of things, kept Europe in a continual ferment. Old associations had no power to hedge in thought; and new combinations of events gave scope to every kind of speculative hardihood. It was the age of sudden political vicissitudes, splendid military achievements, constant social alternations, and fearless inquiry. It was an experimental, irreverent, and unbelieving age; and even at such a time, Manzoni sent forth his calm pictures of rustic life; he revived the primitive in human nature; exhibited the graces of simplicity, the moral value of faith, the charm of spotless integrity, the need of a vista through which, amid the darkness and tumult of life, glimpses could be afforded of heaven; the blessedness of forgiveness; the tranquil joy of expiation, the glory of repentance, and the beauty of holiness. It was like the low warbling of a lute amid the braying of trumpets; or one of the soft sunsets of Claude reflected on a thunder-cloud. It was an enterprise, in its very hopelessness and beauty, worthy of the heart of genius; and the peaceful and sweet manner in which it was achieved, evinces the dignity of scholarship and the self-possession of faith.

It has, indeed, been objected to the *Promessi Sposi,* that it is circumstantial even to tediousness; that it lacks vivacity of tone and variety of interest. Perhaps these and similar faults are inseparable from the author's plan; his first object being truth to nature and history, in order to render his work locally authentic, and give it a national interest; and his second to inculcate certain great principles of life and action, which he saw were lost sight of in an age of preternatural and spasmodic excitement. The polished correctness of the style, too, while on the one hand it has given

the novel a classical rank and caused it to be one of the most approved textbooks in the acquisition of the Italian tongue, on the other, by a certain stiffness and the use of uncommon words, occasioned by the classic fastidiousness of the author, has induced pedantry of style, the very reverse of that colloquial ease, which is so great a requisite in the popular novel. These and other incidental defects do not, however, at all invalidate the well-founded claims of *Promessi Sposi,* as a true picture of Italian life, felicitously conceived and artistically developed.

As the artistic representative of truth and the pleasing stimulant of benign emotions, Fiction thus redeems itself from the serious objections to which it was once far more liable than at present. "It is necessary to our rank as spiritual beings," says a judicious writer, "that we should be able to invent and to behold what is not; and to our rank as moral creatures that we should know and confess that it is not." Hence the unsatisfactory blending of fact and fiction, by the excessive development of any of the elements we have designated, the exaggerations of professedly veritable travellers, the fanciful narratives of historians, as well as grossly illusive pictures of life and nature even in a romance. Such errors offend the integrity of the novelist's art exactly as mean expedients and grotesque combinations in architecture, or untrue drawing and extravagant colour in painting, or want of proportion in statuary; because such blemishes destroy the sentiment and mar the completeness of invention in writing, as well as in form or design. Legitimately produced, however, and truly inspired, fiction interprets humanity, informs the understanding, and quickens the affections. It reflects ourselves, warns us against prevailing social follies, adds rich specimens to our cabinets of character, dramatises life for the unimaginative, daguerreotypes it for the unobservant, multiplies experience for the isolated or inactive, and cheers age, retirement, and invalidism, with an available and harmless solace. A distinguished modern statesman decided a question that arose in a social circle, by very gravely quoting a passage from *Robinson Crusoe.* His friends expressed their surprise that one whose pursuits were so complicated and absorbing should remember the very words of that nursery tale; he assured them he had read it once every year since he was a boy as a mental refreshment. Humboldt pauses in his description of tropical vegetation, to mention with gratitude the fact that it is associated in his mind with the correctly delineated scenery of Paul and Virginia. The philosophic Mackintosh advocates fiction because "it creates and nourishes sympathy;" and the poet Gray declared that it was heaven to pass a rainy day in reading new novels. Thus resorted to as a pastime in the intervals of more exacting studies, and at periods of convalescence or recreation, it is one of the most ready and useful of luxuries, but no more to be relied upon altogether as intellectual food, than champagne, spices, or beautiful fruit, for animal nourishment. It is, therefore, only the abuse of fiction which deadens the zest of truth, for its right office is to heighten its effect. "Matter of fact," says Hunt, "is our perception of the grosser and more external shapes of truth; fiction represents the residuum of the mystery. To love matter of fact is to have a lively sense of the visible and the immediate; to love fiction is to have as lively a sense of the possible and the remote."

The word novel has a much higher signification than formerly. It once conveyed the idea of vapid sentimentalism or irrational romance, only adapted to very weak and morbidly fanciful tastes. It furnished pabulum to imaginary woes, and yielded unhealthy excitement to undisciplined minds. Hence the very justifiable prejudice so long cherished against this kind of reading by vigorous intellects. A half century has effected a complete revolution in this department of literature. Perhaps the first example which led to this auspicious change is the *Caleb Williams* of Godwin. That remarkable work proved that a story may be deeply interesting without being mainly occupied with the tender passion; and it suggested that human nature and human life afforded a boundless and most instructive field for true genius to represent. The English have excelled in fiction, perhaps, in part, from the judgment which they, of all people, know best how to bring to the arrangement of passionate and poetic materials, and thus render them harmonious and effective. If we glance at the number and variety of standard English novels that still maintain their place in select libraries, we cannot but acknowledge that our vernacular is the most prolific source of excellent fiction, in modern times. Consider, also, the important subjects these works illustrate, and how ably they have been made the exponents of grave opinion, social questions, history, philanthropy, art, and morals. The most vivid pictures of London society, in the days of Johnson, are yet to be found in the novels of Miss Burney; and its present absurdities have been most effectually satirized by the novels of Hook. If we desire to realize the life of the East, the Anastasius of Hope is the most available *camera obscura* into which to enter and view its reflection. We are confidently referred to the novels of Smollett for an authentic character of the English navy fifty years ago. The low life of Great Britain is sketched in enduring colours by Dickens. The philosophy of common sense—that trait of national character which chiefly distinguishes the Anglo-Saxon from the southern European, is permanently elaborated in the novels of Maria Edgeworth and Miss Austin. All salient eras of human history and social life have been reproduced by modern novelists. Scottish annals and scenery may be said to have been revealed to the world by the author of Waverley; and Macaulay sustains his description of the condition of the clergy in the reign of Charles the Second, by the parsons Fielding has bequeathed. Miss Ferrier's novels have immortalized the most humorous and characteristic traits of Scotch society. The life of the north of Europe is now familiar to us through the charming tales of Miss Bremer. Lockhart and our own Ware have given adequate pictures whereby the unlearned may be initiated into that memorable epoch when the advent of Christianity introduced a new element into the life of the Roman Empire. Systems of political economy, the questions that divide the Episcopal Church, the social problems involved in the manufacturing enterprise of England, the racy and pathetic aspects of Irish

life, the biography of illustrious men, the arts of diplomacy, principles of taste, government, religion, and science, now, almost daily, find accredited and fascinating interpreters in the guise of popular novelists.

The conditions we have indicated are happily fulfilled in the Romance of Manzoni. Every one at all familiar with the public events of the time, which are made in the novel to lend the dignity of great social phenomena to the humble experiences of the hero and heroine,—will trace a scrupulous authenticity in the narrative; and not less faithful are the incidental glimpses afforded of the laws, customs, and social economy of the period. We seem, as we read, to breathe the atmosphere of that epoch when the feudal spirit yet lingered in Italy, although its practical influence was essentially modified; when haughty lords still kept their armed retainers, and could, with certain precautions, violently outrage individual rights with impunity; when the sanctions of the Church yet exercised an unquestioned authority;—the age of local warfare, of Latin edicts, of gross popular delusions, of scholastic pedantry, and fanciful philosophy. These phases of life in that day and country are brought out with remarkable tact in the course of the story. The war to settle the succession of the ducal states of Gonzaga, and the occurrence of a famine and the plague at Milan, by arousing all the latent elements of society, give ample occasion to indicate the degree of knowledge, the tone of public opinion, and the standard of civilization then and there attained. We are admitted freely to the banquet of the lordly castle, the discussions of the piazza, the domestic life of the palace, the secrets of conventual discipline, the gossip of the *osteria,* the interviews of the archbishop, and the humble colloquies of the village hearth. Attentively regarded, they yield the most clear and reliable impressions; and the amount of positive information thus gleaned from the story, is not less remarkable than the facility with which it is suggested. The more elaborate pictures thus vividly reproduced from the dusty archives of municipal history, will bear a very thoughtful perusal. The description of the bread riots and the various scenes enacted at Milan during the ravages of the plague, have scarcely been equalled for graphic delineation and true pathos, by any of the many brilliant sketches, in the same vein, subsequently attempted by the most eloquent writers. Their beautiful diction in some cases enhances the effect; the minute circumstances and affecting points of view chosen, are such as an actual spectator would naturally have selected; while the light and shade, the impressive fact and the affecting sentiment, are blended with that inimitable skill which is only an intuition of genius. Indeed, the chastened tone of these parts of the romance,—often affording not only room, but temptation to exaggerate, is one of its prominent merits. We do not, for a moment, lose sight of the dreadful reality on account of the melo-dramatic representation. On the contrary, the dangling hair of virgin-bodies piled on the dead-carts; the horrid buffoonery of the *monatti*; the maternal tenderness and care lavished so calmly on an infant's corpse, in the midst of the licentious misery around; the remorseful terrors of the selfish noble, and the heartless cupidity of the base servant, the devotion of the benevolent, and the callous indifference of the hardened;—each individual demonstration of character and every special incident that stand out from the general record of pestilence and famine, are usually so true to the great and authenticated occurrences, that we not only confess that they might have been, but feel that they were. So much for the unity of these ghastly, yet memorable pictures. The author is equally felicitous in minor limning;—the forms of salutation, the classic oaths, the religious adjurations, the proverbs, gestures, and casual provincialisms that occur, have not only authority, but significance. Passed over, by the ordinary reader, without interest, to those familiar with the region and the classes depicted, they have a peculiar meaning and an intrinsic charm.

Manzoni has, also, a concise way of sketching a whole genus in one of the species, of exhibiting what is characteristic of a domain or a class by a single effective specimen. Thus, in the portrait of Federigo Borromeo we have not only an historical personage, but the ideal of the scholar, saint, and gentleman combined, of that age. Perpetua's counterparts may be seen by every traveller who sojourns awhile with an Italian family of the middle class. The plants enumerated as having overgrown Renzo's garden during his banishment, might be classified in a botanical nomenclature of Lombardy. Don Ferrante's philosophical creed illustrates the scientific Quixotism then indulged by speculative minds; and a very adequate idea of the scenery of northern Italy may be derived from the account given of the different journeys of the fugitives between Milan, Monza, and Bergamo.

In the unpretending but significant tales of Dana and Hawthorne we often discover the essence of romance—the most pure and subtle elements of original fiction. Remorse has found no more refined and touching interpreter than the former; and it is rarely that what is adjacent and immediate has been so delicately and suggestively delineated as by the latter. Professional life has revealed some of its most thrilling secrets by the pen of Warren; and popular art is most vividly illustrated in Wilhelm Meister. Many of the profound laws of love and music may be learned in Consuelo; the luxuries and the psychological working of sentiment glow and melt along the pages of Rousseau; fantasy, in its wildest, most sublime and most exquisite play, emanates from the German novelists—now shadowy with the weird genius of Hoffman, and now aerial with the crystal grace of Undine. The iris-hues of the *Midsummer Night's Dream* reappear in the fairy tale; and all the virtues and the comfort of modern civilization are embodied in English stories of domestic life. But the field embraced by this endeared form of literature is too vast for specific comment. The fertility of its resources may be imagined by considering what rich elements are included in the exuberant life of the primitive fiction, the truthful consistency of the standard narrative, and the insight into men and things, of the modern fashionable novel: take, for instance, the tone of Boccaccio—the verisimilitude of De Foe, and the knowledge of the world of Thackeray;—how much of

human life, both inward and outward, how many of the elemental and the manifest principles of our common nature and of universal experience, are therein combined!

Personal familiarity with the country and people described in Manzoni's novel, is almost essential to its complete enjoyment and appreciation. To have seen one of the religious processions, in Tuscany, for instance, bearing the relics of a saint for the purpose of checking a freshet or a drought, and to have watched the hopeful countenances of the rustic throng, renders far more vivid the ceremonial of escorting the gorgeously-decked remains of St. Carlo through the streets of Milan, to stay that awful pestilence. The sight of one of the popular tumults which agitated Sicily when the cholera prevailed there, a few years since, and the ocular proof of the fanaticism of the ignorant wretches in sacrificing so many innocent victims to the suspicion of having poisoned the wells, and thus induced the disease,—brings home to the most unimaginative the frantic delusion of the Milanese, in ascribing the pestilence, whose course is so graphically described by the novelist, to the same cause. The scribes who yet sit in the squares of Palermo and Naples to indite letters for the common people, make the difficulties of Renzo in corresponding with his betrothed, appear very natural. An *habitué* of a *trattoria* in Italy, will recognise the viands the language and bearing of the innkeepers as identical with those of our own day; and a certain extraordinary blending of acuteness and candour, of almost childish simplicity in matters of faith and feeling, and dexterity or evasion in cases involving personal safety or interest, which might appear inconsistent elsewhere, are perfectly true to Italian character. In fact, in many particulars, Hogarth and Crabbe are not more thoroughly literal interpreters of nature than Manzoni.

The monotony of provincial life in Italy, the family dictatorship, which virtually forces superfluous children to enter the cloister, and the more benign aspects of Catholicism, to those who have been in contact with the domestic life of the country, are reproduced in this story with singular truth. It was doubtless no small part of the author's plan to touch the patriotic sensibilities of his countrymen by the nationality of his work; and this, perhaps, account for the fear he seems to have entertained of the slightest extravagance; and the somewhat tiresome historical interludes scattered through the romance. The sentiments unfolded are those of the author himself. He was thoroughly sincere both in his patriotism and his piety; and this is the more honourable to him inasmuch as his origin is noble his associations of the highest kind, and his education superior; but the scholar and the man of rank were not suffered to overlay the Christian and the philanthropist. While other authors of the period scarcely professed any faith whatever, and followed their own vagrant impulses, Manzoni looked to God in meekness, and around upon his country with love. His nature was essentially contemplative; he believed rather in the victories of thought than those of the sword; and relied on the primitive and indestructible sentiments of humanity far more than external violence for the advancement of truth. His first work, **Conte di Carmagnola,** which appeared in 1820, a tragedy embodying the noblest self-devotion and patriotism, excited a deep interest throughout the continent. Other dramas, his famous Ode, entitled **Il Cinque di Maggio,** on the death of Napoleon, and a volume of hymns,—then a rare species of writing in Italy, increased his literary renown.

But his popularity is derived from his novel—**I Promessi Sposi.** He adopted this form of literature as that which gave him the surest and most extensive access to the minds of his countrymen. Scott's unparalleled success in the same department was already the literary phenomenon of the day; and to Manzoni belongs the credit of first effectively introducing the modern novel into Italy. By patient elaboration of authentic facts, by careful limning from original elements of character within his observation, by infusing the genuine sentiments of his own heart into the beings he portrayed, and by a scholar-like finish of style, he laboured to produce an unexceptionable, graphic, interesting, and standard national romance; and, however humble the sphere he chose to illustrate, he accomplished his purpose. It is a curious fact that almost the only trace of his ideal tendencies in this work, is discoverable in some of his comparisons, which, by their fancifulness, betray the poet. Otherwise the design is mainly Flemish, both in subjects and exactitude. The atmosphere, however, of the whole picture, to the view of one whose associations are enlisted, is as soft, attractive, and mellow, as that of spring in Italy. The gentle and tranquil excitements of rural life and primitive manners, touch the heart of the sympathetic reader. The resignation of Lucia, the conversion of the wicked *Innominato,* the sublime patience of Padre Cristofero, the diverting cowardice of Don Abbondio, the shrewishness of Perpetua, the enlarged benevolence of Federigo, with the episodes of extreme human misery, and the final happy fortunes of the humble lovers, gradually win upon our calm attention, and become, at last, endeared to our remembrance.

W. D. Howells (essay date 1887)

SOURCE: "Alessandro Manzoni," in *Modern Italian Poets: Essays and Versions,* Books for Libraries Press, 1972, pp. 126-74.

[*In the following excerpt, originally published in 1887, Howells provides an introduction to European Romanticism, briefly surveys Manzoni's life, and evaluates his verse dramas and poetry—quoting extensively from selected works.*]

I

It was not till the turbulent days of the Napoleonic age were past, that the theories and thoughts of Romance were introduced into Italy. When these days came to an end, the whole political character of the peninsula reverted, as nearly as possible, to that of the times preceding the revolutions. The Bourbons were restored to Naples, the Pope to Rome, the Dukes and Grand Dukes to their several states, the House of Savoy to Piedmont, and the Austrians to Venice and Lombardy; and it was agreed among all these despotic governments that there was to be no Italy save, as Metternich suggested, in a geographical sense. They encouraged a relapse, among their subjects, into the follies and vices of the past, and they largely succeeded. But, after all, the age was against them; and people who have once desired and done great things are slow to forget them, though the censor may forbid them to be named, and the prison and the scaffold may enforce his behest.

With the restoration of the Austrians, there came a tranquillity to Milan which was not the apathy it seemed. It was now impossible for literary patriotism to be openly militant, as it had been in Alfieri and Foscolo, but it took on the retrospective phase of Romance, and devoted itself to the celebration of the past glories of Italy. In this way it still fulfilled its educative and regenerative mission. It dwelt on the victories which Italians had won in other days over their oppressors, and it tacitly reminded them that they were still oppressed by foreign governments; it portrayed their own former corruption and crimes, and so taught them the virtues which alone could cure the ills their vices had brought upon them. Only secondarily political, and primarily moral, it forbade the Italians to hope to be good citizens without being good men. This was Romance in its highest office, as Manzoni, Grossi, and D'Azeglio conceived it. Æsthetically, the new school struggled to overthrow the classic traditions; to liberate tragedy from the bondage of the unities, and let it concern itself with any tragical incident of life; to give comedy the generous scope of English and Spanish comedy; to seek poetry in the common experiences of men and to find beauty in any theme; to be utterly free, untrammeled, and abundant; to be in literature what the Gothic is in architecture. It perished because it came to look for Beauty only, and all that was good in it became merged in Realism which looks for Truth.

These were the purposes of Romance, and the masters in whom the Italian Romanticists had studied them were the great German and English poets. The tragedies of Shakespeare were translated and admired, and the dramas of Schiller were reproduced in Italian verse; the poems of Byron and of Scott were made known, and the ballads of such lyrical Germans as Bürger. But, of course, so quick and curious a people as the Italians had been sensitive to all preceding influences in the literary world, and before what we call Romance came in from Germany, a breath of nature had already swept over the languid elegance of Arcady from the northern lands of storms and mists; and the effects of this are visible in the poetry of Foscolos's period.

The enthusiasm with which Ossian was received in France remained, or perhaps only began, after the hoax was exploded in England. In Italy, the misty essence of the Caledonian bard was hailed as a substantial presence. The king took his spear, and struck his deeply sounding shield, as it hung on the willows over the neatly kept garden-walks, and the Shepherds and Shepherdesses promenading there in perpetual *villeggiatura* were alarmed and perplexed out of a composure which many noble voices had not been able to move. Emiliani-Giudici declares that Melchiorre Cesarotti, a professor in the University of Padua, dealt the first blow against the power of Arcadia. This professor of Greek made the acquaintance of George Sackville, who inflamed him with a desire to read Ossian's poems, then just published in England; and Cesarotti studied the English language in order to acquaint himself with a poet whom he believed greater than Homer. He translated Macpherson into Italian verse, retaining, however, in extraordinary degree, the genius of the language in which he found the poetry. He is said (for I have not read his version) to have twisted the Italian into our curt idioms, and indulged himself in excesses of compound words, to express the manner of his original. He believed that the Italian language had become "sterile, timid, and superstitious," through the fault of the grammarians; and in adopting the blank verse for his translation, he ventured upon new forms, and achieved complete popularity, if not complete success. "In fact," says Giudici, "the poems of Ossian were no sooner published than Italy was filled with uproar by the new methods of poetry, clothed in all the magic of magnificent forms till then unknown. The Arcadian flocks were thrown into tumult, and proclaimed a crusade against Cesarotti as a subverter of ancient order and a mover of anarchy in the peaceful republic—it was a tyranny, and they called it a republic—of letters. Cesarotti was called corrupter, sacrilegious, profane, and assailed with titles of obscene contumely; but the poems of Ossian were read by all, and the name of the translator, till then little known, became famous in and out of Italy." In fine, Cesarotti founded a school; but, blinded by his marvelous success, he attempted to translate Homer into the same fearless Italian which had received his Ossian. He failed, and was laughed at.

Ossian, however, remained a power in Italian letters, though Cesarotti fell; and his influence was felt for romance before the time of the Romantic School. Monti imitated him as he found him in Italian; yet, though Monti's verse abounds, like Ossian, in phantoms and apparitions, they are not northern specters, but respectable shades, classic, well-mannered, orderly, and have no kinship with anything but the personifications, Vice, Virtue, Fear, Pleasure, and the rest of their genteel allegorical company. Unconsciously, however, Monti had helped to prepare the way for romantic realism by his choice of living themes. Louis XVI, though decked in epic dignity, was something that touched and interested the age; and Bonaparte, even in pagan apotheosis, was so positive a subject that the improvvisatore acquired a sort of truth and sincerity in celebrating him. Bonaparte might not be the Sun he was hailed to be, but even in Monti's verse he was a soldier, ambitious, unscrupulous, irresistible, recognizable in every guise.

In Germany, where the great revival of romantic letters took place,—where the poets and scholars, studying their own Minnesingers and the ballads of England and Scotland, reproduced the simplicity and directness of thought characteristic of young literatures,—the life as well as the song of the people had once been romantic. But in Italy there had never been such a period. The people were municipal, mercantile; the poets burlesqued the tales of chivalry, and the traders made money out of the Crusades. In Italy, moreover, the patriotic instincts of the people, as well as their habits and associations, were opposed to those which fostered romance in Germany; and the poets and novelists, who sought to naturalize the new element of literature, were naturally accused of political friendship with the hated Germans. The obstacles in the way of the Romantic School at Milan were very great, and it may be questioned if, after all, its disciples succeeded in endearing to the Italians any form of romantic literature except the historical novel, which came from England, and the untrammeled drama, which was studied from English models. They produced great results for good in Italian letters; but, as usual, these results were indirect, and not just those at which the Romanticists aimed.

In Italy the Romantic School was not so sharply divided into a first and second period as in Germany, where it was superseded for a time by the classicism following the study of Winckelmann. Yet it kept, in its own way, the general tendency of German literature. For the *Sorrows of Werther,* the Italians had the *Last Letters of Jacopo Ortis*; for the brood of poets who arose in the fatherland to defy the Revolution, incarnate in Napoleon, with hymn and ballad, a retrospective national feeling in Italy found the same channels of expression through the Lombard group of lyrists and dramatists, while the historical romance flourished as richly as in England, and for a much longer season.

De Sanctis studies the literary situation in the concluding pages of his history; they are almost the most brilliant pages, and they embody a conception of it so luminous that it would be idle to pretend to offer the reader anything better than a résumé of his work. The revolution had passed away under the horror of its excesses; more temperate ideas prevailed; the need of a religious and moral restoration was felt. "Foscolo died in 1827, and Pellico, Manzoni, Grossi, Berchet, had risen above the horizon. The Romantic School, 'the audacious boreal school,' had appeared. 1815 is a memorable date. . . . It Marks the official manifestation of a reaction, not only political, but philosophical and literary. . . . The reaction was as rapid and violent as the revolution. . . . The white terror succeeded to the red."

Our critic says that there were at this time two enemies, materialism and skepticism, and that there rose against them a spirituality carried to idealism, to mysticism. "To the right of nature was opposed the divine right, to popular sovereignty legitimacy, to individual rights the State, to liberty authority or order. The middle ages returned in triumph. . . . Christianity, hitherto the target of all offense, became the center of every philosophical investigation, the banner of all social and religious progress. . . . The criterions of art were changed. There was a pagan art and a Christian art, whose highest expression was sought in the Gothic, in the glooms, the mysteries, the vague, the indefinite, in a beyond which was called the ideal, in an aspiration towards the infinite, incapable of fruition and therefore melancholy. . . . To Voltaire and Rousseau succeeded Chateaubriand, De Staël, Lamartine, Victor Hugo, Lamennais. And in 1815 appeared the **Sacred Hymns** of the young Manzoni."

II

The Romantic movement was as universal then as the Realistic movement is now, and as irresistible. It was the literary expression of monarchy and aristocracy, as Realism is the literary expression of republicanism and democracy. What De Sanctis shows is that out of the political tempest absolutism issued stronger than ever, that the clergy and the nobles, once its rivals, became its creatures; the prevailing bureaucracy interested the citizen class in the perpetuity of the state, but turned them into office-seekers; the police became the main-spring of power; the office-holder, the priest and the soldier became spies. "There resulted an organized corruption called government, absolute in form, or under a mask of constitutionalism. . . . Such a reaction, in violent contradiction of modern ideas, could not last." There were outbreaks in Spain, Naples, Piedmont, the Romagna; Greece and Belgium rose; legitimacy fell; citizen-kings came in; and a long quiet followed, in which the sciences and letters flourished. Even in Austria-ridden Italy, where constitutionalism was impossible, the middle class was allowed a part in the administration. "Little by little the new and the old learned to live together: the divine right and the popular will were associated in laws and writs. . . . The movement was the same revolution as before, mastered by experience and self-disciplined. . . . Chateaubriand, Lamartine, Victor Hugo, Lamennais, Manzoni, Grossi, Pellico, were liberal no less than Voltaire and Rousseau, Alfieri and Foscolo. . . . The religious sentiment, too deeply offended, vindicated itself; yet it could not escape from the lines of the revolution . . . it was a reaction transmuted into a reconciliation."

The literary movement was called Romantic as against the old Classicism; medieval and Christian, it made the papacy the hero of its poetry; it abandoned Greek and Roman antiquity for national antiquity, but the modern spirit finally informed Romanticism as it had informed Classicism; Parini and Manzoni were equally modern men. Religion is restored, but, "it is no longer a creed, it is an artistic motive. . . . It is not enough that there are saints, they must be beautiful; the Christian idea returns as art. . . . Providence comes back to the world, the miracle reappears in story, hope and prayer revive, the heart softens, it opens itself to gentle influences. . . . Manzoni reconstructs the ideal of the Christian Paradise and reconciles it with the modern spirit. Mythology goes, the classic remains; the eighteenth century is denied, its ideas prevail."

The pantheistic idealism which resulted pleased the citizen-fancy; the notion of "evolution succeeded to that of revolution"; one said civilization, progress, culture, instead of liberty. "Louis Philippe realized the citizen ideal. . . . The problem was solved, the skein untangled. God might rest. . . . The supernatural was not believed, but it was explained and respected. One did not accept Christ as divine, but a human Christ was exalted to the stars; religion was spoken of with earnestness, and the ministers of God with reverence."

A new criticism arose, and bade literature draw from life, while a vivid idealism accompanied anxiety for historical truth. In Italy, where the liberals could not attack the governments, they attacked Aristotle, and a tremendous war arose between the Romanticists and the Classicists. The former grouped themselves at Milan chiefly, and battled through the Conciliatore, a literary journal famous in Italian annals. They vaunted the English and Germans; they could not endure mythology; they laughed the three unities to scorn. At Paris Manzoni had imbibed the new principles, and made friends with the new masters; for Goethe and Schiller he abandoned Alfieri and Monti. "Yet if the Romantic School, by its name, its ties, its studies, its impressions, was allied to German traditions and French fashions, it was at bottom Italian in accent, aspiration, form, and motive. . . . Every one felt our hopes palpitating under the medieval robe; the least allusion, the remotest meanings, were caught by the public, which was in the closest accord with the writers. The middle ages were no longer treated with historical and positive intention; they became the garments of our ideals, the transparent expression of our hopes."

It is this fact which is especially palpable in Manzoni's work, and Manzoni was the chief poet of the Romantic School in that land where it found the most realistic development, and set itself seriously to interpret the emotions and desires of the nation. When these were fulfilled, even the form of Romanticism ceased to be.

III

Alessandro Manzoni was born at Milan in 1784, and inherited from his father the title of Count, which he always refused to wear; from his mother, who was the daughter of Beccaria, the famous and humane writer on Crimes and Punishments, he may have received the nobility which his whole life has shown.

In his youth he was a liberal thinker in matters of religion; the stricter sort of Catholics used to class him with the Voltaireans, and there seems to have been some ground for their distrust of his orthodoxy. But in 1808 he married Mlle. Louisa Henriette Blondel, the daughter of a banker of Geneva, who, having herself been converted from Protestantism to the Catholic faith on coming to Milan, converted her husband in turn, and thereafter there was no question concerning his religion. She was long remembered in her second country "for her fresh blond head, and her blue eyes, her lovely eyes," and she made her husband very happy while she lived. The young poet signalized his devotion to his young bride, and the faith to which she restored him, in his *Sacred Hymns,* published in this devout and joyous time. But Manzoni was never a Catholic of those Catholics who believed in the temporal power of the Pope. He said to Madam Colet, the author of *L'Italie des Italiens,* a silly and gossiping but entertaining book, "I bow humbly to the Pope, and the Church has no more respectful son; but why confound the interests of earth and those of heaven? The Roman people are right in asking their freedom—there are hours for nations, as for governments, in which they must occupy themselves, not with what is convenient, but with what is just. Let us lay hands boldly upon the temporal power, but let us not touch the doctrine of the Church. The one is as distinct from the other as the immortal soul from the frail and mortal body. To believe that the Church is attacked in taking away its earthly possessions is a real heresy to every true Christian."

The *Sacred Hymns* were published in 1815, and in 1820 Manzoni gave the world his first tragedy, *Il Conte di Carmagnola,* a romantic drama written in the boldest defiance of the unities of time and place. He dispensed with these hitherto indispensable conditions of dramatic composition among the Italians eight years before Victor Hugo braved their tyranny in his Cromwell; and in an introduction to his tragedy he gave his reasons for this audacious innovation. Following the *Carmagnola,* in 1822, came his second and last tragedy, *Adelchi.* In the mean time he had written his magnificent ode on the Death of Napoleon, **"Il Cinque Maggio,"** which was at once translated by Goethe, and recognized by the French themselves as the last word on the subject. It placed him at the head of the whole continental Romantic School.

In 1825 he published his romance, *I Promessi Sposi,* known to every one knowing anything of Italian, and translated into all modern languages. Besides these works, and some earlier poems, Manzoni wrote only a few essays upon historical and literary subjects, and he always led a very quiet and uneventful life. He was very fond of the country; early every spring he left the city for his farm, whose labors he directed and shared. His life was so quiet, indeed, and his fate so happy, in contrast with that of Pellico and other literary contemporaries at Milan, that he was accused of indifference in political matters by those who could not see the subtler tendency of his whole life and works. Marc Monnier says, "There are countries where it is a shame not to be persecuted," and this is the only disgrace which has ever fallen upon Manzoni.

When the Austrians took possession of Milan, after the retirement of the French, they invited the patricians to inscribe themselves in a book of nobility, under pain of losing their titles, and Manzoni preferred to lose his. He constantly refused honors offered him by the Government, and he sent back the ribbon of a knightly order with the answer that he had made a vow never to wear any decoration. When Victor Emanuel in turn wished to do him a like honor, he held himself bound by his excuse to the Austrians, but accepted the honorary presidency of the Lombard Institute of Sciences, Letters and Arts. In 1860 he was elected a Senator of the realm; he appeared in order to take the oath and then he retired to a privacy never afterwards broken.

IV

"Goethe's praise," says a sneer turned proverb, "is a brevet of mediocrity." Manzoni must rest under this damaging applause, which was not too freely bestowed upon other Italian poets of his time, or upon Italy at all, for that matter.

Goethe could not laud Manzoni's tragedies too highly; he did not find one word too much or too little in them; the style was free, noble, full and rich. As to the religious lyrics, the manner of their treatment was fresh and individual although the matter and the significance were not new and the poet was "a Christian without fanaticism, a Roman Catholic without bigotry, a zealot without hardness."

The tragedies had no success upon the stage. The *Carmagnola* was given in Florence in 1828, but in spite of the favor of the court, and the open rancor of the friends of the Classic School, it failed; at Turin, where the *Adelchi* was tried, Pellico regretted that the attempt to play it had been made, and deplored the "vile irreverence o the public."

Both tragedies deal with patriotic themes, but they are both concerned with occurrences of remote epochs. The time of the *Carmagnola* is the fifteenth century; that of the *Adelchi* the eighth century; and however strongly marked are the characters,—and they are very strongly marked, and differ widely from most persons of Italian classic tragedy in this respect,—one still feels that they are subordinate to the great contests of elements and principles for which the tragedy furnishes a scene. In the *Carmagnola* the pathos is chiefly in the feeling embodied by the magnificent chorus lamenting the slaughter of Italians by Italians at the battle of Maclodio; in the *Adelchi* we are conscious of no emotion so strong as that we experience when we hear the wail of the Italian people, to whom the overthrow of their Longobard oppressors by the Franks but the signal of a new enslavement. This chorus is almost as fine as the more famous one in the *Carmagnola*; both are incomparably finer than anything else in the tragedies and are much more dramatic than the dialogue. It is in the emotion of a spectator belonging to our own time rather than in that of an actor of those past times that the poet shows his dramatic strength; and whenever he speaks abstractly for country and humanity he moves us in a way that permits no doubt of his greatness.

After all, there is but one Shakespeare, and in the drama below him Manzoni holds a high place. The faults of his tragedies are those of most plays which are not acting plays, and their merits are much greater than the great number of such plays can boast. I have not meant to imply that you want sympathy with the persons of the drama, but only less sympathy than with the ideas embodied in them. There are many affecting scenes, and the whole of each tragedy is conceived in the highest and best ideal.

V

In the ***Carmagnola,*** the action extends from the moment when the Venetian Senate, at war with the Duke of Milan, places its armies under the command of the count, who is a soldier of fortune and has formerly been in the service of the Duke. The Senate sends two commissioners into his camp to represent the state there, and to be spies upon his conduct. This was a somewhat clumsy contrivance of the Republic to give a patriotic character to its armies, which were often recruited from mercenaries and generaled by them; and, of course, the hireling leaders must always have chafed under the surveillance. After the battle of Maclodio, in which the Venetian mercenaries defeated the Milanese, the victors, according to the custom of their trade, began to free their comrades of the other side whom they had taken prisoners. The commissioners protested against this waste of results, but Carmagnola answered that it was the usage of his soldiers, and he could not forbid it; he went further, and himself liberated some remaining prisoners. His action was duly reported to the Senate, and as he had formerly been in the service of the Duke of Milan, whose kinswoman he had married, he was suspected of treason. He was invited to Venice, and received with great honor, and conducted with every flattering ceremony to the hall of the Grand Council. After a brief delay, sufficient to exclude Carmagnola's followers, the Doge ordered him to be seized, and upon a summary trial he was put to death. From this tragedy I give first a translation of that famous chorus of which I have already spoken; I have kept the measure and the movement of the original at some loss of literality. The poem is introduced into the scene immediately succeeding the battle of Maclodio, where the two bands of those Italian *condottieri* had met to butcher each other in the interests severally of the Duke of Milan and the Signory of Venice.

> CHORUS.
>
> On the right hand a trumpet is sounding,
>   On the left hand a trumpet replying,
> The field upon all sides resounding
>   With the trampling of foot and of horse.
>   Yonder flashes a flag; yonder flying
> Through the still air a bannerol glances;
> Here a squadron embattled advances,
>   There another that threatens its course.
>
> The space 'twixt the foes now beneath them
>   Is hid, and on swords the sword ringeth;
> In the hearts of each other they sheathe them;
>   Blood runs, they redouble their blows.
>   Who are these? To our fair fields what bringeth
> To make war upon us, this stranger?
> Which is he that hath sworn to avenge her,
>   The land of his birth, on her foes?

> They are all of one land and one nation,
>   One speech; and the foreigner names them
> All brothers, of one generation;
>   In each visage their kindred is seen;
>   This land is the mother that claims them,
> This land that their life blood is steeping,
> That God, from all other lands keeping,
>   Set the seas and the mountains between.
>
> Ah, which drew the first blade among them
>   To strike at the heart of his brother?
> What wrong, or what insult hath stung them
>   To wipe out what stain, or to die?
>   They know not; to slay one another
> They come in a cause none hath told them;
> A chief that was purchased hath sold them;
>   They combat for him, nor ask why.
>
> Ah, woe for the mothers that bare them,
>   For the wives of these warriors maddened!
> Why come not their loved ones to tear them
>   Away from the infamous field?
>   Their sires, whom long years have saddened,
> And thoughts of the sepulcher chastened,
> In warning why have they not hastened
>   To bid them to hold and to yield?
>
> As under the vine that embowers
>   His own happy threshold, the smiling
> Clown watches the tempest that lowers
>   On the furrows his plow has not turned,
>   So each waits in safety, beguiling
> The time with his count of those falling
> Afar in the fight, and the appalling
>   Flames of towns and of villages burned.
>
> There, intent on the lips of their mothers,
>   Thou shalt hear little children with scorning
> Learn to follow and flout at the brothers
>   Whose blood they shall go forth to shed;
>   Thou shalt see wives and maidens adorning
> Their bosoms and hair with the splendor
> Of gems but now torn from the tender,
>   Hapless daughters and wives of the dead.
>
> Oh, disaster, disaster, disaster!
>   With the slain the earth's hidden already;
> With blood reeks the whole plain, and vaster
>   And fiercer the strife than before!
>   But along the ranks, rent and unsteady,
> Many waver—they yield, they are flying!
> With the last hope of victory dying
>   The love of life rises again.
>
> As out of the fan, when it tosses
>   The grain in its breath, the grain flashes,
> So over the field of their losses
>   Fly the vanquished. But now in their course
>   Starts a squadron that suddenly dashes
> Athwart their wild flight and that stays them,
> While hard on the hindmost dismays them
>   The pursuit of the enemy's horse.
>
> At the feet of the foe they fall trembling,
>   And yield life and sword to his keeping;

In the shouts of the victors assembling,
    The moans of the dying are drowned.
  To the saddle a courier leaping,
Takes a missive, and through all resistance,
Spurs, lashes, devours the distance;
    Every hamlet awakes at the sound.

Ah, why from their rest and their labor
    To the hoof-beaten road do they gather?
Why turns every one to his neighbor
    The jubilant tidings to hear?
Thou know'st whence he comes, wretched father?
And thou long'st for his news, hapless mother?
In fight brother fell upon brother!
    These terrible tidings *I* bring.

All around I hear cries of rejoicing;
    The temples are decked; the song swelleth
From the hearts of the fratricides, voicing
    Praise and thanks that are hateful to God.
    Meantime from the Alps where he dwelleth
The Stranger turns hither his vision,
And numbers with cruel derision
    The brave that have bitten the sod.

Leave your games, leave your songs and exulting;
    Fill again your battalions and rally
Again to your banners! Insulting
    The stranger descends, he is come!
  Are ye feeble and few in your sally,
Ye victors? For this he descendeth!
'T is for this that his challenge he sendeth
    From the fields where your brothers lie dumb!

Thou that strait to thy children appearedst,
    Thou that knew'st not in peace how to tend them,
Fatal land! now the stranger thou fearedst
    Receive, with the judgment he brings!
  A foe unprovoked to offend them
At thy board sitteth down, and derideth,
The spoil of thy foolish divideth,
    Strips the sword from the hand of thy kings.

Foolish he, too! What people was ever
    For bloodshedding blest, or oppression?
To the vanquished alone comes harm never;
    To tears turns the wrong-doer's joy!
  Though he 'scape through the years' long
     progression,
Yet the vengeance eternal o'ertaketh
Him surely; it waiteth and waketh;
    It seizes him at the last sigh!

We are all made in one Likeness holy,
    Ransomed all by one only redemption;
Near or far, rich or poor, high or lowly,
    Wherever we breathe in life's air,
  We are brothers, by one great preëmption
Bound all; and accursed be its wronger,
Who would ruin by right of the stronger,
    Wring the hearts of the weak with despair.

Here is the whole political history of Italy. In this poem the picture of the confronted hosts, the vivid scenes of the combat, the lamentations over the ferocity of the embattled brothers, and the indifference of those that behold their kinsmen's carnage, the strokes by which the victory, the rout, and the captivity are given, and then the apostrophe to Italy, and finally the appeal to conscience—are all masterly effects. I do not know just how to express my sense of near approach through that last stanza to the heart of a very great and good man, but I am certain that I have such a feeling.

The noble, sonorous music, the solemn movement of the poem are in great part lost by its version into English; yet I hope that enough are left to suggest the original. I think it quite unsurpassed in its combination of great artistic and moral qualities, which I am sure my version has not wholly obscured, bad as it is.

VI

The scene following first upon this chorus also strikes me with the grand spirit in which it is wrought; and in its revelations of the motives and ideas of the old professional soldier-life, it reminds me of Schiller's *Wallenstein's Camp*. Manzoni's canvas has not the breadth of that of the other master, but he paints with as free and bold a hand and his figures have an equal heroism of attitude and motive. The generous soldierly pride of Carmagnola, and the strange *esprit du corps* of the mercenaries, who now stood side by side, and now front to front in battle; who sold themselves to any buyer that wanted killing done, and whose noblest usage was in violation of the letter of their bargains, are the qualities on which the poet touches, in order to waken our pity for what has already raised our horror. It is humanity in either case that inspires him—humanity characteristic of many Italians of this century who have studied so long in the school of suffering that they know how to abhor a system of wrong, and yet excuse its agents.

The scene I am to give is in the tent of the great *condottiere*. Carmagnola is speaking with one of the Commissioners of the Venetian Republic, when the other suddenly enters:

> COMMISSIONER: My lord, if instantly
> You haste not to prevent it, treachery
> Shameless and bold will be accomplished, making
> Our victory vain, as 't partly hath already.
> COUNT: How now?
> COM: The prisoners leave the camp in troops!
> The leaders and the soldiers vie together
> To set them free; and nothing can restrain them
> Saving command of yours.
> COUNT: Command of mine?
> COM: You hesitate to give it?
> COUNT: 'T is a use,
> This, of the war, you know. It is so sweet
> To pardon when we conquer; and their hate
> Is quickly turned to friendship in the hearts
> That throb beneath the steel. Ah, do not seek
> To take this noble privilege from those
> Who risked their lives for your sake, and to-day
> Are generous because valiant yesterday.
> COM: Let him be generous who fights for himself,

My lord! But these—and it rests upon their honor-
Have fought at our expense, and unto us
Belong the prisoners.
COUNT: You may well think so,
Doubtless, but those who met them front to front,
Who felt their blows, and fought so hard to lay
Their bleeding hands upon them, they will not
So easily believe it.
COM: And is this
A joust for pleasure then? Doth not Venice
Conquer to keep? And shall her victory
Be all in vain?
COUNT: Already I have heard it.
And I must hear that word again? 'T is bitter;
Importunate it comes upon me, like an insect
That, driven once away, returns to buzz
About my face. . . . The victory is in vain!
The field is heaped with corpses; scattered wide,
And broken are the rest—a most flourishing
Army, with which, if it were still united,
And it were mine, mine truly, I 'd engage
To overrun all Italy! Every design
Of the enemy baffled; even the hope of harm
Taken away from him; and from my hand
Hardly escaped, and glad of their escape,
Four captains against whom but yesterday
It were a boast to show resistance; vanished
Half of the dread of those great names; in us
Doubled the daring that the foe has lost;
The whole choice of the war now in our hands;
And ours the lands they 've left—is 't nothing?
Think you that they will go back to the Duke,
Those prisoners; and that they love him, or
Care more for *him* than *you?* that they have fought
In *his* behalf? Nay, they have combatted
Because a sovereign voice within the heart
Of men that follow any banner cries,
"Combat and conquer!" they have lost and so
Are set at liberty; they 'll sell themselves—
O, such is now the soldier!—to the first
That seeks to buy them—Buy them; they are yours!
1ST COM: When we paid those that were to fight
    with them,
We then believed ourselves to have purchased them.
2D COM: My lord, Venice confides in you; in you
She sees a son; and all that to her good
And to her glory can redound, expects
Shall be done by you.
COUNT: Everything I can.
2D COM: And what can you not do upon this field?
COUNT: The thing you ask. An ancient use, a use
Dear to the soldier, I can not violate.
2D COM: You, whom no one resists, on whom so
    promptly
Every will follows, so that none can say,
Whether for love or fear it yield itself;
You, in this camp, you are not able, you,
To make a law, and to enforce it?
COUNT: I said
I could not; now I rather say, I *will* not!
No further words; with friends this hath been ever
My ancient custom; satisfy at once
And gladly all just prayers, and for all other
Refuse them openly and promptly. Soldier!
COM: Nay—what is your purpose?
COUNT: You will see anon.

[*To a soldier who enters.*]
How many prisoners still remain?
SOLDIER: I think,
My lord, four hundred.
COUNT: Call them hither—call
The bravest of them—those you meet the first;
Send them here quickly. [*Exit soldier.*]
Surely, I might do it—
If I gave such a sign, there were not heard
A murmur in the camp. But these, my children,
My comrades amid peril, and in joy,
Those who confide in me, believe they follow
A leader ever ready to defend
The honor and advantage of the soldier;
I play them false, and make more slavish yet,
More vile and base their calling, than 't is now?
Lords, I am trustful, as the soldier is,
But if you now insist on that from me
Which shall deprive me of my comrades' love,
If you desire to separate me from them,
And so reduce me that I have no stay
Saving yourselves—in spite of me I say it,
You force me, you, to doubt—
COM: What do you say?
[*The prisoners, among them young Pergola, enter.*]
COUNT (TO THE PRISONERS): O brave in vain!
Unfortunate! To you,
Fortune is cruelest, then? And you alone
Are to a sad captivity reserved?
A PRISONER: Such, mighty lord, was never our belief.
When we were called into your presence, we
Did seem to hear a messenger that gave
Our freedom to us. Already, all of those
That yielded them to captains less than you
Have been released, and only we—
COUNT: Who was it,
That made you prisoners?
PRISONER: We were the last
To give our arms up. All the rest were taken
Or put to flight, and for a few brief moments
The evil fortune of the battle weighed
On us alone. At last you made a sign
That we should draw nigh to your banner,—we
Alone not conquered, relics of the lost.
COUNT. You are those? I am very glad, my
    friends,
To see you again, and I can testify
That you fought bravely; and if so much valor
Were not betrayed, and if a captain equal
Unto yourselves had led you, it had been
No pleasant thing to stand before you.
PRISONER: And now
Shall it be our misfortune to have yielded
Only to you, my lord? And they that found
A conqueror less glorious, shall they find
More courtesy in him? In vain we asked
Our freedom of your soldiers—no one durst
Dispose of us without your own assent,
But all did promise it. "O, if you can,
Show yourselves to the Count," they said. "Be sure,
He 'll not embitter fortune to the vanquished;
An ancient courtesy of war will never
Be ta'en away by him; he would have been
Rather the first to have invented it."
COUNT (TO THE COMS): You hear them, lords? Well,
    then, what do you say?

What would you do, you? *(To the prisoners)*
Heaven forbid that any
Should think more highly than myself of me!
You are all free, my friends; farewell! Go, follow
Your fortune, and if e'er again it lead you
Under a banner that 's adverse to mine,
Why, we shall see each other. *(The Count observes*
young Pergola and stops him.)
Ho, young man,
Thou art not of the vulgar! Dress, and face
More clearly still, proclaims it; yet with the others
Thou minglest and art silent?
PERGOLA: Vanquished men
Have nought to say, O captain.
COUNT: This ill-fortune
Thou bearest so, that thou dost show thyself
Worthy a better. What 's thy name?
PERGOLA: A name
Whose fame 't were hard to greaten, and that lays
On him who bears it a great obligation.
Pergola is my name.
COUNT: What! thou 'rt the son
Of that brave man?
PERGOLA: I am he.
COUNT: Come, embrace
Thy father's ancient friend! Such as thou art
That I was when I knew him first. Thou bringest
Happy days back to me! the happy days
Of hope. And take thou heart! Fortune did give
A happier beginning unto me;
But fortune's promises are for the brave,
And soon or late she keeps them. Greet for me
Thy father, boy, and say to him that I
Asked it not of thee, but that I was sure
This battle was not of his choosing.
PERGOLA: Surely,
He chose it not; but his words were as wind.
COUNT: Let it not grieve thee; 't is the leader's shame
Who is defeated; he begins well ever
Who like a brave man fights where he is placed.
Come with me, *(takes his hand)*
I would show thee to my comrades.
I 'd give thee back thy sword. Adieu, my lords;
(To the Coms.)
I never will be merciful to your foes
Till I have conquered them.

A notable thing in this tragedy of ***Carmagnola*** is that the interest of love is entirely wanting to it, and herein it differs very widely from the play of Schiller. The soldiers are simply soldiers; and this singleness of motive is in harmony with the Italian conception of art. Yet the ***Carmagnola*** of Manzoni is by no means like the heroes of the Alfierian tragedy. He is a man, not merely an embodied passion or mood; his character is rounded, and has all the checks and counterpoises, the inconsistencies, in a word, without which nothing actually lives in literature, or usefully lives in the world. In his generous and magnificent illogicality, he comes the nearest being a woman of all the characters in the tragedy. There is no other personage in it equaling him in interest; but he also is subordinated to the author's purpose of teaching his countrymen an enlightened patriotism. I am loath to blame this didactic aim, which, I suppose, mars the æsthetic excellence of the piece.

Carmagnola's liberation of the prisoners was not forgiven him by Venice, who, indeed, never forgave anything; he was in due time entrapped in the hall of the Grand Council, and condemned to die. The tragedy ends with a scene in his prison, where he awaits his wife and daughter, who are coming with one of his old comrades, Gonzago, to bid him a last farewell. These passages present the poet in his sweeter and tenderer moods, and they have had a great charm for me.

SCENE—THE PRISON
COUNT (SPEAKING OF HIS WIFE AND DAUGHTER): By this time
they must know my fate. Ah! why
Might I not die far from them? Dread, indeed,
Would be the news that reached them, but, at least,
The darkest hour of agony would be past,
And now it stands before us. We must needs
Drink the draft drop by drop. O open fields,
O liberal sunshine, O uproar of arms,
O joy of peril, O trumpets, and the cries
Of combatants, O my true steed! 'midst you
'T were fair to die; but now I go rebellious
To meet my destiny, driven to my doom
Like some vile criminal, uttering on the way
Impotent vows, and pitiful complaints.
          . . . . .
But I shall see my dear ones once again
And, alas! hear their moans; the last adieu
Hear from their lips—shall find myself once more
Within their arms—then part from them forever.
They come! O God, bend down from heaven on them
One look of pity.
[*Enter* ANTONIETTA, MATILDE, *and* GONZAGA.]
ANTONIETTA: My husband!
MATILDE: O my father!
ANTONIETTA: Ah, thus thou comest back! Is this the moment
So long desired?
COUNT: O poor souls! Heaven knows
That only for your sake is it dreadful to me.
I who so long am used to look on death,
And to expect it, only for your sakes
Do I need courage. And you, you will not surely
Take it away from me? God, when he makes
Disaster fall on the innocent, he gives, too,
The heart to bear it. Ah! let *yours* be equal
To your affliction now! Let us enjoy
This last embrace—it likewise is Heaven's gift.
Daughter, thou weepest; and thou, wife! Oh, when
I chose thee mine, serenely did thy days
Glide on in peace; but made I thee companion
Of a sad destiny. And it is this thought
Embitters death to me. Would that I could not
See how unhappy I have made thee!
ANTONIETTA: O husband
Of my glad days, thou mad'st them glad! My heart,—
Yes, thou may'st read it!—I die of sorrow! Yet
I could not wish that I had not been thine.
COUNT: O love, I know how much I lose in thee:
Make me not feel it now too much.
MATILDE: The murderers!
COUNT: No, no, my sweet Matilde; let not those
Fierce cries of hatred and of vengeance rise
From out thine innocent soul. Nay, do not mar

These moments; they are holy; the wrong 's great,
But pardon it, and thou shalt see in midst of ills
A lofty joy remaining still. My death,
The cruelest enemy could do no more
Than hasten it. Oh surely men did never
Discover death, for they had made it fierce
And insupportable! It is from Heaven
That it doth come, and Heaven accompanies it,
Still with such comfort as men cannot give
Nor take away. O daughter and dear wife,
Hear my last words! All bitterly, I see,
They fall upon your hearts. But you one day will have
Some solace in remembering them together.
Dear wife, live thou; conquer thy sorrow, live;
Let not this poor girl utterly be orphaned.
Fly from this land, and quickly; to thy kindred
Take her with thee. She is their blood; to them
Thou once wast dear, and when thou didst become
Wife of their foe, only less dear; the cruel
Reasons of state have long time made adverse
The names of Carmagnola and Visconti;
But thou go'st back unhappy; the sad cause
Of hate is gone. Death 's a great peacemaker!
And thou, my tender flower, that to my arms
Wast wont to come and make my spirit light,
Thou bow'st thy head? Aye, aye, the tempest roars
Above thee! Thou dost tremble, and thy breast
Is shaken with thy sobs. Upon my face
I feel thy burning tears fall down on me,
And cannot wipe them from thy tender eyes.
   . . . Thou seem'st to ask
Pity of me, Matilde. Ah! thy father
Can do naught for thee. But there is in heaven,
There is a Father thou know'st for the forsaken;
Trust him and live on tranquil if not glad.
   . . . . .
Gonzaga, I offer thee this hand, which often
Thou hast pressed upon the morn of battle, when
We knew not if we e'er should meet again:
Wilt press it now once more, and give to me
Thy faith that thou wilt be defense and guard
Of these poor women, till they are returned
Unto their kinsmen?
GONZAGA: I do promise thee.
COUNT: When thou go'st back to camp,
Salute my brothers for me; and say to them
That I die innocent; witness thou hast been
Of all my deeds and thoughts—thou knowest it.
Tell them that I did never stain my sword
With treason—I did never stain it—and
I am betrayed.—And when the trumpets blow,
And when the banners beat against the wind,
Give thou a thought to thine old comrade then!
And on some mighty day of battle, when
Upon the field of slaughter the priest lifts
His hands amid the doleful noises, offering up
The sacrifice to heaven for the dead,
Bethink thyself of me, for I too thought
To die in battle.
ANTONIETTA: O God, have pity on us!
COUNT: O wife! Matilde! now the hour is near
We needs must part. Farewell!
MATILDE: No, father—
COUNT: Yet
Once more, come to my heart! Once more, and now,
In mercy, go!

ANTONIETTA: Ah, no! they shall unclasp us
By force!
[*A sound of armed men is heard without.*]
MATILDE: What sound is that?
ANTONIETTA: Almighty God!
[*The door opens in the middle; armed men are seen.
Their
leader advances toward the Count; the women swoon.*]
COUNT: Merciful God! Thou hast removed from them
This cruel moment, and I thank Thee! Friend,
Succor them, and from this unhappy place
Bear them! And when they see the light again,
Tell them that nothing more is left to fear.

VII

In the *Carmagnola* having dealt with the internal wars which desolated medieval Italy, Manzoni in the *Adelchi* takes a step further back in time, and evolves his tragedy from the downfall of the Longobard kingdom and the invasion of the Franks. These enter Italy at the bidding of the priests, to sustain the Church against the disobedience and contumacy of the Longobards.

Desiderio and his son Adelchi are kings of the Longobards, and the tragedy opens with the return to their city Pavia of Ermenegarda, Adelchi's sister, who was espoused to Carlo, king of the Franks, and has been repudiated by him. The Longobards have seized certain territories belonging to the Church, and as they refuse to restore them, the ecclesiastics send a messenger, who crosses the Alps on foot, to the camp of the Franks, and invites their king into Italy to help the cause of the Church. The Franks descend into the valley of Susa, and soon after defeat the Longobards. It is in this scene that the chorus of the Italian peasants, who suffer, no matter which side conquers, is introduced. The Longobards retire to Verona, and Ermenegarda, whose character is painted with great tenderness and delicacy, and whom we may take for a type of the what little goodness and gentleness, sorely puzzled, there was in the world at that time (which was really one of the worst of all the bad times in the world), dies in a convent near Brescia, while the war rages all round her retreat. A defection takes place among the Longobards; Desiderio is captured; a last stand is made by Adelchi at Verona, where he is mortally wounded, and is brought prisoner to his father in the tent of Carlo. The tragedy ends with his death; and I give the whole of the last scene:

Enter CARLO *and* DESIDERIO.
DESIDERIO: Oh, how heavily
Hast thou descended upon my gray head,
Thou hand of God! How comes my son to me!
My son, my only glory, here I languish,
And tremble to behold thee! Shall I see
Thy deadly wounded body, I that should
Be wept by thee? I, miserable, alone,
Dragged thee to this; blind dotard I, that fain
Had made earth fair to thee, I digged thy grave.
If only thou amidst thy warriors' songs
Hadst fallen on some day of victory,
Or had I closed upon thy royal bed
Thine eyes amidst the sobs and reverent grief

Of thy true liegemen, ah; it still had been
Anguish ineffable! And now thou diest,
No kind, deserted, in thy foeman's land,
With no lament, saving thy father's, uttered
Before the man that doth exult to hear it.
CARLO: Old man, thy grief deceives thee. Sorrowful,
And not exultant do I see the fate
Of a brave man and king. Adelchi's foe
Was I, and he was mine, nor such that I
Might rest upon this new throne, if he lived
And were not in my hands. But now he is
In God's own hands, whither no enmity
Of man can follow him.
DES: 'T is a fatal gift
Thy pity, if it never is bestowed
Save upon those fallen beyond all hope—
If thou dost never stay thine arm until
Thou canst find no place to inflict a wound!
(Adelchi is brought in, mortally wounded.)
DES: My son!
ADELCHI: And do I see thee once more, father?
Oh come, and touch my hand!
DES: 'T is terrible
For me to see thee so!
AD: Many in battle
Did fall so by my sword.
DES: Ah, then, this wound
Thou hast, it is incurable?
AD: Incurable.
DES: Alas, atrocious war!
And cruel I that made it. 'T is I kill thee.
AD: Not thou nor he *(pointing to Carlo),* but the
   Lord God of all.
DES: Oh, dear unto those eyes! how far away
From thee I suffered! and it was one thought
Among so many woes upheld me. 'T was the hope
To tell thee all one day in some safe hour
Of peace—
AD: That hour of peace has come to me.
Believe it, father, save that I leave thee
Crushed with thy sorrow here below.
DES: O front
Serene and bold! O fearless hand! O eyes
That once struck terror!
AD: Cease thy lamentations,
Cease, father, in God's name! For was not this
The time to die? But thou that shalt live captive,
And hast lived all thy days a king, oh listen:
Life's a great secret that is not revealed
Save in the latest hour. Thou 'st lost a kingdom;
Nay, do not weep! Trust me, when to this hour
Thou also shalt draw nigh, most jubilant
And fair shall pass before thy thought the years
In which thou wast not king—the years in which
No tears shall be recorded in the skies
Against thee, and thy name shall not ascend
Mixed with the curses of the unhappy. Oh,
Rejoice that thou art king no longer! that
All ways are closed against thee! There is none
For innocent action, and there but remains
To do wrong or to suffer wrong. A power
Fierce, pitiless, grasps the world, and calls itself
The right. The ruthless hands of our forefathers
Did sow injustice, and our fathers then
Did water it with blood; and now the earth
No other harvest bears. It is not meet

To uphold crime, thou 'st proved it, and if 't were,
Must it not end thus? Nay, this happy man
Whose throne my dying renders more secure,
Whom all men smile on and applaud, and serve,
He is a man and he shall die.
DES: But I
That lose my son, what shall console me?
AD: God!
Who comforts us for all things. And oh, thou
Proud foe of mine! *(Turning to Carlo.)*
CARLO: Nay, by this name, Adelchi,
Call me no more; I was so, but toward death
Hatred is impious and villainous. Nor such,
Believe me, knows the heart of Carlo.
AD: Friendly
My speech shall be, then, very meek and free
Of every bitter memory to both.
For this I pray thee, and my dying hand
I lay in thine! I do not ask that thou
Should'st let go free so great a captive—no,
For I well see that my prayer were in vain
And vain the prayer of any mortal. Firm
Thy heart is—must be—nor so far extends
Thy pity. That which thou can'st not deny
Without being cruel, that I ask thee! Mild
As it can be, and free of insult, be
This old man's bondage, even such as thou
Would'st have implored for thy father, if the heavens
Had destined thee the sorrow of leaving him
In others' power. His venerable head
Keep thou from every outrage; for against
The fallen many are brave; and let him not
Endure the cruel sight of any of those
His vassals that betrayed him.
CARLO: Take in death
This glad assurance, Adelchi! and be Heaven
My testimony, that thy prayer is as
The word of Carlo!
AD: And thy enemy,
In dying, prays for thee!
Enter ARVINO.
ARVINO: (IMPATIENTLY) O mighty king, thy warriors
   and chiefs
Ask entrance.
AD: (APPEALINGLY) Carlo!
CARLO: Let not any dare
To draw anigh this tent; for here Adelchi
Is sovereign; and no one but Adelchi's father
And the meek minister of divine forgiveness
Have access here.
DES: O my beloved son!
AD: O my father,
The light forsakes these eyes.
DES: Adelchi,—No!
Thou shalt not leave me!
AD: O King of kings! betrayed
By one of Thine, by all the rest abandoned:
I come to seek Thy peace, and do Thou take
My weary soul!
DES: He heareth thee, my son,
And thou art gone, and I in servitude
Remain to weep.

I wish to give another passage from this tragedy: t[
speech which the emissary of the Church makes to Ca[
when he reaches his presence after his arduous passage

the Alps. I suppose that all will note the beauty and reality of the description in the story this messenger tells of his adventures; and I feel, for my part, a profound effect of wildness and loneliness in the verse, which has almost the solemn light and balsamy perfume of those mountain solitudes:

> From the camp,
> Unseen, I issued, and retraced the steps
> But lately taken. Thence upon the right
> I turned toward Aquilone. Abandoning
> The beaten paths, I found myself within
> A dark and narrow valley; but it grew
> Wider before my eyes as further on
> I kept my way. Here, now and then, I saw
> The wandering flocks, and huts of shepherds. 'T was
> The furthermost abode of men. I entered
> One of the huts, craved shelter, and upon
> The woolly fleece I slept the night away.
> Rising at dawn, of my good shepherd host
> I asked my way to France. "Beyond those heights
> Are other heights," he said, "and others yet;
> And France is far and far away; but path
> There 's none, and thousands are those mountains—
> Steep, naked, dreadful, uninhabited
> Unless by ghosts, and never mortal man
> Passed over them." "The ways of God are many,
> Far more than those of mortals," I replied,
> "And God sends me." "And God guide you!" he said.
> Then, from among the loaves he kept in store,
> He gathered up as many as a pilgrim
> May carry, and in a coarse sack wrapping them,
> He laid them on my shoulders. Recompense
> I prayed from Heaven for him, and took my way.
> Reaching the valley's top, a peak arose,
> And, putting faith in God, I climbed it. Here
> No trace of man appeared, only the forests
> Of untouched pines, rivers unknown, and vales
> Without a path. All hushed, and nothing else
> But my own steps I heard, and now and then
> The rushing of the torrents, and the sudden
> Scream of the hawk, or else the eagle, launched
> From his high nest, and hurtling through the dawn,
> Passed close above my head; or then at noon,
> Struck by the sun, the crackling of the cones
> Of the wild pines. And so three days I walked,
> And under the great trees, and in the clefts,
> Three nights I rested. The sun was my guide;
> I rose with him, and him upon his journey
> I followed till he set. Uncertain still,
> Of my own way I went; from vale to vale
> Crossing forever; or, if it chanced at times
> I saw the accessible slope of some great height
> Rising before me, and attained its crest,
> Yet loftier summits still, before, around,
> Towered over me; and other heights with snow
> From foot to summit whitening, that did seem
> Like steep, sharp tents fixed in the soil; and others
> Appeared like iron, and arose in guise
> Of walls insuperable. The third day fell
> What time I had a mighty mountain seen
> That raised its top above the others; 't was
> All one green slope, and all its top was crowned
> With trees. And thither eagerly I turned
> My weary steps. It was the eastern side,

> Sire, of this very mountain on which lies
> Thy camp that faces toward the setting sun.
> While I yet lingered on its spurs the darkness
> Did overtake me; and upon the dry
> And slippery needles of the pine that covered
> The ground, I made my bed, and pillowed me
> Against their ancient trunks. A smiling hope
> Awakened me at day-break; and all full
> Of a strange vigor, up the steep I climbed.
> Scarce had I reached the summit when my ear
> Was smitten with a murmur that from far
> Appeared to come, deep, ceaseless; and I stood
> And listened motionless. 'T was not the waters
> Broken upon the rocks below; 't was not the wind
> That blew athwart the woods and whistling ran
> From one tree to another, but verily
> A sound of living men, an indistinct
> Rumor of words, of arms, of trampling feet,
> Swarming from far away; an agitation
> Immense, of men! My heart leaped, and my steps
> I hastened. On that peak, O king, that seems
> To us like some sharp blade to pierce the heaven,
> There lies an ample plain that 's covered thick
> With grass ne'er trod before. And this I crossed
> The quickest way; and now at every instant
> The murmur nearer grew, and I devoured
> The space between; I reached the brink, I launched
> My glance into the valley and I saw,
> I saw the tents of Israel, the desired
> Pavilion of Jacob; on the ground
> I fell, thanked God, adored him, and descended.

VIII

I could easily multiply beautiful and effective passages from the poetry of Manzoni; but I will give only one more version, **"The Fifth of May,"** that ode on the death of Napoleon, which, if not the most perfect lyric of modern times as the Italians vaunt it to be, is certainly very grand. I have followed the movement and kept the meter of the Italian, and have at the same time reproduced it quite literally; yet I feel that any translation of such a poem is only a little better than none. I think I have caught the shadow of this splendid lyric; but there is yet no photography that transfers the splendor itself, the life, the light, the color; I can give you the meaning, but not the feeling, that pervades every syllable as the blood warms every fiber of a man, not the words that flashed upon the poet as he wrote, nor the yet more precious and inspired words that came afterward to his patient waiting and pondering, and touched the whole with fresh delight and grace. If you will take any familiar passage from one of our poets in which every motion of the music is endeared by long association and remembrance, and every tone is sweet upon the tongue, and substitute a few strange words for the original, you will have some notion of the wrong done by translation.

"THE FIFTH OF MAY"

> He passed; and as immovable
>   As, with the last sigh given,
> Lay his own clay, oblivious,
>   From that great spirit riven,
> So the world stricken and wondering
>   Stands at the tidings dread:

Mutely pondering the ultimate
   Hour of that fateful being,
And in the vast futurity
   No peer of his foreseeing
Among the countless myriads
     Her blood-stained dust that tread.

Him on his throne and glorious
   Silent saw I, that never—
When with awful vicissitude
   He sank, rose, fell forever—
Mixed my voice with the numberless
     Voices that pealed on high;
Guitless of servile flattery
   And of the scorn of coward,
Come I when darkness suddenly
   On so great light hath lowered,
And offer a song at his sepulcher
     That haply shall not die.

From the Alps unto the Pyramids,
   From Rhine to Manzanares
Unfailingly the thunderstroke
   His lightning purpose carries;
Bursts from Scylla to Tanais,—
     From one to the other sea.
Was it true glory?—Posterity,
   Thine be the hard decision;
Bow we before the mightiest,
   Who willed in him the vision
Of his creative majesty
     Most grandly traced should be.

The eager and tempestuous
   Joy of the great plan's hour,
The throe of the heart that controllessly
   Burns with a dream of power,
And wins it, and seizes victory
     It had seemed folly to hope—
All he hath known: the infinite
   Rapture after the danger,
The flight, the throne of sovereignty,
   The salt bread of the stranger;
Twice 'neath the feet of the worshipers,
     Twice 'neath the altar's cope.

He spoke his name; two centuries,
   Armèd and threatening either,
Turned unto him submissively,
   As waiting fate together;
He made a silence, and arbiter
     He sat between the two.
He vanished; his days in the idleness
   Of his island-prison spending,
Mark of immense malignity,
   And of a pity unending,
Of hatred inappeasable,
     Of deathless love and true.

As on the head of the mariner,
   Its weight some billow heaping,
Falls even while the castaway,
   With strained sight far sweeping,
Scanneth the empty distances
     For some dim sail in vain;
So over his soul the memories

Billowed and gathered ever!
How oft to tell posterity
   Himself he did endeavor,
And on the pages helplessly
     Fell his weary hand again.

How many times, when listlessly
   In the long, dull day's declining—
Downcast those glances fulminant,
   His arms on his breast entwining—
He stood assailed by the memories
     Of days that were passed away;
He thought of the camps, the arduous
   Assaults, the shock of forces,
The lightning-flash of the infantry,
   The billowy rush of horses,
The thrill in his supremacy,
     The eagerness to obey.

Ah, haply in so great agony
   His panting soul had ended
Despairing, but that potently
   A hand, from heaven extended,
Into a clearer atmosphere
     In mercy lifted him.
And led him on by blossoming
   Pathways of hope ascending
To deathless fields, to happiness
   All earthly dreams transcending,
Where in the glory celestial
     Earth's fame is dumb and dim.

Beautiful, deathless, beneficent
   Faith! used to triumphs, even
This also write exultantly:
   No loftier pride 'neath heaven
Unto the shame of Calvary
     Stooped ever yet its crest.
Thou from his weary mortality
   Disperse all bitter passions:
The God that humbleth and hearteneth,
   That comforts and that chastens,
Upon the pillow else desolate
     To his pale lips lay pressed!

IX

Giuseppe Arnaud says that in his sacred poetry Manzoni gave the Catholic dogmas the most moral explanation, in the most attractive poetical language; and he suggests that Manzoni had a patriotic purpose in them, or at least a sympathy with the effort of the Romantic writers to give priests and princes assurance that patriotism was religious, and thus win them to favor the Italian cause. It must be confessed that such a temporal design as this would fatally affect the devotional quality of the hymns, even if the poet's consciousness did not; but I am not able to see any evidence of such sympathy in the poems themselves. I detect there a perfectly sincere religious feeling, and nothing of devotional rapture. The poet had, no doubt, a satisfaction in bringing out the beauty and sublimity of his faith; and, as a literary artist, he had a right to be proud of his work, for its spirit is one of which the tuneful piety of Italy had long been void. In truth, since David, king of Israel, left making psalms, religious songs have been poorer than any other sort of songs; and it is high praise of Manzoni's **Inni Sacri** to say that they are in irreproachable taste, and unite in unaffected poetic appreciation of the grandeur of Christianity as much reason as may coexist with obedience.

The poetry of Manzoni is so small in quantity, that we must refer chiefly to excellence of quality the influence and the fame it has won him, though I do not deny that his success may have been partly owing at first to the errors of the school which preceded him. It could be easily shown, from literary history, that every great poet has appeared at a moment fortunate for his renown, just as we might prove, from natural science, that it is felicitous for the sun to get up about day-break. Manzoni's art was very great, and he never gave his thought defective expression, while the expression was always secondary to the thought. For the self-respect, then, of an honest man, which would not permit him to poetize insincerity and shape the void, and for the great purpose he always cherished of making literature an agent of civilization and Christianity, the Italians are right to honor Manzoni. Arnaud thinks that the school he founded lingered too long on the educative and religious ground he chose; and Marc Monnier declares Manzoni to be the poet of resignation, thus distinguishing him from the poets of revolution. The former critic is the nearer right of the two, though neither is quite just, as it seems to me; for I do not understand how any one can read the romance and the dramas of Manzoni without finding him full of sympathy for all Italy has suffered, and a patriot very far from resigned; and I think political conditions—or the Austrians in Milan, to put it more concretely—scarcely left to the choice of the Lombard school that attitude of aggression which others assumed under a weaker, if not a milder, despotism at Florence. The utmost allowed the Milanese poets was the expression of a retrospective patriotism, which celebrated the glories of Italy's past, which deplored her errors, and which denounced her crimes, and thus contributed to keep the sense of nationality alive. Under such governments as endured in Piedmont until 1848, in Lombardy until 1859, in Venetia until 1866, literature must remain educative, or must cease to be. In the works, therefore, of Manzoni and of nearly all his immediate followers, there is nothing directly revolutionary except in Giovanni Berchet. The line between them and the directly revolutionary poets is by no means to be traced with exactness, however, in their literature, and in their lives they were all alike patriotic.

Manzoni lived to see all his hopes fulfilled, and died two years after the fall of the temporal power, in 1873. "Toward mid-day," says a Milanese journal at the time of his death, "he turned suddenly to the household friends about him, and said: 'This man is failing—sinking—call my confessor!' The confessor came, and he communed with him half an hour, speaking, as usual, from a mind calm and clear. After the confessor left the room, Manzoni called his friends and said to them: 'When I am dead, do what I did every day: pray for Italy—pray for the king and his family—so good to me!' His country was the last thought of this great man dying as in his whole long life it had been his most vivid and constant affection."

S. B. Chandler (essay date 1974)

SOURCE: "Literary Criticism: History and Literature," in *Alessandro Manzoni: The Story of a Spiritual Quest*, Edinburgh University Press, 1974, pp. 69-85.

[*In the following excerpt, Chandler surveys Manzoni's critical writings and his* Fermo e Lucia, *the precursor to* I promessi sposi.]

The early 1820s were the period of Manzoni's intensest creative activity as he moved towards the climax and resolution of his spiritual and artistic quest. The **Lettre à M. Chauvet sur l'unité de temps et de lieu dans la tragédie** belongs to early 1820 and the **Discorso sopra alcuni punti della storia longobardica in Italia** was begun in autumn 1820 and published in 1822; of his creative works, **Marzo 1821, Il Cinque Maggio, Adelchi** and **La Pentecoste** were written in these years. On 24 April 1821, however, Manzoni began work on a historical novel, now referred to as **Fermo e Lucia,** and completed it on 17 September 1823. From this, **I Promessi Sposi** was eventually to emerge.

The **Lettre à M. Chauvet** replies to criticisms from this French critic of the ideas on tragedy expressed and exemplified in **Il conte di Carmagnola**, especially regarding the unities of time and place, but, in fact, goes beyond them to become an important statement of the relationship of tragic poetry to history. It was published in 1823 in Paris together with Fauriel's translations of the two tragedies. Manzoni attacks these two unities as arbitrary concepts unrelated to the nature of a particular action, which should unfold within the period and locations inherent in it and thus necessary for the coherent development of the characters involved—'le système historique', Manzoni calls it. Observance of the unity of time, defined as twenty-four hours, had prompted a predominance of the love motive in French tragedy: in his *Andromaque,* for example, Racine was compelled to elevate the secondary motive of Pyrrhus' love for Andromaque to prominence over the voice of compassion and humanity in the sacrifice of the child Astyanax. In contrast with Shakespeare's *Othello,* Voltaire in his *Zaïre* had been reduced to unconvincing expedients within a single day and A. W. Schlegel had exposed the weakness of his reasoning. If the two unities were enforced, much in Shakespeare's and Goethe's plays would have to be removed in favour of reported narrative: Manzoni examines *Richard II* to prove his point.

The subject-matter of tragic poetry, he writes, must be drawn from the real, the historically true, because mere invention represents the lowliest part of the human mind. The greatest poetry has been based on historical events or what were once regarded as such—Racine, for instance, invented nothing. But how do the roles of the historian and the poet differ? The historian finds a series of events which the human mind through its very nature regards as interconnected with links of cause and effect, precedence and consequence; it brings under one point of view, as by a single intuition, a number of facts separated by the conditions of time and place and discards others connected only by accidental coincidence. The historian presents the essential facts in the order in which the human intellect finds them, but for him the series is indefinite. The poet, on the other hand, stages a detached portion of history, the reason for whose isolation lies in the events composing it, a reason which the spectator can grasp with ease and pleasure. The poet chooses from history interesting and dramatic events, so closely interconnected but so weakly linked with events before and after that the mind takes pleasure in making of them a single spectacle and seeks eagerly to grasp the full extent and depth of their relationship, and to unravel as clearly as possible the governing laws of cause and effect. This unity is more marked and more readily apprehended when interconnected events are grouped around one principal event as means or obstacles: an event that appears at times as the accomplishment of human plans, at others as a stroke of Providence which annuls them, or as a goal glimpsed afar that a man wishes to avoid, yet towards which he rushes by the very road he had taken in order to reach the opposite goal. The poet may be guided to his choice of events by coming upon an imposing character, observation of whom will illuminate an aspect of human nature.

The historian looks at events from the outside, but the poet contemplates not only men's actions but their thoughts, the feelings accompanying their deliberations and designs, successes and failures; the speeches with which they have endeavoured to make their passion and will prevail over those of others, have expressed their anger or sadness, have, in fact, revealed their originality. With his sympathetic imagination, the poet apprehends and communicates the secrets of the human will. Poetry fills out history by restoring its lost parts, imagining facts where history offers only indications, inventing characters to represent the known way of life of an age, but in such a way that invention accords with reality and sets it in greater relief. All this, affirms Manzoni, is 'creation'. Dramatic poetry is the expression, according to their actions, of men's feelings, desires and sufferings, of men regarded as inseparable from history. Conversely, the creation of 'facts' in order to adapt defined feelings to them has dominated the novel since Mlle de Scudéry, though some novelists have, like dramatic poets, created poetic truth.

The poet will strive to render faithfully a dramatic idea from history and thus bring out its moral effect. The portrayal of the true will absolve him from the need to inspire passions in the spectator with the hope of attracting him. It is not in sharing the delirium and anguish, the desires and pride of tragic characters that we feel the highest degree of emotion: above this narrow, agitated sphere, in the pure joys of 'contemplation désintéressée', we are most vividly seized with pity and terror for ourselves when we see the useless sufferings and vain joys of men. The poet should assist us in our development of a moral force through which passions can be mastered and judged. By showing us the passions that have tormented mankind, the poet can make us feel that common basis of misery and weakness which disposes us to an indulgence formed, not of weariness and disdain, but of reason and love. In presenting events to us as witnesses, he can help us acquire the habit of fixing our thoughts on the great and serene ideas which are cancelled out and vanish through the impact of the daily realities of life. The poet may touch our minds strongly but 'en vivifiant, en développant l'idéal de justice et de bonté que chacune [âme] porte en elle, et non en les plongeant à l'étroit dans un idéal de passions factices' [by animating, by developing the ideal of justice and of goodness that each soul bears within it, and not by restricting them to an ideal of artificial passions]; in this procedure, he elevates our reason.

For Manzoni, the true had an intrinsic interest and he believed that an increasing taste for historical studies was finally transforming history into a science. With a clearer view of history, the public would prefer it to single inventions of fiction.

In his rejection of the distinction between the 'bello morale' and the 'bello poetico' (published as **Pensiero XVIII** by Chiari and Ghisalberti in the third volume of **Tutte le opere**), Manzoni insists that poetry is impossible without ideas and that the pleasure felt by readers of a literary work consists of the acquisition of ideas, of assent and of the consequent mental repose. When a work arouses ideas contrary to those suggested by the author, pleasure turns to conflict and mental distress. Poetic beauty ('bello poetico') is identical with moral beauty ('bello morale'). Poetry lacking in moral beauty will be unfavourably judged:

> A misura che gli uomini si coltiveranno, abbandoneranno errori e riconosceranno verità. Quelli che vedranno più verità morali saranno i migliori ragionatori, gli uomini i più avanzati. Ora il giudizio di questi sarà sfavorevole alle opere mancanti del bello morale. Ragione: perchè gli uomini non possono acconsentire a ciò che si oppone ad una verità da essi riconosciuta. [According as men become more cultivated, they will abandon errors and recognize truths. Those who see more moral truths will be the best in using their reason, the most advanced men. Now the judgment of these people will be unfavourable to works lacking moral beauty. Reason: because men are unable to give assent to what is opposed to a truth they recognize.]

Their adverse criticism and indignation will be proportioned to the degree of artifice in the means employed to make immoral ideas triumph. Elsewhere, in his **Postille** to A. W. Schlegel's *Lectures on Dramatic Art and Literature* (in the second volume of the **Opere inedite o rare,** edited by Ruggero Bonghi), Manzoni asserts that a dramatic poet, like everyone else, must desire whatever contributes to the perfecting of society, provided that he regards his art as a means rather than as an end. Manzoni adds that, although a reader is quite willing to transport himself back to a writer's age, there is no doubt that eternally valid themes arouse the deepest feeling and the highest praise.

Turning to the *Materiali estetici,* we find Manzoni insisting that the only greatness in a poet lies in saying things useful to all men: indeed, literature should be considered a branch of the moral sciences. These sciences, he goes on, progress more slowly than other sciences, because convincing the intellect of their valid points does not suffice: the passions that abhor these truths and the habits that will be disturbed by them have first to be overcome. The deeper the penetration into the human heart the more extensive is the discovery of the eternal principles of goodness, which are commonly forgotten in the normal circumstances and passions of everyday life. The dramatic poet should carry his readers with their imagination beyond the ordinary run of life to the infinite region of possible ills where they can realize their weakness and understand that only goodness and an upright conscience, together with God's help, can alleviate their mental and spiritual distress: everybody feels this effect after reading a tragedy of Shakespeare. To conclude these excerpts from the *Materiali estetici,* the following oft-quoted sentence sums up Manzoni's outlook: 'La rappresentazione delle passioni che non eccitano simpatia, ma riflessione sentita, è più poetica d'ogni altra.' [The representation of passions that do not excite sympathy, but a reflection that is felt, is more poetic than any other.]

A similar stress on the true as the only source of noble and lasting pleasure is attributed to the Romantics in Manzoni's *Lettera sul romanticismo* of 22 September 1823 addressed to the Marchese Cesare Taparelli d'Azeglio, father of Massimo, who married Manzoni's eldest daughter, Giulietta, in 1831. Manzoni acknowledges the difficulty of defining the 'vero' as being different in this context from the word's normal connotation. In this letter, he looks back to the Romantic-Classicist controversy that began in Italy in 1816 and reviews the arguments on each side, basing himself on the claim that, in Milan, the term 'Romanticism' had referred to a body of ideas more rational, ordered and general than those in any other Italian centre. Manzoni outlines the negative criticism of neoclassical practice and the positive proposals advanced by the Romantics. He rejects mythology as expressive of a bygone society and as at variance with Christianity, towards which Romanticism tended; imitation, which the admired classical authors had themselves not practised; and the use of rules founded on special facts rather than on the nature of the human mind. In the original letter, but not in the revised text of 1870, Manzoni offered as a general principle, to which all the positive propositions of Romanticism could be reduced, the following: 'che la poesia e la letteratura in genere debba proporsi l'utile per iscopo, il vero per soggetto e l'interessante per mezzo' [that poetry and literature in general should propose for themselves the useful as their purpose, the true as subject matter and the interesting as means]. In a letter of 6 July 1824 to the

critic Paride Zaiotti, who had attacked the Romantics though praising the *Adelchi,* Manzoni emphasized the Romantics' sincerity in examining their own and opposing opinions and the correctness of their views, which had, in fact, prevailed, even if everybody was not yet prepared to concede this point.

The *Discorso sopra alcuni punti della storia longobardica in Italia,* begun in autumn 1820, develops some points made in a letter to Fauriel of 17 October of that year. Scholars in times 'postérieurs à la renaissance des lettres' had amassed facts and theorized on medieval customs but had never discerned 'ce qu'il y avait d'important et de vrai dans les institutions, et dans le caractère de cette époque' [what was important and true in the institutions and in the character of that age], while the 'philosophes' had seen what was not there. Misjudging all the evidence, historians had regarded the Lombards as Italians simply because they had been in Italy for two centuries. 'Les Turcs à ce compte', comments Manzoni, 'doivent être bien Grecs.' [By this count the Turks must certainly be Greeks.] He had consulted the histories collected by Muratori in Italy and Augustin Thierry in France but was seeking a modern work which discussed the condition of the Italians, subjugated and 'possessed'. In due course, he would compose a historical work to show that the history of the barbarians' establishment in Italy was still to be written and to persuade someone to undertake it or at least to destroy many firmly held, but absurd, beliefs.

In the *Discorso,* then, Manzoni investigates several problems arising from his study of Lombard domination in Italy: the fallacy of a union between conquerors and conquered and of a supposed Lombard beneficence towards the Italians, the role of successive popes in invoking Frankish aid against Lombard attacks, and the relevant views of various historians. In a discussion of the approaches of Muratori and Vico, he foresees the advantages accruing from the mass of factual information and specialized judgments of the former if allied with the wide-ranging glance and synthesizing power of the latter. The main point of interest, however, is less his search for exactness than his moral judgment of the facts thus established. Modern criticism of the *Discorso* has tended until recent years to be dominated by Benedetto Croce's stricture that Manzoni's mind was not adapted to the historian's task: he treated history as an instrument, not as an end, in accordance with his eighteenth-century intellectualism, which, in turn, was reinforced by his rather Jansenist Catholicism, meticulous and of extreme moral rigidity. Croce held that we interrogate history, not to estimate the moral goodness or inadequacy of men, but to understand what they accomplished through their virtues and vices, an accomplishment which operates within us and stimulates our thought and action.

Manzoni expresses his viewpoint in the introduction. A series of material, external facts, even if completely authenticated, is not history, nor does it suffice in order to form a dramatic concept of a historical event. In the facts themselves a number of essential features is missing: the climate of laws, customs and opinion in which the leading characters operated; the justice or injustice of their intentions and inclinations, regardless of the human conventions for or against which they acted; the desires, fears and sufferings and, in short, the general condition of the immense number of people who had no active part in events but felt their effects. These considerations form the criteria of the judgment to be made upon the events.

Thus Manzoni inquires which of the forces represented by popes and kings tended to lessen the woes of the multitude and introduce a little more justice; and, after a careful examination of the final contests between the papacy and the Lombards, he assigns to the former the limited justice possible in human affairs. Let the apologists of the Lombards declare what would have been the condition of the Roman people if the Lombard King Astolfo's plans against the Papal States had succeeded, what part equity, security and dignity would have played in the subsequent administration and all the social benefits which make it less difficult for men to be just. By calling in the Franks, the popes consulted the best interests of the subject Italians, for Charlemagne's advent safeguard them from barbarian invasions. Manzoni emphasizes the cardinal moral concept of disapproval of actions and feelings in proportion to the sorrow voluntarily caused by them. The Christian ethic proclaims that injustice is always despicable, whereas paganism forgave and sometimes admired crimes springing from pride. Thus, too, Manzoni condemns writers who not only ridiculed for the benefit of posterity the conquered Italians of the period after the fall of Rome but also excused and praised their persecutors: and yet 'il più forte sentimento d'avversione dovrebb'essere per la volontà che si propone il male degli uomini' [the strongest feeling of aversion should be for the will that proposes evil for men]. Similarly, he expresses surprise that writers, in other respects upright and perceptive, could be so motivated by anti-papal sentiment as to ask posterity to shed tears, not for the grief occasioned by death or for such sufferings as every man laments and may feel personally, but for the loss of power and for the defeat of the ambitious plans of those who had deliberately caused so many tears. To be acceptable, a thought or deed must conform to the duties deriving from equity and universal charity.

Interest in the feelings of all people actually affected by specific events prompts Manzoni to insist on the autonomy in history of each generation. No generation should be deemed a mere stepping-stone to those following nor should a series of events be judged by the interests of posterity rather than of the human beings involved. No man or generation is a mere instrument of another. We have seen that Manzoni imputed to each generation a distinctive 'spirit'. The basic inspiration is the Christian concept of each person's value as a creature of God, but readers of Kant will recall his view of man as an end in himself and the moral impossibility of using another as a means. According to Manzoni, it is neither reasonable nor human— the coupling of these epithets is notable—to consider one generation simply as a means for those succeeding. He is

obviously reacting against the tendency of some Enlightenment thinkers to regard past ages as functions in the evolution of their own lofty times, a tendency inevitable to proponents of the idea of progress. Manzoni's position contrasts sharply with that current in Lombardy and elsewhere in the years after 1830. In his *Del dramma storico* of 1830, for example, Mazzini asserted that the thought and the moral law of the universe are progress: whatever generation passes its time on the earth in idleness without promoting the process of perfection by a single degree has no life in the records of Humanity; the next generation tramples upon it as a traveller tramples the dust. Manzoni reaffirmed his position even more strongly many years later in his *La rivoluzione francese del 1789 e la rivoluzione italiana del 1859.* Since each human action is to be judged according to an eternally valid moral law, such a judgment cannot be postponed so as to take account of the consequences of such an action: each action being subject to an eternal moral law, if it is wrong at the time of its commission, it remains so ever after. Since each man is equally human and created in the image of God, he cannot be subordinated to the supposed needs of some abstract entity called 'humanity' and consequently the people of one period cannot be subordinated to the assumed good of those of a later age; men of the present must be considered: 'Noi persistiamo quindi nel credere che tra gli uomini si devano contare anche quelli che vivono' [Therefore we persist in thinking that, among mankind, those now living must also be counted]. Manzoni does believe, however, that each generation builds on the work of its predecessors, viewing it as capital productive of new directions rather than a wealth to support idleness.

Though eternally valid premises govern Manzoni's judgments on history, a prerequisite is the identification of facts and causes. Thus, the anachronistic pre-dating of a Lombard-Italian union which had, in fact, derived from many causes operating in a long succession of ages, prevented the identification of the origin and development of these causes and the consequent knowledge of an essential part of the 'corso della società'. This Vichian phrase recurs in Manzoni's attack on Muratori's monolithic conception of the Middle Ages: the various periods of which Manzoni saw as exemplifying 'il differente corso della civiltà'.

For Manzoni the past is complete and immutable. Historians must seek out and weigh the evidence—Manzoni seems not to have appreciated the immense difficulty of defining admissible evidence and of obtaining agreement thereon—and then produce the only correct or 'just' interpretation: 'nessun interesse, nessuna considerazione, nessun ostacolo dovrebbe ritenerli dall'essere interamente giusti in parole' [no interest, no consideration, no obstacle should prevent them from being wholly just in their words]. If the facts are known, then only one interpretation—or judgment—is possible: an interpretation based on the Christian ethic. A common attitude and outlook are prescribed for historians just as, in *I promessi sposi*, Manzoni expects in his readers the same outlook and reactions as his own. The historians of any Christian age were re-quired to align themselves with him. If Manzoni shared the Romantic emphasis on the special features of different ages, he also accepted the idea of a basically unchanging man, though he saw the constant factor not as reason in the eighteenth-century sense but as a rational Christian morality. He could not admit a subjective viewpoint governed by the historian's own experience of life and his commitment to a course of action in his own society, which are now generally regarded as operative after the vain attempt at 'scientific' history by the school of Ranke. Manzoni's criticism of modern historians for viewing distant ages by the measure of their own is justified, except that it assumes a single outlook in their age. Croce's opposition is predictable. Manzoni would have rejected outright his concept that the past has no real being, but is something posited by the spirit in a constantly changing present, so that all history is contemporary history.

Despite his preoccupation with Christian ethics and their implication of eternal law, Manzoni rarely alludes to them directly. In one passage, however, he sums the question up succinctly:

> i vari svolgimenti e gli adattamenti della natura umana nel corso della società; di quello stato così naturale all'uomo e così violento, così voluto e così pieno di dolori, che crea tanti scopi dei quali rende impossibile l'adempimento, che sopporta tutti i mali e tutti i rimedj piuttosto che cessare un momento, di quello stato che è un mistero di contraddizioni in cui l'ingegno si perde, se non lo considera come uno stato di prova e di preparazione ad un'altra esistenza [the various developments and the adaptations of human nature in the course of society; of that state so natural to man and so violent, so deliberate and so full of sorrow, which creates so many goals of which it renders impossible the attainment, which endures all ills and all remedies rather than desist for a moment, of that state which is a mystery of contradictions in which the mind gets lost, if it does not consider it as a state of trial and of preparation for another existence].

These words suggest that society, with its sorrows and frustrations, was an inevitable human condition and functioned as a moral proving-ground for mankind. The next life and Christian moral standards were the controlling factors, restored by Manzoni after the Enlightenment repudiation of Christian teleology and its introduction of posterity as a substitute higher tribunal, as in Diderot's 'La postérité pour le philosophe, c'est l'autre monde de l'homme religieux' or Schiller's 'The world's history is the world's court'. [For the philosopher, posterity is the other world of the religious man].

During his stay in Paris in 1819-20, Manzoni established contacts with three friends of Fauriel: the historians Augustin Thierry and Guizot and the philosopher Victor Cousin. In 1820, Thierry began his systematic study of the sources of French history, animated by a desire to illuminate some dark corners of the Middle Ages. With learning, knowledge of life and imagination, a historian could recre-

ate the men and women of the past in their full humanity: indeed, for the imagination there is no past. Thierry's theory of the two races, conquerors and conquered, who later became social classes, is expounded especially in his *La conquête d'Angleterre* and influenced Manzoni in the *Adelchi* and *Discorso*. With his theory that the novel can contain the truest part of history which is excluded from the compilations of historians, Thierry is in harmony with Manzoni's observations on dramatic poetry and history.

The direction of Manzoni's thought is revealed by a letter to Fauriel of 29 January 1821 concerning his friend Tommaso Grossi's narrative poem *I Lombardi alla prima crociata*. Grossi's intention, said Manzoni, was to depict an age through a *fable* of his own invention, more or less as in Scott's *Ivanhoe*; to invent actions so as to develop historical ways of life—'une ressource très heureuse'. Mere historical narration would not permit the inclusion of poetic invention:

> mais, rassembler les traits caractéristiques d'une époque de la société, et les développer dans une action, profiter de l'histoire sans se mettre en concurrence avec elle, sans prétendre faire ce qu'elle fait mieux, voilà ce que me paraît encore accordé à la poésie, et ce qu'à son tour elle peut faire [but, to gather together the characteristic features of an epoch of society and to develop them in an action, to profit from history without putting oneself in competition with it, without claiming to do what it can do better, this is what I think is still granted to poetry and what for her part she is able to do].

It is significant that Manzoni had informed Goethe six days earlier that he had accepted the latter's advice and not divided the characters of the *Adelchi* into historical and ideal.

On 24 April 1821, then, Manzoni began work on *Fermo e Lucia,* which he completed on 17 September 1823, after an interruption for the *Adelchi.* He is reported to have told a friend that he went to his country-house at Brusuglio after the Piedmontese failure to invade Lombardy in March 1821, taking with him the *History of Milan* of the seventeenth-century writer, Giuseppe Ripamonti, and a work which can be identified as the *Sul commercio de' commestibili e caro prezzo del vitto (On the food trade and the high cost of food)* of 1802 by Melchiorre Gioia. Without Sir Walter Scott, he explained, it would not have occurred to him to write a novel, but when he found in Ripamonti the figures of Gertrude, the Innominato and Cardinal Federigo Borromeo, the descriptions of the famine and rioting in Milan, the passage of the mercenaries and the plague and, in Gioia, the edicts of the governors of Milan, he wondered if it would not be possible to invent an action including these characters and events: it was the edict that the lawyer Azzeccagarbugli showed Renzo in which reference is made to threats of violence offered to a priest so as to prevent a marriage that impelled him to invent the action of the novel. From the political economist Gioia, Manzoni derived ideas on the supply and price of food and the two shared ironical attitudes to seventeenth-century governments. A useful commentary is furnished by a letter of 30 April 1821 from Ermes Visconti to Victor Cousin, probably inspired by Manzoni himself. According to Manzoni, says Visconti, Scott's originality lay in showing 'le parti qu'on peut tirer des mœurs, des habitudes domestiques, des idées, qui ont influé sur le bonheur et sur les malheurs de la vie à différentes époques de l'Histoire de chaque pays' [the use that can be made of the customs, of the domestic habits, of the ideas which have influenced the happiness and the unhappiness of life at different ages in the history of each country]. Manzoni would avoid Scott's falsification of history and intended 'conserver dans son intégrité le positif de faits auxquels il doit faire allusion; sauf à ne les effleurer que très rapidement' [to preserve in its integrity the positive feature of facts to which allusion must be made; except that they should be touched upon only very rapidly]. The fictional parts would form the basis of the novel and not conflict with historical fact: 'ces fictions en outre, seront telles que les historiens puissent aisément les avoir ignorées ou négligées '[these fictions besides will be such that the historians may easily have not known or neglected them].

Manzoni's most explicit statement on the historical novel occurs in his letter to Fauriel of 3 November 1821:

> Pour vous indiquer brièvement mon idée sur les romans historiques, et vous mettre ainsi sur la voie de la rectifier, je vous dirai que je les conçois comme une représentation d'un état donné de la société par le moyen de faits et de caractères si semblables à la réalité, qu'on puisse les croire une histoire véritable qu'on viendrait de découvrir. Lorsque des événemens et des personnages historiques y sont mêlés, je crois qu'il faut les représenter de la manière la plus strictement historique; ainsi par exemple Richard cœur-de-lion me paraît défectueux dans *Ivanhoe.* [In order to indicate briefly to you my idea of historical novels and to set you on the way to correcting it, I shall tell you that I conceive them as a representation of a given state of society by means of actions and characters so similar to reality that they could be considered a true history that had just been discovered. When historical events and characters are mixed in, I think that they must be presented in the strictest historical manner; thus, for example, Richard Cœur de Lion seems defective to me in *Ivanhoe.*]

The historical novel is a 'given state of society' in which all classes must obviously be included if the 'state' is to emerge clearly; invented actions and characters must be such as could have existed, inasmuch as they will merge with their historical counterparts. The whole thing presupposes that the novelist has conducted the historical research required to arrive at the 'reality' of the period.

The composition of a serious novel in Italian embodying a profound view of life was a bold undertaking. In the eighteenth century, Italy had not seen a development of the novel comparable with that in Britain and France. Except for a few examples of the philosophical and satirical novel, Italian novels had usually described long series of adventures, often in several countries, with little real characterization or coherence of construction. The novels of Pietro Chiari are typical. Many English and French works were translated into Italian, the former often from already existing French versions. In general, the Italian novel of the eighteenth century had aimed to move its readers by stories of love.

At the turn of the century, Ugo Foscolo's *Le ultime lettere di Jacopo Ortis* marked a new direction. With Goethe's *Sorrows of Young Werther* as its forerunner, it investigated in a series of letters Jacopo's increasingly tormented mind. Unlike Goethe, however, Foscolo introduced political as well as amorous disillusionment: the French, who had been welcomed in Italy as liberators, had handed Venice over to Austria by the Treaty of Campoformio. The *Jacopo Ortis,* however, was a far cry from the kind of novel planned by Manzoni. The first imitations of Sir Walter Scott did not appear until 1827, the year in which the first version of *I promessi sposi* was published. Afterwards, polemic arose in regard to the historical novel. On the whole, then, as they contemplated the novels of the eighteenth century, Italian critics held the novel form in low regard as a rather frivolous intrusion into the traditional literary genres and as mere entertainment suitable mainly for women.

A more serious problem for Manzoni related to language. A novel containing the adventures and dialogue of humble characters and accessible to a wide public could hardly be written in the traditional literary language with its Tuscan basis and its remoteness from popular speech. Manzoni refers to the poverty of the Italian language compared with French, which had been spoken for so long that writers could choose the correct word from personal experience. In Italy, the non-Tuscan writer was forced to use a language he had almost never spoken, which few people indeed did speak, and which some alleged had been corrupted by modern authors: a language little used for works of 'moral science'. General types of expression for modern ideas were lacking; no feeling of communion was possible between writer and reader. No sure criterion existed for judgment of vocabulary. The purists were right in demanding a fixed standard but wrong in identifying it with the Italian classics. A modern writer, says Manzoni, can achieve at best an approximate perfection of style: he should have read the Italian classical authors and works in other languages, especially French, and have conversed on important topics with other Italians. Manzoni concluded that the composition of a novel in Italian is extremely difficult, though the same difficulty existed, to a less degree, for other subjects.

Manzoni informed Fauriel on 29 May 1822 of his conception from the records of the period chosen for his novel—1628-31 in Lombardy—the conception from which the novel grew: an extraordinary social situation with an arbitrary government and feudal and popular anarchy, an astonishing state of legislation, a profound, fierce and pretentious ignorance, classes with opposite interests and outlooks; a plague which had brought out extreme evil, the most absurd prejudices and the most moving virtues. He was striving to immerse himself in the spirit of such an original age. He believed that he could best develop the action and plot of his novel by observing human action in reality and especially its difference from 'l'esprit romanesque'. He would avoid the artificially contrived unity of all the novels he had read, even though readers were conditioned by habit to expect such a unity.

If the reading of Scott provided an example of a new literary form, Manzoni's adoption and elaboration of the historical novel stemmed from both spiritual and artistic reasons. His acceptance of this world with all its shortcomings and the resultant conviction that it is impossible to contract out of life prevented the recurrence of an Adelchi or a Conte di Carmagnola. He no longer sought Providence in history and had moved far from the assured position of Bossuet. In addition, God was no longer a detached observer, operative only after death. Justice—and thus a limited happiness—was sometimes possible in this life. Tragedy had become inappropriate. Manzoni's Romantic and Christian concept of history as embracing all men in a given age, including the humble of whom no trace survived in documents, was incompatible with the traditional characters and language of tragedy and, in any case, the Romantics preached that literature should deal with subjects of interest and concern to the majority. In the tragedies, Manzoni had reserved a 'cantuccio' for his own direct intervention, but the novel permitted many degrees of intervention, not least in the narrative passages between the 'scenes' or dialogues, and yet preserved and adherence to history.

Critics have devoted much attention to *Fermo e Lucia* in their investigation of the creative process of *I promessi sposi* and the charting of Manzoni's artistic and spiritual development, although, as Giacomo Devoto pointed out, *Fermo e Lucia* is really an independent work, since the writer's inspiration, vision of life and, consequently, expression are markedly different. It was still the period of the *Adelchi* and of Manzoni's elaboration of his ideas on history and literature.

Compared with *I promessi sposi, Fermo e Lucia* is an inchoate mass of disparate elements: discussions of narrative technique, sometimes with the reader, in the manner of Fielding, which indicate Manzoni's own uncertainty; protestations that he is transcribing history, not relating invented actions; historical passages as such; psychological analyses; realistic descriptions or lengthy dwelling on sordid themes, as in the episode of Geltrude (as she is called in *Fermo e Lucia*), which fills out the perversity of the age; excessive moralizing; many of these features interrupt the narrative flow and prevent the attainment of a coherent structure founded on various levels of narration. The integration of individual lives into historical backgrounds and events is incomplete and the formulation and motivation of character inadequately worked out. A tendency to gloomy tints and strong contrasts, especially of good and

evil or between humble and powerful, suggestive of the preceding Gothic novel, here expresses a profound pessimism reminiscent of the *Adelchi.* There is no hope of reward in this world for good deeds and, given the conditions of the time, the virtuous Cardinal Borromeo is not appreciated. Padre Cristoforo's parting words to Renzo in the *lazzeretto* foretell worse times to come, for the sons will be more arrogant and violent than their fathers; the plague will not set the world aright since it strikes a vineyard already accursed. Earlier, he had confessed to becoming a friar so as to escape this infamous world, but had discovered that escape comes only with death.

Like the form, the language is somewhat uneven and disorderly. In the second introduction, written on the completion of the work (the first being contemporary with the initial chapters), Manzoni refers to an undigested compound of Lombard, Tuscan, French and Latin elements in his work. *Fermo e Lucia,* that is, uses the artificial, invented language defined in the letter of 3 November 1821 to Fauriel: surviving elements of traditional literary Italian, expressions from current speech and some derived from French, which was open to new terminology and was far richer than Italian. The use of Milanese would have been easy and natural to him, but not for most of his readers. Though acknowledging the superiority of Tuscan, he wonders whether it is adequate for contemporary usage. He has, in fact, reached the fundamental linguistic question; what kind of Italian should be employed in the novel, a literary form of recent origin which reflected changing social conditions? Manzoni had appreciated the crisis in the Italian language as early as 9 February 1806 in a letter to Fauriel: in a fragmented Italy, a widespread inertia and ignorance had separated the written and spoken languages to such an extent that good writers could not instruct the mass of the people. Obviously, a literary non-spoken Italian would not suffice. In *Marzo 1821,* Manzoni had looked for an Italy united in arms, language, religion, memories, blood and hearts: it was he who raised the language question to a social and political level in the context of the Risorgimento and removed it from the exclusive realm of literature. The question remained, however: was there a common Italian language in the peninsula?

Among the various solutions, the purists, as Manzoni had mentioned in his letter of 3 November 1821, advocated a return to the great Tuscan writers of the fourteenth century, although some admitted the sixteenth century also. Among the classicists, Vincenzo Monti could attack their narrowness and admission of outdated words, but he still relied upon the traditional literary language, distinguishing it from speech. The Romantic demand for a literature related to the contemporary world required a simpler, more comprehensible Italian, free from imitation of past works and drawn from current usage in both vocabulary and structure. Since speech was based on an abundance of dialects, however, a selection was needed. At first, in the second introduction to *Fermo e Lucia,* Manzoni goes beyond the artificial compound language defined on 3 November 1821 by positing the need for a language formed from reading 'well written' books and from conversation with cultured people, a language established by convention among numerous writers and speakers, but he did not know whether it existed. Writing to Luigi Rossari in June 1825, he referred to their joint desire for a 'lingua toscana-milanese', that is, a language employing expressions common to both Tuscan and Milanese.

The transformation of *Fermo e Lucia* into the 1825-7 edition of *I promessi sposi* includes the use of this 'Tuscan-Milanese' language. Thereafter, Manzoni concluded that a living language was required and that Tuscan was the only possible candidate, since it alone was at all common among Italians. He believed that the Italian dialects shared a common element with Tuscan. He therefore set himself to Tuscanize the language of his novel with the aid of Cherubini's *Vocabolario milanese-italiano* and of Tuscan friends; but here again there was no guarantee of conformity with actual Tuscan current usage. The only solution was direct contact with the living language in Tuscany itself, as Manzoni later declared in letters to Giuseppe Borghi on 25 February and 7 April 1829. Though at first Manzoni did not differentiate between Florentine and other Tuscan usage, he eventually noticed divergencies. Thus he decided on Florence as the location of his stay in Tuscany and, together with his family, he left Milan on 15 July 1827. He remained in Florence from 29 August to 1 October. He wrote to Tommaso Grossi on 17 September: 'ho settantun lenzuolo da risciaquare, e un'acqua come Arno, e lavandaie come Cioni e Niccolini, fuor di qui non le trovo in nessun luogo' [I have seventy-one sheets to rinse and water like the Arno and washer-women like Cioni and Niccolini, away from here I don't find them anywhere]. While in Florence, Manzoni also met Gianpietro Vieusseux, editor of the periodical *L'Antologia,* which had Romantic leanings, Pietro Giordani, the classicist and friend of Leopardi, Gino Capponi and Leopardi himself, who described him as full of amiability and worthy of his fame. The eventual product of Manzoni's sojourn in Florence was the revised and final edition of *I promessi sposi* published in 1840-2.

Gian Piero Barricelli (essay date 1976)

SOURCE: "Provident Ill-Fortune," in *Alessandro Manzoni,* Twayne Publishers, 1976, pp. 55-83.

[*In the following excerpt, Barricelli offers a thematic and stylistic study of Manzoni's dramas* Il conte di Carmagnola *and* Adelchi.]

"The idea of a performance of my things gives me apprehension together with an insurmountable aversion; if, in my two poor tragedies which you deign to look upon so indulgently, I went contrary to the general taste and experienced the displeasure of hearing myself screamed at [by those who read them], I would at least find comfort in the thought that, given their strangeness, they would never ap-

pear on the stage. Indeed, you see for yourself how they are put together, without any concern for stage effects, uses, or conventions; there is a multiplicity of characters, excessive length, speeches inhuman for the lungs to bear— and even more so for the ears; there are varied and disconnected scenes, and very little of what one commonly means by action, which moves along slowly, obliquely, and in spurts. In short, all those things that can make a performance difficult and boring are gathered there, as if to compile a single study of them. Therefore, concerning those points on which you deign to seek my advice, I must tell you candidly that I have none, nor would I be able to propose anything at all—let alone anything which would be better than what you have yourself proposed, for this could not be possible. . . . Allow me, then, to enjoy the sweet thought of your friendly intention, without my having to witness too risky an effect. And I am not speaking for myself alone—for whom, I must confess, the sound of a hiss would be more bitter than that of a thousand applauses would be welcome; and, as you see, I am imagining an event much more favorable than reason dictates. I am not speaking for those two poor dramas which, if they find just enough air to breathe inside a book, could, if tested on stage, die a violent death; no, I am speaking also for Art, and for those who handle it much better than I."[1]

So Manzoni responded to the proposal by the Supervisor of Theater of the city of Florence to produce *Il Conte di Carmagnola* and *Adelchi.* As he also stated in the letter, his intention had been "to write for readers and nothing more," a kind of armchair theater *à la* Seneca or Musset. We know that *Carmagnola* was performed in Florence in August, 1828, and *Adelchi* in Turin in June, 1843 (neither with scintillating success), but both times Manzoni stayed home. For him, drama was poetry, and tragedy a form of religious art, as it had been originally—which meant a form of meditation, best experienced in the intimacy of one's study instead of in crowded, noisy theaters. Hence the logical transition in his literary output from poetry to drama, to dramas which have always been considered more part of his lyrical production than as a separate genre, and which, even in their most rending moments, deny us the normal use of the word "dramatic." Again, as in the *Inni,* a sense of the human collectivity permeates the atmosphere, and of this collectivity in history, thus renewing our awareness of the basic ties between history and poetry. Orioli suggests that Manzoni's interest stems from the common search for truth which characterizes both pursuits: history as the succession of events and their causes, poetry as the penetration into the secret passions and motives of those who act them out.[2] The preface to *Carmagnola* speaks of a "dialogued poem" which obviates the need for performance, and the *Lettre à M. Chauvet* speaks of tragedy as "explaining what men have felt, wanted, and suffered through their acts," as a recreation of historical moral truth.

Apart from the *Inni* (especially **"La Pentecoste"**), the tragedies remind us of motifs in **"Marzo 1821"** and **"Il cinque maggio,"** of the former's appeal to the Italic community "of arms, of tongue, of altar, / Of memories, of blood and of heart" to cleanse itself of internal conflict and rid itself of foreign masters, and of the latter's philosophy of triumph and death, the recognition of the vanity of human ambition, and the solace of faith. Historical drama afforded Manzoni a broader canvas than poetry for the representation of human reality, for the psychological portrayal of the actions of men in time; if his readings of Goethe and Schiller, Corneille and Racine, Metastasio and Calderón, and above all Shakespeare, had taught him anything they had taught him this. Furthermore, Italy presented a natural backdrop for drama. He lived in a tragic country, whose history since the disappearance of the Roman Empire read like a graveyard's inventory: death by plundering invasions, internecine discordances, political ineptness, death by occupational atrocities, servility, in short, death by ill-fortune. In the adventures and misadventures of his homeland, whose intellectual and moral greatness was systematically strangulated by suffering and corruption, were to be found many subjects worthy of the best writers. Of all the modern tragedians, Shakespeare most felt the tragic pathos of human life and best knew how to dramatize history poetically. Manzoni always retained a keen sensitivity for the mystery of the one and the complexity of the other, so that his attraction to the author of *Coriolanus, Richard II,* and *Henry IV* is easily understood.

Poetry, of course, means style. By virtue of its truth, tragedy moves the reader, but it fails if the characters do not speak "truly," that is, if they speak in the artificial rhetoric of the past. Manzoni clearly is conscious of doing something new for Italian theater, so subserviently bound to the manner of Alfieri. Even if ***Carmagnola*** reflects the historically-centered models of Goethe's *Egmont* and Schiller's *Wallenstein* trilogy, in what concerns the play's linguistic manner Manzoni does innovate, in opposition to his illustrious compatriot:

> I hope to finish a tragedy that I began with great ardor and hope to do at least something new in this country. . . . After having read Shakespeare well, and things that have been written lately about the theater, and after having thought about them, my ideas have really changed regarding certain reputations: I dare not say more. . . . But what pains people have taken to do poorly! . . . What care to make men speak neither as they speak normally nor as they could speak, to separate prose from poetry, and to replace it with the coldest rhetorical language least apt to elicit sympathetic responses![3]

In his quest for subject matter, he came upon the story in Sismondi's *Républiques italiennes* (end of Book 7) of the fifteenth-century *condottiere,* Count Carmagnola (a plebeian who became a soldier of fortune), who left the service of Duke Filippo Maria Visconti of Milan, whose dominions he had reconquered and amplified, disgruntled at the Duke's shabby treatment of him, and entered that of his Venetian enemies, whose armies he led victoriously against the former master, only to be suspected of treason by the

Doge and the Senators, condemned and executed. The fated life of one man, whom Manzoni deemed innocent (though modern historians disagree), and the fratricidal history of a people—these elements shaped Manzoni's inspiration. The Count's innocence coupled with the sharp contrast between his courageous loyalty and the petty distrust of those wielding political power seemed good material for tragedy—for national tragedy, since the destruction wrought by such egoism paved the way for the country's unhappy future. It is significant that the historical tableau reveals what one critic calls "the Italy of the *quattrocento* with her grandeurless discords, passionless wars, crafty politics devoid of daring or magnanimous ambition."[4] This kind of realism was typical of Manzoni's peculiar brand of Romanticism.

How did he construct his play? He did so not only by opposing Alfieri's classical lexicon but also by discarding the unities of time and place, and by considering unity of action not in the Racinian sense of all events leading to and evolving from a central crisis but in the "historical" sense of the events surrounding the life of one man during a single and self-contained period. In the Preface, Manzoni analyzes five objections to the unities; the most succinctly stated is the fifth: "Finally, these rules stand in the way of much beauty and cause many inconveniences." And that says it all. In its five acts, ***Il Conte di Carmagnola*** moves about readily from the Hall of the Senate in Venice to the Count's house to the Duke of Milan's camp, the Count's tent in the opposite camp, and the Hall of the Chieftains again in Venice, back to the Count's tent, then to his house, and finally to his prison, and all of this takes place in over six years of history (1425-1432). The author thus gave the unities "a hard slap in the face."[5]

The play opens with Francesco Foscari, Doge of Venice, discussing with his Senate the Florentine Republic's offer to join forces and wage war against the Duke of Milan. The Doge favors the war, particularly now that he can employ the services of one who had served the Milanese well but who had fled the Duchy when Visconti had attempted to have him murdered. This person is, of course, Carmagnola, who is introduced into the Senate chamber to state his views. Hortatory and eloquent, Carmagnola confidently promises victory.

> . . . of an open enemy
> The open enemy am I now. I shall serve
> Your interests, but do so frankly and with purpose
> Stated, as one who is certain
> That he undertakes a just cause. . . .
> Now is the time to beat him: seize
> This moment: boldness now is prudence.

Upon his leaving, Marino, one of the Chiefs of the Council of Ten, expresses diffidence of the Count, who could turn against Venice just as easily as he now proposes to turn against Milan. But Marino's counsel of prudence, through which the Machiavellian consciousness of Venetian political life is revealed, is opposed by Senator Marco's praise of Carmagnola; as his friend, he can vouch for the Count's integrity. His remarks carry, the Doge's desires are voted, and Marco personally bears the news to Carmagnola's home. The Count joyfully anticipates his revenge over Visconti, despite his friend's admonition to proceed cautiously, since not all Venetians look upon him favorably:

> This is the day that destiny
> Seals my life; for since this holy earth
> In her ancient glorious bosom
> Has welcomed me, and named me her son,
> This will I to be forever, and I consecrate
> This sword forever both to its defense
> And greatness.

The second act is a study in contrast, rising from microcosm to macrocosm, and ending lyrically in a lament over Italian disharmony. First we note the discordance in the Milanese camp among the various mercenary captains (Angelo della Pergola, Guido Torello, Niccolò Piccinino, Francesco Sforza, among others) concerning the feasibility of doing battle, finally resolved by their leader Carlo Malatesti's decision to attack. Then we are taken to Carmagnola's camp where, under his persuasive leadership, all receive without controversy the news of the deployment of Visconti's forces on the plains of Maclodio. In the end, the Chorus intervenes to forecast the Venetian victory, and above all to deprecate fratricidal warfare, thus coloring the old historical story with new political and humanitarian shades:

> Of one land are they all, one tongue
> Do they all speak; the foreigner
> Calls them brothers. . . .
> Oh ill-fortune! Have these foolish warriors
> No wives, have they no mothers? . . .
> Oh ill-fortune! ill-fortune! ill-fortune!
> With dead the land is now already covered. . . .
> As in the air the grain is spread
> From the fully turning airing blade,
> So all about the vast terrain
> The beaten warriors all lie scattered. . . .
> The brothers have killed the brothers. . . .
> Meanwhile from the circling Alps
> The foreigner turns his gaze downward:
> He sees the strong who bite the dirt,
> And counts them each with cruel joy. . . .
> The foreigner descends; and he is here.
> Victors! Are you weak and few?
> But this is why he comes to challenge you,
> And eagerly awaits you on those fields
> Where your brother perished. . . .
> All made in the image of a single One,
> All children of a single Redemption,
> In any hour, on any portion of the land
> That we go through this mortal life,
> We are brothers, tightly bounded in a pact;
> Cursed he who breaks it,
> Who rises up above the weeping weak,
> Who grieves a soul immortal!

In the third act, in which Carmagnola's soldiers free a number of prisoners and he defends their gesture ("This is a custom of war, as well you know") to two objecting

Commissioners of the Venetian Republic, the Count's fortunes begin to wane. His unwillingness to pursue mercilessly the vanquished Milanese and his magnanimity with the prisoners are misinterpreted, and suspicion over his behavior with the foe is heightened when he is seen in polite conversation with those who in former times had ridden by his side. The Commissioners return to Venice to inform the Senate of Carmagnola's suspected treason.

Act IV takes place some years later, during which time the Count, despite several military mishaps, has been able to maintain his proud, sometimes haughty, posture. But the opposition between Marino and Marco erupts when the latter is charged by the former with guilty indulgence toward his friend and patriotic negligence toward the Republic, and when Marco protests his faithfulness to Venice, he is made to prove it by signing an agreement to leave the city to fight the Turks at Thessalonica, without warning the Count who is to be lured back to Venice deceptively and face trial for treason. Marco feels trapped and signs; later he analyzes his action along with his conscience with a fine psychological awareness matched only by his distress and feeling of impotence:

> . . . Before today
> I knew not myself! . . . Oh what a secret
> I came upon today! . . .
> . . . in witness I have summoned heaven
> Of my odious cowardice . . . its sentence
> I have underwritten. . . . I too have my share
> In his blood! Oh what did I do! . . . I let myself
> Be thus terrified? . . . This life? . . . Well, often times
> It can't be spared without a crime:
> Did I not know it? Why then did I promise?
> For whom did I fear? for me? for me? for this
> Dishonored head? . . . or for my friend?
> My refusal would have hastened the blow,
> But not deterred it. Oh my God, Who all discern,
> Unto me reveal Your heart: that I might see at least
> Into which abyss I now have fallen, if I've been
> More foolish or more craven or ill-fortuned. . . .
> . . . I extended him my hand;
> He shook it, gallant man, and at this moment that he sleeps,
> And the foe's upon him, I withdrew it;
> He awakens, seeks me out, and I have fled!
> He scorns me, then he dies! . . .
> . . . And I am yet
> But at the edge of precipice; I see this,
> And I can withdraw. . . . Can I not find
> A way? . . .
> Oh impious ones, in what a net abominable
> You have webbed me! Now there is for me
> No noble counsel; whatever I choose, I'm guilty.
> Oh atrocious doubt! . . . But I do thank them: they have
> Established me a destiny: along a single way
> They have shoved me, and I hasten there; at least
> I'm favored that I never chose it; I choose nothing,
> and whate'er
> I do derives from force and will of others.

Carmagnola receives the Senate invitation. His friend Giovanni Francesco Gonzaga warns him to be on his guard, but in typical fashion the Count, apart from his desire to be reunited with his wife Antonietta and his daughter Matilde, trusts in his own sense of loyalty and in his friend Marco. He returns happily to Venice: "Yet entirely happy / I cannot be: for who could tell me / If I shall ever see so fine a camp again?"

The final act is the most intense of the play. It takes place at night, in the chamber of the Council of the Ten, where the Doge speaks in sibylline tones insinuating accusations as he goes along—all of which makes Carmagnola soon recognize the trap into which he has fallen. He responds righteously, but to no avail. He is sent off to prison, where his final colloquy with Gonzaga and then with his wife and daughter (who faint in anguish) reveals what the author really intended to bring out in his character: magnanimity, pride, nobility, and tragedy.

> . . . Tell my comrades
> That I die innocent: you were the witness
> Of my deeds and of my thoughts, and this you
>   know. . . .
>   . . . I am
> The one betrayed. . . .
> Oh piteous God, in this moment so cruel
> You lead them off, and I do thank You. Friend,
> You succor them; from this ill-omened spot
> You remove them, and when light again they'll see
> Tell them naught remains for them to fear.

Critics have not disagreed in pointing to the tragedy's basic weakness: the psychological incompatibility between great strength of character, displayed to the point of imprudent impetuosity, and small, shrewd, cold, calculating political maneuvers on the part of a suspicious oligarchy of potentates. It was on this irreconcilable dichotomy, however, that Manzoni consciously wanted to build his tragedy: of the noble Carmagnola he asks if "he is [not truly] a dramatic character?"[6] The problem is not the concept but the execution, for the dichotomy remains dramatically unexploited, albeit moving. There is little sense of tragic accumulation of events, mainly because too many of them depend less on an individual flaw than on human weakness generally, and less on tragic consistency than on normal mutability under the dictates of suspicion or self-interest. "The catastrophe," writes one critic about the protagonist, "finds him too different from before; we have two characters: a not too characteristic warrior, and a deeply melancholy man, with no strong bridge between the two."[7] And even if we may counter this argument by noting that there is nothing contradictory about melancholy courage, and that, like Corneille's Polyeucte, there is something abstract about this soldier accustomed to open combat and not covert schemes, we might still refer to the comment of another critic who says that Carmagnola is an adventurer who may be more courageous than shrewd, but who really has no noble ambitions, leaps at the chance of revenge against Visconti, and so becomes "a wolf among wolves"; how is it that this peasant who has risen to power unscrupulously is now so ingenuously trusting and done in by a betrayal the likes of which he must

have witnessed frequently?[8] But apart from Manzoni's insistence on historical accuracy—excessive to the point of dividing his characters formally between "Historical" and "Ideal" (fictional)—it is unfair to step outside the frame of the play. What Manzoni created was a Christian Romantic who ends like the Napoleon of **"Il cinque maggio,"** purified of the need for earthly conquest and glory, and only at this point "naught remains . . . to fear." He may be "unverisimilar," but then again, and *artes poeticae* notwithstanding, what tragic hero finally is not?

In a deeper sense, however, it is Marco who strikes us as the more tragic figure. He is the victim of the capricious twists of worldly events and of his own conflicting perspectives on loyalty; his noble impulses cry for the heroism he does not possess, and his anguish in retrospect stems not from confusion or blindness but from a lucid recognition of his unheroic essence. Marco's long, self-inquisitional monologue in Act IV, in which he plunges as far down to scrutinize his self as any character can, gives us an insight into Manzoni's real dramatic abilities, but the passage is too fleeting and the Count claims (as he should) too much of our attention. Still, in a very necessary way, Marco deepens the tragic tonality of the play, so that it would be hard to conceive it without him.

This tonality is maintained uniformly by the regular, almost military, rhythm of the cadenced endecasyllables. Monti may have found the style, in his words, careless and prosaic, but another contemporary, Pellico, understood Manzoni's attempt to bring the language down from Olympus, and in good Romantic fashion make the work accessible to those untutored in lofty poetic diction (the play is written in blank verse). Therefore, having no linguistic tradition of this sort to back him up, Manzoni experimented with a balanced and simplified, yet musical, language, lest the drama not communicate directly with the public.[9] We must recognize that whatever appeal *Il Conte di Carmagnola* may still have is due in large measure to the sense of immediacy provided by the language.

According to the preface, Manzoni inserted the Chorus concluding Act II in order to have a "little corner" for himself, somewhere for him to enter the play, not in the Classical sense of interpreting the action and alluding to its denouement, but in the sense of a metahistorical comment—more intensely poetic, to be sure—on the ills of Italy and mankind. Apart from standing out because of its different pattern of versification,[10] the Chorus introduces new subject matter which many have deemed too inconsistent with that of the rest of the play. Manzoni's explanation is twofold:

> The Chorus was certainly inserted with the intention of defiling . . . wars. . . . It seems to me that the spectator, or the reader, may bring to a drama two types of interest. The first comes from seeing men and things represented in conformity with that kind of perfection and desire which we all have within us. . . . The other interest comes from a representation closer to the truth, to that mixture of greatness and pettiness, reasonable-

ness and foolishness, which we see in the big and small events of this world. This interest relates to an important and eternal part of man's mind: the desire to know what really is, to see as much as possible in ourselves and our destiny on this earth. Of these two types of interest, I believe that the deeper one, and the one more useful to stimulate, is the second. . . .[11]

Extraneous though it may be in a strict sense, then, the *Carmagnola* Chorus was to allow the useful and "modern" meaning not to go unnoticed, and it was to give the poet himself not so much a role in the play as an opportunity to give vent to his most urgent historical consciousness. Its function combined ethics with aesthetics: in reinterpreting the fundamental character of Greek choruses as he saw them, it was ". . . in no way *a caprice or an enigma* but what he really . . . wanted it to be: 'a personification of the moral thoughts inspired by the action, an organ for the sentiments of the poet who speaks in the name of all humanity.'"[12]

On balance, *Il Conte di Carmagnola* is an acceptable but not an exceptional tragedy. It can be read well, and can be appreciated if the reader interpolates the missing warmth and intensity, for there is more poetry than passion, more lyricism than drama, in it. We need not go as far as Foscolo who deplored it, or as the *Biblioteca Italiana* and London's *Quarterly Review,* which criticized it severely, but we can understand the reservations.[13] Structurally, particularly in the interrelationships between scenes, it is well conceived; otherwise, Manzoni himself recognized repeatedly the weaknesses of his "little romantic monster"[14] and did not need the critics' "open derision."[15] Pellico, however, liked it, though he thought that it dragged somewhat because the characters came too close to the truth. And Goethe praised it, taking up the cudgels in its defense in rebutting the journals. While he did not quite understand the need for Manzoni's distinction between historical and fictional characters, he was clear in his high regard: "I esteem *Carmagnola* very much, very much. . . . It is noteworthy for its depth; and the lyrical part is very beautiful. . . ."[16]

Goethe also extolled *Adelchi,* "something greater by reason of its argument."[17] He had advised Manzoni to choose in the future a subject with deeper pathos, and this the second tragedy has, not necessarily because the subject matter is more moving but because it is handled by the poet with more consistent mastery. It is artistically unified and presents a total poetic experience. But it did not become so painlessly. Manzoni was "not at all happy" with the original version, "and if . . . one ever were to sacrifice some tragedies, this one would not escape suppression. I imagined the character of the protagonist based on historical data . . . but I noted that for all of that there was nothing historical about what I did. . . . The result is something with a romanesque flavor which does not agree with the whole and which shocks even me as it would a badly disposed reader."[18] And when he went about revising it, he erased "perhaps a thousand verses."[19] Indeed, the second version, the one Goethe knew, was "purified": many of the

harsh political allusions, such as to the Pope's greedy temporal ambitions or to the servile alliances with foreign predatory powers, are toned down and diffused throughout the tragedy by innuendo, implication, and overtone, thus permitting the protagonist to stand out in greater relief. This does not mean that the political suggestiveness of the play, with reference to the suffering of contemporary Italy under foreign domination, was erased: we need only read the two choruses to be reminded that Manzoni wanted the analogy with the Risorgimento. As the censor said: "Whom did Mr. Manzoni take us for? Does he perhaps believe that we do not know what he is aiming at?"[20] Manzoni's was not a call to arms, however; his Christian conscience could not permit incitement. Besides, for him the Risorgimento was a spiritual phenomenon, an appeal to men's civic and Christian consciences, and *Adelchi,* as its protagonist unquestionably suggests, stems from Manzoni's disappointment over the pitiful failure of liberal agitations (in Naples, Sicily, and Piedmont during that year, 1821) to make any headway toward independence. In fact, there are those who see Murat's failure in the inspiration of *Carmagnola* as an anticipation of *Adelchi.*[21] This play is so strongly pessimistic that it almost strikes a jarring note in Manzoni's generally unruffled philosophical manner.

Yet this was the ethical result rather than the historical purpose, about which he wrote to Fauriel: "I want [to depict] the fall of the Lombard kingdom . . . ; everybody regards the Lombards as Italians . . . , and you can see that by looking at things this way they judged falsely the facts, laws, people, everything . . . I should like you to send me some modern works (excluding the best known) by those who for better or for worse have tried to disentangle the chaos of practices (of medieval barbarians), and who above all have spoken about the conditions of the natives, subjugated and *owned*—which is the point on which history is the poorest."[22] As usual, his desire for historical accuracy outstripped necessity, and in his intense research he went to great lengths to verify details. A typical example is his letter to Luigi Paroletti, his cousin in Turin:

> French and Italian historians who talk of Charlemagne's descent into Italy in 773, merely say that he took the mountain route and reached the rear of the armies of Desiderio, his enemy and king of the Lombards, who had made camp at the Alpine Chiuse, which he had fortified, and which without doubt is Susa. But the author of a chronicle in the Monastery of the Novalesa, who wrote during the following century and filled his book with stories, goes into greater detail, which, though mixed with fable, still might be worth looking into, since that place where Charlemagne sojourned for a while could contain a parcel of the truth. So then, he says that an unknown passage was indicated to Charlemagne, and that by following his guide he marched from the Novalesa *per crepidinem cuiusdam montis in quo usque in hodiernum diem Via Francorum dicitur* [along the base of a certain mountain which in our day continues to be called the Road of the Franks]. I find a Villafranca in the Aosta valley, which, given the similarity of the names, makes me suspect it to be this *Via Francorum.* Descending from this mountain, according

to the chronicler, Charlemagne arrived in *planitiem Vici, cui nomen erat Gavensis* [on the level ground of Vico, the name of which was Giaveno]. The commentator interprets Giaveno, but I cannot find this Giaveno on my insufficiently detailed maps. Now, I should like to know if, by leaving the Novalesa, there is a road that leads through the mountains to Giaveno, and from there to Susa, and approximately how many days it takes to cover it.[23]

This time, Manzoni not only preceded his tragedy with "Notizie Storiche," as he had done with ***Carmagnola,*** but he also engaged in true historiography with his elaboration of the "Notizie" in the form of *Discorsi sopra alcuni punti della storia longobardica.* The historical situation of ***Adelchi*** (barbarian Longobards lording over the enslaved Latin people who look to the Pope to mitigate their suffering, and the Pope's beckoning the Franks into Italy, thus pitting barbarians against barbarians—not unlike pitting Austrians against French in the nineteenth-century context—but ultimately doing nothing to alleviate the agonies of the weak, oppressed Latins) blends intimately with its poetic inspiration through which the situation is relived. In this case, poetry more than ever becomes the spirit of history, "a vital and indissoluble wedding of history and fantasy, where fantasy is totally incorporated into history, and history dissolves totally into fantasy."[24] The "literary" society evoked—the courageous palladin, his faithful friend, the beautiful suffering lady, the prevaricating traitors, the rash defiance of one king and the obstinate power of the other—acts like an aura rising from the solid substratum of history.

The drama reveals a world presided over by force, by thirst for conquest, in which the conflict for Manzoni is "between the law of the Gospel and the historical necessity of violence."[25] At the beginning of the play, which opens in the royal palace in Pavia, a squire announces the arrival of Longobard King Desiderio's daughter Ermengarda, who has been repudiated by her husband Charlemagne, King of the Franks. Spurred by pride and vengeance, Desiderio's thoughts turn to Pope Adrian who, with the proper inducements, could put Charlemagne's nephews on the Frankish throne (they had been driven out by their uncle and were at Desiderio's court with their mother Gerberga[26]). Prince Adelchi disagrees, urging that his father first regain the Pope's support by restoring to him the lands he had promised years before to restore. Greatly saddened over his sister's treatment, he exclaims:

> . . . Oh bitter price
> Of kingdom! Oh state . . . more woeful
> Than that of subjects, if even their gaze
> We are obliged to fear, and hide our forehead
> For shame; and if we cannot even honor
> The ill-fortune of someone beloved
> In the open sun!
>
> . . . . .
> Remember
> Of whom we are the kings; for in our ranks
> Mingled with the faithful, and perhaps far more than
>   they,

> Lurk our enemies, and that the sight
> Of a foreign banner changes every enemy
> Into a traitor. Oh father, to die the heart
> Alone suffices; but the victory and kingdom
> Are for him who rules over the peaceful.

These last words adumbrate the catastrophe, which seems fated even if by chance the Longobards should win. Nonetheless, his practical nature insists that, if any chance exists, it cannot take place without vacating the Vatican territory: "Let us clear out the Roman lands, and friends / Be of Adrian, for he so wishes." But Desiderio is too fired with the need for immediate military action:

> . . . To perish,
> Perish on the throne or in the dust I would
> Before I suffer such a shame. Let not
> That advice escape your lips again: your father
> So commands you.

Ermengarda's already painful situation is compounded by the king's brash attitude; her words sigh typically with a combination of lassitude and entreaty:

> My sorrow does not ask so much; I only wish
> To forget; this willingly the world accords
> The wretched. Oh, enough! In me
> Let ill-fortune end. I was to wear
> The candid badge of friendship and of peace:
> But heaven willed it not; ah, may it not be said
> I brought discordance everywhere I went
> And tears, for all to whom I was to be
> A pledge of joy.

She asks to retire to a convent, in whose solitude she might through prayer bring peace to her heart. When Charlemagne's ambassador arrives, there is no changing Desiderio's mind, particularly since the legate talks of Longobard restitutions to the Vatican, and the king urges his noblemen to war. A good part of them responds to his rousing words. The act ends, however, with another part of them bent on betraying their king; they meet at the home of Svarto, a common soldier bitter over his commonness and unscrupulous in the method he plans to adopt to overcome it.

> . . . At the bottom of Fate's urn,
> Covered over by a thousand names, my own
> Does lie; if this urn is not shaken, at the bottom
> It will lie forever, and I shall die
> In this obscurity of mine, without anyone ever
> Knowing that I dared to leave it well behind.
> I am naught. . . .
> Who thinks of Svarto? who cares to observe him?
> What foot turns to reach this lowest limit?
> Who hears me? or who fears me? Oh, if boldness
> But bestowed award! If only destiny had not
> Commanded in advance! and if the empire
> Were with swords contested, then you'd see,
> Proud dukes, just who among us would obtain it.
> If only it were up to the adroit! I read your hearts,
> All, but mine is shut to you. Oh! how much
> Astonishment would hit you, and how much disdain
> If you ever were to find out that a single wish,

A single hope, now binds me to you. . . .
Some day to be your equal! You might think
I want my fill of gold. What's gold? to throw it
At your subject's feet, now that is destiny; but humble
And defenseless to extend my hand to grab it,
Like a beggar. . . .

He volunteers to take the message of the duke's betrayal to Charlemagne; the trip is risky, but a nobleman would be detected more readily than he:

If at roll call someone calls my name and asks:
Where is he? let one of you say: Svarto? I saw him
Running long the Ticino; his steed
Got frisky, from his saddle shook him off
Into the waves; he was with arms, and surfaced not
  again.
Hapless one! they'll say; and none
Will speak again of Svarto.

The second act moves to the Frankish camp in Val di Susa, where Charlemagne expresses concern over the feasibility of crossing the Alps. His predicament lasts until the arrival of Martino, Deacon of Ravenna sent by his Archbishop, who informs him of the Longobard position at the Chiuse (". . . there crowded / Are the horses and the arms; there gathered / A whole people stands . . .") and of the existence nearby of a hitherto unknown pass through the mountains—the one he took to slip unnoticed by the Longobards, and the one Charlemagne should take to descend upon the enemy from behind. Once Charlemagne's worries are erased, his true personality is revealed: the dominator, who in the face of conquest can easily discard moral responsibilities such as his repudiation of Ermengarda for purely political expediency:

        . . . I see again
The star which sparkled at my leaving,
Then lay hid some time. What seemed
To push me away from Italy was but
The ghost of error; lying
Was the voice that said inside my heart:
No, never, no, on the soil of Ermengarda's birth
You cannot be king. Oh world! I am
Of your blood. You are alive: why then
Stood you before me stubbornly,
Tacitly, afflicted, in act of rebuke,
Pallidly, as if come from the tomb?
God has damned her house; so was I then
To stay united with her? . . .
        . . . A king cannot
Travel his high road, without having
Someone fall beneath his feet. . . .
        . . . . .
        . . . Three more days,
Then the battle and the victory; and after that
Rest in lovely Italy, amid the fields
Waving with the grain, and in the orchards
Laden with fruit unknown to our fathers;
Among the ancient temples and the palaces,
In that land cheered by song, prized by the sun,
Sheltering in its bosom the world's lords,
And God's martyrs; where the shepherd supreme
Raises both his palms, and blesses

Our banners, where we have as enemies
A puny people, still divided
Among themselves at that, and half-way mine. . . .

The beauty of Italy attracts, and her divided citizenry makes the prey that much more enticing for someone for whom no law exists except success.

Adelchi dominates the third act; he is duty-bound to defend the honor of the kingdom, yet knows deep inside him that all is to no avail, and that an unhappy destiny hovers over the Longobard enterprise. For this reason, when his close and devoted friend Anfrido mentions the word "glory," his melancholy reply fits not only his profile but also the whole temper of the drama:

        . . . Glory? my
Destiny is to crave it, and to die
Never having tasted it.

He fights as he must, for a condemned cause. But he fights valiantly, even while all else crumbles about him, and in so doing offers a sharp contrast with the defecting dukes: Guntigi, Ildechi, Farvaldo, Indolfo, etc. The cowardly sight even revolts a noble, Frankish warrior, Rutlando (alias Orlando, or Roland), who cries his disgust to Charlemagne:

        . . . Oh king, I call you
As witness, and you too, you Counts, for on this
Vile day I unsheathed not my sword; let him today
Wound whome'er he wishes. Frightened, scattered
  flock,
I shan't pursue it. . . .
        . . . . .
        . . . Friends?
This we would have been much more, had we at the
  Chiuse
Crossed arms. They asked me for the king; I turned
My shoulders; you will see them now. No, if I knew
What kind of enemy we marched against, for sure
I would not have moved away from France.

Anfrido dies with honor, and Adelchi chastizes the "Day of infamy and ire," seeking for himself the same kind of honorable death. At this point, Manzoni introduces one of the two Choruses of the tragedy, a pessimistic comment on Italy's destiny:

From the mossy porches and the failing Forums,
From the woods and from the screeching smithies,
From the furrows laved with servile sweat,
A people frequently dispersed arises,
Perks its ears, uplifts its head
Rocking with new rumors rising.
        . . . . .
In their looks and faces, confused and uncertain,
Suffered contempt mixes contrastingly
With the wretched pride of times gone by.
        . . . . .
And on deserters, with sword flaming,
Like ransacking dogs loosed running,
Right and left he sees the warriors come;
He sees them, rapt in a joy unknown

Surveys the battle with lithe hope
And dreams the end of his harsh service.
                    . . . . .

Would the wished prize, promised to the brave,
Be—deluded ones—a shift of fortune,
That a foreign people end your sorrows?
Return to your proud ruins,
To the faint-hearted jobs of your parched workshops,
To the furrows laved with servile sweat.
The stout will mingle with the foe surrendered,
The new lord will mix with the old;
On your neck will ride both nations.
They share the serfs, they share the herds;
They pause together on the blood-soaked fields
Of a dispersed race without a name.

Act IV finds Ermengarda in the monastery of St. Salvator in Brescia where she dies, the fragile victim of her enduring love for Charlemagne and of an irrational, insensitive world which substitutes blood for beauty and violence for peace. Among her dying words, she recalls to the abbess her sister, Ansberga, the happier times of yesteryear:

Smiling days! Do you remember? We crossed over
Mountains, rivers, forests, and with every dawn
The joy of waking grew. What days!
No, speak not of them, I beg you! Heaven knows
If I thought that ever in a mortal heart
So much joy could be contained, and so much sorrow!
You weep for me! Oh, wish you to console me?
Call me daughter: for at this name I feel
A martyr's fullness, and it floods
My heart, and casts it out into oblivion.

The scene concludes with the Chorus returning to sing the death of the afflicted heroine. It is one of the author's finest poetic efforts and, like the previous Chorus, is often included separately among his "lyrics" in the exclusive sense. It may be imagined as a chorus of nuns, to whom Manzoni has lent his most intimate feelings, and contains three parts: the heroine's final moments, the reevocation of her tragedy, and moral reflections on the theme of "provident ill-fortune," the Providential intervention of God in the turmoiled affairs of Ermengarda who through her suffering redeems her Nemesis-plagued race and attains salvation.

With her soft braids spreading
Over her troubled bosom,
Her limbs slow, and bedewed
With death her white visage, she
Pious lies, trembling
Her eyes seeking sky.
                    . . . . .

As dew upon a tuft
Of grass that has turned arid
Makes life again freshly
Flow inside the withered blades,
Which rise once more green
In the tempered dawn;

So into her thoughts, by
Love's ungodly virtue wrought,

Descends the cooling balm
Of a friendly word; her heart
Delights in calm joys
Of another love.
                    . . . . .

Descended from a line
With oppressors blameworthy,
Whose numbers spelled courage,
Whose offense became reason,
Blood their right, and fame
Was in no pity,

Provident ill-fortune
Placed you among the oppressed;
You die lamented, calm,
And descend to sleep with them:
No one will insult
The accused ashes.

You die; may your lifeless
Visage be reformed in peace,
As once it was careless
Of an erring destiny.
It colored only
Slight virginal thoughts.

Thus from the clouds rent through
The setting sun appears,
And behind the mountain
Crimsons now the trembling West,
Boding good farmers
A day more serene.[27]

The scene shifts quickly to the walls of Pavia, the town to which Desiderio has retreated, and where Guntigi prepares the final betrayal in a speech ringing with Shakespearean overtones:

          . . . Loyalty? So let the saddened friend
Of a fallen lord, the one who, stubborn
In his hope, or, say, irresolute, stood
With him until the end, and with him fell,
Cry Loyalty! Hah, Loyalty! and with it
Let him be consoled—all right. For whate'er consoles
In it we wish to trust—no hesitation. But when
We might lose all, and yet we can
Save all; and when the lucky one, the sire
For whom God declares himself, the consecrated
Charles sends me a messenger, wants me his friend,
Invites me not to perish, wants to separate
Me from the cause of misadventure. . . .
What for, though always shunned, does this word
Loyalty return to assail me,
Like a troubling bore? it always hurls itself
In the midst of all my thoughts, consulting them,
Upsetting them? This Loyalty! All destinies
Are fine with her, and death is beautiful. Who says
     so?
The one for whom you die. And so the universe
Repeats it with a single voice, and shouts
That, be he mendicant or derelict, the loyal man
Is honor worthy, more than is the traitor
Leisuring with friends. Ah, is that so? But if he's
     worthy,
What's he doing being mendicant or derelict? . . .

The final act, in the Royal Palace at Verona, seals the end of the Longobardic world. The petulant natures of the two rival monarchs makes it impossible for them to behave toward each other with civility, each only too quick to berate the other. Vanquished, Desiderio begs Charlemagne to spare his son's life and let all other matters rest, not indulge his greed, for "Heaven abhors immoderate desires," and when the Frankish king balks, he erupts:

> I begged you, so I did, though at the test
> I should have known you! You deny it; on your head
> The treasure of revenge grows thicker.
> Deceit has made you victor; let the victory
> Make you proud and merciless.
> Step on the prostrate, and climb; you offend God. . . .

to which the irritated victor responds:

> Silence, you who are defeated. What's this? Just
>   yesterday
> You dreamed my death, and now you beg forgiveness,
> Which would be meet if, in the easy hour
> Of hospitable discourse, delighted I
> Would be rising from your table! . . .

Still, before the nobility of Adelchi, who is carried in mortally wounded from the field of battle, even Charlemagne softens and acquiesces to the Prince's words of friendship. To his father, at whose side he has stood dutifully though in full knowledge of the vanity of the situation, Adelchi utters dying:

> Life has its great secret, and the final hour
> Alone can understand it. . . .
> Rejoice you are not king, rejoice that every course
> Of action is now blocked: no place is there
> For friendly, harmless deeds; all that remains
> Is to do wrong, or suffer it. A force ferocious
> Possesses this world, and it bears the name
> Of Law. The bloodied hand of our ancestors
> Seeded injustice; our own fathers
> Cultivated it with blood; by now this earth
> Will not yield another harvest. . . .

As the final curtain falls, Adelchi gives up his "tired soul" to Heaven.

The plot's underpinning reflects ideas Manzoni derived from French historians like Fauriel and other liberal thinkers of the Restoration, primarily Augustin Thierry.[28] The latter's dualistic vision of conquerors and conquered, oppressors and oppressed, with, in *Adelchi*'s case, Italy representing the Third Estate amid the clash of races bent on domination, gives the play an historical justification in the light of which the characters, fictional or real, engage a dimension of life greater than themselves. As one critic put it, Adelchi is "the soul of exile."[29] More than anyone else, he feels the guilt of his "race" and knows both the Papal diffidence and the reciprocal hatreds separating Longobards from Franks from Italic Latins. In the subtle ways of his restive conscience, he has compassion for the Italians, his serfs, for, as Croce stated, he is aware that the world is not

based on the opposition between good and evil, rather on the shock of vital interests,[30] on whichever side these may lie. He has, then, a pragmatic sense of ruling, which with reference to personal behavior becomes transmuted into exemplary ethics. It is erroneous to try to see in him a typically Romantic hero. True, he is Romantic in his many inner contradictions: his desire for glory, yet his unwillingness to attain it by calculation, hypocrisy, or "politics"; his stern regal bearing, yet his inability to react with justified ferocity against traitors; his will to avenge the insult to Ermengarda, yet his too profound Christianity to throw pity to the winds; his confidence in his courage and in himself, yet his awareness that it will not avail his sister, his realm, or his father. He is Romantic in that he feels he was born for greatness, yet he kills its potential by his unquestioning faith in duty and by the attendant resignation. His stoic front hides a gentle heart. But his world-weariness is not Romantic lassitude in the poetic manner of Novalis' *Heinrich von Ofterdingen;* it is the realization of Christian renunciation, far more convincing than Chateaubriand's attempt to portray it in *René* through the mouth of Father Souël. To say, with De Sanctis,[31] that Adelchi realizes the ideal of the *Inni* (in preparation of Father Cristoforo and Cardinal Borromeo in *I promessi sposi*) strikes us as exaggerated, or needlessly facile. He does, however, represent the apogee of Christian fatalism in the theater; he does not permit himself to withdraw from the historical determinism which affects his duty, and if he obeys the dictates of necessity, he does so with his arm and not with his sword.[32] There may not be in him the agony of doubt, but there is the anguish of engagement. If only for this reason, he has been compared with Alfieri's Ildovaldo in *Rosmunda,* the Marquis de Posa in Schiller's *Don Carlos,* Sophocles' Antigone and Shakespeare's Cordelia, but above all with Hamlet—with the one exception, apart from the unparalleled depth of the Shakespearean hero, that Adelchi's is not a philosophical nature that stifles action but an active nature for which philosophy despairs. Hence he is to some extent a solitary hero in the Shakespearean tradition, but to a larger extent a representative hero, imbued with religiosity, illustrating a particularly symbolic situation.[33] In Western literature, he comes as close to the Christian tragic hero as we may witness; his only rival is Corneille's Polyeucte, but Adelchi's inner travail does not admit comparison with the former's abstract stoicism. We may admire Polyeucte; we feel for Adelchi.

Like her brother, Ermengarda is portrayed not as deluded by life but as a conscience of life. Both are victims, to be sure, but through their openness to justice, love, and charity something of them survives. Manzoni deifies his heroine, for in a sense she is Italy; he makes her ethereal, emerge like an elegy in an epic of armor, or, as Ulivi put it, like "the kind of blended and afflicted musicality we associate with Racine's Phèdre and Athalie."[34] But more than Italy, she is humanity, its drama. Though her emotions bear the stamp of regal refinement, she is more loving than queen,[35] and her passion churns only inwardly; outwardly it is tenderness and sacrifice, that is, an expression of spirituality. When Manzoni inscribed a copy of *I promessi sposi* for his daughter Enrichetta, he wrote in it, recalling his recently deceased wife, what her name meant to him—something which could justifiably apply to Ermengarda (or the novel's Lucia): "faith, purity, wisdom, love of one's own, benevolence toward all, sacrifice, humility, *all that is holy, all that is lovable* (St. Paul)."[36]

Manzoni's genius for characterization is not limited to *I promessi sposi* or to the protoganists of this play, for next to Adelchi and Ermengarda, the other characters do not pale. He knew that he was side-stepping tradition when he created the role of Charlemagne, as he wrote to Cousin: "Charlemagne . . . will be neither Ariosto's leader of the paladins, nor the saint of some ecclesiastical authors, nor the legislator of some great men, nor the wise man of some university faculty, nor the rascal of some philosophers, nor the hero of those who received pensions from his younger brother, but someone who after all that may still turn out to be a poorly conceived character."[37] He turned out well, however, the "most composite" character in the play, the "pure politician and all-time Caesar,"[38] who has as many personalities as there are situations for them in which to function. Indeed, Galletti alludes to "the Caesarian profile of Napoleon,"[39] but a more apt reminiscence would conjure up the Machiavellian prince, for whom the political end is the only rule, necessity must be faced with resoluteness, and power is not to be measured by petty ambition. If his language swells with the pomp of victory, it is because he can still remain human, or rather return to his humanity, after the deed has been accomplished and the power accrued.

Next to him, Desiderio appears less composite than complex, because in his case we cannot speak of a pure Machiavellism but of a confusion between fever of ambition, of dominion, rough pride and petty egoism on the one hand, and on the other genuine paternal compassion and sporadic bursts of magnanimity. Of all the characters who walk Manzoni's stage, he remains the most difficult to grasp, beneath the obvious superstructure of a barbarian prince, and therefore the one who arouses the most curiosity. The broad, ethical dimensions of the crisis escape him; his vision is fragmented by his impulses, good and bad. This is not the case with the leading traitors, Guntigi and Svarto, who bring to mind "the tragic morality of Shakespeare,"[40] without, however, overpowering us with the fearsome evil of the Iagos. Their vision is not fragmented; they have a clear view of "real" life, stripped of idealistic charisms, and use cold logic to legitimize ugly calculation. Guntigi's "Loyalty" monologue drips with sophistry and ably conceals the void of his conscience, while Svarto climbs to become Count of Susa, acting like an elemental incarnation of that earthly "force ferocious" that Adelchi speaks of, before which decency has no chance, and in whose throes "ill-fortune" is merciful when it is "provident." Too bad that both Guntigi and Svarto, limited to their respective corners of the play, do not develop more forcefully throughout it, and that, as Carducci remarked, they are not endowed with a deeper, Michelangelesque or Shakespearean trait or two. Still, in their own corners, they remain impressive.

In the brief lapse of dramatic time from near the end of Act III to near the beginning of Act IV, Manzoni concentrated the lyrical essence of the tragedy in the form of two Choruses, regarded by many as the fruit of his historical and ethical meditation. Structurally, they "peak" the action by revealing its symbolism and by allowing the poet to intervene so as to draw the play out of itself, to summarize and to teach. Their importance in Manzoni's mind cannot be minimized: he talked about having had to "rhyme the two lyrical choruses . . . , in order to draw attention to what is most serious and poetic in the subject matter. . . ."[41] Thus their aesthetic placement serves a philosophical end, for by being juxtaposed they signal once again the tragic dualism in Manzoni's world view, the sense of collective and individual tragedy which underlies his pessimism regarding things of this earth. The first one is Italy's Chorus, or as Russo calls it, "a sorrowful epic of war," the peripeteia of a whole society aroused and dismembered by superior forces and adverse historical traditions. The same critic notes too that the national motif is colored with Manzoni's Christian consciousness, and that while we may speak of a certain "contemplative pessimism," we may also speak of another "active pessimism," that of teaching the people to work and be virtuous for their own inner redemption.[42] The second, Ermengarda's Chorus, points to the ensuing private tragedy, the solitary destiny of the individual, who in the nature of things will always be frail and haplessly suffering if he is going to be honest. Only endurance or forebearance marks the life of the good, at the end of which hope lies in the Providential reward of being removed from it. There is, shall we say, poetry in morality, and in the morality of death.

Before and after the two Choruses, the structure of the tragedy—the scene by scene progression and the feeling of spaciousness emerging from it—adumbrate the narrative artist of the novel. The interrelationship of the parts, rather than tightly confine the play according to Classical norms, yields through the subject matter to a broader, we might suggest cosmic, sense of the whole. Nowhere is this sense more pronounced than in Martino's recounting of his arduous journey across the beautiful Alps. Little knowing that the Franks will turn out to be invaders and not liberators,[43] he represents the Italian people's hope, a hope which becomes lyricized in the form of a sublime account of the country's natural beauty:

> . . . Here
> No trace of man appears, but only forests
> Of firs intact, rivers unknown, and trailless
> Valleys; all was quiet: I heard
> But my own steps, and from time to time
> The torrent's thunder, or the unexpected
> Falcon's screeching, or the eagle's darting
> In early morning from its raised nest, roaring
> Above my head, or in the afternoon
> The sylvan crackling of the pine cones
> Stung by the sun. I journeyed thus three days
> And I spent three nights under tall plants
> Or in the gorges. My guide was the sun;
> With it I arose, and then I followed
> Its course, facing last its setting. I walked

Uncertain of the road, and crossing over
From vale to vale; or if at times I saw
Rising before me the summit of a cliff
Accessible, and I did reach the top,
More peaks more sublime, stood
In front and all around, still others whitened
From crest to base with snow, almost
Like pointed, steep pavilions, pegged
Into the earth; still others, iron-firm,
Like walls erect and insurmountable. The third sun
Was setting when I scaled a lofty mountain
Which raised its forehead higher than the rest
And was one long green slope, its summit
Crowned with trees. . . .

Passages like this one highlight *Adelchi.* They make it Manzoni's lyrical masterpiece and, together with *Il Conte di Carmagnola,* augured well for the future of Romantic theater in a Europe seeking the theatrical ground for its new literature. Goethe alluded to Manzoni's "new dramatic school." But the Romantic "school" of historical drama went in other directions, in those—primarily in Germany and Austria—of Kleist, Hebbel, Grillparzer, and Ludwig (and the little recognized Grabbe and Büchner), while in France, Manzoni's intellectual center, it sank into the soap-opera platitudes of Hugo's *Hernani, Ruy Blas, Lucrèce Borgia, Les Burgraves,* etc. Disenchanted with such productions, Sainte-Beuve looked back to the promise held forth by Manzoni's dramatic works: "When I think of those two beautiful columns which seemed to shape for us in advance the portico of the edifice, providing we followed the example, I can hardly not blush at what, under our very eyes, has happened to this dream of a theatre."[44]

Goethe was correct: Manzoni's theater was "new." While the characters do stand out, they leave an impression on us more through what they do not say than through what they say, and therefore do not overpower us like Phèdre, or Lear, or Oedipus. Manzoni's propensity to write for readers rather than for spectators aided this attenuation which, combined with his ethico-historical concerns, produced what has been called a narrated representation. On this basis, one critic[45] has pointed to Manzoni's modernity, since his conception anticipates Brecht's epic theater, although the latter's objective depiction of events cannot blend with the former's subjective poetization of them. Still, there remains the same "ethical dissatisfaction with the conventions of the traditional stage," and conceived as an epic narrative, *Adelchi* presents possibilities involving stage and public, that is, a collective experience, which would be difficult in the conventional manner of stressing the imposing hero and the impressive heroine.[46]

The underlying pessimism is the same. More pagan and naturalistic, Shakespeare does not concern himself with Christian renunciation; Manzoni does, and Brecht does not know it. Greek Fate became Destiny in Shakespeare and Marxist struggle in Brecht, while Manzoni saw existence more Jansenistically as an infirmity, in which participation means fighting and in which good actions turn to, or are

annulled by, worldly evil. Not the least cause for worry is history's ability to place fine men and women, princes or paupers alike, in the roles of oppressors; necessity makes no allowances for good will, and in short order all hands become soiled. Nonetheless, "fighting and active participation are the primary condition for salvation. . . . Of course, to participate by fighting is not an optimistic solution, and we might say that, along with admiration, a historical *pietas* veils the eyes of the poet when he looks at man's tumultuous incursions."[47] We may either obey reluctantly, like Adelchi, or absorb sacrificially, like Ermengarda. A troubling fatality hovers above our heads; Thierry's racial determinants look, more philosophically, like Jansenistic determinism if we consider, somewhat like Russo, the unreconcilability between the Jansenistic world of Grace inhabited by Adelchi, Ermengarda, and Martino, and the Machiavellian world of Realpolitik inhabited by Desiderio, Svarto, and Charlemagne.[48] Hence the veracious, tragic atmosphere of *Adelchi.* We cannot feel that if the aberrations of the hero's historical age were rectified, all would end well. If tragedy must encourage a metaphysical attitude through a poetic cosmology, then *Adelchi* fits the mode, and the notion that Christian tragedy is not possible because of the promise of salvation does not apply. For Manzoni, Providence operates in the infinite rather than in the finite, preparing salvation with pain and ill-fortune, "but abandoning the earth and the living to the whirlwind of evil and to the anguish of eternal shipwreck."[49]

To be sure, Hamlet, who looks upon his fellow man's hypocrisy and injustice with equal aversion as Adelchi, cannot invite death as confidently as his counterpart because he has no faith in the beyond. But Adelchi is no less anguished and his tone no less pessimistic. For this reason, the play should not be considered an exemplum to which the human traits of its characters are subservient, or in which inspiration drew exclusively from the Christian fountain; in fact, the emphasis rests on the personality, albeit not overpowering, moving as best he can in an evil world toward an attainment, in some cases, of the Christian ideal. If the play's expressiveness stems from a refined religiosity, its humanity stems from a sensitive psychological assessment of human behavior. "The thought that moves the drama is doubtlessly Christian, but the feeling that penetrates every scene is one of horror for universal injustice and disdain for triumphant perfidy."[50] Sansone insists that in its finest moments, *Adelchi* expresses not Manzoni's religious but his secular pessimism, his tragic sense of life,[51] and to this we must add that he does so to the point of near crisis. His "freest poetry" (the expression comes from Croce[52]) may be free in a sense other than versification. For *Adelchi* rings surprisingly with doubt, with the agonizing questions of Job: why do the good suffer?; why do they die without realizing their good?; how can Ermengarda be cast aside so shamelessly?; why are Svarto's ambitions fulfilled?; how can Charlemagne stoop to an acceptance of human fraud when his own knight Rutlando shudders? In other words, where is this divine, Providential justice which ultimately controls human history from above, which shapes the historical design? In the long run, Christianity shows itself in **Adelchi** only in the way its heroes accept death, in the "provident ill-fortune." The rest is cast with bleak thoughts.

Notes

1. Letter to Attilio Zuccagni Orlandini, January 4, 1828, quoted from *Manzoni: tutte le opere* (Roma: Avanzini e Torraca, 1965), pp. 66-67.

2. Giovanni Orioli, in ibid., p. 67.

3. Letter to Fauriel, March 25, 1816, *Epistolario,* I, 140.

4. Galletti, p. 384.

5. Letter to Fauriel, March 25, 1816, *Epistolario,* I, 140.

6. Letter to Gaetano Giudici, February 7, 1820, *Epistolario,* I, 172.

7. Momigliano, p. 177. To the contrary, Francesco Flora sees in Carmagnola's "religious acceptance of death" the culminating sign of an essentially "poetic" character (*Storia della letteratura italiana* [Milano: Mondadori, 1940], III, 204-6).

8. Galletti, pp. 389-90.

9. See Orioli, p. 67.

10. The Chorus is in sixteen octanes (seven decasyllables and a final nonasyllable) and in rhyme: abacbddc.

11. Letter to Gaetano Giudici, February 7, 1820, *Epistolario,* I, 172-73.

12. Alberto Chiari, Introduction to *Il Conte di Carmagnola* (Firenze: Le Monnier, 1947), p. xxxvi.

13. Foscolo actually despaired: "Poor us! Poor *belle lettere*! . . . What a sacrilege!" The *Biblioteca italiana* (February, 1820) said scoffingly: "We have hundreds of such tragedies . . . ," and the *Quarterly Review* urged Manzoni to stick to splendid odes and not disgust the public with weak tragedies (December, 1820). See *Epistolario,* I, 193-96.

14. Used for *Adelchi,* though in his mind the epithet applied also to *Carmagnola*: letter to Fauriel, March 6, 1822, *Epistolario,* I, 228.

15. Letter to Johann Wolfgang Goethe, January 23, 1821, *Epistolario,* I, 191. In this letter of gratitude for the German poet's "favorable judgment," Manzoni expresses surprise that critics "saw almost everything differently from the way I had imagined it; they praised those things to which I had given less importance, and took as oversights and inadvertences . . . those parts which were the fruit of my most sincere and persevering meditation."

16. *Epistolario,* I, 194. Goethe's long analysis was in *Über Kunst und Alterthum* of that year. Manzoni admitted to Goethe that the character distinction was due to "too scrupulous an attachment to his-

torical accuracy" (*Epistolario,* 1, 192), and of Fauriel (March 6, 1822, *Espistolario,* I, 231), who was preparing a French translation, he requested a deletion of the distinction. A German translation was readied by one Arnold.

17. See *Epistolario,* I, 194.

18. Letter to Fauriel, December 3, 1821, *Epistolario,* I, 218.

19. Letter to Fauriel, March 6, 1822, *Epistolario,* I, 228.

20. Quoted in *Epistolario,* I, 197.

21. See Chiari, p. xxxiii.

22. Letter to Fauriel, October 17, 1820, *Epistolario,* I, 187-88.

23. Letter to Luigi Paroletti, 1820(?), *Lettere inedite,* pp. 6-7.

24. Filippo Piemontese, "L'ispirazione storico-religiosa dell'*Adelchi,*" *Convivium* 1 (1949), p. 4.

25. Galletti, p. 391.

26. Manzoni later asked Fauriel, when translating into French, to leave the historical names as they were, for even if they sounded coarse that could not be helped, but to make the fictional ones "less baroque and closer to their Germanic root . . . since I have had to distort them in order to Italianize them" (Letter to Fauriel, March 6, 1822, *Epistolario,* I, 230).

27. While the whole play, like *Carmagnola,* is in endecasyllables, the two Choruses stand out rhythmically through their change in meter. "Italy's Chorus" (the first) contains eleven stanzas of six 12-syllable verses each, rhymed aabccb. It has a slow, deliberate cadence, creating an effect of sad solemnity. "Ermengarda's Chorus" (the second) is made up of twenty stanzas of six 8-syllable lines, with only 2 and 4 rhyming, and 6 with the previous 6. The effect is totally different: it moves along effortlessly, and more lyrically and more serenely than the first.

28. See the study by Cesare De Lollis, *Alessandro Manzoni e gli storici liberali francesi della Restaurazione* (Bari: Laterza, 1926).

29. Bollati, quoted in Orioli, p. 69.

30. Benedetto Croce, "Alessandro Manzoni," in *Saggi e discussioni* (Bari: Laterza, 1952), p. 118.

31. Francesco De Sanctis, *Letteratura italiana nel secolo XIX,* ed. L. Blasucci, 2 vols. (Bari: Laterza, 1953), I, 101.

32. Croce, p. 120.

33. However, we are not of the opinion, held by some, that the characters in *Adelchi* in the long run become rigidified into symbols of Manzoni's thought. In varying degrees, each has his own complexity

34. Ulivi, p. 101.

35. See Emilio Santini, *Il teatro di A. Manzoni* (Palermo: Palumbo, 1940), pp. 79-87 passim.

36. Letter to Coen, May 20, 1834, *Epistolario,* I, 479.

37. Quoted in Galletti, pp. 394-95.

38. Filippo Piemontese, *Manzoni* (Brescia: La Scuola Editrice, 1953), p. 161.

39. Galletti, p. 395.

40. Momigliano, p. 188.

41. Letter to Fauriel, March 6, 1822, *Epistolario,* I, 228.

42. Russo, pp. 19-20.

43. Momigliano (pp. 186-87) suggests that the reason Martino does not reappear in the play after scene 3 of Act II is that he represents the great hope for Italian liberation, to be executed by the Franks, and when this hope is crushed (as Italy's Chorus tells us) by subsequent disillusion, there is no need for him to return on stage. He vanishes with the hope. Russo stresses too heavily the "presence of God" and the "poetry of faith" in this description of nature's wonders (*Alessandro Manzoni: liriche, tragedie, e prose* [Firenze: Sansoni, 1951] p. 180). We see it primarily as a structural device.

44. "M. Fauriel," in *Portraits contemporains* (Paris: Calmann-Lévy, 1889), IV, 206.

45. Nino Borsellino, "Panorama della letteratura critica sull'*Adelchi,*" *Quaderni del teatro popolare italiano,* no. 1 (Torino: Einaudi, 1960), p. 147.

46. See a brief discussion along some of these lines in Luciano Codignola, "Aless. Manzoni: *Adelchi,*" in ibid., p. 142.

47. Ulivi, p. 89.

48. Russo, "Parere sull'*Adelchi,*" in *Ritratti e disegni storici.*

49. Galletti, pp. 405-6.

50. Ibid., p. 396.

51. See his *Opera poetica di Alessandro Manzoni,* the discussion of *Adelchi* which centers around this point of view.

52. Croce, p. 117.

Works Cited

Primary Sources

Alessandro Manzoni: Tutte le opere. Edited by Bruno Cagli, a cura di G. Orioli, E. Allegretti, G. Manacorda, and L. Felici. Roma: Avanzini e Torraca, 1965.

Tutte le poesie di Alessandro Manzoni. A cura di A. L. Castris. Firenze: Sansoni, 1965.

Liriche. A cura di Attilio Momigliano. Torino: Einaudi, 1932.

The Sacred Hymns and the Napoleonic Ode. Translated by Reverend Joel Foote Bingham. London/New York: H. Frowde, 1904.

Alessandro Manzoni: Tragedie. A cura di P. Egidi. Torino: Einaudi, 1921.

Adelchi, tragedia storica. A cura di Giorgio Derzero. Torino: G. B. Paravia, 1947.

Il Conte di Carmagnola. A cura di Alberto Chiari. Firenze: Le Monnier, 1947.

I promessi sposi: storia milanese del secolo XVII scoperta e rifatta da Alessandro Manzoni. Torino: Società Editrice Internazionale, 1933.

I promessi sposi. Edited by L. Gessi. Roma: A Signorelli, 1960.

I promessi sposi. Edited by Pietro Mazzamuto. Palermo: Palumbo, 1955.

I promessi sposi. Edited by Alberto Moravia. Torino: Einaudi, 1960.

I promessi sposi. Edited by Giuseppe Petronio. Torino: Paravia, 1946.

The Betrothed Lovers. With a biographical introduction by G. T. Bettany. London/New York: Ward, Look, 1889.

The Betrothed. With a critical and biographical introduction by Maurice Francis Egan. New York: Appleton, 1900.

The Betrothed. With an introduction by James, cardinal Gibbons. New York: The National Alumni, 1907.

The Betrothed. Edited by Charles W. Eliot. Harvard Classics, vol. 21. New York: Collier, 1909-1910.

The Betrothed. Translated, with a preface by Archibald Colquhoun. London: J. M. Dent, 1951/New York: E. P. Dutton, 1956, 1959.

The Betrothed. Translated by Archibald Colquhoun. New York: E. P. Dutton, 1961.

Epistolario di Alessandro Manzoni. Edited by Giovanni Sforza. Milano: Paolo Carrara, 1882.

Lettere inedite di Alessandro Manzoni. Edited by Ercole Gnecchi. Milano: L. F. Cogliati, 1900.

Carteggio di Alessandro Manzoni. A cura di Giovanni Sforza e Giuseppe Gallavresi. 2 vols. Milano: U. Hoepli, 1912-1921.

Secondary Sources

Chandler, S. B. *Alessandro Manzoni: The Story of a Spiritual Quest.* Edinburgh: Edinburgh University Press, 1974. A general view of Manzoni's works, rich in insights relating to how all of them successively permit a unitary development toward a spiritual view of life.

Chiavacci, Angelica. *Il "Parlato" nei "Promessi sposi"*. Firenze: Sansoni, 1961. A good discussion not only of speech and dialogue but also of how the whole novel is aesthetically and implicitly dialogued.

Colombo, Umberto. *Manzoni e gli "umili"*. Milano: Edizioni Paoline, 1972. Stresses the notion and the meaning of the commoner in the novel, making good use of recent scholarship.

Costa, Sarnio, and Mavaro, Giuseppe. *L'opera del Manzoni nelle pagine dei critici*. Firenze: Le Monnier, 1962. A helpful anthology, with introductory notes, of Manzoni criticism.

Croce, Benedetto. *A. Manzoni*. Bari: Laterza, 1930. A seminal study in Manzoni criticism, relating to questions of historiography, language, aesthetics, didacticism, and the oratorical nature of the novel.

De Lollis, Cesare. *Alessandro Manzoni e gli storici liberali francesi della Restaurazione*. Bari: Laterza, 1926. A look into the intellectual formation of Manzoni and the attitude of "deheroization" of history, along with certain ideas of Thierry.

De Sanctis, Francesco. *Manzoni*. Edited by C. Muscetta and D. Puccini. Torino: Einaudi, 1955. Fundamental observations, in the historical method, focusing on Manzoni's liberal, democratic inspiration, his dramaturgy, the novel as fictionalization of religious, philosophical ideas, and his psychological perceptiveness.

D'ovidio, Francesco. *Nuovi studi manzoniani*. Caserta: Editrice Moderna, 1928. In the lineage of De Sanctis and the historical method, looking into the popular-national character of the novel and its genuine historicity.

Gabbuti, Elena. *Manzoni e gli ideologi francesi*. Firenze: Sansoni, 1936. Manzoni's analytical mind in contact with the Ideologues and the question of the nature of things relative to truth, knowledge, language, and art.

Galletti, Alfredo. *Alessandro Manzoni*. Milano: A. Corticelli, 1944. A capital study on the total Manzoni in a context of intellectual history and what today would be called comparative literature.

Getto, Giovanni. *Manzoni europeo*. Milano: U. Mursia & C., 1971. An excellent compilation of essays from 1960 to 1970 dealing with Manzoni internationally: the baroque novel, France, Rousseau, Schiller, Shakespeare, and Cervantes.

Goffis, Cesare Federico. *La lirica di A. Manzoni*. Bari: Adriatica Editrice, 1967. The maturing continuity of Manzoni's thought, and the possibility of lexical analysis to penetrate the soul of the poet.

Gorra, Marcella. *Manzoni*. Palermo: Palumbo, serie Storia della critica, 1959/1962. A valuable review of the avenues and problems of Manzoni criticism.

Graf, Arturo. *Foscolo, Manzoni, Leopardi*. Torino: Chiantore, 1945. Manzoni's romanticism, his primacy in historiography, and the psychological dimension measured against the presence of the supernatural.

Marcazzan, Mario. "Il paesaggio dei *Promessi sposi*," *Humanitas*, 1198-1203 no. 3, (1948). The relationship between nature, characters, and the novel's meaning.

Mazzamuto, Pietro. *Poetica e stile in Alessandro Manzoni*. Firenze: Le Monier, 1957. The Chauvet letter background of Manzoni's poetics, a fine appreciation of the relationship between irony and his tragicomic direction, and its influence on his realism.

Momigliano, Attilio. *Alessandro Manzoni*. Milano: Principato, 1966. A loosely discoursed but insightfully penetrating appreciation of the total Manzoni, stressing the notions of musicality and of the essential unity of his works.

Montano, Rocco. *Comprendere Manzoni*. Napoli: G. B. Vico Editrice, 1975. A tightly and clearly argued interpretation of Manzoni's realism with reference to the Absolute, the narrative, the problem of history and art, the happy ending, the role of language, the notion of moralism, and the intellectual background of the novel.

Pellizzari, Achille. "Estetica e religione di A. Manzoni," *Studi manzoniani*, edited by G. de Robertis, Vol. 1. Napoli: Perella, 1914. Generally favoring historical criticism over aesthetic approaches to Manzoni, and his tie with Jansenism and its spiritual values.

Petrocchi, Giorgio. *La tecnica manzoniana del dialogo*. Firenze: Le Monnier, 1959. An expert exegesis on the relationship between speech and character (psychological, moral, and otherwise) in the novel.

Reynolds, Barbara. *The Linguistic Writings of A. Manzoni*. Cambridge: Cambridge University Press, 1950. A valuable attempt to direct attention to unedited or insufficiently researched linguistic essays of Manzoni or to the philological problems he raises.

Russo, Luigi. *I personaggi dei "Promessi sposi"*. Bari: Laterza, 1952. A profound, though sometimes too religiously oriented, analysis of the main characters of the novel.

Sansone, Mario. *L'opera poetica di A. Manzoni*. Milano-Messina: Principato, 1947. A convincing look into the coherence of Manzoni's lyricism, or the poetic internalization of his most fundamental ethical convictions.

Ulivi, Ferruccio. *La lirica del Manzoni*. Bari: Adriatica Editrice, 1967. The intellectual background and the aesthetic experiences of the poetry, before and after the conversion, including the tragedies, considered as poetry.

Wall, Bernard. *Alessandro Manzoni*. New Haven: Yale University Press, 1954. A rapid—often too rapid—introduction to Manzoni and the major features of his more important works.

Zottoli, Angelandrea. *Umili e potenti nella poetica del Manzoni*. Roma: Tumminelli, 1942. An illuminating comparison of Manzoni and Thierry with reference to the historyless "subaltern" classes and the implications for the historical novel.

Robert S. Dombroski (essay date 1985)

SOURCE: "Manzoni on the Italian Left," in *Annali d'Italianistica,* Vol. 3, 1985, pp. 97-110.

[*In the following essay, Dombroski considers the ideological character of Manzoni's* I promessi sposi, *particularly as the novel's concerns with social class have been perceived by Marxist critics.*]

A number of themes emerge in the history of Manzoni criticism which enable us to define a nucleus of problems that have a special relevance for the practical concerns of the political Left. By far the most important of these problems, historically speaking, regards Manzoni's attitude toward the popular masses. Much of the work of Italian Marxists on Manzoni consists of showing how the representation of social reality in *I promessi sposi* determines the ideological completeness of Manzoni's narrative system, and within this social reality the place of the humble believer is no doubt of crucial importance. The canonical text on this issue is Gramsci's. His notes have become the subject of a debate in which contending interpreters have sought to defend specific political positions.

Gramsci, we know, was passionately interested in the relationship between culture and society and, as we might well expect, this interest affected the way he discussed literature. Why is Italian literature not popular in Italy? Why do Italians show a definite preference for foreign authors? Gramsci's answer to these questions is consistent throughout the *Quaderni del carcere* and forms the basis for his critique of Manzoni. Simply put, "non esiste in Italia un blocco nazionale intellettuale e morale," and, therefore, there is no national cultural hegemony, which means that Italian intellectuals have failed to respond to the needs, aspirations and emotional make-up of the populace. As a result, the cultured classes exist detached from the people-nation; they produce a literature that—its esthetic qualities aside—is neither popular nor national and thus does not represent the collective social mind. On the other hand, the popularity of foreign novels and their continuing interest result mainly from the fact that the social and intellectual concerns they explore satisfy the people's real, psychological needs (*Quaderni* 1:334).

The issue for Gramsci is not whether works of literature contain an acceptable moral, religious or political ideology, but why they are read, to what degree and by whom. Gramsci knows that readers encounter literary works in particular social and historical contexts and that their response or interpretation is dependent on this fact. He also knows that the historical subject of Manzoni's novel is the "humble believer" who determines the work's potential audience by encoding within himself an image of the kind of human identity its author fosters and is seeking to diffuse. The incontestable fact that the poor in *I promessi sposi* occupy a central place in the action only tells us that Manzoni has acknowledged their importance for historical fiction. More important by far is Manzoni's "attitude" toward the poor: how he reacts to their presence in history.

It is on this point that Gramsci draws an important comparison between Manzoni and Tolstoi. Both are the authors of religious narratives, but while Tolstoi has a "democratic" understanding of the Gospel and views the populace as a genuine source of ethical and religious life, Manzoni is a product of the Counter Reformation: his Christian beliefs are a blend of "aristocratic Jansenism" and, with regard to the poor, "Jesuitic paternalism." In contrast to the candid and spontaneous wisdom expressed by Tolstoi's humble believers, which, according to Gramsci, illuminates the minds of the learned, Manzoni endows only his "great" characters with a profound inner being. Unlike Tolstoi, he does not share in the emotional lives of the poor and, removed as he is from their lot, he writes about them with ironic detachment. His fascination with them, his promoting them to the rank of protagonists in his story, are largely effects of his concern for historical verisimilitude. In other words, although Manzoni's humble believers are the novel's energizing force, they are for Gramsci subordinated to the problem of writing a historical narrative. Tolstoi's religious art, Gramsci implies, is therefore ultimately more "realistic" than Manzoni's for the simple fact that he considers the moral and historical questions as one and the same. The problem of representing God's presence in history becomes essentially for Tolstoi one of showing how God speaks through the poor. Manzoni, on the other hand, "è troppo cattolico per pensare che la voce del popolo sia la voce di Dio: tra il popolo e Dio c'è la chiesa, e Dio non s'incarna nel popolo, ma nella chiesa. Che Dio s'incarni nel popolo può credere il Tolstoi non il Manzoni" (*Quaderni* 3:1703).

It is noteworthy that Gramsci, in expounding his argument on the non-national popular character of *I promessi sposi,* will in another instance take the side of the political reactionary Filippo Crispolti against Angelandrea Zottoli, who in his *Umili e potenti nella poetica del Manzoni* (1931), was among the first of Manzoni's critics to pose the problem of the centrality of the humble believer in *I promessi sposi.* With Crispolti's article in hand ("Nuove indagini sul Manzoni"), Gramsci refuses to frame the question in the pure and simple terms of historical presence and esthetic focus because he recognizes the difficulty of uniting coherently Manzoni's choice of subject matter with the author's psychological posture toward the pure, reiterating his claim that Manzoni depicts his humble believers as being devoid of "vita interiore" and "personalità morale profonda": they—he quotes Crispolti—are "animals" and Manzoni treats them with the "benevolence of a Catholic society for the protection of animals." In sum, between Manzoni and his humble characters stands the Church which conditions an attitude not of equality but of benevolent condescension. In other words, Manzoni, in contrast to Tolstoi, is not concerned with the problem of uniting the great, the poor and the middle classes in a spectrum of human existence that is both national and popular, but rather that of representing the age-old struggle between the strong and the weak, with great complexity and on a large scale (*Quaderni* 2:895-96).

However destructive and incontrovertible, Gramsci's criticisms of Manzoni articulate a problem fundamental to the most basic comprehension of *I promessi sposi*: the question of ideology—what kind of understanding of people and history does the novel express and promote by virtue of its form; what logic of history, class affiliation and biography produces the sequence of events, the characters and their authorial interpretation. For the non-militant, academic Marxist, Manzoni's detachment from the sentiments of the humble may prove to be a moot point, yet it is nevertheless an effect of the author's ideology that cannot be denied or ignored, except with the most astute of exegetical strategies. By this I do not mean that Gramsci's critique of Manzoni is wholly correct, or that its inferences constitute stable meanings indispensable to subsequent Marxist interpretations. Underlying Gramsci's judgments is the simple question "for whom has Manzoni written" and "what framework of assumptions do the author and his audience share." His notes single out an important symptom of a determinate structure, which specifies a particular ideological orientation; it imprints Manzoni's work with a cultural attitude and thus displays it as a social practice. By identifying Manzoni's posture toward his humble characters as "benevolently condescending," Gramsci shows what its practical social uses might be.

What is furthermore inferred by Gramsci's notes is that Manzoni's emotional detachment from his humble characters helps realize a historical narrative in which poetry and history remain distinct. In order to foreground history, Manzoni had to present a source of probability that was specifically historical, and that he did by representing the society, language and events of the Seicento. The effect he promotes through his attitude toward the poor is also largely historical. The unlettered or semi-literate Christians he depicts lived in a world which was that of the Church, and, as there were transcendent reasons for titles of nobility, the humble believer too had his *raison d'être*. Within the divine plan, he was, according to seventeenth-century religious preachings, an object to be fathered by the great and the rich on whom, in the ideal pre-bourgeois Christian social order, his subsistence depended. Gramsci, of course, was not concerned with the degree to which historical probability in *I promessi sposi* becomes structurally prominent. It was sufficient for him to point out why the novel had never become truly popular and why it did not represent a national consciousness.

The question of "national consciousness" is central also to the second most influential of Marxist texts on Manzoni: namely, the pages Georg Lukács devotes to *I promessi sposi* in *The Historical Novel*. But the perspective Lukács deploys is radically different from Gramsci's, although, as we shall see, not necessarily incompatible. As a study of genre, Lukács' work demonstrates how the "historical spirit" and the novel interact to portray the "totality of history," and, particularly, how in the historical process the past becomes a necessary precondition for the present. Unlike Gramsci, who theorized the causes and conditions of the lack of a national cultural unity in Italy, Lukács takes

as his starting point the "objective unfavorableness" of Italian history. In his view, Manzoni's purpose was to write a novel which would "rouse the present," and "which contemporaries would experience as their own prehistory" (70). Lukács leaves untouched the social identity of those contemporaries and, therefore, the meaning of their sense of history's "objective unfavorableness" in relation to the cultural projects they sought to promote. It is thus possible for Lukács to frame the question of "national consciousness" in universal terms, declaring that Manzoni's historical subject was "the critical condition of the entire life of the Italian people resulting from Italy's fragmentation" (70). Gramsci, by contrast, viewed Manzoni's way of rewriting history as a symptom of that very problem of disunity.

In specific terms, Lukács argues that what appears to be at the literal level the simple story of the "love, separation and reunion of a young peasant boy and girl" is symbolic of the "general tragedy of the Italian people in a state of national degradation and fragmentation" (70). The actual historical experience of Renzo and Lucia becomes the allegory of the master narrative of Italian history itself. The novel's actual historical events, for Lukács, are significant insofar as they are figures of a general truth: "the tragedy of the Italian people as a whole." By attributing to the novel a fundamentally allegorical character, Lukács does not run the risk of reducing it to a kind of abstract cause, simply because the history he refers to represents the *natural* condition of an entire humanity. His essential point is, then, that the sameness and immobility, characteristic of Italian history, could only be incorporated in one, grand totalizing scheme, in *one* novel, superbly original and historically profound, yet—for the concept of history it embodies—unable to capture the historically typical in a way comparable to Walter Scott: "Despite all the human and historical authenticity, despite all the psychological depth which their author bestows on them, Manzoni's characters are unable to soar to those historically typical heights which mark the summits of Scott's works" (71).

This brings us to the most important and suggestive point of Lukács' interpretation, one that presents the basic elements of the ideological question in Manzoni, which could not be classified simply in terms of the then current meanings of "conservative," "reactionary" or "liberal." Lukács' observations are important because they apprehend the contradiction underlying Manzoni's historical perspective, the same contradiction that is transformed into "history" in *I promessi sposi*: they show that, while Manzoni writes Italian history by depicting a "concrete episode taken from Italian popular life," he equates that history with a state of being—eternal, absolute, unchangeable and exemplary.

Lukács' discussion of Manzoni, although brief, is acute. For, after he has identified the process by which "history" becomes equated with "eternity" and the "humanity" of Manzoni's popular characters with "nature," he can then point to the absence in *I promessi sposi* of a "world-historical atmosphere" which "manifests itself in a certain limitedness of human horizon on the part of his characters" (71). The fate of Lucia, he argues, "is really no more than an externally menaced idyll, while an inevitable pettiness attaches itself to the negative characters of the novel." The crucial effect of such a mode of representation is that it does not "reveal dialectically the historical limits of the whole period." The romance codes which Lukács refers to function to disrupt the historical process, causing it to become, paradoxically, the *destiny* of Italian history, and, therefore, the novel as the novel of that destiny.

In a general sense, Lukács' perspective indicates that the symbolic lives of Manzoni's characters, in spite of their well-depicted "class-conditioned psychology," prevent them from becoming truly "historically typical": they fail to represent salient aspects of a particular historical milieu. This issue may be seen to involve also Gramsci's criticisms of Manzoni, whose principal fault was found in the lack of genuine sympathy toward his popular characters. Questions about a writer's attitude toward his characters are ultimately questions about what he thinks his characters should be. But the subject itself of historical fiction poses obvious limits to the free reign of fantasy, for it demands that a certain historical probability or verisimilitude be respected in the creation of representative individuals. Gramsci believed that Manzoni's Catholicism caused him to repress his characters' historical individuality. He saw it, moreover, as the generative force behind an irony rooted in the transcendental norm of Divine Providence. Hence, for Gramsci, Lukács' concept of a master narrative at the base of Manzoni's popular story leads inevitably to the impoverishment of actual historical experience. In Gramscian terms, reality, through Manzoni's allegorical rewriting, becomes then divested of its revolutionary potential. Put differently, Lukács' reading of *I promessi sposi* could be said to provide a philosophical framework for understanding Gramsci's criticisms, because the contradictory historical process he defines within the novel can, concretely speaking, only derive from the impulse on Manzoni's part to reconcile two opposing social ideologies: while Manzoni predicts a new society based on reason and human industry as a means of overcoming the backwardness of Italian culture, he also regulates the social and political stimulus by keeping that society within the boundaries set by a transcendent and absolute religious norm. These, in sum, are also the terms of Gramsci's general portrayal of a Manzoni in whom we find elements that are "technically bourgeois" next to the many visible marks left on his Catholicism by the Counter Reformation.

Whether or not the attitudes and observations just discussed meet the needs of a modern criticism, they draw their strength from the stimulus they provide and also from the number of critical problems they bring to light. Especially important to subsequent Marxian approaches to Manzoni is that associated with his social ideology. During the sixties, the Manzoni debate on the Left centered largely around the question of how to define his "bourgeois attitudes": the extent to which they were in fact "bourgeois" and their specific features.

The contending interpretations of this period may be reduced to two fundamental positions. The first, argued by Natalino Sapegno, advocates a return to De Sanctis' idea of a "democratic" Manzoni who, in consolidating the "real" and the "ideal," "poetry" and "history," offers the most highly developed model of the bourgeois outlook. In an attempt to temper Gramsci's judgments, Sapegno updates De Sanctis by maintaining that Manzoni's critique of tradition meets the needs of a progressive bourgeois ideology: "De Sanctis aveva giustamente messo in rilievo la novità dell'opera del Manzoni, in quanto essa si poneva e aveva coscienza di porsi in contrasto con tutta la tradizione precedente, petrarchesca e aulica; aveva pertanto sottolineato il senso profondo della sua poetica realistica, in quanto esigenza e proposta di soluzioni narrative, e cioè antiliriche e prosastiche, e di un linguaggio popolare. In questo senso, Manzoni era per lui lo scrittore moderno per eccellenza, il rappresentante più insigne della cultura borghese uscita dalla rivoluzione, quello che meglio di tutti rispecchiava in sé l'equilibrio e l'umanità di quella cultura."[1] For Sapegno the motivating force behind *I promessi sposi* is a conception of socio-political unity based on Christian principles of human equality. In this sense, Manzoni's choice of humble characters as the story's protagonists, which marks a reversal of traditional esthetic hierarchies, situates him squarely on the side of historical progress.

Two themes of this argument are noteworthy: 1) Manzoni's "bourgeois" perspective is totally compatible with Christian principles which in fact constitute its foundation, and 2) the humble and popular masses, or proletarian strata of society, as represented in the novel, are one and the same. The former is a notion which will draw together otherwise disparate points of view, while the latter will be called immediately into question.

Against this latter assumption and against the general notion of Manzoni as a "progressive bourgeois" Gian Franco Vené argues the opposite case: that Manzoni's strong bourgeois convictions prevent him from creating humble characters who are veritable representatives of the popular masses, that Renzo and Lucia, from the standpoint of class affiliation, are not "common people" but "petty bourgeois." This also involves showing that, in representing the great and the powerful, Manzoni, at the same time, sets forth universally valid ethical standards that go beyond class interests. Furthermore, Vené sees at the thematic center of *I promessi sposi* not the poor and the humble but rather the great and the powerful, whom Manzoni depicts as morally superior. He also argues that the new, categorically egalitarian, bourgeois morality reflected in the novel is in fact the morality of its "powerful" figures, of the Cardinal and the Innominato. Vené provides an adequate historical grounding for his argument, showing that in Italy, in contrast to England and France, bourgeois economic interests were shared by an aristocracy which not only accepted but also worked to foster its own *embourgeoisement*. For Vené, then, Manzoni had no intention whatsoever to oppose aristocratic and middle class values. His cultural project, on the other hand, was to etch out an ideal of Christian virtue and of moral nobility which he hoped would become in the end the virtues of society. From the standpoint of practical politics, this plan did not entail passing the reigns of power from one class to another but restoring degraded values according to a process that was both "revolutionary" and "conservative": "Rivoluzionario nel senso che per la prima volta per società si intende l'insieme di tutti gli uomini; a tutti gli uomini i nuovi prìncipi debbono sapere progere il loro aiuto; conservatore nel senso che si cerca di trasferire nella nuova concezione della società una aristocrazia rinsanguata, despositaria di certi valori morali che non sono di tutti, né da tutti raggiungibili" (120).

So, according to Vené, Manzoni sees the relationship between the great and the humble to be essentially of a functional type: one that enabled the middle class to continue ruling and, in order to safeguard its hegemony, to evolve in the direction of proletarian interests. Finally, these ideological tactics are for him thoroughly consistent with the rise of the bourgeoisie in Italy: "Né servilità né dominazione: questo è il messaggio che i vati della borghesia inviano alla società. Libera e responsabile emancipazione di ogni individuo: è lo stesso messaggio che gli economisti inviano ai detentori del capitale ancora troppo legati alla tradizione delle concessioni monopolistiche; ed è la stessa premessa teorica che gli intellettuali intendono rivolgere al popolo" (108-09).

Although with Vené we have a rather persuasive argument against Sapegno's notion of a "democratically progressive" Manzoni, the argument is not entirely convincing, because (like the one it opposes) it cannot resolve the contradiction posed by the novel's ending. What, in sum, do we make of Lucia's antibourgeois questioning of Renzo's newly acquired secular outlook? Can experience transmit the requisite knowledge for making people self-sufficient? And Lucia's ultimate reliance on God, taken by the narrator as the story's essential meaning—how is this consistent with bourgeois morality? It must be—Vené concludes—that Manzoni himself did not believe that the beneficent intervention of extraordinary individuals, such as the Cardinal and the Innominato, could suffice to bring about social change and thus regulate society according to right moral principles.

If Vené brings much sceptical doubt to bear on the notion of Manzoni as a "progressive bourgeois," he does so in a way that separates the author's social ideology from its esthetic realization. A more substantial criticism of the De Sanctis-Sapegno thesis, and one which is unmistakenly more militant since it seeks to reveal both the ideological and esthetic limitations of *I promessi sposi,* comes interestingly not from the Marxist camp but rather from Alberto Moravia, a literary intellectual who can be best described as "radical bourgeois." What Moravia fastens onto in *I promessi sposi* is Manzoni's "arte di propaganda" which—he remarks—in its effort to produce a kind of "realismo cattolico," anticipates the tactics to be later de-

ployed by Socialist realism (307-08). Polemics aside, Moravia's argument may be read as an attempt to explode the myth of a "bourgeois" Manzoni and the value of his critique may be located precisely in his endeavor to call attention to the political, social and esthetic conservatism mirrored in the novel. Briefly, Manzoni, according to Moravia, has not written a bourgeois novel, but one of Catholic propaganda. He goes on to formulate the relationship of esthetics to politics in *I promessi sposi* as follows: instead of confronting his own time, Manzoni chose to write a historical novel about an episode in the seventeenth century in order to justify "forcing" all of Italian reality into the ideological frame of Catholicism. Manzoni's own age did not permit him to write a novel that was both Catholic and universal; so he looked back to a time when Catholicism and reality were identical, in which the forces hostile to Catholicism could not claim to be positive either historically or esthetically, in which propaganda was poetry and poetry was propaganda. For Moravia, Manzoni's ideology conforms to the Catholic interpretation of life, which has many affinities to the kind of social and political rule fostered by Italian Christian Democracy in the fifties and early sixties.

The problem as Moravia poses it is this: Manzoni does not create his ideology as do, say, Stendhal and Dostoievsky, but rather accepts the preexisting ideology of the Catholic Church. He thus adopts an attitude toward the lower classes which—to echo Gramsci's charge—is notably condescending. At the same time, because he is an accomplished artist, he realizes the art of propaganda in a genuinely poetic way, one which produces a vision of reality antithetic to what were the dominant, bourgeois aspirations of his time, so convincingly expressed in the works of his great European contemporaries.

Moravia's criticisms of Manzoni are developed on a higher level by Guido Bollati in the essay "Un carattere per gli italiani" (1: 987-97), which likewise addresses the question of Manzoni's antibourgeois ideology. However, for Bollati there is no distinction to be made between Manzoni the Catholic propagandist and Manzoni the literary artist, because both of these activities are, in his view, to be subordinated to the author's function as an ideologue. By focussing on Manzoni as a moralist and political thinker, Bollati is able to examine his writings against the background of similar ideological projects at work in post-Restauration Italy. Manzoni occupies a central place in the strategies deployed by the wealthy Lombard landowners in the creation of an independent national state. On the other hand, his work also reflects an entire constellation of themes, which, in one form or another, have dominated bourgeois anti-capitalism: namely, the tendency manifest in certain sectors of the European bourgeoisie to keep in check the democratically progressive impetus provided by the French Revolution. For Bollati these operative concepts constitute the aporia or self-engendered paradox to be found at the ideological base of the Risorgimento: "La sfasatura anacronistica tra i due momenti non ammette, secondo logica, alcuna soluzione intermedia: si tratta o di incanalare la rinascita italiana in un solco di progresso radicale, mettendolo in sintonia con quella spinta rivoluzionaria; o di coordinarla alla spinta opposta, anche a rischio che in ragione dell'arretratezza italiana il progresso di emancipazione ne risulti rallentato fino al limite di un accantonamento, di attesa indefinita" (988). Confronted with such an impasse, Bollati's Manzoni has chosen to subordinate the local and immediate political problem to the more general concern of preserving and restoring in the modern age the society of Christian humanism which the utilitarian reasoning at the basis of the French Revolution threatens to destroy.

At this juncture in Bollati's argument, the positions set forth by Gramsci and Lukács become truly operative. Having singled out in *Le osservazioni sulla morale cattolica* the passage where Manzoni places in opposition Christian ethics and utilitarian political reasoning, Bollati shrewdly points out how Manzoni's choice of renouncing politics for Christian principles blocks off in an eternal and unchangeable historical frame a kind of "conservative Utopia." Here the only desirable change is that which leads from universal warfare to the universal benevolence of a society where social classes are also changeless and absolute. This "Utopia of beneficence," as Bollati calls it (997), was Manzoni's answer to liberalism.

There can be no question that Bollati sees in the Manzonian Utopia an act of rhetorical subterfuge and in his quarrel with utilitarianism a tactic to discredit liberalism and thus prevent any possible transition to democracy and socialism. In fact, at the core of Bollati's argument looms the idea of Manzoni as a "bourgeois reactionary." To the historical nightmare of a proletarian revolution Bollati's Manzoni opposes a culture of universal values; to a starving populace, who could benefit from the social programs inspired by utilitarian thought, the luxury of a Christian civilization. Thus Bollati, in pursuing these ideological sanctions, turns the tables most effectively on previous Left criticism and presents Manzoni in a wholly negative light. His object, however, is not to deny Manzoni the recognition he has deservedly received, but to show how and to what extent his work has contributed to the formation of an "Italian character": the *homo italicus* whose generically conceived, natural (non-historical) existence thrives under the protection of the Christian tradition and the Catholic Church.

Bollati's thesis raises the same problem as the previous interpretations: in its zeal to capture the real identity of Manzoni with his age, it fails to grasp the differences or openings, especially in the novel, which resist the ideological closure forced on them by this kind of reading. Nevertheless, his essay succeeds admirably in providing a historical rationale for both the Gramscian notion of a paternalistic, condescending Manzoni and to Lukács' sense of the absence in *I promessi sposi* of a "world historical atmosphere." By focussing on Manzoni's principal theoretical text, *Le osservazioni sulla morale cattolica,* Bollati calls our attention to its importance in relation to Manzo-

ni's general ideological project. Still, this reading, suggestive as it is, does not go far enough along the lines he proposes. In particular, it does not extend to the novel to show how it too fulfills an ideological function as a hegemonic work which justifies a particular form of class domination. Such an undertaking will be the work of Augusto Simonini. But before the publication of *L'ideologia di Alessandro Manzoni* (1978), Italy's institutionalized Left made another sustained attempt to appropriate Manzoni as a forerunner of a democratically progressive ideology and, now, herald of "historical compromise." The work which best exemplifies this tendency appeared, significantly, in *Critica marxista*: entitled "La struttura ideologica dei *Promessi sposi*," Salinari's essay presents a number of interpretative possibilities which, because of the far-reaching political implications of his argument, deserve careful reading.

Salinari begins his article by citing a passage from the *Quaderni del carcere,* where Gramsci speaks of "spunti più nuovi . . . tecnicamente borghesi" in Manzoni: namely, the novelist's praise of commerce and banking and his denunciation of rhetoric. However, for Salinari we have in Manzoni not just the presence of a few hints, but rather an "organica concezione borghese della società assunta nel momento della sua espansione, con la carica ideale e rinnovatrice che la contraddistingueva in quella prima fase, carica che si esauriva solo più tardi con il processo di stabilizzazione della nuova classe dominante" (183). This being his general thesis, Salinari goes on to single out the following themes in *I promessi sposi*: 1) Manzoni's critique of pre-bourgeois legal norms and institutions, 2) his support of liberal economic principles, as, for example, the law of supply and demand, 3) his condemnation of the worldiness of the Church, and 4) his ideological posture *vis-à-vis* the popular masses. In discussing these themes, Salinari is concerned to stress the fundamentally bourgeois perspective adopted in the structure of the fictional experience recounted in the novel. He sums up Manzoni's ideology as that of "un intellectuale 'organico' della borghesia lombarda nel periodo della restaurazione, vale a dire della classe sociale più progressiva in quel periodo storico, nella regione italiana nella quale essa si era sviluppata con maggiore ampiezza e con caratteristiche autonome. E la sorgente più autentica della sua ispirazione è un impegno etico-politico" (194).

Salinari's major point is not his description of Manzoni's place in Restauration culture or his view of Manzoni's social class as the most progressive of the time, but rather his endeavor to accommodate Manzoni within a Gramscian political perspective. This strategy is often at odds with Gramsci's manifest meaning, as for instance when Salinari draws connections between the cultural project of a "progressive organic intellectual" and his attitude toward the irrational impulses of popular masses. For Gramsci there would be little doubt that Manzoni's censure of the "irrationality" of collective violence shows that he has not assimilated the personal experience of those disinherited and oppressed masses he claims to represent, but rather portrays them as ignorant of their own real interests. To recognize, as Manzoni does, that the masses are motivated by just demands and yet are unconscious of their actions means that the pressures they exert on the ideological structures of society must be diminished. Salinari is undoubtedly correct in showing how Manzoni's morally based pragmatism and anti-Jesuitic religious stance are consistent with the tradition of Lombard Illuminism. The fact that the populace is assigned a "subaltern" role in the political process proves that in the last analysis Manzoni is more concerned with the threat of a proletarian uprising that might arise from a Jacobin-type radicalization of the bourgeois revolution. Indeed, it is hard to see how such a position may be construed as "progressive," when its primary concern is to deny the passions of the oppressed an operational legitimacy.

Salinari becomes even more provocative when in concluding his discussion he contrasts Manzoni and Leopardi: the former a standard bearer of an enlightened, revolutionary class, the latter an isolated pessimist, cut off from the historical process. This position in favor of the cultural strategies of the Lombard bourgeoisie, seen as *the* vital force in modern Italian history, carries with it also a positive reevaluation of the official Romantic movement. For it calls our attention to the cultural politics of major intellectual groups, ascribing a greater importance to the organizational phase of their activities than to the ideological contents of their works.

By contrast, Augusto Simonini, in response to Salinari, undertakes an extensive analysis of the way *I promessi sposi* functions on the ideological level. His purpose is to submit Manzoni's texts, chiefly the novel, to *symptomatic analysis,* that is, a mode of interpretation that points out the specific ways *I promessi sposi* elaborates a socio-political message out of an ostensibly neutral subject matter (the rediscovered manuscript), already inscribed into the course of history. Simonini's methodological starting point is a view of the cultural sphere as an arena of class conflict and revolutionary struggle and the literary work as a strategy designed to shut out of the reader's consciousness certain truths about history. For Simonini Manzoni is not the "democratic thinker" Salinari makes him out to be: neither in the modern sense of the word nor in the meaning given to the term in Manzoni's time. Instead, his ideological orientation was one of the most coherent and intransigent forms of socio-political moderatism. This derived not so much from a conservative desire to restore the past as from the need to place internal controls on the development of liberalism, lest it give rise to a democratic social movement. In other words, Manzoni—here Simonini restates Bollati's position—understood well that the social dangers inherent in liberal egalitarian principles constituted a real threat from the Left. As a result, Manzoni's manifest sympathy toward the humble believers appears only at first glance as the expression of Christian brotherhood.

But where Simonini differs from his predecessors is in the way he reveals the extent to which the ideological func-

tion is present at all levels of the narrative. The sort of interpretation demanded by Manzoni's novel must, in his view, take into consideration two different modes of ideological expression, which produce two different esthetic effects. First, there is Manzoni's critique of the feudal, aristocratic and absolutist ideals and institutions that dominate the historical context chosen as the novel's setting. Here Simonini is in agreement with Salinari (and, for that matter, practically all previous Manzoni criticism) in stating that Manzoni targets an entire world of foreign domination and the social and intellectual evils and personal violence it cultivates. In Manzoni's negative and corrosive portrayal of this society, ideology and style go hand in hand: "In questo versante si hanno le prove migliori della sua arte: ideologia e stile si richiamano e si alimentano a vicenda, fondendosi quasi senza residui" (39). When Manzoni, however, represents the world as he thinks it should be, "si ha invece quasi sempre una sfasatura ricorrente tra nucleo concettuale ed espressione letteraria" (39). For Simonini this separation or disjointedness between ideological manipulation and esthetic production springs objectively from a disalignment between Manzoni the Christian and Manzoni the ideologue who has become the "organic intellectual of moderate liberalism": "L'astuzia, la sagacia dell'uomo di parte, di classe, di consorteria se ne impadronisce e vi svolge dal di dentro un'azione frenante e deviante, da quinta colonna. Nella misura in cui l'uomo cede alla prevaricazione delle sue istanze ideologiche, nei suoi limiti ed eccessi, anche l'artista è travolto. Si hanno allora i momenti più fiacchi, meno autentici della sua arte" (40).

In the last analysis, Simonini argues that there is good and bad ideology in *I promessi sposi*: a "positive" code designed to subvert the old order, existing alongside a "negative" text that seeks to contain human experience and aspirations within the limits imposed by the ideology of Christian right reason. To overcome this opposition, which inescapably recalls the Crocean distinction between poetry and non-poetry or, more precisely, between art and ideology, we must assume that both compositional moments are part of a process of compensatory exchange and that their opposition serves only to censure or devalue their motivating impulse. One easily sees that Manzoni's novel embodies, as Bollati has remarked, a profound Utopian impulse. But to understand the kind of ideological gratification at work in the text we must abandon the wholly negative connotation the phrase "utopia della benevolenza" evokes in Bollati's interpretation.

A useful way of looking at the problem is to follow the very suggestive tact proposed by Federic Jameson in *The Political Unconscious* and view Manzoni's novel as a cultural text whose function as a "legitimizing strategy" for Catholic moderatism cannot be understood simply as the result of the imposition of ideology on the reader. For, if it is to be seen truly as a hegemonic work in the Gramscian sense, we must logically rule out that it exercizes its control by force, but rather that it promotes ideological adherence by offering "substantial incentives" in the form of Utopian impulses. In this light *I promessi sposi* raises the same question Jameson asks of all cultural texts: "how is it possible for a cultural text which fulfills a demonstrably ideological function, as a hegemonic work whose formal categories as well as its content secure the legitimation of this or that form of class domination—how is it possible for such a text to embody a properly Utopian impulse, or to resonate a universal value inconsistent with the narrower limits of class privilege which inform its more immediate ideological vocation?" (288). Jameson's answer is simply that all class consciousness is in its very nature Utopian insofar as it expresses the unity of a collectivity. Whether or not completely satisfying, this response reveals the conceptual limits of the Marxist approaches summarized above. While there can be little doubt that Manzoni's politics were in fact those of moderate liberalism, and while we cannot deny that Manzoni's class affiliation generates the kind of ideological compromise expressed in *I promessi sposi,* we can no longer be content with knowing how the novel, and Manzoni's work in general, carries out its specific ideological task. By this I do not mean that Bollati's and Simonini's political readings cannot be thoroughly substantiated, but rather that their arguments in the final analysis prove what we already take for granted in political criticism: that a side is to be taken against or for a particular form of class consciousness.

In conclusion, it may be helpful to recall one of Gramsci's fundamental precepts: that popular literature represents the collective mind—which is just a simpler way of phrasing Jameson's idea of literature as the "symbolic affirmation of a specific historical and class form of collective unity" (291). The concrete historical problem in Manzoni that I think has yet to be sufficiently noticed by any Marxism regards the psychological character of the audience on which Manzoni so painstakingly has inscribed his work. Lest we view *I promessi sposi* as a mere instrument of class domination, we must integrate the *deconstructive* or *symptomatic analyses,* so well executed in the criticism reviewed above, with a complementary phase of reading. This should be directed at an integral understanding of the *lived system* of meaning and values that constitutes a multilateral hegemonic process, which in the last instance supplies the historical logic for those impulses diffused by the literary text. Along these lines in *L'apologia del vero* I have attempted to give an instructive example of how in *I promessi sposi* the ideological compromise expressed in the accommodation of religious and secular interests may be seen as a strategy aimed at nourishing the utopian longings of a class that was, historically speaking, bourgeois in its aspirations, but still essentially prebourgeois in its effective capacity to realize those aspirations. My purpose is not to divert attention from the profoundly ideological character of the novel, but instead to suggest that its ideology articulates a social unity, concretely reflected in the precariousness dominating a particular historical conjuncture, and that this "lived system" of relations dictates the modalities for the symbolic structuring of experience.

Finally, ideological analyses of the kind reviewed above tend to overlook the complex process by which Manzoni

brought his novel to its final form. The making of *I promessi sposi* did not entail simply the transition from an original concept (realized in *Fermo e Lucia* and later deemed unsatisfactory) to the structurally definitive texts of 1827 and 1840. In fact, it called for a much slower operation, carried out over several intermediate drafts or "minutes," which involved a careful redimensioning of characters and episodes. Recent philological inquiry has illuminated, better than ever before, the ongoing tension between Manzoni and his subject matter: how Manzoni plucked away at his own text, refusing and unraveling previous narrative solutions and repressing certain provisional impulses until his story took on the shape dictated by his changing attitude toward his art and his commitment as a social novelist.[2] This difficult and problematic gestation can never be accounted for totally in the finished product. The struggle involved in the production of *I promessi sposi* is effaced by a deceptive transparency of ideological closure. No matter what ideology is generated by Manzoni's art, or what social and political attitudes the outcome of his story seems to embody, they all exclude the process which, in Manzoni's case at least, was never a simple, coherent fulfillment of preestablished aims and goals. So when we discuss ideology in *I promessi sposi,* let us keep in mind, among other things, that ideology is not simply an end product, fully shaped and seamless, but instead the lived experience of production, contradictory and at times illusive, which indicates a *lived* relation to the social world.

Notes

1. "Manzoni tra De Sanctis e Gramsci," *Ritratto* 107.

2. See, in particular, Toschi, *Si dia un padre a Lucia* and also, at this time in press, by the same author *I tegoli di Casale.*

Works Cited

Bollati, Guido. "Un carattere per gli italiani." *Storia d'Italia.* Torino: Einaudi, 1972.

Crispolti, Filippo. "Nuove indagini sul Manzoni." *Pègaso* (agosto 1931): 129-44.

Dombroski, Robert S. *L'apologia del vero: lettura e interpretazione dei "Promessi sposi."* Padova: Liviana, 1984:

Gramsci, Antonio. *Quaderni del carcere.* Ed. Valentino Gerratana. 4 voll. Edizione critica dell'Istituto Gramsci. Torino: Einaudi, 1975.

Jameson, Federic. *The Political Unconscious: Narrative as a Socially Symbolic Act.* Ithaca: Cornell UP, 1981.

Lukács, Georg. *The Historical Novel.* Trans. Hannah and Stanley Mitchell. Atlantic City: Humanities Press, 1978.

Moravia, Alberto. "Alessandro Manzoni o l'ipotesi di un realismo cattolico." *L'uomo come fine e altri saggi.* Milano: Bompiani, 1964.

Salinari, Carlo. "La struttura ideologica dei *Promessi sposi.*" *Critica marxista* 12.3-4 (1974): 183-200.

Sapegno, Natalino. *Ritratto di Manzoni ed altri saggi.* Bari: Laterza, 1962.

Simonini, Augusto. *L'ideologia di Alessandro Manzoni.* Ravenna: Longo, 1978.

Toschi, Luca. *I tegoli di Casale.* Firenze: Sansoni, 1985.

————. *Si dia un padre a Lucia: studi sugli autografi manzoniani.* Padova: Liviana, 1983.

Vené, Gian Franco. *Letteratura e capitalismo in Italia.* Milano: Sugar, 1983.

Douglas Radcliff-Umstead (essay date 1985)

SOURCE: "Beyond Time and Space in Manzoni's Tragedies," in *Rivista di Studi Italiani,* Vol. 3, No. 2, December, 1985, pp. 68-87.

[*In the following essay, Radcliff-Umstead describes Manzoni's tragedies* Il conte di Carmagnola *and* Adelchi *as dramas of Christian salvation and transcendence.*]

Alessandro Manzoni structured his tragedies **Il Conte di Carmagnola** and **Adelchi** on a dialectic between history and eternity, excessive evaluation of time and transcendence of territorial ambitions. This author aimed at creating Christian tragedies that would represent man's earthly battle for sovereign might and the final realization of the vanity involved in the struggle for control over the world. Following the example of Shakespeare as an historical dramatist, Manzoni sought to understand the centuries-old tragedy of Italy by going back to the records of the internecine warfare of city-states during the Renaissance and the imperial expansionism of the Longobard realm in the eighth century. The Italian writer hoped to portray that moment in the interior life of his dramatic heroes when they would perceive the futility of their violent and vainglorious deeds and would turn their gaze from the battleground of this world to the freedom of Heaven. In this essay I shall explore the dimensions of time and space in **Il Conte di Carmagnola** and **Adelchi** as the major forces working within Manzoni's dramas of eternal Christian fate.[1]

By breaking with the unities of place and time the Italian author allowed himself the opportunity to represent the conflict for dominion as it occurred over a wide range of territory for a period of time that would last several years. Manzoni defended his deliberate violation of neoclassical practice in both the preface to **Il Conte di Carmagnola** and the **Lettre à M. Chauvet,** where he justified the innovations of his first play against the attacks of the French critic Victor Chauvet. By affirming the principles of a "sistema romantico" or "sistema storico," the Italian playwright wishes to found literature upon the truth of established historical facts. Romantic historicist drama would be free of the merely formalistic unity of pseudo-aristotelian rules so as to achieve a superior unity out of

the playwright's understanding of human motives behind the documented deeds of archival records.[2] Manzoni believed that Shakespeare had already created such a Christian historicist drama, in works like *Richard II* that revealed the tormented heart of a ruler whose sense of dignity compelled him to abdicate from his throne.[3] Modern drama, built solidly on history, would lead spectators beyond "cette sphère étroite et agitée" (p. 278) to behold the emptiness of involvement in human time and space while comprehending the need to yield to the force of eternity.

In his desire to be true to history Manzoni prefaced **Il Conte di Carmagnola** with a list of actual historical characters and a list of "invented" characters, and in order to anwer some of the questions raised by **Adelchi** he compiled a **Discorso sopra alcuni punti della storia longobardica in Italia.** The territorial sphere of both plays is not a space of love and joy but one of hatred and warfare.[4] The Count of Carmagnola exemplifies that earthly combativeness in his career as a *condottiere,* first for the Duke of Milan Filippo Maria Visconti and later for the Venetian Senate. Manzoni learned of the mercenary warrior's tragic downfall in reading Sismondi's *Histoire des Républiques italiennes du moyen âge.* The dramatist situates the events of his play from 1425 to 1432, from the time that Carmagnola, out of offended pride against the Milanese lord who had dismissed him, persuaded the Venetian government to enlist him as its military leader against the Lombard forces. Despite the count's initial victories several of the Venetian oligarchs doubted his loyalty and finally succeeded in ordering the general's execution following a series of defeats on the battle-field. The dramatist envisioned Carmagnola as a tragic figure whose faith had met betrayal by ruthless political leaders. The count rose to the height of being a commander-in-chief from a humble origin as a shepherd. Yet he felt no ties to the meadows and wheatfields of his native region. At the play's start Carmagnola is living in Venice as an exile from Lombardy. Having lost all his estates and possessions, this general without a war to fight is seeking a battlefield, his only true space of intimacy as he is a soldier and not a landholder or politician. Only with the declaration of hostilities between Venice and Lombardy does Carmagnola feel at ease as he contemplates vengeance against the monarch who stripped him of rightful honors. Manzoni constructs his drama around a mercenary warrior who holds to a rigid standard of professional loyalty but who faces cynical politicians intent on manipulating and sacrificing those that serve their regimes.

Although the break with unity of place allows the author numerous changes of scene from act to act as well as within the acts themselves, the tragic center of **Il Conte di Carmagnola** remains within the constricting atmosphere of the governmental chambers of the Venetian Republic. In the drama's definitive version the first act opens with a plenary session of the Venetian Senate while the last two acts start in the cabinet of the fearful Council of Ten. The presence of the Venetian government hangs ominously over the otherwise free and open battle-field of Maclodio, where Carmagnola achieves in Act Three his greatest victory only to offend two official commissioners from Venice by releasing all military prisoners. Just in the manner of neoclassical style dramatists like Racine who saw tragedy as a closed avenue ending in destruction, Manzoni concentrates his play upon the fear, treachery, and suspicion hovering over the Venetian governmental chambers. Since Carmagnola's prison cell and the place of his execution are most likely located within the complex of government buildings, the tragedy is always centered in the murderous inclosure of a political institution. Even though the general thinks of himself as the master of his life, it is his enemy, the "invented" character councilor Marino who determines the outcome of time's fatal course.

To maintain the drama's focus on the site of political conspiracy in Venice, Manzoni alters history by moving the place of an assassination attempt against Carmagnola from the actual event at Treviso to the Most Serene City. News of the unsuccessful assassination convinces the Venetian Doge of the count's loyalty to the regime of St. Mark, and in the play's opening address the Doge denounces in words ringing with hypocritical irony the murder attempt as an insult to the peaceful sanctuary provided by Venice:

> Che vile opra di tenebre e di sangue
> Sugli occhi nostri fu tentata, in questa
> Stessa Venezia, inviolato asilo
> Di giustizia e di pace . . .

> (I, ii, 9-12)[5]

But Venice will prove to be for Carmagnola a place of "tenebre e di sangue" and of "perfidio della trama" (I,i,22), where in the very same assembly room where he receives the command of the country's armies he will fall victim to the machinations of his enemies. The dramatist contrasts Carmagnola's loyal service to his adoptive land with its unjust punishment in juxtaposed terms of solar brilliance and conspiratorial darkness in the scene where the count affirms his innocence:

> Ciò che feci per voi, tutto lo feci
> Alla luce del sol; renderne conto
> Tra insidiose tenebre non voglio.

> (V, ii, 91-93)

Within the dark confines of patrician bureaucracy neither justice nor mercy can prevail as the count's accusers succeed in having him condemned to death. Total deprivation of light and life on this earth results from advancing the territorial aggressions of an authoritarian state.[6]

While the dramatist recognizes in the Count of Carmagnola an exceptional being who bound his destiny to the caprices of Fortune, Manzoni also sees in his hero's fate an abiding human situation for all individuals who yield to the temptations of earthly desire and ambition. From his Christian viewpoint the writer beholds the mortal weakness of even those forceful beings who aspire the most to achieve greatness. In the same way that Victor Hugo in the preface to his drama *Cromwell* states his intention to portray the paradoxes of the human soul and the circumstances of life in compromising society,[7] so too does the Italian playwright seek to represent the conflicting forces in his characters and their world:

> quel misto di grande e di meschino, di ragionevole
> e di pazzo che si vede negli avvenimenti grandi e
>   piccoli
> di questo mondo; e questo interesse tiene ad una parte
> importante ed eterna dell'animo umano, il desiderio di
> conoscere quello che è realmente e di vedere più che
>   si può,
> in noi e nel nostro destino su questa terra . . .[8]

For Manzoni the playwrights who succeeded best in depicting the vacillations of the heart and the promises left unfulfilled in society were Shakespeare and Schiller. As a Christian the Italian author acknowledges the moral fragility of the soul born in sin and continually led into sinfulness through the need to dwell in a world thriving on deceptions and petty concessions to expediency. Although Manzoni does not deny the possibility of greatness, he points out the limitations and the ultimate disillusionment of founding hopes on worldly attachments and temporal aspirations.

Carmagnola realizes that illusory victory at the battle of Maclodio. Manzoni constructs all of Act Two in six scenes to illustrate how the count becomes the master of the warring arena and those who have to combat within it. While the first three scenes at the Lombard camp show how the mercenary captains are divided over the decision to initiate hostilities or to perform a strategic withdrawal, the final three brief scences reveal the harmony of spirit in the Venetian camp where all the captains and their soldiers rally around the count's leadership. Carmagnola becomes the battle's *metteur en scene* directing all the moves of the bellicose players. But, as Manzoni stresses, this earth has many battlegrounds that are not all situated on open fields. Although Carmagnola wins the battle, the spying Venetian commissioners who consider him a traitor report his suspicious activities to the Venetian bureaucrats who will in time prove to be the victors in this tragedy by combatting the count's pride and impulsiveness with their guile. For it is the force of time that undermines the general as the envious circle of Venetian conspirators patiently wait for the inevitable reversal of military triumphs, allowing a few years to pass until they lure Carmagnola into a trap of no return. On his last mission to Venice, supposedly to confer with the government on terms of a peace treaty, Carmagnola sets off on what seems a glorious journey across the cities of the realm where deceitful officials vie to pay him every honor. In reality the doomed commander-in-chief is travelling a road of infamy that will end in imprisonment and death.

Statecraft in the world of Manzoni's first drama functions as an art of victimization to destroy the opportunity for a harmonious rapport between government officials and courageous private citizens. The author introduces two "invented" characters to contrast the opposing directions of the Venetian regime: Carmagnola's chief enemy the councilor Marino and the general's friend Senator Marco. The count considered his friendship with Marco as a special favor from Heaven to protect him in his dangerous career, but in the tense atmosphere of Venetian political affairs an agent of *Realpolitik* like Marino possesses every advantage over idealists like Marco who dwell in an unreal time and space. Although at first Carmagnola hoped to become Marco's spiritual double by emulating the senator's noble and generous nature, by the play's close the soldier learns that every man is alone on this earth and the only enduring attachment will be beween man and God. For this tragedy seeks to illustrate the injustice pervading the institutions of society. Marco, Manzoni's "personaggio ideale," will also realize his isolation after the Council of Ten compels him to sign a document promising not to warn the count of the government's intention to arrest him on a charge of treason. The senator perceives that one cannot remain both a loyal citizen and a faithful friend because public service and the absolute obedience it requires call for the sacrifice of private relationships. In defending the count on the floor of the Senate, Marco forgot his own counsel to his friend that they were not born "In luoghi e in tempi ov'uom potesse aperto / Mostrar l'animo in fronte . . ." (I, ii, 400-401). On the highest level of leadership in the Most Serene Republic any rapprochement between individuals might lead to compromise and betrayal to the authorities. The very verb "avvicinarsi" bears the danger of extermination, and when it is used in Act IV, i, 168, to suggest a possible reconciliation between Carmagnola and the Visconti duke that "drawing near" has fatal consequences for the general. Membership in the hierarchy of the state prevents anyone from establishing an "individual distance" to make possible some measure of personal privacy.[9] Only those like Marino who can master dissimulation may hope to survive and prevail in the government's stifling atmosphere since only a brief moment of self-revelation will suffice to fall from lofty rank and perish. Marco's loss is all the more devastating as he not only fails to uphold a personal trust and therein compromises forever his integrity, but his acquiescence to state authority also sends him into a future of exile on a perilous diplomatic mission to Thessalonika. That very nation for which the senator has forfeited freedom of conscience casts him out like a criminal suspect. Remorse over his act of treacherous silence and realization of his immediate exile precipitate an identity crisis for Marco:

> Io prima d'oggi
> Non conoscea me stesso! . . . Oh che segreto
> Oggi ho scoperto! Abbandonar nel laccio
> Un amico io potea. . . .
>
> (IV, ii, 271-274)

The senator has permitted others representing the state to define his identity and to determine the distant space he will occupy in the future. Like Count Carmagnola the senator has been lured into a "laccio" or an "agguato" as he speaks of an "abbominevol rete" that others have stretched out to trap him. Marco sees himself as dangling

"all'orlo . . . del precipizio" (IV, i, 331) or already fallen into the "abisso" (IV, i, 290) of moral compromise. The terms that the senator uses to describe his bewilderment are of a spatial nature as he faces in full isolation his destiny of exile. Marco attempts to place responsibility for his faithlessness to Carmagnola by blaming the Venetian government that denied him any other choice but to sign the document pledging silence. Marco prefers to remain in a zone of consoling inner darkness, rejecting the enlightenment that would come from accepting moral responsibility for his decision.[10]

After his arrest and condemnation to death the Count of Carmagnola undergoes a spiritual conversion where he recognizes the vanity of all his earthly ambitions. At this point in the tragedy, by the final act, the warrior's wife and daughter at last enter into the drama. For it is only at this moment of inner illumination that the two women can have a place in the tragedy. During the first four acts there was room merely for combat, but now that the general's fate has been sealed and every avenue of action has been closed forever to the soldier, he can give free rein to the yearning for tenderness that he has repressed in his heart. Before the last meeting with his wife and daughter—the single intimate scene in the drama—the general surveys his military career and contemplates the honorable death it should have brought him:

> O campi aperti!
> O sol diffuso! o strepito dell'armi
> O gioia de' perigli! o trombe! o grida
> De' combattenti! o mio destrier! tra voi
> Era bello il morir. . . .
>
> (V, ii, 232-236)

Carmagnola now realizes that after the joys of worldly combat there arrives a supreme happiness: death as the consolation that his most powerful enemy cannot take away from him as he finds peace and redemption. The count's final words to his family are of resignation and comfort, not of the tormenting revenge which poisoned his years of exile from Lombardy. This warrior no longer thinks of fighting for thrones, crowns, or realms since his one longing is for the impregnable asylum offered by God. In death as a Christian this fugitive general discovers the shelter which can never fail him. He has seen across the abyss between soul and body, man and God which Victor Hugo defines in the preface to *Cromwell* as the melancholy of separation. A spirit of forgiveness at last elevates Francesco Bussone Count of Carmagnola above this petty world of territorial combat. In the narrow enclosure of his prison cell this *condottiere* who once seemed to hold the destiny of nations in his hands releases himself from all earthly bonds to know Heaven's eternal deliverance.

Manzoni designed still another dimension for his first tragedy than the drama of an innocent soldier condemned to death who finds peace by renouncing the treacherous world. In the play's preface the author explained that the chorus which appears between the second and third acts would serve as a "little corner" where he might make a lyrical comment on the universal meaning of the actions occurring in the drama. The battle of Maclodio gives rise to the chorus, which reflects on the horrors of fratricidal wars. The ground which is disputed in the battle is not a beloved land that soldiers defend against outside enemies but rather an arena for greed and the false ambitions of territorial aggrandizement. Throughout the chorus' account of the battle only fragments of land are visible as the ground vibrates from the friction of hoofs and feet. Sword thrusts move over the entire plain. In attempting to identify the warring phantoms the chorus discovers that they all come from a common fatherland:

> D'una terra son tutti: un linguaggio
> Parlan tutti: fratelli li dice
> Lo straniero: il comune lignaggio
> A ognun d'essi dal volto traspar.
> Questa terra fu a tutti nudrice,
> Questa terra di sangue ora intrisa,
> Che natura dall'altre ha divisa,
> E recinta con l'alpe e col mar.

(Chorus, ii, 17-24)

Despite the boundaries and barriers Nature created to defend the land from foreign invasion the native's rapacity has left it open prey to alien armies. For the country with its internal strife has become a "Fatal terra" (Chorus, i, 107) that will not be able to resist enemy aggression since the inhabitants would never unite against an outside foe. But rejoicing over ruling a divided people will not endure forever as the conquerors will one day experience divine retribution for subjugating the land. The chorus' final message is of the common destiny that awaits both victors and vanquished:

> Tutti fatti a sembianza d'un Solo,
> Figli tutti d'un solo Riscatto,
> In qual ora, in qual parte del suolo
> Trascorriamo quest'aura vital,
> Siam fratelli; siam stretti ad un patto.

(Chorus, ii, 121-125)

No matter what part of the war-torn world different peoples occupy, they are brothers in a single Redemption that promises to lift them to the peace of a celestial home.[11]

That attempt to introduce the destiny of nameless masses into the context of a dramatic work forms the background for Manzoni's second tragedy *Adelchi,* where the confrontation between two Germanic warrior peoples determines the fate of the subject Latin population. Time in *Adelchi* effaces man's dream of domination and glory. Temporal process constantly undermines the efforts of the various characters to define a sphere of sovereign action or tranquil retreat for themselves. The play's action occurs from 772 to 774 when Carlomagno leads his Frankish army to victory in defeating the Longobards who rule northern and central Italy. Within less than two years radical political, social, and legal transformations take place with the fall of the Longobards, who established their control of Italy in

the sixth century. Time's rapid passing compels each major character to behold his or her individual destiny. Movement across time is a passage from the certainty of the past toward the unknown and unexpected. The illusions of the characters who imagine themselves as the makers of history are either shattered on coming into conflict with eternal justice or integrated with the destiny of the nations that are subjected to historical change. Time's ultimate effect would seem to be loss and surrender.

Of all the characters the Longobard monarch Desiderio relies most on time as the force which will confirm him as the supreme arbiter of fate in the Christian world. In his determination to bring Italy completely under Longobard control Desiderio does not hesitate to invade the territory of Pope Adriano even though he realizes that the Franks will probably intervene to protect the Church. The experiences of a lifetime have convinced the king that if he acts swiftly and rapaciously, he will surely overcome every obstacle to triumph. For Desiderio ascended to the throne by usurping the rightful place of Prince Rachi, brother to the previous ruler Astolfo. His power rests on the support of potentially treacherous nobles, who are willing to follow their monarch in wars of territorial conquest so long as they can increase their own fiefdoms. Desiderio understands that time is a force which may bring unforeseen vicissitudes: "E di vicende e di pensier il tempo / impreveduto apportar . . ." (Act I, iii, 260-261). But the king deludes himself that he can remain in control of the temporal process defending his realm from interior and exterior threats. The elderly monarch believes that history is a myth which is remade from day to day and that he is destined to retain the central role of authority in the myth of the Longobards.[12]

Victor in past struggles and ruler of the present, Desiderio intends to take advantage of an affront by Carlo against the honor of the Longobards in order to rally his family and allies in a definitive battle with the Franks. Previously he united his dynasty with that of the Carolingians by having his daughter Ermengarda married to Carlo. But after the Franks repudiated that marriage, Desiderio uses that humiliation as a pretext for war with the Franks:

> Quando all'oltraggio
> Pari fia la mercé, quando la macchia
> fia lavata col sangue; allor, deposti
> i vestimenti del dolor, dall'ombre
> la mia figlia uscirà. . . .
> . . . E il giorno
> lunge non è. . . .

(Act I, ii, 72-76, 79-80)

Desiderio anticipates a future when the uncertainties of the present will vanish through the shedding of Frankish blood to avenge the outrage to his daughter. The stress on temporal conjunctions (*quando*) and adverbs (*allor, lunge*) in the king's speech reveals the explosive tension within Desiderio as he projects himself and his nation toward a perilous destiny.[13] He intends to remove Carlo from the Frankish throne and force the Pope to anoint as the new Frankish monarchs the sons of Gerberga, Carlo's widowed sister-in-law who sought refuge at the Longobard court: "Che le innocenti teste / unga, e sovr'esse proferisca preghi" (Act I, ii, 88-89). The use of the subjunctive mood in "unga" and "proferisca" points out the unreal time zone toward which the king projects his grandiose desires. Prince Adelchi attempts to remind his father that his predecessor Astolfo almost lost his throne after Pope Stefano II asked the Franks to enter Italy and protect the papal states from appropriation by the Longobards. But Desiderio refuses to heed the lessons of the past as he envisions a future where all obstacles will fall before him.

On the afternoon when the Frankish army succeeds in penetrating the Alpine defenses of the Longobard forces, the kingdom which Desiderio built upon brutal exploitation collapses within a few hours. Only then as the king views the ruin of his illusions does he look back to the past, to the hateful time when the first Longobard ruler descended into Italy:

> Maledetto quel dì che sopra il monte
> Alboino salì, che in giù rivolse
> lo sguardo, e disse: questa terra è mia!

(Act III, viii, 319-321)

Desiderio at last comes to see time as a hostile force that can take away all that it has given. By confronting time the monarch understands that the Longobards were always destined to perish by sword and flame. By deluding himself that he could determine the future of dynasties and pontiffs, Desiderio has acted as the agent of temporal change. Then in the course of a few months one Longobard stronghold after another surrenders to Carlo, and Desiderio soon finds himself the prisoner of the Franks. Although the loss of his kingdom and liberty causes the elderly monarch to arrive at an awareness of time as a force of discontinuity effected by divine justice, he acknowledges personal guilt only upon beholding his dying son Adelchi. The prince discloses to his father how the hour of death has permitted him to comprehend life's mysterious destiny: "Gran segreto è la vita, / e nol comprende / che l'ora estrema . . ." (Act V, vii, 342-343). Desiderio's future will now be one of total isolation as he contemplates spending the final years of his life in a faraway Frankish monastery where Carlo will imprison him. The Longobard king is the last figure to be seen on stage, lamenting by the body of his fallen son as he looks forward to the loneliness of his future exile.[14]

Through divine election Carlo emerges the supreme leader over all the Christian realms of western Europe. It is a God-directed destiny rather than his own resoluteness that enables the Frankish ruler to plant the royal lance on Italy's soil. In his first stage appearance Carlo admits to a papal legate his apprehensions about attacking the Longobard fortifications and barriers created by Nature:

> Chiusa è la via? Natura al mio nemico
> il campo preparò, gli abissi intorno

> gli scavò per fossati; e questi monti
> che il Signor fabbricò, son le sue torri
> e i battifredi. . . .

(Act II, i, 36-40)

The Frankish king, wondering if God has intentionally obstructed the way for the invading army, is planning to return to a war against the infidel Saxons where victory would signify the triumph of the Christian faith. Carlo remains unmoved by the legate's predictions of a "secondo regno" until Martino, the deacon of Ravenna, arrives in the camp with news that he has found a path through the mountains. Martino's lengthy description of his hazardous journey through unknown Alpine passes and gorges serves to convince Carlo that God guided the deacon's steps, that nothing can deter the advance of Frankish troops.[15] Once his freedom to move has been secured, Carlo hails the star of his destiny to reign:

> La stella
> che scintillava al mio partir, che ascosa
> stette alcun tempo, io la riveggo. . . .

(Act II, iii, 292-294)

The lingering doubts which are expressed in the imperfect tense of "scintillava" and the past absolute of "stette" give way to the resoluteness of a warrior intent on conquest. Time, as Manzoni also noted in the ode *Il cinque maggio,* is a wave that can carry one on to triumph or pull him down to humiliating defeat. On later confronting the captive Longobard king, Carlo declares that Heaven decided the outcome of the war between them since it chose the Frankish ruler for a glorious destiny that could not be altered: ". . . né lamentar posso un destino, / ch'io non voglio mutar. Tal del mortale / è la sorte quaggiù . . ." (Act V, iv, 151-153). Carlo's use of the adverb "quaggiù" clearly indicates his concern with earthbound warfare. God and religion for this victorious ruler become allies in the conquest of the world.[16] The present and the future belong to Carlo, not as the genuine champion of faith but as a man whose fate has harmoniously coincided with the movement of history.

Triumph comes to Carlo partly because of the fear and greed of the treacherous Longobard nobles who desert their king rather than lose their estates and titles. Most of them are the "fedeli," vassals sworn to defend their lord to the death. But in the third scene of Act IV the warrior Guntigi reflects in a soliloquy that "Fedeltà" brings no material rewards to the loyal vassal who is reduced to begging on account of his devotion to a fallen king. Having already lost the town of Ivrea to one of Carlo's men, Guntigi agrees to betray Desiderio in order to become count of Pavia; and he even risks his son's life as a pledge of "fidelity" to the Franks. The most outstanding example of the worldly honor that an astute traitor can achieve falls to Svarto, who rises from an obscure soldier in Act I to win the title of count of Susa for serving as an intermediary between the Longobard nobles and Carlo. Carlo exploits the fear of territorial dispossession among the Longobard leaders to win them to the Frankish cause. Manzoni's pessimistic view of earthly existence is evident in this drama from the victory of all those venal nobles and soldiers who transfer their allegiance to safeguard their parcels of territory or to gain new holdings. Although an individual like Guntigi tries to rationalize his faithlessness by affirming his bravery and attributing his acts to the need to preserve the integrity of the kingdom, it is attachment to titles and fiefdoms that motivate him and his fellow "fedeli" in deserting their monarch. For while truly courageous warriors perish in the dust of battlefields, traitors like Svarto and Guntigi inherit the land. The future belongs to the faithless.[17]

In the letter to Chauvet the dramatist accused French classical playwrights like Corneille and Racine of having devoted too important a place to love in their works, largely because the unity of time had forced them to describe a violent passion which might explode in a period lasting less than twenty-four hours. But with the character Ermengarda the Italian writer produced as passionate a creature as any Racinian figure like Hermione in *Andromaque*. Throughout the greedy chaos of human savagery where self-interest wins out, Ermengarda remains an innocent who has given herself to love. Never succeeding at breaking her attachment to the past, Ermengarda attempts to find a zone of peace and forgetfulness. In her voluntary exile in a convent at Brescia, the former queen makes a sham appearance of living in resignation to the injustice her husband committed against her. To others she insists she is no longer dwelling in the time of lost happiness: ". . . ogni passata / cosa è nulla per me . . ." (Act I, iii, 231-232). Her passion, however, remains very much alive since she suffers from Carlo's unwillingness to reciprocate her affection. For love is an emotion that must be shared across time, or the unreturned feelings will carry the lover to murderous resentment (as in French classical tragedy) or as here to maddening despair. The years of a loving marriage represent for Ermengarda the high moment of love as analyzed by Benjamin Constant in his novel *Adolphe*: "Love is only a luminous point, and nevertheless it seems to lay hold of all time. A few days ago it did not exist, very soon it will exist no longer; but as long as it exists, it sheds its splendor over the time that must follow."[18] That luminous point in time stays within the cloister of the spirit where Ermengarda harbors a melancholy which will turn to delirium after she learns that Carlo has taken a new queen. Instead of severing ties with the past she has wished to hold onto the memory of her marriage by requesting she be buried with her wedding ring and all her regal insignia. In her heart she has wished to be remembered as Carlo's bride. News of Carlo's second marriage, rather than providing a final release from bonds with the past, plunges her into a frenzy where her tormented imagination goes back to the time when she and her cherished mother-in-law Bertrada used to accompany each other on imperial journeys in full assurance of Carlo's devotion to them. Through her delirium Ermengarda crosses temporal bounds in a frantic attempt to restore in the present the period of her life when she experienced love

and respect. On the verge of death the queen awakens to an awareness of the past as an agonizing nightmare: ". . . Da un triste sogno / io mi risveglio" (Act IV, i, 202-203). Having lost the illusion of a resplendent past, Ermengarda can no longer withstand the oppression of the present and the emptiness of the future, from which she retreats in death.[19]

Between the first and second scenes of Act IV, Manzoni adds his own prayers in a chorus hoping that the dead Ermengarda will know eternal peace. The chorus reviews the queen's entire life in an appeal for her to be free of the burden of memories: arrival in France, Carlo in his glory as a warrior king, the consoling sights of physical Nature. Manzoni's chorus serves to filter the events of the past in order to transcend the passion of unrequited love as it entreats the queen's soul to put behind her earthly emotions:

> Sgombra, o gentil, dall'ansia
> mente i terrestri ardori;
> leva all'Eterno un candido
> pensier d'offerta, e muori:
> fuor della vita è il termine
> del lungo tuo martir.
>
> (Chorus, iii, 13-18)

From having always enjoyed the comforting presence of others, Ermengarda passed to a sterile isolation where memories of a beloved time tortured her. As long as the former queen directed her thoughts to precious images of her earthly existence, she persisted in what was a martyrdom for love and her husband's ruthless political expediency in sacrificing her. In its desire to liberate Ermengarda from the barren past the chorus declares that although Desiderio's daughter was born of a royal family, destiny placed her among the dispossessed of the earth: "te collocò la provvida / sventura in fra gli oppressi" (Chorus, xviii, 103-104). In dying Ermengarda and the masses of the oppressed will find salvation away from the anguish of life in this world. By taking her rightful place among the oppressed Ermengarda will at last realize the tranquility of an eternal realm beyond the bounds of this temporal sphere.[20]

In this play's *Notizie storiche* Manzoni confesses to his dissatisfaction with Adelchi as an overly imaginary character. The playwright's original drafts for the drama emphasize the prince's desire to rectify the wrongs of his father by planning to restore lost papal territory and especially to achieve the unification of Longobards with Latins as a single nation.[21] That dream of justice continues into the drama's definitive version where Adelchi sees time as a constant conflict between filial responsibility and his longing for glory as a builder of a nation. Royal heritage as a warrior had made him a destroyer. Adelchi shares with his father an appreciation of time as the bearer of destiny, and like his sister he wishes to see justice realized within this world. Adelchi views himself as a creature without a clear direction in life. After accepting the "asta reale" from his father, Adelchi became a joint ruler whose exploits on the battlefield reinforced the barbarous hold of the Longobard regime. His past is that of an active partner in bloodshed: ". . . Risponda / il passato per me . . ." (Act I, iii, 286-287). The past possesses an irrevocable quality about it that weighs the prince's actions in the present and immediate future. But Adelchi rebels against his identity as a pitiless conqueror, for he desires to gain for himself lasting fame as a builder rather than a demolisher:

> . . . Oh! mi parea,
> pur mi parea che ad altro io fossi nato,
> che ad esser capo di ladron; che il cielo
> su questa terra altro da far mi desse
> che senza rischio e senza onor, guastarla.

> (Act III, i, 74-78)

The repetition of "mi parea" and the subsequent imperfect subjunctive indicate the appearance that the prince would like to produce in his earthly enterprises to join divinely appointed destiny with well merited honor. Adelchi rejects his father's abuse of regal power to extend the country's territorial bounds and would prefer to remain what Manzoni in his youthful poem *In morte del Carlo Imbonati* calls a "giusto solitario" standing aloof from malefactors.[22] Although he regards the present as a desert of hopelessness, the prince considers his first duty to be obedience to his father. Heaven destined him to be son, prince, and king. If that fate involves participation in the evils of Desiderio's regime, Adelchi will offer no effective resistance. The prince's situation recalls that of Hamlet who cannot escape taking part in the decadent dynasty that will end at his death.

Pride as a warrior and a sense of outrage for the affront to his sister impel Adelchi to the battlefield, where he nearly succeeds in reversing the tide of history against the Frankish troops until the cowardice and greed of Longobard vassals undermine his valorous deeds. Even with the total collapse of his kingdom Adelchi refuses to commit suicide, hoping to flee to Byzantium in order to return one day to renew the struggle. In the midst of defeat this joint monarch remains convinced he has a mission to accomplish in this world, "a far quaggiù" (Act V, ii, 64), and he uses the same adverb ("quaggiù") as Carlo to express his continuing concern to take part in the compromising affairs of statecraft. At this moment in the drama Manzoni significantly departs from history by placing Adelchi's death shortly after the surrender of Verona rather than as actually occurred years later following exile at the Byzantine court. The author's intention is to have the prince share with Desiderio his final receptivity to time as judge and redeemer of human acts.

In the course of events Adelchi would withdraw from his violent participation in his father's belligerent activities so that he might reflect on the historical role he had accepted as unavoidable. His patience in performing the part of an historical agent in wars of aggression must be explained by Adelchi's readiness to live intensely the myth of Longobardic grandeur which Desiderio advanced to inspire his nobles and troops. It would have been the prince's personal choice to be able to modify that myth, reinterpreting the greatness of the Longobards as a people who could rule wisely and fairly over Germanic and Latin subjects alike. But Adelchi yielded to negative destiny, renouncing the opportunity to alter historical necessity. Time is seen here as a negative force compelling individuals to pursue one mythic course instead of another. At the moment that the Longobardic myth completely vanishes around him, Adelchi reaffirms the negativity of the temporal process: ". . . il tempo toglie / e dà . . ." (Act V, ii, 101-102). His kingdom is lost, and the insult to Ermengarda has not been avenged. Although time has indeed taken away more than it has given, Adelchi recalls how earlier in the play he remarked that "Il tempo / porterà la salute . . ." (Act III, ix, 383-384). In dying the prince recognizes that "salvation" is a spiritual and not a temporal concern. He realizes that he is moving out of history toward eternity, from the finite to the infinite. Through death he will leave behind his historical role in violent human time. Adelchi consoles his father by reminding him that loss of the kingdom has also placed the old man outside the passing of events:

> Godi che re non sei; godi che chiusa
> all'oprar t'è ogni via: loco a gentile,
> ad innocente opra non v'è: non resta
> che far torto, o patirlo. Una feroce
> forza il mondo possiede, e fa nominarsi
> dritto: la man degli avi insanguinata
> seminò l'ingiustizia; i padri l'hanno
> coltivata col sangue; e omai la terra
> altra messe non dà. . . .

> (Act V, viii, 351-359).

The prince understands that he too must be cut down together with the blood-stained harvest of injustice. This earth offered only two paths: that of victim or malefactor. While death releases Adelchi from the atavistic heritage of crime, defeat prevents Desiderio from committing further atrocities. For to remain in human time signifies to take part in the commission of injustice and to perpetuate tyranny. Death offers the liberation of the heavenly kingdom.[23]

Eternity is the realm where the voice of earthly desire and ambition never reaches to disturb the harmony of souls who have achieved the reward of peace. The Count of Carmagnola, Ermengarda, and Adelchi in dying all hope to participate in Heaven's unending glory. On this earth warriors like Carmagnola and Prince Adelchi met defeat in their passionate combat for power and renown. Queen Ermengarda experienced that attachment to mortal love marked by an agonizing discontinuity in time from which she could never recover. Manzoni's two tragedies demonstrate how only attachment to divine love would be permanent. The stage representation of military and political history should lead spectators away from hostile space and time to the transcending salvation of Christian destiny in God. In his dramas Alessandro Manzoni moves beyond historical conflict to the serenity of the Eternal.

Notes

1. The present essay combines my observations from previously published studies: "Historical Time and Eternal Fate in *Adelchi*," *La Parola del Popolo,* 24 (August 1974), 71-73; and "The Transcendence of Human Space in Manzonian Tragedy," *Studies in Romanticism,* 13 (Winter 1974), 25-46. As a theoretical guide I have followed some of the lines of investigation suggested by Georges Poulet, *Studies in Human Time,* tr. Elliott Coleman (Baltimore: Johns Hopkins University, 1956).

2. Carlo Cordié, "La recensione di Victor Chauvet al *Carmagnola* del Manzoni," *Convivium,* 25 (1957), 464-474, presents Chauvet's original review from the *Lycée Français* of May 1820 along with an introduction on the French critic's career. Natalino Sapegno, "La *Lettre à Chauvet* e la poetica del Manzoni," *Ritratto di Manzoni ed altri saggi* (Bari: Laterza, 1961), pp. 75-100, regards the letter to Chauvet as surpassing the polemic against dramatic rules and constituting a major advance in the formation of a Romantic poetics for Italian literature. Peter Farina, "A. Manzoni on the Dramatic Unity," *The USF Language Quarterly* 11, No. 1-2 (Fall-Winter 1972), 48-50, examines Manzoni's views on theatrical unities as expressed in the preface to *Il Conte di Carmagnola,* his *Lettre à Chauvet,* and especially the essay *Del Romanzo storico.*

3. For Manzoni's analysis of *Richard II* consult the *Lettre à Chauvet sur l'unité de temps et de lieu dans la tragedie,* in *Tutte le opere di Alessandro Manzoni,* ed. Giuseppe Lesca (Florence: Barbéra, 1946), pp. 257-259. Aside from his rigid neoclassical criteria, Chauvet did render some insightful criticisms about Manzoni's first drama, particularly the weakness of bringing the general's wife and daughter into the play only in the final act, where Carmagnola's religious conversion also comes as a shock to totally unprepared spectators.

4. For the sentimental attachment to human space, place, site or locus see Gaston Bachelard, *The Poetics of Space,* tr. Maria Jolas (New York: Orion, 1964), pp. xxxi-xxxii. While Bachelard's study stresses a joyous space, it will be demonstrated in my essay that earth space for Manzoni is a realm of contention. Robert Ardrey, *The Territorial Imperative* (New York: Atheneum, 1968), p. 116, comments on the primitive human desire to acquire control over land.

5. All quotations from the two tragedies can be found in Vol. I of the omnibus edition of Manzoni's works by Alberto Chiari and Fausto Ghisalberti (Milan: Mondadori, 1957), which includes early drafts for the plays, as in the eighth scene of Act I for *Carmagnola* where the count's peasant father appears on the street in Venice asking directions to his son's house.

6. In the Chauvet letter, pp. 263-264, Manzoni mentions the "lutte entre le pouvoir civil et la force militaire" that caused the count's destruction. A resolutely independent general could never survive the efforts of Venetian oligarchs to bend him to their will.

7. Cf. *Préface du Cromwell* (Oxford: Clarendon Press, 1909), *passim.*

8. From a letter by Manzoni to Gaetano Giudici, February 7, 1820, as cited by S. B. Chandler, *Alessandro Manzoni, The Story of a Spiritual Quest* (Edinburgh: Edinburgh University Press, 1974), pp. 30-31.

9. Ardrey, pp. 158-159 and 162, analyzes the role of "individual distance" to create a zone of withdrawal for reflection.

10. Chandler, *Alessandro Manzoni,* pp. 34-35, argues that Marco never truly looked into the secret chamber of his heart because of his failure to recognize his moral obligation to aid the general. But Luigi Derla, *Il realismo storico di Alessandro Manzoni* (Milano: Cisalpino, 1965), pp. 74-75, claims that Marco's tragic situation rests in the lack of any choice since the Venetian state negated all freedom and forced Marco to obey.

11. Chandler, *ibid.,* p. 35, discusses the wavering between temporal and extratemporal viewpoints in the chorus and Manzoni's inability to reconcile history with eternity. Giorgio Petrocchi, "Il momento letterario del *Carmagnola*," *Giornale storico della letteratura italiana* 147 (1970), 43-66, compares the different versions of the play and judges them as vacillations on Manzoni's part between an early political-historical vision of Carmagnola to a later religious-ethical portrait. Schiller in writing his tragedy of *Mary, Queen of Scots,* also moved from a political to a religious interpretation.

12. In his *Discorso sopra alcuni punti della storia longobardica in Italia,* Manzoni contended that the Longobard rulers and their Latin subjects never constituted a single people. Longobards and Latins had separate legal systems, and it was Longobard count-judges who tyrannically settled all disputes between the two nations. Manzoni feared that Italians would always remain a slave people under foreign domination, and in the chorus following Act III of *Adelchi* the author speaks to all Italians warning them of the heritage of being a "volgo disperso che nome non ha." Claude Lévi-Strauss, "History and Dialectic," *The Savage Mind* (Chicago: University of Chicago Press, 1966), pp. 254-255, acknowledges the role of myth, such as that of the French Revolution, to be an historical agent inspiring practical action in succeeding generations of Frenchmen. Desiderio adroitly manipulates the myth of Longobardic grandeur.

13. Gilberto Lonardi, *L'esperienza stilistica del Manzoni tragico* (Florence: Olschki, 1965), p. 16, in commenting on Desiderio's refusal to learn from

the past notes how words like "quando," "allor," and "lunge" demonstrate the king's mental life in an undetermined future.

14. Manzoni remarks in the play's *Notizie storiche* that according to historical records Desiderio's wife Ansa was alive during the Frankish war and that she accompanied her husband to imprisonment. By placing Ansa's death prior to the tragedy's time span the author heightened the effect of the king's final isolation.

15. Lonardi, *op. cit.,* pp. 32-45, analyzes Martino's speech with its constant repetition of "Dio" or "Iddio" to indicate God's silent presence throughout the Alpine crossing.

16. Luigi Russo, "Parere sull'*Adelchi,*" *Ritratti e disegni storici,* 4th ser. (Florence: Sansoni, 1965), p. 50, considers Carlo's conventional religiosity to be a political ploy. Derla, pp. 133-135, speaks of Manzoni's tendency to devaluate heroes. In the *Discorso sopra alcuni punti della storia longobardica,* pp. 173-177, Manzoni attributes Carlo's military success to his singular ability to unite different ranks of Frankish society into his army.

17. Chandler, *Manzoni,* p. 58, observes how Guntigi justifies his new allegiance by referring to Carlo as the "consacrato" of God, thereby excusing treachery as obedience to divine will. Attilio Momigliano, *Alessandro Manzoni* (Milan: Principato, 1964), pp. 187-188, studies Svarto's desire to lift himself from his lowly post. Eurialo de Michelis, *Studi sul Manzoni* (Milan: Feltrinelli, 1962), p. 124, points out that Svarto seeks personal advantage to gain power in his society, in contrast to the Venetian councilors of *Il Conte di Carmagnola* who act primarily out of a sense of duty to the state. Giuseppe Toffanin, *Sul Manzoni* (Naples: Libreria Scientifica, 1972), pp. 52-53, compares Guntigi and Svarto to Iago.

18. Cited by Poulet, *Human Time,* p. 215.

19. Russo, p. 87, accurately states that Ermengarda's words "ogni passata / cosa" reveal a passion which remains very much alive. I strongly disagree with Russo, pp. 96-100, where he dismisses Ermengarda's delirium as rhetorical artifice. Aurelia Accame Bobbio, *Alessandro Manzoni, segno di contraddizione* (Rome: Studium, 1975), p. 189, judges Ermengarda as an expiatory figure whose suffering in part redeems the wrongs perpetrated by her Longobardic dynasty.

20. Chandler, *Manzoni,* pp. 63-64, analyzes the chorus to show that God stands outside of history as an eternal refuge for tormented individuals like the queen.

21. Arnaldo Fratelli, "Adelchi, personaggio inventato," *Sipario* 15, No. 164 (1960), 4, discusses Manzoni's displeasure at changing the historical facts concerning Adelchi. In Act I, Sc. 2, and the start of Act V for the play's original draft, the dramatist advanced

Adelchi's plans for the union of Latins with Longobards, but then Manzoni broke off noting "Scartate tutto e rifar l'atto in modo più conforme alla storia." While Giacinto Margiotta, *Dalla prima alla seconda stesura dell'"Adelchi," Studio Comparativo* (Florence: Le Monnier, 1956), *passim,* believes the first draft to be related to Manzoni's patriotic aspirations as expressed in the ode *Marzo 1821*; Filippo Piemontese, *Studi sul Manzoni e altri saggi* (Milan: Marzorati, 1952), pp. 86-87, asserts that the playwright's disillusionment with the wars for Italian liberation had little influence on the drama's revision.

22. Chandler, *Manzoni,* pp. 15-17, analyzes the *carme* on Imbonati's death, where the poet points out the unequal warfare between the solitary man of just character and the numerous brotherhood of the evil.

23. Benedetto Croce, *Alessandro Manzoni* (Bari: Laterza, 1946), p. 119, suggests that death revealed nothing to Adelchi but gave him a sense of resignation to the world's injustices. Alfredo Galletti, *Alessandro Manzoni* (Milan: Mursia, 1958), p. 294, illustrates Manzoni's attempt at a Christian drama as a representation of human misery and weakness that only Heaven can relieve.

Gregory L. Lucente (essay date 1986)

SOURCE: "The Uses and Ends of Discourse in *I promessi sposi*: Manzoni's Narrator, His Characters, and Their Author," in *MLN,* Vol. 101, No. 1, January, 1986, pp. 51-77.

[*In the following essay, Lucente asserts that Manzoni's use of language in* I promessi sposi *is central to an understanding of the novel's theme and structure.*]

Questions of language, particularly of its worldly use and abuse, are of major concern in *I promessi sposi*.[1] These questions begin with the book's introduction and continue, though in constantly varying forms and contexts, throughout the novel. In the introduction the narrator states his reasons for reworking the story, which he claims to have found in an anonymous seventeenth-century manuscript, and begins to explain the procedures he has adopted for revising its language. Although toward the end of the introduction the narrator makes an oblique reference to himself as an "author," the guise he assumes actually combines the attributes of two traditional roles, that of the dutiful editor, common to eighteenth-century fiction from Defoe, Richardson, and Laclos to Goethe and Foscolo, and that of the historical novel's more actively creative writer, such as found in the contemporary and highly influential books of Sir Walter Scott.

The introduction opens, of course, with a passage supposedly copied verbatim from the scratched and faded original, which the narrator had intended to transcribe from first to last, word for word. But after a page or so the nar-

Framed profile of Alessandro Manzoni

rator breaks off the transcription of the autograph and gives vent to his doubts about the entire project. As the narrator laments, and as the language of the opening passage amply demonstrates, the original is so full of elaborate conceits, Lombard idioms, incorrect Italian, arbitrary grammar, poorly articulated sentences, Spanish elegance, and inappropriate rhetoric that, even transcribed, no one would ever endure the toil of reading it. Regardless of all of the narrator's efforts at transcription, therefore, the story would remain unread and unknown, in short, useless.

The narrator finds this situation distressing for a single reason: the story itself is too beautiful to lose. Therefore, in order to salvage it from the oblivion of unread texts, he proposes what he has already done, that is, to rework the original, leaving the events and their sequence as they stand while changing what he at first terms the manuscript's "dicitura" and later its "stile" In response to the obvious question of what sort of language or style to adopt instead, the narrator admits that at one point he had actually considered furnishing an account of each and every change along with the logic behind it, but by the time that he began putting the explanations together, he realized that

they would have made up another book all by themselves He accordingly refuses the temptation to explain himsel at such length, and he seems content to let the matter res there, without further clarification beyond the inferences to be drawn from his introductory comments and the evidence of the narrative itself. He excuses this omission by saying that, along with the fact that one book at a time seems quite enough, "un libro impiegato a giustificarne un altro, anzi lo stile d'un altro, potrebbe parer cosa ridicola" (p. 6).

It is well known that Manzoni's work on the novel ex tended over a period of many years and included severa thorough revisions. Both in the unpublished draft of *Ferme e Lucia* (1821-23) and in the first edition of *I promess sposi* (1827), the device of the "found" manuscript and it reworking may have been little more than a literary con ceit—though one of a different sort from those of the text' "anonymous" original—just a convenient and currentl fashionable way to get the story going, insignificant in it self and of little direct relation to the narrative that fol lows. But this is not the case. As the story develops, it be comes increasingly apparent that questions of language ar not only central to the narrative's style but also that the go right to the heart of the story's subject matter. After th openly self-conscious introduction, these issues, which in volve linguistic mastery as well as linguistic hierarchy, ar clearest in the text's treatment of the official state edict: in the salient example of Renzo's linguistic education, i the story of Fra Cristoforo's conversion and his encounte with Don Rodrigo, in the massive effects of the plague and, finally, in Manzoni's overall relation to the product c his own discourse in terms of worldly meaning an worldly use. In the end, no account of the narrative's orga nization and meaning is complete without coming to term with the ways in which the novel presents and attempts t resolve these questions.

The first clear sign that the narrative's concern with lar guage is going to continue past the introduction and int the story itself is the presentation in Chapter 1 of the go ernment edicts, the language and style of which recall th circumlocutory and affectedly "elegant" discourse of th anonymous manuscript quoted at the introduction's begir ning. The "gride," in this case dealing with the vagaboncc and *bravi* of seventeenth-century Lombardy, are indee examples of the inflated rhetoric that Manzoni regularl associates with the upper strata of the dominant Spanis hierarchy. But along with Manzoni's ongoing critique c social behavior, and with the stamp of historical authorit that the proclamations lend to the novel's own discours the "gride" also give Manzoni a way of broaching one c his favorite topics, the relationship between discourse ar worldly action:

> Con tutto ciò, anzi in gran parte a cagion di ciò, quelle gride, ripubblicate e rinforzate di governo in governo, non servivano ad altro che ad attestare ampollosamente l'impotenza de' loro autori; o, se producevan qualche effetto immediato, era principalmente d'aggiunger molte vessazioni a quelle che i pacifici e i deboli già

soffrivano da' perturbatori, e d'accrescer le violenze e l'astuzia di questi.

(pp. 16-17)

The intention of the narrator's commentary on the "gride" is, of course, to account for the continuing corruption and abuse by powerful, though supposedly outlawed or legally restricted, segments of local society. This and contiguous passages thus help to explain how and why the basic mechanism of the narrative—the blocking of Renzo and Lucia's marriage at the capricious whim of Don Rodrigo in his competition with his cousin Attilio—can have occurred at all. Indeed, the passage goes on to describe the hapless state of the peaceful and unprotected ordinary man ("l'uomo bonario"), who is, ironically, subject both to the arbitrarily enforced rules of the official law and to the unofficial but no less real illegal harassment on the part of the outlaws.

But there is a complementary set of thematics at work in this explanation that, in the long run, is equally telling in *I promessi sposi.* These thematics, like those in the introduction, deal with questions of language and utility. What, after all, do the high-flown, often repeated, and elaborately elegant edicts represent if not the "impotence" of their authors? Their meaning seems directed outward, into the world of everyday activity. But in another sense their meaning is reflected back inward, to show the ineffectiveness of their authors' endeavors, and *this* meaning is only underscored by their endless repetition. What, therefore, is the worldly effect of these edicts if not precisely the opposite of that which, at least in practical terms, is intended? The lesson, in this very hierarchical and complexly ordered society, is especially obvious in spite of—or perhaps because of—the well-known ironic detachment with which Manzoni's narrator views it: pompous show goes hand in hand with worldly failure. At best, such overbearing pomposity will end as it began, in vapid rhetoric and "vane proteste" At worst, it will result in the opposite of what is hoped. This is a difficult lesson to learn, since it involves aspects of style in regard both to discourse and to other forms of human behavior; but, as the narrator is already aware (indeed as is demonstrated in the very revisions of his text) and as Renzo must eventually realize, too, this lesson is crucial for anyone who seeks to get along, and possibly even to do well, in human society. It is the narrator's assessment of the "gride," moreover, both in their rhetorical complexity and their worldly ineffectiveness, that ties the thematics of this first chapter to those of the exchange in Chapter 3 between Renzo and the devilishly tricky lawyer, popularly known as Dr. Azzeccagarbugli, and that thus leads to the scene of Renzo's first great failure in the lessons of discourse as presented in the novel.

II

Renzo goes to consult Azzeccagarbugli (at Agnese's instigation) with his hopes high. Both because of Don Rodrigo's interest in Lucia and Don Abbondio's personal shortcomings, Renzo and Lucia are in stormy seas, with their wedding and their happiness in jeopardy, and Renzo knows it. Yet, given the unpleasant situation, Renzo has done all right for himself up to this point. By his directness and the strength of his will, he has forced the necessary information out of Don Abbondio, cutting through the haze of the timorous priest's obfuscations and "latinorum," and, together with Agnese and the less than enthusiastic Lucia, he has decided on the next step to be taken. But unlike Don Abbondio, who is still within the social realm of Renzo's everyday life in the village, the once important Azzeccagarbugli is a figure from another social sphere altogether.[2] In this respect, therefore, the scene between Renzo and Azzeccagarbugli foreshadows Renzo's experiences in Milan after the bread riot, where he is again notably out of his element.

As Manzoni makes clear in the scene between Renzo and the lawyer, the passport that permits passage from one level of society toward the next (though without destroying either the hierarchical levels themselves or the privileges that they protect) is language. Azzeccagarbugli, of course, knows this from the start. His particular professional talent is at using language to defend his clients from the apparent intent of the law. He does this, as his epithet suggests (a name so thoroughly associated with the man's essence that Agnese can no longer recall what his real name is), by turning the language of the law away from its worldly referents and then directing it back into a maze of discourse, so that its worldly, legal sense is nothing more than a conundrum, null and void, and his clients, no matter how miscreant, can go scot free. Azzeccagarbugli's once prodigious skills do not mean that he never makes a mistake (although he perceives Renzo's gift of the capons for what it is, he completely misconstrues the import of Renzo's lack of a forelock, which he considers evidence of Renzo's prudence in shaving off the bravo's customary "ciuffo"). But his abilities do mean that he knows how to recognize his errors and how to act on that recognition in order to recover from them.

When Renzo first enters the lawyer's studio and asks to have a word in confidence, Azzeccagarbugli makes everything seem easy: "Son qui . . . parlate. . . . Ditemi il fatto come sta" (p. 44). But there is a problem that is greater than either of them, at least for the moment, realizes. As Renzo himself admits: "Lei m'ha da scusare: noi altri poveri non sappiamo parlar bene" (p. 44). Renzo finally manages to mention the threats made to the priest and the unfulfilled matrimony, at which point Azzeccagarbugli takes over.

Throughout the lawyer's subsequent comments and his reading of the "gride" that treat forcible interference with marriage, Renzo remains so thoroughly immersed in the "words" themselves (which he is convinced will aid him but which he can read only "un pochino") that it never occurs to him that the lawyer has taken him for a bravo in need of a shrewd defense instead of a poor silk-worker in search of justice. When the truth finally comes out—that Azzeccagarbugli has gotten things exactly reversed—the lawyer has a simple explanation. According to Azzecca-garbugli, the fault is Renzo's because he, along with all those of his class, is ignorant of the uses of language in the world: "Diavolo! . . . Che pasticci mi fate? Tant'è; siete tutti così: possibile che non sappiate dirle chiare le cose?" (p. 49). Now that Azzeccagarbugli has given Renzo a moment to talk, Renzo tells him the rest of the story, stressing that in fact he did make Don Abbondio speak clearly ("io l'ho fatto parlar chiaro") and then coming out with the name of Don Rodrigo. This is quite enough for Azzeccagarbugli, who washes his hands of the entire matter. The lawyer's only advice to Renzo is to leave people of his station alone. If Renzo really wants to tell his story, he should tell it among his equals, who do not know any better than he does how to measure their words: "Fate di questi discorsi tra voi altri, che non sapete misurar le parole; e non venite a farli con un galantuomo che sa quanto valgono" (pp. 49-50).

At this turn of events, Renzo seems intent on justifying himself, but the lawyer, obviously concerned for his own interests now that the name of Don Rodrigo has been mentioned, cuts his ex-client off and shoves Renzo toward the door, insisting to the astounded servant that she return Renzo's capons, since he wants nothing from Renzo or, indeed, anything whatever to do with him. Before pushing Renzo out of his studio, however, Azzeccagarbugli—more from anger and frustration than anything else—gives him one last piece of advice that will turn out to be of special significance in the development both of Renzo's character and of Manzoni's narrative in general: "*Imparate a parlare*: non si viene a sorprender così un galantuomo" (p. 50, my italics).

The importance of language is emphasized in the exchange between Renzo and the hapless Azzeccagarbugli by the narrator's insistent repetition of the word "parola," which resounds like a tattoo throughout the entire scene. It is true that Azzeccagarbugli's type of discourse is not intended in any sense as a model for Renzo to follow, that, because of the lawyer's present condition and his linguistic chicanery, he is actually, as Giorgio De Rienzo has pointed out, a champion of the word who is now "decaduto (e avvilito)."[3] Nevertheless, Azzeccagarbugli's climactic exhortation does provide a clear beginning (after Don Abbondio's latinate preface) to Renzo's *Bildungsroman* in the world of language.[4] Renzo's real education has to wait, however, until after he, Lucia, and Agnese, with the assistance of Fra Cristoforo, have fled to Monza and then split up, and Renzo has arrived, on his own and dejected, in the turbulent atmosphere of Milan.

Following the bread riot, with its heady mixture of confusion, scuffling, and camaraderie and its odd linguistic amalgam of Italian and Spanish, Renzo, having taken a moment to catch his breath, begins to make a speech. But Renzo simply is not yet competent to act profitably on his own in the broader world of society. It is important to see, moreover, the critical role that language plays in Renzo's worldly ineptitude. Everything that happens to Renzo in

this section of the story in Milan—incuding the events to which he will later refer in his final summary of the lessons he has learned—occurs through the medium of discourse. This is not to say that in Manzoni's view discourse itself is somehow superior to other worldly endeavor, but only that there is no action or interaction among human beings that is completely outside of it or that does not depend on it in some fashion or other; which is why language is one thing that Renzo must learn to use if he is to learn others, one key to the kingdom of social wisdom and success.

Renzo begins his harangue after the riot more agitated than agitator, so thoroughly wrapped up in his own predicament that his speech has more to do with the injustice of Don Rodrigo's treachery than with the current availability or price of bread in Milan. But his audience takes him for what he says rather than what he is, and they view him either as a sincere young leader, or as a country lout full of hot air, or, in the eyes of the disguised agent, Ambrogio Fusella, as a dangerous outside agitator to be identified, arrested, and imprisoned for the protection of the State. At the conclusion of what the narrator refers to as Renzo's "predica" (which includes connotations of "sermon" as well as "speech," p. 244), Renzo has ears only for those who voice their support; and he goes off behind the agent, whom he, of course, believes to be his friend, with the end in mind of satisfying his hunger and thirst.

The following scene at the Inn of the Luna Piena, framed by the hustle and bustle of the crowd and presented through the narrator's juggling of various perspectives all at once, is one of the most astutely organized and precisely sketched in all of Manzoni's narrative.[5] The action of this scene proves to be crucial, moreover, for Renzo's progressive education in the ways of discourse and in the limits of social behavior. After a brief introduction, the narrator frames the scene with the thoughts of the innkeeper, who immediately recognizes Renzo's companion and wonders whether Renzo himself is hound or hare, hunter or prey. Renzo orders wine and stew, and, at the innkeeper's apology for the lack of bread, he produces the third and last of his supply of *panini*, raising it high to show the crowd and shouting (amidst a gentle narrative irony over which he has no control) "ecco il pane della *provvidenza*!" (p. 246, my italics). With the approval of his companions and the encouragement of one in particular ("viva il pane a buon mercato!"), Renzo goes on to give his thumbnail sketch of the ideal economic program: "A buon mercato? disse Renzo: *gratis et amore.*" He hurries to add, however, that he really has no intention of revolutionizing the current economic system of sale and payment (since, as was clear in his previous speech, he believes not in overthrowing the present system but in ridding it of injustices); and he goes on to say that, if he could only find whoever owned the bread in the first place, he would be more than willing to pay for it.

With this pronouncement, the narrator distinguishes Renzo's goals from the sort of economic and social program familiar to Manzoni's contemporaries as the basis for the revolution in France. But more than that, he demonstrates Renzo's inability, at this point in the narrative, to formulate and express clear ideas either about his own situation or about that of others. This failing was already apparent in his high-flown pronouncements and exhortations before meeting his "guida"; and, as occurs with regularity throughout the first half of the novel, Manzoni again makes use of lexical indicators to shade Renzo's limitations. During Renzo's encounter with Don Abbondio, one of his primary objections had been to the priest's resorting to the linguistic trickery of Latin (a language that, as Manzoni suggests on several occasions in the story, was not understood by the general populace). Moreover, while still at the inn, Renzo complains obliquely about Don Abbondio's linguistic subterfuge and openly about Ferrer's "qualche parolina in latino" (p. 255), which Renzo attempts to repeat in his own wine-addled discourse ("*siés baraòs trapolorum*"), thereby reflecting both Ferrer's Spanish and Don Abbondio's "latinorum." But to state his economic program, Renzo himself has resorted to a Latin formula, "*gratis et amore.*"

Such inconsistency within Renzo's behavior would not be disturbing in and of itself, but as Renzo continues, the inconsistencies mount. Indeed, it is obvious to the innkeeper and perhaps to others present as well that Renzo is not only a hare, but also (as the narrator already suggested in his comments on Don Rodrigo's schemes in Chapter 11) one that is doing everything possible to get caught. Renzo, of course, knows nothing of this, and therein lies both Renzo's foolishness and his weakness. Earlier, in the street, he thought he had spoken "con un po' di politica, per non dire in pubblico i fatti miei" (p. 244). But at the Inn of Luna Piena, where he is not only urged on by the crowd but also animated by the wine, Renzo lets himself go as though he were indeed inspired by the Full Moon, and he does so at exactly the wrong moment.

Fusella's task at the inn is as precise as it is tricky: to get Renzo's name without arousing either Renzo's suspicions or the ill will of the inn's other customers. After Renzo's assertion of his legal expertise (probably a result of his single disastrous experience with Azzeccagarbugli) and his refusal to give his name and province of origin despite the innkeeper's dutiful citation of the appropriate "gride" under the agent's watchful gaze, Renzo's "guida" is constrained to hold his tongue and wait for his loquacious prey to set his own trap, in which Renzo is quick to oblige. Having thanked his guide and the others who have helped him to avoid the innkeeper's pen, ink, and paper, Renzo once again assumes the attitude of a preacher ("mettendosi di nuovo in attitudine di predicatore") and decries those who rule the world and who always want to make writing enter into everything: "Sempre la penna per aria! Grande smania che hanno que' signori d'adoprar la penna!" (p. 250). One of the gamblers nearby makes a joke of this, saying that once "que' signori" have finished eating their geese, they have to find something to do with all those quills. Here Renzo responds in kind, and the narrator, in

an important aside to which we will return shortly, comments on Renzo's reply. But the matter is more serious than either the gambler's initial jest or Renzo's jocular response, and Renzo continues along the same line he had taken previously, lamenting the close association between writing and power and the use of writing to subject the unlettered: "Ma la ragione giusta la dirò io . . . : è perché la penna la tengon loro: e così, le parole che dicon loro, volan via, e spariscono; le parole che dice un povero figliuolo, stanno attenti bene, e presto presto le infilzan per aria, con quella penna, e te le inchiodano sulla carta, per servirsene, a tempo e luogo." Renzo's lament leads to his complaints about the treacheries of Latin and then once more to the day's affairs, all of which were conducted "in volgare," or the common speech of the local populace, and all, Renzo notes, without recourse to pen, ink, and paper. This brings Renzo back to his expectations for the following day, thereby giving the guileful agent, who up to now has listened in silence, the opening he needs.

The program Fusella outlines for the rectification of the pricing and distribution of bread depends, first, on pen, ink, and paper and, second, on the gathering up of all the names of those involved, as the narrator takes pain to emphasize. But, as the narrator also points out, Renzo, "invaghito del progetto," does not notice any of that; he falls for the ruse without hesitation when asked to participate in a trial run and gives not only his name but also the details of his marital status. With this, the guide has obtained exactly what he wanted, and he departs posthaste, in fact so abruptly that Renzo is left talking to himself, apparently loudly enough that the serving boy thinks Renzo is addressing him rather than the agent's undrained glass (which Renzo then downs in one gulp). When the waiter responds to Renzo, saying he has understood ("Ho inteso"), Renzo seems bemused but not surprised, since he still believes, despite all the lessons of his own experience, that when reasons are just ("giuste"), every reasonable person will understand and agree. For Renzo at this point, when language is used in the service of justice and truth, it is, or should be, transparent, that is, significant but secondary: expression is only a necessary means to a much more important end. Ironically, the more he drinks the more he demonstrates the failures of this belief, since he cannot find the words to finish his well-meant but poorly formed sentences, and by the end of the scene, very nearly insensate, he has become the laughingstock of the inn's earthy clientele.

The narrator handles the description of the entire scene by distancing himself from its presentation both through the use of such screens as the innkeeper and even Fusella and through direct addresses to the reader. As Renzo drinks more and more, the narrator recounts less and less. Early in the scene, during the exchange over the official registration of guests at the inn, Renzo downs his third glass of wine and the narrator, after reporting that fact, adds: "e d'ora in poi ho paura che non li potremo più contare" (p. 248). Later on, just after Fusella's departure and Renzo's oblique exchange with the waiter, the narrator again interrupts the course of his description in order both to provide extra information not discernible from the present scene and to explain the rationale for the gaps in representation that are to follow. While discussing Renzo's excesses in light of his inexperience, the narrator alludes once again to the original manuscript's anonymous author:

> Su questo il nostro anonimo fa una osservazione, che noi ripeteremo: e conti quel che può contare. Le abitudini temperate e oneste, dice, recano anche questo vantaggio, che, quanto più sono inveterate e radicate in un uomo, tanto più facilmente, appena appena se n'allontana, se ne risente subito; dimodoché se ne ricorda poi per un pezzo; e anche uno sproposito gli serve di scola. . . .
>
> Noi riferiremo soltanto alcune delle moltissime parole che [Renzo] mandò fuori, in quella sciagurata sera: le molte più che tralasciamo, disdirebbero troppo; perché, non solo non hanno senso, ma non fanno vista d'averlo: condizione necessaria in un libro stampato.

(pp. 253-54)

Manzoni's narrator thus excuses Renzo's behavior (and quietly asks the reader's complicity) by saying not only that this is Renzo's first indulgence in such excess but also that Renzo will learn from it, and what he will learn, in his movement from inexperience toward maturity, will be the value of honesty and temperance and the dangers of excessive behavior of any sort. At the same time, the narrator reaffirms his own love of truth ("l'amore che portiamo alla verità") and his commitment to representational fidelity (in following the anonymous manuscript's story if not its style), even though he later qualifies this commitment, within his own narrative intended for publication, by subordinating representational fidelity to sense. This valuation in regard to narrative practice is of the same sort that the narrator and, perhaps surprisingly, even the author of the anonymous original make in regard to Renzo's social behavior: it is important to act in the world and to believe in something that is worthy of action, but it is equally important to exercise restraint in all endeavors or chaos will reign in terms of both literary representation and worldly comportment. This attitude toward behavior also recalls the narrator's initial goal in redoing the anonymous manuscript, that is, to rid it of linguistic excesses and, thereby, to make it readable and pleasant so that its story can be followed and understood. The lesson for Manzoni's narrator as well as for the narrative's "primo uomo" is clear: following one's beliefs and even acting on one's impulses can be a benefit and a virtue, but only as they are subordinated to a higher value, that of making sense (and although exactly what *this* value is subordinate to is not yet apparent in Manzoni's text, it will become much more so by the story's end).

If, however, this dual appeal to both behavioral and linguistic discretion, in worldly action as well as in worldly representation, seems too limited, indeed, entirely too sober in view of Renzo's extraordinary spirit and Manzoni's strikingly rich text, it must be remembered that these comments on narrative and linguistic aims and practices are not the only self-consciously literary notations in this portion of the narrative. The other commentary in this vein, produced by Renzo before his fall into drunkenness and explained by the narrator in the aside mentioned previously, comes earlier in the chapter, following the gambler's joke about the geese and the quills. Renzo responds to the gambler's witticism in an especially significant way: "To', disse Renzo: è un poeta costui. Ce n'è anche qui de' poeti: già ne nasce per tutto. N'ho una vena anch'io, e qualche volta ne dico delle curiose . . . ma quando le cose vanno bene" (p. 250). The narrator explains Renzo's remark with the pretense of clarifying the key term's local usage:

> Per capire questa baggianata del povero Renzo, bisogna sapere che, presso il volgo di Milano, e del contado ancora più, poeta non significa già, come per tutti i galantuomini, un sacro ingegno, un abitator di Pindo, un allievo delle Muse; vuol dire un cervello bizzarro e un po' balzano, che, ne' discorsi e ne' fatti, abbia più dell'arguto e del singolare che del ragionevole. Tanto quel guastamestieri del volgo è ardito a manomettere le parole, e a far dir loro le cose più lontane dal loro legittimo significato! Perché, vi domando io, cosa ci ha che fare poeta con cervello balzano?

(p. 250)

As is often true of Manzoni's irony in the novel, this passage is equally as interesting for what it omits as for what it says. It is clear that Renzo's tongue has long since been loosened by the exuberance of the day's events and that his head is light from the wine, and it is also obvious that Renzo's reply is meant as a facetious feint. In both of these respects, it is a "baggianata." But the narrator's explanation of the term "poeta," or indeed his reason for explaining it at all, is far from straightforward. The importance of the quality of behavior in regard to both speech and other forms of action ("ne' discorsi e ne' fatti") is a theme that, as we have seen, runs throughout the entire chapter, so *that* part of the narrator's commentary seems clear enough. But neither of the two definitions of poet that the narrator offers—either the supposedly correct one, cast in the erudite, Neoclassical frame of the gentlemanly allusion to Pindus and the Muses or the popular meaning of "poet" as a term designating an irrational oddball—seems entirely acceptable to the narrator. The first is treated ironically through its inflation, the second through its vulgarity and illegitimacy. The next step, therefore, rather than the outright rejection of the populace's wisdom as contained in language, is the questioning of this wisdom yet without offering any real solution, as though maybe there were some truth, though not the whole truth, in the popular conception of the poet as a singular, exceptionally imaginative individual. Finally, rather than affirming or denying either sense of the word or taking any sort of definite stance on the question—Classical as well as Shakespearean and Romantic—of the relation between poetry and irrationality, the narrator lets the whole matter drop with a question of his own.

Although this approach differs from the narrator's later explicit explanation of his representational procedure in regard to Renzo's drunken discourse, the technique of placing two positions on an issue side by side and then withdrawing from any definite solution (often weighting the second over the first by means of a question that seems merely rhetorical) recurs throughout Manzoni's text, beginning with his pre-publication consideration of stylistic questions as described in the introduction and running all the way to Renzo's and Lucia's closing evaluations of the meaning of their experience. At the inn, the weight seems to fall on the imagination as significant in its own right even if it *is* peculiar and even if, in excess, it, too, is doubtless either hazardous, repugnant, or both. Renzo's depiction of himself as something of a poet (though only in better times) thus joins the other indications of the close relation between the narrator and his character; and it tempers the narrator's sober judgment of Renzo's follies even as Renzo indulges in the excesses for which he will have to pay but from which, eventually, he will learn. That the narrator himself is implicated in this assessment of human discourse and behavior is important, therefore, since this self-reflexive implication demonstrates the ties of sympathy between the narrator and the story's leading man at the same time that it reinforces the narrative bond between action and discourse and again underscores the continuing thematics of excess and restraint in both areas. But however significant the narrator's excursus is, it must also be remembered that, at least at this point, the narrator's reaction to the question he raises is neither affirmation nor denial but instead clever, ironic withdrawal.

Consequent to what the Milanese authorities eventually learn, the notary and his bailiffs arrive at the inn early the following morning to take Renzo into custody. At first it may seem that the change in Renzo's attitude from the night before—from acceptance and unquestioning fellowship to skepticism and recalcitrance—is simply the result of his sobriety, the usual feelings and reactions of the "morning after." But as is typical of the multilayered depth of Manzoni's narrative technique, there is no single logical or psychological explanation for Renzo's sudden enlightenment. Part of his learning has, however, already been explained by the narrator in the lengthy excursus dealing with the limitations of the text's fidelity to complete representation and with the moral effects that extreme behavior has on normally reserved individuals. Within the narrator's earlier scheme of things, therefore, Renzo's awakening into the light (however grim) of knowledge can be explained by his excesses of the previous evening, the very same excesses, in fact, that have got him into the straits in which he now finds himself.

This combination of psychological notation—broadly stated and then subtly developed without further narratorial commentary—and implicit literary "explanation" (in terms of the topos of the reawakening into moral knowledge) is most clearly demonstrated, as is again customary in Manzoni's representationally oriented aesthetics, in the character's deeds. At first Renzo can do little except

watch, look, and think (p. 269). This is the same behavior that, in a later context, is extolled by Manzoni as the exemplary conduct of human beings, who all too often, by separating speech from these other aspects of intelligent behavior and by being too quick to leap to language, manage only to make themselves lamentable rather than admirable (p. 543). As distinct from Renzo's earlier reactions in Milan, his behavior now shows that he no longer indiscriminately believes whatever he hears ("Però, di tante belle parole Renzo non ne credette una" [p. 271]). When Renzo sees and recognizes others who might help him approaching him and his captors on the street, he signals to them by moving his head and coughing; and when the right moment comes, he seizes the opportunity that fortune has provided and states his case in both practical and moral terms: "Se non m'aiuto ora, pensò, mio danno. E subito alzò la voce: figliuoli! mi menano in prigione, perché ieri ho gridato: pane e giustizia. Non ho fatto nulla; son galantuomo: aiutatemi, non m'abbandonate, figliuoli!" (p. 273). So Renzo has begun to learn the importance and utility of language, and he demonstrates what he has learned by using discourse (including body language) in action. His words are skillfully framed, and they play once again on that trickiest of terms, "galantuomo." He seizes the moment and speaks, and shortly thereafter is free. In the narrative organization of these central chapters (14 to 16), the efficacy of the concluding harangue at least in part makes up for the foolishness of the introductory one as well as for the discursive errors in between.

If there is any doubt as to what Renzo has learned in Milan, it is quickly dispelled by his behavior at the inn in Gorgonzola, where the way in which he conducts himself reaffirms his newly acquired wisdom in the uses of discourse. As the Milanese *mercante* begins to relate his version of the story of the previous day's events (in which Renzo figures as a dangerous provocateur), Renzo listens "zitto e attento" (p. 284), paying closer attention than any of the others in the audience while carefully concealing his interest. Along with this cautious, in part fear-driven behavior, he also refrains from the sort of alcoholic indulgence of the evening before (although he does not refuse wine altogether, as he had meanwhile at the rustic inn) and now remains content with a half liter of "vino sincero." Even when the merchant's story becomes most animated and the reactionary slant of his opinions most obvious, Renzo, despite all his perfectly natural desires to flee, continues to sit quietly and restrain himself (as Fusella had done at the Luna Piena and as Fra Cristoforo had also done during another meal). Finally, when Renzo sees the opportunity to depart without giving rise to suspicion, he pays the innkeeper and leaves "senza far altri discorsi" (p. 289), thereby conducting himself in a manner completely different from that of the previous evening in Milan. Renzo has thus begun to learn not only how to use language but also how to refrain from linguistic excess in the interest of his own well-being (though this is just a beginning and nothing more), and his behavior at the inn in Gorgonzola aptly attests to this knowledge.

In this case, of course, Renzo's silence has nothing to do with acquiescence. His fury at the merchant's tale is reflected, however, not in public discourse but in his thoughts to himself as he heads away from the inn towards the Adda. After mentally berating the merchant for the inaccuracies of his report, Renzo concludes with an internally voiced imperative, again directed to the merchant, that both binds Renzo's linguistic experiences together into a consistent process of learning and recalls the beginning of that very process: "*E imparare a parlare un'altra volta*; principalmente quando si tratta del prossimo" (p. 291, my italics). From a beginning pupil, Renzo has, at least in the context of *this* moment, become the master.

At the end of this chapter, there is a codicil to the entire lesson that extends from Renzo's entry into Milan to his arrival at his cousin Bortolo's in the territory of Bergamo in Chapter 17. Bortolo, after praising the *bergamasco* lawyer who has made such an impression in Venice and done so much for his fellows in Bergamo precisely because he "knows how to speak" (304; 271), cautions Renzo that, if he wants to stay and work in the silk industry nearby, there is a local linguistic oddity that he must learn to accept, however repugnant it may be to him at first. This is the *bergamasco* habit of referring to anyone from the territory of Milan as a "baggiano." That Renzo says he is ready to live with this facetious if less than complimentary epithet pleases Bortolo at the same time that it indicates another stage on the way to Renzo's understanding of the ways and the deformations of language in the world. The term itself casts back, furthermore, to the narrator's description of Renzo's own "baggianata" concerning poets at the inn in Milan, and it also casts forth to the novel's conclusion. The narrative is not done, therefore, either with this epithet or with the process of linguistic education signaled by the repetition of the verb "imparare." But before reviewing where these terms lead in the story, it is necessary to trace the development of another set of concerns that are also of crucial significance both within Azzeccagarbugli's initial command and within the order of language itself, those of hierarchy.

III

In *I promessi sposi* hierarchy is important to language both in an external and in an internal sense. Externally, the forms of language correspond to the already hierarchical ordering of society: each class, and each local division within a given class, has its own regular way of expressing meaning in discourse. Internally, language depends on the ordered priorities of hierarchy for its articulation and so for the production of its meaning. These two all-pervasive aspects of linguistic hierarchy—social and grammatical—are already apparent in the novel's introduction, in the narrator's reflection on the "gride," and in Azzeccagarbugli's discussion with Renzo concerning the laws and their meaning; and they are presented with special force in the story of Fra Cristoforo's encounter with the irascible young nobleman in Chapter 4 and in the scene of the friar's exchange with Don Rodrigo in Chapter 6, in each of

which questions of hierarchy assume the primary focus of the narrative.[6] Because of the complexities of the laws of social conduct as explained in the first of these two scenes, the problem between the nobleman and Lodovico (soon to become Cristoforo) may appear to be merely a matter of interpretation, of understanding the differences between the old behavioral codes of chivalry and the new ones of the bourgeoisie. In fact, however, the encounter is due as much to the pettiness and the overbearing pride of *both* parties as to the contradictions within the laws of conduct and the dispute is finally resolved not by intricate interpretation but by the violence that cuts through and thus renders mute all artificial questions of hierarchy and privilege.

It is important to see, in these and other scenes, that Manzoni's polemic is not directed *against* the hierarchical ordering of the rules of human society but rather *toward* the knowledgeable readjustment of such hierarchies along the lines of revealed Christian truth.[7] As becomes apparent in the postprandial exchange between Far Cristoforo and Don Rodrigo, moreover, Manzoni's polemic is actually two-pronged, since it is for worldly use within a hierarchically ordered set of values and against either disuse or incorrectly ordered hierarchies. At the same time, Manzoni's position is further refined by his concern not just for "doing good" but also for avoiding "doing evil."

The exchange between Don Rodrigo and Fra Cristoforo underscores the hierarchical nature of language as a social phenomenon when the angered nobleman describes his usual procedures for teaching his inferiors to speak properly (p. 92). The eventual reversal of fortune in the hierarchy of worldly power between Renzo and Don Rodrigo is also given special linguistic emphasis in Chapter 35 when the Capuchin encourages Renzo to forgive Don Rodrigo through blessing (*bene dire*).[8] But the centra event that demonstrates the importance of linguistic and social hierarchy—and its breakdown through violence—is the arrival of the plague itself and the total disorder and confusion that it brings with it.[9] In Chapter 31, moreover, one of the first institutions portrayed as being affected by the plague is—perhaps not unexpectedly, given the novel's habitual concerns—language itself. As in the novel's initial discussions of the "gride," Manzoni again concentrates on the use and abuse of language in the state's official pronouncements and particularly on its equivocations regarding the name to be given the pestilence, which goes from "non peste" to "febbri pestilenziali" before at last being officially called "peste." After generalizing on the all too common examples of gradually increasing errors in the history of human expression, in which words and ideas often do not coincide in any transparent fashion, Manzoni's narrator concludes, in a passage mentioned earlier in the context of Renzo's escape, by offering first a "metodo" of proceeding that demonstrates Manzoni's confidence in regard to human potential and then a lament that shows his pessimism in regard to actual human practice. This passage is perhaps worth citing in its entirety:

> In principio dunque, non peste, assolutamente no, per nessun conto: proibito anche di proferire il vocabolo.

Poi febbri pestilenziali: l'idea s'ammette per isbieco in un aggettivo. Poi, non vera peste; vale a dire peste sì, ma in un certo senso; non peste proprio, ma una cosa alla quale non si sa trovare un altro nome. Finalmente, peste senza dubbio, e senza contrasto: ma già ci s'è attaccata un'altra idea, l'idea del venefizio e del malefizio, la quale altera e confonde l'idea espressa dalla parola che non si può più mandare indietro.

Non è, credo, necessario d'esser molto versato nella storia dell'idee e delle parole, per vedere che molte hanno fatto un simil corso. Per grazie del cielo, che non sono molte quelle d'una tal sorte, e d'una tal importanza, e che conquistino la loro evidenza a un tal prezzo, e alle quali si possano attaccare accessòri d'un tal genere. Si potrebbe però, tanto nelle cose piccole, come nelle grandi, evitare, in gran parte, quel corso così lungo e così storto, prendendo il metodo proposto da tanto tempo, d'osservare, ascoltare, paragonare, pensare, prima di parlare.

Ma parlare, questa cosa così sola, e talmente più facile di tutte quel-l'altre insieme, che anche noi, dico noi uomini in generale, siamo un po' da compatire.

(p. 542-43)

The damage done to language by man's reaction to the plague is not different in kind from that which periodically afflicts, and progressively contaminates, the relationship between words and ideas, though it is far more severe. Indeed, the temptation to use language too freely, and so to abuse its true meaning and propriety, is one that is shared even by the narrator, as part of the human condition ("anche noi, dico noi uomini in generale" (p. 543). It is probably a simplification to say that, with the passing of the plague, language as well as everything else in the novel is put right again, and that in fact all is better than before. Nevertheless, something of the sort is the case, because this is, of course, the general motion of Manzoni's *commedia.* The absolution of Lucia from her vow, which Fra Cristoforo, as the worldly instrument of God's word (p. 637), accomplishes by placing one good alongside another and choosing between them in the hierarchically ordered Christian system of values, is a part of this process, as had been Renzo's pardoning of Don Rodrigo. It is also true that, after the passing of the plague and the completion of Renzo and Lucia's union, many of the linguistic practices that earlier had presented difficulties are now acceptable as an aspect of the new order of things. Don Abbondio's Latin, now "honest, sacrosanct" rather than guileful, is no longer offensive to Renzo (p. 663), and even the references to Lucia in Bergamo as "quella bella *baggiana*" are taken for honest admiration (as the narrator remarks approvingly, "L'epiteto faceva passare il sostantivo," p. 671).

But despite the temptation to view the plague primarily as a terrifying yet arbitrarily conceived and introduced *deus ex machina,* as an important yet mechanical device that intervenes from outside the story to remove all difficulties and set everything straight, the plague's role in the story should not be taken lightly. Rather than being an external phenomenon in relation to the thematic development of the novel, the plague is part and parcel of a cluster of themes that have been inextricably present since the very beginning of the story (and fairly obvious since Lodovico's death in Chapter 4 and the initially humorous though later deeply serious moral, social, and physical confusion of the attempted but thwarted trickeries in the village in Chapter 8). The primary components of this narrative cluster are, first, various forms of reciprocal violence and, second, the lengthy process of decay that leads to chaos and then to sacrifice before it culminates in the reinstitution of a newly sanctified order. That this process plays itself out on the level of language as well as on those of other social, moral, and religious institutions demonstrates the all encompassing nature of these Girardian thematics in Manzoni's text.[10] The wager voiced between Don Rodrigo and Attilio, his "colleague" and at the same time his rival in libertinism and bullying (p. 78), also shows the power of mimetic desire within Manzoni's story (i.e. Don Rodrigo desires Lucia in large measure because he perceives that Attilio desires her, and Don Rodrigo perseveres in his otherwise unlikely plot because of his pride and his concern for his reputation, which is to say, his concern for the way in which others perceive him). Don Rodrigo thus demonstrates the sort of melodramatically active and profane desire that is the other side of the narrator's own benignly chaste (i.e. idealistically Romantic) though only slightly less obvious feelings for Lucia (p. 256). The disconcerting hubris of Don Rodrigo's attitude toward Attilio's death, moreover, quickly turns him into the uncanny double of all of the plague's other victims, thus extending his role past that of an individual villain into that of the communal scapegoat, at once the embodiment and the carrier of all that is evil in regard to both cruelty and sexual transgression. In Girardian terms, therefore, it is not a coincidence that Don Rodrigo shows the unmistakable signs of the plague immediately after his evening of wine and his hubristic mock eulogy for his dead cousin.[11]

The Unnamed, of course, would have been the prime candidate for this part, especially after the abduction of Lucia and his symbolic usurpation of Don Rodrigo's role, however temporary, in relation to her. But the Unnamed's conversion short-circuits such a fate. It also, surprisingly enough, indicates the eventual turn of the narrative's entire representation of society away from the corrupted hierarchy of chivalry—Spanish, petty, and thoroughly decadent, the type of social order in which the unrestrained treachery of Don Rodrigo, a mediocre man yet one inhabited by the devil (p. 309), could not only exist but also dominate—and toward the newly (re)established power and authority of traditional Christian values.[12] It is important to see, therefore, that what Renzo and Lucia learn from the entire arc of their experience, and are free to express after the plague has first reunited them and then passed, is not a group of lessons adduced by the narrator at the story's conclusion like a handful of morals plucked from the body of the story and tacked onto its conclusion at the last minute. Rather, they represent the lessons embedded in the entire process of decadence, violence, and reestablished (though inherently precarious) hierarchical order that has been an integral part of the narrative's subject matter, in its representation of all levels of society, from the very start.

But what exactly do Renzo and Lucia learn from their "adventures," or, better yet, what are we as readers intended to make of what they say they have learned? The narrator's report of Renzo's recapitulation of his own story and his account of what he has learned from it follows two paragraphs of description of the young couple's current circumstances. According to this passage, Renzo's business is going extremely well, and he and Lucia, as new arrivals in the region of Bergamo, have been granted a special exemption from the local taxes ("Per i nostri fu una nuova cuccagna," p. 672). Before a year of marriage has ended they have a baby girl, named not surprisingly for the Virgin, and thereafter follow others of both sexes, all of whom, Renzo decides, must learn to read and write, "dicendo che, giacché la c'era questa birberia, dovevano almeno profittarne anche loro." Lucia, of course, understands a great deal more than her husband and, despite her usually quiet nature, speaks the crucial lesson at the narrative's conclusion. But before that, at the end of the narrator's telescoped description of the couple's present life, Renzo gets to his list of individual lessons:

> "Ho imparato . . . a non mettermi ne' tumulti: ho imparato a non predicare in piazza: ho imparato a guardare con chi parlo: ho imparato a non alzar troppo il gomito: ho imparato a non tenere in mano il martello delle porte, quando c'è lì d'intorno gente che ha la testa calda: ho imparato a non attaccarmi un campanello al piede, prima d'aver pensato quel che possa nascere." E cent'altre cose.

All of these individual lessons (regardless of Renzo's notable and continuing personal limitations) derive primarily from what is, for Renzo, the story's germinating center, made up of his experiences in Milan in the novel's middle chapters. The *ritornello* of "ho imparato," however, along with its connection to the acts of discourse (making speeches and paying attention to those with whom one speaks) ties this concluding litany to the entire process of linguistic and social education that begins, in regard to Renzo, with the exhortation from Azzeccagarbugli to learn to speak properly, and in regard to the novel as a whole, with the narrator's explanation of his linguistic aims and procedures in the story's introduction. In both cases, though in different ways, the goal of this process has been the attainment of the ability to *use* language and other forms of behavior to make one's way in the world of humanity, in what is now a symbolically and literally purged society.

IV

Manzoni's feelings as a Christian writer demonstrate a further concern for the communicative powers of language in his relation to his own text. As Manzoni's various reflections on the aesthetics of narrative fiction attest (though with markedly differing measures of optimism and pessi-

mism during different periods of his life), in his view the historical novel attempts to unite the effects of two distinct sorts of writing, poetry, broadly defined, and history. Traditionally, this sort of distinction might have lead to a further one, that, roughly speaking, between creating and reporting. But in regard to *I promessi sposi* this was not Manzoni's concept. For Manzoni, history already contained the evidence of divine Providence, and so of the *one* Creator, in its course, however difficult or even impossible to discern this evidence might be. The writer's goal, as Olga Ragusa has pointed out in regard to Manzoni's Romantic aesthetic theories, was not to create but to find the suitable object to *re*-create.[13] The writer's distinctive imaginative skill lay both in conceiving of that object and in imitating it in the most effective manner possible. If he could succeed in getting his re-presentation of "history" right (i.e., both imaginatively effective *and* seemingly transparent), then that representation would contain, and at the same time bear witness to, the immanent signs of truth's meaning with which the Creator, through Providence, had already endowed the world's story.[14] The exceptional ambition of his project, and the responsibility Manzoni felt for it as a devout Christian, suggest some of the reasons for his agonizing over the novel both before and after its publication.

At the same time, the thoroughgoing nature of the novel's representational aesthetic, with its religious as well as artistic rationales, explains in large part why—after the introduction—the tale most often turns back on the manner of its telling only in secondary ways, like the habitual broaching but then stylized curtailment of such topics as fictional representation and the status and fortunes of books in the world of the present as well as in the historical past.[15] In the published versions of the novel, moreover, this same restraint is generally evident in Manzoni's self-reflexive commentaries on authors and their audience, including Manzoni's actual readership, as well as in his invitations, or at times his challenges, to his readers to fill in the novel's gaps in representation (which remain brief *boutades* rather than the harangues or the extended excurses of *Fermo e Lucia*). However, there is a further example of literary self-reflexivity in *I promessi sposi* that is striking both in its openness and in the aura of skepticism surrounding it. The passage in question, which again deals specifically with questions of language, is a lengthy explanation in Chapter 27. It picks up the thread of the narrator's various earlier references to books and writing (and particularly the discussions of Renzo the "poet" and of the requirements of intelligibility for printed books in Chapter 14). In Chapter 27, the narrator's commentary begins with consideration of the inevitable gaps between intention, linguistic reproduction, and meaning in the letters written and interpreted by the "letterati" for Agnese and Renzo. The "letterato," similar to Manzoni's narrator in relation to the story's anonymous manuscript, is not content merely to copy out whatever he is told but feels obliged both to put whatever it is in literary form *and* to improve on it. These considerations would not be so obviously disturbing if they did not go on to include a self-consciously pointed discussion of the language of *published* authors. Such writers—explicitly including Manzoni himself—are in fact prey to the same pitfalls in the relationship between words, things, and human understanding and are thus victims of the same problems in the praxis of writing:

> Con tutto ciò, al letterato suddetto non gli riesce sempre di dire tutto quel che vorrebbe; qualche volta gli accade di dire tutt'altro: *accade anche a noi altri, che scriviamo per la stampa.*

(p. 464, my italics)

That this process of error and confusion is then seen to extend past writing to *reading* and interpretation (including, in this instance, Renzo's fury with the "lettore interprete") confirms our earlier consideration of Manzoni's concerns for his book as a meaningful product in the world of everyday communication even while it casts those concerns in a remarkably uncertain and troubled light.

Once again, part of this uncertainty stems from Manzoni's concept of communication not only in terms of logic but also in terms of religious truth. Even though, within Manzoni's religious system, language's relation to its referents may not finally be accidental or arbitrary (the question occupying the story's anonymous chronicler at the very point at which Manzoni's narrator breaks off his transcription), man cannot *know* the precise nature of the motivation between names and things, signs and referents, since *that* knowledge is restricted to the barred realm of Providence's source. Sometimes, as in "Lucia," the relation may seem to be clear by divine intention, or, as in "Cristoforo," it may appear meaningful both beyond and also within human design; but usually understanding, and in all cases complete certainty, is reserved to one realm alone.

This abdication of final authority on the part of the worldly author helps to account for the fact that ***I promessi sposi,*** even when it is self-conscious of its language, is most often not overly disturbed or disturbing in that regard. Like the organizing effects of Romantic irony itself, moreover, this abdication makes the narrative into a seemingly closed system, though one in which closure is raised to the second power, wherein resides the will of the true Author. But at the same time it is essential to see that this abdication, this very lack of certainty, cuts both ways, since it returns to disrupt Manzoni's text to such a degree that no amount of self-conscious apologetics can finally resolve the continuing doubts about not just the *use* but also the *ends* of novelistic discourse. Given this impasse, all that man can do, as is affirmed by the narrator, Fra Cristoforo, and eventually even Renzo (whose offspring would now in theory be able to read about and thus to follow their forebear's lesson in Manzoni's book), is to learn to use language, despite all its inherent difficulties and pitfalls, as well and therefore as effectively as possible. As far as the novel is concerned, this ability, within the limits of mankind's intellectual and moral capacities and his social opportunities, can help to furnish the keys to the kingdom of this world, if not the next. At the narrative's conclusion, as

for Manzoni himself through the entire novel, this turns out to be no small prize and no meager responsibility, either for the story's characters, striving to live and communicate in their world, or for Manzoni in his.

Notes

1. All references are to *I promessi sposi. Testo critico della edizione definitiva del 1840. Tutte le opere di Alessandro Manzoni,* 2, tome 1, ed. Alberto Chiari and Fausto Ghisalberti, I classici Mondadori (Milan: Mondadori, 1954).

2. This point is also made by Sergio Romagnoli in "Lingua e società nei *Promessi sposi,*" in *Atti del convegno manzoniano di Nimega (16-17-18 ottobre 1973),* ed. Carlo Ballerini. Istituto di lingua e letteratura italiana dell'Università Cattolica di Nimega e Istituto di Cultura per i Paesi Bassi (Florence: Libreria Editrice Fiorentina, 1979), pp. 126-59; rpt. in Romagnoli's *Manzoni e i suoi colleghi,* Nuovi saggi (Florence: Sansoni, 1984), pp. 35-64.

3. In *L'avventura della parola nei "Promessi sposi",* L'ippogrifo, 21 (Rome: Bonacci, 1980), pp. 42-43. De Rienzo, who sees the word as both the entry to and the embodiment of the worldly "regno del possibile," goes on to characterize Don Rodrigo, somewhat too grandiosely, as "l'eroe negativo della parola" (p. 43). He eventually fills out this scheme through consideration of l'Innominato, Fra Cristoforo, Don Abbondio, and Federigo Borromeo, as well as through discussion of Renzo's liguistic education and Lucia's silence. De Rienzo's perspective is limited by his continued emphasis on language as an act in itself, that is, apart from the other wordly gestures and attitudes that are essential to language's meaning and force. Despite this limitation, however, his book is a landmark in the study of linguistic self-consciousness in Manzoni's novel.

4. The term *Bildungsroman* is used by Giovanni Getto, who sees Renzo's experience in Milan (Chapter 14) as the key to his ongoing education in *Letture Manzoniane* (Florence: Sansoni, 1964), p. 241. In this regard, see also Guido Baldi, "La ribellione di Renzo tra Eden e storia," in *Da Dante al Novecento. Studi critici offerti dagli scolari a Giovanni Getto nel suo ventesimo anno di insegnamento universitario* (Milan: Mursia, 1970), pp. 485-512. For more recent treatments of this aspect of Renzo's story see: Romagnoli, "Lingua e società nei *Promessi Sposi*"; Mary Ambrose, "Error and Abuse of Language in the 'promessi sposi,'" *Modern Language Review,* 72 (1977), 62-72; Giorgio Ficara, "Renzo, l'allievo delle Muse," *Lettere italiane,* 29 (1977), 34-58; De Rienzo, pp. 107-37; and Robert S. Dombroski, *L'apologia del vero. Lettura ed interpretazione dei 'Promessi Sposi',* Guide di cultura contemporanea (Padua: Liviana, 1984), pp. 35-66.

5. No one has reacted to this scene more appropriately than Attilio Momigliano, who, with exquisite sensi-

259

bility, describes the innkeeper as Rembrantesque and comments that the visual qualities of the portrayal of the crowd of drinkers bring to mind the paintings of Van Ostade, in *Alessandro Manzoni*, 5th ed. (Milan-Messina: Principato, 1958), p. 267.

6. In a different context, Jean-Pierre Barricelli has noted that the effects of hierarchy, along with elaborate obstruction and closure, are even at work in Manzoni's composition of place, particularly in the novel's description of the path, the walls, and the cliffs and valleys of the opening paragraphs. See "Structure and Symbol in Manzoni's *I Promessi Sposi*," *PMLA* 87 (1972), 499-507.

7. The polemical nature of *I Promessi Sposi*, discussion of which began as soon as the novel was published, led Benedetto Croce (in this instance borrowing his terminology from Giuseppe Citanna, with whom Croce exchanged opinions on Manzoni in *La critica* in the 1920's) to declare Manzoni's novel an "opera oratoria." See: Croce, *Alessandro Manzoni. Saggi e discussioni*, 4th ed., Biblioteca di cultura moderna, 191 (Bari: Laterza, 1952), pp. 105-11, 146; and Citanna, *Storia della letteratura italiana. Volume terzo. Ottocento,* 2nd ed. (Milan: Garzanti, 1954), pp. 40-63. For an important continuation of this once lively discussion, see Luigi Russo, "Alessandro Manzoni poëta an orator?" (1941), in *Ritratti e disegni storici. Serie quarta. Dal Manzoni al De Sanctis e la letteratura dell'Italia unita,* New ed., La civiltà europea (Florence: Sansoni, 1965), pp. 109-47.

8. On the importance of this term in the novel, see Ficara, "Le parole e la peste in Manzoni," *Lettere italiane,* 33 (1981), 3-37.

9. In regard to the chaos and reciprocal violence that the plague in literature (including *I Promessi Sposi*) both symbolizes and further incites, see René Girard, "The Plague in Literature and Myth" (1974), in *"To double business bound": Essays on Literature, Mimesis, and Anthropology* (Baltimore: Johns Hopkins Univ. Press, 1978), pp. 136-54. See also Dombroski, "The Ideological Question in Manzoni," *Studies in Romanticism,* 20 (1981), 497-524, especially pp. 515-24, trans. and rev. in *L'apologia del vero,* pp. 67-96, especially pp. 86-96; and Ficara, "Le parole e la peste in Manzoni."

10. Girard is succinctly explicit on this cluster of themes in "The Plague in Literature and Myth," pp. 148-49. For his most recent treatment of this subject see *Le Bouc émissaire* (Paris: Grasset, 1983), especially pp. 7-36.

11. Girard discusses similar effects of hubristic pride and the communal doubling of sudden victimage in Artaud's work (treated by Girard in the context of Shakespeare and Dostoevski) in "The Plague in Literature and Myth," p. 149.

12. In terms of the *symbolism* of narrative organization, this conversion and shift also help save Lucia's

honor, since one of the primary aspects in certain mythic representations of the scapegoat's role is sexual union with a beautiful maiden prior to his ritual expulsion or murder. The role of the scapegoat in modern literature, including this aspect of it, is discussed by John B. Vickery in his *Myths and Texts: Strategies of Incorporation and Displacement* (Baton Rouge: Louisiana State Univ. Press, 1983), pp. 43-45, 102-47.

13. See Ragusa's "Imitation and Originality in Manzoni's Romantic Theory," *Le parole e le idée,* 6 (1964), 219-28. On the development and the complexity of Manzoni's aesthetic theories, in his own writings as well as in relation to competing theories of the period, see also: Barbara Reynolds, *The Linguistic Writings of Alessandro Manzoni: A Textual and Chronological Reconstruction* (Cambridge: W. Heffer & Sons, 1950); Dante Isella, "Introduzione," in *Postille al vocabolario della Crusca nell'edizione veronese,* ed. Dante Isella. Documenti di filologia, 7 (Milan: Ricciardi, 1964), pp. vii-xviii; and Mario Puppo, *Poesia e verità. Interpretazioni manzoniane,* Biblioteca di cultura contemporanea, 137 (Messina-Florence: D'Anna, 1979). For brief commentaries on the close relation in Manzoni's thought between language and its practical use in society, see: Maria Corti, "Uno scrittore in cerca della lingua," *L'approdo letterario,* 10 (1964), p. 12; and Vittorio Spinazzola, ed., *I promessi sposi,* 3rd ed., I Garzanti, 382 (Milan: Garzanti, 1972), p. 11 (and for more extensive, if also more diffuse treatment, see Spinazzola, *Il libro per tutti. Saggio sui 'Promessi sposi'* Nuova biblioteca di cultura, 246 [Rome: Riuniti, 1983]). On the relation between rhetoric and logic in Manzoni's aesthetic theories, with particular attention to the *Storia della colonna infame,* see Angelo R. Pupino, *"Il vero solo è bello." Manzoni tra retorica e logica,* Saggi, 221 (Bologna: Il Mulino, 1982). Romano Amerio discusses Manzoni's views of the importance of both language's *use* in the world and its potential for *abuse* (as one key to human error) in his extensive commentary on *La morale cattolica, Osservazioni sulla morale cattolica,* ed. Romano Amerio, 3 vols. (Milan-Naples: Ricciardi, 1965), III, 106-17, 125-27.

14. In regard to general questions of Manzoni's style as technique and meaning, see: (on style and the mixture of narrative voices) Giuseppe De Robertis, *Primi studi manzoniani e altre cose,* Quaderni di letteratura e d'arte (Florence: Le Monnier, 1949), pp. 3-110; (on style as both form and sense) Giovanni Nencioni, "Conversazioni dei Promessi Sposi," *La rassegna della letteratura italiana,* 60 (1956), 53-68; (on linguistic parodies) Giorgio Petrocchi, *La tecnica manzoniana del dialogo,* Saggi di letteratura italiana, 10 (Florence: Le Monnier, 1959); (on rhetorical levels and stylistics) Giorgio Bàrberi Squarotti, *Teoria e prove dello stile di Manzoni,* I quaderni di Sigma (Milan: Silva, 1965); (on

literary irony and social class) Guido Guglielmi, *Ironia e negazione,* La ricerca letteraria, Serie critica, 24 (Turin: Einaudi, 1974); and (on irony and metalanguage) Ezio Raimondi, *Il romanzo senza idillio. Saggio sui Promessi Sposi* (Turin: Einaudi, 1974), pp. 223-47, 250-307.

15. The most important treatments of the effects and the implications of self-consciousness in *I Promessi Sposi,* all of which have been mentioned earlier in regard to specific issues, are: Romagnoli; Raimondi; Ambrose; Ficara, "Renzo, l'allievo delle Muse" and "Le parole e la peste in Manzoni"; De Rienzo; and Spinazzola, *Il libro per tutti,* especially pp. 219-76. There is also an early and extremely impressionistic (though lengthy) treatment of the topic by Giuseppe Sertoli, "Lettura metaromanzesca della prima pagina dei 'Promessi Sposi,'" *Il cristallo,* 13 (1971), 67-86. Joanna Richardson's recent structuralist reading of the novel, "Narrative Strategy in *I promessi sponsi,*" *Neophilologus,* 68 (1984), 214-24, points toward (though does not actually provide) another way of treating the "dédoublement" (p. 223) of the nineteenth-century narrator in relation to Manzoni's novel.

Verina R. Jones (essay date 1991)

SOURCE: "Manzoni's Dark Ladies," in *Romance Studies,* Vol. 19, Winter, 1991, pp. 37-52.

[*In the following essay, Jones discusses Manzoni's use of only dark-haired women in* I promessi sposi *as it departs from the canon's tradition of differentiating between virtuous blond-haired and treacherous dark-haired women.*]

> "'I didn't finish the book," said Maggie. ". . . I'm determined to read no more books where the blonde-haired women carry away all the happiness . . . If you could give me some story, now, where the dark woman triumphs, it would restore the balance. I want to avenge Rebecca and Flora MacIvor, and Minna and all the rest of the dark unhappy ones.'"
>
> *(The Mill on the Floss,* Book 5, Chapter 1)

There are no blonde women in Manzoni's novel. Both the heroine, good, sweet, shy, homely Lucia, and the counter-heroine, glamorous, imperious, treacherous Gertrude, are dark. What follows is an investigation of the modes and significance of this infringement of the canon.

That the literary tradition demanded a sharp differentiation between the blonde woman and the dark woman, with the blonde woman representing the positive pole, is well established. It is a differentiation that is all pervasive, at least within European culture. Within this tradition, what celebrations there are of the dark beauty more often than not merely reinforce the stereotype by presenting themselves as infringements of the norm. In this sense, the dark bride in the Song of Songs, who defines herself as 'dark but comely', not 'dark and comely', may constitute an archetype. But on the other hand, different periods and different literary genres appear to confer on this all pervasive stereotype varying patterns and meanings, which are worth outlining.[1]

1. THE CANON

In both Medieval and Renaissance literature blonde hair is always a prerogative of beauty, at least in women. Dark hair, when it is mentioned at all, tends to designate evil and treachery, and because it is taken for granted that goodness equals beauty, then blondeness becomes a sign of both beauty and goodness. Very few ugly women are actually described, and the blonde woman reigns supreme. If we take a random list of famous women in European literature, we find that the colour of their hair is either not specified (such is the case with Dante's Beatrice), or else it is blonde. Blonde are Petrarch's Laura, Sydney's Stella, Ariosto's Angelica, Shakespeare's Desdemona, and many more.

In fact Angelica, daughter of the emperor of Catai, is, as has been said, 'l'unica cinese bionda che sia mai esistita'. This illustrates better than anything the non-referential nature of the blonde/dark dichotomy. Angelica is blonde because she is beautiful, and because the literary tradition demands that beautiful women should be blonde, not because of any link with an extra-textual reality. Equally, the literary tradition imposes the same norm both within cultures where one might expect an abundance of blonde hair in reality, such as in Northern Europe, and in Southern European cultures, where the opposite would be the case. The colour of the hair can be considered therefore the primary element of the literary canon as such. The other feature which is normally mentioned in descriptions of beauty, the eyes, appears to take on more of a mimetic quality: while in Anglo-Saxon literature beauties have blue or grey eyes, in Italian and Spanish literature black eyes are the norm.

Blonde hair as a prerequisite of beauty, in fact pre-dates medieval literature. As M. B. Ogle has commented 'this reign of the blonde in modern literature is but a continuation of her reign in the literature of Greece and Rome . . . the Roman love-poets and the later Greek writers of romance and erotic letters, give to the ladies whom they desire to praise the same golden or auburn hair . . . their models, the Greek Alexandrian poets, praise the same blonde type . . . the Greek heroes and heroines, gods and goddesses, with one or two prominent exceptions, are described as blondes by Homer and the early poets.'[2] The principal channels of distribution of this stereotype, and of the whole complex cluster of conventions that accompanies it, are, according to Ogle, initially the rhetorical schools, and then, with the Renaissance, Italian lyric poetry.[3]

Giovanni Pozzi, in his detailed analyses of the shifting canons presiding over the portrayal of beauty in literature, has argued that, although a body of conventions goes right back to classical antiquity, a proper normative code only comes into being with the Middle Ages, and lasts until about the early seventeenth century, petering out with the Arcadia.[4] In the process of formation of the code a key role was played by Petrarch. After Petrarch the lyrical tradition was controlled by a rigid canon (which Pozzi has designated as 'canone breve'), which only allowed mention of a limited number of anatomical items, chosen mainly from among facial features (hair, eyes, cheeks, lips), with the possible addition of one more item chosen from among neck, hand and breast. This was accompanied by an accentuation of the use of metaphors as against literal designations, and by a reduction of the motivations underlying the metaphors to those of splendour and colour. There was to be only a limited roster of permitted colours (yellow, red, and white), and only a limited number of tropes to designate such colours: gold or amber for yellow, roses for red, with a wider range for white, which included ivory, snow, marble and pearls.

Not only does the golden hair continue to reign supreme, but it is also the most prominent feature in instances of infringement of the code. Very often a dark beauty serves, paradoxically, to reinforce the canon precisely through being, like the dark bride of the Song of Songs, dark *but* beautiful, as in Tasso's 'Bruna sei tu ma bella', which begins in fact with the line 'Bella sei tu, ma bruna'. Or else, it may signal a parodistic intent, or a self-consciously low poetic composition, both of which, of course, can only be defined in opposition to the canon which controls high poetry.[5]

Such appears to be, in its broad outlines, the pattern surrounding the blonde/dark dichotomy in the lyrical tradition. In other types of poetry, such as narrative or allegorical, although the code may function in different and less rigid ways, golden hair still reigns supreme as a sign of beauty.

When it comes to modern narrative the situation is far less clear-cut. While lyric poetry is exquisitely non-referential and self-consciously codified according to rigorously defined patterns, the novel is situated at the opposite pole. By its very nature the modern novel is self-consciously referential, overtly rejecting the mediation of literary codes, indeed of literariness *per se*. And yet the opposition between blonde-haired women and the 'dark unhappy ones' still persists, even though in modified forms, and clearly quite apart from any reference to extra-textual reality.

Unfortunately, the canon, such as it is, governing this aspect of the portrait in the novel, although it is very frequently referred to, tends to be taken for granted rather than investigated, so that in fact surprisingly little is actually known about its pattern (or patterns) and its functioning.

Wellek and Warren have defined the dichotomy in the following terms: 'The blonde is the home-maker, unexciting but steady and sweet. The brunette—passionate, violent, mysterious, alluring, and untrustworthy—gathers up the characteristics of the Oriental, the Jewish, the Spanish, and the Italian as seen from the point of view of the "Anglo-Saxon"'. And Northrop Frye identifies a 'very common convention of the nineteenth-century novel' in the 'use of two heroines, one dark and one light', and then defines the dark heroine as being 'as a rule passionate, haughty, plain, foreign or Jewish, and in some way associated with the undesirable or with some kind of forbidden fruit like incest'. And this is, on the whole, as far as it goes in terms of generalized statements on the issue.[6]

So, the dark woman in the novel can be beautiful, indeed may be more glamorous than the blonde, but cannot be good. But what kind of beauty is the dark beauty?

Much work still remains to be done on this question, but it seems to me that two useful points of departure are Utter and Needham's observations regarding the masculinity of the dark woman, on the one hand, and Mario Praz's notion of the 'tainted beauty' which he discusses in his famous seminal work *The Romantic Agony* on the other.[7]

Starting from an examination of *Waverley*'s Flora McIver (as it happens, one of Maggie Tulliver's 'dark unhappy ones'), Utter and Needham remark on her 'most striking resemblance to her brother Fergus . . . the same dark eyes, eye-lashes, and eye-brows', while 'the haughty and somewhat stern regularity of Fergus's features, was beautifully softened in those of Flora', and come to the conclusion that Scott's 'purpose is . . . to show the brunette as a feminized version of the man', while the 'blonde is every inch the woman in her own right' (pp. 200-201). This raises important questions to do with the construction/reconstruction of the feminine, as opposed to the female character, in the literary tradition, a path fleetingly, and rather obviously, trodden by Gilbert and Gubar.[8]

And it would seem that into the nineteenth-century typology of the dark woman also converges that complex knot of traits investigated by Praz as the syndrome of the 'tainted beauty'. The typical iconographic traits of the *femme fatale,* pale skin and dark hair and eyes, suggesting in their turn pain, corruption, and mystery, originate with that 'fascination of corruption' which develops throughout the eighteenth century, and becomes fixed initially in a series of male figures: Schiller's *Räuber* Karl Moor, Byron's bandits, as well as the more obvious figures of 'banditti' and adventurers of the Gothic novel, of which Radcliffe's Schedoni is probably the most famous (Praz, pp. 51-81).

We will assume, then, that in the novel the blonde woman is normally good and not necessarily beautiful, while the dark woman is evil or unhappy or both, often glamorously endowed with a tainted kind of beauty, often disturbingly ambiguous in her feminine/masculine identification.

How, and why, does Manzoni go against the norm?

2. THE TWO PORTRAITS

Lucia, a peasant girl, is constructed according to the archetype of the persecuted maiden. Her story, which takes place in seventeenth-century Lombardy, is triggered by her persecution by the local feudal lord: her impending marriage to Renzo is prevented, she is forced to flee her village in order to escape kidnapping by her persecutor, and the eventual happy ending happens after a series of further vicissitudes which see her alternately aided and oppressed by a variety of helpers and villains. One such villain is Gertrude, the 'signora' of the convent to which Lucia is first directed in her search for sanctuary, but who in fact betrays her and becomes instrumental in her kidnapping. Gertrude is also the protagonist of a sub-narrative of her own. This consists of a detailed account of the family pressures which led her, the younger daughter of Spanish grandees, to enter the convent against her wishes, and of her subsequent affair with a local thug which triggers both her involvement in the murder of a fellow nun and, later, in the betrayal of Lucia.

Temperamentally as well as diegetically, the two women are the opposite of each other: Lucia is gentle, modest, shy, retiring, unassuming, while Gertrude is arrogant, haughty, sexually aware. Textually, they are constructed as both antithetical and identical: they are in many ways the negative specular image of each other.[9] This opposition/identity is apparent throughout the text of the novel in a variety of ways, not least in their physical portraits.

It is important to keep in mind that Manzoni's novel went through three major stages of re-writing, because this allows us to examine the workshop that lies behind the text. Very often, it is precisely the tortuous history of certain sections of the text that will give a clue to the drift presiding over the construction/reconstruction of our two dark ladies.[10]

Of both women we are given physical portraits at the point when they are first introduced; on the occasion of the wedding that is not to be, in the case of Lucia, and for Gertrude when Lucia first sets eyes on her when entering the convent.[11]

    a. Lucia.

Lucia usciva in quel momento tutta attillata dalle mani della madre. *Le amiche si rubavano la sposa,* e le facevan forza perchè si lasciasse vedere; e lei s'andava schermendo, con quella modestia un po' guerriera delle contadine, facendosi scudo alla faccia col gomito, chinandola sul busto, e aggrottando i lunghi e neri sopraccigli, mentre però *la bocca s'apriva al sorriso.* [neither the eyebrows nor the smile are mentioned in *FL.* (***Fermio e Lucia***)] *I neri* e giovanili *capelli, spartiti sopra la fronte, con una bianca e sottile drizzatura,* si ravvolgevan dietro il capo, in cerchi moltiplici di trecce, trapassate da lunghi spilli d'argento, che si dividevano all'intorno, quasi a guisa de' *raggi d'un'aureola* [*FL*: e ravvolti col resto delle chiome dietro il capo in una treccia tonda e raggomitolata a foggia di tanti cerchi, e trapunta da grossi spilli d'argento che s'aggiravano intorno alla testa in guisa d'una [*sic*] *diadema,* vol. 3, t. I, chapter 2, p. 42] *come ancora usano le contadine nel Milanese.* Intorno al collo aveva un vezzo di granati alternati con bottoni d'oro a filigrana: *portava un bel*

busto di broccato a fiori, con le maniche separate e allacciate da bei nastri: *una corta gonnella* di filaticcio di seta, a pieghe fitte e minute, *due calze vermiglie,* due pianelle, di seta anch'esse, a ricami. Oltre a questo, ch'era l'ornamento particolare del giorno delle nozze, Lucia aveva quello quotidiano d'una *modesta bellezza',* a variant of *FL*: 'quello quotidiano che consisteva in *due occhi neri vivi,* e modesti, e un volto di una regolare e *non comune bellezza',* vol. 3, pp. 791-92] rilevata allora e accresciuta dalle varie affezioni che le si dipingevan sul viso: *una gioia temperata da un turbamento leggiero,* quel *placido accoramento che si mostra di quand' in quando sul volto delle spose,* e, *senza scompor la bellezza,* le dà un carattere particolare.

               (vol. 1, chapter 2, p. 38).

a. At that moment Lucia was just coming, all dressed up, from her mother's hands. *Her friends were bustling round the bride* and making her show herself off; and she was defending herself, with the rather aggressive modesty of peasant girls, shielding her face with her elbow, dropping it over her breast, and drawing her long black eyebrows down in a frown yet with *her lips parted in a smile.* Her *black* young *hair* was *divided over her forehead in a fine white parting,* and wound round behind her head in multiple plaited coils, pierced by long silver hairpins which splayed out almost like *the rays of a halo,* [*FL*: which encompassed her head like a diadem] *as are still worn by the peasant women of Lombardy* Around her neck she had a necklace of garnets alternating with filigree gold beads; *she wore a fine bodice* of flowered *brocade,* with the cuffs open and laced with beautiful ribbons, a *short* silk *skirt* with tiny tight pleats, *scarlet stockings,* and a pair of slippers also embroidered in silk. Apart from these special ornaments for her wedding day, Lucia had the everyday one of her *modest beauty,* [a variant of *FL*: the everyday one which consisted of a pair of *black eyes, lively and modest,* and a face of harmonious and *uncommon beauty*] heightened and brought out at this moment by the various emotions crossing her face: *joy tempered by a slight agitation, and the quiet melancholy which sometimes shows on the faces of brides, and, without marring their beauty,* gives them an air of their own.

    b. Gertrude.

Il suo *aspetto,* che poteva dimostrar venticinque anni, *faceva* a prima vista un'*impressione* di bellezza, ma d'una *bellezza sbattuta, sfiorita* e, direi quasi, *scomposta.* Un *velo nero,* sospeso e stirato orizzontalmente sulla testa, cadeva dalle due parti, discosto alquanto dal viso; sotto il velo, una *bianchissima benda* di lino cingeva, fino al mezzo, una *fronte* di diversa, ma non d'inferiore *bianchezza* [*FL*: sotto il velo una benda di lino stringeva la fronte, al mezzo: e la parte che si vedeva diversamente ma non meno bianca della benda sembrava un *candido avorio* posato in un nitido foglio di carta, vol. 3, t. II, chapter 1, p. 153—*sm* (*seconda minutia*): e la parte che ne rimaneva scoperta, diversamente ma non meno candida della benda, poteva parere un *avorio* ravvolto in un nitido foglio, vol. 2, p. 743]; un'altra benda a pieghe circondava il viso, e terminava sotto il mento in un soggolo, che si stendeva alquanto, sul petto, a coprire *lo scollo d'un nero saio.* Ma quella fronte si raggrinzava spesso, come per una *contrazione dolorosa*; e allora due *sopraccigli neri* si ravvicinavano, con un rapido movimento. Due *occhi, neri neri* anch'essi, si fissavano talora in viso alle persone, con un'*investigazione superba*; talora si chinavano in fretta, come per cercare un nascondiglio; in certi momenti, un attento osservatore avrebbe argomentato che chiedessero affetto, corrispondenza, pietà; altre volte avrebbe creduto coglierci la rivelazione instantanea d'un odio inverterato e compresso, *un non so che di minaccioso e di feroce*: quando restavano immobili e fissi attenzione, chi ci avrebbe immaginato una svogliatezza orgogliosa, chi avrebbe potuto sospettarci il travaglio d'un pensiero nascosto, d'una preoccupazione familiare all'animo, e più forte su quello che gli oggetti circostanti. Le *gote pallidissime* scendevano con un *contorno delicato e grazioso, ma alterato* e reso mancante da una lenta estenuazione. Le labbra, quantunque appena tinte d'un roseo sbiadito, pure, spiccavano in quel pallore [*FL*: Le guance pallidissime, ma delicate scendevano con una *curva* dolce ed *eguale* ad un mento rilevato appena *come quello d'una statua greca*. Le *labbra regolarissime*, dolcemente prominenti, benchè colorate appena d'un roseo tenue, spiccavano pure fra quel pallore, vol. 3, t. II, chapter 1, p. 154—a variant of *FL*: Le *labbra regolari* dolcemente prominenti, colorate d'un roseo vivace spiccavano in quella bianchezza, vol. 3, p. 815]: i loro moti erano, come quelli degli occhi, subitanei, vivi, *pieni d'espressione e di mistero*. La *grandezza ben formata della persona scompariva* in un certo abbandono del portamento, *o compariva sfigurata* in certe *mosse* repentine, irregolari, *o troppo risolute per una donna*, non che per una monaca [no reference to unfeminine qualities in *FL*.] Nel vestire stesso c'era qua e là *qualcosa di studiato e di negletto*, che annunziava una monaca *singolare*: la *vita* era *attillata* con una certa cura secolaresca, e dalla benda usciva sur una tempia una ciocchettina di *neri capelli*; cosa che dimostrava o *dimenticanza o disprezzo della regola* che prescriveva di tenerli sempre corti, da quando erano stati tagliati, nella cerimonia solenne del vestimento.

(vol. 1, chapter 9, pp. 149-50).

b. Her *countenance*, which might be that of a woman of twenty-five, *gave* a first *impression* of beauty; but of a *worn, faded*, and, one might almost say, *ravaged beauty. A black veil*, stretched flat across her head, fell down somewhat away from her face on either side; under the veil a linen *band of snowy white* half-covered a *forehead* of a different but not inferior *whiteness*; [*FL*: that part of the forehead which was visible, of a different but no lesser whiteness than the band, looked like *bleached ivory—sm*: might seem like *ivory*] another pleated band surrounded her face and ended under her chin in a wimple that spread partly over her breast and covered the *neckline of a black habit*. But this forehead was continually puckering up, as if *contracted in pain*, when a *pair of black eyebrows* would draw together with a quick movement. A *pair of eyes—jet black*, too—would sometimes fasten on people's faces with an air of *haughty curiosity*, and sometimes suddenly drop, as if seeking to escape detection; at certain moments an attentive observer might have thought they were asking for affection, sympathy, and pity; at others he might think that he had caught the sudden flash of a long-pent, inveterate hatred, *a hint of something threatening and savage*. When they were at rest, and not

fixed on anything in particular, some might have read in them a proud indifference, others suspected them to be gnawed by a hidden thought, a familiar preoccupation of the mind, which engrossed it more than any object around. Her *cheeks* were *very pale* and *delicately and beautifully shaped, but wasted* and shrunk by gradual emaciation. Her lips stood out against this pallor, though barely suffused with a faint rosy tinge, [*FL*: her very pale but delicate cheeks were *gently and harmoniously curved*, and her *chin* was *reminiscent of a Greek statue. Her lips were perfectly shaped . . .* —A variant of *FL*: her *perfect lips*] and their movements were sudden and lively, like those of her eyes, *full of expression and mystery. The beauty of her well-formed figure was spoiled* by a certain carelessness of carriage, or *disfigured* by certain abrupt, irregular *movements*, which were *too resolute for a woman*, let alone a nun. Even her very dress showed a *mixture of studied attention and neglect* which betokened a *strange* sort of nun: her *waist* was *drawn in* tight with a certain worldly care, and a curl of *black hair* escaped from her headband on to one temple—a sign of either *forgetfulness or contempt of the rule* that the hair was always to be kept short from the moment when it was cut during the solemn ceremony of investiture.

Clearly the two portraits conform to very different, indeed antithetical, stereotypes. And therefore the common features, the dark hair and dark eyebrows, are likely to function as very different signs.

If we agree with Wellek and Warren that the 'blonde is the homemaker, unexciting but steady and sweet' while the dark woman is 'passionate, violent, mysterous, alluring and untrustworthy', then it would seem that dark-haired Lucia conforms to the former stereotype, while equally dark-haired Gertrude conforms with the latter. This raises the possibility of an interesting paradox: textually the two characters would appear to fulfil functions which are the opposite of their characterization within the story. It is Gertrude, the rebellious character, who conforms with the canon, while Lucia, the submissive and retiring one, challenges the canon.

Let us examine the two portraits in more detail, beginning with Gertrude.

Beauty is a clear attribute of Gertrude, but it is a special kind of beauty, qualified through a series of oppositions ('impressione di bellezza, ma d'una bellezza sbattuta', 'contorno delicato e grazioso, ma alterato', 'grandezza ben formata della persona scompariva . . . , o compariva sfigurata'), or outright oxymorons ('qualcosa di studiato e di negletto'). In fact the overt statement of her beauty at the outset of the portrait is itself an oxymoron, pointing clearly to the cliché of the tainted beauty ('bellezza' but 'sbattuta', 'sfiorita', and, most explicit of all, 'scomposta'). The unharmonious, restless, corrupted quality of Gertrude's appearance is also the point of arrival of a gradual process of elimination of adjectives and comparisons present in the initial versions, which could have suggested harmony and regularity: 'curva . . . eguale', 'labbra regolarissime', 'labbra regolari', 'come quello d'una statua greca'.

Paleness and darkness, the typical iconographic traits of the *homme fatal/femme fatale,* also dominate Gertrude's portrait: not only are her dark eyebrows, eyes, and hair contrasted to the pale forehead, and pale (in fact 'pallidissime') cheeks, but this is reinforced by the opposition velo nero/bianchissima benda/nero saio. And the portrait of Gertrude as the typical dark, tainted beauty is made complete by the insistent suggestions of mystery, hidden passions, disturbing and mutually contradictory emotions and pain.

While it is tempting to link Gertrude's 'Spanishness' (she is the scion of 'gente grande, venuta di Spagna') to the exoticism that is often associated with the dark beauty in the nineteenth-century novel, it would be impossible not to recognize the insistent play on the ambiguity between masculinity and femininity that Utter and Needham have put forward as a component of the stereotype of the dark beauty.

In a sense this ambiguity is at the very core of Gertrude's presence. She is a nun, therefore a figure that partakes both of quintessential femininity and of the denial of femininity; not only that, but her monastic being is negated by subtle yet clear erotic traits ('vita . . . attillata', 'scollo d'un saio nero'), this latter produced through a juxtaposition of a word with potentially erotic connotations ('scollo') with the monastic habit. The masculinity emerges fleetingly in the hint of aggression and violence contained in the 'non so che di minaccioso e di feroce', but then also surfaces much more openly in the mention of the over-assertive body movements, which are defined as unfeminine, this time quite overtly, and, it would seem, intentionally, since the detail is introduced after the completion of the first version of the novel.

In this way Gertrude's dark hair, mentioned indirectly in connection with her slack attitude towards the rules of her order, takes on a heightened significance. One might note that the very mention of the colour of her hair is a negation of her monastic being (a nun's head should be both shaven and hidden under the veil), and in *FL* this is what it amounts to, a sign of rebelliousness. But in *PS* [*I promessi sposi*] it acquires the added function of re-affirming the femininity that the text has just negated, and yet this re-affirmation is made possible through a personality trait, assertive rebelliousness, that in itself belongs to the masculine, not the feminine, stereotype. Not only is mysteriousness a trait of Gertrude's characterization, but ambiguity is at the core of her textual presence. And as such she conforms perfectly to the canon of the dark lady.

In other words, Gertrude is the exact opposite of Lucia. While disharmony and irregularity dominate Gertrude's beauty, Lucia's appearance bears the insistent mark of order and regularity: her hair is parted by a 'drizzatura', and is neatly tied up in plaits rolled round the back of her head. The emotions that transpire on her face are mild, normal and straightforward, unlike Gertrude's violently contradictory ones. Indeed she is, overtly, the negation of

Gertrude's tainted beauty: while Gertrude had a 'bellezza . . . scomposta', in the case of Lucia we have 'senza scompor la bellezza'.

In fact Lucia's beauty is rather doubtful: the meanderings of the text through its various versions reveal a clear concern with making her less beautiful, certainly not glamorous. Not only does the definitive version reject the variant 'non comune bellezza' and overtly state that she is only moderately beautiful ('modesta bellezza'), but it also expunges the reference to her eyes ('due occhi neri vivi'), which would be a prerequisite of any portrayal of beauty, according to the traditional rhetorical code.

It would be difficult not to view the portrait of Lucia as that of a 'homemaker, unexciting but steady and sweet', who would therefore be expected to be blonde. Why is Lucia then dark? I think that part, but only part, of the answer lies at the very core of those features of Lucia which conform to the stereotype of the blonde. Behind the clear drift towards her deglamorization, there is a concern with making her unexceptional, ordinary, typical of a whole class of real people (note the reference to the similarity with present-day Lombard peasant women), in other words with making her more like reality, less like literature. And it is perfectly in character for Manzoni, with his sophisticated awareness of literary conventions to want to signal this movement away from literariness towards referentiality through an explicit rejection of the literary canon. This rejection becomes in fact explicit at the end of the novel, when Lucia and Renzo, now married, move to neighbouring Venetia, and their new neighbours are disappointed at Lucia's appearance because they were expecting to see a woman 'con i capelli proprio d'oro'. But I shall return to this later.

3. SOURCES AND INTERTEXTS

I promessi sposi, as a historical novel, is partially based on historical material. On this account also, the two women differ. Gertrude is a semi-historical character, derived from the most famous of Manzoni's historical sources, Ripamonti's *Historiae patriae,*[12] while Lucia is entirely fictional. She is, on the other hand, constructed through a complex network of literary intertexts. An examination of the points of contact between the two portraits and their models uncovers additional layers of meaning to the topic under discussion.

A. GERTRUDE

There are two passages in Ripamonti which function as sources for the portrait of Gertrude. One describes her as a young nun (passage 1), and the other as an old woman doing penance for her sins (passage 2):[13]

> 1. Facile intelligeres, *ex corpore, & ore, animoque illo,* una *cum virginitate, verecundiam quoque excidisse omnem*: nec Virginem iam esse ipsam, nec dignam, quae in coetu Virginum diutius haberetur.

[*From looking at her body and her face, and from her temperament, one could see that she had lost all modesty together with her virginity*; she was neither a virgin herself, nor worthy of being in the company of virgins.]

2. sanctior haec, scribentibus ista nobis, adhuc superstes erat curvae *proceritatis* anus, torrida, macilenta, veneranda, quam *pulchram,* & impudicam aliquando esse potuisse ex adspectu vix fides.

[What remained was an old woman, saintlier than the man who writes these pages, *tall* and bent, shrivelled, emaciated, venerable, she who had been so *beautiful* and sinful.]

Manzoni's description reproduces the reference to beauty and tallness in passage 2. From passage 1, it transforms the generic reference to her aspect into specific details, and conversely makes vague, menacing and mysterious that which is in the source an explicit and straightforward reference to the loss of virginity and modesty. In other words the receiving text constructs features of the dark lady out of historical material through suitable transformations. It is my contention that this transformation happens through the filter of a Gothic intertext, no less than the Gothic portrait par excellence, that is to say Radcliffe's Schedoni, which is, according to Mario Praz, the chief channel of distribution of the stereotype of the contaminated beauty into European literature.

That there are points of contact between Manzoni's Gertrude and Radcliffe's Schedoni has been noticed already by Giovanni Getto, who sees them however in terms of vague similarities.[14] I am arguing instead that Schedoni's portrait (passage 3 below) has functioned as a specific and precise model for the portrait of Gertrude:

3. La sua figura *faceva impressione* . . . era *alta,* e, benchè estremamente magra, le sue membra erano grandi e sgraziate, e, come andava a gran passi, avvolto nelle *nere vesti* del suo ordine, v'era *qualcosa di terribile* nel suo *aspetto*; qualcosa di quasi sovrumano. Il suo *cappuccio,* inoltre, gittando un'ombra sul livido *pallore del suo volto,* ne aumentava la fierezza, e conferiva un carattere quasi d'orrore ai suoi grandi occhi melanconici. La sua non era la melanconia d'un cuore sensitivo ferito, ma apparentemente quella di una tetra *e feroce* natura. V'era nella sua fisionomia un non so che d'estremamente *singolare,* difficile a definire. Portava le tracce di molte passioni . . . i suoi occhi erano così intensi, che con un solo sguardo potevano penetrare nel cuore degli uomini, e leggervi i segreti pensieri; *pochi potevano tollerare la loro indagine,* o perfino sopportare d'incontrarli una seconda volta.[15]

[His figure *was striking* . . . *tall,* and, though extremely thin, his limbs were large and uncouth, and as he stalked along, wrapt in *the black garments* of his order, there was *something terrible* in its *air*; something almost super-human. His *cowl,* too, as it threw a shade over the livid *paleness of his face,* increased his severe character, and gave an effect to his large melancholy eye, which approached to horror. His was not the melancholy of a sensible and wounded heart, but appar-

ently that of a gloomy and *ferocious* disposition. There was something in his physiognomy extremely *singular,* and that can not easily be defined. It bore the traces of many passions . . . his eyes were so piercing that they seemed to penetrate, at a single glance, into the hearts of men, and to read their most secret thoughts; *few persons could support their scrutiny,* or even endure to meet them twice.]

Not only does the receiving text adopt general motifs from the source text: the paleness, the contrast between paleness and darkness, the suggestion of murky emotions, the air of mystery. It also borrows specific words and syntagmatic structures, some of which are re-used literally ('faceva impressione'—'aspetto'—'feroce'—'singolare'), while others are paraphrased, broken up and transposed ('alta' to 'grandezza'—'nere vesti' to 'nero saio'—'qualcosa di terribile' to 'un non so che di minaccioso'—'cappuccio', 'pallore del suo volto' to 'velo', 'fronte', 'bianchezza'—'pochi potevano tollerare la loro indagine' to 'investigazione superba').

In the case of Gertrude, source and intertext serve to confirm and reinforce the canon.

B. LUCIA

The text that must have functioned as the immediate model for the description of Lucia's hair is a section of a poem belonging to the dialect tradition, the 'Lament del Marchionn di gamb avert' written in Milanese dialect in 1816 by the great classic of Milanese dialect poetry, Carlo Porta. The 'Lament' includes a portrait of the Marchionn's own beloved, the lovely Tetton, whose hair is described as follows:[16]

> I cavij a la zoeura
> Spartij in duu sulla front, negher, e folt
>
> (229-30)
>
> Her hair in the style of mountain girls
> parted in the middle of her forehead, black, and thick

This clearly generates, through an almost literal transposition, Lucia's 'neri . . . capelli, spartiti sopra la fronte' And 'a la zoeura', the reference to the style of mountain girls, emerges elsewhere in Manzoni's text, where Lucia is called 'la montanara'.

Both the nature of the source text (a dialect poem), and its topic (a lower-class girl) clearly confirm and reinforce the drift towards realism which, as we have seen, presides over the attribution of dark hair to Manzoni's heroine. But it is interesting to examine the wider context of the immediate source for the description of Lucia's hair. On the one hand this acts as confirmation that Porta's description has been used as a direct source for Manzoni's description surrounded as it is by a cluster of less literal though no less clear borrowings. But on the other hand this brings to light a more complex operation. Porta's text constructs the figure of Tetton through a series of constant and explicit erotic connotations (beginning with her very name), which are notably absent in the construction of Lucia. But by constructing Lucia's portrait through material which is partly borrowed from that of an explicitly erotic portrait, Manzoni's text both censures and alludes to this very eroticism at the same time, thereby casting a subtle air of ambiguity over his overtly saintly heroine.[17] Tetton's attire

> La Gh'eva sù on corsett
> De velù ross scarlatt strengiuu sui fianch
> Con sott on percall bianch
> Ch'el rivava domà al fior di colzett.
>
> (221-24)
>
> She was wearing a corset
> of scarlet red velvet tight on her hips
> above a white petticoat
> which only just reached down to her stockings.

re-emerges, stripped of its erotic connotations, in Lucia's 'portava un bel busto di broccato . . . una corta gonnella . . . due calze vermiglie'. The description of Tetton's lips and teeth:

> E dal lavritt rident
> Compariva ona fira de dencitt
>
> (237-38)
>
> And between her laughing lips
> appeared a row of dainty teeth

appears to generate the less literal 'la bocca s'apriva al sorriso', and one could argue that even Lucia's 'modesta bellezza' derives from the equally average beauty of Tetton:

> La gh'eva anca in sò ajutt
> La bellezza regina di bellezz,
> Desdott annitt e mezz,
> Quel gran roffian che dà mari anca ai brutt.
>
> (253-56)
>
> She also had to her advantage
> that beauty which is the queen of all beauties
> eighteen years and a half
> that great pimp which finds husbands even for the
> plain ones

The points of contact with Porta both confirm the realistic intent as the chief rationale underlying Lucia's dark hair, and add an ambiguous halo of eroticism.

But Lucia's portrait, as it settles into its definitive shape in the final version of the novel, also acquires a symbolic element, focussed precisely on her hair, with a clear religious connotation: the crown of hair-pins which looked like a diadem in *FL* becomes 'raggi d'un'aureola' in *PS*. If we pursue this line of religious connotations we are led to another intertextual trail: Lucia the dark haired bride surrounded by her girl friends ('Le amiche si rubavano la sposa') also contains an allusion to the dark bride of the Song of Songs, who says of herself 'nigra sum sed formosa, filiae Hierusalem'.[18] The Song of Songs: a religious text, but also one of the most powerful pieces of erotic poetry in world literature.

The two intertexts reinforce the two strands present in the surface text of Lucia's portrait, the realistic and the religious, but they both, in their different ways, also add subtly erotic allusions.

And the Song of Songs is also, as I mentioned earlier, a crucial text in the canon that controls the blonde woman/dark woman dichotomy.

4. THE CHALLENGE TO THE CANON

While the dark hair of Manzoni's anti-heroine appears to conform to the canon, such as it is, of the nineteenth-century novel, the dark hair of its heroine clearly goes against it. If we now re-examine the text briefly, we find some elements which suggest that the challenge to the canon is wider than that.

The reference to the paleness of Gertrude's forehead is expressed through a metaphor in *FL* ('un candido avorio': 'bleached ivory'). The metaphor is modified in *sm* ('un avorio': 'ivory'), and eventually eliminated in the final version. The meanderings of the text lead in this case from the metaphor to the literal designation. But *PS* also introduces two metaphors which were absent in *FL*.

When Lucia arrives in Venetia at the end of the story, the dashed expectations of the locals with regard to her beauty are expressed through parodistically used metaphors: 'credevan forse che dovesse avere i capelli proprio d'oro, e le gote proprio di rosa' (chapter 38, p. 669) ['they expected to find her hair all gold, and her cheeks all roses']. If we put this passage side by side with the expunged passage from *FL,* we are left with three canonic tropes (gold, roses, and ivory), and with the three colours permitted by the Petrarchan code (yellow, red, and white).

It would seem that the darkness of the ladies' hair in Manzoni's novel is but the visible pinnacle of a wider and more complex textual operation, amounting to a meta-discourse on the conventions of the lyrical tradition.

Notes

1. The most informative writings on the blonde/dark opposition are still, in my opinion, M. B. Ogle, 'The 'White Hand' as a Literary Conceit', *The Sewanee Review,* XX (1912), 459-69, M. B. Ogle, 'Classical Literary Tradition in Early German and Romance Literature', *Modern Language Notes,* XXVII, 8 (1912), 233-42, and M. B. Ogle, 'The Classical Origin and Tradition of Literary Conceits', *American Journal of Philology,* XXXIV, 2 (1913), 125-52, which deal with various aspects of the stereotype in the European Medieval and Renaissance tradition, and its origins in classical literature, and W. C. Curry, *The Middle English Ideal of Personal Beauty* (Baltimore: J. H. Furst Company, 1916), which is mainly about the Anglo-Saxon tradition. Useful though less systematic information is also to be found in M. R. de la Clavière, *Les femmes de la*

Renaissance (Paris, 1898), E. Rodocanachi, *La femme italienne à l'époque de la Renaissance* (Paris: Librairie Hachette, 1907), M. Lazard, *Images littéraires de la femme à la Renaissance* (Paris: Presses Universitaires de France, 1985), and A. Quondam, 'Il naso di Laura', in *Il ritratto e la memoria,* edited by A. Gentili (Rome: Bulzoni, 1989), 9-44. Invaluable, though not directly focussed on the blonde/dark dichotomy, are Giovanni Pozzi's investigations of the intricacies of literary codes in the poetic tradition: 'Codici, stereotipi, topoi e fonti letterarie', in *Intorno al codice. Atti del III Congresso della Associazione Italiana di Studi Semiotici (AISS)* (Florence: La Nuova Italia, 1976), 'Il ritratto della donna nella poesia d'inizio Cinquecento e la pittura di Giorgione', *Lettere italiane,* XXXI, 1 (1979), 3-30, and 'Temi, τόποι, stereotipi', *Letteratura italiana,* vol. 3, *Le forme del testo,* I, *Teoria e poesia* (Turin: Einaudi, 1984), 391-436. I am grateful to Luciano Cheles for providing me with much relevant material on this issue.

2. Ogle 1913, pp. 126-27.

3. Ogle 1913, p. 127, and Ogle 1912 *(MLN),* p. 241.

4. Pozzi, especially 1979, pp. 6-14, and 1984 pp. 420-21.

5. Particularly poignant instances of praise of the dark beauty, accompanied by polemical references to the norm, are contained in two inscriptions found in Pompei: 'quisquis amat nigra, nigris carbonis ardet. nigra cum video, mora libenter aedeo', and 'candida me docuit nigras / odisse puellas. odero se potero, se non, invitus / amabo. / scripsit Venus fisica Pompeiana.' *(Corpus Inscriptionum Latinarum,* vol. IV, 6892, and 1520). I am grateful to Giulio Lepschy for providing me with this reference, and also for being so helpful and supportive throughout the various phases of this study.

6. R. Wellek & A. Warren, *Theory of Literature* (London: Jonathan Cape, 1949), p. 228. N. Frye, *Anatomy of Criticism* (Princeton: Princeton U.P., 1957), p. 101. Some useful information is also to be found in R. P. Utter and G. B. Needham, *Pamela's Daughters* (London: Lovat Dickson Ltd., 1937), R. Barthes, *Sade, Fourier, Loyola* (Paris: Éditions du Seuil, 1971), F. Portinari, *Le parabole del reale* (Turin: Einaudi, 1976), M. Romano, *Mitologia romantica e letterature popolare. Struttura e sociologia del romanzo d'appendice* (Ravenna: Longo, 1977), S. M. Gilbert and S. Gubar, *The Madwoman in the Attic* (Newhaven & London: Yale U.P., 1979), U. Eco, M. Federzoni, I. Pezzini, & M. P. Pozzato, *Carolina Invernizio, Matilde Serao, Liala* (Florence: La Nuova Italia, 1979), Ph. Perrot, *Le travail des apparences ou les transformations du corps féminin XVIII-XIX siècle.* (Paris: Éditions du Seuil, 1984), and *Le portrait littéraire,* edited by K. Kupisz, G.-A. Pérouse, and J.-Y. Debreuille (Lyon: Presses Universitaires de Lyon, 1988).

7. Utter & Needham, *Pamela's Daughters,* M. Praz *The Romantic Agony* (London: Oxford U. P., 1954 The original appeared with the title *La carne, l morte e il diavolo nella letteratura romantica,* i 1930). For both volumes references will be given i the text.

8. '[The] monster-woman, threatening to replace he angelic sister, embodies intransigent female au tonomy . . . patriarchal texts have traditionall suggested that every angelically selfless Snov White must be hunted, if not haunted, by a wick edly assertive Stepmother . . . assertiveness, ag gressiveness—all characteristics of a male life o "significant action"—are "monstrous" in wome precisely because "unfeminine" and therefore ur suited to a gentle life of "contemplative purity." *The Madwoman in the Attic,* p. 28.

9. On Lucia see N. Busetto, 'La genesi e la composiz ione poetica di Lucia', in *La genesi e la formazion poetica dei Promessi sposi* (Bologna: Zanichell 1921) 190-278, P. Fossi, *La Lucia del Manzoni e altre note critiche* (Florence: Sansoni, 1937), E. D Michelis, 'Lucia', in *Studi sul Manzoni* (Milan: Fe trinelli, 1962), 216-38, G. Getto, *Letture manzi niane* (Florence: Sansoni, 1964), E. De Micheli *La vergine e il drago* (Padua: Marsilio, 1968), C Baldi, 'La ribellione di Renzo tra Eden e storia', *Da Dante al Novecento. Studi critici offerti dag scolari a Giovanni Getto nel suo ventesimo anno insegnamento universitario* (Milan: Mursia, 1970 489-512, G. Livio, 'Manzoni e Sade, ou "les pro pérités de la vertu"', *Utopia,* III (1973), 20-24, De Angelis, *Qualcosa su Manzoni* (Turin: Einaud 1975), A. R. Pupino, 'Manzoni e il male', Nuo argomenti, LIII-LIV (1977), 316-49, R. Salsan *Ritrattistica e mimica nei Promessi sposi* (Rom Palombi, 1979), G. De Rienzo, *Lucia nel labirin dei 'Promessi sposi.'* (Turin: Giappichelli, 1981), Stoppelli, 'Manzoni e il tema di Don Giovanni Belfagor, XXXIX (1984), 501-16, G. Baldi, *promessi sposi. Progetto di società e mito* (Mila Mursia, 1985), G. De Rienzo, *Per amore di Luci* (Milan: Rusconi, 1985), V. R. Jones, 'Towards a r construction of Manzoni's Lucias', *The Italiani* VII (1987), 36-44, and V. R. Jones, 'Lucia and h Sisters: Women in Alessandro Manzoni's *I promes sposi',* in *Women and Italy. Essays on Gender Cu ture and History,* edited by Z. G. Barański and W. Vinall (London: MacMillan, 1991). On the te tual relationship between Lucia and Gertrude, s De Angelis 1975, Pupino 1977, and Jones 1991.

10. The first version, entitled *Fermo e Lucia* (hencefo *FL*), was written between 1821 and 1823, and nev published. Soon after the completion of the fi draft, Manzoni began the revision of the man script. This is known as the *seconda minu* (henceforth *sm*), and eventually came to fruiti between 1825 and 1827, in the first published ve sion, the so-called *ventisettana.* The definitive ve

sion of *I promessi sposi,* the so-called *quarantana* (henceforth *PS*), appeared in 1840. The changes from the *ventisettana* to the *quarantana* are generally limited to single words, and are almost exclusively motivated by Manzoni's wish to move closer to spoken Florentine. The significant changes for our purposes are the ones involved in the transition from the draft to the *ventisettana,* which often involved extensive re-casting and re-writing, additions, and omissions. All references to all versions of the novel will be to the critical edition published by the Casa del Manzoni: *I promessi sposi,* edited by A. Chiari and F. Ghisalberti (Milan: Mondadori, 1954), and will be given in the text.

11. Sections from earlier versions of the novel which differ significantly from the *quarantana* are given in square brackets. Words and phrases that will be the object of discussion are in bold. Translations from the definitive version of *I promessi sposi* are from *The Betrothed,* translated by A. Colquhoun, (London: Dent, 1951), with occasional slight modifications. All other translations, including those from earlier versions of the novel, are my own. The English version of the passage from *The Italian* is of course Radcliffe's own original.

12. Iosephi Ripamonti Canonici Scalensis Chronistae Urbis Mediolani *Historiae Patriae Decadis V Libri VI,* Mediolani, apud Io: Baptistam, et Iulium Caesarem Malatestam, [1641-48].

13. Lib. VI, p. 363, and pp. 375-76. Significant words are in [italic].

14. 'Nell' *Italian or the Black Penitents* il monaco Schedoni . . . anticipa sia pure vagamente qualcuno dei tratti, che saranno poi della monaca di Monza.' G. Getto, *Manzoni europeo* (Milan: Mursia, 1971), p. 88.

15. A. Radcliffe, *The Italian or the Confessional of the Black Penitents* (first published in 1797) (London: Oxford U. P., 1971), chapter 2, pp. 34-35. I am reproducing the passage in Italian translation (taken from Praz, *La carne,* p. 62), since this will, not surprisingly, reveal more clearly the similarities with Manzoni's text. Significant words are in [italic].

16. C. Porta, *Poesie,* edited by D. Isella (Florence: La Nuova Italia, 1955, LXV). Line numbers are given in the text. The similarity between the descriptions of Lucia's hair and Tetton's hair is also mentioned briefly in E. Raimondi and L. Bottoni's commentated edition of *I promessi sposi* (Milan: Principato, 1987). The following are literal translations of the four passages: 1. 'I capelli alla montanara, spartiti in due sulla fronte, neri e folti'. 2. 'aveva su un busto di velluto rosso scarlatto stretto sui fianchi, con sotto un percalle bianco che le arrivava appena all'orlo delle calze'. 3. 'E dai labbrucci ridenti compariva una fila di dentini'. 4. 'Aveva anche in suo aiuto la bellezza regina delle bellezze, diciotto anni e mezzo, quella gran ruffiana che trova marito anche alle brutte'.

17. Something similar happens with borrowings from another of Porta's explicitly erotic female figures, la Ninetta del Verzée, who functions as a partial model for a later section of Lucia's story. I intend to explore this at greater length in a book-length study of Manzoni's women characters.

18. I am quoting from the Vulgate since this is the version with which Manzoni would have been familiar.

Mirto Golo Stone (essay date 1991)

SOURCE: "'He Was Tall, Dark and Bald': Aristocratic Desire and Fantasies of Authority in *I promessi sposi*," in *Forum Italicum,* Vol. 25, No. 1, Spring, 1991, pp. 3-16.

[*In the following essay, Stone probes the pro-aristocratic element in Manzoni's otherwise republican novel* I promessi sposi.]

Like every title, mine too aims at arousing the reader's curiosity: as carefully as it is required by the difficult art of wrapping presents—example or metaphor perhaps not entirely out of place—, what is sought after is a combination of terms able to promise the surprising, the unthought, or at least a modest infringement on the routine of scholarly interpretation, on the *status quo* of every day critical discourse.

Those who are acquainted with traditional and/or recent readings of *I promessi sposi* know how anti-aristocratic this novel is supposed to be: how much it would strive to convey, however problematically, a liberal, progressive, that is, *bourgeois* symbolic vision.[1]

For sure, the heading '*aristocratic* desire' is thus meant as a challenge, announcing the fact that the hypothesis brought forth here will be another, and a contrary one.

Still, the most arresting effect I entrust to my title does not so much concern the proposal of a new and improved definition for the nature of *I promessi sposi*'s desires, but rather the suggestion that terms such as 'fantasies' and 'desire' can indeed be invoked in connection with this novel—that they need to become, in fact, the focus of our inquiry into the specific narrative tradition that Manzoni began, and made *possible*.

Freed from the *Risorgimento* legend according to which the process of political unification and a generic 'rise of the bourgeoisie' had gone hand in hand, contemporary historiography has been recently engaged in a re-thinking of the Italian 19th century which has crucial implications for our work as *literary* historians.

In fact, according to a perspective which has increasingly become more convincing and substantiated, both the "*transizione al moderno,*"[2] and the national enterprise would be characterized, in Italy, by "a renewed and enriched hegemony of the *aristocratic* class."[3]

Following this logic, we could then isolate, in the phenomenon of *Risorgimento,* a specific *historical contradiction*: originating in the need to put into practice a dialectic which simultaneously mandates a motion towards 'progress' and one towards 'conservation'.

A 'new' subject—the 'Italian'—is needed: a subject active enough to participate in the effort of *Risorgimento*—to embrace the cause of a '*resurrection*'—, but who would not translate it into the language of class/social relationships—into an '*insurrection*'. Bollati put it into a nutshell: "In practice, it's a matter of turning a dynamic which is in itself revolutionary to the purposes of an anti-revolutionary defense."[4]

As I wish to suggest, the first Italian novel is born at a particular historical hour: the hour in which the necessity arose to define "Italianness,"[5] to 'give *form*', precisely, to a concept the determination of which cannot be left to just 'anybody's' guess, and speculation.

I promessi sposi, then, as the fulfillment of a specific historical need: a *first* symbolic answer to various dilemmas raised by the complex dynamic I have here attempted to outline; specifically, as I will now illustrate, to the dilemma of *social conservation* within *political progressivism*: a very crucial question to the class which, as historiography tells us, will pull *Risorgimento* off and 'win' it—a question, also, to which the first Italian novelist was by no means indifferent.

Lamenting how "literary critics . . . so susceptible to the suspicion of ideological tampering" would have lost sight of "the unity of Manzoni's experience," Bollati defined it as being "centered on an unflinching will of intervention in his own time," and thus proposed a re-evaluation of Manzoni as *ideologue*: heir of Confalonieri and key figure, in the Lombard, *aristocratic* cultural leadership.[6]

Insofar as *I promessi sposi* is concerned, his invitation has yet to be accepted: and since judging on its merits goes hand in hand with putting my theoretical proposal concerning the origins of the Italian 19th century novel to test, we shall now turn to what stands in the way of both.

In Scalia's summarization, "having freed Gramsci from the intemperance and the severity of his thesis" Manzoni would come to be posited, through the 'neo-realist' years, as "the advanced forefront of the consciousness of the Italian bourgeoisie, sufficiently *anti-aristocratic* to be a progressive bourgeois."[7]

Later, Salinari will go on—and on—with "the idealistic and renovating thrust" of Manzoni's "organic conception of a society taken in the moment of its expansion."[8]

Specifically, the particular 'treatment' of the aristocracy in *I promessi sposi* has constituted the most powerful argument that the critical defense of this novel's anti aristocratic leanings has brought forward: the last bastion as it were, around which this kind of interpretations have fortified themselves.

Thus Spinazzola, for example, argued quite recently that "Manzoni's hostility towards the aristocratic class is generalized to the point of investing with mockery even those of its members who exercise an activity which is, in itself praiseworthy."[9] Hence, as he observes, the narrator' irony—in contrast with "the benevolent and friendly affection towards the common people"—"face to face with the privileged classes . . . becomes satire, inclined toward caricature-like resentment, and thus acquiring a univoca sense of condemnation."[10] In the final analysis, as Spinazzola sees it, "Manzoni, in short, denies any future to the aristocracy as a social class; but he grants a chance of redemption to its single members, as moral individuals."[11]

A far cry from the *letter,* not just the "intemperance" of Gramsci's argument: who would still specify, from his forgotten grave, that Manzoni's "benevolence" towards the "common people" is that of a "catholic society for the protection of animals,"[12] and that his social sympathies lay with those of Shakespeare. To restore, then, Gramsci's thesis in its proper 'severity':

> Shakespeare, in conformity with the tendencies of his time, sides manifestly with the upper classes: his drama is essentially *aristocratic* . . . In Manzoni, the tendency is analogous, although its manifestations are toned down. . . . Shakespeare was not 'morally' superior to his time. . . .[13]

Neither was Manzoni: whose 'greatness' is to be attributed precisely to his ability to interpret correctly his time and the hegemonic spirit of it—not surpass it or outdo it.

The 'problem' which the specific 'treatment' of the aristocracy in *I promessi sposi* appears to raise is actually simple solution: we must however become cognizant within the story's logic, of a differentiation which criticism has failed to appreciate and assess, and which constitutes an integral part of this novel's symbolic effort.

The fictional presentation of the aristocracy is split in *promessi sposi*: there is a 'bad' aristocracy and a 'good' aristocracy—precisely as some liked to think the case was in Lombardy, in the early Nineteen hundreds.

Towards the *former,* the novel's logic is *appropriate* critical, 'severe' if we want, and in fact even *indignant* times: a logic which is, no doubt, 'hostile' enough to strike on occasion, a posture or two of outright mockery. Insofar however, as the *latter* is concerned, the question isn't even one of mere 'sympathy', but rather of utter *delight*; when it comes to its 'good' aristocracy the text does more than simply 'side' with it—it actually turns quite laudatory

tory, thus providing a rather enthusiastic symbolic *celebration* of the leadership of its choice.

While the idea of discriminating between one aristocracy and another has seemingly become alien to the consciousness of today's readers of *I promessi sposi,* for its close contemporaries it rather amounted, in principle and in practice, to something quite obvious: to a matter of fact which will have, in due time, its impact and influence on the history to follow.

According to Meriggi, what the "Italian case discloses with particular evidence" is how the "reformistic practice which characterized the 19th century" produced, within the Austrian sphere of power, an "uprooting of those regional oligarchies which were structurally (and geographically) peripheral"; consequently, "the northern-Italian nobles . . . did not share with the middle-European *communitas* either customs nor codes. The joining tendencies of the Restauration stressed even more their estrangement from that world."[14]

It would be precisely in the terms and progression of such an 'estrangement', as Meriggi's conclusions make clear, where the origins of *Risorgimento* are to be found:

> The Italian nobility found itself, in the age of Restauration, suddenly incorporated in a global system which penalized its autonomistic pride. Already considered during the preceding century a nobility of inferior rank, it had not suffered—at the level of class interests—as long as the centrality of the patrician system had been respected. The 19th century . . . however, deprived it of the influence which it had, until then, exercised in the public sphere; and its divorce from the exercise of power coincided with its withdrawal into the exclusive rituals of the *salon,* from which the Austrian nobles . . . remained excluded until the eve of 1848, to their dismay and awe.[15]

Some went into *salons* (such as that of countess Maffei), and some others, of perhaps less sparkling a disposition, set out to write a novel: and now let's talk about Manzoni's 'severity' towards 'the' aristocracy of *I promessi sposi*; about his 'univocal condemnation' and 'mockery' of it.

If it is true that one can indeed be, in this novel's logic, both noble and bad, it is also certain that, if this is the case, then he must also be *Spanish*; and in turn, a nobleman can indeed be *great*: but then, in this instance, Spanish he is *not*—he's something *else* and 'other': what, exactly, we'll see in a minute. For one marquis who shows—after a plague—some good will (despite his lack of social vision) there are crowds of bad noble *Spaniards* all over the story: in fact, one could even say that belonging to the Spanish nobility constitutes a pre-requisite of sorts for this novel's major and minor villains.

Don Rodrigo, Attilio, the *conte zio* (who will die without his 'promotion' and without seeing his beloved Madrid again), Gertrude's father, and, for that matter, Gertrude herself . . . on don Ferrante we couldn't swear, although

the fact that he refers to Machiavelli and Botero as two "*matadori*" is highly suspicious;[16] the two additional villains, moreover, who do not properly belong to the Spanish nobility are still, nevertheless, unmistakenly presented as enjoying close ties with it, and as gravitating within its sphere of power and interests: and we have an Azzeccagarbugli—with his ridiculous pro-Spanish toasts (V:86)—and a Ferrer—whose show of bilinguism discloses the truth of his politics (XIII:232-39)—both of whom contribute to our 'dear Renzo's' misfortunes, thus eliciting, of course, the reader's dislike.

It is to *this specific* aristocracy that Manzoni "denies any future" as a "social class"—while granting, however, a "chance of redemption to its *single* members" as "moral *individuals*."[17]

A *bad* aristocracy: the locus itself of moral corruption, feudal perversions, cultural backwardness, socio-political inefficiency: who would want something *like that* to govern the Milanese duchy? If the narrator is 'hostile', it is not to our surprise: for he *is* the heir of Confalonieri—a proven liberal and a *progressive* mind. As long, of course, as we are clear as to the *specific* meaning which these terms acquired in early 19th century Lombardy:

> In the first years of the new order in the Lombard-Venetian territory liberal and nostalgic-Napoleonic, or liberal and ex-mason had constituted a pair of synonims . . . but from the early twenties onwards the frame of reference changes drastically: liberal became a synonim for noble, or better yet, for dissident noble. But that liberalism, which radically excluded from itself the idea of political and social equality. . . .[18]

Far from contradicting it, the critical posture which this novel strikes towards its *Spanish* aristocrats is perfectly consistent with the specific socio-ideological dialectic I have been isolating earlier, and of which *I promessi sposi* constitutes a first, and crucial, symbolic document.

Dialectic of *Risorgimento*: mandating, as we have seen, a motion towards 'progress'—as an assist, however, to literary criticism's own contribution (somewhat overdue) to make light on the nature of such 'progress', let us make it clear that this novel's 'univocal condemnation' of so many of its aristocrats serves the purposes not of social, but of *political* progressivism: for it is a change of guard that Manzoni had in mind, not a change of *class* leadership.

Let me then cut the suspense short as to whom and what constitutes the 'good'—indeed the *great*—aristocracy of *I promessi sposi.*

A saint and a christianly converted dissident: the two *proper* heroes of the novel—for a 'hero' the good Tramaglino boy is not: he's only "such a main character; one could almost say the protagonist of our story." (XIV:253)

Federigo Borromeo and the Unnamed: the two characters who bear concrete witness to the validity of Gramsci's observation that Manzoni "finds 'magnanimity', 'high thoughts', 'noble feelings' only in *some* members of the upper class."[19]

Federigo Borromeo and the Unnamed: that is to say, the symbolic forms which Manzoni's fantasies of *authority* take up in the well-devised fiction of *I promessi sposi.*

Spinazzola, who in the text reads only a "general Manzonian impatience with the figures of authority,"[20] or Dombroski, who believes that "the new 'enlightened' upper class has no real representative in the novel, save for the narrator,"[21] must not have been effected by the particular charisma which characterizes these two figures of power: they must have obviously remained untouched and undisturbed by the specific seductive charm with which this fiction endows its saint and its Christian warrior.

Still, it's not for nothing that they are the ones to whom the crowds of *I promessi sposi* cheer, almost in a *delir de toucher*: for if their sights elicits the uncontainable expression of the populace's affection, it is not out of trickery and demagogy, but because of that genuine superiority which alone compels instinctual recognition without seeking it. Appropriately, the image of their entrance, side by side, in chapter XXIII comes to amount to a glimpse at the millennium:

> L'arcivescovo andò avanti, spinse l'uscio, che fu subito spalancato da due servitori, che stavano uno di qua e uno di là: e la mirabile coppia apparve agli sguardi bramosi del clero raccolto nella stanza. . . . E si seppe poi, che a più d'uno dei riguardanti era allora venuto in mente quel detto d'Isaia: *il lupo e l'agnello andranno ad un pascolo; il leone e il bue mangeranno insieme lo strame.*

> (XXIII:393)

The *millennium*: according, for sure, first of all to the desiderata of a *Catholic morality*—to the specific project of religious edification inscribed in the novel: "basic catechism," as Pietro Giordani had called it.[22]

More complex and equally cherished longings, however, are inscribed in this suggestive image, endowing it with its specific power and 'beauty': the longings, for example, of a certain Lombard "catholic-reactionary culture" which was "nostalgic of the centrality the Church had enjoyed in public life . . . during the prerevolutionary era";[23] hence a *cardinal* (a *prince* [!] of the church) as the first half of this novel's 'remarkable couple': of the specific authority which the text proposes as an object of desire.

Consistently, the novel's logic will present Federigo Borromeo as the embodiment of a 'superior' and crucially *alternative* leadership: through famines and plagues, his practice shines with the foresight and efficiency that the Spanish authorities *lack*; while the story of his own *Bildung* (XXII: 372-74) unequivocally confirms the specifically aristocratic character of the ideal he is made to em-

body—the particular nature of a *noblesse,* spiritual as it is, through which Nietzsche was able to see:

> *All spirit in the end becomes bodily visible.* Christianity . . . has chiselled out perhaps the most refined figures in human society that have yet existed: the figures of the higher and highest catholic priesthood, especially when they have descended from a noble race and brought with them an inborn grace of gesture, the eye of command, and beautiful hands and feet. Here the human race attains to that total spiritualization produced by the continual ebb and flow of the two species of happiness (the feeling of power and the feeling of surrender) . . . one takes *pride* in obeying, which is the distinguishing mark of all aristocrats. . . .[24]

Cardinal Federigo: good, *and* beautiful, as the text impresses upon the reader: "tutte le forme del volto indicavano che, in altre età, c'era stata quella che propriamente si chiama *bellezza*; l'abitudine de' pensieri solenni e benevoli . . . vi avevano sostituito una, direi quasi, *bellezza senile*" (XXIII:384, my emphasis); beautiful, *and* good: one of those "rare men" who are to be admired for having poured into "the quest and practice of good" "un ingegno egregio, *tutti i mezzi d'una grand'opulenza,* tutti i vantaggi d'una condizione *privilegiata.*" (XXII:372, my emphasis)

Kalòskaìagathòs: following the specific logic which critical thought has aptly recognized and made manifest:

> *Kalokagathia,* held up by the humanists to modern society as a model of aesthetic-moral harmony, always laid heavy stress on possessions, and Aristotle's *Politics* openly admits the fusion of inner worth with status in its definition of nobility as 'inherited wealth, combined with excellence. . . . Wealth as goodness is an element in the world's mortar: the tenacious illusion of their identity prevents the conforntation of moral ideas with the order in which the rich are right, while at the same time it has been impossible to conceive concrete definitions of morality other than those derived by wealth.[25]

Cardinal Federigo: it takes him only a mere four thousand *scudi* to provide the expedient, 'enlightened' solution to problem of 'social evil' which occupies a prominent place in the novel's concerns—the forced cloistering of girls of noble birth (XXII:378).

Fantasies of authority: and now for the other figure which makes them complete; for it is only the embrace of Federigo with *the Unnamed* which can tell us the entire story of this novel's most cherished socio-political desires.

The *great* aristocracy of *I promessi sposi* can cry and repent: what the text will reflect back to us is still the image of a "wild and fiery nature" (XXXIII:384); for as it set out to elaborate its own model of *kalokagathia* the Manzonian imagination came up with more than a cardinal with the lively eyes and an "almost majestic bearing" (XXIII:384): alongside, in fact, Federigo's 'senile beauty' this novel gives us also to admire *another kind* of handsome:

Era grande, bruno, calvo; bianchi i pochi capelli che gli
rimanevano; rugosa la faccia: a prima vista, gli si
sarebbe dato più de' sessant'anni che aveva; ma il con-
tegno, le mosse, la durezza risentita de' lineamenti, il
lampeggiar sinistro, ma vivo degli occhi, indicavano
una forza di corpo e d'animo, che sarebbe stata straor-
dinaria in un giovine.

(XX:340)

Another kind of handsome: nor should it appear improper
or strange for the Manzonian imagination to be open to its
suggestion. Only a misguided liberal such as Sismondi
could in fact believe that catholic morality entailed a loss
of spiritual backbone, or that by embracing it the Italian
character had lost its vigor, and "*il seme delle grandi
cose.*"[26]

Far from weakening it, Christian enlightenment will provide a more appropriate collocation for the 'vigor' of this
'wild and fiery nature', reproposing it in fact in the terms
of a higher aesthetical logic—for on the same day he converts, the Unnamed becomes a saint:

A nessuno di loro passò per la mente che, per esser lui
convertito, si potesse prendergli il sopravvento, rispon-
dergli come a un altr'uomo. Vedevano in lui un santo,
ma un di que' santi che si dipingono con la testa alta, e
con la spada in pugno.

(XXIV:424)

As Calvino observed, the novel's *conversione risolutrice*
is not Lodovico's (the future "*bourgeois* friar," as Spinazzola has called him[27]), but "it's postponed to a higher level
with the Unnamed":[28] a point which becomes, vis-à-vis the
political fantasies inscribed in this novel, a crucial gear of
its symbolic strategy.

They will both convert, Lodovico and the Unnamed; but
only the latter, this "signore altrettanto potente per ric-
chezze, *quanto nobile per nascita*" (XIX:333, my
emphasis) will get finally to develop appropriately the
genuine potential he *always had* as a protector of the oppressed, a hero of the popular imagination, a leader. (Cfr.
XIX:335)

As Guido Baldi has pointed out, the Unnamed's "condition as an outlaw is a form of adjustment to the modalities
of behavior of that particular society":[29] a bad society, as
the novel's logic repeatedly makes clear; a society which
is in need of political change, and of better authorities.
Hence, if already as one of the products of a bad time "il
suo nome significava qualcosa d'irresistibile, di strano, di
favoloso" (336), once a convert the Unnamed can become
the *proper* object of the love, the affection, the admiration
of the common people—as it should be for the *fit* leaders
who are both noble and christianly enlightened.

In his presence, his men experience "una specie di quella,
dirò così, verecondia, che anche gli uomini più zotici e più
e petulanti provano davanti a una superiorità che hanno
già riconosciuta" (XXIV:425)—precisely as in: "la pre-

senza di Federigo era infatti di quelle che annunziano una
superiorità, e la fanno amare." (XXXIII:383)

Hence once they have witnessed, immediately following
his conversion, "la gioia, la baldanza della popolazione,
l'amore e la venerazione per l'innominato" (XXIV:425),
his men will have no doubts as to bow this Christian noble
dissident ought to be regarded:

nell'uomo che avevan sempre riguardato, per dir così,
di basso in alto . . . vedevano ora la meraviglia, *l'idolo
di una moltitudine*; lo vedevano al di sopra degli altri,
ben diversamente di prima, ma non meno; sempre fuori
dalla schiera comune, sempre *capo.*

(XXIV:425, my emphasis)

Some others can talk about Manzoni's 'impatience with
the figures of authority": for myself, I find his fantasies,
his daydreams on the matter more interesting.

Particularly since, if we return for a moment to the question of the *specific* class which, as the historians tell us,
constituted the leadership of *Risorgimento* and, as it were,
'won' it, we will realize that what marks such a 'victory'
is a particular historical hour: a time of great disappointments and lost illusions:

'The identity of several among those who were now
seizing power was a painful revelation for many. . . .'
With these flaming words the democratic and bourgeois
Cattaneo commented on the *coup de main* by which
the liberal-nobiliary faction lead by Casati excluded
him from the revolutionary government of Milan. . . .
In the following decade the aristocracy . . . maintained
a consistent position of support to the Sardinian crown,
taking it upon itself to assume the direction of a political play in which the bourgeoisie came to be assigned,
and accepted, an utterly instrumental and subordinate
role.[30]

1848: the aristocracy wins the day and its specific aspirations become the political reality of the very first 'Italians';
what had suddenly hit Cattaneo and his friends as a 'painful revelation' could already have been deteted, however,
in the fantasies of authority prophetically inscribed in the
novel that the 'heir of Confalonieri' had written twenty
years earlier, and whose definitive edition dates 1840.

For it is the Unnamed, the most beloved, the most formidable *nobleman* of **I promessi sposi,** the one who ruins it
all for the *Spanish* villain don Rodrigo—not the parvenu
merchant's son: a victory which would cast an even more
suggestive shadow had a certain arresting page of **Fermo
e Lucia** not been deleted in the second version of the
novel. The first time around, in fact, we were made to witness directly the conversation between don Rodrigo and
the Unnamed, in the course of which the latter was given
to display an interesting aspect of his character, which deserves full attention (in **Fermo e Lucia** the Unnamed is
called *Conte del Sagrato,* and he's ten years younger):

—Dovrei scusarmi—cominciò don Rodrigo,—di venir
così a dare *infado* a Vossignoria Illustrissima.—

—Lasci queste *cerimoniacce spagnole,* e mi dica in che posso servirla.— . . .

—A dir vero—riprese don Rodrigo—io mi trovo impegnato in un affare d'onore, e . . . mi son fatto animo a venir a chiedere consiglio, e per dir tutto anche a domandare il suo *amparo.—*

—Al diavolo anche *l'amparo,*—ripose con impazienza il Conte.—Tenga queste *parolacce* per adoprarle in Milano con . . . quei parrucconi impostori che non sapendo essere padroni *in casa loro,* si protestano servitori d'uno *Spagnolo infingardo.—*[31]

Unmistakable the anti-Spanish sentiments of the Count: even though they might be framed in a rather vulgar and base context (any mention of money will be appropriately droppen in *I promessi sposi*):

—Patti chiari—risposte senza titubare il Conte . . .

—Venti miglia . . . un borgo . . . presso Milano . . . un monastero . . . la Signora che spalleggia . . . due cappuccini di mezzo . . . signor mio, questa donna vale dugento doppie.—A queste parole succedette un istante di silenzio . . . Il Conte diceva nella sua mente:

—L'avresti avuta per centocinquanta se non parlavi *d'infado* e *d'amparo.—*[32]

While we might regret that the Unnamed had to be robbed of such overt 'patriotic' sentiments, we need only to turn to one of the last images that *I promessi sposi* gives us of this Christian noble dissident, this warrior-saint and leader of men to console ourselves:

Ma quando, al calar delle bande alemanne, alcuni fuggiaschi di paesi invasi o minacciati capitarono su al castello a chieder ricovero, l'innominato, tutto contento . . . con quel tono naturale di comando ch'esprimeva la certezza dell'ubbidienza . . . fece dire a' suoi contadini e affittuari della valle, che chiunque si sentiva, venisse con armi al castello; a chi non ne aveva, ne diede; scelse alcuni, che fossero come uffiziali . . . Lui intanto non stava mai fermo; dentro e fuori dal castello, su e giù per la salita, in giro per la valle, a stabilire, a rinforzare, a visitar posti . . . e tutti, o l'avessero già visto, o lo vedessero per la prima volta, lo guardavano estatici, dimenticando un momento i guai e i timori che li avevano spinti lassù; e si voltavano ancora a guardarlo, quando, staccandosi da loro, seguitva la sua strada.

(XXIX: 510-11)

Talk about the *fit* kind of leadership; about an *aristocracy* (with his peasants and tenants) which is most great when it is, appropriately, Christianly enlightened: in full consistency with the fantasies of an ideologue who, as Bollati observed in regard to his 'theoretical' production,

happened to bear witness to a miracle which at once fulfilled his expectations both as a patriot and insofar as his moral philosophy was concerned: the unification of Italy (as he himself recounted later) was accomplished thanks to a series of favorable circumstances and to a *deus ex machina* in the figure of Vittorio Emanuele II on horseback, at the head of his army.

Confalonieri's project had thus come true (—Let the prince of Carignano come, Milan shall welcome him—) . . .[33]

Once we read it carefully, it is almost eerie, this difficult *promessi sposi*: a novel which, as I have attempted to illustrate, does not lack in patriotic passion—who knows, i Mazzini, the republican, had read it more attentively, he might have objected to it on *other* grounds than those o which he settled.[34]

Let other, less devout ideologues of *Risorgimento* do bet ter if they can: with the Unnamed dashing from post to post Manzoni had really done *his* utmost. The Unnamed and Federigo Borromeo: if their embrace is meant to giv the reader a quiver, it's not only thanks to the 'basi catechism' inscribed in it; for this alliance symbolicall seals the promise of a historical future which will indee be brought to realization; the promise and the fantasy c an authority which knows how to make itself *obeyed;* of 'stronger', more 'efficient' authority which compels re spect and *admiration*—as it makes itself *loved:* the ido indeed, of the common people and the simple in spiri and it will soon be *1848*—in Lombardy, as in the rest c Europe.

Notes

1. For a succint summarization and discussion of th De Sanctis-Sapegno-Salinari tradition, cfr. Gian Scalia, "Manzoni a sinistra," *Italianistica,* Anno (1973), N. 1, 21-42; for more recent approache cfr.: Robert Dombroski, "The Seicento as Strateg 'Providence' and the 'Bourgeois' in *I promes sposi,*" *MLN,* Vol. 91 (1976), N. 1, 80-100; "Tl Ideological Question in Manzoni," *Studies in R manticism,* Vol. 20 (1981), N. 4, 497-524; *Apolog del vero,* Padua: Liviana, 1985; and Vittorio Spina zola, *Il libro per tutti. Saggio su I promessi spo* (Roma: Editori Riuniti, 1983). Neither of them co tradicts the 'traditional', 'bourgeois' interpretatic of *I promessi sposi* that this article challenges.

2. Cfr. Marco Meriggi, "Czoernig, Mittermaier e società lombarda," *Storia in Lombardia,*" n. 1988, 57-73, 72. Cfr. also his *Amministrazione classi sociali nel Lombardo-Veneto (1814-184* (Bologna: Il Mulino, 1983) and *Il Regno Lombard Veneto* (Milan: UTET, 1987). I would like to ta this opportunity to thank Meriggi for his attenti and helpful reading of my 'work in progress'.

3. Marco Meriggi, *Amministrazione e classi sociali,* 342. All translations from italian editions are own.

4. Giulio Bollati, "L'Italiano," *Storia d'Italia* (Tur Einaudi, 1972), Vol. I, pp. 951-1022, p. 970.

5. *Ibid.,* p. 958.

6. In "L'Italiano" Bollati develops a solid argum on the *Osservazioni sulla morale cattolica* as a bo "which acquires its full meaning only once we re

it against the context of contemporary European culture," that is to say, as Manzoni's admonishment "to that wing of the European bourgeoisie which boldly rides the liberal tiger dashing towards industrialism and revolutions" (p. 991), of which Sismondi was a representative.

7. Gianni Scalia, "Manzoni a sinistra," p. 24.

8. Carlo Salinari, "La struttura ideologica dei Promessi Sposi," *Critica Marxista,* Vol. 2-3 (1974), 183-200.

9. Vittorio Spinazzola, *Il libro per tutti,* p. 163.

10. *Ibid.,* p. 162.

11. *Ibid.,* p. 180.

12. Antonio Gramsci, *Letteratura e vita nazionale* (Rome: Editori Riuniti, 1971), p. 99.

13. *Ibid.,* p. 100.

14. Marco Meriggi, *Amministrazione e classi sociali,* p. 241.

15. *Ibid.,* p. 180.

16. Alessandro Manzoni, *I promessi sposi,* ed. Alberto Chiari and Fausto Ghisalberti (Milan: Mondadori, 1954), XXVII:472.

Chapter and page references to the edition first noted will be thereafter given parenthetically in the text.

17. Like Gertrude, for example, who is, "della costola d'Adamo; e i suoi del tempo antico erano gente grande, venuta di Spagna, dove son *quelli che comandano* . . . e i suoi d'adesso, laggiù a Milano, contan molto, e son di quelli *che han sempre ragione*" (IX:148, my emphasis).

18. Marco Meriggi, *Amministrazione e classi sociali,* p. 328.

19. Antonio Gramsci, *Letteratura e vita nazionale,* p. 100.

20. Vittorio Spinazzola, *Il libro per tutti,* p. 190.

21. Robert Dombroski, "The Ideological Question in Manzoni," p. 524.

22. Cfr. Pietro Giordani, *Lettere inedite a Lazzaro Papi* (Lucca: Tipografia Baccelli, 1951), p. 105.

23. Marco Meriggi, *Il regno lombardo-veneto,* p. 210.

24. Friedrich Nietzsche, *Daybreak. Thoughts on the Prejudices of Morality,* tr. R. J. Holligdale (Cambridge: Cambridge University Press, 1982), pp. 36-37.

25. Theodor W. Adorno, *Minima Moralia,* tr. E. F. N. Jephcott (London: Verso, 1978), p. 184.

26. Sismondo de' Sismondi, quoted in "L'Italiano," p. 993.

27. Vittorio Spinazzola, *Il libro per tutti,* p. 191.

28. Italo Calvino, "Il romanzo dei rapporti di forza," *Atti del Convegno manzoniano di Nimega,* ed. Carlo Ballerini (Florence: Libreria Editrice Fiorentina, 1974), pp. 215-25, p. 222. Now in: *Una pietra sopra* (Turin: Einaudi, 1980), pp. 267-78.

29. Guido Baldi, *Giuseppe Rovani e il problema del romanzo dell'Ottocento* (Florence: Leo Olschki, 1967), p. 21.

30. Marco Meriggi, *Amministrazione e classi sociali,* p. 341.

31. Alessandro Manzoni, *Fermo e Lucia,* ed. Alberto Chiari e Fausto Ghisalberti (Milan: Mondadori, 1954), VIII:255-56.

32. *Ibid.,* p. 257.

33. Giulio Bollati, "L'Italiano," p. 997.

34. According to Giuseppe Mazzini, Manzoni had "abandoned fight for resignation"; cfr. "De l'art en Italie," *Revue Republicaine,* Paris, Vol. V, June 25, 1835, 194-218. Now in: *Scritti letterari editi ed inediti,* Vol. VIII (Imola: Galeati, 1910), p. 46.

Mark Davie (essay date 1992)

SOURCE: "Manzoni After 1848: An 'Irresolute Utopian'?" in *Modern Language Review,* Vol. 87, No. 4, October, 1992, pp. 847-57.

[*In the following essay, Davie explores Manzoni's relationship to Italian nationalism in the nineteenth century.*]

When Manzoni was asked in 1848 to stand as a candidate for the Piedmontese parliament, he wrote to his proposer declining the invitation, and explaining why he considered himself unsuitable for the task:

> Un *utopista* e un irresoluto sono due soggetti inutili per lo meno in una riunione dove si parli per concludere; io sarei l'uno e l'altro nello stesso tempo. Il fattibile le più volte non mi piace, e dirò anzi, mi ripugna; ciò che mi piace, non solo parrebbe fuor di proposito e fuor di tempo agli altri, ma sgomenterebbe me medesimo, quando si trattasse, non di vagheggiarlo o di lodarlo semplicemente, ma di promoverlo in effetto, e d'aver poi sulla coscienza una parte qualunque delle conseguenze.[1]

Many readers of *I promessi sposi* would endorse Manzoni's typically self-deprecating verdict. For all the novel's mordant social satire, so that it has accurately been described as 'from one point of view [. . .] all a searching critique of the *ancien régime*',[2] its political and social message remains ambivalent. In a world where injustice is rife, any attempt by its humble protagonists to assert their rights proves misguided and counter-productive, and the patient submission to Divine Providence which it appears to enjoin has always struck some readers as glib and unconvincing. The much-quoted strictures of Settembrini[3] echo the comment made by Pietro Giannone as early as 1832: 'Nelle circostanze e ne' tempi che corrono, la virtù della rassegnazione non è quella che occorre alla nostra povera patria.'[4]

What is more, Manzoni himself, during the twenty years in which he was occupied with the writing and revision of *I promessi sposi,* apparently followed the example of the characters in his novel, remaining aloof from political involvement. This followed the disappointments of 1815 and 1821, when he had twice greeted what he took to be the dawn of Italy's liberation with an enthusiastic poem, only for his hopes to be rapidly dashed; on both occasions the poems remained unpublished.[5] It was not until the dramatic events of 1848 that he was again provoked into a public expression of support for rebellion against an oppressive government.

It is puzzling, therefore, to read the account by Manzoni's wife Teresa Borri of a scene during the Milan insurrection of March 1848. An enthusiastic crowd gathered outside their house, shouting 'Viva Manzoni!'. Manzoni went out onto a balcony and responded, 'No! No! Viva l'Italia e chi combatte per lei! Io non ho fatto nulla!'. 'No! No!', came the reply from the crowd, 'Lei ha fatto assai! Ha dato l'iniziativa a tutta Italia! Evviva! Evviva Manzoni campione dell'Italia!' A spokesman then added, 'Chiediamo a Manzoni un inno per la Liberazione dell'Italia!', to which Manzoni responded in some embarrassment, 'Lo farò! Lo farò quando potrò!'.[6] According to another witness, Manzoni protested that he was no longer 'buono a far versi', but promised none the less 'che pure qualche cosa farebbe, dando in luce qualche sua poesia inedita', and this was in fact his response to the request: he published the poems of 1815 and 1821 with the title *Pochi versi inediti,* with the proceeds being donated to the relief of refugees from Austrian repression in the Veneto.[7]

On what grounds did the Milanese crowd acclaim Manzoni as 'campione dell'Italia'? It is true that Tommaseo, as early as 1825, had acclaimed his *Adelchi* as a tragedy whose hero was the Italian people, and in the immediate popular success of *I promessi sposi* on its publication in 1827, a few critics had welcomed it as a sign of national renewal.[8] But only from the late 1840s, and consistently only in the 1850s, was there any public discussion of the novel as an indictment of Italian demoralization under foreign occupation.[9] The crowd outside Manzoni's house seems to have been at least as alert as the critics to the book's potential as a patriotic text.

Surprising though the crowd's acclamation may have been, and embarrassing though Manzoni may have found it, he accepted the invitation to identify publicly with the nationalist cause by publishing the *Versi inediti.* Later in 1848 he went further, publishing a polemical article in the Turin journal *La Concordia.*[10] Prompted by a report that the merchants of Prague had petitioned the Austrian government not to give way to pressure for Italian independence because of the damage it would do to trade, he asserts that if Italians thought they were being kept subject to the empire to protect its trade they would respond by boycotting its

goods. But first he has this to say about the manifest inju tice which Austrian occupation in Italy had become:

> Pur troppo, in certi tempi, e forse in ogni tempo, certe ingiustizie paiono così naturali, che nè a chi ne gode, nè a chi ne patisce non viene neppure in mente che debbano cessare. Ma viene un momento in cui questa o quella ingiustizia comparisce così chiaramente ingiustizia, che non può più sostenersi contro la negazione di tutte le menti, contro la riprovazione di tutti gli animi, diventa odiosa e ridicola insieme, e (mi perdonino gli astuti se rimando loro la parola che adoprano come la più tremenda delle ingiurie) diventa un'utopia. Ora la dominazione austriaca in qualsiasi parte d'Italia è una di quelle ingiustizie per le quali un tal momento è venuto.[11]

The impression of Manzoni nailing his colours to the n tionalist mast in this essay is undermined by the accomp nying letter with which he submitted it through a frier insisting firmly on 'il più stretto incognito'.[12] But it is striking passage none the less, especially for its use of ◦ word *utopia,* and the parenthesis with which he draws ◦ tention to it. The essay was submitted on 13 Septemb 1848, and published two days later—less than a month b fore he wrote declining to stand for parliament on t' grounds that he was 'un *utopista* e un irresoluto'. T irony of the latter remark is sharpened by the fact that ◦ had so recently gone out of his way to stress that it w now the defenders of the status quo who were the *utopis* who were out of touch with political reality. Manzoni m still not have seen himself as a practical politician, but tl did not prevent him from seeing Italian independence as matter of practical politics.

Not that it was easy to see, in September 1848, how ind pendence was to be achieved; the months since the N lanese *cinque giornate* had seen Carlo Alberto's Lomba campaign end in defeat and Austrian authority r established. Manzoni himself relapsed, after the bri anonymous outburst of the *Concordia* article, into his cu tomary public silence on political questions. But this d not mean that he was not exercised by the dilemma whi remained after the unsuccessful campaigns of 1848-4 given that the status quo was manifestly unjust, what a tion was it legitimate to take to overcome that injustice? particular, in what circumstances was it permissible ◦ rebel against an established government?

For Manzoni, as for many of his contemporaries, the foc of such questions was the French Revolution of 1789; ◦ outcome of his prolonged reflections on the Revoluti◦ and its consequences is an unfinished historical essay ◦ some 250 pages: *La rivoluzione francese del 1789 e rivoluzione italiana del 1859: Osservazioni comparative* Planned, as the title indicates, as a comparative study ◦ the light of the successful achievement of Italian indepe dence in 1859-60, and written probably between 1862 a 1864,[14] the text does not fulfil the promise of the title; ◦ comparative element is almost wholly lacking, and wh remains is a detailed account of political events in Fran in the single year from August 1788 (the summoning of the Estates General) to 26 August 1789 (the adoption by the National Assembly of the Declaration of the Rights of Man). Anecdotal evidence confirms Manzoni's lifelong interest in and detailed knowledge of the revolutionary period,[15] and a letter of February 1850 asking his stepson to obtain for him a copy of Meillan's *Mémoires* 'per un passo del dialogo che sto terminando'[16] suggests that he was already thinking about the theme of the essay at this time. So although they were written in the early 1860s, the *Osservazioni* seem to reflect his concerns of a decade earlier, and the body of the text makes virtually no reference to the events of 1859-60, which should have provided the final vindication for his long-standing support of the Italian national cause. This gives the *Osservazioni* an oddly one-sided character, for which it hardly seems an adequate explanation to say that Manzoni left the work unfinished because his narrative became bogged down in excessive detail. The author of *I promessi sposi* knew, after all, how to handle a long and complex narrative.

Starting from the premise that 'la grandissima maggioranza della popolazione francese [. . .] volesse delle riforme nel suo governo, e avesse delle ragioni più che giuste di volerle' (I, 1, p. 323), Manzoni asks how this justifiable demand for reform led 'in pochissimo tempo, a uno sconquasso, quale è attestato dalla storia' (I, 23, p. 328). His conclusion, spelt out at length in Chapter IV of the *Osservazioni,* is that the subsequent *sconquasso* was the inevitable consequence of the act of usurpation whereby the Third Estate, in June 1789, declared itself unilaterally to be the 'National Assembly' without reference to the crown or the other two Estates (IV, 3, p. 353); that single act of lawlessness opened the way for all the rest. In an appropriately tortuous passage he paraphrased the implications of such a declaration (IV, 40, p. 360); later in the chapter he made the same point much more succinctly, commenting on the phrase 'la nazione illuminata' which the Assembly had used of itself: 'La formula poi di *nazione illuminata* non esprime, che una contradizione: tutti, vale a dire alcuni' (IV, 189, p. 396). The Third Estate's action met none of the conditions under which it might—politically no less than legally—be justified: it was not necessary in order to bring about reform; it produced a greater evil than it abolished, because it destroyed a government without putting anything in its place; those responsible had neither a popular mandate for their action nor popular approval for the result (IV, 280, p. 418).

At first sight this is little more than a standard conservative critique of the Revolution, saying nothing of substance which had not been said by Edmund Burke within a year of the events themselves. Both Manzoni's fundamental reasons for declaring the Third Estate's actions illegitimate were equally clearly set out by Burke: that the monarchy, far from being incapable of reform, had already moved to initiate it,[17] and that the self-styled National Assembly had no legal standing, having subverted the basis of its own authority.[18] So, too, was his conviction that the

horrors of the Revolution followed inexorably from the Assembly's initial act of rebellion.[19] Given this strongly negative judgement of the French Revolution, it is not surprising to learn from the memoirs of Manzoni's stepson, Stefano Stampa, that he was dismayed when he read a draft of the essay, and urged Manzoni to write an introduction explaining how the Italian case was different. Otherwise, Stampa told him, 'la parte che riguarda la Rivoluzione francese ed il principio d'autorità, sarà sfruttato dal partito clericale-gesuitico, per abbattere appunto e per rovinare la rivoluzione italiana: e tu invece di giovarle le avresti portato il più gran danno'.[20] Manzoni complied, with an introduction which seeks to show how the Italian 'revolution' was legitimate precisely because it had avoided the usurpation of power which had taken place in France.

The result is to make the work even more forthright in its condemnation of the 1789 revolutionaries. Manzoni spells out the two disastrous results of their action: 'L'oppressione del paese, sotto il nome di libertà; e la somma difficoltà di sostituire al governo distrutto un altro governo; che avesse, s'intende le condizioni della durata' (*Introduction*, 3, p. 309). The first consequence was simply the culmination of 'il sopravvento di forze arbitrarie e violente' which had been present from the outset, while the second was apparent from the fact that France had had ten different constitutions in the sixty-one years between 1791 and 1852 (6-9, pp. 309-10). In Italy, on the other hand, neither of these 'tristissimi effetti' had ensued; where France had succumbed to oppression and anarchy, Italy had achieved liberty:

> La libertà davvero, che consiste nell'essere il cittadino, per mezzo di giuste leggi e di stabili istituzioni, assicurato, e contro violenze private, e contro ordini tirannici del potere, e nell'essere il potere stesso immune dal predominio di società oligarchiche, e non sopraffatto dalla pressura di turbe, sia avventizie, sia arrolate.
>
> (10-11, pp. 310-11)

Where no French government in the aftermath of the Revolution had achieved stability, in Italy 'ai governi distrutti poté sottentrare un novo governo, con un'animatissima e insieme pacifica prevalenza e quasi unanimità di liberi voleri'. The reason was that Italy's liberators had observed, while the revolutionaries of 1789 had failed to observe, 'una condizione, non meno imposta dall'equità, che richiesta [. . .] dalla prudenza':

> Che la distruzione del governo, o de' governi esistenti prima della Rivoluzione, fosse un mezzo indispensabile per ottenere un bene essenziale e giustamente voluto dalle rispettive società rette da loro: in altri termini, che que' governi fossero irreformabilmente opposti al bene e alla volontà delle società medesime.
>
> (12-14, p. 311)

While this could not be said of the government of Louis XVI, in Italy the very multiplicity of states was intrinsically unjust, simply because they stood in the way of national unification: 'Erano ugualmente irreformabili, per il loro esser molti' (22, p. 313).

This last sentence abruptly broadens the argument to justify not only the expulsion of the Austrians from Lombardy but the overthrow of all the other governments of the peninsula in the course of unification under the Piedmontese crown. Such a large leap in his normally scrupulous step-by-step argument is indicative of Manzoni's uncritical approach to the recent events in Italy, in marked contrast to his observations on the events of 1789. And although he confidently claimed that the second part of the *Osservazioni,* dealing with Italy, would be straightforward and uncontroversial (*Introduction,* 19, p. 312), it remained unwritten. Indeed, his difficulty in formulating his position is reflected in the existence of at least two abandoned drafts of the introduction, and there is evidence that he continued working on it as late as July 1869, some time after he had given up any idea of completing the *Osservazioni* themselves.[21] Could it be that the Italian case proved on reflection to be less straightforward than he originally thought?

The first of his conditions for justifying revolution—that a government should be overthrown only when it was clearly beyond any hope of reform—is at least acknowledged by the assertion already quoted, that 'erano ugualmente irreformabili, per il loro essere molti'. But what of the second—that those who claims to act in the name of the nation should have a clear legal mandate to do so? Here another passage in Chapter IV of the *Osservazioni* is relevant.

Manzoni comments on the moment, in the dense sequence of events of June 1789, when the King summoned a joint meeting of the three Estates, thereby reconstituting the Estates General which had effectively been dissolved by the earlier unilateral action of the Third Estate: 'E il re al quale solo apparteneva per consenso universale (qual titolo più legittimo?) la facoltà di convocare gli Stati Generali, era naturalmente il solo che potesse avere quella di ristabilirli' (IV, 184, p. 395). The parenthesis in this sentence contains a point of major importance, as he acknowledges a few pages later. The King's declaration added that 'se gli Stati Generali lo avessero abbandonato nella impresa, avrebbe fatto egli solo il bene dei suoi popoli, e solo si sarebbe riguardato come il loro vero rappresentante', and Manzoni underlines the significance of this last phrase:

> Erano, in bocca di un Re di Francia, parole nuove, che prenunziavano e accettavano un tempo nuovo, erano una rinunzia, implicita ma irrepugnabile a quella massima tanto solenne in Francia fino allora, che il re tenesse il suo potere direttamente e immediatamente da Dio, e che, per conseguenza, questo potere fosse indipendente da ogni sindacato, e inamissibile.
>
> (IV, 211-13, pp. 401-02)

Once it is conceded that the King acts 'per consenso universale', as the 'representative' of the people, it be-

comes possible for their *consenso* to be withdrawn, transferred to some other body. Indeed, when on 30 J? the King and the nobility and clergy submitted to the ? mands of the Third Estate, Bailly asserted that the popu? acclamation which followed confirmed the validity of th? actions; Manzoni translates from his *Mémoires:*

> Questi segni di soddisfazione da parte dei nostri commettenti [. . .] sono prove della saggezza della nostra condotta, e stabiliscono la base su di cui si appoggiava l'autorità della Assemblea Nazionale; c'era l'espressione della volontà generale; la forza era nel popolo, che ci osservava.
>
> (IV, 257, p. 412)[22]

Manzoni sees the contradiction into which his argum? has led him: having appealed to 'consenso universale' ? the source of the King's authority (leaving aside the qu? tion of how such *consenso* might be expressed ? measured), how can he now deny its validity as the ? thority for the Third Estate? He answers this objecti? from an imaginary interlocutor by pointing to another c? tradiction. He does not deny a people's right to overthr? a government which no longer promotes the common go? (IV, 260, p. 413), but 'nemmeno un popolo può avere diritto di convalidare un equivoco', which was the imp? cation of the Third Estate's attempt to limit the King power while still retaining the monarchy. 'Ma il potere ? soluto e il governo crano uniti e come compenetrati ne persona del re'; the only person who could limit the King power without fatally weakening his authority was ? King himself. 'Ed era per l'appunto ciò che aveva tent? di fare lo sventurato Luigi', in the declaration which ? Third Estate had rejected on 23 June (IV, 261-65, pp. 4? 14).

Manzoni's argument once more echoes Burke's, a? reaches ostensibly the same conclusion. But when Bur? concludes, 'A state of contempt is not a state for a prin? better get rid of him at once',[23] his tone is heavily ironic the very brutality of the conclusion encourages the rea? to recoil from it. Where Burke firmly believed in the pr? ciple of heredity (and so had to fudge the issue when ? discussed the English 'Glorious Revolution' of 1688? Manzoni is sufficiently a child of the revolution to belie? that a king's power does derive ultimately from popu? consent; for all his sympathy with Louis XVI, his discu? sion never has the instinctive revulsion with which Bur? contemplated the possibility of his being deposed. The ? sult was that Manzoni in his turn had to fudge when ? came to discussing the role of the House of Savoy in t? unification of Italy, stressing the 'consenso universal? which they enjoyed among their subjects.

The stimulus to do so was provided by an invitation whi? came to Manzoni in the last months of his life: to contri? ute to a collection of autographs of 'uomini delle diver? province che in vario modo cooperarono virtualmen? all'indipendenza nazionale' which was being formed ? the city of Turin. With an energy remarkable in a man ?

eighty-eight, he responded by embarking on an account of the events of 1848-49 and the progress they represented towards Italian unification: the essay ***Dell'indipendenza dell'Italia.***[25]

Not surprisingly, in view of the occasion which prompted it, the essay underlines the leading role played by Piedmont in achieving unification; it had, Manzoni declared, been his conviction 'da più d'un mezzo secolo' that 'da codesta parte d'Italia dovesse, potesse, un giorno, venire il risorgimento della, purtroppo, più vasta parte del rimanente' (I, 2, p. 681). The phrase 'da più d'un mezzo secolo', taken literally, dates his faith in Piedmont back to the abortive officers' revolt which had inspired his poem ***Marzo 1821.*** This may well be what he had in mind, for the episode marked the first hesitant appearance on the political scene of the young prince Carlo Alberto, and the greater part of the essay is a highly sympathetic account of Carlo Alberto's role as King of Piedmont in the events of 1848-49.

After briefly praising his military campaigns in Lombardy and commiserating with his lack of success, Manzoni concentrates on the constitutional *Statuto* which Carlo Alberto had granted in February 1848, which had been preserved in his son Vittorio Emmanuele's negotiations with Austria after his defeat in 1849, and which had survived to form the basis of the constitution of the new Kingdom of Italy in 1860. This was the source of Piedmont's political strength:

> Infatti, al Piemonte era rimasta una forza che lo distingueva da tutti gli altri Stati d'Italia [. . .]: la forza che nasceva dalla stima e dalla fiducia reciproca del Re e del paese, da un sentimento concorde, e riguardo ai sacrifizi da farsi, e riguardo alla dignità da mantenersi.
>
> (III, 6, p. 688)

The *Statuto* was too eloquent a testimony to the advantages of freedom and independence for Austria to remain indifferent to it:

> Lo Statuto, il solo che desse indizio di poter prendere radice in Italia, perché il solo voluto concordemente e sinceramente dal principe e dal paese, era un mezzo permanente di combattere il predominio straniero, sia col propalarne, per mezzo della tribuna e della stampa, i dolorosi effetti sull'altre parti d'Italia, sia col mantener vivo in quelle il sentimento dell'indipendenza.
>
> (III, 20, p. 691)

In a discarded draft for the next chapter Manzoni returned to this theme again:

> Si vide in codesta parte d'Italia stabilito in fatto ciò che la grandissima maggioranza degl'Italiani aveva desiderato e vagheggiato per tutta l'Italia; voglio dire uno Statuto con cui erano assicurate e regolate [. . .] le libertà, e pubbliche e individuali.

He concedes that Carlo Alberro was not the first Italian ruler to grant a constitution in 1848, but then continues,

> Ma, (e fu questo l'avvenimento novo,) l'esito della guerra venendo a *interpretar le carte che avevano celato il vero,* costrinse le menti a riconoscere nel fatto del Piemonte, una differenza essenziale dagli altri. Apparve sincero. E ciò per la ragione naturalissima, che era tale.[26]

So central, indeed, was this theme that even before he embarked on writing the essay, Manzoni had responded to the invitation from Turin with an open letter of thanks, explaining his fear that the essay he had in mind 'sarebbe stata fastidiosamente prolissa per l'Onorevole Comitato a cui era diretta', and giving the essence of what he wanted to say in a single sentence:

> Che la concordia nata nel 1849 tra il giovane Re di codesta estrema parte della patria comune, e il suo popolo ristretto d'allora, fu la *prima* cagione d'una tale indipendenza, poiché fu essa, e essa sola, che rese possibile anche il generoso e non mai abbastanza riconosciuto aiuto straniero; e essa sola che fece rimaner privi d'effetto gli sforzi opposti della Potenza allora prevalente in Italia, e fatalmente avversa a questa indipendenza.[27]
>
> (Italics original)

However he rephrased it, Manzoni's claim rested on subjective judgements which by their nature could not be substantiated: 'la stima e la fiducia reciproca del Re e del paese'; 'un sentimento concorde'; 'voluto concordemente e sinceramente'; 'Apparve sincero [. . .] per la ragione naturalissima, che era tale'. It is true that he had a well-placed informant in his son-in-law Massimo d'Azeglio, Prime Minister of Piedmont in 1849-52, whose letters he was able to quote as evidence of the firm stand which he took in the armistice negotiations with Austria.[28] But it is clear that the King did not share d'Azeglio's commitment to constitutionalism,[29] and in any case Manzoni's motives for stressing the popular support for the Piedmontese monarchy are plain: in Carlo Alberto he saw a monarch who succeeded, where Louis XVI had failed, in reaching a constitutional agreement with his subjects; this in turn gave Carlo Alberto's son the legitimacy to justify his annexation of the rest of Italy in 1859-60.

In a letter to d'Azeglio in May 1850, Manzoni had joked that his support for the monarchy was purely opportunistic, unlike that of Stefano Stampa, who had always been a convinced monarchist:

> E io, vecchio come sono, ho dovuto confessargli che aveva avuta più ragione di me; e ora com'ora la penso come lui; me se spuntasse qualcosa che promettesse di meglio (per ora non pare), volto subito casacca; e allora state freschi: vi farò tanto male, quanto bene vi fo ora, che è una cosa immensa.[30]

He never did 'turn his coat'; on the contrary, as I have shown, he claimed at the end of his life to have looked to Piedmont as the source of Italy's renewal for more than half a century. Certainly by 1850 his mind was made up; from then onwards, far from being *irresoluto,* he seems to have been surprisingly ready to brush any doubts aside in his eagerness to identify with a potential national saviour.

The same readiness to commit himself to a position and thereafter to ignore any difficulties it might raise is apparent in his attitude to another controversial aspect of Italian unification: the position of the Papacy. This is the most surprising implication of his cavalier dismissal of all the governments of Italy except Piedmont as 'ugualmente irreformabili, per il loro essere molti'; where, for a Catholic like Manzoni, did this leave the Papal State?

As early as 1819-20 he had concluded that the French Church had benefited spiritually from its loss of temporal power at the Revolution:

> M'ingannerò, ma credo che quando la Religione fu spogliata in Francia dello splendore esterno, quando non ebbe altra forza che quella di Gesù Cristo, poté parlar più alto, e fu più ascoltata; e almeno coloro che sono disposti a pigliare le parti degli oppressi, ebbero contro di essa un pregiudizio di meno.[31]

It would be reasonable to assume that he extended this principle to the temporal power of the Papacy, and the memoirs of several of his acquaintances record remarks which he made to this effect,[32] but he was careful not to commit himself to such a view in print. Again, however, the events of 1848 obliged him to translate the principle into a specific political choice.

The conflict of loyalties between his Catholicism and his patriotism was sharpened by the fact that his friend and mentor, Antonio Rosmini, played a central part in the attempt to enlist the support of Pius IX for a federation of Italian states.[33] In May 1848, at the critical juncture after the Pope's Allocution dissociating his state from the war against Austria, Rosmini wrote to Cardinal Castracane urging him to commit the Papacy unequivocally to the Italian national cause. He made it clear that he started from the orthodox premise that the Pope could not renounce his temporal power:

> Non v'ha dubbio che il Sommo Pontefice dee adempire i doveri ad un tempo di Principe temporale e Capo della Chiesa; e sarebbe un manifesto errore il pretendere che gli uni siano inconciliabili cogli altri. Questo è quello che vogliono i tristi, quelli che macchinano di spogliare la Chiesa de' suoi Stati temporali: Pio IX ha giurato di conservarli alla Chiesa; e però dee dimostrare col fatto che quelle due specie di doveri sono conciliabili, che egli sa realmente adempirli nella loro pienezza. Questo principio dee indubitatamente regolare la condotta del Pontefice: non credo che su di ciò possa cadere alcun dubbio.[34]

Rosmini sent a copy of this letter to Manzoni, asking for his comments; Manzoni replied on 23 May:

> Costretto a portare un giudizio, e un giudizio sommario, dico che la lettera mi pare, in tutti i punti essenziali, concludentissima. [. . .] Avrei poche osservazioni minute, e risguardanti piuttosto la forma che la sostanza.

Characteristically, he suggested toning down Rosmini's more forthright expressions; where Rosmini had written that if he failed to support the Italian cause, 'il Papa perderà tutta la sua riputazione, l'Italia lo esecrerà come Principe temporale', Manzoni commented that e'secrerà 'forse è troppo forte'. His other suggestion was even more restrained:

> E anche, ma questo forse per mio interesse, quel *tristi* [. . .] che pare applicabile anche a chi creda che la soluzione definitiva, e probabilmente lontana, possa portare la separazione del poter temporale, per vie e con compensi preparati dalla Provvidenza, e con l'assentimento dello stesso Pontefice.[35]

Mild though this is (Manzoni clearly counted himself among those whom Rosmini labelled *tristi*) he makes his own position quite plain, and once more he refuses to be deflected from supporting what he has concluded is the best hope of national unification.

A rare glimpse of the real strength of his feelings about the Papal State is provided by his daughter Vittoria's account of his reaction to the news of Garibaldi's occupation of the Romagna, in September 1860:

> Quando in settembre arrivarono le notizie della spedizione di Romagna, papà non stava più in sé dalla contentezza: piangeva, rideva, batteva le mani, gridando ripetutamente: 'Viva Garibaldi! Viva Garibaldi!' Nessuno l'aveva mai visto prima, nè lo rivide mai più dopo, in un tale stato di gioiosa eccitazione.

She goes on to give an accurate summary of the view he had expressed in the *Morale cattolica*:

> Papà era convinto che la perdita del potere temporale dovesse essere una misura provvidenziale per la Chiesa, la quale, liberata da ogni cura terrena, avrebbe potuto—credeva lui—meglio esercitare il suo dominio spirituale, e meglio uniformarsi ai precetti del suo Divino Fondatore.

But she then chooses to stress both the unorthodoxy of this position, and—certainly more than Manzoni himself would have done—the strength of his anti-clericalism:

> Era nel giusto papà? S'ingannava? *Ai posteri* . . . ! Egli stesso, visto l'atteggiamento preso più tardi da Pio IX, dopo il '70, non osava più parlare dello scottante argomento. Ma clericale non fu mai, e ritenne sempre che nessuno meno dei clericali s'ispirasse al Vangelo di Gesù Cristo.[36]

Manzoni was always more circumpsect. But even if the *scottante argomento* was taboo, his actions were unequivocal. From 1848 onwards he was committed to the allegiance which led him to accept a Senatorship in the new kingdom in 1860, and four years later to attend the Chamber for the only time in order to vote for the removal of the national capital from Turin to Florence, as a necessary step on the road to Rome:[37] even more strikingly, in 1872 to accept the freedom of the city of Rome (in recognition, he wrote, of 'le aspirazioni costanti d'una lunga vita all'indipendenza e all'unità d'Italia')[38] at a time when many Catholics believed that the capture of the Eternal City had been an act of sacrilege. There is good reason to believe that the year in which Manzoni described himself as 'un *utopista* e un irresoluto' was the year in which he ceased to be either.

Notes

1. Letter of 7 October 1848 to Giorgio Briano; no. 867 in A. Manzoni, *Lettere,* ed. by C. Arieti, II (*Tutte le opere,* VII) (Milano: Mondadori, 1970), p. 462.

2. K. Foster, 'The Idea of Truth in Manzoni and Leopardi', *Proceedings of the British Academy,* 53 (1967), 243-57 (p. 246).

3. 'Ma nel 1827, nel tempo più scuro e feroce della Reazione, quando i preti spadroneggiavano, l'Austria incrudeliva nel Lombardo Veneto, e i nostri tirannelli infuriavano a straziarci, scrivere e pubblicare un libro che loda i preti e i frati, e consiglia pazienza sommessione perdono, significa (il Manzoni certamente non volle questo, ma questa è la conseguenza necessaria del libro) consigliare la sommessione nella servitù, la negazione della patria e di ogni generoso sentimento civile, significa che Dio vuole l'Austria nella Lombardia e nella Venezia, il Duca a Modena, il Papa a Roma, i Borboni a Napoli, e che li vuole per suoi fini che noi non dobbiamo cercare, e li vuole per nostro bene, per farci soffrire e acquistar merito per una vita migliore' (L. Settembrini, *Lezioni di letteratura italiana,* 2nd edn, 3 vols (Napoli: Morano, 1877), III, 313).

4. Quoted in A. Cottignoli, *Manzoni fra i critici dell'Ottocento* (Bologna: Boni, 1978), p. 68. On this Pietro Giannone (1792-1872), see G. Mazzoni, *L'Ottocento* (Storia Letteraria d'Italia, IX), 2nd edn (Milano: Vallardi, 1934), pp. 726-28; his criticism of Manzoni was published in the Paris journal *L'Esule,* I (1832), 262-302.

5. 'Il proclama di Rimini', on Joachim Murat's proclamation of an independent kingdom of Italy in March 1815, and 'Marzo 1821', prompted by the short-lived promise by the young Carlo Alberto of a liberal constitution in Piedmont.

6. N. Ginzburg, *La famiglia Manzoni* (Torino: Einaudi, 1983), p. 242.

7. See the note to 'Marzo 1821' in A. Manzoni, *Poesie e tragedie,* ed. by F. Ghisalberti (*Tutte le opere,* I) (Milano: Mondadori, 1957), pp. 854-56.

8. N. Tommaseo's review of the *Adelchi* in *Il nuovo raccoglitore,* I (April-June 1825), was reprinted in E. Bellorini, *Discussioni e polemiche sul Romanticismo (1816-1826),* 2nd edn, 2 vols (Bari: Laterza, 1975), II, 217-61. The first appreciations of the civic virtues of *I promessi sposi* are expressed in private letters rather than in print: for example, P. Giordani: 'Gl'impostori e gli oppressori se ne accorgeranno poi (ma tardi) che profonda testa, che potente leva è, chi ha posto tanta cura in apparir semplice, e quasi minchione [. . .]. Oh perché non ha Italia venti libri simili!' (letter to F. Testa, 25 December 1827); and even Sismondi: 'Il y avait du génie dans ses *Promessi sposi,* il y avait en même temps l'exemple du genre de lecture, qui peut, en dépit de la censure, faire l'impression la plus générale et la plus utile sur le public italien' (letter to C. Ugoni, 11 September 1829, both quoted in G. Sforza, 'Le prime accoglienze ai *Promessi sposi*', in *Brani inediti dei 'Promessi sposi'*, 2nd edn, 2 vols (Milano: Hoepli, 1905), II, xxxii-xxxiii, lvi).

9. For the change in published criticism of the novel from the late 1840s onwards, see Cottignoli, pp. 65-82 ('I *Promessi sposi* e la critica patriottica').

10. Published with the title 'Indipendenza politica e liberismo economico', in A. Manzoni, *Saggi storici e politici,* ed. by F. Ghisalberti (*Tutte le opere,* IV) (Milano: Mondadori, 1963), pp. 707-11; also as no. 862 in *Lettere,* II, pp. 453-58.

11. 'Indipendenza politica . . .', 5-6; in *Saggi storici e politici,* p. 708.

12. Letter of 13 September 1848 to Gabrio Casati; no. 861 in *Lettere,* II, pp. 452-53.

13. Published in *Saggi storici e politici,* pp. 307-677 (text, pp. 307-567; drafts and fragments, pp. 571-677). From Chapter IV, 25 (p. 358) onwards the text is based on Manzoni's unrevised draft, and is therefore occasionally unclear or inelegant, as well as containing inconsistencies of spelling. References in the discussion which follows are to chapter, paragraph, and page number in this edition.

14. See *Saggi storici e politici,* pp. 764-68.

15. 'Della Rivoluzione di Francia nessuno conosceva i più minuti particolari meglio di lui. Non v'era piccolo accidente, ch'egli non sapesse a memoria. Non v'era persona che vi avesse avuta parte, della quale non avesse cercato di penetrare le più intime pieghe dell'animo' (R. Bonghi); 'Forse non ci fu opera o opuscoletto sulla rivoluzione francese ch'egli non avesse meditato, al punto che sapeva a memoria il nome di tutti i membri della Convenzione' (S. Stampa, both quoted in *Saggi storici e politici,* p. 764).

16. Letter to Stefano Stampa, no. 920 in *Lettere,* II, pp. 509-10 (12 February 1850). This letter appears to have been overlooked by Ghisalberti in his note on the date of the *Osservazioni*: 'Nell'epistolario peccato non si trovi cenno di un antico proposito di scrivere sul grande avvenimento, soprattutto quando il Manzoni ripiegò la mente sua alla considerazione dei grandi fenomeni della storia. [. . .] Il Manzoni ebbe quindi soltanto dopo gli avvenimenti politici che portarono alla unità della nazione italiana, suo

sogno antichissimo, l'impulso a fare un esame filosofico, per dirlo illuministicamente, dei due grandi momenti storici' (*Saggi storici e politici,* pp. 764-66). Clearly the two 'grandi momenti storici' could not be compared until the second had happened, but it is clear that he had studied the events of 1789 some time before 1859.

17. Edmund Burke, *Reflections on the Revolution in France,* edited by Conor Cruise O'Brien (Harmondsworth: Penguin, 1968), pp. 230-31: 'Is it then true, that the French government was such as to be incapable or undeserving of reform; so that it was of absolute necessity the whole fabric should be at once pulled down, and the area cleared for the erection of a theoretic experimental edifice in its place? All France was of a different opinion in the beginning of the year 1789.'

18. *Reflections,* pp. 275-76: 'I can never consider this assembly as anything else than a voluntary association of men, who have availed themselves of circumstances, to seize upon the power of the state. [. . .] They do not hold the authority they exercise under any constitutional law of the state. They have departed from the instructions of the people by whom they were sent; which instructions, as the assembly did not act in virtue of any antient usage or settled law, were the sole source of their authority.'

19. *Reflections,* p. 126: 'They have seen the French rebel against a mild and lawful monarch, with more fury, outrage, and insult, than ever any people had been known to rise against the most illegal usurper, or the most sanguinary tyrant. Their resistance was made to concession; their revolt was from protection; their blow was aimed at a hand holding out graces, favours, and immunities. This was unnatural. The rest is in order. They have found their punishment in their success.'

20. S. S[tampa], *Alessandro Manzoni, la sua famiglia, i suoi amici* (Milano: Cogliati, 1885), p. 440; quoted in Manzoni, *Saggi storici e politici,* p. 769.

21. See the accounts given by R. Bonghi and G. Rossari of visits to Manzoni in October 1868 and July 1869 respectively, quoted in *Saggi storici e politici,* pp. 769-70; the discarded drafts of the introduction are printed at pages 571-98.

22. For the original, see *Mémoires de Bailly,* 3 vols (Paris: Baudouin, 1821-22), I, 261 (entry for 30 June 1789).

23. *Reflections,* p. 322.

24. *Reflections,* p. 101: 'Unquestionably there was at the Revolution [of 1688], in the person of King William, a small and a temporary deviation from the strict order of a regular hereditary succession; but it is against all genuine principles of jurisprudence to draw a principle from a law made in a special case, and regarding an individual person. *Privilegium non transit in exemplum.* If ever there

was a time favourable for establishing the principle that a king of popular choice was the only legal king, without all doubt it was at the Revolution. Its not being done at that time is a proof that the nation was of opinion it ought not to be done at any time.'

25. *Saggi storici e politici,* pp. 681-702; for the circumstances in which it was written, see page 808.

26. *Saggi storici e politici,* pp. 820-21.

27. Letter to Pio Celestino Agodino, in two drafts, letters 1579 and 1580, in *Lettere,* III, pp. 424-25 (11 February 1873); published in *La Gazzetta Piemontese,* 13 February 1873. Manzoni then drafted several versions of an 'Avviso al lettore' to preface the finished essay, reproducing the substance of this statement (*Saggi storici e politici,* pp. 815-17), but in the end did not use any of them.

28. 'L'uomo che, meglio di qualunque altro, poteva conoscere qual fosse, in un tale affare la volontà determinata del re, poiché ne era l'interprete ufiziale, dico il presidente del suo Consiglio, scriveva, nel forte delle trattative, a un amico di confidenza: "Lavoro per convincer l'Europa, che siamo capaci di fare qualunque pazzia [to defend the *Statuto*]"' (III, 4, p. 688). The 'amico di confidenza' was another of Manzoni's sons-in-law, Giovanni Battista Giorgini; d'Azeglio's letters to him are quoted again in III, 16-17, and 22, pp. 690-91.

29. See the documents cited in D. Mack Smith, *The Making of Italy, 1796-1866,* 2nd edn (London: Macmillan, 1988), pp. 166-71.

30. Letter to d'Azeglio, no. 937 in *Lettere,* II, pp. 526-27 (2 May 1850).

31. *Osservazioni sulla morale cattolica,* ed. by R. Amerio, 3 vols (Milano and Napoli: Ricciardi, 1966), II, 456-57 (Part II, I, 110). Part II of the *Morale cattolica* was unpublished in Manzoni's lifetime, but Amerio concludes that it was substantially written at the same time as Part I, published in 1819 (*Morale cattolica,* I, xviii-xxi). In any case Manzoni expressed similar views on the desirability of the Church's shedding its temporal power in letters to Canon Tosi in December 1819 and April 1820 (nos 126 and 133 in *Lettere,* I, pp. 188-90, 205-08).

32. See, for instance, N. Tommaseo, *Colloquii col Manzoni* (Firenze: Sansoni, 1929), pp. 160-64, 204; Stampa, *Alessandro Manzoni,* pp. 146-47, 168-69; and the discussion in F. Ruffini, *La vita religiosa di Alessandro Manzoni,* 2 vols (Bari: Laterza, 1931), II, 416-40. The relevant extracts are collected in Manzoni, *Opere,* ed. by M. Barbi and F. Ghisalberti, 3 vols (Milano: Centro Nazionale di Studi Manzoniani, 1942-50), III, 669-77.

33. See K. Foster, 'Rosmini in 1848-49', in *God's Tree* (London: Blackfriars, 1957), pp. 93-101.

34. Rosmini to Cardinal Castracane, 17 May 1848, in *Carteggio fra Alessandro Manzoni e Antonio*

Rosmini, ed. by G. Bonola (Milano: Cogliati, 1901), pp. 95-105 (p. 96).

35. No. 853 in *Lettere,* II, p. 447 (23 May 1848).

36. M. Scherillo, *Manzoni intimo. 1: Vittoria e Matilde Manzoni. Memorie di Vittoria Giorgini-Manzoni* (Milano: Hoepli, 1923), p. 138.

37. No doubt Manzoni was also influenced by his belief in the linguistic pre-eminence of Florence (see Tommaseo, *Colloquii col Manzoni,* pp. 130-31), but that he hoped and expected Florence eventually to give way to Rome is made clear in a letter from Giorgini to his wife, Manzoni's daughter Vittoria, when he accompanied Manzoni to Turin for the Senate vote. D'Azeglio and others were irritated by Manzoni's insistence on recording his vote, and hinted that Giorgini should have dissuaded him, but, Giorgini wrote, 'Si vede proprio che questi signori conoscono poco Pappà, che ne hanno un concetto molto inferiore a quello che merita, e che per conseguenza si esagerano grandemente il potere della mia influenza su di lui. Dovrebbero sapere che egli è ben chiaro e ben fermo nelle sue idee e nei suoi propositi, e che poche idee ha più chiare e più ferme di quella di volere che si vada a Roma. Per lui è evidente che l'andare adesso a Firenze significa incamminarsi sulla via di Roma, e non saremmo certo capaci nè io, nè Massimo [d'Azeglio], nè Donna Costanza [Arconati], nè altri, di fargli cambiar rotta: ha in testa più fitto che mai il *chiodo di Roma,* ed è sempre pieno di fiducia che a Roma ci potremo andare col pieno consenso della coscienza cattolica' (5 December 1864; in Manzoni, *Opere,* III, 670-72).

38. Letter to the Mayor of Rome, no. 1559 in *Lettere,* III, p. 412 (28 July 1872).

Susanna Ferlito (essay date 1998)

SOURCE: "Fear of the Mother's Tongue: Secrecy and Gossip in Manzoni's *I Promessi Sposi,*" in *MLN,* Vol. 113, No. 1, January, 1998, pp. 30-51.

[*In the following essay, Ferlito examines the mother-daughter relationship in Manzoni's* I promessi sposi *and the ways in which gossip both defines and undermines female relationships.*]

Victoria Goddard, in her study of women's sexuality and group identity in Naples, rethinks the question of how codes of honor and shame are constructed and defended by examining the importance of women's role as "bearers," perhaps, as "*the* bearers of group identity."[1] Following in the wake of Mary Douglas's work on the body and rituals of pollution,[2] Goddard foregrounds the responsibility that women have in maintaining and perpetuating a group identity:

If women are seen as the boundary markers and the carriers of group identity, it follows that their 'integrity' should be safeguarded. The concept of the group can operate at different levels of inclusion: the family, the kinship group, the village, region, class, or caste. The integrity of the women of a group cannot be understood solely in terms of ensuring appropriate marriage arrangements, which would, however explain many aspects of behavior resulting in the isolation and 'protection' of women. The role of women as carriers of identity has further repercussions of a less obvious nature, which, I would argue, are related to women's role and powers as reproducers. Women may also be seen as the guardians of the 'secrets' of the group. By the very process of their control by men and their relegation to and identification with the domestic sphere, women are in a unique position to provoke a crisis within the group.

(180)

The potential of this crisis that women are in a "unique position" to provoke is powerfully illustrated in a text of fundamental significance for the construction of modern Italian culture and identity, namely Manzoni's *I Promessi Sposi [The Betrothed]* [hereafter **PS**].[3] In the following pages, I focus on how Manzoni's representation of the mother-daughter relationship in the novel implicitly recognizes and keeps at bay the critical potential of this bond and, by extension, the critical potential of a female alliance in the peasant community to which Lucia, her mother Agnese, and Lucia's fiancé Renzo, belong. My analysis shows that Manzoni's representation of Lucia's secret fear of her mother's gossip in a small community governed by face-to-face relations, is indicative of larger social and political questions which the novel fails to articulate but cannot quite suppress and/or efface.

I. The Secret

On the morning of her wedding day, while she is busy being dressed by a group of women from her peasant village, Lucia Mondella is called aside by a little girl who whispers something into her ear. Lucia leaves the group of women, goes downstairs to where Renzo is anxiously waiting for her. He tells her that their parish priest, Don Abbondio, has called off their marriage ceremony because his life has been threatened by the nobleman Don Rodrigo should he marry the two. Intimating that she knows something Renzo doesn't, and with a feeling of terror in her heart, Lucia asks him to wait for her while she goes back upstairs to dismiss the women. In the meantime, roused by her daughter's disappearance, Lucia's mother, Agnese, comes downstairs and Renzo anxiously tells her the little he knows about what has happened while they await Lucia's return. When she enters the room, Agnese rebukes her daughter for not having ever said anything and Lucia, wiping the tears from her eyes, promises to explain everything to her.

A chapter into the novel, this is a crucial scene. It sets in motion the plight of the two 17th-century Lombard peasant protagonists, Lucia Mondella and Renzo Tramaglino, whose marriage plans and hopes for a quiet and predictable future in their village are torn asunder by Don Rodrigo's fancy for Lucia; a fancy that has led him to make a bet with his cousin Attilio that he, Don Rodrigo, will have seduced Lucia by the festive date of Saint Martin. Situated in the context of a Lombardy governed by the Spanish and about to be devastated by famine, war, and the plague of 1630, the **PS** tells the story of what happens to Lucia, Agnese, and Renzo: their forced departure from the village, their separation, and their final reunion and marriage two years later after many trials and adventures.

The scene described above is crucial to the story not just because it introduces the main characters and sets their plight in motion, but because it produces, by way of Lucia's response to her mother, a secret point of entry and critique of the novel's patriarchal subtext. The fact is that Lucia doesn't tell her mother *everything* but what she does say appeases Agnese's resentment at having been left out of her daughter's confidence. The scene would raise few questions if this were all there was to Lucia's response. But the narrator tells us that Lucia had another good reason for not bringing her mother into her confidence and that about this other reason, namely her fear of her mother's gossip, Lucia remains silent. In short, readers are alerted to the fact that Lucia tells her mother only *one* of two good reasons and that the one becomes a secret precisely because the other satisfies Agnese's desire for an explanation. Paradoxically, this secret only constitutes itself as such in the moment of its disappearance: in the moment that Lucia's one good answer renders her other good reason undetectable and therefore secret.[4] Agnese has no reason to suspect that her daughter's answer conceals another "good" reason. Thus, it is in the act of responding that Lucia's mistrust becomes absolutely secret—to her mother. We, however, know; and find ourselves, as readers, in the position of witnessing a secret which excludes the mother and her mode of being in the world. The question is why? What is at stake for the narrator in telling us that Lucia does not tell her mother *everything*? Why does Lucia fear her mother's gossip and how does this secret, which successfully silences the mother's potential for gossip, function both on a narrative and ideological level? As Marianne Hirsch asks: "How do plots and structures of realism rooted as they are in Oedipal forms and preoccupations rest on and benefit from the erasure, trivialization, or objectification of the mother?"[5]

These questions challenge the presuppositions traditionally at work in readings of Lucia's position in the novel. What brings them into focus is a preoccupation with narratives that silence the mother's voice and gloss over the potential for a female entrustment.[6] When read through the lens of entrustment, Lucia's secret mistrust of her mother stands out as the marker of an all too familiar Oedipal scenario depicting the daughter's embrace of the Father's law. One does not have to be a feminist to note the production of Lucia's secret, but a reader engaged in a critical analysis of representations of gender in social and cultural texts is more likely to investigate this detail and question its larger

implications for a text that, like the **PS**, plays such a pivotal role in Italian culture and politics. Lucia Mondella is, without doubt, the most famous female character in modern Italian literature but in spite of the massive and ongoing proliferation of more or less sympathetic "takes" on her character, she remains, in my view, also the least understood. Standing as a symbol of unquestionable virtue and faith, she has acquired the status of a cultural icon and the value of a commodity fetish.

From her first appearance in the novel, in the scene we are examining, Lucia is seen to be enveloped in an soft aura, illuminated by her candor and faith.[7] When noted at all, her response to her mother's question is construed as a sign of filial compassion for her mother's indiscrete nature: by keeping silent about her mistrust, Lucia spares her mother's feelings. Emma Grimaldi, who has argued most persuasively for a benign interpretation of Lucia's secret, supports the compassionate reading with a comparative analysis of the differences between this scene as described in the **PS** and Manzoni's prior draft version of the scene in *Fermo e Lucia* [hereafter **FL**].[8] In that text, which can be thought of as the working draft for **PS**, Lucia Zarella (in the **FL** [*Fermo e Lucia*] she has a different surname from the **PS**) doesn't give her mother an explanation because she can't bring herself to reveal her fear that, had she done so, all the neighborhood would have known.[9] By bursting into tears, she avoids giving any response and in Grimaldi's view, this avoidance is a sign of immaturity. Grimaldi's interpretation of the difference between Lucia's responses raises two questions: the first has to do with the question of responsibility and, the second, with a question of how one reads the relation between two versions of essentially the same story. Grimaldi's interpretation of Lucia's Mondella's silence as compassionate in the **PS**, leaves unread how it deceives Agnese. It presumes Agnese's inability to understand, or change, or respond, or explain, and/or assume responsibility for what she is held incapable of doing; namely protecting Lucia's honor by keeping silent. To be sure, there are cases when keeping silent is sometimes more caring and honest than saying what comes first to one's mind, but Lucia Mondella's secret treats Agnese as if she has a pathological condition which cannot be helped or cured and she, therefore, must be pitied. Lucia Zarella's weeping in the **FL,** on the contrary, does not preclude Agnese from understanding and knowing that her daughter does not trust her. Lucia Zarella's non-response does not downplay Agnese's agency or her capacity to respond and therefore one could say that Lucia Zarella's non-response is more honest and ultimately responsible than Lucia Mondella's careful and "caring" answer.

Interpreting the secret as Lucia's compassionate suppression of a painful truth is a powerful one because it immediately adds to Lucia's portrait the virtue of maturity and compassion. It also has the advantage of glossing over the significance of the daughter's mistrust of her mother. By reading her secrecy as compassionate, one forgets that what is kept from Agnese is not just any secret but one that makes trust impossible. It prevents the mother from knowing anything that really matters—from knowing that her daughter does not want to risk confiding in her.[10] What Grimaldi's intertextual rereading of the **FL** and the **PS** scene suggests, however, is its dependence on a traditional practice of privileging the **PS** as the final and aesthetically superior text over the **FL** as its first draft version.

Susan Stanford Friedman's psychoanalytic approach to intertextuality has helped problematize the impetus towards unidirectional readings of differences between versions of a same story.[11] Friedman proposes a method of "reading texts both ways," that is without privileging the final version as the superior and teleological endpoint of all the others but rather reading each text as a version of a "complex composite text whose parts remain distinct yet interact according to a psycho/political dynamic to which we have some access with the help of Freud's theory of repression and grammar for the dream-work" (166). Read from this perspective, the two scenes and the passage between them yield a much more problematical interpretation of Lucia's response to her mother as well as a more complex understanding of Manzoni's investment in producing it as a secret in the **PS**. One of the things that happens to these episodes, read both ways, is that the seemingly unimportant paradigm of the mother-daughter relation begins to appear as a crucial site for exploring both the construction of Lucia's angelic figure and for examining Manzoni's ambivalence about the power and political potential of trust between mother and daughter. The secret surfaces as the visible marker of Manzoni's ambivalence towards the power of this relation and its potential for articulating in a political way the relation between private and public, individual and society. I can put it this way: the moment one takes note of Lucia's fear of Agnese's mediation, then the possibilities implicit in gossip's "other" positive effects become available to the reader's speculation. Had Lucia confided in her mother, for instance, Agnese might have used gossip to rally her community's defense of her daughter.

From the perspective of entrustment, to gloss over this filial mistrust and its implications for the mother-daughter plot in the novel is like glossing over a crossed-out word, leaving unread an illegible mark, a stain. To understand the politics of this secret Manzoni so casually offers on a platter, only to whisk it away as if it did not matter, requires a re-focusing of the reading lens on the mother-daughter relation and on the question of Lucia's preference for the private (male) world of confession over the mother's world of gossip with its constant blurring of the boundaries between private and public, its constantly making secret affairs public. It means investigating how Lucia's secret mistrust of her mother functions within the economy of a historical novel about three illiterate peasants for whom not only Agnese's gossip, but gossip in general, would be a crucial means for communicating and sharing experiences and knowledge. It means asking why only the negative aspects of gossip are foregrounded when gossip, historically, has invariably offered communities,

and female communities in particular, a powerful tool for shaping, modifying, and regulating behaviors and customs.[12] Stressing the positive aspects of gossip means, as Patricia Meyer Spacks writes, remembering that "its [gossip's] talk may be devoid of malicious intent; it often involves close and emotionally fruitful human association; reflecting intense interest in the personal, it may include subtle judgment and discrimination."[13] Politically, Lucia's rejection of Agnese's networking abilities and her mediation also entails closing off the possibility of a peasant rebellion against the oppressor Don Rodrigo.

II. READING BOTH WAYS

In the **FL,** Lucia tells her mother and Renzo that one evening Don Rodrigo, accompanied by some of his friends, had seen her leaving the silk-mill and had tried to draw her aside and take liberties with her. She had escaped his grasp but heard him say in anger, exacerbated by his friends' laughter, "ci vedremo" [we'll be seeing each other]. "Allora" [so], Lucia explains to Agnese and Renzo: "io pensai di non andar più alla filanda, feci un pò di baruffa colla Marcellina, per avere un pretesto, e vi ricorderete mamma ch'io vi dissi che non ci andrei" [I thought of not going back to the silk mill any more and I provoked a quarrel with Marcellina in order to find a pretext, and you will remember, mother, that I told you I would not be going] (260). Lucia, however, does return to work as the season's work is almost over and she thinks that for the few remaining days she can protect herself from Don Rodrigo by remaining in the midst of her companions. His persecution continues:

> mi aspettava quand'io andava al mercato, e vi ricorderete mamma ch'io vi dissi che aveva paura d'andar sola e non ci andai più: mi aspettava quand'io andava a lavare, ad ogni passo: io non dissi nulla, forse ho fatto male. Ma pregai tanto Fermo che affrettasse le nozze: pensava che quando sarei sua moglie colui non ardirebbe più tormentarmi; ed ora. . . .
>
> (261)
>
> [He waited for me when I went to the market, and you will remember, mother, that I told you that I was afraid of going alone and didn't go anymore: he waited for me when I went to the washing place, at every step: I said nothing, perhaps I did wrong. But I begged Fermo to hurry the wedding plans: thinking that when I would have been his wife he wouldn't have dared torment me anymore; and now . . .]

Lucia at this point bursts into tears and, as we saw before, her sobbing keeps her from having to respond to her mother's question. Agnese, however, insists. She tries a less directly scolding question: "Non ne hai tu fatto parola con nessuno?" [did you not speak of this to anyone?], and when Lucia confesses that she had indeed told Father Galdino in confession, Agnese reluctantly approves her daughter's choice of confessor but reiterates "hai fatto bene; ma dovevi dirlo *anche* a tua madre" [you did well; but you should have *also* told your mother] (my emphasis, 261).

The syncopated rhythm of Lucia's narrative, with its repeated reminders to her mother of the times which she had expressed her fears or acted strangely, conveys a sense of Lucia's anguish as Don Rodrigo's assiduous and relentless pursuit continues over time and she finds him invading the spaces of her everyday life: the market square, the washing place, the road between the silk mill and home. But the focus in Lucia's story-telling is not on Don Rodrigo's pursuit alone. Lucia's litany of "e vi ricorderete mamma che . . ." [and you will remember mama that . . .] draws one's attention to the drama of a failure in communication between mother and daughter. It strongly underlines that while Lucia did not tell her mother openly, she also did not hide her anguish from her mother. Indeed, she desired her mother's attention as much as she feared telling her about Don Rodrigo. Lucia's reminders carry a strong tone of reprimand for her mother's having failed to understand. If Agnese remains in the dark, as we deduce from Lucia's representation of the events, it is because she does not hear her daughter's repeated appeals for help nor does she question the changes in Lucia's behavior.[14] When Lucia tells Agnese that she is not going back to the silk mill, presumably because of a misunderstanding with Marcellina, Agnese doesn't object or intervene. When Lucia tells her of her fear of going back to the market alone and doesn't go, Agnese has no reaction. Lucia's increasing anguish about Don Rodrigo's relentless invasion of the spaces of her everyday life is heightened by her increasing sense of isolation from a mother who doesn't understand. The sense of anguish and drama that exudes from Lucia's story-telling stems from this combination over a long period of time of her mother's failure to understand and of her inability to escape Don Rodrigo's lustful gaze. Within this framework, Lucia's bursting into tears when her mother rebukes her for her silence can be read as the pained response of a daughter reliving the experience of her mother's failure to get the point.

My reading of Lucia's narrative and emphasis on her ambivalent desire for her mother's ear, foregrounds several problems that Manzoni resolves in the course of retelling the story in the **PS.** In the passage between the **FL** and the **PS,** Manzoni suppresses any sense of Lucia's desire for her mother's ear. While in neither version of the story does Lucia actuall turn to her mother for help, in the **PS** there is no trace of her ambivalent desire to do so. The narrator tells the following story:

> pochi giorni prima, mentre tornava dalla filanda, ed era rimasta indietro dalle sue compagne, le era passato innanzi don Rodrigo, in compagnia d'un altro signore; che il primo aveva cercato di trattenerla con chiacchere, com'ella diceva, non punto belle; ma essa, senza dargli retta, aveva affrettato il passo, e raggiunte le compagne; e intanto aveva sentito quell'altro signore rider forte, e don Rodrigo dire: scommettiamo. Il giorno dopo, coloro s'eran trovati ancora sulla strada; ma Lucia era nel mezzo delle compagne, con gli occhi bassi; e l'altro signore sghignazzava, e don Rodrigo diceva: vedremo, vedremo. "Per grazia del cielo," continuò Lucia, "quel giorno era l'ultimo della filanda. Io raccontai subito . . ."

(53)

[A few days before, as she was returning from the silk mill, and had remained behind her companions, Don Rodrigo had passed by her accompanied by another gentleman; the former had tried to entertain her with chatter, as she put it, not at all proper; but she, without paying attention to him, had quickened her pace and caught up with her companions; meanwhile she heard the other gentleman laugh very loudly, and Don Rodrigo say: let's bet. The following day, the two were again at the same site; but Lucia this time was in the middle of her group, keeping her eyes lowered; the other gentleman sniggered and Don Rodrigo said 'we'll see, we'll see.' 'Thank God' Lucia added 'that day was the last [of work] at the silk mill. I immediately told . . .']

Lucia explains that she talked to Fra Cristoforo in confession the last time she and her mother had gone to the convent's church and she reminds her mother of that morning: "se vi ricordate, quella mattina, io andava mettendo mano ora a una cosa, ora a un'altra, per indugiare, tanto che passasse altra gente del paese avviata a quella volta, e far la strada in compagnia con loro; perchè, dopo quell'-incontro, le strade mi facevan tanta paura . . ." [if you remember that morning, I was busy going from one thing to another, lingering, so that others from the village would be going in that direction; because after that encounter, the roads terrified me] (53). This reminder is a visible carry-over from the **FL,** but it is no longer charged with a sense of Lucia's reprimand to her mother for failing to take note of her fears. In the **FL,** the failure in communication between mother and daughter raised implicitly the question of whether Lucia's turn to Fra Galdino (Fra Cristoforo, in the **PS**) came as a consequence of this breakdown, whether Agnese's failure to understand Lucia brought her ultimately, after much hesitation, to opt for the safer and quieter ways of a man-who would-understand.[15] In the **PS,** any sense of hesitation or ambivalence about whether or not to trust Agnese is gone, and gone is any hesitation about whether or not it is proper for her to override Agnese's maternal authority by going directly to Fra Cristoforo. In other words, Lucia's turn to Fra Cristoforo in the **PS** is immediate and unproblematical. In the **PS,** her lingering in order to wait for other people to walk with them to the convent is an "empty" lingering: it does not threaten, slow down, or cause her to rethink her decision to confess Don Rodrigo's pursuit to Fra Cristoforo instead of her mother. Whereas Lucia, in the **FL,** admits "forse ho fatto male" [maybe I did wrong] to have turned to Fra Cristoforo without having first (or also) consulted Agnese, she shows no such hesitation or regret in the **PS.** In the **PS,** Lucia takes no emotional or practical risks. Her dawdling has nothing to do with wanting to get her mother's attention. Thus, while the result of the story in the **FL** scene is no different from that of the **PS** there is a crucial difference between the two representations of Lucia.

Lucia, in the **PS,** is a radically different subject. Manzoni dedramatizes her emotional and affective world. Lucia's inner world, her interiority, bears no signs of time, of a history, of lived experience. Structurally, Manzoni achieves this reduction of drama by concentrating Lucia's encounter with Don Rodrigo into a forty-eight hour period and limiting it to a single site. For readers of the theater, his representation of Lucia's drama is recognizably patterned on the spatial and temporal grid of the classical theatrical unities of time and space. What Manzoni achieves by adopting the theatrical grid which his poetics had rejected is a reduction of drama and an increase of theatricality. By translating into a narrative context the unities of time and place, Manzoni effaces the intensity of Lucia's inner drama and sense of the complexity of her emotional world. Her story is staged as if her only passion were fear. What "happens" to her, what she experiences, can be taken in at a glance: her fear—cut clean of any ambivalence and desire—is projected on to the page without a history. While in his theoretical essay on theatrical representation, the **Lettre à M. C*******,**[16] Manzoni had argued for the need to show how an individual's passions developed gradually and over time, in his revision of Lucia's story he successfully suppresses the complexity of her fear *and* desire for her mother's trust and does so precisely by reducing her experiences into a temporal and spatial grid which eliminates any tension or possibility of misunderstandings between mother and daughter. The story of this suppression remains unread when the **PS** is privileged as the aesthetically superior text, the one that successfully elevates Lucia above the vulgar squalidness of her peasant everyday life.

In comparing the two scenes, critics have focused extensively on Manzoni's shift from direct to indirect speech and his reduction of the historical and social details within which he had located Lucia Zarella's encounter with Don Rodrigo. His rewriting of the **FL** scene is seen as protecting Lucia's innocence from being contaminated by Don Rodrigo's sordid desire. By not having her speak directly, Manzoni reinforces the sense of her as a maiden pure, innocent, and absolutely untouched by evil nature (Grimaldi, 152). In not speaking directly, Lucia is seen to rise above the petulant morality which brought her in the **FL** to explain that she was not the only one harassed by Don Rodrigo and that "purtroppo v'era chi lasciava fare!" [unfortunately there were those who let themselves be touched by him] (261). In the **PS,** as Guido Baldi argues, an aura of perfection envelops Lucia's story from the beginning and makes it unimaginable to think of Lucia making excuses, fighting with her co-workers, creating scenes, and makes it sacrilegious to think of Don Rodrigo actually taking liberties with her.[17] According to Grimaldi, the more energetic and combative Lucia of the **FL** is sacrificed to a figure of candor and purity (161). From her point of view, the most important change between the two representations of Lucia's encounter with Don Rodrigo takes place less on Lucia's side than on the side of the male pursuer. Manzoni's retelling of the story in the **PS** foregrounds the pronouncement of Don Rodrigo's bet and therefore focuses on the value of male virility and honor (152). By privileging this focus on the bet and its pronouncement, what gets ignored or left unseen is the significance of the narrator's pronouncement of Lucia's secret and what it hides. Manzoni's suppression of Lucia's desire for her mother's understanding turns Lucia's encounter with Don Rodrigo not

just into the drama of his objectifying gaze but into a tragedy of her isolation, isolation from her mother, from a community of other women who could and might understand her terrible predicament. The success of Manzoni's production of Lucia's secret consists precisely in offering the daughter's silence towards the mother *as if* it were of no import or consequence to the story. The secret mistrust which divides daughter from mother remains ignored by all but those readers for whom the separation between mother and daughter is never innocent, never simple, and always to the advantage of patriarchal practices and perspective.

III. FEAR OF THE (M)OTHER'S TONGUE

Taking at face value the apparent tranquillity of Lucia's relationship to her mother is to grossly misunderstand the function of Agnese's position at the margins of the story and leave unread the constraints which keep her from being able to speak for her daughter. Agnese is a character of extraordinary interest not in spite of her marginalized position but because of it, because of what her position at the margins makes visible.[18] It, first of all, shows that the strange absence of biological fathers in the text (neither Lucia's nor Renzo's biological father are ever mentioned) does not point to a privileging of the maternal, as for example, Franco Lanza argues.[19] Indeed, not only are neither Lucia's nor Renzo's father ever mentioned, but their deaths do not haunt the protagonists in any way. The striking absence of biological fathers in both the **FL** and the **PS** suggests an interesting, even important, twist in a tradition of nineteenth-century literary plots which tend instead to depict mothers as either dead, absent, overbearing, or wicked, when they are not otherwise just plain uninteresting and trivial. This twist, however, is not enough to sustain the argument that Manzoni privileges the maternal world over the paternal. On the contrary, as Lucia's secret makes visible, it is not Agnese but Fra Cristoforo who occupies the space of authority left empty by the absence of Agnese's husband. Lucia's fear not only marginalizes her mother's voice but reveals the mother's irrelevance in a world where father figures constitute the sole point of reference and voice of authority. It is only when we take note of this marginalization that Agnese's rebuke about her daughter's silence acquires a new significance. Both in the **FL** and in the **PS** Agnese is not just hurt, she is scandalized. Her words to Lucia underline her position as mother: "dovevi dirlo anche a tua madre" [you should have also told your *mother*] (**FL** 261; **PS** 53). Agnese, unlike Lucia in the same passage does not refer to herself with the more private and endearing term *mamma* but with the official and public: *madre*. Appealing to her position as mother, Agnese desires, demands an explanation from her daughter. What is at stake is her sense of propriety, her right—as mother—to know about such important matters regarding her daughter. What upsets Agnese, the FL narrator says, is that she who knows so much about *everyone else* doesn't know about what touches her most intimately (260). The daughter's silence does not just leave a gossipy, curious, mother out of the loop, it makes public the mother's limited value as an authority figure for her daughter. Agnese's right and control, as a single parent of a female only daughter, are diminished by Lucia's act. If Lucia had a father, her immediate turn to Fra Cristoforo instead of to him would have been construed as a gross insult, injury, and betrayal of her father's trust. But because Lucia has no father (or male relatives), her by-passing of Agnese's position is interpreted as a mature and sensible act and not a breach in a hierarchy of authority figures. The word "betrayal" does not come into the picture. Agnese's scandalized reaction to her daughter's silence is read as a sign of her pettiness rather than as a reaction to a public humiliation. Thus, when a reader as attentive as Grimaldi states that Agnese's reaction deserves *at least some mention* (146-47), but then interprets Lucia's secret as compassionate towards her mother's indiscrete ways, what is invariably diminished is Agnese's role: her reaction *as mother* to finding out, in front of another person—Renzo—that she doesn't know the most important things about her daughter's life. Grimaldi deduces from the confessional scene that Agnese's pettiness serves Manzoni's task of underlining Lucia's superiority over her mother.[20] However, when read from the perspective of entrustment, the scene shows that Lucia's docile ways and downcast eyes depend not only on her being progressively silenced and removed from a local and peasant milieu but also upon a leveling out, and marginalization, of the power of another woman—her mother—to offer her a point of reference, authority, and mediation in the world.

Agnese's potential gossip is consistently suggestive of its power of blurring boundaries. As Spacks writes, gossip as a phenomenon raises questions about boundaries, authority, distance, the nature of knowledge (*Gossip,* 12). If Agnese's chatter threatens the boundaries between public and private she also threatens to blur the sexual division of roles which exclude her, as mother, from publicly defending her daughter. Agnese's frustrated relation to the public sphere is visible through her competitive relationship to Renzo. When, in the aftermath of Lucia's explanation, the threesome attempts to find a way to get around Don Rodrigo and Don Abbondio's cowardly acquiescence to his threat, Agnese is the first to come up with a solution. She suggests that Renzo go to Lecco to consult with the not-so-reputable lawyer Azzecca-Garbugli known around town for his ability to get folk out of trouble. Agnese, in other words, doesn't offer to talk with the lawyer. While she competes with Renzo for finding a solution to their problem she lets him take the responsibility and visibility of assuming a public role, thereby reinforcing an implicit gender division of tasks and roles. Indeed, when Renzo fails to convince the lawyer to help him use the law against Don Rodrigo, Agnese implicitly rebukes him for his weakness and, conversely, when Renzo succeeds in his plans to find witnesses for their second plan, a subterfuge marriage, he concludes his report to Agnese and Lucia with the exclamation "*ahn*" which, as the narrator explains, "significa: sono o non sono un uomo io? si poteva trovar di meglio? vi sarebbe venuta in mente? e cento cose simili" [am I or am I not a man? could one have done better? would it have ever come to your mind to do that? and a

hundred other such things] (130). It is in reference to a division of sexual roles that we can understand why Agnese later on in the novel murmurs to herself that Renzo was "un giovine quieto, fin troppo" [a quiet fellow, all too quiet] (130). Agnese's comment which has puzzled critics because it seems so unwarranted by the facts, makes sense when it is placed within the perspective of Agnese's frustrated competitive relation with Renzo.[21] If she takes it for granted that Renzo—as a man—is the one who has to negotiate matters with other men, she nevertheless desires to be the negotiator—behind the scenes.

As mother *and* gossip, Agnese threatens to blur any clear cut division between public and private. She is both an insider and outsider. Her house, located at the margins of the peasant village (between Don Rodrigo's palace and the village) symbolically reinforces her difference from others in the village.[22] While gender, class, and gossip reinforce her ties to the village, Agnese's status as a widow—and as a widow without close male relatives to speak for her—keeps her somewhat at a distance. As the mother of a female only child, and in the absence of a network of close parentage—either her own or her husband's—Agnese is unusually isolated in her world. Manzoni, in telling Agnese's story, departs from the traditional structures of peasant families which used to be, up until the late 18th century, comprised of very large multiple families which sometimes extended to five or six married couples with their accompanying inlaws, children etc.[23] In the absence of brothers, uncles, sons, or male relatives and in-laws to stand and defend the honor of her family, Agnese finds herself in a position of extraordinary responsibility as head of her household and yet, as we have seen, her lack of authority is made obvious both by the narrator's reference to Lucia's secret fear and Lucia's turn to Fra Cristoforo.[24] Agnese's gossip offers a tool for overcoming her distance from the community, Lucia's secret mistrust of her gossip marginalizes Agnese's voice to the periphery of the narrative where she is not only prevented/prohibited from sharing with others of her community her justifiable maternal anger against Don Rodrigo's violation of her daughter's space but where the potential of her chatter for instigating a shared response, a common village rebellion against the oppressor, is kept carefully at bay. It is this threat of Agnese's potentially destabilizing chatter and indeed of the political potential that her gossip might have for rallying support for her daughter's protection that remains unread when Lucia's response to her mother is interpreted as a compassionate gesture of sparing her mother's feelings. Rather, Lucia's silence is based on a fear, turned secret, that her story might enter the village's circuit of knowledge and thereby presumably damage her reputation and taint the honor of her name. To protect her name, she rejects her mother's trust and authority, instead of risking (as she does in the FL) her mother's mediation.[26]

What lies behind Manzoni's production of Lucia's secret fear is a problematic of negotiating between the possibilities of community versus institutional control over individual subjects. The secret, which marks the breakdown trust between mother and daughter, suggests that Manzoni privileges an institutional (religious, in this case, but no less institutionalized) form of control, over gossip as the form of control that a community, Lucia's community, might take. Gossip is a powerful means for a community to control, inform, shape and regulate the behavior of members of the group. Women have historically been known to use gossip as a weapon against aggressive male behavior. As Cavallo and Cerruti point out in their discussion of female honor in the sixteenth and seventeenth centuries, by confiding in her female neighbors, a wife was able to make her husband's misbehavior part of the public domain and thereby exert pressure on him. Husbands feared female gossip, because when reported within other family circles it eventually had an impact on their relations with other men. In moments of conflict, worry about bad-mouthing drove the male to warn his wife to avoid contact with female neighbors (88). Gossip provided women with a language circuit of their own, and the strongest links in this invisible chain of solidarity were those between mother and daughter. But the chains of a female solidarity, and the power of a community, Cavallo and Cerutti argue, depend foremost on the strength of the social ties:

> disseminating the news, judging it, and intervening in behavior were possible only if the social network was characterized by high density or internal cohesiveness, understood as the strength of relationships among its members. The strength of the network did not depend so much on its size as on its cohesion; that is, on the presence of strong bonds that linked its components.
>
> (92)

Lucia's confession to Fra Cristoforo draws attention to Manzoni's representation of Lucia's community. Lucia's fear of having her secret spread to the neighborhood—*her* neighborhood—underlines her distance from her mother and, via her mother, from the village. Fear is the governing emotion among the peasants and, rather than a community, Lucia's village seems an aggregation of individuals who have difficulty thinking publicly, or expressing a public opinion. When describing the social dynamics in Lucia's village, Manzoni privileges a view of gossip's negative and divisive powers. The male peasants, for example, are afraid of gossiping even amongst themselves about Don Rodrigo. Renzo knows he cannot convince his friends to defend him were he to challenge Don Rodrigo. The women of the village are never shown to use gossip as a means for gathering information and/or aiding each other but rather, as in the case of an exchange between Agnese and Don Abbondio's servant Perpetua, gossip becomes a tool for distracting the other's attention. Both men and women fear speaking their minds even to their closest relatives, and their silence, as Manzoni puts it, eventually makes them come to feel less. Manzoni doesn't say explicitly what this lessening or numbing of feeling amounts to, but one deduces that what becomes less felt, in this numbing process, is a sense of a shared community identity. It is only in a moment of extreme crisis—the discovery that Agnese's house has been violently ransacked

and Lucia and Agnese are nowhere to be found that the peasants rally to defend the honor of their women who, they believe, have been abducted from the village (176).[27] The desire for a community rally against the feared oppressor Don Rodrigo immediately dissipates as a (false) rumor spreads among the men that Lucia and Agnese are instead visiting one of their homes. Gossip, again, plays a divisive and dissipating role rather than affirming the bonds of a cohesive peasant community.

It is only among the nobility that gossip is articulated as a cohesive force. Gossip is very much feared by Don Rodrigo's cousin Attilio who speculates on the possibility of a popular uprising against Don Rodrigo. It is precisely the threat of a community rebellion that Attilio uses to convince his powerful uncle, a member of the Milanese Secret Council, that something must be done to protect Don Rodrigo. The solution consists, as he intimates, in asking the head of the religious order to which the friar belongs, the Provincial Father, to send Fra Cristoforo far away to another convent. Attilio's understanding of the potential gossip has for gathering and rallying public opinion also reveals that he does not consider Lucia's village capable of doing so without the aid and instigation of someone (a man) who comes from the outside and is from an educated, albeit not noble, class. From Attilio's view point, "*aizzatori*" [the instigators] and the "*curiosi maligni*" [malicious curious] who would be most susceptible to Fra Cristoforo's prodding are male. The "*ciarlare*" [chatter] he fears is that of men—not women. Men, in his view, have the power to threaten Don Rodrigo or at least seriously to weaken the reputation of his power and control over the territory. Gender as well as class shape Attilio's vision of gossip and its political danger. It is not Agnese's anger—as mother—and the power of her gossip to instigate a community rebellion that are feared or even recognized as an issue of concern, but rather Fra Cristoforo's capacity to speak for and to Agnese's village. While the noble class understands the potential gossip has for gathering and rallying public opinion, the lower peasant class seems oblivious to its power and political potential.

If it were not for Lucia's secret there would be no sign of the power of Agnese's voice to threaten the status quo in the peasant community. Her secret opens a space of ambiguity and ambivalence that critical readings have constantly and unconsciously closed. For example, Ezio Raimondi and Luciano Bottoni in their critical edition of the **PS** clarify with a footnote Lucia's announcement to her mother about her confession to Fra Cristoforo:

> Al padre Cristoforo, in confessione: il vincolo della confessione esclude, senza offenderlo, lo spirito di interferenza della madre. Al Manzoni si è rimproverato che, stando alle leggi canoniche, i cappuccini non avrebbero potuto confessare persone estranee all'Ordine, ma uno studioso autorevole come M. Barbi replicava che di fatto essi non furono mai privati della facoltà di confessare i laici. Certo, Lucia, per ragioni di logica artistica, non poteva confidarsi con don Abbondio.
>
> (53)

[To father Cristoforo in confession: the bond of confession excludes, but without offending, Agnese's interventionist spirit. Manzoni has often been reproached that according to the canonical laws, the Capuchins would not have been allowed to confess individuals outside of their Order but in reality, as a scholar as authoritative as M. Barbi replies, in practice friars were not denied the possibility of confessing lay individuals. Certainly, for the sake of artistic reasons, Lucia could hardly have gone to Don Abbondio for confession]

The note illustrates, on the one hand, the impetus to explain the artistic and practical reasons motivating Manzoni's reference to a confessional practice not officially sanctioned by the Church while, on the other hand, the lack of interest in explaining Lucia's secret mistrust for her mother's voice and mediation. In other words, the footnote preempts any such question about the function of Lucia's secret from being raised by stating that Lucia's confessional bond to Fra Cristoforo "excludes, but does not offend" Agnese's desire for intervention. The interpretation thereby leads us back to a reading of Lucia's secret as a compassionate act of filial silence: reading which glosses over any of the tensions, ambivalences, and political implications of choosing to speak—or not—in and through the mother's tongue. Manzoni's suppression of Lucia's ambivalent desires to confide in her mother, leads to a refocusing of the lens on how Lucia's secret mistrust, occasionally underlined by her silencing glares, keeps Agnese's maternal tongue from speaking for her. This potential voice, kept at bay, draws attention to the need for rethinking the relations between margins/center, private/public, insider/outsider, community control/institutional control in the novel. Agnese's position makes visible the possibilities of the desire, possibilities, and limits, to challenging a division of gender roles and spheres.[28] As Lorraine Code writes, "gossip, in its workings, shatters the monolithic definition of 'knowledge' that governs standard epistemologies both honorifically and regulatively. It appeals, convincingly, to hitherto disreputable locations as sites where knowledge that is implicated in life-altering power can be made."[29] The suppression of Lucia's ambivalent desire for a maternal / community mediation (suppression which we have seen is constitutive to the difference between the Lucias in the **FL** and the **PS**) invites readers to rethink radically the narrative as well as the ideological implications of a novel considered so neutral in its representation of women and men as to make moot the question of a Manzonian feminism or anti-feminism.[30] Under the scrutiny of my feminist lens, Lucia's secret stands out like an illegible mark, an undecipherable scribble, a detail-under-erasure in a scene which makes trust between mother and daughter impossible.[31] The secret, in other words, exudes a secret appeal. In her reading of fetishism, Emily Apter writes that the detail has the "tendency to prick consciousness, to encroach on the terrain of inner feelings, to expand to the point of obsession."[32] What emerges from my insistent remarking of Lucia's secret is the knowledge of how fundamentally interwoven it is with a text itself so interwoven with the construction of modern Italian identity and culture that its stains and blemishes, while noted,

remain unread. Lucia's secret reproduces, at a textual and experiential level, the same visual effect and fetishistic experience which Manzoni describes as being constitutive to his writing of the novel. The **PS** begins, as Manzoni explains in his prefatory remarks to the **PS,** with the story of his discovery of a seventeenth century anonymous manuscript which he decides diligently to transcribe and is in the process of so doing when he comes across a blot in the text which he cannot decipher. In front of this illegible mark he pauses and begins to reflect on the purpose of his transcription of the baroque seventeenth century prose:

> Ma, quando io avrò durata l'eroica fatica di trascriver questa storia da questo dilavato e graffiato autografo, e l'avrò data, come si suol dire, alla luce, si troverà poi chi duri la fatica di leggerla?—Questa riflessione dubitativa, nata nel travaglio del decifrare uno scarabocchio che veniva dopo *accidenti,* mi fece sospendere la copia, e pensar più seriamente a quello che convenisse di fare
>
> (3)

> But when I will have labored through the task of transcribing this story from this faded and messy manuscript, and I will have brought it, so to speak, to light, who will have the energy to read through it? This doubt, born in the process of trying to decipher a large scribble which came after the word *accidents,* made me suspend the transcribing, and think more seriously about what ought to be done.

As a result of this reflection, Manzoni decides to translate (instead of transcribe) the story. The blot has, in other words, disrupted the flow of his writing and reading: its jolting unintelligibility produces a moment of critical reflection, a moment of distance and, ultimately, the opportunity to translate and rewrite a story that otherwise would be unreadable to a modern audience. For a different audience, Lucia's secret reproduces the same need to stop and rethink the premises of a story that begins with the daughter's exclusion of her mother from a position of knowledge and power. The secret invites us to rethink those spaces and discourses of knowledge kept from the center, kept from the telling of Lucia's story, kept from "threatening" the stability of Lucia's iconic position. It would be simplistic, at this point, to assume under the aegis of a feminist gesture this disruptive textual moment, this fascinating secret which immediately appeals to a feminist's eye. Manzoni was not a feminist or, for that matter, an anti-feminist. The more complicated and demanding task is capitalizing on the leverage of this secret, magnifying its ambivalent position in the novel, its disruptive power, its constant potential for opening "a view from elsewhere" within the novel's Oedipal scripting of Lucia's silent betrayal.[33] Manzoni, in the first drafted preface to the **FI** suggests that women are, generally speaking, better readers than men because they read for the plot and if it bores them, they don't hesitate to throw the book aside. Unlike men, he argues, women do not thrive on the pleasure of teasing out the author's mistakes, errors, and failures (241). In other words, men read fetishistically and are involved in a competitive relation with the author, while women remain libidinally uninvested in the novels they enjoy. Seen through his gendering of the reading process, Manzoni's blatant parading of Lucia's secret takes on an added, last provocative dimension.

Notes

1. Victoria Goddard, "Honour and Shame: the Control of Women's Sexuality and Group Identity in Naples." *The Cultural Construction of Sexuality* ed. Pat Caplan (London: Tavistock Publications, 1987) 180.

2. See: Mary Douglas, *Purity and Danger: An Analysis of Concepts of Pollution and Taboo* (London: Routledge and K. Paul, 1969).

3. Hereafter referred to as PS. All citations to the PS are from: Alessandro Manzoni *I Promessi Sposi* eds. Ezio Raimondi and Luciano Bottoni (Milano: Principato, 1988). All translations into English are my own.

4. On this paradoxical logic of the secret see Louis Marin, "Logiques du secret," *Traverses* (1984): 30-31.

5. Marianne Hirsch, *The Mother/Daughter Plot: Narrative, Psychoanalysis, Feminism* (Bloomington: Indiana University Press, 1989) 46.

6. By entrustment I mean the relationship which Italian feminists have defined as *affidamento*: "one woman gives her trust or entrusts herself symbolically to another woman, who thus becomes her guide, mentor or point of reference—in short the figure of symbolic mediation between her and the world." See: *Sexual Difference: A Theory of Social-Symbolic Practice.* The Milan Woman's Bookstore Collective trans Patricia Cicogna and Teresa De Lauretis (Bloomington: Indiana UP, 1987) 9.

7. See Sergio Romagnoli, *Fermo e Lucia*, (Milano: Fratelli Fabbri, 1973).

8. Emma Grimaldi, *Dentro il romanzo: strutture narrative e registri simbolici tra il Fermo e Lucia e I Promessi Sposi* (Messina: Sicania, 1992).

9. The *Fermo e Lucia* (hereafter FL) is written between 1821-1823 but not published. In 1825 Manzoni rewrites it, changes its title to *Sposi Promessi*, and then publishes it in 1827 with the title *I Promessi Sposi*. For an edition of *Fermo e Lucia* see: *Tutte le Opere* ed. Mario Martelli. Vol 1. (Firenze: Sansoni editori, 1973).

10. It is not the only secret Lucia will keep from her mother. For example, she doesn't immediately tell Agnese about her vow of chastity which she makes during her night of captivity in the palace of the Unnamed prince. Fearing her mother's disapproval and/or attempt to get her out of it, Lucia doesn't tell her until it becomes necessary to explain her assumed indifference towards Renzo.

11. Susan Stanford Friedman, "Weavings: Intertextuality and the (Re)Birth of the Author." *Influence and Intertextuality in Literary History* eds. Jay Clayton and Eric Rothstein (Madison: Wisconson UP, 1991).

12. On gossip as creating a female circuit of language see: Lucetta Scaraffia "Essere uomo, essere donna." *La famiglia Italiana dall'Ottocento a oggi* ed. Piero Melograni (Bari: Editori Laterza, 1988). Also, S. Cavallo and S. Cerutti, "Female Honor and the Social Control of Reproduction."

13. Patricia Meyer Spacks, *Gossip* (New York: Alfred A. Knopp, 1985) 34.

14. It is important to note that Agnese's failure to notice her daughter's strange behavior is in direct contrast with the cruel and subtle surveillance to which Gertrude, the other main female character in the novel, is subjected by her father. When Gertrude, who is trying to resist her father's pressure to enter the monastery of Monza, becomes much calmer and quieter as a result of her infatuation with a young page who is serving her, her father has her surveilled by a servant. Thus, unlike Agnese, Gertrude's father immediately perceives that his daughter's behavior is different and thus significant.

15. See Marianne Hirsch, *Mother-Daughter Plot: Narrative, Psychoanalysis, Feminism* (Bloomington: Indiana UP, 1989).

16. Alessandro Manzoni, "Lettre à M. C*** sur l'unité de temps et de lieu dans la tragédie." *Tutte le opere*, ed. M. Martelli. Vol. 2. (Firenze: G.C. Sansoni, 1973).

17. Guido Baldi, *I Promessi Sposi: progetto di società e mito* (Milano: Mursia, 1985) 308.

18. Critics have found Agnese a much less interesting counterpart to Lucia than the more glamorous nun Gertrude. Giuliana Katz suggests that Manzoni displaces his libidinous and aggressive feelings onto Gertrude while Lucia becomes the angelic and healing figure, the receptive figure for his affection. See: Giuliana Katz Sanguinetti, "*I Promessi Sposi e la psicanalisi,*" ed Guido Pugliese *Perspectives on the Nineteenth-Century Italian Novels* (Ottawa: Dovehouse, 1989) 77-88. For a discussion of Gertrude/Lucia, see also: Verina Jones, "Lucia and Her Sisters: Women in Alessandro Manzoni's *I Promessi Sposi*" *Women and Gender, Culture and History*, eds. Zygmunt G. Baranski and Shirley W. Vinall (New York: St. Martin's Press, 1991) 209-23.

19. Franco Lanza, "Antilucia nella critica e nella pubblicistica" *Otto/Novecento* 1.3 (1977): 55-66.

20. "Agnese risponde allo stereotipo piu' frequente, è affettuosa e protettiva, quantunque il narratore la mostri non molto scrupolosa sotto il profilo morale, affinche' acquisti maggior risalto la coscienza particolarmente delicata della figlia." Elena Sala di Felice, *Manzoni/Grossi: congresso nazionale di Studi Manzoniani* (Milano: Centro Nazionale di Studi Manzoniani, 1991) 255.

21. Giorgio de Rienzo asks whether this is not a lapsus on Manzoni's part and whether Agnese has some precise notion of facts we don't have any knowledge of: "forse e' concesso a lei—attraverso questo lapsus manzoniano—di avere qualche nozione precisa dei fatti, che per il lettore sono solo sospetti?" *Per amore di Lucia* (Milano: Rusconi, 1987) 52.

22. There are various changes in the location of Agnese's and Renzo's respective houses between FL and PS. In the PS40, Renzo's house is in the middle of the village and "Lucia's house at the other side of the village in fact slightly outside it" ("passato davanti a casa sua [di Renzo], ch'era nel mezzo del villaggio, e, attraversatolo, s'avvio' a quella di Lucia ch'era in fondo, *anzi un po' fuori*." The italics here indicates what Manzoni adds to the PS 40 from the PS 27 version. 45). See *I Promessi Sposi di Alessandro Manzoni raffrontati due edizioni del 1825 e 1840* ed Policarpo Petrocchi (Firenze: Casa Editrice le Lettere, 1992).

23. Anna Cento Bull, "Introduction." *From Peasant to Entrepreneur: The Survival of the Family Economy in Italy* eds. Anna Cento Bull and Paul Corner (Oxford: Berg, 1993).

24. For an interesting account of the conditions for women head of households in the 18th-century, see Maura Palazzi "Abitare da sole: donne capofamiglie alla fine del Settecento." 37-57 *Memoria* 18:3 (1986).

25. Ironically, the only time Agnese is required to mediate for Lucia and correspond with Renzo who is now living in Bergamo, she must find another person—a man—to write her letters and to read for her Renzo's (also mediated) replies. Agnese never mediates directly for her daughter.

26. With regards to trusting her community Lucia Mondella takes to heart Bettina's lesson in the FL. Bettina was one of Lucia's girl-friends who let herself be flattered by Don Rodrigo and blatantly paraded his presents in front of her community. When he later shuns her because he has caught sight of Lucia, Bettina understands her delusion and runs from her village.

27. Lucetta Scaraffia points out in her studies on the construction of gender identities in Italy in the nineteenth century that the honor of a woman coincided with that of the original or acquired family, and that her body was the symbol of the unity and prestige of this family and in particular, of the men who "possessed" her, the father, the husband, the brother ("Essere uomo, essere donna," 212). It is only when Lucia is thought to be abducted that the men of an extended family-community feel that the honor of their village has been threatened.

28. "Woman's position has always been dual, both outside of dominant values and inside the society that lives by them. Often enough women have been complicit with dominant values, and women's culture exists as a 'muted' subculture at the margins of the dominant culture. The analysis of woman's position as ("ambiguously") non-hegemonic, is more subtle than that of woman as simply Other or Outsider." Judith Kegan Gardiner, "Gender, Values, and Lessing's Cats." *Feminist Issues in Literary Scholarship* ed. Shari Benstock. (Bloomington: Indiana UP, 1987) 112-13.

29. Lorraine Code, "Gossip, or In Praise of Chaos." *Rhetorical Spaces and Gendered Locations* (New York: Routledge, 1995) 149.

30. Pietro Gibellini, "Le piccole donne dei *Promessi Sposi*" *Otto/Novecento* XVI:6 (1992).

31. On fetishism of reading, see Naomi Schor, *Reading in Detail: Aesthetics and the Feminine* (New York: Methuen, 1987). Also Frank Kermode's use of the distinction between overreaders and ordinary readers in "Secrets and Narrative Sequence" *On Narrative* ed W. J. T. Mitchell (Chicago: Chicago UP, 1980) 79-98.

32. Emily Apter, *Feminizing the Fetish: Psychoanalysis and Narrative Obsession in Turn-of-the-Century France* (Ithaca: Cornell UP 1991) xi.

33. See on this point Teresa de Lauretis, *Technologies of Gender: Essays on Theory, Film, and Fiction* (Bloomington: Indiana UP, 1987) 25.

FURTHER READING

Biography

Kennard, Joseph Spencer. "Alexander Manzoni." In *Italian Romance Writers,* pp. 81-115. New York: Brentano's, 1906.

Biographical sketch of Manzoni that focuses particularly on the sources for and composition of *I promessi sposi.*

Criticism

Biasin, Gian-Paolo. "The Juice of the Story: Alessandro Manzoni, *I promessi sposi.*" In *The Flavors of Modernity: Food and the Novel,* pp. 29-42. Princeton, N.J.: Princeton University Press, 1993.

Considers alimentary metaphors and other concerns with hunger, food, and eating in *I promessi sposi.*

Chandler, S. Bernard. "The Voice of Conscience in Alessandro Manzoni and Some of His Predecessors." *Rivista di Studi Italiani* 12, No. 1 (June 1994): 130-33.

Briefly surveys instances of religious guilt and internal conflict in *I promessi sposi.*

Cro, Stelio. "Cavour and Manzoni's 'Liberalism.'" In *Romance Languages Annual* 5 (1993): 188-93.

Mentions Manzoni's contribution to the doctrine of Italian liberalism in chapter 12 of *I promessi sposi* and the novelist's ideological affinity with Camillo Benso di Cavour in regard to this subject.

De Lucca, Robert. "Revealed Truth and Acquired Knowledge: Considerations on Manzoni and Gadda." In *MLN* 111, No. 1 (January 1996): 58-73.

Probes the impact of Manzoni's theory of poetic verisimilitude on the writings of Carlo Emilio Gadda.

Ferlito, Susanna. "Mapping European Philosophy: The Coy Politics of Manzoni's 'Lettera a Victor Cousin.'" In *Modern Language Quarterly* 59, No. 2 (June 1998): 195-226.

Analyzes the rhetorical stance and effectiveness of Manzoni's critique of philosophical eclecticism in his *"Lettera a Victor Cousin."*

Gatti-Taylor, Marisa and Steven Taylor. "The God-Man and the Man-God: The Scriptural Matrix of Napoleonic Images in Two Odes by Manzoni and Hugo." In *Nineteenth-Century French Studies* 18, Nos. 3-4 (Spring-Summer 1990): 454-62.

Traces biblical allusions in Manzoni's *Il cinque maggio* and Victor Hugo's "Lui."

Gladfelder, Hal. "Seeing Black: Alessandro Manzoni Between Fiction and History." In *MLN* 108, No. 1 (January 1993): 59-86.

Views Manzoni's *Storia della colonna infame* and subsequent works of historical fiction as about both the reconstruction of and the reconstruction of truth from earlier works.

Godt, Clareece G. *The Mobile Spectacle: Variable Perspective in Manzoni's* I promessi sposi. New York: Peter Lang, 1998, 167 p.

In-depth study of shifting points of view in *I promessi sposi* that additionally comments on Manzoni's treatment of history, landscape, and human psychology in the work.

Haraguchi, Jennifer. "Historical Fact and Literary Invention: The Medical and Social Plagues of *I promessi sposi.*" In *Romance Languages Annual* 7 (1995): 268-72.

Enumerates thematic and structural parallels between historical and metaphorical plagues in *I promessi sposi.*

Illiano. A. "On Manzoni's Disillusionment with Literature." In *Forum Italicum* 24, No. 1 (Spring 1990): 111-15.

Discusses Manzoni's departure from literature in favor of historiography as a superior means of accessing moral truth.

Jones, Verina R. "Counter-Reformation and Popular Culture in *I promessi sposi*: A Case of Historical Censorship." In *Renaissance & Modern Studies* 36 (1993): 36-51.

Explores Manzoni's rewriting of the history of the Catholic Church in *I promessi sposi.*

Papini, Giovanni. "Alessandro Manzoni." In *Labourers in the Vineyard,* pp. 131-89. London: Sheed & Ward, 1930.

Studies Manzoni's *apologia* for the Catholic Church, *Osservazioni sulla morale cattolica,* his novel *I promessi sposi,* and his contribution to the Italian *Risorgimento.*

Pierce, Glenn Palen. "Further Considerations on Manzoni and the Literature of the *Seicento milanese*: A Note on Don Ferrante's Library." In *Italica* 66, No. 1 (Spring 1989): 35-41.

Comments on Manzoni's literary indebtedness to the Milanese playwright Carlo Maria Maggi.

————. *Manzoni and the Aesthetics of the Lombard* Seicento: *Art Assimilated into the Narrative of* I promessi sposi. Cranbury, N.J.: Associated University Presses, 1998, 253 p.

Full-length investigation of the influence of sixteenth- and seventeenth-century Lombard drama on Manzoni's novel *I promessi sposi.*

Catharine Maria Sedgwick
1789-1867

American novelist. For further information on Sedgwick's life and career, see *NCLC,* Volume 19.

INTRODUCTION

A popular as well as critically acclaimed writer in her own time, Sedgwick is best remembered for her novels depicting colonial and early nineteenth-century New England life. Contemporary critics admired Sedgwick for her use of distinctly American settings and themes in her writing, including the use of American characters, history, morals, values, and ideals. She was also noted for her realistic descriptions of domestic detail and regional culture. Sedgwick's first novel, *A New-England Tale* was published in 1822, and she is numbered among a group of nineteenth-century writers who helped found a uniquely American body of literature. Although she was neglected by scholars and critics for many years, Sedgwick's work was rediscovered in the 1970s, and since then most attention has been focused on *Hope Leslie; or, Early Times in the Massachusetts* (1827), a historical novel that deals with such varied subjects as Puritan attitudes towards religion, women's role in the new American republic, and the relationship between whites and Native Americans.

BIOGRAPHICAL INFORMATION

Sedgwick was born into a prestigious family in Stockbridge, Massachusetts. Her father, Theodore Sedgwick, was an early and prominent member of the newly-formed U.S. Congress, and his political obligations kept him from home for long periods of time. Left to manage the large household by herself, Sedgwick's mother, Pamela, suffered debilitating bouts of mental illness. Consequently, the responsibility for raising Sedgwick and her younger brother often fell upon the older siblings, to whom she remained deeply attached all her life. Offered the best education available to girls at the time, Sedgwick nevertheless always felt disadvantaged because of the poor educational opportunities open to girls—even girls from the most prominent backgrounds. She attended a local grammar school, which offered a meager curriculum, and later went to boarding schools in Albany and Boston. When her mother died in 1807, Sedgwick went to live with relatives in New York, where she became friends with a number of literary figures, including poet William Cullen Bryant and the noted theologian and Unitarian minister William Ellery Channing, whose liberal beliefs left a strong impression on her. Sedgwick returned to her family home in Stockbridge

following her father's death in 1813. His conversion from Calvinism to Unitarianism shortly before his death, as well as her own admiration for Channing, fueled Sedgwick's already strong interest in religion; in 1821 she also converted to the Unitarian faith. The hostile reaction to her conversion from conservative friends and relatives helped inspire her lifelong quest for religious tolerance and also prompted her to begin writing. In 1822, she composed a tract about religious persecution, which, with her brother's encouragement, she eventually developed into her first novel, *A New-England Tale.* Sedgwick continued to write throughout most of her life, composing moral tracts and didactic tales as well as novels. She divided her time between New York City and Massachusetts, where she became renowned for her tea parties. These gatherings brought together some of the leading American writers, including Herman Melville, Nathaniel Hawthorne, Ralph Waldo Emerson, and James Fenimore Cooper. Sedgwick also became involved with social causes, helping to promote improvements in prisons and schools. Although involved in numerous social and political causes, Sedgwick avoided taking controversial stances, leading biographers to comment on her ambivalent attitudes. For example, she opposed slavery, but considered the abolitionists too extreme in their views; she remained unmarried, but idealized matrimony; and she supported women's right to own property, but not women's right to vote. Sedgwick continued to champion social reform until late into her seventies when she became ill and moved to Boston. There a niece cared for her until her death at the age of seventy-eight.

MAJOR WORKS

Sedgwick wrote both fiction and nonfiction and there is a didactic tone in all her work that stresses the need for religious and racial tolerance, as well as social and political reform. Her first novel, *A New-England Tale,* focuses on the evils of organized religion. Set in the early nineteenth century, the work tells the story of a noble young woman who is the victim of corrupt church leaders. Because most novels written in America at this time were modeled on the works of English authors, this novel garnered special critical attention for its American setting and characters. In addition, the focus on moral concerns and domestic themes also met with immediate acclaim and Sedgwick soon became one of the country's most popular authors. Her work, titled *Redwood* (1824), was equally well received. Featuring a highly-principled protagonist, Debby Lenox, and again focusing on religious concerns, the work has often been praised for the creation of one of the most realistically-drawn women characters in early American literature. Despite the success of these two novels, it is Sedgwick's fourth novel, *Hope Leslie,* that is considered by most critics to be her best work. In this historical romance situated in New England, Sedgwick describes the customs of the Native American Pequot tribe. It follows the relations between whites and Native Americans, and introduces the theme of miscegenation into American literature. She followed this publication with several others, including *Clarence* (1830), *The Linwoods* (1835), and *Married or Single?* (1857). After the mid-1830s, Sedgwick primarily wrote nonfiction prose, including several moral tales and essays to help teach children in Sunday school. In addition, she also wrote her autobiography, unpublished during her lifetime, and later titled *The Power of Her Sympathy* (1871; 1993).

CRITICAL RECEPTION

Sedgwick's works were considered innovative during her own time because she was one of the first American writers to use local scenery, customs, and characters. And while many contemporaries considered her writing style awkward and her works overbearingly didactic, she was universally praised for her well-realized characters and lively plots. Additionally, she was lauded for the realism of her work. Critical interest in her writing, however, began diminishing soon after the publication of her last novel, *Married or Single?,* and as other authors began writing novels about American locales, customs, and char-

acters, her work began to appear less innovative. It was not until the mid-twentieth century that Sedgwick's work once again gained critical attention, and with the new edition of *Hope Leslie* in the late 1980s critics began focusing on her historical significance. This novel in particular has garnered the most attention from modern critics, who universally praise Sedgwick's innovative writing style and subjects. In this historical romance, she told the story of Hope Leslie, her sister Faith, and Magawisca, a Pequot Indian. Through the stories of these women and within the boundaries of the romance tradition, Sedgwick skillfully confronted authorized versions of history, and offered an alternate perspective to the Puritans' largely ethnocentric view of the Pequot War and the displacement of Native Americans during the early years of the American republic. Critics such as Philip Gould, who examines this work in the context of other contemporary historical accounts of the Pequot War, have praised Sedgwick's revisionist interpretation of Puritan historiography through the eyes of those traditionally marginalized or oppressed by it, such as women and Native Americans. Similarly, examining the work as a political text that reflects the social concerns of its time, Douglas Ford notes that Sedgwick used *Hope Leslie* to explore the possibilities of a more inclusive definition of American identity and culture. Carol J. Singley agrees, noting that while Sedgwick wrote within the confines of the traditional frontier romance tradition, she used her writing to offer an alternative vision of the American woman and American culture. In fact, Singley feels that while she seemed to be following romantic conventions, Sedgwick actually undercut many of the assumptions upon which the romance in her tale is organized, instead opting to teach by adhering to facts of history and depicting authentic characters and events. Despite a gap of many years in the critical attention given to her work, contemporary and modern critics alike have acknowledged Sedgwick as one of the first American writers to focus on moral themes that address issues of both social and political significance for nineteenth-century America. She has also been praised for her terse prose style and the creation of courageous, independent female characters. Perhaps most importantly, however, Sedgwick is now acknowledged by literary historians for her contribution to the development of a national literature in America.

PRINCIPAL WORKS

A New-England Tale; or, Sketches of New England Character and Manners (novel) 1822; revised as *A New England Tale, and Miscellanies* 1852

Mary Hollis: An Original Tale (novel) 1822

Redwood: A Tale 2 vols. (novel) 1824

Hope Leslie; or, Early Times in the Massachusetts (novel) 1827

Clarence; or, A Tale of Our Own Times (novel) 1830

Home (novel) 1835

The Linwoods; or, "Sixty Years Since" in America (novel)
1835

Tales and Sketches 2 vols. (short stories) 1835-44

The Poor Rich Man, and the Rich Poor Man (novel) 1836

Live and Let Live; or, Domestic Service Illustrated (novel)
1837

Means and Ends; or, Self-Training (essays) 1839

Letters from Abroad to Kindred at Home (letters) 1841

Married or Single? (novel) 1857

Life and Letters of Catharine M. Sedgwick (unfinished
autobiography and letters) 1871; revised as *The Power
of Her Sympathy: The Autobiography and Journal of
Catharine Maria Sedgwick* [edited by Mary Kelley]
1993

CRITICISM

Sister Mary Michael Welsh (essay date 1937)

SOURCE: "An Analysis of Miss Sedgwick's Novels," in
*Catharine Maria Sedgwick: Her Position in the Literature
and Thought of Her Time Up to 1860,* Catholic University
of America, 1937, pp. 21-34.

[*In the following essay, Welsh offers an overview of Sedgwick's best known novels, including* A New England Tale,
Hope Leslie, *and* The Linwoods.]

Since it would hardly serve any great purpose to consider
the work of Miss Sedgwick chronologically, it seems better to examine her work by forms. In the matter of importance her novels come first. It is through her six novels
that she is best known by the critics of American literature. Especially important are **Hope Leslie,** 1827, and **The
Linwoods,** 1835; but the analysis will proceed not according to their importance, but in the order of their publication. The plan is to give a brief summary of the plot, then,
to consider the various elements contained in each novel,
and, finally, to apply these elements to the generally accepted standards of novel construction.

A New England Tale

Her first novel, **A New England Tale,** 1822, is set in her
own familiar Berkshires. Here she was perfectly at home;
she knew the country and she understood the people. Her
thorough knowledge of New England characters, and her
complete understanding of their strength and weakness
were powerful aids in the development of her tale, and in
this respect she far surpasses the skill of Maria Edgeworth,
who wrote of a locale to which she was alien. The story
was written shortly after Miss Sedgwick's renunciation of
Calvinism and her acceptance of the new Unitarianism.
The pharisaical judgments of some of her neighbors had
given her considerable annoyance, and she wrote the tale
with the hope of acquainting them, through delightful sat-

ire, with the fact that the religious motives and sentiments
of some of their number were sometimes actuated by hypocrisy.

Her intention when she began to write the tale was to produce a simple tract for Sunday school classes, but as she
wrote she became so interested in the work that she continued adding further incidents until it had outgrown the
length of the sketch she had intended and had reached the
proportions of a novel. It is always placed with her novels
but, strictly speaking, it is more correctly a tale as the author herself designates it in her title. Briefly, the plot is
this: Jane Elton, a twelve year old girl, is a destitute orphan. Her three maternal aunts try to shift responsibility in
adopting her. Crazy Bet, a town character, upbraids them.
Thus the author has used Crazy Bet as a means of castigating the Puritanical character. The only sincere friend of
the orphan is Mary Hull, a servant, who is the example of
genuine charity and sterling piety. There are three men:
Mr. Lloyd, a Quaker of sound principle; Mr. Erskine, weak
and vacillating; and David Wilson, hypocrite and libertine.
The story ends in the happy marriage of Jane and Mr.
Lloyd.

The material of this novel is familiar and the treatment
idealistic. It is not romantic in the sense of history or of
customs, but there is a small touch of the Gothic element.
The plot is simple with but little interest—what interest is
there is in the didactic purpose. There is a seduction incident, a little more hideous in its consequences than those
incidents found in similar novels of the day. There is also
a duel. Poetic justice is meted out to evil doers and the
virtuous are rewarded. With the exception of Mrs. Wilson,
the characters are not self-revealing; they do not stand out.
The narration is fair—somewhat impeded by the ever
present desire to satirize and preach. The unity of impression is blurred by too many unnecessary details not vitally
connected. There is a definite harmony between the characters and the material, but the balance among the characters themselves is sadly lacking. Jane is too good; the Wilson girls are too bad. The integrity of Mr. Lloyd far
outweighs the rascality of David Wilson. There is no organic rhythm to the book—no proportion. Too much attention is given to one aunt with but a passing reference to
the other two. There is no particular quality of style, and
the method is a form, occasionally that of letters, too well
worn at that time to be considered worth while. The whole
story is so positively didactic, so replete with satire, that
no memorable reading of life comes down to us.

Yet this novel was a success—financially speaking. In
spite of this fact Miss Sedgwick was loathe to rush into a
literary career. She made no pretensions to authorship. Her
novel, she said, was not for the erudite of Boston, but for
the young and the humble. The tale, however, was a daring adventure in satirizing the accepted religion of the
place and period. The author showed courage in publishing it. The book was later reprinted in England and translated into German. To the literary historian it is of interest

both because of its being her first novel and because of its setting forth the material in which she was later to do her best work.

REDWOOD

Two years afterwards, 1824, the second novel *Redwood* appeared. This was a tale of domestic life and dealt with such events that ordinarily occur in all well-regulated communities. The treatment of this material is a vivid idealization, and the result, an unusual amount of interest.

Mr. Redwood and his daughter, Caroline, arrive in the midst of an electric storm at a little town in Vermont. Redwood has his arm broken when his frightened horses wreck the carriage. Mr. Lennox and his sister, Aunt Debby, offer him the hospitality of their house. While Redwood is convalescing the plot develops.

Redwood, when young, was a high-principled man but he lost his religion and morality through his association with an atheist. In this state he had contracted a clandestine marriage with Mary Erwine, a pious governess, but socially inferior. His father insisted on his marrying a rich girl—his cousin. He broke with Mary and his infidelity killed her. He knew nothing of her death until he reached Rome. On his return he married his cousin who lived but a few years. Before she died she left him a daughter, Caroline, who grew to be the epitome of the social uselessness of the time.

In the Lennox family there was an Ellen Bruce. Ellen was all that a model ward should be, but there is in addition an air of mystery about her. She owns a casket which is not to be opened until she is twenty-one.

Other visitors appear at the Lennox household. The two Shakers, Susan Allen and her niece Emily, make a fleeting visit, leaving a sense of future tragedy in their wake. The Westalls, mother and son, stop on their return to Virginia. Redwood and Mrs. Westall are anxious to arrange a marriage between their children. This marriage would please Caroline, but Charles Westall's choice rests on Ellen Bruce.

The meeting at Lebanon Springs of all the principal characters brings the story to a rapid conclusion. Caroline elopes with an English officer, Ellen Bruce turns out to be the daughter of Redwood and Mary Erwine, Mr. Redwood regains his lost faith, Charles Westall marries Ellen, and Aunt Debby rescues Emily from the influence of the Shakers.

The plot, easily penetrated at the outset, is, nevertheless, filled with many complications, and the general effect is that it holds the interest.

The character development is exceptionally good. The proud, selfish, envious Caroline is thoroughly revealed to us, and toward the end she shows some good development. The gentle, generous, trustful character of Ellen

Bruce is perhaps too good to be real, but the contrast between her and Caroline is convincing. So, too, is the contrast between Susan Allen and her niece Emily. Above all, though, Aunt Debby Lennox stands out—practical, childlike, yet wise in the ways of the world, a counsellor to the needy—a character unique in American literature at that time. These women are far superior to the women we find in Cooper's novels at the same date.

The narrative is good—better than that of the contemporary women writers. The unity is strong yet relieved by variety of interests all held in restraint. The story is in harmony with the setting, and the balance of characters and groups of characters is acceptable. The story lacks an appreciable rhythm, but the proportion of the book is excellent. There is as yet no evidence of a distinct style—no lyric quality, and the method Miss Sedgwick follows is one found in almost every contemporary novel. Deep pathos pervades some parts of the story, while others display a keen sense of humor. The dialogue is easy, natural, and appropriate.

The mystery surrounding Ellen's birth, the casket which she may not open, the meeting with her father under such peculiar circumstances—all seem extraordinary. These are, however, in accordance with the style of the fiction of the period. Sir Walter Scott and Miss Edgeworth made use of such expedients, and the readers of the day accepted them without question.

The moral, which is a religious one, is well worked into the texture of the story and does not stare officiously from its pages. Miss Sedgwick shows how plentiful and how valuable are the materials to be found in the lives of her people, and how readily they adapt themselves to the pages of fiction. The story is decidedly romantic in its descriptions of scenery, and this romance is deepened by many of the incidents—the electric storm, the accident at the lake, the abduction, and the imprisonment in the hut of the Indian. The sentimentality of the author's predecessors is apparent, too, in the secret marriage of Mary Erwine and in Redwood's desertion of her. The incident of the visits of Ellen to the blind child and the operation which gave her sight, is used some years later by Mrs. Augusta Evans Wilson in *St. Elmo,* 1835.

The novel was reprinted in England and translated into French. A notice of *Redwood* in *The Constitionnel,* a Paris newspaper, attributed the authorship to Cooper.

HOPE LESLIE

Redwood, 1824, was followed by *Hope Leslie; or, Early Times in Massachusetts,* 1827. This novel, an historical one, was probably suggested by a review of *Redwood* which appeared in the *North American Review,* after the publication of that novel. While commending *Redwood,* the review points out the wonderful material available to the writer who would go back to the infancy of the colonies, to the fearless lives of the pioneers, the unknown terrors of the forests, and the mingled kindness and treachery of the savage tribes by whom the settlers were surrounded.[1]

The plot was suggested by an incident connected with the Indian massacre at Deerfield, Massachusetts. A young girl was taken captive by the Indians and married to a chief. She was, after some years, discovered by her relatives; but she refused to return to them, preferring to remain with her Indian husband.

Springfield, Massachusetts, and the city of Boston are used as the chief settings for the novel. William Fletcher, confident of the safety of his little family, leaves his wife and two sons in Springfield while he travels to Boston to meet his cousin, Mrs. Leslie, who is arriving from England. When the vessel reaches port, he learns that Mrs. Leslie died at sea, leaving her two little daughters, Faith and Hope, to his guardianship. He is obliged to remain in Boston for some days but sends Faith to Springfield, keeping Hope with him. Shortly after Faith arrives at the settlement, the father of two young Indians held in service at the Fletcher homestead, attacks the family, kills Mrs. Fletcher and her infant son, and takes Faith and Mrs. Fletcher's elder son, Everell, captive with the intention of sacrificing him. As the ax descends to take his life, Everell is saved by Magawisca, the chief's daughter, who, like Pocahontas, throws herself between him and the ax and receives the blow which severs her arm.

After Everell's escape the story passes over the intervening years to present Everell and Hope grown to manhood and womanhood. The scene changes to Boston. Here in a few months events throng thick and fast upon one another. Hope meets her sister Faith; but the meeting is interrupted by the villain of the story, Sir Philip Gardiner, who leads a guard to the meeting place and takes captive Magawisca, who accompanied Faith. Oneco, Faith's Indian husband, and the old chief Ononotto then take Hope prisoner, believing she has acted as a decoy. Hope evades them and is rescued by an Italian sailor who supposes her to be his patron saint. Magawisca is tried for conspiracy, and in this trial occurs the most tragic scene introduced in an American novel up to this period. Here in open court the Indian maiden produces the crucifix dropped by Gardiner and asks him to swear upon it to the truth of his statements.

Faith steals back to her Indian husband. Hope plans the escape of Magawisca by disguising her in the clothes of her old tutor whom she leaves in the cell in her stead, knowing the gentle old man will not be made to suffer. The awful catastrophe of the blowing up of the vessel on which Gardiner had planned to carry off Hope ends the story. All the evil ones meet their punishment in the explosion, and the good are safe from their further machinations. Everell and Hope, as is expected, are happily married.

The novel is decidedly romantic. The author has used material that is historical and has treated it idealistically. On several occasions the sentiment of terror adds a Gothic touch. The plot does not stand out; it is so involved in minor plots, that the main one is, at times, obscured. These minor incidents, however, are all so stirring and thrilling that the interest aroused is intense. Hope's escape, first from the Indians, then from the outlaws, and finally from the treachery of Sir Philip Gardiner—all keep alive the interest awakened at the beginning of the novel when the massacre occurred. The characters are too strongly idealized. In Magawisca we have a high idealization of the Indian, but the character seems overdrawn. Both Everell and Hope are also idealized. They hold too perfectly to a happy mean, scarcely attainable at their age and period. The Puritan character is presented in a more favorable light than in *A New England Tale.* Governor Winthrop and Mr. Fletcher, though strict adherents, are both free from the blight of Puritan severity. The story is told in an easy, familiar style, with few interruptions for the sake of sermonizing, and with frequent passages of subtle humor. Again, the author rises to the heights of eloquence, as in Magawisca's dramatic trial scene. The narration will bear comparison with that of any other writer of the time. Even with the numerous incidents, many so vivid that they almost hide the chief plot, the unity of the story is intact; and a strong restraining influence is exercised. The harmony between characters is perfect. The story is quite in keeping with the setting, and thus, harmony is preserved. The author appears to leave, to some extent at least, the more open didacticism of her predecessors, and writes in a smooth, natural style. Miss Sedgwick gives evidence of much originality in this novel. Her introduction of the crucifix and Hope's rescue of Magawisca are incidents new to the American novel. For these she had no precedent.

CLARENCE; OR A TALE OF OUR OWN TIMES

Three years after the publication of *Hope Leslie,* in 1830 *Clarence* appeared.

The story begins with the friendship established between Mr. Flavel, an aged man, and Frank Carroll, an attractive young boy. The old man becomes ill, and Frank persuades his parents to take him into their house, to nurse him through his illness. Flavel, whose real name is Clarence, turns out to be the father of Mr. Carroll and the grandfather of Frank. When a young child, Mr. Carroll had been lost through the villainy of John Smith, a clerk, to whom Clarence had entrusted him. Flavel dies shortly after the relationship has been established and leaves his immense wealth to Mr. Carroll who from now on is known by his true name of Clarence. The happiness of becoming the possessor of this fortune is changed to grief when Frank dies suddenly.

The tenth chapter really begins the plot. The tale is rather complicated, presenting two pairs of lovers, Gerald Rosco and Gertrude Clarence; Emilie Layton and Randolph Marion, whose love affairs run anything but smoothly. Two villains, John Smith, the faithless clerk, and Pedrillo an adventurer, masquerading as a wealthy gentleman, add to the complication of the plot.

Mr. Clarence and his daughter move to their country house. Here they meet Mrs. Layton. She is a cultured woman of the world, but one who does not hesitate to sacrifice her daughter's happiness in order to avoid the loss of their wealth. This daughter, Emilie, is a lovable girl; and the idea of her marriage with the adventurer, Pedrillo, is most repugnant. Louis Seton, the timid, sensitive artist, deeply in love with Gertrude Clarence, is also introduced.

In the second part of the novel, the scene changes to New York City and city life is vividly and truly described throughout the remainder of the book. The author's own life was spent partly in the country and partly in the city and her affections seem to be equally divided between the two. She is one of the first to indicate clearly the city, as such, in the novel, Hugh Breckenridge and Charles Brockden Brown alone preceding her. The attitude of city life interested her, and she was the first to present real social situations as they are found actually existing in the city. The first real account of a church service in a novel occurs in *Clarence.*

She is one of the first to introduce into a novel an incident that permits her to express her sentiments and those of her contemporaries regarding the folly of duelling.

In spite of the romanticism of *Clarence,* the novel presents in its descriptions of social life in New York City, a realism that is true and accurate in all its details. Different grades of society are depicted: the newly rich with their over-crowded, gaudily furnished rooms; the intolerant many, who, sure of their own position in society, scorn their less fortunate neighbors who are seeking entrance; the genuinely refined, who, although bereft of their fortunes, still retain their graciousness and culture.

There is also in *Clarence* a condemnation of the shallowness of the city's social standards. It is an indictment against the artificiality of fashionable life. A fine sarcasm prevails.

Clarence, though one of the most romantic of Miss Sedgwick's novels, is developed from material thoroughly realistic. Scenes depicting the most extravagant romance are, however, generously sprinkled throughout the novel. As is usual with the author, she has so deluged her story with interesting events, that, while the plot itself seems weakened, it is never lost sight of; although it runs along in danger of eclipse by some of the minor plots. The novel is strong in character portrayal, but lacks character development. All are either good or bad at the beginning, and the good remain unchanged; while the bad become more wicked as the plot develops. Yet, the characters are splendidly drawn and are individuals, not types. Mrs. Layton is beautiful, polished, charming, yet so selfish she would sacrifice everything and everyone to satisfy her slightest whim. Gertrude Clarence is in direct contrast to Mrs. Layton. Gertrude is not beautiful, but charming in her simplicity, her honesty, and her goodness. She is willing to sacrifice herself in order to bring comfort to others. Gerald

Roscoe corresponds in character to Gertrude and forms a marked contrast to the dishonest profligate, Pedrillo. The narration is splendid. The story abounds in effective, appropriate dialogues; and the depression some sections of the novel would produce is tempered by a tactful introduction of mild humor. The unity of impression is weak, owing chiefly to the strength of minor plots. While these incidents seem to confuse those of the chief plot, they furnish, nevertheless, a restraint that excites interest. The contrast in characters makes for harmony and presents a perfect balance. In this novel, the author makes her nearest approach to lyrical style. She makes frequent use of the epistolary Richardsonian method to bring events up to date, and in these letters she excels. In adopting this style she is in keeping with the writers of her time, but takes the initiative in introducing new incidents—church services and duelling.

Interwoven side by side are the romantic and the dramatic. Miss Sedgwick has not forgotten her purpose in writing which was both to entertain and to instruct. Throughout the book she has injected, quietly and effectively, the moral she wished to instill. One lesson which she brings home very strongly is that one's death depends upon the life the individual has led. This is brought out very plainly in the contrast between the death of Pedrillo and that of Seton.

THE LINWOODS; OR SIXTY YEARS SINCE IN AMERICA

Five years elapsed after the publication of *Clarence,* 1830, before Miss Sedgwick gave to the public another novel. This was *The Linwoods; or Sixty Years Since in America,* 1835, an historical romance which carries the reader back sixty years to the stirring events of the Revolution. The scene is laid in New York, but the New England farm life is introduced in the home of Eliot Lee and his sister Bessie. In *Clarence,* the New York of the 1830's plays an important rôle, while *The Linwoods* acquaints the reader with the colonial city of the Dutch settlement.

The review of *Redwood* already referred to, published in the *North American Review* in 1825, seems to have suggested the writing of *The Linwoods* as well as the writing of *Hope Leslie.*

The *Review* calls attention to the wealth of material open to writers of fiction, if they would go back to the incidents of the Revolution; to the policies that divided families and separated friends; and to the volunteers who came from foreign shores to aid the struggling colonists.

Although *The Linwoods* was not written until ten years after this Review, it seems probable that it had its influence on the creation of this novel; for all the incidents suggested in it are made use of by Miss Sedgwick. She does not, however, go deeply into the events of the war, nor bring out as heroes our great historic figures. General Washington is introduced several times but he is by no means the principal character. The reader meets Lafayette but he disappears before one really knows he is there.

General Putnam, also, opportunely arrives at the decisive moment only to be lost sight of immediately. Mrs. Washington appears for the first time in a novel and delights the reader with her kindly manner and her gracious aid in assisting with the wedding preparations of Eliot Lee, the hero of the romance. The mercenary and military adventures so scorned by the Rebels have their place in the story; the Tory also plays his part. The nobility of the colonists in their privations and sufferings endured so uncomplainingly, is contrasted with the selfishness and feastings of the enemy.

The very first chapter of the book introduces the chief characters; Bessie Lee, the daughter of a New England farmer, Isabella Linwood and her brother Herbert, children of a wealthy Tory, and Jasper Meredith, the friend of young Linwood. When the war opens, Herbert Linwood, in opposition to the command of his father, joins the rebel forces and is disowned in consequence. Eliot Lee becomes an officer and is in close attendance on General Washington. Bessie Lee, deceived by Jasper Meredith, gradually becomes mad and wanders from her New England home to New York to return his trinkets to him, believing that by doing so she will be freed from the love she has had for him. Here at the close of the war all are united and, as usual, rewarded or punished as poetic justice demands. Throughout the story one exciting event follows another, so that there is not a dull moment to be disposed of.

As usual Miss Sedgwick is not strong in building up her plot. Incidents without number are gathered around it. This is true of **The Linwoods** as well as of all her other novels. This does not, however, seem to detract from the interest of the plot but rather adds to it, for the author is always felicitous in her selection of incidents, and so ingenious in weaving them into the story that one overlooks the lack of plot unity.

Again, as is usual with Miss Sedgwick, the women characters are exceedingly well-drawn. The heroine, Isabella Linwood, is an excellent character, beautiful, intelligent, loyal—lovable in every way. The gentle, trusting Bessie Lee is a most pathetic figure. The beautiful traitorous Ruthven sisters present a woeful contrast with their miserable duplicity. Herbert Linwood and Eliot Lee are noble types of colonial youths, while Jasper Meredith may well be placed in the same category with the Ruthven girls. All these characters are real; the only suggestion of idealization is in Eliot Lee, or in the devotion to Eliot of the poor unfortunate Kissel. The story is told in a fascinating manner. Incidents crowd in such quick succession and from such unsuspected sources that, while the interest is intense, the unity of impression is sometimes marred. Naturally the many changes in these minor events provide a restraining influence. There is always harmony between characters and settings, whether these be the New England farm house or the Clinton mansion. Miss Sedgwick's use of contrast inevitably tends to balance in characters—a balance that she preserves in all her novels. The same simple ease in writing which seems natural to the author is evi-

dent here. Letters are frequently used to advance the plo and explain situations. The proportion is good, althougl prominent historical figures are lightly passed over. In thi Miss Sedgwick is probably influenced by Scott, in givin₁ minor places to these characters. Her purpose is didactic for she states in her Preface that she is presenting this pic ture of the sufferings of their ancestors in the hope that he young readers may be faithful to the free institutions trans mitted to them. In spite of this, however, one could no call the novel really didactic. Miss Sedgwick is unique i being the first to introduce Mrs. Washington into a novel.

MARRIED OR SINGLE?

Passing over her didactic tales for the present, we go on t her last novel which was not published until twenty-tw years later. In 1857, however, she produced another nove entitled **Married or Single?** In her Preface to this story th author openly proclaims her purpose in writing. She say that it is a woman's right to shape her own course and tha she would feel that the novel had not been written in vai if it did anything to lessen the stigma attached by the vu gar to the title of "old maid."

As a novel it does not bear comparison with either **Th Linwoods** or **Hope Leslie.** The author has piled into th tale all kinds of incidents and grouped them together i this story. There are several pairs of lovers, three or fou characters with a mysterious past, a seduction with i usual tragedy in the death of the victim, the inevitable tr angle, and a young man unjustly imprisoned for forger. The main theme of the novel is a woman's right to enjc an independent life.

Grace Herbert, the heroine of the story, after discoverir the villainy of Copeland, her betrothed, determines to le a single life. She proves her ability to support herself a though her girlhood had been passed in a home of wealt Her resolution to remain single weakens when she fin that she is loved by Archibald Lisle, an ideal character ar the hero of the novel. The tale leaves her at twenty-thr years of age betrothed to the hero with the promise of happy life before her.

There are many passages in the novel, however, that gi the reader much knowledge of the author's philosophy life, and her position on some of the questions of the da There is a little satire on transcendentalism which shov her lack of confidence in this philosophy. She places th term in the mouth of one of her characters to designa anything he cannot explain—its meaning seems to be o scure and cloudy. The uncultured wealthy, who invi friends to see their portraits painted by one of the old ma ters, come in for their share of the satire. The introducti of the runaway slave and her little child afford an opport nity for expressing her sentiments about this question.

There are so many plots in this story, it is difficult to d termine just which is the real one. The love story Archibald Lisle and Grace Herbert, however, appears to the principal one, and their experiences which end in their final union constitute the plot. The characters, like the plots, are numerous, and are of all kinds. Miss Sedgwick fails to make her woman characters convincing, as she has done in her earlier novels. Her idealization of hero and heroine has resulted in rendering both rather vapid. No particular character in the book stands out. Her narration is excellent, for she is a finished story-teller; and even in an inferior tale, can hold the interest of the reader. Unity of impression is lacking, however, lost in the multiplicity of minor plots which obscure the main issue. The restraint is too forced. There is a certain harmony between characters and material, but balance among the characters is wanting. The good far exceed all others, and the villain, Copeland, stands absolutely alone. The book lacks proportion, many of the minor plots exceeding the interest of the main plot. There is no particular style to the writing—the author does not appear to have acquired any special style. Nor does this tale exhibit any originality of method; it follows her usual manner, weaving incidents around a group of characters. At times, these incidents seem introduced simply because the author wanted to write about them, not that they aided the plot.

As a novel, the work is a failure. Its value and importance lie in the fact that it helps to place the author in the issues of her day, since she has given expression to her sentiments regarding many current questions.

Summing up this analysis of her novels, we find that while her material has been divided between the familiar and the historical, the treatment has been invariably idealistic. This is quite in keeping with the authors of her day. We find, however, that her plot construction, with the exception of the last novel, improves with each new one; but that intrigue and complications tend toward obscuring the unity of impression so much desired. In this particular, Miss Sedgwick ranks on a par with most of her contemporaries, but is inferior to both Cooper and Simms.

Her best characterization comes out in her second novel, **Redwood,** in the personage of Aunt Debby Lennox. A comparison of Miss Sedgwick's characterizations with those of Cooper will show, especially in regard to women, a far more human group of heroines. But not even Aunt Debby can be classified in the same category with Harvey Birch, Long Tom Coffin, or Natty Bumpo.

It seems safe to say that Miss Sedgwick's dialogue is the equal of the best of her contemporaries, and that for the most part it maintains a consistent level of excellence.

Another interesting point lies in her inventiveness. She is particularly rich in adding unique situations and incidents to her stories, and in this respect she has anticipated Cooper, Dickens, Motley, and the Brontes. Seldom does she look forward to the newer realism. All too frequently she looks backward to the sentimentalism and the Gothic materials of an earlier time.

That she is something of a social historian is apparent in **Clarence.** Although she was not a pioneer in the social

materials of city life, still she did far better work in that field than any other writer up to the coming of Willis in his *Paul Fane.*

The ever prevailing shadow of didacticism is over her work, and for this reason alone her novels make no appeal to the modern reader. In almost every other respect she takes her place in the literary world among such early novelists as Cooper, Neale, Bird, Simms, Cooke, Willis, and Holmes. The didacticism which kills our interest in her novels marked her as an author whose work was in great demand in the journals and publications of her day. Her faults were the faults of the age.

Note

1. *North American Review,* "Review of *Redwood*" (Boston, 1825), XX, 245.

Thomas H. Fick (essay date 1990)

SOURCE: "Catharine Sedgwick's 'Cacoethes Scribendi': Romance in Real Life," in *Studies in Short Fiction,* Vol. 27, No. 4, Fall, 1990, pp. 567-76.

[*In the following essay, Fick examines Sedgwick's short story "Cacoethes Scribendi" as a protorealistic piece dealing with antebellum conceptions of literary realism.*]

Although Catharine Sedgwick was one of the most respected and popular authors writing before the Civil War, until recently she has been largely ignored by twentieth-century critics. In an 1835 review of **The Linwoods,** Edgar Allan Poe wrote that "of American *female* writers we must consider [Catharine Sedgwick] the first" (95), but after her death in 1867 she came to merit only passing references in literary histories and critical works. During the past few years, however, her literary reputation has undergone a minor revaluation, at least in part because her work shows a remarkable sensitivity to literary modes and conventions. Her first novel—**A New England Tale** (1822)—established the major conventions of what Nina Baym calls "woman's fiction" and, as Michael D. Bell points out, in **Hope Leslie** she demonstrated an unusual knack for working with existing conventions. It is therefore not surprising to find that two recent collections of women's fiction open with exemplary stories by Sedgwick: Judith Fetterley begins *Provisions: A Reader from 19th-Century American Women* with **"Cacoethes Scribendi"** (1830) and Susan Koppelman chooses **"Old Maids"** (1834) to introduce her anthology *Old Maids: Short Stories by Nineteenth Century U.S. Women Writers.* Koppelman goes so far as to claim, with considerable justification, that not only does **"Old Maids"** set "the classic pattern for a story written in defense of old maids," it also introduces "the major themes characteristic of women's short fiction" (9, 10). Clearly, Sedgwick's fiction is attractive both for its graceful execution and for its articulation of formal and thematic concerns—the implicit (and sometimes explicit) commentary on operative conventions as well as subjects. For these reasons, Sedgwick's works are interesting both for themselves and for what they can tell us about the development of modes and genres.

In this essay I want to consider **"Cacoethes Scribendi,"** one of Sedgwick's most rewarding short fictions, for what it reveals about antebellum conceptions of realism in literature. This "protorealistic" writing shares some characteristics with formula fiction and is often marked by interventive authorial commentary—a narrative strategy virulently attacked by almost all American proponents of realism since Henry James.[1] Yet despite such narratological *faux pas,* protorealistic fiction explicitly presents itself as engaged in exploring "reality" both by the structure of the story (which like Mark Twain's *Adventures of Huckleberry Finn* centers on an opposition between reality and aristocratic romance) and by the authorial voice. It is my contention that we must grant a tentative legitimacy to these structural and authorial assertions of realism if we are to understand how the real is conceived and portrayed in antebellum literature.

"Cacoethes Scribendi" (Latin: writer's itch) is a compact tale that explores the opposition between the "real" and the ideal through two converging lines of development. On the one hand, the story is about women and writing. Mrs. Courland (the matriarch of an all-female household) and her sisters indulge their passion for writing with an exuberance that, as Judith Fetterley rightly observes, suggests no trace of the "anxiety of authorship" that Gilbert and Gubar find central to the woman writer's experience (5). On the other hand, the story concerns the subjects of women's fiction: while Mrs. Courland is engaged in the act of writing, her daughter Alice acts out a courtship and marriage that exemplifies the sort of fiction Mrs. Courland should write. Thus **"Cacoethes Scribendi"** explores both the act of writing and one subject of writing, in this case the unfolding romance between Alice and her cousin Ralph—a text-book example of true love.

While the parallel plots clearly indicate that the story has something to say about the relation between writing and living—technique and subject—modern readers can easily be deceived about the precise nature of that relation. In her introduction to the story, for example, Fetterley argues that Alice's lover Ralph emerges "as the genuine writer" because "His is a 'true story,' based on real feelings," and because when he writes his declaration of love for Alice "he writes only what he has to say." In this view, the story endorses a conception of reality, and of realistic writing, that stands opposed to what are presumed to be the sentimental and formulaic productions of Mrs. Courland, who presumably writes standard odes to romantic love. Yet Fetterley's notion of realism is both tautological and ahistorical: Ralph's is an ostensibly "real" story because it is based on "real" feelings, with the unexamined assumption that real feelings (in this case love) are spontaneous, unmediated—presumably the result of something like "instinct" or nature, and that hence endure as transhistorical

constants. Yet real feelings, like right actions or even true love, are products of their times and are expressed in different ways: one *"has* to say" what one has learned is possible and appropriate to say. Further, "true stories" about real feelings are recognized as true only within the literary conventions that define the consensus about what constitutes reality. (Literary realism is itself determined by conventions, as critics have long acknowledged.) We should resist the temptation to find **"Cacoethes Scribendi"** significant to the extent that it anticipates the particular conventions of postbellum literary realism—a teleological conception of genre. If we move beyond vague, incantatory evocations of "true stories" and "real feelings," we find that Ralph's feelings, and hence the truth of his story (a very conventional love story), have a logic of their own.

In the literary economy of this tale, "reality" emerges as reflection of moral codes and social formulae—a collective human construction that bestows meaning upon the actions of the individual. (In contrast, the post-Darwinian notion of realism posits an individual working out the imperatives of impersonal and inhuman forces; the world of conventional morality is frequently considered unscientific, artificial, and hence irrelevant.) As one consequence, the characters and plots in antebellum realism tend to be portrayed in broadly representative terms—as what might seem to us now as stereotypical or formulaic. What I am suggesting is that we look for the "real" story in antebellum fiction not in the portrayal of thorough-going individuality, but in characters and plots that explicitly represent shaping conditions and expectations, and that thus often appear to the modern reader to be formulaic in the case of plot and conventional in the case of character. By adhering to a moral and collective notion of the "real," Sedgwick performs an essentially conservative cultural function that is upsetting both to liberal critics who look for an enlightened ideology (or literary practice), and formalist critics who value intricate aesthetic shape, complex verbal resonance, and moral ambiguity. Yet for antebellum writers the portrayal of what Sedgwick elsewhere calls the "beau actual" (**"First Love"** 83) was the dominant form of representing contemporary conditions, and to read such tales as **"Cacoethes Scribendi"** as a justification of Howellsian realism is quite simply untrue to the narrative. We can see how the "real" operates in much antebellum fiction by looking closely at Sedgwick's carefully crafted tale.

Mrs. Courland's profession of authorship begins when Frank returns from Boston with two annual collections of poetry and fiction, a form of publication then extremely popular among middle-class readers.[2] Although intended for Alice, these collections have their most immediate and obvious effect on Mrs. Courland: "she *felt a call* to become an author, and before she retired to bed she obeyed the call, as if it had been, in truth, a divinity stirring within her" (53). She inspires her three unmarried sisters to follow her writerly example, and together they turn out examples of almost every form of popular prose: religious tracts, treatises on botany and child rearing, with an en-

phasis on romantic sketches. There are several other consequences of this obsessive "itch." First, in her search for
subjects Mrs. Courland cannibalizes her daughter's public
life with such energy that Alice grows "afraid to speak or
to act, and from being the most artless . . . little creature
in the world, she became as silent and as stiff as a statue"
(56). A comic version of the tortured artists that appear in
Nathaniel Hawthorne's tales, Mrs. Courland violates her
subject's public and private self, but she changes her
daughter from artless girl to statuary rather than, like Ethan
Brand, her own heart to stone.

The other results of writing are in some ways more positive. A hundred years before Virginia Woolf called for a
room of one's own, Mrs. Courland and her three sisters
abandon the parlor for their separate bedrooms, and their
retreat from the space of domestic action turns the parlor
from "a sort of village exchange" to a "tower of Babel after the builders had forsaken it" (56). Writing silences the
sort of social discourse that comprises the typical
nineteenth-century woman's world and substitutes another
whose lack of conviviality is at least partly balanced by an
increase in authority. But the story does not validate the
romantic notion of an isolated Promethean creator. Indeed,
most antebellum fiction by women portrays the community of the parlor in positive terms and conversation as an
alternative to the linear masculine narratives of business
and adventure—as Sedgwick's play on "village exchange"
neatly suggests. The true "bluestocking," as Sedgwick indicates in another short story, is as unpretentious, social,
and neighborly as any other member of her community.[3]
Since Mrs. Courland separates herself from the community it is reasonable to conclude that her fiction may also
be misconceived: Mrs. Courland seeks inspiration not in
her world but apart from it. The anxiety of authorship is
therefore not an issue, but the nature of what Mrs. Courland authors most certainly is.

While Mrs. Courland easily enlists her sisters in a life of
joyous scribbling, neither example nor exhortation can
convince her daughter Alice to write a line. Yet in an important sense Alice's refusal to touch a pen doesn't cut her
off from the subjects of fiction as Mrs. Courland cuts herself off when she abandons the hospitable "village exchange." Indeed, while Mrs. Courland pursues her writing,
in the now-empty parlor Alice and her cousin Frank are
enacting the age-old tale of true love—a literal rather than
a literary endeavor. The women's withdrawal to their un-
social space clears a space for acting out a flesh and blood
social drama: "Not a sound was heard [in the parlor] save
Ralph's and Alice's voices, mingling in soft and suppressed murmurs" (56)—and these are murmurs Sedgwick
has no need to translate for her audience. This, as we shall
see, is the real story that Ralph and Alice enact—a story
that is real precisely because it represents the common and
expected lot.

The drama of the young couple's lovemaking stands in
contrast to Mrs. Courland's literary apprenticeship, for the
annual has a different but equally powerful effect on Alice

and Frank. Unlike her mother, Alice responds to the meaning of the stories rather than the idea of writing, to the
presence of desire rather than the desire to write. When
Frank first brings the annuals that trigger Mrs. Courland's
"itch," Alice is particularly affected by one tale about "two
tried faithful lovers, and married at last!" and she calls
Frank's special attention to the ending: "I hate love stories
that don't end in marriage" (52). Frank passionately agrees,
and "for the first time Alice felt her cheeks tingle at his
approach" (52). Ralph and Alice's love is given shape and
direction by the conventional story in the annual: love becomes real because fiction makes its habitual and accepted
plot available to the two participants. As one young woman
comments in a story by Susan Pindar, "If I could only hear
one *true* love story, something that I knew had really occurred—then it would serve as a kind of text for all the
rest. Oh! how I long to hear a real story of actual life"
(54). Similarly, before Ralph and Alice found their own
"text" they "had always lived on terms of cousinly affection—an affection of a neutral tint that they never thought
of being shaded into the deep dye of a more tender passion" (52). A later exchange between Ralph and Mrs. Courland clarifies the relationship between the activity and the
subjects of writing that is suggested by the annual's double
effect. When Mrs. Courland asks Ralph to corroborate her
opinion that Alice is a fool to fear being called a "blue-
stocking," he answers "It would be a pity, aunt, to put blue
stockings on such pretty feet as Alice's" (57). The conversation continues for a while in the same vein, with Ralph
converting "blue-stocking" into clumsy compliments about
Alice's dainty feet. His word play mimics the relationship
between the two narrative lines: **"Cacoethes Scribendi"** is
a story about literary women—about bluestockings—but it
is also about well-turned ankles and lovers' compliments.
The relationship between the two plots is further explored
in the episode that moves Ralph and Alice's passion from
the private to the public realm, reinscribing their drama in
the social world and bringing the story to its anticipated
conclusion. Mrs. Courland has been pestering Ralph to
write about his experiences, and he finally gives in: "I will
sit down this moment, and write a story—a true story—
true from beginning to end" (57). He takes up his pen and
with much labor writes a single scratched and interlined
paragraph that presents a "short and true story of his love
for his sweet cousin Alice."

Ralph's single act of authorship raises one of the central
questions of the story: in what way is Ralph's story true?
Does Ralph emerge, as Fetterley maintains, "as the genuine writer" because "His is a 'true story,' based on real
feelings, and [because] he writes only what he has to say"?
On the one hand Ralph's paragraph is not a fiction; it represents his actual feelings and evokes a response that
shapes the rest of his life. In a more important way, however, both his written and lived stories are—or become—
"literary" and conventional: as we have seen, the courtship
was given shape and bodied forth from the nebulous realm
of adolescent affection by a sentimental story whose plot it
mirrors from beginning to end. Ralph becomes an adult
when he learns accurately to "read" the conventional plot

of true love. Indeed, **"Cacoethes Scribendi"** concludes with a one-sentence paragraph describing Alice's nuptials and the young lover's disappearance into the space of generic bliss: "her mother and aunts saw her the happy mistress of the Hepburn farm, and the happiest of wives."

As my discussion of the story should make clear, Fetterley is right but for the wrong reasons: Ralph's story *is* a "true story," not because it conveys his special feelings in contrast to conventional ones—for clearly it does not—but precisely because it fulfills common expectations about the course of events.[4] The truth of this story is therefore confirmed partly by the difficulty with which Ralph writes it, and partly by the confidence with which he lives it, a confidence generated by seeing it as repeating a cultural formula. We miss this notion of what constitutes real life if we insist on judging **"Cacoethes Scribendi"** by postbellum definitions of realism, which are profoundly suspicious of predictable narrative shape.[5] We miss it also if we equate realism with biological or sociological pessimism (the great descending curve of the naturalists). By all indications Mrs. Courland is a bad writer not because she writes "romance" but because her fiction pays no attention to the form, balance, and restraint of common plots such as the one that unfolds in her parlor—**"The Romance in Real Life,"** as Sedgwick titles another of her short stories.

It is easy to misread the indications of Mrs. Courland's weakness as a writer. We might, for example, decide that her error lies in composing romantic tales of love rather than realistic ones of misery or thwarted affection. This possibility is first suggested when Mrs. Courland reminds Ralph of three encounters he could make into wonderful articles, "founded on fact, all romantic and pathetic." Here she appears to be the sentimental romancer, cut off from the conditions of everyday life and lost in romantic haze. Indeed, Alice not-so-gently counters that:

> The officer drank too much; and the mysterious lady turned out to be a runaway milliner; and the man in black—oh! what a theme for a pathetic story!—the man in black was a widower, on his way to Newhaven, where he was to select his third wife from three *recommended* candidates.

To this objection Mrs. Courland brashly responds, "do you suppose it is necessary to tell things precisely as they are?" In this exchange Alice seems to function as the voice of modern realism, reminding her mother that desire must not overpower fact, and urging attention to the dark side of life. From a post-Jamesian perspective, therefore, it is tempting to see Mrs. Courland as the misguided romancer who distorts the available topics of everyday life; in this view Mrs. Courland is a bad writer because she doesn't recognize the marvelously gritty topics that would attract, say, Stephen Crane or Theodore Dreiser (if not W. D. Howells).

But such a reading just won't do. After all, Sedgwick herself does not give us the "realist's" (more properly the naturalist's) story of a drunken officer or fugitive milliner

or hardhearted, mercenary widower, but a tale of courtship and marriage. When evaluated according to the criteria of antebellum realism, the "romantic" content of the story subverts its supposed realism and hence we must consider the story hopelessly confused. However, **"Cacoethes Scribendi"** does not define unrealistic writing as stories of true love rather than drunken soldiers. Within the tale's world "things precisely as they are" (as demonstrated by Alice and Ralph's courtship) can be remarkably conventional, even what we might now consider sentimental. Mrs. Courland's fault lies not in the desire to write of true love rather than drunken soldiers, but in her inability to see such plots when they unfold in her own parlor, and to render them with appropriate decorum and proportion—something that Sedgwick most emphatically does. **"Cacoethes Scribendi"** offers several examples of the sort of writing Mrs. Courland should but cannot do. Take, for example, the narrator's description of Ralph—the actual lover to Mrs. Courland's fictional ones: "Ralph was no prodigy; none of his talents were in excess, but all in moderate degree" (51). Alice perfectly complements her lover no girl of seventeen, the narrator remarks, "was ever more disinterested, unassuming, unostentatious, and unspoiled" (52). None, all—the language of absolutes humorously characterizes the perfectly average lover in contrast to the extravagant pretensions of aristocratic romance.

What I am suggesting may be hard to stomach—that we take authorial claims to represent the real seriously, rather than as excuses for writing fiction.[6] This means entertaining the possibility that a structured social and moral world—which can appear to us as formulaic—can be the reality to which earlier writers respond, the one they wish to represent as the primary experience of their lives. At issue is not whether we consider such a world to be true but whether the writers did—and clearly the oppositional structure of the tales tells us that this is the case. Another attempt to understand realism seems to me culturally and temporally limited. There is obviously much about Sedgwick's conception of the "real" that the modern reader must find unacceptable. As the product of a white middle class woman, it downplays, even if it does not entirely ignore, suffering, injustice, prejudice, disease—the dark panoply of human misery. These are indeed large omissions. However, I maintain that we cannot disregard repeated assertions of what constitutes part of the author's "reality" when such assertions occur within an oppositional structure pitting real against ideal—that is, when the work clearly recognizes that the nature of reality is a primary issue. The difficulty of recognizing the relation between the reality of protorealism and the conditions it ostensibly reflects is that we expect realism to be mimetic in a particular way: always to reflect the *consequences* as well as the *conditions* of society—in short, structurally to contain a commentary as well as a vision of the world. Prose which does not contain such commentary is considered documentary if it is not fiction, or romance if it is literature that uncritically and unselfconsciously expresses how a society would *like* to see itself. But fiction like **"Cacoethes Scribendi"** can be considered neither documentary nor romance—hence our discomfort with its generic indeterminacy. While presented as an explicit alternative to dangerously deceptive romantic expectations, this vision of the real is not scientific or "natural" but subjective and human: one hears nothing of the impersonal forces that scholars of realism have seen as the focus of postbellum realism.[7] Instead, something is real to the extent that it functions as a *representative* text, one agreed upon and validated, a reality of consensus rather than objective inquiry. This sort of common text, rather than the scientific and essentially dehumanizing realism of post-Civil War America, marks the "protorealism" of much fiction by antebellum women. Sedgwick's exemplary tale helps us to understand the very different conventions of this mode.

Notes

1. As John Cawelti remarks: "Two central aspects of formulaic structures have been generally condemned in the serious artistic thought of the last hundred years: the essential standardization and their primary relation to the needs of escape and relaxation" (8). Protorealistic prose is frequently standardized, but within this cultural standardization it attacks rather than promotes escape. Robyn Warhol's recent work on narrative strategies in nineteenth-century women's fiction suggests one way of reconciling the intrusive narrator and literary realism. In "Toward a Theory of the Engaging Narrator," Warhol proposes to add the term "engaging narrator" to our critical lexicon; unlike the "distancing narrator" the engaging narrator addresses a narratee directly in order to stir her to sympathy and ultimately to action in the extratextual world. Elsewhere she argues that Stowe's explicit didacticism and direct addresses to the reader do not violate verisimilitude but promote a sense of continuity between textual and extratextual worlds ("Poetics and Persuasion").

2. "Cacoethes Scribendi" appeared in just such a collection (*The Atlantic Souvenir*) in 1830.

3. In a story published in 1832, Sedgwick defends literary women against charges of desexing themselves by describing a visit by the "bluestocking" Mrs. Rosewell to the home of one of her admirers. Mrs. Rosewell is revealed to be modest, sociable, and adept in smoothing the course of true love— not at all the terrible literary lion and "mannish writer of reviews" (336) the company anticipates. Indeed, it is her dilettantish host Mrs. Laight who delves into ponderous tomes and produces an unreadable essay on "the intellectual faculties" (344). Sedgwick's strategy is to justify Mrs. Rosewell's writing by promoting her participation in daily activities; to one questioner Mrs. Rosewell responds that "my last work was cutting out some vests for my boys" (341). This is a culturally conservative strategy that appears frequently in antebellum fiction: writing and women's traditional activities are shown to be complementary and authorship is re

duced to an affirmation of the status quo. Given these values, Mrs. Courland's retreat from social space must be considered an inappropriate move, since she defines her literary "work" as separate from the middle-class woman's domestic work.

4. A number of recent scholars have shown that what Alfred Habegger calls "domestic bitterness" (34-37) was of great interest to antebellum writers. David Reynolds, for example, discusses "the literature of misery"—works that focus on the dark side of women's experience, which frequently focus on nightmarish and even savage fantasies of violence and revenge against conventional patriarchal society (340, 352).

5. William B. Stone's formulation of the problem is typical: "For a work to be termed an example of literary realism it must be able to impose an aesthetic order on its materials, but it must do so *unobtrusively*" (48; original emphasis).

6. For a discussion of the eighteenth- and early nineteenth-century suspicion of fiction, see Martin. On antebellum responses to fiction see Nina Baym, *Novels, Readers, and Reviewers*, especially Chapter 2, "The Triumph of the Novel," in which Baym argues that the supposed hostility to fiction in nineteenth-century America has been greatly exaggerated.

7. George J. Becker, for example, writes of "the sense of blind, impersonal force which is the mark of the great realistic novels" (130).

Works Cited

Baym, Nina. *Novels, Readers, and Reviewers; Responses to Fiction in Antebellum America.* Ithaca: Cornell UP, 1984.

———. *Woman's Fiction: A Guide to Novels by and about Women in America, 1820-1870.* Ithaca: Cornell UP, 1978.

Becker, George J., ed. *Documents of Modern Literary Realism.* Princeton: Princeton UP, 1963.

Bell, Michael Davitt. "History and Romance Convention in Catharine Sedgwick's *Hope Leslie.*" *American Quarterly* 22 (1970): 213-21.

Cawelti, John. *Adventure, Mystery, and Romance.* Chicago: U of Chicago P, 1976.

Fetterley, Judith, ed. *Provisions: A Reader from 19th-Century American Women.* Bloomington: Indiana UP, 1985.

Habegger, Alfred. *Gender, Fantasy, and Realism in American Literature.* New York: Columbia UP, 1982.

Koppelman, Susan, ed. *Old Maids: Short Stories by Nineteenth Century U.S. Women Writers.* Boston: Pandora, 1984. 53-61.

Martin, Terence. *The Instructed Vision: Scottish Common Sense Philosophy and the Origins of American Fiction.* Bloomington: Indiana UP, 1961.

Pindar, Susan. "Aunt Mable's Love Story." Koppelman 53-61.

Poe, Edgar Allan. Review of *The Linwoods,* by Catharine Sedgwick. *The Complete Works of Edgar Allan Poe.* Ed. James A. Harrison. New York: AMS, 1965.

Reynolds, David. *Beneath the American Renaissance: The Subversive Imagination in the Age of Emerson and Melville.* New York: Knopf, 1988.

Sedgwick, Catharine Maria. "Cacoethes Scribendi." Fetterley 49-59.

———. "First Love." *Sartain's Magazine* 4 (1849): 81-84.

———. "A Sketch of a Blue Stocking." *The Token: A Christmas and New Year Present.* Ed. S. G. Goodrich. Boston, 1832. 334-46.

Stone, William B. "Towards a Definition of Literary Realism." *Centrum* I (Spring 1973): 47-60.

Warhol, Robyn. "Poetics and Persuasion: Uncle Tom's Cabin as a Realist Novel."

———. "Toward a Theory of the Engaging Narrator: Earnest Interventions in Gaskell, Stowe, and Eliot." *PMLA* 101 (1986): 811-18.

Carol J. Singley (essay date 1992)

SOURCE: "Catharine Maria Sedgwick's *Hope Leslie*: Radical Frontier Romance," in *Desert, Garden, Margin, Range: Literature on the American Frontier,* edited by Eric Heyne, Twayne Publishers, 1992, pp. 110-22.

[*In the following essay, Singley examines* Hope Leslie *as a frontier romance that offers an alternative vision of American women and culture.*]

Hope Leslie, published in 1827, was Catharine Maria Sedgwick's third and most successful novel. A historical romance set in the early colonial period, it centers on the adventures of a spirited, independent young woman, Hope Leslie, who energetically resists traditional conventions imposed by her Puritan world, yet who ends the novel in the most typical of ways, married to the young colonial hero, Everell Fletcher. Like many American novels of its time, *Hope Leslie* has a convoluted, somewhat contrived plot, with many doubling structures, cliff-hanging chapter endings, and narratorial intrusions. The novel primarily focuses on three issues: the friendship, romance, and eventual marriage of Hope to her foster brother and childhood friend, Everell Fletcher; a rigid and intolerant Puritan system, intent on order and suppression of women and Indians; and the complex relationship of settlers, land, and Native American culture, represented chiefly through Magawisca, the young Pequod woman who risks her life to save Everell's and who forms an indissoluble bond of friendship with Hope.

As historical romance, *Hope Leslie* combines mythic aspects of the American frontier, a fictional marriage plot and historical accuracy. Several events in the novel—the Pequod attack on the Fletcher family, Magawisca's rescue of Everell, the villainy of Tory sympathizer Sir Philip Gardiner—are based on documented historical data that Sedgwick culled from her reading,[1] but the novel is primarily fiction, intended, as Sedgwick says in her preface to *Hope Leslie,* to "illustrate not the history, but the character of the times" ([*Hope Leslie,* hereafter,] *HL,* 5). The novel has from the very beginning been compared with the frontier romances of James Fenimore Cooper. Sedgwick's contemporary, Sarah Hale, called *Hope Leslie* Sedgwick' "most popular tale; and indeed, no other novel written by an American, except, perhaps, the early work of Cooper ever met with such success" (quoted in Foster, 95). Reflecting the biases of the day, one reviewer noted that Sedgwick "had fallen into the error, so apparent in the works of Cooper . . . that have anything to do with Indians" (*HL,* x), but most applauded Sedgwick's depiction of American Indians, some granting that Sedgwick's novel contained "pictures of savage life more truthful than that of Cooper" (quoted in Foster, 95). Transcendentalist Margaret Fuller, noting Cooper's faults, also praised his fiction for its "redemption from oblivion of our forest-scenery and the noble romance of the hunter-pioneer's life," and in her next paragraph gave Sedgwick—the only American woman novelist she ever cited by name—tempered praise for writing "with skill and feeling, scenes and personages from the revolutionary time." Sedgwick's work, Fuller wrote, "has permanent value."[2] Alexander Cowie, indicating the direction that critical opinion of Sedgwick would assume by the end of the nineteenth century, compared the fiction of the two writers, implying that Sedgwick "modestly" and wisely did not try to compete with Cooper.[3]

Despite Sedgwick's extraordinary popularity, by the end of the nineteenth-century she was practically unread, excluded from the anthologies that canonized Cooper and formed the literary myths of Adam in the New World—the "melodramas of beset manhood," as Nina Baym has called them.[4] We have little trouble recognizing this process of marginalization. At one time thought to be *the* American literary form, the historical romance gave way to the more imaginative, abstract romances of Cooper, Hawthorne, Melville, and other male writers. Men's narratives assumed the status of the universal while the domestic novel became associated with the particularized, narrow interest of "scribbling women." By 1936 Van Wyck Brooks could write of Sedgwick, "No one could have supposed that her work would live."[5]

But live it has. Newly reprinted and accessible to a new generation of readers, *Hope Leslie* stands ready to take its place in the American literary tradition. I argue here that Sedgwick deserves as prominent a place in an American canon as Cooper, not only for the comparable literary value of her fiction—after all, the same "threadbare formulas" and assortment of escapes, rescues, and pursuits that Robert Spiller cites in Cooper's fiction are no more egregious in Sedgwick's novel,[6] and, furthermore, Sedgwick's prose is often cleaner and clearer in expression than Cooper's (Foster, 94)—but for the alternative vision of the American woman, American culture, and the relationship to nature that she provides. While following romantic conventions, Sedgwick in fact undercuts many of the assumptions upon which the romance is organized. Also, while apparently obeying the moral and literary dictum that literature teach by adhering to the facts of history and by depicting authentic characters and events—Gov. and Margaret Winthrop, the Reverend John Eliot, the Pequod Chief Mononotto, for example—Sedgwick provides an alternative literary history, one that exposes injustice against women, Native Americans, and the land. Finally, while Cooper works in the realm of the abstract, indulging the masculine fantasy of escape into some past golden age or into timelessness,[7] Sedgwick engages both the social and the natural realms, suggesting a transcendental ideal achievable in society as well as nature.

Critics of American literature have persistently favored a mythology that David Levin has described as "a movement from the 'artificial' toward the 'natural.'"[8] This practice celebrates the individual white man either alone in nature—whether he be Natty Bumppo, Ishmael, Thoreau, or Huck Finn—or in union with a same-sexed other.[9] For example, writing about the second of Cooper's *The Leatherstocking Tales, The Last of the Mohicans*—the novel in which the hero, Natty Bumppo supposedly "matures"—D. H. Lawrence is exuberant: "In his immortal friendship of Chingachgook and Natty Bumppo, Cooper dreamed the nucleus of a new society . . . A stark stripped human relationship of two men, deeper than the deeps of sex. Deeper than property, deeper than fatherhood, deeper than marriage, deeper than Love."[10] With its "wish-fulfillment vision" (Lawrence, 73) and yearning for escape, the male-defined main-stream American romance has been constructed around impossibility. Sedgwick shows us the damage that results from insistence on this impossibility: the very fabric of society and nature itself is jeopardized. Order turns to confusion; America's promise is unfulfilled.

Because Sedgwick utilizes the conservative form of the romance—the so-called "woman's novel"—readers have generally read her fiction as reinforcing the conventional nineteenth-century notions that woman's fulfillment is found in the domestic sphere[11] and as validating the notion of the progress of history (Bell). Only recently has attention been given to the deeply critical qualities of Sedgwick's novel. Sandra Zagarell, for example, reads Sedgwick's treatment of women and Indians as two sides of the same repressive Puritan coin, noting not only Sedgwick's domesticity but her concern "with the foundations and organization of public life."[12] Contrary to critical consensus, *Hope Leslie* is not "an extraordinary conventional novel" (Bell, 213-14), nor is its comic marriage plot, as Frye explains, one "that brings hero and heroine together [and] causes a new society to crystallize around the hero."[13] Despite the conservative requirements of its genre, *Hope Leslie* exhibits signs of its own unraveling, as if to suggest the unworkability of its own romantic conventions. The novel replicates the chaos and contradiction inherent in the Puritan conception of its "errand in the wilderness," addressing problems that fall outside the accepted sphere of historical romance. It also posits a heroine who resists what Leslie Rabine calls the "totalizing structure" of romantic narrative, and who struggles, valiantly and sometimes successfully, to sustain herself as an autonomous subject rather than become absorbed into the male quest for identity and mythic unity with himself.[14]

On some levels, Catharine Maria Sedgwick and James Fenimore Cooper have much in common. Both choose fictional contexts to express concern over the rapid, careless encroachment of civilization on the wilderness and the extinction of the Native Americans. Both also depart from their privileged, Federalist backgrounds to advocate egalitarian notions of democracy. We see important differences, however, when comparing *Hope Leslie* with a Leatherstocking novel written just one year earlier, during a period when the Jackson Indian Removal Policy had effectively cleared the eastern United States of Native American presence. *The Last of the Mohicans,* published in 1826 and set in 1740, is only tangentially colonial in that it depicts a chapter from the nine-year French and Indian War. In contrast, *Hope Leslie* focuses specifically on a nine-year colonial period from 1636 to 1645 and, as Mary Kelley notes in her introduction, explores "the roots of American moral character" (*HL,* xiii). Cooper's characters seldom leave the forest or evince concern with the political, economic, or social aspects of the law; Sedgwick's characters directly confront Puritan social, religious, and legal systems, finding in them the basis for discord and injustice. In Cooper's novels, the American hero can thrive only outside the constraints of civilization. Sedgwick addresses questions both of culture *and* nature, criticizing the "Law" of the Founding Fathers that enforces policies of actual repression and thereby fosters patterns of imaginative escape.[15]

If the character of Hope Leslie can be read as the "spirit of American history" (Bell, 221), it is history with a revisionary spirit. Hope's adventurous and generous nature contrasts with the repression and self-absorption of the Puritans; her many "doubles" in the novel challenge dichotomous views of womanhood and warn of the fragmented nature of the American psyche, split in such ways that fusion of the individual, nature, and society is impossible.

The force of Sedgwick's critique is suggested by her biography as well as by her fiction published before *Hope Leslie.* "The country is condemned to the ministration of inferior men," she wrote in a letter to her brother Robert in 1814.[16] In 1821, Sedgwick changed her membership from the Calvinist to the Unitarian church. Her first novel, *A New England Tale* (1822), is a blatant attack on Puritan hypocrisy; after venturing into a novel of manners with *Redwood* (1824), she returns to a critique of Puritanism with *Hope Leslie,* this time linking the present-day concerns about American expansion to the original project of the Puritan founders. Feeding the nation's appetite for historical fiction, **Hope Leslie** became an instant success. But it is by no means a book of reconciliation or progress. Below its seemingly accepting surface are deep fissures that throw into question not only the American project in the new land but also the romance literature that since Richard Chase has been synonymous with the American project.

The novel opens in England with a tale of thwarted romance—that of Hope's mother, Alice, and Alice's liberal-thinking cousin, William Fletcher. Alice's father, also named William Fletcher, prevents her from eloping to the New World with her cousin. Under pressure from her father, Alice marries Charles Leslie instead, but when her husband dies, she sets sail for the New World on her own. She dies at sea, leaving her two daughters to the guardianship of her former lover William Fletcher, who has since married a "meek" and "godly maiden and dutiful helpmate" (**HL,** 14), followed John Winthrop and John Eliot to America, and settled on the western frontier near Springfield, Massachusetts. When Fletcher meets the two orphaned girls in Boston, he renames them Hope and Faith, and sends Faith on ahead to Springfield. In a surprise Pequod attack on the Fletcher homestead, Faith and the Fletchers' son Everell are captured, Mrs. Fletcher and her infant son are killed, and two Indian children, Magawisca and Oneco, captives from a previous battle, are reunited with their tribe. Hope and William Fletcher, some distance away, are spared. The Pequod chief, Mononotto, intends to kill Everell, but Magawisca heroically saves his life and effects his escape; Faith, however, remains a captive, eventually converting to Catholicism and marrying Oneco.

As their names suggest, religious "Faith" of the Puritans is lost to the Indians, while the more secular "Hope" remains to confront the Puritan intolerance and repression spearheaded by Gov. Winthrop and his docile, subservient wife. And although the younger William Fletcher embodies a more liberal Puritanism than his stern elders, he is by name indistinguishable from the authoritarian uncle he has left in England. With this naming, Sedgwick suggests that Old World repression is simply transferred to the New World, at least so far as Native Americans and women are concerned. Themes of imprisonment, captivity and family disruption, rather than the comic restoration of social order associated with romance, pervade the novel. And despite epigraphs from *A Midsummer Night's Dream* and *As You Like It,* in **Hope Leslie** unlike in Shakespearean romantic comedy, there will be no return to a green world at the end of the story. Society is not rejuvenated.

After the Pequod attack and escape sequence, Sedgwick resumes the narrative nine years later. Everell is being educated in England; writing to him, Hope describes her own "education" in nature as well as an incident in which an Indian woman, Nelema, saves her tutor's life by curing a snakebite. The Boston authorities respond to the news of Nelema's kindness by imprisoning her for witchcraft and removing Hope from Fletcher's custody so that she can profit from the more ordered training at the Winthrop residence. Here Hope shares a room with Winthrop's newly

arrived niece, Esther Downing. Undaunted by Puritan restrictions, Hope manages to free not only Nelema but Magawisca, who has been imprisoned as a result of a scheme by Sir Philip Gardiner to overthrow the Puritan government. The plot then follows a comedy of manners formula, with Hope escaping the seductions of Gardiner and his hired sailors and finally marrying Everell after predictable mistaken identities and confused affections. At the end of the novel, Esther returns to England and Magawisca to the forest.

Although Sedgwick bases the major elements of her narrative on documented history, it is not her adherence to facts but her departure from them that is so intriguing. Sedgwick's subject, set in "an age of undisputed masculine supremacy" (**HL,** 16), attempts an alternative history from a woman's perspective, a perspective also sympathetic to the plight of the Native American, whom she sees in an oppression parallel to woman's. This woman's history which as Rabine tells us, takes place outside "dominant frameworks," is deeply critical and seeks "to subvert romantic ideology" (107). Thus, while the Springfield settlement is historically accurate, Sedgwick dramatizes with particular sensitivity the vulnerability of Margaret Fletcher and the children as they sit helpless and ignorant on the porch while the Pequods stealthily plan their attack. Women, the scene demonstrates, are powerless pawns in masculine battles. Whereas in the annals of history, Philip Gardiner's mistress lives on to marry, Sedgwick has her die in a fiery explosion, graphically depicting society's intolerance of sexually experienced unmarried women. And while no exact historical figure exists for Esther, Sedgwick invents her as the submissive, dull counterpart to Hope, model of passivity that only a masculinist ideology like Winthrop's could endorse.

Sedgwick's rewriting of the Indian attack is most telling. The attack on the Fletcher homestead is preceded by narrative by Magawisca, in which it is clear that the Puritans—not the Indians—precipitated the violence by first attacking the sleeping, unsuspecting Pequod village. During this brutal raid, the Indian children Magawisca and Oneco are captured and their mother and brother killed. The structural symmetry of the two attacks—in each battle a mother and son are killed and two children are taken captive—renders the acts of male violence morally indistinguishable and underlines the falsity of assigning blame to the Indians. The one inescapable difference, however, is that in the end the Puritans will prevail and the Indian tribes will be eradicated. Reinforcing this imbalance of power, Sedgwick depicts Magawisca raising and losing her arm to protect Everell from her father's axe, and noting later in the novel that the Indians cannot "grasp in friendship the hand raised to strike us" (**HL,** 292).

The parallel massacres by the Puritans and the Pequods—the first a "ghost chapter" in the novel—haunt the narrative, undermining dreams of harmony and unity that sent the Puritans to America. Kelley writes that the romance "interwoven with the narrative of Indian displacement

(*HL,* xxi). In fact, the massacre threatens to displace the romance altogether, just as role inversions in the novel subvert the gender system in which the male provides and protects and the female submits and obeys. The Indian attacks actually set into motion an alternative narrative of redemption, not through Calvinist devotion to doctrine but through the wits and magnanimity of the female characters. Hope and Magawisca, more generous in spirit than their male counterparts, attempt to undo the wrongs of their male leaders, fundamentally challenging the precepts upon which the Puritan, male world is constructed. They do not offer a Cooperian escape or romantic/comic affirmation.

Like Natty Bumppo in *The Leatherstocking Tales,* Hope takes "counsel from her own heart" (*HL,* xxiv), but her independence is unlike his because she is female. Hope's power extends beyond domestic morality and the woman's sphere. And if she exemplifies the selflessness that Kelley associates with nineteenth-century femininity (*HL,* xxiii), she also embodies the traits attributed to men, acting on behalf of her own advancement as well as others'. Hope, as Bell remarks, "seems to specialize in freeing Indians" (216); this observation is true both in the terms of the novel's plot and Hope's larger project of social justice. An "unfettered soul," Hope does not hesitate to commit "a plain transgression of a holy law" (*HL,* 280, 311).

If Hope stands for the white woman's resourcefulness and defiance of male restrictiveness, Magawisca represents the integrity of the Native American woman. But unlike Natty Bumppo's noble savages, who slay in order to achieve peace, Magawisca engages in no violence, whatever the personal risk. Foster (77) and Bell (216-17) speculate on Sedgwick's use of local town history for Magawisca's amputation, with Bell suggesting a source in the Captain John Smith—Pocahontas story. But Sedgwick tells us in her preface that with respect to Magawisca, "we are confined not to the actual, but the possible" (6). Magawisca, her Indian double, Nelema, and her white double, Hope Leslie—all of whom save lives even when it means their own captivity—are Sedgwick's "hope" for a revised American history and new literary mythology. The magnitude of their heroism is Sedgwick's version of what Levin calls the movement from the "artificial" to the "natural." In Sedgwick's view, society should move away from the "artificial" imposition of violence and oppression and toward the "natural" coexistence of peace and mutuality.

Despite Hope's rebellions, the novel ends in the heroine's marriage to the young Puritan Everell Fletcher, seemingly validating Rabine's observation that women's protests and assertions occurring in the middle of romances are often negated by their endings. Marriage is an outcome Cooper assiduously avoids for his own heroes, but a more realistic Sedgwick reminds the reader that no matter how independent the heroine, marriage is not easily renegotiated.

Family is the mainstay of the woman's romance as well as the "familiar" domain appropriated by American male writers to contrast with the fears and unknowns of the American wilderness. And the family, Gossett and Bardes assert in their study of *Hope Leslie,* is the central building block of a democratic republic. Although Sedgwick's reputation rests on her domestic writing, and Kelley describes her as "a divinely appointed reformer within the confines of domesticity,"[17] in *Hope Leslie* no home is glorified. The Fletcher homestead is exposed and vulnerable, the Winthrop home is repressive, and Digby's parlor is the setting for mistaken identities and mismatched lovers. Families are repeatedly torn apart in this novel; women and children are not protected by men but become victims of their battles. Home, then, is not a comforting haven, with "good living under almost every roof," as de Crèvecoeur would have it,[18] but a precarious site of danger.

Ann Snitow notes that the "one socially acceptable moment of transcendence [for women] is romance;"[19] that is, conventional love between men and women leading to marriage. As her name implies, Hope Leslie is "hopelessly" committed to this bourgeois romantic ending. Yet Hope is also an individual—a "pathfinder" in her own right, to use Cooper's term, and through her, Sedgwick goes farther than most previous American writers in exposing Puritan hypocrisy and affirming the value of Native American and female culture. Hope breaks the boundaries of normal expectation for young women as she treks through nature, befriends Indians, frees political prisoners, and eludes drunken sailors. Her most inspiring and affecting experience is not marrying Everell but climbing a mountain with her tutor to survey an expanse of undeveloped land. "Gaz[ing] on the beautiful summits of this mountain," Hope writes in a letter to Everell, who is receiving his education in England, not in nature, "I had an irrepressible desire to go to them" (*HL,* 99). Hope resists romantic seduction, political captivity, and traditional domesticity throughout the novel; she will not become a Mrs. Winthrop, who "like a horse easy on the bit . . . was guided by the slightest intimation from him who held the rein" (*HL,* 145).

Forever the adventurous youth, never the adult, Hope not only challenges conventional notions of what it means for a woman to grow up; she also resists Puritan mandates to be "hardened for the cross-accidents and unkind events . . . the wholesome chastisements of life" (*HL,* 160). Hope, in fact, achieves a fantasy of indulgence *and* sacrifice, of selfishness *and* doing for others, proving as she moves undaunted through one escapade after another that, contrary to Calvinist doctrine, good deeds on earth *can* bring joy. Emerging from virtually every situation unscathed, Hope subverts Puritan ethics and behavior; and although she marries Everell at the end of the novel, the major events in her life revolve not around romance but around nature and the sense of fair play.

Neither is Everell Fletcher romantic or heroic in the traditional sense. Well-meaning but weak, he is an example of the dilution of the bloodline that so worried the Founding Fathers, a parallel to that most famous of feeble Puritan sons, Arthur Dimmesdale. Everell has more tolerance than his stern male forebears, but he lacks vision and capability to put thought into action. His capture during the Pequod raid of the Fletcher farm inverts the traditional female captivity narrative: a white man, he must be saved by an Indian woman. Everell's significant instruction comes not from the Bible or England, but from Magawisca's narrative about her own people's plight. When Magawisca later is imprisoned because Puritan officials mistakenly think her guilty of inciting an attack on Boston, Everell fails to free her because of his fears: the hapless young man struggles outside the jail with a ladder while Hope successfully schemes for Magawisca's release. Passive and ineffectual, Everell is the hero because he marries the heroine.

The true bond—and the real romance—in this novel is between Hope and Magawisca. It is a same-sex bond that Fiedler has found essential to American romance. In constructing same-sex friendship between Magawisca and Hope, Sedgwick creates a parallel of the relationship between Natty Bumppo and Chingachgook in *The Leatherstocking Tales*—but with a difference. Doubles throughout the novel, Hope and Magawisca are drawn together by, and in spite of, the destructive acts of their fathers. Both have lost their mothers through war, both are torn between obedience to their fathers and the dictates of their own minds, and both oppose Puritan law, finding inspiration and guidance in nature or their own consciences. In prison the two learn the meaning of trust and betrayal, and in a secret meeting in a cemetery—symbol of death by male order—where their mothers are buried, they seal their bond: "Mysteriously have our destinies been interwoven. Our mothers brought from a far distance to rest here together—their children connected in indissoluble bonds" (*HL,* 192). The union of Magawisca and Hope represents the waste caused by masculine violence as well as the need for feminine healing—a healing not between the Old World of England and the New World of America, as traditional American romances have it, but between the original world of the Native Americans and the new, intrusive world of the Puritans. Unlike Natty and Chingachgook, Hope and Magawisca do not retreat into nature together, isolated but free. They participate in society, serving as its critics, mediators, and healers. When their relationship is sundered, Hope's marriage to Everell can only be a partial substitute.

Women, Sedgwick suggests, must play active and essential, not passive or secondary, roles in American society. In Cooper's fiction, in service to the American Adam mythology, women are rendered dichotomously. As Fiedler notes (21), Cooper establishes the "pattern of female Dark and Light that is to become the standard form" in American literature: an innocent, passive woman juxtaposed with a vibrant, sexualized one, whether Alice and Cora in *The Last of the Mohicans,* Hetty and Judith in *The Deerslayer,* or Inez and Ellen in *The Prairie.* While women in nature figure as tokens of exchange in elaborate captivity sequences engineered by men in *The Leatherstocking Tales,*

Cooper fundamentally endorses the standard nineteenth century view of separate spheres for men and women with women "the repositories of the better principles of our nature."[20] This dichotomous view of women has its corollary in the male view of nature: a lone male figure either seeks a lover's alliance in nature as replacement for the relationship he fails to achieve with woman, or he views nature as a fearful object he must conquer or destroy in order to validate his own existence.

Sedgwick rejects these dichotomies for her female characters. Magawisca and Hope are as capable as their male counterparts of participating in nature and society. As sisters, Hope and Faith represent active and passive aspects of the female principle, but this distinction is never expressed in terms of sexual and spiritual purity or innocence. No female in *Hope Leslie* exhibits the "yearning felt by a presumably experienced woman to return to the pristine state of the innocent virgin" that Porte finds in Cooper (21), a view that incidentally reads all female sexuality as a fall into sin requiring redemption or escape. Faith, on the one hand, not only marries, she marries a "red-blooded" Native American; Hope, on the other hand, a virgin throughout the novel, romps from adventure to adventure unaffected by salacious sailors and villainous seducers. And Magawisca, who according to the Cooper paradigm must be "wild and dangerous" because Indian (Bell, 218), is, in fact, peaceable and socially oriented. Only Rosa, seduced and abandoned in the New World, appears as a stock character—a desperate reminder of romance's failure to accommodate women's sexuality. A prototype of Bertha Rochester, she takes vengeance on her oppressor, destroying herself in the process. Rosa gives angry expression to the female energy that her more socially integrated counterpart, Hope, channels into minor rebellions.

Hope Leslie forbids a reductionist view of women and the romance. It rejects patriarchal concepts of female submissiveness and purity, instead presenting women as complex models of democracy, adventure, mutuality, and sympathy. Sedgwick, in fact, presents not just one double of Hope but many, demonstrating multiple rather than dichotomous ways of womanhood. Hope, Magawisca, and Esther all love Everell, but Magawisca and Esther give him up. Hope marries, but her union with her foster brother is more friendship than a romance, modeled perhaps on Sedgwick's own relationship with her brothers.[21] Esther's single status endorses autonomous womanhood: "Marriage is not *essential* to the contentment, the dignity, or the happiness of woman," Sedgwick writes in defense of Esther's decision (*HL,* 350, italics in original), and her own life is testimony that a single woman can find satisfaction as friend or sister.

The doublings become uneasy where Native Americans are involved, however. By eschewing a retreat into nature that Natty Bumppo achieves with Chingachgook, Sedgwick emphasizes the crucial difference between the races: the inevitable decimation of the Native American to make way for white expansion and greed. "We are commanded to do good to all," Hope explains to her tutor as she works to free Magawisca (*HL*, 312). But she cannot prevent the inevitable. Esther, prevented by Puritan conscience from helping Magawisca escape from prison, essentially gives herself up to the rigid law-of-the-father; and Magawisca, "first to none" (Kelley 1978, 224), returns to a nature that is blighted and a people "spoiled." Dichotomies reemerge with Magawisca's declaration, "The Indian and the white man can no more mingle, and become one, than day and night" (*HL*, 330).

In *The Prairie,* published in 1827, the same year as *Hope Leslie,* Cooper uses a tree as a symbol to describe the natural cycles of growth, ripening, and death, comparing the monumentality of nature to the works of humans: "It is the fate of all things to ripen and then to decay. The tree blossoms and bears its fruit, which falls, rots, withers, and even the seed is lost! There does the noble tree fill its place in the forests. . . . It lies another hundred years. . . ."[22] Sedgwick also presents such a Pantheistic notion of nature, giving Magawisca words that fuse the natural and the human: 'The Great Spirit is visible in the life-creating sun. I perceive Him in the gentle light of the moon that steals through the forest boughs. I feel Him here,' she continued, pressing her hand on her breast" (*HL*, 189). But this notion of nature has been negated by white encroachment. Sedgwick uses the familiar nineteenth-century symbol of the blasted tree, which Mononotto points to as representative of his race at the hands of the white men, to signify not only the decimation of the Native Americans but also the assault against women and nature. Thus Magawisca's body, the right arm missing, is truncated like the blasted tree. Hawthorne uses the same symbol in "Roger Malvin's Burial" to convey the guilty conscience of Reuben, who fails to send a rescue party to his dying father-in-law. Hawthorne's message, anticipated by Sedgwick, is that the strong and able have responsibility to succor those in need.

Hope's sister Faith, another double, also goes off into the wilderness, married to chief Mononotto's son Oneco in one of the few cases of miscegenation in early American fiction—certainly one that Cooper disallows in *The Last of the Mohicans.* The relationship of Faith and Oneco is mutually loving, gentle, and respectful. The bird imagery associated with the couple throughout the novel communicates a spirit of openness and freedom in nature. But just as Magawisca is mateless, the marriage of Oneco and Faith has a sterile, frozen quality about it. Faith speaks no English, and the couple is without children.

Constrained by her own position in history, Sedgwick perhaps could not conceive of an ending that both subverts and rewrites the white patriarchal plot. Were she able to do so, the pressure to produce salable fiction most likely would have prevented its articulation. Nonetheless, *Hope Leslie* strains against its conventions as surely as its female characters struggle against unjust imprisonment.

Hope Leslie is discomfiting for literary critics and readers who prefer retreat into a fantasy world where one can ignore the injustices to nature by escaping further into the wilderness. In this novel, the frontier myth does not seem to be, as Annette Kolodny has outlined it in *The Lay of the Land,* a fantasy of the land as a domesticated garden.[23] It is, to some extent, what Leland Person suggests in his essay on miscegenation: a successful intermarriage of races, an Eden where the white woman is included and the white man excluded.[24] The point is not that women ultimately prove superior—as they inevitably do, both in romance and in this novel—but that the pact with power engineered by men has jeopardized men, women, and nature. Cooper's paradisiacal wilderness is a profound and evocative symbol in American literature, but Sedgwick, while valuing nature, forbids an egocentric or overly romantic view of it. She does not let us forget that we are usurpers and that there will be no regeneration through violence. Her view more closely resembles what David Mogen calls "a gothic tradition of frontier narrative" that expresses, among other meanings, "despair about our history and our future."[25]

The American literary hero feminizes the land, seeking in it a validation of his own creative principle. He wants to be the sole possessor of the virgin soil, which he penetrates with axe or gun and seeks to make pregnant with unresolved possibility.[26] Sedgwick tells us that this pregnancy is a false one and that woman/land will not be reduced to a medium for man's self-glorification. The white man will, like Everell, inevitably find himself its captive rather than its victor. A possessive relationship with the land only results in estrangement from it. Thus Fussell writes, "Cooper's heart was in his writing," but a "habitual need for recessive withdrawal . . . sprang from [his] fundamental alienation from his country" (28, 29).

If the male fantasy is escapist, the female fantasy is integrationist, inclusive of the whole of woman's traits—religious, sexual, adventurous, heroic. Without this integration, there can only be fragmentation. Governor Winthrop's household "move[s] in a world of his own" (*HL*, 301), cut off from the very unity of nature, God, individual, and society that it seeks.

This transcendental vision of unity, suggested in Sedgwick's historical and romantic critique, is developed some years later, not in the individualistic transcendentalism of Ralph Waldo Emerson, but in the social transcendentalism of Margaret Fuller. Like Emerson, Fuller embraces the ideal of the individual in nature, but while valuing the abstract, she also advocates social awareness. Looking out at the western territory near the Great Lakes in the summer of 1843, Fuller seeks "by reverent faith to woo the mighty meaning of the scene, perhaps to foresee the law by which a new order, a new poetry, is to be evoked." Hope enjoys this same personal and transcendental relationship when she visits Mount Holyoke with her tutor and Nelema. But Fuller's fantasy is modified by the "distaste I must experience at its mushroom growth": development "is scarce less wanton than that of warlike invasion," and the land bears "the rudeness of conquest." Emerson sought to unify technology and transcendental philosophy into a seamless fabric of hopeful expansion, but Fuller notes not transcendental insight but blindness: "Seeing the traces of the Indians . . . we feel as if they were the rightful lords of the beauty they forbore to deform. But most of these settlers do not see at all" (Chevigny, 318, 322).

The first writers, as Fussell notes, gave the West its mythology, finding in it their own dreams of possession and control. For women, identified with and through nature, the myth spells death and defeat. Sedgwick quietly but radically alters that mythology, transcending the limits of romance and history to establish her own yearning for social and natural unity.

Notes

1. For detailed discussions of Sedgwick's uses of historical sources, see Michael Davitt Bell, "History and Romance Convention in Catharine Maria Sedgwick's *Hope Leslie,*" *American Quarterly* 22 (1970): 216-18; hereafter cited in text; Edward Halsey Foster, *Catharine Maria Sedgwick* (New York: Twayne, 1974), 73-80; hereafter cited in text; and Mary Kelley, ed. and intro., *Hope Leslie; Or, Early Times in the Massachusetts* (1827; reprint, New Brunswick, N.J.: Rutgers University Press, 1987), xxi-xxxiii; hereafter cited in text as *HL*. Sedgwick also explains her fictional use of these materials in the preface to her novel (5-6).

2. Bell Gale Chevigny, ed., *The Woman and the Myth: Margaret Fuller's Life and Writings* (Old Westbury, N.Y.: Feminist Press, 1976), 190; hereafter cited in text.

3. Alexander Cowie, *The Rise of the American Novel* (New York: American Book, 1948), 204. Readers sometimes had difficulty distinguishing Sedgwick's and Cooper's fiction. Published anonymously in 1824, Sedgwick's *Redwood* was attributed to Cooper and actually appeared in France and Italy with Cooper's name on the title page. See Harold E. Mantz, *French Criticism of American Literature Before 1850* (New York: Columbia University Press, 1917), 43.

4. Nina Baym, "Melodramas of Beset Manhood: How Theories of American Fiction Exclude Women Authors," *American Quarterly* 33 (1981): 123-39.

5. Van Wyck Brooks, *The Flowering of New England* (New York: E. P. Dutton, 1936), 188.

6. Robert E. Spiller et al., *Literary History of the United States,* 3d ed., rev., vol. 1 (New York: Macmillan, 1963), 256.

7. See, for example, Joel Porte, *The Romance in America: Studies in Cooper, Poe, Hawthorne, Melville, and James* (Middletown, Conn.: Wesleyan University Press, 1969); hereafter cited in text: "Natty is the epic hero par excellence" (43), with *The Last of the Mohicans* and *The Pioneers* serving as Cooper's *Iliad* and *Odyssey* (39-52); and Georg

Lukacs, *The Historical Novel* (New York: Humanities Press, 1965), who finds "an almost epic-like magnificence" in Cooper's portrayals (64). Addressing Cooper's aesthetics, H. Daniel Peck, *A World by Itself: The Pastoral Moment in Cooper's Fiction* (New Haven: Yale University Press, 1927), finds in his landscapes not so much a frontier consciousness but a timeless, classic pastoral ideal. Robert E. Spiller, *Fenimore Cooper: Critic of His Times* (New York: Minton, Balch, 1931); John McWilliams, *Political Justice in a Republic: James Fenimore Cooper's America* (Berkeley: University of California Press, 1972); George Dekker, *The American Historical Romance* (New York: Cambridge University Press, 1987); and others have noted Cooper's social and political criticism, but these interests appear mainly in Cooper's middle and late novels, not his early fiction, which is more appropriately compared with *Hope Leslie.* As Yvor Winters, *In Defense of Reason* (Denver: University of Denver Press, 1947) writes, "In the Leatherstocking Series . . . we have nothing whatever to do with social criticism, or at least nothing of importance" (185).

8. David Levin, *History as Romantic Art* (Stanford: Stanford University Press, 1959), ix.

9. See Leslie Fiedler, *Love and Death in the American Novel,* rev. ed. (New York: Stein & Day, 1975); hereafter cited in text; and R. W. B. Lewis, *The American Adam: Innocence, Tragedy, and Tradition in the Nineteenth Century* (Chicago: University of Chicago Press, 1955).

10. D. H. Lawrence, *Studies in Classic American Literature* (1923; reprint, New York: Viking, 1964), 78; hereafter cited in text.

11. Suzanne Gossett and Barbara Ann Bardes, "Women and Political Power in the Republic: Two Early American Novels," *Legacy* 2 (Fall 1985): 13-30; hereafter cited in text.

12. Sandra A. Zagarell, "Expanding 'America': Lydia Sigourney's *Sketch of Connecticut,* Catharine Sedgwick's *Hope Leslie,*" *Tulsa Studies in Women's Literature* 6 (Fall 1987): 225.

13. Northrop Frye, *Anatomy of Criticism: Four Essays* (Princeton: Princeton University Press, 1957), 163.

14. Leslie Rabine, *Reading the Romantic Heroine: Text, History, Ideology* (Ann Arbor: University of Michigan Press, 1985), 7; hereafter cited in text.

15. Philip Fisher, *Hard Facts: Setting and Form in the American Novel,* New York: (Oxford University Press, 1985), argues that *The Last of the Mohicans* captures the spirit of the 1640s (39-40); but Cooper does not, like Sedgwick, take on the Puritan system of life in this novel. While one might argue that with its portrayal of the early stage of a hero's life *The Deerslayer,* published in 1841, is a more appropriate companion text for *Hope Leslie,* the novel, even more than *The Last of the Mohicans*

reflects a timelessness and abstract yearning for lost origins and freedoms. Wayne Franklin, *The New World of James Fenimore Cooper* (Chicago: University of Chicago Press, 1982), even while defending Cooper's involvement with history, admits "even in *The Deerslayer,* as far back as he could push Natty, [Cooper] . . . introduced Tom Hutter and Harry March. . . . This bite of realism upsets what otherwise might become pure dream" (107-108).

16. Catharine Maria Sedgwick, *Life and Letters of Catharine Maria Sedgwick,* ed. Mary E. Dewey (New York: Harper & Brothers, 1872), 101.

17. Mary Kelley, "A Woman Alone: Catharine Maria Sedgwick's Spinsterhood in Nineteenth-Century America," *The New England Quarterly* 51 (June 1978): 209; hereafter cited in text.

18. Michel-Guillaume Jean de Crèvecoeur, *Letters From an American Farmer* (1782; reprint, New York: Dutton, 1957), 64.

19. Ann Barr Snitow, "Mass Market Romance: Pornography for Women is Different," *Radical History Review* 20 (Spring-Summer 1979): 150.

20. Quoted in Marvin Meyers, *The Jacksonian Persuasion: Politics and Belief* (Stanford: Stanford University Press, 1957), 52.

21. Unmarried, Sedgwick sublimated her erotic energies into an ethos of sibling love and comradeship: "The affection others have given to husbands and children I have given to brothers," she wrote (Kelley 1978, 213).

22. James Fenimore Cooper, *The Prairie* (1827; reprint, New York: Signet, 1964), 250.

23. Annette Kolodny, *The Lay of the Land* (Chapel Hill: University of North Carolina Press), 1975.

24. Leland Person, "The American Eve: Miscegenation and a Feminist Frontier Fiction," *American Quarterly* 37 (Winter 1985): 668-85.

25. David Mogen, "Frontier Myth and American Gothic," *Genre* 14 (Fall 1981): 330-31.

26. See, for example, *Wyandote; or, The Hutted Knoll* (1843), where Cooper's language is explicitly sexual and generative: "There is a pleasure in diving into a virgin forest and commencing the labours of civilization. . . . [This diving] approaches nearer to the feeling of creating, and is far more pregnant with anticipation and hopes. . . ." Quoted in Edwin Fussell, *Frontier: American Literature and the American West* (Princeton: Princeton University Press, 1965), 28; hereafter cited in text.

Mary Kelley (essay date 1993)

SOURCE: "Negotiating a Self: The Autobiography and Journals of Catharine Maria Sedgwick," in *New England Quarterly,* Vol. 66, No. 3, September, 1993, pp. 366-98.

[In the following essay, Kelley appraises Sedgwick's autobiography and journals in the context of the larger contemporary political and ideological landscape in which they were written.]

In a letter written on 5 October 1851, Catharine Maria Sedgwick responded to a proposal made by William Minot, the husband of her beloved niece and namesake, Kate. William had suggested that Sedgwick, a nationally acclaimed author of novels, tales, and sketches, undertake her autobiography. Had William appealed to her on the basis of her literary achievements, this inveterately modest woman almost certainly would have declined. Not surprisingly, then, William asked that the autobiography be written for his and Kate's daughter Alice, a child to whom Sedgwick was devoted.

Nonetheless, the project seemed daunting. A woman who had remained unmarried despite the protestations of suitors, Sedgwick told William she had "'boarded round' so much, had my home in so many houses and so many hearts," indeed had her life "so woven into the fabric of others that I seem to have had no separate individual existence." Nowhere else in the entire body of Sedgwick's writings did she reveal more about the character of her richly textured relationships with her parents, her brothers and sisters, her nieces and nephews than in this letter to Minot. Nowhere else did she signal more strikingly the impact those relationships had upon her sense of self. Ironically, this conception of herself as intertwined with the lives of those whom she cherished also meant that she would not refuse William's request, that she would consider it her "filial duty." Telling him that "perhaps I might tell a short and pleasant story to my darling Alice," Sedgwick displayed her typical modesty. Just as typically, she achieved much more than she promised in her autobiography of a childhood and adolescence that had spanned the opening years of the early republic. Gathering together the threads of memory, Sedgwick wove together a deeply personal narrative and an illuminating portrayal of a newly independent America.[1]

Sedgwick also kept a journal throughout much of her adult life. Beginning in the summer of 1821, when she was thirty-one, Sedgwick filled twelve volumes with meditations upon the author as an adult and the world she shared with other antebellum Americans. Taken together, the autobiography and the journals constitute Sedgwick's self-representation, child to adult. Moreover, they offer readers a dramatic representation of both the changes and the continuities characterizing relations of power in the decades between America's Revolution and its Civil War. More than a century before historians did so, Sedgwick situated power in its broadest context. Her autobiography and journals extended the meaning of power to include gender relations, and they addressed with equal insight social and political relations.

Ranked in the nineteenth century with Washington Irving, James Fenimore Cooper, and William Cullen Bryant as a founder of her nation's literature, Sedgwick published six novels and nearly one hundred tales and sketches in a career that spanned the four decades prior to the Civil War. Ranging from a revisionary portrayal of the conflict between Puritans and Indians to a dissection of a Jacksonian America dominated by commercialism, Sedgwick's fiction dealt with issues decidedly social and political in character. Portrayals of movements for reform, discourses on class relations, doctrinal debates between Congregationalists and Unitarians—all these issues and more were incorporated into a body of literature that spoke to the felt realities of early nineteenth-century Americans. Equally concerned with issues of gender, Sedgwick placed strong, independent, and articulate heroines at the center of her fiction. Sedgwick's model of gender relations presumed different roles for women and men. Nonetheless, she accorded women signal status as central social and cultural actors.

In the opening sentence of her autobiography, Sedgwick describes her project as a collection of "memories."[2] Begun in the sixty-fourth year of her life, Sedgwick's autobiography in the narrowest sense is exactly that—a commemorative text designed to inscribe the past upon the present. However, the design, the effort "to brighten the links of the chain that binds us to those who have gone before, and to keep it fast and strong," has significance beyond this objective. Perhaps most important, Sedgwick departs from an autobiographical tradition in which the self moves inexorably toward separation and individuation. In sanctioning connection, in stressing reciprocal commitment, Sedgwick stood in contrast to other notable American autobiographers such as Benjamin Franklin, Ralph Waldo Emerson, and Henry Adams, each of whom presents the self on a trajectory toward autonomy.[3] Sedgwick's emphasis upon an identity constructed in relation to others locates her narrative in an alternative tradition initiated by the fourteenth-century Englishwoman Dame Julian of Norwich. Julian's *Revelations,* Margery Kempe's fifteenth-century *Book of Margery Kempe,* and Margaret Cavendish's *True Relation* two centuries later all define the self in relation to others. New Englander Anne Bradstreet inscribed the same relational self in her seventeenth-century "To My Dear Children." So too did Sedgwick in the middle of the nineteenth century.[4]

Born in Stockbridge, Massachusetts, on 28 December 1789, Catharine Maria was the third daughter and sixth child of the Sedgwicks. Descended from one of the most distinguished families in the Connecticut River Valley, Pamela Dwight had married Theodore Sedgwick in 1774. She had chosen a husband who rapidly achieved the standing of her parents, the socially prominent Joseph and Abigail Dwight. Theodore's election to the Massachusetts legislature, first the house and then the senate, had elevated the Sedgwicks to one of the state's leading families prior to their daughter's birth. The next decade brought national distinction. Elected to the United States House of Representatives, in which he served as speaker, and the Senate, Theodore became one of the early republic's most

influential Federalists. His proud daughter recalled that Theodore and his allies in the "Federal party loved their country and were devoted to it, as virtuous parents are to their children."

However much these powerful Federalists may have been dedicated to their nation, they found their claims to leadership in a newly independent America challenged by those who sought a more egalitarian society. The hierarchy, the finely graded stratification, and the deference to a gentlemanly elite that had prevailed in colonial society no longer seemed secure.[5] In the description of her mother's parents, Sedgwick illustrated the contrast between that earlier world and the one being born in the years following the American Revolution. A "gentleman par excellence of his time," Joseph Dwight had been a highly successful lawyer and land speculator in the Connecticut River Valley. One of Stockbridge's prominent residents and trustee of its Indian school, Joseph's status had been conveyed to posterity in a painting that displayed his "most delicately beautiful hands." Sedgwick presumed that her grandfather had simply wanted to show his descendants that he "had kept 'clean hands,' a commendable virtue, physically or morally speaking." Perhaps he did, but those hands, free of the marks of hard labor, also served to distinguish Joseph as a member of the elite, a leader among his contemporaries. Virtually everything about Abigail Dwight had performed the same service. Described in terms of readily identifiable signifiers of status, the woman who shared in the management of the Indian school was "dignified," "benevolent," and "pleasing." Like the hands that her husband displayed, the apparel that Abigail donned confirmed her social standing. The "dress, of rich silk, a high-crowned cap, with plaited border, and a watch, then so seldom worn as to be a distinction, all marked the gentlewoman, and inspired respect."

In the midst of a transformation that was altering their nation's social and political premises, a post-revolutionary elite continued to defend the prerogatives that had set Joseph and Abigail apart even as challenges to their authority escalated. Infuriated that forms of deference signifying a hierarchical society were being cast aside, Theodore Sedgwick's brow had lowered when emboldened artisans presented themselves at the *front* door of his home. He did more than glower when a still more presumptuous representative of the coming order stood at the same door and refused to remove his hat. The lad had been forcibly removed by the elder Sedgwick, albeit with the hat still securely on his head. Clearly, as his daughter remarked wryly, Theodore had been "born too soon to relish the freedoms of democracy." The same might be said for Pamela Sedgwick. She had insisted that the family and the servants be segregated—household help, Catharine recalled, had been "restricted to the kitchen table." Sedgwick's recollections documented the increasing resistance to Pamela's practice. "Now Catha*rine*," said a local resident when the young Sedgwick had been sent to recruit the woman's daughter for a servant, "'we are all made out of the same clay, we have got one Maker and one Judge, and we' got to lay down in the grave side by side. Why can't you sit down to the table together?"

The conflict between those defending the older order and their challengers took on a political cast in the competition between the nation's parties, the Federalists and the Democratic-Republicans.[6] The political philosophy of loyal Federalist Theodore bore all the marks of a party committed to the maintenance of a traditional hierarchy—a paternalistic approach to politics, a belief that only elite leadership could sustain the nation, and a haughty distrust of the lower orders. Theodore's commitment to the republican experiment was not the issue. Service as a legislator in the Massachusetts General Court, leadership in the nation's Congress, and tenure on the Massachusetts Supreme Court all testified to his dedication to republican government founded under the Constitution. Instead, it was the very meaning of republicanism that was being contested during the three decades of Theodore's career. Sedgwick recalled that her father and other prominent Federalists "hoped a republic might exist and prosper." Indeed, they entertained the hope that it might "be the happiest government in the world, but not without a strong aristocratic element." It was that last caveat, that insistence upon a "strong aristocratic element," that separated leading Federalists from those dedicated to a republicanism in which all of the enfranchised played a role in the conduct of politics.

The Federalists' opposition to increased popular participation was informed by their allegiance to a traditional social structure that divided the world into gentlemen and lower orders. Men like Theodore who identified "all sound principles, truth, justice, and patriotism" with a gentlemanly elite had no truck with the lower orders, at least as political entities. They, as Sedgwick recalled, were dismissed by her father "as 'Jacobins,' 'sans culottes,' and 'miscreants.'" Theodore's epithets notwithstanding, he surely recognized, as his daughter did, that the forces opposing him possessed an "intense desire to grasp the power and place that had been denied to them, and a determination to work out the theories of the government." With the election of 1800, Theodore believed they had accomplished exactly that. The defeat of his party at the polls and the rejection of the republicanism with which he identified led Theodore to resign his Congressional seat. Still in control of Massachusetts, the Federalists appointed him to the state's highest court. Disillusioned but still eager to wield influence, he remained there until his death in 1813.

Despite the highly publicized hostility between the rival parties, politics in the early republic was not without a lighter side. And despite Theodore's sober sense of purpose, his daughter caught the pranks, the lampoons, and the unpretentious humor of the times. She recorded these memories in her autobiography. They also became the subject of **"A Reminiscence of Federalism,"** a story Sedgwick based upon a summer she spent in Bennington, Vermont, during the last decade of the eighteenth century. Bennington's main street, as she noted in the autobiography, "extended a long way, some mile and a half, from a

hill at one end to a plain at the other," a section of town where the old horse Clover was left to graze. Clover was no ordinary horse. His distinction was that his superannuated sides had been "pasted over with lampoons in which the rival factions vented their wit or their malignity safe from personal responsibility, for Clover could tell no tales." Daily, indeed hourly, Clover "trudged from the hill, a walking gazette, his ragged and grizzled sides covered with the militant missives, and returned bearing the responses of the valley, as unconscious of his hostile burden, as the mail is of its portentous contents." In her story, which she published in 1835, Sedgwick allows one Democratic-Republican to voice his opinion that "distrust of the people was the great error of the Federalists"; the narrator responds that that perspective "will now perhaps be admitted with truth."[7] Sedgwick had come to the same opinion only in adulthood. The younger Sedgwick, as she readily admitted in her autobiography, had aligned herself with her father, looking upon every member of the opposition as "grasping, dishonest, and vulgar." Every member of the rival party had been cast as "an enemy to his country."

The hierarchy and deference under assault in the social and political relations of the early republic had also characterized gender relations in colonial society. Whether gentlewoman or member of the lower orders, a woman had been considered a man's subordinate. In a hierarchy that divided the world into the feminine and the masculine, a woman had been expected to defer to male authority in the household and in the world beyond its doors. Many of the underpinnings of this system remained intact in the years after the Revolution. Women were still subject to coverture, a legal tradition that submerged a wife's property in her husband's. They were still denied participation in the nation's body politic either as voters or as jurors. Simultaneously, however, subtle but discernible changes were becoming evident.

Enhanced opportunities for female education began to erase the disparity in literacy between white women and white men. Building upon the basic literacy taught in public schools, an increasing number of private academies and seminaries provided women a more extended and diversified education. Republican motherhood, an ideology that ascribed political significance to domestic responsibilities, made women's education critical to the survival of the newly independent nation. Expected to foster the necessary elements of virtue in their sons and to encourage the same in their husbands, mothers and wives became the educators of their nation's citizens. In fulfilling this obligation, women participated, albeit indirectly, in civil and political life. Standing as an archetype of gender relations, the institution of marriage registered continuity and change in the early republic. Women did remain subject to the intersecting strands of subordination and authority that had marked colonial marriages. Nonetheless, the practice of more egalitarian relations in some households signaled modifications in this pattern. Not least, the idea that a woman might remain unmarried and still have a meaningful life was glimpsed as a possibility. Within a generation, Catharine Maria Sedgwick would count herself among the women who made that idea a reality.[8]

The marriages of Theodore Sedgwick illustrated the persistence of older patterns of gender relations. Before he had reached the age of twenty-eight, Theodore had married twice, enhancing his status both times. In 1768 he married Eliza Mason, a member of a prominent family in Franklin, Connecticut. When he contracted smallpox three years after their marriage, Theodore immediately removed himself from the household and returned only after he had been certified as recovered. These precautions notwithstanding, Eliza, whose pregnancy had made inoculation inadvisable, became infected. The smallpox that her husband had barely survived killed her. Although Catharine Sedgwick believed that only "the canonized 'year and a day'" had elapsed before her parents' marriage, Theodore actually married Pamela Dwight in 1774, three years after Eliza's death. Whatever their individual differences, Eliza and Pamela both practiced the deference toward Theodore that traditional gender relations mandated. And, as if to signify the wifely role she and Eliza shared, Pamela enshrined the memory of her predecessor in the name of her eldest child, Eliza Mason.

In characterizing her mother as "modest," "humble," and "reserved," Sedgwick described the posture that Pamela had adopted toward her husband. Their conversations when Theodore was deciding whether to continue his political career betray the same deference. In a letter Sedgwick included in her autobiography, Pamela suggested that her husband consider the toll exacted by his career. "'A wish to serve the true interests of our country is certainly a laudable ambition,'" she recognized, but should not Theodore consider that "'the intention brings many cares with it.'" With striking ease and confidence, Pamela commented on the political realities her husband faced in the waning years of the eighteenth century—the government was as yet untried, the citizenry as yet untested. Both ease and confidence disappeared, however, when she enumerated the costs that mattered most to her. She could say only hesitantly that "'your family deserves some attention.'" She could not say at all that *she* merited consideration: "'I have not a distant wish you should sacrifice your happiness to mine, or your inclination to my opinion.'" Instead, should Theodore decide to continue to pursue a career that took him away from his family at least half of each year, Pamela duly assured him that "'submission is my duty, and, however hard, I will try to practice what reason teaches me I am under obligation to do.'" At the top of the letter, which was deposited with the family's correspondence at the Massachusetts Historical Society, Sedgwick wrote in her own hand: "a beautiful and characteristic letter from my beloved mother, wise and tender."[9]

Her daughter's sentiments notwithstanding, Pamela found the separations from her husband very hard indeed. Sedgwick herself acknowledged that her mother had been "left for many months in this cold northern country, with young children, a large household, and complicated concerns, and the necessity of economy." Pamela's letters to her husband focused upon the isolation, the longing for companionship; indeed, her letters were a litany of loneliness. Theodore's departure occasioned a "very sensible pain," although she had tried to conceal it so as not to distress him. Disappointed that his return was delayed yet again, she told him in another letter: "I sicken at the thought of your being absent for so long a time." She found almost intolerable "this vale of Widowhood." Perhaps most tellingly, Pamela confided in still another letter, "we are all like a body without a soul."[10]

The costs of separation increased as Pamela's fragile health grew more precarious and her struggle with depression more desperate. In December 1791, she pleaded with her husband to return home and the next moment ordered him to stay away. The letter was short. It told Theodore that she had sunk deeply into herself. Friends had tried to tell her that she was ill, "but this I have no reason to believe." Yet as the words tumbled from her pen she made Theodore believe: "But shall I tell, can I tell you that I have lost my understanding." What was she to think, what could she think, she wondered, "what is my shame, what is my pain, what is my confusion to think of this what evils [a]wait my poor family without a guide, without a head." She wanted him to return for the children, "for their sakes," but surely not for his or for hers, "for your sake I wish you not to come, you must not come. It would only make us both more wretched."[11] Although Pamela rallied from that attack, others that followed were still more severe. In a letter that Sedgwick included in her autobiography, Theodore told his other daughters, Eliza and Frances, that as Pamela's condition deteriorated, he had struggled to decide whether to remain in Congress or resign his office: "'I most sincerely endeavored to weigh all circumstances, and to discover what I ought to do.'" Theodore chose his career. Pamela's attacks of depression ended only with her death in 1807.

Ostensibly, Sedgwick defended her father's decision, declaring in the autobiography that Theodore's letters had been filled with the "most thoughtful love for my mother, the highest appreciation of her character." Only devotion to his country had persuaded him to persist in his career; he had "felt it to be his duty to remain in public life at every private sacrifice." Perhaps most important, Pamela's suffering had ended with her death. And his daughter insisted, Theodore's contribution "to establish the government, and to swell the amount of that political virtue which makes the history of the Federal party the record of the purest patriotism the world has known—*that remains.*"

Simultaneously, however, Sedgwick subverted this defense of her father. In some of the most moving passages in the autobiography, she tallies the costs of Theodore's choice. Surely the largest toll had been exacted from Pamela. Acknowledging the pain her mother had suffered, Sedgwick notes that the separations seemed "to have been almost cruel to her." She had been "oppressed with cares and responsibilities." She had borne the "terrible weight of do-mestic cares." But Sedgwick did not stop there. The daughter also exposed her own deeply ambivalent response. She also had her litany. She recalls her first words, "Theodore" and "Philadelphia," words signifying her father's absence. She recalls childhood's sorrows and joys, matched to "Papa's going away" and "Papa's coming home." She recalls the suffering she endured at the time of Pamela's death. "Beloved mother," she exclaims, "even at this distance of time, the thought of what I suffered when you died thrills my soul!" And there is the decision to include the wrenchingly powerful eulogy. Penned by her brother Harry shortly after Pamela's death, it testified to their mother's endurance. Declaring that "her sufferings, in degree and duration, have been perhaps without a parallel," Harry emphasized that she had nonetheless displayed "the invincible meekness and the gentleness of her heavenly temper." Meekness, gentleness, in a word, subordination, highlighted the gender relations that Pamela practiced. It was the costs inherent in those relations that led Sedgwick to undermine the defense of her father. Unable to elide the evidence of her ambivalence, Theodore and Pamela's daughter scattered its traces through the text of her autobiography.

Theodore's absence and Pamela's illness obliged Catharine to look elsewhere for daily care, support, and guidance. She found all that and more in Elizabeth Freeman, an African-American who was the family's servant for twenty-six years. In the passage in the autobiography that describes "Mah Bet," or Mumbet, Sedgwick remarks to Alice that those "who surround us in our childhood, whose atmosphere infolds us, as it were, have more to do with the formation of our characters than all our didactic and preceptive education." It was Mumbet's "perception of justice," her "uncompromising honesty," her "conduct of high intelligence" that had left an indelible impression on Theodore and Pamela's daughter. When she described my "Mother—my nurse—my faithful friend" in a journal entry made only a month before Mumbet's death on 28 December 1829, Sedgwick had listed the qualities that would emerge later in the autobiography: a "strong love of justice," "incorruptible integrity," and "intelligent industry." Mumbet also exhibited "strong judgment," had an "iron resolution," and demonstrated "quick and firm decision." Embodying a power that sets her apart from other individuals in the autobiography and the journals, Mumbet emerges as the most exceptional individual encountered there, regardless of sex. Still more tellingly, she emerges as the woman with whom Sedgwick most deeply identifies, and, in turn, Sedgwick declares that Mumbet had "clung to us with a devotion and tenacity of love seldom equalled."[12]

In the autobiography, however, Sedgwick is oblivious to the structural limitations of her relationship with the beloved Mumbet. Presented as if untouched by the disabilities of the racially based institution of slavery dominating late eighteenth-century America, the loyal servant is constructed exclusively in relation to Catharine and her family. It is almost as if the racial difference between Mumbet and Catharine, between black and white, were erased. Notwithstanding Sedgwick's devotion, racial difference did privilege Catharine and render Mumbet her subordinate.[13]

But Mumbet was also Elizabeth Freeman, the African-American who had challenged slavery's legality in the newly independent state of Massachusetts. It is Freeman whom Sedgwick celebrates in **"Slavery in New England,"** a chronicle published in *Bentley's Miscellany* in 1853. Here Sedgwick acknowledges the difference between herself and Mumbet; here too she acknowledges Mumbet's agency. Having decided that the Declaration of Independence applied to all Americans, the slave Freeman had approached Theodore Sedgwick early in 1781. "Won't the law give me my freedom?" she had asked Berkshire County's most prominent lawyer. After Freeman enlisted Theodore as her counsel and challenged the constitutionality of slavery in the county's court, the law did exactly that. Freeman's achievement established the precedent for slavery's abolition throughout Massachusetts. Immediately after the court's decision, Freeman joined the Sedgwicks as the family's servant. It was *Mumbet's* personal strength, her determination, her force, all of which had been highlighted in the autobiography and journals, that made possible *Freeman's* public pursuit of liberation, an act that Sedgwick applauded in **"Slavery in New England."**[14]

Sedgwick's older siblings also played an influential role in her childhood. Deeply attached to all of her brothers and sisters, Sedgwick developed the strongest ties with her four brothers, Theodore, Harry, Robert, and Charles. Sharing with them "an intimate companionship and I think as true and loving a friendship as ever existed between brothers and sister," she considered them her "chiefest blessing in life." Long after her childhood had ended, Sedgwick told a friend that she had "no recollection beyond the time when they made my happiness."[15] Nearly a decade older and already away at school, the younger Theodore had little impact on his sister's early years. Of the others, Harry's "loving, generous disposition," his "domestic affections," strongly impressed his sister. Robert, designated as her "favorite," served as "protector and companion." And Charles, born two years after Sedgwick, "was the youngest of the family, and so held that peculiar relation to us all as junior." That status made him no less beloved. Charles, as Sedgwick made clear in her autobiography and journals, was "a joy and thanksgiving to me."

Born fourteen and eleven years before their younger sister, Eliza and Frances had a less decisive influence upon Catharine's childhood. Both, as Sedgwick reflected, "were just at that period when girls' eyes are dazzled with their own glowing future." That future was marriage, of course. And it was the relationship between marital union and sibling separation that Sedgwick remembered about her sisters. In recalling her oldest sister, who had played a maternal role in her early childhood, Sedgwick focused upon the separation occasioned by Eliza's marriage. The ceremony that might have been regarded as a celebration of a newly formed union left the seven-year-old Catharine with "the impression that a wedding was rather a sundering than a forming of ties." Deeply upset, she had cried at the wedding and had been taken away. Mumbet had tried to calm her, whispering "her 'hush' but for the first time it was impotent." Later the bridegroom, Thaddeus Pomeroy, had come to her and, trying to soothe her, had said, "'Your sister may stay with you this summer!'" Five decades later, Sedgwick had not forgotten her reaction: "*May!* How my whole being revolted at the word. He had the power to bind or loose my sister!" The significance of this incident cannot be lost on readers of the autobiography, for Sedgwick repeats it almost verbatim and in equally impassioned tones just two pages later.

As Sedgwick and her siblings prepared for their lives as adults, both their family status and their gender shaped the education their parents provided for them. Theodore, Harry, Robert, and Charles were all sent to preparatory schools that trained them in the classical languages, then the basic requirement for higher education. With the exception of Charles, the brothers all attended college before they began their apprenticeships as lawyers. These opportunities marked them as sons of an elite family. Less than one percent of the male population attended institutions of higher learning as late as 1840. None of the female population did so, at least in the eighteenth century. Oberlin, which did welcome women, did not open its doors until 1832.[16] The family's standing also shaped the education offered Eliza, Frances, and Catharine, each of whom was provided the most advanced instruction then available to women: they attended a series of private schools in New York City, Albany, and Boston, where their programs combined a smattering of academics with preparation in social accomplishments.[17]

Sedgwick herself sharply distinguished between her formal and informal education. Her "school life," she stated bluntly in her autobiography, "was a waste, my home life my only education." This disclaimer notwithstanding, she did receive the formal schooling considered appropriate for the daughter of an elite family. Catharine first attended the local school in rural Stockbridge. When Catharine was eight, Pamela wrote to Theodore that she had sent their daughter to Bennington, Vermont, "as our school here is worse than none."[18] Catharine's letters to Theodore suggest that Pamela's opinion was at least slightly exaggerated. But in the autobiography Sedgwick did say that if there was "any other school a little more select or better chanced, I went to that." Whatever the particular school, however, she noted wryly, "our minds were not weakened by too much study." The demands were relatively insignificant and the curricula restricted to reading, spelling, geography, and arithmetic.

The family then enrolled their daughter in a series of schools in three different cities. Here, too, Catharine found the challenges slight. Recalling her experience in New York City with a mixture of levity and regret, she noted that as early as the age of eleven she had been sent there

and "had the very best teaching of an eminent Professor of Dancing!" Her schooling at Mrs. Bell's in Albany continued in like fashion. Sedgwick commented that Mrs. Bell herself "rose late, was half the time out of her school, and did very little when in it." Considering the instruction she offered when there, that may not have been a serious loss. In a letter written to her mother on 6 October 1803, the thirteen-year-old Catharine noted that she had "begun another piece of embroidery, a landscape. It has a very cultivated and rather a romantic appearance." But the daughter had begun to take a stand regarding the relative merits of her education. Little time would be devoted to embroidery in the future, she told her mother. The study of geography and the practice of writing were much more important.[19] So too was the mastery of a foreign language. In 1804, four years after she had begun French while in New York City, Catharine wrote to each parent describing her progress at Mrs. Payne's in Boston. In November she told Pamela that she was "very well contented and pleased with my new situation" and that she was pleased as well with her French instructor, "a very excellent one, I assure you."[20] Nearly two months later, on the day after her fifteenth birthday, she answered Theodore's inquiry about her progress in French: "I hardly find time to attend to anything else; I am very fond of it and it is *my opinion* that I come on very well."[21] Nonetheless, the cumulative experience was judged inadequate, and years later Sedgwick registered her intense and lasting disappointment in the autobiography: "I have all my life felt the want of more systematic training."

Although it was equally unsystematic, Sedgwick regarded her informal education far more positively. Noting that her father and her brothers had "uncommon mental vigor," she emphasizes that "their daily habits, and pursuits, and pleasures were intellectual, and I naturally imbided from them a kindred taste." She pays particular tribute to her father who read aloud to the family. She remembers listening at the age of eight to passages from Cervantes, Shakespeare and Hume. The father who read aloud also pressed the daughter to read to herself. Telling her that he hoped she would "find it in your power to devote your mornings to reading," he reminded Catharine that hers was a privileged position—"there are few who can make such improvements by it and it would to be lamented if this precious time should be lost."[22] The girl heeded her father's counsel. Indeed, the "love of reading" he had instilled in her became to her "'education.'" By the age of eleven, she was reading constantly, "chiefly novels." When she was twelve, Catharine added Rollin's multi-volume *Ancient History,* which introduced her to "Cyrus's greatness." Lighter fare included the increasingly popular children's miscellanies collected by Anna Barbauld and Arnaud Berquin.

Sedgwick, then, had little education in the "common sense," but there were "peculiar circumstances in [her] condition that in some degree supplied these great deficiencies." They were peculiar circumstances. Sedgwick was basically untutored and undirected, but as the result of living in a cultured household, "there was much chance seed dropped in the fresh furrow, and some of it was good seed." She also boldly adds, "some of it, I may say, fell on good ground." Sedgwick's metaphor highlights the paradoxical character of her education. Arbitrary, unstructured, and unpredictable as that education was, it had been obtained from a family that valued learning and considered the transmission of culture a responsibility, its possession a birthright.

Whether formal or informal, however, Sedgwick's education had not been designed to prepare her for a public career. Presuming that a woman's existence would be centered in the home, elite families focused on preparing their daughters for the roles of wife and mother. Companion to husband and instructor to children, the educated woman was expected to dedicate herself to her family. This ideal of the wife and mother aside, the physical and emotional demands of domesticity made it difficult to engage in other pursuits. Ideology and circumstance, then, located a woman within the household and made the role she played there central to her identity. Any career beyond the home was decidedly unlikely. In contrast to nine out of ten women in the nineteenth century, Sedgwick remained unmarried. However, that unusual status did not make her eligible for a career. Instead, it was assumed that an unmarried woman would either remain with her parental family or attach herself to her siblings' families. Whatever the familial locus, the single woman's life was still defined in the context of domesticity.

Nonetheless, Sedgwick challenged prevailing experience and expectation. Her siblings, female and male, played significant, albeit starkly different, roles in their sister's decision to remain single. The experiences of Eliza and Frances were cautionary tales. Each of their marriages made tangible a gender hierarchy in which women were relatively powerless. The consequences for Frances were disastrous. Although Sedgwick describes the marriage only sparingly in her autobiography, she captures its tone and temper in a single phrase—Frances "endured much heroically." In letters written to her other siblings, Sedgwick elaborated upon her sister's desperately unhappy union with Ebenezer Watson. The reason for Frances's distress was simple. As Sedgwick wrote to Eliza about Frances's husband, "Mr. Watson is *brutal* in his conduct to her and does and has for a long time rendered her miserable." With a demeanor that Sedgwick described as "oppressive," as "essentially diabolical," Ebenezer tyrannized over Frances. Why, then, did Frances remain with her husband? Again the answer was simple. Frances, as Sedgwick told Eliza in the same letter, "would leave him—but she cannot bear a separation from the children." This was no idle concern. Nineteenth-century legislation governing custody of children in the event of separation or divorce accorded the husband almost exclusive rights. Frances's situation was, then, "one of those hopeless miseries over which we must mourn without being able to remove it."[23] Throughout the crises that beset the marriage, Frances's brothers and sisters continued to provide sympathy and support. A re-

signed Frances remained in the marriage. Shortly before her elder sister's death in June 1842, Sedgwick wrote to a friend that Frances had been "through a life of vexing trials that would have cooled any love, exhausted any enthusiasm but hers."[24] The evidence suggests that was only a slight exaggeration.

In contrast to her sister Frances's experience, Eliza sustained a deeply caring marriage with Thaddeus Pomeroy. Nonetheless, this union as well entailed hardship. Eliza, Sedgwick recalls in the autobiography, had a "hard life of it—indifferent health and the painful drudgery of bearing and nurturing twelve children." Just as important, nineteenth-century gender relations dictated that the resolution of marital incompatibilities was Eliza's responsibility. Thaddeus, as Sedgwick described him, "was a man after the old pattern—resolute, fearless, enduring, generous, with alterations of tenderness and austerity, of impulsiveness and rigidity." Unfortunately, some of these characteristics "were trying to [Eliza's] gentle disposition and unvarying and quiet devotion to duty." Four months before her sister's death in 1827, Sedgwick testified to Eliza's success in adapting to a marriage that resembled her parents'. Eliza, she declared in her journals, "can look back upon a life in which her duties have been well sustained." Her sister had been "an example of a Christian daughter and *sister*—wife and mother—friend and benefactor."[25] Sedgwick praised the obvious constancy. She commended the effort well performed. Only later, in the autobiography, did she remark upon the costs. Only then did she attribute those costs to patriarchal gender relations.

While the experiences of Frances and Eliza contributed to Sedgwick's decision not to marry, her brothers, all of whom welcomed her into their households, played the crucial role. Offering care, affection, and companionship, Theodore, Harry, Robert, and Charles provided their sister with a familial base and made it possible for Sedgwick to create a marriage of circumstance. In a letter that she wrote when she was fifty-one, Sedgwick told her close friend Louisa Minot (mother of William; mother-in-law of Kate) that "the affection that others give to husbands and children I have given to my brothers." She recognized that hers was an unusual situation. "Few," she noted, "can understand the dependence and intensity of my love for them."[26] Developed in childhood, that dependence and intensity increased in the wake of Theodore Sedgwick's death, which occurred shortly after his youngest daughter's twenty-third birthday. Writing to her eldest brother ten days after their father had died on 24 January 1813, Sedgwick told Theodore II that she longed to see him, longed to tell him that she felt "for all my brothers new sensations of love and dependence."[27]

In the decade following her father's death, Sedgwick's bond with two of her brothers increased in depth and strength. Each of these relationships had its particular character, each its particular expression of affection. Playfulness, remarkable wit, and shared sensibilities marked the intimacy Catharine shared with Harry. The attachment with Robert was charged with passion. Writing to him six months after their father's death, Sedgwick proclaimed, "I do love you, with a love surpassing at least the ordinary love of woman." Six years later, she described him as "as much a part of me as the lifeblood that flows through my heart." Robert's declarations of affection were equally intense, his need for her equally strong. "My dear Kate," he told her on more than one occasion, "I know not how I could live without you."[28]

The trajectory of these relationships changed sharply in the 1820s, however. The years of mental illness that eventually cost Harry his life transformed all his relationships, not least the one that he had established with his sister Catharine. From 1827 until Harry's death late in 1831, Sedgwick's journals are filled with expressions of overwhelming loss. In one of the many entries commenting on Harry's deteriorating condition, she lamented his "darkened mind," his "troubled spirit." Still another entry described that once powerful mind as "a broken instrument." The spontaneity, the clarity, the discernment were gone forever. "Oh, it is too much," his sister cried out.[29]

Sedgwick's desolation was sharpened by another loss she had experienced earlier in the decade. The situation was very different, although the impact seemed only slightly less. In December 1821, Robert had told his sister that he had decided to marry Elizabeth Ellery. "We cannot walk so close together as we have done," Sedgwick responded. That recognition devastated her: "No one can ever know all that I have, and must feel, because no one has ever felt the sheltering love, the tenderness, the friendship that left me nothing to desire." Despite Robert's efforts to dissuade his sister, Sedgwick tried to lessen her dependence upon him. At the time of his marriage, Robert complained that she no longer spoke in "that language of the heart, by which you are accustomed so faithfully to interpret its emotions." Nearly a year passed before Sedgwick felt sufficiently detached to acknowledge that her reticence had been motivated by the need to have his presence and professions of affection become "less necessary."[30] The connection, the sense of reciprocal commitment, established between sister and brother had become essential to Sedgwick; the process of disengagement had been extremely painful.

Ultimately, Sedgwick achieved her objective of lessened dependence, although a deep attachment clearly persisted. After Harry's declining health required him and his wife Jane to leave New York City, Sedgwick spent her winters there with Robert and his family. She also traveled with them in Europe for fifteen months. But the intimacy, the mutual reliance Catharine and Robert expressed in their letters prior to Robert's marriage, disappeared from their correspondence. Sedgwick herself alluded to the difference in a journal entry dated 2 December 1837. The passage describes her relationships with members of her family, including Robert. But the sentences about him have been carefully inked out. In the margin alongside the passage, Sedgwick added the following on 24 July 1846, nearly

five years after her brother's death: "Here I had written a lamentation over the transference of the first place in my dear brother Robert's heart. He had been father, lover as well as brother to me, and when in the inevitable concentration of a closer tie I felt an aching void, I expressed it as I should not."[31] Sedgwick immediately added, "years passed on and I had proof that the love of our early years for a time without its usual demonstrations was there in that tenderest of hearts." That restored intimacy was Robert's gift to his sister in the final months before his death in September 1841.

The vacuum left by Harry and Robert was increasingly filled by Charles. The bond Sedgwick developed with the only brother younger than herself is documented in a correspondence that spans nearly half a century. Theirs became a relationship in which reciprocity was perhaps the strongest hallmark. It seems appropriate that Sedgwick, an individual who had constituted herself in relation to others, should have experienced an exceptional mutuality in the sibling relationship that lasted the longest. Charles would express to his sister his desire to "make my house myself, my all as conducive to your happiness as it is possible it should be." Catharine prefigured the success of his endeavor in her earlier comment that she had known "nothing of love—of memory—of hope—of which you are no an essential part."[32]

The losses and shifting intensities notwithstanding, Sedgwick established deeply meaningful relationships with her brothers that sustained her until Charles's death in 1856. Still, in entry upon entry in her journal, Sedgwick considered the consequences of her decision to remain single. As each of her brothers married, she became "first to none," as she phrased it in one of the early volumes. Being "second best" was inevitably difficult. It caused her the "keenest suffering." It surely constituted the "chief misery of single life." And, as she recorded in the journal's last entry on 28 December 1854, she still felt "so acutely—so unworthily the inevitable change from the time when I was first in many hearts to being first in none."[33]

But if Sedgwick chose to highlight the costs of her decision in most of her journal entries, she also left meditations there that located that decision in a larger and more balanced context. Yes, she had "suffered," she noted on 2 December 1834, the day after her forty-fifth birthday. But her life's more positive dimension was openly acknowledged—"for the most part I can look back upon a very happy life." Her literary career had brought her "far more of the world's respect than I ever expected." Her cherished friendships had extended, undiminished, through the years. The most important ties, the connections upon which she had constructed her core identity, had been more complicated. The marriages of her brothers had meant that "a portion of what was mine has been diverted into other channels." Resignedly she commented, "my heart has ached and *does ache*." Resignation was balanced by resolution, however. She would not "repine," she would not be "exacting."[34] In another entry recorded two years later

Sedgwick mediated upon the alternative. The death of William Jarvis, one of her former suitors, provided the occasion. Whatever loneliness she had suffered, whatever pain her secondary status had entailed, Jarvis's death reminded Sedgwick of her conviction that a successful marriage required much more than the "liking" she had felt for the then "young man of five and twenty."[35]

It was not so much that Sedgwick regretted her decision to remain single; indeed, evidence indicates that she did not. And yet a relentlessly honest Sedgwick meditated upon the consequences of her choice throughout her life. That she vacillated, this time calmly accepting those consequences, that time lamenting them, suggests ambivalence. But Sedgwick was no simple woman, and neither was her ambivalence simple. Its complicated character she herself expressed concisely, profoundly, and perhaps unconsciously. "From my own experience," she said, "I would not advise any one to remain unmarried." For, she immediately added, "my experience has been a singularly happy one."[36]

Sedgwick's brothers were central to the choice she made about marriage. They were no less important in their sister's literary career. Strongly and consistently supportive, Theodore, Harry, Robert, and Charles encouraged the initially reluctant author, applauded the novels and stories, and negotiated with the publishers. In a letter written a decade before Sedgwick's appearance as a novelist, Harry displayed the enthusiasm with which he and his brothers fostered her career. Telling Catharine that he had agreed to edit Boston's *Weekly Messenger* every third week, he declared that he intended to print a portion of her recent letter—"a delightful scrap of yours on the sacred character of a *pastor.*" In his effort to bolster the confidence of female authors, he needed the "ammunition of a petticoated youth of high and early promise." None other than his sister would provide the necessary armament: "How confidently shall I claim for 'my fair countrywomen' the need of their genius; how triumphantly shall I prove their precocity of intellect."[37] Harry's confidence in his sister was manifest. So too was his determination that she cultivate her talent. In asserting that the country must no longer neglect the genius of its women, he laid claim upon Sedgwick to display her own. Harry was also the first brother to persuade her to enlarge the form and scope of a religious tract she had begun shortly after she left orthodox Congregationalism for Unitarianism.

Theodore and Robert then joined forces with Harry, and they convinced their sister that the novel that emerged from the tract should be published. Having read 130 pages of *A New England Tale* shortly after its publication in 1822, Theodore told Sedgwick that the novel "exceeds all my expectations, fond and flattering as they were." He had never doubted her abilities, but having seen them confirmed, his heart was filled with "pride and pleasure." With the publication of Sedgwick's second novel two years later, Robert delighted in recounting to his sister that "wherever I go I receive compliments, felicitations, and

even homage for the honor I have come to, by my relation to the author of *Redwood.*" Charles "rejoiced beyond all expression at the progress of the book" he was reading in manuscript. The volume this time was *Hope Leslie,* Sedgwick's third novel, which appeared shortly after his heartening letter in the spring of 1827. Three years later, he told Sedgwick in mock horror that she must end her literary career or his "family will be ruined." Adults and children alike were locked away in their rooms absorbed with *Clarence,* Sedgwick's fourth novel.[38] So long as each was able, all of Sedgwick's brothers stayed the course, prompting, bolstering, and persuading their sister that her talent demanded literary expression. Dedicating *Clarence* "To my Brothers—my best friends," Sedgwick acknowledged their signal importance to her career.

The elite standing of her family and the gender conventions of her century intersected in Sedgwick's career. The daughter of an influential Federalist, she nonetheless discarded the political convictions of her father and came to support the more egalitarian democracy he had found so threatening. However, two letters, both expressing Sedgwick's pleasure at favorable reactions to her fiction, highlight a lingering elitism that qualified her support for egalitarian democracy. "In this country," she succinctly informed her friend Louisa Minot, "we must do everything for the *majority.*"[39] Later elaborating upon her responsibilities to those who were numerically dominant, Sedgwick expressed her opinion to clergyman William Ellery Channing that "there is an immense moral field opening demanding laborers." She, of course, defined herself as one of those laborers; "neither pride nor humility should withold [*sic*] us from the work to which we are clearly 'sent.'"[40]

In suggesting that elite status entailed particular responsibilities to the larger society, Sedgwick had to address a basic question: Was there any role for individuals of privilege in an increasingly democratic antebellum America? Despite the claims that resonated through these decades, America's democracy remained decidedly limited—barriers to participation either as voters or as jurors remained in place for African-American men and for women of all races. Universal suffrage for white men had made them equal at the polls. In defining the elite's obligations as cultural rather than political, then, Sedgwick envisioned a privileged class that might yet be critical to the success of a society that defined itself as democratic. Those who could no longer expect to dominate at the polls could retain power and authority in the domain of culture. And there they could continue to "do everything for the *majority.*" But was it possible for a *woman* to invest herself with the obligations she had accorded an elite? Entitled by her family's status to enrich herself intellectually and culturally, Sedgwick took a further step and defined herself as a participant in the construction of culture. Had she clung to the political model of elite dominance, she, like all women regardless of status, would have been excluded from participation in the national project. In combining the increasingly popular idea that women should be moral guardians with the long-standing conviction that culture should be informed by moral as well as aesthetic purpose, Sedgwick was able to circumvent barriers based on gender and to transform the legacy that Theodore Sedgwick had intended only for his sons. She could, therefore, see herself as Channing's equal and insist that they both dedicate themselves to the "work to which we are clearly 'sent.'"[41]

The consequences of the obligations Sedgwick so willingly embraced were not always welcomed, however. Ranked with the early nineteenth century's most prominent writers, Sedgwick acknowledged the pleasure of distinction. Yes, she conceded in a journal entry recorded shortly after the publication of *Hope Leslie,* she delighted in being one of antebellum America's most notable literary figures, in "being able to command a high station wherever I go." But that distinction also entailed what her brother Charles aptly termed "Lafayettism," a condition in which the subject became the possession of her public. Having been "introduced to multitudes at [Saratoga] Springs who paid this compliment to what they deemed my literary success," Sedgwick found the experience distasteful. She had "to fritter away in general courtesies time and thought and feeling." It was a "disadvantage" that she felt deeply. That Sedgwick sought the betterment of those same multitudes was obvious. That she sought influence as a cultural arbiter was equally so. Nonetheless, she still longed for the deference that would have insulated her from the claims an increasingly aggressive public made upon its famous. She still longed to be aloof.[42]

The moral nature of the cultural obligations Sedgwick assigned elite women is evident in the reflections on literary women that are scattered throughout her autobiography and journals. Sometimes the subject she chooses is herself. Shortly after the publication of *Hope Leslie,* Sedgwick recorded a meditation on the meaning of fame. Noting in her journal that "my fond friends expect a great accession of fame to me," she asked herself that spring of 1827, "fame—what is it?" The praise that had marked the publication of her novel was dismissed as nothing more than the transient "breath of man." Fame was welcomed only if it was endowed with purpose, only if her achievements "produced some good feeling."[43] Almost as frequently, the subject is other women who have broken ground as participants in the construction of culture. Sedgwick's meditations in this regard appear almost as reflections in a mirror. In contemplating other literary women, this participant in her nation's intellectual and cultural enterprise contemplated herself. Nonetheless, Sedgwick had to look abroad for counterparts during the formative decades of her career. In contrast to the Englishwomen with whom she compared herself, she stood nearly alone as a prominent American writer who happened to be a woman.

The English writer Harriet Martineau, who visited the United States in the early 1830s, is the subject of one of the journals' longer entries. Considering Sedgwick's earlier reservations about the political economist, the impression Martineau made upon her when they met is all the more telling. At first Sedgwick had thought that the pursuit of such a masculine enterprise "was not the loveliest manifestation of woman." But Martineau, whom Sedgwick calls "extraordinary," had allayed this concern almost immediately. She had been "so modest, gentle, and kind." She had exhibited such a venerable combination of "genius and virtue." That Sedgwick considered virtue more important becomes obvious in a second entry comparing Martineau to Anna Barbauld, Maria Edgeworth, Anna Jameson, and Felicia Hemans, all of whom had been successful in their literary careers. None, however, had achieved Martineau's prominence. Sedgwick asks herself why. Certainly, the others had "shown as powerful a genius as hers"; indeed, Sedgwick considers some of them superior in this regard. Martineau had distinguished herself, rather, by her singular commitment of "God's good gifts to the use of his creatures." She had made the common good the sine qua non of her career. Martineau had also been decidedly inclusive in her definition of those creatures. Leaving to others "the intellectual amusement or advancement of the gifted and educated," Martineau had focused upon the multitudes. That egalitarianism had made "us all cry Hail thou favored among women!"[44]

The two entries reveal at least as much about Sedgwick as about Martineau, their putative subject. Perhaps most notably, they demonstrate the remarkable agility with which Sedgwick was able to negotiate antebellum America's gender conventions. Erasing her initial suspicion that political economy is most properly a masculine undertaking, Sedgwick makes its practitioner the embodiment of femininity. Still more tellingly, she complicates the common premise that men alone are lords of creation, a popular phrase that signals the gender conventions limiting participation in the construction of culture. In ascribing creativity, or "genius," to Martineau, Barbauld, Edgeworth, Jameson, and Hemans, Sedgwick openly contradicts those who locate generative power exclusively in the masculine. Yet for all the boldness of her challenge, the burden of Sedgwick's commentary is more in keeping with than set against prevailing gender conventions. Most strikingly Sedgwick makes "virtue," a concept increasingly associated with women, an equally important qualification for participation in the construction of culture. Although the precise meaning of virtue was contested among antebellum Americans, all generally agreed that dedication to the common good was central to its definition and that women's potential for such dedication exceeded men's. Negotiating the highly charged gender conventions and designing a readily identifiable persona from those conventions Sedgwick had made culture Martineau's domain. Simultaneously, she had done the same for herself.

In a letter that is emblematic of the devotion Sedgwick inspired in virtually everyone with whom she shared herself, the youngest of her siblings told her that she had been the recipient of many gifts. By far the one for which she should be most grateful was the most obvious—"the power of your sympathy," as Charles described his sister's deep and sustaining identification with others.[45] The designation was appropriate for Sedgwick the individual as well as for the gender conventions of her century. In her autobiography, in her journals, in her fiction, in short, in all of her writings, she had insisted upon the signal importance of connectedness. Indeed, she had presented her life as entirely interwoven with the lives of others dear to her. Nineteenth-century gender conventions, which located in women a special capacity for selflessness, also privileged such connection as feminine.

Yet Charles neglected to mention the equal significance Sedgwick attached to the freedom to choose. Based on the premise that women had a claim on individual fulfillment, choice had enormous implications for women in a century in which they were expected to subordinate themselves to the needs and desires of men. In her writings and in the most important decisions taken in her life, Sedgwick made those implications tangible. The issues she selected covered a broad spectrum—decisions regarding religious affiliation, vocational commitment, and marital identity were included in her domain. The gender conventions of her century constructed connection and choice almost as a binary opposition. Inflected as feminine and masculine, choice appeared possible only for men. But Sedgwick deconstructed this opposition and made connection and choice complementary imperatives for both sexes. Insisting that women should freely and fully choose a life for themselves, she suggested that only then could they just as freely and fully practice connection. No longer marked as exclusively feminine, connection could be a mutual practice for women and men. In this as in so much else, she displayed the insight, or as Charles phrased it, the power of her sympathy, which made her autobiography and her journals compelling.

Notes

1. Catharine Maria Sedgwick to William Minot, 5 October 1851, Catharine Maria Sedgwick Papers, Massachusetts Historical Society, Boston, Mass. All quotations from MHS collections are by permission.

2. Autobiography of Catharine Maria Sedgwick, C. M. Sedgwick Papers, Massachusetts Historical Society. Unless otherwise noted, all subsequent references derive from this source.

3. This point was made by Georges Gusdorf, in "Conditions and Limits of Autobiography," an influential essay published in 1956 (trans. James Olney, in his edition *Autobiography: Essays Theoretical and Critical* [Princeton: Princeton University Press, 1980], pp. 28-48). Autobiography, as Gusdorf has defined it, entails a "conscious awareness of the singularity of each individual life" (p. 30). Whatever its merits for analysis of the male autobiographical self, Gusdorf's theory is based solely upon an analysis of men's experiences. Susan Stanford Friedman has highlighted the gendered character of this individualistic theory in "Women's Autobiographical Selves: Theory and Practice" (in *The Private Self: Theory and Practice of Women's Au-*

tobiographical Writings, ed. Shari Benstock [Chapel Hill: University of North Carolina Press, 1988], pp. 34-62). Until recently, scholarship on autobiography has focused almost exclusively on male texts. As her title suggests, Sidonie Smith's *A Poetics of Women's Autobiography: Marginality and the Fictions of Self-Representation* (Bloomington: Indiana University Press, 1987) shifts the angle of vision. I have found Smith's commentary on current theories of women's autobiography very useful. She has explored the complicated relationship between experience and representation in women's autobiography in the highly suggestive "Construing Truths in Lying Mouths: Truthtelling in Women's Autobiography," *Studies in the Literary Imagination* 23 (1990): 145-63. See also Estelle Jelinek, *The Tradition of Women's Autobiography: From Antiquity to the Present* (Boston: Twayne, 1986); Carolyn Heilbrun, *Writing a Woman's Life* (New York: W. W. Norton, 1988); Personal Narratives Group, ed., *Interpreting Women's Lives: Feminist Theory and Personal Narratives* (Bloomington: Indiana University Press, 1989); Margo Cully, ed., *American Women's Autobiography: Fea(s)ts of Memory* (Madison: University of Wisconsin Press, 1992). For commentary on the varied forms of life writing, including letters, journals, and autobiographies analyzed in this article, see Susan Groag Bell and Marilyn Yalom, eds., *Revealing Lives: Autobiography, Biography, and Gender* (Albany: State University of New York Press, 1990), pp. 1-11.

4. In her analysis of the autobiographies of Dame Julian of Norwich, Margery Kempe, Margaret Cavendish, and Anne Bradstreet, Mary Mason highlights characteristics that distinguish women's from men's construction of the self ("The Other Voice: Autobiographies of Women Writers," in *Autobiography: Essays Theoretical and Critical,* pp. 207-35). Carol Holly has employed a similar strategy in analyzing the autobiographies of Sedgwick and Lucy Larcom ("Nineteenth-Century Autobiographies of Affiliation: The Case of Catharine Sedgwick and Lucy Larcom," in *American Autobiography: Retrospect and Prospect,* ed. Paul John Eakin [Madison: University of Wisconsin Press, 1991], pp. 216-34). See also Rose Norman, "New England Girlhoods in Nineteenth-Century Autobiography," *Legacy: A Journal of American Women Writers* 8 (1991): 104-17.

5. The unparalleled social and political changes that occurred in the decades following the Revolution are insightfully explored in Gordon S. Wood's "The Democratization of Mind in the American Revolution," in *Leadership in the American Revolution: Papers Presented at the Third Symposium, May 9 and 10, 1974* (Washington: Library of Congress, 1974), pp. 63-89. These changes have received extended treatment in Wood's recently published *The Radicalism of the American Revolution* (New York:

Alfred A. Knopf, 1992). Robert E. Shalhope has analyzed the same phenomenon in his incisive "Republicanism, Liberalism, and Democracy: Political Culture in the Early Republic," *Proceedings of the American Antiquarian Society* 102 (1992): 99-152.

6. The conduct and character of Massachusetts politics are described by Ronald P. Formisano, in *The Transformation of Political Culture: Massachusetts Parties, 1790s-1840s* (New York: Oxford University Press, 1983). The Federalists are analyzed in James M. Banner Jr.'s *To the Hartford Convention: The Federalists and the Origins of Party Politics in Massachusetts, 1789-1815* (New York: Alfred A. Knopf, 1970). Paul Goodman does the same for the opposition in *The Democratic-Republicans of Massachusetts: Politics in a Young Republic* (Cambridge: Harvard University Press, 1964). See also Linda K. Kerber's analysis of the Federalist ideology in *Federalists in Dissent: Imagery and Ideology in Jeffersonian America* (Ithaca: Cornell University Press, 1970).

7. Catharine Maria Sedgwick, "A Reminiscence of Federalism," in *Tales and Sketches* (Philadelphia, 1835), pp. 24, 30.

8. There is now a considerable body of scholarship that examines the Revolution in relation to women. Linda Kerber has written extensively on the Revolution's legal and political implications. She also identified Republican Motherhood in her pathbreaking article "The Republican Mother: Women and the Enlightenment—An American Perspective," *American Quarterly* 28 (1976): 187-205. See also Rosemarie Zagarri, "Morals, Manners, and the Republican Mother," *American Quarterly* 44 (1992): 192-215. Jan Lewis commented upon a republican wife's responsibility to her husband in "The Republican Wife: Virtue and Seduction in the Early Republic," *William and Mary Quarterly*, 3rd ser. 44 (1987): 696-721. Both Kerber and Mary Beth Norton have addressed the significance of women's increased educational opportunities. More recently, I have done the same in "'Vindicating the Equality of Female Intellect': Women and Authority in the Early Republic," *Prospects: An Annual Journal of American Cultural Studies* 17 (1992): 1-27. Norton suggested that the choice to remain unmarried became viable in the years after the Revolution. See Kerber, *Women of the Republic: Intellect and Ideology in Revolutionary America* (Chapel Hill: University of North Carolina Press, 1980); "The Paradox of Women's Citizenship in the Early Republic: The Case of Martin vs. Massachusetts, 1805," *American Historical Review* 97 (1992): 349-78; Norton, *Liberty's Daughters: The Revolutionary Experience of American Women, 1750-1800* (Boston: Little, Brown, 1980).

9. Pamela Dwight Sedgwick to Theodore Sedgwick, 18 November [179?], Sedgwick IV, Massachusetts Historical Society.

10. Pamela Dwight Sedgwick to Theodore Sedgwick, 31 January 1789, 26 June 1790, 14 February 1791, Sedgwick III.

11. Pamela Dwight Sedgwick to Theodore Sedgwick, 4 December 1791, Sedgwick III.

12. Journals of Catharine Maria Sedgwick, 29 November 1829, C. M. Sedgwick Papers, Massachusetts Historical Society.

13. In her illuminating essay on the neglected dimensions of difference, Elsa Barkley Brown has analyzed the relational character of difference. See "'What Has Happened Here': The Politics of Difference in Women's History and Feminist Politics," *Feminist Studies* 18 (1992): 295-312. See also Nell Irvin Painter's introduction to *The Secret Eye: The Journal of Ella Gertrude Clanton Thomas, 1848-1889* (Chapel Hill: University of North Carolina Press, 1990), pp. 1-67.

14. Catharine Maria Sedgwick, "Slavery in New England," *Bentley's Miscellany* 34 (1853): 417-24. Freeman's challenge to the constitutionality of slavery is the subject of Arthur Zilversmit's "Quok Walker, Mumbet, and the Abolition of Slavery in Massachusetts," *William and Mary Quarterly*, 3rd ser. 25 (1968): 614-24. See also William O'Brien, "Did the Jennison Case Outlaw Slavery in Massachusetts," *William and Mary Quarterly*, 3rd ser. 17 (1960): 219-41; John D. Cushing, "The Cushing Court and the Abolition of Slavery in Massachusetts: More Notes on the Quok Walker Case," *American Journal of Legal History* 5 (1961): 118-44; and Elaine MacEacheren, "Emancipation of Slavery in Massachusetts: A Reexamination, 1770-1790," *Journal of Negro History* 55 (1970): 289-306.

15. Catharine Maria Sedgwick to Orville Dewey, 7 September 1841, in *Life and Letters of Catharine M. Sedgwick*, ed. Mary E. Dewey (New York: Harper & Brothers, 1872), p. 278.

16. Maris Vinovskis and Richard Bernard have demonstrated that only a tiny percentage of the population attended college before the Civil War. Basing their findings on federal censuses, they show that 0.8% were enrolled in 1840, 0.8% in 1850, and 1.0% in 1860. See Vinovskis and Bernard, "Beyond Catharine Beecher: Female Education in the Antebellum Period," *Signs: Journal of Women in Culture and Society* 3 (1978): 859. Lawrence Cremin addresses education more generally in *American Education: The Colonial Experience, 1607-1783* (New York: Harper & Row, 1970). Imaginative in approach and convincing in argument, Cremin's volume nonetheless suffers from a failure to distinguish between education offered females and males; only men receive extensive consideration.

17. Women's education is the subject of Thomas Woody, *A History of Women's Education in the*

United States (New York: Science Press, 1929). Published more than fifty years ago, Woody's two volumes remain the basic source, although they are more descriptive than analytic. Barbara Miller Solomon's insightful study *In The Company of Educated Women: A History of Women and Higher Education in America* (New Haven: Yale University Press, 1985) focuses on higher education.

18. Pamela Dwight Sedgwick to Theodore Sedgwick, 9 July 1798, Sedgwick III.

19. Catharine Maria Sedgwick to Pamela Dwight Sedgwick, 6 October 1803, Sedgwick IV.

20. Catharine Maria Sedgwick to Pamela Dwight Sedgwick, 11 November 1803, Sedgwick IV.

21. Catharine Maria Sedgwick to Theodore Sedgwick, 29 December 1804, Sedgwick IV.

22. Theodore Sedgwick to Catharine Maria Sedgwick, 23 April 1806, Sedgwick III.

23. Catharine Maria Sedgwick to Eliza Pomeroy, 1 December 1822, Sedgwick IV.

24. Catharine Maria Sedgwick to Orville Dewey, 12 June 1842, in *Life and Letters,* pp. 281-82.

25. Sedgwick, Journals, 9 July [1827].

26. Catharine Maria Sedgwick to Louisa Minot, 5 September 1841, Sedgwick IV.

27. Catharine Maria Sedgwick to Theodore Sedgwick II, 3 February 1813, Sedgwick III.

28. Catharine Maria Sedgwick to Robert Sedgwick, 2 July 1813, C. M. Sedgwick Papers; Catharine to Robert, 21 November 1819, C. M. Sedgwick Papers; Robert to Catharine, 20 November 1813, Sedgwick IV.

29. Sedgwick, Journals, 10 June [1827] and 31 December 1828.

30. Catharine Maria Sedgwick to Robert Sedgwick, December 1821, C. M. Sedgwick Papers; Robert to Catharine, 9 August 1822, Sedgwick IV; Catharine to Robert, 11 June 1823, C. M. Sedgwick Papers.

31. Sedgwick, Journals, 2 December 1837.

32. Charles Sedgwick to Catharine Maria Sedgwick, 2 April 1848, Sedgwick IV; Catharine to Charles, 2 February 1829, C. M. Sedgwick Papers.

33. Sedgwick, Journals, 18 May [1828], 5 August [1830], 2 December 1837, and 28 December 1854.

34. Sedgwick, Journals, 29 December 1834. She made another notable entry in this regard on 2 December 1837.

35. Sedgwick, Journals, 12 October 1836.

36. Sedgwick, Journals, 18 May [1828].

37. Harry Sedgwick to Catharine Maria Sedgwick, 22 June 1812, Sedgwick IV.

38. Theodore Sedgwick to Catharine Maria Sedgwick, 6 May 1822, *Life and Letters,* p. 152; Robert Sedg-

wick to Catharine, 17 July 1824, Sedgwick IV; Charles Sedgwick to Catharine, 28 March 1827, Sedgwick IV; Charles to Catharine, 21 May 1830, Sedgwick IV.

39. Catharine Maria Sedgwick to Louisa Minot, 26 November 1836, Sedgwick IV.

40. Catharine Maria Sedgwick to William Ellery Channing, 24 August 1837, C. M. Sedgwick Papers. The perspective of post-Revolutionary writers is the subject of Emory Elliott's *Revolutionary Writers: Literature and Authority in the New Republic, 1725-1810* (New York: Oxford University Press, 1982). Positing a crisis of authority as the signal experience of these writers, Elliott suggests that they forged an identity more in keeping with the democratizing tendencies of the early republic. The historical context for this development is provided in Joseph J. Ellis's *After the Revolution: Profiles of Early American Culture* (New York: W. W. Norton, 1979). Elliott and Ellis, each of whom considers only men, do not include gender as an analytical category. Gender is central to Cathy Davidson's highly suggestive study of these decades. See *Revolution and the Word: The Rise of the Novel in America* (New York: Oxford University Press, 1986), esp. pp. 3-79. I have discussed gender and its relationship to literary authority in antebellum America in *Private Woman, Public Stage: Literary Domesticity in Nineteenth-Century America* (New York: Oxford University Press, 1984), esp. pp. 111-214. Michael Warner analyzes the implications of transformations in print discourse and reading that took place in eighteenth-century America in *The Letters of the Republic: Publication and the Public Sphere in Eighteenth-Century America* (Cambridge: Harvard University Press, 1990). Richard Brown's study of the same phenomenon extends the analysis into the nineteenth century; see his *Knowledge Is Power: The Diffusion of Information in Early America, 1700-1865* (New York: Oxford University Press, 1989).

41. In a study published nearly sixty years ago, William Charvat identified how antebellum Americans linked the aesthetic and the moral when defining the purpose of culture. The importance that Unitarian leaders such as William Ellery Channing attached to this linkage has been explored by Daniel Walker Howe; Lawrence Buell has done the same for New England's writers more generally. The related tie between the moral and the feminine has received consideration from scholars studying women and antebellum reform. Lori Ginzberg's recent study of elite women's participation in organized benevolence is particularly insightful in this regard. Perhaps most notably, she has highlighted a strategy justifying female participation that is remarkably similar to Sedgwick's. See Charvat, *The Origins of American Critical Thought, 1810-1835* (Philadelphia: University of Pennsylvania Press,

1936); Howe, *The Unitarian Conscience: Harvard Moral Philosophy, 1805-1861* (Cambridge: Harvard University Press, 1970); Buell, *New England Literary Culture: From Revolution through Renaissance* (Cambridge: Cambridge University Press, 1986); Ginzberg, *Women and the Work of Benevolence: Morality, Politics and Class in the 19th-Century United States* (New Haven: Yale University Press, 1990).

42. Michael T. Gilmore's analysis of Emerson, Hawthorne, Thoreau, and Melville identifies a similar ambivalence in their reaction to popularity; they simultaneously sought to cultivate a larger and less elite public and to resist its claims. Donald M. Scott has examined the changing relationship between knowledge and the marketplace. No longer the possession of an elite, knowledge itself had become a commodity available for purchase by any literate American. Stow Persons's insightful study explores the implications of all these changes. See Gilmore, *American Romanticism and the Marketplace* (Chicago: University of Chicago Press, 1985), esp. pp. 1-17; Scott, "Knowledge and the Marketplace," in *The Mythmaking Frame of Mind: Social Imagination and American Culture,* ed. James Gilbert et al. (Belmont, Calif.: Wadsworth, 1992), pp. 99-112; Persons, *The Decline of American Gentility* (New York: Columbia University Press, 1973).

43. Sedgwick, Journals, 10 June 1827.

44. Sedgwick, Journals, 8 October [1834] and 9 August 1835.

45. Charles Sedgwick to Catharine Maria Sedgwick, [June 1837], Sedgwick IV.

T. Gregory Garvey (essay date 1994)

SOURCE: "Risking Reprisal: Catharine Sedgwick's *Hope Leslie* and the Legitimation of Public Action by Women," in *American Transcendental Quarterly,* Vol. 8, No. 4, December, 1994, pp. 287-98.

[*In the following essay, Garvey assesses* Hope Leslie *as a text that dramatizes the pressures of female authorship in nineteenth-century America while also displaying the advantages of expanding women's responsibility for moral values in the public arena.*]

Writing on the cusp of nineteenth-century activism for women's rights, Catharine Sedgwick played a central role in legitimating the presence of women on the literary stage. As recent critics of nineteenth-century women's writing have noted, Sedgwick serves as a kind of "breakthrough" figure, an author who holds the distinction of standing near the beginning of a line of writers that would dominate the antebellum era. Nina Baym comments on Sedgwick's unique position by pointing out that "Sedgwick's career was not typical, . . . She achieved considerable

prestige in her own time, was ranked with James Fenimore Cooper for her historical writing, and continued to produce actively for more than thirty years" (54). Also, Mary Kelley, whose interests are more psychological than Baym's, accounts for Sedgwick's ability to make peace with her own transgression of gender norms by arguing that Sedgwick "had been able to transgress traditional boundaries and enter the world beyond the home by denying to herself and to the world that she had committed any transgression at all" (287). Early in her career, though, Sedgwick's growing public acclaim created anxieties that had to be faced before they could be resolved or suppressed.

Sedgwick's major works appeared well before women authors came to dominate the marketplace in the 1850s. Her first novel, *A New-England Tale,* was published in 1822, and her second, *Redwood,* appeared two years later. The recognition that these novels received by the time that she published *Hope Leslie* in 1827 placed Sedgwick in the public spotlight. This publicity created private anxieties that Sedgwick was compelled to address even though she sought to minimize her own presence as a public figure. In her letters, repeated allusions to the tension that authorship created underscore the uniqueness of her position. Shortly after the publication of *A New-England Tale,* Sedgwick received a letter from her brother Harry which chided her to "have done with" the "womanish fears" that she had been expressing. In the letter, he assumes that his sister's fears were caused by the risk that her book would be unpopular and consoles her by claiming that "I don't know of anything which now gives me so much excitement as the certain prospect of your future eminence" (Dewey 152).

Ironically, this prospect of eminence seems to have been the main source of Sedgwick's fears. In an undated letter to a female friend, Sedgwick refers to her just-published novel: "I am more anxious than I can express to you to remain unknown, but, that, I fear, is impossible now" (154). Another shows Sedgwick dealing with her anxieties somewhat differently. Responding to an invitation to stay with friends in Boston during the summer of 1822, Sedgwick speaks directly of the pressures that her fame was creating:

> I should be delighted to visit Boston in the course of the summer, but I should neither go nor stay with any reference to my little tract. I protest against being supposed to make any pretensions as an author; my production is a very small affair any way, and only intended for the young and the humble and not for you erudite, pro-di-g-ous Boston folks.

> (156)

This brief passage reveals a variety of sensitivities; a knee-jerk resistance to being forced into the public spotlight, indignation at inflated expectations regarding her personality, and finally, a sarcastic self-justification that displays her wit even as it situates her motivation within a traditionally feminine realm.

All of these reactions represent different tactics for dealing with a changed relationship to the public realm. Kelley goes to the heart of the psychological aspect of this change by observing that a fundamental tension informing Sedgwick's novels is between her sense of social vulnerability and her desire to play a role in the life of the young nation. Kelley concludes that Sedgwick's ability to champion an expansion of woman's sphere beyond domestic settings was blunted by "deep inner restraints" that derived from her own socialization (*Private* 167). By Kelley's logic, these "inner" restraints ironically mirrored "outer" normative pressures and created the private psychological context in which Sedgwick strove to pursue her career as an author.

On an equally personal level, there was also a set of pressures that worked against general expectations of feminine passivity and submissiveness. In important ways, Sedgwick's impulse to participate in the public life of the nation reflects the experiences of her childhood. Sedgwick seems to have regarded public service as the duty, if not the birthright, of her family. Indeed, she perceived her own literary career as a manifestation of an ongoing family tradition. Her father, Theodore Sedgwick, had been Speaker of the House of Representatives during George Washington's presidency. Her three brothers were also active in national politics.

Even as the favorite daughter of a blue-blooded New England family though, Sedgwick knew that the forms of service open to her father and brothers were closed to her. In a searching letter that she sent to her father in 1812, she considers the different types of fulfillment society held out to men and women:

> I have regarded your life to find some rules of action to apply to my own, but I have relinquished the scrutiny with the same feeling of disappointment that the humble architect of a cottage would have, turning from the survey of a lofty palace, in which he had almost absurdly hoped to find a model for his little dwelling. A life dignified by usefulness, in which it has been the object of delight to do good, and the happiness to do it in an extended sphere, does, however, furnish some points of imitation for the most limited routine of domestic life. Wisdom and virtue are never at a loss for occasions and time for their exercise, and the same light that lightens the world is applied to individual use and gratification. You may benefit a nation, my dear papa, and I may improve the condition of a fellow-being.
>
> (Dewey 91)

This letter marks Sedgwick's emerging awareness that her own realm of action is "most limited." Not only do "lofty palace" and "little dwelling" serve as architectural metaphors which contrast her father's and her own spheres of action, but Sedgwick's musing throughout the letter conveys an uneasy tone, as if she is trying to reconcile herself to the circumscribed boundaries of domesticity when she clearly would prefer to act "in an extended sphere."

Working in a world where women authors had yet to fully justify their place on the shelves of booksellers, the relationship between Sedgwick's desire to act in public and the conventional impulses that this letter also reveals takes on a heightened significance. Sedgwick's conventionality stands in tension with the subtle dangers that would coincide with any attempt to participate in the public life of the nation. In *Hope Leslie,* this tension is displaced onto Sedgwick's heroines who balance their desire to act against their equally strong fears of male reprisal. Nonetheless, the two heroines of the novel, Hope Leslie and the Indian princess Magawisca, disregard social conventions and intervene in the political affairs of their societies. Though successful and morally justified, these interventions are met by a variety of punishments—Hope is placed under overlordship; Magawisca is imprisoned and physically maimed.

Most importantly, though, even as Sedgwick dramatizes the fears that were generated by her own role as a woman author, she also defines a set of conditions under which women's intervention in political affairs becomes not only legitimate, but necessary. By making a desire to avoid impending moral crises the dominant motivational impulse of her heroines, Sedgwick justifies their interventions into male realms of power. In effect, she asserts that the female conscience is as valid a source of social authority as is the legal power held by men. Thus through the effort to legitimate her own transgression of gender norms, *Hope Leslie* both dramatizes the pressure that authorship created and seeks to release those pressures by exploring the advantages that American culture stood to gain by expanding women's responsibility for moral values into the public arena.

Even her decision to locate the novel in seventeenth-century New England underscores this basic tension between her desire to serve the public and the internalized impulses which made such service appear inappropriate and potentially dangerous. In the Puritan society which she portrays, the terms of women's containment prefigure the conditions of early nineteenth-century America. The Puritan "helpmeet" was ideally pious, modest, submissive, and invisible to the public eye (Ulrich 5-10). The elements of true womanhood in the nineteenth century that Barbara Welter describes in her classic essay almost duplicate these criteria. Welter defines the "four cardinal virtues" of femininity in Sedgwick's age as piety, purity, submissiveness, and domesticity (20ff). Nonetheless, by portraying her women characters as civic-minded individuals who are unjustly persecuted as witches and spies, Sedgwick also revises the history of Puritan New England. In this way Sedgwick not only provides herself with the safety of an historically distant stage on which to investigate the tensions that were embedded in the world of her experience, but also reinvents the earlier context by redefining the motivations that impelled her seventeenth-century women characters to transgress the boundaries of acceptable behavior. Despite the psychological inhibitions that her own socialization imposed on her, Sedgwick thus makes *Hope*

Leslie an instrument of social progress. In it, she models the terms on which women might legitimately enter the political arena.

Using the war between the Puritans and the Pequod Indians to establish a background of social disorder, the basic struggle of *Hope Leslie* is a contest over the foundations on which legitimate authority ought to rest. Though the patriarchs of both cultures hold legal authority, their willingness to make moral compromises in the name of political expediency precipitates social crises in each society. As a counterbalance, Sedgwick establishes conscience as a structuring principle in the moral economies of both the Puritan and the Pequod communities. The role that conscience plays as a motivation to action is introduced in the prefatory scenes of the novel. Hope's adoptive father, Fletcher, emigrates to Massachusetts Bay during the mid-seventeenth-century English civil wars in order to avoid complicity in what he considers an unjust conflict. He then establishes a homestead on the wooded outskirts of Boston where Hope, the orphaned daughter of his first love, is placed in his care. The pastoral home that they establish, though, is disturbed by the outbreak of war. Magawisca, the Indian Princess who had been captured by the Puritans, is placed in the Fletcher household as a servant. While Fletcher and Hope are in Boston, his homestead is attacked by Magawisca's father, Chief Mononotto, who rescues his daughter, but also kills Fletcher's wife and infant son. Fletcher's surviving son, Everell, is taken hostage by the Indians. It is against this chaotic background that Hope and Magawisca form an alliance and work to preserve the moral integrity of their two communities.

Though the cultural differences between Hope and Magawisca's experience are central features of the novel, Sedgwick makes little distinction between the impulses on which the leaders of the Puritan and Indian societies act. However, she does distinguish the impulses that motivate action in men from those that motivate action in women. As various intrigues develop, political, rather than moral or ethical considerations lead Governor Winthrop of Boston and Chief Mononotto of the Pequod Indians to make potentially disastrous errors in judgment. Winthrop's first concern is to preserve the established norms of the Puritan community. He contrives to "put jesses on" the unruly Hope by arranging her betrothal to the rakish Sir Gardiner. Later, Winthrop subordinates ethics to the exigencies of practical politics by insisting that Magawisca be placed in prison, even though he understands that she might die as a result. Within the Pequod community, Chief Mononotto is equally guilty of misusing legal authority. Mononotto cynically decides to sacrifice his captive, Everell Fletcher, as a means of silencing critics within his own tribe: "Brothers," says Mononotto, "My people have told me I bore a woman's heart towards the enemy. Ye shall see. I will pour out this English boy's blood to the last drop, and give his flesh and bones to the dogs and wolves" (92).

The threats which male authorities pose to the moral order of both communities ultimately compel women to inter-

vene on behalf of the innocent. Sedgwick's portrait of a public realm in which political considerations come before moral ones prepares the way for woman's entrance not only onto the public stage, but into the realm of politics. The conditions under which Hope and Magawisca intercede in public affairs, though, make it clear that their motivation is not a desire to participate in public life for its own sake. Rather, they are motivated by a desire to redress the moral inequities that the warring patriarchs create. Hope, for example, takes "counsel only in her heart," which tells her that "the rights of innocence [are] paramount to all other rights" (120).

Thus, even as Sedgwick uses conscience to justify openly subversive action by women, she draws on conventional beliefs by ascribing the motivation for women's action to a morally driven desire to resolve crises (Bardes and Gossett 22). Women's intervention is given a regulatory and reactive function. It only becomes legitimate when legally constituted authority fails to function properly. But despite its reactive quality, Sedgwick sees woman's conscience as an authoritative source of public justice, the court of last appeal which authorizes Hope's intervention in political affairs.

Hope and Magawisca's interventions serve to dissipate the threats that are created by potentially tragic situations. As the agents of crisis resolution, they work to reassert the primacy of moral justice over political expediency. In a study of romance conventions in this novel, Michael Davitt Bell observed that Northrop Frye's definition of comic drama captures the pattern through which Sedgwick compels moral/female authority to struggle against legal/male authority: "At the beginning of the [novel] the obstructing characters are in charge of the [novel's] society, and the audience recognizes that they are usurpers. At the end of the [novel] the device in the plot that brings hero and heroine together causes a new society to crystallize around the hero[ine]" (163). Throughout *Hope Leslie* the patriarchs function as "obstructing characters" threatening to reduce their communities to moral chaos as they pursue political ends. This danger demands that someone from outside the legal power structure intervene to ensure that moral standards will be upheld. The "device in the plot" which ultimately "causes a new society to crystallize around the hero[ine]" is a pattern of direct public action by women.

In one episode, Hope literally saves the life of an Indian herbalist who is unjustly sentenced to hang because the Puritan court concluded that only through sorcery could she have saved the victim of a rattlesnake bite. The herbalist Nelema views her act of mercy altruistically, musing "I, the last of my race, [am] bidden to heal a servant in the house of our enemies" (104). Hope perceives the injustice of the old woman's condemnation, but when she confronts magistrate Pynchon, the judge scolds her as "forward" and admonishes Hope to leave Nelema's fate to the legal authorities. Yet Magistrate Pynchon's refusal to give her voice in the process of "justice" fails to render Hope ineffectual. Rather, it compels her to realize the "rights of innocence" through subterfuge. She masterminds a jailbreak and sets Nelema free.

In addition to illustrating the justificatory force of conscience, this clandestine rescue also illustrates the reactive nature of Sedgwick's legitimation of intervention by women. Although Hope takes the law into her own hands, she does so only after all conventional means of rescuing Nelema have been exhausted. Sedgwick thus implicitly casts the context in which women can enter the public realm as a breakdown in the functioning of women's moral influence. By Sedgwick's logic, moral insight is rooted in woman's conscience. This conscience ideally functions to structure interaction between men and women such that standards of moral, ethical, and social behavior pass from women into the male subconscious. Being thus continually "influenced" by the women around them, men are to embody the content of the female conscience in the structure of public institutions. According to this schema, women's authority transcends categories of public and private because men become the vehicle for extending female authority throughout public institutions. Ideally, then, women's intervention in the public realm would become unnecessary.

However, in **Hope Leslie,** the patriarchs have become corrupted by the very public realm that they are responsible for managing. The link that carries women's influence into the public arena has broken down, and women must repair it lest the entire structure collapse. The Nelema episode is typical of the pattern that Sedgwick establishes: a problematic exercise of legal authority by the patriarchs threatens to rupture the moral order of the community, whereupon one of the novel's heroines risks her own punishment by circumventing male authority and independently bringing the demands of her conscience into reality. It is in these moments of social crisis that Sedgwick's reliance on conscience as a legitimation of political action comes into sharp focus.

Aptly enough, Sedgwick chooses legal trials as the settings in which she dramatizes the Puritan authorities' inability to cope with situations where moral and legal justice are in conflict. The crisis situations that emerge from misuses of authority in **Hope Leslie** function to call the legitimacy of the established social order into question and create what Jurgen Habermas refers to as a "legitimation crisis." In practice, Habermas asserts, "If governmental crisis management fails, it lags behind practical demands. The penalty for this failure is withdrawal of legitimation. Thus, the scope for action [by the established government] contracts precisely at those moments when it needs to be drastically expanded" (69).

For example, when the Puritans put Magawisca on trial for espionage, the court becomes enmeshed in a thicket of conflicting loyalties. The villainous Sir Gardiner proves willing to lie under a Protestant oath, but he balks at lying under a Catholic oath. Reverend John Elliot eloquently ar-

gues that the law of mercy should rule. But a magistrate from the bench contends that the court should not stay "the course of justice" (293). Even though the magistrates scrupulously follow all conventional legal procedures, they prove incapable of discerning truth from falsehood in order to arrive at the appropriate verdict of "not guilty." The narrator sums up the confusion between legal and moral justice: "Their reason, guided by the best lights they possessed, decided against her—the voice of nature crying out for her" (294). The court, being unable to arrive at a verdict, sends Magawisca to languish in prison until she can be retried. In this situation of paralysis, Hope intervenes to free Magawisca and resolve the crisis.

Thus Sedgwick manipulates the legitimation crisis that her male protagonists create so that legal resolution becomes impossible. In such situations of legal paralysis, moral action by Hope and Magawisca, despite its risks, becomes the instrument of final justice. In effect, female intervention is justified as both a moral and a practical necessity.

These interventions, though, are paid for both by fear of male reprisal and by actual punishment. The competing demands that social prescription and conscience place on Sedgwick's heroines reflect a conflict between external expectations and internal impulses that mirrors contradictions inherent in the polarization of society into private and public realms. Out of this polarization emerges the primary practical dilemma which Hope and Magawisca must resolve, a dilemma that dramatizes the conflicting aspiration and trepidation that Sedgwick felt in her own consciousness. In the seventeenth-century world that Sedgwick reconstructs, as in the New England of her day, external normative forces demanded that women be passive. Yet if women were to heed the voice of conscience, they would be compelled to intervene. Still, as the dangers that Hope and Magawisca face make clear, when women respond to the demands of their consciences, they risk becoming victims themselves.

Each time that Hope or Magawisca violates the boundaries of her place as a Puritan or Indian maiden, she risks punishment not because of the harm her actions create, but because she crosses the line into traditionally male realms of power. Magistrate Pynchon, for example, recognizes that Hope's clandestine rescue of Nelema poses a greater threat to existing social norms than the Indian's "sorcery": "While [Pynchon] easily reconciled himself to the loss of the prisoner, he felt the necessity of taking instant and efficient measures to subdue to becoming deference and obedience, the rash and lawless girl, who had dared to interpose between justice and its victim" (121). The reactions against female action that Sedgwick attributes to her male characters imply a fear of reprisal that underscores the vulnerability of all women who presume to intervene in public affairs. Magistrate Pynchon's reaction to Nelema's escape can be regarded as a reflection of Sedgwick's own sense of vulnerability as one of her nation's first women novelists.

The danger of male reprisal that Sedgwick's heroines encounter takes its most extreme form as Magawisca subverts the summary trial and condemnation of Everell Fletcher. Everell's execution has "the air of hasty preparation" as the Pequod gather "to witness what they believed to be" the course of "exact and necessary justice" (91). Yet Everell is an innocent captive, and ironically, of all the Puritan characters, he is the most sympathetic to the Pequod cause. Sedgwick makes it clear that the execution is politically motivated and manifestly unjust. The prospect of this crime compels Magawisca to risk her own life in order to save Everell. She leaps in front of the condemned man as her father's tomahawk swings toward Everell's neck. The tragic result is—as Sedgwick phrases it—that her arm is "lopped" off.

Like her heroines, Sedgwick legitimated her own public career by portraying herself as a moral counselor. But for a woman to insinuate her authority beyond the range of passive, domestic influence by projecting a voice onto the public stage was still a politically radical act. Joanne Dobson sums up the terms of this conceptual division between the private and public spheres by noting that mid-nineteenth-century opinion ascribed to women, "the unique and awesome, yet seductively flattering, responsibility of mediating moral values in a morally deficient society, and that their divinely ordained arena for doing so was a domestic one" (224). One wishes that Dobson had chosen "but" rather than "and" to introduce the final clause of her sentence. For it is this geographical restriction that generated Sedgwick's "deep inner restraints" as well as her anxiety concerning direct male reprisal for public action.

Changing social conditions added to the delicacy of Sedgwick's position on the margin of both the private and the public realms. For during the period of Sedgwick's rise to prominence, barriers preventing women from circumventing traditional norms were being vigorously debated. Under the pressure of urbanization, industrialization, and democratization, Jacksonian Americans were compelled to revaluate a host of legal, social, and domestic conventions. Many of these had traditionally regulated gender relations (Smith-Rosenberg 79-87). As this period of upheaval progressed, ideals of womanhood came into more and more obvious conflict with the actual conditions of women's lives. Women were entering the public realm as factory operatives, authors, and advocates for moral reform. But they were also being encouraged to marry and subsume their identities into those of their husbands. Once married, women still could not sign contracts, nor could they control their own earnings or property. Given the contradictions between the conditions of women's lives and prevailing cultural demands that women remain both passive and dependent, one can see how the triumphs and punishments of her heroines enact Sedgwick's desire to loosen restrictions on female action. One can also sense the dangers that Sedgwick would have perceived in this same desire.

As a single woman, Sedgwick sought to balance these tensions in her own life, constructing an identity that had both private and public components. Not only did her public career as an author span thirty years, but she approxi-

mated a conventional private life by maintaining close connections with the families of her brothers. Although striking this balance between private and public lives allowed her an unusual degree of personal independence, it also entailed an almost hypersensitive awareness of her own anomalous position within the social structure. Kelley considers Sedgwick's choice to remain single but also stay within the orbit of her siblings' families an "effective compromise" which permitted her to maintain both "intimacy and autonomy" ("Woman" 213). One wonders, though, how effective this compromise could have been. Even though it seems to have been a source of genuine happiness in Sedgwick's life, it also must have created a set of tensions that revolved around the act of maintaining the balance between autonomy and intimacy. Her brothers' willingness to accept her into their households provided Sedgwick with a high level of security, but by living in such close proximity to their families, she must also have been acutely conscious that her position was both marginal and vulnerable. There are times when she seemed to feel the need to withdraw in order to gain a degree of distance from her own conflicting desires. When her brother Robert married, for example, Sedgwick felt compelled to temporarily withdraw from the family circle in order to make his affection "less Necessary" (Dewey 160).

The delicate and imperfect balance that Sedgwick sustained between her private and public presences is reflected in the nuanced contradictions through which Sedgwick resolves various plot lines in *Hope Leslie.* Despite her justification of women's presence in political affairs, Sedgwick almost certainly would have denied that *Hope Leslie* was seeking to transform prevailing constructions of womanhood. The advice that she would give to young women in *Means and Ends* and *Live and Let Live* bears witness to the continuing conventionality of her attitudes. Indeed, if her later writings can be taken as an indication, she became increasingly conservative during the 1850s and 1860s.

In many respects it is this tension between Sedgwick's competing impulses to accept and reject traditional constructions of femininity that gives *Hope Leslie* enduring value. Sedgwick's desire to resolve this tension by imagining women who could integrate the private and public realms is reflected in the futures that she envisions for the characters in the novel. In Hope, Sedgwick seems to provide the model for a new, woman-centered, social order. Hope marries Everell but does not then recede into domestic oblivion. Instead, she incorporates most of the community into her family. Minor characters such as Mister Craddock and Dame Grafton are accepted as "life-members" of the new household. Even Barnaby Tuttle, a jailer Hope tricked to gain Magawisca's freedom, is given an "annual stipend from our heroine" so that he could pass his old age "versifying psalms." Hope thus becomes the moral—and economic—center of a small community. In essence, the public sphere is subsumed into the private, where Hope's "influence" can reach beyond Everell and pervade the entire community.

But is it really Hope who prefigures the future? Sedgwick gives the last word in the novel to Hope's cousin Esther Downing, the "pattern maiden of the republic." The future Sedgwick imagines for Esther complicates the vision with which she completes her picture of Hope. Esther forgoes marriage and symbolically sacrifices private intimacy in order to bestow her "disinterested devotion" on all "mankind" (350). This resolution is especially telling as it is a projection of the conditions of Sedgwick's own life as a single woman and a writer. In this scenario, the private woman is co-opted by the public sphere where she can serve as moral ballast. In neither Hope's nor Esther's case, then, does Sedgwick's expansion of women's moral authority finally break down the boundary which was a primary source of her own anxiety as a writer, the boundary between the "extended sphere" of the public realm and the "limited routine" of the private realm. These resolutions, such as they are, suggest the depth of Sedgwick's ambivalence regarding the transgressive nature of her own chosen career. Ultimately, they suggest the irreconcilability of the tensions that Sedgwick experienced as an actor on both the public and private stages.

Though Sedgwick is understandably incapable of even imagining a world where women can hold equal influence in their houses and in the town hall, she does identify a set of conditions that justify women's presence in political affairs. However, in 1827, despite the legitimating power of woman's conscience, even legitimate intervention does not preclude the possibility of reprisal. Further, according to Sedgwick's vision, the woman who hopes to affect morals in an "extended sphere" must either accept the community into her household—as Hope does—or she must sacrifice domestic pleasures and have her moral influence coopted by the public realm—as Esther does. Although woman's conscience offers a legitimate motivation for public action, in practice, Sedgwick sees it enacted only through secret circumventions of the boundary between the private and public realms—a boundary that compels the demands of conscience to struggle against deeply seated fears of retribution.

Works Cited

Bardes, Barbara Ann, and Suzanne Gossett. *Declarations of Independence: Women and Political Power in Nineteenth-Century American Fiction.* New Brunswick: Rutgers University Press, 1990.

Baym, Nina. *Woman's Fiction: A Guide to Novels by and about Women in America, 1820-1870.* Ithaca: Cornell University Press, 1982.

Bell, Michael Davitt. "Historical Romance Convention in Catharine Sedgwick's *Hope Leslie.*" American Quarterly 22 (1970): 313-321.

Berg, Barbara. *The Remembered Gate: Origins of American Feminism.* New York: Oxford University Press, 1978.

Dewey, Mary E., ed. *Life and Letters of Catharine Maria Sedgwick.* New York: Harper and Brothers, 1871.

Dobson, Joanne. "The Hidden Hand: Subversion of Cultural Ideology in Three Mid-Nineteenth Century American Women's Novels." *American Quarterly* 33 (1986): 224.

Frye, Northrop. *Anatomy of Criticism: Four Essays.* Princeton: Princeton University Press, 1957.

Habermas, Jurgen. *Legitimation Crisis.* Trans. Thomas McCarthy. Boston: Beacon Press, 1975.

Kelley, Mary. *Private Woman, Public Stage: Literary Domesticity in Nineteenth-Century America.* New York: Oxford University Press, 1984.

————. "A Woman Alone: Catharine Maria Sedgwick's Spinsterhood in Nineteenth Century America." *New England Quarterly* 51 (1978): 209-225.

Sedgwick, Catharine. *Hope Leslie.* New Brunswick: Rutgers University Press, 1987 [1827].

————. *A New-England Tale; or, Sketches of New-England Character and Manners.* New York: E. Bliss and White, 1822.

————. *Redwood; A Tale.* New York: E. Bliss and White, 1824.

————. *Means and Ends; or, Self-Training.* Boston: Marsh, Capen, Lyon and Webb, 1840.

————. *Live and Let Live; or, Domestic Service Illustrated.* New York: Harper and Brothers, 1837.

Smith-Rosenberg, Carol. *Disorderly Conduct: Visions of Gender in Victorian America.* New York: Alfred A. Knopf, 1985.

Ulrich, Laura. *Good Wives: Image and Reality in the lives of Women in Northern New England, 1650-1750.* New York: Alfred A. Knopf, 1982.

Welch, Richard E. Theodore Sedgwick. *Federalist.* Middletown, Connecticut: Wesleyan University Press, 1965.

Welter, Barbara. *Dimity Convictions: The American Woman in the Nineteenth Century.* Athens: Ohio University Press, 1976.

Maria Lamonaca (essay date 1995)

SOURCE: "'She Could Make a Cake as Well as Books . . .': Catharine Sedgwick, Anna Jameson, and the Construction of the Domestic Intellectual," in *Women's Writing,* Vol. 2, No. 3, 1995, pp. 235-49.

[*In the following essay, Lamonaca examines and compares the impact of Catharine Sedgwick's and Anna Jameson's "domestic advice manuals" and "conduct books" on nineteenth century women.*]

> . . . *I resolved to form Dora's mind.*

I began immediately. When Dora was very childish . . . I tried to be grave—and disconcerted her, and myself too. I talked to her on the subjects which occupied my thoughts; and I read Shakespeare to her—and fatigued her to the last degree. I accustomed myself to giving her, as if it were quite casually, little scraps of useful information, or sound opinion—and she started from them when I let them off, as if they had been crackers. No matter how incidentally or naturally I endeavored to form my little wife's mind, I could not help seeing that she always had an instinctive perception of what I was about, and became prey to the keenest apprehensions. In particular, it was clear to me, that she thought Shakespeare a terrible fellow . . .

(Charles Dickens, *David Copperfield*)

This description of David Copperfield's attempts to "form" his wife's mind highlights issues of female education in Victorian society, particularly anxieties over the preparation—or lack thereof—of young women for marriage and motherhood. Dora, deprived of the benefits of motherly instruction, wreaks havoc on the Copperfield household. She can neither cook, nor manage servants, nor maintain the household accounts. Copperfield's gift of a domestic advice manual—a "Cookery-book"—comes to naught; it functions mainly as a perch for a dog. Most troubling to Copperfield, however, is not Dora's domestic ineptitude, but rather her unsuitability as an intellectual companion. While mentally accomplished, highly literate Victorian women were often derided as "strong-minded women" and "bluestockings," an opposing current of thought attempted to justify female intellectual prowess. Such writers as Sarah Ellis viewed the mental cultivation of a woman essential to her calling as a future wife; the educated woman would be "a companion who will raise the tone of his mind . . . from low anxieties and vulgar cares."[1] This paper attempts to examine the nineteenth-century construction of an ideal, highly literate woman—woman as accomplished reader—particularly as it is presented in domestic advice manuals and conduct books of the era. This inquiry will focus on two conduct books, *Means and Ends; or Self-Training* (1840) by Catharine Maria Sedgwick, and *Characteristics of Women* (1832) by Anna Jameson. While the texts themselves reveal much about contemporary thought on the subject of literate/intellectual women, equally revealing are the motives and circumstances behind Sedgwick's and Jameson's work.

An especially important consideration in this study is how Sedgwick's and Jameson's conduct manuals "market" literacy. What is their conception of female literacy, and why do they endorse it? A major question posed by historical literacy studies, as Karl Kaestle phrases it, is: "Does literacy have a liberating or constraining effect on individuals' lives?"[2] Do Jameson and Sedgwick portray literacy as a means of self-discipline or as a strategy of empowerment? It is all too easy, it seems, to label conduct manuals solely as an example of the "constraining effect" of literacy. A close reading of Sedgwick's and Jameson's books, however, reveals a multidimensional construction of literacy, one which seems to embody the personal concerns and ambivalences of the authors themselves.

The fact that Victorian conduct manuals *encouraged* literate practices in women often becomes obscured by other aspects of the genre. Much contemporary scholarship emphasizes the repressive nature of these books as a means of social control. "Although a female genre, often written by women and directed at female readers," states Nancy Armstrong, "conduct books of the eighteenth and nineteenth centuries . . . were attuned to the economic interests that they designated as the domain of the male."[3] Both Nancy Armstrong and Mary Poovey interpret the conduct book genre as an ideological tool of the rising middle class. The ideal woman of the conduct book, a submissive household angel, supported her husband's endeavors in the workplace, thereby affirming capitalist values.[4] Viewed in strictly economic terms, the conduct book becomes a means of commodifying women. It defines a woman whose "sexual identity has been suppressed by a class that values her chiefly for material reasons."[5] These arguments are entirely plausible; what, after all, could be more repressive to women than the cult of the Household Angel? An important consideration, however, is whether conduct books, despite their political implications, advanced the abilities or position of Victorian women in any respect.[6]

The view of conduct books as a means of social control emphasizes their role in regulating women's literacy, restricting and silencing the woman reader/writer. These books discussed, often in exhaustive detail, what specifically women should and should not read. Along with the spread of literacy in the nineteenth century, Carla Peterson points out, a persistent suspicion of books as moral "poison" remained embedded in European culture.[7] Fictional literature—novels and romances—posed the greatest threat to the highly impressionable minds of young women. Thomas Broadhurst, in his *Advice to Young Ladies on the Improvement of the Mind and Conduct of Life* (1810), warns against the woman who "to the culpable neglect of the most important obligations, is daily absorbed by philosophic and literary speculations, or soaring aloft amid the enchanted regions of fiction and romance."[8] Some writers, like Broadhurst, felt that imaginative literature drew women away from household duties; others worried that it gave women false, deceptively glamorous views of the world. Others condemned the novel—with its scenes of passion—as a threat to the purity and innocence of young girls.[9] Conduct manuals devoted less attention, it seems, to the regulation of writing practices, but some issued admonitions against the "literary woman." The woman writer, once published, abandoned the private sphere and immodestly thrust herself into the public arena. Hannah More, *Strictures on the Modern System of Female Education* (1799), argues that women's knowledge "is not often like the learning of men, to be reproduced in some literary composition, nor ever in any learned profession, but comes out in conduct."[10]

Conduct manuals simultaneously encouraged and restrained women's reading practices, for "reading was once the most useful and the most dangerous way to take up a woman's time."[11] A woman could read romance not els, and neglect her housework or she could read the Bible, and instruct her children. Reading, furthermore, was an activity which kept the woman within the confines of her home, and out of the contaminating public sphere. It could (as the immense popularity of conduct books shows) instruct women in appropriate feminine behaviour and duties, and thus contribute to the formation of the private, domestic sphere. Undoubtedly, what was considered "acceptable" reading for women varied, but conduct manuals frequently recommended the Bible, devotional works, poetry, various forms of non-fiction, and certain "polite novels" by "lady novelists."[12] Conduct books, although strictly regulating women's reading, at once encouraged it as a duty. Typically, they justified women's reading as education for marriage and motherhood. Sarah Newton considers such mixed messages in regard to women's literacy, ultimately, as restrictive ones. "These anti-intellectual messages," she states; "even when they seem contradictory, become powerful arguments for the woman to focus her curiosity within rigorously guarded role limitations."[13] While many conduct books undoubtedly sought to limit women's intellectual development, elements of Catharine Sedgwick's and Anna Jameson's works seem to encourage women to cultivate interests in matters outside the domestic sphere. These writers, in many respects, embraced highly conventional views of women's place in society. At the same time, however, they evince a keen awareness of social inequalities between the sexes, and argue for improvements in women's education and social status. This current of thought, arguably, contributed to the growth of a female intellectual elite which sought social and political reform. Furthermore, later in the century, educational reformers applied conduct book ideology—the belief that educated women made better wives and mothers—to their appeals for higher education for women. The conduct book ideal of the literate woman, therefore, was not a liberating end in itself for women, but part of a gradual process of social enlightenment and reform.

This paper's assessment of Jameson's and Sedgwick's books differs from the general perception of conduct books as overwhelmingly conservative in character. Conduct books, Newton argues, stubbornly resisted the growing current of female political activism in the mid- to late-nineteenth century. "As women become more vocal and political," she states, "American conduct writers continue to find both mission and market . . . these later writers find that their task is to affirm and defend it [women's traditional place in society]."[14] Although conduct books did, to a large extent, serve a conservative political agenda through their construction of a conventional feminine ideal, many conduct book writers—by virtue of their identity as female authors—were unconventional women who upheld progressive ideas. In the early nineteenth century, women were overwhelmingly denied "access to the means of literary production."[15] Women such as Sedgwick and Jameson, then, as published women writers, were through this fact alone quite extraordinary. Catharine Maria Sedgwick (1789-1867), an American novelist ranked in her day with leading male writers, published ***Means and Ends; or Self-***

Training in 1840. Anna Jameson (1794-1860), a British writer, wrote essays, art criticism and travel narratives, along with the 1832 *Characteristics of Women*. These two writers make for an interesting parallel study. Although Sedgwick was American and Jameson British, the writings of each were well received in the other's native country. The women, only 5 years apart in age, were contemporaries and personal friends. Each greatly admired the work of the other; they met in 1837 during Anna's trip to the USA and Canada, and kept up a correspondence thereafter. Both Sedgwick and Jameson were, in many respects, nonconformists to the Victorian feminine ideal. Their education, while largely informal and self-directed, was unusually broad for a woman of the period. Both received extraordinary support from male relatives in pursuing their literary work. While marriage and motherhood was the ideal, both women remained independent—Sedgwick through choice, and Jameson by way of a failed marriage. Although Sedgwick and Jameson, in their books, constructed a female intellectual along the lines of polarized gender roles, each called for the improvement of women's social and political status.

Catharine Maria Sedgwick was born in 1789 in Stockholm, Massachusetts. She was the third of six children in a highly distinguished family. Her father, Theodore Sedgwick, served in the Massachusetts legislature, both houses of Congress, and sat on the bench of the Massachusetts Supreme Court. Her family life, it seems, was somewhat troubled by her mother's recurrent bouts of depression and mental illness. Sedgwick was therefore left much to herself as a child; later, she lamented the "want of female supervision" in her early years. Perhaps this lack inspired Sedgwick to act, through her writing, as a moral guide to other young women. Sedgwick also expressed regret over the inadequacy of her formal education. Of the district schools she attended, she states, "Our minds were not weakened by too much study—reading, spelling, and Dwight's Geography were the only paths of knowledge into which we were led."[16] At the age of 11 Sedgwick attended a boarding school in Albany where she learned a smattering of "accomplishments"—dancing and French.

Although Sedgwick deplored the inadequacy of her formal education, she appreciated her home schooling. "I was reared in an atmosphere of high intelligence," she remarks. "My father had uncommon mental vigor. So had my brothers. Their daily habits, and pursuits, and pleasures were intellectual, and I naturally imbibed from them a kindred taste."[17] Sedgwick's father regularly read Hume, Shakespeare, Cervantes and Hudibras to the family. Sedgwick also recalls reading *Rollin's Ancient History* to herself at the tender age of 10. "My school life was a waste," Sedgwick concludes, "my home life my only instruction."[18] She also read less scholarly texts. Another passage from her letters states: "I read constantly, *but* chiefly novels [italics mine]. I remember little of that winter, but falling romantically in love with a handsome young man . . . It was the fancy of a few weeks of a girl of eleven! I knew him afterwards, a cold selfish but still handsome man."[19] Here

Sedgwick seems to imply that novel-reading had a direct effect on her foolish fancies; she would have behaved differently, the reader infers, if she had known better.

In the course of her literary career, Sedgwick wrote numerous didactic tales and sketches, but she is best known for her six novels: *A New England Tale* (1822), *Redwood* (1824), *Hope Leslie* (1827), *Clarence* (1830), *The Linwoods* (1835), and *Married or Single?* (1847). Sedgwick, initially, published with reluctance; probably she wished to avoid public notoriety as a female author. Interestingly, her four brothers had the greatest influence on her writing. Charles, Harry, Theodore and Robert praised Catharine's work, and conducted transactions with her publishers. In 1821, Catharine wrote to a friend, "My dear brother Theodore makes a most extravagant estimate of my powers. It is one thing to write a spurt of a letter, and another to write a book."[20] Shortly afterwards, Harry persuaded Catharine to expand a religious tract she had written—originally intended for Sunday School instruction—into a full-length novel. The result, *A New England Tale,* was published anonymously in 1822, but her identity became known in due course. From the very beginning, the public received her work enthusiastically.

Although Sedgwick wrote only a few works explicitly designed as conduct or advice manuals, "everything she wrote," states Mary Walsh, "had a lesson to convey."[21] She seemed to view herself less as a writer of imaginative literature than as an educator and moral guide. After the publication of a domestic manual in 1837, *Live and Let Live*—a discussion on how to secure competent servants—Sedgwick writes, "I thank heaven that I am not now working for the poor and perishable rewards of literary ambition . . . Neither pride nor humility should withhold us from the work to which we are clearly "sent." . . . There is much sin from mere ignorance . . ."[22] One Reverend Dr Channing praised Sedgwick for this same book; in a letter to her he writes, "Thousands will be the better and happier for it; thousands, as they read it, will feel their deficiencies, and resolve to do better."[23] This seems like unduly exalted praise for a manual on domestic help, but the sanctity of the Victorian home, after all, was at stake. It should be no surprise, furthermore, that Sedgwick's novels are highly moralistic as well. This moralism, argues Walsh, ultimately compromises Sedgwick's writings. "The ever prevailing shadow of didacticism is over her work," she states, "and for this reason alone her novels make no appeal to the modern reader."[24]

In the first chapter of *Means and Ends; or Self-Training,* Sedgwick clearly states her authorial intent. She means to address an audience of fellow "young countrywomen," 10 to 16 years in age: "I have written the following pages to aid you in your *self-education* . . . [The book] has been written with a deep interest for your welfare and improvement, and I should be sorry if it proved a total failure" (pp. 10, 12).[25] Sedgwick defines her conception of education for women: "It is not enough, believe me, to get hard lessons in arithmetic, grammar, and geography, French,

Italian, and Music . . . More than all this is required to make you a good wife and mother" (p. 16). Although Sedgwick stresses the necessary moral dimension of a woman's training, she encourages intellectual development as well. In Chapter XI, "What to Read, How to Read," Sedgwick eloquently praises the book: "What is a book, my young friends? Is it not a cabinet which contains the most interesting creation of God, the mind of a human being, a portion of the Divine mind?" (p. 222). She discusses the importance of reading in the formation of good character. "Resolve to devote a portion of every day, for a year to come, to reading," she advises (p. 226).

Sedgwick spends a goodly portion of the chapter advising what girls should and should not read, but "The selection of books is *next* in importance to a love for reading" (p. 226, italics mine). Clearly, she stresses the importance of reading first and attempts to regulate it only afterwards. Interestingly, Sedgwick—a writer of didactic tales herself—actually discourages the reading of religious tracts. Many are badly written, she feels, and thus, "You are attracted by a story, and, to get a little pure gold, you receive a great deal of dross" (p. 227). Rather, she encourages her audience to read the Bible daily. In addition, she recommends histories of the USA, travel narratives, good biographies, and certain works of "English Literature," including Shakespeare. "In the wide department of fictitious writing," she warns, "let your consciences restrain and direct your inclination . . ." (p. 229). Sedgwick, however, gives her readers a few hints. "You have no excuse for reading the profligate and romantic novels of the last century, or the no less profligate and far more insidious romances of the present day, such as Mr Bulwer's, and the trash that fills the circulating libraries" (p. 232). She concludes the chapter with advice on the care of texts, including the strict rejoinder, "Do not wet the fingers to turn over the leaves of books!" (p. 232).

Although Sedgwick, like many of her contemporaries, attempts to regulate women's reading practices, she nonetheless encourages her audience to read widely, educate themselves, and develop critical thinking skills. Furthermore, in her final chapter, "Might Makes Right," she addresses the issue of women's rights. Sedgwick condemns those who agitate for equality with men. "It has been well and truly said," she states, "that when a woman claims the rights of a man, she surrenders her own rights" (p. 253). Sedgwick has no wish to see women voting or sitting in legislatures, but she does acknowledge the need to improve women's lot in society. In particular, she mentions laws which deny a married woman's right to hold property, and prevent a separated woman from taking custody of her own children.

Sedgwick proposes that women attain certain rights not by demanding them outright, but by educating themselves and thereby proving themselves worthy. "Women as yet, for the most part, have exercised but half their powers." Sedgwick expresses confidence that if women but prove their rational and intellectual capabilities, men will grant them their rights. Hence her chapter title, "Might Makes Right." While this view seems anything but enlightened in the present day, it was, arguably, progressive for the times. Although Sedgwick advocates different duties for men and women, she never ranks women's intellectual abilities below those of men. Furthermore, she encourages women to cultivate an interest in topics traditionally considered male terrain, such as politics. She argues,

> Make yourself acquainted thoroughly with [your country's] institutions, its past and present condition, its extent, climate laws, productions, and commerce. All these subjects come within our own sphere—they may be called domestic matters. Think you, if a woman was well instructed and well read on these topics, would she be as incapable of business, and therefore as dependent as she now is?

> (p. 229)

Sedgwick expresses concern over a woman's ability to depend on herself. As an unmarried woman (albeit a financially secure one) herself, she realized that despite the ideal, not all women would become wives and mothers. Thus she upheld self-education also as a preparation for earning a living.

In *Means and Ends*, Sedgwick presents mental acuity as a natural, desirable, even essential feminine trait. When women are highly (self-) educated, men "may hold more communion on their great social duties with their mothers, wives and sisters" (p. 254). In this manner, she implies, women can have an enormous influence upon social and political reform, all without leaving their appropriate sphere. The female intellectual, then, is always a domestic intellectual. Sedgwick saw herself, as a "literary woman" in a similar light. In 1835, Sedgwick wrote in her journal, "My *author's* existence has always seemed something accidental, extraneous, and independent of my inner self. My books have been a pleasant occupation . . . But they constitute no portion of my happiness—that is such I derive from the dearest relations of life".[26] Although Sedgwick never married, she remained with her family all her life. As she implies here, she regarded her true calling not as an author, but as a devoted sister and aunt. Mary Dewey, Sedgwick's earliest biographer, wrote admiringly of her in 1871, "She could make a cake as well as books, and provide for all the household exigencies as ingeniously as she could conduct a story . . .".[27]

Like Catharine Sedgwick, Anna Jameson idealized a distinctly feminine intellectual as well. This author was born Anna Murphy, in Dublin, in 1794. Her father, who shortly thereafter moved his family to London, was a miniature portrait painter who struggled to support his wife and five daughters. Nonetheless, the girls had a governess who supervised their education. When she left the family in 1806, Anna, at age 12, took charge over the education of herself and her sisters. Geraldine MacPherson, Anna's niece and earliest biographer, states that, "Anna's education progressed, chiefly at her own will and pleasure, with an extensive breadth and desultory character as conspicuous as

its ambition."[28] She was encouraged by her father, who took pride in his intellectually precocious oldest daughter. Anna studied French, Italian and Spanish, developed a passion for poetry, as well as Sir William Jones's Indian and Persian romances. Her reading varied from classical works such as *The Odyssey* and *The Iliad*, to religious tracts by Hannah More. Interestingly, Jameson's opinion of such didactic tracts is as negative as Sedgwick's, although for different reasons: "It is most certain that more moral mischief was done to me by some of those than by all Shakespeare's plays together. These so-called pious tracts first introduced me to the knowledge of the vices of vulgar life, and the excitements of a vulgar religion . . .".[29]

Regarding Jameson's mention of Shakespeare, he was, according to Clara Thomas, "on the forbidden shelf" in the Jameson home. This is especially interesting in relation to the Sedgwick household, which endorsed the reading of Shakespeare. Although a significant number of conduct manuals recommended the author as well, others worried about his influence on young, impressionable readers. In *The Young Ladies' Reader* (1845), Sarah Ellis states, "It is scarcely possible to imagine a prudent and judicious mother allowing the unrestrained and private reading of Shakespeare amongst her children . . .".[30] However, she continues, a mother "thoroughly imbibed with a sense of the beautiful and pure" could read aloud *selected* passages "to improve the taste of those around her." Anna, however, read Shakespeare in secret, and considered herself no worse for the experience. "I had read him all through between seven and ten years old," she recalls. "He never did me any moral mischief. He never soiled my mind with any disordered image. What was exceptional and coarse in language I passed by without attracting any meaning whatever to."[31] Jameson, in fact, seems to feel that regulating a child's reading achieves little, if anything. Drawing upon her own experience, she states, "it was not the forbidden books that did the mischief, except in their being read furtively." Rather, certain "approved" reading disturbed her as a child, religious tracts, for example, and violent passages from the Old Testament and Goldsmith's *History of England*.

Jameson, obliged to help support her family financially, took three successive positions as a governess between 1810 and 1825. Later, in 1845, she complained bitterly about her former profession in a work entitled *On Mothers and Governesses*. "I have never in my life heard of a governess who was such by choice," she states.[32] This is the only avenue for impoverished middle-class women, she points out, and laments the fact that governesses are held in such low esteem. The proper education of governesses, she argues, would raise the status of their profession in the eyes of society. "A college expressly to teach women the art of teaching would be very useful; we want good and efficient female teachers for all classes . . .".[33] As much as Jameson later disparaged the profession, her tenure as governess provided the springboard for her subsequent writing career. In 1821 she accompanied her employers on a European tour. Her experiences and observations on this tour served as the material for her first book, *The Diary of an Ennuyee* (1826), which was expanded and reissued in 1834 as *Visits and Sketches.*

Jameson, much like Catharine Sedgwick, was at first a reluctant author. In 1825 she left her position to marry Robert Jameson, a barrister. Although the marriage was a miserable failure, Robert did encourage his wife's literary abilities. At his prompting, she wrote short pieces of her travels, published anonymously, for *London Magazine*; shortly thereafter, he secured the office of an "eccentric cobbler-bookseller" to publish Anna's *Diary*.[34] Anna seemed to embark on the venture as a joke. Geraldine MacPherson describes her attitude: "'You may print it if you like,' said Mrs Jameson, adding, half in jest, "if it sells for anything more than will pay the expenses, you shall give me a Spanish guitar for my share of the profits.'"[35] Jameson and her publisher, nonetheless, took an extreme measure to protect the author's identity. 'A final paragraph was added . . . Herein it was stated that "the writer died on her way home at Autun, in her twenty-sixth year, and had been buried in the garden of the Capuchin Monastery near that city."'[36] Despite Anna's reluctance to draw attention to herself as a female author, her identity became known along with the success of her first book. Once Anna separated from Robert in 1829, writing became more a necessity than a hobby. In order to support herself, her parents, and two unmarried sisters, Jameson wrote well over a dozen books in her lifetime. She was best known as an art critic, although her criticism, like Sedgwick's novels, contains a heavy dose of moral didacticism. This strand runs throughout her oeuvre, as certain titles of her books reveal: *Memoirs and Essays on Art, Literature and Social Morals* (1846), *Legends of the Madonna* (1852), *The History of Our Lord, as Exemplified in Works of Art* (published posthumously, 1864).

Jameson's *Characteristics of Women, Moral, Poetical, and Historical* (1832) is technically literary criticism; however, the work presents literary analysis in a sort of conduct manual format. Despite the ambiguity of its genre, Jameson clearly wrote the book—a study of Shakespeare's heroines—in order to define a womanly ideal. At the very outset, the author denies any motives for writing which would be considered unfeminine. "Accident made me an authoress," she states, "and not now, nor ever, have I written to flatter any prevailing fashion of the day for the sake of profit . . . This little book was undertaken without the thought of fame or money . . ." (p. ii).[37] According to this disclaimer, Jameson writes not for public display, nor as a means to earn her own living (a less believable claim, however). Rather, her purpose is to enlighten and instruct, but in as unobtrusive a manner as possible. "I do not choose presumptuously to fling . . . opinions in the face of the world, in the form of essays on morality, or treatises on education. I have rather chosen to illustrate certain positions by examples, and leave my readers to deduce the moral themselves, and draw their own inferences" (p. v). Jameson, obviously, feels it necessary to preface her work with an apology for the female author/intellectual.

Jameson's *Characteristics,* unlike **Means and Ends,** does not explicitly discuss women's reading practices. Its use of Shakespearean heroines for moral examples, however, assumes a thorough grounding in Shakespeare (and a fairly high degree of literacy) among its audience. Furthermore, its primary concern is the state of women's education and contemporary views of the female intellectual. "It appears to me that the condition of women in society," she states, "as at present constituted, is false in itself and injurious to them,—that the education of women . . . at present conducted, is founded in mistaken principles, and tends to increase fearfully the sum of misery and error in both sexes . . ." (p. v). Jameson is not concerned here with a lack of opportunity for women's intellectual development. Rather, she fears that women are becoming educated at the expense of their moral instincts and sympathies. The current system of education, she argues, "inundates us with hard clever, sophisticated girls . . . with whom vanity and expediency take place of conscience and affection" (p. xxxi). While the poorly-taught woman, as Sedgwick emphasizes, is an unfit wife and mother, problems can develop from the wrong sort of education also. A woman's education, Jameson argues, must not neglect her moral development. "A time is coming perhaps," she states, "when the education of women will be considered with a view to their future destination as the mother and nurses of legislatures and statesmen; and the cultivation of their powers of reflection and moral feelings supersede the . . . [means] by which they are now crammed with knowledge and accomplishments" (p. xxxi).

Through her discussion of Shakespeare's heroines, Jameson means "to illustrate the various modifications of which the female character is susceptible, with their causes and results" (p. iv). She has chosen Shakespeare's work, because in his plays "the male and female characters bear precisely the same relation to each other that they do in nature and society—they are not equal in prominence or power" (p. xv). For example, Shakespeare's women are capable of great emotion, but men surpass them even in this: "Juliet is the most impassioned of his female characters," she writes, "but what are *her* passions to those that shake the soul of Othello?" (p. xv). Still, Shakespeare's heroines exhibit a superior moral sensibility. While Lady Macbeth and Richard III are both depraved characters, Lady Macbeth suffers womanly pangs of remorse, while Richard, as a male villain, "has neither pity, love nor fear" (p. xvi). This technique of Jameson's shows itself most amusingly in her discussion of *Much Ado About Nothing.* She describes the scene where Beatrice orders Benedict to kill Claudio as having a "comic effect," for she thinks that Beatrice, as a good, virtuous woman, must surely be joking.

Jameson divides Shakespeare's heroines into four types: characters of intellect, characters of passion and imagination, characters of the affections, and characters of history. She discusses "characters of intellect" first however; and since her preface addresses questions of women's education, this appears as her greatest interest. Women's intelects, Jameson states explicitly, are inferior to those of men. They are also qualitatively different. "In man the intellectual faculties exist more self-posed and self-directed—more indifferent of the rest of the character." Women's intellect, however, is "modified by the sympathies and moral qualities" (p. 39). This "feminine" quality of the intellect, however, is natural and desirable in a woman. Male authors, argues Jameson, have traditionally misrepresented women of intellect. "Men of genius have committed some signal mistakes . . . they could form no conception of intellect which was not masculine, and therefore have either suppressed the feminine element altogether and drawn coarse caricatures, or they have made them completely artificial" (p. 40).

Jameson lauds Shakespeare because, she argues, he presents realistic, believable portraits of intellectual women. She discusses four heroines in this chapter, those "at once distinguished by their mental superiority": Portia (*Merchant of Venice*), Isabella (*Measure for Measure*), Beatrice (*Much Ado About Nothing*) and Rosalind (*As You Like It*). "The wit which is lavished on each," she declares, "is profound, or pointed, or sparkling, or playful—but always feminine; like spirits distilled from flowers, it always reminds us of its origin;—it is volatile essence, sweet as powerful" (p. 41). Jameson, incidentally, praises all Shakespeare's heroines in this same flowery and effusive vein, for two volumes. As part of her discussion on Portia, Jameson implies that women's intellect is *inherently* feminine. "I never yet met in real life, nor ever read in tale or history, of any woman, distinguished for intellect of highest order, who was not also remarkable for [feminine qualities] . . . which is compatible with the most serious habits of thought, and the most profound sensibility . . . ." (p. 50). This statement seems directly to contradict the concerns Jameson states in her preface. If all intellectual women are inherently feminine, how can any form of education remove this quality? Despite Jameson's ambivalence in this passage, she obviously believes that intellect and femininity are highly compatible. In this respect, her views on female intellect are analogous to Sedgwick's in *Means and Ends.*

As Jameson's argument in *Characteristics* indicates, her views on the position of women are highly conservative to a modern day reader. Nonetheless, her construction of the female intellectual, like Sedgwick's, is an attempt to bridge traditional views of women with women's increasing literacy and educational opportunity. Although Jameson does not explicitly address the subject of women's rights in this book, she became increasingly outspoken on the topic in succeeding years. Her lifelong concern for the education and welfare of women is particularly evident in *On Mothers and Governesses* (1845), and *The Communion of Labor: A Second Lecture on the Social Employments of Women* (1856). One of her most scathing criticisms of women's position in society appears in *Winter Studies and Summer Rambles in Canada* (1838), the result of a 9 month North American tour. Jameson describes the Native American women she encountered, and states that their lot, in some ways, is superior to that of European women. The Native American woman, she argues, "is sure of protection, sure of maintenance, at least while the man has it; sure of kind treatment; sure that she will never have her children taken from her but by death . . . ."[38] Jameson's observation did not pass uncriticized by male reviewers.

It is interesting to consider how Jameson's view of herself as a female intellectual and writer compares with that of Catharine Sedgwick. While Sedgwick saw her identity as an author as secondary and extraneous to her family life, Jameson was much less tied, by dint of frequent travel, to her family. Furthermore, writing for Jameson must have taken a far more central role, as she made her livelihood from it. Although Jameson originally published with reluctance, she later vigorously defends the role of the woman writer. In *Winter Sketches,* she depicts writing as a necessary means of advancement for women. "Women *must* find means to fill up the void of existence. Men, our natural protectors, our lawgivers, our masters, throw us upon our own resources . . . We have gone away from nature, and we must—if we can, substitute another nature. Art, literature and science, remain to us . . . ."[39] Here Jameson views the role of female intellectual as an inevitable response to social inequalities. She expresses contempt for those who ridicule female writers. During her visit to Toronto in 1837, she describes the society she encountered: "The cold narrow minds, the confined ideas, the by-gone prejudices of the society, are hardly conceivable . . . The women here express, vulgarly enough, an extreme fear of the "authoress" and I am anything but popular."[40]

Catharine Maria Sedgwick and Anna Jameson were but two contributors to an enormous body of conduct literature for women in nineteenth-century England and the USA. As scholars have noted, these books served a highly conservative purpose. By encouraging women to conform to a womanly ideal, conduct books prescribed rigid norms of behaviour which confined women to a domestic sphere, and thus reinforced Victorian patriarchal structures. The books addressed all aspects of a woman's life: dress, household training, manners, morals, health (*Means and Ends* devotes a chapter to "Care of the Skin"), and mental development. Very often, this last topic referred primarily to women's self-education, or private reading practices. Regarding the subject of women's literacy, conduct books often sent mixed messages to their readers. Like everything else in a woman's life, reading must serve a morally edifying purpose and conform to certain standards. Women's minds, then, were to be molded and shaped by the "right" sort of reading. This attitude took for granted a woman who was mentally docile, easily impressionable and likely to be swayed by any argument. The literate woman, having read the proper books, would be a suitable companion for her husband, and thus strengthen the power of the domestic sphere and perpetuate the *status quo*. In Catharine Sedgwick's *Means and Ends,* however, this strand of thought coexists with the idea of female intellectual development as a politically powerful force. Sedgwick encourages her readers to develop critical thinking skills and cultivate interests not traditionally regarded as part of a woman's sphere. In this manner, women can improve their position in society. Furthermore, she acknowledges the economic necessity of independent, self-supporting women. Anna Jameson, in *Characteristics of Women,* regards women's intellects as inferior to those of men. Nonetheless, by praising Shakespeare's "Women of Intellect," she portrays strength of mind as an admirable and necessary quality in a woman. In other of her didactic works, Jameson, like Sedgwick, calls for reforms in women's social, educational and economic positions.

A closer examination of the multiple constructions of literacy in **Means and Ends** and *Characteristics of Women* reveals four primary definitions. For both Jameson and Sedgwick, female literacy was a means of self-discipline and training; it contributed to the formation of a "good character." A woman of "good character" reinforced a conservative, patriarchal social order. The second construction of literacy in these books is an economic one. Literacy was portrayed as an economic investment; after all, the literate woman made a more desirable wife and mother, thus improving her chances for a good match. Although this dimension served a conservative agenda as well, an "economic" definition of literacy could also challenge the *status quo.* Sedgwick and Jameson both evince an awareness of literacy's importance for the single, unsupported woman. Literate women, they recognize, could more easily support themselves as part of a growing female workforce divorced from the domestic sphere. The third definition of literacy, as it appears in these conduct manuals, reinforces class hierarchies, and helps define a growing middle class. Literacy is a badge of wealth and social status, as the mistress of a comfortable, well-staffed household would have more leisure, and thus greater opportunity, to read all Shakespeare's plays, for example, or set aside an hour a day for reading. Sedgwick and Jameson, after all, were upper middle-class women writing for an upwardly mobile segment of society. The fourth of Sedgwick's and Jameson's definitions is literacy as a means of empowerment. Sedgwick encouraged women to educate themselves, and thus effect social reform through their fathers, brothers and husbands. Jameson used much of her didactic writing as an outlet for her concerns over women's role and welfare in society.

The multiple roles of literacy set forth by Jameson and Sedgwick highlight their complex ideological positions. Although both authors were progressive in their social/political outlook, they upheld the ideal of an intelligent yet traditionally feminine woman—a "domestic intellectual" of sorts. For these writers, women's literacy promised both continuity and change. Through perusal of the Bible, for example, a woman might read about the necessity of wifely submissiveness—and learn to conform to an age-old feminine ideal—while also developing a political consciousness through reading the newspapers. This construction of the domestic intellectual—at once progressive and highly traditional—seems to reflect the personal ambivalence of the authors themselves. Sedgwick and Jameson both shied away, at least initially, from the role of female writer, a persona typically mocked in the contemporary press as that of a masculinized woman. Both used writing, however, to carry out an acceptable female duty—the moral and spiritual edification of society. Both were highly intelligent, independent, and keenly aware of women's social and political wrongs—yet they never, in any respect, viewed themselves as crusaders for women's rights. Rather, Sedgwick and Jameson, as self-constructed domestic intellectuals, attempted to effect political change through quiet persuasion. Their conduct books cannot be interpreted so much as bulwarks of a conservative social order, but as the products of women living in a complex era and a rapidly changing society.

Notes

1. Ellen Jordan (1991) "'Making Good Wives and Mothers'? The Transformation of Middle-Class Girls' Education in Nineteenth-Century Britain", p. 477, *History of Education Quarterly,* 31, pp. 439-462.

2. Karl Kaestle (1988) "The History of Literacy and the History of Readers", in Eugene R. Kintgen, Barry M. Kroll & Mike Rose (Eds) *Perspectives on Literacy,* p. 97 (Carbondale: Southern Illinois University Press).

3. Nancy Armstrong (1987) *Desire and Domestic Fiction: a political history of the novel,* p. 94 (New York: Oxford University Press).

4. Mary Poovey (1984) *The Proper Lady and the Woman Writer,* p. 10 (Chicago: University of Chicago Press).

5. Armstrong, *Desire and Domestic Fiction,* p. 95.

6. We should acknowledge at this point the existence of a parallel conduct book tradition for men. Nancy Armstrong, in *Desire and Domestic Fiction,* notes that by the mid-eighteenth century, "the number of books specifying the qualities of a new kind of woman had well outstripped the number of those devoted to describing the aristocratic male" (p. 62). Conduct literature for men, she argues, evolved into other forms (such as political satire) while women's conduct books retained their popularity well into the nineteenth century. Nonetheless, Sarah Newton, in *Learning to Behave,* lists well over a hundred conduct books for men published in the USA in the nineteenth-century. While women's conduct literature prepared its readers for marriage and motherhood, men's advice manuals often patterned themselves after *Poor Richard's Almanack,* encouraging ambition and industrious habits as the means to economic success.

7. Carla Peterson (1987) *The Determined Reader,* p. 13 (New Brunswick: Rutgers University Press).

8. Quoted in Poovey, *The Proper Lady,* p. 68.

9. Kate Flint (1993) *The Woman Reader: 1837-1914,* p. 214 (New York: Oxford University Press).

10. Quoted in Poovey, *The Proper Lady*, p. 35.

11. Armstrong, *Desire and Domestic Fiction*, p. 100.

12. Poovey, *The Proper Lady*, p. 97.

13. Sarah E. Newton (1994) *Learning to Behave*, p. 76 (Westport: Greenwood Press).

14. Ibid., p. 78.

15. John Guillory (1993) *Cultural Capital*, p. 19 (Chicago: University of Chicago Press).

16. Mary Kelly (Ed.) (1993) *The Power of Her Sympathy: the autobiography and journal of Catharine Maria Sedgwick*, p. 11 (Boston: The Massachusetts Historical Society).

17. Ibid., p. 76.

18. Ibid., p. 84.

19. Ibid., p. 92.

20. Mary E. Dewey (1871) *The Life and Letters of Catharine M. Sedgwick*, p. 150 (New York: Harper & Brothers).

21. Sister Mary Michael Walsh (1937) *Catharine Maria Sedgwick*, p. 6 (Washington: Catholic University of America).

22. Dewey, *The Life and Letters of Catharine M. Sedgwick*, p. 271.

23. Ibid., p. 270.

24. Walsh, *Catharine Maria Sedgwick*, p. 34.

25. Catharine Maria Sedgwick (1840) *Means and Ends, or Self-Training* (Boston: Marsh, Capen Lyon & Webb)

26. Kelly, *The Power of Her Sympathy*, p. 151.

27. Dewey, *The Life and Letters of Catharine M. Sedgwick*, p. 330.

28. Geraldine MacPherson (1878) *Memoirs of the Life of Anna Jameson*, p. 12 (London: Longman, Green & Co.).

29. Quoted in Clara Thomas (1967) *Love and Work Enough: the life of Anna Jameson*, p. 6 (Toronto: University of Toronto Press).

30. Flint, *The Woman Reader*, p. 83.

31. Quoted in Thomas, *Love and Work Enough*, p. 6.

32. Ibid., p. 18.

33. Ibid.

34. Ibid., p. 28.

35. Quoted in MacPherson, *Memoirs of the Life of Anna Jameson*, p. 41.

36. Ibid., p. 42.

37. Anna Jameson (1833) *Characteristics of Women* (Annapolis: J Hughes).

38. Quoted in Thomas, *Love and Work Enough*, p. 138.

39. Elizabeth Helsinger, Robin Lauterbach Sheets & William Veeder (Eds.) (1983) *The Woman Question: Literary Issues*, p. 24 (Chicago: University of Chicago Press).

40. Quoted in Mrs Steuart Erskine (Ed.) (1915) *Anna Jameson: letters and friendships*, p. 150 (London: T. Fisher Unwin).

Philip Gould (essay date 1996)

SOURCE: "Catharine Sedgwick's 'Recital' of the Pequot War," in *Covenant and Republic: Historical Romance and the Politics of Puritanism*, Cambridge University Press, 1996, pp. 61-90.

[*In the following essay, Gould illustrates how Sedgwick uses a revisionist account of the Pequot War to present a larger cultural debate over the nature of citizenship in the early American republic.*]

> I hope my dear Mrs. Embry [sic] you will go on to enrich your native country and to elevate the just pride of your country women.
>
> —Catharine Sedgwick to Emma Embury, January 29, 1829[1]

> It has been the fate of all the tribes to be like the Carthaginians, in having their history written by their enemies. Could they now come up from their graves, and tell the tale of their own wrongs, reveal their motives, and describe their actions, Indian history would put on a different garb from the one it now wears, and the voice of justice would cry much louder in their behalf than it has yet done.
>
> —"Materials for American History," *North American Review* (1826)

Shortly before Catharine Sedgwick published her third novel, **Hope Leslie**, in 1827, she wrote a letter home to her brother, Charles, recounting a recent trip to Boston that she had made by stagecoach. Along the way, as Sedgwick described it, she encountered an aged veteran of the Revolutionary War who somehow charmed her. To Sedgwick the incident was worthy of detail:

> One old soldier I shall never forget. He was not like most of our old pensioners, a subject of pity on account of (perhaps) accidental virtue, but everything about him looked like the old age of humble frugal industrious virtue. And then he was so patient under the severest of all physical evils . . . so cheerful and bright, so confiding in kindness, and so trustful in his fellow-creatures. . . . [He wore] famous green mittens, knit as he said, with a tear in his eye, "by his youngest *darter*," leaning on his cane, the horrid cancer decently dressed and sheltered, talking with a benign expression of his old friends, but his eye kindling, and his form straightening with a momentary vigor as he spoke of the heroic deeds of his youthful companions, and the serenity and meekness, and philosophy with which he spoke of the sufferings and the progress of them.[2]

On its surface, Sedgwick's encounter seems to be nothing more than a sentimental account of an endearing old man. Yet her narrative of the incident, I would argue, suggests her relation—specifically through *writing*—to a living, cultural symbol of Revolutionary republicanism. What kind of "man" is this? Or better yet: What kind of manhood does Sedgwick manage to re-create here? By claiming both his unique and ordinary qualities, Sedgwick locates this "old soldier" both within and without the fold of a identifiable type. This immediately raises the issue of his representativeness. As a masculine legacy of the Revolution, he is transformed, albeit subtly, by Sedgwick's pen into an androgynous ideal. The passage's rhetoric welds together his meekness and vigor, his tears and heroic deeds, figuring a new symbol of republican manhood whose classical virtues are subsumed by his capacity for feeling. His daughter's mittens—a domestic production, after all—literally and symbolically cover his hands. So the scene translates power from male subject to female writer, from classical vigor to sentimental pathos, and devilishly suggests that the very icon of Revolutionary manhood is itself diseased, and perhaps on its last leg. This is the theme of *Hope Leslie*'s "recital" of the Pequot War.

The successful revision of this icon depends on the negotiation of the masculine language and ideology we examined in the preceding chapter. As I began to show, republican language of "virtue" was layered densely with gendered meaning during the transitional era of the early republic. "Virtue" signified not only the tenets of classical republicanism and liberal individualism but also the precepts of affect, benevolence, and pious, universal love that descended in large part from eighteenth-century Scottish Common Sense philosophy. As the word began to signify new, modern republican adhesives of sociability and Christian benevolence, these traits became increasingly associated in early national America with women themselves and evolved into an ideology of domesticity during the antebellum era. The crucial point here is that during this era the gendered meanings of republican virtue could lend instability to the nature of "masculine" and "feminine" behavior. And as Sedgwick's letter to her brother shows, such instability afforded the chance to refashion the terms of civic ethics in a republic. By manipulating language, one could redefine along the lines of gender the very meaning of a "republic."

In the next two chapters I take up the issue of gender politics in women's historical romance by situating two of the era's most popular historical romances, *Hope Leslie* and Lydia Child's *Hobomok* (1824), in this cultural and historical context. As I argued at the outset of this study, literary critics of all sorts have placed women's historical romance of the 1820s in context of the American Renaissance. In this schema, these texts are either failures that mark Hawthorne's later success or credible novels that should be considered part of the nation's literary flowering. In each case, the critical trajectory points forward, ignoring the specifically *post-Revolutionary* nature of the language and thematics of women's writing. Moreover,

women's historical romance emerged during the 1820s in the context of an established, masculinized genre of nationalist history. Historians like Hannah Adams and Emma Willard were extraordinary women even to cultivate literary careers for themselves at this time. Yet there was little room for "revisionist" historiography at this time. Why, then, we should ask, did women writers even take up the subject of Puritanism? How do their historical productions about Puritanism compare to those of male "historians"? How did they engage contemporary, nationalist histories—and what were the cultural stakes of writing revisionary history via the medium of historical romance?

Virtually everyone recognizes the "antipatriarchal" nature of women's historical fiction. Yet this theme is made even more significant when recast as part of a larger gendered struggle over the nature of the republic, a struggle, I would argue, taking place in part through the medium of Puritan history. The transitional nature of the early republic, with all of its cultural and rhetorical instability, made such a struggle particularly resonant. Indeed, it made it possible. In this chapter and the next, I unravel the languages of republicanism in women's historical romance as a way of demonstrating that the political nature of Sedgwick's and Child's novels descends from the cultural experience of the American Revolution. This chapter demonstrates the immediate significance of *Hope Leslie*'s revisionary history of the Pequot War, where Sedgwick thematizes the incompatibility of gendered forms of "republican" virtue. It provides a segue to Chapter 3, a more comprehensive reconsideration of the literary "conventions" of women's historical romance in the context of this period's changing political culture. Puritanism provided an arena in which to debate the protean, gendered meanings of republican "virtue," a debate that directly involved a struggle over language itself.

HOPE LESLIE, THE PEQUOT WAR, AND
REPUBLICAN VIRTUE

The Pequot War has produced more than its share of historiographic controversy. This, as we shall see, is much more the case with present-day interpretations of the war than those current in early national America. In the aftermath of Watergate and the Vietnam War, revisionist historians began with renewed fervor to question the reliability of Puritan accounts of the attack on the Pequot in 1637. Francis Jennings led the charge during the mid-1970s by pointing out a regional bias that supposedly had distorted an entire historiographic tradition: "During the nineteenth century and much of the twentieth, the whole historical profession was dominated by historians who were not only trained in New England but at the same time were steeped in the accepted traditions of that region. Our histories generally show their imprint."[3] The revisionist refusal, however, to treat Puritan sources "as gospel" (as Jennings put it) has itself come under attack. For instance, one critic of the revisionists' "radicalizing polemics" has argued that they tend to oversimplify ambiguities in Puritan histories and thereby unfairly assail Puritan military tactics and political motives alike.[4] These historiographic debates are characterized by deep animosities, but more importantly, they reduce themselves to two crucial questions: Did Captain John Mason's attack on one of the two Pequot forts at Mystic constitute a "massacre"? And did the leaders of Connecticut and Massachusetts Bay undertake a defensive operation, or a war of conquest? This debate continues to occupy early Americanists, presenting the vexing problem of how we interpret Puritan sources.[5]

As critics of **Hope Leslie** have noted, it is just this issue that lies at the heart of Catharine Sedgwick's revisionary history of the Pequot War. In the novel's crucial fourth chapter, which recounts the war from the point of view of Magawisca, a young Native American woman who witnessed the Puritan attack, Sedgwick interrogates seventeenth-century accounts of the conflict found in William Hubbard's *A Narrative of the Troubles with the Indians in New England* (1677) and John Winthrop's *The History of New England* (1630-49), both of which had been reprinted in the decade before **Hope Leslie**'s publication.[6] Mary Kelley rightly admires Sedgwick for strategically "[m]ining the early histories": "Sedgwick simultaneously turned the [Puritan] witnesses against themselves and introduced an alternative interpretation."[7] Sandra Zagarell similarly has concluded that **Hope Leslie** "challenges the official history of original settlement by exposing the repositories of the nation's early history, the Puritan narratives, as justifications of genocide."[8] More recently, Dana D. Nelson has extended and complicated antipatriarchal approaches by claiming that, taken together, Puritan and Native American versions of the war in **Hope Leslie** testify to "the political aspect of [all] historical representation": "Thus through a sympathetic frame of reference, Sedgwick is able to establish a historical dialogue that had been suppressed from the Puritan accounts."[9]

Whether **Hope Leslie** contains, then, a radical attack on Puritan histories or an uncannily prescient exercise in historical dialogics, the line of continuity in these readings locates Sedgwick vis-à-vis seventeenth-century historiography. None considers the novel primarily in an early republican cultural context—that is, by reading its history of the war in the context of post-Revolutionary discourse about the conflict. What were, in other words, the contemporary political and cultural issues imbedded within early national narratives about colonial military history? By comparing Sedgwick's history to those of her own era, rather than simply to the likes of Hubbard, Winthrop, and others, we might reconceive of **Hope Leslie** as an exercise in contemporary cultural criticism. This significantly lends new meanings to its "antipatriarchal" theme. In the context of contemporary histories, **Hope Leslie** both critiques the viability of masculine, classical republicanism and participates in a larger cultural debate over the nature of citizenship in the early American republic.

This debate was facilitated by the potently ambiguous meanings of "virtue." As several historians of Revolutionary America have noted, during the eighteenth century nu-

merous intellectual-historical pressures transformed the traditionally masculine meanings of "virtue." Its classical context, of course, was *exclusively* masculine. "Virtue" derived from the Roman concept of *virtu* (the source of "virility"), signifying the austerity, patriotic vigilance, and martial valor theoretically requisite to republican life. Citizenship, as the ancient Romans conceived of it, was the ideal medium for men to express their collective personalities; the *vivere civile*—the ideal of active citizenship—generally described a situation whereby rulers served dutifully in politics and the masses in military defense. However, in a landmark essay exerting wide influence on scholars of women's history, Ruth Bloch has traced a number of intellectual developments during the eighteenth century that gradually feminized traditionally masculine meanings of virtue.[10] "Virtue," Bloch concludes, "if still regarded as essential to the public good in a republican state, became ever more difficult to distinguish from private benevolence, personal manners, and female sexual propriety."[11] Gordon Wood similarly has argued for the modern forms of love and benevolence that gradually emerged as the new adhesives of a republican order: "Virtue became less the harsh self-sacrifice of antiquity and more the willingness to get along with others for the sake of peace and prosperity. Virtue became identified with decency. Whereas the ancient classical virtue was martial and masculine . . . the new virtue was soft and feminized and capable of being expressed by women as well as men; some, in fact, thought it was even better expressed by women."[12]

Changes in eighteenth-century civic culture later coalesced into what one historian has called the "discernible social theory" of domesticity.[13] The view that women were the "natural" stewards of national morality helped to create what Linda Kerber has, in a now famous (and debated) phrase, called "republican motherhood."[14] From its Revolutionary-era genesis, as Kerber noted, this role imposed upon American women "the contradictory demands of domesticity and civic activism."[15] The republic's new guardians of civic ethics were at once politically valued and politically disenfranchised. While historians today have come to view with suspicion the gendered dichotomy of "private" and "public" spheres,[16] the home theoretically became the site of inculcating republican virtue.[17] For example, Benjamin Rush, the Revolutionary generation's most prolific writer on republican education, specifically stated that American women (and by this, of course, he meant white, middle- and upper-class women) "must concur in our plans of education for young men, or no laws will ever render them effectual."[18] One should recognize as well that Rush's gendered construction of republican morality and pedagogy (a subject I pursue at greater length in the next chapter) was premised on the same understanding of cyclical history as the New Ebenezer of Puritanism: "In the ordinary course of human affairs," as Rush put it, "we shall probably too soon follow the footsteps of the nations of Europe in manners and vices. The first marks we shall see of our declension, will appear among our women."[19] Hence republican womanhood derived from those anxieties in Whiggish thinking that cast the republic as a fragile, fated thing.

Born from such anxieties, the cultural role of the republican woman helped to legitimate women's writing during this era. The image of the republican woman writer, however, pen in hand, righteously invested in America's civic and political health, was only tenuously empowering. Writers like Catharine Sedgwick certainly carried the "political" authority of moral propriety into the public sphere. Even as a very young woman, a decade before she wrote her first book, *A New-England Tale* (1822), Sedgwick appeared to be aware of the personal, literary, and ideological leverage that republican womanhood afforded. In 1812 she wrote a letter to her father, Theodore Sedgwick, the Speaker of the U.S. House of Representatives, which declared with ostensible humility, "You may benefit a nation, my dear papa, and I may improve the condition of a fellow being."[20] Despite her use of the metaphors of "cottage" and "palace," to distinguish her sphere from her father's, Sedgwick subtly implied a gendered equivalence of their roles: "Wisdom and virtue are never at a loss for occasions and time for their exercise, and *the same light* that lightens the world is applied to individual use and gratification."[21] Throughout her literary career, Sedgwick's moral role, with its enabling and sometimes radical possibilities, was premised on the "light" that symbolically marks the beginnings of the evolution of republican womanhood into domesticity. Years later, an anonymous writer for the *North American Review* began his evaluation of *Hope Leslie* by legitimating women's writing in much the same way. "We hold it to be a fortunate thing for any country, that a portion of its literature should fall into the hands of the female sex; because their influence, in any walk of letters, is almost sure to be powerful and good."[22] In "the interests of virtue," women's writing "nurture[d] the growth . . . of youthful intellect and feeling."[23] At the same time, however, he delimited women's writing to the "proper walks"—"the lighter kinds of literature"[24]—thereby circumscribing its politics within domestic space.

This newfound "political" role for women, however, raised a troubling question buried within the cant of republican motherhood. Which kind of "virtue" were women supposed to teach husbands and sons at home? This issue crucially involves the substance of republican citizenship. Male political theorists, of course, glossed over it, recognizing little problem in ideologically reconciling classical and domestic virtue. Men, after all, ideally incorporated benevolence and love into their social relations, even if times of political crisis demanded an exclusively "masculine" response of patriotic duty and martial courage (a subject taken up in Chapter 5). But the opposite was not true. Women had no access to the classical norms of republican citizenship. One should recognize that a lingering ideology of austere manhood contained misogynistic overtones (the abhorrence of "effeminacy," for example, or the negatively feminine connotations of "luxury" and "indolence"). Moreover, masculine republicanism undervalued the *affective* ways in which women could forge

truly political identities. How, then, did women writer[s] treat a masculine ideology that in large part underwrot[e] their own legal and political disenfranchisement? Diveste[d] of true representation, if not always political expression[,] women writers waged a cultural and ideological struggl[e] within the republic by exploiting the contradictions i[n] their political role.

Nowhere in early national culture was masculine republi[-] canism more pronounced than in the heroic subject o[f] military history. To put it simply, military history wa[s] meant to "inspire virtue" and "instill patriotism" in mal[e] citizens.[25] Exploits of the American Revolution, the man[y] frontier conflicts with Native Americans, and, to come t[o] the issue at hand, the Pequot War, all helped codify a nar[-] rowly masculine understanding of citizenship that effec[-] tively heightened the difference between men and wome[n] as political beings. This is the cultural politics of *Hop[e] Leslie*'s revisionary history. Soaked in a rhetoric of Ro[-] man masculinity, the subject of the war in Sedgwick['s] own day served to memorialize classical *virtu*. Her nove[l,] then, addresses decidedly contemporary issues of the re[-] public by debunking an entire tradition of masculine ico[-] nography derived immediately (though not exclusively[)] from Revolutionary-era political culture. *Hope Leslie['s]* fourth chapter is just what she calls Magawisca'a narra[-] tive—a "recital," or performance, of history, which com[-] peted with other contemporaneous performances over th[e] meaning of virtue in early America.

THE "STORY" OF 1637

Hope Leslie's "recital" of the Pequot War confronts [a] long-standing historiographic tradition. Puritan versions o[f] the conflict tell the larger story of God's Providence i[n] New England, and they typically begin with the murde[r] during the 1630s of three Englishmen—John Stone, Walt[er] Norton, and John Oldham—as a way of justifying Ma[-] son's expedition against the Pequot in what is now Mysti[c,] Connecticut, in the spring of 1637. New England's earl[y] historians virtually ignored the fact that these three me[n] were anything but saintly figures (Stone, for example, p[i-] rated a Plymouth ship, nearly stabbed Plymouth's gover[-] nor, and was exiled from Massachusetts Bay for adulte[ry] and threats of violence; Oldham, as Bradford's *Of Ply[-] mouth Plantation* attests, was quarrelsome enough to b[e] called "Mad Jack" by the likes of Thomas Morton).[26] In[-] stead, they turned these three rogues into martyrs in ord[er] to confirm Native American "savagery" and thereby justi[fy] the war. In one of the most important firsthand accounts [of] the war, John Mason himself unwittingly confirms th[is] rhetorical strategy by claiming that "the Beginning is th[e] Moiety of the Whole."[27] Even providential history, Maso[n] suggests, is manipulable: "If the Beginning be but ob[-] scure, and the Ground uncertain, its Continuance ca[n] hardly persuade to purchase belief: or if Truth be wanti[ng] in History, it proves but a fruitless Discourse."[28]

From the seventeenth to the nineteenth century, this narr[a-] tive framing device for the war aimed "to purchase belie[f] and hold the moral high ground. The four histories by the actual participants in the war—Mason, John Underhill, Lion Gardiner, and Philip Vincent[29]—deftly contextualize the Puritan massacre in this way. Mason, for example, begins by recounting the fate of the "cruelly murdered" John Stone, who fell into the "bloody Design" of the Pequot,[30] while Underhill similarly laments Oldham's death: "The Indians [the Eastern Niantics, a tributary of the Narragansetts] . . . knocked him in the head, and martyred him most barbarously, to the great grief of his poor distressed servants."[31] Gardiner and Vincent focused instead on Pequot "mischief" in Connecticut at Fort Saybrook and Wethersfield, but the narrative effect remains the same.[32] Later Puritan historians, such as William Hubbard, easily adopted this narrative strategy because it worked so well in casting the war as a defensive operation against a most "fierce, cruel, and warlike People" who "treacherously and cruelly murthered Captain Stone, and Captain Norton."[33] Ever since the nineteenth-century antiquarian James Savage disparaged his abilities as a historian, most critics have noted how Hubbard's *A General History of New England* borrows extensively from John Winthrop's *Journal*. But what better way to stir up passions than the gruesome account of Oldham's murder that Winthrop provides: "[The Puritans] found John Oldham under the seine stark naked, his head cleft to the brains, and his hands and legs cut as if they had been cutting them off, yet warm."[34] Founded upon the dichotomy between "saint" and "savage," the sensationalist rhetoric of Puritan narrative would seem to belie John Mason's claim that reliable history need not "stir up the affections of men."[35] Puritan history works affectively, consuming, like the flames of Mystic Fort, whatever sympathy readers might later have for the Pequot themselves.

Early nationals easily appropriated this narrative scheme. The deaths of these three "martyrs" later served the nationalistic bias of early republican historiography quite well. Connecticut's premier history-writer, Benjamin Trumbull, merely reinscribed the Puritan line as it was found in Mason and Hubbard by beginning his chapter on the war with the accusation that the "Indians in general were ever jealous of the English, from the first settlement of New-England, and wished to drive them from the country."[36] The "brutal" murders of Stone and Oldham soon follow, as they do in Abiel Holmes, Jedidiah Morse, and Epaphras Hoyt.[37] Moreover, the subject of the war further demonstrates ways in which sectarian rivalries of post-Revolutionary New England collapse under the pressures of nationalist piety. No less than her orthodox adversary, Jedidiah Morse, Hannah Adams argued that the New England Fathers "had still an arduous task to secure themselves from the malevolence and jealousy of the natives . . . [taking] every precaution to avoid a war."[38]

The perpetuation of this rhetorical frame for the war helps to explain the historiographic design of *Hope Leslie*. One might otherwise overlook Sedgwick's inversion of the chronological sequence of an entire historiographic tradition, as she transplants what she realizes are the embel-

lished "stories" of the deaths of Norton, Stone, and Oldham to a moment *after* the massacre has occurred.[39] In the preface to the novel, she manipulates uncertain generic distinctions and gender stereotypes by assuming with all humility the persona of the inadequate historian. Yet this very act devilishly signals her historiographic maneuver: "The antiquarian reader will perceive that some liberties have been taken with the received accounts of Sir Philip [or Sir Christopher] Gardiner, and a slight variation has been allowed in the chronology of the Pequod war" (5). By dislodging these stories from their traditional placement, Sedgwick is able to emancipate readerly sympathy for the Pequot, and thereby recover that element of pathos—that humanitarian impulse at the core of domestic ideology—which both Puritan historians and their early national descendents successfully suppress.

In lieu of the murders of the Big Three, Sedgwick reframes Magawisca's narrative with a scene between Everell Fletcher, a Puritan boy who is the novel's future hero, and Digby, an actual veteran of the war, which functions to invalidate masculine historiography. Indeed, as Digby dutifully guards the Fletcher freehold against the possibility of Indian conspiracies, he stands as a trope for the virtue of Puritan and republican vigilance. And as he begins to rehash the war for Everell, he becomes a living metaphor for a historiographic tradition with which *Hope Leslie* now competes:

> The subject of the Pequod war once started, Digby and Everell were in no danger of sleeping at their post. Digby loved, as well as another man, and particularly those who have had brief military experience, to fight his battles o'er again; and Everell was at an age to listen with delight to tales of adventure and danger. They thus wore away the time till the imaginations of both relater and listener were at that pitch, when every shadow is embodied, and every passing sound bears a voice to the quickened sense.
>
> (43)

In this instance Sedgwick wryly criticizes the historical reliability of status quo historiography, since even eyewitness accounts (what William Hubbard called "the mouths of some faithful witnesses")[40] derive from romantic imaginations. At stake here are the Horatian tenets that history offer both pleasure and instruction, the cultural foundations for historical print that Sedgwick problematizes by transferring supposedly "female" faculty psychology to male sensibilities.[41] Both Digby and Everell are stirred up by the "adventure and danger" of a romantic, masculine history, which places them in an imaginative "pitch" distorting "sense" itself.

The ambiguous meaning of "sense" here exploits thematic possibilities arising from the complex legacies of Lockean epistemology and Common Sense morality. Sensation signifies a number of things: immediate impression, the (failed) capacity for reason, and sensibility as the affective source of moral behavior. After pontificating to Everell on the vulnerability of the senses, Digby is unable to recognize Magawisca as she emerges from the forest shadows—a fact that parallels his inability to recognize the ethical implications—because of his lack of moral feeling—of the Puritan massacre at Mystic. Digby fails, then, on simultaneously moral and epistemological counts: Magawisca he mistakes for a man and the Pequot for "a kind of beast" (42). Confounded by his own misperception at the moment Magawisca emerges from the woods, Digby asks, completely dumbfounded, "'Could I have been so deceived?'" (44). As a representative male historian, his inadequacy devolves upon a deformed moral sense. Sedgwick thus dramatizes a larger defect in masculine historiography by destabilizing the rigid categorical oppositions (reality and illusion, male and female, history and romance) upon which it is founded. Both Everell and *Hope Leslie*'s contemporary reader clearly need another historian.

REPUBLICANISM AND REVISIONARY HISTORY

But what kind of historian? And what was at stake in rewriting this kind of history?

These issues involve the nature of the war's representation in Sedgwick's own era as well as the historiographic and ideological relations between commonwealth and republic. Certainly early national antiquarians, both textbook writers and more "original" historians, naturally borrowed from Puritan sources. The theory and method surrounding their historiographic practice, however, should be understood in its immediate context, for too often critics mystify how and why nineteenth-century historians borrow from their predecessors. George H. Callcott, for example, has argued for the increasing scholarly rigor and sophistication with which nineteenth-century historians approached primary sources, suggesting that the ideal antebellum historian was a "lawyer" or a "judge" of historical evidence: "To use the sources was a simple dictum, but to criticize them, weigh their authenticity, and use them discretely was an art."[42] But Callcott simultaneously admits that the historian "felt no need to argue for originality, and he would not have understood why he should make a fetish of reworking material when what he wanted to say already had been better said by another."[43] Together, these two assessments only muddle the issue of historiography as a cultural and political practice. Why, one might ask, did early national history-writers assume that the narrative of the war "had been better said" by their Puritan ancestors?

Early nationals thematized the war principally in two ways, both of which involved important ideological relations between Puritan commonwealth and early American republic: the validation of American exceptionalism and the recovery of Revolutionary *virtu*. Didactic historians during Sedgwick's day co-opted the Puritan theological concept of "special Providences," the rare intervention of divine agency to determine events, which was in this case apparent in Mason's success despite being greatly outnumbered. To dramatize the divinely miraculous nature of this underdog victory, they followed their Puritan forebears in mis-

leadingly casting the Pequot as a rising power.[44] Hannah Adams, for one, marveled at the "interposition of Divine Providence [that] was visible in restraining the savages from their [the Puritans'] infant settlements."[45] Trumbull emphasized the day of thanksgiving that the Puritans held afterward, noting that "in all the churches of New-England devout and animated praises were addressed to him, who giveth his people the victory, and causes them to dwell safely."[46] Such rhetoric deliberately blurred the meaning of the "people," transferring its eschatological promise from commonwealth to republic.

Such a transferral involved translation as well. Much more dramatically than in Puritan histories, early national narrative of the war occasioned the opportunity to instruct readers in the political necessity of republican *virtu*. Early nationals mediated the Pequot War through a cultural discourse of Revolutionary republicanism. Even as Americans gradually sloughed off the atavistic codes of classical republicanism, they still periodically invoked it as a source of masculine identity. Its cultural use, of course, was contingent on rhetorical context. Even a proponent for a wholly "modern" Constitution, such as James Madison, could resort to it, declaring, for example, in the *Federalist* #57 that the "vigilant and and manly spirit" of the people must safeguard the republic against the power of the House of Representatives.[47] This masculine ethos also informed Andrew Jackson's cultivation of the persona of "Old Hickory," the hero of the War of 1812 who had saved the republic at the Battle of New Orleans. Timothy Dwight's handling of his ancestors' run-in with the Pequot begins to show how the period's historical discourse was shaped by a resilient ideology of masculine republicanism. In *Travel in New-England and New-York,* Dwight concluded:

> Few efforts, made by man have been more strongly marked with wisdom in the projection, or with superior courage and conduct, in the execution. Every step appears to have been directed by that spirit, and prudence, which mankind have, with one voice, regarded with admiration and applause in the *statesman and the hero.*[48]

In this same vein, Benjamin Trumbull's history reveals an affinity with an older ideal of republicanism, where the selfless virtue of volunteer yeoman-citizens (as opposed to standing armies) ensures political survival: "The importance of the crisis was now come, when the very existence of Connecticut, under providence, was to be determined by the sword, in a single action; and to be decided by the good conduct of less than eighty brave men."[49] This is more than the clichéd patriotism it might initially appear to be. Trumbull's rhetoric mediates syntactically between passivity and activity, between the agencies, in other words, of divine providence and republican heroism. The phrase "by the sword" allies this militarism metonymically with a distinctly premodern mode of warfare.

The political logic of this historical metaphor is apparent as well in the association of colonial New England with an ancient myth of republican purity. In a Forefathers Da oration of 1820, for example, an Orthodox minister from Connecticut concluded that the "valour" of Mason's expedition prevented "an extermination of the rising colonies."[50] In his *History of the Indian Wars* (1824) Epaphras Hoyt employs a similar language: "Finding war unavoidable, the Connecticut people acted with vigour."[51] As we have seen, in the aftermath of the Revolution these words lent an exclusively masculine resonance to the historical trope of Puritanism. Here, specifically within the context of military history, their meanings draw upon an Anglo-Saxon mythology of manhood. In the 1828 *American Dictionary,* Noah Webster significantly noted that "vigor" derived from the Saxon word *wigan,* which meant to "carry on war," and that (to recall Dwight's emphasis above on both wisdom and fortitude) it meant both "[s]trength of mind" and "force of body."[52] At least theoretically, then, these masculine qualities ensured one's ability to preserve one's property and hence one's independence. Moreover, the word's lexical origins place Puritan militarism within a larger mythology of the ancient purity of the Anglo-Saxon constitution, which to many American Revolutionaries had provided the historical roots of American "liberties" and hence a justification for independence. Revolutionary theorists as diverse as Thomas Jefferson (in "A Summary View of the Rights of British America" [1774]) and Noah Webster (in his conceptualization of the relation between politics and a national language) looked to the mythic purity of the ancient Germanic tribes as the source of English liberties. The Norman invasion in 1066 disrupted Saxon liberties which the American struggle of 1776 in effect recovered.[53] The submerged lexical associations between Puritanism and Saxonism thus further place colonial history within the framework of Whig ideology.

Surprisingly enough, in light of the period's overt racism, what might be called the valor/ization of Puritanism was paralleled by the Pequot themselves. As Neal Salisbury has noted, to Puritan historians "the Pequot's most offensive traits were their 'pride' and their 'insolence.'"[54] Early nationals easily marshaled these racist epithets to reinforce the saint/sinner dichotomy upon which the narrativity of the war was constructed.[55] Lion Gardiner was careful to include a scene where, during an interlude in the fighting, the Pequot approached the Puritan patrol outside Fort Saybrook and asked "if we did use to kill women and children?" Gardiner's blunt reply, "We said they should see that hereafter," supposedly elicited a moment of Pequot bravado: "We are Pequits, and have killed Englishman, and can kill them as mosquetoes, and we will go to Conectecott and kill men, women, and children."[56] The subtext of contesting masculinities in these Puritan histories (apparent, for example, in Winthrop's and Hubbard's account of John Gallop's heroism, or Mason's bristling over the Narragansett slights upon Puritan valor) endured into early national discourse. Jedidiah Morse, for one, noted how the Pequot became cocky with their initial successes and mocked the Puritans, calling them "'all one sqaw.'"[57]

Paradoxically, however, the Pequot stood as a model of republican virtue. Juggling their admiration for the Pequot's "manly resistance," and the obvious benefit of the war's outcome, historians refashioned the Pequot according to conflicting imperatives of gender and race. After narrating their utter defeat, historians such as David Ramsay uncannily refashioned savage pride into civic valor: "In this first essay of their arms, the colonists of New England displayed both courage and perseverance; but instead of treating a vanquished foe with the respect due to an independent people, who made a gallant effort to defend their property, the rights and the freedom of their nation, the victors urged upon them the desolations of war."[58] In this context, the Pequot sachem Sassacus could be transformed from the most ignoble of savages to the paragon of patriotism. "In an enlightened age and country," Timothy Dwight maintained, Sassacus "might perhaps have been a Charles, or an Alexander."[59] Once they were defeated, the Pequot exemplified, according to Hannah Adams, "the spirit of a people contending for their country and existence."[60] And Abiel Holmes's claim that the Pequot refused "dependence"[61] suggests more than one might at first expect. This code word derives specifically from Revolutionary political assumptions juxtaposing liberty and enslavement, and signals the need for arms to ensure freedom. Such an odd configuration of Native American republicanism was, of course, not restricted to the Pequot alone. Cadwallader Colden, after all, had done virtually the same thing in his *History of the Five Nations* (1727), and the praise Washington Irving heaped upon the Wampanoag sachem, Metacom, in "Philip of Pokanoket" was typical (as I discuss in Chapter 4) of post-Revolutionary histories about King Philip's War. Most important here is the double bind into which the Pequot were narratively placed by early republican history-writers. Alternatively cast as satanic savages and vigilant republicans, the Pequot were "othered" in simultaneously countervailing ways, bearing the early national inscriptions of both an ideal of citizenship and a foil for civilization.

This context helps explain the structural and rhetorical design of *Hope Leslie.* The novel's "recital" of the war consists of twin massacre scenes dramatizing a cyclical pattern of history in which gendered equivalences model a pattern of "savagery" transcending race. The symmetry of the two massacres—one Puritan, one Pequot—crucially works to subvert an ethos of masculine republicanism, specifically in the equivalence history-writers drew between Puritan and Pequot *virtu.* The novel's parallel massacre scenes invert this equivalence, disfigure it by redefining republican valor as male "savagery." *Hope Leslie* shows that it is self-consciously engaged with the masculine cultural formulas surrounding narratives of the war. I should at this point distinguish my reading of this section of *Hope Leslie* from those who have noted Sedgwick's revision of racial stereotypes.[62] Others duly have suggested the limitations of such a revision but have overlooked or simply ignored the ways in which Sedgwick substitutes gendered stereotypes for racial ones. Native American men in this instance become no less "savage" than their Puritan counterparts; they show that "masculine savage quality" Sedgwick attributed to Indian nature in her autobiography written later in life.[63] Gender, in other words, distills race. And the context of republicanism in early national culture helps to explain why.

The issue is this: *Hope Leslie*'s dual massacre scenes thematize the incompatibility of the gendered forms of republican "virtue." The Puritan attack on Mystic, and Mononotto's revenge against the Fletcher household at Bethel, constitute analogous violations of the *home*. Sedgwick takes her cue from the repressed guilt in both Puritan and early national accounts about the killing of innocent women and children (Mason's tortuous insistence, for example, justifying his decision to attack that particular fort; or Jedidiah Morse's paradoxically titillated disgust with "a scene of sublimity and horror indescribably dreadful").[64] In this context, Magawisca describes the fort as a "nest, which the eagles of the tribe had built for their mates and their young" (47). She specifies that the torch used to light it on fire "was taken from our hearth-stone" (49), thus lending the massacre a particularly dark irony rooted in an emergent antebellum ideology of the home. More importantly, since the historical record located Sassacus and the rest of the ruling elders at another fort nearby, Sedgwick's placement of them at a council of chiefs implicitly argues that the public sphere of political duty (the *vivere civile* in classical terms) leaves the home tragically unprotected. Only the maternal figure Monoco can sense its imminent destruction. There is no middle ground here: The twin republican tenets of valor and duty together precipitate an inevitable disaster for domestic life. Later, as Pequot fugitives flee to a Connecticut swamp for protection, the final Puritan attack culminates in an explicit violation of sacred domestic space, as "the wailings of the dying children" resound after the English "penetrated the forest-screen" (53).

Virtually the same domestic idyll becomes the victim of the Pequot attack on Bethel. "All was joy in Mrs. Fletcher's dwelling" (60), the narrator notes as the family prepares for the arrival of Mr. Fletcher and Hope Leslie. Even as Sedgwick in this scene suggests that a wife's vanity may result from an unhealthy desire to please her husband ("in obedience to matrimonial duty, or, it may be, from some lingering of female vanity . . ." [61]), Sedgwick still idealizes the moment distinctly in terms of familial harmony: "A mother, encircled by her children, is always a beautiful spectacle" (61). Sedgwick here deploys a romantic trope whose sentimental surface almost obscures its political potency: "like diligent little housewives," the minstrel birds seek "materials for their housekeeping" (61). The affinities between the "natural" and the domestic, however, are complicated by the scene's emphasis on the cultivated order of Anglo domestic space—a trait that significantly distinguishes the Fletcher home from the Pequot one. In light of what we have seen as the period's discourse of Puritan enterprise, Mrs. Fletcher's house tellingly reflects "the neatness of English taste"; "a rich bed of clover that overspread the lawn . . . *rewarded the industry of the cultivators*" (61, italics mine). What appears to be a series of replicating images, then, is subject to slippage, as the Pequot fort, Fletcher home, and house of Na-

ture vary in degrees of cultivation, together demonstratin[g] both the sanctity of domestic space and a liberal mythol[ogy] of property rights.

In Chapter 4, I take up the importance of this ideology i[n] reading James Fenimore Cooper's novel of the Connecti[ot] cut frontier, *The Wept of Wish-ton-Wish* (1829), but fo[r] now we might recognize that similar details surroundin[g] these two massacre scenes reinforce this gendered equiva[nce] lence and suggest its empowering claims to universality[.] First of all, both patriarchal heads are significantly absen[t] during the respective massacres. Second, Magawisca['s] desperate plea during the murder of Mrs. Fletcher and he[r] child—"'the mother—the children—oh they are all good[—] take vengeance on your enemies—but spare—spare ou[r] friends—our benefactors," (63)—strikes the same cords o[f] domestic pathos ringing out earlier at the attack on Mysti[c.] Moreover, there is a biographical context for all of this. I[n] her autobiography written to her niece, Sedgwick admitte[d] as much: "There was a traditionary story of my mother['s] childhood which used to affect my imagination, for in m[y] youth, dear Alice, the dark shadows of the Indians ha[d] hardly passed off our valleys, and tales about them mad[e] the stock terrors of our nurseries."[65] The real terror (th[e] vulnerability of the "nurseries") lies in the imagined viola[tion of domestic space that *Hope Leslie* dramatizes i[n] symmetrical scenes of massacre.

The difference here between Puritan and Pequot men di[s]solves almost entirely. Although the Pequot sache[m] Mononotto experiences a momentary pulse of feeling f[or] his victims, his "obdurate heart" only really awakens [at] the "courage of the heroic girl." At this moment, the Na[tive American sachem significantly bears one of the earl[y] national era's most common epithets for the Puritan Fa[thers] when he silences his daughter "sternly" (75).[66] Sed[g]wick thus inverts the equivalence which her own cultu[re] drew between Puritan and Pequot valor, recasting repub[li]can manhood as a "savage" code of civic ethics.[67] Th[is] thematic maneuver implicitly mocks those ethical and ra[cial discrepancies in status quo historiography which faile[d] to see the obvious equivalence between "white" and "re[d] savagery. For if Puritan histories unwittingly dramati[zed] vengeful behavior on both sides, early nationals were u[n]willing to recognize an equivalence that would hav[e] shaken their moral high ground. David Ramsay in this re[spect merely parroted the Word of the Fathers on Pequ[ot] "nature": "Revenge is the darling passion of savages, [to] secure the indulgence of which, there is no present adva[n]tage that they will not sacrifice, and no future consequen[ce] they will not totally disregard."[68] "When determined up[on] revenge," Charles Goodrich assured his readers in 182[3,] "no danger would deter them; neither absence nor tim[e] could cool them."[69] Morse shuddered at the image of fi[ve] Pequot heads perched on poles at Fort Saybrook, a res[ult] of vengeance taken by Lion Gardiner's men: "So cont[a]gious are malignant passions."[70] The hollowness of th[e] racist dichotomy between saint and savage, which Mor[se] cannot bear to admit but cannot completely hide eithe[r,] gets a biting rebuttal by Sedgwick in an earlier scene the novel where Digby and a Mohawk are traveling together to deliver Sassacus's scalp to the Puritan magistrates. In a moment of unforgiving irony, Sedgwick has Digby comment that the dried, bloody scalp "'is an abomination to the soul and eye of a christian'" (25). Transporting the badge of Puritan triumph, Digby and the "fierce savage" are indubitably equated.

The gendered project of *Hope Leslie*'s revision of military history is coterminous with a critique of America's millennial destiny constructed upon the smoldering ashes of Mystic Fort. Sedgwick's exposure of masculine republicanism subverts a theory of exceptional, progressive history by, oddly enough, invoking the Whiggish concept of cyclical time. If Puritans relied on typology (in Hubbard's reading of New England, for example, via the Israelites' victory over Amalek) to explain the war's meaning, early nationals perpetuated the theory of providential destiny. In this context, the symmetry of *Hope Leslie*'s narrative design suggests a view of cyclical history that disrupts the historical teleology of nationalist narrative. Male vengeance occurs and reoccurs in inexorable cycles of retribution that parade falsely as republican virtue. The macabre image of Mrs. Fletcher's blood "trickling, *drop by drop*, from the edge of the flooring to the step" (67, italics added) not only gothically refigures the true nature of Revolutionary *virtu* but resonates as well, especially in light of these quid pro quo retributions, with a sense of inevitability. Historical process is key to gendered revision. As we have seen, the subject of Puritanism during the early republic was emplotted to fulfill both cyclical and progressive history. In this regard *Hope Leslie*'s revisionism at once inscribes and redeploys this ambiguity. The novel bears the markings of its own historical emergence at the very moment it displaces progressive with cyclical history—at the very moment, in other words, when the trope of the home's destruction displaces that of the American Israel.

The novel's treatment of race, however, complicates its gendered intentions. Consider, for example, a moment during *Hope Leslie*'s preface:

> The Indians of North America are, perhaps, the only race of men of whom it may be said, that though conquered, they were never enslaved. They could not submit, and live. When made captives, they courted death and exulted in torture. These traits of their character will be viewed by an impartial observer, in a light very different from that in which they were regarded by our ancestors. In our histories, it was perhaps natural that they should be represented as "surly dogs," who preferred to die rather than to live, from no other motives than a stupid or malignant obstinacy. Their own historians or poets, if they had such, would as naturally, and with more justice, have extolled their high-souled courage and patriotism.
>
>   (6)

The first part of the passage could be culled from the period's nationalist historiography. (How similar, for example, is Salma Hale's claim that Pequot "resistance was brave

and obstinate" and that "for bravery in battle and fortitude in suffering [the Pequot] were not surpassed by any of the English troops.").[71] At this moment *Hope Leslie* participates in the cant of Revolutionary America by arguing in effect that the Pequot chose, in the words of New Hampshire's state motto, to live free or die. The new historian whom her reader presumably needs—the "impartial observer"—thus humanizes the Pequot within the sanctioned terms of masculine republican heroism. Her self-conscious departure from Puritan racism (in the brief but stinging allusion to William Hubbard in quotation marks in the excerpt above) rescues the racial other in a way that partakes in a cultural apotheosis of "republican" Native Americans.

What, then, one might ask, is the ethical status of the two massacre scenes? A close reading of Magawisca's history shows that this trope of Pequot valor actually problematizes the thematic trajectory of these scenes, their subversion of classical republican virtue. First of all, Magawisca refers to the Pequot as a "proud and prosperous" tribe (56). As a wavering heroine in the tradition of Sir Walter Scott, her unwillingness to inform Mrs. Fletcher of Mononotto's presence results from kinship ties, specifically because her "pride" is "enlisted on the side of her people" (55). Most importantly, Magawisca's actual account of a massacre of domestic innocents loses its initial intention. What at first looks like a "home" inhabited by women and children uncannily becomes a battleground where the Pequot braves "fought as if each man had a hundred lives" (48). William Bradford, Sedgwick argues to reinforce this point, mistook Pequot "courage" and "fortitude" for savagery. Interestingly enough, these textual inconsistencies actually create a parallel to issues raised by today's historians about the Pequot War. Sedgwick in effect prepares her reader for the kind of massacre that Francis Jennings and other revisionists have argued, but then quickly changes frequency during the conflict to emphasize the "manly spirit" of Samoset, who defends the home "with a prince-like courage" (49).[72] Why?

The contradictions surrounding *Hope Leslie*'s history of the Pequot War—the simultaneous appropriation and subversion of classical republicanism—derive from Sedgwick's complex relationship both to her immediate audience and to her period's prevailing ideologies of race. Her revisionary history belies the difficulty of carrying on simultaneous revisions of gender and race. A historiographic and ethical problem faced her: How does one both critique republican manhood and fully humanize the Pequot for a potentially dubious audience? In *The First Settlers of New England* (1829), Lydia Child faced a similar dilemma and marshaled the trope of Pequot manliness to similar ends. In Child's series of domestic dialogues, a mother/historian informs her children/readers that had "the Pequods quietly submitted to have their country ravaged, and fortresses built in their immediate vicinity to awe them into immediate subjection, they must have been less than men."[73] Both Sedgwick and Child in these instances resort to a culturally specific brand of ethnocentrism, which if they did not at least partly embrace, they nonetheless deployed to sway their readers *on their readers' own terms.* Revolutionary republicanism was apparently too misogynistic an ideology to embrace as a modern standard of civic behavior, and yet too powerful a polemical tool to resist. Hence the Pequot warrior himself emerges from this era as a protean text, a sign of cultural and gendered ambivalence, and the object of psychological and ideological projections of Anglo authors. The Pequot War becomes the fictive site of a thematic fracture between gender and race revealing in this case the cultural legacy of the American Revolution.

ROMANTIC HISTORY AND HISTORICAL ROMANCE

These thematic inconsistencies in *Hope Leslie* coincide with theoretical issues surrounding the very status of historical narrative. Indeed, this section of the novel raises the issue of the representational status of all history-writing; it does so within the context of the changing relations between "history" and historical "fiction" during this early republic. Sedgwick's narrative strategies obviously fulfill her objections to an exclusively masculine form of republicanism. But these strategies also expose an irrepressible (and yet unacknowledged) sense of the impossibility of composing "objective" history. The ideological disruption Sedgwick creates as a historian, of sorts, actually complicates her claims to authenticity. Her revisionary history, after all, manipulates narrative to defamiliarize readers. To put this in present-day theoretical terms, Sedgwick "reemplots"[74] the Pequot War, divesting the deaths of Stone, Norton, and Oldham of their narrative power (which Jennings and others have recognized) to rationalize the later massacre at Mystic. By reframing the massacre at Mystic, and constructing parallel massacre scenes, Sedgwick's engagement in gender politics ultimately exposes the metahistorical status of *Hope Leslie.* Her novel's fourth chapter is exactly what she calls Magawisca's narrative—a "recital," or performance, of history. So despite her intentions to award Magawisca narrative authority, the text's performative qualities suggest the inevitability of historical relativism.

A close look at the relationship between Magawisca's and Digby's histories bears this out. From the outset of Magawisca's narrative, Sedgwick complicates the subject of historical truth by suggesting that her Indian angel's history is an enumeration of events *and* an artistic performance. "[Magawisca] paused for a few moments, sighed deeply, and then began the recital of the last acts in the tragedy of her people; the principal circumstances of which are detailed in the chronicles of the times by the witnesses of the bloody scenes" (47). Through her own eyewitness, Sedgwick aims to compete with Puritan ones like John Mason and John Underhill, who, via William Hubbard and others, influenced early national discourse about the war. Yet she creates at this moment uncertainties about the status of "history." Is it a dramatic performance—or merely an enumeration of facts? Magawisca's performance is implied by her need as an artist to pause and capture the moment, to marshall her resources before she stands and delivers. Magawisca's description recalls the generic

ambiguity established in the novel's Preface when Sedgwick states that hypothetically either Pequot "historians or poets" (6) could have defended their people's cause.

Magawisca's performance further suggests the power of historical romance as a medium for revisionary history. The crucial point here is that Digby's and Magawisca's histories metaphorically express an increasing competitiveness (and familiarity) between history and historical romance, a subject that I addressed in the Introduction. In this instance the text of *Hope Leslie* inscribes its own context—that is, the discursive practices surrounding the production of all history-writing during this particular era. Everell Fletcher thus can be situated as the early republic's implied reader for whom the genres of history and historical fiction are competing. And this implied reader, *Hope Leslie* suggests, already has been corrupted by masculine nationalist historiography. The reader (perhaps unknowingly) comes to historical romance in need of help.

Like *Hope Leslie*'s reader, Everell becomes easily seduced into the scene's paradoxically liberating and debilitating pathos: "'Did they so rush on sleeping women and children?' asked Everell, who was unconsciously lending all his interest to the party of the narrator" (48). As Magawisca's story progresses, Everell unwittingly loses his capacity to object to her "version," and helplessly asks instead for more details about the fate of Sassacus. So the power of historical narrative would seem to lie along the axis of feeling and imagination. Yet the logical extension of such thinking destabilizes the authenticity of Magawisca's history. Sedgwick's apparent desire to authorize Magawisca is frustrated by language belying an irrepressible sense of the artificiality (as in "art" or "artifice") of historical romance:

> It [the war] was an important event to the infant colonies, and its magnitude probably somewhat heightened to the imaginations of the English . . . and Everell had heard [the events] detailed with the interest and particularity that belongs to recent adventures; but he had heard them in the language of the enemies and conquerors of the Pequods; and from Magawisca's lips they took a new form and hue; she seemed, to him, to embody nature's best gifts, and her feelings to be the inspiration of heaven. This new version of an old story reminded him of the man and the lion in the fable. But here it was not merely changing sculptors to give the advantage of one or another of the artist's subjects; but it was putting the chisel into the hand of truth, and giving it to whom it belonged.

(53)

The metaphor of the chisel at once legitimates *Hope Leslie*'s artistic achievement and undermines the historicity of such a performance. The language surrounding this achievement suggests its purely representational quality. Magawisca's account is "a new *version* of an old story," possessing only a new "hue and form" rather than a new substance. Compare this language to the epigraph at the start of this chapter. The reviewer of an early national history defending the Pequot (which tellingly equates the Pu-ritans to the Ancient Romans) rhetorically raises the same theoretical problem: a "different garb" suggests form rather than substance, the inevitable dressings and redressings of language that we inevitably bestow upon the past. Histori-cal narrative would seem to face the problem that the claim to "the hand of truth" is complicated by the lurking sense that only new "versions" can be told.

Sedgwick's intentions here would appear to be open to de-bate. Dana D. Nelson recently has argued against the no-tion that Magawisca's history simply subverts the patriar-chal Word. In her view Sedgwick juxtaposes Digby's and Magawisca's histories in order to show the inevitably dia-logic character of historical narrative.[75] My argument coin-cides with Nelson so far as both of us recognize the repre-sentational nature of the two histories. But her understanding of Sedgwick's intentions ignores the cul-tural and historiographic contexts in which *Hope Leslie* emerged. First of all, the ideological stakes of writing his-tory in this case—the gendered meanings of republicanism during this era—make it difficult for one to believe that Sedgwick stood so theoretically detached from Magawis-ca's account.

Moreover, the view that Sedgwick self-consciously up-holds historical relativism depends on Everell's unreliabil-ity (because of his excessive emotionalism) as a standard for judging the "truth" of Magawisca's history. Yet to read Bakhtin backward, as Nelson does, in order to find an ava-tar of dialogism in Catharine Sedgwick herself, elides early national assumptions about the nature of historical writing. The romanticization of historiography during the antebellum era is crucial to gauging the relative status in *Hope Leslie* of Digby's and Magawisca's narratives. Early nationals increasingly understood historiography to be an affective and imaginative process. "You will struggle in vain," Samuel Knapp declared in the preface to *Lectures on American Literature* (1829), "to make American history well understood by your pupils, unless biographical sketches, anecdotes and literary selections, are mingled with the mass of general facts. The heart must be affected, and the imagination seized, to make lasting impressions upon the memory."[76] Reviews of nationalist histories in-creasingly called for a work of "genius" that could but-tress the nation's artistic reputation at home and abroad.[77] The year of *Hope Leslie*'s publication, a writer for the *American Journal of Education* defined a new American history in just these terms: "Our country is the monument of our great men. Our history is our national poetry. . . . If we are an intellectual people, it is to be hoped we are not merely so. It is hoped that we have [in the composi-tion of history] imagination and feeling. Then let this his-tory have an interesting form . . . let those parts of it ap-pear which address the moral sentiments."[78]

In this emergently romantic era Sedgwick herself under-stood Everell's response to Magawisca's "history" to ap-proximate an affective ideal that she elsewhere endorsed. Indeed, the exchange between Magawisca and Everell ac-

tually models a dynamic of *all* history-writing that Sedg-wick espoused in a letter (written the year after *Hope Le-slie*'s publication) to the renowned Swiss historian Jean-Charles-Leonard Simonde de Sismondi, author of the multivolumed *History of the Italian Republics in the Middle Ages* (1809-18):

> But, after all, you cannot estimate the benefit, for you are not aware of the homage your writings have in-spired . . . that you infuse into them a moral life, that you breathe your own soul into them, impart to them . . . a portion of your own identity. This seems to me to be one of their attractive and attaching peculiarities. It is this that makes us feel them to be the production of a being, whose affections and sympathies are kin-dred to our own.[79]

The passage marks an ostensibly odd moment where a writer of historical fiction tells a historian that she admires him *as* a historian because his work appeals to faculties associated with imaginative writing. Sedgwick situates history-writing's didacticism within a psychological, emo-tive dynamic allying the "affections and sympathies" of both reader and writer. The net result not only blurs the genres of history and romance (as we saw in the earlier scene with Digby and Everell) but also obviates the idea that, in Sedgwick's view, Everell's response somehow problematizes the reliability of Magawisca's historical nar-rative. Just the opposite: It further validates it.

An affective epistemology helps to explain the equivalence *Hope Leslie* draws between Digby's and Magawisca's "histories." *Hope Leslie* registers both the performative nature of *all* history-writing and the increasing competi-tion between the genres of history and fiction expressed in the juxtaposition of Digby's and Magawisca's accounts. Both historical narratives have the same audience; they produce essentially the same effects. Moreover, *Hope Le-slie* reveals the instability of generic borders. The reasons for this lie in the convergence of two important trends during the early republic: the proliferation of historical ro-mance in the 1820s and the gradual romanticization of his-tory. Chapter 5 explores the politics of faculty psychology in histories of the Salem witchcraft trials, and locates the uncertainty with which early nationals viewed the imagi-nation, but here I wish to emphasize that during this tran-sitional era historiography was increasingly subjected to romantic literary standards.

The similar cultural space that these dual genres inhabited in the early republic is metaphorically apparent in the equivalent receptions that Digby's and Magawisca's narra-tives elicit. If we recall the scene between Digby and Ever-ell, where masculine war stories produce only "heightened imaginations," revisionary history in the form of female romance produces much the same thing: "Everell's imagi-nation, touched by the wand of feeling, presented a very different picture of those defenseless families of savages . . ."; he "did not fail to express to Magawisca with all the eloquence of a heated imagination, his sympathy and admiration of her heroic and suffering people" (54). Moreover, the power of imagination (as in the letter to Sismondi) involves both historian and audience. For the "wand of feeling" with which Magawisca touches Everell ambiguously refers to their mutually affected sensibilities. Through Magawisca, then, Sedgwick anticipates a principle of romantic historiography which valued the historian's passionate involvement in historical subject matter.[80] The interaction leaves Magawisca and Everell in the same kind of "romantic abstraction" (54) that Digby and Everell earlier had experienced. And so if Digby's history manages to invalidate itself as nothing more than a specifically masculine romanticism, its feminized revision in Magawisca's performance similarly relies upon the purely manipulative function of language. As history and romance metaphorically vie for authority in *Hope Leslie,* they expose only an equivalent performativity.

In this context, then, *Hope Leslie* stages dual modes of history-writing whose epistemological claims inevitably are compromised by the very qualities of affect and imagination that lend them narrative power. Yet *Hope Leslie*'s "recital" at least suggests the problematic implications of history-as-performance that early national histories generally suppressed. Most history-writers used the term simply to signify an enumeration of historical facts. The title of Jeremy Belknap's *American Biography,* for example, includes the phrase, "Comprehending a Recital of the Events connected with their Lives and Actions." Those, like Belknap, who claimed historical accuracy refused to acknowledge how nationalist pieties may have complicated those claims. "Where is the American," one orator asked in 1826, "who has not felt a glow of enthusiasm in listening to a recital of those events that led to our national emancipation?"[81] David Ramsay similarly claimed a scrupulous fidelity to the facts: "The history of a war on the frontiers can be little else than a recital of the exploits, the sufferings, the escapes and deliverances of individuals, of single families, or small parties."[82] Ironically, the *North American Review* found that Ramsay was too close to the contemporary materials treated in the third volume of his history "to admit of a cool, philosophical recital."[83] Yet even here its signification slips as the reviewer in the next breath calls Ramsay's history a "performance." Thus, predominantly male writers and reviewers alike deployed the term to denote a scrupulous fidelity to the facts, the kind of research that enhanced one's narrative and political authority.[84]

Hope Leslie's performance calls attention to yet another meaning of "recital." The first entry for the word in Webster's 1828 *American Dictionary* defined it as a "Rehearsal; the repetition of the words of another or of a writing; as of the *recital* of a deed; the *recital* of testimony." This suggests an act of ventriloquy. Certainly, as we have seen, this process aptly characterizes the transmission of Puritan narrative into early national historical discourse. Early nationals, in effect, followed the biblical epigraph to William Hubbard's *A Narrative of the Troubles with the Indians,* taken from Exodus 17.14, after God had granted the Israelites a victory over the tribe of Amalek: "And the Lord said unto Moses, Write this for a Memorial in a Book, and rehearse it in the ears of Joshua, for I will utterly put out the Remembrance of Amalek from under heaven." From John Mason's account of the assault on Mystic Fort, through William Hubbard's paraphrasing of it, to its virtual ventriloquy in Benjamin Trumbull and his contemporaries, the Puritan story of the Pequot War continuously was "rehearsed." Like Joshua himself, early nationals were reminded of the sacredness of national destiny and the purely secular means by which the republic would survive. In the very act of engaging the subject of the Pequot War, then, Sedgwick confronted—and disrupted—the word of the Fathers as it was "rehearsed" from the commonwealth to the republic.

WOMEN'S WRITING AND REVISIONARY HISTORY

The appearance of the Pequot War in *Hope Leslie* is thus no accident at all. The subject of the war in early national culture was laden with the masculine ideologies of Revolutionary republicanism, and it carried, like the Y chromosome, the genetic inheritance of a misogynistic understanding of the "republic," which presumably would be passed on (through narrative) to future generations. Sedgwick's treatment of the war was impelled by a gender-specific republican politics of exclusion rooted in classical ideology, which understood the republic in terms of the capacity of male citizens to express their identities fully through active citizenship. Sedgwick's manufacturing of domestic pathos, and her redefinition of "savagery" along the lines of gender—as opposed strictly to race—should be understood in this context. Classical republican ideology merely highlighted the political and ethical inconsistencies in the Revolutionary settlement of 1787-8, ones that excluded women from citizenship and yet still asked them to contribute to the making of good citizens. Women had a political role with no political rights.

So the thinly veiled contest taking place in *Hope Leslie* between nationalist history and historical romance actually shows Sedgwick interrogating the ethical viability of her culture's association of Puritanism with "republicanism"—a word she already is begining to redefine in the early part of the novel. This crucial section of *Hope Leslie* signals her controversy with a political and cultural metaphor, her dismantling of what I have called the New Ebenezer of the early republic. In the next chapter, I explore this process of historical revision as cultural criticism, a process that further brings into focus the contemporary historicity of the "Puritans" in women's historical romance.

The representational status of Puritanism has important consequences for redefining the very terms of the debate about women's history-writing in general. In *The Feminization of American Culture* (1977), Ann Douglas argues that nineteenth-century female romance represented an "escape" from masculine history.[85] Douglas noted that ministers like Jared Sparks turned away from the feminized province of the Unitarian pulpit in order to pursue the more masculine avocation of history. As Douglas saw it, this was a way for men to escape feminine "influence" and reassert their masculinity. Recent critics justifiably have argued that Douglas failed to see the seriousness of domestic politics in antebellum women's writing.[86] Yet the typical corrective that women's history-writing represented anything but an "escape from history" misses the point. A contemporary reviewer of *Hope Leslie* rightly claimed that Sedgwick "has had the industry to study the early history of New England,"[87] but today we should not define the novel's historicity so narrowly. *Hope Leslie* represents its own emergence in post-Revolutionary culture. And this explains why Douglas objected to Sedgwick's anachronistic language, which presumably reflected an "apostasy from history" and a "confused conscience,"[88]—traits characterizing, for Douglas, women's historical writing in general. What she (and many others) fail to see is the secondary importance of Puritanism in *Hope Leslie.* The novel's anachronistic language and thematics of "virtue" testify to its preeminent concerns with the status of civic ethics in the republic.

The "recital" that *Hope Leslie* offers begins to suggest the competition between alternative forms of "history" during this era. Published in 1827, the very year in which Massachusetts legislated the study of history into the public school curriculum, *Hope Leslie* registers a hyper self-consciousness about the discursive field of history-writing into which it enters. Much later in life, in her autobiography addressed to her niece's daughter, Sedgwick would time and again juxtapose the state and the home as contending spheres of education, emphasizing, of course, the superiority of the latter: "I believe, my dear Alice, that the people who surround us in our childhood, whose atmosphere infolds us, as it were, have more to do with the formation of our characters than all our didactic and preceptive education."[89] The antagonistic power relations between the state and the home are inscribed in *Hope Leslie* in the contest between Digby's and Magawisca's tales, or, in effect, masculine nationalist historiography and women's historical romance. Eight years after *Hope Leslie,* Sedgwick again suggested this tension in *The Linwoods* (1835), a historical novel set in Revolutionary America. While lightly chastising the "duty" that the meekly obedient Bessie Lee performs by "so virtuously" reading histories, the novel's heroine, Isabella Linwood, asks her, "If history then is mere fiction, why may we not read romances of our own choosing? My instincts have not misguided me, after all."[90] Isabella's iconoclasm toward status quo historiography expresses ex post facto Sedgwick's own in *Hope Leslie.* Isabella here testifies to Sedgwick's underlying assumptions about the competition for an immediate reading audience. The story of the Pequot War introduces narrative strategies that work ideally to emancipate the implied reader of the day who, like Everell, presumably has been corrupted.

Like Hope Leslie, who, we should remember, nearly married William Hubbard, Catharine Sedgwick vented herself "upon the ungainly ways of scholars" (154). But these scholars were not really the dead ghosts of John Mason

and William Hubbard, but the very real, living spectres of Benjamin Trumbull, Jedidiah Morse, and others who exerted significant cultural power in early-nineteenth-century New England. In the next chapter I explore the narrative strategies with which both Sedgwick and Child conduct cultural criticism, articulating along the way the ambiguous ideological relations between republicanism and domesticity. Such criticism was made possible by the very instability of "virtue" itself during this transitional era. What did it mean—masculine vigilance or affectional benevolence? Who were the real stewards of republican virtue? Like the old war veteran of her letter to Charles, the "republican" heroes of *Hope Leslie* and *Hobomok* are subjected to complex surgical procedures in which the language and ideas of republicanism are forever changed.

Notes

1. This unpublished letter comes from the Emma Embury Collection, which is in the inventory of the 19th-Century Shop in Baltimore, Maryland. I would like to thank Stephen Loewentheil for his cooperation in allowing me to consult and use this material.

2. Letter to Charles Sedgwick, October 27, 1826, in *Life and Letters of Catharine M. Sedgwick,* ed. Mary Dewey (New York: Harper & Bros., 1872), 179-80.

3. Francis Jennings, *The Invasion of America: Indians, Colonialism, and the Cant of Conquest* (New York: Norton, 1976), 181. Other important revisionist studies include Richard Drinnon, *Facing West: The Metaphysics of Indian-Hating and Empire-Building* (Minneapolis: University of Minnesota Press, 1980), 35-45; and Neal Salisbury, *Manitou and Providence: Indians, Europeans, and the Making of New England, 1500-1643* (New York: Oxford University Press, 1982), 203-35. These historians address traditional accounts of the war, which place greater faith in the reliability of Puritan sources, such as found in Alden T. Vaughan's *New England Frontier: Puritans and Indians, 1620-1675* (Boston: Little, Brown, 1965). For an even earlier tradition of revisionist historians, see Vaughan, 134.

4. Stephen T. Katz, "The Pequot War Reconsidered," *New England Quarterly* 64 (June 1991), 207.

5. See, for example, Alfred A. Cave's "Who Killed John Stone: A Note on the Origins of the Pequot War," *William and Mary Quarterly,* 3rd ser. 49 (July 1992), 509-21. For an even more recent interpretation of whether or not the expedition qualifies as an act of genocide, see Michael Freeman, "Puritans and Pequots: The Question of Genocide," *New England Quarterly* 68 (June 1995), 278-93.

6. See Edwin Halsey Foster, *Catharine Maria Sedgwick* (New York: Twayne, 1974), 73-80.

7. Mary Kelley, "Introduction" to *Hope Leslie; or Early Times in the Massachusetts* (New Brunswick, NJ: Rutgers University Press, 1987), xxix, xxxi.

8. Sandra Zagarell, "Expanding 'America': Lydia Sigourney's *Sketch of Connecticut,* Catharine Sedgwick's *Hope Leslie," Tulsa Studies in Women's Literature* 6 (Fall 1987), 235. For commentary that is less specific on Sedgwick's relationship to Puritan historiography but that still notes the novel's "subversion of male myth/history," see Christopher Castiglia, "In Praise of Extra-vagant Women: *Hope Leslie* and the Captivity Romance," *Legacy* 6 (1989), 12, and Lucy Maddox, *Removals: Nineteenth-Century American Literature and the Politics of Indian Affairs* (New York: Oxford University Press, 1991), 105 and n. 14, 191.

9. Dana Nelson, *The Word in Black and White: Reading "Race" in American Literature, 1638-1867* (New York: Oxford University Press, 1992), 72.

10. Ruth H. Bloch, "The Gendered Meanings of Virtue in Revolutionary America," *Signs: Journal of Women in Culture and Society* 13 (1987), 37-58. Bloch argues that through the affective epistemology of Edwardsian religion, Scottish Common Sense thinkers such as Francis Hutcheson who posited an emotional moral sense, and the rise of literary sentimentalism, virtue became increasingly associated with the workings of the heart and hence with women themselves. See also Jay Fliegelman, *Prodigals and Pilgrims: The American Revolution against Partiarchal Authority, 1750-1800* (Cambridge: Cambridge University Press, 1982).

11. Bloch, "Gendered Meanings," 56.

12. Gordon Wood, *The Radicalism of the American Revolution* (New York: Vintage, 1993), 216. See the entire section on "Benevolence," 213-25, for this change.

13. Nancy Cott, *The Bonds of Womanhood: "Woman's Sphere" in New England, 1780-1835* (New Haven: Yale University Press, 1977), 96.

14. Linda Kerber, *Women of the Republic: Intellect and Ideology in Revolutionary America* (Chapel Hill: University of North Carolina Press, 1980; New York: Norton, 1986). See also Mary Beth Norton's *Liberty's Daughters: The Revolutionary Experience of American Women* (New York, 1980). Rosemarie Zagarri recently has traced the intellectual roots of republican womanhood to the "civil jurisprudential school" of the Scottish Enlightenment. See "Morals, Manners, and the Republican Mother," *American Quarterly* 44 (June 1992), 192-215. For the importance of liberalism to women's political status, see Kerber's "The Republican Ideology of the Revolutionary Generation," *American Quarterly* 37 (Fall 1985), 474-95, esp. 485.

15. Kerber, *Women of the Republic,* 288.

16. The very notion of "separate spheres" has come under increasing scrutiny by historians of American women. In this chapter and the next, I treat this issue as an ideological construct rather than as an accurate description of social and political reality. For recent challenges to the concept of "woman' sphere," see Linda Kerber, "Separate Spheres, Female Worlds, Woman's Place: The Rhetoric of Woman's History," *Journal of American History* 7. (1988), 9-39, "Politics and Culture in Women' History: A Symposium," *Feminist Studies* 6 (Spring 1980), 26-64; Kathy Peiss, "Going Public: Women in Nineteenth-Century Cultural History," *ALH* (December 1991), 817-28; Lori D. Ginzberg *Women and the Work of Benevolence: Morality Politics, and Class in the Nineteenth-Century United States* (New Haven: Yale University Press 1990); and Mary Ryan, *Women in Public: Between Banners and Ballots, 1825-1880* (Baltimore: John Hopkins University Press, 1990).

17. As Cott has shown, a number of factors made the home the "natural" place for the formation of virtuous citizens. See *Bonds,* 19-62, for changes that gradually devalued the home as a site of economic production. In this regard, see also Gerda Lerner "The Lady and the Mill Girl: Changes in the Status of Women in the Age of Jackson," in *The Majority Finds its Place: Placing Women in History* (New York: Oxford University Press, 1979), 15-30, esp 17-18, 25, 29. For the ideological legacy of Lockean and Rousseauist educational theories emphasizing the importance of nurturance, see Fliegelman *Prodigals and Pilgrims,* 9-36.

18. Benjamin Rush, "A Plan for the Establishment of Public Schools and the Diffusion of Knowledge in Pennsylvania; to which are added Thoughts upon the Mode of Education Proper in a Republic. Addressed to the Legislature and Citizens of the State, 1786. In *Essays, Literary, Moral and Philosophical* (Philadelphia: Thomas and Samuel Bradford, 1798)

19. Rush, "Thoughts Upon Female Education Accommodated to the Present State of Society, Manner and Government in the United States of America in *Essays,* 89.

20. *Life and Letters,* ed. Dewey, 91.

21. Ibid., 91, italics added.

22. *North American Review* 26 (April 1828), 403-2(403 for citation.

23. Ibid., 408.

24. Ibid., 406.

25. George H. Callcott, *History in United States, 1800 1860: Its Practice and Purpose* (Baltimore: John Hopkins University Press, 1970), 104.

26. William Bradford gives some account of the machinations of John Lyford and John Oldham. See *C Plymouth Plantation,* rev. ed., ed. Samuel Eli Morison (New York: Knopf, 1991), 147-69, esp. 8, 149-50. See also Jennings, 188-90, and Vaughan 123-4.

27. John Mason's "A Brief History of the Pequot Wa was edited by Thomas Prince, who brought it

publication in Boston in 1736. It was reprinted in the *Collections of the Massachusetts Historical Society,* 2nd ser. 8 (1826), 120-53, 126 for citation. All future citations refer to this edition. As others have shown, *Hope Leslie* reveals Sedgwick's familiarity with Winthrop, Hubbard, and Bradford. I suspect that she likely was familiar with the *MHSC* reprinting of John Mason, but its virtual transmission in William Hubbard effectively skirts this problem. Let me say here, however, that my discussion in this chapter concerns the intertextual relations of these Puritan (and early national) histories. My references to the reprinted narratives of Gardiner, Underhill, and Vincent—all of which postdate the publication of *Hope Leslie*—are premised on those rhetorical and ideological features *common* to Puritan historians.

28. Mason, "Brief History," 129.

29. John Underhill, "Newes from America; or a New and Experimental Discoverie of New England," *Collections of the Massachusetts Historical Society,* 3rd ser. 6 (1837), 1-28. Lion Gardiner, "Leift Lion Gardiner his Relation of the Pequot Warres" in *Collections of the Massachusetts Historical Society* 3rd ser. 3 (1833), 131-60, and in *A History of the Pequot War* (Cincinnati: William Dodge, 1860), 5-32. All citations in the essay come from the 1860 edition; P[hilip] Vincent, "A True Relation of the Late Battell Fought in New-England, between the English and the Pequet Salvages: In which were Slaine and Taken Prisoners about 700 of the Salvages, and Those which Escaped Had Their Heads Cut Off by the Mohocks; with the Present State of Things There" (London: Thomas Harper, 1638), reprinted with Underhill's narrative in *Collections of the Massachusetts Historical Society,* 3rd ser. 6 (1837), 29-43.

30. Mason, "Brief History," 130.

31. Underhill, "Newes from America," 4.

32. See Gardiner, "Relation," 12-14, and Vincent, "True Relation," 35-7.

33. William Hubbard, *The Present State of New England. Being a Narrative of the Troubles with the Indians in New-England, from the First Planting Therof in the Year 1607 to this Present Year 1677: But Chiefly of the Late Troubles in the Last Two Years, 1675 and 1676; to which is added a Discourse about the Warre with the Pequods in the Year 1637* (London: Thomas Parkhurst, 1677), 116-17.

34. John Winthrop, *The History of New England from 1630 to 1649,* ed. James Savage (Boston: Phelps & Farnham, 1825), 190; Hubbard's account is virtually the same. See *A General History of New England from the Discovery to MDCLXXX* (Cambridge, MA: Hilliard & Metcalf, 1815), 249.

35. Mason, "Brief History," 129.

36. Benjamin Trumbull, *A Complete History of Connecticut, Civil and Ecclesiastical* (Hartford: Hudson & Goodwin, 1797), I:59-60.

37. Abiel Holmes, *American Annals* (Cambridge, MA: Hilliard & Brown, 1829), I:235; Jedidiah Morse and Elijah Parish, *A Compendious History of New England* (London: William Burton, 1808), 93; Epaphras Hoyt, *Antiquarian Researches: Comprising a History of the Indian Wars in the Country Bordering Connecticut River and Parts Adjacent* (Greenfield, MA: Ansel Phelps, 1824), 44. Even the famous antiquarian Samuel Drake, who initially argued that the English settlers "were too proud to court the favor of the natives," went on to recount the deaths of Norton, Stone, and Oldham. See the Appendix to his edition of Thomas Church's *The History of King Philip's War* (Exeter, NH: J&B Williams, 1829), 302-9.

38. Hannah Adams, *A Summary History of New England* (Dedham, MA: H. Mann & J. H. Adams, 1799), 68.

39. Catharine Maria Sedgwick, *Hope Leslie; or Early Times in the Massachusetts,* ed. Mary Kelley (New Brunswick, NJ: Rutgers University Press, 1987), 56. All quotations come from this edition and will be cited parenthetically in the text.

40. Hubbard, *Narrative of the Trouble with the Indians,* 116.

41. See Callcott, *History in the United States,* 139-47.

42. Ibid., 125.

43. Ibid., 136.

44. For a corrective to this commonly held misconception, see Salisbury, *Manitou and Providence,* 211.

45. Adams, *Summary History,* 68.

46. Trumbull, *Complete History of Connecticut,* 87.

47. *The Federalist Papers,* ed. Clinton Rossiter (New York: NAL Penguin, 1961), 353.

48. Timothy Dwight, *Travels in New-England and New-York* (New Haven: T. Dwight, 1821-2), III:19, italics added.

49. Trumbull, *Complete History of Connecticut,* 76.

50. Noah Porter, "A Discourse on the Settlement and Progress of New England" (Hartford: Peter Gleason, 1821), 10.

51. Epaphras Hoyt, *Antiquarian Researches,* 46.

52. Noah Webster, *An American Dictionary of the English Language* (New York: S. Converse, 1828), unpaginated.

53. See Merrill D. Peterson, *Thomas Jefferson and the New Nation* (New York: Oxford University Press, 1970), 57-61, and David P. Simpson, *The Politics of American English, 1776-1850* (New York: Oxford University Press, 1986), 81-90.

54. Salisbury, *Manitou and Providence,* 224.

55. See, for example, Adams, *Summary History,* 69; Trumbull, *Complete History of Connecticut,* 62; Dwight, *Travels,* III:12, and Morse and Parish, *Compendious History,* 95.

56. Gardiner, "Relation" (1860), 17. See Jennings, *Invasion of America,* 211-13, for European and Native American codes of warfare and the false stereotypes that have been pinned on the Pequot in this regard.

57. Morse and Parish, *Compendious History,* 95.

58. Ramsay, *History of the United States,* I:85.

59. Dwight, *Travels in New-England,* III:11.

60. Adams, *Summary History,* 70.

61. *American Annals,* I:241.

62. See, for example, Kelley, "Introduction," xxix, and Zagarell, "Expanding 'America,'" 233, 237.

63. See *The Power of Her Sympathy: The Autobiography and Journal of Catharine Maria Sedgwick,* ed. Mary Kelley (Boston: Northeastern University Press, 1993), 49.

64. Morse and Parish, *Compendious History,* 97.

65. See Kelley, ed., *Power of Her Sympathy,* 49.

66. See, for example, Isaac Goodwin's "An Oration Delivered at Lancaster," *Worcester Magazine and Historical Journal* 1 (Worcester: Rogers & Griffin, 1826), 327. Hawthorne's "Endicott and the Red Cross" investigates the ambiguities of Puritan rigor, as Endicott is described in this language. See *The Centenary Edition of the Works of Nathaniel Hawthorne,* vol. IX, ed. William Charvat, Roy Harvey Pearce, and Claude M. Simpson (Columbus: Ohio State University Press, 1974), 431, 444.

67. Ann Kibbey has argued for the "interchangeable" quality of Puritan and Pequot women as a way of showing the intimacy between Puritan racism and sexism. I would argue that despite the ostensible similarities, Sedgwick does not anticipate Kibbey's argument. Sedgwick issues much less of an indictment against "Puritan" sexism per se and more of one aimed at a political-cultural metaphor between Puritanism and republicanism that was popular during her own time. Sedgwick's feminization of Mystic Fort comments on the destructive capacity of male *virtu,* in which *both* Puritan and Native American men are implicated. Much of Kibbey's argument rests on the dubious conclusion that the diagram at the end of John Underhill's narrative symbolizes a vagina that "portrays both the Puritan men's genocidal violence and the sexual symbolism of their act" (110). Readers also might be warned that Kibbey gives an idiosyncratic interpretation of Underhill's narrative to make it evidence of the "association between the violence of the war and [Puritan] men's attitudes toward women" (109).

Underhill's reference to his wife mocks his *own* stubbornness. Kibbey also misreads Underhill's treatment of two captive, Puritan women, whom he mentions certainly not to serve misogynistic ends but only to show that the Lord chastens whom He loves. This fulfills the promotional dimension of the narrative: "You that intend to go to New England, fear not a little trouble" (22). One also wonders how Kibbey so easily associates Hutchinson with all Puritan women, and Puritan women with Pequot women in Underhill's narrative. See *The Interpretation of Material Shapes in Puritanism: A Study of Rhetoric, Prejudice, and Violence* (Cambridge: Cambridge University Press, 1986).

68. Ramsay, *History of the United States,* I:84.

69. Charles A. Goodrich, *A History of the United States of America* (New York: G. C. Smith, 1829), 15.

70. Morse and Parish, *Compendious History,* 96.

71. Salma Hale, *History of the United States* (London: John Miller, 1826), 43, 86.

72. Sedgwick likely read Philip Vincent's "A True Relation of the Late Batell Fought in New England," first published in 1638 and yet not reprinted in the *Massachusetts Historical Society Collections* until 1837. The description of Samoset's valor bears an uncanny resemblance to a passage in Vincent which is not present in any other of the firsthand Puritan accounts. Sedgwick reads as follows: "Samoset, the noble boy, defended the entrance with a prince-like courage, till they struck him down; prostrate and bleeding he again bent his bow, and had taken deadly aim at the English leader, when a sabre-blow severed his bowstring" (49).

And Vincent: "A stout Pequet encounters [an English soldier at the entrance], shoots his arrow, drawn to the head, into his right arm, where it stuck. He slashed the salvage betwixt the arm and the shoulder, who, pressing towards the door, was killed by the English" (37).

Edward Johnson's *Wonder-Working Providence of Sions Saviour in New-England* (1654), with which, as Mary Kelley has demonstrated, Sedgwick was familiar, does specify that there were bowmen at the entrances to the fort who "wounded the foremost of the English in the shoulder" but gives nothing of the particular details found in both Vincent and Sedgwick. See *Wonder-Working Providence of Sions Savior in New England* (1653), ed. J. Franklin Jameson (New York: Charles Scribner's Sons, 1910), 167, and Kelley, n.5, 359, for Sedgwick and Edward Johnson.

73. Lydia Maria Child, *The First Settlers of New England: or, Conquest of the Pequods, Narragansetts and Pokanokets. As Related by a Mother to her Children. By a Lady of Massachusetts* (Boston: Munroe & Francis, 1829), 24.

74. The term comes, of course, from Hayden White *Metahistory* (Baltimore and London: Johns Hop-

kins University Press, 1973). White argues that "The same event [the attack upon Mystic Fort in this case] can serve as a different kind of element of many different historical stories, depending upon the role it is assigned in a specific motific characterization of the set to which it belongs" (7). See also "The Historical Text as Literary Artifact," in *The Writing of History: Literary Form and Historical Understanding,* ed. Robert H. Canary and Henry Kozicki (Madison: University of Wisconsin Press, 1978), 41-62. Selected essays have been compiled in *The Content of the Form: Narrative Discourse and Historical Representation* (Baltimore: Johns Hopkins University Press, 1987). While White has incurred the wrath of many historians, a more balanced theoretical dissent stressing the continuity between narrative and reality may be found in David Carr, *Time, Narrative and History* (Bloomington: Indiana University Press, 1986).

75. See Nelson, *The Word in Black and White,* n.13, 159.

76. Knapp, *Lectures,* unpaginated.

77. I have taken up this issue in part in my Introduction. See, for example, the review of David Ramsay's *History of the United States* in the *North American Review* 6 (1818), 335-7, and the review of Charles Goodrich's *History of the United States* in the *American Journal of Education* 2 (1827), 683-7.

78. *American Journal of Education,* 686.

79. Dewey, ed., *Life and Letters,* 192.

80. "History only becomes dramatic on two conditions: it must either have the passion of the politician or the imagination of the poet." Quoted from the *Edinburgh Review* 105 (January 1857), 23, in Callcott, *History in the United States,* 148-9. See 147-50 for the importance of emotion to the efficacy of historical narrative. David Levin also noted the "vital feeling of the past" with which the romantic historian was imbued: "One concentrated on responding emotionally to its [in this case, European ruins'] sound, on putting oneself or one's reader in proper imaginative relation with it." See *History as Romantic Art: Bancroft, Prescott, Motley and Parkman* (Stanford, CA: Stanford University Press, 1959), 7-8.

81. See Goodwin in *The Worcester Magazine and Historical Journal,* 327.

82. Ramsay, *History of the United States,* I:137.

83. *North American Review,* 340.

84. The entry for "recital" in the 1828 *American Dictionary* further suggests this lexical instability. Webster first distinguishes between an "enumeration" and a "narrative"; the latter he calls "a telling of the particulars of an adventure or of a series of events." But this distinction collapses because it fails to distinguish between an "enumeration" and a "telling." Another instance of this sense of "recital" may be found in one of the period's orations, where the speaker argues that war stories of the veterans of the War of 1812 actually swayed naive farmers and thus promoted a kind of dangerous militarism: "The poor inhabitant of a remote retreat, who listens with enthusiasm to the *recital* of the exploits of his countrymen, and associates himself in interest with those who never regarded him, discovers a patriotism which we cannot but esteem. . . . Let them be better informed, and know that the country which they love, demands their zeal only for its rights . . . and that those who excite it in behalf of their own personal renown, impose on their affections and betray their interest." See Andrew Ritchie, "An Address Delivered to the Massachusetts Peace Society at their Third Anniversary" (Boston: Wells & Lilly, 1819), 14-15.

85. Ann Douglas, *The Feminization of American Culture* (New York: Knopf, 1977; Anchor, 1988), 165-99.

86. The extent of this rebuttal to Douglas is vast, but it originated principally in Nina Baym's *Women's Fiction: A Guide to Novels by and about Women in America, 1820-1870* (Ithaca, NY: Cornell University Press, 1978) and Jane Tompkins's *Sensational Designs: The Cultural Work of American Fiction, 1790-1860* (New York: Oxford University Press, 1986). For a recent contribution to the politics of sentiment, see Shirley Samuels, ed., *The Culture of Sentiment: Race, Gender and Sentimentality in Nineteenth-Century America* (New York: Oxford University Press, 1992), esp. 10-15, for a reassessment of the Douglas-Tompkins debate.

87. *North American Review* 26 (April 1828), 413.

88. Douglas, *Feminization,* 185.

89. Kelley, ed., *Power of Her Sympathy,* 69-70.

90. *The Linwoods: or "Sixty Years Since" in America* (New York: Harper & Bros., 1835), 64.

Douglas Ford (essay date 1997)

SOURCE: "Inscribing the 'Impartial Observer' in Sedgwick's *Hope Leslie*," in *Legacy,* Vol. 14, No. 2, 1997, pp. 81-92.

[*In the following essay, Ford discusses the manner in which* Hope Leslie *addresses the repressive treatment of women and Native Americans.*]

Taken together, recent criticism discussing Catharine Maria Sedgwick's ***Hope Leslie*** constructs a dialogue concerning not only Sedgwick's neglected position in the canon, but also what most critics agree to be her unconventional portrayal of both women and Native American characters. In fact, several critics have pointed out the manner in which Sedgwick's novel questions the repressive treatment of both women and Native Americans,[1] which leads to a question I hope to address: Does the novel negotiate race and gender within the context of domesticity in the same way, to the same ends? The novel's remarkable preface pushes race to the forefront, as it positions the narrative to challenge the dominant racist assumptions of nineteenth-century America by arguing that "the enlightened and accurate observer of human nature, will admit that the difference of character among the various races of the earth, arises mainly from difference of condition" (6). This statement assigns a bold mission for the novel, as it must contend with the discourses which produce the negative images of race which inform the literature of Sedgwick's period. Additionally, this preface introduces a complex preoccupation with language which this paper will explore, particularly in the crucial images the novel constructs for an "enlightened" reader, images bearing conflicting levels of signification.

Several critics have praised Sedgwick's narrative for transcending racist and sexist notions, an assessment based largely upon the protagonist, who acts decisively and independently upon a Puritan power structure that not only marginalizes her, but treats Native Americans unjustly. However, a schism opens between what Sedgwick's narrator says and how Sedgwick's readers—today as well as in antebellum America—may read the actions and statements of the text's characters. In effect, the novel's preface suggests a certain degree of faith that the "accurate" reader will fill this schism in a desirable manner. Suzanne Gossett and Barbara Bardes provide the sort of reading which reveals how this schism opens largely out of discursive conditions during Sedgwick's time:

> Hope never speaks against male authority, but her actions demonstrate a similar sense of being exempt from its application. Of course she is a romantic projection, and her actions go unpunished because Sedgwick chooses that they shall. In 1827 Sedgwick could not assert that women are oppressed by their exclusion from the political process, but she designs her plot to drive the reader to this conclusion.
>
> (23)

However, even as the textual events "drive the reader" toward a progressive conclusion concerning gender equality, the novel reveals a deeper, more problematic nature concerning questions of race. Indeed, Sedgwick's novel opens gaps where the cultural assumptions of Sedgwick's period sneak through, resulting in a tension in the text that operates contrary to the intentions Sedgwick outlines in her preface. The voice of Hope herself reveals anxiety, even some horror, at the crossing of the racial boundaries prescribed by the European settlers. This embedded conflict raises questions concerning how Sedgwick's audience may have envisioned an "accurate observer," and for contemporary readers, the text continues to raise questions: Does such a position actually exist, and if so, in what form?

Signs of this tension have not gone unnoticed by the novel's commentators. In her reading of the text, Sandra

Zagarell notices "forces" which *Hope Leslie* presents "stubbornly and openly unresolved," such as Faith's refusal to return to the Puritan community (239). Indeed, Faith's presence in the text causes much of the novel's buried tension to rise to the surface. This tension reaches a particularly urgent pitch in the middle of the text, when Magawisca reunites Hope with Faith, whom the Pequods, led by Mononotto, had kidnapped in a raid upon the Fletcher home in the novel's first volume. This kidnapping results in a cultural transformation for Faith: she grows up neither speaking nor understanding English, she appears in "savage attire," and as Hope learns, she has married Oneco (227). Furthermore, she responds to Hope's emotional embrace by "remain[ing] passive in her arms. Her eye was moistened, but she seemed rather abashed and confounded" (227). The manner in which Faith's response to the reunion differs from Hope's plays into what Louise K. Barnett in *The Ignoble Savage* outlines as "a characteristic common to all [Indian] stereotypes," namely stoicism which "ranges from a habitual failure to register facial expression to control over all forms of physical reaction during moments of intense stress" (76). Sedgwick's reunion scene bears traces of the overall pattern Barnett detects in other representations. While Faith's eye appears "moistened," the narrator quickly qualifies this response by noting that her appearance suggests confusion and embarrassment; in other words, Faith's need to control her own emotion, and her confusion over her own disconcertment might signify to the nineteenth-century reader "Indian" or "Other" as much as her attire or her language.

However, the complexity of this scene becomes evident in light of the multiple possibilities of interpretation it contains simultaneously, each affected by the cultural conditions which arrange perceptions of both the embarrassment and the "moistened" eye. That is, read through the lens which Barnett's scholarship provides, Faith's embarrassment exhibits itself, as I have suggested above, as a response to her own tear. In effect, the Indian that Faith has become shows embarrassment at the old feelings which Hope awakens in her. A reading of this kind leaves the "stoic Indian" stereotype intact within Sedgwick's novel. Or the tear itself represents Sedgwick's dismantling of racial stereotypes, affirming emotional expression as a capacity of Native Americans and not one limited to white European settlers. Faith herself, being a "conditioned" Indian and not Indian by birth, adds a further dimension of uncertainty to this scene; again, the extent to which we read her Otherness as reversible—as Hope does when she entertains methods of bribing Faith back into Puritan society—affects the way we read Sedgwick's handling of racial stereotypes. Does Faith embody Sedgwick's belief that race actually involves conditioning, as suggested in the preface, or does the tear signal that Faith lacks the "essence" of being Indian?

Before looking further into Sedgwick's negotiation of race within this scene and the rest of the text, the novel's preface warrants another look. As I have noted earlier, this preface suggests that racial differences occur "mainly from difference of condition." Elsewhere, Sedgwick criticizes the way Puritan settlers represented Indians in their own writing:

> These traits of their character will be viewed by an impartial observer, in a light very different from that in which they were regarded by our ancestors. In our histories, it was perhaps natural that they should be represented as "surly dogs," who preferred to die rather than live, from no other motives than a stupid or malignant obstinacy.
>
> (6)

The resurfacing of Faith in the narrative bears textual witness not only to Sedgwick's statement concerning racial conditioning, but also to the narrative's search for the type of impartial observation which Sedgwick describes above. In a sense, Faith becomes the site which Sedgwick installs for such an observer; yet this scene's instability, borne out of the conflicting meanings which occupy the same narrative space, demonstrates how different discourses overlap, including remnants of the Puritan discourses which Sedgwick sets her novel against in the preface. The scene of Hope's reunion with Faith becomes charged with a tension which reverberates through the rest of the novel, shifting the ground beneath the impartial observer, who, ideally, would embody a stable consciousness somehow outside the discourses which produce negative stereotypes.

Hope's difficulty in accepting Faith's cultural transformation becomes equally problematic, particularly when read in the context of her later actions, which involve her challenges to unjust Puritan rulings against Native American subjects: first Nelema, an old woman who saves Craddock from a snake bite, and later Magawisca. Twentieth-century critics read these later actions and rightly point out, as Carol J. Singley has, that the novel "undercuts" several romance conventions, specifically by "exposing injustice to women, American Indians, and the land"; these injustices, of course, perpetuate themselves through the discourses of a repressive Puritan power base, and as the conventions of the antebellum frontier romance suggest, some of these discourses survive into Sedgwick's era (40).

By looking for ways in which *Hope Leslie* "expos[es] injustices," we tend to read the novel as subverting a single, monolithic ideology of a repressive mechanism, thus obstructing our view of the plurality of *discourses* which produce power. Michel Foucault draws a helpful distinction between the two in "Truth and Power." Of three reasons why the "notion of ideology appears . . . to be difficult to make use of," Foucault says of the first that,

> like it or not, [ideology] always stands in virtual opposition to something else which is supposed to count as truth. Now I believe that the problem does not consist in drawing the line between that in a discourse which falls under the category of scientificity or truth, and that which comes under some other category, but in seeing historically two effects of truth are produced within discourses which in themselves are neither true nor false.
>
> (60)

Thus it becomes helpful to view how *Hope Leslie* represents individual discourses which produce conflicting versions of "truth," rather than a single, over-arching ideology. Such a view reveals that the novel internalizes such conflict and engages in processes more problematic than the straightforward correction of injustices brought about by a monolithic form of power. In other words, the novel's consideration of Native Americans and women as (to borrow an image employed by Singley) "two sides of the same coin" appears more complicated (41).[2] Indeed, Foucault's explanation provides a reading lens which helps melt, so to speak, this coin—an image of wholeness, solidity, impregnability; we can then note ways in which the text, by incorporating a range of discourses, often inadvertently undercuts the progressive mission its preface has outlined.

Even as Sedgwick focuses her novel upon establishing a position for an "impartial observer," her text becomes subject to the discursive materials of its era.[3] In the first volume of the novel, the narrator says of Hope, "It has been seen that Hope Leslie was superior to some of the prejudices of the age," suggesting that she serves as the point where this "impartial observer" becomes inscribed in the text (123). As the second volume begins, the text continues to inscribe around Hope a design by which its readers can decipher "truth" and "falsehood"; yet this design begins to show increased signs of unraveling as Hope finds herself needing to invent an explanation for her absence and the time she spent meeting Magawisca and Faith in the cemetery. Simple oppositions—such as "truth" or "falsehood"—show their limitations as Hope must develop skills of "diplomacy," which the novel describes as "that art that contrives to give such a convenient indistinctness to the boundary line between truth and falsehood" (175). The novel increasingly scrutinizes how the notion of "truth" constructs itself while Hope serves as the voice through which more lines of discourse enter the novel, blurring the "boundary line between truth and falsehood." The notion of an "impartial observer" thus shows signs of stress, as the novel struggles to locate the position for such a vista among the truth-shaping processes of diplomacy that go on throughout the novel.

To return to the usefulness of Singley's coin metaphor, the text confounds itself with Hope's eventual dilemma concerning her sister's transformation, to the crucial point that "truth" becomes increasingly subject to negotiating and bargaining. Philip Gould has already pointed out the ways in which Sedgwick's "recital" of the Pequot War bargains in a sense for the reader's sympathy by challenging the chronology of events leading up to the war, as described in Puritan accounts.[4] The confrontation between Magawisca and Hope over Faith's cultural transformation reveals further instances of negotiation, particularly when Hope offers to buy her sister back into Puritan society with jewels and feathers; however, the true bargaining in this scene occurs in determining the very *language* suitable in describing the extent of that transformation. This bargaining puts Hope's diplomacy skills to the test, as she reveals some negative cultural assumptions when learning of Faith's marriage to Oneco: "'God forbid!' exclaimed Hope, shuddering as if a knife had been plunged in her bosom. 'My sister married to an Indian!'" (188). Magawisca's response challenges the implied construction of "Indian" in Hope's outburst with an alternative construction:

> "An Indian!" exclaimed Magawisca, recoiling with a look of proud contempt, that showed she reciprocated with full measure, the scorn expressed for her race. "Yes—an Indian, in whose veins runs the blood of the strongest, the fleetest of the children of the forest, who never turned their backs on friends or enemies, and whose souls have returned to the Great Spirit, stainless as they came from him. Think ye that your blood will be corrupted by mingling with this stream?"
>
> (188)

In constructing an idealized vision of the Indian, this passage echoes the cadences of the preface's description of the Indians who "were never enslaved," who "could not submit, and live," and who "courted death, and exulted in torture" after being "made captives" (6).

In effect, Magawisca assumes the voice of the "liberal philanthropist" who, Sedgwick writes in her preface, "will not be offended by a representation which supposes that the elements of virtue and intellect are not withheld from any branch of the human family" (6). Nevertheless, nothing Magawisca says registers with Hope until the negotiation turns to the delicate weighing of religious terms: "'Listen to me,' [Magawisca] said; 'your sister is of what you call the christian family. I believe ye have *many names* in that family. She hath been signed with the cross by a holy father from France; she bows to the crucifix'" (189, emphasis added). Hope finally responds with some degree of hesitance, reasoning that "any christian faith was better than none" (189). In effect, acceptance of Faith's marriage comes with conditions—conditions which, at their root level, hinge upon what to *call* Faith and agreement upon a proper signifier; indeed, Faith needs to belong to what Hope may "call the christian family."

Price in Sedgwick's novel frequently revolves around language, and words often become a form of currency accepted for payment. When Magawisca becomes imprisoned thanks to the sinister manipulations of Sir Philip Gardiner, she can escape prison by verbally exchanging one set of principles for another. Hope overhears these conditions, which hinge upon Magawisca's being "induced to renounce her heathenish principles, and promise, instead of following her father to the forest, to remain here, and join the catechised Indians" (279). Like the novel's Puritan leaders, Hope also places considerable weight upon Christianity in the novel's represented systems of weights, balances, and exchanges. Yet, Sedgwick's novel also highlights the need for Hope to develop the ability to see value as it exists *outside* of these systems. An indication of this need comes in a scene in which Magawisca reappears after a period of absence, disguised and pretending to sell moccasins. When Mrs. Grafton walks in, wanting to know

how much the moccasins cost, Hope claims not to know. Mrs. Grafton chides her, "Do not know! that's peculiar of you, Hope Leslie; you never inquire the price of any thing" (184). This statement becomes ironic in light of the fact that Hope actually seeks the price that will buy her sister back into Puritan culture. After Hope's diamond ring catches Faith's eye during their reunion scene, Hope tells Magawisca that if Faith "will come home with me, she shall be decked with jewels from head to foot, she shall have feathers from the most beautiful birds that wing the air, and flowers that never fade—tell her that all I possess shall be hers" (229-30).

This scene illustrates Hope's difficulty in looking beyond value as her culture prescribes it, and it dramatizes in remarkable fashion the attempt to locate and define Otherness beyond popular, sensational images. Indeed, elsewhere in this scene, Faith (or Mary, as the novel sometimes refers to her) reveals her own cultural signifier—a mantle, which emphasizes the finality of her cultural transformation:

> [Hope] thought that if Mary's dress, which was singularly and gaudily decorated, had a less savage aspect, she might look more natural to her; and she signed to her to remove the mantle she wore, made of birds' feathers, woven together with threads of the wild nettle. . . . The removal of the mantle, instead of the effect designed, only served to make more striking the aboriginal peculiarities.
>
> (228)

This scene poses the need to perceive Faith outside of the debilitating discourses which distort identity. By removing the mantle, Hope believes she can remove Faith's Otherness; yet, the persistence of Faith's "aboriginal peculiarities" unhinges this hope and, more important, complicates the novel's own representation of Faith to the impartial observer. While Hope needs the mantle removed in order to see Faith with a "less savage aspect," Sedgwick actually needs the mantle to portray Faith's Otherness. In other words, the novel finds itself caught at cross purposes: it insists that Faith's mantle does not contain her cultural identity, that this identity exists as something apart from it; yet, the novel *requires* the mantle to make Faith's Otherness visible to its reader.

Sedgwick's novel dares to imagine a discourse which can make cultural distinctions clear and draw sympathy from its reader, but it ultimately finds itself confined by the limiting discourses actually available. Recent scholarship suggests that the prevalent forms of writing during Sedgwick's era reflect this situation, bearing witness to the unavailability of a truly liberating discourse. In "The Literary Debate Over 'the Indian' in the Nineteenth Century," Sherry Sullivan analyzes two modes of writing—writing sympathetic to the Indian and antiprimitivist writing—but she argues that ultimately the two discourses "were one and the same."[5] She observes that "[b]oth interpreted 'the Indian' in terms of white civilization and ignored the actual, historical Indians before them. Both also agreed that white civilization was morally superior to 'primitive' Indian culture, as they understood it (though they disagreed as to whether it was a relative or an absolute superiority)" (25). Clearly sympathetic to the native inhabitants of North America, Sedgwick's novel dramatizes through Magawisca the conflict which Sullivan notices at large in sympathetic writing. Indeed, by the end of the novel, Magawisca must leave the settlement for the wilderness, despite the consternation of Hope and Everell, who desire her to remain and become assimilated into the Christian community. Of course, Magawisca does not choose to remain, the novel thus maintaining Magawisca's strong, independent nature. Yet, expressing Magawisca's virtue becomes problematic, for the novel finds such expression only in terms valued by the white Puritan culture which she rejects. Filtered through Hope's eyes, Magawisca's belief in a "Great Spirit" invites "the thought that a mind so disposed to religious impressions and affections might enjoy the brighter light of Christian revelation—a revelation so much higher, nobler, and fuller, than that which proceeds from the voice of nature" (332). The novel asks us to sympathize with Magawisca, but by and large this sympathy comes by understanding Magawisca's virtue as Christian-like.

Furthermore, the novel provides a rare, though not solitary, example of interracial marriage in antebellum fiction, but even such an example comes with conditions. Barnett once again assesses an overall pattern in fiction of this period, and she notes the rules by which sexual relations could—or to be more specific, could *not*—take place: "Because whites are depicted as superior in all ways, they must be more sexually desirable than Indians." Barnett goes on to explain that as a result, "fictive male Indians often desire white women," though only "exceptional cases" occur in which these Indians "succeed in possessing them" (113). Barnett's generalization provides a context for Faith's marriage to Oneco, suggesting that even in this "exceptional case," Sedgwick's novel on a surface level actually subscribes to a discourse which constructs superiority in whiteness. Adding support to this notion, the novel hints at the possibility of romance between Magawisca, an Indian, and Everell, a European, but this romance never develops. Barnett's analysis of antebellum literature uncovers the improbability of such a union: "In keeping with the aggressive and passive stereotypes of sex role [sic] which are little altered by race, Indian males— but not females—can actively pursue whites" (119).[6] In fact, Magawisca herself expresses the complications of a union between European and Indian when she observes that "the Indian and the white man can no more mingle, and become one, than day and night" (330).

However, a direct reading of Magawisca's statement as articulating the novel's complicity with an unwritten rule of literature disregards how ***Hope Leslie*** maintains itself as a provocative, if conflicted, text. Indeed, even when Sedgwick's novel adheres superficially to the discursive "rules" governing the treatment of race during this period, it also manages to unsettle and call attention to those rules. Magawisca's comment concerning the impossibility of unity

between the Native American and the European contains metafictional resonances, as if to direct readerly attention toward the (im)possibilities depicted in the fiction of this period, including even representations found in Sedgwick's novel. In other words, no such union could take place *in fiction*. As the preface to the novel powerfully suggests, Sedgwick's interest rests largely in representation itself, while implying that her own set of representations will correct the unsavory Puritan depictions of America's natives. Magawisca and Everell maintain a fictional impossibility in frontier fiction, but Sedgwick also has Magawisca *articulate* this sort of impossibility, placing the power of commentary and perspective in the hands of a normally marginalized character: a Native American woman.

Significantly, at least one of the novel's early commentators found Magawisca disagreeable for her allegedly non-Indian characteristics. A review originally published in the *Western Review* in 1827 refers to Magawisca as "the first genuine Indian angel" and goes on to say that "[t]his angel, as she stands, is a very pretty fancy; but no more like a squaw, than the croaking of a sandhill crane is like the sweet, clear and full note of the redbird." The writer continues by defining the role of a fiction writer in matters of race: "Dealers in fiction have privileges; but they ought to have for foundations, some slight resemblance to nature" (qtd. in Foster 86). This decree for "some slight resemblance to nature" hearkens back to Foucault's statement concerning how ideology "always stands in virtual opposition to something else which is supposed to count as truth." A survey of the frontier literature of the nineteenth century, such as Sullivan provides, suggests that a significant degree of disagreement existed over just what form this "nature" should take. Sullivan dismantles the notion that the "Indian hater fiction," which first became popular in the 1820s, accurately reflects "a broad negative consensus of [white] views about the Indian," but indicates instead "a wide divergence and a persistent debate" (14). As Sullivan points out, perception in the early nineteenth century shifted away from the negative portrayals predominantly found in Puritan texts and captivity narratives, to a portrayal influenced by Romanticism wherein the Native American "became less an object of fear and disgust than a source of both pity and admiration" (16).

Even ***Hope Leslie,*** a sympathetic text constructed for the "impartial observer," finds itself negotiating with the multiplicity of attitudes which Sullivan detects. Clearly aware of "Indian hater fiction," Sedgwick incorporates such discourse into her novel, particularly through Digby, a veteran of the Pequot war, which preceded the events of the novel. After witnessing Magawisca running through the woods, he expresses himself in language appropriate to "Indian hater fiction": "I had rather meet a legion of French men than a company of these savages. They are a kind of beast we don't comprehend—out of range of God's creatures—neither angel, man, nor yet quite devil" (42). Richard Drinnon has pointed out that "[i]n times of trouble natives were always wild animals that had to be rooted out of their dens, swamps, jungles," and Digby's language in the passage enforces this line of thought to some degree (53).[7] However, even in expressing his distaste for Indians as a "kind of beast," Digby runs into a problem depicted frequently in **Hope Leslie,** a problem rooted in the limitations of language, specifically in the lack of a *name* for that which disturbs him. Indeed, Digby's confusion suggests that for the European-American, the Indian exists not just "out of range of God's creatures," but somehow "out of range" of available language.

Comparisons to other texts help illuminate the degree to which naming the Other constitutes a concern for Sedgwick in the writing of **Hope Leslie.** For instance, in 1703, when the French began aligning themselves with the Abenaki Indians, Solomon Stoddard wrote a letter to Massachusetts governor Joseph Dudley outlining a proposal to use dogs to hunt Indians "as they do bears" (373). "They act like wolves and are to be dealt withal as wolves," Stoddard's letter states (374). Additionally, a canonical text, Mary Rowlandson's *A True History of the Captivity and Restoration,* creates an image of the Narragansett Indians as "a company of hell-hounds," and in an image with parallels to Digby's, it includes a striking image of "the roaring, and singing, and dancing, and yelling of those black creatures in the night, which made the place a lively resemblance of hell!" (29). Both Stoddard and Rowlandson's texts help reveal Sedgwick's method of interrogating such imagery through Digby, who becomes perplexed over not just the physical reality of the Indians he fears, but the linguistic category in which to place them. In struggling to name the danger, no such "lively resemblance" makes itself apparent to him, as it seems to in the case of Rowlandson's narrator.

Not only does the novel confront preexisting semiotic challenges in representing Native American characters, but it relies upon some familiarity with the genre of the captivity romance in creating sympathy for Indians within its largely white readership. In a paper recently presented at a meeting of the Southeastern Society for Eighteenth-Century Studies, Kathryn Zabelle Derounian-Stodola observes, "In Indian captivity narratives by and about women the main metonymy is the decisive fracturing of the original family unit which, after the attack by Native Americans, rarely reconstructed itself intact" (4). This generalization helps illuminate the manner in which Sedgwick constructs a striking reversal of the captivity romance—specifically by exploring the integration of the Indian captive into the white family unit. Early on, the novel concerns itself with efforts to assimilate Magawisca and Oneco into the Fletcher household, and, in a sense, the novel becomes for this time *their* narrative of captivity. They do not simply become adopted by the Fletchers, as in the case of Faith and Hope, but rather Sedgwick embeds their stories with a sense of dislocation.

Enforcing this idea, Magawisca's background includes the crucial detail that she learned English through the instruction of "an English captive, who for a long time dwelt with their tribe" (21). This bit of information implies an embedded text within **Hope Leslie,** one borne out of the writing popularized by figures such as Rowlandson. Far beyond simply explaining Magawisca's ability to speak English, this detail implies that there exist multiple subject positions from which to view captivity and that the experience does not limit itself to the white subject. Language again plays a significant role, however, as the *expression* of the "captivity" story of Magawisca and Oneco becomes the property, in a sense, of Mr. Fletcher. As he tells Mrs. Fletcher their story, he includes the negative tropes of representation one finds in Puritan writing, particularly in the way he describes the manner in which their "wolfish tribe were killed, or dislodged from their dens" (21). This negative language creates friction with further sections of his narrative where he expresses regret over the fate of other captives: "Some, by a christian use of money were redeemed; and others, I blush to say it, for 'it is God's gift that every man should enjoy the good of his own labour,' were sent into slavery in the West Indies" (21). Even as he brings to light the tragic reality of slavery, Fletcher bases his concern for its victims upon a biblical authority, the same authority, in fact, which becomes an object of resistance in the case of Monoca, the mother of Oneco and Magawisca. Fletcher describes her resistance to conversion elsewhere in his narrative, noting that "she would not even consent that the holy word should be interpreted to her; insisting, in the pride of her soul, that all the children of the Great Spirit were equal objects of His favour; and that He had not deemed the book he had withheld, needful to them" (22).

In the above passage, the novel once again places emphasis upon *translation,* as Monoca refuses an interpretation of the "holy word," highlighting a concern for language as not simply a means of bridging cultural understanding but also as a source of disruption. Contributing to this complexity, this passage also presents a conflict which resonates throughout the novel as a whole: Sedgwick would expect her readers to share some of Fletcher's religious sensibility, despite the counter-purpose of her prose which also inspires admiration for Monoca's transgressive actions. Clearly, Sedgwick includes several instances of transgression—particularly those performed by Hope herself—which have become the subject of recent commentaries of the novel's place(s) among other domestic novels and frontier romances of its period. One of the strongest such commentaries comes from Carol J. Singley, who proposes the intriguing notion that as a frontier romance, the "real romance [in the novel] . . . is between Hope and Magawisca" (47). Inevitably, the impartial observer which Sedgwick imagines for her text would be informed by such literary forms and would find her or his perceptions affected by them.

Understanding the novel's notion of the location of this impartiality comes in part by understanding the novel's relationship to these forms, including a preoccupation with powerful conflicts emerging where these forms intersect within the novel. In fact, the novel restructures the monolithic categories of "Indian" and "Christian" prevalent in

Puritan writing into an opposition between domesticity and the wilderness. This opposition becomes evident in the case of Magawisca, who becomes an object of domestication within the Fletcher household. In a letter to her husband, Mrs. Fletcher describes Magawisca's response to this process:

> I have, in vain, attempted to subdue her to the drudgery of domestic service, and make her take part with Jennet; but as hopefully might you yoke a deer with an ox. It is not that she lacks obedience to me—so far as it seems she can command her duty, she is ever complying; but it appeareth impossible to her to *clip the wings of her soaring thoughts,* and keep them down to household matters.
>
> (32, emphasis added)

The complexity of this passage presents itself in light of the intersection it creates between domestic fiction, whose conventions appear in the novel, and the genre of the frontier romance, which Sedgwick helped popularize. Conflicting meanings emerge within these shifting, and not altogether harmonious, contexts. As a character in domestic fiction, Magawisca's "wings" in this passage suggest the "angel" which, for the critic in the *Western Review* mentioned previously, put her authenticity as an "Indian" at risk. As a frontier romance contributing to white representations of Native Americans, however, the figuration in this passage reorients itself to construct an image of Magawisca complicit with other popular images. Indeed, in this case, the "wings" associated with her thoughts suggest animal characteristics, a romantic image which nonetheless duplicates the antiprimitivist inclination to paint Indians as animal in nature.

This discourse emerges earlier in the novel—again through the voice of Mrs. Fletcher. In this case, she tells Magawisca and Oneco that they "will soon perceive that our civilized life is far easier—far better and happier than your wild wandering ways, which are indeed, as you will presently see, but little superior to those of the wolves and foxes" (24). Everell, Magawisca's champion through much of the novel, upbraids his mother for this remark, but he does so in language that appears conciliatory to the "wild animal" discourse. He says, "hunted, as the Indians are, to their own dens, I am sure, mother, they *need* the fierceness of the wolf, and the cunning of the fox" (24, Sedgwick's emphasis). Everell corrects his mother's racism, but he does so in a manner which maintains her language and, by applying new connotations, confirms its suitability. In this manner, Everell echoes a passage from Sedgwick's preface: "[I]t was perhaps natural that [Indians] should be represented as 'surly dogs,' who preferred to die rather than live, from no other motives than a stupid or malignant obstinacy" (6). These passages illustrate the novel's dissatisfaction with the existing discourse available for the representation of Native Americans, as well as the difficulty of creating a place outside of it. Negotiating with this discourse ultimately entails entering it, and inevitably, the novel reinscribes it to a degree.

Much of the novel's criticism has focused upon its more affirmative characteristics, noting the remarkable degree to which Sedgwick constructs a "sisterhood" between Magawisca and Hope that transcends conventional depictions.[8] Singley identifies the "union" between Magawisca and Hope as one which counters "masculine violence" with "the need for feminine healing—a healing not between the Old World of England and the New World of America, as traditional American romances have it, but between the original culture of the Native Americans and the new intrusive society of the Puritans" (47). Even while maintaining this powerful vision, the novel preoccupies itself with the problematic nature of representing this Native American culture; furthermore, while the images this paper has focused upon might, in one sense, point out the novel's short-comings, I argue that Sedgwick, as a skilled artist and a woman in a male-dominated culture, maintained an awareness of language as a medium which distorts even as it fosters the possibility of unity and understanding. Her text, far from simply remaining subject to discursive constraints, becomes a commentary upon those constraints.

The novel's treatment of marriage becomes an important arena in which to explore these constraints, particularly as Sedgwick challenges her culture's assumptions concerning the necessity of marriage in the lives of women. As Singley points out, the novel does conform with the conventions of the period by ending with the marriage of Hope and Everell, indicating that Sedgwick "could not conceive of an ending that would both subvert *and* rewrite the white patriarchal plot" (49-50, Singley's emphasis). However, the novel also depicts Esther Downing, who chooses to stay single, a decision the narrator supports with a biting statement: "She illustrated [the] truth . . . that marriage is not *essential* to the contentment, the dignity, or the happiness of woman" (350, Sedgwick's emphasis). This statement also underscores where the novel's treatments of race and gender diverge. That is, marriage between Everell and Magawisca becomes not a matter of choice, but a matter of "nature." At one point in the novel, Everell explains to Digby his feelings for Magawisca: "I might have loved her—might have forgotten that nature had put barriers between us" (214). The surface events of the novel leave this construction of nature intact: Everell marries Hope, thus serving as the means by which the novel conforms to conventions which call for a female protagonist to marry at a novel's conclusion. Together, Everell's statement concerning "nature," the novel's adherence to certain conventions, as well as Sedgwick's preface calling attention to "condition" as a determining factor in cultural differences, generate textual conflict; yet out of this conflict comes the novel's most provocative "statement" concerning race. Indeed, by conforming to conventions on the surface, Sedgwick actually reveals the degree to which Everell's notion of "nature" exists as a construction of language.

I want to conclude by returning to the reunion scene between Hope and Faith. Here, Hope confronts a newly constructed Faith, literally a product of a language new and unfamiliar to Hope. With Magawisca acting as translator,

Hope makes significant use of the negative tropes which occur throughout the narrative: "Ask her . . . if she remembers the day when the wild Indians sprung upon the family at Bethel, like wolves upon a fold of lambs?" (229). Again, Indians act like "wolves." But here, these tropes must become translated into the language of the very people denied humanity *by* such tropes. Magawisca's translation of Hope's question remains outside the reader's realm; we have only Magawisca's translation of Faith's confirmation that she does, in fact, remember the incident. We never know what Magawisca translates—that is, whether or not, or in what form, her translation recreates images of Indians as wild animals.

The importance of the language barrier then becomes paramount, from the moment that Faith's response to Hope's emotional entreaties—"No speak Yengees"—proves halting to the line of communication Hope would take. "Oh what shall I do! what shall I say!" Hope says in response (228). It becomes easy to imagine Hope speaking for Sedgwick's novel, which preoccupies itself with the limitations of language and asks itself similar questions. With Faith no longer sharing Hope's own language, Hope finds herself in the narrow and unknown passageway between languages, an unwritten passageway, in effect, where transformations could and likely do take place. Indeed, this scene of translation becomes the novel's center of gravity in its attempt to imagine an impartial observer, one who can negotiate between the disparate effects produced by conflicting discourses. Just as Magawisca leaves Hope and Everell with the declaration that "the Indian and the white man can no more mingle, and become one, than day and night" (330), so too does this elusive passageway between languages represent a potential mingling of day and night, a crosscultural point of connection.

Notes

1. Sandra Zagarell's excellent reading presents a particularly clear view of the many ways in which Sedgwick's text links gender and race issues. Zagarell points out how the text succeeds in "problematizing the Puritan founders' beliefs and policies," including "their attitudes towards white women as the domestic analogy of their view of Indians" (236). Likewise, Suzanne Gossett and Barbara Ann Bardes note that "[t]he dilemmas faced by Hope and Magawisca allow Sedgwick to question the legitimacy of a political authority which excludes certain groups in the population, in this case women and Indians" (23). Also, in her introduction to the edition of the novel published in the American Women Writers Series, Mary Kelley elaborates upon Sedgwick's textual perception of Native Americans: "[Sedgwick] dismissed the idea that Indians were inherently inferior and made them as fully human as those who clothed themselves in the mantle of civilization" (xxix).

2. Singley derives this coin metaphor from her own reading of Zagarell's article, "Expanding 'America': Lydia Sigourney's *Sketch of Connecticut,* Catharine Sedgwick's *Hope Leslie.*"

3. Zagarell acknowledges that the novel "has its share of conventional formulas and stereotypes," but her reading revolves around the notion that the novel "casts light on the collusion between the established narrative structures and racist, patriarchal definitions of the nation" (233).

4. Gould provides the following detailed explanation: "By dislodging the traditional narrative frame for the attack on Mystic, Sedgwick effectively emancipates readerly sympathy for the Pequots consumed by the flames, and hence recovers the humanitarian pathos at the core of domestic virtue which Puritan historians—and their early national descendants—successfully repress" (646).

5. As Sullivan points out, Roy Harvey Pearce had made this point earlier in *Savagism and Civilization: A Study of the Indian and the American Mind* (U of California P, 1988), which in 1953 was originally titled *The Savages of America: A Study of the Indian and the Idea of Civilization.*

6. In her survey of this trend, Barnett notes that "[a]mong major characters in the frontier romance, no Indian girl acquires a white husband" (113).

7. In "Catharine Sedgwick's 'Recital' of the Pequot War," Philip Gould gives close attention to Digby and the role he plays as a "living metaphor for a masculine historiography with which *Hope Leslie* now competes" (646). Gould concludes this arresting section by pointing out how Digby's epistemology "fails," and thus, "Everell—and Sedgwick's reader—clearly need another historian" (647). For more on Sedgwick's revision of the Puritan account of the Pequot War, see Gould's essay.

8. Zagarell points out one particularly noteworthy way in which Sedgwick undercuts such depictions. Because of Hope's dark hair, Sedgwick "revises the prevalent tendency, racist as well as gynophobic, to split women characters into the sexual and the chaste, the dark and light" (237).

Works Cited

Barnett, Louise J. *The Ignoble Savage: American Literary Racism, 1790-1890.* Westport: Greenwood, 1975.

Derounian-Stodola, Kathryn Zabelle. "Troping Captivity in Early American Women's Fiction: Rowson, Foster, and Bleecker." Southeastern American Society for Eighteenth-Century Studies. February 1995.

Drinnon, Richard. *Facing West: The Metaphysics of Indian-Hating and Empire Building.* Minneapolis: U of Minnesota P, 1980.

Foster, Edward Halsey. *Catharine Maria Sedgwick.* New York: Twayne, 1974.

Foucault, Michel. "Truth and Power." *The Foucault Reader.* Ed. Paul Rabinow. New York: Pantheon, 1984. 51-75.

Gossett, Suzanne, and Barbara Ann Bardes. "Women and Political Power in the Republic: Two Early American Novels." *Legacy: A Journal of Nineteenth-Century American Women Writers* 2.2 (1985): 13-30.

Gould, Philip. "Catharine Sedgwick's 'Recital' of the Pequot War." *American Literature* 66 (1994): 641-62.

Kelley, Mary. Introduction. *Hope Leslie.* By Catharine Maria Sedgwick. New Brunswick: Rutgers UP, 1987. ix-xxxix.

Rowlandson, Mary. *A True History of the Captivity and Restoration of Mrs. Mary Rowlandson. Classic American Autobiographies.* Ed. William L. Andrews. New York: Penguin, 1992. 20-69.

Sedgwick, Catharine Maria. *Hope Leslie.* 1827. Ed. Mary Kelley. New Brunswick: Rutgers UP, 1987.

Singley, Carol J. "Catharine Maria Sedgwick's *Hope Leslie:* Radical Frontier Romance." *The (Other) American Traditions: Nineteenth-Century Women Writers.* Ed. Joyce W. Warren. New Brunswick: Rutgers UP, 1993. 39-53.

Stoddard, Solomon. "Letter to Governor Joseph Dudley." 1703. *Remarkable Providences: Readings on Early American History.* Ed. John Demos. Boston: Northeastern UP, 1991. 372-74.

Sullivan, Sherry. "The Literary Debate over 'the Indian' in the Nineteenth-Century." *American Indian Culture and Research Journal* 9 (1985): 13-31.

Zagarell, Sandra A. "Expanding 'America': Lydia Sigourney's *Sketch of Connecticut,* Catharine Sedgwick's *Hope Leslie." Tulsa Studies in Women's Literature* 6 (1987): 225-45.

Judith Fetterley (essay date 1998)

SOURCE: "'My Sister! My Sister!': The Rhetoric of Catherine Sedgwick's *Hope Leslie,*" in *American Literature,* Vol. 70, No. 3, September, 1998, pp. 491-516.

[*In the following essay, Fetterley contends that* Hope Leslie *is a novel that examines and reflects the political, feminist, and ideological contradictions of its time.*]

Hope Leslie is arguably one of the most under-analyzed texts of nineteenth-century American literature. While sales figures from the Rutgers University Press American Women Writers series indicate its extensive use in classrooms across the country, and perhaps its interest for the general reader as well, scholarly and professional readings of the text have not developed proportionately.[1] This lag gains further resonance if we recognize that in little over a decade Sedgwick wrote five major novels—a fictional output equaled only by Cooper. Responding, like Cooper, to the call for a distinctively American literature, she rivaled him in her own day as the writer who could answer Sydney Smith's sneering question, "[W]ho in the four quarters of the globe reads an American book?" by putting America on the literary map. Moreover, like her contemporary, Lydia Huntley Sigourney, she created a space for the woman writer to participate in creating an American literature and hence in constructing the new Republic. While Nina Baym claims that if Sigourney "had not existed, it would have been necessary to invent her," Catharine Sedgwick could never have been made up, for she exceeds the imagination that did, in fact, as Baym goes on to point out, invent Sigourney as the "epitome of the specifically *female* author in her range of allowed achievements and required inadequacies."[2] In a certain sense, Catharine Sedgwick is too good to make up, and if she could not have been invented in her own day, neither has she been successfully reinvented in our own.

An essay seeking to explain this phenomenon would, I believe, work against efforts to "reinvent" Catharine Sedgwick, for it would inevitably address the conversations surrounding the construction and reconstruction of nineteenth-century American literary history more than Sedgwick's own texts. In an earlier essay on American women writers and the politics of recovery, I argued that "those of us interested in nineteenth-century American women writers may need to find ways to revitalize modes of criticism no longer fashionable because these modes may represent stages in the process of literary evaluation that we cannot do without," and I referred specifically to the techniques of close reading associated with the New Criticism of the 1950s and 1960s.[3] While those techniques were designed to establish and justify the canonization of a limited set of texts, I believe it is possible to disengage the methodology of New Criticism from its ideology and to use that methodology to serve very different political ends. Indeed, in recovering and reading women's texts from the last century, I think it is not only possible but desirable to use the master's tools to dismantle the master's house. For if a primary effect of New Critical methodology was to accord value to the objects of its attention—to find them worthy of intensive, sustained analysis, to assign them, in a word, the status of the analyzable—then to apply this methodology to texts that the ideology of New Criticism rejected as unworthy has a potentially radical effect. I would argue further that it is essential to undertake this activity at this moment in the construction of American literary history in order to prevent the possibility that a text such as ***Hope Leslie*** will be "re-vanished" on the grounds that there was really nothing to say about it anyway. It is in the effort to prevent such a disappearance that I offer the following unabashedly close reading.

I offer this essay as well as a way of reading texts by nineteenth-century American women that balances the polarity between the hagiography characteristic of the first phase of recovery, a hagiography directly proportional to the misogyny informing previous treatment of these writers and texts, and the critique associated with the second phase, a critique that implicates these writers and their texts in a variety of nineteenth-century racist, classist, and imperialist projects.[4] Like other late-twentieth-century readers of these texts, themselves recovering from the intensity associated with the alternating phases of celebration and critique, I want to move beyond the binary opposition of these impulses by proposing that what is admirable about **Hope Leslie** cannot be separated from what is problematic, and that, moreover, it is this very entanglement that makes the text worth recovering in the first place. In proposing this approach, I am also writing against what has been a primary model for the work of recovery, namely, the assumption that these works can be best understood in terms of a dominant text and a subtext—a conventional surface text that covers and contains a radical subtext (or vice versa, depending on the reader's politics). While such a model may indeed be useful for reading certain works, it tends to produce a false sense of coherence and to rationalize too readily what are clearly incompatible stories. My own approach, based on rhetorical analysis and informed by Joan Scott's work on French feminists, relies more on the concept of paradox than on coherence. Given Scott's analysis of the importance of coherence to the legitimation of ideological/political systems such as the French and American republics, and given her understanding of the role played by the production of "sexual difference" in achieving such coherence in the face of women's actual exclusion from the categories of individual and citizen, we may well conclude that those texts that have "only paradoxes to offer" are the ones we should most work to recover.[5]

PRE-TEXT

Sedgwick opens **Hope Leslie** in England with the words of William Fletcher the elder, who represents all that is "old"—loyalty, obedience, sovereignty, authority, law:

> "Take good heed that the boy be taught unquestioning and unqualified loyalty to his sovereign—the Alpha and Omega of political duty. . . . One inquiry should suffice for a loyal subject. 'What is established?' and that being well ascertained, the line of duty is so plain, that he who runs may read. . . . Liberty, what is it! Daughter of disloyalty and mother of all misrule— who, from the hour that she tempted our first parents to forfeit paradise, hath ever worked mischief to our race."[6]

Fletcher's admonitions construct a "pre-text" that enables Sedgwick to propose her own theory for the origins of America. In contrast to the efforts of some of her contemporaries who gendered the nation's origins in intensely masculine terms—heroic forefathers battling a howling wilderness and warring against savage enemies—and equated republican America with manliness, Sedgwick offers a different vision of the relation of gender to the new nation. A good rhetorician, Fletcher places his most powerful argument last, convinced that by gendering "Liberty" feminine he will have created a natural and hence insuperable barrier to his nephew's identification with the concept. In the context of Sedgwick's text, however, Fletcher's strategy serves to associate the gendering of America, whether as feminine or masculine, with a specific set of

political interests understood as emphatically un-American. Thus, for Sedgwick, America begins with the history of men like the younger William Fletcher who refuse to accept the gendering of "liberty" and are therefore immune to the gender terrorism of being labeled "women." Though her initial emphasis is on those men willing to pass as "women," Sedgwick's real agenda is the construction of a rhetoric that will enable women in America to become "men."

The pre-text of **Hope Leslie** provides Sedgwick with a pretext for beginning her work as well. Through the story of Alice Fletcher, forcibly prevented from joining her lover in passage to America, returned to her father's home against her will and ordered to marry a man of her father's choosing, Sedgwick represents the fate of biological women in a country where they have no chance of becoming "men." Though William Fletcher the younger is no seducer, Alice's attempted elopement to America evokes the history of Charlotte Temple. In **Hope Leslie,** Sedgwick defines *Charlotte Temple,* one of the most popular stories in America, even in 1827, as essentially un-American, a story of the old country, for whether dragged off by a seducer or dragged home by a father, women in stories like *Charlotte Temple* are subject to patriarchal control. Committed to the structures of heterosexual romantic love, both Charlotte and Alice seek America for the wrong reasons. In preventing Alice from reaching America, Sedgwick in effect reverses and undoes the story of Charlotte Temple, clearing the ground for a new and different story based on a different understanding of America. Moreover, Sedgwick embeds *Charlotte Temple* in the text of **Hope Leslie** through the story of Rosa and Sir Philip, and, as Christopher Castiglia has observed, when she concludes her own novel with an explosion that blows up both seduced and seducer, we recognize her desire to annihilate romantic love with its plot of "seduced and abandoned" as a basis for the story of America.[7]

Romantic love stands between women and the possibility of becoming "men" in part because it reifies the separation of public and private by gender, thus supporting a model of the civic in which events in the private sphere cannot or need not have any effect on the public sphere. In challenging this model, Sedgwick not only goes beyond the postulates of Enlightenment liberal feminism that did not, for the most part, challenge the division between public and private but only argued for women's larger inclusion in the public sphere; she also rewrites her own family history. As Mary Kelley has noted in her introduction to **The Power of Her Sympathy,** Sedgwick's father, whom she admired, even adored, assumed that service to one's country required putting aside the claims of the domestic and the private, even when doing so led to the depression, illness, and death of his wife.[8] According to Kelley, in the autobiographical memoir Sedgwick began when she was in her sixties, she articulates, however indirectly, the cost to women like her mother of her father's definition of citizenship, one that led him to serve twelve years in Congress and to be absent from home for long periods of time despite the evident distress this caused his wife. Much earlier, however, in *Hope Leslie,* Sedgwick had argued that there can be no meaningful understanding of public good separate from a recognition of its "private" cost, that in fact the true America cannot be built by men and women like her father and mother. Rather, the construction of America falls to the decidedly antiromantic Hope Leslie and to her "brother" Everell, whose understanding of citizenship makes no distinction between the public and private. When Everell rejects Governor Winthrop's argument for refusing to release Magawisca—namely, that "private feelings must yield to the public good"—he does so because he recognizes that in such formulations one person's private needs are in fact recast as public good (234).[9]

REPUBLICAN SISTERHOOD

When the younger William Fletcher arrives in Boston, he almost immediately finds it necessary to move further west to achieve the condition of liberty for which he left the mother country. When the new so quickly becomes the old, when here becomes there, "America" emerges as a future possibility, perhaps an ever-receding one, but certainly one not yet realized in colonial Boston or the early republic of the United States. In this context the ahistoricity of Hope Leslie, a republican heroine two hundred years before her time who still occupies a space of future possibility in relation to "the girls of today," becomes legible as well. And if "America" is essentially a future possibility, then fiction provides an appropriate space for its construction through an imaginative act that might move the present toward that desired future. In *Women of the Republic,* Linda Kerber argues persuasively that in the years between 1790 and 1820 American women "were left to invent their own political character" and that they did so primarily by devoting their political imagination and energy to the construction of Republican motherhood.[10] Writing some few years after the end of the period Kerber analyzes, Sedgwick proposes in *Hope Leslie* a different and more radical model for the inclusion of women in the American republic, a model I call "Republican sisterhood." While Republican motherhood brought women into the public and political sphere by focusing on a woman's role as the mother of sons and hence a producer of the nation's future citizens, *Hope Leslie* emphasizes the figure left out of this picture, the daughter, and holds out the hope that a daughter need not be a mother. Indeed, if Republican motherhood left the daughter out of the picture, absorbing her into the figure of the mother by conceiving of her as merely a mother in the making, *Hope Leslie* reverses the image, imagining the disappearance of the mother through her absorption into the daughter. Equally significant, the removal of the mother allows the son to be reconfigured as brother and substitutes the relation of brother and sister for the iconography of mother and son. In *Hope Leslie,* then, the daughter imagined primarily as a sister occupies the center of the picture, and because she inhabits the same subject position as her brother—in contrast to the Republican mother, whose subject position differs significantly from that of her son—she offers a different basis and hence an alternative model for women's inclusion in the American republic.

Sedgwick begins the text proper of her novel with Hope Leslie writing a very long letter to her absent "brother," Everell Fletcher. Since letters in *Hope Leslie* figure as the site where one's "true" identity is revealed (for example, when we read Sir Philip's letters we discover who he "really" is), introducing Hope Leslie through letters authenticates her character, giving the reader grounds for believing that she really is what she appears to be. Moreover, if letters provide evidence of one's "true" identity, they by necessity provide evidence of identity itself. By writing, Hope reveals not only who she *really* is but that she really *is*; she establishes her ability to construct a coherent and functioning "I" and hence her possession of the kind of literacy that matters for citizenship—the literacy of subjectivity that makes her capable of writing her own version of "history." Further, with this epistolary opening the narrative voice is displaced by a character's voice, signaling from the outset the degree to which character voice and narrative voice are one and the same. In this text, then, whose pre-text includes not only the removal of Hope's biological mother but also of her potential surrogate mother, Mrs. Fletcher, the attack on Republican motherhood implicit in the violence of Mrs. Fletcher's removal extends even to narrative strategy, for in *Hope Leslie* there will be no "mother" voice to cover and contain the daughter.

Though the logic of Republican sisterhood requires the prior existence of the brother as ground for the claims of the sister, Sedgwick's narrative imaginatively inverts this priority to create a subliminal argument more radical still than the one she makes explicitly. This opening scene presents Everell as removed: Hope writes to him on the anniversary of his "recovery" from his first removal because he is once again removed, this time to England. Thus Sedgwick positions Hope as the original American, Eve preceding Adam in the garden.[11] Though this American Eve clearly needs her Adam/Everell, this need is not the need of romantic love, of opposites attracting and completing each other; rather, it is the need to discover someone just like her, someone who will identify with and be identical to her, who will mirror and support her. Though Hope possesses the literacy of subjectivity without Everell, her ability to construct him as identical to her plays a considerable part in her ability to construct herself through writing. Reporting her testimony to the magistrates on the question of Nelema's escape, Hope writes, "What I would fain call courage, Mr. Pynchon thought necessary to rebuke as presumption:—'Thou art somewhat forward, maiden,' he said, 'in giving thy opinion; but thou must know, that we regard it but as the whistle of a bird; withdraw, and leave judgment to thy elders'" (109). Clearly speech can be equivalent to silence, depending on who listens; and just as clearly Hope's literacy—her ability to write her own history, in which defending Nelema is understood as courage, not presumption—depends upon Everell's sympathetic ear.

Sedgwick's argument for the inclusion of women as equal partners in the American republic, whether now or in the future, depends upon the rhetoric of identity between brother and sister, a key component of Enlightenment liberal feminism. Thus Sedgwick carefully positions Everell as Hope's brother—his father should have been hers, her mother should have been his, they are raised together, and Hope signs her letter "sister," addressing him as "brother." Moreover, Sedgwick's initial description of Everell could easily describe Hope as well: "His smooth brow and bright curling hair, bore the stamp of the morning of life; hope and confidence and gladness beamed in the falcon glance of his keen blue eye; and love and frolic played about his lips. . . . [H]is quick elastic step truly expressed the untamed spirit of childhood" (22). We hardly need the word "hope" here to recognize the identity of this boy to the girl who bounds from the litter carrying her to Bethel and dashes forward to be reunited with her sister.

When, in the second half of the text, Sedgwick reintroduces her characters to each other upon Everell's return from England, she is even more careful to employ the rhetoric of sameness. She describes Hope as "open, fearless, and gay," with a face that reflects her "sportive, joyous, and kindly" feelings. Physically, Hope has the "elastic step and ductile grace which belongs to all agile animals"; intellectually, she has "permitted her mind to expand beyond the contracted boundaries of sectarian faith" (122, 123). In Everell, we find "a youth in manhood's earliest prime, with a frank, intelligent, and benevolent countenance over which . . . joy and anxiety flitted with rapid vicissitude" (124). Later we hear of his "unsubdued gaiety," his "unconstrained freedom," and the charm of his "ease, simplicity, and frankness" (136). Thus Hope is open and Everell frank; Everell is intelligent and Hope has an expanded mind; Hope is filled with kindly feelings and Everell is benevolent—the list could be expanded but the point is clear.

Though Sedgwick creates an escape hatch that will allow her to conform at the eleventh hour to the conventions of the novel and specifically of the historical romance, the relationship between Hope and Everell is decidedly antiromantic. Moreover, Everell's "universal" desirability—all the girls adore him—leads one to suspect that he functions less as an object of love than as the sign of a desired state of being, a desired subjectivity. He is what girls want to be more than to have, the brother as mirror and ground for what the American sister can also become, the point of comparison that enables women in America to imagine themselves as "men."

WHAT THEN IS THE AMERICAN, THIS NEW
PERSON?

Writing to Everell, Hope describes how she managed, despite the initial resistance of her "father" and aunt, to become one of a party of men venturing to climb a nearby mountain: "I urged, that our new country develops faculties that young ladies, in England, were unconscious of

possessing" (98). In this carefully crafted comment, Sedgwick indicates the difference America makes: young women in England possess the same faculties as young women in America, but England keeps women unconscious and therefore undeveloped. America allows a woman like Hope Leslie to recognize in herself the same faculties developed and promoted in her "brother"— namely, those quintessential American virtues of independence, self-reliance, and self-determination. America develops in women the ability to think critically and hence to challenge established authority. Hope insists not only on the physical freedom to climb mountains and visit graveyards alone at night; she insists on intellectual freedom as well, having learned from the arguments of those around her to doubt all dogma and to let her mind expand "like the bird that spreads his wings and soars above the limits" (123). Perhaps most crucially, America develops in women that "reverence of self" that Judith Sargent Murray claimed was essential for the success of the new Republic in her essay of 1784, "Desultory Thoughts upon the Utility of Encouraging a Degree of Self-Complacency, Especially in Female Bosoms." Proposing that she "would early impress under proper regulations, a reverence of self . . . , that dignity, which is ever attendant upon self-approbation, arising from the genuine source of innate rectitude," Murray further suggests that such reverence for self would cure the "depression of soul" that she, like Mary Wollstonecraft, saw as afflicting many women "all their life long."[12]

Though Sedgwick gives Murray's concept a far more radical cast, Hope Leslie is clearly characterized by a "reverence of self . . . arising from the genuine source of innate rectitude." As Aunt Grafton puts it, "It's what everybody knows, who knows Hope, that she never did a wrong thing" (177)—and her hopefulness can be directly linked to her self-approbation. Moreover, Hope's reverence for self leads her to a decided lack of reverence for established authority, simply because it is established. Though rebuked for her "levity" and irreverence in suggesting to Mr. Holioke that they name the mountain they have just climbed after him, she observes that "the good man has never since spoken of his name-sake, without calling it 'Mount Holioke,'" an observation designed to indicate to Everell that she has taken the measure of such men (101).

Hope's lack of reverence for authority manifests itself more seriously, however, in her willingness to challenge decisions on matters pertaining to the state and the "public good." Despite the disapproval of authority, Hope speaks out in defense of Nelema and when she fails to be heard takes matters into her own hands, releasing the prisoner and effecting her escape. Similarly, Hope agrees to participate in Everell's plan to free Magawisca, thereby risking her freedom and even her life by putting herself in the way of Sir Philip Gardiner and his plot. Indeed, Hope's courage in choosing to challenge the authority of the state becomes more pronounced when we recognize the degree to which the state perceives itself to be in danger and is willing to mobilize against such danger, whether real or apparent. References to treason and sedition, to plots against the state, appear with considerable frequency in *Hope Leslie,* a story that takes place against the background of the English Civil War with its monitory icon of a beheaded king. Within the text we have the multiply treacherous Sir Philip, the imprisoned Thomas Morton, instances of treachery within and among Indian tribes and between Indians and whites, and the threat of a possible conspiracy among the Indians to annihilate the English settlers. Though Sedgwick minimizes the reality of the last threat by portraying the Indian tribes as weak, dispirited, and internally divided, Hope's decision to free Magawisca suggests that she is indeed willing to take treason as her text in order to realize the possibility of America.[13] Thus the model of citizenship Sedgwick proposes as necessary to actualize the rhetorical premise of the equality of brother and sister requires acts of civil disobedience that may be labeled treason. Founded in the original treason of defying gender terrorism, the true and gender-neutral America may require continued acts of treason for its ultimate realization.

Sedgwick refrains, however, from making this claim an overt part of her text, for Magawisca's release in fact provokes no reprisal. Though Governor Winthrop does occasional duty as a patriarchal heavy, "impatient to put jesses on this wild bird of yours, while she is on our perch" by marrying her to William Hubbard, future author of the infamous portrayal of the slaughter of the Pequods whom Sedgwick quotes in her text, he also figures as the reconstructed father, reborn during the passage to America because he is willing to embrace the identity of "mother" and "daughter" in the pursuit of America (155). Thus we are led to believe that Winthrop too secretly desires Magawisca's release and approves of, even identifies with, Hope's act. In *Hope Leslie,* then, Sedgwick accomplishes nothing less than the deployment of biological woman as the representative American. Witty, smart, compassionate, gutsy, Hope Leslie is a lover of self and a challenger of arbitrary authority who, while insisting on her physical and intellectual freedom, is willing to take extreme risks for what she believes. She is a remarkably "American" figure, yet one whom we will not see again in American fiction for a long time. And despite the treasonous implications of her text, Sedgwick manages to keep Hope out of jail, both literally and figuratively. Yet we might well be justified in asking at what cost Sedgwick has produced this amazingly hopeful story. I turn now to a complex answer to this question, one that will, not surprisingly, present a far more complicated and less hopeful story.

SLIPPAGE AND MODULATION

Hope Leslie is clearly meant to be hopeful, yet whether by design or slip its title acknowledges the existence of a different tonality and a text that might as accurately be named *Hope-lessly.* As Dana Nelson observes in her own analysis, "tension and ambivalence mark the [text]," and "*Hope Leslie* is finally equivocal."[14] While Nelson locates this ambivalence partly in Sedgwick's investment in "Anglo-

America's historical inheritance" and partly in the uneven developments of critique ("cultural hegemony is pervasive, and enlightenment not always foolproof"),[15] reading Sedgwick as both radical and conservative, I wish to argue that contradictions are an inevitable element of Sedgwick's project and that one cannot separate *Hope Leslie* from *Hope-lessly.* Slippages occur in the hope-ful text that operate as a kind of modulation, enabling us to move from one tonal register to another and to recognize that they are both part of the same composition. Writing to Everell, Hope remarks, "As you already know, Everell, therefore it is no confession, I love to have my own way" (114). While this phrase can seem a gender-neutral assertion of independence, a version of that "universal" American quality celebrated, for example, in Thoreau's "different drummer," in this context it has overtones of the willful, the self-indulgent, and the personal that can make it seem gender-specific, not indeed the locution of a "brother." Later, when Hope insists on remaining alone overnight on the island where Digby, the former family servant now himself modulated into the independent supervisor of the Governor's garden, resides, he situates her desire to have her own way in the context of America: "Why this having our own way, is what every body likes; it's the privilege we came to this wilderness world for" (225). Yet he also subtly undercuts the legitimacy of Hope's insistence by suggesting the potential irresponsibility of her willfulness: "I always said, Miss Hope, it was a pure mercy you chose the right way, for you always had yours" (225). Moreover, as events unfold, it becomes clear that Hope does not always choose the right way and that her insistence on having her own way places others as well as herself in danger. "Having my own way" becomes similarly gendered still later when Hope has recourse to methods of manipulation that can easily be labeled "feminine." In order to persuade Barnaby to let her visit Magawisca even though she does not have the authorizing pass, she bursts into tears, knowing that Barnaby will be unable to refuse "this little kindness" to "one who had been an angel of mercy to his habitation" (308).

Sedgwick similarly problematizes Hope's "reverence of self." In one of the novel's strangest scenes, she acknowledges certain anxieties on the subject of Hope's self-love, anxieties perhaps aggravated by her refusal to create a narrative voice that would itself put "jesses" on her character through narrative distance. Hope escapes being raped by the drunken sailors she encounters on her flight from Oneco by impersonating a Catholic saint; and while she justifies her act by claiming that the woman who became a saint "might not have been a great deal better than myself" (271), the excessiveness of her claim reminds readers that, where women are concerned, it may be hard to distinguish between an appropriate reverence for self and an inappropriate willingness to let the self be reverenced, for in a historical context in which self-love is specifically proscribed for women and in which women are socially constructed as selfless, self-love may seem, and even be, narcissistic. Thus while Sedgwick does present the rhetoric of "sister equals brother" as fixed and absolute, providing the theoretical ground for a gender-neutral America, she also, like Scott's French feminists who argue both "for the identity of all individuals and the difference of women,"[16] allows gender to function as a powerful field of force, destabilizing the rhetoric of equality and suggesting significant distinctions between sisters and brothers. If we return to the scene in question for a moment, we can move still closer to an understanding of the rhetorical complexity of *Hope Leslie,* for the very mechanism Sedgwick uses to restabilize her rhetoric of equality points to and opens up the central rhetorical fissure of the text.

When Esther rebukes Hope for taking her rescue out of the hands of providence and into her own, and for supporting superstition even to save her own life, Everell turns "disappointed away," recognizing only the difference between Esther and Hope (272). Implicitly asserting his identification with Hope, his response returns her reverence of self to the gender-neutral context of American self-reliance. In this scene, however, Esther becomes the scapegoat, attracting all the negative energy that might otherwise be directed at Hope. Indeed, throughout the text Hope is compared explicitly and implicitly to various "sisters" and, with the exception of Magawisca, always to her advantage. Primary among these sisters are, of course, the "English" twins, Rosa and Esther. Both are women who accept male authority and see their own position as subordinate, who regard romance and religion as the main concerns of women, and who accept the separation of public and private, which entails their own confinement to the latter. Though superficially Rosa appears the opposite of the severe, chaste, and religious Esther, their equal susceptibility to romantic love, with its attendant addiction to masculine authority and consequent lack of self-reverence, links them and distinguishes them from Hope.

But what are we to make of a text in which the logic of the sister-sister relationship is so different from the logic of the sister-brother relationship? What are we to make of a text that seeks to establish equality between brother and sister while insisting on distinctions among sisters, thus presumably arguing that only some sisters get to be equal to brothers, only some women get to be sisters? What are we to make of a text that is so hard on "sisters," in which Rosa commits suicide, Jennet is blown up, and Esther is exiled? This question becomes particularly acute and particularly painful when we turn our attention to the real sisters in the text. But it is only when we turn our attention to these figures that we can begin to grasp the complexity of *Hope Leslie* and to comprehend the extent of Sedgwick's "hopelessness."

"MY SISTER! MY SISTER!"

Perhaps no scene in *Hope Leslie* is so troubling as the one in which Hope is temporarily reunited with her long-lost sister, Mary/Faith/White Bird. (This sister, we might note, has another name, the Indian words translated as White Bird, that even Sedgwick recognizes cannot be uttered within her text.) This scene becomes less strange, however, if we read it as the moment when "Hope Leslie" encounters "Hope-lessly," when Sedgwick confronts the contradictory impulses of her text and her own rhetorical dilemma. In this scene, we see a different Hope, one who is revolted by rather than respectful of difference, one who cannot imagine that her sister has made choices or even that she has any life at all. Hope seems desperate to recover her sister, yet her efforts place that sister in actual danger; she is obsessed with keeping her sister, yet she loses her by resorting to cheap tricks. While we may understand why Hope views her sister as lost, we are less able to see why she should care so much, since she has been separated from this sister for years and has lived quite hopefully without her. Nor can we readily understand why she finds her sister's Indianness sickening and disgusting, since up to this point Hope's interactions with Indians have fallen within the liberal humanist and unitarian position of respect, recognition of essential sameness, and, in the case of Nelema, one might argue, even covert identification. Here, as elsewhere, Sedgwick's narrative voice doubles Hope's perspective, for Hope too constructs Mary as simply not there, without language or memory: her face "pale and spiritless was only redeemed from absolute vacancy by an expression of gentleness and modesty" (229). Though one might expect Sedgwick to recognize the implications of the word "vacant," echoing as it does the phrase *vacuum domicilium* used by the English to justify their appropriation of Native American lands (126), like Hope she seems suddenly to be confronted with a difference so profound that she can only represent the fact that she can not represent it.[17] But the difference of this scene, its strangeness and excessiveness, as well as its obvious contradictions—Hope wants to keep her sister but goes about it in a way guaranteed to lose her—forces us to confront extraordinary embedded questions: Why does Hope wish to recover her sister, why is she unsuccessful, and why is the experience of loss and failure so traumatic, placing her in both literal and spiritual danger? Answers to these questions become clearer if we raise another query: Who is the sister whom Hope has really lost and seeks to recover?

When Hope first encounters Magawisca, disguised as a stranger selling moccasins who shows her a "necklace of hair and gold entwined together," she exclaims, "'My sister! my sister!'" (183). As Sandra Zagarell has observed, Sedgwick carefully constructs the relation of Hope and Magawisca as that of "metaphoric sisters. Their first meeting takes place in the Boston cemetery in which their mothers are buried. . . . In Winthrop, Magawisca and Hope share a symbolic Puritan father, . . . and they are literal sisters-in-law."[18] Moreover, when Hope finally meets Magawisca she is in effect recovering her "brother's" lost "sister." In this context we might be justified in reading Mary's "vacantness" as a sign that she represents a space actually occupied by someone else; she is not there because she is in fact not the "true" sister. If we imagine this sister to be Magawisca, then indeed we can begin to understand Hope's hopelessness.

In her preface, Sedgwick identifies Magawisca as the figure who represents her own creativity; in imagining Magawisca she allowed herself to move from the "actual" to the "possible." Given that in this text America itself is conceived as the possible, we might reasonably assume that for Sedgwick the fate of America is inextricably linked to the fate of Magawisca. Rhetorically speaking, Magawisca's function in the text is clear; she makes the argument, articulated by Sedgwick in her preface, "that the elements of virtue and intellect are not withheld from any branch of the human family" and "that the difference of character among the various races of the earth, arises mainly from difference of condition" (6). In other words, she makes the argument that "red equals white," just as Hope makes the argument that "sister equals brother." Moreover, Magawisca realizes the more radical implications of Sedgwick's rhetoric, for having "obtained an ascendancy over her father's mind by her extraordinary gifts and superior knowledge," she has acquired substantial political power in the world of the fathers, effectively displacing her brother in her father's affection and, more significantly, in his council (326). In a word, she is the daughter understood as son.

Presumably, when Magawisca returns to Boston, Hope has the opportunity to recover this sister as well as her birth sister, but ultimately Magawisca is as lost to her as Mary. We must then ask the final and most painful question: Why can't Hope keep this sister; why, like Rachel seeking her lost children, must she continue to lament, "'Oh, my sister! my sister!'" (188)?

INTERLUDE

At the end of **Hope Leslie** both Hope and Everell beg Magawisca to remain in Boston and become "American," and to the degree that Sedgwick's rhetorical model has constructed her as same and equal this plea seems eminently reasonable. During Magawisca's trial, Sir Philip has been noticeably unsuccessful in his effort to render her as "other," since she so clearly possesses those virtues understood as "universal" and particularly those understood as universal to women (note, for example, the reference to "the modesty of her sex" [282]). Yet from the outset Sedgwick has also constructed Magawisca under the mark of difference. Though introduced as one "beautiful even to an European eye," in contrast to Everell, who "bore the stamp of the morning of life; hope and confidence and gladness," Magawisca's expression is one of "thoughtfulness, and deep dejection . . . , the legible record of her birth and wrongs" (23, 22, 23). Indeed, it is Magawisca's difference as much as her sameness that makes her attractive to Everell. In describing the interaction of Everell and Magawisca to her absent husband, Mrs. Fletcher describes a relationship that we might now identify as ideally multicultural:

"The boy doth greatly affect the company of the Pequod girl, Magawisca. If, in his studies, he meets with any trait of heroism, (and with such, truly, her mind doth seem naturally to assimilate) he straightway calleth for her and rendereth it into English, in which she

hath made such marvellous progress, that I am sometimes startled with the beautiful forms in which she clothes her simple thoughts. She, in her turn, doth take much delight in describing to him the customs of her people, and relating their traditionary tales, which are like pictures, captivating to a youthful imagination."

(31-32)

Similar enough to inhabit the same world, Magawisca and Everell are yet different enough to provide opportunities for each other's growth. Indeed, one could argue that Everell's and Hope's "expanded" minds depend upon Magawisca's difference, for they could not present themselves as open, tolerant, and unprejudiced if there were no differences to overcome. Yet Sedgwick's rhetorical model has no way of recognizing difference as an argument for equality. If Magawisca were to agree at the end to remain in "America," she would not in fact be able to retain those differences of race, religion, and culture that actually constitute her value. For if one argues for citizenship by invoking the rhetoric of equality, how can one at the same time promote a respect for difference? In thus confronting the limitations of her rhetorical model, Sedgwick indicates that political situations are actually far more complex than the rhetorical models designed to address them. We might recognize the persistence of this problem today in the language of affirmative action, for the phrase "women and minorities," by making women white and minorities male, excludes minority women. Since in the rhetoric of liberalism white men are understood as grounding all claims for equality, those who cannot be equated with them by either race or gender have no basis for their claims. One could make the affirmative action phrase inclusive by specifying "white women and minorities" or "women and minority males," but only at the cost of rhetorical power and the risk of being meaningless.

In this context we might acknowledge Sedgwick's courage in seeking to accomplish the rhetorically difficult and culturally unimaginable move of equating the racialized woman with the white man. Though her primary energy is clearly devoted to the equation of white women with white men, the relationship of Magawisca and Everell actually precedes that of Hope and Everell and constitutes an unprecedented and unduplicated moment in American literary history. That such an extraordinary equation should ultimately prove unstable and the strategy for accomplishing it unworkable is hardly surprising. Indeed, I have already indicated the inherent incompatibility of the value of difference with the rhetoric of equality. If we consider as well the issue of rhetorical power, we will find a further source of difficulty, for the rhetorical power of the equation of sister and brother finds its ground in the nonnegotiable privilege of the brother. To argue for the equation of sister with brother so as to make gender the sole and hence potentially insignificant variable requires from the outset a certain occlusion of race and class privilege. In making this argument, Sedgwick inevitably commits herself to a construction of the sister and brother as equally privileged except in the area of gender. Like Everell, Hope is rich, white, literate, and the beloved child of a member of the ruling elite. If we return for a moment to our first encounter with her, we may discover that her understanding of the privilege attendant upon difference is as powerful as her recognition of the privilege to be gained from similarity.

We first see Hope exercising her American sense of independence, which is also her feminine insistence on having her own way, when, over the protests of the Indian men who are carrying her, she leaps from the litter, giving each a tap on his ear "for," as she puts it, "your sulkiness" (70). That Hope's motive for exercising the privilege of race is her overwhelming desire to be reunited with her sister who has in fact just then "gone native" only underscores the extraordinary complexity of this text. Placing the problematic of the sister-sister relationship at the heart of a text designed to propose optimistically and even breezily the nonproblematic equation of brother and sister requires Sedgwick to critique the very rhetoric that structures her text. For a rhetoric designed to bring privileged white women into citizenship may not do much for their differently raced (or classed) sisters. To put it slightly differently, as long as the rhetoric of equality begins from the ground of the "brother," there will be no place in America for "my sister! my sister!"

Hopelessly

We might, however, be advisedly suspicious of an argument that explains Hope's loss solely in terms of the limitations of a rhetorical model, for hopelessness seems an excessive response to rhetorical frustration. To understand the text of *Hope-lessly,* we must look more closely at the relationship of Magawisca and Everell and at the reasons for the instability of this particular equation. In so doing we may discover not only an additional rhetorical complexity; we may also uncover the more profound emotional and political causes of this complexity and instability, for such an investigation leads inevitably to a recognition of the difference between the sister-sister relationship and the brother-sister equation.

Though Sedgwick clearly constructs **Hope Leslie** as an alternate history of relations between whites and Native Americans with Magawisca as an alternative to the image of both the savage savage (she is noble) and the noble savage (she is "white"), nothing in her text suggests that Sedgwick can imagine a future for Magawisca within America. Indeed, as we have noted, while Everell is introduced in terms of future possibility ("the morning of life"), Magawisca is consistently described by images that suggest the "evening" of life—something fading, disappearing. In her final exchange with Everell and Hope, Magawisca herself points to the impossibility, and perhaps even the speciousness of their hopes: "It cannot be—it cannot be. . . . [T]he Indian and the white man can no more mingle, and become one, than day and night" (330). While we surely would not fault Sedgwick for failing to imagine what no one of her time seemed capable of imag-

ining—that is, how there could be a nation within a nation, persons who could be at once Indians and Americans—we might well fault her for participating in the "cult of the Vanishing American," that "elegiac mode" so common to the literature of the period that by asserting the inevitability of Indian removal naturalizes as it deplores it. Sedgwick's text could be said to accomplish what Lora Romero has called "the historical sleight-of-hand crucial to the topos of the doomed aboriginal: it represents the disappearance of the native as not just natural but as having already happened."[19] Though Sedgwick acknowledges at various points within **Hope Leslie** the actual motive behind the removal of native Americans (the desire for their land), and though she herself may well have protested the Indian Removal Act of 1830, she does not choose to use her text as an opportunity to challenge American complacency and complicity in removal or to propose that the failure to solve the conundrum of difference lies more in a lack of commitment than in the limitations of rhetorical models or a failure of imagination. Given the extent of Sedgwick's investment in Magawisca, we might well ask why she is willing to let her go. Or, to put it somewhat differently, we might ask whether or not Magawisca's removal serves interests still more powerful than those that would be served by her inclusion.

In the scene that begins a sequence of events that by their strangeness, their difference bring all the problems of the text to the surface, Digby makes an observation that seems to come out of nowhere: "Time was," says Digby, speaking to Everell, "when I viewed you as good as mated with Magawisca"; and Everell himself acknowledges, "I might have loved her" (214). Digby continues, however, by observing that it was just as well that Magawisca had "disappeared" before Hope's arrival at Bethel, "for I believe it would have broken [her] heart, to have been put in that kind of eclipse by Miss Leslie's coming between you and her," and he concludes by saying, "Now all is as it should be" (214). Digby's sense of resolution is, of course, premature, as it precipitates Hope's announcement of Everell and Esther's "engagement." In her haste to give Everell away to someone else, we might read an acknowledgment of Hope's discomfort with Digby's model of "natural" succession; indeed, we might read her response as evidence of her sense of the "unnaturalness" of her displacement of Magawisca and of the violence required to bring about the "should be" of her possession of Everell. While, as I have argued, the text of **Hope Leslie** is decidedly antiromantic, it may be more than just the conventions of the novel that brings about the intrusion of romance at this point in the text. Indeed, it may be that romance here serves to identify the heart of the problem in the relationship of sister to sister. For if Hope and Magawisca are constructed as rivals for the possession of Everell, then the relationship of sister to sister becomes antagonistic to that of sister to brother. And if this is so, we might expect to see as much effort directed to disrupting as to constructing the equation between sister and sister. In this context, we can better understand the relentless construction of difference between Hope and her sisters—Rosa, Esther, and

Jennet—for this cumulative construction of difference supports the key distinction between Magawisca and Hope, which is muddled by the presentation of Magawisca as the red who equals white yet is clearly essential to removing Magawisca from competition with Hope.

To return, then, to the question of why Hope is unsuccessful in recovering her sister, we might say that the answer lies in the fact that as much as she wishes to recover her she equally wishes to remove her. And if we reconsider what Hope sees when she looks at her sister, we may understand more fully why she might desire her removal. In Mary's "vacantness" Hope confronts the terror of nonidentity—that absence of and from self she hopes to escape through identification with her brother—to which her identification with her sister inevitably leads. And in Mary's "degradation" Hope confronts the reality of her position as a woman, whether white or red, in the American republic of then and now. In this context, Sedgwick's assumption of the insignificance of gender, so essential to the hopeful part of *Hope Leslie,* turns into a fantasy designed to obscure the actual fact of women's radical inequality. References to the degraded condition of women break through the text in figures like Mrs. Fletcher, Madam Winthrop, Rosa, Esther, and even Magawisca, for in this context Magawisca's "redness" can be read less as a sign of race and more as a sign of gender. The rhetoric of sibling equality, then, works differently for sister and sister than for brother and sister; indeed, the one destabilizes the other as it threatens to reinforce the actual inequality of sister and brother by underscoring the significance of gender. For sisterhood, however powerful it may become, begins with the recognition of mutual misery, perhaps the reason that Hope flees the weeping Rosa. If equation with the brother represents for the sister a securing of identity and an accession to power, and if equation with the sister represents a potential threat to these possibilities, then we can appreciate the value of the construction of difference between sisters, for such difference provides the sole protection against the disintegration of identity embodied in sister Mary, "gone native."

Yet we must finally return to the implications of Sedgwick's decision to racialize the figure I have been calling the "real" sister. If we assume that her primary goal was to equate Hope and Everell and secondarily to equate Magawisca and Everell, and that these two equations would result in a third, that of Hope and Magawisca, we must ask what went wrong. The answer to this question lies not simply in the limitations of a rhetorical model that cannot at once argue for equality through sameness and promote a recognition of the value of cultural difference as an alternative basis for equality. Nor does it lie simply in the fact that the claim for the insignificance of gender is compromised by the equation of sister with sister. Rather, it also lies in the fact that Sedgwick had ultimately to confront her fear that her case for the equality of white women would be undermined if she made the same case for racially other women, that her argument for gender would be hopelessly compromised by the issue of race. Unable to

imagine how she could both be and have her brother if she must also serve as the ground for her sister's equation with the brother, indeed if she must share him with her sister, Hope chooses to lose her sister.[20] In *Hope Leslie,* then, racial passing comes to seem as impossible and incomprehensible as gender passing seems obvious and simple, and the opportunity to become "men" is reserved for white women. And since the text imaginatively presents racial passing as more possible than gender passing—sister Mary becomes Indian, Magawisca could be white, but Rosa is unconvincingly male—we might argue that the construction of racial difference implicit in Hope's losing her sister is in fact essential to the argument for gender equality. If such be the case, then the rhetoric of *Hope Leslie* is hopelessly at odds with itself.[21]

REMOVAL?

Hope Leslie provides powerful evidence of the anxiety that accompanies an argument for the equality of white middle-class "American" women. When Sir Philip Gardiner visits Magawisca in jail and is accidentally locked up in a cell with Thomas Morton, he experiences a terror out of proportion to either his situation or his character. We might therefore be justified in reading this terror symptomatically—somebody is afraid of being caught, imprisoned, and driven mad as the consequence of challenging the state. In *Declarations of Independence,* Bardes and Gossett acknowledge "the repeated concern with prisons and imprisonment found in Sedgwick's novels," and suggest that this pattern derives from Sedgwick's recognition that those who challenge authority, particularly women, may well end up in prison.[22] Indeed, within the text of *Hope Leslie* we find a representation of the woman whose claim to equality met with banishment and death, not indulgence and acceptance. This figure serves to remind us of the radical nature of *Hope Leslie*'s rhetoric of gender equality and of the potential danger in making such a claim. I refer, of course, to the figure of Anne Hutchinson, who makes her appearance almost immediately in the America of *Hope Leslie.* When Mr. Fletcher haltingly tries to tell his wife that the two children of his beloved Alice have arrived in Boston, she is "perplexed by his embarrassment," and immediately inquires, "[H]as poor deluded Mrs. Hutchinson again presumed to disturb the peace of God's people?" (19). That Hope Leslie's arrival in America should be marked by a reference to Anne Hutchinson seems hardly accidental. Although, according to Amy Lang, the view of Anne Hutchinson as "prompted to dissent by her resentment of the lowly status assigned women in New England" is "doubtful on a number of counts," what is clear, as Lang further observes, is that she came to be seen as the embodiment of the radical possibilities for women of the American experiment, the transformation attendant upon that North Atlantic passage.[23] In this light, her fate came to be understood as representing the danger attendant upon the argument for gender equality because it exposed the lengths to which male authority would go to protect its own interest.

This reading of Anne Hutchinson was, of course, particularly true for the early nineteenth century, and to find

Hutchinson so immediately on the threshold of our text suggests that she provides a powerful interpretive frame for what follows, just as she does later for Hawthorne. Her significance is further underscored by the prominence in **Hope Leslie** of Governor Winthrop, historically the architect of her persecution, and by the fact that the trial of Magawisca corresponds with the date of Anne Hutchinson's death. Since the supporters of Hutchinson refused to take part in the expedition against the Pequods, we might be justified in reading the trial of Magawisca as a coded representation of the trial of Anne Hutchinson. But what, then, would we make of this "fact"?

For one thing, as previously suggested, the presence of Anne Hutchinson signals the radical nature of Sedgwick's argument for gender equality and identifies the dangers of taking up such an argument. For another, the displacement of the figure of Anne Hutchinson from Hope Leslie to Magawisca suggests that Sedgwick determined to handle this danger by removal, creating a text that potentially argues for the equality of race but ultimately abandons that potential to participate in the ideology of removal, the "inevitable" and "natural" disappearance of the Indian. That such a move serves the purpose of making the argument for gender equality look less radical by comparison seems clear. However, that the price Sedgwick pays for this strategy may be so extreme as to call into question the value of her entire rhetorical enterprise seems equally clear, for the identities of Catharine Sedgwick, Hope Leslie, Magawisca, and Anne Hutchinson are hopelessly entangled in this text, and to exclude Magawisca from the rhetoric of equality leaves a text as disfigured and disarmed as Magawisca herself. Yet the power of **Hope Leslie** lies in this very entanglement, and Sedgwick's most radical act may be to propose that a text so disfigured and disarmed is the only meaningful, whole text possible for an author willing to risk engagement with the actual mess of America in the effort to realize its potential. Textually speaking, Sedgwick refuses a model of separation and removal, insisting instead on a single text whose contradictions, compromises, and complicities she thrusts upon us, exposed and raw.

Notes

1. Paperback sales for *Hope Leslie* from the date of publication by Rutgers Univ. Press (June 1987) to December 1997 are listed at 17,182. In the same series, comparable texts and figures include Fanny Fern's *Ruth Hall* (June 1986) at 17,775; Maria Cummins's *The Lamplighter* (October 1988) at 2,906; and Caroline Kirkland's *A New Home, Who'll Follow?* (April 1990) at 3,547.

2. Nina Baym, "Reinventing Lydia Sigourney," *American Literature* 62 (September 1990): 385.

3. Judith Fetterley, "Nineteenth-Century American Women Writers and the Politics of Recovery," *American Literary History* 6 (Fall 1994): 605.

4. For an analysis of these two phases of recovery, see June Howard, "Unraveling Regions, Unsettling Periods: Sarah Orne Jewett and American Literary

History," *American Literature* 68 (June 1996): 365-84. For examples of what I am calling the hagiographic phase as applied to *Hope Leslie,* see Christopher Castiglia, "In Praise of Extra-vagant Women: *Hope Leslie* and the Captivity Romance," *Legacy* 6 (Fall 1989): 3-16; and Sandra Zagarell, "Expanding 'America': Lydia Sigourney's *Sketch of Connecticut,* Catharine Sedgwick's *Hope Leslie,*" *Tulsa Studies in Women's Literature* 6 (Fall 1987): 225-45. For readings of nineteenth-century American women and their texts as "complicit," see Richard Brodhead, *Cultures of Letters* (Chicago: Univ. of Chicago Press, 1993); Lori Merish, "'The Hand of Refined Taste' in the Frontier Landscape: Caroline Kirkland's *A New Home, Who'll Follow?* and the Feminization of American Consumerism," *American Quarterly* 45 (December 1993): 485-523; and more recently, Rosemarie Garland Thomson, "Benevolent Maternalism and Physically Disabled Figures: Dilemmas of Female Embodiment in Stowe, Davis, and Phelps," *American Literature* 68 (September 1996): 555-86.

5. See Joan Wallach Scott, *Only Paradoxes to Offer: French Feminists and the Rights of Man* (Cambridge, Mass: Harvard Univ. Press, 1996), 1-18.

6. Catharine Maria Sedgwick, *Hope Leslie; or, Early Times in the Massachusetts* (1827; reprint, New Brunswick, N.J.: Rutgers Univ. Press, 1987), 7-8. All future references are to this edition and will be cited parenthetically in the text.

7. Castiglia, "Extra-vagant Women," 9-10.

8. *The Power of Her Sympathy: The Autobiography and Journal of Catharine Maria Sedgwick,* ed. Mary Kelley (Boston: Massachusetts Historical Association, 1993), 12-15.

9. Sedgwick identifies the public nature of "private" space at various points within her text. For example, the Indian guests of Governor Winthrop refuse their placement at a side table during a family dinner, aware that this apparently private act has major implications for public policy.

10. Linda K. Kerber, *Women of the Republic* (Chapel Hill: Univ. of North Carolina Press, 1980), 269. See especially Kerber's introduction, 7-12.

11. In arguing for the existence in the 1820s of "an admittedly short-lived female alternative" to the male construction of the genre of frontier fiction, Leland Person proposes as one of its components "an alternative, female, frontier fantasy—a pact between Indians and women, an Eden from which Adam rather than Eve has been excluded" ("The American Eve: Miscegenation and A Feminist Frontier Fiction," *American Quarterly* 37 [Winter 1985]: 670). While I share Person's recognition of Sedgwick's manipulation of the Edenic myth, I do not see her as seeking to exclude Adam/Everell since he is so essential

to the larger rhetorical strategy of her text. Indeed, it is his necessary inclusion that finally disrupts "the pact between Indians and women."

12. *Selected Writings of Judith Sargent Murray,* ed. Sharon M. Harris (New York: Oxford Univ. Press, 1995), 48.

13. The phrase "treason as her text" is intended to evoke the title and content of Lillian Robinson's "Treason Our Text: Feminist Challenges to the Literary Canon," *Tulsa Studies in Women's Literature* 2 (Spring 1983): 83-98.

14. Dana D. Nelson, "Sympathy as Strategy in Sedgwick's *Hope Leslie,*" in *The Culture of Sentiment,* ed. Shirley Samuels (New York: Oxford Univ. Press, 1992), 200, 202.

15. Ibid., 202, 199.

16. Scott, "Only Paradoxes," 11.

17. While one might argue, as would Nina Baym, that Hope's reaction stems from her belief that Christianity is the only true faith and that she cannot bear to think of her sister as other than Christian, in the graveyard scene in which Hope and Magawisca meet to arrange for Hope to see her sister, Sedgwick actually distances herself from Hope's position. While Hope is relieved to discover that her sister is at least a Catholic, "for," as the narrator observes, "she thought that any Christian faith was better than none," Sedgwick does not indicate that this is her position and indeed she gives Magawisca the last word in the exchange (189). See Nina Baym, *American Women Writers and the Work of History, 1790-1860* (New Brunswick, N.J.: Rutgers Univ. Press, 1995), 156-62, and chap. 2.

18. Zagarell, "Expanding 'America,'" 237-38.

19. Lora Romero, "Vanishing Americans: Gender, Empire, and New Historicism," *American Literature* 63 (September 1991): 385.

20. Though I am focusing here on the rhetorical interests at stake, one might argue that Sedgwick's text is haunted by the economic interests at stake as well. In a footnote to the text of Sedgwick's *Autobiography,* Mary Kelley points out that the socioeconomic standing of Sedgwick's maternal grandparents was achieved by the profit they made from their management of the Stockbridge Indian School. If this is the case, then Sedgwick's own socioeconomic standing, essential to her career as author, indirectly derived from the act of Indian removal. See Kelley, *Autobiography,* 46.

21. In "Catharine Sedgwick's 'Recital' of the Pequot War" (*American Literature* 66 [December 1994]: 641-62), Philip Gould arrives at a similar analysis of Sedgwick's rhetorical dilemma, though from a rather different if not necessarily oppositional understanding of her purpose. Arguing that Sedgwick's primary agenda in *Hope Leslie* is to redefine Republican manhood as savagery and to replace this definition of virtue with one that reflected feminine values, he suggests that this gender agenda is subverted by her equal desire to humanize and defend the Pequots through an appeal to the very rhetoric of manhood she is seeking to displace. Therefore she presents them as people who "admirably chose to live free or die" and valorizes them "within the culturally sanctioned terms of masculine republican heroism." Thus he concludes that Sedgwick's text "demonstrates the difficulty of carrying on simultaneous revisions of gender and race." For Gould's discussion of this issue, see 651-52.

22. Barbara Bardes and Suzanne Gossett, *Declarations of Independence* (New Brunswick, N.J.: Rutgers Univ. Press, 1990), 35.

23. Amy Schrager Lang, *Prophetic Woman: Anne Hutchinson and the Problem of Dissent in the Literature of New England* (Berkeley and Los Angeles: Univ. of California Press, 1987), 41, 42.

Gustavus Stadler (essay date 1999)

SOURCE: "Magawisca's Body of Knowledge: Nation-Building in *Hope Leslie,*" in *The Yale Journal of Criticism,* Vol. 12, No. 1, Spring, 1999, pp. 41-56.

[*In the following essay, Stadler explains that, by investing narrative authority in the figure of Magawisca, Sedgwick uses an individual to dramatize public issues of conflict between the colonists and Native Americans in her novel* Hope Leslie.]

It has now become something of a critical commonplace in American cultural and literary studies to argue that the conceptual division between public and private spheres—a paradigm which has been particularly influential in work on the antebellum era—is artificial, ideological, and largely designed to enforce a social hierarchy between the genders. It has even been persuasively argued that the repeated critique of this binarism by feminist and other critics has unintentionally helped to maintain its authority.[1] But before doing away with this dualism as a frame of analysis, we might be wise to attend to our writers' and critics' continuing preoccupation with it (and with its deconstruction), one which I believe dates back to the earliest decades of the nation. By "preoccupation" I mean to emphasize the service these categories have provided for a rhetoric of *fantasy,* of imaginations of the self and its ability (or lack of ability) to act and to speak as a citizen, as an American self, in an American nation and culture. A particular branch of this genealogy of fantasy, usually found in work by liberal Euro-American writers, constructs people of color as mediating, critical figures in the always already problematic scheme of public and private life.[2] For a liberal, white writer, such a figure is embedded with deconstructive force, because he or she appears to wear the social on his or her skin—his or her very body is infused with a degree of cultural conflict which threatens the distinction between politics and the personal before s/he has uttered a word. Within this tradition, these characters of color, by means of the sensations and particularities that make up their selfhood, become the means of the author's general critique of the national configuration of public and private.

This usually means, more nearly, framing an issue as confined to the private sphere of individual deliberation—a sphere which masks the fact that certain individuals' deliberations are taken more seriously than others—and demanding the interposition of a public debate, a public conscience. Thus, in *Uncle Tom's Cabin,* the horrific spectacle of whipped black bodies, especially Uncle Tom's, is meant to dramatize the inappropriateness of leaving the slavery question up to individuals, individual families, or individual regions of the nation. Catherine Sedgwick's 1827 novel **Hope Leslie** is a still earlier instance of a slightly different take on the private/public dualism. By investing remarkable narrative authority in an Indian woman, Magawisca, this historical novel of early New England dramatizes public issues, primarily the colony's relations with native people, as foundational for the actualization of a model of private subjectivity suited to the proto-United States. The novel tells a revisionary history of the nation to its antebellum readership, one in which the privacy of Americans was secured through fascination with, and attacks on, the bodies of Indians. It thus attempts to ensure a place for corporeality, for embodied struggle, in the history of the nation.

Sedgwick, the daughter of one-time Speaker of the House of Representatives Theodore Sedgwick, was intimate with the public life of the young nation, and grew up in a house which offered her many more opportunities for cultural growth than most families and schools of the time.[3] Influenced like many of her contemporaries by the writings of Maria Edgeworth, her first two novels followed the parameters of "literary domesticity," a phrase coined by Mary Kelley to describe the interest of many antebellum female writers in fiction set in the home, often telling the story of a young girl's rise into virtuous womanhood.[4] In 1826, perhaps buoyed by readings of Lydia Maria Child's *Hobomok* (1824) and the early volumes of James Fenimore Cooper's Leatherstocking Tales, Sedgwick set out to write a novel of early America turning on the presence of native characters. While the novel is set in the colonial era that many writers of the antebellum era found so appealing, it also alludes implicitly to the debates taking place in her time over forced Indian removal, especially of the Cherokees. As Lucy Maddox has argued, these debates were not simply a forum in which the ethics of removal were discussed, but "a wide-spread public reexamination of the terms in which the nation wished to define itself."[5] Thus **Hope Leslie,** which would make Sedgwick the most eminent American woman writer until Stowe's publication of *Uncle Tom's Cabin,* was situated within current public debates over the shape of the nation, of where it began and ended, of who belonged and who didn't.[6]

Hope Leslie takes place in a transparently fantastic seventeenth-century Massachusetts during a period of particularly violent clashes with the native Pequot people. It narrates the story of the Fletcher family, whose son, Everell, befriends a Pequot girl, Magawisca, and essentially adopts her as a surrogate sister. Magawisca's liminal position, we will see, between inclusion in the Fletcher family and exclusion from the entire English community, makes her into an important marker of the limits of the new white nation. When Hope Leslie, daughter of the woman Mr. Fletcher had once loved in England, arrives from overseas, she becomes almost instantly taken with Magawisca, and her attempt to defend Magawisca from accusations that she is conspiring against the colony is one cornerstone of the novel's plot.

Throughout the novel, the two girls are identified with one another. Each mourns a lost mother. Each is an adopted member of the Fletcher family—Mr. Fletcher brings the young Hope and her sister over from England upon the death of their mother, his one true love, whom he had been forbidden to marry. Both Hope and Magawisca are involved in passionate relationships with their fathers. Each openly desires Everell. In comparison to Magawisca, however, Hope is nervous, excitable and often agitated. Under the burden of holding a secret, she struggles to contain her information in a manner the text implicitly juxtaposes with Magawisca's composed body of knowledge. Having arranged, through the Pequot girl, a secret visit with her sister, kidnapped during the initial Pequot raid, Hope finds herself caught between her "duties" to the white community and the "obligation of her promise to Magawisca":

> She would waver and resolve to disclose her secret appointment; but the form of Magawisca would rise to her recollection with its expression of truth and sweetness and confidence, as if to check her treacherous purpose.[7]

Magawisca's "form" becomes a node of identification for Hope, by which she can mimic the Indian girl's own capacity to resist disclosure. Magawisca's iconicity—not her self but her "form," not truth but its "expression"—releases Hope from a crisis of interior conflict. Throughout the novel, Magawisca's "form" helps the English characters—especially female characters—to regulate their psychological states. And while Magawisca exits the novel before its end, her work apparently done, Sedgwick ultimately attempts to embed some of her power in the body of Hope's friend Esther Downing, a young English woman who comes to resist the demands of the marriage plot which increasingly encroaches on the narrative.

The novel positions Magawisca, and her particular control of colonial New England's ability to "read" its fate, at the center of the making of the American nation. The surface of her body continually comes under scrutiny as the settlers attempt to decipher the relationship of her inner, private self—which knows whether her people, led by her father, plan to attack the settlement, but which also feels a sizable degree of emotional attachment to the Fletchers—to her outward, public appearance and what it can tell them about the safety and status of their proto-national community. With its dialectical relationship between Magawisca's public spectacularity and the interior absorption of the individual members of the Massachussetts colony, *Hope Leslie* delineates the constant mediations of the public in the private. It simultaneously presses this process into one that serves the formation of the American nation.

Hope Leslie, the character, is a heroine to the proto-nation to the extent that she acts to allow Magawisca to remain to some degree *unreadable* to the settlers; toward the end of the novel, she engineers the Indian woman's escape from prison, thereby ending the colony's effort to force her to signify her people's intentions. On the one hand, the novel is thus a remarkable instance of a radical skepticism toward humanism, of the philosophical and aesthetic doctrines of moral sympathy which so underwrote novels at this period in their history.[8] Magawisca, Hope affirms, has a right to secrecy, a right to privacy, a right to difference. On the other hand, Sedgwick does something which we would today call appropriation; she makes Magawisca a figure modeled very much on her own interests as a white, bourgeois woman. This is not to say, exactly, that she "whitens" Magawisca, or projects traits and behaviors esteemed by her own culture onto the figure of the Pequot girl. She specifically uses Magawisca not so much to represent positive, definitive *qualities* with which she would like herself to be associated, but rather to make certain that through Magawisca the text registers a protest against the body politics of early republican citizenship—politics which Michael Warner has shown to extend a privileged disembodiment to white, male property owners, and to consign "others" to the ghetto of the "particular."[9] The principle of abstraction on which documents like the Constitution and Bill of Rights are written contains an invisible but powerful subtext excluding those with certain bodily traits—certain genitals, certain skin colors. Sedgwick, the daughter of one of the early republic's most powerful national politicians, finds it useful to go back more than a century before the writing of these documents and locate a different national origin, one in which bodily presence and pain help cement the state. More than to act as an ideal or heroine *per se,* the character Magawisca is largely present to provide the corpo-reality in this revisionary process of nation-building.

Sedgwick's apparent interest in native people—however fantastic it rendered itself in *Hope Leslie*—has led a number of critics to remark upon her difference from the bulk of the American women writers we have come to associate, perhaps too hastily, with "literary domesticity."[10] Much of the last two or so decades' effort to "reclaim" this fiction, the bestselling literature of its time, has focused on the novels' construction in the home of a kind of alternative world outside the vicissitudes of capitalism and public politics *per se.* What I find especially remarkable about *Hope Leslie* is the extent to which, when viewed as addressing antebellum gender politics, it takes a very different tack.[11] Rather than trying to politicize privacy by sanctifying it, Sedgwick's novel attempts to undermine the status of privacy by revealing, in what will prove an ambivalent political gesture, its construction on the grounds of history and the forced removal of native peoples. The novel thus levels a critique against the contemporary antebellum gendered politics of citizenship and against the increasingly privately defined domain of women. It certainly achieves the latter by showing female characters like Magawisca and Hope as active, spirited agents in an important foundational period for the American nation. But it also uses their relationship to posit the public force of fantasy, of identification, and, I would argue, of novel-reading.

Foreshadowing late-twentieth-century readings of the novel, a number of contemporary reviews of *Hope Leslie,* positive and negative, criticized Sedgwick's Magawisca as an implausible portrayal of a Native American woman. The *Western Monthly Review* objected that "we should have looked in any place for such a character, rather than in an Indian wigwam."[12] The *New-England Magazine* urged its readers to remember that although Sedgwick's historical novel placed her in the first class of American writers, its portrayal of Indians meant it could be regarded at best as a "beautiful fiction."[13] Many reviewers of the time had also condemned James Fenimore Cooper's *The Last of the Mohicans,* published a year before *Hope Leslie,* for its romanticization of Indian character. Both Sedgwick and Cooper had, to varying degrees, placed their Indian characters in authoritative roles in their novels. For Cooper, Chingachgook and Uncas were fading figures of innocent, benevolent patriarchy in a landscape blighted by European greed. For Sedgwick, Magawisca provided many of the same qualities: morality, honor, martyrdom. Moreover, she offered an unfamiliar historical narrative of Indian victimization to compete with the versions of seventeenth-century history proffered by the Puritan fathers themselves.[14]

Cooper responded to this criticism by explicitly referring to his subsequent works as "romances" and announcing in the preface to *The Deerslayer* that: "It is the privilege of all writers of fiction, more particularly when their works aspire to the elevation of romances, to present the *beau-ideal* of their characters to the reader."[15] Sedgwick, however, had responded to these charges in advance. In her preface to *Hope Leslie,* she issued what to some may have seemed an irresponsible disclaimer:

> The writer is aware that it may be thought that the character of Magawisca has no prototype among the aborigines of this country. Without citing Pocohontas [*sic*], or any other individual, as authority, it may be sufficient to remark, that in such delineations, we are not confined to the actual, but the possible.
>
> (6)

This seems to me, more than a disclaimer, a reclamation of the "possible," of the fantasy work of the novel. Unlike Cooper, Sedgwick frames her fictional liberty-taking as a representational strategy from the beginning. Moreover, she explicitly posits the potential problem as one not of literary genre, but of authority.[16] From the onset, Sedgwick's writing arises out of the question, who is going to authorize the discourse at hand? Pocahontas? The Puritan histories?[17] Writing as a woman, Sedgwick's own authority comes under scrutiny from which Cooper and other male heirs of Walter Scott are protected. Her consciousness of the way the particularity of her gender could or could not make certain discourse make sense in certain spheres permeates *Hope Leslie*. A white woman writing a historical novel with a noble, honorable, erotically attractive, powerful Indian female character did not quite make sense to the bourgeois public sphere of 1827. Sedgwick is eminently conscious that to speak publicly she needs to cite authority; however, this consciousness, which she makes evident in this foreword-like paragraph, will grant her the liberty to create Magawisca, and it will form the basis of her portrayal of Magawisca.

Sedgwick immediately identifies this portrayal with the tenets of what we have come to call cultural relativism. She identifies her writing specifically with "liberal philanthrop[y]," and elegantly outlines her credo that the world's outer appearance makes it clear to the discerning eye that difference, as we say today, is relative:

> The liberal philanthropist will not be offended by a representation which supposes that the elements of virtue and intellect are not withheld from any branch of the human family; and the enlightened and accurate observer of human nature, will admit that the difference of character among the various races of the earth, arises mainly from difference of condition.
>
> (6)

Interestingly, this eloquent paean to Enlightenment moral and political philosophy, writing which underwrote many of the documents of the American Revolution, is itself underwritten by an emphasis on appearance, and on the necessity that the "liberal" subject have a discerning eye. Sedgwick embeds this eye in *Hope Leslie,* placing it at various points in the foreheads of various members of the Puritan community, and directing it largely toward Magawisca's body, which forms (rather than on which will be written) a series of questions about knowledge, disclosure, and the power of secrecy. The text pays an indulgent amount of attention to her body, continually mapping its specificities and dramatizing the efforts of the English settlers to read her corporeality as a series of signs. In fact, it is Magawisca's body which comes to serve as the dominant authority shaping the novel's events.

At first, the expressive power of Magawisca's body seems largely to reflect a willfulness and personal integrity Sedgwick is attributing to the character's own "self." The radicalness of her public utterances is at times remarkable, as when, on trial for fomenting Indian hostilities against English communities, she announces, "I deny your right to judge me. My people have never passed under your yoke— not one of my race has ever acknowledged your authority"

(286). But Magawisca's force of enunciation is consistently mirrored in the force of her physicality. The most dramatic and, for the novel, most resonant example of this is the force of a violently physical *absence*—the arm she loses defending Everell Fletcher from the vengeance of her father's blade. After a skirmish near the Fletcher household, Everell is kidnapped by Chief Mononotto, Magawisca's father, for purposes of execution, a deadly exchange for the killing of Magawisca's brother in a previous battle. Magawisca begs her father for mercy toward Everell, whom she has in effect already exchanged for her biological brother. Mononotto refuses his daughter's pleas, leading her to "interpose[] her arm." The result is a gruesome corporeal spectacle:

> It was too late. The blow was levelled—force and direction given—the stroke aimed at Everell's neck, severed his defender's arm, and left him unharmed. The lopped quivering member dropped over the precipice. Mononotto staggered and fell senseless, and all the savages, uttering horrible yells, rushed toward the fatal spot.
>
> (93)

Brought about by the assumption that it is better her arm than Everell's head, Magawisca's paternally administered amputation becomes the mark of her loyalty to the sympathetic bonds offered in the proto-antebellum-domestic-space of the Fletcher household. The dynamic associated with Magawisca throughout the novel is most succinctly portrayed here; her body protects the colonial mind. Consequently, mirroring the larger historical force of Indian removal, accelerating during the time of Sedgwick's writing, a violently inflicted Indian *absence* becomes the marker of the native role in American nation-building.[18]

The amputation returns with Magawisca later in the novel as a publicly effective force which will augment the force of her body to cement the colony's proto-national bonds. Yet Magawisca's physical authority shapes the novel virtually from its beginning. Recently captured in a battle between white settlers and the Pequot tribe led by her father, Magawisca makes her first appearance in *Hope Leslie* when she arrives to take up a position as a servant in the Fletcher household. As she emerges into the clearing around the house, which lies removed from the town (called Bethel, on the border of the colony), William Fletcher immediately makes note of her appearance to his wife:

> "Here comes the girl, Magawisca, clothed in her Indian garb, which the governor has permitted her to retain, not caring, as he wisely says, to interfere with their innocent peculiarities; and she, in particular, having shown a loathing of English dress."
>
> (22)

Immediately, the novel grants Magawisca control over her self-representation. She has successfully fought to keep her physical appearance in the manner she desires. And while the narrator here establishes a likely ahistorical ethic of liberal tolerance that will permeate the novel (the hegemonic acceptance of "innocent peculiarities"), the text has also established a continuum between the "look" of the native characters and that of the white characters.[19] The appearance of Magawisca conjures a description of her white male compatriot/pseudo-sibling Everell Fletcher's body and physical presence, which in turn flows into a delineation of Magawisca's corporeality, all in the space of two packed paragraphs. It is as if Magawisca and her will to maintain her "peculiarities" construct a lens through which the peculiarities, or at least particularities, of the young white male Everell come into view. Everell, "a fair ruddy boy of fourteen," is noted for his frame, which lends him the "muscle of manhood," his "quick elastic step," which lends him the "spirit of childhood," and finally for his dress, whose details include an "awkward space" of bareness around the forearms (22-23). Our picture of Everell emphasizes his brimming energy and adolescent *esprit*—a description not distant from the idyllic adolescent portrayals of Natty Bumppo in Cooper's later volumes of the *Leatherstocking Tales*. But it also places him within the discourse of bodily willfulness instigated by Magawisca's appearance.

The parallel between Magawisca and Everell is most evident when the text tells us, as she enters the Fletcher parlor behind him, that "she and her conductor were no unfit *representatives* of the people from whom they sprung [my emphasis]." In both characters, in other words, the wealth of psychic will and physical energy is meant to be identified with a wealth of signification—a degree of significance which makes them not simply instances of two "people[s]," but representative of them.[20] Sedgwick is here citing another antebellum inheritance of Puritanism, what Sacvan Bercovitch has identified as the notion of the errand, through which "to assert oneself in the right way, here in the American wilderness, was to embody the goals of New England" and later America.[21] Sedgwick's text corporealizes this model, lingering over its "representative" characters' bodies as it prepares to use them as signs of a national symbolic.

In its initial description of Magawisca's physical presence, the text goes to great lengths to emphasize how much the girl is there to be read, and to keep being read. Whereas Everell was overflowing with erratic motion and energy, his Indian female counterpart is all harmony, stillness and solidity. Her arms are described as a "model for sculpture," and the text makes further, repeated references to her as statuesque, placing her within the neoclassicist approach to representing Indians at this time in both visual and literary arts.[22] More importantly, the passage shows just what is involved in rendering her "peculiarities" "innocent" to the white reader:

> Her form . . . expressed a consciousness of high birth.
> Her face, although marked by the peculiarities of her
> race, was beautiful even to an European eye . . . there
> must be something beyond symmetry of feature to fix
> the attention, and it was an expression of dignity,

thoughtfulness, and deep dejection that made the eye linger on Magawisca's face, as if it were perusing there the legible record of her birth and wrongs.

(23)

Despite the difference embedded in her racial "peculiarities," and beyond the mere fact of their "symmetry," Magawisca as a whole coheres as a representation of qualities like "nobility," "thoughtfulness," and "dejection" which are "legible" to a "European eye." Her bodily surface, engraven with her past—"the legible record of her birth and wrongs"—is brought into being as an accessible text to be read, "perused," by a Western gaze.

Magawisca is thus something of a known quantity in the cultural symbology of early-nineteenth-century America, what Robert Tilton has called the "Romantic Indian."[23] She is aligned with a host of traits which on the one hand idealize her and on the other make her an aestheticized outlet for liberal guilt over the Indian removals taking place as Sedgwick was writing. What I want to press here, however, is the text's insistence on Magawisca's utility for figurative purposes, her capacity for making meaning by becoming a physical object of interpretation. She is not only the repository of a host of cultural stereotypes like those outlined by Tilton, Joy Kasson, Brian Dippie, and others. She is also an indicator of what becomes useful and compelling knowledge to the "European eye." Indeed, the phrase "model for sculpture" fashions the girl not as sculpture itself, but as the medium through which the shaping of some object or symbol might take place.

Hope Leslie shows the attention Magawisca's physical appearance inspires in the "European eye" not merely as exoticism but as a determining factor in the formation of the modern American nation. The novel does this, mainly, in two ways: by positioning Magawisca, almost literally, as the national border dividing and marking the difference between the colonists' and the Pequots' communities; and by inducing a model of subjectivity, a mode of individual mediation between public event and private interiority, which fits the requirements of the modern Western nation. Because Magawisca's position in the text is so ambiguous—she is, as we have seen, a virtual sibling to Everell, a state reinforced when Hope, upon encountering Magawisca for the first time, utters the words "My sister!" (183)—she becomes an important locus of interpretation for determining what constitutes sameness and difference.[24] The early chapters of the novel most directly thematize this function, as the Fletchers, in their house on the edge of the settlement, await the possible appearance of Mononotto and his troops, bent (importantly, as we will see) on avenging the death of his son at the hands of the settler community. Magawisca spends much of this time moving in and out of the woods which extend from the frontier, where the Fletchers' domesticity is situated, into the "unknown." Everell and the loyal white servant Digby ambivalently eye the girl's "abstractness of manner and . . . the efforts she made to maintain a calm demeanor" (40). Simultaneously, they debate the possibility that Magawisca's motives may be less than loyal to her adoptive family. Magawisca has taken a voluntary vow of silence with regard to her father, his plans, and his whereabouts. Everell and Digby can only attempt to determine, by surveying her countenance and general appearance, whether she is in fact a spy for her biological father. As if needing to physically locate the national border, Everell and Digby move to the very edge of the Fletcher house's grounds to watch for a Pequot attack, and begin to watch Magawisca's movements for any clue she may give as to the imminence of an attack. Digby's narration conveys her power as spectacle: "See how she looks all around her . . . Stand close, observe her, see . . ." (42).

Here and throughout the novel, Magawisca's relation to the Puritan power structure hinges on the question, "What does she know?" The actions and motivations of the white colonists continually turn on the question of what Magawisca knows about her father's plans to avenge himself on them. Throughout the book, she refuses to divulge this information, to empty her interiority into the waiting ears of white subjects (except, to some extent, Hope Leslie). Moreover, she refuses to allow her knowledge to betray itself on the surface of her body. Instead she skulks silently about the house like a more generally symbolic "bird of ill-omen." Despite her love for the Fletchers and her very apparent fear for their safety, which bring renewed attention to her body, she refuses to become anything other than the ambiguous reading surface which defines the border of white knowledge.

Magawisca's resistance to the appeals made to her for knowledge, often by the members of her pseudo-family, permits the novel to use her as a critique of early-nineteenth-century ideals of domesticity, privacy, and intimacy. When Mrs. Fletcher presses Magawisca for information on a rattlesnake skin and rattle mysteriously left in the house, the girl stays mute after merely identifying the tokens as symbols of approaching danger and death. "Why, Magawisca, are these fearful tokens given to me? Dost thou know, girl, aught of a threatening enemy—of an ambushed foe?" asks Mrs. Fletcher. The girl responds, "I have said all that I may say" (39). Although she has ostensibly become a member of the Fletcher family, she refuses to submit to the imperatives around privacy and publicity in the white bourgeois sphere. She will not address the symbols as they obtain *individually* to either Mrs. Fletcher or herself. She does briefly experience some inner turmoil, "but after a short struggle with conflicting feelings," she proclaims: "That which I may speak without bringing down on me the curse of my father's race, I will speak" (39). The illocutionary force of this utterance constitutes her as outside the white domestic economy of intimacy and privacy. She makes clear that the enunciative conditions of her own relation to the public and the private are different from those of the settler community; there is no safety for her in the Fletchers' benevolent hearth. Magawisca's knowledge and the drama around her potential

disclosure thematize for Sedgwick a manner in which privacy can become strategic. Individuality, interiority, and confession are not social *imperatives*. They are performative enunciations to be *deployed*, in the service of collective interests. Magawisca's liminal relationship to the Fletcher family thus allows her to become a fantasy of national, public efficacy constituted within the space and discourse of domesticity.

Magawisca is figured from the outset as the border of the white nation. She delineates its physical boundaries and frays the edges of its assumptions regarding the rights of domestic intimacy. A gap of seven years, during which Magawisca, Hope, and Everell become young adults, intervenes before the next series of events in the novel's narrative. This transformation mobilizes a number of energies in the plot. The adolescent spirit that characterized each character must now be made to make sense through the terms that dictate adult private life. Put directly, the issue of who is to marry whom must be resolved. This is, of course, not a question for Magawisca; although there was a subcategory of antebellum literature in which mixed marriages took place, Sedgwick's heroine was doubly marked—not only by her racial particularity, but by her amputation.[25] Magawisca spends much of the latter half of the novel inside a prison cell, arrested on the basis of suspicions concerning her role in another spate of Indian attacks on colonial settlements. But this confinement only works to bring Magawisca further into the center of the English community; it places her in a privileged space from which to continue to mediate the building of the young proto-nation. Granted access to one man's sexual secrets, she serves to channel the sexual energies of the white characters, energies which were largely dissolute in the first half, left to churn in an ambiguous mix of pseudo-sibling relationships. She helps bring Hope and Everell together, to make them marriageable.[26]

The centerpiece of the latter half of the book is Magawisca's trial on suspicion of conspiring against the colony. However, what is supposed to be a disciplinary procedure addressing the political threat Magawisca has supposedly posed to the colonists quickly becomes focused on the privilege to hold sexual secrets. The seven-year gap allows the introduction of a new character, Sir Philip Gardiner, who has fled England to escape from a shady "series of ill-luck" and infiltrated the Puritan community, disguised as a devout, upstanding follower, with his former mistress Rosa in tow. The forlorn Rosa, whom Sir Philip has seduced and attempted to abandon, has insisted on making the transatlantic trip with him in disguise as his servant boy. Sir Philip, meanwhile, has transferred his affections—and marital hopes—to Hope Leslie, whose "generous rashness" arouses his interest. Judith Fetterley has usefully described this subplot as the novel's explicit effort to exile from its domain the dominant plot of the eighteenth-century novel—the seduction story.[27] But the novel also employs this subplot to scrutinize the privileges of privacy which make it possible for an individual male to act as seducer—privileges based on the entitlement to abstraction from one's physical, sexual behavior.

Convinced that her race and her precarious state will make her vulnerable to manipulation, Sir Philip visits Magawisca in prison with a deal to offer: he will give her a file to use on the cell bars if she will subsequently take his ex-mistress off to the Indian wilds. Of course, Magawisca refuses, on grounds of principle; significantly, though, the incident fortifies her with a piece of private knowledge to be strategically deployed, a privileged bit of information which has come her way specifically because of her bodily specificity. When Magawisca's trial for her role in the Pequot nation's attacks on the colony commences, the public spectacle around Indian national secrets allows, for Sedgwick, the figuring of a spectacle around the (supposedly private) sexual secret.[28] Shifting the grounds of what can constitute public discourse, or what can and cannot be discussed in public spaces, Magawisca inspires an inner crisis in Sir Philip, as he notices the reverence in which the trial audience seems to hold her. In a sense, she forces on him an unwanted degree of interiority, a process of deliberation over his personal situation, a type of mental processing which it has previously only been the burden of female characters to assume. He begins to worry that she might actually be taken at her word should she reveal the content of their prison interview, and plans an offense-as-defense strategy eerily reminiscent of that articulated in present-day legal cases of sexual harassment and rape:

> He had no time to deliberate on the most prudent course to be pursued. The most obvious was to inflame the prejudices of Magawisca's judges, and by anticipation discredit her testimony; and quick of invention, and unembarrassed by the instincts of humanity, he proceeded . . . to detail the following gratuitous particulars.
>
> (285)

The "particulars" the narrator refers to here are from a false tale told by one of the Fletcher servants of having seen Magawisca "kneeling on the bare wet earth, making those monstrous and violent contortions, which all who heard them, well knew characterized the devil-worship of powwows" (285-86). Philip's strategy is to re-embody and re-racialize Magawisca, to bring a set of corporeally excessive "particulars," a term reminiscent of the "peculiarities" cited earlier in the novel, into a sphere in which utter disembodiment—the equal value of each individual's testimony itself—is the projected ideal. He attempts to discredit Magawisca on the basis of what has been serving her so powerfully in the novel, the power of her body as a spectacle.

Magawisca responds to Philip's attempt to scandalously embody her by requiring that he take an oath before his testimony, an act not typically mandatory for a "member of the congregation." Although she has previously denied the jurisdiction of the court, and although the narrative itself credits the native "principle of retaliation" as responsible for this demand, it is important to note a specific message sent by the call for an oath: under oath, it is clear that the speaking subject is *citing* authority when s/he speaks. Sir Philip, the novel tells us, "was far enough from having one of those religious consciences that regard truth as so sacred that no ceremonies can add to its authority" (288). He requires the extra boost of authority to be persuasive. And Magawisca dramatically complicates this issue by producing a crucifix Philip dropped during his visit to her prison cell. The court is therefore thrown into a crisis as to which authority should be cited—secular or religious, court or church. The novel dramatizes a conflict of two types of traditional, male-dominated structures of authority. By this logic, the novel's confinement of its female characters within patriarchal structures becomes not so much retrograde, as some critics argue, as much as it is a mapping of the crises that ensue from the needs of all utterances to be authorized.[29] The trial scene thus becomes a crucial enactment of the drama of authority staged by Sedgwick, the author, at the beginning of the novel, as she sought to justify what some would surely take as a fantastic portrayal of an Indian woman.

But the authority most in play is that of the *public*—the spectators in the courtroom—whose "every eye was turned toward Magawisca, in the hope that she might make an explanation." For the moment, the judges are aligned with this authority: "[the audience's] motions of curiosity coinciding with the dictates of justice, in the bosoms of the sage judges themselves, were very likely to counteract the favour any of them might have felt for Sir Philip" (289). Magawisca is able to turn the attention Philip has brought to her body back against itself, into a generative, submissive "curiosity." She increases the authority of publicity when she dramatically unveils her amputation and paraphrases Patrick Henry: "I demand of thee death or liberty!" Through the process of unveiling, she once again stages a drama of embodiment. She juxtaposes nationalist discourse with the most peculiar "peculiarity" of her body. The eminently manipulable public responds with cries of "Liberty!" When Magawisca anachronistically alludes to Patrick Henry, whom Jay Fliegelman has identified as the most important early national icon of political oratory, she becomes not simply heroic, but more specifically an embodied voice in the young United States' discourse of nation-founding.[30]

Her dramatic courtroom appearance in a sense instigates the system of privacy, of individuality that these fictional colonists will need in order to become a modern American nation. Having stuck a dagger in the once abstracted privacy of a respected Puritan male, Magawisca exits the courtroom "leaving in the breasts of a great majority of the audience, a strange contrariety of feelings and opinions." It is as if the threat to Philip's privacy mobilizes interiority within the members of the public at large, the public which has begun to turn its judgment in Magawisca's favor. The following chapter further thematizes the degree to which Magawisca's performance in the public space of the courtroom has made it possible for the settlers to become individual, private selves:

> The day of Magawisca's trial was eventful, and long remembered in the annals of the Fletcher family. Indeed, every one in any way associated with them, seems to have participated in the influences of their ruling star. Each member of Governor Winthrop's household appeared to be moving in a world of his own, and to be utterly absorbed in his own projects and hopes.
>
> (301)

What I wish to emphasize here is the degree to which the novel employs the spectacle of Magawisca to bring into being the private life of its white subjects. She seems to be making the American nation possible, forcing the Puritan community to become a conglomeration of individuals who may very well each have their own opinions and, importantly, emotions about Magawisca's trial. As the novel moves at a rapid clip, from here on, to make marriage between Hope and Everell possible, and to seamlessly remove Magawisca from the fabric of the white community, it would seem that the novel's nation-making work essentially concludes with the trial scene. Indeed, the fate of Magawisca the character is that of her "real" referents— exile to the West, conveniently represented here as self-imposed. The single countering force to the novel's conservatism here, its need to expunge the emptied signifier of Magawisca's body, is the supplemental plot it produces, surprisingly, via the presence of Esther Downing, who is exiled from the heterosexual contract when brother and sister become man and wife.[31] The unmarried Sedgwick seems to have found, in the recuperation of this unmarried character, a vehicle for making Magawisca's embodied performativity continue to work, this time in a form more fully available to white, female readers for identification.

Rejecting Everell's claim that "the present difference of the English with the Indians, is but a vapour that has, even now, nearly passed away," Magawisca relinquishes her role as border guard and departs for an unnamed place. By leaving the place anonymous, the novel makes it clear that she is not exiled to some other national space existing in simultaneity with the colony; effectively, the colony has triumphed and already become America, a country which subsumes a continent, which leaves no space adjacent to it.[32] Effectively, Magawisca dies. Her last performative act is to bless the marriage of Hope and Everell, turning over her authority to their bourgeois sexual contract:

> "Oh! yes, Magawisca," urged Everell, "come back to us and teach us to be happy, as you are, without human help or agency."
>
> "Ah!" she replied, with a faint smile, "ye need not the lesson, ye will each be to the other a full stream of happiness. May it be fed from the fountain of love, and grow broader and deeper through all the passage of life."
>
> (333)

When Magawisca leaves, her effects seem to have been memorialized through the double signs of the (hetero)sexual contract and the American nation. But the work the novel does toward this apparent culmination leaves a significant bit of residue at its very core. This is Esther Downing, who receives the lion's share of attention as the novel closes and comes to serve as heir to Magawisca, registering as she does the border of the marriage bond. Once a relatively minor character defined almost exclusively by her nervous, doomed passion for Everell, this young woman becomes the novel's most unlikely heroine. She gently berates Hope and Everell for their inattention to her feelings, and quietly leaves the town, only to return a few years later to reestablish bonds with her former companions, "without any other emotions, on either side, than those which belong to warm and tender friendship" (349). Given Esther's newly refined, attractive character, "[h]er hand was often and eagerly sought," the narrator coyly informs us in the novel's final paragraph (which I quote in full):

> but she appears never to have felt a second engrossing attachment. The current of her purposes and affections had set another way. She illustrated a truth, which, if more generally received by her sex, might save a vast deal of misery: that marriage is not *essential* to the contentment, the dignity, or the happiness of woman. Indeed, those who saw on how wide a sphere her kindness shone, how many were made better or happier by her disinterested devotion, might have rejoiced that she did not "Give to a party what was meant for mankind."
>
> (348-49)

Staunchly refusing the demands of the bourgeois sexual contract, in the end, it is Esther who becomes most like Magawisca. She is the final embodiment of Magawisca's iconic ability to endure the demands of physical "peculiarity"; here, such "peculiarity" is associated with the desire to take on a permanent heterosexual mate. Esther illustrates the ultimate fantasy of the antebellum white woman, forced to have undergone a "vast deal of misery" in her sexual role, become safe, yet authoritative in a wide "sphere," once her place in the community is mediated not by a husband or potential husband, but by a woman of color. And while that woman of color has also mediated and brought into being the traditional novel-ending-in-marriage, it is this Esther, this unrecuperated fantasy with which the novel leaves us.

The way most of us have read the nineteenth-century domestic novel, of which Sedgwick, in the U.S., was a founding figure, has been to imagine its characters as idealized representations of "real" selves, available for readerly identification. In his book *The Letters of the Republic*, Michael Warner opposes the dominant literary assumptions of the eighteenth and nineteenth centuries in America, finding in the former a focal, constitutive concern for the national public good, and in the latter a focus on individual, private experiences of fantasy and identification. In the early nineteenth century, he writes, it became possible to "be a member of a nation, attributing its agency to yourself in imaginary identification, without . . . exercising any agency in the public sphere."[33] In other words, one was a citizen just in the personal, interiorized act of reading, the basis of what Benedict Anderson has famously called an "imagined community." Warner's argument suggests a shift in the technology of literary narrative toward private readerly identification, essentially toward realism, toward inviting readers to locate samenesses between their selves and those portrayed in the fiction at hand.[34]

The legacy of *Hope Leslie*'s Magawisca should be to question the degree to which such identifications took place neatly and uncritically. Certainly, Hope, Esther, and Magawisca are all characters with whom readers, especially young, white, female readers, are asked to identify themselves. Yet Sedgwick's novel also maps the process by which Hope, and most surprisingly, Esther, come into being through Magawisca's presence as figures for identification. A liminal force, largely constituted through public histories and public events, and embodied in this Pequot woman, makes private identification possible for the white, female citizens of the antebellum republic. Although Magawisca certainly embodies idealized qualities with which most readers would like to identify themselves—emotional strength, physical stamina, adherence to principle, etc.— what the novel seeks to emphasize throughout is the preoccupation the "European eye" has with her. She is always signifying, even if what she signifies doesn't always make sense to the English characters. Thus she is not simply an icon of a woman who speaks and acts powerfully. She is a marker of Euro-American preoccupation with embodying national fantasy, and Sedgwick's novel uses her as such to retell the story of the nation. This would suggest that women's novels of the antebellum period ought to be evaluated as much for the ways they depict and critique the dynamics of fantasy, of "imaginary identification," as for the ways they enact them.

Notes

1. See Lora Romero, *Home Fronts: Antebellum Domesticity and Its Critics* (Durham, NC: Duke University Press, 1997), chapter one, and Cathy Davidson, "Preface: No More Separate Spheres!," *American Literature* 70 (Sept. 1998): 443-63.

2. Here is a very preliminary working list of such characters/figures, beyond the one discussed in this essay: Lydia Maria Child's Hobomok, who sacrifices his marriage to a Puritan woman and the son they share, when her white husband, presumed dead, returns; Stowe's Uncle Tom, who, as a number of critics have shown, is essentially an emotionally overwrought domestic heroine writ large over the nation-defining issues of slavery and abolition; the famous tearful Indian of the 1970s anti-littering campaign, whose sentiment served to stand in for the loss of a supposedly once-pure national landscape; Latrell Sprewell, the once ostracized NBA player whose recent ad campaign spectacularizes his corn-rowed hair in the service of the slogan, "I'm the American dream." Within recent work in cultural studies, Lauren Berlant's notion of the "diva citizen" can be seen both to expostulate on and embody something akin to what I am describing. See the chapter "Notes on Diva Citizenship" in *The Queen of America Goes to Washington City* (Durham, NC: Duke University Press, 1997).

3. The best biographical work on Sedgwick to date is Mary Kelley, "Introduction" to Catharine Maria Sedgwick, *The Power of Her Sympathy: The Autobiography and Journal of Catharine Maria Sedgwick,* ed. Kelley (Boston: Massachussetts Historical Society, 1993).

4. See Mary Kelley, *Private Woman, Public Stage: Literary Domesticity in Nineteenth-Century America* (New York: Oxford University Press, 1984).

5. Lucy Maddox, *Removals: Nineteenth-Century American Literature and the Politics of Indian Affairs* (New York: Oxford University Press, 1991), 17.

6. It is important to note the degree to which *Hope Leslie* is still shaped by literary and political discourses of domesticity; I do not wish to argue that it is exceptional, or exceptionally politically engaged, by virtue of its historical and race plots.

7. Catharine Maria Sedgwick, *Hope Leslie* (New Brunswick, NJ: Rutgers University Press, 1987), 207. Hereafter, page numbers of citations are from this edition and will appear parenthetically in the body of the text.

8. For the early history of this literary and intellectual legacy in America, see Julia A. Stern, *The Plight of Feeling: Sympathy and Dissent in the Early American Novel* (Chicago: University of Chicago Press, 1997).

9. Michael Warner, "The Mass Public and the Mass Subject," in *Habermas and the Public Sphere,* ed. Craig Calhoun (Cambridge, MA: MIT Press, 1992), 377-401.

10. The canon of critical work on middle-class female writers of the antebellum period has expanded dramatically in the past few years. The foundational works in this canon are generally taken to be Ann Douglas, *The Feminization of American Culture* (New York: Knopf, 1977); Nina Baym, *Woman's Fiction: A Guide to Novels By and About Women in America, 1820-1870* (Ithaca, NY: Cornell University Press, 1978); and Jane Tompkins, *Sensational Designs: The Cultural Work of American Fiction* (New York: Oxford University Press, 1985). The most compelling critique of the shape this criticism has taken, and of the debates that have developed within it, appears in Romero, *Home Fronts.*

11. Also see Nina Baym, *American Women Writers and the Work of History 1790-1860* (New Brunswick, NJ: Rutgers University Press, 1995).

12. *Western Monthly Review* I (1828): 289. Quoted in Mary Kelley's introduction to Sedgwick, *Hope Leslie,* x.

13. *New-England Magazine* 8 (1835): 489-90. Quoted in Maddox, *Removals,* 45.

14. The racist disavowal of Sedgwick's portrayal of Magawisca has been echoed as recently as the 1970s, when Edward Halsey Foster wrote that "Miss Sedgwick's 'noble savages' . . . are very much the creation of her own imagination; for there are few surviving records of the Puritan epoch which suggest that the savages were fully as noble as they appear to be in the novel." See Foster, *Catharine Maria Sedgwick* (New York: Twayne, 1974), 77. Foster's comment is also remarkable in its resistance to recognizing the degree to which the novel throws into question the authority of the "few surviving records of the Puritan epoch."

15. Quoted in Maddox, *Removals,* 45.

16. Philip Gould argues that this constitutes the book's criticism of the narrativization of history: "Sedgwick enacts exactly that which she calls Magawisca's narrative: a 'recital'—a *performance*—of history . . . the text itself dramatizes the inevitability of historical relativism [Gould's emphasis]." See Gould, "Catharine Sedgwick's 'Recital' of the Pequot War," *American Literature* 66:4 (Dec. 1994): 653.

17. For the most concise account of Sedgwick's researches in Puritan history, see Foster, *Catharine Maria Sedgwick.* For a reading of the relationship between *Hope Leslie* and the story of Pocahontas, see Robert Tilton, *Pocahontas: The Evolution of an American Narrative* (Cambridge: Cambridge University Press, 1994), 77-81.

18. That the absence is here inflicted by another Indian, Magawisca's own father, contributes to the degree to which the portrayal of Magawisca is at least partially informed by the myth of the "vanishing American," the Indian who is always already dying and/or leaving, even before contact with white settlers. See Brian Dippie, *The Vanishing American: White Attitudes and U.S. Indian Policy* (Middletown, CT: Wesleyan University Press, 1982).

19. The nineteenth century is everywhere embedded in the novel, from the benevolent intimacy of the Fletchers' domestic hearth, to the smooth-around-the-edges liberality attributed to strict Puritan patriarchs like Governor Winthrop and the minister John Eliot, to forthright reminders from Sedgwick like:

"We forget that the noble pilgrims lived and endured for us." Maddox specifically upbraids Sedgwick for her "beatification" of Eliot, whose writings belie a fairly faithful upholding of Puritan orthodoxy in the matter of race relations. See Maddox, *Removals,* 109. The novel creates an imagined historical community by extending a narrative bridge from Puritan culture to that of her present-day, nineteenth-century bourgeois readership. This national present is explicitly built on the graves of those who died fighting in the Pequot wars.

20. The word "people" renders the referent of Magawisca's representativity ambiguous; it blurs the distinctions between categories such as family, nation, and race; it works toward the dehistoricization and decontextualization of her status as representative. It makes her available as representative of a host of qualities and ideals, and of a type of collectivity (this ambiguous notion of "people") which she can share with Everell Fletcher.

21. See Bercovitch, *The Rites of Assent: Transformations in the Symbolic Construction of America* (New York: Routledge, 1993), 33.

22. This mode of description is another strategy *Hope Leslie* shares with the *Leatherstocking Tales.*

23. See also Joy Kasson, *Marble Queens and Captives: Women in Nineteenth-Century American Sculpture* (New Haven: Yale University Press, 1990).

24. For an excellent reading of the novel as an imagination of "republican sisterhood," see Judith Feterley's recent article, "'My Sister! My Sister!': The Rhetoric of Catharine Sedgwick's *Hope Leslie,*" *American Literature* 70 (Sept. 1998): 491-516.

25. For a summary of such novels see Eric Sundquist, "The Literature of Expansion and Race," in *The Cambridge History of American Literature,* vol. 2, ed. Sacvan Bercovitch (Cambridge: Cambridge University Press, 1995), 223-25.

26. The novel's plot here reverses the racial logic of the genre of the captivity narrative. For an insightful reading of *Hope Leslie* as caught up in, and critiquing, this genre, see Christopher Castiglia, *Bound And Determined: Captivity, Culture-Crossing, And White Womanhood From Mary Rowlandson To Patty Hearst* (Chicago: University of Chicago Press, 1996).

27. Fetterley, "'My Sister!,'" 495.

28. Berlant's essay "Notes on Diva Citizenship" describes "women who have sought . . . to transform the horizons and the terms of authority that mark both personal and national life in America by speaking about sexuality as the fundamental and fundamentally repressed horizon of national identity, legitimacy, and affective experience" (458). Although

in a full study many differences would need to be attended to, I see Magawisca working within this tradition, which Berlant associates with Harriet Jacobs, Frances Harper's Iola Leroy, and Anita Hill.

29. Important readings of the novel's configurations of patriarchy appear in Maddox, *Removals,* and Dana Nelson, "Sympathy as Strategy in Sedgwick's *Hope Leslie,*" in *The Culture of Sentiment,* ed. Shirley Samuels (New York: Oxford University Press, 1992).

30. See Fliegelman, *Declaring Independence: Jefferson, Natural Language, and the Culture of Performance* (Stanford: Stanford University Press, 1993).

31. One might seek to establish a connection between this move and Sedgwick's own lifelong unmarried status. Such a possibility is worth musing upon, but I am hesitant to reinforce what I consider to be the burdensome autobiographical, experiential assumptions often placed upon women's writing of this era. For more on this see Judith Fetterley, "Commentary: Nineteenth-Century American Women Writers and the Politics of Recovery," *American Literary History* 6 (Fall 1994): 600-611, and my dissertation, "Obscene Sentiments: Reading, Effects, and Sentimental Form in Fanny Fern, Louisa May Alcott, and Henry James" (Ph.D. diss., Duke University, 1997).

32. This firmly places Magawisca within what has been called the "cult of the Vanishing American" recurrent in antebellum literature representing native peoples. See Dippie, *The Vanishing American.*

33. Warner, *The Letters of the Republic: Publication and the Public Sphere in Eighteenth-Century America* (Cambridge, MA: Harvard University Press, 1990), 173. It could well be argued that Warner takes a counterposition to this overly simplified version of literary history in his "The Mass Public and the Mass Subject," in which he argues for the centrality of the mass public witness specifically to citizens who bear "embodied particularities."

34. For different critiques of Warner see Fliegelman, *Declaring Independence* and Davidson, "Preface."

FURTHER READING

Biography

Foster, Edward Halsey. *Catharine Maria Sedgwick.* New York: Twayne Publishers, 1974, 171 p.

A full-length biography of Sedgwick.

Criticism

Bauermeister, Erica R. "*The Lamplighter, The Wide, Wide, World,* and *Hope Leslie*: Reconsidering the Recipes for Nineteenth-Century American Women's Novels." In *Legacy* 8, No. 1 (Spring 1991): 17-28.

A comparative study of three novels written by prominent nineteenth-century women writers, commenting on their standing as autonomous works of literature.

Castiglia, Christopher. "In Praise of Extra-Vagrant Women: *Hope Leslie* and the Captivity Romance." In *Legacy* 6, No. 2 (Fall 1989): 3-16.

An analysis of *Hope Leslie* as a frontier romance that subverts racial and gender stereotypes.

Gossett, Suzanne and Barbara Ann Bardes. "Women and Political Power in the Republic: Two Early American Novels." In *Legacy* 2, No. 2 (Fall 1985): 13-30.

An analysis and comparison of *Hope Leslie* and Sarah Josepha Hale's *Northwood* as fictive expressions of the contemporary political culture.

Gould, Philip. "Catharine Sedgwick's 'Recital' of the Pequot War." In *American Literature* 66, No. 4 (December 1994): 641-62.

Examines Sedgwick's revisionary history of the Pequot War in *Hope Leslie* and discusses the significance of its "anti-patriarchalism."

Holly, Carol. "Nineteenth-Century Autobiographies of Affiliation: The Case of Catharine Sedgwick and Lucy Larcom." In *American Autobiography: Retrospect and Prospect,* edited by Paul John Eakin, pp. 216-34. Madison: University of Wisconsin Press, 1991.

A discussion of nineteenth-century women's autobiographies as texts of affiliation that present the autobiographical act as an intimate, interactive, and female event.

Karafilis, Maria. "Catherine Maria Sedgwick's *Hope Leslie*: The Crisis between Ethical Political Action and U.S. Literary Nationalism in the New Republic." In *American Transcendental Quarterly* 12, No. 4 (December 1998): 327-44.

Proposes that a conflict exists in *Hope Leslie* between Sedgwick's desire for an alternative model of governance and her desire to foster a domestic national literature.

Nelson, Dana. "Sympathy as Strategy in Sedgwick's *Hope Leslie.*" In *The Culture of Sentiment: Race, Gender, and Sentimentality in Nineteenth-Century America,* edited by Shirley Samuels, pp. 191-202. New York: Oxford University Press, 1992.

Contends that the sympathetic frame of reference employed by Sedgwick and other female authors in their frontier romances fostered a more positive cultural vision by attempting to promote similarities between races and cultures.

Ross, Cheri Louise. "(Re)Writing the Frontier Romance: Catharine Maria Sedgwick's *Hope Leslie*." In *College Language Association Journal* 39, No. 3 (March 1996): 320-40.

Examination of *Hope Leslie* as a frontier romance that transforms the genre by giving it a feminist, non-racist nature.

Zagarell, Sandra A. "Expanding 'America': Lydia Sigourney's *Sketch of Connecticut* and Catharine Sedgwick's *Hope Leslie*." In *Tulsa Studies in Women's Literature* 6, No. 2 (Fall 1987): 225-45.

Discussion of Sedgwick and Sigourney's works as examples of women's writing that offers an expanded view of America as a nation grounded in inclusiveness and a sense of community.

Additional coverage of Sedgwick's life and career is contained in the following sources published by the Gale Group: *Dictionary of Literary Biography,* **Vols. 1, 74, and 183.**

How to Use This Index

The main references

> **Calvino, Italo**
> 1923-1985 .... CLC **5, 8, 11, 22, 33, 39,**
> **73; SSC 3**

list all author entries in the following Gale Literary Criticism series:

BLC = *Black Literature Criticism*
CLC = *Contemporary Literary Criticism*
CLR = *Children's Literature Review*
CMLC = *Classical and Medieval Literature Criticism*
DA = *DISCovering Authors*
DAB = *DISCovering Authors: British*
DAC = *DISCovering Authors: Canadian*
DAM = *DISCovering Authors: Modules*
     DRAM: *Dramatists Module;* *MST:* *Most-Studied Authors Module;*
     MULT: *Multicultural Authors Module;* *NOV:* *Novelists Module;*
     POET: *Poets Module;* *POP:* *Popular Fiction and Genre Authors Module*
DC = *Drama Criticism*
HLC = *Hispanic Literature Criticism*
LC = *Literature Criticism from 1400 to 1800*
NCLC = *Nineteenth-Century Literature Criticism*
NNAL = *Native North American Literature*
PC = *Poetry Criticism*
SSC = *Short Story Criticism*
TCLC = *Twentieth-Century Literary Criticism*
WLC = *World Literature Criticism, 1500 to the Present*

The cross-references

> See also CANR 23; CA 85-88;
> obituary CA116

list all author entries in the following Gale biographical and literary sources:

AAYA = *Authors & Artists for Young Adults*
AITN = *Authors in the News*
BEST = *Bestsellers*
BW = *Black Writers*
CA = *Contemporary Authors*
CAAS = *Contemporary Authors Autobiography Series*
CABS = *Contemporary Authors Bibliographical Series*
CANR = *Contemporary Authors New Revision Series*
CAP = *Contemporary Authors Permanent Series*
CDALB = *Concise Dictionary of American Literary Biography*
CDBLB = *Concise Dictionary of British Literary Biography*
DLB = *Dictionary of Literary Biography*
DLBD = *Dictionary of Literary Biography Documentary Series*
DLBY = *Dictionary of Literary Biography Yearbook*
HW = *Hispanic Writers*
JRDA = *Junior DISCovering Authors*
MAICYA = *Major Authors and Illustrators for Children and Young Adults*
MTCW = *Major 20th-Century Writers*
SAAS = *Something about the Author Autobiography Series*
SATA = *Something about the Author*
YABC = *Yesterday's Authors of Books for Children*

Literary Criticism Series
Cumulative Author Index

Akst, Daniel 1956- .... **CLC 109**
See also CA 161
Aksyonov, Vassily (Pavlovich)
1932- .... **CLC 22, 37, 101**
See also CA 53-56; CANR 12, 48, 77;
CWW 2
Akutagawa Ryunosuke 1892-1927 . **TCLC 16**
See also CA 117; 154; DLB 180
Alain 1868-1951 .... **TCLC 41**
See also CA 163
Alain-Fournier TCLC 6
See also Fournier, Henri Alban
See also DLB 65
Alarcon, Pedro Antonio de
1833-1891 .... **NCLC 1**
Alas (y Urena), Leopoldo (Enrique Garcia)
1852-1901 .... **TCLC 29**
See also CA 113; 131; HW 1
Albee, Edward (Franklin III) 1928- . **CLC 1,
2, 3, 5, 9, 11, 13, 25, 53, 86, 113; DA;
DAB; DAC; DAM DRAM, MST; DC
11**
See also AITN 1; AW; CA 5-8R; CABS 3;
CANR 8, 54, 74; CDALB 1941-1968;
DA3; DLB 7; INT CANR-8; MTCW 1, 2
Alberti, Rafael 1902-1999 .... **CLC 7**
See also CA 85-88; 185; CANR 81; DLB
108; HW 2
Albert the Great 1193(?)-1280 ...... **CMLC 16**
See also DLB 115
Alcala-Galiano, Juan Valera y
See Valera y Alcala-Galiano, Juan
Alcayaga, Lucila Godoy
See Godoy Alcayaga, Lucila
Alcott, Amos Bronson 1799-1888 .... **NCLC 1**
See also DLB 1, 223
Alcott, Louisa May 1832-1888 . **NCLC 6, 58,
83; DA; DAB; DAC; DAM MST, NOV;
SSC 27**
See also AAYA 20; AMWS 1; AW; CDALB
1865-1917; CLR 1, 38; DA3; DLB 1, 42,
79, 223, 239, 242; DLBD 14; JRDA;
MAICYA; SATA 100
Aldanov, M. A.
See Aldanov, Mark (Alexandrovich)
Aldanov, Mark (Alexandrovich)
1886(?)-1957 .... **TCLC 23**
See also CA 118; 181
Aldington, Richard 1892-1962 .... **CLC 49**
See also CA 85-88; CANR 45; DLB 20, 36,
100, 149
Aldiss, Brian W(ilson) 1925- . **CLC 5, 14, 40;
DAM NOV; SSC 36**
See also CA 5-8R; CAAE 190; CAAS 2;
CANR 5, 28, 64; DLB 14; MTCW 1, 2;
SATA 34
Alegria, Claribel 1924- .... **CLC 75; DAM
MULT; HLCS 1; PC 26**
See also CA 131; CAAS 15; CANR 66, 94;
CWW 2; DLB 145; HW 1; MTCW 1
Alegria, Fernando 1918- .... **CLC 57**
See also CA 9-12R; CANR 5, 32, 72; HW
1, 2
Aleichem, Sholom TCLC 1, 35; SSC 33
See also Rabinovitch, Sholem
Aleixandre, Vicente 1898-1984
See also CANR 81; HLCS 1; HW 2
Alepoudelis, Odysseus
See Elytis, Odysseus
See also CWW 2
Aleshkovsky, Joseph 1929-
See Aleshkovsky, Yuz
See also CA 121; 128
Aleshkovsky, Yuz CLC 44
See also Aleshkovsky, Joseph

Alexander, Lloyd (Chudley) 1924- ... **CLC 35**
See also AAYA 1, 27; CA 1-4R; CANR 1,
24, 38, 55; CLR 1, 5, 48; DLB 52; JRDA;
MAICYA; MTCW 1; SAAS 19; SATA 3,
49, 81
Alexander, Meena 1951- .... **CLC 121**
See also CA 115; CANR 38, 70
Alexander, Samuel 1859-1938 .... **TCLC 77**
Alexie, Sherman (Joseph, Jr.)
1966- .... **CLC 96; DAM MULT**
See also AAYA 28; CA 138; CANR 95;
DA3; DLB 175, 206; MTCW 1; NNAL
Alfau, Felipe 1902-1999 .... **CLC 66**
See also CA 137
Alfred, Jean Gaston
See Ponge, Francis
Alger, Horatio, Jr. 1832-1899 .... **NCLC 8, 83**
See also DLB 42; SATA 16
Algren, Nelson 1909-1981 ..... **CLC 4, 10, 33;
SSC 33**
See also CA 13-16R; 103; CANR 20, 61;
CDALB 1941-1968; DLB 9; DLBY 81,
82; MTCW 1, 2
Ali, Ahmed 1908-1998 .... **CLC 69**
See also CA 25-28R; CANR 15, 34
Alighieri, Dante
See Dante
Allan, John B.
See Westlake, Donald E(dwin)
Allan, Sidney
See Hartmann, Sadakichi
Allan, Sydney
See Hartmann, Sadakichi
Allard, Janet CLC 59
Allen, Edward 1948- .... **CLC 59**
Allen, Fred 1894-1956 .... **TCLC 87**
Allen, Paula Gunn 1939- .... **CLC 84; DAM
MULT**
See also AMWS 4; CA 112; 143; CANR
63; DA3; DLB 175; MTCW 1; NNAL
Allen, Roland
See Ayckbourn, Alan
Allen, Sarah A.
See Hopkins, Pauline Elizabeth
Allen, Sidney H.
See Hartmann, Sadakichi
Allen, Woody 1935- .... **CLC 16, 52; DAM
POP**
See also AAYA 10; CA 33-36R; CANR 27,
38, 63; DLB 44; MTCW 1
Allende, Isabel 1942- . **CLC 39, 57, 97; DAM
MULT, NOV; HLC 1**
See also AAYA 18; AW; CA 125; 130;
CANR 51, 74; CWW 2; DA3; DLB 145;
HW 1, 2; INT 130; MTCW 1, 2
Alleyn, Ellen
See Rossetti, Christina (Georgina)
Alleyne, Carla D. CLC 65
Allingham, Margery (Louise)
1904-1966 .... **CLC 19**
See also CA 5-8R; 25-28R; CANR 4, 58;
DLB 77; MTCW 1, 2
Allingham, William 1824-1889 ...... **NCLC 25**
See also DLB 35
Allison, Dorothy E. 1949- .... **CLC 78**
See also CA 140; CANR 66; DA3; MTCW
1
Alloula, Malek CLC 65
Allston, Washington 1779-1843 .... **NCLC 2**
See also DLB 1, 235
Almedingen, E. M. CLC 12
See also Almedingen, Martha Edith von
See also SATA 3
Almedingen, Martha Edith von 1898-1971
See Almedingen, E. M.
See also CA 1-4R; CANR 1

Almodovar, Pedro 1949(?)- .... **CLC 114;
HLCS 1**
See also CA 133; CANR 72; HW 2
Almqvist, Carl Jonas Love
1793-1866 .... **NCLC 42**
Alonso, Damaso 1898-1990 .... **CLC 14**
See also CA 110; 131; 130; CANR 72; DLB
108; HW 1, 2
Alov
See Gogol, Nikolai (Vasilyevich)
Alta 1942- .... **CLC 19**
See also CA 57-60
Alter, Robert B(ernard) 1935- .... **CLC 34**
See also CA 49-52; CANR 1, 47
Alther, Lisa 1944- .... **CLC 7, 41**
See also CA 65-68; CAAS 30; CANR 12,
30, 51; GLL 2; MTCW 1
Althusser, L.
See Althusser, Louis
Althusser, Louis 1918-1990 .... **CLC 106**
See also CA 131; 132; DLB 242
Altman, Robert 1925- .... **CLC 16, 116**
See also CA 73-76; CANR 43
Alurista
See Urista, Alberto H.
See also DLB 82; HLCS 1
Alvarez, A(lfred) 1929- .... **CLC 5, 13**
See also CA 1-4R; CANR 3, 33, 63; DLB
14, 40
Alvarez, Alejandro Rodriguez 1903-1965
See Casona, Alejandro
See also CA 131; 93-96; HW 1
Alvarez, Julia 1950- .... **CLC 93; HLCS 1**
See also AAYA 25; AMWS 7; CA 147;
CANR 69; DA3; MTCW 1
Alvaro, Corrado 1896-1956 .... **TCLC 60**
See also CA 163
Amado, Jorge 1912- .... **CLC 13, 40, 106;
DAM MULT, NOV; HLC 1**
See also CA 77-80; CANR 35, 74; DLB
113; HW 2; MTCW 1, 2
Ambler, Eric 1909-1998 .... **CLC 4, 6, 9**
See also BRWS 4; CA 9-12R; 171; CANR
7, 38, 74; DLB 77; MTCW 1, 2
Amichai, Yehuda 1924-2000 .. **CLC 9, 22, 57,
116**
See also CA 85-88; 189; CANR 46, 60;
CWW 2; MTCW 1
Amichai, Yehudah
See Amichai, Yehuda
Amiel, Henri Frederic 1821-1881 .... **NCLC 4**
Amis, Kingsley (William)
1922-1995 ...... **CLC 1, 2, 3, 5, 8, 13, 40,
44, 129; DA; DAB; DAC; DAM MST,
NOV**
See also AITN 2; BRWS 2; CA 9-12R; 150;
CANR 8, 28, 54; CDBLB 1945-1960;
DA3; DLB 15, 27, 100, 139; DLBY 96;
INT CANR-8; MTCW 1, 2
Amis, Martin (Louis) 1949- .... **CLC 4, 9, 38,
62, 101**
See also BEST 90:3; BRWS 4; CA 65-68;
CANR 8, 27, 54, 73, 95; DA3; DLB 14,
194; INT CANR-27; MTCW 1
Ammons, A(rchie) R(andolph)
1926-2001 ...... **CLC 2, 3, 5, 8, 9, 25, 57,
108; DAM POET; PC 16**
See also AITN 1; CA 9-12R; CANR 6, 36,
51, 73; DLB 5, 165; MTCW 1, 2
Amo, Tauraatua i
See Adams, Henry (Brooks)
Amory, Thomas 1691(?)-1788 .... **LC 48**
Anand, Mulk Raj 1905- .. **CLC 23, 93; DAM
NOV**
See also CA 65-68; CANR 32, 64; MTCW
1, 2
Anatol
See Schnitzler, Arthur

Anaximander c. 611B.C.-c. 546B.C. .... **CMLC 22**

Anaya, Rudolfo A(lfonso) 1937- ...... **CLC 23; DAM MULT, NOV; HLC 1**
See also AAYA 20; CA 45-48; CAAS 4; CANR 1, 32, 51; DLB 82, 206; HW 1; MTCW 1, 2

Andersen, Hans Christian 1805-1875 .... **NCLC 7, 79; DA; DAB; DAC; DAM MST, POP; SSC 6**
See also AW; CLR 6; DA3; MAICYA; SATA 100

Anderson, C. Farley
See Mencken, H(enry) L(ouis); Nathan, George Jean

Anderson, Jessica (Margaret) Queale 1916- .... **CLC 37**
See also CA 9-12R; CANR 4, 62

Anderson, Jon (Victor) 1940- . **CLC 9; DAM POET**
See also CA 25-28R; CANR 20

Anderson, Lindsay (Gordon) 1923-1994 .... **CLC 20**
See also CA 125; 128; 146; CANR 77

Anderson, Maxwell 1888-1959 .... **TCLC 2; DAM DRAM**
See also CA 105; 152; DLB 7, 228; MTCW 2

Anderson, Poul (William) 1926- .... **CLC 15**
See also AAYA 5, 34; CA 1-4R, 181; CAAE 181; CAAS 2; CANR 2, 15, 34, 64; CLR 58; DLB 8; INT CANR-15; MTCW 1, 2; SATA 90; SATA-Brief 39; SATA-Essay 106; SCFW 2

Anderson, Robert (Woodruff) 1917- .... **CLC 23; DAM DRAM**
See also AITN 1; CA 21-24R; CANR 32; DLB 7

Anderson, Sherwood 1876-1941 ..... **TCLC 1, 10, 24; DA; DAB; DAC; DAM MST, NOV; SSC 1**
See also AAYA 30; AW; CA 104; 121; CANR 61; CDALB 1917-1929; DA3; DLB 4, 9, 86; DLBD 1; GLL 2; MTCW 1, 2

Andier, Pierre
See Desnos, Robert

Andouard
See Giraudoux, (Hippolyte) Jean

Andrade, Carlos Drummond de CLC 18
See also Drummond de Andrade, Carlos

Andrade, Mario de 1893-1945 .... **TCLC 43**

Andreae, Johann V(alentin) 1586-1654 .... **LC 32**
See also DLB 164

Andreas-Salome, Lou 1861-1937 ... **TCLC 56**
See also CA 178; DLB 66

Andress, Lesley
See Sanders, Lawrence

Andrewes, Lancelot 1555-1626 .... **LC 5**
See also DLB 151, 172

Andrews, Cicily Fairfield
See West, Rebecca

Andrews, Elton V.
See Pohl, Frederik

Andreyev, Leonid (Nikolaevich) 1871-1919 .... **TCLC 3**
See also CA 104; 185

Andric, Ivo 1892-1975 .... **CLC 8; SSC 36**
See also CA 81-84; 57-60; CANR 43, 60; DLB 147; MTCW 1

Androvar
See Prado (Calvo), Pedro

Angelique, Pierre
See Bataille, Georges

Angell, Roger 1920- .... **CLC 26**
See also CA 57-60; CANR 13, 44, 70; DLB 171, 185

Angelou, Maya 1928- .... **CLC 12, 35, 64, 77; BLC 1; DA; DAB; DAC; DAM MST, MULT, POET, POP; PC 32**
See also AAYA 7, 20; AMWS 4; AW; BW 2, 3; CA 65-68; CANR 19, 42, 65; CDALBS; CLR 53; DA3; DLB 38; MTCW 1, 2; SATA 49

Anna Comnena 1083-1153 .... **CMLC 25**

Annensky, Innokenty (Fyodorovich) 1856-1909 .... **TCLC 14**
See also CA 110; 155

Annunzio, Gabriele d'
See D'Annunzio, Gabriele

Anodos
See Coleridge, Mary E(lizabeth)

Anon, Charles Robert
See Pessoa, Fernando (Antonio Nogueira)

Anouilh, Jean (Marie Lucien Pierre) 1910-1987 .... **CLC 1, 3, 8, 13, 40, 50; DAM DRAM; DC 8**
See also CA 17-20R; 123; CANR 32; MTCW 1, 2

Anthony, Florence
See Ai

Anthony, John
See Ciardi, John (Anthony)

Anthony, Peter
See Shaffer, Anthony (Joshua); Shaffer, Peter (Levin)

Anthony, Piers 1934- .... **CLC 35; DAM POP**
See also AAYA 11; AW; CA 21-24R; CANR 28, 56, 73; DLB 8; MTCW 1, 2; SAAS 22; SATA 84

Anthony, Susan B(rownell) 1916-1991 .... **TCLC 84**
See also CA 89-92; 134

Antoine, Marc
See Proust, (Valentin-Louis-George-Eugene-)Marcel

Antoninus, Brother
See Everson, William (Oliver)

Antoninus, Marcus Aurelius 121-180 .... **CMLC 45**

Antonioni, Michelangelo 1912- .... **CLC 20**
See also CA 73-76; CANR 45, 77

Antschel, Paul 1920-1970
See Celan, Paul
See also CA 85-88; CANR 33, 61; MTCW 1

Anwar, Chairil 1922-1949 .... **TCLC 22**
See also CA 121

Anzaldua, Gloria (Evanjelina) 1942-
See also CA 175; DLB 122; HLCS 1

Apess, William 1798-1839(?) .... **NCLC 73; DAM MULT**
See also DLB 175; NNAL

Apollinaire, Guillaume 1880-1918 .. **TCLC 3, 8, 51; DAM POET; PC 7**
See also CA 152; MTCW 1

Appelfeld, Aharon 1932- ... **CLC 23, 47; SSC 42**
See also CA 112; 133; CANR 86; CWW 2

Apple, Max (Isaac) 1941- .... **CLC 9, 33**
See also CA 81-84; CANR 19, 54; DLB 130

Appleman, Philip (Dean) 1926- .... **CLC 51**
See also CA 13-16R; CAAS 18; CANR 6, 29, 56

Appleton, Lawrence
See Lovecraft, H(oward) P(hillips)

Apteryx
See Eliot, T(homas) S(tearns)

Apuleius, (Lucius Madaurensis) 125(?)-175(?) .... **CMLC 1**
See also DLB 211

Aquin, Hubert 1929-1977 .... **CLC 15**
See also CA 105; DLB 53

Aquinas, Thomas 1224(?)-1274 ..... **CMLC 33**
See also DLB 115

Aragon, Louis 1897-1982 .. **CLC 3, 22; DAM NOV, POET**
See also CA 69-72; 108; CANR 28, 71; DLB 72; GLL 2; MTCW 1, 2

Arany, Janos 1817-1882 .... **NCLC 34**

Aranyos, Kakay 1847-1910
See Mikszath, Kalman

Arbuthnot, John 1667-1735 .... **LC 1**
See also DLB 101

Archer, Herbert Winslow
See Mencken, H(enry) L(ouis)

Archer, Jeffrey (Howard) 1940- ...... **CLC 28; DAM POP**
See also AAYA 16; BEST 89:3; CA 77-80; CANR 22, 52, 95; DA3; INT CANR-22

Archer, Jules 1915- .... **CLC 12**
See also CA 9-12R; CANR 6, 69; SAAS 5; SATA 4, 85

Archer, Lee
See Ellison, Harlan (Jay)

Archilochus c. 7th cent. B.C.- .... **CMLC 44**
See also DLB 176

Arden, John 1930- .... **CLC 6, 13, 15; DAM DRAM**
See also BRWS 2; CA 13-16R; CAAS 4; CANR 31, 65, 67; DLB 13; MTCW 1

Arenas, Reinaldo 1943-1990 . **CLC 41; DAM MULT; HLC 1**
See also CA 124; 128; 133; CANR 73; DLB 145; GLL 2; HW 1; MTCW 1

Arendt, Hannah 1906-1975 .... **CLC 66, 98**
See also CA 17-20R; 61-64; CANR 26, 60; DLB 242; MTCW 1, 2

Aretino, Pietro 1492-1556 .... **LC 12**

Arghezi, Tudor CLC 80
See also Theodorescu, Ion N.
See also CA 167; DLB 220

Arguedas, Jose Maria 1911-1969 .... **CLC 10, 18; HLCS 1**
See also CA 89-92; CANR 73; DLB 113; HW 1

Argueta, Manlio 1936- .... **CLC 31**
See also CA 131; CANR 73; CWW 2; DLB 145; HW 1

Arias, Ron(ald Francis) 1941-
See also CA 131; CANR 81; DAM MULT; DLB 82; HLC 1; HW 1, 2; MTCW 2

Ariosto, Ludovico 1474-1533 .... **LC 6**

Aristides
See Epstein, Joseph

Aristophanes 450B.C.-385B.C. .... **CMLC 4; DA; DAB; DAC; DAM DRAM, MST; DC 2**
See also AW; DA3; DLB 176

Aristotle 384B.C.-322B.C. .... **CMLC 31; DA; DAB; DAC; DAM MST**
See also AW; DA3; DLB 176

Arlt, Roberto (Godofredo Christophersen) 1900-1942 .... **TCLC 29; DAM MULT; HLC 1**
See also CA 123; 131; CANR 67; HW 1, 2

Armah, Ayi Kwei 1939- .... **CLC 5, 33, 136; BLC 1; DAM MULT, POET**
See also BW 1; CA 61-64; CANR 21, 64; DLB 117; MTCW 1

Armatrading, Joan 1950- .... **CLC 17**
See also CA 114; 186

Arnette, Robert
See Silverberg, Robert

Arnim, Achim von (Ludwig Joachim von Arnim) 1781-1831 ..... **NCLC 5; SSC 29**
See also DLB 90

Arnim, Bettina von 1785-1859 .... **NCLC 38**
See also DLB 90

Arnold, Matthew 1822-1888 ..... **NCLC 6, 29, 89; DA; DAB; DAC; DAM MST, POET; PC 5**
See also AW; CDBLB 1832-1890; DLB 32, 57

Arnold, Thomas 1795-1842 .... **NCLC 18**
See also DLB 55
Arnow, Harriette (Louisa) Simpson
1908-1986 .... **CLC 2, 7, 18**
See also CA 9-12R; 118; CANR 14; DLB
6; MTCW 1, 2; SATA 42; SATA-Obit 47
Arouet, Francois-Marie
See Voltaire
Arp, Hans
See Arp, Jean
Arp, Jean 1887-1966 .... **CLC 5**
See also CA 81-84; 25-28R; CANR 42, 77
Arrabal
See Arrabal, Fernando
Arrabal, Fernando 1932- ... **CLC 2, 9, 18, 58**
See also CA 9-12R; CANR 15
Arreola, Juan Jose 1918- .... **SSC 38; DAM**
MULT; HLC 1
See also CA 113; 131; CANR 81; DLB 113;
HW 1, 2
Arrian c. 89(?)-c. 155(?) .... **CMLC 43**
See also DLB 176
Arrick, Fran CLC 30
See also Gaberman, Judie Angell
Artaud, Antonin (Marie Joseph)
1896-1948 . **TCLC 3, 36; DAM DRAM;**
DC 14
See also CA 104; 149; DA3; MTCW 1
Arthur, Ruth M(abel) 1905-1979 ..... **CLC 12**
See also CA 9-12R; 85-88; CANR 4; SATA
7, 26
Artsybashev, Mikhail (Petrovich)
1878-1927 .... **TCLC 31**
See also CA 170
Arundel, Honor (Morfydd)
1919-1973 .... **CLC 17**
See also CA 21-22; 41-44R; CAP 2; CLR
35; SATA 4; SATA-Obit 24
Arzner, Dorothy 1900-1979 .... **CLC 98**
Asch, Sholem 1880-1957 .... **TCLC 3**
See also CA 105; GLL 2
Ash, Shalom
See Asch, Sholem
Ashbery, John (Lawrence) 1927- .. **CLC 2, 3,**
4, 6, 9, 13, 15, 25, 41, 77, 125; DAM
POET; PC 26
See Berry, Jonas
See also AMWS 3; CA 5-8R; CANR 9, 37,
66; DA3; DLB 5, 165; DLBY 81; INT
CANR-9; MTCW 1, 2
Ashdown, Clifford
See Freeman, R(ichard) Austin
Ashe, Gordon
See Creasey, John
Ashton-Warner, Sylvia (Constance)
1908-1984 .... **CLC 19**
See also CA 69-72; 112; CANR 29; MTCW
1, 2
Asimov, Isaac 1920-1992 ..... **CLC 1, 3, 9, 19,**
26, 76, 92; DAM POP
See also AAYA 13; AW; BEST 90:2; CA
1-4R; 137; CANR 2, 19, 36, 60; CLR 12;
DA3; DLB 8; DLBY 92; INT CANR-19;
JRDA; MAICYA; MTCW 1, 2; SATA 1,
26, 74; SCFW 2
Assis, Joaquim Maria Machado de
See Machado de Assis, Joaquim Maria
Astley, Thea (Beatrice May) 1925- .. **CLC 41**
See also CA 65-68; CANR 11, 43, 78
Aston, James
See White, T(erence) H(anbury)
Asturias, Miguel Ángel 1899-1974 .... **CLC 3,**
8, 13; DAM MULT, NOV; HLC 1
See also CA 25-28; 49-52; CANR 32; CAP
2; DA3; DLB 113; HW 1; MTCW 1, 2
Atares, Carlos Saura
See Saura (Atares), Carlos
Atheling, William
See Pound, Ezra (Weston Loomis)

Atheling, William, Jr.
See Blish, James (Benjamin)
Atherton, Gertrude (Franklin Horn)
1857-1948 .... **TCLC 2**
See also CA 104; 155; DLB 9, 78, 186;
TCWW 2
Atherton, Lucius
See Masters, Edgar Lee
Atkins, Jack
See Harris, Mark
Atkinson, Kate CLC 99
See also CA 166
Attaway, William (Alexander)
1911-1986 .... **CLC 92; BLC 1; DAM**
MULT
See also BW 2, 3; CA 143; CANR 82; DLB
76
Atticus
See Fleming, Ian (Lancaster); Wilson,
(Thomas) Woodrow
Atwood, Margaret (Eleanor) 1939- ... **CLC 2,**
3, 4, 8, 13, 15, 25, 44, 84, 135; DA;
DAB; DAC; DAM MST, NOV, POET;
PC 8; SSC 2
See also AAYA 12; AW; BEST 89:2; CA
49-52; CANR 3, 24, 33, 59, 95; DA3;
DLB 53; INT CANR-24; MTCW 1, 2;
SATA 50
Aubigny, Pierre d'
See Mencken, H(enry) L(ouis)
Aubin, Penelope 1685-1731(?) .... **LC 9**
See also DLB 39
Auchincloss, Louis (Stanton) 1917- .. **CLC 4,**
6, 9, 18, 45; DAM NOV; SSC 22
See also AMWS 4; CA 1-4R; CANR 6, 29,
55, 87; DLB 2; DLBY 80; INT CANR-
29; MTCW 1
Auden, W(ystan) H(ugh) 1907-1973 . **CLC 1,**
2, 3, 4, 6, 9, 11, 14, 43, 123; DA; DAB;
DAC; DAM DRAM, MST, POET; PC
1
See also AAYA 18; AMWS 2; AW; CA
9-12R; 45-48; CANR 5, 61; CDBLB
1914-1945; DA3; DLB 10, 20; MTCW 1,
2
Audiberti, Jacques 1900-1965 .... **CLC 38;**
DAM DRAM
See also CA 25-28R
Audubon, John James 1785-1851 . **NCLC 47**
Auel, Jean M(arie) 1936- .... **CLC 31, 107;**
DAM POP
See also AAYA 7; BEST 90:4; CA 103;
CANR 21, 64; DA3; INT CANR-21;
SATA 91
Auerbach, Erich 1892-1957 .... **TCLC 43**
See also CA 118; 155
Augier, Emile 1820-1889 .... **NCLC 31**
See also DLB 192
August, John
See De Voto, Bernard (Augustine)
Augustine 354-430 .... **CMLC 6; DA; DAB;**
DAC; DAM MST
See also AW; DA3; DLB 115
Aurelius
See Bourne, Randolph S(illiman)
Aurobindo, Sri
See Ghose, Aurabinda
Austen, Jane 1775-1817 ...... **NCLC 1, 13, 19,**
33, 51, 81, 95; DA; DAB; DAC; DAM
MST, NOV
See also AAYA 19; AW 1; CDBLB 1789-
1832; DA3; DLB 116
Auster, Paul 1947- .... **CLC 47, 131**
See also CA 69-72; CANR 23, 52, 75; DA3;
DLB 227; MTCW 1
Austin, Frank
See Faust, Frederick (Schiller)
See also TCWW 2

Austin, Mary (Hunter) 1868-1934 . **TCLC 25**
See also Stairs, Gordon
See also CA 109; 178; DLB 9, 78, 206, 221;
TCWW 2
Averroes 1126-1198 .... **CMLC 7**
See also DLB 115
Avicenna 980-1037 .... **CMLC 16**
See also DLB 115
Avison, Margaret 1918- .... **CLC 2, 4, 97;**
DAC; DAM POET
See also CA 17-20R; DLB 53; MTCW 1
Axton, David
See Koontz, Dean R(ay)
Ayckbourn, Alan 1939- ...... **CLC 5, 8, 18, 33,**
74; DAB; DAM DRAM; DC 13
See also BRWS 5; CA 21-24R; CANR 31,
59; DLB 13; MTCW 1, 2
Aydy, Catherine
See Tennant, Emma (Christina)
Ayme, Marcel (Andre) 1902-1967 ... **CLC 11;**
SSC 41
See also CA 89-92; CANR 67; CLR 25;
DLB 72; SATA 91
Ayrton, Michael 1921-1975 .... **CLC 7**
See also CA 5-8R; 61-64; CANR 9, 21
Azorin CLC 11
See also Martinez Ruiz, Jose
Azuela, Mariano 1873-1952 . **TCLC 3; DAM**
MULT; HLC 1
See also CA 104; 131; CANR 81; HW 1, 2;
MTCW 1, 2
Baastad, Babbis Friis
See Friis-Baastad, Babbis Ellinor
Bab
See Gilbert, W(illiam) S(chwenck)
Babbis, Eleanor
See Friis-Baastad, Babbis Ellinor
Babel, Isaac
See Babel, Isaak (Emmanuilovich)
Babel, Isaak (Emmanuilovich)
1894-1941(?) .... **TCLC 2, 13; SSC 16**
See also Babel, Isaac
See also CA 104; 155; MTCW 1
Babits, Mihaly 1883-1941 .... **TCLC 14**
See also CA 114
Babur 1483-1530 .... **LC 18**
Baca, Jimmy Santiago 1952-
See also CA 131; CANR 81, 90; DAM
MULT; DLB 122; HLC 1; HW 1, 2
Bacchelli, Riccardo 1891-1985 .... **CLC 19**
See also CA 29-32R; 117
Bach, Richard (David) 1936- .... **CLC 14;**
DAM NOV, POP
See also AITN 1; BEST 89:2; CA 9-12R;
CANR 18, 93; MTCW 1; SATA 13
Bachman, Richard
See King, Stephen (Edwin)
Bachmann, Ingeborg 1926-1973 .... **CLC 69**
See also CA 93-96; 45-48; CANR 69; DLB
85
Bacon, Francis 1561-1626 .... **LC 18, 32**
See also CDBLB Before 1660; DLB 151,
236
Bacon, Roger 1214(?)-1294 .... **CMLC 14**
See also DLB 115
Bacovia, George 1881-1957 .... **TCLC 24**
See also Bacovia, G.; Vasiliu, Gheorghe
See also DLB 220
Badanes, Jerome 1937- .... **CLC 59**
Bagehot, Walter 1826-1877 .... **NCLC 10**
See also DLB 55
Bagnold, Enid 1889-1981 ...... **CLC 25; DAM**
DRAM
See also CA 5-8R; 103; CANR 5, 40; DLB
13, 160, 191; MAICYA; SATA 1, 25
Bagritsky, Eduard 1895-1934 .... **TCLC 60**
Bagrjana, Elisaveta
See Belcheva, Elisaveta

Brentano, Clemens (Maria)
1778-1842 .... **NCLC 1**
See also DLB 90

Brent of Bin Bin
See Franklin, (Stella Maria Sarah) Miles (Lampe)

Brenton, Howard 1942- .... **CLC 31**
See also CA 69-72; CANR 33, 67; DLB 13; MTCW 1

Breslin, James 1935-1996
See Breslin, Jimmy
See also CA 73-76; CANR 31, 75; DAM NOV; MTCW 1, 2

Breslin, Jimmy CLC 4, 43
See also Breslin, James
See also AITN 1; DLB 185; MTCW 2

Bresson, Robert 1901(?)-1999 .... **CLC 16**
See also CA 110; 187; CANR 49

Breton, Andre 1896-1966 .. **CLC 2, 9, 15, 54; PC 15**
See also CA 19-20; 25-28R; CANR 40, 60; CAP 2; DLB 65; MTCW 1, 2

Breytenbach, Breyten 1939(?)- .. **CLC 23, 37, 126; DAM POET**
See also CA 113; 129; CANR 61; CWW 2; DLB 225

Bridgers, Sue Ellen 1942- .... **CLC 26**
See also AAYA 8; AW; CA 65-68; CANR 11, 36; CLR 18; DLB 52; JRDA; MAICYA; SAAS 1; SATA 22, 90; SATA-Essay 109

Bridges, Robert (Seymour)
1844-1930 ... **TCLC 1; DAM POET; PC 28**
See also CA 104; 152; CDBLB 1890-1914; DLB 19, 98

Bridie, James TCLC 3
See also Mavor, Osborne Henry
See also DLB 10

Brin, David 1950- .... **CLC 34**
See also AAYA 21; CA 102; CANR 24, 70; INT CANR-24; SATA 65; SCFW 2

Brink, Andre (Philippus) 1935- . **CLC 18, 36, 106**
See also CA 104; CANR 39, 62; DLB 225; INT 103; MTCW 1, 2

Brinsmead, H(esba) F(ay) 1922- ...... **CLC 21**
See also CA 21-24R; CANR 10; CLR 47; MAICYA; SAAS 5; SATA 18, 78

Brittain, Vera (Mary) 1893(?)-1970 .. **CLC 23**
See also CA 13-16; 25-28R; CANR 58; CAP 1; DLB 191; MTCW 1, 2

Broch, Hermann 1886-1951 .... **TCLC 20**
See also CA 117; DLB 85, 124

Brock, Rose
See Hansen, Joseph
See also GLL 1

Brodkey, Harold (Roy) 1930-1996 ... **CLC 56**
See also CA 111; 151; CANR 71; DLB 130

Brodsky, Iosif Alexandrovich 1940-1996
See Brodsky, Joseph
See also AITN 1; CA 41-44R; 151; CANR 37; DAM POET; DA3; MTCW 1, 2

Brodsky, Joseph CLC 4, 6, 13, 36, 100; PC 9
See also Brodsky, Iosif Alexandrovich
See also CWW 2; MTCW 1

Brodsky, Michael (Mark) 1948- .... **CLC 19**
See also CA 102; CANR 18, 41, 58

Brodzki, Bella ed. CLC 65

Brome, Richard 1590(?)-1652 .... **LC 61**
See also DLB 58

Bromell, Henry 1947- .... **CLC 5**
See also CA 53-56; CANR 9

Bromfield, Louis (Brucker)
1896-1956 .... **TCLC 11**
See also CA 107; 155; DLB 4, 9, 86

Broner, E(sther) M(asserman)
1930- .... **CLC 19**
See also CA 17-20R; CANR 8, 25, 72; DLB 28

Bronk, William (M.) 1918-1999 .... **CLC 10**
See also CA 89-92; 177; CANR 23; DLB 165

Bronstein, Lev Davidovich
See Trotsky, Leon

Brontë, Anne 1820-1849 .... **NCLC 4, 71**
See also DA3; DLB 21, 199

Brontë, Charlotte 1816-1855 ...... **NCLC 3, 8, 33, 58; DA; DAB; DAC; DAM MST, NOV**
See also AAYA 17; AW; CDBLB 1832-1890; DA3; DLB 21, 159, 199

Brontë, Emily (Jane) 1818-1848 ... **NCLC 16, 35; DA; DAB; DAC; DAM MST, NOV, POET; PC 8**
See also AAYA 17; AW; CDBLB 1832-1890; DA3; DLB 21, 32, 199

Brontës
See Brontë

Brooke, Frances 1724-1789 .... **LC 6, 48**
See also DLB 39, 99

Brooke, Henry 1703(?)-1783 .... **LC 1**
See also DLB 39

Brooke, Rupert (Chawner)
1887-1915 .... **TCLC 2, 7; DA; DAB; DAC; DAM MST, POET; PC 24**
See also AW; BRWS 3; CA 104; 132; CANR 61; CDBLB 1914-1945; DLB 19; GLL 2; MTCW 1, 2

Brooke-Haven, P.
See Wodehouse, P(elham) G(renville)

Brooke-Rose, Christine 1926(?)- ...... **CLC 40**
See also BRWS 4; CA 13-16R; CANR 58; DLB 14, 231

Brookner, Anita 1928- . **CLC 32, 34, 51, 136; DAB; DAM POP**
See also BRWS 4; CA 114; 120; CANR 37, 56, 87; DA3; DLB 194; DLBY 87; MTCW 1, 2

Brooks, Cleanth 1906-1994 . **CLC 24, 86, 110**
See also CA 17-20R; 145; CANR 33, 35; DLB 63; DLBY 94; INT CANR-35; MTCW 1, 2

Brooks, George
See Baum, L(yman) Frank

Brooks, Gwendolyn 1917-2000 . **CLC 1, 2, 4, 5, 15, 49, 125; BLC 1; DA; DAC; DAM MST, MULT, POET; PC 7**
See also AAYA 20; AITN 1; AMWS 3; AW; BW 2, 3; CA 1-4R; CANR 1, 27, 52, 75; CDALB 1941-1968; CLR 27; DA3; DLB 5, 76, 165; MTCW 1, 2; SATA 6

Brooks, Mel CLC 12
See also Kaminsky, Melvin
See also AAYA 13; DLB 26

Brooks, Peter 1938- .... **CLC 34**
See also CA 45-48; CANR 1

Brooks, Van Wyck 1886-1963 .... **CLC 29**
See also CA 1-4R; CANR 6; DLB 45, 63, 103

Brophy, Brigid (Antonia)
1929-1995 .... **CLC 6, 11, 29, 105**
See also CA 5-8R; 149; CAAS 4; CANR 25, 53; DA3; DLB 14; MTCW 1, 2

Brosman, Catharine Savage 1934- ..... **CLC 9**
See also CA 61-64; CANR 21, 46

Brossard, Nicole 1943- .... **CLC 115**
See also CA 122; CAAS 16; CCA 1; CWW 2; DLB 53; GLL 2

Brother Antoninus
See Everson, William (Oliver)

The Brothers Quay
See Quay, Stephen; Quay, Timothy

Broughton, T(homas) Alan 1936- ..... **CLC 19**
See also CA 45-48; CANR 2, 23, 48

Broumas, Olga 1949- .... **CLC 10, 73**
See also CA 85-88; CANR 20, 69; GLL 2

Broun, Heywood 1888-1939 .... **TCLC 104**
See also DLB 29, 171

Brown, Alan 1950- .... **CLC 99**
See also CA 156

Brown, Charles Brockden
1771-1810 .... **NCLC 22, 74**
See also AMWS 1; CDALB 1640-1865; DLB 37, 59, 73

Brown, Christy 1932-1981 .... **CLC 63**
See also CA 105; 104; CANR 72; DLB 14

Brown, Claude 1937- .... **CLC 30; BLC 1; DAM MULT**
See also AAYA 7; BW 1, 3; CA 73-76; CANR 81

Brown, Dee (Alexander) 1908- . **CLC 18, 47; DAM POP**
See also AAYA 30; CA 13-16R; CAAS 6; CANR 11, 45, 60; DA3; DLBY 80; MTCW 1, 2; SATA 5, 110; TCWW 2

Brown, George
See Wertmueller, Lina

Brown, George Douglas
1869-1902 .... **TCLC 28**
See also CA 162

Brown, George Mackay 1921-1996 ... **CLC 5, 48, 100**
See also CA 21-24R; 151; CAAS 6; CANR 12, 37, 67; DLB 14, 27, 139; MTCW 1; SATA 35

Brown, (William) Larry 1951- .... **CLC 73**
See also CA 130; 134; INT 133

Brown, Moses
See Barrett, William (Christopher)

Brown, Rita Mae 1944- .... **CLC 18, 43, 79; DAM NOV, POP**
See also CA 45-48; CANR 2, 11, 35, 62, 95; DA3; INT CANR-11; MTCW 1, 2

Brown, Roderick (Langmere) Haig-
See Haig-Brown, Roderick (Langmere)

Brown, Rosellen 1939- .... **CLC 32**
See also CA 77-80; CAAS 10; CANR 14, 44

Brown, Sterling Allen 1901-1989 ...... **CLC 1, 23, 59; BLC 1; DAM MULT, POET**
See also BW 1, 3; CA 85-88; 127; CANR 26; DA3; DLB 48, 51, 63; MTCW 1, 2

Brown, Will
See Ainsworth, William Harrison

Brown, William Wells 1815-1884 ... **NCLC 2, 89; BLC 1; DAM MULT; DC 1**
See also DLB 3, 50

Browne, (Clyde) Jackson 1948(?)- ... **CLC 21**
See also CA 120

Browning, Elizabeth Barrett
1806-1861 ...... **NCLC 1, 16, 61, 66; DA; DAB; DAC; DAM MST, POET; PC 6**
See also AW; CDBLB 1832-1890; DA3; DLB 32, 199

Browning, Robert 1812-1889 . **NCLC 19, 79; DA; DAB; DAC; DAM MST, POET; PC 2**
See also AW; CDBLB 1832-1890; DA3; DLB 32, 163

Browning, Tod 1882-1962 .... **CLC 16**
See also CA 141; 117

Brownson, Orestes Augustus
1803-1876 .... **NCLC 50**
See also DLB 1, 59, 73

Bruccoli, Matthew J(oseph) 1931- ... **CLC 34**
See also CA 9-12R; CANR 7, 87; DLB 103

Bruce, Lenny CLC 21
See also Schneider, Leonard Alfred

Bruin, John
See Brutus, Dennis

Brulard, Henri
See Stendhal

Carroll, James P. 1943(?)- .... **CLC 38**
See also CA 81-84; CANR 73; MTCW 1
Carroll, Jim 1951- .... **CLC 35**
See also AAYA 17; CA 45-48; CANR 42
Carroll, Lewis NCLC **2, 53; PC 18**
See also Dodgson, Charles Lutwidge
See also AW; CDBLB 1832-1890; CLR 2,
18; DLB 18, 163, 178; DLBY 98; JRDA
Carroll, Paul Vincent 1900-1968 ..... **CLC 10**
See also CA 9-12R; 25-28R; DLB 10
Carruth, Hayden 1921- ..... **CLC 4, 7, 10, 18,
84; PC 10**
See also CA 9-12R; CANR 4, 38, 59; DLB
5, 165; INT CANR-4; MTCW 1, 2; SATA
47
Carson, Rachel Louise 1907-1964 ... **CLC 71;
DAM POP**
See also CA 77-80; CANR 35; DA3;
MTCW 1, 2; SATA 23
Carter, Angela (Olive) 1940-1992 ...... **CLC 5,
41, 76; SSC 13**
See also BRWS 3; CA 53-56; 136; CANR
12, 36, 61; DA3; DLB 14, 207; MTCW
1, 2; SATA 66; SATA-Obit 70
Carter, Nick
See Smith, Martin Cruz
Carver, Raymond 1938-1988 ..... **CLC 22, 36,
53, 55, 126; DAM NOV; SSC 8**
See also AMWS 3; CA 33-36R; 126; CANR
17, 34, 61; DA3; DLB 130; DLBY 84,
88; MTCW 1, 2; TCWW 2
Cary, Elizabeth, Lady Falkland
1585-1639 .... **LC 30**
Cary, (Arthur) Joyce (Lunel)
1888-1957 .... **TCLC 1, 29**
See also CA 104; 164; CDBLB 1914-1945;
DLB 15, 100; MTCW 2
Casanova de Seingalt, Giovanni Jacopo
1725-1798 .... **LC 13**
Casares, Adolfo Bioy
See Bioy Casares, Adolfo
Casely-Hayford, J(oseph) E(phraim)
1866-1903 ...... **TCLC 24; BLC 1; DAM
MULT**
See also BW 2; CA 123; 152
Casey, John (Dudley) 1939- .... **CLC 59**
See also BEST 90:2; CA 69-72; CANR 23
Casey, Michael 1947- .... **CLC 2**
See also CA 65-68; DLB 5
Casey, Patrick
See Thurman, Wallace (Henry)
Casey, Warren (Peter) 1935-1988 .... **CLC 12**
See also CA 101; 127; INT 101
Casona, Alejandro **CLC 49**
See also Alvarez, Alejandro Rodriguez
Cassavetes, John 1929-1989 .... **CLC 20**
See also CA 85-88; 127; CANR 82
Cassian, Nina 1924- .... **PC 17**
See also CWW 2
Cassill, R(onald) V(erlin) 1919- ... **CLC 4, 23**
See also CA 9-12R; CAAS 1; CANR 7, 45;
DLB 6
Cassiodorus, Flavius Magnus c. 490(?)-c.
583(?) .... **CMLC 43**
Cassirer, Ernst 1874-1945 .... **TCLC 61**
See also CA 157
Cassity, (Allen) Turner 1929- .... **CLC 6, 42**
See also CA 17-20R; CAAS 8; CANR 11;
DLB 105
Castaneda, Carlos (Cesar Aranha)
1931(?)-1998 .... **CLC 12, 119**
See also CA 25-28R; CANR 32, 66; HW 1;
MTCW 1
Castedo, Elena 1937- .... **CLC 65**
See also CA 132
Castedo-Ellerman, Elena
See Castedo, Elena

Castellanos, Rosario 1925-1974 .... **CLC 66;
DAM MULT; HLC 1; SSC 39**
See also CA 131; 53-56; CANR 58; DLB
113; HW 1; MTCW 1
Castelvetro, Lodovico 1505-1571 .... **LC 12**
Castiglione, Baldassare 1478-1529 ...... **LC 12**
Castiglione, Baldesar
See Castiglione, Baldassare
Castle, Robert
See Hamilton, Edmond
Castro (Ruz), Fidel 1926(?)-
See also CA 110; 129; CANR 81; DAM
MULT; HLC 1; HW 2
Castro, Guillen de 1569-1631 .... **LC 19**
Castro, Rosalia de 1837-1885 ... **NCLC 3, 78;
DAM MULT**
Cather, Willa
See Cather, Willa Sibert
See also TCWW 2
Cather, Willa Sibert 1873-1947 ...... **TCLC 1,
11, 31, 99; DA; DAB; DAC; DAM
MST, NOV; SSC 2**
See also Cather, Willa
See also AAYA 24; AW; CA 104; 128;
CDALB 1865-1917; DA3; DLB 9, 54, 78;
DLBD 1; MTCW 1, 2; SATA 30
Catherine, Saint 1347-1380 .... **CMLC 27**
Cato, Marcus Porcius
234B.C.-149B.C. .... **CMLC 21**
See also DLB 211
Catton, (Charles) Bruce 1899-1978 . **CLC 35**
See also AITN 1; CA 5-8R; 81-84; CANR
7, 74; DLB 17; SATA 2; SATA-Obit 24
Catullus c. 84B.C.-c. 54B.C. .... **CMLC 18**
See also DLB 211
Cauldwell, Frank
See King, Francis (Henry)
Caunitz, William J. 1933-1996 .... **CLC 34**
See also BEST 89:3; CA 125; 130; 152;
CANR 73; INT 130
Causley, Charles (Stanley) 1917- .... **CLC 7**
See also CA 9-12R; CANR 5, 35, 94; CLR
30; DLB 27; MTCW 1; SATA 3, 66
Caute, (John) David 1936- ... **CLC 29; DAM
NOV**
See also CA 1-4R; CAAS 4; CANR 1, 33,
64; DLB 14, 231
Cavafy, C(onstantine) P(eter) TCLC **2, 7;
DAM POET**
See also Kavafis, Konstantinos Petrou
See also CA 148; DA3; MTCW 1
Cavallo, Evelyn
See Spark, Muriel (Sarah)
Cavanna, Betty **CLC 12**
See also Harrison, Elizabeth Cavanna
See also JRDA; MAICYA; SAAS 4; SATA
1, 30
Cavendish, Margaret Lucas
1623-1673 .... **LC 30**
See also DLB 131
Caxton, William 1421(?)-1491(?) .... **LC 17**
See also DLB 170
Cayer, D. M.
See Duffy, Maureen
Cayrol, Jean 1911- .... **CLC 11**
See also CA 89-92; DLB 83
Cela, Camilo Jose 1916- .... **CLC 4, 13, 59,
122; DAM MULT; HLC 1**
See also BEST 90:2; CA 21-24R; CAAS
10; CANR 21, 32, 76; DLBY 89; HW 1;
MTCW 1, 2
Celan, Paul CLC **10, 19, 53, 82; PC 10**
See also Antschel, Paul
See also DLB 69
Celine, Louis-Ferdinand CLC **1, 3, 4, 7, 9,
15, 47, 124**
See also Destouches, Louis-Ferdinand
See also DLB 72
Cellini, Benvenuto 1500-1571 .... **LC 7**

Cendrars, Blaise CLC **18, 106**
See also Sauser-Hall, Frederic
Centlivre, Susanna 1669(?)-1723 .... **LC 65**
See also DLB 84
Cernuda (y Bidon), Luis
1902-1963 .... **CLC 54; DAM POET**
See also CA 131; 89-92; DLB 134; GLL 1;
HW 1
Cervantes, Lorna Dee 1954-
See also CA 131; CANR 80; DLB 82;
HLCS 1; HW 1
Cervantes (Saavedra), Miguel de
1547-1616 .. **LC 6, 23; DA; DAB; DAC;
DAM MST, NOV; SSC 12**
See also AW
Cesaire, Aime (Fernand) 1913- . **CLC 19, 32,
112; BLC 1; DAM MULT, POET; PC
25**
See also BW 2, 3; CA 65-68; CANR 24,
43, 81; DA3; MTCW 1, 2
Chabon, Michael 1963- .... **CLC 55**
See also CA 139; CANR 57, 96
Chabrol, Claude 1930- .... **CLC 16**
See also CA 110
Challans, Mary 1905-1983
See Renault, Mary
See also CA 81-84; 111; CANR 74; DA3;
MTCW 2; SATA 23; SATA-Obit 36
Challis, George
See Faust, Frederick (Schiller)
See also TCWW 2
Chambers, Aidan 1934- .... **CLC 35**
See also AAYA 27; AW; CA 25-28R; CANR
12, 31, 58; JRDA; MAICYA; SAAS 12;
SATA 1, 69, 108
Chambers, James 1948-
See Cliff, Jimmy
See also CA 124
Chambers, Jessie
See Lawrence, D(avid) H(erbert Richards)
See also GLL 1
Chambers, Robert W(illiam)
1865-1933 .... **TCLC 41**
See also CA 165; DLB 202; SATA 107
Chamisso, Adelbert von
1781-1838 .... **NCLC 82**
See also DLB 90
Chandler, Raymond (Thornton)
1888-1959 .... **TCLC 1, 7; SSC 23**
See also AAYA 25; AMWS 4; CA 104; 129;
CANR 60; CDALB 1929-1941; DA3;
DLB 226; DLBD 6; MTCW 1, 2
Chang, Eileen 1921-1995 .... **SSC 28**
See also CA 166; CWW 2
Chang, Jung 1952- .... **CLC 71**
See also CA 142
Chang Ai-Ling
See Chang, Eileen
Channing, William Ellery
1780-1842 .... **NCLC 17**
See also DLB 1, 59, 235
Chao, Patricia 1955- .... **CLC 119**
See also CA 163
Chaplin, Charles Spencer
1889-1977 .... **CLC 16**
See also Chaplin, Charlie
See also CA 81-84; 73-76
Chaplin, Charlie
See Chaplin, Charles Spencer
See also DLB 44
Chapman, George 1559(?)-1634 .... **LC 22;
DAM DRAM**
See also DLB 62, 121
Chapman, Graham 1941-1989 .... **CLC 21**
See also Monty Python
See also CA 116; 129; CANR 35, 95
Chapman, John Jay 1862-1933 .... **TCLC 7**
See also CA 104

Clarin
See Alas (y Urena), Leopoldo (Enrique Garcia)
Clark, Al C.
See Goines, Donald
Clark, (Robert) Brian 1932- .... **CLC 29**
See also CA 41-44R; CANR 67
Clark, Curt
See Westlake, Donald E(dwin)
Clark, Eleanor 1913-1996 .... **CLC 5, 19**
See also CA 9-12R; 151; CANR 41; DLB 6
Clark, J. P.
See Clark Bekederemo, J(ohnson) P(epper)
See also DLB 117
Clark, John Pepper
See Clark Bekederemo, J(ohnson) P(epper)
Clark, M. R.
See Clark, Mavis Thorpe
Clark, Mavis Thorpe 1909- .... **CLC 12**
See also CA 57-60; CANR 8, 37; CLR 30; MAICYA; SAAS 5; SATA 8, 74
Clark, Walter Van Tilburg
1909-1971 .... **CLC 28**
See also CA 9-12R; 33-36R; CANR 63; DLB 9, 206; SATA 8
Clark Bekederemo, J(ohnson) P(epper)
1935- .. **CLC 38; BLC 1; DAM DRAM, MULT; DC 5**
See also Clark, J. P.; Clark, John Pepper
See also BW 1; CA 65-68; CANR 16, 72; MTCW 1
Clarke, Arthur C(harles) 1917- .... **CLC 1, 4, 13, 18, 35, 136; DAM POP; SSC 3**
See also AAYA 4, 33; AW; CA 1-4R; CANR 2, 28, 55, 74; DA3; JRDA; MAICYA; MTCW 1, 2; SATA 13, 70, 115
Clarke, Austin 1896-1974 ... **CLC 6, 9; DAM POET**
See also CA 29-32; 49-52; CAP 2; DLB 10, 20
Clarke, Austin C(hesterfield) 1934- .. **CLC 8, 53; BLC 1; DAC; DAM MULT**
See also BW 1; CA 25-28R; CAAS 16; CANR 14, 32, 68; DLB 53, 125
Clarke, Gillian 1937- .... **CLC 61**
See also CA 106; DLB 40
Clarke, Marcus (Andrew Hislop)
1846-1881 .... **NCLC 19**
See also DLB 230
Clarke, Shirley 1925-1997 .... **CLC 16**
See also CA 189
Clash, The
See Headon, (Nicky) Topper; Jones, Mick; Simonon, Paul; Strummer, Joe
Claudel, Paul (Louis Charles Marie)
1868-1955 .... **TCLC 2, 10**
See also CA 104; 165; DLB 192
Claudius, Matthias 1740-1815 .... **NCLC 75**
See also DLB 97
Clavell, James (duMaresq)
1925-1994 .. **CLC 6, 25, 87; DAM NOV, POP**
See also CA 25-28R; 146; CANR 26, 48; DA3; MTCW 1, 2
Clayman, Gregory CLC 65
Cleaver, (Leroy) Eldridge
1935-1998 . **CLC 30, 119; BLC 1; DAM MULT**
See also AW; BW 1, 3; CA 21-24R; 167; CANR 16, 75; DA3; MTCW 2
Cleese, John (Marwood) 1939- .... **CLC 21**
See also Monty Python
See also CA 112; 116; CANR 35; MTCW 1
Cleishbotham, Jebediah
See Scott, Walter
Cleland, John 1710-1789 .... **LC 2, 48**
See also DLB 39

Clemens, Samuel Langhorne 1835-1910
See Twain, Mark
See also AW 2; CA 104; 135; CDALB 1865-1917; DA; DAB; DAC; DAM MST, NOV; DA3; DLB 11, 12, 23, 64, 74, 186, 189; JRDA; MAICYA; SATA 100
Clement of Alexandria
150(?)-215(?) .... **CMLC 41**
Cleophil
See Congreve, William
Clerihew, E.
See Bentley, E(dmund) C(lerihew)
Clerk, N. W.
See Lewis, C(live) S(taples)
Cliff, Jimmy CLC 21
See also Chambers, James
Cliff, Michelle 1946- .... **CLC 120; BLCS**
See also BW 2; CA 116; CANR 39, 72; DLB 157; GLL 2
Clifton, (Thelma) Lucille 1936- .... **CLC 19, 66; BLC 1; DAM MULT, POET; PC 17**
See also BW 2, 3; CA 49-52; CANR 2, 24, 42, 76; CLR 5; DA3; DLB 5, 41; MAICYA; MTCW 1, 2; SATA 20, 69
Clinton, Dirk
See Silverberg, Robert
Clough, Arthur Hugh 1819-1861 ... **NCLC 27**
See also DLB 32
Clutha, Janet Paterson Frame 1924-
See Frame, Janet
See also CA 1-4R; CANR 2, 36, 76; MTCW 1, 2; SATA 119
Clyne, Terence
See Blatty, William Peter
Cobalt, Martin
See Mayne, William (James Carter)
Cobb, Irvin S(hrewsbury)
1876-1944 .... **TCLC 77**
See also CA 175; DLB 11, 25, 86
Cobbett, William 1763-1835 .... **NCLC 49**
See also DLB 43, 107, 158
Coburn, D(onald) L(ee) 1938- .... **CLC 10**
See also CA 89-92
Cocteau, Jean (Maurice Eugene Clement)
1889-1963 .... **CLC 1, 8, 15, 16, 43; DA; DAB; DAC; DAM DRAM, MST, NOV**
See also AW; CA 25-28; CANR 40; CAP 2; DA3; DLB 65; MTCW 1, 2
Codrescu, Andrei 1946- .... **CLC 46, 121; DAM POET**
See also CA 33-36R; CAAS 19; CANR 13, 34, 53, 76; DA3; MTCW 2
Coe, Max
See Bourne, Randolph S(illiman)
Coe, Tucker
See Westlake, Donald E(dwin)
Coen, Ethan 1958- .... **CLC 108**
See also CA 126; CANR 85
Coen, Joel 1955- .... **CLC 108**
See also CA 126
The Coen Brothers
See Coen, Ethan; Coen, Joel
Coetzee, J(ohn) M(ichael) 1940- ...... **CLC 23, 33, 66, 117; DAM NOV**
See also AAYA 37; CA 77-80; CANR 41, 54, 74; DA3; DLB 225; MTCW 1, 2
Coffey, Brian
See Koontz, Dean R(ay)
Coffin, Robert P(eter) Tristram
1892-1955 .... **TCLC 95**
See also CA 123; 169; DLB 45
Cohan, George M(ichael)
1878-1942 .... **TCLC 60**
See also CA 157
Cohen, Arthur A(llen) 1928-1986 ...... **CLC 7, 31**
See also CA 1-4R; 120; CANR 1, 17, 42; DLB 28

Cohen, Leonard (Norman) 1934- ...... **CLC 3, 38; DAC; DAM MST**
See also CA 21-24R; CANR 14, 69; DLB 53; MTCW 1
Cohen, Matt(hew) 1942-1999 .... **CLC 19; DAC**
See also CA 61-64; 187; CAAS 18; CANR 40; DLB 53
Cohen-Solal, Annie 19(?)- .... **CLC 50**
Colegate, Isabel 1931- .... **CLC 36**
See also CA 17-20R; CANR 8, 22, 74; DLB 14, 231; INT CANR-22; MTCW 1
Coleman, Emmett
See Reed, Ishmael
Coleridge, Hartley 1796-1849 .... **NCLC 90**
See also DLB 96
Coleridge, M. E.
See Coleridge, Mary E(lizabeth)
Coleridge, Mary E(lizabeth)
1861-1907 .... **TCLC 73**
See also CA 116; 166; DLB 19, 98
Coleridge, Samuel Taylor
1772-1834 .... **NCLC 9, 54; DA; DAB; DAC; DAM MST, POET; PC 11**
See also AW; CDBLB 1789-1832; DA3; DLB 93, 107
Coleridge, Sara 1802-1852 .... **NCLC 31**
See also DLB 199
Coles, Don 1928- .... **CLC 46**
See also CA 115; CANR 38
Coles, Robert (Martin) 1929- .... **CLC 108**
See also CA 45-48; CANR 3, 32, 66, 70; INT CANR-32; SATA 23
Colette, (Sidonie-Gabrielle)
1873-1954 . **TCLC 1, 5, 16; DAM NOV; SSC 10**
See also Willy, Colette
See also CA 104; 131; DA3; DLB 65; MTCW 1, 2
Collett, (Jacobine) Camilla (Wergeland)
1813-1895 .... **NCLC 22**
Collier, Christopher 1930- .... **CLC 30**
See also AAYA 13; CA 33-36R; CANR 13, 33; JRDA; MAICYA; SATA 16, 70
Collier, James L(incoln) 1928- .... **CLC 30; DAM POP**
See also AAYA 13; CA 9-12R; CANR 4, 33, 60; CLR 3; JRDA; MAICYA; SAAS 21; SATA 8, 70
Collier, Jeremy 1650-1726 .... **LC 6**
Collier, John 1901-1980 .... **SSC 19**
See also CA 65-68; 97-100; CANR 10; DLB 77
Collingwood, R(obin) G(eorge)
1889(?)-1943 .... **TCLC 67**
See also CA 117; 155
Collins, Hunt
See Hunter, Evan
Collins, Linda 1931- .... **CLC 44**
See also CA 125
Collins, (William) Wilkie
1824-1889 .... **NCLC 1, 18, 93**
See also CDBLB 1832-1890; DLB 18, 70, 159
Collins, William 1721-1759 . **LC 4, 40; DAM POET**
See also DLB 109
Collodi, Carlo NCLC 54
See also Lorenzini, Carlo
See also CLR 5
Colman, George
See Glassco, John
Colt, Winchester Remington
See Hubbard, L(afayette) Ron(ald)
Colter, Cyrus 1910- .... **CLC 58**
See also BW 1; CA 65-68; CANR 10, 66; DLB 33

Damas, Leon-Gontran 1912-1978 .... **CLC 84**
See also BW 1; CA 125; 73-76

Dana, Richard Henry Sr.
1787-1879 .... **NCLC 53**

Daniel, Samuel 1562(?)-1619 .... **LC 24**
See also DLB 62

Daniels, Brett
See Adler, Renata

Dannay, Frederic 1905-1982 . **CLC 11; DAM POP**
See also Queen, Ellery
See also CA 1-4R; 107; CANR 1, 39; DLB 137; MTCW 1

D'Annunzio, Gabriele 1863-1938 ... **TCLC 6, 40**
See also CA 104; 155

Danois, N. le
See Gourmont, Remy (-Marie-Charles) de

Dante 1265-1321 .... **CMLC 3, 18, 39; DA; DAB; DAC; DAM MST, POET; PC 21**
See also AW; DA3

d'Antibes, Germain
See Simenon, Georges (Jacques Christian)

Danticat, Edwidge 1969- .... **CLC 94, 139**
See also AAYA 29; AW; CA 152; CANR 73; MTCW 1

Danvers, Dennis 1947- .... **CLC 70**

Danziger, Paula 1944- .... **CLC 21**
See also AAYA 4, 36; AW; CA 112; 115; CANR 37; CLR 20; JRDA; MAICYA; SATA 36, 63, 102; SATA-Brief 30

Da Ponte, Lorenzo 1749-1838 .... **NCLC 50**

Dario, Ruben 1867-1916 .... **TCLC 4; DAM MULT; HLC 1; PC 15**
See also CA 131; CANR 81; HW 1, 2; MTCW 1, 2

Darley, George 1795-1846 .... **NCLC 2**
See also DLB 96

Darrow, Clarence (Seward)
1857-1938 .... **TCLC 81**
See also CA 164

Darwin, Charles 1809-1882 .... **NCLC 57**
See also DLB 57, 166

Daryush, Elizabeth 1887-1977 ...... **CLC 6, 19**
See also CA 49-52; CANR 3, 81; DLB 20

Dasgupta, Surendranath
1887-1952 .... **TCLC 81**
See also CA 157

Dashwood, Edmee Elizabeth Monica de la
Pasture 1890-1943
See Delafield, E. M.
See also CA 119; 154

Daudet, (Louis Marie) Alphonse
1840-1897 .... **NCLC 1**
See also DLB 123

Daumal, Rene 1908-1944 .... **TCLC 14**
See also CA 114

Davenant, William 1606-1668 .... **LC 13**
See also DLB 58, 126

Davenport, Guy (Mattison, Jr.)
1927- .... **CLC 6, 14, 38; SSC 16**
See also CA 33-36R; CANR 23, 73; DLB 130

Davidson, Avram (James) 1923-1993
See Queen, Ellery
See also CA 101; 171; CANR 26; DLB 8

Davidson, Donald (Grady)
1893-1968 .... **CLC 2, 13, 19**
See also CA 5-8R; 25-28R; CANR 4, 84; DLB 45

Davidson, Hugh
See Hamilton, Edmond

Davidson, John 1857-1909 .... **TCLC 24**
See also CA 118; DLB 19

Davidson, Sara 1943- .... **CLC 9**
See also CA 81-84; CANR 44, 68; DLB 185

Davie, Donald (Alfred) 1922-1995 .... **CLC 5, 8, 10, 31; PC 29**
See also CA 1-4R; 149; CAAS 3; CANR 1, 44; DLB 27; MTCW 1

Davies, Ray(mond Douglas) 1944- ... **CLC 21**
See also CA 116; 146; CANR 92

Davies, Rhys 1901-1978 .... **CLC 23**
See also CA 9-12R; 81-84; CANR 4; DLB 139, 191

Davies, (William) Robertson
1913-1995 .... **CLC 2, 7, 13, 25, 42, 75, 91; DA; DAB; DAC; DAM MST, NOV, POP**
See also Marchbanks, Samuel
See also AW; BEST 89:2; CA 33-36R; 150; CANR 17, 42; DA3; DLB 68; INT CANR-17; MTCW 1, 2

Davies, Walter C.
See Kornbluth, C(yril) M.

Davies, William Henry 1871-1940 ... **TCLC 5**
See also CA 104; 179; DLB 19, 174

Da Vinci, Leonardo 1452-1519 ..... **LC 12, 57, 60**

Davis, Angela (Yvonne) 1944- .... **CLC 77; DAM MULT**
See also BW 2, 3; CA 57-60; CANR 10, 81; DA3

Davis, B. Lynch
See Bioy Casares, Adolfo; Borges, Jorge Luis

Davis, B. Lynch
See Bioy Casares, Adolfo

Davis, Gordon
See Hunt, E(verette) Howard, (Jr.)

Davis, H(arold) L(enoir) 1896-1960 . **CLC 49**
See also CA 178; 89-92; DLB 9, 206; SATA 114

Davis, Rebecca (Blaine) Harding
1831-1910 .... **TCLC 6; SSC 38**
See also CA 104; 179; DLB 74, 239

Davis, Richard Harding
1864-1916 .... **TCLC 24**
See also CA 114; 179; DLB 12, 23, 78, 79, 189; DLBD 13

Davison, Frank Dalby 1893-1970 ..... **CLC 15**
See also CA 116

Davison, Lawrence H.
See Lawrence, D(avid) H(erbert Richards)

Davison, Peter (Hubert) 1928- .... **CLC 28**
See also CA 9-12R; CAAS 4; CANR 3, 43, 84; DLB 5

Davys, Mary 1674-1732 .... **LC 1, 46**
See also DLB 39

Dawson, Fielding 1930- .... **CLC 6**
See also CA 85-88; DLB 130

Dawson, Peter
See Faust, Frederick (Schiller)
See also TCWW 2, 2

Day, Clarence (Shepard, Jr.)
1874-1935 .... **TCLC 25**
See also CA 108; DLB 11

Day, Thomas 1748-1789 .... **LC 1**
See also AW 1; DLB 39

Day Lewis, C(ecil) 1904-1972 . **CLC 1, 6, 10; DAM POET; PC 11**
See also Blake, Nicholas
See also BRWS 3; CA 13-16; 33-36R; CANR 34; CAP 1; DLB 15, 20; MTCW 1, 2

Dazai Osamu **TCLC 11; SSC 41**
See also Tsushima, Shuji
See also CA 164; DLB 182

de Andrade, Carlos Drummond
See Drummond de Andrade, Carlos

Deane, Norman
See Creasey, John

Deane, Seamus (Francis) 1940- ...... **CLC 122**
See also CA 118; CANR 42

de Beauvoir, Simone (Lucie Ernestine Marie
Bertrand)
See Beauvoir, Simone (Lucie Ernestine
Marie Bertrand) de

de Beer, P.
See Bosman, Herman Charles

de Bergerac, Savinien Cyrano
1619-1655 .... **LC 65**

de Brissac, Malcolm
See Dickinson, Peter (Malcolm)

de Campos, Alvaro
See Pessoa, Fernando (Antonio Nogueira)

de Chardin, Pierre Teilhard
See Teilhard de Chardin, (Marie Joseph)
Pierre

Dee, John 1527-1608 .... **LC 20**

Deer, Sandra 1940- .... **CLC 45**
See also CA 186

De Ferrari, Gabriella 1941- .... **CLC 65**
See also CA 146

Defoe, Daniel 1660(?)-1731 .... **LC 1, 42; DA; DAB; DAC; DAM MST, NOV**
See also AAYA 27; AW; CDBLB 1660-1789; CLR 61; DA3; DLB 39, 95, 101; JRDA; MAICYA; SATA 22

de Gourmont, Remy(-Marie-Charles)
See Gourmont, Remy (-Marie-Charles) de

de Hartog, Jan 1914- .... **CLC 19**
See also CA 1-4R; CANR 1

de Hostos, E. M.
See Hostos (y Bonilla), Eugenio Maria de

de Hostos, Eugenio M.
See Hostos (y Bonilla), Eugenio Maria de

Deighton, Len **CLC 4, 7, 22, 46**
See also Deighton, Leonard Cyril
See also AAYA 6; BEST 89:2; CDBLB
1960 to Present; DLB 87

Deighton, Leonard Cyril 1929-
See Deighton, Len
See also CA 9-12R; CANR 19, 33, 68;
DAM NOV, POP; DA3; MTCW 1, 2

Dekker, Thomas 1572(?)-1632 . **LC 22; DAM DRAM; DC 12**
See also CDBLB Before 1660; DLB 62, 172

Delafield, E. M. **TCLC 61**
See also Dashwood, Edmee Elizabeth
Monica de la Pasture
See also DLB 34

de la Mare, Walter (John)
1873-1956 ..... **TCLC 4, 53; DAB; DAC; DAM MST, POET; SSC 14**
See also AW; CA 163; CDBLB 1914-1945;
CLR 23; DA3; DLB 162; MTCW 1;
SATA 16

Delaney, Franey
See O'Hara, John (Henry)

Delaney, Shelagh 1939- .... **CLC 29; DAM DRAM**
See also CA 17-20R; CANR 30, 67; CD-
BLB 1960 to Present; DLB 13; MTCW 1

Delany, Martin Robinson
1812-1885 .... **NCLC 93**
See also DLB 50

Delany, Mary (Granville Pendarves)
1700-1788 .... **LC 12**

Delany, Samuel R(ay), Jr. 1942- . **CLC 8, 14, 38, 141; BLC 1; DAM MULT**
See also AAYA 24; BW 2, 3; CA 81-84;
CANR 27, 43; DLB 8, 33; MTCW 1, 2

De La Ramee, (Marie) Louise 1839-1908
See Ouida
See also SATA 20

de la Roche, Mazo 1879-1961 .... **CLC 14**
See also CA 85-88; CANR 30; DLB 68;
SATA 64

De La Salle, Innocent
See Hartmann, Sadakichi

Delbanco, Nicholas (Franklin)
1942- .... **CLC 6, 13**
See also CA 17-20R; CAAE 189; CAAS 2;
CANR 29, 55; DLB 6, 234

del Castillo, Michel 1933- .... **CLC 38**
See also CA 109; CANR 77

Deledda, Grazia (Cosima)
1875(?)-1936 .... **TCLC 23**
See also CA 123

Delgado, Abelardo (Lalo) B(arrientos) 1930-
See also CA 131; CAAS 15; CANR 90;
DAM MST, MULT; DLB 82; HLC 1; HW
1, 2

Delibes, Miguel CLC 8, 18
See also Delibes Setien, Miguel

Delibes Setien, Miguel 1920-
See Delibes, Miguel
See also CA 45-48; CANR 1, 32; HW 1;
MTCW 1

DeLillo, Don 1936- ..... **CLC 8, 10, 13, 27, 39,
54, 76; DAM NOV, POP**
See also AMWS 6; BEST 89:1; CA 81-84;
CANR 21, 76, 92; DA3; DLB 6, 173;
MTCW 1, 2

de Lisser, H. G.
See De Lisser, H(erbert) G(eorge)
See also DLB 117

De Lisser, H(erbert) G(eorge)
1878-1944 .... **TCLC 12**
See also de Lisser, H. G.
See also BW 2; CA 109; 152

Deloney, Thomas 1543(?)-1600 .... **LC 41**
See also DLB 167

Deloria, Vine (Victor), Jr. 1933- ...... **CLC 21,
122; DAM MULT**
See also CA 53-56; CANR 5, 20, 48; DLB
175; MTCW 1; NNAL; SATA 21

Del Vecchio, John M(ichael) 1947- .. **CLC 29**
See also CA 110; DLBD 9

de Man, Paul (Adolph Michel)
1919-1983 .... **CLC 55**
See also CA 128; 111; CANR 61; DLB 67;
MTCW 1, 2

DeMarinis, Rick 1934- .... **CLC 54**
See also CA 57-60, 184; CAAE 184; CAAS
24; CANR 9, 25, 50

Dembry, R. Emmet
See Murfree, Mary Noailles

Demby, William 1922- .... **CLC 53; BLC 1;
DAM MULT**
See also BW 1, 3; CA 81-84; CANR 81;
DLB 33

de Menton, Francisco
See Chin, Frank (Chew, Jr.)

Demetrius of Phalerum c.
307B.C.- .... **CMLC 34**

Demijohn, Thom
See Disch, Thomas M(ichael)

Deming, Richard 1915-1983
See Queen, Ellery
See also CA 9-12R; CANR 3, 94; SATA 24

de Molina, Tirso 1580(?)-1648 .... **DC 13**
See also HLCS 2

de Montherlant, Henry (Milon)
See Montherlant, Henry (Milon) de

Demosthenes 384B.C.-322B.C. ...... **CMLC 13**
See also DLB 176

de Natale, Francine
See Malzberg, Barry N(athaniel)

de Navarre, Marguerite 1492-1549 ..... **LC 61**

Denby, Edwin (Orr) 1903-1983 .... **CLC 48**
See also CA 138; 110

Denis, Julio
See Cortazar, Julio

Denmark, Harrison
See Zelazny, Roger (Joseph)

Dennis, John 1658-1734 .... **LC 11**
See also DLB 101

Dennis, Nigel (Forbes) 1912-1989 ...... **CLC 8**
See also CA 25-28R; 129; DLB 13, 15, 233;
MTCW 1

Dent, Lester 1904(?)-1959 .... **TCLC 72**
See also CA 112; 161

De Palma, Brian (Russell) 1940- ...... **CLC 20**
See also CA 109

De Quincey, Thomas 1785-1859 ..... **NCLC 4,
87**
See also CDBLB 1789-1832; DLB 110; 144

Deren, Eleanora 1917(?)-1961
See Deren, Maya
See also CA 111

Deren, Maya CLC 16, 102
See also Deren, Eleanora

Derleth, August (William)
1909-1971 .... **CLC 31**
See also CA 1-4R; 29-32R; CANR 4; DLB
9; DLBD 17; SATA 5

Der Nister 1884-1950 .... **TCLC 56**

de Routisie, Albert
See Aragon, Louis

Derrida, Jacques 1930- .... **CLC 24, 87**
See also CA 124; 127; CANR 76; DLB 242;
MTCW 1

Derry Down Derry
See Lear, Edward

Dersonnes, Jacques
See Simenon, Georges (Jacques Christian)

Desai, Anita 1937- ..... **CLC 19, 37, 97; DAB;
DAM NOV**
See also BRWS 5; CA 81-84; CANR 33,
53, 95; DA3; MTCW 1, 2; SATA 63

Desai, Kiran 1971- .... **CLC 119**
See also CA 171

de Saint-Luc, Jean
See Glassco, John

de Saint Roman, Arnaud
See Aragon, Louis

Desbordes-Valmore, Marceline
1786-1859 .... **NCLC 97**
See also DLB 217

Descartes, Rene 1596-1650 .... **LC 20, 35**

De Sica, Vittorio 1901(?)-1974 .... **CLC 20**
See also CA 117

Desnos, Robert 1900-1945 .... **TCLC 22**
See also CA 121; 151

Destouches, Louis-Ferdinand
1894-1961 .... **CLC 9, 15**
See also Celine, Louis-Ferdinand
See also CA 85-88; CANR 28; MTCW 1

de Tolignac, Gaston
See Griffith, D(avid Lewelyn) W(ark)

Deutsch, Babette 1895-1982 .... **CLC 18**
See also CA 1-4R; 108; CANR 4, 79; DLB
45; SATA 1; SATA-Obit 33

Devenant, William 1606-1649 .... **LC 13**

Devkota, Laxmiprasad 1909-1959 . **TCLC 23**
See also CA 123

De Voto, Bernard (Augustine)
1897-1955 .... **TCLC 29**
See also CA 113; 160; DLB 9

De Vries, Peter 1910-1993 ..... **CLC 1, 2, 3, 7,
10, 28, 46; DAM NOV**
See also CA 17-20R; 142; CANR 41; DLB
6; DLBY 82; MTCW 1, 2

Dewey, John 1859-1952 .... **TCLC 95**
See also CA 114; 170

Dexter, John
See Bradley, Marion Zimmer
See also GLL 1

Dexter, Martin
See Faust, Frederick (Schiller)
See also TCWW 2

Dexter, Pete 1943- .. **CLC 34, 55; DAM POP**
See also BEST 89:2; CA 127; 131; INT 131;
MTCW 1

Diamano, Silmang
See Senghor, Leopold Sedar

Diamond, Neil 1941- .... **CLC 30**
See also CA 108

Diaz del Castillo, Bernal 1496-1584 .. **LC 31;
HLCS 1**

di Bassetto, Corno
See Shaw, George Bernard

Dick, Philip K(indred) 1928-1982 ... **CLC 10,
30, 72; DAM NOV, POP**
See also AAYA 24; CA 49-52; 106; CANR
2, 16; DA3; DLB 8; MTCW 1, 2

Dickens, Charles (John Huffam)
1812-1870 .... **NCLC 3, 8, 18, 26, 37, 50,
86; DA; DAB; DAC; DAM MST, NOV;
SSC 17**
See also AAYA 23; CDBLB 1832-1890;
DA3; DLB 21, 55, 70, 159, 166; JRDA;
MAICYA; SATA 15

Dickey, James (Lafayette)
1923-1997 .... **CLC 1, 2, 4, 7, 10, 15, 47,
109; DAM NOV, POET, POP**
See also AITN 1, 2; AMWS 4; CA 9-12R;
156; CABS 2; CANR 10, 48, 61; CDALB
1968-1988; DA3; DLB 5, 193; DLBD 7;
DLBY 82, 93, 96, 97, 98; INT CANR-10;
MTCW 1, 2

Dickey, William 1928-1994 .... **CLC 3, 28**
See also CA 9-12R; 145; CANR 24, 79;
DLB 5

Dickinson, Charles 1951- .... **CLC 49**
See also CA 128

Dickinson, Emily (Elizabeth)
1830-1886 ..... **NCLC 21, 77; DA; DAB;
DAC; DAM MST, POET; PC 1**
See also AAYA 22; CDALB 1865-1917;
DA3; DLB 1; SATA 29

Dickinson, Peter (Malcolm) 1927- .. **CLC 12,
35**
See also AAYA 9; CA 41-44R; CANR 31,
58, 88; CLR 29; DLB 87, 161; JRDA;
MAICYA; SATA 5, 62, 95

Dickson, Carr
See Carr, John Dickson

Dickson, Carter
See Carr, John Dickson

Diderot, Denis 1713-1784 .... **LC 26**

Didion, Joan 1934- .... **CLC 1, 3, 8, 14, 32,
129; DAM NOV**
See also AITN 1; AMWS 4; CA 5-8R;
CANR 14, 52, 76; CDALB 1968-1988;
DA3; DLB 2, 173, 185; DLBY 81, 86;
MTCW 1, 2; TCWW 2

Dietrich, Robert
See Hunt, E(verette) Howard, (Jr.)

Difusa, Pati
See Almodovar, Pedro

Dillard, Annie 1945- .. **CLC 9, 60, 115; DAM
NOV**
See also AAYA 6; AMWS 6; CA 49-52;
CANR 3, 43, 62, 90; DA3; DLBY 80;
MTCW 1, 2; SATA 10

Dillard, R(ichard) H(enry) W(ilde)
1937- .... **CLC 5**
See also CA 21-24R; CAAS 7; CANR 10;
DLB 5

Dillon, Eilis 1920-1994 .... **CLC 17**
See also AW; CA 9-12R, 182; 147; CAAE
182; CAAS 3; CANR 4, 38, 78; CLR 26;
MAICYA; SATA 2, 74; SATA-Essay 105;
SATA-Obit 83

Dimont, Penelope
See Mortimer, Penelope (Ruth)

Dinesen, Isak CLC 10, 29, 95; SSC 7
See also Blixen, Karen (Christentze
Dinesen)
See also MTCW 1

Ding Ling CLC 68
See also Chiang, Pin-chin

Diphusa, Patty
See Almodovar, Pedro
Disch, Thomas M(ichael) 1940- ... **CLC 7, 36**
See also AAYA 17; CA 21-24R; CAAS 4;
CANR 17, 36, 54, 89; CLR 18; DA3;
DLB 8; MAICYA; MTCW 1, 2; SAAS
15; SATA 92
Disch, Tom
See Disch, Thomas M(ichael)
d'Isly, Georges
See Simenon, Georges (Jacques Christian)
Disraeli, Benjamin 1804-1881 ... **NCLC 2, 39, 79**
See also DLB 21, 55
Ditcum, Steve
See Crumb, R(obert)
Dixon, Paige
See Corcoran, Barbara
Dixon, Stephen 1936- .... **CLC 52; SSC 16**
See also CA 89-92; CANR 17, 40, 54, 91;
DLB 130
Doak, Annie
See Dillard, Annie
Dobell, Sydney Thompson
1824-1874 .... **NCLC 43**
See also DLB 32
Doblin, Alfred **TCLC 13**
See also Doeblin, Alfred
Dobrolyubov, Nikolai Alexandrovich
1836-1861 .... **NCLC 5**
Dobson, Austin 1840-1921 .... **TCLC 79**
See also DLB 35; 144
Dobyns, Stephen 1941- .... **CLC 37**
See also CA 45-48; CANR 2, 18
Doctorow, E(dgar) L(aurence)
1931- .... **CLC 6, 11, 15, 18, 37, 44, 65, 113; DAM NOV, POP**
See also AAYA 22; AITN 2; AMWS 4;
BEST 89:3; CA 45-48; CANR 2, 33, 51,
76; CDALB 1968-1988; DA3; DLB 2, 28,
173; DLBY 80; MTCW 1, 2
Dodgson, Charles Lutwidge 1832-1898
See Carroll, Lewis
See also AW 2; CLR 2; DA; DAB; DAC;
DAM MST, NOV, POET; DA3; MAI-
CYA; SATA 100
Dodson, Owen (Vincent)
1914-1983 .... **CLC 79; BLC 1; DAM MULT**
See also BW 1; CA 65-68; 110; CANR 24;
DLB 76
Doeblin, Alfred 1878-1957 .... **TCLC 13**
See also Doblin, Alfred
See also CA 110; 141; DLB 66
Doerr, Harriet 1910- .... **CLC 34**
See also CA 117; 122; CANR 47; INT 122
Domecq, H(onorio Bustos)
See Bioy Casares, Adolfo
Domecq, H(onorio) Bustos
See Bioy Casares, Adolfo; Borges, Jorge
Luis
Domini, Rey
See Lorde, Audre (Geraldine)
See also GLL 1
Dominique
See Proust, (Valentin-Louis-George-Eugene-
)Marcel
Don, A
See Stephen, SirLeslie
Donaldson, Stephen R. 1947- .. **CLC 46, 138; DAM POP**
See also AAYA 36; CA 89-92; CANR 13,
55; INT CANR-13; SATA 121
Donleavy, J(ames) P(atrick) 1926- .... **CLC 1, 4, 6, 10, 45**
See also AITN 2; CA 9-12R; CANR 24, 49,
62, 80; DLB 6, 173; INT CANR-24;
MTCW 1, 2

Donne, John 1572-1631 .... **LC 10, 24; DA; DAB; DAC; DAM MST, POET; PC 1**
See also AW; CDBLB Before 1660; DLB
121, 151
Donnell, David 1939(?)- .... **CLC 34**
Donoghue, P. S.
See Hunt, E(verette) Howard, (Jr.)
Donoso (Yanez), Jose 1924-1996 ... **CLC 4, 8, 11, 32, 99; DAM MULT; HLC 1; SSC 34**
See also CA 81-84; 155; CANR 32, 73;
DLB 113; HW 1, 2; MTCW 1, 2
Donovan, John 1928-1992 .... **CLC 35**
See also AAYA 20; AW; CA 97-100; 137;
CLR 3; MAICYA; SATA 72; SATA-Brief
29
Don Roberto
See Cunninghame Graham, Robert
(Gallnigad) Bontine
Doolittle, Hilda 1886-1961 . **CLC 3, 8, 14, 31, 34, 73; DA; DAC; DAM MST, POET; PC 5**
See also H. D.
See also AMWS 1; AW; CA 97-100; CANR
35; DLB 4, 45; GLL 1; MTCW 1, 2
Dorfman, Ariel 1942- ...... **CLC 48, 77; DAM MULT; HLC 1**
See also CA 124; 130; CANR 67, 70; CWW
2; HW 1, 2; INT 130
Dorn, Edward (Merton)
1929-1999 .... **CLC 10, 18**
See also CA 93-96; 187; CANR 42, 79;
DLB 5; INT 93-96
Dor-Ner, Zvi **CLC 70**
Dorris, Michael (Anthony)
1945-1997 .... **CLC 109; DAM MULT, NOV**
See also AAYA 20; AW; BEST 90:1; CA
102; 157; CANR 19, 46, 75; CLR 58;
DA3; DLB 175; MTCW 2; NNAL; SATA
75; SATA-Obit 94; TCWW 2
Dorris, Michael A.
See Dorris, Michael (Anthony)
Dorsan, Luc
See Simenon, Georges (Jacques Christian)
Dorsange, Jean
See Simenon, Georges (Jacques Christian)
Dos Passos, John (Roderigo)
1896-1970 ... **CLC 1, 4, 8, 11, 15, 25, 34, 82; DA; DAB; DAC; DAM MST, NOV**
See also AW; CA 1-4R; 29-32R; CANR 3;
CDALB 1929-1941; DA3; DLB 4, 9;
DLBD 1, 15; DLBY 96; MTCW 1, 2
Dossage, Jean
See Simenon, Georges (Jacques Christian)
Dostoevsky, Fedor Mikhailovich
1821-1881 . **NCLC 2, 7, 21, 33, 43; DA; DAB; DAC; DAM MST, NOV; SSC 2, 33, 44**
See also AW; DA3; DLB 238
Doughty, Charles M(ontagu)
1843-1926 .... **TCLC 27**
See also CA 115; 178; DLB 19, 57, 174
Douglas, Ellen **CLC 73**
See also Haxton, Josephine Ayres; William-
son, Ellen Douglas
Douglas, Gavin 1475(?)-1522 .... **LC 20**
See also DLB 132
Douglas, George
See Brown, George Douglas
Douglas, Keith (Castellain)
1920-1944 .... **TCLC 40**
See also CA 160; DLB 27
Douglas, Leonard
See Bradbury, Ray (Douglas)
Douglas, Michael
See Crichton, (John) Michael

Douglas, (George) Norman
1868-1952 .... **TCLC 68**
See also CA 119; 157; DLB 34, 195
Douglas, William
See Brown, George Douglas
Douglass, Frederick 1817(?)-1895 .. **NCLC 7, 55; BLC 1; DA; DAC; DAM MST, MULT**
See also AMWS 3; AW; CDALB 1640-
1865; DA3; DLB 1, 43, 50, 79; SATA 29
Dourado, (Waldomiro Freitas) Autran
1926- .... **CLC 23, 60**
See also CA 25-28R; 179; CANR 34, 81;
DLB 145; HW 2
Dourado, Waldomiro Autran
See Dourado, (Waldomiro Freitas) Autran
See also CA 179
Dove, Rita (Frances) 1952- .... **CLC 50, 81; BLCS; DAM MULT, POET; PC 6**
See also AMWS 4; BW 2; CA 109; CAAS
19; CANR 27, 42, 68, 76; CDALBS;
DA3; DLB 120; MTCW 1
Doveglion
See Villa, Jose Garcia
Dowell, Coleman 1925-1985 .... **CLC 60**
See also CA 25-28R; 117; CANR 10; DLB
130; GLL 2
Dowson, Ernest (Christopher)
1867-1900 .... **TCLC 4**
See also CA 105; 150; DLB 19, 135
Doyle, A. Conan
See Doyle, Arthur Conan
Doyle, Arthur Conan 1859-1930 .... **TCLC 7; DA; DAB; DAC; DAM MST, NOV; SSC 12**
See also Doyle, Sir Arthur Conan
See also AAYA 14; AW; CA 104; 122; CD-
BLB 1890-1914; DA3; DLB 18, 70, 156,
178; MTCW 1, 2; SATA 24
Doyle, Conan
See Doyle, Arthur Conan
Doyle, John
See Graves, Robert (von Ranke)
Doyle, Roddy 1958(?)- .... **CLC 81**
See also AAYA 14; BRWS 5; CA 143;
CANR 73; DA3; DLB 194
Doyle, Sir A. Conan
See Doyle, Arthur Conan
Doyle, Sir Arthur Conan
See Doyle, Arthur Conan
See also BRWS 2
Dr. A
See Asimov, Isaac; Silverstein, Alvin
Drabble, Margaret 1939- ...... **CLC 2, 3, 5, 8, 10, 22, 53, 129; DAB; DAC; DAM MST, NOV, POP**
See also BRWS 4; CA 13-16R; CANR 18,
35, 63; CDBLB 1960 to Present; DA3;
DLB 14, 155, 231; MTCW 1, 2; SATA 48
Drapier, M. B.
See Swift, Jonathan
Drayham, James
See Mencken, H(enry) L(ouis)
Drayton, Michael 1563-1631 ..... **LC 8; DAM POET**
See also DLB 121
Dreadstone, Carl
See Campbell, (John) Ramsey
Dreiser, Theodore (Herman Albert)
1871-1945 .... **TCLC 10, 18, 35, 83; DA; DAC; DAM MST, NOV; SSC 30**
See also AW; CA 106; 132; CDALB 1865-
1917; DA3; DLB 9, 12, 102, 137; DLBD
1; MTCW 1, 2
Drexler, Rosalyn 1926- .... **CLC 2, 6**
See also CA 81-84; CANR 68
Dreyer, Carl Theodor 1889-1968 ...... **CLC 16**
See also CA 116

Engel, Marian 1933-1985 .... **CLC 36**
    See also CA 25-28R; CANR 12; DLB 53;
    INT CANR-12
Engelhardt, Frederick
    See Hubbard, L(afayette) Ron(ald)
Engels, Friedrich 1820-1895 .... **NCLC 85**
    See also DLB 129
Enright, D(ennis) J(oseph) 1920- .. **CLC 4, 8,**
    31
    See also CA 1-4R; CANR 1, 42, 83; DLB
    27; SATA 25
Enzensberger, Hans Magnus
    1929-................................ **CLC 43; PC 28**
    See also CA 116; 119
Ephron, Nora 1941- .... **CLC 17, 31**
    See also AAYA 35; AITN 2; CA 65-68;
    CANR 12, 39, 83
Epicurus 341B.C.-270B.C. .... **CMLC 21**
    See also DLB 176
Epsilon
    See Betjeman, John
Epstein, Daniel Mark 1948- .... **CLC 7**
    See also CA 49-52; CANR 2, 53, 90
Epstein, Jacob 1956- .... **CLC 19**
    See also CA 114
Epstein, Jean 1897-1953 .... **TCLC 92**
Epstein, Joseph 1937- .... **CLC 39**
    See also CA 112; 119; CANR 50, 65
Epstein, Leslie 1938- .... **CLC 27**
    See also CA 73-76; CAAS 12; CANR 23,
    69
Equiano, Olaudah 1745(?)-1797 .... **LC 16;**
    BLC 2; DAM MULT
    See also DLB 37, 50
Erasmus, Desiderius 1469(?)-1536 ...... **LC 16**
Erdman, Paul E(mil) 1932- .... **CLC 25**
    See also AITN 1; CA 61-64; CANR 13, 43,
    84
Erdrich, Louise 1954- .... **CLC 39, 54, 120;**
    DAM MULT, NOV, POP
    See also AAYA 10; AMWS 4; BEST 89:1;
    CA 114; CANR 41, 62; CDALBS; DA3;
    DLB 152, 175, 206; MTCW 1; NNAL;
    SATA 94; TCWW 2
Erenburg, Ilya (Grigoryevich)
    See Ehrenburg, Ilya (Grigoryevich)
Erickson, Stephen Michael 1950-
    See Erickson, Steve
    See also CA 129
Erickson, Steve CLC 64
    See also Erickson, Stephen Michael
    See also CANR 60, 68
Ericson, Walter
    See Fast, Howard (Melvin)
Eriksson, Buntel
    See Bergman, (Ernst) Ingmar
Ernaux, Annie 1940- .... **CLC 88**
    See also CA 147; CANR 93
Erskine, John 1879-1951 .... **TCLC 84**
    See also CA 112; 159; DLB 9, 102
Eschenbach, Wolfram von
    See Wolfram von Eschenbach
Eseki, Bruno
    See Mphahlele, Ezekiel
Esenin, Sergei (Alexandrovich)
    1895-1925 .... **TCLC 4**
    See also CA 104
Eshleman, Clayton 1935- .... **CLC 7**
    See also CA 33-36R; CAAS 6; CANR 93;
    DLB 5
Espriella, Don Manuel Alvarez
    See Southey, Robert
Espriu, Salvador 1913-1985 .... **CLC 9**
    See also CA 154; 115; DLB 134
Espronceda, Jose de 1808-1842 ..... **NCLC 39**

Esquivel, Laura 1951(?)- .... **CLC 141;**
    HLCS 1
    See also AAYA 29; CA 143; CANR 68;
    DA3; MTCW 1
Esse, James
    See Stephens, James
Esterbrook, Tom
    See Hubbard, L(afayette) Ron(ald)
Estleman, Loren D. 1952- ..... **CLC 48; DAM**
    NOV, POP
    See also AAYA 27; CA 85-88; CANR 27,
    74; DA3; DLB 226; INT CANR-27;
    MTCW 1, 2
Euclid 306B.C.-283B.C. .... **CMLC 25**
Eugenides, Jeffrey 1960(?)- .... **CLC 81**
    See also CA 144
Euripides c. 485B.C.-406B.C. .... **CMLC 23;**
    DA; DAB; DAC; DAM DRAM, MST;
    DC 4
    See also AW; DA3; DLB 176
Evan, Evin
    See Faust, Frederick (Schiller)
Evans, Caradoc 1878-1945 ... **TCLC 85; SSC**
    43
Evans, Evan
    See Faust, Frederick (Schiller)
    See also TCWW 2
Evans, Marian
    See Eliot, George
Evans, Mary Ann
    See Eliot, George
Evarts, Esther
    See Benson, Sally
Everett, Percival
    See Everett, Percival L.
Everett, Percival L. 1956- .... **CLC 57**
    See also Everett, Percival
    See also BW 2; CA 129; CANR 94
Everson, R(onald) G(ilmour)
    1903-1992 .... **CLC 27**
    See also CA 17-20R; DLB 88
Everson, William (Oliver)
    1912-1994 .... **CLC 1, 5, 14**
    See also CA 9-12R; 145; CANR 20; DLB
    212; MTCW 1
Evtushenko, Evgenii Aleksandrovich
    See Yevtushenko, Yevgeny (Alexandrovich)
Ewart, Gavin (Buchanan)
    1916-1995 .... **CLC 13, 46**
    See also CA 89-92; 150; CANR 17, 46;
    DLB 40; MTCW 1
Ewers, Hanns Heinz 1871-1943 ..... **TCLC 12**
    See also CA 109; 149
Ewing, Frederick R.
    See Sturgeon, Theodore (Hamilton)
Exley, Frederick (Earl) 1929-1992 .... **CLC 6,**
    11
    See also AITN 2; CA 81-84; 138; DLB 143;
    DLBY 81
Eynhardt, Guillermo
    See Quiroga, Horacio (Sylvestre)
Ezekiel, Nissim 1924- .... **CLC 61**
    See also CA 61-64
Ezekiel, Tish O'Dowd 1943- .... **CLC 34**
    See also CA 129
Fadeyev, A.
    See Bulgya, Alexander Alexandrovich
Fadeyev, Alexander TCLC 53
    See also Bulgya, Alexander Alexandrovich
Fagen, Donald 1948- .... **CLC 26**
Fainzilberg, Ilya Arnoldovich 1897-1937
    See Ilf, Ilya
    See also CA 120; 165
Fair, Ronald L. 1932- .... **CLC 18**
    See also BW 1; CA 69-72; CANR 25; DLB
    33
Fairbairn, Roger
    See Carr, John Dickson

Fairbairns, Zoe (Ann) 1948- .... **CLC 32**
    See also CA 103; CANR 21, 85
Fairman, Paul W. 1916-1977
    See Queen, Ellery
    See also CA 114
Falco, Gian
    See Papini, Giovanni
Falconer, James
    See Kirkup, James
Falconer, Kenneth
    See Kornbluth, C(yril) M.
Falkland, Samuel
    See Heijermans, Herman
Fallaci, Oriana 1930- .... **CLC 11, 110**
    See also CA 77-80; CANR 15, 58; MTCW
    1
Faludi, Susan 1959- .... **CLC 140**
    See also CA 138; MTCW 1
Faludy, George 1913- .... **CLC 42**
    See also CA 21-24R
Faludy, Gyoergy
    See Faludy, George
Fanon, Frantz 1925-1961 ... **CLC 74; BLC 2;**
    DAM MULT
    See also BW 1; CA 116; 89-92
Fanshawe, Ann 1625-1680 .... **LC 11**
Fante, John (Thomas) 1911-1983 ..... **CLC 60**
    See also CA 69-72; 109; CANR 23; DLB
    130; DLBY 83
Farah, Nuruddin 1945- .. **CLC 53, 137; BLC**
    2; DAM MULT
    See also BW 2, 3; CA 106; CANR 81; DLB
    125
Fargue, Leon-Paul 1876(?)-1947 .... **TCLC 11**
    See also CA 109
Farigoule, Louis
    See Romains, Jules
Farina, Richard 1936(?)-1966 .... **CLC 9**
    See also CA 81-84; 25-28R
Farley, Walter (Lorimer)
    1915-1989 .... **CLC 17**
    See also AW; CA 17-20R; CANR 8, 29, 84;
    DLB 22; JRDA; MAICYA; SATA 2, 43
Farmer, Philip Jose 1918- .... **CLC 1, 19**
    See also AAYA 28; CA 1-4R; CANR 4, 35;
    DLB 8; MTCW 1; SATA 93
Farquhar, George 1677-1707 ... **LC 21; DAM**
    DRAM
    See also DLB 84
Farrell, J(ames) G(ordon)
    1935-1979 .... **CLC 6**
    See also CA 73-76; 89-92; CANR 36; DLB
    14; MTCW 1
Farrell, James T(homas) 1904-1979 . **CLC 1,**
    4, 8, 11, 66; SSC 28
    See also CA 5-8R; 89-92; CANR 9, 61;
    DLB 4, 9, 86; DLBD 2; MTCW 1, 2
Farrell, Warren (Thomas) 1943- ...... **CLC 70**
    See also CA 146
Farren, Richard J.
    See Betjeman, John
Farren, Richard M.
    See Betjeman, John
Fassbinder, Rainer Werner
    1946-1982 .... **CLC 20**
    See also CA 93-96; 106; CANR 31
Fast, Howard (Melvin) 1914- .. **CLC 23, 131;**
    DAM NOV
    See also AAYA 16; AW; CA 1-4R, 181;
    CAAE 181; CAAS 18; CANR 1, 33, 54,
    75; DLB 9; INT CANR-33; MTCW 1;
    SATA 7; SATA-Essay 107; TCWW 2
Faulcon, Robert
    See Holdstock, Robert P.

Garfield, Leon 1921-1996 .... **CLC 12**
See also AAYA 8; AW; CA 17-20R; 152;
CANR 38, 41, 78; CLR 21; DLB 161;
JRDA; MAICYA; SATA 1, 32, 76; SATA-
Obit 90

Garland, (Hannibal) Hamlin
1860-1940 .... **TCLC 3; SSC 18**
See also CA 104; DLB 12, 71, 78, 186;
TCWW 2

Garneau, (Hector de) Saint-Denys
1912-1943 .... **TCLC 13**
See also CA 111; DLB 88

Garner, Alan 1934- ...... **CLC 17; DAB; DAM POP**
See also AAYA 18; AW; CA 73-76, 178;
CAAE 178; CANR 15, 64; CLR 20; DLB
161; MAICYA; MTCW 1, 2; SATA 18,
69; SATA-Essay 108

Garner, Hugh 1913-1979 .... **CLC 13**
See also Warwick, Jarvis
See also CA 69-72; CANR 31; CCA 1; DLB
68

Garnett, David 1892-1981 .... **CLC 3**
See also CA 5-8R; 103; CANR 17, 79; DLB
34; MTCW 2

Garos, Stephanie
See Katz, Steve

Garrett, George (Palmer) 1929- .. **CLC 3, 11, 51; SSC 30**
See also AMWS 7; CA 1-4R; CAAS 5;
CANR 1, 42, 67; DLB 2, 5, 130, 152;
DLBY 83

Garrick, David 1717-1779 .... **LC 15; DAM DRAM**
See also DLB 84

Garrigue, Jean 1914-1972 .... **CLC 2, 8**
See also CA 5-8R; 37-40R; CANR 20

Garrison, Frederick
See Sinclair, Upton (Beall)

Garro, Elena 1920(?)-1998
See also CA 131; 169; CWW 2; DLB 145;
HLCS 1; HW 1

Garth, Will
See Hamilton, Edmond; Kuttner, Henry

Garvey, Marcus (Moziah, Jr.)
1887-1940 ...... **TCLC 41; BLC 2; DAM MULT**
See also BW 1; CA 120; 124; CANR 79

Gary, Romain CLC 25
See also Kacew, Romain
See also DLB 83

Gascar, Pierre CLC 11
See also Fournier, Pierre

Gascoyne, David (Emery) 1916- .... **CLC 45**
See also CA 65-68; CANR 10, 28, 54; DLB
20; MTCW 1

Gaskell, Elizabeth Cleghorn
1810-1865 .... **NCLC 5, 70, 97; DAB; DAM MST; SSC 25**
See also CDBLB 1832-1890; DLB 21, 144,
159

Gass, William H(oward) 1924- . **CLC 1, 2, 8, 11, 15, 39, 132; SSC 12**
See also AMWS 6; CA 17-20R; CANR 30,
71; DLB 2, 227; MTCW 1, 2

Gassendi, Pierre 1592-1655 .... **LC 54**

Gasset, Jose Ortega y
See Ortega y Gasset, Jose

Gates, Henry Louis, Jr. 1950- .... **CLC 65; BLCS; DAM MULT**
See also BW 2, 3; CA 109; CANR 25, 53,
75; DA3; DLB 67; MTCW 1

Gautier, Theophile 1811-1872 .. **NCLC 1, 59; DAM POET; PC 18; SSC 20**
See also DLB 119

Gawsworth, John
See Bates, H(erbert) E(rnest)

Gay, John 1685-1732 .. **LC 49; DAM DRAM**
See also DLB 84, 95

Gay, Oliver
See Gogarty, Oliver St. John

Gaye, Marvin (Penze) 1939-1984 ..... **CLC 26**
See also CA 112

Gee, Maggie (Mary) 1948- .... **CLC 57**
See also CA 130; DLB 207

Gee, Maurice (Gough) 1931- .... **CLC 29**
See also CA 97-100; CANR 67; CLR 56;
SATA 46, 101

Gelbart, Larry (Simon) 1928- .... **CLC 21, 61**
See also Gelbart, Larry
See also CA 73-76; CANR 45, 94

Gelbart, Larry 1928-
See Gelbart, Larry (Simon)

Gelber, Jack 1932- .... **CLC 1, 6, 14, 79**
See also CA 1-4R; CANR 2; DLB 7, 228

Gellhorn, Martha (Ellis)
1908-1998 .... **CLC 14, 60**
See also CA 77-80; 164; CANR 44; DLBY
82, 98

Genet, Jean 1910-1986 .. **CLC 1, 2, 5, 10, 14, 44, 46; DAM DRAM**
See also CA 13-16R; CANR 18; DA3; DLB
72; DLBY 86; GLL 1; MTCW 1, 2

Gent, Peter 1942- .... **CLC 29**
See also AITN 1; CA 89-92; DLBY 82

Gentile, Giovanni 1875-1944 .... **TCLC 96**
See also CA 119

Gentlewoman in New England, A
See Bradstreet, Anne

Gentlewoman in Those Parts, A
See Bradstreet, Anne

Geoffrey of Monmouth c.
1100-1155 .... **CMLC 44**
See also DLB 146

George, Jean Craighead 1919- .... **CLC 35**
See also AAYA 8; AW; CA 5-8R; CANR
25; CLR 1; DLB 52; JRDA; MAICYA;
SATA 2, 68

George, Stefan (Anton) 1868-1933 . **TCLC 2, 14**
See also CA 104

Georges, Georges Martin
See Simenon, Georges (Jacques Christian)

Gerhardi, William Alexander
See Gerhardie, William Alexander

Gerhardie, William Alexander
1895-1977 .... **CLC 5**
See also CA 25-28R; 73-76; CANR 18;
DLB 36

Gerstler, Amy 1956- .... **CLC 70**
See also CA 146

Gertler, T. CLC 134
See also CA 116; 121

Ghalib NCLC 39, 78
See also Ghalib, Hsadullah Khan

Ghalib, Hsadullah Khan 1797-1869
See Ghalib
See also DAM POET

Ghelderode, Michel de 1898-1962 ..... **CLC 6, 11; DAM DRAM; DC 15**
See also CA 85-88; CANR 40, 77

Ghiselin, Brewster 1903- .... **CLC 23**
See also CA 13-16R; CAAS 10; CANR 13

Ghose, Aurabinda 1872-1950 .... **TCLC 63**
See also CA 163

Ghose, Zulfikar 1935- .... **CLC 42**
See also CA 65-68; CANR 67

Ghosh, Amitav 1956- .... **CLC 44**
See also CA 147; CANR 80

Giacosa, Giuseppe 1847-1906 .... **TCLC 7**
See also CA 104

Gibb, Lee
See Waterhouse, Keith (Spencer)

Gibbon, Lewis Grassic TCLC 4
See also Mitchell, James Leslie

Gibbons, Kaye 1960- .... **CLC 50, 88; DAM POP**
See also AAYA 34; CA 151; CANR 75;
DA3; MTCW 1; SATA 117

Gibran, Kahlil 1883-1931 .... **TCLC 1, 9; DAM POET, POP; PC 9**
See also CA 104; 150; DA3; MTCW 2

Gibran, Khalil
See Gibran, Kahlil

Gibson, William 1914- .. **CLC 23; DA; DAB; DAC; DAM DRAM, MST**
See also AW; CA 9-12R; CANR 9, 42, 75;
DLB 7; MTCW 1; SATA 66; SCFW 2

Gibson, William (Ford) 1948- ... **CLC 39, 63; DAM POP**
See also AAYA 12; CA 126; 133; CANR
52, 90; DA3; MTCW 1

Gide, Andre (Paul Guillaume)
1869-1951 . **TCLC 5, 12, 36; DA; DAB; DAC; DAM MST, NOV; SSC 13**
See also AW; CA 104; 124; DA3; DLB 65;
MTCW 1, 2

Gifford, Barry (Colby) 1946- .... **CLC 34**
See also CA 65-68; CANR 9, 30, 40, 90

Gilbert, Frank
See De Voto, Bernard (Augustine)

Gilbert, W(illiam) S(chwenck)
1836-1911 .... **TCLC 3; DAM DRAM, POET**
See also CA 104; 173; SATA 36

Gilbreth, Frank B., Jr. 1911-2001 .... **CLC 17**
See also CA 9-12R; SATA 2

Gilchrist, Ellen 1935- ...... **CLC 34, 48; DAM POP; SSC 14**
See also CA 113; 116; CANR 41, 61; DLB
130; MTCW 1, 2

Giles, Molly 1942- .... **CLC 39**
See also CA 126

Gill, Eric 1882-1940 .... **TCLC 85**

Gill, Patrick
See Creasey, John

Gillette, Douglas CLC 70

Gilliam, Terry (Vance) 1940- .... **CLC 21, 141**
See also Monty Python
See also AAYA 19; CA 108; 113; CANR
35; INT 113

Gillian, Jerry
See Gilliam, Terry (Vance)

Gilliatt, Penelope (Ann Douglass)
1932-1993 .... **CLC 2, 10, 13, 53**
See also AITN 2; CA 13-16R; 141; CANR
49; DLB 14

Gilman, Charlotte (Anna) Perkins (Stetson)
1860-1935 .... **TCLC 9, 37; SSC 13**
See also CA 106; 150; DLB 221; MTCW 1

Gilmour, David 1949- .... **CLC 35**
See also CA 138, 147

Gilpin, William 1724-1804 .... **NCLC 30**

Gilray, J. D.
See Mencken, H(enry) L(ouis)

Gilroy, Frank D(aniel) 1925- .... **CLC 2**
See also CA 81-84; CANR 32, 64, 86; DLB
7

Gilstrap, John 1957(?)- .... **CLC 99**
See also CA 160

Ginsberg, Allen 1926-1997 .... **CLC 1, 2, 3, 4, 6, 13, 36, 69, 109; DA; DAB; DAC; DAM MST, POET; PC 4**
See also AAYA 33; AITN 1; AMWS 2; AW;
CA 1-4R; 157; CANR 2, 41, 63, 95;
CDALB 1941-1968; DA3; DLB 5, 16,
169; GLL 1; MTCW 1, 2

Ginzburg, Eugenia CLC 59

Ginzburg, Natalia 1916-1991 .... **CLC 5, 11, 54, 70**
See also CA 85-88; 135; CANR 33; DLB
177; MTCW 1, 2

Giono, Jean 1895-1970 .... **CLC 4, 11**
See also CA 45-48; 29-32R; CANR 2, 35;
DLB 72; MTCW 1

Giovanni, Nikki 1943- .... **CLC 2, 4, 19, 64,
117; BLC 2; DA; DAB; DAC; DAM
MST, MULT, POET; PC 19**
See also AAYA 22; AITN 1; AW; BW 2, 3;
CA 29-32R; CAAS 6; CANR 18, 41, 60,
91; CDALBS; CLR 6; DA3; DLB 5, 41;
INT CANR-18; MAICYA; MTCW 1, 2;
SATA 24, 107

Giovene, Andrea 1904- .... **CLC 7**
See also CA 85-88

Gippius, Zinaida (Nikolayevna) 1869-1945
See Hippius, Zinaida
See also CA 106

Giraudoux, (Hippolyte) Jean
1882-1944 .... **TCLC 2, 7; DAM DRAM**
See also CA 104; DLB 65

Gironella, Jose Maria 1917- .... **CLC 11**
See also CA 101

Gissing, George (Robert)
1857-1903 .... **TCLC 3, 24, 47; SSC 37**
See also CA 105; 167; DLB 18, 135, 184

Giurlani, Aldo
See Palazzeschi, Aldo

Gladkov, Fyodor (Vasilyevich)
1883-1958 .... **TCLC 27**
See also CA 170

Glanville, Brian (Lester) 1931- .... **CLC 6**
See also CA 5-8R; CAAS 9; CANR 3, 70;
DLB 15, 139; SATA 42

Glasgow, Ellen (Anderson Gholson)
1873-1945 .... **TCLC 2, 7; SSC 34**
See also CA 104; 164; DLB 9, 12; MTCW
2

Glaspell, Susan 1882(?)-1948 . **TCLC 55; DC
10; SSC 41**
See also AMWS 3; AW 2; CA 110; 154;
DLB 7, 9, 78, 228; TCWW 2

Glassco, John 1909-1981 .... **CLC 9**
See also CA 13-16R; 102; CANR 15; DLB
68

Glasscock, Amnesia
See Steinbeck, John (Ernst)

Glasser, Ronald J. 1940(?)- .... **CLC 37**

Glassman, Joyce
See Johnson, Joyce

Glendinning, Victoria 1937- .... **CLC 50**
See also CA 120; 127; CANR 59, 89; DLB
155

Glissant, Edouard 1928- . **CLC 10, 68; DAM
MULT**
See also CA 153; CWW 2

Gloag, Julian 1930- .... **CLC 40**
See also AITN 1; CA 65-68; CANR 10, 70

Glowacki, Aleksander
See Prus, Boleslaw

Gluck, Louise (Elisabeth) 1943- .. **CLC 7, 22,
44, 81; DAM POET; PC 16**
See also AMWS 5; CA 33-36R; CANR 40,
69; DA3; DLB 5; MTCW 2

Glyn, Elinor 1864-1943 .... **TCLC 72**
See also DLB 153

Gobineau, Joseph Arthur (Comte) de
1816-1882 .... **NCLC 17**
See also DLB 123

Godard, Jean-Luc 1930- .... **CLC 20**
See also CA 93-96

Godden, (Margaret) Rumer
1907-1998 .... **CLC 53**
See also AAYA 6; CA 5-8R; 172; CANR 4,
27, 36, 55, 80; CLR 20; DLB 161; MAI-
CYA; SAAS 12; SATA 3, 36; SATA-Obit
109

Godoy Alcayaga, Lucila
1899-1957 .... **TCLC 2; DAM MULT;
HLC 2; PC 32**
See also BW 2; CA 104; 131; CANR 81;
HW 1, 2; MTCW 1, 2

Godwin, Gail (Kathleen) 1937- ..... **CLC 5, 8,
22, 31, 69, 125; DAM POP**
See also CA 29-32R; CANR 15, 43, 69;
DA3; DLB 6, 234; INT CANR-15;
MTCW 1, 2

Godwin, William 1756-1836 .... **NCLC 14**
See also CDBLB 1789-1832; DLB 39, 104,
142, 158, 163

Goebbels, Josef
See Goebbels, (Paul) Joseph

Goebbels, (Paul) Joseph
1897-1945 .... **TCLC 68**
See also CA 115; 148

Goebbels, Joseph Paul
See Goebbels, (Paul) Joseph

Goethe, Johann Wolfgang von
1749-1832 ...... **NCLC 4, 22, 34, 90; DA;
DAB; DAC; DAM DRAM, MST,
POET; PC 5; SSC 38**
See also AW; DA3; DLB 94

Gogarty, Oliver St. John
1878-1957 .... **TCLC 15**
See also CA 109; 150; DLB 15, 19

Gogol, Nikolai (Vasilyevich)
1809-1852 . **NCLC 5, 15, 31; DA; DAB;
DAC; DAM DRAM, MST; DC 1; SSC
4, 29**
See also AW; DLB 198

Goines, Donald 1937(?)-1974 . **CLC 80; BLC
2; DAM MULT, POP**
See also AITN 1; BW 1, 3; CA 124; 114;
CANR 82; DA3; DLB 33

Gold, Herbert 1924- .... **CLC 4, 7, 14, 42**
See also CA 9-12R; CANR 17, 45; DLB 2;
DLBY 81

Goldbarth, Albert 1948- .... **CLC 5, 38**
See also CA 53-56; CANR 6, 40; DLB 120

Goldberg, Anatol 1910-1982 .... **CLC 34**
See also CA 131; 117

Goldemberg, Isaac 1945- .... **CLC 52**
See also CA 69-72; CAAS 12; CANR 11,
32; HW 1

Golding, William (Gerald)
1911-1993 ..... **CLC 1, 2, 3, 8, 10, 17, 27,
58, 81; DA; DAB; DAC; DAM MST,
NOV**
See also AAYA 5; AW; BRWS 1; CA 5-8R;
141; CANR 13, 33, 54; CDBLB 1945-
1960; DA3; DLB 15, 100; MTCW 1, 2

Goldman, Emma 1869-1940 .... **TCLC 13**
See also CA 110; 150; DLB 221

Goldman, Francisco 1954- .... **CLC 76**
See also CA 162

Goldman, William (W.) 1931- ...... **CLC 1, 48**
See also CA 9-12R; CANR 29, 69; DLB
44; IDFW 3

Goldmann, Lucien 1913-1970 .... **CLC 24**
See also CA 25-28; CAP 2

Goldoni, Carlo 1707-1793 .... **LC 4; DAM
DRAM**

Goldsberry, Steven 1949- .... **CLC 34**
See also CA 131

Goldsmith, Oliver 1730-1774 . **LC 2, 48; DA;
DAB; DAC; DAM DRAM, MST, NOV,
POET; DC 8**
See also AW; CDBLB 1660-1789; DLB 39,
89, 104, 109, 142; SATA 26

Goldsmith, Peter
See Priestley, J(ohn) B(oynton)

Gombrowicz, Witold 1904-1969 .... **CLC 4, 7,
11, 49; DAM DRAM**
See also CA 19-20; 25-28R; CAP 2

Gomez de la Serna, Ramon
1888-1963 .... **CLC 9**
See also CA 153; 116; CANR 79; HW 1, 2

Goncharov, Ivan Alexandrovich
1812-1891 .... **NCLC 1, 63**
See also DLB 238

Goncourt, Edmond (Louis Antoine Huot) de
1822-1896 .... **NCLC 7**
See also DLB 123

Goncourt, Jules (Alfred Huot) de
1830-1870 .... **NCLC 7**
See also DLB 123

Gontier, Fernande 19(?)- .... **CLC 50**

Gonzalez Martinez, Enrique
1871-1952 .... **TCLC 72**
See also CA 166; CANR 81; HW 1, 2

Goodman, Paul 1911-1972 ..... **CLC 1, 2, 4, 7**
See also CA 19-20; 37-40R; CANR 34;
CAP 2; DLB 130; MTCW 1

Gordimer, Nadine 1923- ...... **CLC 3, 5, 7, 10,
18, 33, 51, 70, 123; DA; DAB; DAC;
DAM MST, NOV; SSC 17**
See also AW; BRWS 2; CA 5-8R; CANR 3,
28, 56, 88; DA3; DLB 225; INT CANR-
28; MTCW 1, 2

Gordon, Adam Lindsay
1833-1870 .... **NCLC 21**
See also DLB 230

Gordon, Caroline 1895-1981 . **CLC 6, 13, 29,
83; SSC 15**
See also CA 11-12; 103; CANR 36; CAP 1;
DLB 4, 9, 102; DLBD 17; DLBY 81;
MTCW 1, 2

Gordon, Charles William 1860-1937
See Connor, Ralph
See also CA 109

Gordon, Mary (Catherine) 1949- .... **CLC 13,
22, 128**
See also AMWS 4; CA 102; CANR 44, 92;
DLB 6; DLBY 81; INT 102; MTCW 1

Gordon, N. J.
See Bosman, Herman Charles

Gordon, Sol 1923- .... **CLC 26**
See also CA 53-56; CANR 4; SATA 11

Gordone, Charles 1925-1995 .... **CLC 1, 4;
DAM DRAM; DC 8**
See also BW 1, 3; CA 93-96; 180; 150;
CAAE 180; CANR 55; DLB 7; INT 93-
96; MTCW 1

Gore, Catherine 1800-1861 .... **NCLC 65**
See also DLB 116

Gorenko, Anna Andreevna
See Akhmatova, Anna

Gorky, Maxim TCLC 8; DAB; SSC 28
See also Peshkov, Alexei Maximovich
See also AW; MTCW 2

Goryan, Sirak
See Saroyan, William

Gosse, Sir Edmund (William)
1849-1928 .... **TCLC 28**
See also CA 117; DLB 57, 144, 184

Gotlieb, Phyllis Fay (Bloom) 1926- .. **CLC 18**
See also CA 13-16R; CANR 7; DLB 88

Gottesman, S. D.
See Kornbluth, C(yril) M.; Pohl, Frederik

Gottfried von Strassburg fl. c.
1170-1215 .... **CMLC 10**
See also DLB 138

Gould, Lois CLC 4, 10
See also CA 77-80; CANR 29; MTCW 1

Gourmont, Remy (-Marie-Charles) de
1858-1915 .... **TCLC 17**
See also CA 109; 150; MTCW 2

Govier, Katherine 1948- .... **CLC 51**
See also CA 101; CANR 18, 40; CCA 1

Goyen, (Charles) William
1915-1983 .... **CLC 5, 8, 14, 40**
See also AITN 2; CA 5-8R; 110; CANR 6,
71; DLB 2; DLBY 83; INT CANR-6

Goytisolo, Juan 1931- .... **CLC 5, 10, 23, 133; DAM MULT; HLC 1**
See also CA 85-88; CANR 32, 61; CWW 2; GLL 2; HW 1, 2; MTCW 1, 2

Gozzano, Guido 1883-1916 .... **PC 10**
See also CA 154; DLB 114

Gozzi, (Conte) Carlo 1720-1806 .... **NCLC 23**

Grabbe, Christian Dietrich
1801-1836 .... **NCLC 2**
See also DLB 133

Grace, Patricia Frances 1937- .... **CLC 56**
See also CA 176

Gracian y Morales, Baltasar
1601-1658 .... **LC 15**

Gracq, Julien **CLC 11, 48**
See also Poirier, Louis
See also CWW 2; DLB 83

Grade, Chaim 1910-1982 .... **CLC 10**
See also CA 93-96; 107

Graduate of Oxford, A
See Ruskin, John

Grafton, Garth
See Duncan, Sara Jeannette

Graham, John
See Phillips, David Graham

Graham, Jorie 1951- .... **CLC 48, 118**
See also CA 111; CANR 63; DLB 120

Graham, R(obert) B(ontine) Cunninghame
See Cunninghame Graham, Robert (Gallnigad) Bontine
See also DLB 98, 135, 174

Graham, Robert
See Haldeman, Joe (William)

Graham, Tom
See Lewis, (Harry) Sinclair

Graham, W(illiam) S(idney)
1918-1986 .... **CLC 29**
See also CA 73-76; 118; DLB 20

Graham, Winston (Mawdsley)
1910- .... **CLC 23**
See also CA 49-52; CANR 2, 22, 45, 66; DLB 77

Grahame, Kenneth 1859-1932 ...... **TCLC 64; DAB**
See also AW 1; CA 108; 136; CANR 80; CLR 5; DA3; DLB 34, 141, 178; MAICYA; MTCW 2; SATA 100

Granger, Darius John
See Marlowe, Stephen

Granin, Daniil **CLC 59**

Granovsky, Timofei Nikolaevich
1813-1855 .... **NCLC 75**
See also DLB 198

Grant, Skeeter
See Spiegelman, Art

Granville-Barker, Harley
1877-1946 .... **TCLC 2; DAM DRAM**
See also Barker, Harley Granville
See also CA 104

Granzotto, Gianni
See Granzotto, Giovanni Battista

Granzotto, Giovanni Battista
1914-1985 .... **CLC 70**
See also CA 166

Grass, Guenter (Wilhelm) 1927- ... **CLC 1, 2, 4, 6, 11, 15, 22, 32, 49, 88; DA; DAB; DAC; DAM MST, NOV**
See also AW; CA 13-16R; CANR 20, 75, 93; DA3; DLB 75, 124; MTCW 1, 2

Gratton, Thomas
See Hulme, T(homas) E(rnest)

Grau, Shirley Ann 1929- . **CLC 4, 9; SSC 15**
See also CA 89-92; CANR 22, 69; DLB 2; INT CANR-22; MTCW 1

Gravel, Fern
See Hall, James Norman

Graver, Elizabeth 1964- .... **CLC 70**
See also CA 135; CANR 71

Graves, Richard Perceval
1895-1985 .... **CLC 44**
See also CA 65-68; CANR 9, 26, 51

Graves, Robert (von Ranke)
1895-1985 .. **CLC 1, 2, 6, 11, 39, 44, 45; DAB; DAC; DAM MST, POET; PC 6**
See also CA 5-8R; 117; CANR 5, 36; CD-BLB 1914-1945; DA3; DLB 20, 100, 191; DLBD 18; DLBY 85; MTCW 1, 2; SATA 45

Graves, Valerie
See Bradley, Marion Zimmer

Gray, Alasdair (James) 1934- .... **CLC 41**
See also CA 126; CANR 47, 69; DLB 194; INT 126; MTCW 1, 2

Gray, Amlin 1946- .... **CLC 29**
See also CA 138

Gray, Francine du Plessix 1930- .... **CLC 22; DAM NOV**
See also BEST 90:3; CA 61-64; CAAS 2; CANR 11, 33, 75, 81; INT CANR-11; MTCW 1, 2

Gray, John (Henry) 1866-1934 ...... **TCLC 19**
See also CA 119; 162

Gray, Simon (James Holliday)
1936- .... **CLC 9, 14, 36**
See also AITN 1; CA 21-24R; CAAS 3; CANR 32, 69; DLB 13; MTCW 1

Gray, Spalding 1941- ..... **CLC 49, 112; DAM POP; DC 7**
See also CA 128; CANR 74; MTCW 2

Gray, Thomas 1716-1771 .... **LC 4, 40; DA; DAB; DAC; DAM MST; PC 2**
See also AW; CDBLB 1660-1789; DA3; DLB 109

Grayson, David
See Baker, Ray Stannard

Grayson, Richard (A.) 1951- .... **CLC 38**
See also CA 85-88; CANR 14, 31, 57; DLB 234

Greeley, Andrew M(oran) 1928- ..... **CLC 28; DAM POP**
See also CA 5-8R; CAAS 7; CANR 7, 43, 69; DA3; MTCW 1, 2

Green, Anna Katharine
1846-1935 .... **TCLC 63**
See also CA 112; 159; DLB 202, 221

Green, Brian
See Card, Orson Scott

Green, Hannah
See Greenberg, Joanne (Goldenberg)

Green, Hannah 1927(?)-1996 .... **CLC 3**
See also CA 73-76; CANR 59, 93

Green, Henry **CLC 2, 13, 97**
See also Yorke, Henry Vincent
See also BRWS 2; CA 175; DLB 15

Green, Julian (Hartridge) 1900-1998
See Green, Julien
See also CA 21-24R; 169; CANR 33, 87; DLB 4, 72; MTCW 1

Green, Julien **CLC 3, 11, 77**
See also Green, Julian (Hartridge)
See also MTCW 2

Green, Paul (Eliot) 1894-1981 .... **CLC 25; DAM DRAM**
See also AITN 1; CA 5-8R; 103; CANR 3; DLB 7, 9; DLBY 81

Greenberg, Ivan 1908-1973
See Rahv, Philip
See also CA 85-88

Greenberg, Joanne (Goldenberg)
1932- .... **CLC 7, 30**
See also AAYA 12; AW; CA 5-8R; CANR 14, 32, 69; SATA 25

Greenberg, Richard 1959(?)- .... **CLC 57**
See also CA 138

Greenblatt, Stephen J(ay) 1943- ...... **CLC 70**
See also CA 49-52

Greene, Bette 1934- .... **CLC 30**
See also AAYA 7; AW; CA 53-56; CANR 4; CLR 2; JRDA; MAICYA; SAAS 16; SATA 8, 102

Greene, Gael **CLC 8**
See also CA 13-16R; CANR 10

Greene, Graham (Henry)
1904-1991 .... **CLC 1, 3, 6, 9, 14, 18, 27, 37, 70, 72, 125; DA; DAB; DAC; DAM MST, NOV; SSC 29**
See also AITN 2; AW; BRWS 1; CA 13-16R; 133; CANR 35, 61; CDBLB 1945-1960; DA3; DLB 13, 15, 77, 100, 162, 201, 204; DLBY 91; MTCW 1, 2; SATA 20

Greene, Robert 1558-1592 .... **LC 41**
See also DLB 62, 167

Greer, Germaine 1939- .... **CLC 131**
See also AITN 1; CA 81-84; CANR 33, 70; MTCW 1, 2

Greer, Richard
See Silverberg, Robert

Gregor, Arthur 1923- .... **CLC 9**
See also CA 25-28R; CAAS 10; CANR 11; SATA 36

Gregor, Lee
See Pohl, Frederik

Gregory, Isabella Augusta (Persse)
1852-1932 .... **TCLC 1**
See also CA 104; 184; DLB 10

Gregory, J. Dennis
See Williams, John A(lfred)

Grekova, I. **CLC 59**

Grendon, Stephen
See Derleth, August (William)

Grenville, Kate 1950- .... **CLC 61**
See also CA 118; CANR 53, 93

Grenville, Pelham
See Wodehouse, P(elham) G(renville)

Greve, Felix Paul (Berthold Friedrich)
1879-1948
See Grove, Frederick Philip
See also CA 104; 141, 175; CANR 79; DAC; DAM MST

Grey, Zane 1872-1939 . **TCLC 6; DAM POP**
See also CA 104; 132; DA3; DLB 212; MTCW 1, 2; TCWW 2

Grieg, (Johan) Nordahl (Brun)
1902-1943 .... **TCLC 10**
See also CA 107; 189

Grieve, C(hristopher) M(urray)
1892-1978 ..... **CLC 11, 19; DAM POET**
See also MacDiarmid, Hugh; Pteleon
See also CA 5-8R; 85-88; CANR 33; MTCW 1

Griffin, Gerald 1803-1840 .... **NCLC 7**
See also DLB 159

Griffin, John Howard 1920-1980 ..... **CLC 68**
See also AITN 1; CA 1-4R; 101; CANR 2

Griffin, Peter 1942- .... **CLC 39**
See also CA 136

Griffith, D(avid Lewelyn) W(ark)
1875(?)-1948 .... **TCLC 68**
See also CA 119; 150; CANR 80

Griffith, Lawrence
See Griffith, D(avid Lewelyn) W(ark)

Griffiths, Trevor 1935- .... **CLC 13, 52**
See also CA 97-100; CANR 45; DLB 13

Griggs, Sutton (Elbert)
1872-1930 .... **TCLC 77**
See also CA 123; 186; DLB 50

Grigson, Geoffrey (Edward Harvey)
1905-1985 .... **CLC 7, 39**
See also CA 25-28R; 118; CANR 20, 33; DLB 27; MTCW 1, 2

Grillparzer, Franz 1791-1872 .. **NCLC 1; DC 14; SSC 37**
See also DLB 133

Hall, James Norman 1887-1951 ..... **TCLC 23**
  See also CA 123; 173; SATA 21
Hall, (Marguerite) Radclyffe
  1880-1943 .... **TCLC 12**
  See also CA 110; 150; CANR 83; DLB 191
Hall, Radclyffe 1880-1943
  See Hall, (Marguerite) Radclyffe
  See also MTCW 2
Hall, Rodney 1935- .... **CLC 51**
  See also CA 109; CANR 69
Halleck, Fitz-Greene 1790-1867 .... **NCLC 47**
  See also DLB 3
Halliday, Michael
  See Creasey, John
Halpern, Daniel 1945- .... **CLC 14**
  See also CA 33-36R; CANR 93
Hamburger, Michael (Peter Leopold)
  1924- .... **CLC 5, 14**
  See also CA 5-8R; CAAS 4; CANR 2, 47;
  DLB 27
Hamill, Pete 1935- .... **CLC 10**
  See also CA 25-28R; CANR 18, 71
Hamilton, Alexander
  1755(?)-1804 .... **NCLC 49**
  See also DLB 37
Hamilton, Clive
  See Lewis, C(live) S(taples)
Hamilton, Edmond 1904-1977 .... **CLC 1**
  See also CA 1-4R; CANR 3, 84; DLB 8;
  SATA 118
Hamilton, Eugene (Jacob) Lee
  See Lee-Hamilton, Eugene (Jacob)
Hamilton, Franklin
  See Silverberg, Robert
Hamilton, Gail
  See Corcoran, Barbara
Hamilton, Mollie
  See Kaye, M(ary) M(argaret)
Hamilton, (Anthony Walter) Patrick
  1904-1962 .... **CLC 51**
  See also CA 176; 113; DLB 191
Hamilton, Virginia 1936- ...... **CLC 26; DAM
  MULT**
  See also AAYA 2, 21; AW; BW 2, 3; CA
  25-28R; CANR 20, 37, 73; CLR 1, 11,
  40; DLB 33, 52; INT CANR-20; JRDA;
  MAICYA; MTCW 1, 2; SATA 4, 56, 79
Hammett, (Samuel) Dashiell
  1894-1961 .... **CLC 3, 5, 10, 19, 47; SSC
  17**
  See also AITN 1; AMWS 4; CA 81-84;
  CANR 42; CDALB 1929-1941; DA3;
  DLB 226; DLBD 6; DLBY 96; MTCW 1,
  2
Hammon, Jupiter 1720(?)-1800(?) . **NCLC 5;
  BLC 2; DAM MULT, POET; PC 16**
  See also DLB 31, 50
Hammond, Keith
  See Kuttner, Henry
Hamner, Earl (Henry), Jr. 1923- ...... **CLC 12**
  See also AITN 2; CA 73-76; DLB 6
Hampton, Christopher (James)
  1946- .... **CLC 4**
  See also CA 25-28R; DLB 13; MTCW 1
Hamsun, Knut **TCLC 2, 14, 49**
  See also Pedersen, Knut
Handke, Peter 1942- .... **CLC 5, 8, 10, 15, 38,
  134; DAM DRAM, NOV**
  See also CA 77-80; CANR 33, 75; CWW
  2; DLB 85, 124; MTCW 1, 2
Handy, W(illiam) C(hristopher)
  1873-1958 .... **TCLC 97**
  See also BW 3; CA 121; 167
Hanley, James 1901-1985 ..... **CLC 3, 5, 8, 13**
  See also CA 73-76; 117; CANR 36; DLB
  191; MTCW 1
Hannah, Barry 1942- .... **CLC 23, 38, 90**
  See also CA 108; 110; CANR 43, 68; DLB
  6, 234; INT 110; MTCW 1

Hannon, Ezra
  See Hunter, Evan
Hansberry, Lorraine (Vivian)
  1930-1965 ..... **CLC 17, 62; BLC 2; DA;
  DAB; DAC; DAM DRAM, MST,
  MULT; DC 2**
  See also AAYA 25; AMWS 4; BW 1, 3; CA
  109; 25-28R; CABS 3; CANR 58;
  CDALB 1941-1968; DA3; DLB 7, 38;
  MTCW 1, 2
Hansen, Joseph 1923- .... **CLC 38**
  See also Brock, Rose; Colton, James
  See also CA 29-32R; CAAS 17; CANR 16,
  44, 66; DLB 226; GLL 1; INT CANR-16
Hansen, Martin A(lfred)
  1909-1955 .... **TCLC 32**
  See also CA 167; DLB 214
Hansen and Philipson eds. **CLC 65**
Hanson, Kenneth O(stlin) 1922- .... **CLC 13**
  See also CA 53-56; CANR 7
Hardwick, Elizabeth (Bruce)
  1916- .... **CLC 13; DAM NOV**
  See also AMWS 3; CA 5-8R; CANR 3, 32,
  70; DA3; DLB 6; MTCW 1, 2
Hardy, Thomas 1840-1928 .. **TCLC 4, 10, 18,
  32, 48, 53, 72; DA; DAB; DAC; DAM
  MST, NOV, POET; PC 8; SSC 2**
  See also AW; CA 104; 123; CDBLB 1890-
  1914; DA3; DLB 18, 19, 135; MTCW 1,
  2
Hare, David 1947- .... **CLC 29, 58, 136**
  See also BRWS 4; CA 97-100; CANR 39,
  91; DLB 13; MTCW 1
Harewood, John
  See Van Druten, John (William)
Harford, Henry
  See Hudson, W(illiam) H(enry)
Hargrave, Leonie
  See Disch, Thomas M(ichael)
Harjo, Joy 1951- ...... **CLC 83; DAM MULT;
  PC 27**
  See also CA 114; CANR 35, 67, 91; DLB
  120, 175; MTCW 2; NNAL
Harlan, Louis R(udolph) 1922- .... **CLC 34**
  See also CA 21-24R; CANR 25, 55, 80
Harling, Robert 1951(?)- .... **CLC 53**
  See also CA 147
Harmon, William (Ruth) 1938- .... **CLC 38**
  See also CA 33-36R; CANR 14, 32, 35;
  SATA 65
Harper, F. E. W.
  See Harper, Frances Ellen Watkins
Harper, Frances E. W.
  See Harper, Frances Ellen Watkins
Harper, Frances E. Watkins
  See Harper, Frances Ellen Watkins
Harper, Frances Ellen
  See Harper, Frances Ellen Watkins
Harper, Frances Ellen Watkins
  1825-1911 ...... **TCLC 14; BLC 2; DAM
  MULT, POET; PC 21**
  See also BW 1, 3; CA 111; 125; CANR 79;
  DLB 50, 221
Harper, Michael S(teven) 1938- ... **CLC 7, 22**
  See also BW 1; CA 33-36R; CANR 24;
  DLB 41
Harper, Mrs. F. E. W.
  See Harper, Frances Ellen Watkins
Harris, Christie (Lucy) Irwin
  1907- .... **CLC 12**
  See also CA 5-8R; CANR 6, 83; CLR 47;
  DLB 88; JRDA; MAICYA; SAAS 10;
  SATA 6, 74; SATA-Essay 116
Harris, Frank 1856-1931 .... **TCLC 24**
  See also CA 109; 150; CANR 80; DLB 156,
  197
Harris, George Washington
  1814-1869 .... **NCLC 23**
  See also DLB 3, 11

Harris, Joel Chandler 1848-1908 ... **TCLC 2;
  SSC 19**
  See also AW 1; CA 104; 137; CANR 80;
  CLR 49; DLB 11, 23, 42, 78, 91; MAI-
  CYA; SATA 100
**Harris, John (Wyndham Parkes Lucas)
  Beynon** 1903-1969
  See Wyndham, John
  See also CA 102; 89-92; CANR 84; SATA
  118
Harris, MacDonald **CLC 9**
  See also Heiney, Donald (William)
Harris, Mark 1922- .... **CLC 19**
  See also CA 5-8R; CAAS 3; CANR 2, 55,
  83; DLB 2; DLBY 80
Harris, Norman **CLC 65**
Harris, (Theodore) Wilson 1921- ..... **CLC 25**
  See also BW 2, 3; CA 65-68; CAAS 16;
  CANR 11, 27, 69; DLB 117; MTCW 1
Harrison, Elizabeth Cavanna 1909-
  See Cavanna, Betty
  See also AW; CA 9-12R; CANR 6, 27, 85
Harrison, Harry (Max) 1925- .... **CLC 42**
  See also CA 1-4R; CANR 5, 21, 84; DLB
  8; SATA 4; SCFW 2
Harrison, James (Thomas) 1937- ...... **CLC 6,
  14, 33, 66; SSC 19**
  See also Harrison, Jim
  See also CA 13-16R; CANR 8, 51, 79;
  DLBY 82; INT CANR-8
Harrison, Jim
  See Harrison, James (Thomas)
  See also TCWW 2
Harrison, Kathryn 1961- .... **CLC 70**
  See also CA 144; CANR 68
Harrison, Tony 1937- .... **CLC 43, 129**
  See also BRWS 5; CA 65-68; CANR 44;
  DLB 40; MTCW 1
Harriss, Will(ard Irvin) 1922- .... **CLC 34**
  See also CA 111
Harson, Sley
  See Ellison, Harlan (Jay)
Hart, Ellis
  See Ellison, Harlan (Jay)
Hart, Josephine 1942(?)- .... **CLC 70; DAM
  POP**
  See also CA 138; CANR 70
Hart, Moss 1904-1961 .... **CLC 66; DAM
  DRAM**
  See also CA 109; 89-92; CANR 84; DLB 7
Harte, (Francis) Bret(t)
  1836(?)-1902 ... **TCLC 1, 25; DA; DAC;
  DAM MST; SSC 8**
  See also AMWS 2; AW; CA 104; 140;
  CANR 80; CDALB 1865-1917; DA3;
  DLB 12, 64, 74, 79, 186; SATA 26
Hartley, L(eslie) P(oles) 1895-1972 ... **CLC 2,
  22**
  See also CA 45-48; 37-40R; CANR 33;
  DLB 15, 139; MTCW 1, 2
Hartman, Geoffrey H. 1929- .... **CLC 27**
  See also CA 117; 125; CANR 79; DLB 67
Hartmann, Sadakichi 1869-1944 ... **TCLC 73**
  See also CA 157; DLB 54
Hartmann von Aue c. 1170-c.
  1210 .... **CMLC 15**
  See also DLB 138
Hartmann von Aue 1170-1210 ...... **CMLC 15**
Haruf, Kent 1943- .... **CLC 34**
  See also CA 149; CANR 91
Harwood, Ronald 1934- .... **CLC 32; DAM
  DRAM, MST**
  See also CA 1-4R; CANR 4, 55; DLB 13
Hasegawa Tatsunosuke
  See Futabatei, Shimei
Hasek, Jaroslav (Matej Frantisek)
  1883-1923 .... **TCLC 4**
  See also CA 104; 129; MTCW 1, 2

Herbert, George 1593-1633 ..... LC 24; DAB;
DAM POET; PC 4
See also CDBLB Before 1660; DLB 126
Herbert, Zbigniew 1924-1998 ..... CLC 9, 43;
DAM POET
See also CA 89-92; 169; CANR 36, 74;
CWW 2; DLB 232; MTCW 1
Herbst, Josephine (Frey)
1897-1969 .... CLC 34
See also CA 5-8R; 25-28R; DLB 9
Herder, Johann Gottfried von
1744-1803 .... NCLC 8
See also DLB 97
Heredia, Jose Maria 1803-1839
See also HLCS 2
Hergesheimer, Joseph 1880-1954 ... TCLC 11
See also CA 109; DLB 102, 9
Herlihy, James Leo 1927-1993 .... CLC 6
See also CA 1-4R; 143; CANR 2
Hermogenes fl. c. 175- .... CMLC 6
Hernandez, Jose 1834-1886 .... NCLC 17
Herodotus c. 484B.C.-429B.C. .... CMLC 17
See also DLB 176
Herrick, Robert 1591-1674 .... LC 13; DA;
DAB; DAC; DAM MST, POP; PC 9
See also DLB 126
Herring, Guilles
See Somerville, Edith
Herriot, James CLC 12; DAM POP
See Wight, James Alfred
See also AAYA 1; CA 148; CANR 40;
MTCW 2; SATA 86
Herris, Violet
See Hunt, Violet
Herrmann, Dorothy 1941- .... CLC 44
See also CA 107
Herrmann, Taffy
See Herrmann, Dorothy
Hersey, John (Richard) 1914-1993 .... CLC 1,
2, 7, 9, 40, 81, 97; DAM POP
See also AAYA 29; CA 17-20R; 140; CANR
33; CDALBS; DLB 6, 185; MTCW 1, 2;
SATA 25; SATA-Obit 76
Herzen, Aleksandr Ivanovich
1812-1870 .... NCLC 10, 61
Herzl, Theodor 1860-1904 .... TCLC 36
See also CA 168
Herzog, Werner 1942- .... CLC 16
See also CA 89-92
Hesiod c. 8th cent. B.C.- .... CMLC 5
See also DLB 176
Hesse, Hermann 1877-1962 ... CLC 1, 2, 3, 6,
11, 17, 25, 69; DA; DAB; DAC; DAM
MST, NOV; SSC 9
See also AW; CA 17-18; CAP 2; DA3; DLB
66; MTCW 1, 2; SATA 50
Hewes, Cady
See De Voto, Bernard (Augustine)
Heyen, William 1940- .... CLC 13, 18
See also CA 33-36R; CAAS 9; DLB 5
Heyerdahl, Thor 1914- .... CLC 26
See also CA 5-8R; CANR 5, 22, 66, 73;
MTCW 1, 2; SATA 2, 52
Heym, Georg (Theodor Franz Arthur)
1887-1912 .... TCLC 9
See also CA 106; 181
Heym, Stefan 1913- .... CLC 41
See also CA 9-12R; CANR 4; CWW 2;
DLB 69
Heyse, Paul (Johann Ludwig von)
1830-1914 .... TCLC 8
See also CA 104; DLB 129
Heyward, (Edwin) DuBose
1885-1940 .... TCLC 59
See also CA 108; 157; DLB 7, 9, 45; SATA
21
Heywood, John 1497-1580 .... LC 65

Hibbert, Eleanor Alice Burford
1906-1993 .... CLC 7; DAM POP
See also BEST 90:4; CA 17-20R; 140;
CANR 9, 28, 59; MTCW 2; SATA 2;
SATA-Obit 74
Hichens, Robert (Smythe)
1864-1950 .... TCLC 64
See also CA 162; DLB 153
Higgins, George V(incent)
1939-1999 .... CLC 4, 7, 10, 18
See also CA 77-80; 186; CAAS 5; CANR
17, 51, 89, 96; DLB 2; DLBY 81, 98; INT
CANR-17; MTCW 1
Higginson, Thomas Wentworth
1823-1911 .... TCLC 36
See also CA 162; DLB 1, 64
Higgonet, Margaret ed. CLC 65
Highet, Helen
See MacInnes, Helen (Clark)
Highsmith, (Mary) Patricia
1921-1995 .... CLC 2, 4, 14, 42, 102;
DAM NOV, POP
See also Morgan, Claire
See also BRWS 5; CA 1-4R; 147; CANR 1,
20, 48, 62; DA3; MTCW 1, 2
Highwater, Jamake (Mamake)
1942(?)- .... CLC 12
See also AAYA 7; CA 65-68; CAAS 7;
CANR 10, 34, 84; CLR 17; DLB 52;
DLBY 85; JRDA; MAICYA; SATA 32,
69; SATA-Brief 30
Highway, Tomson 1951- .... CLC 92; DAC;
DAM MULT
See also CA 151; CANR 75; CCA 1;
MTCW 2; NNAL
Hijuelos, Oscar 1951- .... CLC 65; DAM
MULT, POP; HLC 1
See also AAYA 25; BEST 90:1; CA 123;
CANR 50, 75; DA3; DLB 145; HW 1, 2;
MTCW 2
Hikmet, Nazim 1902(?)-1963 .... CLC 40
See also CA 141; 93-96
Hildegard von Bingen 1098-1179 . CMLC 20
See also DLB 148
Hildesheimer, Wolfgang 1916-1991 .. CLC 49
See also CA 101; 135; DLB 69, 124
Hill, Geoffrey (William) 1932- ...... CLC 5, 8,
18, 45; DAM POET
See also BRWS 5; CA 81-84; CANR 21,
89; CDBLB 1960 to Present; DLB 40;
MTCW 1
Hill, George Roy 1921- .... CLC 26
See also CA 110; 122
Hill, John
See Koontz, Dean R(ay)
Hill, Susan (Elizabeth) 1942- .... CLC 4, 113;
DAB; DAM MST, NOV
See also CA 33-36R; CANR 29, 69; DLB
14, 139; MTCW 1
Hillard, Asa G. III CLC 70
Hillerman, Tony 1925- . CLC 62; DAM POP
See also AAYA 6; AW; BEST 89:1; CA 29-
32R; CANR 21, 42, 65; DA3; DLB 206;
SATA 6; TCWW 2
Hillesum, Etty 1914-1943 .... TCLC 49
See also CA 137
Hilliard, Noel (Harvey) 1929-1996 ... CLC 15
See also CA 9-12R; CANR 7, 69
Hillis, Rick 1956- .... CLC 66
See also CA 134
Hilton, James 1900-1954 .... TCLC 21
See also CA 108; 169; DLB 34, 77; SATA
34
Himes, Chester (Bomar) 1909-1984 .. CLC 2,
4, 7, 18, 58, 108; BLC 2; DAM MULT
See also BW 2; CA 25-28R; 114; CANR
22, 89; DLB 2, 76, 143, 226; MTCW 1, 2
Hinde, Thomas CLC 6, 11
See also Chitty, Thomas Willes

Hine, (William) Daryl 1936- .... CLC 15
See also CA 1-4R; CAAS 15; CANR 1, 20;
DLB 60
Hinkson, Katharine Tynan
See Tynan, Katharine
Hinojosa(-Smith), Rolando (R.) 1929-
See also CA 131; CAAS 16; CANR 62;
DAM MULT; DLB 82; HLC 1; HW 1, 2;
MTCW 2
Hinton, S(usan) E(loise) 1950- .... CLC 30,
111; DA; DAB; DAC; DAM MST,
NOV
See also AAYA 2, 33; CA 81-84; CANR
32, 62, 92; CDALBS; CLR 3, 23; DA3;
JRDA; MAICYA; MTCW 1, 2; SATA 19,
58, 115
Hippius, Zinaida TCLC 9
See also Gippius, Zinaida (Nikolayevna)
Hiraoka, Kimitake 1925-1970
See Mishima, Yukio
See also CA 97-100; 29-32R; DAM DRAM;
DA3; MTCW 1, 2
Hirsch, E(ric) D(onald), Jr. 1928- .... CLC 79
See also CA 25-28R; CANR 27, 51; DLB
67; INT CANR-27; MTCW 1
Hirsch, Edward 1950- .... CLC 31, 50
See also CA 104; CANR 20, 42; DLB 120
Hitchcock, Alfred (Joseph)
1899-1980 .... CLC 16
See also AAYA 22; CA 159; 97-100; SATA
27; SATA-Obit 24
Hitler, Adolf 1889-1945 .... TCLC 53
See also CA 117; 147
Hoagland, Edward 1932- .... CLC 28
See also CA 1-4R; CANR 2, 31, 57; DLB
6; SATA 51; TCWW 2
Hoban, Russell (Conwell) 1925- . CLC 7, 25;
DAM NOV
See also CA 5-8R; CANR 23, 37, 66; CLR
3, 69; DLB 52; MAICYA; MTCW 1, 2;
SATA 1, 40, 78
Hobbes, Thomas 1588-1679 .... LC 36
See also DLB 151
Hobbs, Perry
See Blackmur, R(ichard) P(almer)
Hobson, Laura Z(ametkin)
1900-1986 .... CLC 7, 25
See also Field, Peter
See also CA 17-20R; 118; CANR 55; DLB
28; SATA 52
Hoch, Edward D(entinger) 1930-
See Queen, Ellery
See also CA 29-32R; CANR 11, 27, 51
Hochhuth, Rolf 1931- .. CLC 4, 11, 18; DAM
DRAM
See also CA 5-8R; CANR 33, 75; CWW 2;
DLB 124; MTCW 1, 2
Hochman, Sandra 1936- .... CLC 3, 8
See also CA 5-8R; DLB 5
Hochwaelder, Fritz 1911-1986 .... CLC 36;
DAM DRAM
See also CA 29-32R; 120; CANR 42;
MTCW 1
Hochwalder, Fritz
See Hochwaelder, Fritz
Hocking, Mary (Eunice) 1921- .... CLC 13
See also CA 101; CANR 18, 40
Hodgins, Jack 1938- .... CLC 23
See also CA 93-96; DLB 60
Hodgson, William Hope
1877(?)-1918 .... TCLC 13
See also CA 111; 164; DLB 70, 153, 156,
178; MTCW 2
Hoeg, Peter 1957- .... CLC 95
See also CA 151; CANR 75; DA3; MTCW
2
Hoffman, Alice 1952- ... CLC 51; DAM NOV
See also AAYA 37; CA 77-80; CANR 34,
66; MTCW 1, 2

Hrabal, Bohumil 1914-1997 .... **CLC 13, 67**
See also CA 106; 156; CAAS 12; CANR
57; CWW 2; DLB 232

Hroswitha of Gandersheim c. 935-c.
1000 .... **CMLC 29**
See also DLB 148

Hsi, Chu 1130-1200 .... **CMLC 42**

Hsun, Lu
See Lu Hsun

Hubbard, L(afayette) Ron(ald)
1911-1986 .... **CLC 43; DAM POP**
See also CA 77-80; 118; CANR 52; DA3;
MTCW 2

Huch, Ricarda (Octavia)
1864-1947 .... **TCLC 13**
See also CA 111; 189; DLB 66

Huddle, David 1942- .... **CLC 49**
See also CA 57-60; CAAS 20; CANR 89;
DLB 130

Hudson, Jeffrey
See Crichton, (John) Michael

Hudson, W(illiam) H(enry)
1841-1922 .... **TCLC 29**
See also CA 115; 190; DLB 98, 153, 174;
SATA 35

Hueffer, Ford Madox
See Ford, Ford Madox

Hughart, Barry 1934- .... **CLC 39**
See also CA 137

Hughes, Colin
See Creasey, John

Hughes, David (John) 1930- .... **CLC 48**
See also CA 116; 129; DLB 14

Hughes, Edward James
See Hughes, Ted
See also DAM MST, POET; DA3

Hughes, (James) Langston
1902-1967 .... **CLC 1, 5, 10, 15, 35, 44,**
108; BLC 2; DA; DAB; DAC; DAM
DRAM, MST, MULT, POET; DC 3;
PC 1; SSC 6
See also AAYA 12; AMWS 1; AW; BW 1,
3; CA 1-4R; 25-28R; CANR 1, 34, 82;
CDALB 1929-1941; CLR 17; DA3; DLB
4, 7, 48, 51, 86, 228; JRDA; MAICYA;
MTCW 1, 2; SATA 4, 33

Hughes, Richard (Arthur Warren)
1900-1976 .... **CLC 1, 11; DAM NOV**
See also CA 5-8R; 65-68; CANR 4; DLB
15, 161; MTCW 1; SATA 8; SATA-Obit
25

Hughes, Ted 1930-1998 . **CLC 2, 4, 9, 14, 37,**
119; DAB; DAC; PC 7
See also Hughes, Edward James
See also AW; BRWS 1; CA 1-4R; 171;
CANR 1, 33, 66; CLR 3; DLB 40, 161;
MAICYA; MTCW 1, 2; SATA 49; SATA-
Brief 27; SATA-Obit 107

Hugo, Richard F(ranklin)
1923-1982 .... **CLC 6, 18, 32; DAM**
POET
See also CA 49-52; 108; CANR 3; DLB 5,
206

Hugo, Victor (Marie) 1802-1885 .... **NCLC 3,**
10, 21; DA; DAB; DAC; DAM DRAM,
MST, NOV, POET; PC 17
See also AAYA 28; AW; DA3; DLB 119,
192; SATA 47

Huidobro, Vicente
See Huidobro Fernandez, Vicente Garcia

Huidobro Fernandez, Vicente Garcia
1893-1948 .... **TCLC 31**
See also CA 131; HW 1

Hulme, Keri 1947- .... **CLC 39, 130**
See also CA 125; CANR 69; INT 125

Hulme, T(homas) E(rnest)
1883-1917 .... **TCLC 21**
See also CA 117; DLB 19

Hume, David 1711-1776 .... **LC 7, 56**
See also BRWS 3; DLB 104

Humphrey, William 1924-1997 .... **CLC 45**
See also CA 77-80; 160; CANR 68; DLB
212; TCWW 2

Humphreys, Emyr Owen 1919- .... **CLC 47**
See also CA 5-8R; CANR 3, 24; DLB 15

Humphreys, Josephine 1945- ..... **CLC 34, 57**
See also CA 121; 127; INT 127

Huneker, James Gibbons
1860-1921 .... **TCLC 65**
See also DLB 71

Hungerford, Pixie
See Brinsmead, H(esba) F(ay)

Hunt, E(verette) Howard, (Jr.)
1918- .... **CLC 3**
See also AITN 1; CA 45-48; CANR 2, 47

Hunt, Francesca
See Holland, Isabelle

Hunt, Howard
See Hunt, E(verette) Howard, (Jr.)

Hunt, Kyle
See Creasey, John

Hunt, (James Henry) Leigh
1784-1859 .... **NCLC 1, 70; DAM POET**
See also DLB 96, 110, 144

Hunt, Marsha 1946- .... **CLC 70**
See also BW 2, 3; CA 143; CANR 79

Hunt, Violet 1866(?)-1942 .... **TCLC 53**
See also CA 184; DLB 162, 197

Hunter, E. Waldo
See Sturgeon, Theodore (Hamilton)

Hunter, Evan 1926- .... **CLC 11, 31; DAM**
POP
See also CA 5-8R; CANR 5, 38, 62; DLBY
82; INT CANR-5; MTCW 1; SATA 25

Hunter, Kristin (Eggleston) 1931- .... **CLC 35**
See also AITN 1; AW; BW 1; CA 13-16R;
CANR 13; CLR 3; DLB 33; INT CANR-
13; MAICYA; SAAS 10; SATA 12

Hunter, Mary
See Austin, Mary (Hunter)

Hunter, Mollie 1922- .... **CLC 21**
See also McIlwraith, Maureen Mollie
Hunter
See also AAYA 13; AW; CANR 37, 78;
CLR 25; DLB 161; JRDA; MAICYA;
SAAS 7; SATA 54, 106

Hunter, Robert (?)-1734 .... **LC 7**

Hurston, Zora Neale 1891-1960 .. **CLC 7, 30,**
61; BLC 2; DA; DAC; DAM MST,
MULT, NOV; DC 12; SSC 4
See also AAYA 15; AW; BW 1, 3; CA 85-
88; CANR 61; CDALBS; DA3; DLB 51,
86; MTCW 1, 2

Husserl, E. G.
See Husserl, Edmund (Gustav Albrecht)

Husserl, Edmund (Gustav Albrecht)
1859-1938 .... **TCLC 100**
See also CA 116; 133

Huston, John (Marcellus)
1906-1987 .... **CLC 20**
See also CA 73-76; 123; CANR 34; DLB
26

Hustvedt, Siri 1955- .... **CLC 76**
See also CA 137

Hutten, Ulrich von 1488-1523 .... **LC 16**
See also DLB 179

Huxley, Aldous (Leonard)
1894-1963 .... **CLC 1, 3, 4, 5, 8, 11, 18,**
35, 79; DA; DAB; DAC; DAM MST,
NOV; SSC 39
See also AAYA 11; AW; CA 85-88; CANR
44; CDBLB 1914-1945; DA3; DLB 36,
100, 162, 195; MTCW 1, 2; SATA 63;
SCFW 2

Huxley, T(homas) H(enry)
1825-1895 .... **NCLC 67**
See also DLB 57

Huysmans, Joris-Karl 1848-1907 ... **TCLC 7,**
69
See also CA 104; 165; DLB 123

Hwang, David Henry 1957- .. **CLC 55; DAM**
DRAM; DC 4
See also CA 127; 132; CANR 76; DA3;
DLB 212; INT 132; MTCW 2

Hyde, Anthony 1946- .... **CLC 42**
See also Chase, Nicholas
See also CA 136; CCA 1

Hyde, Margaret O(ldroyd) 1917- ..... **CLC 21**
See also CA 1-4R; CANR 1, 36; CLR 23;
JRDA; MAICYA; SAAS 8; SATA 1, 42,
76

Hynes, James 1956(?)- .... **CLC 65**
See also CA 164

Hypatia c. 370-415 .... **CMLC 35**

Ian, Janis 1951- .... **CLC 21**
See also CA 105; 187

Ibanez, Vicente Blasco
See Blasco Iba

Ibarbourou, Juana de 1895-1979
See also HLCS 2; HW 1

Ibarguengoitia, Jorge 1928-1983 ...... **CLC 37**
See also CA 124; 113; HW 1

Ibsen, Henrik (Johan) 1828-1906 ... **TCLC 2,**
8, 16, 37, 52; DA; DAB; DAC; DAM
DRAM, MST; DC 2
See also AW; CA 104; 141; DA3

Ibuse, Masuji 1898-1993 .... **CLC 22**
See also CA 127; 141; DLB 180

Ichikawa, Kon 1915- .... **CLC 20**
See also CA 121

Ichiyo, Higuchi 1872-1896 .... **NCLC 49**

Idle, Eric 1943-2000 .... **CLC 21**
See also Monty Python
See also CA 116; CANR 35, 91

Ignatow, David 1914-1997 .. **CLC 4, 7, 14, 40**
See also CA 9-12R; 162; CAAS 3; CANR
31, 57, 96; DLB 5

Ignotus
See Strachey, (Giles) Lytton

Ihimaera, Witi 1944- .... **CLC 46**
See also CA 77-80

Ilf, Ilya TCLC 21
See also Fainzilberg, Ilya Arnoldovich

Illyes, Gyula 1902-1983 .... **PC 16**
See also CA 114; 109; DLB 215

Immermann, Karl (Lebrecht)
1796-1840 .... **NCLC 4, 49**
See also DLB 133

Ince, Thomas H. 1882-1924 .... **TCLC 89**

Inchbald, Elizabeth 1753-1821 ...... **NCLC 62**
See also DLB 39, 89

Inclan, Ramon (Maria) del Valle
See Valle-Inclan, Ramon (Maria) del

Infante, G(uillermo) Cabrera
See Cabrera Infante, G(uillermo)

Ingalls, Rachel (Holmes) 1940- .... **CLC 42**
See also CA 123; 127

Ingamells, Reginald Charles
See Ingamells, Rex

Ingamells, Rex 1913-1955 .... **TCLC 35**
See also CA 167

Inge, William (Motter) 1913-1973 ..... **CLC 1,**
8, 19; DAM DRAM
See also CA 9-12R; CDALB 1941-1968;
DA3; DLB 7; MTCW 1, 2

Ingelow, Jean 1820-1897 .... **NCLC 39**
See also DLB 35, 163; SATA 33

Ingram, Willis J.
See Harris, Mark

Innaurato, Albert (F.) 1948(?)- ... **CLC 21, 60**
See also CA 115; 122; CANR 78; INT 122

Innes, Michael
See Stewart, J(ohn) I(nnes) M(ackintosh)

Innis, Harold Adams 1894-1952 .... **TCLC 77**
See also CA 181; DLB 88

Kerrigan, (Thomas) Anthony 1918- .. **CLC 4, 6**
See also CA 49-52; CAAS 11; CANR 4
Kerry, Lois
See Duncan, Lois
Kesey, Ken (Elton) 1935- ..... **CLC 1, 3, 6, 11, 46, 64; DA; DAB; DAC; DAM MST, NOV, POP**
See also AAYA 25; AW; CA 1-4R; CANR 22, 38, 66; CDALB 1968-1988; DA3; DLB 2, 16, 206; MTCW 1, 2; SATA 66
Kesselring, Joseph (Otto) 1902-1967 .... **CLC 45; DAM DRAM, MST**
See also CA 150
Kessler, Jascha (Frederick) 1929- ...... **CLC 4**
See also CA 17-20R; CANR 8, 48
Kettelkamp, Larry (Dale) 1933- .... **CLC 12**
See also CA 29-32R; CANR 16; SAAS 3; SATA 2
Key, Ellen (Karolina Sofia) 1849-1926 .... **TCLC 65**
Keyber, Conny
See Fielding, Henry
Keyes, Daniel 1927- ...... **CLC 80; DA; DAC; DAM MST, NOV**
See also AAYA 23; CA 17-20R, 181; CAAE 181; CANR 10, 26, 54, 74; DA3; MTCW 2; SATA 37
Keynes, John Maynard 1883-1946 .... **TCLC 64**
See also CA 114; 162, 163; DLBD 10; MTCW 2
Khanshendel, Chiron
See Rose, Wendy
Khayyam, Omar 1048-1131 .... **CMLC 11; DAM POET; PC 8**
See also DA3
Kherdian, David 1931- .... **CLC 6, 9**
See also CA 21-24R; CAAS 2; CANR 39, 78; CLR 24; JRDA; MAICYA; SATA 16, 74
Khlebnikov, Velimir TCLC 20
See also Khlebnikov, Viktor Vladimirovich
Khlebnikov, Viktor Vladimirovich 1885-1922
See Khlebnikov, Velimir
See also CA 117
Khodasevich, Vladislav (Felitsianovich) 1886-1939 .... **TCLC 15**
See also CA 115
Kielland, Alexander Lange 1849-1906 .... **TCLC 5**
See also CA 104
Kiely, Benedict 1919- .... **CLC 23, 43**
See also CA 1-4R; CANR 2, 84; DLB 15
Kienzle, William X(avier) 1928- ..... **CLC 25; DAM POP**
See also CA 93-96; CAAS 1; CANR 9, 31, 59; DA3; INT CANR-31; MTCW 1, 2
Kierkegaard, Soren 1813-1855 ..... **NCLC 34, 78**
Kieslowski, Krzysztof 1941-1996 .... **CLC 120**
See also CA 147; 151
Killens, John Oliver 1916-1987 .... **CLC 10**
See also BW 2; CA 77-80; 123; CAAS 2; CANR 26; DLB 33
Killigrew, Anne 1660-1685 .... **LC 4**
See also DLB 131
Killigrew, Thomas 1612-1683 .... **LC 57**
See also DLB 58
Kim
See Simenon, Georges (Jacques Christian)
Kincaid, Jamaica 1949- ..... **CLC 43, 68, 137; BLC 2; DAM MULT, NOV**
See also AAYA 13; AMWS 7; AW; BW 2, 3; CA 125; CANR 47, 59, 95; CDALBS; CLR 63; DA3; DLB 157, 227; MTCW 2

King, Francis (Henry) 1923- .... **CLC 8, 53; DAM NOV**
See also CA 1-4R; CANR 1, 33, 86; DLB 15, 139; MTCW 1
King, Kennedy
See Brown, George Douglas
King, Martin Luther, Jr. 1929-1968 .... **CLC 83; BLC 2; DA; DAB; DAC; DAM MST, MULT**
See also AW; BW 2, 3; CA 25-28R; CANR 27, 44; CAP 2; DA3; MTCW 1, 2; SATA 14
King, Stephen (Edwin) 1947- .... **CLC 12, 26, 37, 61, 113; DAM NOV, POP; SSC 17**
See also AAYA 1, 17; AMWS 5; AW 1; BEST 90:1; CA 61-64; CANR 1, 30, 52, 76; DA3; DLB 143; DLBY 80; JRDA; MTCW 1, 2; SATA 9, 55
King, Steve
See King, Stephen (Edwin)
King, Thomas 1943- ... **CLC 89; DAC; DAM MULT**
See also CA 144; CANR 95; CCA 1; DLB 175; NNAL; SATA 96
Kingman, Lee CLC 17
See also Natti, (Mary) Lee
See also SAAS 3; SATA 1, 67
Kingsley, Charles 1819-1875 .... **NCLC 35**
See also AW 2; DLB 21, 32, 163, 190
Kingsley, Sidney 1906-1995 .... **CLC 44**
See also CA 85-88; 147; DLB 7
Kingsolver, Barbara 1955- .... **CLC 55, 81, 130; DAM POP**
See also AAYA 15; AMWS 7; CA 129; 134; CANR 60, 96; CDALBS; DA3; DLB 206; INT CA-134; MTCW 2
Kingston, Maxine (Ting Ting) Hong 1940- .... **CLC 12, 19, 58, 121; DAM MULT, NOV**
See also AAYA 8; AW; CA 69-72; CANR 13, 38, 74, 87; CDALBS; DA3; DLB 173, 212; DLBY 80; INT CANR-13; MTCW 1, 2; SATA 53
Kinnell, Galway 1927- ..... **CLC 1, 2, 3, 5, 13, 29, 129; PC 26**
See also AMWS 3; CA 9-12R; CANR 10, 34, 66; DLB 5; DLBY 87; INT CANR-34; MTCW 1, 2
Kinsella, Thomas 1928- .... **CLC 4, 19, 138**
See also BRWS 5; CA 17-20R; CANR 15; DLB 27; MTCW 1, 2
Kinsella, W(illiam) P(atrick) 1935- . **CLC 27, 43; DAC; DAM NOV, POP**
See also AAYA 7; CA 97-100; CAAS 7; CANR 21, 35, 66, 75; INT CANR-21; MTCW 1, 2
Kinsey, Alfred C(harles) 1894-1956 .... **TCLC 91**
See also CA 115; 170; MTCW 2
Kipling, (Joseph) Rudyard 1865-1936 .... **TCLC 8, 17; DA; DAB; DAC; DAM MST, POET; PC 3; SSC 5**
See also AAYA 32; AW; CA 105; 120; CANR 33; CDBLB 1890-1914; CLR 39, 65; DA3; DLB 19, 34, 141, 156; MAICYA; MTCW 1, 2; SATA 100
Kirkland, Caroline M. 1801-1864 . **NCLC 85**
See also DLB 3, 73, 74; DLBD 13
Kirkup, James 1918- .... **CLC 1**
See also CA 1-4R; CAAS 4; CANR 2; DLB 27; SATA 12
Kirkwood, James 1930(?)-1989 .... **CLC 9**
See also AITN 2; CA 1-4R; 128; CANR 6, 40; GLL 2
Kirshner, Sidney
See Kingsley, Sidney
Kis, Danilo 1935-1989 .... **CLC 57**
See also CA 109; 118; 129; CANR 61; DLB 181; MTCW 1

Kissinger, Henry A(lfred) 1923- ..... **CLC 137**
See also CA 1-4R; CANR 2, 33, 66; MTCW 1
Kivi, Aleksis 1834-1872 .... **NCLC 30**
Kizer, Carolyn (Ashley) 1925- ... **CLC 15, 39, 80; DAM POET**
See also CA 65-68; CAAS 5; CANR 24, 70; DLB 5, 169; MTCW 2
Klabund 1890-1928 .... **TCLC 44**
See also CA 162; DLB 66
Klappert, Peter 1942- .... **CLC 57**
See also CA 33-36R; DLB 5
Klein, A(braham) M(oses) 1909-1972 . **CLC 19; DAB; DAC; DAM MST**
See also CA 101; 37-40R; DLB 68
Klein, Norma 1938-1989 .... **CLC 30**
See also AAYA 2, 35; AW; CA 41-44R; 128; CANR 15, 37; CLR 2, 19; INT CANR-15; JRDA; MAICYA; SAAS 1; SATA 7, 57
Klein, T(heodore) E(ibon) D(onald) 1947- .... **CLC 34**
See also CA 119; CANR 44, 75
Kleist, Heinrich von 1777-1811 ...... **NCLC 2, 37; DAM DRAM; SSC 22**
See also DLB 90
Klima, Ivan 1931- .... **CLC 56; DAM NOV**
See also CA 25-28R; CANR 17, 50, 91; CWW 2; DLB 232
Klimentov, Andrei Platonovich 1899-1951 .... **TCLC 14; SSC 42**
See also CA 108
Klinger, Friedrich Maximilian von 1752-1831 .... **NCLC 1**
See also DLB 94
Klingsor the Magician
See Hartmann, Sadakichi
Klopstock, Friedrich Gottlieb 1724-1803 .... **NCLC 11**
See also DLB 97
Knapp, Caroline 1959- .... **CLC 99**
See also CA 154
Knebel, Fletcher 1911-1993 .... **CLC 14**
See also AITN 1; CA 1-4R; 140; CAAS 3; CANR 1, 36; SATA 36; SATA-Obit 75
Knickerbocker, Diedrich
See Irving, Washington
Knight, Etheridge 1931-1991 . **CLC 40; BLC 2; DAM POET; PC 14**
See also BW 1, 3; CA 21-24R; 133; CANR 23, 82; DLB 41; MTCW 2
Knight, Sarah Kemble 1666-1727 .... **LC 7**
See also DLB 24, 200
Knister, Raymond 1899-1932 .... **TCLC 56**
See also CA 186; DLB 68
Knowles, John 1926- . **CLC 1, 4, 10, 26; DA; DAC; DAM MST, NOV**
See also AAYA 10; AW; CA 17-20R; CANR 40, 74, 76; CDALB 1968-1988; DLB 6; MTCW 1, 2; SATA 8, 89
Knox, Calvin M.
See Silverberg, Robert
Knox, John c. 1505-1572 .... **LC 37**
See also DLB 132
Knye, Cassandra
See Disch, Thomas M(ichael)
Koch, C(hristopher) J(ohn) 1932- .... **CLC 42**
See also CA 127; CANR 84
Koch, Christopher
See Koch, C(hristopher) J(ohn)
Koch, Kenneth 1925- .... **CLC 5, 8, 44; DAM POET**
See also CA 1-4R; CANR 6, 36, 57; DLB 5; INT CANR-36; MTCW 2; SATA 65
Kochanowski, Jan 1530-1584 .... **LC 10**
Kock, Charles Paul de 1794-1871 . **NCLC 16**

La Guma, (Justin) Alex(ander)
1925-1985 .... **CLC 19; BLCS; DAM NOV**
See also BW 1, 3; CA 49-52; 118; CANR 25, 81; DLB 117, 225; MTCW 1, 2

Laidlaw, A. K.
See Grieve, C(hristopher) M(urray)

Lainez, Manuel Mujica
See Mujica Lainez, Manuel
See also HW 1

Laing, R(onald) D(avid) 1927-1989 . **CLC 95**
See also CA 107; 129; CANR 34; MTCW 1

Lamartine, Alphonse (Marie Louis Prat) de
1790-1869 . **NCLC 11; DAM POET; PC 16**

Lamb, Charles 1775-1834 ..... **NCLC 10; DA; DAB; DAC; DAM MST**
See also AW; CDBLB 1789-1832; DLB 93, 107, 163; SATA 17

Lamb, Lady Caroline 1785-1828 ... **NCLC 38**
See also DLB 116

Lamming, George (William) 1927- ... **CLC 2, 4, 66; BLC 2; DAM MULT**
See also BW 2, 3; CA 85-88; CANR 26, 76; DLB 125; MTCW 1, 2

L'Amour, Louis (Dearborn)
1908-1988 ...... **CLC 25, 55; DAM NOV, POP**
See also Burns, Tex; Mayo, Jim
See also AAYA 16; AITN 2; BEST 89:2; CA 1-4R; 125; CANR 3, 25, 40; DA3; DLB 206; DLBY 80; MTCW 1, 2

Lampedusa, Giuseppe (Tomasi) di TCLC 13
See also Tomasi di Lampedusa, Giuseppe
See also CA 164; DLB 177; MTCW 2

Lampman, Archibald 1861-1899 ... **NCLC 25**
See also DLB 92

Lancaster, Bruce 1896-1963 .... **CLC 36**
See also CA 9-10; CANR 70; CAP 1; SATA 9

Lanchester, John CLC 99

Landau, Mark Alexandrovich
See Aldanov, Mark (Alexandrovich)

Landau-Aldanov, Mark Alexandrovich
See Aldanov, Mark (Alexandrovich)

Landis, Jerry
See Simon, Paul (Frederick)

Landis, John 1950- .... **CLC 26**
See also CA 112; 122

Landolfi, Tommaso 1908-1979 .... **CLC 11, 49**
See also CA 127; 117; DLB 177

Landon, Letitia Elizabeth
1802-1838 .... **NCLC 15**
See also DLB 96

Landor, Walter Savage
1775-1864 .... **NCLC 14**
See also DLB 93, 107

Landwirth, Heinz 1927-
See Lind, Jakov
See also CA 9-12R; CANR 7

Lane, Patrick 1939- ... **CLC 25; DAM POET**
See also CA 97-100; CANR 54; DLB 53; INT 97-100

Lang, Andrew 1844-1912 .... **TCLC 16**
See also CA 114; 137; CANR 85; DLB 98, 141, 184; MAICYA; SATA 16

Lang, Fritz 1890-1976 .... **CLC 20, 103**
See also CA 77-80; 69-72; CANR 30

Lange, John
See Crichton, (John) Michael

Langer, Elinor 1939- .... **CLC 34**
See also CA 121

Langland, William 1332(?)-1400(?) ... **LC 19; DA; DAB; DAC; DAM MST, POET**
See also DLB 146

Langstaff, Launcelot
See Irving, Washington

Lanier, Sidney 1842-1881 ..... **NCLC 6; DAM POET**
See also AMWS 1; DLB 64; DLBD 13; MAICYA; SATA 18

Lanyer, Aemilia 1569-1645 .... **LC 10, 30**
See also DLB 121

Lao-Tzu
See Lao Tzu

Lao Tzu fl. 6046th cent. B.C.-490 ... **CMLC 7**

Lapine, James (Elliot) 1949- .... **CLC 39**
See also CA 123; 130; CANR 54; INT 130

Larbaud, Valery (Nicolas)
1881-1957 .... **TCLC 9**
See also CA 106; 152

Lardner, Ring
See Lardner, Ring(gold) W(ilmer)

Lardner, Ring W., Jr.
See Lardner, Ring(gold) W(ilmer)

Lardner, Ring(gold) W(ilmer)
1885-1933 .... **TCLC 2, 14; SSC 32**
See also CA 104; 131; CDALB 1917-1929; DLB 11, 25, 86, 171; DLBD 16; MTCW 1, 2

Laredo, Betty
See Codrescu, Andrei

Larkin, Maia
See Wojciechowska, Maia (Teresa)

Larkin, Philip (Arthur) 1922-1985 ... **CLC 3, 5, 8, 9, 13, 18, 33, 39, 64; DAB; DAM MST, POET; PC 21**
See also BRWS 1; CA 5-8R; 117; CANR 24, 62; CDBLB 1960 to Present; DA3; DLB 27; MTCW 1, 2

Larra (y Sanchez de Castro), Mariano Jose
de 1809-1837 .... **NCLC 17**

Larsen, Eric 1941- .... **CLC 55**
See also CA 132

Larsen, Nella 1893-1963 .... **CLC 37; BLC 2; DAM MULT**
See also BW 1; CA 125; CANR 83; DLB 51

Larson, Charles R(aymond) 1938- ... **CLC 31**
See also CA 53-56; CANR 4

Larson, Jonathan 1961-1996 .... **CLC 99**
See also AAYA 28; CA 156

Las Casas, Bartolome de 1474-1566 ... **LC 31**

Lasch, Christopher 1932-1994 .... **CLC 102**
See also CA 73-76; 144; CANR 25; MTCW 1, 2

Lasker-Schueler, Else 1869-1945 ... **TCLC 57**
See also CA 183; DLB 66, 124

Laski, Harold J(oseph) 1893-1950 . **TCLC 79**
See also CA 188'

Latham, Jean Lee 1902-1995 .... **CLC 12**
See also AITN 1; AW; CA 5-8R; CANR 7, 84; CLR 50; MAICYA; SATA 2, 68

Latham, Mavis
See Clark, Mavis Thorpe

Lathen, Emma CLC 2
See also Hennissart, Martha; Latsis, Mary J(ane)

Lathrop, Francis
See Leiber, Fritz (Reuter, Jr.)

Latsis, Mary J(ane) 1927(?)-1997
See Lathen, Emma
See also CA 85-88; 162

Lattimore, Richmond (Alexander)
1906-1984 .... **CLC 3**
See also CA 1-4R; 112; CANR 1

Laughlin, James 1914-1997 .... **CLC 49**
See also CA 21-24R; 162; CAAS 22; CANR 9, 47; DLB 48; DLBY 96, 97

Laurence, (Jean) Margaret (Wemyss)
1926-1987 . **CLC 3, 6, 13, 50, 62; DAC; DAM MST; SSC 7**
See also CA 5-8R; 121; CANR 33; DLB 53; MTCW 1, 2; SATA-Obit 50

Laurent, Antoine 1952- .... **CLC 50**

Lauscher, Hermann
See Hesse, Hermann

Lautreamont, Comte de
1846-1870 .... **NCLC 12; SSC 14**

Laverty, Donald
See Blish, James (Benjamin)

Lavin, Mary 1912-1996 . **CLC 4, 18, 99; SSC 4**
See also CA 9-12R; 151; CANR 33; DLB 15; MTCW 1

Lavond, Paul Dennis
See Kornbluth, C(yril) M.; Pohl, Frederik

Lawler, Raymond Evenor 1922- .... **CLC 58**
See also CA 103

Lawrence, D(avid) H(erbert Richards)
1885-1930 .... **TCLC 2, 9, 16, 33, 48, 61, 93; DA; DAB; DAC; DAM MST, NOV, POET; SSC 4, 19**
See also Chambers, Jessie
See also AW; CA 104; 121; CDBLB 1914-1945; DA3; DLB 10, 19, 36, 98, 162, 195; MTCW 1, 2

Lawrence, T(homas) E(dward)
1888-1935 .... **TCLC 18**
See also Dale, Colin
See also BRWS 2; CA 115; 167; DLB 195

Lawrence of Arabia
See Lawrence, T(homas) E(dward)

Lawson, Henry (Archibald Hertzberg)
1867-1922 .... **TCLC 27; SSC 18**
See also CA 120; 181; DLB 230

Lawton, Dennis
See Faust, Frederick (Schiller)

Laxness, Halldor CLC 25
See also Gudjonsson, Halldor Kiljan

Layamon fl. c. 1200- .... **CMLC 10**
See also DLB 146

Laye, Camara 1928-1980 ... **CLC 4, 38; BLC 2; DAM MULT**
See also BW 1; CA 85-88; 97-100; CANR 25; MTCW 1, 2

Layton, Irving (Peter) 1912- .... **CLC 2, 15; DAC; DAM MST, POET**
See also CA 1-4R; CANR 2, 33, 43, 66; DLB 88; MTCW 1, 2

Lazarus, Emma 1849-1887 .... **NCLC 8**

Lazarus, Felix
See Cable, George Washington

Lazarus, Henry
See Slavitt, David R(ytman)

Lea, Joan
See Neufeld, John (Arthur)

Leacock, Stephen (Butler)
1869-1944 .... **TCLC 2; DAC; DAM MST; SSC 39**
See also CA 104; 141; CANR 80; DLB 92; MTCW 2

Lear, Edward 1812-1888 .... **NCLC 3**
See also CLR 1; DLB 32, 163, 166; MAICYA; SATA 18, 100

Lear, Norman (Milton) 1922- .... **CLC 12**
See also CA 73-76

Leautaud, Paul 1872-1956 .... **TCLC 83**
See also DLB 65

Leavis, F(rank) R(aymond)
1895-1978 .... **CLC 24**
See also CA 21-24R; 77-80; CANR 44; DLB 242; MTCW 1, 2

Leavitt, David 1961- ..... **CLC 34; DAM POP**
See also CA 116; 122; CANR 50, 62; DA3; DLB 130; GLL 1; INT 122; MTCW 2

Leblanc, Maurice (Marie Emile)
1864-1941 .... **TCLC 49**
See also CA 110

Lebowitz, Fran(ces Ann) 1951(?)- ... **CLC 11, 36**
See also CA 81-84; CANR 14, 60, 70; INT CANR-14; MTCW 1

Levin, Meyer 1905-1981 .... **CLC 7; DAM POP**
See also AITN 1; CA 9-12R; 104; CANR 15; DLB 9, 28; DLBY 81; SATA 21; SATA-Obit 27

Levine, Norman 1924- .... **CLC 54**
See also CA 73-76; CAAS 23; CANR 14, 70; DLB 88

Levine, Philip 1928- .. **CLC 2, 4, 5, 9, 14, 33, 118; DAM POET; PC 22**
See also AMWS 5; CA 9-12R; CANR 9, 37, 52; DLB 5

Levinson, Deirdre 1931- .... **CLC 49**
See also CA 73-76; CANR 70

Levi-Strauss, Claude 1908- .... **CLC 38**
See also CA 1-4R; CANR 6, 32, 57; DLB 242; MTCW 1, 2

Levitin, Sonia (Wolff) 1934- .... **CLC 17**
See also AAYA 13; AW; CA 29-32R; CANR 14, 32, 79; CLR 53; JRDA; MAICYA; SAAS 2; SATA 4, 68, 119

Levon, O. U.
See Kesey, Ken (Elton)

Levy, Amy 1861-1889 .... **NCLC 59**
See also DLB 156, 240

Lewes, George Henry 1817-1878 ... **NCLC 25**
See also DLB 55, 144

Lewis, Alun 1915-1944 .... **TCLC 3; SSC 40**
See also CA 104; 188; DLB 20, 162

Lewis, C. Day
See Day Lewis, C(ecil)

Lewis, C(live) S(taples) 1898-1963 .... **CLC 1, 3, 6, 14, 27, 124; DA; DAB; DAC; DAM MST, NOV, POP**
See also AAYA 3; BRWS 3; CA 81-84; CANR 33, 71; CDBLB 1945-1960; CLR 3, 27; DA3; DLB 15, 100, 160; JRDA; MAICYA; MTCW 1, 2; SATA 13, 100

Lewis, Janet 1899-1998 .... **CLC 41**
See also Winters, Janet Lewis
See also CA 9-12R; 172; CANR 29, 63; CAP 1; DLBY 87; TCWW 2

Lewis, Matthew Gregory
1775-1818 .... **NCLC 11, 62**
See also DLB 39, 158, 178

Lewis, (Harry) Sinclair 1885-1951 . **TCLC 4, 13, 23, 39; DA; DAB; DAC; DAM MST, NOV**
See also AW; CA 104; 133; CDALB 1917-1929; DA3; DLB 9, 102; DLBD 1; MTCW 1, 2

Lewis, (Percy) Wyndham
1884(?)-1957 .. **TCLC 2, 9, 104; SSC 34**
See also CA 104; 157; DLB 15; MTCW 2

Lewisohn, Ludwig 1883-1955 .... **TCLC 19**
See also CA 107; DLB 4, 9, 28, 102

Lewton, Val 1904-1951 .... **TCLC 76**
See also IDFW 3

Leyner, Mark 1956- .... **CLC 92**
See also CA 110; CANR 28, 53; DA3; MTCW 2

Lezama Lima, Jose 1910-1976 .... **CLC 4, 10, 101; DAM MULT; HLCS 1**
See also CA 77-80; CANR 71; DLB 113; HW 1, 2

L'Heureux, John (Clarke) 1934- ...... **CLC 52**
See also CA 13-16R; CANR 23, 45, 88

Liddell, C. H.
See Kuttner, Henry

Lie, Jonas (Lauritz Idemil)
1833-1908(?) .... **TCLC 5**
See also CA 115

Lieber, Joel 1937-1971 .... **CLC 6**
See also CA 73-76; 29-32R

Lieber, Stanley Martin
See Lee, Stan

Lieberman, Laurence (James)
1935- .... **CLC 4, 36**
See also CA 17-20R; CANR 8, 36, 89

Lieh Tzu fl. 7th cent. B.C.-5th cent.
B.C. .... **CMLC 27**

Lieksman, Anders
See Haavikko, Paavo Juhani

Li Fei-kan 1904-
See Pa Chin
See also CA 105

Lifton, Robert Jay 1926- .... **CLC 67**
See also CA 17-20R; CANR 27, 78; INT CANR-27; SATA 66

Lightfoot, Gordon 1938- .... **CLC 26**
See also CA 109

Lightman, Alan P(aige) 1948- .... **CLC 81**
See also CA 141; CANR 63

Ligotti, Thomas (Robert) 1953- ...... **CLC 44; SSC 16**
See also CA 123; CANR 49

Li Ho 791-817 .... **PC 13**

Liliencron, (Friedrich Adolf Axel) Detlev von 1844-1909 .... **TCLC 18**
See also CA 117

Lilly, William 1602-1681 .... **LC 27**

Lima, Jose Lezama
See Lezama Lima, Jose

Lima Barreto, Afonso Henrique de
1881-1922 .... **TCLC 23**
See also CA 117; 181

Lima Barreto, Afonso Henriques de
See Lima Barreto, Afonso Henrique de

Limonov, Edward 1944- .... **CLC 67**
See also CA 137

Lin, Frank
See Atherton, Gertrude (Franklin Horn)

Lincoln, Abraham 1809-1865 .... **NCLC 18**

Lind, Jakov CLC 1, 2, 4, 27, 82
See also Landwirth, Heinz
See also CAAS 4

Lindbergh, Anne (Spencer) Morrow
1906-2001 .... **CLC 82; DAM NOV**
See also CA 17-20R; CANR 16, 73; MTCW 1, 2; SATA 33

Lindsay, David 1878(?)-1945 .... **TCLC 15**
See also CA 113; 187

Lindsay, (Nicholas) Vachel
1879-1931 . **TCLC 17; DA; DAC; DAM MST, POET; PC 23**
See also AMWS 1; AW; CA 114; 135; CANR 79; CDALB 1865-1917; DA3; DLB 54; SATA 40

Linke-Poot
See Doeblin, Alfred

Linney, Romulus 1930- .... **CLC 51**
See also CA 1-4R; CANR 40, 44, 79

Linton, Eliza Lynn 1822-1898 .... **NCLC 41**
See also DLB 18

Li Po 701-763 .... **CMLC 2; PC 29**

Lipsius, Justus 1547-1606 .... **LC 16**

Lipsyte, Robert (Michael) 1938- ..... **CLC 21; DA; DAC; DAM MST, NOV**
See also AAYA 7; CA 17-20R; CANR 8, 57; CLR 23; JRDA; MAICYA; SATA 5, 68, 113

Lish, Gordon (Jay) 1934- ... **CLC 45; SSC 18**
See also CA 113; 117; CANR 79; DLB 130; INT 117

Lispector, Clarice 1925(?)-1977 .... **CLC 43; HLCS 2; SSC 34**
See also CA 139; 116; CANR 71; DLB 113; HW 2

Littell, Robert 1935(?)- .... **CLC 42**
See also CA 109; 112; CANR 64

Little, Malcolm 1925-1965
See Malcolm X
See also BW 1, 3; CA 125; 111; CANR 82; DA; DAB; DAC; DAM MST, MULT; DA3; MTCW 1, 2

Littlewit, Humphrey Gent.
See Lovecraft, H(oward) P(hillips)

Litwos
See Sienkiewicz, Henryk (Adam Alexander Pius)

Liu, E 1857-1909 .... **TCLC 15**
See also CA 115

Lively, Penelope (Margaret) 1933- .. **CLC 32, 50; DAM NOV**
See also CA 41-44R; CANR 29, 67, 79; CLR 7; DLB 14, 161, 207; JRDA; MAICYA; MTCW 1, 2; SATA 7, 60, 101

Livesay, Dorothy (Kathleen)
1909-1996 . **CLC 4, 15, 79; DAC; DAM MST, POET**
See also AITN 2; CA 25-28R; CAAS 8; CANR 36, 67; DLB 68; MTCW 1

Livy c. 59B.C.-c. 17 .... **CMLC 11**
See also DLB 211

Lizardi, Jose Joaquin Fernandez de
1776-1827 .... **NCLC 30**

Llewellyn, Richard
See Llewellyn Lloyd, Richard Dafydd Vivian
See also DLB 15

Llewellyn Lloyd, Richard Dafydd Vivian
1906-1983 .... **CLC 7, 80**
See also Llewellyn, Richard
See also CA 53-56; 111; CANR 7, 71; SATA 11; SATA-Obit 37

Llosa, (Jorge) Mario (Pedro) Vargas
See Vargas Llosa, (Jorge) Mario (Pedro)

Lloyd, Manda
See Mander, (Mary) Jane

Lloyd Webber, Andrew 1948-
See Webber, Andrew Lloyd
See also AAYA 1; CA 116; 149; DAM DRAM; SATA 56

Llull, Ramon c. 1235-c. 1316 .... **CMLC 12**

Lobb, Ebenezer
See Upward, Allen

Locke, Alain (Le Roy) 1886-1954 . **TCLC 43; BLCS**
See also BW 1, 3; CA 106; 124; CANR 79; DLB 51

Locke, John 1632-1704 .... **LC 7, 35**
See also DLB 101

Locke-Elliott, Sumner
See Elliott, Sumner Locke

Lockhart, John Gibson 1794-1854 .. **NCLC 6**
See also DLB 110, 116, 144

Lodge, David (John) 1935- ...... **CLC 36, 141; DAM POP**
See also BEST 90:1; BRWS 4; CA 17-20R; CANR 19, 53, 92; DLB 14, 194; INT CANR-19; MTCW 1, 2

Lodge, Thomas 1558-1625 .... **LC 41**
See also DLB 172

Lodge, Thomas 1558-1625 .... **LC 41**

Loennbohm, Armas Eino Leopold 1878-1926
See Leino, Eino
See also CA 123

Loewinsohn, Ron(ald William)
1937- .... **CLC 52**
See also CA 25-28R; CANR 71

Logan, Jake
See Smith, Martin Cruz

Logan, John (Burton) 1923-1987 .... **CLC 5**
See also CA 77-80; 124; CANR 45; DLB 5

Lo Kuan-chung 1330(?)-1400(?) .... **LC 12**

Lombard, Nap
See Johnson, Pamela Hansford

Lomotey (editor), Kofi CLC 70

London, Jack TCLC 9, 15, 39; SSC 4
See also London, John Griffith
See also AAYA 13; AITN 2; AW; CDALB 1865-1917; DLB 8, 12, 78, 212; SATA 18; TCWW 2

Middleton, Richard (Barham)
1882-1911 .... **TCLC 56**
See also CA 187; DLB 156

Middleton, Stanley 1919- .... **CLC 7, 38**
See also CA 25-28R; CAAS 23; CANR 21,
46, 81; DLB 14

Middleton, Thomas 1580-1627 .... **LC 33;
DAM DRAM, MST; DC 5**
See also DLB 58

Migueis, Jose Rodrigues 1901- .... **CLC 10**

Mikszath, Kalman 1847-1910 .... **TCLC 31**
See also CA 170

Miles, Jack CLC 100

Miles, Josephine (Louise)
1911-1985 .. **CLC 1, 2, 14, 34, 39; DAM
POET**
See also CA 1-4R; 116; CANR 2, 55; DLB
48

Militant
See Sandburg, Carl (August)

Mill, John Stuart 1806-1873 .... **NCLC 11, 58**
See also CDBLB 1832-1890; DLB 55, 190

Millar, Kenneth 1915-1983 ... **CLC 14; DAM
POP**
See also Macdonald, Ross
See also CA 9-12R; 110; CANR 16, 63;
DA3; DLB 2, 226; DLBD 6; DLBY 83;
MTCW 1, 2

Millay, E. Vincent
See Millay, Edna St. Vincent

Millay, Edna St. Vincent
1892-1950 .... **TCLC 4, 49; DA; DAB;
DAC; DAM MST, POET; PC 6**
See also Boyd, Nancy
See also AW; CA 104; 130; CDALB 1917-
1929; DA3; DLB 45; MTCW 1, 2

Miller, Arthur 1915- ...... **CLC 1, 2, 6, 10, 15,
26, 47, 78; DA; DAB; DAC; DAM
DRAM, MST; DC 1**
See also AAYA 15; AITN 1; AW 1; CA
1-4R; CABS 3; CANR 2, 30, 54, 76;
CDALB 1941-1968; DA3; DLB 7;
MTCW 1, 2

Miller, Henry (Valentine)
1891-1980 .... **CLC 1, 2, 4, 9, 14, 43, 84;
DA; DAB; DAC; DAM MST, NOV**
See also AW; CA 9-12R; 97-100; CANR
33, 64; CDALB 1929-1941; DA3; DLB
4, 9; DLBY 80; MTCW 1, 2

Miller, Jason 1939(?)-2001 .... **CLC 2**
See also AITN 1; CA 73-76; DLB 7

Miller, Sue 1943- .... **CLC 44; DAM POP**
See also BEST 90:3; CA 139; CANR 59,
91; DA3; DLB 143

Miller, Walter M(ichael, Jr.)
1923-1996 .... **CLC 4, 30**
See also CA 85-88; DLB 8

Millett, Kate 1934- .... **CLC 67**
See also AITN 1; CA 73-76; CANR 32, 53,
76; DA3; GLL 1; MTCW 1, 2

Millhauser, Steven (Lewis) 1943- .... **CLC 21,
54, 109**
See also CA 110; 111; CANR 63; DA3;
DLB 2; INT 111; MTCW 2

Millin, Sarah Gertrude 1889-1968 ... **CLC 49**
See also CA 102; 93-96; DLB 225

Milne, A(lan) A(lexander)
1882-1956 ..... **TCLC 6, 88; DAB; DAC;
DAM MST**
See also AW 1; CA 104; 133; CLR 1, 26;
DA3; DLB 10, 77, 100, 160; MAICYA;
MTCW 1, 2; SATA 100

Milner, Ron(ald) 1938- .... **CLC 56; BLC 3;
DAM MULT**
See also AITN 1; BW 1; CA 73-76; CANR
24, 81; DLB 38; MTCW 1

Milnes, Richard Monckton
1809-1885 .... **NCLC 61**
See also DLB 32, 184

Milosz, Czeslaw 1911- ...... **CLC 5, 11, 22, 31,
56, 82; DAM MST, POET; PC 8**
See also AW; CA 81-84; CANR 23, 51, 91;
CWW 2; DA3; MTCW 1, 2

Milton, John 1608-1674 .... **LC 9, 43; DA;
DAB; DAC; DAM MST, POET; PC 19,
29**
See also AW; CDBLB 1660-1789; DA3;
DLB 131, 151

Min, Anchee 1957- .... **CLC 86**
See also CA 146; CANR 94

Minehaha, Cornelius
See Wedekind, (Benjamin) Frank(lin)

Miner, Valerie 1947- .... **CLC 40**
See also CA 97-100; CANR 59; GLL 2

Minimo, Duca
See D'Annunzio, Gabriele

Minot, Susan 1956- .... **CLC 44**
See also AMWS 6; CA 134

Minus, Ed 1938- .... **CLC 39**
See also CA 185

Miranda, Javier
See Bioy Casares, Adolfo
See also CWW 2

Miranda, Javier
See Bioy Casares, Adolfo

Mirbeau, Octave 1848-1917 .... **TCLC 55**
See also DLB 123, 192

Miro (Ferrer), Gabriel (Francisco Victor)
1879-1930 .... **TCLC 5**
See also CA 104; 185

Misharin, Alexandr CLC 59

**Mishima, Yukio CLC 2, 4, 6, 9, 27; DC 1;
SSC 4**
See also Hiraoka, Kimitake
See also DLB 182; GLL 1; MTCW 2

Mistral, Frederic 1830-1914 .... **TCLC 51**
See also CA 122

Mistral, Gabriela
See Godoy Alcayaga, Lucila

Mistry, Rohinton 1952- .... **CLC 71; DAC**
See also CA 141; CANR 86; CCA 1

Mitchell, Clyde
See Ellison, Harlan (Jay); Silverberg, Robert

Mitchell, James Leslie 1901-1935
See Gibbon, Lewis Grassic
See also CA 104; 188; DLB 15

Mitchell, Joni 1943- .... **CLC 12**
See also CA 112; CCA 1

Mitchell, Joseph (Quincy)
1908-1996 .... **CLC 98**
See also CA 77-80; 152; CANR 69; DLB
185; DLBY 96

Mitchell, Margaret (Munnerlyn)
1900-1949 . **TCLC 11; DAM NOV, POP**
See also AAYA 23; AW 1; CA 109; 125;
CANR 55, 94; CDALBS; DA3; DLB 9;
MTCW 1, 2

Mitchell, Peggy
See Mitchell, Margaret (Munnerlyn)

Mitchell, S(ilas) Weir 1829-1914 .... **TCLC 36**
See also CA 165; DLB 202

Mitchell, W(illiam) O(rmond)
1914-1998 .. **CLC 25; DAC; DAM MST**
See also CA 77-80; 165; CANR 15, 43;
DLB 88

Mitchell, William 1879-1936 .... **TCLC 81**

Mitford, Mary Russell 1787-1855 ... **NCLC 4**
See also DLB 110, 116

Mitford, Nancy 1904-1973 .... **CLC 44**
See also CA 9-12R; DLB 191

Miyamoto, (Chujo) Yuriko
1899-1951 .... **TCLC 37**
See also CA 170, 174; DLB 180

Miyazawa, Kenji 1896-1933 .... **TCLC 76**
See also CA 157

Mizoguchi, Kenji 1898-1956 .... **TCLC 72**
See also CA 167

Mo, Timothy (Peter) 1950(?)- ... **CLC 46, 134**
See also CA 117; DLB 194; MTCW 1

Modarressi, Taghi (M.) 1931- .... **CLC 44**
See also CA 121; 134; INT 134

Modiano, Patrick (Jean) 1945- .... **CLC 18**
See also CA 85-88; CANR 17, 40; CWW
2; DLB 83

Moerck, Paal
See Roelvaag, O(le) E(dvart)

Mofolo, Thomas (Mokopu)
1875(?)-1948 .. **TCLC 22; BLC 3; DAM
MULT**
See also CA 121; 153; CANR 83; DLB 225;
MTCW 2

Mohr, Nicholasa 1938- .... **CLC 12; DAM
MULT; HLC 2**
See also AAYA 8; AW; CA 49-52; CANR
1, 32, 64; CLR 22; DLB 145; HW 1, 2;
JRDA; SAAS 8; SATA 8, 97; SATA-Essay
113

Mojtabai, A(nn) G(race) 1938- ..... **CLC 5, 9,
15, 29**
See also CA 85-88; CANR 88

Moliere 1622-1673 .... **LC 10, 28, 64; DA;
DAB; DAC; DAM DRAM, MST; DC
13**
See also AW; DA3

Molin, Charles
See Mayne, William (James Carter)

Molnár, Ferenc 1878-1952 .. **TCLC 20; DAM
DRAM**
See also CA 109; 153; CANR 83; DLB 215

Momaday, N(avarre) Scott 1934- ...... **CLC 2,
19, 85, 95; DA; DAB; DAC; DAM
MST, MULT, NOV, POP; PC 25**
See also AAYA 11; AMWS 4; AW; CA 25-
28R; CANR 14, 34, 68; CDALBS; DA3;
DLB 143, 175; INT CANR-14; MTCW 1,
2; NNAL; SATA 48; SATA-Brief 30

Monette, Paul 1945-1995 .... **CLC 82**
See also CA 139; 147; GLL 1

Monroe, Harriet 1860-1936 .... **TCLC 12**
See also CA 109; DLB 54, 91

Monroe, Lyle
See Heinlein, Robert A(nson)

Montagu, Elizabeth 1720-1800 .... **NCLC 7**

Montagu, Mary (Pierrepont) Wortley
1689-1762 .... **LC 9, 57; PC 16**
See also DLB 95, 101

Montagu, W. H.
See Coleridge, Samuel Taylor

Montague, John (Patrick) 1929- ..... **CLC 13,
46**
See also CA 9-12R; CANR 9, 69; DLB 40;
MTCW 1

Montaigne, Michel (Eyquem) de
1533-1592 .... **LC 8; DA; DAB; DAC;
DAM MST**
See also AW

Montale, Eugenio 1896-1981 ... **CLC 7, 9, 18;
PC 13**
See also CA 17-20R; 104; CANR 30; DLB
114; MTCW 1

Montesquieu, Charles-Louis de Secondat
1689-1755 .... **LC 7**

Montessori, Maria 1870-1952 ...... **TCLC 103**
See also CA 115; 147

Montgomery, (Robert) Bruce 1921(?)-1978
See Crispin, Edmund
See also CA 179; 104

Montgomery, L(ucy) M(aud)
1874-1942 .... **TCLC 51; DAC; DAM
MST**
See also AAYA 12; CA 108; 137; CLR 8;
DA3; DLB 92; DLBD 14; JRDA; MAI-
CYA; MTCW 2; SATA 100

Mueller, Lisel 1924- .... **CLC 13, 51; PC 33**
See also CA 93-96; DLB 105
Muir, Edwin 1887-1959 .... **TCLC 2, 87**
See also CA 104; DLB 20, 100, 191
Muir, John 1838-1914 .... **TCLC 28**
See also CA 165; DLB 186
Mujica Lainez, Manuel 1910-1984 ... **CLC 31**
See also Lainez, Manuel Mujica
See also CA 81-84; 112; CANR 32; HW 1
Mukherjee, Bharati 1940- .... **CLC 53, 115;
DAM NOV; SSC 38**
See also BEST 89:2; CA 107; CANR 45,
72; DLB 60; MTCW 1, 2
Muldoon, Paul 1951- .... **CLC 32, 72; DAM
POET**
See also BRWS 4; CA 113; 129; CANR 52,
91; DLB 40; INT 129
Mulisch, Harry 1927- .... **CLC 42**
See also CA 9-12R; CANR 6, 26, 56
Mull, Martin 1943- .... **CLC 17**
See also CA 105
Muller, Wilhelm NCLC 73
Mulock, Dinah Maria
See Craik, Dinah Maria (Mulock)
Munford, Robert 1737(?)-1783 .... **LC 5**
See also DLB 31
Mungo, Raymond 1946- .... **CLC 72**
See also CA 49-52; CANR 2
Munro, Alice 1931- .... **CLC 6, 10, 19, 50, 95;
DAC; DAM MST, NOV; SSC 3**
See also AITN 2; AW; CA 33-36R; CANR
33, 53, 75; CCA 1; DA3; DLB 53; MTCW
1, 2; SATA 29
Munro, H(ector) H(ugh) 1870-1916
See Saki
See also AW; CA 104; 130; CDBLB 1890-
1914; DA; DAB; DAC; DAM MST, NOV;
DA3; DLB 34, 162; MTCW 1, 2
Murdoch, (Jean) Iris 1919-1999 ... **CLC 1, 2,
3, 4, 6, 8, 11, 15, 22, 31, 51; DAB;
DAC; DAM MST, NOV**
See also BRWS 1; CA 13-16R; 179; CANR
8, 43, 68; CDBLB 1960 to Present; DA3;
DLB 14, 194, 233; INT CANR-8; MTCW
1, 2
Murfree, Mary Noailles 1850-1922 ... **SSC 22**
See also CA 122; 176; DLB 12, 74
Murnau, Friedrich Wilhelm
See Plumpe, Friedrich Wilhelm
Murphy, Richard 1927- .... **CLC 41**
See also BRWS 5; CA 29-32R; DLB 40
Murphy, Sylvia 1937- .... **CLC 34**
See also CA 121
Murphy, Thomas (Bernard) 1935- ... **CLC 51**
See also CA 101
Murray, Albert L. 1916- .... **CLC 73**
See also BW 2; CA 49-52; CANR 26, 52,
78; DLB 38
Murray, Judith Sargent
1751-1820 .... **NCLC 63**
See also DLB 37, 200
Murray, Les(lie) A(llan) 1938- .... **CLC 40;
DAM POET**
See also CA 21-24R; CANR 11, 27, 56
Murry, J. Middleton
See Murry, John Middleton
Murry, John Middleton
1889-1957 .... **TCLC 16**
See also CA 118; DLB 149
Musgrave, Susan 1951- .... **CLC 13, 54**
See also CA 69-72; CANR 45, 84; CCA 1
Musil, Robert (Edler von)
1880-1942 .... **TCLC 12, 68; SSC 18**
See also CA 109; CANR 55, 84; DLB 81,
124; MTCW 2
Muske, Carol CLC 90
See also Muske-Dukes, Carol (Anne)

Muske-Dukes, Carol (Anne) 1945-
See Muske, Carol
See also CA 65-68; CANR 32, 70
Musset, (Louis Charles) Alfred de
1810-1857 .... **NCLC 7**
See also DLB 192
Mussolini, Benito (Amilcare Andrea)
1883-1945 .... **TCLC 96**
See also CA 116
My Brother's Brother
See Chekhov, Anton (Pavlovich)
Myers, L(eopold) H(amilton)
1881-1944 .... **TCLC 59**
See also CA 157; DLB 15
Myers, Walter Dean 1937- ..... **CLC 35; BLC
3; DAM MULT, NOV**
See also AAYA 4, 23; AW; BW 2; CA 33-
36R; CANR 20, 42, 67; CLR 4, 16, 35;
DLB 33; INT CANR-20; JRDA; MAI-
CYA; MTCW 2; SAAS 2; SATA 41, 71,
109; SATA-Brief 27
Myers, Walter M.
See Myers, Walter Dean
Myles, Symon
See Follett, Ken(neth Martin)
Nabokov, Vladimir (Vladimirovich)
1899-1977 .... **CLC 1, 2, 3, 6, 8, 11, 15,
23, 44, 46, 64; DA; DAB; DAC; DAM
MST, NOV; SSC 11**
See also AW; CA 5-8R; 69-72; CANR 20;
CDALB 1941-1968; DA3; DLB 2; DLBD
3; DLBY 80, 91; MTCW 1, 2
Naevius c. 265B.C.-201B.C. .... **CMLC 37**
See also DLB 211
Nagai, Kafu TCLC 51
See also Nagai, Sokichi
See also DLB 180
Nagai, Sokichi 1879-1959
See Nagai, Kafu
See also CA 117
Nagy, Laszlo 1925-1978 .... **CLC 7**
See also CA 129; 112
Naidu, Sarojini 1879-1949 .... **TCLC 80**
Naipaul, Shiva(dhar Srinivasa)
1945-1985 .... **CLC 32, 39; DAM NOV**
See also CA 110; 112; 116; CANR 33;
DA3; DLB 157; DLBY 85; MTCW 1, 2
Naipaul, V(idiadhar) S(urajprasad)
1932- .... **CLC 4, 7, 9, 13, 18, 37, 105;
DAB; DAC; DAM MST, NOV; SSC 38**
See also BRWS 1; CA 1-4R; CANR 1, 33,
51, 91; CDBLB 1960 to Present; DA3;
DLB 125, 204, 206; DLBY 85; MTCW 1,
2
Nakos, Lilika 1899(?)- .... **CLC 29**
Narayan, R(asipuram) K(rishnaswami)
1906-2001 .... **CLC 7, 28, 47, 121; DAM
NOV; SSC 25**
See also CA 81-84; CANR 33, 61; DA3;
MTCW 1, 2; SATA 62
Nash, (Frediric) Ogden 1902-1971 . **CLC 23;
DAM POET; PC 21**
See also CA 13-14; 29-32R; CANR 34, 61;
CAP 1; DLB 11; MAICYA; MTCW 1, 2;
SATA 2, 46
Nashe, Thomas 1567-1601(?) .... **LC 41**
See also DLB 167
Nashe, Thomas 1567-1601 .... **LC 41**
Nathan, Daniel
See Dannay, Frederic
Nathan, George Jean 1882-1958 .... **TCLC 18**
See also Hatteras, Owen
See also CA 114; 169; DLB 137
Natsume, Kinnosuke 1867-1916
See Natsume, Soseki
See also CA 104
Natsume, Soseki TCLC 2, 10
See also Natsume, Kinnosuke
See also DLB 180

Natti, (Mary) Lee 1919-
See Kingman, Lee
See also CA 5-8R; CANR 2
Naylor, Gloria 1950- .... **CLC 28, 52; BLC 3;
DA; DAC; DAM MST, MULT, NOV,
POP**
See also AAYA 6; AW; BW 2, 3; CA 107;
CANR 27, 51, 74; DA3; DLB 173;
MTCW 1, 2
Neff, Debra CLC 59
Neihardt, John Gneisenau
1881-1973 .... **CLC 32**
See also CA 13-14; CANR 65; CAP 1; DLB
9, 54
Nekrasov, Nikolai Alekseevich
1821-1878 .... **NCLC 11**
Nelligan, Emile 1879-1941 .... **TCLC 14**
See also CA 114; DLB 92
Nelson, Willie 1933- .... **CLC 17**
See also CA 107
Nemerov, Howard (Stanley)
1920-1991 .... **CLC 2, 6, 9, 36; DAM
POET; PC 24**
See also CA 1-4R; 134; CABS 2; CANR 1,
27, 53; DLB 5, 6; DLBY 83; INT CANR-
27; MTCW 1, 2
Neruda, Pablo 1904-1973 .. **CLC 1, 2, 5, 7, 9,
28, 62; DA; DAB; DAC; DAM MST,
MULT, POET; HLC 2; PC 4**
See also AW; CA 19-20; 45-48; CAP 2;
DA3; HW 1; MTCW 1, 2
Nerval, Gerard de 1808-1855 ... **NCLC 1, 67;
PC 13; SSC 18**
Nervo, (Jose) Amado (Ruiz de)
1870-1919 .... **TCLC 11; HLCS 2**
See also CA 109; 131; HW 1
Nessi, Pio Baroja y
See Baroja (y Nessi), Pio
Nestroy, Johann 1801-1862 .... **NCLC 42**
See also DLB 133
Netterville, Luke
See O'Grady, Standish (James)
Neufeld, John (Arthur) 1938- .... **CLC 17**
See also AAYA 11; AW; CA 25-28R; CANR
11, 37, 56; CLR 52; MAICYA; SAAS 3;
SATA 6, 81
Neumann, Alfred 1895-1952 .... **TCLC 100**
See also CA 183; DLB 56
Neumann, Ferenc
See Moln
Neville, Emily Cheney 1919- .... **CLC 12**
See also AW; CA 5-8R; CANR 3, 37, 85;
JRDA; MAICYA; SAAS 2; SATA 1
Newbound, Bernard Slade 1930-
See Slade, Bernard
See also CA 81-84; CANR 49; DAM
DRAM
Newby, P(ercy) H(oward)
1918-1997 .... **CLC 2, 13; DAM NOV**
See also CA 5-8R; 161; CANR 32, 67; DLB
15; MTCW 1
Newlove, Donald 1928- .... **CLC 6**
See also CA 29-32R; CANR 25
Newlove, John (Herbert) 1938- .... **CLC 14**
See also CA 21-24R; CANR 9, 25
Newman, Charles 1938- .... **CLC 2, 8**
See also CA 21-24R; CANR 84
Newman, Edwin (Harold) 1919- ...... **CLC 14**
See also AITN 1; CA 69-72; CANR 5
Newman, John Henry 1801-1890 .. **NCLC 38**
See also DLB 18, 32, 55
Newton, (Sir)Isaac 1642-1727 .... **LC 35, 52**
Newton, Suzanne 1936- .... **CLC 35**
See also CA 41-44R; CANR 14; JRDA;
SATA 5, 77
New York Dept. of Ed. CLC 70
Nexo, Martin Andersen
1869-1954 .... **TCLC 43**
See also DLB 214

Ōe, Kenzaburō 1935- .... **CLC 10, 36, 86; DAM NOV; SSC 20**
See also CA 97-100; CANR 36, 50, 74; DA3; DLB 182; DLBY 94; MTCW 1, 2

O'Faolain, Julia 1932- .... **CLC 6, 19, 47, 108**
See also CA 81-84; CAAS 2; CANR 12, 61; DLB 14, 231; MTCW 1

O'Faolain, Sean 1900-1991 ...... **CLC 1, 7, 14, 32, 70; SSC 13**
See also CA 61-64; 134; CANR 12, 66; DLB 15, 162; MTCW 1, 2

O'Flaherty, Liam 1896-1984 .... **CLC 5, 34; SSC 6**
See also CA 101; 113; CANR 35; DLB 36, 162; DLBY 84; MTCW 1, 2

Ogilvy, Gavin
See Barrie, J(ames) M(atthew)

O'Grady, Standish (James) 1846-1928 .... **TCLC 5**
See also CA 104; 157

O'Grady, Timothy 1951- .... **CLC 59**
See also CA 138

O'Hara, Frank 1926-1966 .... **CLC 2, 5, 13, 78; DAM POET**
See also CA 9-12R; 25-28R; CANR 33; DA3; DLB 5, 16, 193; MTCW 1, 2

O'Hara, John (Henry) 1905-1970 . **CLC 1, 2, 3, 6, 11, 42; DAM NOV; SSC 15**
See also CA 5-8R; 25-28R; CANR 31, 60; CDALB 1929-1941; DLB 9, 86; DLBD 2; MTCW 1, 2

O Hehir, Diana 1922- .... **CLC 41**
See also CA 93-96

Ohiyesa 1858-1939
See Eastman, Charles A(lexander)

Okigbo, Christopher (Ifenayichukwu) 1932-1967 ... **CLC 25, 84; BLC 3; DAM MULT, POET; PC 7**
See also BW 1, 3; CA 77-80; CANR 74; DLB 125; MTCW 1, 2

Okri, Ben 1959- .... **CLC 87**
See also BRWS 5; BW 2, 3; CA 130; 138; CANR 65; DLB 157, 231; INT 138; MTCW 2

Olds, Sharon 1942- ... **CLC 32, 39, 85; DAM POET; PC 22**
See also CA 101; CANR 18, 41, 66; DLB 120; MTCW 2

Oldstyle, Jonathan
See Irving, Washington

Olesha, Yuri (Karlovich) 1899-1960 .. **CLC 8**
See also CA 85-88

Oliphant, Laurence 1829(?)-1888 .. **NCLC 47**
See also DLB 18, 166

Oliphant, Margaret (Oliphant Wilson) 1828-1897 .... **NCLC 11, 61; SSC 25**
See also Oliphant
See also DLB 18, 159, 190

Oliver, Mary 1935- .... **CLC 19, 34, 98**
See also AMWS 7; CA 21-24R; CANR 9, 43, 84, 92; DLB 5, 193

Olivier, Laurence (Kerr) 1907-1989 . **CLC 20**
See also CA 111; 150; 129

Olsen, Tillie 1912- .... **CLC 4, 13, 114; DA; DAB; DAC; DAM MST; SSC 11**
See also CA 1-4R; CANR 1, 43, 74; CDALBS; DA3; DLB 28, 206; DLBY 80; MTCW 1, 2

Olson, Charles (John) 1910-1970 .. **CLC 1, 2, 5, 6, 9, 11, 29; DAM POET; PC 19**
See also AMWS 2; CA 13-16; 25-28R; CABS 2; CANR 35, 61; CAP 1; DLB 5, 16, 193; MTCW 1, 2

Olson, Toby 1937- .... **CLC 28**
See also CA 65-68; CANR 9, 31, 84

Olyesha, Yuri
See Olesha, Yuri (Karlovich)

Ondaatje, (Philip) Michael 1943- .... **CLC 14, 29, 51, 76; DAB; DAC; DAM MST; PC 28**
See also CA 77-80; CANR 42, 74; DA3; DLB 60; MTCW 2

Oneal, Elizabeth 1934-
See Oneal, Zibby
See also CA 106; CANR 28, 84; MAICYA; SATA 30, 82

Oneal, Zibby **CLC 30**
See also Oneal, Elizabeth
See also AAYA 5; CLR 13; JRDA

O'Neill, Eugene (Gladstone) 1888-1953 .... **TCLC 1, 6, 27, 49; DA; DAB; DAC; DAM DRAM, MST**
See also AITN 1; AW; CA 110; 132; CDALB 1929-1941; DA3; DLB 7; MTCW 1, 2

Onetti, Juan Carlos 1909-1994 ... **CLC 7, 10; DAM MULT, NOV; HLCS 2; SSC 23**
See also CA 85-88; 145; CANR 32, 63; DLB 113; HW 1, 2; MTCW 1, 2

O Nuallain, Brian 1911-1966
See O'Brien, Flann
See also CA 21-22; 25-28R; CAP 2; DLB 231

Ophuls, Max 1902-1957 .... **TCLC 79**
See also CA 113

Opie, Amelia 1769-1853 .... **NCLC 65**
See also DLB 116, 159

Oppen, George 1908-1984 ...... **CLC 7, 13, 34**
See also CA 13-16R; 113; CANR 8, 82; DLB 5, 165; TCLC 107

Oppenheim, E(dward) Phillips 1866-1946 .... **TCLC 45**
See also CA 111; DLB 70

Opuls, Max
See Ophuls, Max

Origen c. 185-c. 254 .... **CMLC 19**

Orlovitz, Gil 1918-1973 .... **CLC 22**
See also CA 77-80; 45-48; DLB 2, 5

Orris
See Ingelow, Jean

Ortega y Gasset, Jose 1883-1955 ... **TCLC 9; DAM MULT; HLC 2**
See also CA 106; 130; HW 1, 2; MTCW 1, 2

Ortese, Anna Maria 1914- .... **CLC 89**
See also DLB 177

Ortiz, Simon J(oseph) 1941- . **CLC 45; DAM MULT, POET; PC 17**
See also AMWS 4; CA 134; CANR 69; DLB 120, 175; NNAL

Orton, Joe **CLC 4, 13, 43; DC 3**
See also Orton, John Kingsley
See also BRWS 5; CDBLB 1960 to Present; DLB 13; GLL 1; MTCW 2

Orton, John Kingsley 1933-1967
See Orton, Joe
See also CA 85-88; CANR 35, 66; DAM DRAM; MTCW 1, 2

Orwell, George **TCLC 2, 6, 15, 31, 51; DAB**
See also Blair, Eric (Arthur)
See also AW; CDBLB 1945-1960; CLR 68; DLB 15, 98, 195; SCFW 2

Osborne, David
See Silverberg, Robert

Osborne, George
See Silverberg, Robert

Osborne, John (James) 1929-1994 .... **CLC 1, 2, 5, 11, 45; DA; DAB; DAC; DAM DRAM, MST**
See also AW; BRWS 1; CA 13-16R; 147; CANR 21, 56; CDBLB 1945-1960; DLB 13; MTCW 1, 2

Osborne, Lawrence 1958- .... **CLC 50**
See also CA 189

Osbourne, Lloyd 1868-1947 .... **TCLC 93**

Oshima, Nagisa 1932- .... **CLC 20**
See also CA 116; 121; CANR 78

Oskison, John Milton 1874-1947 .. **TCLC 35; DAM MULT**
See also CA 144; CANR 84; DLB 175; NNAL

Ossian c. 3rd cent. - .... **CMLC 28**
See also Macpherson, James

Ossoli, Sarah Margaret (Fuller marchesa d') 1810-1850 .... **NCLC 5, 50**
See also Fuller, Margaret; Fuller, Sarah Margaret
See also CDALB 1640-1865; DLB 1, 59, 73, 183, 223, 239; SATA 25

Ostriker, Alicia (Suskin) 1937- .... **CLC 132**
See also CA 25-28R; CAAS 24; CANR 10, 30, 62; DLB 120

Ostrovsky, Alexander 1823-1886 .. **NCLC 30, 57**

Otero, Blas de 1916-1979 .... **CLC 11**
See also CA 89-92; DLB 134

Otto, Rudolf 1869-1937 .... **TCLC 85**

Otto, Whitney 1955- .... **CLC 70**
See also CA 140

Ouida **TCLC 43**
See also De La Ramee, (Marie) Louise
See also DLB 18, 156

Ousmane, Sembene 1923- ... **CLC 66; BLC 3**
See also Sembene, Ousmane
See also BW 1, 3; CA 117; 125; CANR 81; CWW 2; MTCW 1

Ovid 43B.C.-17 . **CMLC 7; DAM POET; PC 2**
See also DA3; DLB 211

Owen, Hugh
See Faust, Frederick (Schiller)

Owen, Wilfred (Edward Salter) 1893-1918 .... **TCLC 5, 27; DA; DAB; DAC; DAM MST, POET; PC 19**
See also AW; CA 104; 141; CDBLB 1914-1945; DLB 20; MTCW 2

Owens, Rochelle 1936- .... **CLC 8**
See also CA 17-20R; CAAS 2; CANR 39

Oz, Amos 1939- ...... **CLC 5, 8, 11, 27, 33, 54; DAM NOV**
See also CA 53-56; CANR 27, 47, 65; CWW 2; MTCW 1, 2

Ozick, Cynthia 1928- ...... **CLC 3, 7, 28, 62; DAM NOV, POP; SSC 15**
See also AMWS 5; BEST 90:1; CA 17-20R; CANR 23, 58; DA3; DLB 28, 152; DLBY 82; INT CANR-23; MTCW 1, 2

Ozu, Yasujiro 1903-1963 .... **CLC 16**
See also CA 112

Pacheco, C.
See Pessoa, Fernando (Antonio Nogueira)

Pacheco, Jose Emilio 1939-
See also CA 111; 131; CANR 65; DAM MULT; HLC 2; HW 1, 2

Pa Chin **CLC 18**
See also Li Fei-kan

Pack, Robert 1929- .... **CLC 13**
See also CA 1-4R; CANR 3, 44, 82; DLB 5; SATA 118

Padgett, Lewis
See Kuttner, Henry

Padilla (Lorenzo), Heberto 1932-2000 .... **CLC 38**
See also AITN 1; CA 123; 131; 189; HW 1

Page, Jimmy 1944- .... **CLC 12**

Page, Louise 1955- .... **CLC 40**
See also CA 140; CANR 76; DLB 233

Page, P(atricia) K(athleen) 1916- ...... **CLC 7, 18; DAC; DAM MST; PC 12**
See also Cape, Judith
See also CA 53-56; CANR 4, 22, 65; DLB 68; MTCW 1

Page, Stanton
See Fuller, Henry Blake

Sedgwick, Catharine Maria
1789-1867 .... **NCLC 19, 98**
See also DLB 1, 74, 239
Seelye, John (Douglas) 1931- .... **CLC 7**
See also CA 97-100; CANR 70; INT 97-100; TCWW 2
Seferiades, Giorgos Stylianou 1900-1971
See Seferis, George
See also CA 5-8R; 33-36R; CANR 5, 36; MTCW 1
Seferis, George CLC 5, 11
See also Seferiades, Giorgos Stylianou
Segal, Erich (Wolf) 1937- . **CLC 3, 10; DAM POP**
See also BEST 89:1; CA 25-28R; CANR 20, 36, 65; DLBY 86; INT CANR-20; MTCW 1
Seger, Bob 1945- .... **CLC 35**
Seghers, Anna CLC 7
See also Radvanyi, Netty
See also DLB 69
Seidel, Frederick (Lewis) 1936- .... **CLC 18**
See also CA 13-16R; CANR 8; DLBY 84
Seifert, Jaroslav 1901-1986 .. **CLC 34, 44, 93**
See also CA 127; DLB 215; MTCW 1, 2
Sei Shonagon c. 966-1017(?) .... **CMLC 6**
Sejour, Victor 1817-1874 .... **DC 10**
See also DLB 50
Sejour Marcou et Ferrand, Juan Victor
See Sejour, Victor
Selby, Hubert, Jr. 1928- .... **CLC 1, 2, 4, 8; SSC 20**
See also CA 13-16R; CANR 33, 85; DLB 2, 227
Selzer, Richard 1928- .... **CLC 74**
See also CA 65-68; CANR 14
Sembene, Ousmane
See Ousmane, Sembene
See also CWW 2
Senancour, Etienne Pivert de
1770-1846 .... **NCLC 16**
See also DLB 119
Sender, Ramon (Jose) 1902-1982 ...... **CLC 8; DAM MULT; HLC 2**
See also CA 5-8R; 105; CANR 8; HW 1; MTCW 1
Seneca, Lucius Annaeus c. 4B.C.-c. 65 .... **CMLC 6; DAM DRAM; DC 5**
See also DLB 211
Senghor, Leopold Sedar 1906- .... **CLC 54, 130; BLC 3; DAM MULT, POET; PC 25**
See also BW 2; CA 116; 125; CANR 47, 74; MTCW 1, 2
Senna, Danzy 1970- .... **CLC 119**
See also CA 169
Serling, (Edward) Rod(man)
1924-1975 .... **CLC 30**
See also AAYA 14; AITN 1; CA 162; 57-60; DLB 26
Serna, Ramon Gomez de la
See Gomez de la Serna, Ramon
Serpieres
See Guillevic, (Eugene)
Service, Robert
See Service, Robert W(illiam)
See also DAB; DLB 92
Service, Robert W(illiam)
1874(?)-1958 .... **TCLC 15; DA; DAC; DAM MST, POET**
See also Service, Robert
See also AW; CA 115; 140; CANR 84; SATA 20
Seth, Vikram 1952- .... **CLC 43, 90; DAM MULT**
See also CA 121; 127; CANR 50, 74; DA3; DLB 120; INT 127; MTCW 2
Seton, Cynthia Propper 1926-1982 .. **CLC 27**
See also CA 5-8R; 108; CANR 7

Seton, Ernest (Evan) Thompson
1860-1946 .... **TCLC 31**
See also CA 109; CLR 59; DLB 92; DLBD 13; JRDA; SATA 18
Seton-Thompson, Ernest
See Seton, Ernest (Evan) Thompson
Settle, Mary Lee 1918- .... **CLC 19, 61**
See also CA 89-92; CAAS 1; CANR 44, 87; DLB 6; INT 89-92
Seuphor, Michel
See Arp, Jean
Sevigne, Marie (de Rabutin-Chantal)
Marquise de 1626-1696 .... **LC 11**
Sewall, Samuel 1652-1730 .... **LC 38**
See also DLB 24
Sexton, Anne (Harvey) 1928-1974 ..... **CLC 2, 4, 6, 8, 10, 15, 53, 123; DA; DAB; DAC; DAM MST, POET; PC 2**
See also AMWS 2; AW; CA 1-4R; 53-56; CABS 2; CANR 3, 36; CDALB 1941-1968; DA3; DLB 5, 169; MTCW 1, 2; SATA 10
Shaara, Jeff 1952- .... **CLC 119**
See also CA 163
Shaara, Michael (Joseph, Jr.)
1929-1988 .... **CLC 15; DAM POP**
See also AITN 1; CA 102; 125; CANR 52, 85; DLBY 83
Shackleton, C. C.
See Aldiss, Brian W(ilson)
Shacochis, Bob CLC 39
See also Shacochis, Robert G.
Shacochis, Robert G. 1951-
See Shacochis, Bob
See also CA 119; 124; INT 124
Shaffer, Anthony (Joshua) 1926- ..... **CLC 19; DAM DRAM**
See also CA 110; 116; DLB 13
Shaffer, Peter (Levin) 1926- .. **CLC 5, 14, 18, 37, 60; DAB; DAM DRAM, MST; DC 7**
See also BRWS 1; CA 25-28R; CANR 25, 47, 74; CDBLB 1960 to Present; DA3; DLB 13, 233; MTCW 1, 2
Shakey, Bernard
See Young, Neil
Shalamov, Varlam (Tikhonovich)
1907(?)-1982 .... **CLC 18**
See also CA 129; 105
Shamlu, Ahmad 1925-2000 .... **CLC 10**
See also CWW 2
Shammas, Anton 1951- .... **CLC 55**
Shandling, Arline
See Berriault, Gina
Shange, Ntozake 1948- .... **CLC 8, 25, 38, 74, 126; BLC 3; DAM DRAM, MULT; DC 3**
See also AAYA 9; AW; BW 2; CA 85-88; CABS 3; CANR 27, 48, 74; DA3; DLB 38; MTCW 1, 2
Shanley, John Patrick 1950- .... **CLC 75**
See also CA 128; 133; CANR 83
Shapcott, Thomas W(illiam) 1935- .. **CLC 38**
See also CA 69-72; CANR 49, 83
Shapiro, Jane CLC 76
Shapiro, Karl (Jay) 1913-2000 ...... **CLC 4, 8, 15, 53; PC 25**
See also AMWS 2; CA 1-4R; 188; CAAS 6; CANR 1, 36, 66; DLB 48; MTCW 1, 2
Sharp, William 1855-1905 .... **TCLC 39**
See also CA 160; DLB 156
Sharpe, Thomas Ridley 1928-
See Sharpe, Tom
See also CA 114; 122; CANR 85; DLB 231; INT 122
Sharpe, Tom CLC 36
See also Sharpe, Thomas Ridley
See also DLB 14
Shatrov, Mikhail CLC 59

Shaw, Bernard
See Shaw, George Bernard
See also BW 1; MTCW 2
Shaw, G. Bernard
See Shaw, George Bernard
Shaw, George Bernard 1856-1950 .. **TCLC 3, 9, 21, 45; DA; DAB; DAC; DAM DRAM, MST**
See also Shaw, Bernard
See also AW; CA 104; 128; CDBLB 1914-1945; DA3; DLB 10, 57, 190; MTCW 1, 2
Shaw, Henry Wheeler 1818-1885 .. **NCLC 15**
See also DLB 11
Shaw, Irwin 1913-1984 .... **CLC 7, 23, 34; DAM DRAM, POP**
See also AITN 1; CA 13-16R; 112; CANR 21; CDALB 1941-1968; DLB 6, 102; DLBY 84; MTCW 1, 21
Shaw, Robert 1927-1978 .... **CLC 5**
See also AITN 1; CA 1-4R; 81-84; CANR 4; DLB 13, 14
Shaw, T. E.
See Lawrence, T(homas) E(dward)
Shawn, Wallace 1943- .... **CLC 41**
See also CA 112
Shea, Lisa 1953- .... **CLC 86**
See also CA 147
Sheed, Wilfrid (John Joseph) 1930- . **CLC 2, 4, 10, 53**
See also CA 65-68; CANR 30, 66; DLB 6; MTCW 1, 2
Sheldon, Alice Hastings Bradley
1915(?)-1987
See Tiptree, James, Jr.
See also CA 108; 122; CANR 34; INT 108; MTCW 1
Sheldon, John
See Bloch, Robert (Albert)
Sheldon, Walter J. 1917-1996
See Queen, Ellery
See also AITN 1; CA 25-28R; CANR 10
Shelley, Mary Wollstonecraft (Godwin)
1797-1851 ..... **NCLC 14, 59; DA; DAB; DAC; DAM MST, NOV**
See also AAYA 20; AW; BRWS 3; CDBLB 1789-1832; DA3; DLB 110, 116, 159, 178; SATA 29
Shelley, Percy Bysshe 1792-1822 .. **NCLC 18, 93; DA; DAB; DAC; DAM MST, POET; PC 14**
See also AW; CDBLB 1789-1832; DA3; DLB 96, 110, 158
Shepard, Jim 1956- .... **CLC 36**
See also CA 137; CANR 59; SATA 90
Shepard, Lucius 1947- .... **CLC 34**
See also CA 128; 141; CANR 81; SCFW 2
Shepard, Sam 1943- .... **CLC 4, 6, 17, 34, 41, 44; DAM DRAM; DC 5**
See also AAYA 1; AMWS 3; CA 69-72; CABS 3; CANR 22; DA3; DLB 7, 212; IDFW 3; MTCW 1, 2
Shepherd, Michael
See Ludlum, Robert
Sherburne, Zoa (Lillian Morin)
1912-1995 .... **CLC 30**
See also AAYA 13; AW; CA 1-4R; 176; CANR 3, 37; MAICYA; SAAS 18; SATA 3
Sheridan, Frances 1724-1766 .... **LC 7**
See also DLB 39, 84
Sheridan, Richard Brinsley
1751-1816 .... **NCLC 5, 91; DA; DAB; DAC; DAM DRAM, MST; DC 1**
See also AW; CDBLB 1660-1789; DLB 89
Sherman, Jonathan Marc CLC 55
Sherman, Martin 1941(?)- .... **CLC 19**
See also CA 116; 123; CANR 86

Sherwin, Judith Johnson
See Johnson, Judith (Emlyn)
See also CANR 85

Sherwood, Frances 1940- .... **CLC 81**
See also CA 146

Sherwood, Robert E(mmet)
1896-1955 .... **TCLC 3; DAM DRAM**
See also CA 104; 153; CANR 86; DLB 7,
26

Shestov, Lev 1866-1938 .... **TCLC 56**

Shevchenko, Taras 1814-1861 .... **NCLC 54**

Shiel, M(atthew) P(hipps)
1865-1947 .... **TCLC 8**
See also Holmes, Gordon
See also CA 106; 160; DLB 153; MTCW 2

Shields, Carol 1935- .... **CLC 91, 113; DAC**
See also AMWS 7; CA 81-84; CANR 51,
74; CCA 1; DA3; MTCW 2

Shields, David 1956- .... **CLC 97**
See also CA 124; CANR 48

Shiga, Naoya 1883-1971 ..... **CLC 33; SSC 23**
See also CA 101; 33-36R; DLB 180

Shikibu, Murasaki c. 978-c. 1014 ... **CMLC 1**

Shilts, Randy 1951-1994 .... **CLC 85**
See also AAYA 19; CA 115; 127; 144;
CANR 45; DA3; GLL 1; INT 127; MTCW
2

Shimazaki, Haruki 1872-1943
See Shimazaki Toson
See also CA 105; 134; CANR 84

Shimazaki Toson TCLC 5
See also Shimazaki, Haruki
See also DLB 180

Sholokhov, Mikhail (Aleksandrovich)
1905-1984 .... **CLC 7, 15**
See also CA 101; 112; MTCW 1, 2; SATA-
Obit 36

Shone, Patric
See Hanley, James

Shreve, Susan Richards 1939- .... **CLC 23**
See also CA 49-52; CAAS 5; CANR 5, 38,
69; MAICYA; SATA 46, 95; SATA-Brief
41

Shue, Larry 1946-1985 .... **CLC 52; DAM
DRAM**
See also CA 145; 117

Shu-Jen, Chou 1881-1936
See Lu Hsun
See also CA 104

Shulman, Alix Kates 1932- .... **CLC 2, 10**
See also CA 29-32R; CANR 43; SATA 7

Shuster, Joe 1914-1992 .... **CLC 21**

Shute, Nevil CLC 30
See also Norway, Nevil Shute
See also MTCW 2

Shuttle, Penelope (Diane) 1947- .... **CLC 7**
See also CA 93-96; CANR 39, 84, 92; DLB
14, 40

Sidney, Mary 1561-1621 .... **LC 19, 39**

Sidney, SirPhilip 1554-1586 . **LC 19, 39; DA;
DAB; DAC; DAM MST, POET; PC 32**
See also CDBLB Before 1660; DA3; DLB
167

Siegel, Jerome 1914-1996 .... **CLC 21**
See also CA 116; 169; 151

Siegel, Jerry
See Siegel, Jerome

Sienkiewicz, Henryk (Adam Alexander Pius)
1846-1916 .... **TCLC 3**
See also CA 104; 134; CANR 84

Sierra, Gregorio Martinez
See Martinez Sierra, Gregorio

Sierra, Maria (de la O'LeJarraga) Martinez
See Martinez Sierra, Maria (de la
O'LeJarraga)

Sigal, Clancy 1926- .... **CLC 7**
See also CA 1-4R; CANR 85

Sigourney, Lydia Howard (Huntley)
1791-1865 .... **NCLC 21, 87**
See also DLB 1, 42, 73, 239

Sigüenza y Gongora, Carlos de
1645-1700 .... **LC 8; HLCS 2**

Sigurjonsson, Johann 1880-1919 ... **TCLC 27**
See also CA 170

Sikelianos, Angelos 1884-1951 ...... **TCLC 39;
PC 29**

Silkin, Jon 1930-1997 .... **CLC 2, 6, 43**
See also CA 5-8R; CAAS 5; CANR 89;
DLB 27

Silko, Leslie (Marmon) 1948- .... **CLC 23, 74,
114; DA; DAC; DAM MST, MULT,
POP; SSC 37**
See also AAYA 14; AMWS 4; AW; CA 115;
122; CANR 45, 65; DA3; DLB 143, 175;
MTCW 2; NNAL

Sillanpaa, Frans Eemil 1888-1964 ... **CLC 19**
See also CA 129; 93-96; MTCW 1

Sillitoe, Alan 1928- ... **CLC 1, 3, 6, 10, 19, 57**
See also AITN 1; BRWS 5; CA 9-12R;
CAAS 2; CANR 8, 26, 55; CDBLB 1960
to Present; DLB 14, 139; MTCW 1, 2;
SATA 61

Silone, Ignazio 1900-1978 .... **CLC 4**
See also CA 25-28; 81-84; CANR 34; CAP
2; MTCW 1

Silone, Ignazione
See Silone, Ignazio

Silver, Joan Micklin 1935- .... **CLC 20**
See also CA 114; 121; INT 121

Silver, Nicholas
See Faust, Frederick (Schiller)
See also TCWW 2

Silverberg, Robert 1935- .... **CLC 7, 140;
DAM POP**
See also AAYA 24; CA 1-4R, 186; CAAE
186; CAAS 3; CANR 1, 20, 36, 85; CLR
59; DLB 8; INT CANR-20; MAICYA;
MTCW 1, 2; SATA 13, 91; SATA-Essay
104; SCFW 2

Silverstein, Alvin 1933- .... **CLC 17**
See also CA 49-52; CANR 2; CLR 25;
JRDA; MAICYA; SATA 8, 69

Silverstein, Virginia B(arbara Opshelor)
1937- .... **CLC 17**
See also CA 49-52; CANR 2; CLR 25;
JRDA; MAICYA; SATA 8, 69

Sim, Georges
See Simenon, Georges (Jacques Christian)

Simak, Clifford D(onald) 1904-1988 . **CLC 1,
55**
See also CA 1-4R; 125; CANR 1, 35; DLB
8; MTCW 1; SATA-Obit 56

Simenon, Georges (Jacques Christian)
1903-1989 .... **CLC 1, 2, 3, 8, 18, 47;
DAM POP**
See also CA 85-88; 129; CANR 35; DA3;
DLB 72; DLBY 89; MTCW 1, 2

Simic, Charles 1938- .... **CLC 6, 9, 22, 49, 68,
130; DAM POET**
See also CA 29-32R; CAAS 4; CANR 12,
33, 52, 61, 96; DA3; DLB 105; MTCW 2

Simmel, Georg 1858-1918 .... **TCLC 64**
See also CA 157

Simmons, Charles (Paul) 1924- .... **CLC 57**
See also CA 89-92; INT 89-92

Simmons, Dan 1948- ...... **CLC 44; DAM POP**
See also AAYA 16; CA 138; CANR 53, 81

Simmons, James (Stewart Alexander)
1933- .... **CLC 43**
See also CA 105; CAAS 21; DLB 40

Simms, William Gilmore
1806-1870 .... **NCLC 3**
See also DLB 3, 30, 59, 73

Simon, Carly 1945- .... **CLC 26**
See also CA 105

Simon, Claude 1913- .... **CLC 4, 9, 15, 39;
DAM NOV**
See also CA 89-92; CANR 33; DLB 83;
MTCW 1

Simon, (Marvin) Neil 1927- ... **CLC 6, 11, 31,
39, 70; DAM DRAM; DC 14**
See also AAYA 32; AITN 1; AMWS 4; CA
21-24R; CANR 26, 54, 87; DA3; DLB 7;
MTCW 1, 2

Simon, Paul (Frederick) 1941(?)- ..... **CLC 17**
See also CA 116; 153

Simonon, Paul 1956(?)- .... **CLC 30**

Simonson, Rick ed. CLC 70

Simpson, Harriette
See Arnow, Harriette (Louisa) Simpson

Simpson, Louis (Aston Marantz)
1923- ...... **CLC 4, 7, 9, 32; DAM POET**
See also CA 1-4R; CAAS 4; CANR 1, 61;
DLB 5; MTCW 1, 2

Simpson, Mona (Elizabeth) 1957- .... **CLC 44**
See also CA 122; 135; CANR 68

Simpson, N(orman) F(rederick)
1919- .... **CLC 29**
See also CA 13-16R; DLB 13

Sinclair, Andrew (Annandale) 1935- . **CLC 2,
14**
See also CA 9-12R; CAAS 5; CANR 14,
38, 91; DLB 14; MTCW 1

Sinclair, Emil
See Hesse, Hermann

Sinclair, Iain 1943- .... **CLC 76**
See also CA 132; CANR 81

Sinclair, Iain MacGregor
See Sinclair, Iain

Sinclair, Irene
See Griffith, D(avid Lewelyn) W(ark)

Sinclair, Mary Amelia St. Clair 1865(?)-1946
See Sinclair, May
See also CA 104

Sinclair, May TCLC 3, 11
See also Sinclair, Mary Amelia St. Clair
See also CA 166; DLB 36, 135

Sinclair, Roy
See Griffith, D(avid Lewelyn) W(ark)

Sinclair, Upton (Beall) 1878-1968 ..... **CLC 1,
11, 15, 63; DA; DAB; DAC; DAM
MST, NOV**
See also AMWS 5; AW; CA 5-8R; 25-28R;
CANR 7; CDALB 1929-1941; DA3; DLB
9; INT CANR-7; MTCW 1, 2; SATA 9

Singer, Isaac
See Singer, Isaac Bashevis

Singer, Isaac Bashevis 1904-1991 .. **CLC 1, 3,
6, 9, 11, 15, 23, 38, 69, 111; DA; DAB;
DAC; DAM MST, NOV; SSC 3**
See also AAYA 32; AITN 1, 2; AW; CA
1-4R; 134; CANR 1, 39; CDALB 1941-
1968; CLR 1; DA3; DLB 6, 28, 52;
DLBY 91; JRDA; MAICYA; MTCW 1,
2; SATA 3, 27; SATA-Obit 68

Singer, Israel Joshua 1893-1944 .... **TCLC 33**
See also CA 169

Singh, Khushwant 1915- .... **CLC 11**
See also CA 9-12R; CAAS 9; CANR 6, 84

Singleton, Ann
See Benedict, Ruth (Fulton)

Sinjohn, John
See Galsworthy, John

Sinyavsky, Andrei (Donatevich)
1925-1997 .... **CLC 8**
See also Tertz, Abram
See also CA 85-88; 159

Sirin, V.
See Nabokov, Vladimir (Vladimirovich)

Sissman, L(ouis) E(dward)
1928-1976 .... **CLC 9, 18**
See also CA 21-24R; 65-68; CANR 13;
DLB 5

Sisson, C(harles) H(ubert) 1914- .... CLC 8
  See also CA 1-4R; CAAS 3; CANR 3, 48,
  84; DLB 27
Sitwell, DameEdith 1887-1964 ...... CLC 2, 9,
  67; DAM POET; PC 3
  See also CA 9-12R; CANR 35; CDBLB
  1945-1960; DLB 20; MTCW 1, 2
Siwaarmill, H. P.
  See Sharp, William
Sjoewall, Maj 1935- .... CLC 7
  See also Sjowall, Maj
  See also CA 65-68; CANR 73
Sjowall, Maj
  See Sjoewall, Maj
Skelton, John 1460-1529 .... PC 25
Skelton, Robin 1925-1997 .... CLC 13
  See also Zuk, Georges
  See also AITN 2; CA 5-8R; 160; CAAS 5;
  CANR 28, 89; CCA 1; DLB 27, 53
Skolimowski, Jerzy 1938- .... CLC 20
  See also CA 128
Skram, Amalie (Bertha)
  1847-1905 .... TCLC 25
  See also CA 165
Skvorecky, Josef (Vaclav) 1924- ...... CLC 15,
  39, 69; DAC; DAM NOV
  See also CA 61-64; CAAS 1; CANR 10,
  34, 63; DA3; DLB 232; MTCW 1, 2
Slade, Bernard CLC 11, 46
  See also Newbound, Bernard Slade
  See also CAAS 9; CCA 1; DLB 53
Slaughter, Carolyn 1946- .... CLC 56
  See also CA 85-88; CANR 85
Slaughter, Frank G(ill) 1908- .... CLC 29
  See also AITN 2; CA 5-8R; CANR 5, 85;
  INT CANR-5
Slavitt, David R(ytman) 1935- ..... CLC 5, 14
  See also CA 21-24R; CAAS 3; CANR 41,
  83; DLB 5, 6
Slesinger, Tess 1905-1945 .... TCLC 10
  See also CA 107; DLB 102
Slessor, Kenneth 1901-1971 .... CLC 14
  See also CA 102; 89-92
Slowacki, Juliusz 1809-1849 .... NCLC 15
Smart, Christopher 1722-1771 .. LC 3; DAM
  POET; PC 13
  See also DLB 109
Smart, Elizabeth 1913-1986 .... CLC 54
  See also CA 81-84; 118; DLB 88
Smiley, Jane (Graves) 1949- ...... CLC 53, 76;
  DAM POP
  See also AMWS 6; CA 104; CANR 30, 50,
  74, 96; DA3; DLB 227, 234; INT
  CANR-30
Smith, A(rthur) J(ames) M(arshall)
  1902-1980 .... CLC 15; DAC
  See also CA 1-4R; 102; CANR 4; DLB 88
Smith, Adam 1723-1790 .... LC 36
  See also DLB 104
Smith, Alexander 1829-1867 .... NCLC 59
  See also DLB 32, 55
Smith, Anna Deavere 1950- .... CLC 86
  See also CA 133
Smith, Betty (Wehner) 1896-1972 .... CLC 19
  See also CA 5-8R; 33-36R; DLBY 82;
  SATA 6
Smith, Charlotte (Turner)
  1749-1806 .... NCLC 23
  See also DLB 39, 109
Smith, Clark Ashton 1893-1961 .... CLC 43
  See also CA 143; CANR 81; MTCW 2
Smith, Dave CLC 22, 42
  See also Smith, David (Jeddie)
  See also CAAS 7; DLB 5
Smith, David (Jeddie) 1942-
  See Smith, Dave
  See also CA 49-52; CANR 1, 59; DAM
  POET

Smith, Florence Margaret 1902-1971
  See Smith, Stevie
  See also CA 17-18; 29-32R; CANR 35;
  CAP 2; DAM POET; MTCW 1, 2
Smith, Iain Crichton 1928-1998 .... CLC 64
  See also CA 21-24R; 171; DLB 40, 139
Smith, John 1580(?)-1631 .... LC 9
  See also DLB 24, 30
Smith, Johnston
  See Crane, Stephen (Townley)
Smith, Joseph, Jr. 1805-1844 .... NCLC 53
Smith, Lee 1944- .... CLC 25, 73
  See also CA 114; 119; CANR 46; DLB 143;
  DLBY 83; INT 119
Smith, Martin
  See Smith, Martin Cruz
Smith, Martin Cruz 1942- .... CLC 25; DAM
  MULT, POP
  See also BEST 89:4; CA 85-88; CANR 6,
  23, 43, 65; INT CANR-23; MTCW 2;
  NNAL
Smith, Mary-Ann Tirone 1944- .... CLC 39
  See also CA 118; 136
Smith, Patti 1946- .... CLC 12
  See also CA 93-96; CANR 63
Smith, Pauline (Urmson)
  1882-1959 .... TCLC 25
  See also DLB 225
Smith, Rosamond
  See Oates, Joyce Carol
Smith, Sheila Kaye
  See Kaye-Smith, Sheila
Smith, Stevie CLC 3, 8, 25, 44; PC 12
  See also Smith, Florence Margaret
  See also BRWS 2; DLB 20; MTCW 2
Smith, Wilbur (Addison) 1933- .... CLC 33
  See also CA 13-16R; CANR 7, 46, 66;
  MTCW 1, 2
Smith, William Jay 1918- .... CLC 6
  See also CA 5-8R; CANR 44; DLB 5; MAI-
  CYA; SAAS 22; SATA 2, 68
Smith, Woodrow Wilson
  See Kuttner, Henry
Smolenskin, Peretz 1842-1885 .... NCLC 30
Smollett, Tobias (George) 1721-1771 ... LC 2,
  46
  See also CDBLB 1660-1789; DLB 39, 104
Snodgrass, W(illiam) D(e Witt)
  1926- .... CLC 2, 6, 10, 18, 68; DAM
  POET
  See also CA 1-4R; CANR 6, 36, 65, 85;
  DLB 5; MTCW 1, 2
Snow, C(harles) P(ercy) 1905-1980 ... CLC 1,
  4, 6, 9, 13, 19; DAM NOV
  See also CA 5-8R; 101; CANR 28; CDBLB
  1945-1960; DLB 15, 77; DLBD 17;
  MTCW 1, 2
Snow, Frances Compton
  See Adams, Henry (Brooks)
Snyder, Gary (Sherman) 1930- . CLC 1, 2, 5,
  9, 32, 120; DAM POET; PC 21
  See also CA 17-20R; CANR 30, 60; DA3;
  DLB 5, 16, 165, 212; MTCW 2
Snyder, Zilpha Keatley 1927- .... CLC 17
  See also AAYA 15; AW; CA 9-12R; CANR
  38; CLR 31; JRDA; MAICYA; SAAS 2;
  SATA 1, 28, 75, 110; SATA-Essay 112
Soares, Bernardo
  See Pessoa, Fernando (Antonio Nogueira)
Sobh, A.
  See Shamlu, Ahmad
Sobol, Joshua CLC 60
  See also CWW 2
Socrates 470B.C.-399B.C. .... CMLC 27
Soderberg, Hjalmar 1869-1941 ...... TCLC 39
Södergran, Edith (Irene)
  See Soedergran, Edith (Irene)

Soedergran, Edith (Irene)
  1892-1923 .... TCLC 31
Softly, Edgar
  See Lovecraft, H(oward) P(hillips)
Softly, Edward
  See Lovecraft, H(oward) P(hillips)
Sokolov, Raymond 1941- .... CLC 7
  See also CA 85-88
Sokolov, Sasha CLC 59
Solo, Jay
  See Ellison, Harlan (Jay)
Sologub, Fyodor TCLC 9
  See also Teternikov, Fyodor Kuzmich
Solomons, Ikey Esquir
  See Thackeray, William Makepeace
Solomos, Dionysios 1798-1857 .... NCLC 15
Solwoska, Mara
  See French, Marilyn
Solzhenitsyn, Aleksandr I(sayevich)
  1918- .. CLC 1, 2, 4, 7, 9, 10, 18, 26, 34,
  78, 134; DA; DAB; DAC; DAM MST,
  NOV; SSC 32
  See also AITN 1; AW; CA 69-72; CANR
  40, 65; DA3; MTCW 1, 2
Somers, Jane
  See Lessing, Doris (May)
Somerville, Edith 1858-1949 .... TCLC 51
  See also DLB 135
Somerville & Ross
  See Martin, Violet Florence; Somerville,
  Edith
Sommer, Scott 1951- .... CLC 25
  See also CA 106
Sondheim, Stephen (Joshua) 1930- . CLC 30,
  39; DAM DRAM
  See also AAYA 11; CA 103; CANR 47, 67
Song, Cathy 1955- .... PC 21
  See also CA 154; DLB 169
Sontag, Susan 1933- .... CLC 1, 2, 10, 13, 31,
  105; DAM POP
  See also AMWS 3; CA 17-20R; CANR 25,
  51, 74; DA3; DLB 2, 67; MTCW 1, 2
Sophocles 496(?)B.C.-406(?)B.C. .... CMLC 2;
  DA; DAB; DAC; DAM DRAM, MST;
  DC 1
  See also AW; DA3; DLB 176
Sordello 1189-1269 .... CMLC 15
Sorel, Georges 1847-1922 .... TCLC 91
  See also CA 118; 188
Sorel, Julia
  See Drexler, Rosalyn
Sorokin, Vladimir CLC 59
Sorrentino, Gilbert 1929- .. CLC 3, 7, 14, 22,
  40
  See also CA 77-80; CANR 14, 33; DLB 5,
  173; DLBY 80; INT CANR-14
Soto, Gary 1952- .... CLC 32, 80; DAM
  MULT; HLC 2; PC 28
  See also AAYA 10, 37; AW; CA 119; 125;
  CANR 50, 74; CLR 38; DLB 82; HW 1,
  2; INT 125; JRDA; MTCW 2; SATA 80,
  120
Soupault, Philippe 1897-1990 .... CLC 68
  See also CA 116; 147; 131
Souster, (Holmes) Raymond 1921- .... CLC 5,
  14; DAC; DAM POET
  See also CA 13-16R; CAAS 14; CANR 13,
  29, 53; DLB 88; SATA 63
Southern, Terry 1924(?)-1995 .... CLC 7
  See also CA 1-4R; 150; CANR 1, 55; DLB
  2; IDFW 3
Southey, Robert 1774-1843 .... NCLC 8, 97
  See also DLB 93, 107, 142; SATA 54
Southworth, Emma Dorothy Eliza Nevitte
  1819-1899 .... NCLC 26
  See also DLB 239
Souza, Ernest
  See Scott, Evelyn

Thakura, Ravindranatha
  See Tagore, Rabindranath
Thames, C. H.
  See Marlowe, Stephen
Tharoor, Shashi 1956- .... **CLC 70**
  See also CA 141; CANR 91
Thelwell, Michael Miles 1939- .... **CLC 22**
  See also BW 2; CA 101
Theobald, Lewis, Jr.
  See Lovecraft, H(oward) P(hillips)
Theocritus c. 310B.C.-c. 250B.C. .. **CMLC 45**
  See also DLB 176
Theodorescu, Ion N. 1880-1967
  See Arghezi, Tudor
  See also CA 116; DLB 220
Theriault, Yves 1915-1983 .... **CLC 79; DAC;**
    DAM MST
  See also CA 102; CCA 1; DLB 88
Theroux, Alexander (Louis) 1939- .... **CLC 2,**
    25
  See also CA 85-88; CANR 20, 63
Theroux, Paul (Edward) 1941- ..... **CLC 5, 8,**
    11, 15, 28, 46; DAM POP
  See also AAYA 28; BEST 89:4; CA 33-36R;
    CANR 20, 45, 74; CDALBS; DA3; DLB
    2; MTCW 1, 2; SATA 44, 109
Thesen, Sharon 1946- .... **CLC 56**
  See also CA 163
Thevenin, Denis
  See Duhamel, Georges
Thibault, Jacques Anatole Francois
    1844-1924
  See France, Anatole
  See also CA 106; 127; DAM NOV; DA3;
    MTCW 1, 2
Thiele, Colin (Milton) 1920- .... **CLC 17**
  See also AW; CA 29-32R; CANR 12, 28,
    53; CLR 27; MAICYA; SAAS 2; SATA
    14, 72
Thomas, Audrey (Callahan) 1935- .... **CLC 7,**
    13, 37, 107; SSC 20
  See also AITN 2; CA 21-24R; CAAS 19;
    CANR 36, 58; DLB 60; MTCW 1
Thomas, Augustus 1857-1934 .... **TCLC 97**
Thomas, D(onald) M(ichael) 1935- . **CLC 13,**
    22, 31, 132
  See also BRWS 4; CA 61-64; CAAS 11;
    CANR 17, 45, 75; CDBLB 1960 to
    Present; DA3; DLB 40, 207; INT CANR-
    17; MTCW 1, 2
Thomas, Dylan (Marlais)
    1914-1953 ...... **TCLC 1, 8, 45, 105; DA;**
    DAB; DAC; DAM DRAM, MST,
    POET; PC 2; SSC 3, 44
  See also AW; BRWS 1; CA 104; 120;
    CANR 65; CDBLB 1945-1960; DA3;
    DLB 13, 20, 139; MTCW 1, 2; SATA 60
Thomas, (Philip) Edward
    1878-1917 .... **TCLC 10; DAM POET**
  See also CA 106; 153; DLB 98
Thomas, Joyce Carol 1938- .... **CLC 35**
  See also AAYA 12; AW; BW 2, 3; CA 113;
    116; CANR 48; CLR 19; DLB 33; INT
    116; JRDA; MAICYA; MTCW 1, 2;
    SAAS 7; SATA 40, 78
Thomas, Lewis 1913-1993 .... **CLC 35**
  See also CA 85-88; 143; CANR 38, 60;
    MTCW 1, 2
Thomas, M. Carey 1857-1935 .... **TCLC 89**
Thomas, Paul
  See Mann, (Paul) Thomas
Thomas, Piri 1928- .... **CLC 17; HLCS 2**
  See also CA 73-76; HW 1
Thomas, R(onald) S(tuart)
    1913-2000 . **CLC 6, 13, 48; DAB; DAM**
    POET
  See also CA 89-92; 189; CAAS 4; CANR
    30; CDBLB 1960 to Present; DLB 27;
    MTCW 1

Thomas, Ross (Elmore) 1926-1995 .. **CLC 39**
  See also CA 33-36R; 150; CANR 22, 63
Thompson, Francis (Joseph)
    1859-1907 .... **TCLC 4**
  See also CA 104; 189; CDBLB 1890-1914;
    DLB 19
Thompson, Francis Clegg
  See Mencken, H(enry) L(ouis)
Thompson, Hunter S(tockton)
    1939- ... **CLC 9, 17, 40, 104; DAM POP**
  See also BEST 89:1; CA 17-20R; CANR
    23, 46, 74, 77; DA3; DLB 185; MTCW
    1, 2
Thompson, James Myers
  See Thompson, Jim (Myers)
Thompson, Jim (Myers)
    1906-1977(?) .... **CLC 69**
  See also CA 140; DLB 226
Thompson, Judith CLC 39
Thomson, James 1700-1748 ... **LC 16, 29, 40;**
    DAM POET
  See also BRWS 3; DLB 95
Thomson, James 1834-1882 .... **NCLC 18;**
    DAM POET
  See also DLB 35
Thoreau, Henry David 1817-1862 .. **NCLC 7,**
    21, 61; DA; DAB; DAC; DAM MST;
    PC 30
  See also AW; CDALB 1640-1865; DA3;
    DLB 1, 223
Thorndike, E. L.
  See Thorndike, Edward L(ee)
Thorndike, Edward L(ee)
    1874-1949 .... **TCLC 107**
  See also CA 121
Thornton, Hall
  See Silverberg, Robert
Thucydides c. 460B.C.-399B.C. ..... **CMLC 17**
  See also DLB 176
Thumboo, Edwin 1933- .... **PC 30**
Thurber, James (Grover)
    1894-1961 .... **CLC 5, 11, 25, 125; DA;**
    DAB; DAC; DAM DRAM, MST, NOV;
    SSC 1
  See also AMWS 1; CA 73-76; CANR 17,
    39; CDALB 1929-1941; DA3; DLB 4, 11,
    22, 102; MAICYA; MTCW 1, 2; SATA
    13
Thurman, Wallace (Henry)
    1902-1934 .... **TCLC 6; BLC 3; DAM**
    MULT
  See also BW 1, 3; CA 104; 124; CANR 81;
    DLB 51
Tibullus c. 54B.C.-c. 18B.C. .... **CMLC 36**
  See also DLB 211
Ticheburn, Cheviot
  See Ainsworth, William Harrison
Tieck, (Johann) Ludwig
    1773-1853 .... **NCLC 5, 46; SSC 31**
  See also DLB 90
Tiger, Derry
  See Ellison, Harlan (Jay)
Tilghman, Christopher 1948(?)- .... **CLC 65**
  See also CA 159
Tillich, Paul (Johannes)
    1886-1965 .... **CLC 131**
  See also CA 5-8R; 25-28R; CANR 33;
    MTCW 1, 2
Tillinghast, Richard (Williford)
    1940- .... **CLC 29**
  See also CA 29-32R; CAAS 23; CANR 26,
    51, 96
Timrod, Henry 1828-1867 .... **NCLC 25**
  See also DLB 3
Tindall, Gillian (Elizabeth) 1938- ...... **CLC 7**
  See also CA 21-24R; CANR 11, 65
Tiptree, James, Jr. CLC 48, 50
  See also Sheldon, Alice Hastings Bradley
  See also DLB 8

Titmarsh, Michael Angelo
  See Thackeray, William Makepeace
Tocqueville, Alexis (Charles Henri Maurice
    Clerel 1805-1859 .... **NCLC 7, 63**
Tolkien, J(ohn) R(onald) R(euel)
    1892-1973 .. **CLC 1, 2, 3, 8, 12, 38; DA;**
    DAB; DAC; DAM MST, NOV, POP
  See also AAYA 10; AITN 1; BRWS 2; CA
    17-18; 45-48; CANR 36; CAP 2; CDBLB
    1914-1945; CLR 56; DA3; DLB 15, 160;
    JRDA; MAICYA; MTCW 1, 2; SATA 2,
    32, 100; SATA-Obit 24
Toller, Ernst 1893-1939 .... **TCLC 10**
  See also CA 107; 186; DLB 124
Tolson, M. B.
  See Tolson, Melvin B(eaunorus)
Tolson, Melvin B(eaunorus)
    1898(?)-1966 .... **CLC 36, 105; BLC 3;**
    DAM MULT, POET
  See also BW 1, 3; CA 124; 89-92; CANR
    80; DLB 48, 76
Tolstoi, Aleksei Nikolaevich
  See Tolstoy, Alexey Nikolaevich
Tolstoy, Alexey Nikolaevich
    1882-1945 .... **TCLC 18**
  See also CA 107; 158
Tolstoy, Count Leo
  See Tolstoy, Leo (Nikolaevich)
Tolstoy, Leo (Nikolaevich)
    1828-1910 .. **TCLC 4, 11, 17, 28, 44, 79;**
    DA; DAB; DAC; DAM MST, NOV;
    SSC 9, 30
  See also AW; CA 104; 123; DA3; DLB 238;
    SATA 26
Tomasi di Lampedusa, Giuseppe 1896-1957
  See Lampedusa, Giuseppe (Tomasi) di
  See also CA 111
Tomlin, Lily CLC 17
  See also Tomlin, Mary Jean
Tomlin, Mary Jean 1939(?)-
  See Tomlin, Lily
  See also CA 117
Tomlinson, (Alfred) Charles 1927- .... **CLC 2,**
    4, 6, 13, 45; DAM POET; PC 17
  See also CA 5-8R; CANR 33; DLB 40
Tomlinson, H(enry) M(ajor)
    1873-1958 .... **TCLC 71**
  See also CA 118; 161; DLB 36, 100, 195
Tonson, Jacob
  See Bennett, (Enoch) Arnold
Toole, John Kennedy 1937-1969 ..... **CLC 19,**
    64
  See also CA 104; DLBY 81; MTCW 2
Toomer, Jean 1892-1967 .... **CLC 1, 4, 13, 22;**
    BLC 3; DAM MULT; PC 7; SSC 1
  See also Pinchback, Eugene; Toomer, Eu-
    gene; Toomer, Eugene Pinchback; Toomer,
    Nathan Jean; Toomer, Nathan Pinchback
  See also AMWS 3; AW; BW 1; CA 85-88;
    CDALB 1917-1929; DA3; DLB 45, 51;
    MTCW 1, 2
Torley, Luke
  See Blish, James (Benjamin)
Tornimparte, Alessandra
  See Ginzburg, Natalia
Torre, Raoul della
  See Mencken, H(enry) L(ouis)
Torrence, Ridgely 1874-1950 .... **TCLC 97**
  See also DLB 54
Torrey, E(dwin) Fuller 1937- .... **CLC 34**
  See also CA 119; CANR 71
Torsvan, Ben Traven
  See Traven, B.
Torsvan, Benno Traven
  See Traven, B.
Torsvan, Berick Traven
  See Traven, B.
Torsvan, Berwick Traven
  See Traven, B.

Urdang, Constance (Henriette)
1922-1996 .... **CLC 47**
See also CA 21-24R; CANR 9, 24

Uriel, Henry
See Faust, Frederick (Schiller)

Uris, Leon (Marcus) 1924- .... **CLC 7, 32; DAM NOV, POP**
See also AITN 1, 2; BEST 89:2; CA 1-4R; CANR 1, 40, 65; DA3; MTCW 1, 2; SATA 49

Urista, Alberto H. 1947-
See Alurista
See also CA 45-48, 182; CANR 2, 32; HLCS 1; HW 1

Urmuz
See Codrescu, Andrei

Urquhart, Guy
See McAlmon, Robert (Menzies)

Urquhart, Jane 1949- .... **CLC 90; DAC**
See also CA 113; CANR 32, 68; CCA 1

Usigli, Rodolfo 1905-1979
See also CA 131; HLCS 1; HW 1

Ustinov, Peter (Alexander) 1921- .... **CLC 1**
See also AITN 1; CA 13-16R; CANR 25, 51; DLB 13; MTCW 2

U Tam'si, Gerald Felix Tchicaya
See Tchicaya, Gerald Felix

U Tam'si, Tchicaya
See Tchicaya, Gerald Felix

Vachss, Andrew (Henry) 1942- .... **CLC 106**
See also CA 118; CANR 44, 95

Vachss, Andrew H.
See Vachss, Andrew (Henry)

Vaculik, Ludvik 1926- .... **CLC 7**
See also CA 53-56; CANR 72; CWW 2; DLB 232

Vaihinger, Hans 1852-1933 .... **TCLC 71**
See also CA 116; 166

Valdez, Luis (Miguel) 1940- .. **CLC 84; DAM MULT; DC 10; HLC 2**
See also CA 101; CANR 32, 81; DLB 122; HW 1

Valenzuela, Luisa 1938- .... **CLC 31, 104; DAM MULT; HLCS 2; SSC 14**
See also CA 101; CANR 32, 65; CWW 2; DLB 113; HW 1, 2

Valera y Alcala-Galiano, Juan
1824-1905 .... **TCLC 10**
See also CA 106

Valery, (Ambroise) Paul (Toussaint Jules)
1871-1945 ... **TCLC 4, 15; DAM POET; PC 9**
See also CA 104; 122; DA3; MTCW 1, 2

Valle-Inclan, Ramon (Maria) del
1866-1936 .... **TCLC 5; DAM MULT; HLC 2**
See also CA 106; 153; CANR 80; DLB 134; HW 2

Vallejo, Antonio Buero
See Buero Vallejo, Antonio

Vallejo, Cesar (Abraham)
1892-1938 .. **TCLC 3, 56; DAM MULT; HLC 2**
See also CA 105; 153; HW 1

Valles, Jules 1832-1885 .... **NCLC 71**
See also DLB 123

Vallette, Marguerite Eymery
1860-1953 .... **TCLC 67**
See also CA 182; DLB 123, 192

Valle Y Pena, Ramon del
See Valle-Inclan, Ramon (Maria) del

Van Ash, Cay 1918- .... **CLC 34**

Vanbrugh, Sir John 1664-1726 .... **LC 21; DAM DRAM**
See also DLB 80

Van Campen, Karl
See Campbell, John W(ood, Jr.)

Vance, Gerald
See Silverberg, Robert

Vance, Jack CLC 35
See also Vance, John Holbrook
See also DLB 8; SCFW 2

Vance, John Holbrook 1916-
See Queen, Ellery; Vance, Jack
See also CA 29-32R; CANR 17, 65; MTCW 1

Van Den Bogarde, Derek Jules Gaspard Ulric Niven 1921-1999 .... **CLC 14**
See also CA 77-80; 179; DLB 19

Vandenburgh, Jane CLC 59
See also CA 168

Vanderhaeghe, Guy 1951- .... **CLC 41**
See also CA 113; CANR 72

van der Post, Laurens (Jan)
1906-1996 .... **CLC 5**
See also CA 5-8R; 155; CANR 35; DLB 204

van de Wetering, Janwillem 1931- ... **CLC 47**
See also CA 49-52; CANR 4, 62, 90

Van Dine, S. S. TCLC 23
See also Wright, Willard Huntington

Van Doren, Carl (Clinton)
1885-1950 .... **TCLC 18**
See also CA 111; 168

Van Doren, Mark 1894-1972 .... **CLC 6, 10**
See also CA 1-4R; 37-40R; CANR 3; DLB 45; MTCW 1, 2

Van Druten, John (William)
1901-1957 .... **TCLC 2**
See also CA 104; 161; DLB 10

Van Duyn, Mona (Jane) 1921- ...... **CLC 3, 7, 63, 116; DAM POET**
See also CA 9-12R; CANR 7, 38, 60; DLB 5

Van Dyne, Edith
See Baum, L(yman) Frank

van Itallie, Jean-Claude 1936- .... **CLC 3**
See also CA 45-48; CAAS 2; CANR 1, 48; DLB 7

van Ostaijen, Paul 1896-1928 .... **TCLC 33**
See also CA 163

Van Peebles, Melvin 1932- .... **CLC 2, 20; DAM MULT**
See also BW 2, 3; CA 85-88; CANR 27, 67, 82

Vansittart, Peter 1920- .... **CLC 42**
See also CA 1-4R; CANR 3, 49, 90

Van Vechten, Carl 1880-1964 .... **CLC 33**
See also AMWS 2; CA 183; 89-92; DLB 4, 9, 51

Van Vogt, A(lfred) E(lton)
1912-2000 .... **CLC 1**
See also CA 21-24R; CANR 28; DLB 8; SATA 14

Varda, Agnes 1928- .... **CLC 16**
See also CA 116; 122

Vargas Llosa, (Jorge) Mario (Pedro)
1936- .... **CLC 3, 6, 9, 10, 15, 31, 42, 85; DA; DAB; DAC; DAM MST, MULT, NOV; HLC 2**
See also CA 73-76; CANR 18, 32, 42, 67; DA3; DLB 145; HW 1, 2; MTCW 1, 2

Vasiliu, Gheorghe
See Bacovia, George
See also CA 123; 189; DLB 220

Vassa, Gustavus
See Equiano, Olaudah

Vassilikos, Vassilis 1933- .... **CLC 4, 8**
See also CA 81-84; CANR 75

Vaughan, Henry 1621-1695 .... **LC 27**
See also DLB 131

Vaughn, Stephanie CLC 62

Vazov, Ivan (Minchov) 1850-1921 . **TCLC 25**
See also CA 121; 167; DLB 147

Veblen, Thorstein B(unde)
1857-1929 .... **TCLC 31**
See also AMWS 1; CA 115; 165

Vega, Lope de 1562-1635 .... **LC 23; HLCS 2**

Vendler, Helen (Hennessy) 1933- ... **CLC 138**
See also CA 41-44R; CANR 25, 72; MTCW 1, 2

Venison, Alfred
See Pound, Ezra (Weston Loomis)

Verdi, Marie de
See Mencken, H(enry) L(ouis)

Verdu, Matilde
See Cela, Camilo Jose

Verga, Giovanni (Carmelo)
1840-1922 .... **TCLC 3; SSC 21**
See also CA 104; 123

Vergil 70B.C.-19B.C. .... **CMLC 9, 40; DA; DAB; DAC; DAM MST, POET; PC 12**
See also AW; DA3; DLB 211

Verhaeren, Emile (Adolphe Gustave)
1855-1916 .... **TCLC 12**
See also CA 109

Verlaine, Paul (Marie) 1844-1896 .. **NCLC 2, 51; DAM POET; PC 2, 32**

Verne, Jules (Gabriel) 1828-1905 ... **TCLC 6, 52**
See also AAYA 16; CA 110; 131; DA3; DLB 123; JRDA; MAICYA; SATA 21

Verus, Marcus Annius
See Antoninus, Marcus Aurelius

Very, Jones 1813-1880 .... **NCLC 9**
See also DLB 1

Vesaas, Tarjei 1897-1970 .... **CLC 48**
See also CA 190; 29-32R

Vialis, Gaston
See Simenon, Georges (Jacques Christian)

Vian, Boris 1920-1959 .... **TCLC 9**
See also CA 106; 164; DLB 72; MTCW 2

Viaud, (Louis Marie) Julien 1850-1923
See Loti, Pierre
See also CA 107

Vicar, Henry
See Felsen, Henry Gregor

Vicker, Angus
See Felsen, Henry Gregor

Vidal, Gore 1925- ...... **CLC 2, 4, 6, 8, 10, 22, 33, 72, 142; DAM NOV, POP**
See also Box, Edgar
See also AITN 1; AMWS 4; BEST 90:2; CA 5-8R; CANR 13, 45, 65; CDALBS; DA3; DLB 6, 152; INT CANR-13; MTCW 1, 2

Viereck, Peter (Robert Edwin)
1916- .... **CLC 4; PC 27**
See also CA 1-4R; CANR 1, 47; DLB 5

Vigny, Alfred (Victor) de
1797-1863 .. **NCLC 7; DAM POET; PC 26**
See also DLB 119, 192

Vilakazi, Benedict Wallet
1906-1947 .... **TCLC 37**
See also CA 168

Villa, Jose Garcia 1914-1997 .... **PC 22**
See also CA 25-28R; CANR 12

Villarreal, Jose Antonio 1924-
See also CA 133; CANR 93; DAM MULT; DLB 82; HLC 2; HW 1

Villaurrutia, Xavier 1903-1950 ...... **TCLC 80**
See also HW 1

Villehardouin 1150(?)-1218(?) .... **CMLC 38**

Villiers de l'Isle Adam, Jean Marie Mathias Philippe Auguste, Comte de
1838-1889 .... **NCLC 3; SSC 14**
See also DLB 123

Villon, François 1431-1463(?) . **LC 62; PC 13**
See also DLB 208

Vine, Barbara CLC 50
See also Rendell, Ruth (Barbara)
See also BEST 90:4

Vinge, Joan (Carol) D(ennison)
1948- .... **CLC 30; SSC 24**
See also AAYA 32; AW; CA 93-96; CANR 72; SATA 36, 113

Ward, Peter
See Faust, Frederick (Schiller)
Warhol, Andy 1928(?)-1987 .... **CLC 20**
See also AAYA 12; BEST 89:4; CA 89-92; 121; CANR 34
Warner, Francis (Robert le Plastrier) 1937- .... **CLC 14**
See also CA 53-56; CANR 11
Warner, Marina 1946- .... **CLC 59**
See also CA 65-68; CANR 21, 55; DLB 194
Warner, Rex (Ernest) 1905-1986 ...... **CLC 45**
See also CA 89-92; 119; DLB 15
Warner, Susan (Bogert) 1819-1885 .... **NCLC 31**
See also DLB 3, 42, 239
Warner, Sylvia (Constance) Ashton
See Ashton-Warner, Sylvia (Constance)
Warner, Sylvia Townsend 1893-1978 .... **CLC 7, 19; SSC 23**
See also CA 61-64; 77-80; CANR 16, 60; DLB 34, 139; MTCW 1, 2
Warren, Mercy Otis 1728-1814 ..... **NCLC 13**
See also DLB 31, 200
Warren, Robert Penn 1905-1989 .. **CLC 1, 4, 6, 8, 10, 13, 18, 39, 53, 59; DA; DAB; DAC; DAM MST, NOV, POET; SSC 4**
See also AITN 1; AW; CA 13-16R; 129; CANR 10, 47; CDALB 1968-1988; DA3; DLB 2, 48, 152; DLBY 80, 89; INT CANR-10; MTCW 1, 2; SATA 46; SATA-Obit 63
Warshofsky, Isaac
See Singer, Isaac Bashevis
Warton, Thomas 1728-1790 ..... **LC 15; DAM POET**
See also DLB 104, 109
Waruk, Kona
See Harris, (Theodore) Wilson
Warung, Price TCLC 45
See also Astley, William
Warwick, Jarvis
See Garner, Hugh
See also CCA 1
Washington, Alex
See Harris, Mark
Washington, Booker T(aliaferro) 1856-1915 ...... **TCLC 10; BLC 3; DAM MULT**
See also BW 1; CA 114; 125; DA3; SATA 28
Washington, George 1732-1799 .... **LC 25**
See also DLB 31
Wassermann, (Karl) Jakob 1873-1934 .... **TCLC 6**
See also CA 104; 163; DLB 66
Wasserstein, Wendy 1950- .. **CLC 32, 59, 90; DAM DRAM; DC 4**
See also CA 121; 129; CABS 3; CANR 53, 75; DA3; DLB 228; INT 129; MTCW 2; SATA 94
Waterhouse, Keith (Spencer) 1929- . **CLC 47**
See also CA 5-8R; CANR 38, 67; DLB 13, 15; MTCW 1, 2
Waters, Frank (Joseph) 1902-1995 .. **CLC 88**
See also CA 5-8R; 149; CAAS 13; CANR 3, 18, 63; DLB 212; DLBY 86; TCWW 2
Waters, Mary C. CLC 70
Waters, Roger 1944- .... **CLC 35**
Watkins, Frances Ellen
See Harper, Frances Ellen Watkins
Watkins, Gerrold
See Malzberg, Barry N(athaniel)
Watkins, Gloria Jean 1952(?)-
See hooks, bell
See also BW 2; CA 143; CANR 87; MTCW 2; SATA 115
Watkins, Paul 1964- .... **CLC 55**
See also CA 132; CANR 62

Watkins, Vernon Phillips 1906-1967 .... **CLC 43**
See also CA 9-10; 25-28R; CAP 1; DLB 20
Watson, Irving S.
See Mencken, H(enry) L(ouis)
Watson, John H.
See Farmer, Philip Jose
Watson, Richard F.
See Silverberg, Robert
Waugh, Auberon (Alexander) 1939-2001 .... **CLC 7**
See also CA 45-48; CANR 6, 22, 92; DLB 14, 194
Waugh, Evelyn (Arthur St. John) 1903-1966 .. **CLC 1, 3, 8, 13, 19, 27, 44, 107; DA; DAB; DAC; DAM MST, NOV, POP; SSC 41**
See also AW; CA 85-88; 25-28R; CANR 22; CDBLB 1914-1945; DA3; DLB 15, 162, 195; MTCW 1, 2
Waugh, Harriet 1944- .... **CLC 6**
See also CA 85-88; CANR 22
Ways, C. R.
See Blount, Roy (Alton), Jr.
Waystaff, Simon
See Swift, Jonathan
Webb, Beatrice (Martha Potter) 1858-1943 .... **TCLC 22**
See also CA 117; 162; DLB 190
Webb, Charles (Richard) 1939- .... **CLC 7**
See also CA 25-28R
Webb, James H(enry), Jr. 1946- ...... **CLC 22**
See also CA 81-84
Webb, Mary Gladys (Meredith) 1881-1927 .... **TCLC 24**
See also CA 182; 123; DLB 34
Webb, Mrs. Sidney
See Webb, Beatrice (Martha Potter)
Webb, Phyllis 1927- .... **CLC 18**
See also CA 104; CANR 23; CCA 1; DLB 53
Webb, Sidney (James) 1859-1947 .. **TCLC 22**
See also CA 117; 163; DLB 190
Webber, Andrew Lloyd CLC 21
See also Lloyd Webber, Andrew
Weber, Lenora Mattingly 1895-1971 .... **CLC 12**
See also CA 19-20; 29-32R; CAP 1; SATA 2; SATA-Obit 26
Weber, Max 1864-1920 .... **TCLC 69**
See also CA 109; 189
Webster, John 1580(?)-1634(?) ... **LC 33; DA; DAB; DAC; DAM DRAM, MST; DC 2**
See also AW; CDBLB Before 1660; DLB 58
Webster, Noah 1758-1843 .... **NCLC 30**
See also DLB 1, 37, 42, 43, 73
Wedekind, (Benjamin) Frank(lin) 1864-1918 .... **TCLC 7; DAM DRAM**
See also CA 104; 153; DLB 118
Wehr, Demaris CLC 65
Weidman, Jerome 1913-1998 .... **CLC 7**
See also AITN 2; CA 1-4R; 171; CANR 1; DLB 28
Weil, Simone (Adolphine) 1909-1943 .... **TCLC 23**
See also CA 117; 159; MTCW 2
Weininger, Otto 1880-1903 .... **TCLC 84**
Weinstein, Nathan
See West, Nathanael
Weinstein, Nathan von Wallenstein
See West, Nathanael
Weir, Peter (Lindsay) 1944- .... **CLC 20**
See also CA 113; 123
Weiss, Peter (Ulrich) 1916-1982 .. **CLC 3, 15, 51; DAM DRAM**
See also CA 45-48; 106; CANR 3; DLB 69, 124

Weiss, Theodore (Russell) 1916- ... **CLC 3, 8, 14**
See also CA 9-12R; CAAE 189; CAAS 2; CANR 46, 94; DLB 5
Welch, (Maurice) Denton 1915-1948 .... **TCLC 22**
See also CA 121; 148
Welch, James 1940- ..... **CLC 6, 14, 52; DAM MULT, POP**
See also CA 85-88; CANR 42, 66; DLB 175; NNAL; TCWW 2
Weldon, Fay 1931- . **CLC 6, 9, 11, 19, 36, 59, 122; DAM POP**
See also BRWS 4; CA 21-24R; CANR 16, 46, 63; CDBLB 1960 to Present; DLB 14, 194; INT CANR-16; MTCW 1, 2
Wellek, Rene 1903-1995 .... **CLC 28**
See also CA 5-8R; 150; CAAS 7; CANR 8; DLB 63; INT CANR-8
Weller, Michael 1942- .... **CLC 10, 53**
See also CA 85-88
Weller, Paul 1958- .... **CLC 26**
Wellershoff, Dieter 1925- .... **CLC 46**
See also CA 89-92; CANR 16, 37
Welles, (George) Orson 1915-1985 .. **CLC 20, 80**
See also CA 93-96; 117
Wellman, John McDowell 1945-
See Wellman, Mac
See also CA 166
Wellman, Mac CLC 65
See also Wellman, John McDowell; Wellman, John McDowell
Wellman, Manly Wade 1903-1986 ... **CLC 49**
See also CA 1-4R; 118; CANR 6, 16, 44; SATA 6; SATA-Obit 47
Wells, Carolyn 1869(?)-1942 .... **TCLC 35**
See also CA 113; 185; DLB 11
Wells, H(erbert) G(eorge) 1866-1946 . **TCLC 6, 12, 19; DA; DAB; DAC; DAM MST, NOV; SSC 6**
See also AAYA 18; AW; CA 110; 121; CDBLB 1914-1945; CLR 64; DA3; DLB 34, 70, 156, 178; MTCW 1, 2; SATA 20
Wells, Rosemary 1943- .... **CLC 12**
See also AAYA 13; AW; CA 85-88; CANR 48; CLR 16, 69; MAICYA; SAAS 1; SATA 18, 69, 114
Welty, Eudora 1909- ...... **CLC 1, 2, 5, 14, 22, 33, 105; DA; DAB; DAC; DAM MST, NOV; SSC 1, 27**
See also AW; CA 9-12R; CABS 1; CANR 32, 65; CDALB 1941-1968; DA3; DLB 2, 102, 143; DLBD 12; DLBY 87; MTCW 1, 2
Wen I-to 1899-1946 .... **TCLC 28**
Wentworth, Robert
See Hamilton, Edmond
Werfel, Franz (Viktor) 1890-1945 ... **TCLC 8**
See also CA 104; 161; DLB 81, 124
Wergeland, Henrik Arnold 1808-1845 .... **NCLC 5**
Wersba, Barbara 1932- .... **CLC 30**
See also AAYA 2, 30; AW; CA 29-32R; 182; CAAE 182; CANR 16, 38; CLR 3; DLB 52; JRDA; MAICYA; SAAS 2; SATA 1, 58; SATA-Essay 103
Wertmueller, Lina 1928- .... **CLC 16**
See also CA 97-100; CANR 39, 78
Wescott, Glenway 1901-1987 .. **CLC 13; SSC 35**
See also CA 13-16R; 121; CANR 23, 70; DLB 4, 9, 102
Wesker, Arnold 1932- ... **CLC 3, 5, 42; DAB; DAM DRAM**
See also CA 1-4R; CAAS 7; CANR 1, 33; CDBLB 1960 to Present; DLB 13; MTCW 1

Literary Criticism Series
Cumulative Topic Index

This index lists all topic entries in Gale's *Classical and Medieval Literature Criticism, Contemporary Literary Criticism, Literature Criticism from 1400 to 1800, Nineteenth-Century Literature Criticism,* and *Twentieth-Century Literary Criticism.*

NCLC Cumulative Nationality Index

NCLC-98 Title Index

ISBN 0-7876-4553-2

9 780787 645533